ELEVENTH EDITION

ACCOUNTANTS' HANDBOOK

VOLUME TWO:

SPECIAL INDUSTRIES AND SPECIAL TOPICS

Subscriber Update Service

BECOME A SUBSCRIBER!

Did you purchase this product from a bookstore?

If you did, it's important for you to become a subscriber. John Wiley & Sons, Inc., may publish, on a periodic basis, supplements and new editions to reflect the latest changes in the subject matter that you **need to know** in order to stay competitive in this ever-changing industry. By contacting the Wiley office nearest you, you'll receive any current update at no additional charge. In addition, you'll receive future updates and revised or related volumes on a 30-day examination review.

If you purchased this product directly from John Wiley & Sons, Inc., we have already recorded your subscription for this update service.

To become a subscriber, please call **1-800-225-5945** or send your name, company name (if applicable), address, and the title of the product to:

mailing address: **Supplement Department**
John Wiley & Sons, Inc.
One Wiley Drive
Somerset, NJ 08875

e-mail: **subscriber@wiley.com**
fax: **1-732-302-2300**
online: **www.wiley.com**

For customers outside the United States, please contact the Wiley office nearest you:

Professional & Reference Division
John Wiley & Sons Canada, Ltd.
22 Worcester Road
Rexdale, Ontario M9W 1L1
CANADA
(416) 675-3580
Phone: 1-800-567-4797
Fax: 1-800-565-6802
canada@jwiley.com

Jacaranda Wiley Ltd.
PRT Division
P.O. Box 174
North Ryde, NSW 2113
AUSTRALIA
Phone: (02) 805-1100
Fax: (02) 805-1597
headoffice@jacwiley.com.au

John Wiley & Sons, Ltd.
Baffins Lane
Chichester
West Sussex, PO19 1UD
ENGLAND
Phone: (44) 1243 779777
Fax: (44) 1243 770638
cs-books@wiley.co.uk

John Wiley & Sons (SEA) Pte., Ltd.
2 Clementi Loop #02-01
SINGAPORE 129809
Phone: 65 463 2400
Fax: 65 463 4605; 65 463 4604
wiley@singnet.com.sg

For updates to the chapters prior to the availability of the supplements, please go to www.wiley.com/go/accountantshandbook11E.

ELEVENTH EDITION

ACCOUNTANTS' HANDBOOK

VOLUME TWO:
SPECIAL INDUSTRIES AND SPECIAL TOPICS

D. R. CARMICHAEL
O. RAY WHITTINGTON
LYNFORD GRAHAM

JOHN WILEY & SONS, INC.

Library of Congress Cataloging-in-Publication Data:

ISBN 978-0-471-79039-6

Printed in the United States of America.

10 9 8 7 6 5 4 3 2 1

ABOUT THE EDITORS

Ray Whittington, PhD, CPA, CMA, CIA, is the Dean of the College of Commerce at DePaul University. Prior to joining the faculty at DePaul, Professor Whittington was the Director of Accountancy at San Diego State University. From 1989 through 1991, he was the Director of Auditing Research for the American Institute of Certified Public Accountants (AICPA), and he previously was on the audit staff of KPMG. He was a member of the Auditing Standards Board of the AICPA and has previously served as a member of the Accounting and Review Services Committee and the Board of Regents of the Institute of Internal Auditors. Professor Whittington has published numerous textbooks, articles, monographs, and continuing education courses.

Lynford Graham, CPA, PhD, CFE is a Certified Public Accountant with more than 25 years of public accounting experience in audit practice and national policy development groups. He was a Partner and the Director of Audit Policy for BDO Seidman, LLP, and was a National Accounting & SEC Consulting Partner for Coopers & Lybrand, responsible for the technical issues research function and database, auditing research, audit automation and audit sampling techniques. Prior to joining BDO Seidman LLP, Dr. Graham was an Associate Professor of Accounting and Information Systems and a Graduate Faculty Fellow at Rutgers University in Newark, New Jersey, where he taught primarily financial accounting courses. Dr. Graham is a member of the American Institute of Certified Public Accountants, and a recent past member of the AICPA Auditing Standards Board. He is a Certified Fraud Examiner and a member of the Association of Certified Fraud Examiners. Throughout his career he has maintained an active profile in the academic as well as the business community. In 2002 he received the Distinguished Service Award of the Auditing Section of the AAA. His numerous academic and business publications span a variety of topical areas including information systems, internal controls, expert systems, audit risk, audit planning, fraud, sampling, analytical procedures, audit judgment, and international accounting and auditing. Dr. Graham holds an MBA in Industrial Management and PhD in Business and Applied Economics from the University of Pennsylvania (Wharton School).

ABOUT THE CONTRIBUTORS

James R. Adler, PhD, CPA, CFE, is founder of Adler Consulting Ltd., which specializes in forensic accounting. He has over 40 years of public accounting and academic experience working with generally accepted accounting principles (GAAP) and generally accepted auditing standards (GAAS). He has had a diversified clientele, including public and private entities as well as governmental bodies such as the SEC, the U.S. Department of Justice, and the FDIC. He has written and lectured extensively on the professional standards and other accounting and economic issues.

Juan Aguerrebere, Jr., CPA, is a founding member of Perez-Abreu, Aguerrebere, Sueiro LLC in Coral Gables, Florida. He has served on numerous AICPA and FICPA committees, including the AICPA Technical Issues Committee, Group of 100, AICPA Joint Trial Board, and FICPA Accounting and Auditing Committee. He has over 13 years of experience in public accounting and auditing and over 20 years of experience in accounting for financial institutions. He has lectured on numerous accounting and auditing issues. He is a member of the AICPA, FICPA, a Diplomat of the American Board of Forensic Accounting, and a Neutral/Arbitrator for the American Arbitration Association.

Vincent Amoroso, FSA, is a principal in the employee benefits section of Deloitte & Touche LLP's Washington National Office. He has published and spoken frequently in the employee benefits accounting area, both on pensions and retiree medical care.

Ian J. Benjamin, CPA, is a managing director in the Not-for-Profit Services Group of American Express Tax and Business Services, Inc. Prior to joining American Express, Mr. Benjamin was a partner at Deloitte & Touche in their Tri-State Not-for-Profit and Higher Education Services Group. He is currently a member of the FASB working group on not-for-profit organizations and the Professional Ethics Committee of the New York State Society of CPAs. He is a former member of the International Accounting Committee and the Not-for-Profit Organizations Committee of the New York State Society of CPAs.

Martin Benis, PhD, CPA, is a professor and former chairman of The Stan Ross Department of Accountancy at the Zicklin School of Business, Bernard M. Baruch College, CUNY. He is currently a consultant on accounting and auditing matters to more than 50 accounting firms and organizations throughout the United States. His articles have appeared in major accounting and auditing journals.

Andrew J. Blossom, CPA, is a senior manager in the Public Services line of business of KPMG Peat Marwick LLP. He is assigned to KPMG's Department of Professional Practice, where he is responsible for handling technical inquiries related to governmental accounting, auditing, and reporting. Mr. Blossom is a member of the AICPA Government Accounting and Auditing Committee. He received his BS degree from the University of Kansas.

William B. Boles, CPA/ABV, ASA, CFP, is a shareholder in the Harrisburg, PA Certified Public Accounting firm of Boles Metzger Brosius & Ritter, PC since it was formed in 1978. He works primarily with business valuation consulting engagements and taxation issues. Prior to 1978 he was the Director of Tax Services for the Harrisburg office of Laventhol & Horwath. As a former

Internal Revenue Agent, those experiences along with the other client work have provided practical insight on tax, accounting and valuation issues.

Stephen Bryan, MBA, PhD, is an associate professor of the Stan Ross Department of Accountancy at the Zicklin School of Business, Bernard M. Baruch College, CUNY. He received his doctorate in accounting from New York University.

Luis E. Cabrera, CPA, is a technical manager with the AICPA's Professional Standards and Services Team. Mr. Cabrera was previously responsible for technical research activities as a senior accountant in the national office of Pannell Kerr Forster, PC. He was also an audit senior with Coopers & Lybrand and has served as an adjunct professor of Accountancy at the Zicklin School of Business in the Stan Ross Department of Accountancy at Bernard M. Baruch College, CUNY.

Joseph V. Carcello, PhD, CPA, CMA, CIA, is a William B. Stokely Distinguished Scholar and an associate professor in the Department of Accounting and Business Law at the University of Tennessee. Dr. Carcello is the coauthor of the *2003 Miller GAAP Practice Manual.* Dr. Carcello has taught professional development courses and conducted funded research for three of the Big 4 firms. He also has taught continuing professional education courses for the AICPA, the Institute of Internal Auditors, the Institute of Management Accountants, and the Tennessee and Florida Societies of CPAs.

Peter T. Chingos, CPA, is a principal in the New York office of Mercer Human Resource Consulting and a member of the firm's Worldwide Partners Group. He is the U.S. leader for the firm's Executive Compensation Consulting Practice. For more than 25 years he has consulted with senior management, compensation committees, and boards of directors of leading global corporations on executive compensation and strategic business issues. He is a frequent keynote speaker at professional conferences, writes extensively on all aspects of executive compensation, and is often quoted in the press. He is a member of the advisory Board of the National Association of Stock Plan Professionals and currently teaches basic and advanced courses in executive compensation in the certification program for compensation professionals sponsored by Worldatwork.

Walton T. Conn, Jr., CPA, is a partner in the Department of Professional Practice of KPMG Peat Marwick LLP, where he works in the information, communication, and entertainment practice. He has spent four years in his firm's Department of Professional Practice in New York and is a former practice fellow of the AICPA Auditing Standards Board.

John R. Deming, CPA, is a partner in the Department of Professional Practice of KPMG Peat Marwick LLP in New York. He is a former member of the AICPA Accounting Standards Executive Committee and has served on a number of FASB task forces and EITF working groups. Mr. Deming has written numerous articles on a variety of accounting issues, including leases, business combinations, pensions, and employee stock-based compensation.

Brent W. Emrick, CPA/ABV, CFP, is a shareholder in the Harrisburg, PA Certified Public Accounting firm of Boles Metzger Brosius & Ritter PC. He joined the firm in 1980 as a Staff Accountant. He works primarily with taxation issues, business valuations, financial and estate planning.

Jason Flynn, FSA, is a senior manager in the employee benefits section of Deloitte & Touche LLP's Detroit office.

Sydney Garmong, CPA, is an Executive in the Financial Institution Group at Crowe, Chizek and Company LLC. Her primary responsibility is to address accounting and regulatory issues affecting financial institutions. Ms. Garmong is a member of the AICPA's Depository Institutions Expert Panel and several other industry committees which maintain an ongoing liaison with various regulators and standard setters including the FDIC, NCUA, OCC, OTS, Federal Reserve, SEC, and the FASB. In addition to addressing technical issues, Ms. Garmong is a frequent speaker at industry and regulatory conferences. Prior to joining Crowe Chizek, she was a senior manager at the AICPA in Washington, DC. During her three years with the AICPA, she addressed financial institution and financial instrument accounting, auditing, and regulatory matters. She served as the staff liaison to the AICPA's Financial Services Expert Panel, and worked on other related projects with AcSEC, an AICPA senior technical committee.

Martha Garner, CPA, is a director in the national office of PricewaterhouseCoopers LLP, where she is the firm's industry specialist for healthcare accounting and financial reporting matters. She has served on numerous AICPA, FASB, and Healthcare Financial Management Association task forces and committees dealing with healthcare financial reporting issues. She is a contributing author on healthcare matters for *Montgomery's Auditing* and the *Financial and Accounting Guide for Not-for-Profit Organizations*, and has authored numerous healthcare articles and publications.

Frederick Gill, CPA, is senior technical manager on the Accounting Standards Team at the AICPA, where he provides broad technical support to the Accounting Standards Executive Committee. During 19 years with the AICPA, he participated in the development of numerous AICPA Statements of Position, Audit and Accounting Guides, Practice Bulletins, issues papers, journal articles, and practice aids. He was a member of the U.S. delegation to the International Accounting Standards Committee, represented the U.S. accounting profession on the United Nations Intergovernmental Working Group of Experts on International Standards of Accounting and Reporting, and was a member of the National Accounting Curriculum Task Force. Previously he held several accounting faculty positions.

Alan S. Glazer, PhD, CPA, Named to the Henry P. and Mary B. Stager Professorship, is professor of Business Administration at Franklin & Marshall College, Lancaster, Pennsylvania. He was associate director of the Independence Standards Board's conceptual framework project and has been a consultant to several AICPA committees. His articles on auditor independence, not-for-profit organizations, and other issues have been published in academic and professional journals.

Andrew F. Gottschalk, CPA, is a senior manger in the public services practice of KPMG Peat Marwick LLP. He has over 15 years of experience serving state and local governments. He is a member of the Government Finance Officers Association, the Association of Government Accountants, and the New York and Illinois Societies of CPAs.

Richard P. Graff, CPA, is CEO of The Graff Consulting Group. He serves as a financial and business adviser to the natural resources industry and has coauthored numerous publications. Prior to that, he was a partner in the international accounting firm of PricewaterhouseCoopers LLP, where he served as audit leader of the U.S. Mining Industry Group.

Dan M. Guy, PhD, CPA, is a writer and consultant. Formerly he served as a vice-president of Professional Standards and Services at the AICPA. He is a coauthor of *Practitioner's Guide to GAAS* and *Ethics for CPAs* (John Wiley & Sons); *Guide to Compilation and Review Engagements* (Practitioners Publishing Company, 1988); and has published numerous articles in professional journals, an auditing textbook (Dryden Press), and an audit sampling textbook (John Wiley & Sons).

Wendy Hambleton, CPA, is an audit partner working in the National SEC Department in BDO Seidman LLP's Chicago office. Prior to joining the SEC Department, Ms. Hambleton worked in the firm's Washington, DC, practice office. She works extensively with clients and engagement teams to prepare SEC filings and resolve related accounting and reporting issues. Ms. Hambleton coauthors a number of internal and external publications, including the AICPA's *Guide to SEC Reporting* and Warren Gorham & Lamont's *Controller's Handbook* chapter on public offering requirements.

Philip M. Herr, JD, CPA, is the director of Advanced Planning of Kingsbridge Financial Group, Inc., Point Pleasant Beach, New Jersey, and is an adjunct professor at Fairleigh Dickinson University, School of Continuing Education, Certified Employee Benefits Specialist Program and Certified Financial Planner Program. He is admitted to the New York and U.S. Tax Court Bars and is a member of the New York State Bar Association, New York State Society of CPAs, New Jersey Society of CPAs, and Association for Advanced Life Underwriting. He specializes in the areas of: tax; estates and trusts; estate, business, and financial planning; ERISA issues and transactions; retirement, employee benefit, and executive compensation planning; and use of life insurance and insurance products. He also holds the NASD 7, 24, 63, and 65 securities licenses.

Karen L. Hooks, PhD, CPA, is a professor of accountancy at Florida Atlantic University (FAU). Her primary research areas are the public accounting work environment, sociology of professions, gender, ethics, and communication. She teaches undergraduate classes, as well as in the Master of Accounting, MBA, and Master of Science in International Business at FAU. Professor Hooks has been published in *Accounting Organizations and Society, Behavioral Research in Accounting, Auditing: A Journal of Practice and Theory, Accounting Horizons, Critical Perspectives on Accounting, Advances in Accounting, Advances in Public Interest Accounting, Journal of Accountancy*, among others. She received her PhD from Georgia State University.

Keith M. Housum, CPA, is a senior manager in the tax consulting practice of Ernst & Young LLP. He specializes in the Financial Services area. Mr. Housum has over six years of experience assisting financial services clients with a variety of tax issues. Clients have ranged in size from small community-based banks to large regional financial institutions. He began his career with Ernst & Young LLP upon graduation from Case Western Reserve University with a bachelor's degree in Accounting. He is a member of the Ohio Society of Certified Public Accountants.

Henry R. Jaenicke, PhD, CPA, was the C. D. Clarkson Professor of Accounting at Drexel University. He is the author of *Survey of Present Practiced in Recognizing Revenues, Expenses, Gains, and Losses* (FASB, 1981) and is the coauthor of the 12th edition of *Montgomery's Auditing* (John Wiley & Sons, 1998). He has served as a consultant to several AICPA committees, the Independence Standards Board, and the Public Oversight Board.

Richard C. Jones, PhD, CPA, is an associate professor in the Accounting/Taxation/Business Law Department of Hofstra University. Dr. Jones's teaching interests include managerial accounting and financial reporting. His research interests focus on auditing and the international self-regulatory accounting environment. Dr. Jones has also contributed extensively to AICPA publications.

Richard R. Jones, CPA, is a senior partner in the National Accounting Standards Professional Practice Group of Ernst & Young LLP, where he is responsible for assisting the firm's clients in understanding and implementing today's complex accounting requirements. Mr. Jones's particular fields of expertise are in the areas of impairments, equity accounting, real estate, leasing, and various financing arrangements.

Allyn A. Joyce has been a business appraiser for 40 years. He is principal of Allyn A. Joyce & Co., Inc., which specializes in litigation support appraisals and litigation support appraisal reviews.

Alan M. Kall is a principal in the tax consulting practice of Ernst & Young LLP specializing in the Financial Services area. Mr. Kall has over 17 years of experience assisting financial services clients with a variety of tax and accounting issues. His clients' range in size from small community-based banks to large regional financial institutions. He began his career with Ernst & Young LLP upon graduation from Cleveland State University with a BBA in Accounting. He is a CPA and a member of the Ohio Society of Certified Public Accountants.

Eric Klis, ASA, is a manager in the employee benefits section of Deloitte & Touche LLP's Minneapolis office.

Margaret R. Kolb, CPA, is a senior manager in Litigation Consulting Department of the New York office of American Express Tax and Business Services, Inc., where she provides litigation consulting, forensic accounting, and expert witness services to law firms and insurance companies. She has prepared expert reports and provided testimony in a variety of forums. Ms. Kolb is a certified public accountant in the State of New York, a member of the American Institute of Certified Public Accountants and the New York State Society of Certified Public Accountants. She recently served for two years on the Litigation Consulting Committee of the New York State Society of Certified Public Accountants.

Debra J. MacLaughlin, CPA, is a partner and the Deputy National SEC Director in BDO Seidman LLP's Chicago office. She has over 23 years of professional accounting experience and has served clients in both the public and private sectors. As Deputy National SEC Director, Ms. MacLaughlin assists the firm's clients and engagement teams in preparing SEC filings, performs prerelease reviews of registration statements and selected Form 10-Ks, and consults on related accounting and reporting issues.

Susan McElyea, CPA, is a director in PricewaterhouseCoopers Transaction Services Group. Her 22 years of industry experience includes corporations owning real estate not used in their business, commercial and industrial developers, home-builders, hotel owners, operators, syndicators, property managers, and retail clients with substantial real estate properties. Experience includes off balance sheet structuring, lease and transaction structuring, lease analysis, securitization and bulk sales transactions, cash flow modeling, due diligence services, private and public debt offerings, development of cash flow projections related to real estate syndications, and consultation regarding accounting and reporting matters with clients in structuring various real estate transactions. Additionally, she has served as an instructor for many real estate accounting and auditing continuing education courses and contributed significantly to the 1995 John Wiley & Sons technical research book entitled *Real Estate Accounting and Reporting*.

Benjamin A. McKnight III, CPA, is a retired partner at Arthur Andersen LLP in its Chicago office. He specializes in services to regulated enterprises, is a frequent speaker, and provides expert testimony on utility and telecommunication accounting and regulatory topics.

Francine Mellors, CPA, is a director in Ernst & Young's National Department of Professional Practice in New York. Her duties include consulting and writing on various accounting topics, including employee benefit issues, as well as serving as knowledge leader and publications director for the National AABS Practice. Prior to this role, Ms. Mellors served as a vice-president in the Accounting Policy Group at the Chase Manhattan Bank and as an auditor at Deloitte and Touche. She holds a BA and an MA in Hispanic Studies and an MBA in Accounting and Management.

John R. Miller, CPA, CGFM, is a partner and member of the board of directors of KPMG LLP. He is partner-in-charge of the firm's Public Services Assurance and Resource Management Services. Mr. Miller is a member of the Comptroller General's Audit Advisory Committee and a former chairman of the AICPA's Government and Auditing Committee and is a recognized authority on governmental financial management.

Lailani Moody, CPA, MBA, is a partner in Grant Thornton LLP's Professional Standards Group. Her responsibilities are primarily in the area of accounting and financial reporting, and, in particular, stock compensation, equity transactions, and newly issued accounting pronouncements from the FASB and the FASB's Emerging Issues Task Force. She was formerly a technical manager in the AICPA's Accounting Standards Division.

Richard H. Moseley, CPA, is a managing director in the Chicago Metro office of American Express Tax and Business Services, Inc. and the co-director of the Quality Assurance Department. Mr. Moseley is responsible for providing consultation services on accounting technical issues and preparing implementation guidance for new accounting standards. He was a member of the AICPA's Accounting Standards Executive Committee and a former member of the PCPS Technical Issues Committee.

Anthony J. Mottola, CPA, CFE, is president of Mottola & Associates, Inc., a consulting firm in areas such as litigation support, financial services, strategic planning, corporate oversight, transactions structuring, and systems and business evaluation. Previously he was a partner with Coopers & Lybrand, Spicer & Oppenheim, and EVP, and a member of the board of directors of Shearson Lehman. He was special assistant to New York City's Deputy Mayor of Finance during its fiscal crises and served as the first Practice Fellow at FASB.

Dennis S. Neier, CPA, is a partner in the accounting firm of Goldstein Golub Kessler LLP, a managing director in the New York office of American Express Tax and Business Services, Inc., and the associate director of the New York Litigation Consulting Department. Mr. Neier provides litigation consulting and support, expert witness, and forensic accounting services to law firms, insurance companies, and in-house counsel. He assists in all phases of the litigation process, from precomplaint through posttrial, and has testimony experience in a variety of forums. He is certified in New York and Louisiana and is a member of the American Institute of Certified Public Accountants, the New York State Society of Certified Public Accountants, the American Arbitration Association, the Association of Certified Fraud Examiners, and the American College of Forensic Examiners, and is a diplomat of the American Board of Forensic Accounting.

Grant W. Newton, PhD, CPA, CMA, is a professor of accounting at Pepperdine University. He is the author of the two-volume set *Bankruptcy and Insolvency Accounting: Practice and Procedures: Forms and Exhibits, Sixth Edition* (John Wiley & Sons, 2006), and coauthor of *Bankruptcy and Insolvency Taxation, Second Edition* (John Wiley & Sons, 1994). He is a frequent contributor to professional journals and has lectured widely to professional organizations on bankruptcy-related topics.

Paul Pacter, PhD, CPA, is director, Deloitte Touche Tohmatsu IAS Global Office, Hong Kong. His responsibilities include IAS technical questions, developing his firm's comment letters to the IASB, advising the Ministry of Finance of China on developing accounting standards, and managing the web site, *www.iasplus.com.* From 1996 to 2000 he was International Accounting Fellow at the International Accounting Standards Committee, London. In that capacity, he managed a number of IASC's agenda projects, including financial instruments recognition and measurement, interim financial reporting, segment reporting, and discontinued operations. Previously Mr. Pacter worked for the U.S. FASB from its inception in 1973 and, for seven years, as commissioner of Finance of the City of Stamford, Connecticut. He has published nearly 100 professional monographs and articles. He received his PhD from Michigan State University and has taught in several MBA programs for working business managers.

Don M. Pallais, CPA, has his own practice in Richmond, Virginia. He is a former member of the AICPA Auditing Standards Board and the AICPA Accounting and Review Services Committee. He has written a host of books, articles, and CPE courses on accounting topics.

Ronald J. Patten, PhD, CPA, is the dean emeritus of the College of Commerce and Kellstadt Graduate School at DePaul University. He was the first director of research for the FASB and a former associate in the firm of Arthur D. Little International. He is the coauthor of *CPA Review: Practice, Theory, Auditing and Law, First and Second Edition* (John Wiley & Sons, 1974, 1978).

Laura J. Phillips, CPA, is a senior manager in the Cleveland office of Ernst & Young LLP. She was formerly assigned to the firm's national offices in New York and Cleveland, specializing in the financial services industry. She has been a Technical Audit Advisor to the Auditing Standards Board of the AICPA as well as a member of the AICPA Auditing Financial Instruments Task Force.

Her articles have appeared in *Bank Accounting* and *Finance and Commercial Lending Review*. She currently serves commercial banking clients.

Michael Ramos, was an auditor with KPMG. Since 1991 he has worked primarily as an author, corporate trainer, and consultant, specializing in emerging accounting and auditing matters. He is now a Vice President at AuditWatch. He has published eight books including *How to Comply with the Sarbanes-Oxley Section 404, Second Edition, and The Sarbanes-Oxley Section 404 Toolkit.*

Ronald F. Ries, CPA, is the managing director in charge of the Not-for-Profit Services Group in the New York office of the American Express Tax and Business Services, Inc. Prior to joining American Express, Mr. Ries was controller, treasurer, and vice president of finance for Spiral Metal Company, Inc. He is an active member of the Accounting for Non-Profit Organizations Committee of the New York State Society of Certified Public Accountants and active in the AICPA. He is a contributing editor to *The Practical Accountant* and lectures and writes frequently on various business and financial matters in both the commercial and not-for-profit sectors.

Lisa A. Ritter, CPA, CFE is a shareholder and member of the Executive Committee of Boles Metzger Brosius & Ritter PC. She joined the firm as a Supervisor of the Audit Department in 1989. She works primarily with audits, reviews, and compilations for businesses, government, and non-profit agencies, and also provides litigation support services. She is a member of the AICPA's Auditing Standards Board.

Jacob P. Roosma, CPA, is director of the New York office of Willamette Management Associates, specializing in business valuation. He was previously a partner in the New York office of Deloitte & Touche LLP and, before that, vice president of Management Planning, Inc.

Mark R. Rouchard, CPA, MBA, is a partner in Ernst & Young's financial services practice. Mr. Rouchard has spent his entire career serving financial institution clients and has provided a wide range of accounting and auditing services to some of Ernst & Young's largest banking clients. Mark currently serves on the AICPA's Regulatory Task Force. He has spoken at AICPA conferences and written for *Bank Accounting and Finance* magazine.

Robert L. Royall II, CPA, CFA, MBA, is a partner in Ernst & Young's National Professional Practices Group in New York City, specializing in accounting for derivatives and hedging activities and financial instruments. Mr. Royall has authored or edited all of his firm's technical literature related to FASB Statement No. 133, *Accounting for Derivative Instruments and Hedging Activities.* He regularly works with the FASB staff and SEC regulators to monitor emerging interpretations in this rapidly changing area. Mr. Royall is a member of the Association for Investment Management and Research.

Steven Rubin, CPA, is a firm director in the national assurance, accounting and advisory services department of Deloitte & Touche LLP. Previously he was the director of accounting at another national firm and a principal and the director of quality control at a local firm. Prior to that he held key staff positions at the AICPA and taught accounting as an adjunct assistant professor at Brooklyn College of CUNY, his alma mater. A frequent writer and lecturer, he is active in the New York State Society of Certified Public Accountants, where he chairs its Financial Accounting Standards Committee, and is former member of its board of directors.

Warren Ruppel, CPA, was the assistant comptroller for accounting of the City of New York, where he was responsible for all aspects of the city's accounting and financial reporting. He has over 20 years of experience in governmental and not-for-profit accounting and financial reporting. He began his career at KPMG after graduating from St. John's University, New York, in 1979. His involvement with governmental accounting and auditing began with his first audit assignment—the second audit ever performed of the financial statements of the City of New York. After that he served many governmental and commercial clients until he joined Deloitte & Touche in 1989 to specialize in audits of governments and not-for-profit organizations. Mr. Ruppel has also served as the CFO of an international not-for-profit organization. Mr. Ruppel has served as instructor for many training courses, including specialized governmental and not-for-profit programs and seminars. He has also been an adjunct lecturer of accounting at the Bernard M. Baruch College, CUNY. He is the author of four books, *OMP Circular A-133 Audits, Wiley GAAP for Governments, Not-for-Profit Organization Audits,* and *Not-for-Profit Accounting Made Easy.* Mr. Ruppel is a member of the AICPA as well as the New York State Society of Certified Public Accountants, where he serves on the Governmental Accounting and Auditing and Not-for-Profit Organizations committees. He is also a member of the Institute of Management Accountants and is a past president of the New York chapter. Mr. Ruppel is a member of the Government Financial Officers Association and serves on its Special Review Committee.

Clifford H. Schwartz, CPA, is a consultant. Formerly he served as a senior technical manager at the AICPA and a manager at Price Waterhouse LLP (now PricewaterhouseCoopers LLP).

E. Raymond Simpson, CPA, was a project manager at the FASB. He served as project manager for SFAS No. 109, "Accounting for Income Taxes," and SFAS No. 52, "Foreign Currency Translation."

Gary L. Smith, CPA, is an Ernst & Young senior manager in the National Accounting Standards Professional Practice group with over 13 years of experience serving clients in a wide variety of industries and development stages. He is responsible for assisting the firm's clients in understanding and implementing today's complex accounting requirements. His particular fields of expertise are in the areas of inventories, income taxes, consolidations, financial instruments, pensions, and commitments and contingencies. Prior to joining national, he spent 10 years working in the Washington, DC area serving multinational, middle market, and entrepreneurial clients in the technology, communications, manufacturing, distribution, professional services, and real estate industries.

Ashwinpaul C. Sondi, PhD, is president of A. C. Sondi & Associates, LLC, a financial consulting firm and a member of the Accounting Standards Executive Committee (AcSEC) of the AICPA. He is a coauthor with G. I. White and Dov Fried of *The Analysis and Use of Financial Statements, Third Edition,* 2001. His consulting and research activities include the analysis of financial statements, use of accounting data in capital markets, analysis of the financial industry, and international accounting differences.

Joel O. Steinberg, CPA, is partner at Goldstein Golub Kessler LLP in New York City, where he specializes in accounting and auditing standards. He is a member of the New York State Society of CPA's Financial Accounting Standards Committee. He has authored several articles, and he provides continuing professional education in accounting and auditing.

Reva Steinberg, CPA, is a partner in the National SEC Department in BDO Seidman LLP's Chicago office. She has over 30 years of professional accounting experience and has served clients in both the public and private sectors. She works extensively with clients and engagement teams to prepare SEC filings and resolve related accounting and reporting issues.

Reed K. Storey, PhD, CPA, had more than 30 years of experience on the framework of financial accounting concepts, standards, and principles, working with both the Accounting Principles Board, as director of Accounting Research of the AICPA, and the FASB, as senior technical adviser. He was also a member of the accounting faculties of the University of California, Berkeley, the University of Washington, Seattle, and Bernard M. Baruch College, CUNY, and a consultant in the executive offices of Coopers & Lybrand (now PricewaterhouseCoopers LLP) and Haskins & Sells (now Deloitte & Touche, LLP).

Dale K. Thompson, CPA, is a senior manager in the Asset Management Services Group at Ernst &Young. He is responsible for accounting, regulatory, and business analysis of current developments effecting mutual fund, alternative products, and investment advisory organizations.

He is a frequent speaker on regulatory matters at industry and firm-sponsored events. He is a member of the AICPAs and the Massachusetts Society of CPAs.

Judith Weiss, CPA, received her MS in Accounting from Long Island University, Greenvale, New York, and holds an MS in Education from Queens College, CUNY. After several years in public accounting and private industry, she became a technical manager in the AICPA's Accounting Standards Division, where she worked with industry committees in the development of Audit and Accounting Guides and Statements of Position. As a senior manager in the national offices of Deloitte & Touche LLP and Grant Thornton LLP, she was involved in projects related to standard setting by the FASB and the AICPA. Since 1993 Ms. Weiss has contributed to several books in the area of accounting and auditing. She has coauthored articles on accounting standards for several publications, including the *Journal of Accountancy, The CPA Journal*, and *The Journal of Real Estate Accounting and Taxation.*

Gerald I. White, CFA, is the president of Grace & White, Inc., an investment counsel firm located in New York City. During the past 30 years he has engaged in numerous professional activities relating to the use of accounting information in making investment decisions. He is coauthor of *The Analysis and Use of Financial Statements, Third Edition* (John Wiley & Sons, 2003).

Jan R. Williams, PhD, CPA, is the Ernst & Young Professor and Dean, College of Business Administration, at the University of Tennessee. He is past president of the American Accounting Association and a frequent contributor to academic and professional literature on financial reporting and accounting education. Most recently he has been involved in the redesign of the CPA examination and is a frequent speaker on this and other topics of professional significance.

Alan J. Winters, PhD, CPA, is professor in the School of Accountancy and Legal Studies at Clemson University. Previously the director of auditing research at the AICPA, he has written many articles for professional and academic journals and an auditing textbook. He is a former member of the AICPA's Accounting and Review Services Committee.

Margaret M. Worthington, CPA, is a government contracts consultant. Prior to her retirement from PricewaterhouseCoopers LLP, she was a partner in the firm's Government Contract Consulting Services practice. She has over 35 years of experience in federal contracting matters. She is coauthor of *Contracting with the Federal Government, Fourth Edition* (John Wiley & Sons, 1998) and has published numerous articles on a variety of federal contracting topics. She earned her BS at UCLA.

Gerard L. Yarnall, CPA, is a partner in the New York Office Dispute Consulting and Forensic Investigations Practice of Deloitte & Touche LLP. Mr. Yarnall was previously Director of Audit and Accounting Publications at the AICPA. He has published and spoken frequently on a wide variety of accounting and auditing topics.

Michael W. Zelko, CPA/ABV is a Manager of the Business Valuation Department of Boles Metzger Brosius & Ritter PC. He joined the firm in 1987 as a member of the Professional staff. He works primarily with business valuation engagements and taxation issues.

PREFACE

The eleventh edition of *Accountants' Handbook* continues the tradition established in the first edition over 82 years ago of providing a comprehensive single reference source for understanding current financial statement and reporting issues. It is directed to accountants, auditors, executives, bankers, lawyers, and other preparers and users of accounting information. Its presentation and format facilitates the quick comprehension of complex accounting-related subjects updated for today's rapidly changing business environment.

This edition of the *Handbook* continues the presentation of two soft-cover volumes; this edition contains a total of 49 chapters. To provide a resource with the encyclopedic coverage that has been the hallmark of this *Handbook* series, this edition again focuses on financial accounting and related topics, including those auditing standards and audit reports that are the common ground of interest for accounting and business professionals.

In the period since the last edition we have witnessed the initial wave of changes to accounting and auditing standards in response to the bankruptcies and frauds that prompted the Sarbanes-Oxley Act of 2002. Issues of earnings management, off-the-balance-sheet related business entities, unrecognized liabilities and the expensing of stock option grants are the focus of reinvigorated standard setting. Similarly, sweeping changes in the auditing environment such as the newly required audits of internal control (see Chapter 5 and the new structures for regulating public company auditors that have been put in place. This edition of the *Handbook* places those events and changes in context, and provides transition and understanding of the events that have led up to these reforms.

This edition provides expanded chapters on fraud and fraud-related issues, as these topics have become more prominent in the business literature and in practice, and management and auditors have by law and regulation, assumed, greater responsibility for preventing and detecting fraud.

In the period since the last edition, the harmonization of accounting and auditing principles has become an important element in the direction of standards setting, both for accounting and auditing. Few major accounting or auditing standards projects are undertaken without involvement or collaboration with the international counterpart standards group. While some may be concerned that this process may slow the standards setting process somewhat, the greater input from a broader cross section of business environment and the broader focus of the standards that are being set, may indeed provide a firmer foundation for promulgating more comprehensive and enduring standards.

Although the FASB continues to be the primary source of authoritative accounting guidance, other sources of guidance are important in today's practice. Pronouncements by the SEC, GASB, and EITF are important, particularly in specialized areas. It is necessary to look to the EITF and to the AICPA audit and accounting guides for guidance in industry-related or special-transaction areas. All of those sources of accounting guidance are included in the scope of this edition of the *Handbook*.

This edition of the *Handbook* is divided into two convenient volumes:

Volume One: *Financial Accounting and General Topics* includes:

- A comprehensive review of the framework of accounting guidance today and the organizations involved in its development, including the development of international standards
- A compendium of specific guidance on general aspects of financial statement presentation, disclosure, and analysis, including SEC filing regulations

- Encyclopedic coverage of each specific financial statement area from cash through shareholders' equity, including coverage of financial instruments

Volume Two: *Special Industries and Special Topics* includes:

- Comprehensive single-source coverage of the specialized environmental and accounting considerations for key industries, including a chapter on the film industry
- Coverage of accounting standards applying to pension plans, retirement plans, and employee stock compensation and other capital accumulation plans
- Diverse topics, including reporting by partnerships, estates and trusts, and valuation, bankruptcy, and forensic accounting

The specialized expertise of the individual authors remains the critical element of this edition as it was in all prior editions. The editors worked closely with the authors, reviewing and critically editing their manuscripts. However, in the final analysis, each chapter is the work and viewpoint of the individual author or authors.

Content of the chapters in this edition have been prepared and/or reviewed by professionals practicing in accounting firms, financial executives, university professors, and financial analysts and executives. Every major international accounting firm is represented among the authors. These professionals bring to bear their own and their firms' experiences in dealing with accounting practice problems. All of the authors and technical reviewers are recognized authorities in their fields and have made significant contributions to the eleventh edition of the *Handbook*.

Our greatest debt is to the authors and reviewers of this edition. We deeply appreciate the value and importance of their time and efforts. We also acknowledge our debt to the editors of and contributors to ten earlier editions of the *Handbook*. This edition draws heavily on the accumulated knowledge of those earlier editions. Finally, we wish to thank John DeRemigis and Judy Howarth at John Wiley & Sons, Inc., for handling the many details of organizing and coordinating this effort.

For convenience, the pronoun "he" is used in this book to refer nonspecifically to the accountant and the business person. We intend this pronoun to include women.

D. R. Carmichael
R. Whittington
L. Graham

CONTENTS

CHAPTER **29**

OIL, GAS, AND OTHER NATURAL RESOURCES

Richard P. Graff, CPA

The Graff Consulting Group

Joseph B. Feiten, CPA

This chapter was updated from the Ninth Edition by Richard Graff and the editors.

29.1 INTRODUCTION

Accounting for oil and gas activities can be extremely complex because it encompasses a wide variety of business strategies and vehicles. The industry's diversity developed in response to the risk involved in the exploration process, the volatility of prices, and the fluctuations in supply and demand for oil and gas. In addition to having a working knowledge of accounting procedures, the oil and gas accountant should be familiar with the operating characteristics of companies involved in oil and gas activities and understand the impact of individual transactions.

Oil and gas activities cover a wide spectrum—ranging from exploration and production activities to the refining, transportation, and marketing of products to consumers. Special accounting rules exist for exploration and production activities. Accounting for refining activities is similar in many ways to other process manufacturing businesses. Likewise, transportation and marketing do not differ significantly from one end product to another. This chapter focuses on the special accounting rules for petroleum exploration and production.

The same may be said for the mining and processing of minerals except that the accounting rules for mineral exploration and production are not so formalized as for petroleum.

29.2 OIL AND GAS EXPLORATION AND PRODUCING OPERATIONS

Oil- and gas-producing activities begin with the search for prospects—parcels of acreage that management thinks may contain economically viable oil or gas formations. For the most likely prospects, the enterprise may contract with a geological and geophysical (G&G) company to test and assess the subsurface formations and their depths. Three-dimensional (3-D) seismic studies send sound waves thousands of feet below the earth's surface, record the million echoes from underground strata, and use powerful computers to read the echoes to create 3-D electronic images of the underground formations. With these ultrasounds of Mother Earth, the enterprise evaluates the various prospects, rejecting some and accepting others as suitable for acquisition of lease rights (prospecting may be done before or after obtaining lease rights).

Specialists called *landmen* may be used to obtain lease rights. A landman is in effect a lease broker who searches titles and negotiates with property owners. Although the landman may be part of the company's staff, oil and gas companies often acquire lease rights to properties through independent landmen. Consideration for leasing the mineral rights usually includes a bonus (an immediate cash payment to the lessor) and a royalty interest retained by the lessor (a specified percentage of subsequent production minus applicable production taxes).

Once the leases have been obtained and the rights and obligations of all parties have been determined, exploratory drilling begins. Because drilling costs run to hundreds of thousands or millions of dollars, many companies reduce their capital commitment and related risks by seeking others to participate in joint venture arrangements. Participants in a joint venture are called *joint interest owners*; one owner, usually the enterprise that obtained the leases, acts as operator. The operator manages the venture and reports to the other, nonoperator participants. The operator initially pays the drilling costs and then bills those costs to the nonoperators. In some cases, the operator may collect these costs from nonoperators in advance.

The operator acquires the necessary supplies and subcontracts with a drilling company for drilling the well. The drilling time may be a few days, several months, or even a year or longer depending on many factors, particularly well depth and location. When the hole reaches the desired depth, various instruments are lowered that "log the well" to detect the presence of oil or gas. The joint interest owners evaluate the drilling and logging results to determine whether sufficient oil or gas can be extracted to justify the cost of completing the well. If the evaluation is negative, the well is plugged and abandoned as a dry hole. If sufficient quantities of crude oil or natural gas (hydrocarbons) appear to be present, the well is completed and equipment is installed to extract and separate the hydrocarbons from the water coming from the underground reservoir. Completion costs are substantial and may even exceed the initial drilling costs.

Before production begins (sometimes even before the well is drilled), the enterprise selects oil and gas purchasers and negotiates sales contracts. To transport the oil or gas from the well, a trunk line may be built to the nearest major pipeline; crude oil also may be stored in tanks at the production site and removed later by truck. The production owner and purchasers prepare and sign division orders, which are revenue distribution contracts specifying each owner's share of revenues. If the division order specifies that the purchaser is to pay all revenues to the operator, the operator must distribute the appropriate amounts to the other joint interest owners and the lessor(s).

The various factors that determine the success or failure of oil and gas exploration activities include many uncertainties. These factors set the oil and gas industry apart from many other capital-intensive industries. Some of these factors include the following:

- *Anticipated Success of Drilling.* Even with the recent technological advances in 3-D seismic, there is still substantial risk of not finding a commercial petroleum reservoir after spending hundreds of thousands of dollars (or more) drilling a well to the target formation. Exploration success is also affected by drilling risks such as stuck drill pipes, blowouts, and improper completions.

- *Taxation.* A substantial portion of the revenues from the sale of crude oil and natural gas goes directly or indirectly to the federal and state governments in the form of severance taxes, ad valorem taxes, and income taxes. In the late 1970s, Congress enacted the Windfall Profit Tax on domestic crude oil. On August 25, 1988, the Windfall Profit Tax was repealed for all crude oil removed after that date. After the various taxes, royalties to the landowner, and production costs have been deducted, the producer's income from the sale of crude oil and natural gas may be only a small percentage of gross revenues. Except for certain tax credits relating to "Tight Sands" and coalbed methane gas production, most tax-related incentives have been eliminated through tax legislation since 1986.

- *Product Price and Marketability.* U.S. crude oil production meets only half of the country's demand and is readily marketable. The United States imports crude oil from Venezuela, Canada, and other countries. For the past several years, U.S. prices of crude oil have fluctuated widely due to numerous factors including world politics, economic conditions, and technology advances. High-quality crude oil sold for $42 per barrel in late 1979, $12 briefly in 1986, $40 briefly in 1990, in the $20 range in 1991, $18 at the end of 1995, $24 at the end of 1996, $15.50 at the end of 1997, and under $14 by spring of 1997. Oil prices also vary due to the quality of the oil and the location of the oil field. In a given month, heavy sour crude oil in California may sell for half or two-thirds the price of light, sweet crude oil produced in Oklahoma.

  In the 1990s, natural gas price volatility exceeded that of crude oil. U.S. natural gas production met substantially all of the country's needs, after competition from gas imported from Canada. Demand for natural gas is seasonal in the United States—high in the winter months for space heating and low in the summer for most areas of the country. Significant quantities of gas produced in the summer are transported by pipelines to underground formations for temporary storage until the winter season. Such temporary storage helps to reduce the seasonal price fluctuations.

  Because of the volatility in oil and gas prices, a number of price hedging mechanisms have been developed, including futures contracts, long-term hedging arrangements, and product swaps.

- *Timing of Production.* How quickly oil and gas are produced directly affects the payback period of an investment and its financial success or failure. The timing of production varies with the geologic characteristics of the reservoir and the marketability of the product. Reservoirs may contain the same gross producible reserves, yet the timing of production causes significant differences in the present value of the future revenue stream.

- *Acreage and Drilling Costs.* Many U.S. companies are focusing on exploration outside the United States. The United States is a mature exploration area producing 10 percent of the world's oil production from 63 percent of the world's oil wells. The global availability of quality exploration acreage, drilling personnel, and supplies has increased, whereas the related costs have dropped significantly since the boom period of the late 1970s and early 1980s.

29.3 ACCOUNTING FOR JOINT OPERATIONS

Oil- and gas-producing activities are recorded in the same general manner as most other activities that use manual or automated revenue, accounts payable, and general ledger systems. There are significant differences in the data gathering and reporting requirements, however, depending on whether the entity is an operator or a nonoperator for a given joint venture. The two major accounting systems unique to oil- and gas-producing activities are the joint interest billing system and the revenue distribution system. The operator's joint interest billing system must properly calculate and record the operator's net cost as well as the costs to be billed to the nonoperators. Likewise, the revenue distribution system should properly allocate cash receipts among venture participants; this entails first recording the amounts payable to the participants and later making the appropriate payments.

As discussed previously, joint interest operations evolved because of the need to share the financial burden and risks of oil- and gas-producing activities. Joint operations typically take the form of a simple joint venture evidenced by two formal agreements, generally referred to as an *exploration agreement* and an *operating agreement*. These agreements define the geographic area involved, designate which party will act as operator of the venture, define how revenue and expenses will be divided, and set forth the rights and responsibilities of all parties to the agreement. The operating agreement also establishes how the operator is to bill the nonoperators for joint venture expenditures and provides nonoperators with the right to conduct "joint interest audits" of the operator's accounting records.

Accounting for joint operations is basically the same as accounting for operations when a property is completely owned by one party, except that in joint operations, revenues and expenses are divided among all of the joint venture partners. The following section discusses accounting for joint operations, first from the operator's standpoint and then from the nonoperators' perspective.

(a) OPERATOR ACCOUNTING.   The operator typically records revenue and expenses for a well on a 100 percent, or "gross," basis and then allocates the revenue and expenses to the nonoperators based on ownership percentages maintained in the division order and joint interest master files. One approach is to record the full invoice or remittance advice amount and use contra or clearing accounts that set up the amounts due from or to the nonoperators. Recording transactions by means of contra accounts facilitates generation of information that management uses to review operations on a gross basis.

Before drilling and completing a well, the operator prepares an authorization for expenditure (AFE) itemizing the estimated costs to drill and complete the well. Although AFEs are normally required by the operating agreement, they are so useful as a capital budgeting tool that they are routinely used for all major expenditures by oil and gas companies, even if no joint venture exists. In addition to AFEs, the operator's field supervisor or engineer at the well site prepares a daily drilling report, which is an abbreviated report of the current status and the drilling or completion activity of the past 24 hours. That report may be compared with a drilling report prepared by the drilling company (also called a *tour* report). Some daily drilling reports indicate estimated cumulative costs incurred to date.

For shallow wells that are quickly and easily drilled, the AFE subsidiary ledger, combined with the daily drilling report, may provide the basis for the operator's estimate of costs incurred but not invoiced. For other wells, however, the engineering department prepares an estimate of cumulative costs incurred through year end as a basis for recording the accrual and, if material, the commitments for future expenditures.

The operator normally furnishes the nonoperators with a monthly summary billing that shows the amount owed the operator on a property-by-property basis. The summary billing is accompanied by a separate joint operating statement for each property. The joint operating statement contains a description of each expenditure and shows the total expenditures for the property. The statement also shows the allocation of expenditures among the joint interest participants. The operator usually does not furnish copies of third-party invoices supporting items appearing on the joint interest billing, but the third-party invoices can be examined and copied during the nonoperators' audit of the joint account. The operator may also furnish the nonoperators a production report and at a later date remit checks to the nonoperators for their share of production.

(b) NONOPERATOR ACCOUNTING. From the nonoperators' standpoint, the accounting for joint operations is basically the same as that followed by the operator. It is not unusual for a company to act as an operator on some properties and a nonoperator on others. To be able to make comparisons and evaluations that include both types of properties, nonoperators should also record items on a gross basis. A nonoperator should develop a control procedure for reviewing the joint operating statement to determine whether the operator is complying with the joint operating agreement, is billing the nonoperator only valid charges at the appropriate percentages, and is distributing the appropriate share of revenue.

(c) OTHER ACCOUNTING PROCEDURES. The operating agreement may permit the operator to charge the joint venture a monthly fixed fee to cover its internal costs incurred in operating the joint venture. Alternatively, the agreement may provide for reimbursement of the operator's actual costs.

The parties in a joint operation may agree either to share costs in a proportion that is different from that used for sharing revenue or to change the sharing percentages after a specific event takes place. Typically, that event is "payout," the point at which certain venturers have recovered their initial investment or an agreed-upon multiple of the investment. All parties involved in joint operations encounter payout situations at some time. Controls must be designed to monitor payout status to ensure that all parties are satisfied that revenues and costs have been properly allocated in accordance with the joint operating agreement.

(d) OVERVIEW OF ACCOUNTING STANDARDS. The following pronouncements set forth generally accepted accounting principles (GAAP) unique to oil and gas producing activities:

- Statement of Financial Accounting Standards (SFAS) No. 19, which describes a "successful efforts" method of accounting
- SFAS No. 25, which recognizes that other methods may be appropriate
- Securities and Exchange Commission (SEC) Regulation S-X, Article 4, Section 10 (also referred to as *S-X Rule 4-10*), which prescribes two acceptable methods for public entities—either the successful efforts method described in SFAS No. 19 or a "full cost" method, as described in S-X Rule 4-10
- SFAS No. 69, which requires supplementary disclosures of oil- and gas-producing activities

Additional guidance and interpretations are found in Financial Accounting Standards Board (FASB) Interpretations, SEC Staff Accounting Bulletins (SABs), surveys in industry accounting practices, and petroleum accounting journals and petroleum accounting textbooks.

The primary differences between the successful efforts and full cost methods center around costs to be capitalized and those to be expensed. As the name implies, under the successful efforts method, only those costs that lead to the successful discovery of reserves are capitalized, while the costs of unsuccessful exploratory activities are charged directly to expense. Under the full cost method, all exploration efforts are treated as capital costs under the theory that the reserves found are the result of all costs incurred. Both methods are widely used; however, larger companies tend to follow the successful efforts method.

Under income tax law and regulations, all exploration and development costs, except leasehold and equipment costs, are generally expensed as incurred. Petroleum producing companies with significant refining or marketing activities (called *integrateds* as opposed to "independents") must capitalize 30 percent of intangible well costs to be amortized over 60 months. Leasehold costs are expensed by complex depletion deductions that, for independents, can exceed actual costs. Equipment costs are depreciated using accelerated methods. Many independent U.S. oil- and gas-producing companies pay the alternative minimum tax.

29.4 ACCEPTABLE ACCOUNTING METHODS

(a) THE SUCCESSFUL EFFORTS METHOD.

(i) Basic Rules. The following points summarize the major aspects of the *successful efforts method* of accounting for oil and gas property costs:

- The costs of all G&G studies to find reserves are charged to expense as incurred.
- Lease acquisition costs for unproved properties are initially capitalized. Unproved properties are those on which no economically recoverable oil or gas has been demonstrated to exist. Unproved properties are to be assessed for impairment at least annually.
- If an unproved property becomes impaired because of such events as pending lease expiration or an unsuccessful exploratory well (dry hole), the loss is recognized and a valuation allowance is established to reflect the property's impairment. Two approaches to impairment are used: (1) Property by property (typically used by small companies or situations involving significant acreage costs), or (2) a formula approach based on factors such as historical success ratios and average lease terms (typically used by larger companies with a significant number of smaller properties).
- Once proved reserves are found on a property, the property is considered proved and the acquisition costs are amortized on a unit-of-production basis over the property's producing life based on total proved reserves (both developed and undeveloped reserves). The SFAS No. 25 definition of proved reserves may be summarized as the estimated volumes of oil and gas that geological and engineering data demonstrate with reasonable certainty to be recoverable in future years from known reservoirs under existing economic and operating conditions.
- If both oil and gas are produced from the property, the unit is normally equivalent barrels or mcfs, whereby gas is converted to equivalent barrels (or barrels are converted to equivalent mcfs) based on relative energy content. A common conversion factor is 5.6 mcf to 1 equivalent barrel.
- For a property containing both oil and gas, the unit may reflect either oil or gas if:
  - The relative property of oil and gas extracted in the current period is expected to continue in the future, or
  - The reflected mineral clearly dominates the other for both current production and reserves.
- Carrying costs required to retain rights to unproved properties (delay rentals, ad valorem taxes, etc.) are charged to expense.
- Exploratory wells are capitalized initially as wells-in-progress and expensed if proved reserves are not found. Successful exploratory wells are capitalized, as are their completion costs (setting casing and other costs necessary to begin producing the well).
- Costs of drilling development wells (even the rare dry ones) are capitalized.

- Costs of successful exploratory wells, along with the costs of drilling development wells on the lease, are amortized on a unit-of-production basis over the property's proved developed reserves on:
  - ○ A property-by-property basis, or
  - ○ The basis of some reasonable aggregation of properties with a common geologic or structural feature or stratigraphic condition, such as a reservoir or field.
- Once production has begun, all regular production costs are charged to expense.
- Capitalized interest, under the requirements of SFAS 34, would also be capitalized as part of the cost of unevaluated properties during the evaluation phase.

(ii) Exploratory versus Development Well Definition. Because Reg. S-X requires that the costs of dry exploratory wells be charged to expense, whereas the costs of dry development wells are capitalized, it is important to properly classify wells. Regulation S-X Rule 4-10, defines the two categories of wells as follows:

1. *Development Well.* A well drilled within the proved area of an oil or gas reservoir to the depth of a stratigraphic horizon known to be productive.
2. *Exploratory Well.* A well drilled to find and produce oil or gas in an unproved area, to find a new reservoir in a field previously found to be productive of oil or gas in another reservoir, or to extend a known reservoir. Generally, an exploratory well is any well that is not a development well, a service well, or a stratigraphic test well.

These definitions may not coincide with those that have been commonly used in the industry (typically, the industry definition of a development well is more liberal than Reg. S-X, Rule 4-10). This results in two problems:

1. Improper classification of certain exploratory dry holes as development wells (the problem occurs primarily with stepout or delineation wells drilled at the edge of a producing reservoir)
2. Inconsistencies between the drilling statistics found in the forepart of Form 10-K (usually prepared by operational personnel) and the supplementary financial statement information required by SFAS No. 69 (usually prepared by accounting personnel)

(iii) Treatment of Costs of Exploratory Wells Whose Outcome Is Undetermined. As set out below, SFAS No. 19 effectively curtails extended deferral of the costs of an exploratory well whose outcome has not yet been determined.

Accounting When Drilling of an Exploration Well Is Completed.

Par. 31: ... the costs of drilling an exploratory well are capitalized as part of the enterprise's uncompleted wells, equipment, and facilities pending determination of whether the well has found proved reserves. That determination is usually made on or shortly after completion of drilling the well, and the capitalized costs shall either be charged to expense or be reclassified as part of the costs of the enterprise's wells and related equipment and facilities at that time. Occasionally, however, an exploratory well may be determined to have found oil and gas reserves, but classification of those reserves as proved cannot be made when drilling is completed. In those cases, one or the other of the following subparagraphs shall apply depending on whether the well is drilled in an area requiring a major capital expenditure, such as a trunk pipeline, before production from that well could begin:

a. Exploratory wells that find oil and gas reserves in an area requiring a major capital expenditure, such as a trunk pipeline, before production could begin. On completion of drilling, an exploratory well may be determined to have found oil and gas reserves, but classification of those reserves as proved depends on whether a major capital expenditure can be justified which, in turn, depends on whether additional exploratory wells find a sufficient quantity of additional reserves. That situation arises principally with exploratory wells drilled in a remote area for which production would require constructing a trunk pipeline. In that case, the cost of drilling the exploratory well shall continue to be carried as an asset pending determination of whether proved reserves have been found only as long as both of the following conditions are met:

(1) The well has found a sufficient quantity of reserves to justify its completion as a producing well if the required capital expenditure is made.

(2) Drilling of the additional exploratory wells is under way or firmly planned for the near future.

Thus, if drilling in the area is not under way or firmly planned, or if the well has not found a commercially producible quantity of reserves, the exploratory well shall be assumed to be impaired, and its costs shall be charged to expense.

b. All other exploratory wells that find oil and gas reserves. In the absence of a determination as to whether the reserves that have been found can be classified as proved, the costs of drilling such an exploratory well shall not be carried as an asset for more than one year following completion of drilling. If, after that year has passed, a determination that proved reserves have been found cannot be made, the well shall be assumed to be impaired, and its costs shall be charged to expense.

Par 32: Paragraph 32 is intended to prohibit, in all cases, the deferral of the costs of exploratory wells that find some oil and gas reserves merely on the chance that some event totally beyond the control of the enterprise will occur, for example, on the chance that the selling prices of oil and gas will increase sufficiently to result in classification of reserves as proved that are not commercially recoverable at current prices.

Accounting When Drilling of an Exploratory-Type Stratigraphic Test Well Is Completed.

Par 33: As specified in paragraph 110, the costs of drilling an exploratory-type stratigraphic test well are capitalized as part of the enterprise's uncompleted wells, equipment, and facilities pending determination of whether the well has found proved reserves. When that determination is made, the capitalized costs shall be charged to expense if proved reserves are not found or shall be reclassified as part of the costs of the enterprise's wells and related equipment and facilities if proved reserves are found.

Par 34: Exploratory-type stratigraphic test wells are normally drilled on unproved offshore properties. Frequently, on completion of drilling, such a well may be determined to have found oil and gas reserves, but classification of those reserves as proved depends on whether a major capital expenditure—usually a production platform—can be justified which, in turn, depends on whether additional exploratory-type stratigraphic test wells find a sufficient quantity of additional reserves. In that case, the cost of drilling the exploratory-type stratigraphic test well shall continue to be carried as an asset pending determination of whether proved reserves have been found only as long as both of the following conditions are met:

(1) The well has found a quantity of reserves that would justify its completion for production had it not been simply a stratigraphic test well.

(2) Drilling of the additional exploratory-type stratigraphic test wells is under way or firmly planned for the near future.

Thus, if associated stratigraphic test drilling is not under way or firmly planned, or if the well has not found a commercially producible quantity of reserves, the exploratory-type stratigraphic test well shall be assumed to be impaired, and its costs shall be charged to expense.

(iv) Successful Efforts Impairment Test.   SFAS No. 121 on impairment of long-lived assets amends SFAS No. 19 and requires application of SFAS No. 121 impairment rules to capitalized costs of proved oil and gas properties for companies following the successful efforts method of accounting.

(v) Conveyances. SFAS No. 19 and Reg. S-X Rule 4-10(m) provides rules to account for mineral property conveyances and related transactions. Conveyances of "production payments" repayable in fixed monetary terms, that is, loans in substance, are accounted for as loans. Conveyances of production payments repayable in fixed production volumes from specified production are deemed to be property sales whereby proved reserves are reduced but the proceeds from sale of a production payment are credited to deferred revenue to be recognized as revenue as the seller delivers future petroleum volumes to the holder of the production payment. Gain or loss is not recognized for conveyances of (1) a pooling of assets in a joint venture to find, develop, or produce oil and gas or (2) such assets in exchange for other assets used in oil- and gas-producing activities. Gain is not recognized (but loss is) for conveyance of a partial property interest when substantial uncertainty exists as to the recovery of costs for the retained interest portion or when the seller has substantial obligation for future performance such as drilling a well. For other conveyances, gain or loss is recognized unless prohibited under accounting principles applicable to enterprises in general.

(b) THE FULL COST METHOD.

(i) Basic Rules. Under Reg. S-X Rule 4-10, oil and gas property costs are accounted for as follows:

- All costs associated with property acquisition, exploration and development activities shall be capitalized by *country-wide* cost center. Any internal costs that are capitalized shall be limited to those costs that can be *directly* identified with the acquisition, exploration and development activities undertaken by the reporting entity for its own account, and shall not include any costs related to production, general corporate overhead or similar activities.
- Capitalized costs within a cost center shall be amortized on the unit-of-production basis using proved oil and gas reserves, as follows:
  - Costs to be amortized shall include (A) all capitalized costs, less accumulated amortization, excluding the cost of certain unevaluated properties not being amortized; (B) the estimated future expenditures (based on current costs) to be incurred in developing proved reserves; and (C) estimated dismantlement and abandonment costs, net of estimated salvage values. [The current rule is referring to undiscounted future decommissioning, restoration and abandonment costs, net of estimated salvage values ("net abandonment costs"). In early 1996, the FASB issued an exposure draft for a proposed SFAS on accounting for certain liabilities related to closure or removal of long-lived assets. If adopted as drafted, the new SFAS would amortize capitalized costs that include a charge corresponding to the accrued liability for net abandonment costs. The liability reflects a present value discounted at a safe rate of interest.]
  - Amortization shall be computed on the basis of physical units, with oil and gas converted to a common unit of measure on the basis of their approximate relative energy content, unless economic circumstances (related to the effects of regulated prices) indicated that use of revenue is a more appropriate basis of computing amortization. In the latter case, amortization shall be computed on the basis of current gross revenues from production in relation to future gross revenues (excluding royalty payments and net profits disbursements) based on current prices from estimated future production of proved oil and gas reserves (including consideration of changes in existing prices provided for only by contractual arrangements). The effect on estimated future gross revenues of a significant price increase during the year shall be reflected in the amortization provision only for the period after the price increase occurs.

  In some cases it may be more appropriate to depreciate natural gas cycling and processing plants by a method other than the unit-of-production method.

Amortization computations shall be made on a consolidated basis, including investees accounted for on a proportionate consolidation basis. Investees accounted for on the equity method shall be treated separately.

(ii) Exclusion of Costs from Amortization.   SEC Financial Report Reg. S-X Rule 4-10, allows two alternatives:

1. Immediate inclusion of all costs incurred in the amortization base
2. Temporary exclusion of *all* acquisition and exploration costs incurred that directly relate to unevaluated properties and certain costs of major development projects

Unevaluated properties are defined as those for which no determination has been made of the existence or nonexistence of proved reserves. Costs that may be excluded are all those costs directly related to the unevaluated properties (i.e., leasehold acquisitions costs, delay rentals, G&G, exploratory drilling, and capitalized interest). The cost of exploratory dry holes should be included in the amortization base as soon as the well is deemed dry.

These excluded costs must be assessed for impairment annually, either:

- Individually for each significant property (i.e., capitalized cost exceeds 10 percent of the net full cost pool), or
- In the aggregate for insignificant properties (i.e., by transferring the excluded property costs into the amortization base ratably on the basis of such factors as the primary lease terms of the properties, the average holding period, and the relative proportion of properties on which proved reserves have been found previously).

(iii) The Full Cost Ceiling Test.   SFAS No. 121 impairment rules are effectively superseded by the following full cost "ceiling test" specified in Reg. S-X Rule 4-10(e)(4):

- For each cost center capitalized costs, less accumulated amortization and related deferred income taxes, shall not exceed an amount (the cost center ceiling) equal to the sum of:

   (A) The present value of estimated future net revenues computed by applying current prices of oil and gas reserves (with consideration of price changes only to the extent provided by contractual arrangements) to estimated future production of proved oil and gas reserves as of the date of the latest balance sheet presented, less estimated future expenditures (based on current costs) to be incurred in developing and producing the proved reserves computed using a discount factor of ten percent and assuming continuation of existing economic conditions; plus (B) the cost of properties not being amortized pursuant to paragraph (c)(3)(ii) of this section; plus (C) the lower of cost or estimated fair value of unproven properties included in the costs being amortized; less (D) income tax effects related to differences between the book and tax basis of the properties referred to in paragraphs (c)(4)(i)(B) and (C) of this section.

- If unamortized costs capitalized within a cost center, less related deferred income taxes, exceed the cost center ceiling, the excess shall be charged to expense and separately disclosed during the period in which the excess occurs. Amounts thus required to be written off shall not be reinstated for any subsequent increase in the cost center ceiling.

Part D, income tax effects, is poorly worded and refers to the income tax effects related to the ceiling components in parts A, B, and C allowing for consideration of the oil and gas properties' tax bases and related depletion carryforwards and related net operating loss carryforwards.

Two other unique aspects of the full cost ceiling test are:

1. *Ceiling Test Exemption for Purchases of Proved Properties.* A petroleum producing company might purchase proved properties for more than the present value of estimated future net revenues, causing net capitalized costs to exceed the cost center ceiling on the date of purchase.

To avoid the write down, the company may request from the SEC staff a temporary (usually one year) waiver of applying the ceiling test. The company must be prepared to demonstrate that the purchased properties' additional value exists beyond reasonable doubt. For more details see SAB No. 47, Topic 12, D-3a.

2. *Effect of Subsequent Event.* If, after year end but prior to the audit report date, either (a) additional reserves are proved up on properties owned at year end, or (b) price increases become known, then such subsequent events may be considered in the year-end ceiling test to mitigate a write down of capitalized costs.

The avoidance of a writedown must be adequately disclosed, but the subsequent events should not be considered in the required disclosures of the company's proved reserves and standardized measure of discounted future net cash flows relating to such reserves (as further described here in Section 29.11, "Financial Statement Disclosures"). For more details, see SAB No. 47, Topic 12, D-3b.

(iv) Conveyances.   Reg. S-X, Rule 4-10(c)(6), provides that accounting for conveyances will be the same as for successful efforts accounting except that sales of oil and gas properties are to be accounted for as adjustments of capitalized costs with no recognition of gain or loss ("unless such adjustments would significantly alter the relationship between capitalized costs and proved reserves"). Exceptions are also made in some circumstances for property sales to partnerships and joint ventures in that (1) proceeds that are reimbursements of identifiable, current transaction expenses may be credited to income and (2) a petroleum company may recognize in income "management fees" from certain types of managed limited partnerships. When a company acquires an oil and gas property interest in exchange for services (such as drilling wells), income may be recognized in limited circumstances.

29.5 ACCOUNTING FOR NATURAL GAS IMBALANCES

Accounting techniques are basically the same whether revenue is generated by selling crude oil or natural gas. However, joint venture participants usually sell their crude oil collectively but may individually market and sell their shares of natural gas production. When a joint venture owner physically takes and sells more or less gas than its entitled share, a "gas imbalance" is created that is later reversed by an equal, but opposite, imbalance or by settlement in cash.

For example, if two joint venture participants each own 50 percent working interests in a well, and one company decides to sell gas on the spot market but the other company declines to sell due to a low spot price (or other factors), the company selling gas will receive 100 percent of revenue after paying the royalty interests. The selling company is in an overproduced capacity with respect to the well (the company is entitled to 50 percent of the gas after royalties but had received 100 percent). A gas imbalance can also occur between a gas producer and the gas transmission company that receives the producer's gas but delivers a different volume to the producer's customer.

Gas-producing companies account for gas imbalances under either the sales method or the entitlements method.

(a) SALES METHOD.   Under the sales method, the company recognizes revenue and a receivable for the volume of gas sold, regardless of ownership of the property. For example, if Company A owns a 50 percent net revenue interest in a gas property but sells 100 percent of the production in a given month, the company would recognize 100 percent of the revenue generated. In a subsequent month, if Company A sells no gas (and the other owners "make up" the imbalance), Company A would recognize zero revenue. Company A would reduce its estimate of proved reserves for any future production that it must give up to meet a gas imbalance obligation and increase proved reserves for any additional future production it has a right to receive from other joint venture participants to eliminate an existing gas imbalance.

Although this method is rather simple from a revenue accounting standpoint, it presents other problems. Regardless of the revenue method chosen, the operator will issue joint interest billing statements for expenses based on the ownership of the property. Depending on the gas-balancing situation, the sales method may present a problem with the matching of revenues and expenses in a period. If a significant imbalance exists at the end of an accounting period, the accountant may be required to analyze the situation and record additional expenses (or reduce expenses depending on whether the property is overproduced or underproduced).

(b) ENTITLEMENTS METHOD.   Under the entitlements method, the company recognizes revenue based on the volume of sales to which it is entitled by its ownership interest. For example, if Company A owns a 50 percent net revenue interest but sells 100 percent of the production in a given month, the company would recognize 50 percent of the revenue generated. Company A would recognize a receivable for 100 percent of the revenue with the difference being recorded in a payable (or deferred revenue) account. When the imbalance is corrected, the payable account will become zero, thus indicating that the property is "in balance."

This method correctly matches revenues and expenses but presents another accounting issue. If a property is significantly imbalanced, Company A may find itself in a position that reserves are insufficient to bring the well back to a balanced condition. If Company A is underproduced in this situation, a receivable (or deferred charge) may be recorded in the asset category that has a questionable realization. In addition, the company is really under- or overproduced in terms of volumes (measured in cubic feet) of gas. A value per cubic foot is assigned based on the sale price at the period of imbalance. If the price is significantly different when the correction occurs, the receivable may not show a zero balance in the accounting records.

(c) GAS BALANCING EXAMPLE.

Facts: Company A owns a 50 percent net revenue.
Gas sales for January are 5,000 mcf @ $2.00 per Mcf.
Gas sales for February are 5,000 mcf @ $2.00 per Mcf.
In January, Company A sells 100 percent of gas production to its purchaser.
In February, Company A sells zero gas to its purchaser.

JANUARY ACCOUNTING ENTRIES

Under the Sales Method	Debit	Credit
Accounts receivable, gas sales	$10,000	
Gas revenue		$10,000
Under the Entitlements Method		
Accounts receivable, gas sales	$10,000	
Gas revenue		$ 5,000
Payable		$ 5,000

FEBRUARY ACCOUNTING ENTRIES

Under the Sales Method	No entries are recorded	
Under the Entitlements Method		
Payable	$ 5,000	
Gas revenue		$ 5,000

29.6 HARD-ROCK MINING

(a) MINING OPERATIONS.   The principal difference between hard-rock mining companies and companies involved in oil- and gas-producing activities, previously discussed in this chapter, relates to the nature, timing, and extent of expenditures incurred for exploration, development, production, and processing of minerals.

Generally in the mining industry, a period of as long as several years elapses between the time exploration costs are incurred to discover a commercially viable body of ore and the expenditure of development costs, which are usually substantial, to complete the project. Therefore, the economic benefits derived from a project are long term and subject to the uncertainties inherent in the passage of time. In contrast, the costs related to exploring for deposits of oil and gas are expended generally over a relatively short time. Major exceptions would be offshore and foreign petroleum exploration and development.

Like petroleum exploration and production, the mining industry is capital intensive. Substantial investments in property, plant, and equipment are required; usually they represent more than 50 percent of a mining company's total assets. The significant capital investments of mining companies and the related risks inherent in any long-term major project may affect the recoverability of capitalized costs.

The operational stages in mining companies vary somewhat depending on the type of mineral, because of differences in geological, chemical, and economic factors. The basic operations common to mining companies are exploration, development, mining, milling, smelting, and refining.

Exploration is the search for natural accumulations of minerals with economic value. Exploration for minerals is a specialized activity involving the use of complex geophysical and geochemical equipment and procedures. There is an element of financial risk in every decision to pursue exploration, and explorers generally seek to minimize the costs and increase the probability of success. As a result, before any fieldwork begins, extensive studies are made concerning which types of minerals are to be sought and where they are most likely to occur. Market studies and forecasts, studies of geological maps and reports, and logistical evaluations are performed to provide information for use in determining the economic feasibility of a potential project.

Exploration can be divided into two phases, prospecting and geophysical analysis. *Prospecting* is the search for geological information over a broad area. It embraces such activities as geological mapping, analysis of rock types and structures, searches for direct manifestations of mineralization, taking samples of minerals found, and aeromagnetic surveys. *Geophysical analysis* is conducted in specific areas of interest localized during the prospecting phase. Rock and soil samples are examined, and the earth's crust is monitored directly for magnetic, gravitational, sonic, radioactive, and electrical data. Based on the analysis, targets for trenching, test pits, and exploratory drilling are identified. Drilling is particularly useful in evaluating the shape and character of a deposit. Analysis of samples is necessary to determine the grade of the deposit.

Once the grade and quantity of the deposit have been estimated, the mining company must decide whether developing the deposit is technically feasible and commercially viable. The value of a mineral deposit is determined by the intrinsic value of the minerals present and by the nature and location of their occurrence. In addition to the grade and quality of the ore, such factors as the physical accessibility of the deposit, the estimated costs of production, and the value of joint products and by-products are key elements in the decision to develop a deposit for commercial exploitation.

The *development* stage of production involves planning and preparing for commercial operation. Development of surface mines is relatively straightforward. For open-pit mines, which are surface mines, the principal procedure is to remove sufficient overburden to expose the ore. For strip mines, an initial cut is made to expose the mineral to be mined. For underground mines, data resulting from exploratory drilling is evaluated as a basis for planning the shafts and tunnels that will provide access to the mineral deposit.

Substantial capital investment in mineral rights, machinery and equipment, and related facilities generally is required in the development stage.

Mining breaks up the rock and ore to the extent necessary for loading and removal to the processing location. A variety of mining techniques exists to accomplish this. The drilling and blasting technique is utilized frequently; an alternative is the continuous mining method, in which a boring or tearing machine is mounted on a forward crawler to break the material away from the rock face.

After removal from the mine site, the ore is ready for *milling*. The first phase of the milling stage involves crushing and grinding the chunks of ore to reduce them to particle size. The second milling procedure is concentration, which involves the separation of the mineral constituents from the rock.

Smelting is the process of separating the metal from impurities with which it may be chemically bound or physically mixed too closely to be removed by concentration. Most smelting is accomplished through fusion, which is the liquefaction of a metal under heat. In some cases, chemical processes are used instead of, or in combination with, heating techniques.

Refining is the last step in isolating the metal. The primary methods utilized are fire refining and electrolytic refining. Fire refining is similar to smelting. The metal is kept in a molten state and treated with pine logs, hydrocarbon gas, or other substances to enable impurities to be removed. Fire refining generally does not allow the recovery of by-products. Electrolytic refining uses an electrical current to separate metals from a solution in such a way that by-products can be recovered.

(b) SOURCES OF GENERALLY ACCEPTED ACCOUNTING PRINCIPLES.   Accounting and reporting issues in the mining industry are discussed in American Institute of Certified Public Accountants (AICPA) Accounting Research Study No. 11, "Financial Reporting in the Extractive Industries" (1969). In 1976, the FASB issued a discussion memorandum, "Financial Accounting and Reporting in the Extractive Industries," which analyzed issues relevant to the extractive industries. Neither of these attempts, however, culminated in the issuance of an authoritative pronouncement for mining companies. SFAS No. 19, "Financial Accounting and Reporting by Oil and Gas Producing Companies," established standards of financial accounting and reporting for companies that are engaged in oil and gas exploration, development, and production activities. As this publication goes to print, a steering committee of the International Accounting Standards Steering Board has produced an issues paper as the first stage in the development of international accounting standards in the mining industry. Absent accounting standards specific to the mining industry, mining companies rely on the guidance provided by authoritative pronouncements, the specific GAAP guidance in SFAS No. 19 for natural resource companies engaged in exploration, development, and production of oil and gas, and the accounting policies followed by mining companies as the basis for GAAP in the mining industry.

29.7 ACCOUNTING FOR MINING COSTS

(a) EXPLORATION AND DEVELOPMENT COSTS.   Exploration and development costs are major expenditures of mining companies. The characterization of expenditures as exploration, development, or production usually determines whether such costs are capitalized or expensed. For accounting purposes, it is useful to identify five basic phases of exploration and development: prospecting, property acquisition, geophysical analysis, development before production, and development during production.

Prospecting usually begins with obtaining (or preparing) and studying topographical and geological maps. Prospecting costs, which are generally expensed as incurred, include (1) options to lease or buy property; (2) rights of access to lands for geophysical work; and (3) salaries, equipment, and supplies for scouts, geologists, and geophysical crews.

Property acquisition includes both the purchase of property and the purchase or lease of mineral rights. Costs incurred to purchase land (including mineral rights and surface rights) or to lease mineral rights are capitalized. Acquisition costs may include lease bonus and lease extension costs, lease brokers commissions, abstract and recording fees, filing and patent fees, and other related expenses.

Geophysical analysis is conducted to identify mineralization. The related costs are generally expensed as exploration costs when incurred. Examples of exploration costs include exploratory drilling, geological mapping, and salaries and supplies for geologists and support personnel.

A body of ore reaches the development stage when the existence of an economically and legally recoverable mineral reserve has been established through the completion of a feasibility study. Costs incurred in the development stage before production begins are capitalized. Development costs include expenditures associated with drilling, removing overburden (waste rock), sinking shafts, driving tunnels, building roads and dikes, purchasing processing equipment and equipment used in developing the mine, and constructing supporting facilities to house and care for the workforce. In many respects, the expenditures in the development stage are similar to those incurred during exploration. As a result, it is sometimes difficult to distinguish the point at which exploration ends and development begins. For example, the sinking of shafts and driving of tunnels may begin in the exploration stage and continue into the development stage. In most instances, the transition from the exploration to the development stage is the same for both accounting and tax purposes.

Development also takes place during the production stage. The accounting treatment of development costs incurred during the ongoing operation of a mine depends on the nature and purpose of the expenditures. Costs associated with expansion of capacity are generally capitalized; costs incurred to maintain production are normally included in production costs in the period in which they are incurred. In certain instances, the benefits of development activity will be realized in future periods, such as when the "block caving" and open-pit mining methods are used. In the block caving method, entire sections of a body of ore are intentionally collapsed to permit the mass removal of minerals; extraction may take place two to three years after access to the ore is gained and the block prepared. In an open-pit mine, there is typically an expected ratio of overburden to mineral-bearing ore over the life of the mine. The cost of stripping the overburden to gain access to the ore is expensed in those periods in which the actual ratio of overburden to ore approximates the expected ratio. In certain instances, however, extensive stripping is performed to remove the overburden in advance of the period in which the ore will be extracted. When the benefits of either development activity are to be realized in a future accounting period, the costs associated with the development activity should be deferred and amortized during the period in which the ore is extracted or the product produced.

SFAS No. 7, "Accounting and Reporting by Development Stage Enterprises" (Accounting Standards Section D04), states that "an enterprise shall be considered to be in the development stage if it is devoting substantially all of its efforts to establishing a new business" and "the planned principal operations have not commenced" or they "have commenced, but there has been no significant revenue therefrom." Although SFAS No. 7 specifically excludes mining companies from its application, the definition of a development stage enterprise is helpful in defining the point in time at which a mine's development phase ends and its production phase begins. It is not uncommon for incidental and/or insignificant mineral production to occur before either economic production per the mine plan or other commercial basis for measurement is achieved. Expenditures during this time frame are commonly referred to as *costs incurred in the start-up period*. Statement of Position (SOP) 98-5, "Reporting on the Costs of Start-up Activities," provides guidance for mining companies as to when development stops and commercial operations begin. Start-up activities are defined broadly in SOP 98-5 as "those one-time activities related to opening a new facility, introducing a new product or service, conducting business in a new territory, conducting business with a new class of customer or beneficiary, initiating a new process in an existing facility, or commencing some new operation." The SOP precludes the capitalization of start-up costs that are incurred during the period of insignificant mineral production and before normal productive capacity is achieved.

(b) PRODUCTION COSTS.   When the mine begins production, production costs are expensed. The capitalized property acquisition, and development costs are recognized as costs of production through their depreciation or depletion, generally on the unit-of-production method over the expected productive life of the mine.

The principal difference between computing depreciation in the mining industry and in other industries is that useful lives of assets that are not readily movable from a mine site must not exceed the estimated life of the mine, which in turn is based on the remaining economically recoverable ore reserves. In some instances, this may require depreciating certain mining equipment over a period that is shorter than its physical life.

Depreciation charges are significant because of the highly capital-intensive nature of the industry. Moreover, those charges are affected by numerous factors, such as the physical environment, revisions of recoverable ore estimates, environmental regulations, and improved technology. In many instances, depreciation charges on similar equipment with different intended uses may begin at different times. For example, depreciation of equipment used for exploration purposes may begin when it is purchased and use has begun, while depreciation of milling equipment may not begin until a certain level of commercial production has been attained.

Depletion (or depletion and amortization) of property acquisition and development costs related to a body of ore is calculated in a manner similar to the unit-of-production method of depreciation. The cost of the body of ore is divided by the estimated quantity of ore reserves or units of metal or mineral to arrive at the depletion charge per unit. The unit charge is multiplied by the number of units extracted to arrive at the depletion charge for the period. This computation requires a current estimate of economically recoverable mineral reserves at the end of the period.

It is often appropriate for different depletion calculations to be made for different types of capitalized development expenditures. For instance, one factor to be considered is whether capitalized costs relate to gaining access to the total economically recoverable ore reserves of the mine or only to specific portions.

Usually, estimated quantities of economically recoverable mineral reserves are the basis for computing depletion and amortization under the unit-of-production method. The choice of the reserve unit is not a problem if there is only one product; if, however, as in many extractive operations, several products are recovered, a decision must be made whether to measure production on the basis of the major product or on the basis of an aggregation of all products. Generally, the reserve base is the company's total proved and probable ore reserve quantities; it is determined by specialists, such as geologists or mining engineers. Proved and probable reserves typically are used as the reserve base because of the degree of uncertainty surrounding estimates of possible reserves. The imprecise nature of reserve estimates makes it inevitable that the reserve base will be revised over time as additional data becomes available. Changes in the reserve base should be treated as changes in accounting estimates in accordance with Accounting Principles Board (APB) Opinion No. 20, "Accounting Changes" (Accounting Standards Section A06), and accounted for prospectively.

(c) INVENTORY.   A mining company's inventory generally has two major components— (1) metals and minerals and (2) materials and supplies that are used in mining operations.

(i) Metals and Minerals.   Metal and mineral inventories usually comprise broken ore; crushed ore; concentrate; materials in process at concentrators, smelters, and refineries; metal; and joint and by-products. The usual practice of mining companies is not to recognize metal inventories for financial reporting purposes before the concentrate stage, that is, until the majority of the nonmineralized material has been removed from the ore. Thus, ore is not included in inventory until it has been processed through the concentrator and is ready for delivery to the smelter. This practice evolved because the amounts of broken ore before the concentrating process ordinarily are relatively small, and consequently the cost of that ore and of concentrate in process generally is not significant. Furthermore, the amount of broken ore and concentrate in process is relatively constant at the end of each month, and the concentrating process is quite rapid—usually a matter of hours. In the case of leach operations, generally the mineral content of the ore is estimated and costs are inventoried. However, practice varies, and some companies do not inventory costs until the leached product is introduced into the electrochemical refinery cells.

Determining inventory quantities during the production process is often difficult. Broken ore, crushed ore, concentrate, and materials in process may be stored in various ways or enclosed in vessels or pipes.

Mining companies carry metal inventory at the lower of cost or market value, with cost determined on a last-in, first out (LIFO), first-in, first out (FIFO), or average basis.

Valuation of product inventory is also affected by worldwide imbalances between supply and demand for certain metals. Companies sometimes produce larger quantities of a metal than can be absorbed by the market. In that situation, management may have to write the inventory down to its net realizable value; determining that value, however, may be difficult if there is no established market or only a thin market for the particular metal.

Product costs for mining companies usually reflect all normal and necessary expenditures associated with cost centers such as mines, concentrators, smelters, and refineries. Inventory costs comprise not only direct costs of production, but also an allocation of overhead, including mine and other plant administrative expenses. Depreciation, depletion, and amortization of capitalized exploration, and development costs also should be included in inventory.

If a company engages in tolling (described in Subsection 29.8(b)), it may have significant production inventories on hand that belong to other mining companies. Usually it is not possible to physically segregate inventories owned by others from similar inventories owned by the company. Memorandum records of tolling inventories should be maintained and reconciled periodically to physical counts.

(ii) Materials and Supplies.   Materials and supplies usually constitute a substantial portion of the inventory of most mining companies, sometimes exceeding the value of metal inventories. This is because a lack of supplies or spare parts could cause the curtailment of operations. In addition to normal operating supplies, materials and supplies inventories often include such items as fuel and spare parts for trucks, locomotives, and other machinery. Most mining companies use perpetual inventory systems to account for materials and supplies because of their high unit value.

Materials and supplies inventories normally are valued at cost minus a reserve for surplus items and obsolescence.

(d) COMMODITIES, FUTURES TRANSACTIONS.   Mining companies usually have significant inventories of commodities that are traded in worldwide markets, and frequently enter into long-term forward sales contracts specifying sales prices based on market prices at time of delivery. To protect themselves from the risk of loss that could result from price declines, mining companies often "hedge" against price changes by entering into futures contracts. Companies sell contracts when they expect selling prices to decline or are satisfied with the current price and want to "lock in" the profit (or loss) on the sale of their inventory. To establish a hedge when it has or expects to have a commodity (e.g., copper) in inventory, a company sells a contract that commits it to deliver that commodity in the future at a fixed price.

SFAS No. 133, "Accounting for Derivative Instruments and Hedging Activities," which is effective for quarters of fiscal years beginning after June 15, 2000, requires derivative instruments, including those which qualify as hedges, to be reported on the balance sheet at fair value. To qualify for hedge accounting, the derivative must satisfy the requirements of a "cash flow hedge," "fair value hedge," or "foreign currency hedge" as defined by SFAS No. 133. The Statement provides that certain criteria be met for a derivative to be accounted for as a hedge for financial reporting purposes. These criteria must be formally documented prior to entering the transaction and include risk-management objectives and an assessment of hedge effectiveness. Financial instruments commonly used in the mining industry include forward sales contracts, spot deferred contracts, purchased puts, and written calls. Additional financial instruments that should be reviewed for statement applicability include commodity loans, tolling agreements, take or pay contracts, and royalty agreements.

(e) RECLAMATION AND REMEDIATION.   The mining industry is subject to federal and state laws for reclamation and restoration of lands after the completion of mining. Historically, costs to reclaim and restore these lands, which can be defined as asset retirement obligations, were recognized using a cost accumulation model on an undiscounted basis. For financial reporting purposes, the environmental and closure expenses and related liabilities were recognized ratably over the mine life using the units-of-production method. SFAS No.143, "Accounting for Asset

Retirement Obligations," which is effective for fiscal years beginning after June 15, 2002, requires that an asset retirement obligation be recognized in the period in which it is incurred. This Statement defines reclamation of a mine at the end of its productive life to be an obligating event that requires liability recognition. The asset retirement costs, which include reclamation and closure costs, are capitalized as a component of the long-lived assets of the mineral property and depreciated over the mine life using the units-of-production method. This Statement requires that the liability for these obligations be recorded at its fair value using the guidance in FASB Concepts Statement No. 7, "Using Cash Flow Information and Present Value in Accounting Measurements," to estimate that liability. This Statement also requires that the liability be discounted and accretion expense be recognized using the credit-adjusted risk-free interest rate in effect at recognition date.

Environmental contamination and hazardous waste disposal and clean up is regulated by the Resource Conservation and Recovery Act of 1976 (RCRA) and the Comprehensive Environmental Response, Compensation and Liability Act of 1980 (CERCLA or Superfund). SOP 96-1, "Environmental Remediation Liabilities," provides accounting guidance for the accrual and disclosure of environmental remediation liabilities. This Statement requires that environmental remediation liabilities be accrued when the criteria of FASB No. 5, "Accounting for Contingencies," have been met. However, if the environmental remediation liability is incurred as a result of normal mining operations and relates to the retirement of the mining assets, the provisions of SFAS No. 143 probably apply.

(f) SHUTDOWN OF MINES.   Volatile metal prices may make active operations uneconomical from time to time, and, as a result, mining companies will shut down operations, either temporarily or permanently. When operations are temporarily shut down, a question arises as to the carrying value of the related assets. If a long-term diminution in the value of the assets has occurred, a write-down of the carrying value to net realizable value should be recorded. This decision is extremely judgmental and depends on projections of whether viable mining operations can ever be resumed. Those projections are based on significant assumptions as to prices, production, quantities, and costs; because most minerals are worldwide commodities, the projections must take into account global supply and demand factors.

When operations are temporarily shut down, the related facilities usually are placed in a "standby mode" that provides for care and maintenance so that the assets will be retained in a reasonable condition that will facilitate resumption of operations. Care and maintenance costs are usually recorded as expenses in the period in which they are incurred. Examples of typical care and maintenance costs are security, preventive and protective maintenance, and depreciation.

A temporary shutdown of a mining company's facility can raise questions as to whether the company can continue as a going concern.

(g) ACCOUNTING FOR THE IMPAIRMENT OF LONG-LIVED ASSETS.   SFAS No. 121, "Accounting for the Impairment of Long-Lived Assets and Long-Lived Assets to Be Disposed Of," provided definitive guidance on when the carrying amount of long-lived assets should be reviewed for impairment. Long-lived assets of a mining company, for example, plant and equipment and capitalized development costs, should be reviewed for recoverability when events or changes in circumstances indicate that carrying amounts may not be recoverable. For mining companies, factors such as decreasing commodity prices, reductions in mineral recoveries, increasing operating and environmental costs, and reductions in mineral reserves are events and circumstances that may indicate an asset impairment. SFAS No. 121 also established a common methodology for assessing and measuring the impairment of long-lived assets. SFAS No. 144, which is effective for fiscal years beginning after December 15, 2001, supercedes SFAS No. 121 but retains the fundamental recognition and measurement provisions of SFAS No. 121. This Statement addresses significant issues relating to the implementation of SFAS No. 121 and develops a single accounting model, based on the framework established in SFAS No. 121, for long-lived assets to be disposed of by sale, whether previously held and used or newly acquired. This Statement defines impairment as "the condition that exists when the carrying amount of a long-lived asset (asset group) exceeds its fair value." An impairment loss is reported only if the carrying amount of the long-lived asset (asset group) (1) is not recoverable, that is, if it exceeds the sum of the undiscounted cash flows expected to result from the use and eventual disposition of the asset (asset group), assessed based on the carrying amount of the asset in use or under development when it is tested for recoverability, and (2) exceeds the fair value of the asset (asset group).

For mining companies, the cash flows should be based on the proven and probable reserves that are used in the calculation of depreciation, depletion, and amortization. The estimates of cash flows should be based on reasonable and supportable assumptions. For example, the use of commodity prices other than the spot price would be permissible if such prices were based on futures prices in the commodity markets. If an impairment loss is warranted, the revised carrying amount of the asset, which is based on the discounted cash flow model, is the new cost basis to be depreciated over its remaining useful life. A previously recognized impairment loss may not be restored.

29.8 ACCOUNTING FOR MINING REVENUES

(a) SALES OF MINERALS.   Generally, minerals are not sold in the raw-ore stage because of the insignificant quantity of minerals relative to the total volume of waste rock. (There are, however, some exceptions, such as iron ore and coal.) The ore is usually milled at or near the mine site to produce a concentrate containing a significantly higher percentage of mineral content. For example, the metal content of copper concentrate typically is 25–30 percent, as opposed to between. 5 and 1 percent for the raw ore. The concentrate is frequently sold to other processors; occasionally mining companies exchange concentrate to reduce transportation costs. After the refining process, metallic minerals may be sold as finished metals, either in the form of products for remelting by final users (e.g., pig iron or cathode copper) or as finished products (e.g., copper rod or aluminum foil).

Sales of raw ore and concentrate entail determining metal content based initially on estimated weights, moisture content, and ore grade. Those estimates are subsequently revised, based on the actual metal content recovered from the raw ore or concentrate.

The SEC has provided guidance for revenue recognition under GAAP in SAB No. 101, which was issued in December 1999. The staff noted that accounting literature on revenue recognition included both conceptual discussions and industry-specific guidance. SAB No. 101 provides a summary of the staff's views on revenue recognition and should be evaluated by mining companies in recording revenues. Revenue should be recognized when the following conditions are met:

- A contractual agreement exists (a documented understanding between the buyer and seller as to the nature and terms of the agreed-upon transaction).
- Delivery of the product has occurred (FOB shipping) or the services have been rendered.
- The price of the product is fixed or determinable.
- Collection of the receivable for the product sold or services rendered is reasonably assured.

For revenue to be recognized, it is important that the buyer has to have taken title to the mineral product and assumed the risks and rewards of ownership.

Sales prices are often based on the market price on a commodity exchange such as the New York Commodity Exchange (COMEX) or London Metal Exchange (LME) at the time of delivery, which may differ from the market price of the metal at the time that the criteria for revenue recognition have been satisfied. Revenue may be recognized on these sales based on a provisional pricing mechanism, the spot price of the metal at the date on which revenue recognition criteria have been satisfied. The estimated sales price and related receivable should be subsequently marked to market through revenue based on the commodity exchange spot price until the final settlement.

(b) TOLLING AND ROYALTY REVENUES. Companies with smelters and refineries may also realize revenue from tolling, which is the processing of metal-bearing materials of other mining companies for a fee. The fee is based on numerous factors, including the weight and metal content of the materials processed. Normally, the processed minerals are returned to the original producer for subsequent sale. To supplement the recovery of fixed costs, companies with smelters and refineries frequently enter into tolling agreements when they have excess capacity.

For a variety of reasons, companies may not wish to mine certain properties that they own. Mineral royalty agreements may be entered into that provide for royalties based on a percentage of the total value of the mineral or of gross revenue, to be paid when the minerals extracted from the property are sold.

The accounting for commodity futures contracts depends on whether the contract qualifies as a hedge under SFAS No. 133, "Accounting for Derivative Instruments and Hedging Activities." In order to qualify for hedging of mineral reserves, management will be required to determine how it measures hedge effectiveness and to formally document the hedging relationship and the entity's risk management objective and strategy for undertaking the hedge. Such documentation will include identification of the hedging instrument, the related hedged item, the nature of the risk being hedged, and how the hedging instrument's effectiveness in offsetting the exposure to changes in the hedged item's fair value attributable to the hedged risk will be assessed. See Chapter 26 for a complete discussion of the requirements for hedge accounting.

29.9 SUPPLEMENTARY FINANCIAL STATEMENT INFORMATION—ORE RESERVES

SFAS No. 89, "Financial Reporting and Changing Prices" (Accounting Standards Section C28), eliminated the requirement that certain publicly traded companies meeting specified size criteria must disclose the effects of changing prices and supplemental disclosures of ore reserves. However, Item 102 of SEC Regulation S-K requires that publicly traded mining companies present information related to production, reserves, locations, developments, and the nature of the registrant's interest in properties.

29.10 ACCOUNTING FOR INCOME TAXES

Chapter 24 addresses general accounting for income taxes. Tax accounting for oil and gas production as well as hard rock mining is particularly complex and cannot be fully covered in this chapter. However, two special deductions need to be mentioned—percentage depletion and immediate deduction of certain development costs.

Many petroleum and mining production companies are allowed to calculate depletion as the greater of cost depletion or percentage depletion. Cost depletion is based on amortization of property acquisition costs over estimated recoverable reserves. Percentage depletion is a statutory depletion deduction that is a specified percentage of gross revenue at the well-head (15 percent for oil and gas) or mine for the particular mineral produced and is limited to a portion of the property's taxable income before deducting such depletion. Percentage depletion may exceed the depletable cost basis.

For purposes of computing the taxable income from the mineral property, gross income is defined as the value of the mineral before the application of nonmining processes. Selling price is generally determined to be the gross value for tax purposes when the mineral products are sold to third parties prior to nonmining processes. For an integrated mining company where nonmining processes are used, gross income for the mineral is generally determined under a proportionate profits method whereby an allocation of profit is made based on the mining and nonmining costs incurred.

For both petroleum and mining companies, exploration and development costs other than for equipment are largely deductible when incurred. However, the major integrated petroleum companies and mining companies must capitalize a percentage of these exploration and development expenditures, which are then amortized over a period of 60 months. Mining companies must recapture the previously deducted exploration costs if the mineral property achieves commercial production. Property impairments, which are expensed currently for financial reporting purposes, do not generate a taxable deduction until such property is abandoned, sold, or exchanged.

29.11 FINANCIAL STATEMENT DISCLOSURES

The SFAS No. 69 details supplementary disclosure requirements for the oil and gas industry, most of which are required only by public companies. Both public and nonpublic companies, however, must provide a description of the accounting method followed and the manner of disposing of capitalized costs. Audited financial statements filed with the SEC must include supplementary disclosures, which fall into four categories:

1. Historical cost data relating to acquisition, exploration, development, and production activity.
2. Results of operations for oil- and gas-producing activities.
3. Proved reserve quantities.
4. Standardized measure of discounted future net cash flows relating to proved oil and gas reserve quantities (also known as *SMOG* [standardized measure of oil and gas]). For foreign operations, SMOG also relates to produced quantities subject to certain long-term purchase contracts held by a party involved in producing the quantities.

The supplementary disclosures are required of companies with significant oil- and gas-producing activities; significant is defined as 10 percent or more of revenue, operating results, or identifiable assets. The Statement provides that the disclosures are to be provided as supplemental data; thus they need not be audited. The disclosure requirements are described in detail in the Statement, and examples are provided in an appendix to SFAS No. 69. If the supplemental information is not audited, it must be clearly labeled as unaudited. However, auditing interpretations (Au Section 9558) require the financial statement auditor to perform certain limited procedures to these required, unaudited supplementary disclosures.

Proved reserves are inherently imprecise because of the uncertainties and limitations of the data available.

Most large companies and many medium-sized companies have qualified engineers on their staffs to prepare oil and gas reserve studies. Many also use outside consultants to make independent reviews. Other companies, which do not have sufficient operations to justify a full-time engineer, engage outside engineering consultants to evaluate and estimate their oil and gas reserves. Usually, reserve studies are reviewed and updated at least annually to take into account new discoveries and adjustments of previous estimates.

The standardized measure is disclosed as of the end of the fiscal year. The SMOG reflects future revenues computed by applying unescalated, year-end oil and gas prices to year-end proved reserves. Future price changes may only be considered if fixed and determinable under year-end sales contracts. The calculated future revenues are reduced for estimated future development costs, production costs, and related income taxes (using unescalated, year-end cost rates) to compute future net cash flows. Such cash flows, by future year, are discounted at a standard 10 percent per annum to compute the standardized measure.

Significant sources of the annual changes in the year-end standardized measure and year-end proved oil and gas reserves should be disclosed.

29.12 SOURCES AND SUGGESTED REFERENCES

Brock, Horace R., Jennings, Dennis R., and Feiten, Joseph B., *Petroleum Accounting—Principles, Procedures, and Issues,* Fourth Edition. Professional Development Institute, Denton, TX, 1996.

Council of Petroleum Accountants Societies, *Bulletin No. 24, Producer Gas Imbalances* as revised. Kraftbilt Products, Tulsa, 1991.

PricewaterhouseCoopers, *Financial Reporting in the Mining Industry for the 21st Century*, 1999.

Financial Accounting Standards Board, "Financial Accounting and Reporting by Oil and Gas Producing Companies," Statement of Financial Accounting Standards No. 19. FASB, Stamford, CT, 1977.

"Suspension of Certain Accounting Requirements for Oil and Gas Producing Companies," Statement of Financial Accounting Standards No. 25. FASB, Stamford, CT, 1979.

"Disclosures about Oil and Gas Producing Activities," Statement of Financial Accounting Standards No. 69. FASB, Stamford, CT, 1982.

O'Reilly, V. M., *Montgomery's Auditing,* Twelfth Edition. John Wiley & Sons, New York, 1996.

Securities and Exchange Commission, "Financial Accounting and Reporting for Oil and Gas Producing Activities Pursuant to the Federal Securities Laws and the Energy Policy and Conservation Act of 1975," Regulation S-X, Rule 4-10, as currently amended. SEC, Washington, DC, 1995.

"Interpretations Relating to Oil and Gas Accounting," SEC Staff Accounting Bulletins, Topic 12. SEC, Washington, DC, 1995.

CHAPTER **30**

REAL ESTATE AND CONSTRUCTION

Clifford H. Schwartz, CPA
PricewaterhouseCoopers LLP

Suzanne McElyea, CPA
PricewaterhouseCoopers LLP

30.1 THE REAL ESTATE INDUSTRY

(a) OVERVIEW.   Real estate encompasses a variety of interests (developers, investors, lenders, tenants, homeowners, corporations, conduits, etc.) with a divergence of objectives (tax benefits, security, long-term appreciation, etc.). The industry is also a tool of the federal government's income tax policies (evidenced by the rules on mortgage interest deductions and restrictions on "passive" investment deductions). The real estate industry consists primarily of private developers and builders.

Other important forces in the industry include pension funds and insurance companies and large corporations, whose occupancy (real estate) costs generally are the second largest costs after personnel costs.

After a decade of growth spurred by steadily falling interest rates in an expanding economy, the new millennium brought in its wake a series of traumatic events that highlighted the uncertainties inherent in the real estate industry:

- *Collapse of the dot-coms.* The sudden rise and dramatic collapse of the Internet-related economy delivered the first shock to real estate markets since the banks scandals of the 1980s. A seller's market was turned on end as rapid retrenchment left behind a glut of office space.

- *The attacks on the World Trade Center and the Pentagon.* The attacks dealt a hard blow to an already declining economy and real estate market. It exposed the vulnerability of the United States to terrorist attacks and made planning for such attacks a central part of real estate management. It was followed by a sharp rise in unemployment and severe weakness in financial markets. It also called into question long time practices of concentrating corporate functions and resources in one location.

- *Enron.* The collapse of Enron led investors and regulators to seriously question the use of off-balance sheet financing vehicles, such as conduits and synthetic leasing, which had become the darlings of Wall Street financiers, growing to more than $5.2 trillion over the last 30 years.

Overbuilding, accounting reform, terrorist threats, and weak markets will continue to plague the recovery of many real estate markets. The sources and extent of available capital for financings and construction will be a concern. This concern will be centered on the ability and willingness of financing institutions to continue lending in an uncertain market, and lenders will increasingly require creditworthiness or enhancements to reduce to their exposure to real estate risk.

30.2 SALES OF REAL ESTATE

(a) ANALYSIS OF TRANSACTIONS.   Real estate sales transactions are generally material to the entity's financial statements. "Is the earnings process complete?" is the primary question that must be answered regarding such sales. In other words, assuming a legal sale, have the risks and rewards of ownership been transferred to the buyer?

(b) ACCOUNTING BACKGROUND.   Prior to 1982, guidance related to real estate sales transactions was contained in two American Institute of Certified Public Accountants (AICPA) Accounting Guides: "Accounting for Retail Land Sales" and "Accounting for Profit Recognition on Sales of Real Estate." These guides had been supplemented by several AICPA Statements of Position that provided interpretations

In October 1982, Statement of Financial Accounting Standards (SFAS) No. 66, "Accounting for Sales of Real Estate," was issued as part of the Financial Accounting Standards Board (FASB) project to incorporate, where appropriate, AICPA Accounting Guides into FASB Statements. This Statement adopted the specialized profit recognition principles of the above guides.

The FASB formed the Emerging Issues Task Force (EITF) in 1984 for the early identification of emerging issues. The EITF has dealt with many issues affecting the real estate industry, including issues that clarify or address SFAS No. 66.

Regardless of the seller's business, SFAS No. 66 covers all sales of real estate, determines the timing of the sale and resultant profit recognition, and deals with seller accounting only. This Statement does not discuss nonmonetary exchanges, cost accounting, and most lease transactions or disclosures.

The two primary concerns under SFAS No. 66 are:

1. Has a sale occurred?

2. Under what method and when should profit be recognized?

The concerns are answered by determining the buyer's initial and continuing investment and the nature and extent of the seller's continuing involvement. The guidelines used in determining these criteria are complex and, within certain provisions, arbitrary. Companies dealing with these types of transactions are often faced with the difficult task of analyzing the exact nature of a transaction in order to determine the appropriate accounting approach. Only with a thorough understanding of the details of a transaction can the accountant perform the analysis required to decide on the appropriate accounting method.

(c) CRITERIA FOR RECORDING A SALE.   SFAS No. 66 (pars. 44–50) discussed separate rules for retail land sales (see Subsection 30.2(h)). The following information is for all real estate sales other than retail land sales. To determine whether profit recognition is appropriate, a test must first be made to determine whether a sale may be recorded. Then additional tests are made related to the buyer's investment and the seller's continued involvement.

Generally, real estate sales should not be recorded prior to closing. Since an exchange is generally required to recognize profit, a sale must be consummated. A sale is consummated when all the following conditions have been met:

- The parties are bound by the terms of a contract.
- All consideration has been exchanged.
- Any permanent financing for which the seller is responsible has been arranged.
- All conditions precedent to closing have been performed.

Usually all those conditions are met at the time of closing. On the other hand, they are not usually met at the time of a contract to sell or a preclosing.

Exceptions to the "conditions precedent to closing" have been specifically provided for in SFAS No. 66. They are applicable where a sale of property includes a requirement for the seller to perform future construction or development. Under certain conditions, partial sale recognition is permitted during the construction process because the construction period is extended. This exception usually is not applicable to single-family detached housing because of the shorter construction period.

Transactions that should not be treated as sales for accounting purposes because of continuing seller's involvement include the following:

- The seller has an option or obligation to repurchase the property.
- The seller guarantees return of the buyer's investment.
- The seller retains an interest as a general partner in a limited partnership and has a significant receivable.
- The seller is required to initiate or support operations or continue to operate the property at its own risk for a specified period or until a specified level of operations has been obtained.

If the criteria for recording a sale are not met, the deposit, financing, lease, or profit sharing (co-venture) methods should be used, depending on the substance of the transaction.

(d) ADEQUACY OF DOWN PAYMENT.   Once it has been determined that a sale can be recorded, the next test relates to the buyer's investment. For the seller to record full profit recognition, the buyer's down payment must be adequate in size and in composition.

(i) Size of Down Payment. The minimum down payment requirement is one of the most important provisions in SFAS No. 66. Appendix A of this pronouncement, reproduced here as Exhibit 30.1, lists minimum down payments ranging from 5 percent to 25 percent of sales value based on usual loan limits for various types of properties. These percentages should be considered as specific requirements because it was not intended that exceptions be made. Additionally, EITF Consensus No. 88-24, "Effect of Various Forms of Financing under FASB Statement No. 66," discusses the impact of the source and nature of the buyer's down payment on profit recognition. Exhibit A to EITF No. 88-24 has been reproduced here as Exhibit 30.2.

If a newly placed permanent loan or firm permanent loan commitment for maximum financing exists, the minimum down payment must be the higher of (1) the amount derived from Appendix A

	Minimum Initial Investment Payment Expressed as a Percentage of Sales Value
Land:	
Held for commercial, industrial, or residential development to commence within two years after sale	20%
Held for commercial, industrial, or residential development after two years	25%
Commercial and industrial property:	
Office and industrial buildings, shopping centers, and so forth:	
Properties subject to lease on a long-term lease basis to parties having satisfactory credit rating; cash flow currently sufficient to service all Indebtedness	10%
Single-tenancy properties sold to a user having a satisfactory credit rating	15%
All other	20%
Other income-producing properties (hotels, motels, marinas, mobile home parks, and so forth):	
Cash flow currently sufficient to service all indebtedness	15%
Start-up situations or current deficiencies in cash flow	25%
Multifamily residential property:	
Primary residence:	
Cash flow currently sufficient to service all indebtedness	10%
Start-up situations or current deficiencies in cash flow	15%
Secondary or recreational residence:	
Cash flow currently sufficient to service all indebtedness	10%
Start-up situations or current deficiencies in cash flow	25%
Single-family residential property (including condominium or cooperative housing)	
Primary residence of buyer	5%[a]
Secondary or recreational residence	10%[a]

[a]As set forth in Appendix A of SFAS No. 66, if collectibility of the remaining portion of the sales price cannot be supported by reliable evidence of collection experience, the minimum initial investment shall be at least 60% of the difference between the sales value and the financing available from loans guaranteed by regulatory bodies, such as the FHA or the VA, or from independent financial institutions.

This 60% test applies when independent first mortgage financing is not utilized and the seller takes a receivable from the buyer for the difference between the sales value and the initial investment. If independent first mortgage financing is utilized, the adequacy of the initial investment on sales of single-family residential property should be determined as described in Subsection 30.2(d) (i).

Exhibit 30.1   Minimum initial investment requirements. (*Source:* SFAS No. 66, "Accounting for Sales of Real Estate" (Appendix A), FASB, 1982. Reprinted with permission of FASB.)

Situation	Cash Received by Seller at Closing	Components of Cash Received by Seller at Closing		Assumption of Seller's Nonrecourse Mortgage
		Buyer's Initial Investment	Buyer's Independent First Mortgage	
1.	100	20	80	
2.	100	0	100	
3.	20	20		80
4.	0	0		100
5.	20	20		
6.	20	20		
7.	80	20	60	
8.	20	20		60
9.	20	20		
10.	0	0		
11.	0	0		
12.	0	0		
13.	80	0	80	
14.	10	10		
15.	10	10		
16.	90	10	80	
17.	10	10		80
18.	10	10		

Assumptions:
Sales price: $100.
Seller's basis in property sold: $70.
Initial investment requirement: 20%.
All mortgage obligations meet the continuing investment requirements of Statement 66.

Exhibit 30.2   Examples of the application of the EITF consensus on Issue No. 88-24. *Source:* **EITF Issue No. 88-24, "Effect of Various Forms of Financing under FASB Statement No. 66" (Exhibit 88-24A), FASB, 1988. (Reprinted with permission of FASB.)**

or (2) the excess of sales value over 115 percent of the new financing. However, regardless of this test, a down payment of 25 percent of the sales value of the property is usually considered sufficient to justify the recognition of profit at the time of sale.

An example of the down payment test—Appendix A compared to the newly placed permanent loan test—is given in the following:

ASSUMPTIONS

Initial payment made by the buyer to the seller on sale of an apartment building	$ 200,000
First mortgage recently issued and assumed by the buyer	1,000,000
Second mortgage given by the buyer to the seller at prevailing interest rate	200,000
Stated sales price and sales value	$1,400,000
115% of first mortgage (1.15 × $1,000,000)	1,150,000
Down payment necessary	$ 250,000

RESULT

Although the down payment required under Appendix A is only $140,000 (10% of $1,400,000), the $200,000 actual down payment is inadequate because the test relating to the newly placed first mortgage requires $250,000.

Seller Financing[1]	Assumption of Seller's Recourse Mortgage[2]	Recognition under Consensus Paragraph	Profit Recognized at Date of Sale[3]		
			Full Accrual	Installment	Cost Recovery
		#1	30		
		#1	30		
		#1	30		
		#1	30		
80(1)		#2	30		
	80	#2	30		
20(2)		#2	30		
20(2)		#2	30		
20(2)	60	#2	30		
	100	#3		0	0
100(1)		#3		0	0
20(2)	80	#3		0	0
20(2)		#3		10	10
90(1)		#3		3	0
	90	#3		3	0
10(2)		#3		20	20
10(2)		#3		20	20
10(2)	80	#3		3	0

[1] First or second mortgage indicated in parentheses.

[2] Seller remains contingently liable.

[3] The profit recognized under the reduced profit method is dependent on various interest rates and payment terms. An example is not presented due to the complexity of those factors and the belief that this method is not frequently used in practice. Under this method, the profit recognized at the consummation of the sale would be less than under the full accrual method, but normally more than the amount under the installment method.

Exhibit 30.2   *Continued.*

The down payment requirements must be related to sales value, as described in SFAS No. 66 (par. 7). Sales value is the stated sales price increased or decreased for other consideration that clearly constitutes additional proceeds on the sale, services without compensation, imputed interest, and so forth.

Consideration payable for development work or improvements that are the responsibility of the seller should be included in the computation of sales value.

(ii) Composition of Down Payment.   The primary acceptable down payment is cash, but additional acceptable forms of down payment are:

- Notes from the buyer (only when supported by irrevocable letters of credit from an independent established lending institution)
- Cash payments by the buyer to reduce previously existing indebtedness
- Cash payments that are in substance additional sales proceeds, such as prepaid interest that by the terms of the contract is applied to amounts due the seller

Examples of other forms of down payment that are not acceptable are:

- Other noncash consideration received by the seller, such as notes from the buyer without letters of credit or marketable securities. Noncash consideration constitutes down payment only at the time it is converted into cash.

- Funds that have been or will be loaned to the buyer builder/developer for acquisition, construction, or development purposes or otherwise provided directly or indirectly by the seller. Such amounts must first be deducted from the down payment in determining whether the down payment test has been met. An exemption from this requirement was provided in paragraph 115 of SFAS No. 66, which states that if a future loan on normal terms from a seller who is also an established lending institution bears a fair market interest rate and the proceeds of the loan are conditional on use for specific development of or construction on the property, the loan need not be subtracted in determining the buyer's investment.

- Funds received from the buyer from proceeds of priority loans on the property. Such funds have not come from the buyer and therefore do not provide assurance of collectibility of the remaining receivable; such amounts should be excluded in determining the adequacy of the down payment. In addition, EITF Consensus No. 88-24 provides guidelines on the impact that the source and nature of the buyer's initial investment can have on profit recognition.

- Marketable securities or other assets received as down payment will constitute down payment only at the time they are converted to cash.

- Cash payments for prepaid interest that are not in substance additional sales proceeds.

- Cash payments by the buyer to others for development or construction of improvements to the property.

(iii) Inadequate Down Payment.   If the buyer's down payment is inadequate, the accrual method of accounting is not appropriate, and the deposit, installment, or cost recovery method of accounting should be used.

When the sole consideration (in addition to cash) received by the seller is the buyer's assumption of existing nonrecourse indebtedness, a sale could be recorded and profit recognized if all other conditions for recognizing a sale were met. If, however, the buyer assumes recourse debt and the seller remains liable on the debt, he has a risk of loss comparable to the risk involved in holding a receivable from the buyer, and the accrual method would not be appropriate.

EITF Consensus No. 88-24 states that the initial and continuing investment requirements for the full accrual method of profit recognition of SFAS No. 66 are applicable unless the seller receives one of the following as the full sales value of the property:

- Cash, without any seller contingent liability on any debt on the property incurred or assumed by the buyer

- The buyer's assumption of the seller's existing nonrecourse debt on the property

- The buyer's assumption of all recourse debt on the property with the complete release of the seller from those obligations

- Any combination of such cash and debt assumption

(e) RECEIVABLE FROM THE BUYER.   Even if the required down payment is made, a number of factors must be considered by the seller in connection with a receivable from the buyer. They include:

- Collectibility of the receivable
- Buyer's continuing investment—amortization of receivable
- Future subordination
- Release provisions
- Imputation of interest

(i) Assessment of Collectibility of Receivable.   Collectibility of the receivable must be reasonably assured and should be assessed in light of factors such as the credit standing of the buyer (if recourse), cash flow from the property, and the property's size and geographical location. This requirement may be particularly important when the receivable is relatively short term and collectibility is questionable because the buyer will be required to obtain financing. Furthermore, a basic principle of real estate sales on credit is that the receivable must be adequately secured by the property sold.

(ii) Amortization of Receivable.   Continuing investment requirements for full profit recognition require that the buyer's payments on its total debt for the purchase price must be at least equal to level annual payments (including principal and interest) based on amortization of the full amount over a maximum term of 20 years for land and over the *customary term of a first mortgage* by an independent established lending institution for other property. The annual payments must begin within one year of recording the sale and, to be acceptable, must meet the same composition test as used in determining adequacy of down payments. The customary term of a first mortgage loan is usually considered to be the term of a new loan (or the term of an existing loan placed in recent years) from an independent financial lending institution.

All indebtedness on the property need not be reduced proportionately. However, if the seller's receivable is not being amortized, realization may be in question and the collectibility must be more carefully assessed. Lump-sum (balloon) payments do not affect the amortization requirement as long as the scheduled amortization is within the maximum period and the minimum annual amortization tests are met.

For example, if the customary term of the mortgage by an independent lender required amortizing payments over a period of 25 years, then the continuing investment requirement would be based on such an amortization schedule. If the terms of the receivable required principal and interest payments on such a schedule only for the first five years with a balloon at the end of year 5, the continuing investment requirements are met. In such cases, however, the collectibility of the balloon payment should be carefully assessed.

If the amortization requirements for full profit recognition as set forth above are not met, a reduced profit may be recognized by the seller if the annual payments are at least equal to the total of:

- Annual level payments of principal and interest on a maximum available first mortgage
- Interest at an appropriate rate on the remaining amount payable by the buyer

The reduced profit is determined by discounting the receivable from the buyer to the present value of the lowest level of annual payments required by the sales contract excluding requirements to pay lump sums. The present value is calculated using an appropriate interest rate, but not less than the rate stated in the sales contract.

The amount calculated would be used as the value of the receivable for the purpose of determining the reduced profit. The calculation of reduced profit is illustrated in Exhibit 30.3.

The requirements for amortization of the receivable are applied cumulatively at the closing date (date of recording the sale for accounting purposes) and annually thereafter. Any excess of down payment received over the minimum required is applied toward the amortization requirements.

(iii) Receivable Subject to Future Subordination.   If the receivable is subject to future subordination to a future loan available to the buyer, profit recognition cannot exceed the amount determined under the cost recovery method (see Subsection 30.2(j)(iii)) unless proceeds of the loan are first used to reduce the seller's receivable. Although this accounting treatment is controversial, the cost recovery method is required because collectibility of the sales price is not reasonably assured. The future subordination would permit the primary lender to obtain a prior lien on the property, leaving only a secondary residual value for the seller, and future loans could indirectly finance the buyer's initial cash investment. Future loans would include funds received by the buyer arising from a permanent loan commitment existing at the time of the transaction unless such funds were first applied to reduce the seller's receivable as provided for in the terms of the sale.

Assumptions:		
Down payment (meets applicable tests)		$ 150,000
First mortgage note from independent lender at market rate of interest (new, 20 years—meets required amortization)		750,000
Second mortgage notes payable to seller, interest at a market rate is due annually, with principal due at the end of the 25th year (the term exceeds the maximum permitted)		100,000
Stated selling price		$1,000,000

Adjustment required in valuation of receivable from buyer:		
Second mortgage payable to seller	$100,000	
Less: present value of 20 years annual interest payments on second mortgage (lowest level of annual payments over customary term of first mortgage—thus 20 years not 25)	70,000	30,000
Adjusted sales value for profit recognition		$ 970,000

The sales value as well as profit is reduced by $30,000.
In some situations profit will be entirely eliminated by this calculation.

Exhibit 30.3   Calculation of reduced profit.

The cost recovery method is not required if the receivable is subordinate to a previous mortgage on the property existing at the time of sale.

(iv) Release Provisions.   Some sales transactions have provisions releasing portions of the property from the liens securing the debt as partial payments are made. In this situation, full profit recognition is acceptable only if the buyer must make, at the time of each release, cumulative payments that are adequate in relation to the sales value of property not released.

(v) Imputation of Interest.   Careful attention should be given to the necessity for imputation of interest under Accounting Principles Board (APB) Opinion No. 21, "Interest on Receivables and Payables," since it could have a significant effect on the amount of profit or loss recognition. As stated in the first paragraph of APB Opinion No. 21: "The use of an interest rate that varies from prevailing interest rates warrants evaluation of whether the face amount and the stated interest rate of a note or obligation provide reliable evidence for properly recording the exchange and subsequent related interest."

If imputation of interest is necessary, the mortgage note receivable should be adjusted to its present value by discounting all future payments on the notes using an imputed rate of interest at the prevailing rates available for similar financing with independent financial institutions. A distinction must be made between first and second mortgage loans because the appropriate imputed rate for a second mortgage would normally be significantly higher than the rate for a first mortgage loan. It may be necessary to obtain independent valuations to assist in the determination of the proper rate.

(vi) Inadequate Continuing Investment.   If the criteria for recording a sale have been met but the tests related to the collectibility of the receivable as set forth herein are not met, the accrual method of accounting is not appropriate and the installment or cost recovery method of accounting should be used. These methods are discussed in Subsection 30.2(j) of this chapter.

(f) SELLER'S CONTINUED INVOLVEMENT.   A seller sometimes continues to be involved over long periods of time with property legally sold. This involvement may take many forms such as participation in future profits, financing, management services, development, construction, guarantees, and options to repurchase. With respect to profit recognition when a seller has continued involvement, the two key principles are as follows:

1. A sales contract should not be accounted for as a sale if the seller's continued involvement with the property includes the same kinds of risk as does ownership of property.

2. Profit recognition should follow performance and in some cases should be postponed completely until a later date.

(i) Participation Solely in Future Profits. A sale of real estate may include or be accompanied by an agreement that provides for the seller to participate in future operating profits or residual values. As long as the seller has no further obligations or risk of loss, profit recognition on the sale need not be deferred. A receivable from the buyer is permitted if the other tests for profit recognition are met, but no costs can be deferred.

(ii) Option or Obligation to Repurchase the Property. If the seller has an option or obligation to repurchase property (including a buyer's option to compel the seller to repurchase), a sale cannot be recognized (SFAS No. 66, par. 26). However, neither a commitment by the seller to assist or use his best efforts (with appropriate compensation) on a resale nor a right of first refusal based on a bona fide offer by a third party would preclude sale recognition. The accounting to be followed depends on the repurchase terms. EITF Consensus No. 86-6 discusses accounting for a sale transaction when antispeculation clauses exist. A consensus was reached that the contingent option would not preclude sale recognition if the probability of buyer noncompliance is remote.

When the seller has an obligation or an option that is reasonably expected to be exercised to repurchase the property at a price higher than the total amount of the payments received and to be received, the transaction is a financing arrangement and should be accounted for under the financing method. If the option is not reasonably expected to be exercised, the deposit method is appropriate.

In the case of a repurchase obligation or option at a lower price, the transaction usually is, in substance, a lease or is part lease, part financing and should be accounted for under the lease method. Where an option to repurchase is at a market price to be determined in the future, the transaction should be accounted for under the deposit method or the profit-sharing method.

(iii) General Partner in a Limited Partnership with a Significant Receivable. When the seller is a general partner in a limited partnership and has a significant receivable related to the property, the transaction would not qualify as a sale. It should usually be accounted for as a profit-sharing arrangement. A significant receivable is one that is in excess of 15 percent of the maximum first lien financing that could be obtained from an established lending institution for the property sold.

(iv) Lack of Permanent Financing. The buyer's investment in the property cannot be evaluated until adequate permanent financing at an acceptable cost is available to the buyer. If the seller must obtain or provide this financing, obtaining the financing is a prerequisite to a sale for accounting purposes. Even if not required to do so, the seller may be presumed to have such an obligation if the buyer does not have financing and the collectibility of the receivable is questionable. The deposit method is appropriate if lack of financing is the only impediment to recording a sale.

(v) Guaranteed Return of Buyer's Investment. SFAS No. 66 (par. 28) states: "If the seller guarantees return of the buyer's investment, . . . the transaction shall be accounted for as a financing, leasing, or profit-sharing arrangement."

Accordingly, if the terms of a transaction are such that the buyer may expect to recover the initial investment through assured cash returns, subsidies, and net tax benefits, even if the buyer were to default on debt to the seller, the transaction is probably not in substance a sale.

(vi) Other Guaranteed Returns on Investment—Other than Sale-Leaseback. When the seller guarantees cash returns on the buyer's investment, the accounting method to be followed depends on whether the guarantee is for an extended or limited period and whether the seller's expected cost of the guarantee is determinable.

Extended Period.   SFAS No. 66 states that when the seller contractually guarantees cash returns on investments to the buyer for an extended period, the transaction should be accounted for as a financing, leasing, or profit-sharing arrangement. An "extended period" was not defined but should at least include periods that are not limited in time or specified lengthy periods, such as more than five years.

Limited Period.   If the guarantee of a return on the buyer's investment is for a limited period, SFAS No. 66 indicates that the deposit method of accounting should be used until such time as operation of the property covers all operating expenses, debt service, and contractual payments. At that time, profit should be recognized based on performance (see Subsection 30.2(j)). A "limited period" was not defined but is believed to relate to specified shorter periods, such as five years or less.

Irrespective of the above, if the guarantee is determinable or limited, sale and profit recognition may be appropriate if reduced by the maximum exposure to loss as described below.

Guarantee Amount Determinable.   If the amount can be reasonably estimated, the seller should record the guarantee as a cost at the time of sale, thus either reducing the profit or increasing the loss on the transaction.

Guarantee Amount Not Determinable.   If the amount cannot be reasonably estimated, the transaction is probably in substance a profit-sharing or co-venture arrangement.

Guarantee Amount Not Determinable But Limited.   If the amount cannot be reasonably estimated but a maximum cost of the guarantee is determinable, the seller may record the maximum cost of the guarantee as a cost at the time of sale, thus either reducing the profit or increasing the loss on the transaction. Alternatively, the seller may account for the transaction as if the guarantee amount is not determinable. Implications of a seller's guarantee of cash flow on an operating property that is not considered a sale-leaseback arrangement are discussed in Subsection 30.2(f)(x).

(vii) Guaranteed Return on Investment—Sale-Leaseback.   A guarantee of cash flow to the buyer sometimes takes the form of a leaseback arrangement. Since the earnings process in this situation has not usually been completed, profits on the sale should generally be deferred and amortized.

Accounting for a sale-leaseback of real estate is governed by SFAS No. 13, "Accounting for Leases," as amended by SFAS No. 28, "Accounting for Sales with Leasebacks," SFAS No. 98, "Accounting for Leases: Sale-Leaseback Transactions Involving Real Estate," and SFAS No. 66. SFAS No. 98 specifies the accounting by a seller-lessee for a sale-leaseback transaction involving real estate, including real estate with equipment. SFAS No. 98 provides that:

- A sale-leaseback transaction involving real estate, including real estate with equipment, must qualify as a sale under the provisions of SFAS No. 66 as amended by SFAS No. 98, before it is appropriate for the seller-lessee to account for the transaction as a sale. If the transaction does not qualify as a sale under SFAS No. 66, it should be accounted for by the deposit method or as a financing transaction (see Subsection 30.2(j)(v)).

- A sale-leaseback transaction involving real estate, including real estate with equipment, that includes any continuing involvement other than a normal leaseback in which the seller-lessee intends to actively use the property during the lease should be accounted for by the deposit method or as a financing transaction.

- A lease involving real estate may not be classified as a sales-type lease unless the lease agreement provides for the transfer of title to the lessee at or shortly after the end of the lease term. Sales-type leases involving real estate should be accounted for under the provisions of SFAS No. 66.

Profit Recognition. Profits should be deferred and amortized in a manner consistent with the classification of the leaseback:

- If the leaseback is an operating lease, deferred profit should be amortized in proportion to the related gross rental charges to expense over the lease term.
- If the leaseback is a capital lease, deferred profit should be amortized in proportion to the amortization of the leased asset. Effectively, the sale is treated as a financing transaction. The deferred profit can be presented gross, but normally is offset against the capitalized asset for balance sheet classification purposes.

In situations where the leaseback covers only a minor portion of the property sold or the period is relatively minor compared to the remaining useful life of the property, it may be appropriate to recognize all or a portion of the gain as income. Sales with minor leasebacks should be accounted for based on the separate terms of the sale and the leaseback unless the rentals called for by the leaseback are unreasonable in relation to current market conditions. If rentals are considered to be unreasonable, they must be adjusted to a reasonable amount in computing the profit on the sale.

The leaseback is considered to be minor when the present value of the leaseback based on reasonable rentals is 10 percent or less of the fair value of the asset sold. If the leaseback is not considered to be minor (but less than substantially all of the use of the asset is retained through a leaseback) profit may be recognized to the extent it exceeds the present value of the minimum lease payments (net of executory costs) in the case of an operating lease or the recorded amount of the leased asset in the case of a capital lease.

Loss Recognition. Losses should be recognized immediately to the extent that the undepreciated cost (net carrying value) exceeds the fair value of the property. Fair value is frequently determined by the selling price from which the loss on the sale is measured. Many sale-leasebacks are entered into as a means of financing, or for tax reasons, or both. The terms of the leaseback are negotiated as a package. Because of the interdependence of the sale and concurrent leaseback, the selling price in some cases is not representative of fair value. It would not be appropriate to recognize a loss on the sale that would be offset by future cost reductions as a result of either reduced rental costs under an operating lease or depreciation and interest charges under a capital lease. Therefore, to the extent that the fair value is greater than the sale price, losses should be deferred and amortized in the same manner as profits.

(viii) Services without Adequate Compensation. A sales contract may be accompanied by an agreement for the seller to provide management or other services without adequate compensation. Compensation for the value of the services should be imputed, deducted from the sales price, and recognized over the term of the contract. See discussion of implied support of operations in Subsection 30.2(f)(x) if the contract is noncancelable and the compensation is unusual for the services to be rendered.

(ix) Development and Construction. A sale of undeveloped or partially developed land may include or be accompanied by an agreement requiring future seller performance of development or construction. In such cases, all or a portion of the profit should be deferred. If there is a lapse of time between the sale agreement and the future performance agreement, deferral provisions usually apply if definitive development plans existed at the time of sale and a development contract was anticipated by the parties at the time of entering into the sales contract.

In addition, SFAS No. 66 (par. 41) provides that "The seller is involved with future development or construction work if the buyer is unable to pay amounts due for that work or has the right under the terms of the arrangement to defer payment until the work is done."

If the property sold and being developed is an operating property (such as an apartment complex, shopping center, or office building) as opposed to a nonoperating property (such as a land lot, condominium unit, or single-family detached home), Subsection 30.2(f)(x) may also apply.

Completed Contract Method.   If a seller is obligated to develop the property or construct facilities and total costs and profit cannot be reliably estimated (e.g., because of lack of seller experience or nondefinitive plans), all profit, including profit on the sale of land, should be deferred until the contract is completed or until the total costs and profit can be reliably estimated. Under the completed contract method, all profit, including profit on the sale of land, is deferred until the seller's obligations are fulfilled.

Percentage of Completion Method (Cost-Incurred Method).   If the costs and profit can be reliably estimated, profit recognition over the improvement period on the basis of costs incurred (including land) as a percentage of total costs to be incurred is required. Thus, if the land was a principal part of the sale and its market value greatly exceeded cost, part of the profit that can be said to be related to the land sale is deferred and recognized during the development or construction period.

The same rate of profit is used for all seller costs connected with the transaction. For this purpose, the cost of development work, improvements, and all fees and expenses that are the responsibility of the seller should be included. The buyer's initial and continuing investment tests, of course, must be met with respect to the total sales value. Exhibit 30.4 illustrates the cost incurred method.

(x) Initiation and Support of Operations.   If the property sold is an operating property, as opposed to a nonoperating property, deferral of all or a portion of the profit may be required under SFAS No. 66 (pars. 28–30). These paragraphs establish guidelines not only for stated support but also for implied support.

Although the implied support provisions do not usually apply to undeveloped or partially developed land, they do apply if the buyer has commitments to construct operating properties and there is stated or implied support.

Assuming that the criteria for recording a sale and the test of buyer's investment are met, the following sets forth guidelines for profit recognition where there is stated or implied support.

Assumptions:

1. Sale of land for commercial development—$475,000.
2. Development contract—$525,000.
3. Down payment and other buyer investment requirements met.
4. Land costs—$200,000.
5. Development costs $500,000 (reliably estimated)—$325,000 incurred in initial year.

Calculation of profit to be recognized in initial year:

Sale of land	$ 475,000
Development contract price	525,000
Total sales price	1,000,000
Costs:	
Land	200,000
Development	500,000
Total costs	700,000
Total profit anticipated	$ 300,000
Cost incurred through end of initial year:	
Land	200,000
Development	$ 325,000
Total	$ 525,000
Profit to be recognized in initial year—525,000 4 700,000 × 300,000 =	$ 225,000

Exhibit 30.4   Percentage of completion, or cost-incurred, method.

Stated Support.   A seller may be required to support operations by means of a guaranteed return to the buyer. Alternatively, a guarantee may be made to the buyer that there will be no negative cash flow from the project, buy may not guarantee a positive return on the buyer's investment. For example, EITF Consensus No. 85-27 "Recognition of Receipts from Made-Up Rental Shortfalls," considers the impact of a master lease guarantee. The broad exposure that such a guarantee creates has a negative impact on profit recognition.

Implied Support.   The seller may be presumed to be obligated to initiate and support operations of the property sold, even in the absence of specified requirements in the sale contract or related document. The following conditions under which support is implied are described in footnote 10 of SFAS No. 66:

- A seller obtains an interest as general partner in a limited partnership that acquires an interest in the property sold.
- A seller retains an equity interest in the property, such as an undivided interest or an equity interest in a joint venture that holds an interest in the property.
- A seller holds a receivable from a buyer for a significant part of the sales price and collection of the receivable is dependent on the operation of the property.
- A seller agrees to manage the property for the buyer on terms not usual for the services to be rendered and which is not terminable by either seller or buyer.

Stated or Implied Support.   When profit recognition is appropriate in the case of either stated or implied support, the following general rules apply:

- Profit is recognized on the ratio of costs incurred to total costs to be incurred. Revenues for gross profit purposes include rent from operations during the rent-up period; costs include land and operating expenses during the rent-up period as well as other costs.
- As set forth in SFAS No. 66 (par. 30):

  > [S]upport shall be presumed for at least two years from the time of initial rental unless actual rental operations cover operating expenses, debt service, and other contractual commitments before that time. If the seller is contractually obligated for a longer time, profit recognition shall continue on the basis of performance until the obligation expires.

- Estimated rental income should be adjusted by reducing estimated future rent receipts by a safety factor of $33^1/_3$ percent unless signed lease agreements have been obtained to support a projection higher than the rental level thus computed. As set forth in SFAS No. 66 (par. 29), when signed leases amount to more than $66^2/_3$ percent of estimated rents, no additional safety factor is required but only amounts under signed lease agreements can be included.

(xi) Partial Sales.   A partial sale includes the following:

- A sale of an interest in real estate
- A sale of real estate where the seller has an equity interest in the buyer (e.g., a joint venture or partnership)
- A sale of a condominium unit

Sale of an Interest in Real Estate.   Except for operating properties, profit recognition is appropriate in a sale of a partial interest if all the following conditions exist:

- Sale is to an independent buyer.
- Collection of sales price is reasonably assured.

- The seller will not be required to support the property, its operations, or related obligations to an extent greater than its proportionate interest.
- Buyer does not have preferences as to profits or cash flow. (If the buyer has such preferences, the cost recovery method is required.)

In the case of a sale of a partial interest in operating properties, if the conditions set forth in the preceding paragraph are met, profit recognition must reflect an adjustment for the implied presumption that the seller is obligated to support the operations.

Seller Has Equity Interest in Buyer.   No profit may be recognized if the seller controls the buyer. If seller does not control the buyer, profit recognition (to the extent of the other investors' proportionate interests) is appropriate if all other necessary requirements for profit recognition are satisfied. The portion of the profit applicable to the equity interest of the seller/investor should be deferred until such costs are charged to operations by the venture. Again, with respect to a sale of operating properties, a portion of the profit relating to other investors' interests may have to be spread as described in Subsection 30.2(f)(x) because there is an implied presumption that the seller is obligated to support the operations.

(g) SALES OF CONDOMINIUMS.   Although the definition of "condominium" varies by state, the term generally is defined as a multiunit structure in which there is fee simple title to individual units combined with an undivided interest in the common elements associated with the structure. The common elements are all areas exclusive of the individual units, such as hallways, lobbies, and elevators.

A cooperative is contrasted to a condominium in that ownership of the building is generally vested in the entity, with the respective stockholders of the entity having a right to occupy specific units. Operation, maintenance, and control of the building are exercised by a governing board elected by the owners. This section covers only sales of condominium units.

(i) Criteria for Profit Recognition.   The general principles of accounting for profit on sales of condominiums are essentially those previously discussed for sales of real estate in general. The following criteria must be met prior to recognition of any profit on the sale of a dwelling unit in a condominium project:

- All parties must be bound by the terms of the contract. For the buyer to be bound, the buyer must be unable to require a refund. Certain state and federal laws require appropriate filings by the developer before the sales contract is binding; otherwise, the sale may be voidable at the option of the buyer.
- All conditions precedent to closing, except completion of the project, must be performed.
- An adequate cash down payment must be received by the seller. The minimum down payment requirements are 5 percent for a primary residence and 10 percent for a secondary or recreational residence.
- The buyer must be required to adequately increase the investment in the property annually; the buyer's commitment must be adequately secured. Typically, a condominium buyer pays the remaining balance from the proceeds of a permanent loan at the time of closing. If, however, the seller provides financing, the same considerations as other sales of real estate apply concerning amortization of the buyer's receivable.
- The developer must not have an option or obligation to repurchase the property.

(ii) Methods of Accounting.   Sales of condominium units are accounted for by using the closing (completed contract) method or the percentage of completion method. Most developers use the closing method.

Additional criteria must be met for the use of the percentage of completion method:

- The developer must have the ability to estimate costs not yet incurred.
- Construction must be beyond a preliminary stage of completion. This generally means at least beyond the foundation stage.
- Sufficient units must be sold to assure that the property will not revert to rental property.
- The developer must be able to reasonably estimate aggregate sales proceeds.

Closing Method.   This method involves recording the sale and related profit at the time a unit closes. Since the unit is completed, actual costs are used in determining profit to be recognized.

All payments or deposits received prior to closing are accounted for as a liability. Direct selling costs may be deferred until the sale is recorded. Where the seller is obligated to complete construction of common areas or has made guarantees to the condominium association, profit should be recognized based on the relationship of costs already incurred to total estimated costs, with a portion deferred until the future performance is completed.

Percentage of Completion Method.   This method generally involves recording sales at the date a unit is sold and recognizing profit on units sold as construction proceeds. As a result, this method allows some profit recognition during the construction period. Although dependent on estimates, this method may be considered preferable for some long-term projects. A lack of reliable estimates, however, would preclude the use of this method.

Profit recognition is based on the percentage of completion of the project multiplied by the gross profit arising from the units sold. Percentage of completion may be determined by using either of the following alternatives:

- The ratio of costs incurred to date to total estimated costs to be incurred. These costs could include land and common costs or could be limited to construction costs. The costs selected for inclusion should be those that most clearly reflect the earnings process.
- The percentage of completed construction based on architectural plans or engineering studies.

Under either method of accounting, if the total estimated costs exceed the estimated proceeds, the total anticipated loss should be charged against income in the period in which the loss becomes evident so that no anticipated losses are deferred to future periods. See further discussion of this method in Section 30.6, "Construction Contracts."

(iii) Estimated Future Costs.   As previously mentioned, future costs to complete must be estimated under either the closing method or the percentage of completion method. Estimates of future costs to complete are necessary to determine net realizable value of unsold units. Estimated future costs should be based on adequate architectural and engineering studies and should include reasonable provisions for:

- Unforeseen costs in accordance with sound cost estimation practices
- Anticipated cost inflation in the construction industry
- Costs of offsite improvements, utility facilities, and amenities (to the extent that they will not be recovered from outside third parties)
- Operating losses of utility operations and recreational facilities (Such losses would be expected to be incurred for a relatively limited period of time—usually prior to sale of facilities or transfer to some public authority.)
- Other guaranteed support arrangements or activities to the extent that they will not be recovered from outside parties or be the responsibility of a future purchaser

Estimates of amounts to be recovered from any sources should be discounted to present value as of the date the related costs are expected to be incurred.

Estimated costs to complete and the allocation of such costs should be reviewed at the end of each financial reporting period, with costs revised and reallocated as necessary on the basis of current estimates, as recommended in SFAS No. 67, "Accounting for Costs and Initial Rental Operations of Real Estate Projects." How to record the effects of changes in estimates depends on whether full revenues have been recorded or whether reporting of the revenue has been deferred due to an obligation for future performance or otherwise.

When sales of condominiums are recorded in full, it may be necessary to accrue certain estimated costs not yet incurred and also related profit thereon. Adjustments of accruals for costs applicable to such previously recognized sales, where deferral for future performance was not required, must be recognized and charged to costs of sales in the period in which they become known. See Subsection 30.2(g)(ii) for further discussion.

In many cases, sales are not recorded in full (such as when the seller has deferred revenue because of an obligation for future performance to complete improvements and amenities of a project). In these situations, the adjustments should not affect previously recorded deferred revenues applicable to future improvements but should be recorded prospectively in the current and future periods. An increase in the estimate of costs applicable to deferred revenues will thus result in profit margins lower than those recorded on previous revenues from the project.

An exception exists, however, when the revised total estimated costs exceed the applicable deferred revenue. If that occurs, the total anticipated loss should be charged against income in the period in which the need for adjustment becomes evident.

In addition, an increase in estimated costs to complete without comparable increases in market value could raise questions as to whether the estimated total costs of the remaining property exceed the project's net realizable value.

APB Opinion No. 20, "Accounting Changes," has been interpreted to permit both the cumulative catch-up method and the prospective method of accounting for changes in accounting estimates. It should be noted that SFAS No. 67 (pars. 42–43) requires the prospective method.

(h) RETAIL LAND SALES. Retail land sales, a unique segment of the real estate industry, is the retail marketing of numerous lots subdivided from a larger parcel of land. The relevant accounting guidance originally covered by the AICPA Industry Accounting Guide, "Accounting for Retail Land Sales," and now included in SFAS No. 66, applies to retail lot sales on a volume basis with down payments that are less than those required to evaluate the collectibility of casual sales of real estate. Wholesale or bulk sales of land and retail sales from projects comprising a small number of lots, however, are subject to the general principles for profit recognition on real estate sales.

(i) Criteria for Recording a Sale.   Sales should not be recorded until:

- The customer has made all required payments and the period of cancellation with refund has expired.
- Aggregate payments (including interest) equal or exceed 10 percent of contract sales price.
- The selling company is clearly capable of providing land improvements and offsite facilities promised as well as meeting all other representations it has made.

If these conditions are met, either the accrual or the installment method must be used. If the conditions are not met, the deposit method of accounting should be used.

(ii) Criteria for Accrual Method.   The following tests for the use of accrual method should be applied on a project-by-project basis:

- The seller has fulfilled the obligation to complete improvements and to construct amenities or other facilities applicable to the lots sold.

- The receivable is not subject to subordination to new loans on the property, except subordination for home construction purposes under certain conditions.
- The collection experience for the project indicates that collectibility of receivable balances is reasonably predictable and that 90 percent of the contracts in force six months after sales are recorded will be collected in full. A down payment of at least 20 percent shall be an acceptable indication of collectibility.

To predict collection results of current sales, there must be satisfactory experience on prior sales of the type of land being currently sold in the project. In addition, the collection period must be sufficiently long to allow reasonable estimates of the percentage of sales that will be fully collected. In a new project, the developers' experience on prior projects may be used if they have demonstrated an ability to successfully develop other projects with the same characteristics (environment, clientele, contract terms, sales methods) as the new project.

Collection and cancellation experience within a project may differ with varying sales methods (such as telephone, broker, and site visitation sales). Accordingly, historical data should be maintained with respect to each type of sales method used.

Unless all conditions for use of the accrual method are met for the entire project, the installment method of accounting should be applied to all recorded sales of the project.

(iii) Accrual Method. Revenues and costs should be accounted for under the accrual method as follows:

- The contract price should be recorded as gross sales.
- Receivables should be discounted to reflect an appropriate interest rate using the criteria established in APB Opinion No. 21.
- An allowance for contract cancellation should be recorded and deducted from gross sales to derive net sales.
- Cost of sales should be calculated based on net sales after reductions for sales reasonably expected to cancel.

(iv) Percentage of Completion Method. Frequently, the conditions for use of the accrual method are met, except the seller has not yet completed the improvements, amenities, or other facilities required by the sales contract. In this situation the percentage of completion method should be applied provided both of the following conditions are met:

- There is a reasonable expectation that the land can be developed for the purposes represented.
- The project's improvements have progressed beyond preliminary stages, and there are indications that the work will be completed according to plan. Indications that the project has progressed beyond the preliminary stage include the following:
  - Funds for the proposed improvements have been expended.
  - Work on the improvements has been initiated.
  - Engineering plans and work commitments exist relating to the lots sold.
  - Access roads and amenities such as golf courses, clubhouses, and swimming pools have been completed.

In addition, there shall be no indication of significant delaying factors such as the inability to obtain permits, contractors, personnel, or equipment, and estimates of costs to complete and extent of progress toward completion shall be reasonably dependable.

The following general procedures should be used to account for revenues and costs under the percentage of completion method of accounting:

- The amount of revenue recognized (discounted where appropriate pursuant to APB Opinion No. 21) is based on the relationship of costs already incurred to the total estimated costs to be incurred.
- Costs incurred and to be incurred should include land, interest and project carrying costs incurred prior to sale, selling costs, and an estimate for future improvement costs.

Estimates of future improvement costs should be reviewed at least annually. Changes in those estimates do not lead to adjustment of deferred revenue applicable to future improvements that has been previously recorded unless the adjusted total estimated costs exceeds the applicable revenue. When cost estimates are revised, the relationship of the two elements included in the revenue not yet recognized—cost and profit—should be recalculated on a cumulative basis to determine future income recognition as performance takes place. If the adjusted total estimated cost exceeds the applicable deferred revenue, the total anticipated loss should be charged to income. When anticipated losses on lots sold are recognized, the enterprise should also consider recognizing a loss on land and improvements not yet sold.

Future performance costs such as roads, utilities, and amenities may represent a significant obligation for a retail land developer. Estimates of such costs should be based on adequate engineering studies, appropriately adjusted for anticipated inflation in the local construction industry, and should include reasonable estimates for unforeseen costs.

(v) Installment and Deposit Methods.   If the criteria for the accrual or percentage of completion methods are not satisfied, the installment or deposit method may be used. See Subsection 30.2(j) for a general discussion of these methods.

When the conditions required for use of the percentage of completion method are met on a project originally recorded under the installment method, the percentage of completion method of accounting should be adopted for the entire project (current and prior sales). The effect should be accounted for as a change in accounting estimate due to different circumstances. See Subsection 30.2(g)(iii) for further discussion of methodology.

(i) ACCOUNTING FOR SYNDICATION FEES.   On February 6, 1992, the AICPA issued Statement of Position (SOP) 92-1, which provides guidance on accounting for real estate syndication income.

Syndicators expect to earn fees and commissions from a variety of sources: up-front fees such as lease-up fees, construction supervision fees, and financing fees; fees serving as an incentive; property management; participation in future profit or appreciation. At the time of the syndication, partnerships usually pay cash to the syndicator for portions of their up-front fees. These fees are usually paid from investor contributions or the proceeds of borrowings. Subsequent fees are expected to be paid from operations, refinancings, sale of property, or remaining investor payments.

The SOP states that SFAS No. 66 applies to the recognition of profit on the sales of real estate by syndicators to partnerships. It concludes that profit on real estate syndication transactions be accounted for in accordance with SFAS No. 66, even if the syndicator never had ownership interests in the properties acquired by the real estate partnerships.

The SOP states that fees charged by syndicators (except for syndication fees and fees for future services) should be included in the determination of "sales value" in conformity with SFAS No. 66. It further states that SFAS No. 66 does not apply to the fees excluded from "sales value." Fees for future services should be recognized when the earning process is complete and collection of the fee is reasonably assured.

This SOP requires that income recognition on syndication fees and fees for future services be deferred if the syndicator is exposed to future losses or costs from material involvement with the properties, partnerships or partners, or uncertainties regarding the collectibility of partnership notes. The income should be deferred until the losses or costs can be reasonably estimated.

The SOP requires that for the purpose of determining whether buyers' initial and continuing investments satisfy the requirements for recognizing full profit in accordance with SFAS No. 66, cash received by syndicators should be allocated to unpaid syndication fees before being allocated to the initial and continuing investment. After the syndication fee is fully paid, additional cash received should first be allocated to unpaid fees for future services, to the extent those services have been performed by the time the cash is received, before being allocated to the initial and continuing investment.

(j) ALTERNATE METHODS OF ACCOUNTING FOR SALES. As previously discussed, in some circumstances the accrual method is not appropriate and other methods must be used. It is not always clear which method should be used or how it should be applied. Consequently, it is often difficult to determine the appropriate method and whether alternative ones are acceptable.

The methods prescribed where the buyer's initial or continuing investment is inadequate are the deposit, installment, cost recovery, and reduced profit methods.

The methods prescribed for a transaction that cannot be considered a sale because of the seller's continuing involvement are the financing, lease, and profit sharing (or co-venture) methods.

(i) Deposit Method. When the substance of a real estate transaction indicates that a sale has not occurred, for accounting purposes, as a result of the buyer's inadequate investment, recognition of the sale should be deferred and the deposit method used. This method should be continued until the conditions requiring its use no longer exist. For example, when the down payment is so small that the substance of the transaction is an option arrangement, the sale should not be recorded.

All cash received under the deposit method (including down payment and principal and interest payments by the buyer to the seller) should be reported as a deposit (liability). An exception is interest received that is not subject to refund may appropriately offset carrying charges (property taxes and interest on existing debt) on the property. Note also the following related matters:

- Notes receivable arising from the transaction should not be recorded.
- The property and any related mortgage debt assumed by the buyer should continue to be reflected on the seller's balance sheet, with appropriate disclosure that such properties and debt are subject to a sales contract. Even nonrecourse debt assumed by the buyer should not be offset against the related property.
- Subsequent payments on the debt assumed by the buyer become additional deposits and thereby reduce the seller's mortgage debt payable and increase the deposit liability account until a sale is recorded for accounting purposes.
- Depreciation should be continued.

Under the deposit method, a sale is not recorded for accounting purposes until the conditions in SFAS No. 66 are met. Therefore, for purposes of the down payment tests, interest received and credited to the deposit account can be included in the down payment and sales value at the time a sale is recorded.

If a buyer defaults and forfeits his nonrefundable deposit, the deposit liability is no longer required and may be credited to income. The circumstances underlying the default should be carefully reviewed since such circumstances may indicate deteriorating value of the property. In such a case it may be appropriate to treat the credit as a valuation reserve. These circumstances may require a provision for additional loss. See Section 30.5 for further discussion.

(ii) Installment Method. When the substance of a real estate transaction indicates that a sale has occurred for accounting purposes, but that collectibility of the total sales price cannot be reasonably estimated (i.e., inadequate buyer's investment), the installment method may be appropriate. However, circumstances may indicate that the cost recovery method is required or is otherwise more appropriate. For example, when the deferred gross profit exceeds the net carrying value of the related receivable, profit may have been earned to the extent of such excess.

Profit should be recognized on cash payments, including principal payments by the buyer on any debt assumed (either recourse or nonrecourse), and should be based on the ratio of total profit to total sales value (including a first mortgage debt assumed by the buyer, if applicable). Interest received on the related receivable is properly recorded as income when received.

The total sales value (from which the deferred gross profit should be deducted) and the cost of sales should be presented in the income statement. Deferred gross profit should be shown as a deduction from the related receivable, with subsequent income recognition presented separately in the income statement.

(iii) Cost Recovery Method.   The cost recovery method must be used when the substance of a real estate transaction indicates that a sale has occurred for accounting purposes but no profit should be recognized until costs are recovered. This may occur when (1) the receivable is subject to future subordination, (2) the seller retains an interest in the property sold and the buyer has preferences, (3) uncertainty exists as to whether all or a portion of the cost will be recovered, or (4) there is uncertainty as to the amount of proceeds. As a practical matter, the cost recovery method can always be used as an alternative to the installment method.

Under the cost recovery method, no profit is recognized until cash collections (including principal and interest payments) and existing debt assumed by the buyer exceed the cost of the property sold. Cash collections in excess of cost should be recorded as revenue in the period of collection.

Financial statement presentation under the cost recovery method is similar to that for the installment method.

(iv) Reduced Profit Method.   When the substance of a real estate transaction indicates that a sale has occurred for accounting purposes, but the continuing investment criteria for full profit recognition is not met by the buyer, the seller may sometimes recognize a reduced profit at the time of sale (see additional discussion in Subsection 30.2(e)(ii)). This alternative is rarely used since a full accrual of anticipated costs of continuing investment will permit full accrual of the remaining profit.

(v) Financing Method.   A real estate transaction may be, in substance, a financing arrangement rather than a sale. This is frequently the case when the seller has an obligation to repurchase the property (or can be compelled by the buyer to repurchase the property) at a price higher than the total amount of the payments received and to be received. In such a case the financing method must be used.

Accounting procedures under the financing method should be similar to the accounting procedures under the deposit method, with one exception. Under the financing method, the difference between (1) the total amount of all payments received and to be received and (2) the repurchase price is presumed to be interest expense. As such, it should be accrued on the interest method over the period from the receipt of cash to the date of repurchase. As in the deposit method, cash received is reflected as a liability in the balance sheet. Thus, at the date of repurchase, the full amount of the repurchase obligation should be recorded as a liability.

In the case of a repurchase option, if the facts and circumstances at the time of the sale indicate a presumption or a likelihood that the seller will exercise the option, interest should be accrued as if there were an obligation to repurchase. This presumption could result from the value of the property, the property being an integral part of development, or from management's intention. If such a presumption does not exist at the time of the sale transaction, interest should not be accrued and the deposit method is appropriate.

(vi) Lease Method.   A real estate transaction may be, in substance, a lease rather than a sale. Accounting procedures under the lease method should be similar to the deposit method, except as follows:

- Payments received and to be received that are in substance deferred rental income received in advance should be deferred and amortized to income over the presumed lease period. Such amortization to income should not exceed cash paid to the seller.

- Cash paid out by the seller as a guarantee of support of operations should be expensed as paid.

The seller may agree to make *loans* to the *buyer* in support of operations, for example, when cash flow does not equal a predetermined amount or is negative. In such a situation, deferred rental income to be amortized to income should be reduced by all the loans made or reasonably anticipated to be made to the buyer, thus reducing the periodic income to be recognized. Where the loans made or anticipated exceed deferred rental income, a loss provision may be required if the collectibility of the loan is questionable.

(vii) Profit-Sharing or Co-Venture Method.   A real estate transaction may be, in substance, a profit-sharing arrangement rather than a sale. For example, a sale of real estate to a limited partnership in which the seller is a general partner or has similar characteristics is often a profit-sharing arrangement. If such a transaction does not meet the tests for recording a sale, it usually would be accounted for under the profit-sharing method. This accounting method should also be followed when it is clear that the buyer is acting merely as an agent for the seller.

Under the profit-sharing method, giving consideration to the seller's continued involvement, the seller would be required to account for the operations of the property through its income statement as if it continued to own the properties.

30.3 COST OF REAL ESTATE

(a) CAPITALIZATION OF COSTS.   In October 1982, the FASB issued SFAS No. 67. This Statement incorporates the specialized accounting principles and practices from the AICPA SOPs No. 80-3, "Accounting for Real Estate Acquisition, Development and Construction Costs," and No. 78-3, "Accounting for Costs to Sell and Rent, and Initial Rental Operations of Real Estate Projects," and those in the AICPA Industry Accounting Guide, "Accounting for Retail Land Sales," that address costs of real estate projects. SFAS No. 67 establishes whether costs associated with acquiring, developing, constructing, selling, and renting real estate projects should be capitalized. Guidance is also provided on the appropriate methods of allocating capitalized costs to individual components of the project.

SFAS No. 67 also established that a rental project changes from nonoperating to operating when it is substantially completed and held available for occupancy, but not later than one year from cessation of major construction activities.

What are the general precepts? Costs incurred in real estate operations range from brick-and-mortar costs that clearly should be capitalized to general administrative costs that clearly should not be capitalized. Between these two extremes lies a broad range of costs that are difficult to classify. Therefore, judgmental decisions must be made as to whether such costs should be capitalized.

(b) PREACQUISITION COSTS.   These costs include payments to obtain options to acquire real property and other costs incurred prior to acquisition such as legal, architectural, and other professional fees, salaries, environmental studies, appraisals, marketing and feasibility studies, and soil tests. Capitalization of costs related to a property that are incurred before the enterprise acquires the property, or before the enterprise obtains an option to acquire it, is appropriate provided all of the following conditions are met:

- The costs are directly identifiable with the specific property.
- The costs would be capitalized if the property had already been acquired.
- Acquisition of the property or of an option to acquire the property is probable (i.e., likely to occur). This condition requires that the prospective purchaser is actively seeking acquisition of the property and has the ability to finance or obtain financing for the acquisition. In addition, there should be no indication that the property is not available for sale.

Capitalized preacquisition costs should be included as project costs on acquisition of the property or should be charged to expense when it is probable that the property will not be acquired. The charge to expense should be reduced by the amount recoverable by the sale of the options, plans, and so on.

(c) LAND ACQUISITION COSTS.   Costs directly related to the acquisition of land should be capitalized. These costs include option fees, purchase cost, transfer costs, title insurance, legal and other professional fees, surveys, appraisals, and real estate commissions. The purchase cost may have to be increased or decreased for imputation of interest on mortgage notes payable assumed or issued in connection with the purchase, as required under APB Opinion No. 21.

(d) LAND IMPROVEMENT, DEVELOPMENT, AND CONSTRUCTION COSTS.   Costs directly related to improvements of the land should be capitalized by the developer. They may include:

- Land planning costs, including marketing and feasibility studies, direct salaries, legal and other professional fees, zoning costs, soil tests, architectural and engineering studies, appraisals, environmental studies, and other costs directly related to site preparation and the overall design and development of the project
- On-site and off-site improvements, including demolition costs, streets, traffic controls, side-walks, street lighting, sewer and water facilities, utilities, parking lots, landscaping, and related costs such as permits and inspection fees
- Construction costs, including onsite material and labor, direct supervision, engineering and architectural fees, permits, and inspection fees
- Project overhead and supervision, such as field office costs
- Recreation facilities, such as golf courses, clubhouse, swimming pools, and tennis courts
- Sales center and models, including furnishings

General and administrative costs not directly identified with the project should be accounted for as period costs and expensed as incurred.

Construction activity on a project may be suspended before a project is completed for reasons such as insufficient sales or rental demand. These conditions may indicate an impairment of the value of a project that is other than temporary, which suggests valuation issues (see Section 30.5).

(e) ENVIRONMENTAL ISSUES.   In EITF Issue No. 90-8, "Capitalization of Costs to Treat Environmental Contamination," the EITF reached a consensus that, in general, costs incurred as a result of environmental contamination should be charged to expense. Such costs include costs to remove contamination, such as that caused by leakage from underground tanks; costs to acquire tangible property, such as air pollution control equipment; costs of environmental studies; and costs of fines levied under environmental laws. Nevertheless, those costs may be capitalized if recoverable but only if any one of the following criteria is met:

- The costs extend the life, increase the capacity, or improve the safety or efficiency of property owned by the company, provided that the condition of the property after the costs are incurred must be improved as compared with the condition of the property when originally constructed or acquired, if later.
- The costs mitigate or prevent environmental contamination that has yet to occur and that otherwise may result from future operations or activities. In addition, the costs improve the property compared with its condition when constructed or acquired, if later.
- The costs are incurred in preparing for sale that property currently held for sale.

In EITF Issue No. 93-5, "Accounting for Environmental Liabilities," the EITF reached a consensus that an environmental liability should be evaluated independently from any potential claim for recovery (a two-event approach) and that the loss arising from the recognition of an environmental liability should be reduced only when it is probable that a claim for recovery will be realized.

The EITF also reached a consensus that discounting environmental liabilities for a specific clean-up site to reflect the time value of money is allowed, but not required, only if the aggregate amount of the obligation and the amount and timing of the cash payments for that site are fixed or reliably determinable.

The EITF discussed alternative rates to be used in discounting environmental liabilities but did not reach a consensus on the rate to be used. However, the Securities and Exchange Commission (SEC) observer stated that SEC registrants should use a discount rate that will produce an amount at which the environmental liability theoretically could be settled in an arm's-length transaction with a third party. That discount rate should not exceed the interest rate on monetary assets that are essentially risk-free and have maturities comparable to that of the environmental liability. In addition, SEC Staff Accounting Bulletin (SAB) 92 requires registrants to separately present the gross liability and related claim recovery in the balance sheet. SAB 92 also requires other accounting and disclosure requirements relating to product or environmental liabilities.

In October 1996, the AICPA issued SOP 96-1, "Environmental Remediation Liabilities." The SOP has three parts. Part I provides an overview of environmental laws and regulations. Part II provides authoritative guidance on the recognition, measurement, display, and disclosure of environmental liabilities. And part III (labeled as an appendix) provides guidance for auditors. A major objective of the SOP is to articulate a framework for the recognition, measurement, and disclosure of environmental liabilities. That framework is derived from SFAS No. 5, "Accounting for Contingencies."

The accounting guidance in the SOP is generally applicable when an entity is mandated to remediate a contaminated site by a governmental agency. However, the SOP does not address the following:

- Accounting for pollution control costs with respect to current operations, which is addressed in EITF Issue No. 90-8, "Capitalization of Costs to Treat Environmental Contamination"
- Accounting for costs with respect to asbestos removal, which is addressed in EITF Issue No. 89-13, "Accounting for the Costs of Asbestos Removal"
- Accounting for costs of future site restoration or closure that are required upon the cessation of operations or sale of facilities, which is the subject of the FASB's project, "Obligations Associated with Disposal Activities"
- Accounting for environmental remediation actions that are undertaken at the sole discretion of management and that are not undertaken by the threat of assertion of litigation, a claim, or an assessment
- Recognizing liabilities of insurance companies for unpaid claims, which is addressed in SFAS No. 60, "Accounting and Reporting by Insurance Enterprises"
- Asset impairment issues discussed in SFAS No. 144, "Accounting for the Impairment or Disposal of Long-Lived Assets," and EITF Issue No. 95-23, "The Treatment of Certain Site Restoration/Environmental Exit Costs When Testing a Long-Lived Asset for Impairment"

(f) INTEREST COSTS.   Prior to 1979, many developers capitalized interest costs as a necessary cost of the asset in the same way as bricks-and-mortar costs. Others followed an accounting policy of charging off interest cost as a period cost on the basis that it was solely a financing cost that varied directly with the capability of a company to finance development and construction through equity funds. This long-standing debate on capitalization of interest cost was resolved in October 1979 when the FASB published SFAS No. 34, "Capitalization of Interest Cost," which provides specific guidelines for accounting for interest costs.

SFAS No. 34 requires capitalization of interest cost as part of the historical cost of acquiring assets that need a period of time in which to bring them to that condition and location necessary for their intended use. The objectives of capitalizing interest are to obtain a measure of acquisition cost that more closely reflects the enterprise's total investment in the asset and to charge a cost that relates to the acquisition of a resource that will benefit future periods against the revenues of the periods benefited. Interest capitalization is not required if its effect is not material.

(i) Assets Qualifying for Interest Capitalization.   Assets qualifying for interest capitalization in conformity with SFAS No. 34 include real estate constructed for an enterprise's own use or real estate intended for sale or lease. Qualifying assets also include investments (equity, loans, and advances) accounted for by the equity method while the investee has activities in progress necessary to commence its planned principal operations, but only if the investee's activities include the use of such to acquire qualifying assets for its operations.

Capitalization is not permitted for assets in use or ready for their intended use, assets not undergoing the activities necessary to prepare them for use, assets that are not included in the consolidated balance sheet, or investments accounted for by the equity method after the planned principal operations of the investee begin. Thus land that is not undergoing activities necessary for development is not a qualifying asset for purposes of interest capitalization. If activities are undertaken for developing the land, the expenditures to acquire the land qualify for interest capitalization while those activities are in progress.

(ii) Capitalization Period.   The capitalization period commences when:

- Expenditures for the asset have been made.
- Activities that are necessary to get the asset ready for its intended use are in progress.
- Interest cost is being incurred.

Activities are to be construed in a broad sense and encompass more than just physical construction. All steps necessary to prepare an asset for its intended use are included. This broad interpretation includes administrative and technical activities during the preconstruction stage (such as developing plans or obtaining required permits).

Interest capitalization must end when the asset is substantially complete and ready for its intended use. A real estate project should be considered substantially complete and held available for occupancy upon completion of major construction activity, as distinguished from activities such as routine maintenance and cleanup. In some cases, such as in an office building, tenant improvements are a major construction activity and are frequently not completed until a lease contract is arranged. If such improvements are the responsibility of the developer, SFAS No. 67 indicates that the project is not considered substantially complete until the earlier of (1) completion of improvements or (2) one year from cessation of major construction activity without regard to tenant improvements. In other words, a one-year grace period has been provided to complete tenant improvements.

If substantially all activities related to acquisition of the asset are suspended, interest capitalization should stop until such activities are resumed. However, brief interruptions in activities, interruptions caused by external factors, and inherent delays in the development process do not necessarily require suspension of interest capitalization.

Under SFAS No. 34, interest capitalization must end when the asset is substantially complete and ready for its intended use. For projects completed in parts, where each part is capable of being used independently while work continues on other parts, interest capitalization should stop on each part that is substantially complete and ready for use. Examples include individual buildings in a multiphase or condominium project. For projects that must be completed before any part can be used, interest capitalization should continue until the entire project is substantially complete and ready for use. Where an asset cannot be used effectively until a particular portion has been completed, interest capitalization continues until that portion is substantially complete and ready for use. An example would be an island resort complex with sole access being a permanent bridge to the project. Completion of the bridge is necessary for the asset to be used effectively.

Interest capitalization should not stop when the capitalized costs exceed net realizable value. In such instances, a valuation reserve should be recorded or appropriately increased to reduce the carrying value to net realizable value (see Subsection 30.3(l)).

(iii) Methods of Interest Capitalization. The basic principle is that the amount of interest cost to be capitalized should be the amount that theoretically could have been avoided during the development and construction period if expenditures for the qualifying asset had not been made. These interest costs might have been avoided either by forgoing additional borrowing or by using the funds expended for the asset to repay existing borrowings in the case where no new borrowings were obtained.

The amount capitalized is determined by applying a capitalization rate to the average amount of accumulated capitalized expenditures for the asset during the period. Such expenditures include cash payments, transfer of other assets, or incurrence of liabilities on which interest has been recognized, and they should be net of progress payments received against such capitalized costs. Liabilities such as trade payables, accruals, and retainages, on which interest is not recognized, are not expenditures. Reasonable approximations of net capitalized expenditures may be used.

In general, the capitalization rate should be based on the weighted average of the rates applicable to borrowings outstanding during the period. If a specific new borrowing is associated with an asset, the rate on that borrowing may be used. If the average amount of accumulated expenditures for the asset exceeds the amounts of specific new borrowings associated with the asset, a weighted average interest rate of all other borrowings must be applied to the excess. Under this alternative, judgment will be required to select the borrowings to be included in the weighted average rate so that a reasonable measure will be obtained of the interest cost incurred that could otherwise have been avoided. It should be remembered that the principle is not one of capitalizing interest costs incurred for a specific asset, but one of capitalizing interest costs that could have been avoided if it were not for the acquisition, development, and construction of the asset.

The amount of interest cost capitalized in an accounting period is limited to the total amount of interest cost incurred in the period. However, interest cost should include amortization of premium or discount resulting from imputation of interest on certain types of payables in accordance with APB Opinion No. 21 and that portion of minimum lease payments under a capital lease treated as interest in accordance with SFAS No. 13.

(iv) Accounting for Amount Capitalized. Interest cost capitalized is an integral part of the cost of acquiring a qualifying asset, and therefore its disposition should be the same as any other cost of that asset. For example, if a building is subsequently depreciated, capitalized interest should be included in the depreciable base the same as bricks and mortar.

In the case of interest capitalized on an investment accounted for by the equity method, its disposition should be made as if the investee were consolidated. In other words, if the assets of the investee were being depreciated, the capitalized interest cost should be depreciated in the same manner and over the same lives. If the assets of the investee were developed lots being sold, the capitalized interest cost should be written off as the lots are sold.

(g) TAXES AND INSURANCE. Costs incurred on real estate for property taxes and insurance should be treated similarly to interest costs. They should be capitalized only during periods in which activities necessary to get the property ready for its intended use are in progress. Costs incurred for such items after the property is substantially complete and ready for its intended use should be charged to expense as incurred.

(h) INDIRECT PROJECT COSTS. Indirect project costs that relate to a specific project, such as costs associated with a project field office, should be capitalized as a cost of that project. Other indirect project costs that relate to several projects, such as the costs associated with a construction administration department, should be capitalized and allocated to the projects to which the cost related. Indirect costs that do not clearly relate to projects under development or construction should be charged to expense as incurred.

The principal problem is defining and identifying the cost to be capitalized. It is necessary to consider all of the following points:

- Specific information should be available (such as timecards) to support the basis of allocation to specific projects.
- The costs incurred should be incremental costs; that is, in the absence of the project or projects under development or construction, these costs would not be incurred.
- The impact of capitalization of such costs on the results of operations should be consistent with the pervasive principle of matching costs with related revenue.
- The principle of conservatism should be considered.

Indirect costs related to a specific project that should be considered for capitalization include direct and indirect salaries of a field office and insurance costs. Costs that are not directly related to the project should be charged to expense as incurred.

(i) GENERAL AND ADMINISTRATIVE EXPENSES.   Real estate developers incur various types of general and administrative expenses, including officers' salaries, accounting and legal fees, and various office supplies and expenses. Some of these expenses may be closely associated with individual projects, whereas others are of a more general nature. For example, a developer may open a field office on a project site and staff it with administrative personnel, such as a field accountant. The expenses associated with the field office are directly associated with the project and are therefore considered to be overhead. On the other hand, the developer may have a number of expenses associated with general office operations that benefit numerous projects and for which specifically identifiable allocations are not reasonable or practicable. Those administrative costs that cannot be clearly related to projects under development or construction should be charged to current operations.

(j) AMENITIES.   Real estate developments often include *amenities* such as golf courses, utilities, clubhouses, swimming pools, and tennis courts. The accounting for the costs of these amenities should be based on management's intended disposition as follows:

- *Amenity to Be Sold or Transferred with Sales Units.* All costs in excess of anticipated proceeds should be allocated as common costs because the amenity is clearly associated with the development and sale of the project. Common costs should include estimated net operating costs to be borne by the developer until they are assumed by buyers of units in the project.
- *Amenity to Be Sold Separately or Retained by Developer.* Capitalizable costs of the amenity in excess of its estimated fair value on the expected date of its substantial physical completion should be allocated as common costs. The costs capitalized and allocated to the amenity should not be revised after the amenity is substantially completed and available for use. A later sale of the amenity at more or less than the determined fair value as of the date of substantial physical completion, less any accumulated depreciation, should result in a gain or loss in the period in which the sale occurs.

(k) ABANDONMENTS AND CHANGES IN USE.   Real estate, including rights to real estate, may be abandoned, for example, by allowing a mortgage to be foreclosed or by allowing a purchase option to lapse. Capitalized costs, including allocated common costs, of real estate abandoned should be written off as current expenses or, if appropriate, to allowances previously established for that purpose. They should not be allocated to other components of the project or to other projects, even if other components or other projects are capable of absorbing the losses.

Donation of real estate to municipalities or other governmental agencies for uses that will benefit the project are not abandonment. The cost of real estate donated should be allocated as a common cost of the project.

Changes in the intended use of a real estate project may arise after significant development and construction costs have been incurred. If the change in use is made pursuant to a formal plan that is expected to produce a higher economic yield (as compared to its yield based on use before change), the project costs should be charged to expense to the extent the capitalized costs incurred and to be incurred exceed the estimated fair value less cost to sell of the revised project when it is substantially completed and ready for its intended use.

(l) SELLING COSTS.   Costs incurred to sell real estate projects should be accounted for in the same manner as, and classified with, construction costs of the project when they meet both of the following criteria:

- The costs incurred are for tangible assets that are used throughout the selling period or for services performed to obtain regulatory approval for sales.
- The costs are reasonably expected to be recovered from sales of the project or incidental operations.

Examples of costs incurred to sell real estate projects that ordinarily meet the criteria for capitalization are costs of model units and their furnishings, sales facilities, legal fees for the preparation of prospectuses, and semipermanent signs.

SFAS No. 67 states that other costs incurred to sell real estate projects should be capitalized as prepaid costs if they are directly associated with and their recovery is reasonably expected from sales that are being accounted for under a method of accounting other than full accrual. Costs that do not meet the criteria for capitalization should be expensed as incurred.

Capitalized selling costs should be charged to expense in the period in which the related revenue is recognized as earned. When a sales contract is canceled (with or without refund) or the related receivable is written off as uncollectible, the related unrecoverable capitalized selling costs are charged to expense or to an allowance previously established for that purpose.

(m) ACCOUNTING FOR FORECLOSED ASSETS.   AICPA SOP 92-3, "Accounting for Foreclosed Assets," provides guidance on determining the balance sheet treatment of foreclosed assets after foreclosure.

The SOP contains a rebuttable presumption that foreclosed assets are held for sale, rather than for the production of income. That presumption may be overcome if (1) management intends to hold a foreclosed asset, (2) laws and regulations as applied permit management to hold the asset, and (3) management's intent is supported by a preponderance of the evidence.

(i) Foreclosed Assets Held for Sale.   After foreclosure, foreclosed assets held for sale should be carried at the lower of (a) fair value less estimated costs to sell or (b) cost (fair value at the time of foreclosure). The SOP states that, if the fair value of the asset less the estimated cost to sell is less than the asset's cost, the deficiency should be recognized as a valuation allowance. However, that provision has been superseded by SFAS No. 121 and SFAS No. 144, which prohibit the subsequent restoration of previously recognized impairment losses.

The amount of any senior debt (principal and accrued interest) to which the asset is subject should be reported as a liability at the time of foreclosure and should not be deducted from the carrying amount of the asset.

(ii) Foreclosed Assets Held for Production of Income.   After foreclosure, assets determined to be held for the production of income (and not held for sale) should be accounted for in the same way that they would have been had the asset been acquired other than through foreclosure.

(n) PROPERTY, PLANT, AND EQUIPMENT.   At the time of this book's publication, the AICPA's Accounting Standards Executive Committee (AcSEC) was considering a proposed SOP,

"Accounting for Certain Costs and Activities Related to Property, Plant and Equipment," which would address accounting and disclosure issues related to PP&E&E, including those for initial acquisition, construction, improvements, betterments, additions, and repairs and maintenance.

The proposed SOP tentatively sets forth a four-stage accounting framework for PP&E: preliminary, preacquisition, acquisition-or-construction, and in-service.

During the preliminary stage, an option to acquire PP&E would be carried at the lower of fair value less cost to sell. Once the purchase is probable, the option would be included in the cost of PP&E and no longer carried at the lower of cost or fair value less cost to sell. An option not deemed probable of exercise would be carried at the lower of cost or fair value less cost to sell until sale or expiration.

Costs related to PP&E that are incurred during the preacquisition stage would be charged to expense as incurred unless the costs are directly identifiable with the specific PP&E.

Costs incurred during the acquisition-or-construction stage would be charged to expense as incurred unless they are directly identifiable with the specific PP&E or meet a set of criteria to be determined by AcSEC.

The in-service stage begins once PP&E is substantially complete or ready for its intended use. Once this stage is reached, most costs related to PP&E would be charged to expense as incurred. Exceptions would be costs incurred for (1) the acquisition of additional PP&E or (2) the replacement of existing PP&E.

The individual costs incurred for planned major maintenance activities would be evaluated to determine whether they should be capitalized as (1) the acquisition of additional components of PP&E or (2) the replacement of existing components of PP&E. All other costs incurred in a planned major maintenance activity would be charged to expense as incurred.

30.4 ALLOCATION OF COSTS

After it has been determined what costs are capitalized, it becomes important to determine how the costs should be allocated, because those costs will enter into the calculation of cost of sales of individual units. Although a number of methods of allocation can be used in different circumstances, judgment often must be used to make sure that appropriate results are obtained.

(a) METHODS OF ALLOCATION.   Capitalized costs of real estate projects should first be assigned to individual components of the project based on specific identification. If specific identification on an overall basis is not practicable, capitalized costs should be allocated as follows:

- Land costs and all other common costs should be allocated to each land parcel benefited. Allocation should be based on the relative fair value before construction.
- Construction costs should be assigned to buildings on a specific identification basis and allocated to individual units on the basis of relative value of each unit.

In the usual situation, sales prices or rentals are available to compute relative values. In rare situations, however, where relative value is impracticable, capitalized costs may be allocated based on the area method/or the relative cost method as appropriate under the circumstances.

The following sections describe the specific identification, value, and area methods of cost allocation.

(i) Specific Identification Method.   This method of cost allocation is based on determining actual costs applicable to each parcel of land. It rarely is used for land costs because such costs usually encompass more than one parcel. However, it frequently is used for direct construction costs because these costs are directly related to the property being sold. This method should be used wherever practicable.

(ii) Value Method.   The relative value method is the method usually used after costs have been assigned on a specific identification basis. Under this method, the allocation of common costs should be based on relative fair value (before value added by on-site development and construction activities) of each land parcel benefited. In multiproject developments, common costs are normally allocated based on estimated sales prices net of direct improvements and selling costs. This approach is usually the most appropriate because it is less likely to result in deferral of losses.

With respect to condominium sales, certain units will usually have a higher price because of location. With respect to time-sharing sales, holiday periods such as Easter, Fourth of July, and Christmas traditionally sell at a premium. Depending on the resort location, the summer or winter season will also sell at a premium as compared with the rest of the year. Caution should be exercised to ensure that the sales values utilized in cost allocation are reasonable.

(iii) Area Method.   This method of cost allocation is based on square footage, acreage, or frontage. The use of this method will not always result in a logical allocation of costs. When negotiating the purchase price for a large tract of land, the purchaser considers the overall utility of the tract, recognizing that various parcels in the tract are more valuable than others. For example, parcels on a lake front are usually more valuable than those back from the lake. In this situation, if a simple average based on square footage or acreage is used to allocate costs to individual parcels, certain parcels could be assigned costs in excess of their net realizable value.

Generally, the area method should be limited to situations where each individual parcel is estimated to have approximately the same relative value. Under such circumstances, the cost allocations as determined by either the area or value methods would be approximately the same.

30.5 VALUATION ISSUES

In October 2001, the FASB issued SFAS No. 144, "Accounting for the Impairment or Disposal of Long-Lived Assets," which supersedes SFAS No. 121, "Accounting for the Impairment of Long-Lived Assets and for Long-Lived Assets to Be Disposed Of." SFAS No. 144 retains many of the fundamental provisions of SFAS No. 121, particularly that long-lived assets be measured at the lower of carrying amount or fair value less cost to sell.

A major change to previous practice is that the accounting model for long-lived assets to be disposed of by sale applies to all long-lived assets, including discontinued operations, thus superseding provisions of APB Opinion No. 30, "Reporting Results of Operations—Reporting the Effects of Disposal of a Segment of a Business." Discontinued operations no longer are measured at net realizable value, nor do they include amounts for operating losses that have not yet occurred. However, SFAS No. 144 retains the requirement in APB Opinion No. 30 to report separately discontinued operations and extends the reporting of discontinued operations to include all components of an entity with operations that can be distinguished from the rest of the entity and that will be eliminated from the ongoing operations of the entity in a disposal transaction. The new reporting requirements are intended to more clearly communicate in the financial statements a change in its business that results from a decision to dispose of operations and, thus, provide users with information needed to better focus on the ongoing activities of the entity.

In another major change from SFAS No. 121, the scope of SFAS No. 144 does not encompass goodwill. That is, goodwill will not be written down as a result of applying the Statement, but goodwill may be included in the carrying amount of an asset group for purposes of applying the Statement's provisions if that group is a reporting unit or includes a reporting unit. SFAS No. 144 also does not address impairment of other intangible assets that are not amortized; SFAS No. 142, "Goodwill and Other Intangible Assets," issued in July 2001, addresses impairment of goodwill and intangible assets that are not amortized.

(a) ASSETS TO BE HELD AND USED.   SFAS No. 144 establishes the following three steps for recognizing and measuring impairment on long-lived assets and certain identifiable intangibles to be held and used:

1. *Indicators*: The Statement provides a list of indicators that serve as a warning light when the value of an asset to be held and used may have been impaired. The presence of any of the following indicators evidence a need for additional investigation:

   — A significant decrease in the market value of an asset

   — A significant change in the extent or manner in which an asset is used or a significant change in an asset

   — A significant adverse change in legal factors or in business climate that could affect the value of an asset or an adverse action or assessment by a regulator

   — An accumulation of costs significantly in excess of the amount originally expected to acquire or construct an asset

   — A current period operating or cash flow loss combined with a history of operating or cash flow losses or a projection or forecast that demonstrates continuing losses associated with an asset used for the purpose of producing revenue

   — A current expectation that it is more likely than not (greater than 50 percent likelihood) that an asset will be sold or otherwise disposed of significantly before the end of its previously estimated useful life

   The list of indicators is not intended to be all-inclusive. Other events or changes in circumstances may indicate that the carrying amount of an asset that an entity expects to hold and use may not be recoverable.

2. *Gross Cash Flow Analysis.* An entity that detects one or more of the indicators discussed above should evaluate whether the sum of the expected future net cash flows (undiscounted and without interest charges) associated with an asset to be held and used is at least equal to the asset's carrying amount. The FASB imposed a high threshold for triggering the impairment analysis. The selection of a cash flow test based on undiscounted amounts will trigger the recognition of an impairment loss less frequently than would a test based on fair value.

3. *Measurement.* For assets to be held and used, the Statement requires an impairment loss to be measured as the amount by which the carrying amount of the impaired asset exceeds its fair value. The distinction between the recognition process, which uses undiscounted cash flows, and the measurement process, which uses fair value or discounted cash flows, is significant. As a result of a relatively minor change in undiscounted cash flows, the impairment measurement process might kick in, thus causing the balance sheet amount to drop off suddenly in any period in which undiscounted cash flows fall below a long-lived asset's carrying amount. Once assets to be held and used are written down, the Statement does not permit them to be written back up. Thus, a new depreciable cost basis is established after a write-down, and subsequent increases in the value or recoverable cost of the asset may not be recognized until its sale or disposal. In addition, an asset that is assessed for impairment should be evaluated to determine whether a change to the useful life or salvage value estimate is warranted under APB Opinion No. 20, "Accounting Changes." SFAS No. 144 thus forces entities to immediately record a loss on an impaired asset instead of shortening the depreciable life or decreasing the salvage value of the asset.

(b) ASSETS TO BE DISPOSED OF.   SFAS No. 144 requires long-lived assets held for sale to be reported at the lower of carrying amount or fair value less cost to sell regardless of whether the assets previously were held for use or recently acquired with the intent to sell. The cost to sell generally includes the incremental direct costs to transact the sale, such as broker commissions, legal and title transfer fees, and closing costs. Costs generally excluded from cost to sell include insurance, security services, utility expenses, and other costs of protecting or maintaining the asset. Subsequent upward adjustments to the carrying amount of an asset to be disposed of may not exceed the carrying amount of the asset before an adjustment was made to reflect the decision to dispose of it. A long-lived asset that is classified as held for sale is not depreciated during the holding period.

While SFAS No. 121 required an entity's management to be committed to a disposal plan before it could classify that asset as held for sale, it did not specify other factors that an entity should consider before reclassifying the asset. SFAS No. 144 lists six criteria that must be met in order to classify an asset as held for sale:

1. Management with the authority to do so commits to a plan to sell the asset (disposal group).

2. The asset (disposal group) is available for immediate sale in its present condition subject only to terms that are usual and customary for sales of such assets (disposal groups). This criterion does not preclude an entity from using an asset while it is classified as held for sale nor does it require a binding agreement for future sale as a condition of reporting an asset as held for sale.

3. The entity initiates an active program to locate a buyer and other actions that are required to complete the plan to sell the asset (disposal group).

4. The entity believes that the sale of the asset (disposal group) is probable (i.e., likely to occur), and, in general, it expects to record the transfer of the asset (disposal group) as a completed sale within one year.

5. The entity actively is marketing the asset (disposal group) for sale at a price that is reasonable in relation to its current fair value.

6. Actions required to complete the plan indicate that it is unlikely that significant changes to the plan will be made or that the plan will be withdrawn.

SFAS No. 144 requires an asset or group that will be disposed of other than by sale to continue to be classified as held for use until the disposal transaction occurs. As a result, the asset continues to be depreciated until the date of disposal. Dispositions other than by sale include abandonment or a transaction that will be accounted for at the asset's carrying amount, such as an exchange for a similar productive long-lived asset or a distribution to owners in a spinoff.

(c) REAL ESTATE DEVELOPMENT. For homebuilders and other real estate developers, SFAS No. 144 classifies land to be developed and projects under development as assets to be held and used until the six criteria for reclassification as held for sale are met (see previous subsection). As a result, unlike assets to be disposed of, such assets are analyzed in light of the impairment indicator list and gross cash flows generated before any consideration is given to measuring an impairment loss. In the absence of such a provision, nearly all long-term projects, regardless of their overall profitability, would be subject to write-downs in their early stages of development, only to be reversed later in the life of the project. Upon completion of development, the project is reclassified as an asset to be disposed of.

30.6 CONSTRUCTION CONTRACTS

Although most real estate developers acquire land in order to develop and construct improvements for their own use or for sale to others, some develop and construct improvements solely for others. There are also many general contractors whose principal business is developing and constructing improvements for others and rarely, if ever, do they own the land.

This section covers guidelines for accounting for development and construction contracts where the contractor does not own the land but is providing such services for others. The principal issue in accounting for construction contracts is when to record income. Construction contracts are generally of two types: fixed price and cost-plus. Under fixed price contracts, a contractor agrees to perform services for a fixed amount. Although the contract price is fixed, it may frequently be revised as a result of change orders as construction proceeds. If the contract is longer than a few months, the contractor usually receives advances from the customer as construction progresses.

Cost-plus contracts are employed in a variety of forms, such as cost plus a percentage of cost or cost plus a fixed fee. Sometimes defined costs may be limited and penalties provided in situations where stated maximum costs are exceeded. Under cost-plus agreements, the contractor is usually reimbursed for its costs as costs are incurred and, in addition, is paid a specified fee. In most cases, a portion of the fee is retained until the construction is completed and accepted. The method of recording income under cost-plus contracts generally is the same as for fixed price contracts and is described below.

(a) AUTHORITATIVE LITERATURE.   In 1955, the AICPA Committee on Accounting Procedures issued ARB No. 45 "Long-Term Construction-Type Contracts." This document described the generally accepted methods of accounting for long-term construction-type contracts for financial reporting purposes and described the circumstances in which each method is preferable.

In 1981, the AICPA issued SOP 81-1, "Accounting for Performance of Construction-Type and Certain Production-Type Contracts." This Statement culminated extensive reconsideration by the AICPA of construction-type contracts. The recommendations set forth therein provide guidance on the application of ARB No. 45 but do not amend that Bulletin. In 1982, the FASB issued SFAS No. 56, "Contractor Accounting" which states that the specialized accounting and reporting principles and practices contained in SOP 81-1 are preferable accounting principles for purposes of justifying a change in accounting principles.

Prior to the issuance of SOP 81-1, authoritative accounting literature used the terms *long term* and *short term* in identifying types of contracts. SOP 81-1 chose not to use those terms as identifying characteristics because other characteristics were considered more relevant for identifying the types of contracts covered. The guidelines set forth below are based largely on SOP 81-1.

(b) METHODS OF ACCOUNTING.   The determination of the point or points at which revenue should be recognized as earned and costs should be recognized as expenses is a major accounting issue common to all business enterprises engaged in the performance of construction contracting. Accounting for such contracts is essentially a process of measuring the results of relatively long-term events and allocating those results to relatively short-term accounting periods. This involves considerable use of estimates in determining revenues, costs, and profits and in assigning the amounts to accounting periods. The process is complicated by the need to continually evaluate the uncertainties that are inherent in the performance of contracts and by the need to rely on estimates of revenues, costs, and the extent of progress toward completion.

There are two generally accepted methods of accounting for construction contracts: the percentage of completion method and the completed contract method. The determination of the preferable method should be based on an evaluation of the particular circumstances, as the two methods are not acceptable alternatives for the same set of circumstances. The method used and circumstances describing when it is used should be disclosed in the accounting policy footnote to the financial statements.

(i) Percentage of Completion Method.   The use of this approach depends on the ability of the contractor to make reasonably dependable estimates. The percentage of completion method should be used in circumstances in which reasonably dependable estimates can be made and in which all the following conditions exist:

- The contract is clear about goods or services to be provided, the consideration to be exchanged, and the manner and terms of settlement.
- The buyer can be expected to pay for the services performed.
- The contractor can be expected to be able to perform his contractual obligations.

The percentage of completion method presents the economic substance of activity more clearly and in a more timely manner than does the completed contract method. It should be noted that estimates of revenues, costs, and percentage of completion are the primary criteria for income recognition. Billings may have no real relationship to performance and generally are not a suitable basis for income recognition.

(ii) Completed Contract Method. This method may be used in circumstances in which an entity's financial position and results of operations would not vary materially from those resulting from the percentage of completion method. The completed contract method should be used when reasonably dependable estimates cannot be made or when there are inherent hazards that cause forecasts to be doubtful.

(iii) Consistency of Application. It is possible that a contractor may use one method for some contracts and the other for additional contracts. There is no inconsistency, since consistency in application lies in using the same accounting treatment for the same set of conditions from one accounting period to another. The method used, and circumstances when it is used, should be disclosed in the accounting policy footnote to the financial statements.

(c) PERCENTAGE OF COMPLETION METHOD. The percentage of completion method recognizes the legal and economic results of contract performance on a timely basis. Financial statements based on the percentage of completion method present the economic substance of a company's transactions and events more clearly and more timely than financial statements based on the completed contract method, and they present more accurately the relationships between gross profit from contracts and related period costs. The percentage of completion method informs the users of the general purpose financial statements concerning the volume of a company's economic activity.

In practice, several methods are used to measure the extent of progress toward completion. These methods include the cost-to-cost method, the efforts-expended method, the units-of-delivery method and the units-of-work-performed method. These methods are intended to conform to the recommendations of ARB 45 (par. 4), which states:

> . . . that the recognized income be that percentage of estimated total income, either:
>
> **a.** that incurred costs to date bear to estimated total costs after giving effect to estimates of costs to complete based upon most recent information, or
> **b.** that may be indicated by such other measure of progress toward completion as may be appropriate having due regard to work performed.

One generally accepted method of measuring such progress is the stage of construction, as determined through engineering or architectural studies.

When using the "cost incurred" approach, there may be certain costs that should be excluded from the calculation. For example, substantial quantities of standard materials not unique to the project may have been delivered to the job site but not yet utilized. Or engineering and architectural fees incurred may represent 20 percent of total estimated costs whereas only 10 percent of the construction has been performed.

The principal disadvantage of the percentage of completion method is that it is necessarily dependent on estimates of ultimate costs that are subject to the uncertainties frequently inherent in long-term contracts.

The estimation of total revenues and costs is necessary to determine estimated total income. Frequently a contractor can estimate total contract revenue and total contract cost in single amounts. However, on some contracts a contractor may be able to estimate only total contract revenue and total contract cost in ranges of amounts. In such situations, the most likely amounts within the range should be used, if determinable. If not, the least favorable amounts should be used until the results can be estimated more precisely.

(i) Revenue Determination. Estimating revenue on a contract is an involved process. The major factors that must be considered in determining total estimated revenue include the basic contract price, contract options, change orders, claims, and contract provisions for incentive payments and penalties. All these factors and other special contract provisions must be evaluated throughout the life of a contract in estimating total contract revenue.

(ii) Cost Determination.   At any time during the life of a contract, total estimated contract cost consists of two components: costs incurred to date and estimated cost to complete the contract. A company should be able to determine costs incurred on a contract with a relatively high degree of precision. The other component, estimated cost to complete, is a significant variable in the process of determining income earned and is thus a significant factor in accounting for contracts. SOP 81-1 states that the following five practices should be followed in estimating costs to complete:

1. Systematic and consistent procedures that are correlated with the cost accounting system should be used to provide a basis for periodically comparing actual and estimated costs.

2. In estimating total contract costs the quantities and prices of all significant elements of cost should be identified.

3. The estimating procedures should provide that estimated cost to complete includes the same elements of cost that are included in actual accumulated costs; also, those elements should reflect expected price increases.

4. The effects of future wage and price escalations should be taken into account in cost estimates, especially when the contract performance will be carried out over a significant period of time. Escalation provisions should not be blanket overall provisions but should cover labor, materials, and indirect costs based on percentages or amounts that take into consideration experience and other pertinent data.

5. Estimates of cost to complete should be reviewed periodically and revised as appropriate to reflect new information.

(iii) Revision of Estimates.   Adjustments to the original estimates of the total contract revenue, cost, or extent of progress toward completion are often required as work progresses under the contract, even though the scope of the work required under the contract has not changed. Such adjustments are changes in accounting estimates as defined in APB Opinion No. 20. Under this Opinion, the cumulative catch-up method is the only acceptable method. This method requires the difference between cumulative income and income previously recorded to be recorded in the current year's income.

Exhibit 30.5 illustrates the percentage of completion method.

The amount of revenue, costs, and income recognized in the three periods would be as follows:

A contracting company has a lump-sum contract for $9 million to build a bridge at a total estimated cost of $8 million. The construction period covers three years. Financial data during the construction period is as follows:

(thousands of dollars)	Year 1	Year 2	Year 3
Total estimated revenue	$9,000	$9,100	$9,200
Cost incurred to date	$2,050	$6,100	$8,200
Estimated cost to complete	6,000	2,000	—
Total estimated cost	$8,050	$8,100	$8,200
Estimated gross profit	$ 950	$1,000	$1,000
Billings to date	$1,800	$5,500	$9,200
Collections to date	$1,500	$5,000	$9,200
Measure of progress	25%	75%	100%

(d) COMPLETED CONTRACT METHOD.   This method recognizes income only when a contract is completed or substantially completed, such as when the remaining costs to be incurred are not significant. Under this method, costs and billings are reflected in the balance sheet, but there are no charges or credits to the income statement.

	To Date	Recognized Prior Year (thousands of dollars)	Current Year
Year 1 (25% completed)			
Earned revenue ($9,000,000 × 0.25)	$2,250.0		$2,250.0
Cost of earned revenue			
($8,050,000 × 0.25)	2,012.5		2,012.5
Gross profit	$ 237.5		$ 237.5
Gross profit rate	10.5%		10.5%
Year 2 (75% completed)			
Earned revenue ($9,100,000 × 0.75)	$6,825.0	$2,250.0	$4,575.0
Cost of earned revenue			
($8,100,000 × 0.75)	6,075.0	2,012.5	4,062.5
Gross profit	$ 750.0	$ 237.5	$ 512.5
Gross profit rate	11.0%	10.5%	11.2%
Year 3 (100% completed)			
Earned revenue	$9,200.0	$6,825.0	$2,375.0
Cost of earned revenue	8,200.0	6,075.0	2,125.0
Gross profit	$1,000.0	$0,750.0	$0,250.0
Gross profit rate	10.9%	11.0%	10.5%

Exhibit 30.5   Percentage of completion, three-year contract. (*Source*: AICPA.)

As a general rule, a contract may be regarded as substantially completed if remaining costs and potential risks are insignificant in amount. The overriding objectives are to maintain consistency in determining when contracts are substantially completed and to avoid arbitrary acceleration or deferral of income. The specific criteria used to determine when a contract is substantially completed should be followed consistently. Circumstances to be considered in determining when a project is substantially completed include acceptance by the customer, departure from the site, and compliance with performance specifications.

The completed contract method may be used in circumstances in which financial position and results of operations would not vary materially from those resulting from use of the percentage of completion method (e.g., in circumstances in which an entity has primarily short-term contracts). In accounting for such contracts, income ordinarily is recognized when performance is substantially completed and accepted. For example, the completed contract method, as opposed to the percentage of completion method, would not usually produce a material difference in net income or financial position for a small contractor that primarily performs relatively short-term contracts during an accounting period.

If there is a reasonable assurance that no loss will be incurred on a contract (e.g., when the scope of the contract is ill-defined but the contractor is protected by a cost-plus contract or other contractual terms), the percentage of completion method based on a zero profit margin, rather than the completed contract method, should be used until more precise estimates can be made.

The significant difference between the percentage of completion method applied on the basis of a zero profit margin and the completed contract method relates to the effects on the income statement. Under the zero profit margin approach to applying the percentage of completion method, equal amounts of revenue and cost, measured on the basis of performance during the period, are presented in the income statement and no gross profit amount is presented in the income statement until the contract is completed. The zero profit margin approach to applying the percentage of completion method gives the users of general purpose financial statements an indication of the volume of a company's business and of the application of its economic resources.

The principal advantage of the completed contract method is that it is based on results as finally determined, rather than on estimates for unperformed work that may involve unforeseen costs and possible losses. The principal disadvantage is that it does not reflect current performance when the period of the contract extends into more than one accounting period. Under these circumstances, it may result in irregular recognition of income.

(e) PROVISION FOR LOSSES.   Under either of the methods above, provision should be made for the entire loss on the contract in the period when current estimates of total contract costs indicate a loss. The provision for loss should represent the best judgment that can be made in the circumstances.

Other factors that should be considered in arriving at the projected loss on a contract include target penalties for late completion and rewards for early completion, nonreimbursable costs on cost-plus contracts, and the effect of change orders. When using the completed contract method and allocating general and administrative expenses to contract costs, total general and administrative expenses that are expected to be allocated to the contract are to be considered together with other estimated contract costs.

(f) CONTRACT CLAIMS.   Claims are amounts in excess of the agreed contract price that a contractor seeks to collect from customers or others for customer-caused delays, errors in specifications and designs, unapproved change orders, or other causes of unanticipated additional costs. Recognition of amounts of additional contract revenue relating to claims is appropriate only if it is probable that the claim will result in additional contract revenue and if the amount can be reliably estimated.

These requirements are satisfied by the existence of all the following conditions:

- The contract or other evidence provides a legal basis for the claim.
- Additional costs are caused by circumstances that were unforeseen at the contract date and are not the result of deficiencies in the contractor's performance.
- Costs associated with the claim are identifiable and are reasonable in view of the work performed.
- The evidence supporting the claim is objective and verifiable.

If the foregoing requirements are met, revenue from a claim should be recorded only to the extent that contract costs relating to the claim have been incurred. The amounts recorded, if material, should be disclosed in the notes to the financial statements.

Change orders are modifications of an original contract that effectively change the provisions of the contract without adding new provisions. They may be initiated by either the contractor or the customer. Many change orders are unpriced; that is, the work to be performed is defined, but the adjustment to the contract price is to be negotiated later. For some change orders, both scope and price may be unapproved or in dispute. Accounting for change orders depends on the underlying circumstances, which may differ for each change order depending on the customer, the contract, and the nature of the change. Priced change orders represent an adjustment to the contract price and contract revenue, and costs should be adjusted to reflect these change orders.

Accounting for unpriced change orders depends on their characteristics and the circumstances in which they occur. Under the completed contract method, costs attributable to unpriced change orders should be deferred as contract costs if it is probable that aggregate contract costs, including costs attributable to change orders, will be recovered from contract revenues. For all unpriced change orders, recovery should be deemed probable if the future event or events necessary for recovery are likely to occur. Some factors to consider in evaluating whether recovery is probable are the customer's written approval of the scope of the change order, separate documentation for change order costs that are identifiable and reasonable, and the entity's favorable experience in negotiating change orders (especially as it relates to the specific type of contract and change order being evaluated). The following guidelines should be used in accounting for unpriced change orders under the percentage of completion method:

- Costs attributable to unpriced change orders should be treated as costs of contract performance in the period in which the costs are incurred if it is not probable that the costs will be recovered through a change in the contract price.

- If it is probable that the costs will be recovered through a change in the contract price, the costs should be deferred (excluded from the cost of contract performance) until the parties have agreed on the change in contract price, or, alternatively, they should be treated as costs of contract performance in the period in which they are incurred, and contract revenue should be recognized to the extent of the costs incurred.

- If it is probable that the contract price will be adjusted by an amount that exceeds the costs attributable to the change order and the amount of the excess can be reliably estimated, the original contract price should also be adjusted for that amount when the costs are recognized as costs of contract performance if its realization is probable. However, since the substantiation of the amount of future revenue is difficult, revenue in excess of the costs attributable to unpriced change orders should only be recorded in circumstances in which realization is assured beyond a reasonable doubt, such as circumstances in which an entity's historical experience provides assurance or in which an entity has received a bona fide pricing offer from the customer and records only the amount of the offer as revenue.

If change orders are in dispute or are unapproved in regard to both scope and price, they should be evaluated as claims.

30.7 OPERATIONS OF INCOME-PRODUCING PROPERTIES

(a) RENTAL OPERATIONS.   Operations of income-producing properties represent a distinct segment of the real estate industry. Owners are often referred to as *real estate operators*. Income-producing properties include office buildings, shopping centers, apartments, industrial buildings, and similar properties rented to others. A lease agreement is entered into between the owner/operator and the tenant for periods ranging from one month to many years, depending on the type of property. Sometimes an investor will acquire an existing income-producing property or alternatively will have the builder or developer construct the property. Some developers, frequently referred to as *investment builders*, develop and construct income properties for their own use as investment properties.

SFAS No. 13 is the principal source of standards of financial accounting and reporting for leases. Under SFAS No. 13, a distinction is made between a capital lease and an operating lease. The lessor is required to account for a capital lease as a sale or a financing transaction. The lessee accounts for a capital lease as a purchase. An operating lease, on the other hand, requires the lessor to reflect rent income, operating expenses, and depreciation of the property over the lease term; the lessee must record rent expense.

Accounting for leases is discussed in Chapter 23 and therefore is not covered in depth here. Certain unique aspects of accounting for leases of real estate classified as operating leases, however, are covered below.

(b) RENTAL INCOME.   Rental income from an operating lease should usually be recorded by a lessor as it becomes receivable in accordance with the provisions of the lease agreement

FTB No. 85-3 provides that the effects of scheduled rent increases, which are included in minimum lease payments under SFAS No. 13, should be recognized by lessors and lessees on a straight-line basis over the lease term unless another systematic and rational allocation basis is more representative of the time pattern in which the leased property is physically employed. Using factors such as the time value of money, anticipated inflation, or expected future revenues to allocate scheduled rent increases is inappropriate because these factors do not relate to the time pattern of the physical usage of the leased property. However, such factors may affect the periodic reported rental income or expense if the lease agreement involves contingent rentals, which are excluded from minimum lease payments and accounted for separately under SFAS No. 13, as amended by SFAS No. 29.

A lease agreement may provide for scheduled rent increases designed to accommodate the lessee's projected physical use of the property. In these circumstances, FTB No. 88-1 provides for the lessee and the lessor to recognize the lease payments as follows:

a. If rents escalate in contemplation of the lessee's physical use of the leased property, including equipment, but the lessee takes possession of or controls the physical use of the property at the beginning of the lease term, all rental payments including the escalated rents, should be recognized as rental expenses or rental revenue on a straight-line basis in accordance with paragraph 15 of Statement No. 13 and Technical Bulletin 85-3 starting with the beginning of the lease term.

b. If rents escalate under a master lease agreement because the lessee gains access to and control over additional leased property at the time of the escalation, the escalated rents should be considered rental expense or rental revenue attributable to the leased property and recognized in proportion to the additional leased property in the years that the lessee has control over the use of the additional leased property. The amount of rental expense or rental revenue attributed to the additional leased property should be proportionate to the relative fair value of the additional property, as determined at the inception of the lease, in the applicable time periods during which the lessee controls its use.

(i) Cost Escalation. Many lessors require that the lessee pay operating costs of the leased property such as utilities, real estate taxes, and common area maintenance. Some lessors require the lessee to pay for such costs when they escalate and exceed a specified rate or amount. In some cases, the lessee pays these costs directly. More commonly, however, the lessor pays the costs and is reimbursed by the lessee. In this situation, the lessor should generally record these reimbursement costs as a receivable at the time the costs are accrued, even though they may not be billed until a later date. Since these costs are sometimes billed at a later date, collectibility from the lessee should, of course, be considered.

(ii) Percentage Rents. Many retail leases, such as those on shopping centers, enable the lessor to collect additional rents, based on the excess of a stated percentage of the tenant's gross sales over the specified minimum rent. While the minimum rent is usually payable in periodic level amounts, percentage rents (sometimes called *overrides*) are usually based on annual sales, often with a requirement for periodic payments toward the annual amount.

SFAS No. 29 (par. 13), "Determining Contingent Rentals," states: "Contingent rentals shall be includable in the determination of net income as accruable."

(c) RENTAL COSTS. The following considerations help determine the appropriate accounting for project rental costs.

(i) Chargeable to Future Periods. Costs incurred to rent real estate should be deferred and charged to future periods when they are related to and their recovery is reasonably expected from future operations. Examples include initial direct costs such as commissions, legal fees, costs of credit investigations, costs of preparing and processing documents for new leases acquired, and that portion of compensation applicable to the time spent on consummated leases. Other examples include costs of model units and related furnishings, rental facilities, semipermanent signs, grand openings, and unused rental brochures, but not rental overhead, such as rental salaries (see "Period Costs" below).

For leases accounted for as operating leases, deferred rental costs that can be directly related to revenue from a specific operating lease should be amortized over the term of the related lease in proportion to the recognition of rental income. Deferred rental costs that cannot be directly related to revenue from a specific operating lease should be amortized to expense over the period of expected benefit. The amortization period begins when the project is substantially completed and held available for occupancy. Estimated unrecoverable deferred rental costs associated with a lease or group of leases should be charged to expense when it becomes probable that the lease(s) will be terminated.

For leases accounted for as sales-type leases, deferred rental costs must be charged against income at the time the sale is recognized.

(ii) Period Costs.   Costs that are incurred to rent real estate projects that do not meet the above criteria should be charged to expense as incurred. SFAS No. 67 specifically indicates that rental overhead, which is defined in its glossary to include rental salaries, is an example of such period costs. Other examples of expenditures that are period costs are initial indirect costs, such as that portion of salaries and other compensation and fees applicable to time spent in negotiating leases that are not consummated, supervisory and administrative expenses, and other indirect costs.

(d) DEPRECIATION.   Under generally accepted accounting principles (GAAP), the costs of income-producing properties must be depreciated. Depreciation, as defined by GAAP, is the systematic and rational allocation of the historical cost of depreciable assets (tangible assets, other than inventory, with limited lives of more than one year) over their useful lives.

In accounting for real estate operations, the most frequently used methods of depreciation are straight-line and decreasing charge methods. The most common decreasing charge methods are the declining balance and sum-of-the-years-digits methods. Increasing charge methods, such as the sinking fund method, are not generally accepted in the real estate industry in the United States.

The major components of a building, such as the plumbing and heating systems, may be identified and depreciated separately over their respective lives. This method, which is frequently used for tax purposes, usually results in a more rapid write-off.

(e) INITIAL RENTAL OPERATIONS.   When a real estate project is substantially complete and held available for occupancy, the procedures listed here should be followed:

- Rental revenue should be recorded in income as earned.
- Operating costs should be charged to expense currently.
- Amortization of deferred rental costs should begin.
- Full depreciation of rental property should begin.
- Carrying costs, such as interest and property taxes, should be charged to expense as accrued.

If portions of a rental project are substantially completed and occupied by tenants or held available for occupancy and other portions have not yet reached that stage, the substantially completed portions should be accounted for as a separate project. Costs incurred should be allocated between the portions under construction and the portions substantially completed and held available for occupancy.

(f) RENTAL EXPENSE.   Rental expense under an operating lease normally should be charged to operations by a lessee over the lease term on a basis consistent with the lessor's recording of income, with the exception of periodic accounting for percentage rent expense, which should be based on the estimated annual percentage rent.

30.8 ACCOUNTING FOR INVESTMENTS IN REAL ESTATE VENTURES

(a) ORGANIZATION OF VENTURES.   The joint venture vehicle—the sharing of risk—has been widely utilized for many years in the construction, mining, and oil and gas industries as well as for real estate developments. Real estate joint ventures are typically entered into in recognition of the need for external assistance, for example, financing or market expertise. The most common of these needs is capital formation.

Real estate ventures are organized either as corporate entities or, more frequently, as partnerships. Limited partnerships are often used because of the advantages of limited liability. The venture is typically formed by a small group, with each investor actively contributing to the success of the venture and participating in overall management, and with no one individual or corporation controlling its operations. The venture is usually operated separately from other activities of the investors. Regardless of the legal form of the real estate venture, the accounting principles for recognition of profits and losses should be the same.

(b) ACCOUNTING BACKGROUND. Accounting practices in the real estate industry in general and, more specifically, accounting for investments in real estate ventures have varied. The result was lack of comparability and, in some cases, a lack of comprehension. Therefore, the following relevant pronouncements were issued:

- *APB Opinion No. 18*. In response to the wide variation in accounting for investments, the APB, in March 1971, issued Opinion No. 18, "The Equity Method of Accounting for Investments in Common Stock." This opinion became applicable to investments in unincorporated ventures, including partnerships, because of an interpretation promulgated in November 1971.

- *AICPA Statement of Position SOP No. 78-9*. The AICPA recognized the continuing diversity of practice and in December 1978 issued SOP 78-9, "Accounting for Investments in Real Estate Ventures." This statement was issued to narrow the range of alternative practices used in accounting for investments in real estate ventures and to establish industry uniformity. The AICPA currently is reconsidering the guidance in SOP 78-9 as part of a broader project, "Equity Method Investments."

- *SFAS No. 94*. In response to the perceived problem of off-balance sheet financing, of which unconsolidated majority-owned subsidiaries were deemed to be the most significant aspect, the FASB issued SFAS No. 94, "Consolidation of All Majority-Owned Subsidiaries," in October 1987. SFAS No. 94 eliminates the concept of not consolidating nonhomogeneous operations and replaces it with the concept that the predominant factor in determining whether an investment requires consolidation should primarily be control rather than ownership of a majority voting interest. This Statement is also applicable to investments in unincorporated ventures, including partnerships.

- *AICPA Notice to Practitioners, ADC acquisition, development, and construction (ADC) Loans, February 1986*. Recognizing that financial institutions needed guidance on accounting for real estate acquisition, development, and construction (ADC) arrangements, the AICPA issued this notice (also known as the *Third Notice*). The notice provides accounting guidance on ADC arrangements that have virtually the same risks and potential rewards as those of joint ventures. It determined that accounting for such arrangements as loans would not be appropriate and provides guidance on the appropriate accounting.

  The SEC incorporated the notice into SAB No. 71 "Views Regarding Financial Statements of Properties Securing Mortgage Loans." SAB No. 71, and its amendment SAB No. 71A, provide guidance to registrants on the required reporting under this notice. Also, EITF Issue Nos. 84-4 and 86-21, as well as SAB No. 71, extend the provisions of this notice to all entities, not just financial institutions.

- *Proposed FASB Interpretation, Consolidation of Certain Special-Purpose Entities (SPEs)*. The FASB has approved for issuance an Exposure Draft of a proposed Interpretation that establishes accounting guidance for consolidation of SPEs. The proposed Interpretation, "Consolidation of Certain Special-Purpose Entities," would apply to any business enterprise—both public and private companies—that has an ownership interest, contractual relationship, or other business relationship with an SPE. Under current practice, two enterprises generally have been included in consolidated financial statements because one enterprise controls the other through voting ownership interests. The proposed Interpretation would explain how to identify an SPE that is not subject to control through voting ownership interests and would require each enterprise involved with such an SPE to determine whether it provides financial support to the SPE through a variable interest. Variable interests may arise from financial instruments, service contracts, nonvoting ownership interests, or other arrangements. If an enterprise holds (1) a majority of the variable interests in the SPE or (2) a significant variable interest that is significantly more than any other party's variable interest, that enterprise would be the primary beneficiary. The primary beneficiary would be required to include the assets, liabilities, and results of the activities of the SPE in its consolidated financial statements.

(c) INVESTOR ACCOUNTING ISSUES.   The accounting literature mentioned above covers many of the special issues investors encounter in practice. The major areas are:

- Investor accounting for results of operations of ventures
- Special accounting issues related to venture losses
- Investor accounting for transactions with a real estate venture, including capital contributions
- Financial statement presentation and disclosures

A controlling investor should account for its income and losses from real estate ventures under the principles that apply to investments in subsidiaries, which usually require consolidation of the venture's operations. A noncontrolling investor should account for its share of income and losses in real estate ventures by using the equity method. Under the equity method, the initial investment is recorded by the investor at cost; thereafter, the carrying amount is increased by the investor's share of current earnings and decreased by the investor's share of current losses or distributions.

In accounting for transactions with a real estate venture, a controlling investor must eliminate all intercompany profit. When the investor does not control the venture, some situations require that all intercompany profit be eliminated, whereas in others, intercompany profit is eliminated by the investor only to the extent of its ownership interest in the venture. For example, as set forth in AICPA SOP 78-9, even a noncontrolling investor is precluded from recognizing any profit on a contribution of real estate or services to the venture. Accounting for other transactions covered by SOP 78-9 includes sales of real estate and services to the venture, interest income on loans and advances to the venture, and venture sales of real estate or services to an investor.

With regard to financial statement presentation, a controlling investor is usually required to consolidate venture operations. A noncontrolling investor should use the equity method, with the carrying value of the investment presented as a single amount in the balance sheet and the investor's share of venture earnings or losses as a single amount in the income statement. The proportionate share approach, which records the investor's share of each item of income, expense, asset, and liability, is not considered acceptable except for legal undivided interests.

The material above is only a very brief summary of comprehensive publications, and there are exceptions to some of those guidelines. In accounting for real estate venture operations and transactions, judgment must be exercised in applying the principles to ensure that economic substance is fairly reflected no matter how complex the venture arrangements.

(d) ACCOUNTING FOR TAX BENEFITS RESULTING FROM INVESTMENTS IN AFFORD-ABLE HOUSING PROJECTS.   The Revenue Reconciliation Act of 1993 provides tax benefits to investors in entities operating qualified affordable housing projects. The benefits take the form of tax deductions from operating loses and tax credits. In EITF Issue No. 94-1, "Accounting for Tax Benefits Resulting from Investments in Affordable Housing Projects," the EITF reached a consensus that a limited partner in a qualified low income housing project may elect to use the effective yield method (described below) if the following three conditions are met:

1. The availability of the limited partner's share of the tax credits is guaranteed by a credit-worthy entity through a letter of credit, tax indemnity agreement or other arrangement.

2. The limited partner's projected yield based solely on the cash flows from the guaranteed tax credits is positive.

3. The limited partner's liability for both legal and tax purposes is limited to its capital investment.

Under the effective yield method, the investor recognizes tax credits as they are allocated and amortizes the initial cost of the investment to provide a constant effective yield over the period that tax credits are allocated to the investor. The effective yield is the internal rate of return on the investment, based on the cost of the investment and the guaranteed tax credits allocated to the investor. Any expected residual value of the investment should be excluded from the effective yield calculation. Cash received from operations of the limited partnership or sale of the property, if any, should be included when realized or realizable.

Under the effective yield method, the tax credit allocated, net of the amortization of the investment in the limited partnership, is recognized in the income statement as a component of income taxes attributable to continuing operations. Any other tax benefits received should be accounted for pursuant to FASB Statement No. 109, "Accounting for Income Taxes."

An investment that does not qualify for accounting under the effective yield method should be accounted for under SOP 78-9, which requires use of the equity method unless the limited partner's interest is so minor as to have virtually no influence over partnership operating and financial policies. The EITF did not establish a "bright line" as to what percentage ownership threshold is required under SOP 78-9 for selecting between the cost and equity methods. The AICPA is currently reconsidering the guidance in SOP 78-9 in its project titled, "Equity Method Investments."

If the cost method is used, the excess of the carrying amount of the investment over its residual value should be amortized over the period in which the tax credits are allocated to the investor. Annual amortization should be based on the proportion of tax credits received in the current year to total estimated tax credits to be allocated to the investor. The residual value should not reflect anticipated inflation.

During the deliberations of EITF Issue No. 94-1, the staff of the SEC announced that they had revised their position on accounting for investments in limited partnerships. Previously, the SEC had not objected to the use of the cost method for limited partnership investments of up to 20 percent, provided the investor did not have significant influence as defined in APB Opinion No. 18, "The Equity Method of Accounting for Investments in Commons Stock." However, the revised position is that the equity method should be used to account for limited partnership investments, unless the investment is "so minor that the limited partner may have virtually no influence over partnership operating and financial policies." In practice, investments of more than three to five percent would be considered more than minor. For public companies, this guidance is to be applied to any limited partnership investment made after May 18, 1995. This would include not only the investments in low income housing projects, but all real estate partnerships and any other types of limited partnership investments (such as oil and gas, etc.).

30.9 FINANCIAL REPORTING

(a) FINANCIAL STATEMENT PRESENTATION.   There are matters of financial statement presentation—as opposed to footnote disclosures—that are unique to the real estate industry. The financial reporting guidelines in this section are based on the principles set forth in authoritative literature and reporting practice.

(i) Balance Sheet.   Real estate companies frequently present nonclassified balance sheets; that is, they do not distinguish between current and noncurrent assets or liabilities. This is because the operating cycle of most real estate companies exceeds one year.

Real estate companies normally list their assets on the balance sheet in the order of liquidity, in the same manner as other companies. A second popular method, however, is to list the real estate assets first, to demonstrate their importance to the companies. In either case, real estate assets should be disclosed in the manner that is most demonstrative of the company's operations. These assets are often grouped according to the type of investment or operation as follows:

- Unimproved land
- Land under development
- Residential lots
- Condominium and single-family dwellings
- Rental properties

(ii) Statement of Income.   Revenues and costs of sales are generally classified in a manner consistent with that described for real estate investments. In 1976, the FASB issued SFAS No. 14, "Financial Reporting for Segments of a Business Enterprise," which states that the financial statements of an enterprise should include certain information about the industry segments of the enterprise. An industry segment is defined in paragraph 10(a) as "a component of an enterprise engaged in providing a product or service or a group of related products and services primarily to unaffiliated customers (i.e. customers outside the enterprise) for profit." Some developers, however, have traditionally considered themselves to be in only one line of business.

In June 1997, the FASB issued SFAS No. 131, "Disclosures about Segments of an Enterprise and Related Information." SFAS No. 131 supersedes SFAS No. 14, although it retains the requirement to report information about major customers. SFAS No. 131 also amends SFAS No. 94, "Consolidation of All Majority-Owned Subsidiaries," to eliminate the disclosure requirements for subsidiaries that were not consolidated prior to the effective date of SFAS No. 94. SFAS No. 131 does not apply to nonpublic entities. SFAS No. 131 adopts a "management approach" to identifying segments and permits entities to aggregate operating segments if certain attributes are present.

(b) ACCOUNTING POLICIES.   Because of the alternatives currently available in accounting for real estate developments, it is especially important to follow the guidelines of APB Opinion No. 22, "Disclosure of Accounting Policies." The Opinion states (par. 12) that disclosures should include the accounting principles and methods that involve any of the following:

A selection from existing acceptable alternatives.

Principles and methods peculiar to the industry in which the reporting entity operates, even if such principles and methods are predominantly followed in that industry.

Unusual or innovative applications of GAAP (and, as applicable, of principles and methods peculiar to the industry in which the reporting entity operates).

The following lists four accounting policy disclosures that are appropriate in the financial statements of a real estate company, as opposed to a manufacturing or service enterprise.

1. *Profit Recognition.* The accounting method used to determine income should be disclosed. Where different methods are used, the circumstances surrounding the application of each should also be disclosed. Similarly, a comment should be included indicating the timing of sales and related profit recognition.
2. *Cost Accounting.* The method of allocating cost to unit sales should be disclosed (e.g., relative market values, area, unit, specific identification). Financial statement disclosure should include, where applicable, capitalization policies for property taxes and other carrying costs, and policies with respect to capitalization or deferral of start-up or preoperating costs (selling costs, rental costs, initial operations).
3. *Impairment of Long-lived Assets.* Real estate held for development and sale, including property to be developed in the future as well as that currently under development, should follow

the recognition and measurement principles set forth in SFAS No. 121 for assets to be held and used. A real estate project, or parts thereof, that is substantially complete and ready for its intended use shall be accounted for at the lower of carrying amount or fair value less cost to sell.

4. *Investment in Real Estate Ventures.* Disclosures of the following accounting policies should be made:

   a. Method of inclusion in investor's accounts (e.g., equity or consolidation)

   b. Method of income recognition (e.g., equity or cost)

   c. Accounting principles of significant ventures

   d. Profit recognition practices on transactions between the investor and the venture

(c) NOTE DISCLOSURES.   The following list describes other financial statement disclosures that are appropriate in the notes to the financial statements of a real estate developer.

Real Estate Assets. If a breakdown is not reflected on the balance sheet, it should be included in the footnotes. Disclosure should also be made of inventory subject to sales contracts that have not been recorded as sales and the portion of inventory serving as collateral for debts.

Inventory Write-Downs. Summarized information or explanations with respect to significant inventory write-downs should be disclosed in the footnotes because write-downs are generally important and unusual items.

Nonrecourse Debt. Although it is not appropriate to offset nonrecourse debt against the related asset, a note to the financial statements should disclose the amount and interrelationship of the nonrecourse debt with the cost of the related property.

Capitalization of Interest. SFAS No. 34 requires the disclosure of the amount of interest expensed and the amount capitalized.

Deferral of Profit Recognition. When transactions qualify as sales for accounting purposes but do not meet the tests for full profit recognition and, as a result, the installment or cost recovery methods are used, disclosure should be made of significant amounts of profit deferred, the nature of the transaction, and any other information deemed necessary for complete disclosure.

Investments in Real Estate Ventures. Typical disclosures with respect to significant real estate ventures include names of ventures, percentage of ownership interest, accounting and tax policies of the venture, the difference, if any, between the carrying amount of the investment and the investor's share of equity in net assets and the accounting policy regarding amortization of the difference, summarized information as to assets, liabilities, and results of operations or separate financial statements, and investor commitments with respect to joint ventures.

Construction Contractors. The principal reporting considerations for construction contractors relate to the two methods of income recognition: the percentage of completion method and the completed contract method.

When the completed contract method is used, an excess of accumulated costs over related billings should be shown in a classified balance sheet as a current asset and an excess of accumulated billings over related costs should be shown as a current liability. If costs exceed billings on some contracts and billings exceed costs on others, the contracts should ordinarily be segregated so that the asset side includes only those contracts on which costs exceed billings, and the liability side includes only those on which billings exceed costs.

Under the percentage of completion method, assets may include costs and related income not yet billed, with respect to certain contracts. Liabilities may include billings in excess of costs and related income with respect to other contracts.

The following disclosures, which are required for SEC reporting companies should generally be made by a nonpublic company whose principal activity is long-term contracting:

- Amounts billed but not paid by customers under retainage provisions in contracts, and indication of amounts expected to be collected in various years

- Amounts included in receivables representing the recognized sales value of performance under long-term contracts where such amounts had not been billed and were not billable at the balance sheet date, along with a general description of the prerequisites for billing and an estimate of the amount expected to be collected in one year
- Amounts included in receivables or inventories representing claims or other similar items subject to uncertainty concerning their determination or ultimate realization, together with a description of the nature and status of principal items, and amounts expected to be collected in one year
- Amount of progress payments (billings) netted against inventory at the balance sheet date

(d) FAIR VALUE AND CURRENT VALUE. The traditional accounting model does not permit the recognition of appreciation of real estate assets. This most affects depreciable income properties, but it also affects land. Using the historical cost model, appreciation of good investments cannot be used to offset losses on unsuccessful projects. Real estate companies have thus been among the strongest proponents of fair value and current value reporting, particularly during periods of rapid appreciation in property values.

(i) Financial Accounting Standards Board Fair Value Project. The FASB has on its agenda a project to provide guidance for measuring and reporting essentially all financial assets and liabilities and certain related assets and liabilities at fair value in the financial statements. The active phases of this project as they relate to the real estate industry have addressed the valuation of financial instruments. Some of the more significant documents that have been issued are SFAS No. 107, "Disclosures about Fair Value of Financial Instruments," SFAS No. 115, "Accounting for Certain Investments in Debt and Equity Securities," and SFAS No. 133, "Accounting for Derivative Instruments and Hedging Activities." A full discussion of these projects and how they affect accounting for the real estate industry is beyond the scope of this chapter. Nevertheless, many advanced forms of real estate financing may be considered financial instruments and are thus subject to the guidance set forth in those documents.

A primary example of such a financing form is the real estate conduit. Conduits are organizations that originate commercial and multifamily mortgage loans for the purpose of issuing collateralized mortgage-backed securities (CMBS) instead of holding the loans in their loan portfolio. Conduits are intermediaries between real estate borrowers and investors that buy CMBS. Conduits are usually special capital market groups, which are subsidiaries of financial institutions such as commercial banks and security firms.

(ii) AICPA Current Value Project. The AICPA had a project on current value reporting by real estate companies that was shelved after issuance of an October 10, 1994, exposure draft of a proposed SOP, "Reporting by Real Estate Companies of Supplemental Current-Value Information." As described in the exposure draft, the measurement of current value would consider the entity's intent and ability to realize asset values and settle liabilities. In addition, the reported amounts would represent the values of specific balance sheet elements—not the value of the entity as a whole. The AICPA attempted to ensure that the guidance would serve solely as the basis for optional supplemental disclosure and not as the framework for an "other comprehensive basis of accounting" (OCBOA).

The exposure draft was developed from the AICPA Real Estate Committee's 1984 "Guidance for an Experiment on Reporting Current Value Information for Real Estate," which provided for a comprehensive approach and a piecemeal approach to the presentation of current value information. Although the piecemeal approach is not discouraged, the current value project focuses primarily on the comprehensive approach, in which all assets and liabilities are reported at their current amounts in balance sheet form.

Both the Experiment and the exposure draft recommend presentation of current value information side by side with the corresponding GAAP information in comparative form. Although the Experiment discussed the idea of including current value statements of operating performance and changes in equity, those statements are not addressed in the exposure draft. Instead, the exposure draft focuses on the disclosure of interperiod changes in revaluation equity—the difference between (1) the net current value of assets and liabilities and (2) the corresponding net carrying amount determined in conformity with GAAP.

(iii) Deferred Taxes.   The reporting of the deferred income tax liability in the current value balance sheet has been controversial. The exposure draft would permit either of the following two methods to be used in determining the deferred income tax liability to be reported in the current value balance sheet:

- Method 1—The reported deferred income tax liability is equal to the discounted amount of the estimated future tax payments, adjusted for the use of existing net operating loss carryforwards or other carryforwards. The determination of the deferred income tax liability is based on the enacted income tax rates and regulations at the balance sheet date (even if not in effect at that date). The exposure draft contains a deemed sale provision at the end of the fifteenth year, with the discounted amount of the tax that would be paid on such a sale included in the reported liability.

- Method 2—The reported deferred income tax liability is based on enacted rates and regulations at the balance sheet date (even if not in effect at that date). The enacted rate is multiplied by the difference between the current value of total net assets and liabilities and their tax bases, adjusted for the use of existing net operating loss carryforwards or other carryforwards. Although this method of determining the anticipated tax liability is conceptually inconsistent with the principle of determining current value based on the discounted amount of estimated future cash flows, the method was included in the exposure draft because it is easy to apply as a result of the fact that it reflects the effect of an immediate and complete liquidation of the reporting entity's portfolio.

(e) ACCOUNTING BY PARTICIPATING MORTGAGE LOAN BORROWERS.   In May 1997, the AICPA issued SOP 97-1, *Accounting by Participating Mortgage Loan Borrowers.* The SOP establishes the borrower's accounting when a mortgage lender participates in either or both of the following:

- Increases in the market value of the mortgaged real estate project
- The project's results of operations

If a lender participates in the market appreciation of the mortgaged property, the borrower must determine the fair value of the appreciation feature at the inception of the loan. A liability equal to the appreciation feature is recognized with a corresponding charge to a debt discount account. The debt discount should be amortized using the interest method.

Interest expense in participating mortgage loans consists of the following items:

- Amounts designated in the mortgage agreement as interest
- Amounts related to the lender's participation in operations
- Amounts representing amortization of the debt discount related to the lender's participation in the project's appreciation

The borrower remeasures the participation liability each period. Any revisions to the participation liability resulting from the remeasurement results in an adjustment to the participation liability via a debit or credit to the related debt discount. The revised debt discount should be amortized prospectively using the effective interest rate.

(f) GUARANTEES. The FASB has on its agenda a project on "Guarantees" that promises to significantly affect real estate financiers. A proposed Interpretation will elaborate on the disclosures to be made by a guarantor in its financial statements about its obligations under certain guarantees that it has issued. It also will require a guarantor to recognize, at the inception of a guarantee, a liability for the fair value of the obligations it has undertaken in issuing the guarantee. The proposed Interpretation does not address the subsequent measurement of the guarantor's recognized liability over the term of the related guarantee.

30.10 SOURCES AND SUGGESTED REFERENCES

Accounting Principles Board, "The Equity Method of Accounting for Investments in Common Stock," APB Opinion No. 18, Interpretation No. 18-2. AICPA, New York, November 1971.

———, "The Equity Method of Accounting for Investments in Common Stock," APB Opinion No. 18. AICPA, New York, March 1971.

———, "Accounting Changes," APB Opinion No. 20. AICPA, New York, 1971.

———, "Interest on Receivables and Payables," APB Opinion No. 21. AICPA, New York, August 1971.

———, "Disclosure of Accounting Policies," APB Opinion No. 22. AICPA, New York, April 1972.

American Institute of Certified Public Accountants, "Inventory Pricing," "Restatement and Revision of Accounting Research Bulletins," Accounting Research Bulletin No. 43. AICPA, New York, June 1953.

———, "Long-Term Construction-Type Contracts," Accounting Research Bulletin No. 45. AICPA, New York, October 1955.

———, "Audit and Accounting Guide for Construction Contractors," Accounting Guide. AICPA, New York, 1981.

———, "Guide for the Use of Real Estate Appraisal Information," Accounting Guide. AICPA, New York, 1987.

———, Issues Paper, "Accounting for Allowances for Losses on Certain Real Estate and Loans and Receivables Collateralized by Real Estate." AICPA, New York, June 1979.

———, "Accounting Practices of Real Estate Investment Trusts," Statement of Position No. 75-2. AICPA, New York, June 27, 1975.

———, "Accounting for Costs to Sell and Rent, and Initial Real Estate Operations of, Real Estate Projects," Statement of Position No. 78-3. AICPA, New York, 1978.

———, "Accounting for Investments in Real Estate Ventures," Statement of Position No. 78-9. AICPA, New York, December 29, 1978.

———, "Accounting for Real Estate Acquisition, Development and Construction Costs," Statement of Position No. 80-3. AICPA, New York, 1980.

———, "Accounting for Performance of Construction-Type and Certain Production-Type Contracts," Statement of Position 81-1. AICPA, New York, July 15, 1981.

———, Third Notice to Practitioners, "Accounting for Real Estate Acquisition, Development, and Construction Arrangements." AICPA, New York, February 10, 1986.

"Accounting for Real Estate Syndication Income," Statement of Position No. 92-1. AICPA, New York, 1992.

"Accounting for Foreclosed Assets," Statement of Position 92-3. AICPA, New York, 1992.

———, "Accounting by Participating Mortgage Loan Borrowers," Statement of Position 97-1. AICPA, New York, 1997.

"Proposed Statement of Position: Accounting for Certain Costs and Activities Related to Property, Plant, and Equipment." AICPA, New York, June 29, 2001.

Financial Accounting Standards Board, "Acquisition, Development, and Construction Loans," EITF Issue No. 84-4. FASB, Stamford, CT, 1984.

———, "Recognition of Receipts from Made-Up Rental Shortfalls," EITF Issue No. 85-27. FASB, Stamford, CT, 1985.

———, "Antispeculation Clauses in Real Estate Sales Contracts," EITF Issue No. 86-6. FASB, Stamford, CT, 1986.

_____ , "Application of the AICPA Notice to Practitioners Regarding Acquisition, Development, and Construction Arrangements to the Acquisition of an Operating Property," EITF Issue No. 86-21. FASB, Stamford, CT, 1986.

_____ , EITF Abstracts: A Summary of Proceedings of the FASB Emerging Issues Task Force, "Profit Recognition on Sale of Real Estate with Insurance Mortgages on Surety Bonds," EITF Issue No. 87-9. FASB, Norwalk, CT, 1988.

_____ , "Effect of Various Forms of Financing under Statement of Financial Accounting Standards No. 66," EITF Issue No. 88-24. FASB, Norwalk, CT, 1988.

_____ , "Accounting for Tax Benefits Resulting from Investments in Affordable Housing Projects," EITF Issue No. 94-1. FASB, Norwalk, CT, 1994.

_____ , "Accounting for Leases," Statement of Financial Accounting Standards No. 13. FASB, Stamford, CT, November 1976.

_____ , "Financial Reporting for Segments of a Business Enterprise," Statement of Financial Accounting Standards No. 14. FASB, Stamford, CT, 1976.

_____ , "Accounting for Sales with Leasebacks (an amendment of FASB Statement No. 13)," Statement of Financial Accounting Standards No. 28. FASB, Stamford, CT, 1979.

_____ , "Determining Contingent Rentals (an amendment of FASB Statement No. 13)," Statement of Financial Accounting Standards No. 29. FASB, Stamford, CT, 1979.

_____ , "Capitalization of Interest Cost," Statement of Financial Accounting Standards No. 34. FASB, Stamford, CT, October 1979.

_____ , "Designation of AICPA Guide and Statement of Position (SOP) 81-1 on Contractor Accounting and SOP 81-2 Concerning Hospital-Related Organizations as Preferable for Purposes of Applying APB Opinion 20," Statement of Financial Accounting Standards No. 56. FASB, Stamford, CT, February 1982.

_____ , "Accounting for Sales of Real Estate," Statement of Financial Accounting Standards No. 66. FASB, Stamford, CT, October 1982.

_____ , "Accounting for Costs and Initial Rental Operations of Real Estate Projects," Statement of Financial Accounting Standards No. 67. FASB, Stamford, CT, October 1982.

_____ , "Consolidation of All Majority-Owned Subsidiaries," Statement of Financial Accounting Standards No. 94. FASB, Stamford, CT, October 1987.

_____ , "Statement of Cash Flows," Statement of Financial Accounting Standards No. 95. FASB, Stamford, CT, November 1987.

_____ , "Accounting for the Impairment of Long-Lived Assets and for Long-Lived Assets to Be Disposed Of," Statement of Financial Accounting Standards No. 121. FASB, Norwalk, CT, March 1995.

_____ , "Accounting for Leases," Statement of Financial Accounting Standards No. 98. FASB, Norwalk, CT, May 1988.

_____ , "Disclosures About Segments of an Enterprise and Related Information," Statement of Financial Accounting Standards No. 131. FASB, Norwalk, CT, 1997.

_____ , "Goodwill and Other Intangible Assets," Statement of Financial Accounting Standards No. 142. FASB, Norwalk, CT, 2001.

_____ , "Accounting for the Impairment or Disposal of Long-Lived Assets," Statement of Financial Accounting Standards No. 144. FASB, Norwalk, CT, 2001.

_____ , "Accounting for Operating Leases with Scheduled Rent Increases." FASB Technical Bulletin No. 85-3. FASB, Stamford, CT, November 1985.

_____ , "Issues Relating to Accounting for Leases," FASB Technical Bulletin No. 88-1. FASB, Norwalk, CT, December 1988.

Cammavano, Jr., Nicholas, and Klink, James J., _Real Estate Accounting and Reporting: A Guide for Developers, Investors, and Lenders,_ Third Edition. John Wiley & Sons, New York, 1995.

Price Waterhouse, "Accounting for Condominium Sales." New York, 1984.

_____ , "Accounting for Sales of Real Estate." New York, 1983.

_____ , "Cost Accounting for Real Estate." New York, 1983.

_____ , "Investor Accounting for Real Estate Ventures." New York, 1979.

Securities and Exchange Commission, "Reporting Cash Flow and Other Related Data," Financial Reporting Policy 202. SEC, Washington, DC.

_____ , "Requirement for Financial Statements of Special Purpose Limited Partnerships," Financial Reporting Policy 405. SEC, Washington, DC.

_____ , "Preparation of Registration Statements Relating to Interests in Real Estate Limited Partnerships," Guide 5. SEC, Washington, DC.

_____ , "Special Instructions for Real Estate Operations to Be Acquired," Regulation S-X, Article 3, Rule 3–14. SEC, Washington, DC.

_____ , "Consolidation of Financial Statements of the Registrant and its Subsidiaries," Regulation S-X, Article 3A, Rule 3A-02. SEC, Washington, DC.

_____ , "Views on Financial Statements of Properties Securing Mortgage Loans," Staff Accounting Bulletin 71-71A (Topic No. 1I). SEC, Washington, DC.

_____ , "Offsetting Assets and Liabilities," Staff Accounting Bulletin Topic No. 11D. SEC, Washington, DC.

Henriques, Diana B. "The Brick Stood Up Before. But Now?" _New York Times_, March 10, 2002, p. 1.

CHAPTER **31**

FINANCIAL INSTITUTIONS

Laura J. Phillips CPA
Ernst & Young LLP

Mark R. Rouchard, CPA
Ernst & Young LLP

Dale K. Thompson, CPA
Ernst & Young LLP

Alan M. Kall, CPA
Ernst & Young LLP

Keith M. Housum, CPA
Ernst & Young LLP

31.1 OVERVIEW

(a) CHANGING THE ENVIRONMENT.   The financial institutions industry has changed significantly in the last decade. Regulatory changes and increased competition have further blurred the lines among depository institutions, mortgage banking activities, investment companies, credit unions, investment banks, insurance companies, finance companies, and securities brokers and dealers.

Competition has increased as all types of financial entities conduct business directly with potential depositors and borrowers. Transactions traditionally executed through depository institutions are now handled by all types of financial institutions. Increased competition has heightened the depository institutions' desire for innovative approaches to attracting depositors and borrowers. Institutions are seeking higher levels of noninterest income, restructuring banking operations to reduce costs, and continuing consolidation within the industry.

(b) ROLE IN THE ECONOMY.   Financial institutions in their basic role provide a medium of exchange; however, they may also serve as a tool to regulate the economy. In a complex financial and economic environment, the regulation of financial institutions—directly and indirectly—is used to impact economic activity.

(c) TYPES OF FINANCIAL INSTITUTIONS.   Many types of financial institutions exist. The more common types are described. In view of the range and diversity within financial institutions, this chapter will focus on three major types of entities/activities: banks and savings institutions, mortgage banking activities, and investment companies.

(i) Banks and Savings Institutions.   Banks and savings institutions (including thrifts) continue in their traditional role as financial intermediaries. They provide a link between entities that have capital and entities that need capital, while also providing an efficient means for payment and transfer of funds between these entities. Banks also provide a wide range of services to their customers, including cash management and fiduciary services.

Financial modernization and financial reform legislation continues to change the way banks and savings institutions conduct business. Banks and savings institutions have developed sophisticated products to meet customer needs and technological advances to support such complex and specialized transactions. Continued financial reform may change the types and nature of permissible banking activities and affiliations.

(ii) Mortgage Banking Activities.   Mortgage banking activities include the origination, sale, and servicing of mortgage loans. Mortgage loan origination activities are performed by entities such as mortgage banks, mortgage brokers, credit unions, and commercial banks and savings institutions. Mortgages are purchased by government-sponsored entities, sponsors of mortgage-backed security (MBS) programs, and private companies such as insurance companies, other mortgage banking entities, and pension funds.

(iii) Investment Companies.   Investment companies pool shareholders' funds to provide the shareholders with professional investment management. Typically, an investment company sells its capital shares to the public, invests the proceeds to achieve its investment objectives, and distributes to its shareholders the net income and net gains realized on the sale of its investments. The types of investment companies include management investment companies, unit investment trusts, collective trust funds, investment partnerships, certain separate accounts of insurance companies, and offshore funds. Investment companies grew significantly in the early 1990s, primarily due to growth in mutual funds.

(iv) Credit Unions.   Credit unions are member-owned, not-for-profit cooperative financial institutions, organized around a defined membership. The members pool their savings, borrow funds, and obtain other related financial services. A credit union relies on volunteers who represent the members. Its primary objective is to provide services to its members, rather than to generate earnings for its owners.

More recently, many credit unions have made arrangements to share branch offices with other credit unions and depository institutions to reduce operating costs.

(v) Investment Banks.   Investment banks or merchant banks deal with the financing requirements of corporations and institutions. They may be organized as corporations or partnerships.

(vi) Insurance Companies.   The primary purpose of insurance is the spreading of risks. The two major types of insurance are life, and property and casualty. The primary purpose of life insurance is to provide financial assistance at the time of death. It typically has a long period of coverage. Property and casualty insurance companies provide policies to individuals (personal lines) and to business enterprises (commercial lines). Examples of personal lines include homeowner's and individual automobile policies. Examples of commercial lines include general liability and workers' compensation. Banks, mutual funds, and health maintenance organizations are aggressively trying to expand into products traditionally sold by insurance companies. In recent years the insurance industry benefited from the strong stock and bond markets; however, slow premium growth and the increased competition continued to pressure insurers to reduce costs and improve profitability.

(vii) Finance Companies.   Finance companies provide lending and financing services to consumers (consumer financing) and to business enterprises (commercial financing). The more common types of consumer financing include mortgage loans, retail sales contracts, and insurance service. The more common types of commercial financing include factoring, revolving loans, installment, term and floor plan loans, portfolio purchase agreements, and lease financing. Captive finance entities represent manufacturers, retailers, wholesalers, and other business enterprises who provide financing to encourage customers to buy their products and services. Many captive finance companies also finance third-party products. More recently, mortgage finance companies and diversified finance companies have increased their presence by increasing the number of loans made to higher risk niches at higher yields.

(viii) Securities Brokers and Dealers.   Securities brokers and dealers serve in various roles within the securities industry. Brokers, acting in an agency capacity, buy and sell securities, commodities, and related financial instruments for their customers and charge a commission. Dealers or traders, acting in a principal capacity, buy and sell for their own account and trade with customers and other dealers. Broker-dealers perform a wide range of both types of activities, such as assisting with private placements, underwriting public securities, developing new products, facilitating international investment activity, serving as a depository for customers' securities, extending credit, and providing research and advisory services.

(ix) Real Estate Investment Trusts.   The new class of Real Estate Investment Trusts (REITs), formed since 1991, are basically self-contained real estate companies. They are designed to align the interests of active management and passive investors, generate cash flow growth, and create long-term value. Traditionally, REITs relied on mortgage debt to finance their development and acquisition activities. Today many REITs are taking advantage of their large market capitalization and strong balance sheets to raise cash by issuing debt on an unsecured basis.

31.2 BANKS AND SAVINGS INSTITUTIONS

(a) PRIMARY RISKS OF BANKS AND SAVINGS INSTITUTIONS.   General business and economic risk factors exist for many industries; however, increased competition among banks and savings institutions has resulted in the industry's aggressive pursuit of profitable activities. Techniques for managing assets and liabilities and financial risks have been enhanced in order to maximize income levels. Technological advances have accommodated increasingly complex transactions such as the sale of securities backed by cash flows from other financial assets. Regulatory policy has radically changed the business environment for banks, savings, and other financial institutions. Additionally, there are other risk factors common to most banks and savings institutions, based on their business activities. The other primary risk factors are described next.

(i) Interest-Rate Risk.   This is the risk that adverse movements in interest rates may result in loss of profits since banks and savings institutions routinely earn on assets at one rate and pay on liabilities at another rate. Techniques used to minimize interest-rate risk are a part of asset/liability management.

(ii) Liquidity Risk.   This is the risk that an institution may be unable to meet its obligations as they become due. An institution may acquire funds short term and lend funds long term to obtain favorable interest rate spreads, thus creating liquidity risk if depositors or creditors demand repayment.

(iii) Asset-Quality Risk.   This is the risk that the loss of expected cash flows due to, for example, loan defaults and inadequate collateral will result in significant losses. Examples include credit losses from loans and declines in the economic value of mortgage servicing rights, resulting from prepayments of principal during periods of falling interest rates.

(iv) Fiduciary Risk.   This is the risk of loss arising from failure to properly process transactions or handle the custody, management, or both, of financial related assets on behalf of third parties. Examples include administering trusts, managing mutual funds, and servicing the collateral behind asset-backed securities.

(v) Processing Risk.   This is the risk that transactions will not be processed accurately or timely, due to large volumes, short periods of time, unauthorized access of computerized records, or the demands placed on both computerized and manual systems. Examples include electronic funds transfers, loan servicing, and check processing.

(b) REGULATION AND SUPERVISION OF BANKS AND SAVINGS INSTITUTIONS. The legal system that governed the financial services industry in the United States was created in response to the stock market crash of 1929 and the resulting Great Depression. Thousands of banks went out of business and, in response, Congress passed the Glass-Steagall Act in 1933. Glass-Steagall prohibited commingling the businesses of commercial and investment banking. Its intent was to restrict banks from engaging in business activities that allegedly contributed to and accelerated the stock market crash. In the view of legislators, the way to do this was to confine banks to certain strictly defined activities.

In 1945, Congress enacted the McCarran-Ferguson Act as comprehensive legislation governing the insurance industry. McCarran-Ferguson effectively delegated the responsibility for regulating the business of insurance to the states. Since then, the states have maintained autonomy in their regulatory role with relatively minor, but increasing, exceptions. With the Bank Holding Company Act of 1956 and amendments in 1970, Congress limited affiliations between bank and nonbank businesses.

Section 20 of the Glass-Steagall Act took on a life of its own. Section 20 limited banks' ability to own subsidiaries "principally engaged" in securities underwriting. Over time, that section evolved from being considered a prohibition against any securities underwriting to permitting banks to do so through a subsidiary, as long as underwriting revenues did not exceed 25 percent of total revenues of that subsidiary—thus allowing them to meet the "not principally engaged" test. Over the years, the effective relaxation of those restrictions enabled numerous acquisitions of securities firms by U.S. bank holding companies and by foreign banks.

These barriers also eroded over time through a combination of changes in customer demands and market activities, the increasing use of more sophisticated financial management techniques, advances in technology, regulatory interpretations, and legal decisions. Product innovation played a role, as the industry learned how to rapidly bundle and unbundle risk, creating new securitization products and accessing the capital markets in ways that had not been contemplated under the then-existing regulatory framework.

As banks assumed a larger role in insurance sales, brokerage, and securities underwriting activities, products began to converge in the marketplace, and the perceived benefits from the convergence of these and related activities instilled a new urgency in the effort to modernize and clarify the regulatory framework governing financial services companies.

The Gramm-Leach-Bliley Act of 1999 (GLB Act) amended the Bank Holding Company Act to allow a bank holding company or foreign bank that qualifies as a financial holding company to engage in a broad range of activities that are defined by the GLB Act to be financial in nature or incidental to a financial activity, or that the Federal Reserve Board (FRB), in consultation with the Secretary of the Treasury, determines to be financial in nature or incidental to a financial activity. The GLB Act also allows a financial holding company to seek Board approval to engage in any activity that the FRB determines both to be complementary to a financial activity and not to pose a substantial risk to the safety and soundness of depository institutions or the financial system generally. Bank holding companies that do not qualify as financial holding companies are limited to engaging in those nonbanking activities that were permissible for bank holding companies before the GLB Act was enacted.

(c) REGULATORY BACKGROUND. Banks and savings institutions have special privileges and protections granted by government. These incentives, such as credit through the Federal Reserve System and federal insurance of deposits, have not been similarly extended to commercial enterprises. Accordingly, the benefits and responsibilities associated with their public role as financial intermediaries have brought banks and savings institutions under significant governmental oversight.

As a result of the financial repercussions of the Great Depression, the government took certain measures to maintain the stability of the country's financial system. Several new regulatory and supervisory agencies were created to promote economic stability, particularly in the banking industry, and to strengthen the regulatory and supervisory agencies that were in existence at the time.

Among the agencies created were the Federal Deposit Insurance Corporation (FDIC), the Securities and Exchange Commission (SEC), the Federal Home Loan Bank Board (FHLBB), and the Federal Savings and Loan Insurance Corporation (FSLIC). The agencies that were strengthened included the Office of the Comptroller of the Currency (OCC) and the FRB. These entities were responsible for designing and establishing policies and procedures for the regulation and supervision of national and state banks, foreign banks doing business in the United States, and other depository institutions. This regulatory and supervisory structure, created during the 1930s, was in place for almost 60 years. In 1989, Congress enacted the Financial Institutions Reform, Recovery and Enforcement Act (FIRREA), which changed the regulatory and supervisory structure of thrift institutions. The FIRREA eliminated the FHLBB and the FSLIC. In their place, it created the Office of Thrift Supervision (OTS) as the primary regulator of the thrift industry and the Savings Association Insurance Fund (SAIF) as the thrift institutions' insurer to be administered by the FDIC.

Even though several of the aforementioned federal agencies have overlapping regulatory and supervisory responsibilities over depository institutions, in general terms, the OCC has primary responsibility for national banks; the FRB has primary responsibility over state banks that are members of the FRB, all financial holding companies and bank holding companies and their non-bank subsidiaries, and most U.S. operations of foreign banks; the FDIC has primary responsibility for all state-insured banks that are not members of the FRB (nonmember banks); and the OTS has primary responsibility for thrift institutions. Exhibit 31.1 lists these regulatory responsibilities.

(i) Office of the Comptroller of the Currency. The Office of the Comptroller of the Currency (OCC) charters, regulates, and supervises all national banks. It also supervises the federal branches and agencies of foreign banks. Headquartered in Washington, D.C., the OCC has six district offices plus an office in London to supervise the international activities of national banks.

The OCC was established in 1863 as a bureau of the U.S. Department of the Treasury. The OCC is headed by the comptroller, who is appointed by the president, with the advice and consent of the Senate, for a five-year term. The comptroller also serves as a director of the FDIC and a director of the Neighborhood Reinvestment Corporation.

The OCC's nationwide staff of examiners conducts on-site reviews of national banks and provides sustained supervision of bank operations. The agency issues rules, legal interpretations, and corporate decisions concerning banking, bank investments, bank community development activities, and other aspects of bank operations.

National bank examiners supervise domestic and international activities of national banks and perform corporate analyses. Examiners analyze a bank's loan and investment portfolios, funds management, capital, earnings, liquidity, sensitivity to market risk, and compliance with consumer

Bank Classifications*	OTS	OCC	State Banking Department	Federal Reserve	FDIC
National banks		X			
State banks and trust companies					
Federal Reserve members			X	X	
Nonmembers					
FDIC insured			X		X
Noninsured			X		
Bank holding companies				X	
Thrift holding companies	X				
Savings Banks	X			X	X
Savings and Loan Associations	X				

*All national banks are members of the Federal Reserve Board. All national banks and state chartered member banks are insured by the FDIC.

Exhibit 31.1   Supervisor and regulator.

banking laws, including the Community Reinvestment Act. They review the bank's internal controls, internal and external audit, and compliance with law. They also evaluate bank management's ability to identify and control risk.

In regulating national banks, the OCC has the power to:

- Examine the banks.
- Approve or deny applications for new charters, branches, capital, or other changes in corporate or banking structure.
- Take supervisory actions against banks that do not comply with laws and regulations or that otherwise engage in unsound banking practices. The agency can remove officers and directors, negotiate agreements to change banking practices, and issue cease-and-desist orders as well as civil money penalties.
- Issue rules and regulations governing bank investments, lending, and other practices.

(ii) Federal Reserve Board.   The Federal Reserve Board (FRB) was created by Congress in 1913 by the Federal Reserve Act. The primary role of the FRB as the nation's central bank is to establish and conduct monetary policy, as well as to regulate and supervise a wide range of financial activities. The structure of the FRB includes a board of governors, 12 Federal Reserve banks, and the member banks. The board of governors consists of seven members appointed by the president, subject to Senate confirmation. National banks must be members of the FRB. State banks are not required to, but may elect to, become members. Member banks and other depository institutions are required to keep reserves with the FRB, and member banks must subscribe to the capital stock of the reserve bank in the district to which they belong.

Since all national banks are supervised by the OCC, the FRB primarily regulates and supervises member state banks, including administering the registration and reporting requirements of the 1934 Act.

The regulatory and supervisory functions and other services provided by the FRB include:

- Examining the Federal Reserve banks, state member banks, bank holding companies and their nonbank subsidiaries, and state licensed U.S. branches of foreign banks
- Requiring reports of member and other banks
- Setting the discount rate
- Providing credit facilities to members and other depository institutions for liquidity and other purposes
- Monitoring compliance with the money-laundering provisions contained in the Bank Secrecy Act
- Regulating transactions between banking affiliates
- Approving or denying applications by state banks to become members and to branch or merge with nonmember banks
- Approving or denying applications to become bank holding companies and for bank holding companies to acquire bank or nonbank subsidiaries
- Approving or denying applications by foreign banks to establish representative offices, branches, agencies, or bank subsidiaries in the United States
- Supplying currency when needed
- Regulating the establishment of foreign operations of national and state member banks and the operations of foreign banks doing business in the United States
- Enforcing legislation and issuing rules and regulations dealing with consumer protection
- Operating the nation's payment system

(iii) Federal Deposit Insurance Corporation. The Federal Deposit Insurance Corporation (FDIC) was created under the Banking Act of 1933. The main purpose for its creation was to insure bank deposits in order to maintain economic stability in the event of bank failures. FIRREA restructured the FDIC during 1989 to carry out broadened functions by insuring thrift institutions as well as banks. The FDIC now insures all depository institutions except credit unions.

The FDIC is an independent agency of the U.S. government, managed by a five-member board of directors, consisting of the Comptroller of the Currency, the Director of the OTS, and three other members, including a chairman, appointed by the president, subject to Senate confirmation.

The FDIC insures deposits under two separate funds: the Bank Insurance Fund (BIF) and the SAIF. From its BIF, the FDIC insures national and state banks that are members of the FRB. These institutions are required to be insured. Also insured from this fund are state nonmember banks and a limited number of insured branches of foreign banks (after 1991 foreign bank branches could no longer apply for FDIC insurance).

From its SAIF, the FDIC insures all federal savings and loan associations and federal savings banks. These institutions are required to be insured. State thrift institutions are also insured from this fund.

Currently, each account, subject to certain FDIC rules, in an insured depository institution is insured to a maximum of $100,000. Other responsibilities of the FDIC include:

- Supervising the liquidation of insolvent insured depository institutions
- Providing financial support and additional measures to prevent insured depository institution failures
- Supervising state nonmember insured banks by conducting bank examinations, regulating bank mergers, consolidations and establishment of branches, and establishing other regulatory controls
- Administering the registration and reporting requirements of the 1934 Act as applied to state nonmember banks

(iv) Office of Thrift Supervision. In 1989, FIRREA created the Office of Thrift Supervision (OTS) under the Department of the Treasury. The OTS regulates federal and state thrift institutions and thrift holding companies. As a principal rule maker, examiner, and enforcement agency, OTS exercises primary regulatory authority to grant federal thrift institution charters, approve branching applications, and allow mutual-to-thrift charter conversions. OTS is headed by a presidentially appointed director. The 12 district Federal Home Loan Banks (FHLBs) continue to be the primary source of credit for thrift institutions.

(d) REGULATORY ENVIRONMENT. The early 1980s were marked by the removal of interest-rate ceilings, the applications of reserve requirements to all depository institutions, expanded thrift powers, and related deregulatory actions. However, the failures of a large number of thrift institutions and commercial banks caused legislators in 1989 and 1991 to increase regulatory oversight. Both FIRREA and the Federal Deposit Insurance Corporation Improvement Act of 1991 (FDICIA) were directed toward protection of federal deposit insurance funds through early detection of an intervention in problem institutions with an emphasis on capital adequacy. FIRREA also established the Resolution Trust Corporation (RTC), which took over the conservatorship and liquidation of a large number of failed thrift institutions due to the bankruptcy of the FSLIC. The RTC completed its mission in 1996 at a net cost of approximately $150 billion to the federal government.

In addition to safety and soundness considerations, current banking regulations recognize economic issues, such as the desire for banks and savings institutions to successfully compete with other, less regulated financial services providers, as well as to address social issues, such as community reinvestment, nondiscrimination, and fair treatment in consumer credit, including residential lending. Costs and benefits of regulations are weighed as the approach to regulation of the industry is redefined.

(e) FEDERAL DEPOSIT INSURANCE CORPORATION IMPROVEMENT ACT SECTION 112.
Regulations implementing Section 36 of the Federal Deposit Insurance Act (FDI Act), as added by Section 112 of FDICIA, became effective July 2, 1993. These regulations imposed additional audit, reporting, and attestation responsibilities on management, directors (especially the audit committee), internal auditors, and independent accountants of banks and savings institutions with $500 million or more in total assets. The reporting requirements were effective for fiscal years ending on or after December 31, 1993. Congress amended the law in 1996 to eliminate attestation reports concerning compliance with certain banking laws; however, management is still required to report on compliance with such laws.

(i) The Regulation and Guidelines.   The regulation itself is short, only about 1,000 words. However, it is accompanied by Appendix A to Part 363—Guidelines and Interpretations—that contain 36 guidelines, providing an explanation to its meaning and operation. The guidelines often leave discretion with an institution or its board, while simultaneously providing guidance that, if followed, would provide a safe harbor from examiner criticism.

(ii) Basic Requirements.   Each FDIC-insured depository institution with assets in excess of $500 million at the beginning of its fiscal year ("covered institutions") is subject to the following requirements:

Annual Report.   Covered institutions must file an annual report, within 90 days of its fiscal year end, with the FDIC and its other appropriate state or federal bank regulator. The annual report must include:

(a) Audited financial statements prepared in accordance with generally accepted accounting principles (GAAP) and audited by an Independent Public Accountant (IPA) meeting the qualifications.

(b) A management report signed by its chief executive and chief financial officer or chief accounting officer containing:
- A statement of management's responsibilities for:
  - Preparing the annual financial statements
  - Establishing and maintaining an adequate internal control structure and procedures for financial reporting
  - Complying with particular laws designated by the FDIC as affecting the safety and soundness of insured depositories
- Assessment by management of:
  - The effectiveness of the institution's internal control structure and procedures for financial reporting as of the end of the fiscal year.
  - The institution's compliance, during the fiscal year, with the designated safety and soundness laws. The FDIC designated only two kinds of safety and soundness laws to be addressed in the compliance report: (1) federal statutes and regulations concerning transactions with insiders and (2) federal and state statutes and regulations restricting the payment of dividends.

(c) An attestation report, by an IPA, on internal control structure and procedures for financial reporting. The institution's IPA must examine, attest to, and report separately on management's assertions about internal controls and about compliance. The attestations are to be made in accordance with generally accepted standards for attestation engagements.

In FIL No. 86-94, the FDIC indicated that financial reporting, at a minimum, includes financial statements prepared under GAAP and the schedules equivalent to the basic financial statements that are included in the institution's appropriate regulatory report (e.g., Schedules RC, RI, and RI-A in the Call Report).

On February 6, 1996, the Board of the FDIC amended the procedures that IPAs follow in testing compliance to streamline the procedures and to reduce regulatory burden.

Audit Committee. Covered institutions must establish an independent audit committee composed of directors who are independent of management. The entire board of directors annually is required to adopt a resolution documenting its determination that the audit committee has met all FDIC-imposed requirements.

The audit committee of any "large" IDI (i.e., total assets of more than $3 billion, measured as of the beginning of each fiscal year) shall include members with banking or related financial management expertise, have access to its own outside counsel, and not include any large customers of the institution. If a large institution is a subsidiary of a holding company and relies on the audit committee of the holding company to comply with this rule, the holding company audit committee shall not include any members who are large customers of the subsidiary institution. Appendix A to Part 363 provides guidelines in determining whether the audit committee meets the above criteria.

The audit committee is required to review with management and the IPA the basis for the reports required by the FDIC's regulation. FDIC suggests, but does not mandate, additional audit committee duties, including overseeing internal audit, selecting the IPA, and reviewing significant accounting policies.

Each subject institution must provide its independent accountant with copies of the institution's most recent reports of condition and examination; any supervisory memorandum of understanding or written agreement with any federal or state regulatory agency; and a report of any action initiated or taken by federal or state banking regulators.

(iii) Holding Company Exception. The requirements of the FDIC's regulation, in some instances, may be satisfied by a bank's or savings association's parent holding company. The requirement for audited financial statements always may be satisfied by providing audited financial statements of the consolidated holding company. The requirements for other reports, as well as for an independent audit committee, may be satisfied by the holding company if:

- The holding company's services and functions are comparable to those required of the depository institution.
- The depository institution has total assets as of the beginning of the fiscal year either of less than $5 billion or equal to or greater than $5 billion and a CAMELS composite rating of 1 or 2. Section 314(a) of the Riegle Community Development and Regulatory Improvement Act of 1994 amended Section 36(i) of the FDI Act to expand the holding company exception to be equal to or greater than $5 billion. The requirement that the institution must have a CAMELS composite rating of 1 or 2 remained unchanged.

The appropriate federal banking agency may revoke the exception for any institution with total assets in excess of $9 billion for any period of time during which the appropriate federal banking agency determines that the institution's exception would create a significant risk to the affected deposit insurance fund.

(iv) Availability of Reports. All of management's reports are made publicly available. The independent accountant's report on the financial statements and attestation report on financial reporting controls is also made publicly available.

(f) CAPITAL ADEQUACY GUIDELINES.   Capital is one of the primary tools used by regulators to monitor the financial health of insured banks and savings institutions. Statutorily mandated supervisory intervention is focused primarily on an institution's capital levels relative to regulatory standards. The federal banking agencies detail these requirements in their respective regulations under capital adequacy guidelines. The capital adequacy requirements are implemented through quarterly regulatory financial reporting ("Call Reports" and "Thrift Financial Reports [TFRs]").

(i) Risk-Based and Leverage Ratios.   Capital adequacy is measured mainly through two risk-based capital ratios and a leverage ratio, with thrifts subject to an additional tangible capital ratio.

(ii) Tier 1, Tier 2, and Tier 3 Components.   Regulatory capital may be composed of three components: core capital or Tier 1, supplementary capital or Tier 2, and for those institutions meeting market risk capital requirements, Tier 3. Tier 1 capital includes elements such as common stock, surplus, retained earnings, minority interest in consolidated subsidiaries and qualifying preferred stock, adjustments for foreign exchange translation, and unrealized losses on equity securities available for sale with readily determinable market values. Tier 2 capital includes, with certain limitations, elements such as general loan loss reserves, certain forms of preferred stock, long-term preferred stock, qualifying intermediate-term preferred stock and term subordinated debt, perpetual debt, and other hybrid debt/equity instruments; Tier 3 capital consists of short-term subordinated debt that meets certain conditions and may be used only by institutions subject to market-risk capital requirements to the extent that Tier 1 and Tier 2 capital elements do not provide adequate Tier 1 and total risk-based capital ratio levels.

Specifically, Tier 3 capital must have an original maturity of at least two years; it must be unsecured and fully paid up; it must be subject to a lock-in clause that prevents the issuer from repaying the debt even at maturity if the issuer's capital ratio is, or with repayment would become, less than the minimum eight percent risk-based capital ratio; it must not be redeemable before maturity without the prior approval of the institution's supervisor; and it must not contain or be covered by any covenants, terms, or restrictions that may be inconsistent with safe and sound banking practices. Tier 2 capital elements individually and together are variously restricted in proportion to Tier 1 capital, which is intended to be the dominant capital component.

Certain deductions are made to determine regulatory capital, including goodwill and other disallowed intangibles, excess portions of qualifying intangibles and deferred tax assets, investments in unconsolidated subsidiaries, and reciprocal holdings of other bank's capital instruments. Certain adjustments made to equity under GAAP for unrealized gains and losses on debt and equity securities available for sale under Financial Accounting Standards Board (FASB) Statement No. 115, mainly unrealized gains, are excluded from Tier 1 and Total Capital. Portions of qualifying, subordinated debt, and limited-life preferred stock exceeding 50 percent of a bank's Tier 1 capital are also deducted. Any regulatory capital deduction is also made to average total assets for ratio computation purposes. The new market-risk capital guidelines discussed below also contained further capital constraints, by stating that the sum of Tier 2 and Tier 3 capital allocated for market risk may not exceed 250 percent of Tier 1 capital allocated for market risk. A thrift's tangible capital is generally defined as Tier 1 capital less intangibles.

(iii) Risk-Weighted Assets.   The capital ratios are calculated using the applicable regulatory capital component in the numerator and either risk-weighted assets or total adjusted on-balance sheet assets as the denominator, as appropriate. Risk-weighted assets are ascertained pursuant to the regulatory guidelines that allocate gross average assets among four categories of risk weights (0%, 20%, 50%, and 100%). The allocations are based mainly on type of asset, type of obligor, and nature of collateral, if any. Gross assets include on-balance sheet assets, credit equivalents of certain off-balance exposures, and credit equivalents of certain assets sold with recourse, limited recourse, or that are treated as financings for regulatory reporting purposes.

Credit equivalents of off-balance-sheet exposures are determined by the nature of the exposure. For example, direct credit substitutes (e.g., standby letters of credit) are credit converted at 100 percent of the face amount. Other off-balance-sheet activities are subject to the current exposure method, which is composed of the positive mark-to-market value (if any) and an estimate of the potential increase in credit exposure over the remaining life of the contract. These "add-ons" are estimated by applying defined credit conversion factors, differentiated by type of instrument and remaining maturity, to the contract's notional value. The nature and extent of recourse impacts the calculation of credit equivalents amounts of assets sold or securitized. In December 2001, the banking agencies issued a final rule amending the agencies' regulatory capital standards to align more closely the risk-based capital treatment of recourse obligations and direct credit substitutes. The rule also varies the capital requirements for position in securitized transactions and certain other exposures according to their relative credit risk and requires capital commensurate with the risks associated with residual interests.

(iv) Capital Calculations and Minimum Requirements. The capital ratios, calculations, and minimum requirements are presented in Exhibit 31.2.

(v) Interest Rate Risk and Capital Adequacy. OTS capital rules require that certain savings associations with excessive interest rate risk exposure (as defined) must deduct 50 percent of the estimated decline in its net portfolio value resulting from a 200 basis point change in market interest rates in excess of 2 percent of the estimated economic value of portfolio assets. In August 1995, the banking agencies amended their minimum capital requirements explicitly to include consideration of interest rate risk, but established no means for quantifying that risk to a specific amount of additional capital. During 1996, the federal bank regulatory agencies approved a policy statement on sound practices for managing interest rate risk in commercial banks, but did not include a standardized framework for measuring interest rate risk. The agencies elected not to pursue a standardized measure and explicit capital charge for interest rate risk, due to concerns about the burden, accuracy, and complexity of a standardized measure and recognition that industry techniques for measuring interest rate risk are continuing to evolve.

(vi) Capital Allocated for Market Risk. In September 1996, the federal bank regulatory agencies (OCC, FDIC, FRB) amended their respective risk-based capital standards to address market risk. Specifically, an institution subject to the market risk capital requirement must adjust its risk-based capital ratio to take into account the general market risk of all positions located in its trading account and foreign exchange and commodity positions, wherever located and for the specific risk of debt and equity positions located in its trading account. Market risk capital requirements generally apply to any bank or bank holding company whose trading activities equal 10 percent or more of its total assets, or whose trading activity equals $1 billion or more. In addition, on a case-by-case basis, an agency may require an institution that does not meet the applicability criteria to comply with the market risk guidelines, if the agency deems it necessary for safety and soundness purposes, or may exclude an institution that meets the applicability criteria.

Capital Ratio	Calculation	Minimum Requirement
Total risk-based ratio:		
Unadjusted	Tier 1 + Tier 2/Risk-weighted assets	≥ 8.0%
Adjusted for marked risk	Tier 1 + Tier 2 + Tier 3/Risk-weighted assets plus market-risk equivalent assets	≥ 8.0%
Tier 1 risk-based ratio	Tier 1/Risk-weighted assets	≥ 4.0%
Tier 1 leverage capital ratio	Tier 1/Average on-balance sheet assets	≥ 4.0%*
Tangible ratio (Thrifts)	Tangible capital/on-balance sheet assets	≥ 1.5%
*3.0% for institutions CAMELS/MACRO rated "1" (overall).		

Exhibit 31.2   Capital ratio calculations and minimum requirements.

No later than January 1, 1998, institutions with significant market risk were required to:

- Maintain regulatory capital on a daily basis at an overall minimum of eight percent ratio of total qualifying capital to risk-weighted assets, adjusted for market risk
- Include a supplemental market-risk capital charge in their risk-based capital calculations and quarterly regulatory reports
- Maintain appropriate internal measurement, reporting, and risk management systems to generate and monitor the basis for the value-at-risk (VAR) and the associated capital charge

The institution's risk-based capital ratio adjusted for market risk is its risk-based capital ratio for purposes of prompt corrective action and other statutory and regulatory purposes.

Institutions are permitted to use different assumptions and modeling techniques reflecting distinct business strategies and approaches to risk management. The agencies do not specify VAR modeling parameters for internal risk management purposes; however, they do specify minimum qualitative requirements for internal risk management processes, as well as certain quantitative requirements for the parameters and assumptions for internal models used to measure market risk exposure for regulatory capital purposes.

Backtesting.   Institutions must perform backtests of their VAR measures as calculated for internal risk management purposes. The backtests must compare daily VAR measures calibrated to a one-day movement in rates and prices and a 99 percent (one-tailed) confidence level against the institution's actual daily net trading profit or loss (trading outcome) for each of the preceding 250 business days. The backtests must be performed once each quarter. An institution's obligation to backtest for regulatory capital purposes does not arise until the institution has been subject to the final rule for 250 business days (approximately one year) and, thus, has accumulated the requisite number of observations to be used in backtesting. Institutions that are found not to have appropriate models and backtesting programs or if backtesting results reflect insufficient accuracy likely will be required to incorporate more conservative calculation factors that would result in a higher capital charge for market risk.

(g) PROMPT CORRECTIVE ACTION.   The federal banking agencies are statutorily mandated to assign each FDIC insured depository institution to one of five capital categories, quantitatively defined by the risk-based and leverage capital ratios.

1. *Well Capitalized.* If capital level significantly *exceeds* the required minimum level for each relevant capital category.
2. *Adequately Capitalized.* If capital level *meets* the minimum level.
3. *Undercapitalized.* If capital level *fails to meet one or more* of the minimum levels.
4. *Significantly Undercapitalized.* If capital level is *significantly below one or more* of the minimum levels.
5. *Critically Undercapitalized.* If the ratio of *tangible equity* (as statutorily defined) *to total assets is 2 percent or less.*

Institutions falling into the last three categories are subject to a variety of "prompt corrective actions," such as limitations on dividends, prohibitions on acquisitions and branching, restrictions on asset growth, and removal of officers and directors. Irrespective of the ratios reported, the agencies may downgrade an institution's capital category based on adverse examination findings.

The regulatory capital ratio ranges defining the "prompt corrective action" capital categories are summarized in Exhibit 31.3.

Capital Category	Total Risk-Based Ratio		Tier 1 Risk-Based Ratio		Tier 1 Leverage Capital Ratio
Well capitalized	≥ 10%	and	≥ 6%	and	≥ 5%
Adequately capitalized	≥ 8%	and	≥ 4%	and	≥ 4%*
Undercapitalized	< 8%	or	< 4%	or	< 4%*
Significantly undercapitalized	< 6%	or	< 3%	or	< 3%
Critically undercapitalized	If the ratio of tangible equity (as statutorily defined) to total assets is 2% or less				
*3% for institutions that have a rating of "1" under the regulatory CAMELS, MACRO, or related rating system; that are not anticipating or experiencing significant growth; and that have well-diversified risk.					

Exhibit 31.3   Regulatory capital categories

(h) REGULATORY EXAMINATIONS. Federally insured banks and savings institutions are required to have periodic full-scope, on-site examinations by the appropriate agency. In certain cases, an examination by a state regulatory agency is accepted. Full-scope and other examinations are intended primarily to provide early identification of problems at insured institutions rather than as a basis for expressing an opinion on the fair presentation of the institution's financial statements.

(i) Scope. The scope of an examination is generally unique to each institution based on risk factors assessed by the examiner and some examinations are targeted to a specific area of operations, such as real estate lending or trust operations. Separate compliance examination programs also exist to address institutions' compliance with laws and regulations in areas such as consumer protection, insider transactions, and reporting under the Bank Secrecy Act.

(ii) Regulatory Rating Systems. Regulators use regulatory rating systems to assign ratings to banks, thrifts, holding companies, parents of foreign banks, and U.S. branches and agencies of foreign banking organizations. The rating scales vary, although each is based on a 5-point system, with "1" (or "A") being the highest rating. The rating systems are presented in Exhibit 31.4. Additionally, in November 1995, the FRB issued SR No. 95-51, "Rating the Adequacy of Risk Management Processes and Internal Controls at State Member Banks and Bank Holding Companies" stating that Federal Reserve System examiners, beginning in 1996, are instructed to assign a formal supervisory rating to the adequacy of an institution's risk management processes, including its internal controls.

(iii) Risk-Focused Examinations. Over the last several years, the banking agencies have been developing and implementing a risk-focused examination/supervisory program that focuses on the business activities that pose the greatest risks to the institutions and an assessment of an organization's management systems to identify, measure, monitor, and control its risks.

(i) ENFORCEMENT ACTIONS. Regulatory enforcement is carried out through a variety of informal and formal mechanisms. Informal enforcement measures are consensual between the bank and its regulator but not legally enforceable. Formal measures carry the force of law and are issued subject to certain legal procedures, requirements, and penalties. Examples of formal enforcement measures include ordering an institution to cease and desist from certain practices of violations, removing an officer, prohibiting an officer from participating in the affairs of the institution or the industry, assessing civil money penalties, and terminating insurance of an institution's deposits. As previously discussed, other mandatory and discretionary actions may be taken by regulators under "prompt corrective action" provisions of the Federal Deposit Insurance Act.

Entity	Assigns Rating	Rating Scale	Rating Components
Banks and Thrifts	OCC, FDIC, OTS, and FRB	**CAMELS** Ratings 1-5	**C**apital adequacy **A**sset quality **M**anagement's performance **E**arnings **L**iquidity **S**ensitivity to Market Risk
Bank holding companies	FRB	**BOPEC** Ratings 1-5	**B**ank's CAMELS rating **O**peration of nonbanking subs. **P**arent's strength **E**arnings **C**apital adequacy
Parents of foreign banks with U.S. branches or agencies	FRB	**SOSA*** (**S**trength **o**f **S**upport **A**ssessment) Ratings A–E.	Effectiveness of home country supervision and other country factors Institution-specific issues Ability of parent to maintain adequate internal controls and compliance with procedures in United States
U.S. branches and agencies of foreign banking organizations	FRB, OCC, and FDIC	**ROCA** Ratings 1-5	**R**isk management **O**perational controls **C**ompliance **A**sset quality

*SOSA ratings will not be disclosed to the bank, branch, or home supervisor. Ratings are for U.S. internal supervisory use only.

Exhibit 31.4   Regulatory rating systems

(j) DISCLOSURE OF CAPITAL MATTERS. Beginning in 1996, the American Institute of Certified Public Accountants (AICPA)'s *Audit Guide for Banks and Savings Institutions* required that the GAAP financial statements of banks and savings associations include footnote disclosures of regulatory capital adequacy/prompt corrective action categories. The following describes the five minimum disclosures:

1. A description of the regulatory capital requirements (a) for capital adequacy purposes and (b) established by the prompt corrective action provisions
2. The actual or possible material effects of noncompliance with such requirements
3. Whether the institution is in compliance with the regulatory capital requirements, including, as of each balance sheet date presented: (1) the institution's required and actual ratios and amounts of Tier 1 leverage, Tier 1 risk-based, total risk-based capital, and, for savings institutions, tangible capital, and (for certain banks and bank holding companies) Tier 3 capital for market risk and (2) factors that may significantly affect capital adequacy such as potentially volatile components of capital, qualitative factors, and regulatory mandates
4. The prompt corrective action category in which the institution was classified as of its most recent notification, as of each balance sheet date presented
5. Whether management believes any conditions or events since notification have changed the institution's category, as of the most recent balance sheet date

If, as of the most recent balance sheet date presented, the institution is either (1) not in compliance with capital adequacy requirements, (2) considered less than adequately capitalized under the prompt corrective action provisions, or (3) both, the possible material effects of such conditions and events on amounts and disclosures in the financial statements should be disclosed.

Additional disclosures may be required where there is substantial doubt about the institution's ability to continue as a going concern.

The disclosures described above should be presented for all significant subsidiaries of a holding company. Bank holding companies should also present the disclosures as they apply to the holding company, except for the prompt corrective disclosure required by item 4.

As with all footnotes to the financial statements, any management representations included in the footnotes, such as with respect to capital matters, would be subject to review by the independent accountant.

(k) SECURITIES AND EXCHANGE COMMISSION

(i) Background. The Securities and Exchange Commission (SEC) was created by Congress in 1934 to administer the Securities Act of 1933 (1933 Act) and the Securities Exchange Act of 1934 (1934 Act). The SEC is an independent agency of the U.S. government, consisting of five commissioners appointed by the president, subject to Senate confirmation.

The 1933 Act requires companies to register securities with the SEC before they may be sold, unless the security or the transaction is exempt. Banks are exempt from the registration requirements of the 1933 Act; however, bank holding companies and their nonbank subsidiaries are not.

(ii) Reporting Requirements. SEC registrants are required to comply with certain industry-specific financial statement requirements, set forth in Article 9 for Bank Holding Companies of SEC Regulation S-X. In addition, they must comply with other nonfinancial disclosures required by Guide 3 for Bank Holding Companies of Regulation S-K.

In 1997, the SEC amended rules and forms for domestic and foreign issuers to clarify and expand existing disclosure requirements for market risk-sensitive instruments. Refer to Financial Reporting Release No. 48 "Disclosure of Accounting Policies for Derivative Financial Instruments and Derivative Commodity Instruments and Disclosure of Quantitative and Qualitative Information About Market Risk Inherent in Derivative Financial Instruments, Other Financial Instruments," for further discussion. Other SEC guidance is listed in "Sources and Suggested References." Additionally, the SEC is undertaking a review of Guide 3 to evaluate potential changes to improve the usefulness of financial institution disclosures.

On December 12, 2001, the SEC issued a financial reporting release, FR-60, "Cautionary Advice Regarding Disclosure About Critical Policies" (FR-60). The SEC's Cautionary Advice alerts public companies to the need for improved disclosures about critical accounting policies. FR-60 defines "critical accounting policies" as those most important to the financial statement presentation and that require the most difficult, subjective, complex judgments.

Perhaps because FR-60 was released late in the year, the Management's Discussion and Analysis (MD&A) disclosures made by registrants in response to FR-60 did not meet the SEC's expectations. As a result, on May 10, 2002, the SEC published a proposed rule, "Disclosure in Management's Discussion and Analysis about the Application of Critical Accounting Policies." The proposed rule would mandate the MD&A disclosure about critical accounting estimates that was encouraged in FR-60, but it is much more specific than FR-60 as to the nature of the disclosures and the basis for the sensitivity analysis. Readers should be alert for any final rules.

On January 22, 2002, the SEC issued a financial reporting release, FR-61, which provides specific considerations for MD&A disclosures. The SEC issued FR-61 to remind public companies of existing MD&A disclosure requirements and to suggest steps for meeting those requirements in 2001 annual reports. The SEC action responds to a December 31 petition from the Big Five firms, which was endorsed by the AICPA. FR-61 is largely consistent with the MD&A interpretive guidance suggested by the Big Five petition.

FR-61 focuses on MD&A disclosure about liquidity and off-balance-sheet arrangements (including special purpose entities (SPE)), trading activities that include nonexchange traded commodity contracts accounted for at fair value, and the effects of transactions with related and certain other parties. These areas are receiving particular public and regulatory scrutiny following the collapse of Enron. The SEC believes that the quality of information provided by public companies in these areas should be improved. The SEC expects registrants to consider FR-61 when preparing year-end and interim financial reports, effective immediately.

(l) FINANCIAL STATEMENT PRESENTATION.

(i) Income Statements. Banks and savings institutions place heavy emphasis on the interest margin, that is, the difference between interest earned and the cost of funds. Accordingly, a specialized income statement format has evolved that focuses on net interest income. Supplemental income statement information may be provided separately to show the impact of investing in certain tax-exempt securities. Such "taxable equivalent" data purports to illustrate income statement data as if such tax-exempt securities were fully taxable.

(ii) Balance Sheets. The balance sheets of banks and savings institutions are not classified into short-term and long-term categories for assets and liabilities, but are generally presented in descending order of maturity. Supplemental information is also presented by many banking institutions showing average balances of assets and liabilities and the associated income or expense and average rates paid or earned.

(iii) Statements of Cash Flow. The statements of cash flow are presented in accordance with Statement of Financial Accounting Standards (SFAS) No. 95, "Statement of Cash Flows," amended by SFAS No. 102, "Statement of Cash Flows—Exemption of Certain Enterprises and Classification of Cash Flows from Certain Securities Acquired for Resale (an Amendment of FASB Statement No. 95)," and SFAS No. 104, "Statement of Cash Flows—Net Reporting of Certain Cash Receipts and Cash Payments and Classification of Cash Flows for Hedging Transactions (an amendment of FASB Statement No. 95)." The amendments permit certain financial institutions, such as banks and savings institutions, to net the cash flows for selected activities such as trading, deposit taking, and loan activities.

(iv) Commitments and Off-Balance-Sheet Risk. Banks and savings institutions offer a variety of financial services, and, accordingly, they enter into a wide range of financial transactions and issue a variety of financial instruments. Depending on the nature of these transactions, they may not appear on the balance sheet and are only disclosed in the footnotes to the financial statements.

(v) Disclosures of Certain Significant Risks and Uncertainties. AICPA Statement of Position (SOP) 94-6, "Disclosure of Certain Significant Risks and Uncertainties," requires institutions to include in their financial statements disclosures about the nature of their operations and the use of estimates in the preparation of their financial statements.

SOP 94-6 also requires disclosure regarding:

Certain Significant Estimates. Estimates used in the determination of the carrying amounts of assets or liabilities or in gain or loss contingencies is required to be disclosed when information available prior to issuance of the financial statements indicates that (a) it is at least reasonably possible that the estimate of the effect on the financial statements of a condition, situation or set of circumstances that existed at the date of the financial statements will change in the near term due to one or more future confirming events, and (b) the effect of the change would be material to the financial statements.

SOP 94-6 further states that (a) the disclosure should indicate the nature of the uncertainty and include an indication that it is at least reasonably possible that a change in the estimate will occur in the near term and (b) if the estimate involves a loss contingency covered by SFAS No. 5, "Accounting for Contingencies," the disclosure should also include an estimate of the possible loss or range of loss, or state that such an estimate cannot be made.

Current Vulnerability Due to Certain Concentrations. Institutions are required to disclose concentrations, as defined in the Statement, if, based on information known to management prior to issuance of the financial statements, (a) the concentration exists at the date of the financial statements, (b) the concentration makes the institution vulnerable to the risk of a near-term severe impact, and (c) it is at least reasonably possible that the events that could cause the severe impact will occur in the near term.

(m) ACCOUNTING GUIDANCE. In addition to the main body of professional accounting literature that comprises GAAP, more specific industry guidance is provided in the industry-specific Audit and Accounting Guides published by the AICPA, specifically "Banks and Savings Institutions" issued in 2000. Additionally, the Emerging Issues Task Force (EITF) of the FASB addresses current issues.

(n) GENERALLY ACCEPTED ACCOUNTING PRINCIPLES VERSUS REGULATORY ACCOUNTING PRINCIPLES. Under the Federal Financial Institutions Examination Council (FFIEC), the three federal banking agencies have developed uniform reporting standards for commercial banks that are used in the preparation of the Reports of Condition and Income (Call Report). The FDIC has also applied these uniform Call Report standards to savings banks under its supervision. Effective with the March 31, 1997, reports, the reporting standards set forth for the Call Report are based on GAAP for banks, and, as a matter of law, many deviate to a more stringent requirement than GAAP only in those instances where statutory requirements or overriding supervisory concerns warrant a departure from GAAP. The OTS maintains its own separate reporting forms for the savings institutions under its supervision. The reporting form used by savings institutions, known as the *TFR*, is based on GAAP as applied by savings institutions, which differs in some respects from GAAP for banks.

Certain differences between GAAP and regulatory accounting principles (RAP) remain after the amendments to the March 1997 Call Report Instructions. Many of these differences remain because the agencies generally default to SEC reporting principles for registrants. The more significant remaining differences between Call Report Instructions and GAAP are related to the following areas: impaired collateral-dependent loans; pushdown accounting; credit losses on off-balance sheet commitments and contingencies; related party transactions; and the application of accounting changes.

(o) LOANS AND COMMITMENTS. Loans generate the largest proportion of most bank and saving institutions' revenues. Institutions originate, purchase and sell (in whole or in part), and securitize loans. The parameters used to create the loan portfolio include many of the institution's key strategies, such as credit risk strategy, diversification strategy, liquidity, and interest rate margin strategy. Accordingly, the composition of the loan portfolio varies by institution. The loan portfolio is critical to the institutions' overall asset/liability management strategy.

(i) Types of Loans. Loans are offered on a variety of terms to meet the needs of the borrower and of the institution. The following are the types of loan arrangements normally issued.

Commercial Loans. Institutions have developed different types of credit facilities to address the needs of commercial customers. Some of the characteristics that distinguish these facilities are: security (whether the loan is collateralized or unsecured); term (whether the loan matures in the short term, long term, on demand, or on a revolving credit arrangement); variable or fixed interest rates, and currency (whether the loan is repayable in the local currency or in a foreign currency).

Loan facilities can be tailored to match the needs of commercial borrowers and may include many combinations of specific loan terms. Some of the common general types are described next.

Secured Loans. Collateral (security) to a loan is usually viewed as a characteristic of any type of loan rather than as a loan category itself. Nevertheless, it is not uncommon for institutions to analyze their loan portfolios in part by looking at the proportion of secured credits and the entire balance.

A significant portion of bank lending is not supported by specific security. The less creditworthy a potential borrower, however, the more likely it becomes that an institution will require some form of collateral in order to minimize its risk of loss.

Loan security is normally not taken with the intention of liquidating it in order to obtain repayment. Maintenance and liquidation of collateral is, in fact, often time consuming and unprofitable for the foreclosing bank. Most loan security takes the form of some kind of fixed or floating claim over specified assets or a mortgage interest in property.

Lines of Credit.   Lines of credit, including facilities that are referred to as *revolving lines of credit*, originate with an institution extending credit to a borrower with a specified maximum amount and a stated maturity. The borrower then draws and repays funds through the facility in accordance with its requirements. Lines of credit are useful for short-term financing of working capital or seasonal borrowings. A commitment fee is usually charged on the unused portion of the facility.

Demand Loans.   Demand loans are short-term loans that may be "called" by the institution at any time, hence the term *demand*. Demand loans are often unsecured and are normally made to cover short-term funding requirements. There is usually no principal reduction during the loan term, the entire balance coming due at maturity.

Term Loans.   Term loans are often used to finance the acquisition of capital assets such as plant and equipment. Due to their longer term, they involve greater credit risk than short-term advances (all other things being equal). To reduce the credit risk, these loans typically are secured and require amortization of principal over the loan term. Loan agreements often contain restrictive covenants that require the borrower to maintain specified financial ratios and to refrain from defined types of transactions for as long as the loan is outstanding.

Asset-Based Lending.   Asset-based lending is a form of revolving line of credit that is related directly to the value of specific underlying assets (typically accounts receivable or inventory). The primary difference between asset-based lending and a simple line of credit is the direct correlation, upon which the institution insists, between the funds advanced and the underlying security. While funds may be advanced on a line of credit up to the approved maximum amount, they may be drawn under an asset-based lending arrangement only to the extent allowed by predetermined formulas related to collateral value. Requests for funds are normally monitored closely and repayments may be demanded where collateral values fall.

Syndications.   A syndicated loan is one where a number of institutions, in a form of joint venture, provide funds they would individually be unwilling or unable to provide. Syndications are used for customers requiring large scale financing, too great for any single institution to accommodate without distorting its loan portfolio. In addition, consortium banks group together banks from different countries to specialize in and centralize large-scale finance for specific projects.

The members of a syndicate appoint one or more of themselves as the managing bank for the syndicate. In certain cases, the borrower might appoint the managing bank, in which case the other members would commonly appoint an agent bank to act on their behalf. The managing bank is responsible for negotiating with the borrower, preparing the appropriate documentation, collecting the loan funds from the syndicate and disbursing them to the borrower, and collecting amounts due from the borrower and distributing them to the syndicate members.

Apart from the managing bank, the syndicate members will not necessarily have any direct dealings with the borrower, although the borrower is aware of the existence of the syndicate. Credit risk rests with each syndicate member to the extent of its participation.

Participations.   Banks sell loans, or part shares in loans, to other financial institutions for a number of reasons: to serve large customers whose financing needs exceed their lending ability; to diversify their loan portfolios; to alter the maturity structure of their loan portfolios; or to increase their liquidity. Participation agreements usually specify such matters as the method of payment of proceeds from the borrower, responsibilities in the event of default, and interest in collateral. Loans may be sold with or without recourse and on terms that may or may not agree with those of the underlying loan.

Loans that are "participated out" (i.e., sold) are normally reported on the seller's balance sheet net of the sold portion (which is reported with other loan assets by the buyer). The fact that another institution has researched and agreed to extend the loan does not reduce the risk of the purchasing bank.

Loans Held for Resale.   Loans may be originated by an institution that intends to resell them to other parties. They may be purchased with the intention to resell. The reasons for such transactions vary. Some institutions wish to provide a type of loan service to their customers, which they do not wish to retain in their portfolio. Some institutions use loan origination as a source of fee income. Some purchase debt to use as securitization for other instruments that they package and sell to specialized markets.

Real Estate Loans.   Real estate loans may be made for commercial or personal purposes, and most banks differentiate their portfolios between the two uses. The rationale for this segregation lies in the fact that while both are classified as real estate lending, the portfolios are subject to different types of risk and/or different degrees of risk. Also, the type and level of expertise required to successfully manage residential and commercial real estate loan portfolios differs just like the type of financing provided to the homeowner is typically not the same as to an owner or developer of commercial real estate.

Incremental knowledge with respect to the particular financing provided must be obtained and constantly updated to successfully manage commercial real estate property lending. For example, construction loan monitoring, appraisal methods, comparable properties in the area, the status of the economy, use of the property, future property developments, occupancy rates, and projected operating cash flows are all important factors in reaching lending decisions.

Mortgage Loans.   Real estate mortgage loans are term loans collateralized by real estate. The loans are generally fairly long term, though some are short term with a large principal ("balloon") payment due at maturity. The loan commitments usually involve a fee to be paid by the borrower upon approval or upon closing.

Some institutions originate residential mortgage loans for sale to investors. Under these arrangements, the bank usually continues to service the loans on a fee basis. The sale allows the bank to provide mortgage financing services for its customers without funding a large volume of loans.

Construction Loans.   Construction loans are used to finance the construction of particular projects and normally mature at the scheduled completion date. They are generally secured by a first mortgage on the property and are backed by a purchase (or "takeout") agreement from a financially responsible permanent lender. They may include the financing of loan interest through the construction period.

Construction loans are vulnerable to a number of risks related to the uncertainties that are characteristic of building projects. Examples of risks associated with construction loans include construction delays, nonpayment of material bills or subcontractors, and the financial collapse of the project contractor prior to project completion.

Construction loan funds are generally disbursed on a standard payment plan (for relatively small, predictable projects) or a progress payment plan (for more complex projects). Extent of completion may be verified by an architect's certification or by evidence of labor and material costs.

In certain construction loans, consideration should be given to accounting for the loan as an investment in real estate if the lender is subject to virtually the same risks and rewards as the owner.

Direct Lease Financing.   Leasing is a form of debt financing for fixed assets that, although differing in legal form, is similar to substance to term lending. Like a more conventional loan, the institution's credit concerns in extending lease financing are ones of cash flow, credit history, management, and projections of future operations. The type of property to be leased and its marketability in the event of default or termination of the lease are concerns quite parallel to the bank's evaluation of collateral. In a leasing arrangement, the bank formally owns the property rather than having a lien on it.

Lease financing arrangements may be accounted for either as financings (i.e., as loans) or as operating leases depending upon the precise terms of the transaction and on the applicable accounting principles.

Consumer Loans.   Consumer loans—personal loans to individual borrowers—can originate through a bank's own customers (direct loans) or through merchants with whom the borrowers deal (indirect loans). They may relate specifically to the purchase of items that can serve as collateral for the borrowing (e.g., vehicles, mobile homes, boats, furniture) or to other needs that provide no basis for a security interest (e.g., vacations, income tax payments, medical expenses, educational costs). Consumer loans may be made on an installment, single payment, or demand basis. They are often broken down into classifications that describe the purpose of the financing (student loans or home equity loans) or the terms of disbursement and repayment (installment loans, credit card loans, check credit).

Installment Loans.   Installment loans are the most common type of consumer credit. Their terms normally include repayment over a specified period of time with fixed minimum periodic (usually monthly) payments. Interest rates are generally fixed on origination but may be variable over the term of the loan. The term is generally determined by the type of purchase being financed and is usually relatively short—10 years or less.

Standby Letters of Credit.   A standby letter of credit is a promise made by an institution to provide compensation to a third party on behalf of its customer in the event that the customer fails to perform in accordance with the terms specified by an underlying contract. Standby letters of credit may be available under a credit facility or may be issued for a specified amount with an expiration date. Normally, payment under such agreements depends on performance or lack of performance of some act required by the underlying contract.

Standby letters of credit are typically recorded as contingent liabilities in memorandum records and are offset by customer liability memorandum accounts. In the event that funds are disbursed under a standby letter of credit agreement, the drawing would be recorded as a loan.

Sovereign Risk.   Sovereign risk lending involves the granting of credit facilities to foreign governments or to companies based in foreign countries. The facilities are normally denominated in a currency other than the domestic currency of the borrower and are typically used to finance imports or to refinance existing foreign currency debt.

In addition to all of the customary considerations surrounding credit risk, sovereign risk lending involves economic, social, and political considerations that bear on the ability of the borrower to repay foreign currency obligations.

Trade Finance

- *Letters of Credit.* Letters of credit are instruments used to facilitate trade (most commonly international trade) by substituting an institution's credit for that of a commercial importing company. A letter of credit provides assurance to a seller that he will be paid for goods shipped. At the same time, it provides assurance to the buyer that payment will not be made until conditions specified in the sales contract have been met.

Letter of credit transactions can vary in any number of ways. The issuing and advising institutions may deal with each other through their own local correspondent banks. Some of the documents may flow in different patterns. The requirements for payment and security will certainly vary from transaction to transaction. One of the attractive features of letter of credit financing from the customer's point of view is its flexibility. Facilities can be tailored to individual transactions or groups of transactions.

- *Bankers' Acceptances.* A bankers' acceptance is like a letter of credit in that it provides a seller of goods with a guarantee of payment, thus facilitating trade. The institution's customer is the buyer who, having established an acceptance facility with the bank, notifies the seller to draw up a bill of exchange. The bank "accepts" that bill (by physically stamping "accepted" on its face and having an authorized bank officer sign it) and, in so doing, commits itself to disburse funds on the bill's due date.

A banker's acceptance represents both an asset and a liability to the accepting bank. The asset is a receivable from the bank's customer, the buyer in the transaction. The liability is a payable to the holder of the acceptance. The bank's accounting for open acceptances varies from country to country. In some countries, the asset and liability are both reflected on the bank's balance sheet. In others, they are netted against each other and thus become, in effect, off-balance-sheet items. In European Union (EU) countries, they appear as memorandum items on the face of the balance sheet.

By substituting its own credit for that of the buying company, the accepting bank creates a financial instrument that is readily marketable. Bankers' acceptances trade as bearer paper on active secondary markets.

(ii) Accounting for Loans

Principal. Loans expected to be held until maturity should be reported as outstanding principal, net of charge-offs, specific valuation accounts and any deferred fees or costs, or unamortized premiums or discounts on purchased loans. Total loans should be reduced by the allowance for credit losses.

Loans held for sale should be reported at the lower of cost or market value. Mortgage loans held for sale should be reported at the lower of cost or market value in conformity with SFAS No. 65, "Accounting for Certain Mortgage Banking Activities." Mortgage-backed securities held for sale in conjunction with mortgage banking activities shall be classified as trading securities and reported at fair value in conformity with SFAS No. 115, "Accounting for Certain Investments in Debt and Equity Securities."

Interest. Interest income on all loans should be accrued and credited to interest income as it is earned using the interest method. Interest income on certain impaired loans should be recognized in accordance with SFAS No. 114, "Accounting by Creditors for Impairment of a Loan," as amended by SFAS No. 118, "Accounting by Creditors for Impairment of a Loan-Income Recognition and Disclosures."

The accrual of interest is usually suspended on loans that are in excess of 90 days past due, unless the loan is both well secured and in the process of collection. When a loan is placed on such nonaccrual status, interest that has been accrued but not collected is reversed, and interest subsequently received is recorded on a cash basis or applied to reduce the principal balance depending on the bank's assessment of ultimate collectibility of the loan. An exception to this rule is that many banks do not place certain types of consumer loans on nonaccrual since they automatically charge off such loans within a relatively short period of becoming delinquent—generally within 120 days.

Loan Fees. Various types of fees are collected by banks in connection with lending activities. SFAS No. 91, "Accounting for Nonrefundable Fees and Costs Associated with Originating or Acquiring Loans and Initial Direct Costs of Leases (an Amendment of FASB Statements No. 13,

60, and 65 and a Rescission of FASB Statement No. 17)," requires that the majority of such fees and associated direct origination costs be offset. The net amount must be deferred as part of the loan (and reported as a component of loans in the balance sheet) and recognized in interest income over the life of the loan and/or loan commitment period as an adjustment of the yield on the loan. The requirements for cost deferral under this standard are quite restrictive and require direct linkage to the loan origination process. Activities for which costs may be deferred include: (1) evaluating the borrower, guarantees, collateral, and other security; (2) preparation and processing of loan documentation for loan origination, and (3) negotiating and closing the loan. Certain costs are specifically precluded from deferral, for example, advertising and solicitation, credit supervision and administration, costs of unsuccessful loan originations, and other activities not directly related to the extension of a loan.

Loan fees and costs for loans originated or purchased for resale are deferred and are recognized when the related loan is sold.

Commitment fees to purchase or originate loans, net of direct origination costs, are generally deferred and amortized over the life of the loan when it is extended. If the commitment expires, then the fees are recognized in other income on expiration of the commitment. There are two main exceptions to this general treatment:

1. If past experience indicates that the extension of a loan is unlikely, then the fee is recognized over the commitment period.

2. Nominal fees, which are determined retroactively, on a commitment to extend funds at a market rate may be recognized in income at the determination date.

Certain fees may be recognized when received, primarily loan syndication fees. Generally, the yield on the portion of the loan retained by the syndicating bank must at least equal the yield received by the other members of the syndicate. If this is not the case, a portion of the fees designated as a syndication fee must be deferred and amortized to income to achieve a yield equal to the average yield of the other banks in the syndicate. EITF Issue No. 97-3, "Accounting for Fees and Costs Associated with Loan Syndication's and Loan Participation's after the Issuance of FASB Statement No. 125," states that loan participation should be accounted for in accordance with the provision of SFAS No. 140, and loan syndication's should be accounted for in accordance with the provision of SFAS No. 91.

Purchased loans are recorded at cost net of fees paid/received. The difference between this recorded amount and the principal amount of the loan is amortized to income over the life of the loan to produce a level yield. Acquisition costs are not deferred, but are expensed as incurred. The AICPA's Accounting Standards Executive Committee has a project under way that is expected to result in a new SOP entitled "Accounting for Certain Purchased Loans." Readers should be alert for a final pronouncement. Additional EITFs have been issued to address purchases of credit card portfolios.

Acquisition, Development, and Construction Arrangements.   Certain transactions that appear to be loans are considered effectively to be investments in the real estate property financed. These transactions are required to be presented separately from loans and accounted for as real estate investments using the guidance set forth in the AICPA Notice to Practitioners dated February 1986. Factors indicating such treatment include six arrangements whereby the financial institution:

1. Provides substantially all financing to acquire, develop, and construct the property, that is, borrower has little or no equity in the property

2. Funds the origination or commitment fees through the loan

3. Funds substantially all interest and fees through the loan

4. Has security only in the project with no recourse to other assets or guarantee of the borrower

5. Can recover its investment only through sale to third parties, refinancing, or cash flow of the project

6. Is unlikely to foreclose on the project during development since no payments are due during this period and therefore the loan cannot normally become delinquent

Troubled Debt Restructurings and Impaired Loans. Banks may routinely restructure loans to meet a borrower's changing circumstances. The new loan terms are reflected in the financial statements essentially as if a new loan has been made. However, if "a creditor for economic or legal reasons related to the debtor's financial difficulties grants a concession ... that it would not otherwise consider," then SFAS No. 15, "Accounting by Debtors and Creditors for Troubled Debt Restructurings," as amended by FASB Statements No. 114, No. 121, "Accounting for Impairment of Long-Lived Assets and Long-Lived Assets to Be Disposed Of," and No. 144, "Accounting for the Impairment or Disposal of Long-Lived Assets," applies.

TROUBLED DEBT RESTRUCTURINGS.   Troubled debt restructurings may include one or more of the following:

- Transfers of assets of the debtor or an equity interest in the debtor to partially or fully satisfy a debt
- Modification of debt terms, including reduction of one or more of the following: (1) interest rates with or without extensions of maturity date(s), (2) face or maturity amounts, and (3) accrued interest

Prior to the release of SFAS No. 114, under a SFAS No. 15 restructuring involving a modification of terms, the creditor accumulated the undiscounted total future cash receipts and compared them to the recorded investment in the loan. If these cash receipts exceeded the recorded investment in the loan, no loss or impairment was deemed to exist; however, if the total cash receipts did not exceed the recorded investment, the recorded investment was adjusted to reflect the total undiscounted future cash receipts. For restructurings involving a modification of terms that occurred before the effective date of SFAS No. 114, this accounting still applies as long as the loan does not become impaired relative to the restructured terms. Restructurings involving a modification of terms after the effective date of SFAS No. 114 must be accounted for in accordance with SFAS No. 114.

IMPAIRED LOANS.   In May 1993, SFAS No. 114, "Accounting by Creditors for Impairment of a Loan (an Amendment of FASB Statements No. 5 and 15)," was issued primarily to provide more consistent guidance on the application of SFAS No. 5 loss criteria and to provide additional direction on the recognition and measurement of loan impairment in determining credit reserve levels. The application of this statement was required beginning in 1995.

SFAS No. 114 applies to all impaired loans, uncollateralized as well as collateralized, except: large groups of smaller balance homogeneous loans that are collectively evaluated for impairment such as credit card, residential mortgage, and consumer installment loans; loans that are measured at fair value or at the lower of cost or fair value; leases; and debt securities, as defined in SFAS No. 115, "Accounting for Certain Investments in Debt and Equity Securities."

A loan is impaired when, based on current information and events, it is probable (consistent with its use in SFAS No. 5—an area within a range of the likelihood that a future event or events will occur confirming the fact of the loss) that a creditor will be unable to collect all amounts due according to the contractual terms of the loan agreement. As used in SFAS No. 114 and in SFAS No. 5, as amended, all amounts due according to the contractual terms means that both the contractual interest payments and the contractual principal payments of a loan will be collected as scheduled in the loan agreement.

It is important to note that an insignificant delay or insignificant shortfall in the amount of payments does not require application of SFAS No. 114. A loan is not impaired during a period of delay in payment if the creditor expects to collect all amounts due including interest accrued at the contractual interest rate for the period of delay.

SFAS No. 114 provides that the measurement of impaired value should be based on one of the following methods:

- Present value of expected cash flows discounted at the loan's effective interest rate
- The observable value of the loan's market price
- The fair value of the collateral if the loan is collateral dependent

The effective rate of a loan is the contractual interest rate adjusted for any net deferred loan fees or costs, premium, or discount existing at the origination or acquisition of the loan. For variable rate loans, the loan's effective interest rate may be calculated based on the factor as it changes over the life of the loan, or it may be fixed at the rate in effect at the date the loan meets the SFAS No. 114 impairment criterion. However, that choice should be applied consistently for all variable rate loans.

All impaired loans do not have to be measured using the same method; the method selected may vary based on the availability of information and other factors. However, the ultimate valuation should be critically evaluated in determining whether it represents a reasonable estimate of impairment.

If the measure of the impaired loan is less than the recorded investment in the loan (including accrued interest, net deferred loan fees or costs, and unamortized premium or discount), a creditor should recognize an impairment by creating a valuation allowance with a corresponding charge to bad-debt expense.

Subsequent to the initial measurement of impairment, if there is a significant change (increase or decrease) in the amount or timing of an impaired loan's expected future cash flows, observable market price, or fair value of the collateral, a creditor should recalculate the impairment by applying the procedures described above and by adjusting the valuation allowance. However, the net carrying amount of the loan should at no time exceed the recorded investment in the loan.

Any restructurings performed under the provisions of SFAS No. 15 need not be reevaluated unless the borrower is not performing in accordance with the contractual terms of the restructuring.

EITF Issue No. 96-22, "Applicability of the Disclosures Required by FASB Statement No. 114 When a Loan Is Restructured in a Troubled Debt Restructuring into Two (or More) Loans," states that when a loan is restructured in a troubled debt restructuring into two (or more) loan agreements, the restructured loans should be considered separately when assessing the applicability of the disclosures in years after the restructuring because they are legally distinct from the original loan. However, the creditor would continue to base its measure of loan impairment on the contractual terms specified by the original loan agreements.

In-Substance Foreclosures.   SFAS No. 114 clarified the definition of in-substance foreclosures as used in SFAS No. 15, "Accounting by Debtors and Creditors for Troubled Debt Restructurings," by stating that the phrase "foreclosure by the creditor" in paragraph 34 should be read to mean "*physical* possession of debtor's assets regardless of whether formal foreclosure proceedings take place." Further, until foreclosure occurs, these assets should remain as loans in the financial statements.

(p) CREDIT LOSSES.   Credit loss estimates are subjective and, accordingly, require careful judgments in assessing loan collectibility and in estimating losses.

(i) Accounting Guidance.   SFAS No. 114, "Accounting by Creditors for Impairment of a Loan (an Amendment of FASB Statements No. 5 and 15)" and SFAS No. 5, "Accounting for Contingencies (as amended by SFAS No. 118, 'Accounting by Creditors for Impairment of Loan-Income Recognition and Disclosures')" are the primary sources of guidance on accounting for the allowance for loan losses. SFAS No. 5 requires that an estimated loss from a contingency should be accrued by a charge to income if both of the following conditions are met:

- Information available prior to issuance of the financial statements indicates that it is probable that an asset had been impaired or a liability had been incurred at the date of the financial statements. It is implicit in this condition that it must be probable that one or more future events will occur confirming the fact of the loss.
- The amount of loss can be reasonably estimated.

SFAS No. 5 states that when a loss contingency exists, the likelihood that the future event or events will confirm the loss or impairment of an asset (whether related to contractual principal or interest) can range from remote to probable. Probable means the future event or events are likely to occur; however, the conditions for accrual are not intended to be so rigid that they require virtual certainty before a loss is accrued.

The allowance for loan losses should be adequate to cover probable credit losses related to specifically identified loans, as well as probable credit losses inherent in the remainder of the loan portfolio that have been incurred as of the balance sheet date. Credit losses related to off-balance sheet instruments should also be accrued if the conditions of SFAS No. 5 are met.

Actual credit losses should be deducted from the allowance, and the related balance should be charged off in the period in which they are deemed uncollectible. Recoveries of loans previously charged off should be added to the allowance when received.

SFAS No. 114 addresses the accounting by creditors for impairment of certain loans, as discussed in Subsection 31.2(o)(ii).

(ii) Regulatory Guidance.   The regulatory agencies issued the "Interagency Policy on the Allowance for Loan and Lease Losses (ALLL)" in December 1993. The policy statement provides guidance with respect to the nature and purpose of the allowance; the related responsibilities of the board of directors, management, and the bank examiners; adequacy of loan review systems; and issues related to international transfer risk. The policy statement also includes an analytical tool to be used by bank examiners for assessing the reasonableness of the allowance; however, the policy statement cautions the bank examiners against placing too much emphasis on the analytical tool, rather than performing a full and thorough analysis.

The OCC also provides guidance in its "Comptrollers' Handbook, Allowance for Loan and Lease Losses," issued in June 1996.

In separate releases on July 6, 2001, the SEC and the FFIEC issued guidance on methodologies and documentation related to the allowance for loan losses. In Staff Accounting Bulletin (SAB) No. 102, "Selected Loan Loss Allowance Methodology and Documentation Issues," the SEC staff expressed certain of their views on the development, documentation, and application of a systematic methodology as required by Financial Reporting Release No. 28 for determining allowances for loan and lease losses in accordance with GAAP. In particular, the guidance focuses on the documentation the staff normally would expect registrants to prepare and maintain in support of their allowances for loan losses. Concurrent with the release of SAB No. 102, the federal banking agencies issued related guidance through the FFIEC entitled "Policy Statement on Allowance for Loan and Lease Losses (ALLL) Methodologies and Documentation for Banks and Savings Institutions." The Policy Statement, developed in consultation with the SEC staff, provides guidance on the design and implementation of ALLL methodologies and supporting documentation practices. Both SAB No. 102 and the Policy Statement reaffirm the applicability of existing accounting guidance; neither attempts to overtly change GAAP as they relate to the ALLL.

(iii) Allowance Methodologies.   An institution's method of estimating credit losses is influenced by many factors, including the institution's size, organization structure, business environment and strategy, management style, loan portfolio characteristics, loan administration procedures, and management information systems.

Common Factors to Consider.   Although allowance methodologies may vary between institutions, the factors to consider in estimating credit losses are often similar. Both SAB No. 102 and the Policy Statement require that when developing loss measurements, banks consider the effect of current environmental factors and then document which factors were used in the analysis and how those factors affected the loss measurements. The following are examples of factors that should be considered:

- Levels of and trends in delinquencies and impaired loans
- Levels of and trends in charge-offs and recoveries

- Trends in volume and terms of loans
- Effects of any changes in risk selection and underwriting standards, and other changes in lending policies, procedures, and practices
- Experience, ability, and depth of lending management and other relevant staff
- National and local economic trends and conditions
- Industry conditions
- Effects of changes in credit concentrations

Supplemental data, such as historical loss rates or peer group analyses, can be helpful; however, they are not, by themselves, sufficient basis for an allowance methodology.

Portfolio Segments.   Another common practice is dividing the loan portfolio into different segments. Each segment typically includes similar characteristics, such as risk classification and type of loan. Segments typically include large problem loans by industry or collateral type and homogeneous pools of smaller loans, such as credit cards, automobile loans, and residential mortgages.

Credit Classification Process.   A credit classification process involves categorizing loans into risk categories and is often applied to large loans that are evaluated individually. The categorization is based on conditions that may affect the ability of borrowers to service their debt, such as current financial information, historical payment experience, credit documentation, public information, and current trends. Many institutions classify loans using a rating system that incorporates the regulatory classification system. These definitions are as follows:

SPECIAL MENTION.   Some loans are considered criticized but not classified. Such loans have potential weaknesses that deserve management's close attention. If left uncorrected, these potential weaknesses may result in deterioration of the repayment prospects for the assets or of the institution's credit position at some future date. Special mention loans are not adversely classified and do not expose an institution to sufficient risk to warrant adverse classification.

SUBSTANDARD.   Loans classified as substandard are inadequately protected by the current sound worth and paying capacity of the obligor or of the collateral pledged, if any. Loans so classified must have a well-defined weakness or weaknesses that jeopardize the liquidation of the debt. They are characterized by the distinct possibility that the institution will sustain some loss if the deficiencies are not corrected.

DOUBTFUL.   Loans classified as doubtful have all the weaknesses inherent in those classified as substandard, with the added characteristic that the weaknesses make collection or liquidation in full, on the basis of currently existing facts, conditions, and values, highly questionable and improbable.

LOSS.   Loans classified as loss are considered uncollectible and of such little value that their continuance as bankable assets is not warranted. This classification does not mean that the loan has absolutely no recovery or salvage value, but rather that it is not practical or desirable to defer writing off this basically worthless asset even though partial recovery may be effected in the future.

Pools of Smaller-Balance Homogeneous Loans.   Loans not evaluated individually are included in pools and loss rates are derived for each pool.

The loss rates to be applied to the pools of loans are typically derived from the combination of a variety of factors. Examples of the factors include: historical experience, expected future performance, trends in bankruptcies and troubled collection accounts, and changes in the customer's performance patterns.

Foreign Loans. The Interagency Country Exposure Risk Committee (ICERC) requires certain loans to have allocated transfer risk reserves (ATRRs). ATRRs are minimum specific reserves related to loans in particular countries and, therefore, must be reviewed by each institution. The ICERC's supervisory role is pursuant to the International Supervision Act of 1983. The collectibility of foreign loans that do not have ATRRs should be assessed in the same way as domestic loans.

Documentation, Completeness, and Frequency. The institution's allowance methodology should be based on a comprehensive, adequately documented, and consistently applied analysis. The analysis should consider all significant factors that affect collectibility of the portfolio and should be based on an effective loan review and credit grading (classification) system. Additionally, the evaluation of the adequacy of the allowance should be performed as of the end of each quarter, and appropriate provisions should be made to maintain the allowance at an adequate level.

SAB No. 102 and the 2001 Policy Statement specifically require, for any adjustments of loss measurements for environmental factors, that banks maintain sufficient *objective* evidence (1) to support the amount of the adjustment and (2) to explain why the adjustment is necessary to reflect current information, events, circumstances, and conditions in the loss measurements.

(q) LOAN SALES AND MORTGAGE BANKING ACTIVITIES. Banks may originate and sell loans for a variety of reasons, such as generating income streams from servicing and other fees, increasing liquidity, minimizing interest rate exposure, enhancing asset/liability management, and maximizing their use of capital.

(i) Underwriting Standards. When loans are originated for resale, the origination process includes not only finding an investor, but also preparing the loan documents to fit the investor's requirements. Loans originated for resale must normally comply with specific underwriting standards regarding items such as borrower qualifications, loan documentation, appraisals, mortgage insurance, and loan terms. Individual loans that do not meet the underwriting standards are typically eliminated from the pool of loans eligible for sale. Generally, the originating institutions may be subject to recourse by the investor for underwriting exceptions identified subsequent to the sale of the loans and any related defaults by borrowers.

(ii) Securitizations. A common method of transforming real estate assets into liquid marketable securities is through securitization. Securitization is where loans are sold to a separate entity which finances the purchase through the issuance of debt securities or undivided interest in the loans. The real estate securities are backed by the cash flows of the loans.

Securitization of residential mortgages has expanded to include commercial and multifamily mortgages, auto and home equity loans, credit cards, and leases.

The accounting guidance for sales of loans through securitizations is discussed in Section 31.3, "Mortgage Banking Activities."

(iii) Loan Servicing. When loans are sold, the selling institution sometimes retains the right to service the loans for a servicing fee, which is collected over the life of the loans as payments are received. The servicing fee is often based on a percentage of the principal balance of the outstanding loans. A typical servicing agreement requires the servicer to perform the billing, collection, and remittance functions, as well as maintain custodial bank accounts. The servicer may also be responsible for certain credit losses.

(iv) Regulatory Guidance. Regulatory guidance with respect to loan sales and mortgage banking activities continues to evolve with the increased activity by institutions. In December 1997, the OCC issued regulatory guidance for national banks in its *Comptrollers' Handbook: Asset Securitization.* The FRB issued a Supervision and Regulation Letter, "Risk Management and Capital Adequacy of Exposures Arising from Secondary Market Credit Activities."

(v) Accounting Guidance. The accounting guidance for purchasing, acquiring, and selling mortgage servicing rights is discussed in Section 31.3.

(vi) Valuation. The accounting guidance addressing the valuation of loans held for sale is discussed in Section 31.3.

(r) REAL ESTATE INVESTMENTS, REAL ESTATE OWNED, AND OTHER FORECLOSED ASSETS. The type and nature of assets included in real estate investments, former bank premises, and other foreclosed assets can vary significantly. Such assets are described next.

(i) Real Estate Investments. Certain institutions make direct equity investments in real estate projects, and other institutions may grant real estate loans that have virtually the same risks and rewards as those of joint venture participants. Both types of transactions are considered to be real estate investments, and such arrangements are treated as if the institution has an ownership interest in the property.

Specifically, GAAP for real estate investments is established in the following authoritative literature:

- AICPA SOP 78-9, "Accounting for Investments in Real Estate Ventures"
- SFAS No. 34, "Capitalization of Interest Cost"
- SFAS No. 58, "Capitalization of Interest Cost in Financial Statements That Include Investments Accounted for by the Equity Method"
- SFAS No. 66, "Accounting for Sales of Real Estate"
- SFAS No. 67, "Accounting for Costs and Initial Rental Operations of Real Estate Projects"
- SFAS No. 144, "Accounting for the Impairment or Disposal of Long-Lived Assets"

(ii) Former Bank Premises. Many institutions have former premises that are no longer used in operations. Such former bank premises may be included in real estate owned.

(iii) Foreclosed Assets. Foreclosed assets include all assets received in full or partial satisfaction of a receivable and include real and personal property; equity interests in corporations, partnerships, and joint ventures; and beneficial interests in trusts. However, the largest component of real estate owned by banks and savings institutions is comprised of foreclosed real estate assets.

Guidance on accounting for and reporting of foreclosed assets is established in the following authoritative literature:

- SFAS No. 15, "Accounting by Debtors and Creditors for Troubled Debt Restructurings"
- SFAS No. 144, "Accounting for the Impairment or Disposal of Long-Lived Assets"
- SOP 92-3, "Accounting for Foreclosed Assets"

In October 2001, the FASB issued SFAS No. 144, "Accounting for the Impairment or Disposal of Long-Lived Asset," (SFAS No. 144, or the Statement). The Statement supersedes FASB Statement No. 121, "Accounting for the Impairment of Long-Lived Assets and for Long-Lived Assets to Be Disposed Of"; however, it retains the fundamental provisions of that Statement related to the recognition and measurement of the impairment of long-lived assets to be "held and used." In addition, the Statement provides more guidance on estimating cash flows when performing a recoverability test, requires that a long-lived asset (group) to be disposed of other than by sale (e.g., abandoned) be classified as "held and used" until it is disposed of, and establishes more restrictive criteria to classify as asset (group) as "held for sale."

The Statement is effective for year ends beginning after December 15, 2001 (e.g., January 1, 2002, for a calendar year entity) and interim periods within those fiscal years. Earlier application is encouraged. Transition is prospective for committed disposal activities that are initiated after the effective date of the Statement or an entity's initial application of the Statement. The Statement also provides transition provisions for assets "held for sale" that were initially recorded under previous models (Accounting Principles Board (APB) No. 30 or FAS No. 121) and do not meet the new "held for sale" criteria within one year of the initial application of the Statement (e.g., December 31, 2002, for a calendar year-end entity that adopts the Statement effective January 1, 2002).

(s) INVESTMENTS IN DEBT AND EQUITY SECURITIES. Banks use a variety of financial instruments for various purposes, primarily to provide a source of income through investment or resale and to manage interest-rate and liquidity risk as part of an overall asset/liability management strategy.

Institutions purchase U.S. government obligations, such as U.S. Treasury bills, notes, and bonds, in addition to the debt of U.S. government agencies and government-sponsored enterprises, such as the U.S. Government National Mortgage Association (Ginnie Mae) and Federal Home Loan Mortgage Corporation (Freddie Mac). Institutions also purchase municipal obligations, such as municipal bonds and tax anticipation notes.

Another common form of investments, which can be tailored to a wide variety of needs, are called *asset-backed securities* (ABSs). Banks can hold ABSs as securities, or they can be the issuer of ABSs along with both governmental and private issuers. The ABSs are repaid from the underlying cash flow generated from other financial instruments, such as mortgage loans, credit card receivables, and mobile home loans. ABSs secured by real estate mortgages are often called *mortgage-backed securities* (MBSs).

The level of risk related to ABSs is often related to the level of risk in the collateral. For example, securitized subprime auto loans, experiencing a decline in credit quality, may also cause a reduction in the value of the ABS, if receipt of the underlying cash flow becomes questionable.

ABSs often include a credit enhancement designed to reduce the degree of credit risk to the holder of the ABS security. Examples of credit enhancement include guarantees, letters of credit, overcollateralization, private insurance, and senior/subordinate structures. The degree of protection provided by the credit enhancement depends on the nature of the collateral and the type and extent of the credit enhancement.

ABSs are structured into a variety of products, many of which are complex. Risk variables, such as prepayment risk, changes in prevailing interest rates, and delayed changes in indexed interest rates, make the forecasting of future cash flows more difficult. ABSs with several investment classes may have varying terms such as maturity dates, interest rates, payment schedules, and residual rights, which further complicates an analysis of the investment. Collateralized mortgage obligations (CMOs) and real estate mortgage investment conduits (REMICs) are two examples of multiclass mortgage securities. The underlying objective of all types of ABSs and mortgage securities is to redistribute the cash flows generated from the collateral to all security holders, consistent with their contractual rights, without a shortfall or an overage.

Banks are generally restricted in the types of financial instruments they may deal in, underwrite, purchase, or sell. Essentially banks may only deal in U.S. government and U.S. government agency securities, municipal bonds, and certain other bonds, notes, and debentures. These restrictions are also limited based on capitalization. The FFIEC policy statement issued in February 1992 addresses the selection of securities dealers, policies and strategies for securities portfolios, unsuitable investment practices, and mortgage derivations.

(i) Accounting for Investments in Debt and Equity Securities. Investment securities are classified in three categories: held-to-maturity, trading, and available-for-sale. SFAS No. 115, "Accounting for Certain Investments in Debt and Equity Securities," addresses the accounting and reporting for investments in equity securities that have readily determinable fair values and for all investments in debt securities. Such securities are classified in three categories and accounted for as follows:

Held-to-Maturity. Securities for which an institution has both the ability and positive intent to hold to maturity are classified as held-to-maturity and are carried at amortized cost. (Any difference between cost and fair value is recorded as a premium or discount, which is amortized to income using the level yield method over the life of the security.)

Trading.   Securities that are purchased and held principally for the purpose of selling them in the near term are carried at fair value with unrealized gains and losses included in earnings.

Available-for-Sale.   All other securities are classified as available-for-sale and carried at fair value with unrealized gains and losses included as a separate component of equity.

SFAS No. 115 addresses changes in circumstances that may cause an enterprise to change its intent to hold a certain security to maturity without calling into question its intent to hold other debt securities to maturity in the future.

For individual securities classified as either available-for-sale or held-to-maturity, entities are required to determine whether a decline in fair value below the amortized cost basis is other than temporary. If such a decline is judged to be other than temporary, the cost basis of the individual security should be written down to fair value as the new cost basis. The amount of the write-down should be treated as a realized loss and recorded in earnings. The new cost basis shall not be changed for subsequent recoveries.

Investment securities are required to be recorded on a trade date basis. Interest income on investment securities is recorded separately as a component of interest income. Realized gains and losses on available-for-sale securities and realized and unrealized gains and losses on trading securities are recorded as a separate component of noninterest income or loss. Upon the sale of an available-for-sale security, any unrealized gain or loss previously recorded in the separate component of equity is reversed and recorded as a separate component of noninterest income or loss.

Discounts and premiums should be accreted or amortized using the interest method in accordance with SFAS No. 91, "Accounting for Nonrefundable Fees and Costs Associated with Originating or Acquiring Loans and Initial Direct Costs of Leases." The interest method provides for a periodic interest income at a constant effective yield on the net investment. The amortization or accretion period should be from the purchase date to the maturity date rather than an earlier call date, except for large numbers of similar loans where prepayments are expected and can be reasonably estimated, such as with certain ABSs.

Transfers among the three categories are performed at fair value. Transfers out of held-to-maturity should be rare.

(ii) Wash Sales.   If the same financial asset is purchased shortly before or after the sale of a security, it is called a *wash sale*. SFAS No. 140 addresses wash sales, stating that unless there is a concurrent contract to repurchase or redeem the transferred financial assets from the purchaser, the seller does not maintain effective control over the transferred assets, and, therefore, the sale should be recorded. SFAS No. 140 provides the accounting guidance for recognizing gains and losses from wash sales, as more fully discussed in Section 31.3.

(iii) Short Sales.   An institution may sell a security it does not own with the intention of buying or borrowing securities at an agreed-upon future date to cover the sale. Given the nature of these transactions, such sales should be within the trading portfolio. Obligations incurred in these short sales should be reported as liabilities and recorded at fair value at each reporting date with change in fair value recorded through income.

(iv) Securities Borrowing and Lending.   An institution may borrow securities from a counterparty to fulfill its obligations and may advance cash, pledge other securities, or issue letters of credit as collateral for borrowed securities. If cash is pledged as collateral, the institution that loans the securities typically earns a return by investing that cash at rates higher than the rate paid or "rebated" back to the institution that borrows the securities. If the collateral is other than cash, the institution that loans the collateral typically receives a fee. Because most securities lending transactions are short term, the value of the pledged collateral is usually required to be higher than the value of the securities borrowed, and collateral is usually valued daily and adjusted frequently for changes in the market price, most securities lending transactions by themselves do not represent significant credit risks. However, other risks exist in securities lending transactions, such as market and credit risks, relative to the maintenance and safeguarding of the collateral. For example, the manner in which cash collateral is invested could present market and credit risk.

SFAS No. 140 addresses the accounting for securities lending transactions. It provides that if the transferor (institution loaning the securities) surrenders control over those securities, the transfer shall be accounted for as a sale, to the extent that consideration (other than beneficial interest) is received in exchange. SFAS No. 140 states that the transferor has surrendered control over the transferred asset only if *all* three of the following conditions have been met:

1. The transferred assets have been isolated from the transferor—put presumptively beyond the reach of the transferor and its creditors, even in bankruptcy or other receivership (pars. 27 and 28).

2. Each transferee (or, if the transferee is a qualifying SPE (par. 35), each holder of its beneficial interests) has the right to pledge or exchange the assets (or beneficial interests) it received, and no condition both constrains the transferee (or holder) from taking advantage of its right to pledge or exchange and provides more than a trivial benefit to the transferor (pars. 29–34).

3. The transferor does not maintain effective control over the transferred assets through either (1) an agreement that both entitles and obligates the transferor to repurchase or redeem them before their maturity (pars. 47–49) or (2) the ability to unilaterally cause the holder to return specific assets, other than through a cleanup call (pars. 50–54).

If all three of the above conditions are met, the securities lending transaction shall be accounted for as a sale, in the following manner:

- *Institution loaning the securities.* Recognizes the sale of the loaned securities, proceeds consisting of the collateral. Also recognizes the forward repurchase commitment.
- *Institution borrowing the securities.* Recognizes the purchase of the borrowed securities, consideration representing the collateral. Also recognizes the forward resale commitment.

Lending securities transactions accompanied by an agreement that entitles and obligates the institution loaning the securities to repurchase or redeem them before their maturity should be accounted for as secured borrowings. The cash (or securities) received as collateral is considered the amount borrowed, and the securities loaned are considered pledged as collateral against the cash borrowed. Any rebate paid to the institution borrowing the securities is treated as interest on the cash borrowed.

When the transfer is recorded as a sale, the cash (or securities) received in conjunction with loaning securities should be recognized as an asset and a corresponding liability established, recording the obligation to return the cash (or securities).

However, most securities lending transactions are accompanied by an agreement that entitles and obligates the securities lender to repurchase or redeem the transferred assets before their maturity. Such transactions will not typically be reported as sales under SFAS No. 140 because of the obligation of the transferor to repurchase the transferred assets. However, the provisions of SFAS No. 140 relating to the recognition of collateral could require that the transfer of securities and related collateral be recorded. The principal criterion to determine whether the collateral will be required to be recorded are whether the parties to the arrangement have the right to sell or repledge it. If such a right is present, the securities lender records the cash or noncash collateral received as its own asset as well as a corresponding obligation to return it. If the securities lender sells the collateral, it would recognize the proceeds and derecognize the collateral. The securities borrower will typically not record the securities received or an obligation to return them unless they are sold. Additionally, the securities borrower will not typically be required to reclassify the collateral provided, if such collateral is in the form of securities.

Additional guidance on accounting for and reporting of investments in debt and equity securities is established in the following:

- FASB Technical Bulletin (TB) No. 94-1, "Application of SFAS No. 115 to Debt Securities Restructured in a Troubled Debt Restructuring," which clarifies that any loan that was restructured in a troubled debt restructuring involving a modification of terms would be subject to SFAS No. 115 if the debt instrument meets the definition of a security
- SFAS No. 91, "Accounting for Nonrefundable Fees and Costs Associated with Originating or Acquiring Loans and Initial Direct Costs of Leases," which specifies that discounts or premiums associated with the purchase of debt securities should be accreted or amortized using the interest method
- SFAS No. 15, "Accounting by Debtors and Creditors for Troubled Debt Restructurings," which applies to troubled debt restructurings involving debt securities
- SFAS No. 114, "Accounting by Creditors for Impairment of a Loan (an Amendment, FASB No. 5 and 15)," which addresses troubled debt restructurings involving a modification of terms of a receivable

(t) DEPOSITS.   Generally, the most significant source of a bank's funding is customer deposits. Institutions now offer a wide range of deposit products having a variety of interest rates, terms, and conditions. The more common types of deposits are described in the following:

(i) Demand Deposits.   Customer deposit accounts from which funds may be withdrawn on demand. Checking and negotiable order of withdrawal (NOW) accounts are the most common form of demand deposits. Deposits and withdrawals are typically made through a combination of deposits, check writing, automatic teller machines (ATMs), point-of-sale terminals, electronic funds transfers (EFTs), and preauthorized deposits and payment transactions, such as payroll deposits and loan payments.

(ii) Savings Deposits.   Interest-bearing deposit accounts that normally carry with them certain access restrictions or minimum balance requirements. Passbook and statement savings accounts and money market accounts are the most common form of savings accounts. Deposits and withdrawals are typically made at teller windows, ATMs, by electronic funds transfers, or by preauthorized payment. Money market accounts often permit the customer to write checks, although the number of checks that may be written is limited.

(iii) Time Deposits.   Interest-bearing deposit accounts that are subject to withdrawal only after a fixed term. Certificates of deposit (CDs), individual retirement accounts (IRAs), and open accounts are the most common form of time deposits.

CDs may be issued in bearer form or registered form and may be negotiable and nonnegotiable. Negotiable CDs, for which there is an active secondary market, are generally short term and are most commonly sold to corporations, pension funds, and government bodies in large denominations, such as $100,000 to $1 million. Nonnegotiable CDs are generally in smaller denominations, and depositors are subject to a penalty fee if they elect to withdraw their funds prior to the stated maturity.

Individual retirement accounts, Keogh accounts, and self-employed-person accounts (SEPs) are generally maintained as CDs; however, due to the tax benefits to depositors, they typically have longer terms than most CDs.

Brokered deposits are third-party time deposits placed by or through the assistance of a deposit broker. Deposit brokers sometimes sell interests in placed deposits to third parties. Federal law restricts the acceptance and renewal of brokered deposits by an institution based on its capitalization.

(u) FEDERAL FUNDS AND REPURCHASE AGREEMENTS. Federal funds and repurchase agreements are often used as a source of liquidity and as a cost-effective source of funds.

(i) Federal Funds Purchased. Generally, short-term funds maturing overnight bought between banks that are members of the Federal Reserve System. Federal funds transactions can be secured or unsecured. If the funds are secured, U.S. government securities are placed in a custody account for the seller.

(ii) Repurchase Agreements. Repurchase agreements, or repos, occur when an institution sells securities and agrees to repurchase the identical (or substantially the same) securities at a specified date for a specified price. The institution may be a seller or a buyer. Most repo transactions occur with other depository institutions, dealers in securities, state and local governments, and customers (retail repurchase agreements), and involve obligations of the federal government or its agencies, commercial paper, bankers' acceptances, and negotiable CDs. The difference between the sale and repurchase price represents interest for the use of the funds. There are also several types of repurchase agreements, such as collar repurchase agreements, fixed-coupon agreements, and yield-maintenance agreements. The terms of the agreements are often structured to reflect the substance of the transaction, such as a borrowing and lending of funds versus a sale and purchase of securities. Some repurchase agreements are similar to securities lending transactions, whereby the seller may (or may not) have the right to sell or repledge the securities to a third party during the term of the repurchase agreement.

SFAS No. 140 provides the accounting guidance for repurchase agreements. In general, SFAS No. 140 uses the three conditions discussed previously in Subsection 31.2(s)(iv), "Securities Borrowing and Lending," when accounting for repurchase agreements. If all three conditions specified in SFAS No. 140 are met, the seller shall account for the repurchase agreement as a sale of financial assets and a forward repurchase commitment, and the buyer shall account for the agreement as a purchase of financial assets and a forward resale commitment.

Also similar to the treatment for securities lending transactions, repurchase agreements where the institution selling the securities maintains effective control over the securities (and thereby not meeting the three sale conditions, described previously, provided by SFAS No. 140) should be accounted for as secured borrowings.

(v) DEBT. Banks and savings institutions use long- and short-term borrowings as a source of funds.

(i) Long-Term Debt. Debentures and notes are the most common form of long-term debt; however, institutions also use long-term mortgages, obligations, commitments under capital leases, and mandatorily redeemable preferred stock to provide long-term funding. Funds are also borrowed through Eurodollar certificates, CMOs, and REMICs; mortgage-backed bond (MBBs), mortgage-revenue bonds, and FHLB advances. The terms of long-term debt vary; they may be secured or unsecured, and they may be convertible.

(ii) Short-Term Debt. Repurchase agreements and federal funds purchased are the most common form of the short-term debt described earlier. Commercial paper is another common source of short-term funding. Commercial paper is an unsecured short-term promissory note typically issued by bank or savings institution holding companies.

MBBs are any borrowings (other than those from an FHLB) collateralized in whole or in part by one or more real estate loans.

Member institutions may borrow from their regional Federal Reserve Bank in the form of discounts and advances, which are primarily used to cover shortages in the required reserve account and also in times of liquidity problems.

(iii) Accounting Guidance. In general, the accounting for debt is the same for banks and savings institutions as for other enterprises although banks and savings institutions have unclassified balance sheets. SFAS Statement No. 140 provides guidance for transfers of financial assets and extinguishments of liabilities.

(w) TAXATION. Taxation of financial institutions is extremely complex; specific discussion is therefore beyond the scope of this book. However, certain significant factors affecting bank and thrift taxation are discussed below.

(i) Loan Loss Reserves.

Banks. Prior to the Tax Reform Act of 1986 (1986 Act), banks were permitted to deduct loan loss provisions based on either the experience method or on a percentage of eligible loans method. The 1986 Act modified Internal Revenue Code Section 585, which now allows only a "small" bank with $500 million or less in average assets (calculated by taking into account the average assets of all other members of an institution's controlled group, if applicable) to calculate an addition to the bad debt reserve using the experience method.

A "large" bank with over $500 million in assets may not use the reserve method. It is limited to the specific charge-off method under IRC Section 166. If a bank becomes a large bank, it is required to recapture its reserve, usually over a four-year period. A deduction under Section 166 is generally allowed for wholly or partially worthless debt for the year in which the worthlessness occurs. The total or partial worthlessness of a debt is a facts-and-circumstances, loan-by-loan determination. A bank may make a conformity election, however, which provides a presumptive conclusion of worthlessness for charge-offs made for regulatory purposes.

In comparison to GAAP, the specific charge-off method generally results in an unfavorable temporary difference (i.e., the book expense is recognized prior to the tax deduction being allowed) because the actual charge-off of a loan usually occurs later than the time the reserve is established for it.

Thrifts. Effective for tax years beginning after December 31, 1995, thrift institutions are subject to the same loan loss rules as banks. Thrifts that qualify as "small" banks (average assets of $500 million or less) can use the experience-based reserve method described above. Thrifts that are treated as "large" banks must use the specific charge-off method.

A thrift that is treated as either a large or small bank is required to recapture or recognize as income its "applicable excess reserves." Such income is generally recognized ratably over a six-year period beginning with the first tax year beginning after 1995.

If a thrift becomes a large bank, the amount of the thrift's applicable excess reserves is generally the excess of (1) the balance of its reserves as of the close of its last taxable year beginning before January 1, 1996, over (2) the balance of its reserves as of the close of its last taxable year beginning before January 1, 1988 (its "pre-1988" or "base year" reserve). Thus, a thrift treated as a large bank generally is required to recapture all post-1987 additions to it bad debt reserves.

In the case of a thrift becoming a small bank, the thrift's applicable excess reserves is the excess of (1) the balance of its reserves as of the close of its last taxable year beginning before January 1, 1996, over (2) the greater of the balance of (a) its pre-1988 reserves, or (b) what the thrift's reserves would have been at the close of its last taxable year beginning before January 1, 1996, had the thrift always used the experience method. Thus, a thrift treated as a small bank may not have any applicable excess reserves (and therefore no recapture) if it had always used the experience method.

A special rule, the "residential loan requirement," may allow the six-year recapture period to be delayed for one or two years, that is, recapture could actually start as late as the first taxable year beginning after 1997. An institution meets the requirement for a taxable year if the principal amount of residential loans made by the institution during the year is not less than its "base amount," defined generally as the average of the principal amounts of residential loans made by the institution during the six most recent tax years beginning before January 1, 1996.

A "residential loan" is generally defined as a loan secured by residential real property, but only to the extent the loan is made to the property owner to acquire, construct, or improve the property. Thus, mortgage refinancings and home equity loans are not considered to be residential loans, except to the extent the proceeds of the loan are used to acquire, construct, or improve qualified real property. Other rules govern the calculation of the base amount for purposes of the requirement.

The residential loan requirement is applicable only for taxable years beginning after December 31, 1995, and before January 1, 1998, and must be applied separately with respect to each such year. Thus, all institutions are required to recapture their applicable excess reserves within the first six, seven, or eight taxable years beginning after December 31, 1995.

(ii) Mark-to-Market. Contrary to normal realization-based tax accounting principles, IRC Section 475 requires "dealers in securities" to recognize gain or loss through "marking-to-market" their securities holdings, unless such securities are validly identified by the taxpayer as excepted from the provisions.

As used in this context, the terms "dealer" and "securities" have very broad application. Virtually all financial institutions are considered dealers in securities for mark-to-market purposes though regulations provide exceptions for certain institutions not engaging in more than de minimus dealer activities. Securities required to be marked (unless validly identified as excepted) include notes, bonds, and other evidences of indebtedness; stock; notional principal contracts; or any evidence of an interest in or a derivative of such security (other than Section 1256(a) contracts); and any clearly identified hedge of such security.

Securities that may be identified as excepted from the mark-to-market provisions are:

- Securities "held for investment," and property identified as such for tax purposes.
- Notes and other evidences of indebtedness (and obligations to acquire such) that are acquired or originated by the taxpayer in the ordinary course of a trade or business that are "not held for sale."
- Hedges of positions or liabilities that are not securities in the hands of the taxpayer, and hedges of positions or liabilities that are exempt from mark-to-market under the two foregoing provisions. This does not apply for hedges held as a dealer.

To be excepted from mark-to-market, the security must be identified by the taxpayer on a contemporaneous basis (generally, day of acquisition) as meeting one of the exceptions.

Whether or not a security is required to be marked-to-market for financial accounting purposes is *not* dispositive for purposes of determining whether such security is treated as "held for investment" or "not held for sale."

Some financial institutions identify all or a significant portion of their loans to customers as excepted from the mark-to-market provisions because they intend to hold those loans to maturity. A possible exception are mortgages that are originated for sale (pipeline or warehoused loans), which do not meet the exception criteria and must be marked-to-market.

(iii) Tax-Exempt Securities. For tax purposes, gross income does not include interest on any obligation of a state or political subdivision thereof (e.g., county, city). Interest on certain non-qualified private activity bonds, unregistered bonds, and arbitrage bonds does not qualify for this exemption.

A deduction is not allowed for interest expense on indebtedness incurred to purchase or carry tax-exempt obligations. Deposit-taking financial institutions (banks and thrifts) are subject to a special two-part formula to determine how much of the total interest expense of an institution is disallowed interest expense.

Interest expense related to tax-exempt obligations acquired after August 1986 is disallowed and is calculated by multiplying total interest expense by the ratio of the tax basis of such obligations to the tax basis of all assets.

Interest expense related to tax-exempt obligations acquired between January 1983 and August 1986 is 20 percent disallowed and is calculated in a manner similar to that just described.

Certain qualified tax-exempt obligations (generally, obligations issued by an entity that will not issue more than $10 million of tax-exempt obligations during the year and that are not private activity bonds) issued after August 1986 are treated as if issued prior to that date (i.e., subject to the 20 percent disallowance rule rather than the 100 percent disallowance rule).

(iv) Nonaccrual Loans.   Generally, interest on a loan must be accrued as income unless the taxpayer can demonstrate that the interest is uncollectible at the time of accrual. The tax rule is dependent on the facts and circumstances for the nonaccrual loans at issue. The FAS No. 114 uses a "probable" test in determining when a loan is impaired. When it is probable that a creditor will be unable to collect all amounts due according to the contractual terms of the loan agreement, the loan is considered impaired. Use of this analysis may now provide substantiation of the tax treatment for impairment of loans.

(v) Hedging.   Financial institutions that are involved in hedging transactions treat the gain or loss from these transactions as ordinary for tax purposes. A hedging transaction must be entered into primarily to manage a taxpayer's risk of interest rate changes, price changes, or currency fluctuations. A taxpayer must also have risk on an overall (or macro) basis. A hedge of a single ordinary asset or liability will be respected if it is reasonably expected to manage the taxpayer's overall risk. Hedges entered into as part of an overall risk reduction program also will qualify.

"Fixed to floating" hedges (e.g., hedges that convert a fixed-rate liability into a floating-rate liability) may satisfy the risk management requirement if, for example, a taxpayer's income varies with interest rates. In addition, hedges entered into to reverse or counteract another hedging transaction may qualify for ordinary gain or loss treatment. Because tax hedges are permissible only with ordinary property, hedges of mortgage servicing rights generally do not qualify as tax hedges, since mortgage servicing rights are generally capital assets.

Hedges of ordinary liabilities qualify as "hedging transactions" regardless of the use of the proceeds from the borrowing. Consequently, gain or loss from a hedge of a liability used to fund the purchase of a capital asset will be ordinary. However, recent guidance in the form of final Treasury regulations provide that the purchase or sale of a debt instrument, an equity security, or an annuity contract is not hedging a transaction even if the transaction limits or reduces the taxpayer's risk.

The timing of the gain or loss from a hedging transaction must reasonably be "matched" with the gain or loss of the item being hedged. This applies to global hedges and other hedges of aggregate risk.

If a taxpayer disposes of a hedged item but retains the hedge, the taxpayer may redesignate the hedge. The taxpayer generally must mark-to-market the hedge on the date that the taxpayer disposes of the hedged item.

There are detailed contemporaneous identification and record-keeping requirements with which an institution must comply to support its treatment of hedging transactions. Failure to comply could lead to characterization of losses from these transactions as capital losses (which may only be used to offset capital gains).

(vi) Loan Origination Fees and Costs.   For financial accounting purposes, SFAS No. 91 requires that all loan origination fees (including loan commitment fees and points) be deferred and generally recognized over the life of the related loan or commitment period as an adjustment of yield. For tax accounting purposes, loan fees received as cash payments incident to a lending transaction (e.g., points) that represent an amount charged for the use of forbearance of money (rather than payment for services) are deferred. Points received in connection with a lending transaction are applied as a reduction to the issue price of the loan and generally create original issue discount (OID) to be recognized over the life of the loan on a constant yield method. In instances where the OID on a loan is de minimus (as defined in regulations), the de minimus OID is recognized in proportion to principal payments received.

For book purposes, the costs associated with origination of a loan are deferred and recognized over the life of the loan together with the origination fees. For tax purposes, institutions generally deduct these costs currently because to date there has been no published guidance requiring capitalization. However, in January 2002, the Treasury issued an Advance Notice of Proposed Rule Making (ANPRM), providing notice that it plans to issue future guidance for loan origination costs. The Notice suggest further guidance will permit a current deduction for de minimis internal costs (e.g., employee salaries) in connection with the origination of intangible assets (e.g., loans).

(vii) Foreclosed Property

Banks.   Generally, a bank recognizes gain or loss on foreclosure of property securing a loan, but is not permitted to deduct any further decrease in or impairment of value. Any decrease in value occurring after foreclosure is recognized when the property is disposed of by the institution. If real property acquired through foreclosure is operated in a trade or business after foreclosure (e.g., as rental property), the institution may deduct depreciation (and other operating expenses) computed in accordance with general tax depreciation provisions.

Thrifts.   Effective for taxable years beginning after December 31, 1995, thrift institutions are subject to the same rules as banks.

Under prior law, a special rule treated the acquisition of property by a thrift as a nontaxable event, with no gain or loss recognized at time of foreclosure and no depreciation allowed on the property. A subsequent write-down charge to the bad debt reserve was allowed if the fair market value of the property was less than the tax basis of the loan. Upon final disposition, the gain or loss was credited or charged to the bad debt reserve.

(viii) Leasing Activities.   Direct financing activities may qualify as financings for tax purposes. As a result, a bank will be considered the owner of the leased property for tax purposes. Accordingly, rental income and depreciation deductions on the leased asset will be recognized for tax purposes but not for financial reporting purposes. This will result in a difference between book and tax accounting under SFAS No. 109.

(ix) FHLB Dividends.   Banks and savings institutions may become members of the FHLB by purchasing stock in individual FHLB member banks. Banks generally become a member of the FHLB for access to additional funding for borrowed funds. The FHLB member banks, of which there are 12, generally pay cash or stock dividends to shareholders, depending on the member bank. Cash dividends paid on FHLB stock that was issued prior to March 28, 1942, are exempt from federal income taxes. This exemption applied even for such stock that was subsequently acquired through merger or otherwise. Cash dividends on FHLB stock issued on or after March 28, 1942, are not exempt from taxation. Stock dividends on FHLB stock are generally not taxable when distributed. These stock dividends create a book/tax difference that is recognized on the sales or redemption of the FHLB shares.

(x) Bank-Owned Life Insurance.   Bank-owned life insurance (BOLI) is commonly used by financial institutions for its financial benefits to help fund benefit programs and to offset certain costs typically incurred when losing key employees of the bank. BOLI is life insurance purchased by a financial institution on the lives of specific employees. The economically beneficial aspects of BOLI are tax-free growth in the cash surrender value of the policy and a tax-tree treatment of the death proceeds, which are both realized by the bank as the owner of a given policy. Insurance premiums on life insurance policies are not tax deductible.

(xi) Original Issue Discount.   Original Issue Discount (OID) rules apply to all debt instruments after July 1, 1982, with certain exceptions. Generally, OID is the excess of what a borrower is obligated to repay when the loan comes due over the amount borrowed. More technically, OID is the excess of the stated redemption price at maturity over its issue price. Under OID rules, the holder of the debt must accrue stated interest under the constant yield method.

(xii) Market Discount. The primary difference between OID and market discount is that purchase of a security at its original purchase versus the secondary market, respectively. Generally, if a debt instrument has declined in value from the time when it was originally issued (other than as a result of principal payments), a purchaser of the bond will acquire it with market discount.

A holder of a market discount may choose between two methods of recognizing accrued market discount. Market discount accrues under a ratable method, in proportion to the payment of principal, unless a constant interest method is elected. The primary difference between market discount and OID is that the borrower is not required to include accrued market discount in taxable income currently, but may elect to do so. Instead, the market discount rules require borrowers to recognize accrued market discount only on receipt of the proceeds of a disposition or a principal payment is made.

(x) FUTURES, FORWARDS, OPTIONS, SWAPS, AND SIMILAR FINANCIAL INSTRUMENTS.
Futures, forwards, swaps, and options and other financial instruments with similar characteristics (collectively, derivatives) have become important financial management tools for banks. The complexity and volume of derivatives and derivatives trading has increased significantly in recent years. Institutions continue to enhance risk management systems to enable them to monitor the risks involved. Bank regulatory agencies continue to encourage institutions to upgrade policies and procedures, risk measurement and reporting systems, and independent oversight and internal control processes. Senior management has increased its knowledge of the derivative products and how risks are monitored.

Derivatives are receiving considerable attention primarily due to the underlying volatility in the markets, relatively large size of the transactions, and the potential for significant earnings fluctuations. Derivatives have many similar risk characteristics as other credit products, such as credit risk, market risk, legal risk, and control risk. The specific risks in a derivatives portfolio are often difficult to identify due to the complexity of the transactions. For example, two or more basic risks are often used in combination, which may be further complicated by the fact that economic interaction between various positions within an institution (on- and off-balance sheet) may be difficult to assess.

Underlying cash flows for derivatives are often referenced to such items as rates, indexes (which measure changes in specific markets), value of underlying positions in financial instruments, in equity instruments, in foreign currencies, commodities, or other derivatives.

Derivatives can generally be described as either forward-based or option-based, or combinations of the two. A forward-based contract (futures, forwards, and swap contracts) obligates one party to buy and a counterparty to sell an underlying financial instrument, foreign currency, or commodity at a future date at an agreed-upon price. An option-based derivative (options, interest rate caps, and interest rate floors) are one-sided in that if the right is exercised, only the holder can have a favorable outcome and the writer can have only an unfavorable outcome. Most derivatives are generally combinations of these two types of contracts.

Derivatives traded through an organized exchange typically have standardized contracts, such as futures and certain options, and the risk characteristics are more related to market risk than to credit risk. Alternatively, derivatives traded over-the-counter are customized to meet certain objectives or needs and often vary in structure, such as swaps and forward contracts. Customized derivative products traded privately typically present a greater degree of credit risk and liquidity risk, depending on the counterparty's financial strength, value of the collateral, if any, and the liquidity of the specific instrument.

The complexity of derivative instruments is largely the result of the pricing mechanisms, flexibility and options features, and value calculation formulas. In addition, derivatives can be structured to be more sensitive to general price movements than the cash market instruments from which their value is derived. The types of derivatives products available varies considerably; however, the following is a brief description of the basic types of contracts.

(i) Futures.   A futures contract is an agreement to make or take delivery of a financial instrument (interest rate instrument, currency, and certain stock indices) at a future date. Most futures contracts are closed out prior to the delivery date by entering into an offsetting contract.

The type of financial instrument delivered depends on the type of futures contract. For example: Investment-grade financial instruments, such as U.S. Treasury securities or mortgage-backed securities are delivered under interest rate futures; foreign currency (in the currency specified) is delivered under foreign currency futures contracts; and commodities such as oil, gold bullion, or coffee are delivered under commodities futures contracts.

Buyers and sellers are required to deposit assets (such as cash, government securities, or letters of credit) with a broker. The assets are called a *margin* and are subject to increases and decreases, if losses or gains are incurred on the open position.

(ii) Forwards.   A forward contract is a contract between two parties to purchase and sell a specified quantity of a financial instrument, foreign currency, or commodity at a specified price, with delivery and settlement at a specified future date. Such contracts are not traded on exchanges and therefore may have a high degree of credit and liquidity risk. Forward rate agreements are forward contracts used to manage interest-rate risk.

(iii) Options.   Option contracts provide the purchaser of the option with the right, but not the obligation, to buy (or sell) a specified instrument, such as currencies, interest rate products, or futures. They also put the seller under the obligation to deliver (or take delivery of) the instrument to the buyer of the option but only at the buyer's option.

A premium is typically paid to the seller of the option, representing both the time value of money and any intrinsic value. Intrinsic value, which cannot be less than zero, is derived from the excess of market price for the underlying item in the contract over the price specified in the contract (strike price).

Holders of option contracts can minimize downside price risks because the loss on a purchased option contracts is limited to the amount paid for the option. On the other hand, while the profit on written option contracts is limited to the premium received, the loss potential is unlimited because the writer is obligated to settle at the strike price if the option is exercised. Options are often processed through a clearinghouse, which guarantees the writer's performance and minimizes credit risk.

Option-based derivative contracts, such as caps, floors, collars, and swaptions, can be combined to transfer risks form one entity to another. The following describes each type of contract.

- *Interest rate caps.* These are contracts in which a cap writer, in return for a premium, agrees to make cash payments to the cap holder equal to the excess of the market rate over the strike price multiplied by the notional principal amount if rates go above specified interest rate (strike price). The cap holder has the right, not the obligation, to exercise the option, and if rates move down, the cap holder will lose only the premium paid. The cap writer has virtually unlimited risk resulting from increases in interest rates above the cap rate.

- *Interest rate floors.* These are contracts in which a floor writer, in return for a premium, agrees to limit the risk of declining interest rates based on a notional amount such that if rates go below a specified interest rate (strike price), the floor holder will receive cash payments equal to the difference between the market rate and the strike price multiplied by the notional principal amount. As with interest rate caps, the floor holder has the right, not the obligation, to exercise the option, and if rates move up, the floor holder will lose only the premium paid. The floor writer has risk resulting from decreases in interest rates below the floor rate.

- *Interest rate collars.* These are combinations of interest rate caps and interest rate floors, that is, one held and one written. Such contracts are often used by institutions to lock a floating rate contract into a predetermined interest rate range.

- *Swaptions.* These are option contracts to enter into an interest rate swap contract at some future date or to cancel an existing swap in the future.

(iv) Swaps. These are contracts between parties to exchange sets of cash flows based on a predetermined notional principal; only the cash flows are exchanged (usually on a net basis) with no principal exchanged. Swaps are used to change the nature or cost of existing transactions, for example, exchanging fixed-rate debt cash flows for floating rate cash flows. Swap contracts are not exchange-traded, therefore they are not as liquid as futures contracts. The principal types of swaps are interest rate swaps and currency swaps. However, there are also basis swaps, equity swaps, commodity swaps, and mortgage swaps. A brief description of seven swaps follows:

1. *Interest rate swaps.* Interest rate swaps are used to manage interest rate risks, such as from floating to fixed or fixed to floating. Periodic fixed payments are made by one party, while another counterparty is obligated to make variable payments, depending on a market interest rate. Master netting agreements are used to permit entities to legally set off related payable and receivable swap contract positions for settlement purposes.

2. *Foreign currency swaps.* Foreign currency swaps are used to fix the value of foreign currency exchange transactions that will occur in the future. Typically, principal is exchanged at inception, interest is paid in accordance with the agreed upon rate and term, and principal is re-exchanged at maturity.

3. *Fixed-rate currency swaps.* Fixed-rate currency swaps occur when two counterparties exchange fixed-rate interest in one currency for fixed-rate interest in another currency.

4. *Basis swaps.* Basis swaps represent a variation on interest-rate swap contracts where both rates are variable but tied to different index rates.

5. *Equity swaps.* Equity swaps occur when counterparties exchange cash flow streams tied to an equity index with a fixed or floating interest.

6. *Commodity swaps.* Commodity swaps occur when counterparties exchange cash flow streams tied to the difference between a commodity's agreed upon price and its variable price, applied to an agreed-upon price of the commodity.

7. *Mortgage swaps.* Typical mortgage swaps occur when an investor exchanges interest payments tied to a short-term floating rate, for cash flows based an a generic class of mortgage-backed securities over a specified period. The cash flows received by the investor include the fixed coupon on the generic class or mortgage-backed securities and any discount or premium. The notional amount of the mortgage swap is adjusted monthly, based on amortization and prepayment experience of the generic class of mortgage-backed securities. When the contract expires, the investor may either have to take physical delivery of the mortgages (at a predetermined price) or settle in cash for the difference between the predetermined price and the current market value for the mortgages. Collateral may be posted to reduce counterparty credit risk.

(v) Foreign Exchange Contracts. These contracts are used both to provide a service to customers and as a part of the institution's trading or hedging activities. The bank profits by maintaining a margin between the purchase price and sale price. Contracts may be for current trades (spot contract), future dates (forward contract), or swap contracts. The bank may also enter into these contracts to hedge a foreign currency exposure.

(vi) Other Variations. Other types of derivative products are discussed in Chapter 26, "Derivatives and Hedge Accounting."

(vii) Accounting Guidance. The FASB issued Statement No. 133, "Accounting for Derivative Instruments and Hedging Activities," in June 1998. Statement No. 133 provides a comprehensive and consistent standard for the recognition and measurement of derivatives and hedging activities.

The Statement resolves the inconsistencies that existed with respect to accounting for derivatives and changes considerably the way many derivatives transactions and hedged items are reported.

SFAS No. 133 requires all derivatives to be recorded on the balance sheet at fair value and establishes "special accounting" for the following three different types of hedges: hedges of changes in the fair value of assets, liabilities, or firm commitments (referred to as *fair value hedges*); hedges of the variable cash flows of forecasted transactions (cash flow hedges); and hedges of foreign currency exposures of net investments in foreign operations. The accounting treatment and criteria for each of the three types of hedges are unique. Changes in fair value of derivatives that do not meet the criteria of one of these three categories of hedges are included in income.

The four basic underlying premises of the new approach are:

1. Derivatives represent rights or obligations that meet the definitions of assets (future cash inflows due from another party) or liabilities (future cash outflows owed to another party) and should be reported in the financial statements.

2. Fair value is the most relevant measure for financial instruments and the only relevant measure for derivatives. Derivatives should be measured at fair value, and adjustments to the carrying amount of hedged items should reflect changes in their fair value (i.e., gains and losses) attributable to the risk being hedged arising while the hedge is in effect.

3. Only items that are assets or liabilities should be reported as such in the financial statements. (The Board believes gains and losses from hedging activities are not assets or liabilities and, therefore, should not be deferred.)

4. Special accounting for items designated as being hedged should be provided only for qualifying transactions, and one aspect of qualification should be an assessment of the expectation of the effectiveness of the hedge (i.e., offsetting changes in fair values or cash flows).

See Chapter 26 for further guidance on SFAS No. 133.

(y) FIDUCIARY SERVICES AND OTHER FEE INCOME

(i) Fiduciary Services   In their fiduciary capacity, banks must serve their clients' interests and must act in good faith at a level absent in most other banking activities. In view of this high degree of fiduciary responsibility, banks usually segregate the responsibilities of the trust department from that of the rest of the bank. This segregation is designed to maintain a highly objective viewpoint in the fiduciary area. Fiduciary services range from the simple safekeeping of valuables to the investment management of large pension funds.

Custodial, safekeeping, and safe deposit activities involve the receipt, storage, and issuance of receipts for a range of valuable assets. This may involve the holding of bonds, stocks, and currency in escrow pending the performance under a contract, or merely the maintenance of a secure depository for valuables or title deeds. As custodian, the bank may receive interest and dividends on securities for the account of customers.

Investment management may be discretionary, whereby the bank has certain defined powers to make investments, or nondiscretionary, whereby the bank may only execute investment transactions based on customers' instructions. The former obviously involves a higher degree of risk to the institution and creates an obligation to make prudent investment decisions.

Other fiduciary services include trust administration, stock and bond registrar, and bank trustee. Trust administration involves holding or management of property, such as pension funds and estates for the benefit of others. Stock and bond registrar and bank trustee functions include the maintenance of records and execution of securities transactions, including changes in ownership and payment of dividends and interest.

Since the assets and liabilities of the trust department of the bank are held in an agency capacity, they are not recorded on the balance sheet of the bank. These activities can, however, generate significant fee income, which is recorded when earned in the statement of income.

(ii) Other Fee Income.   Emphasis on fee income-generating activities has increased in response to both the risk-based capital guidelines, which created more pressure to reduce the size of the balance sheet, and a general increase in competition in the financial services industry.

Some of the principal forms of fee-generating activity include the following:

- *Annuities.* Banks sell fixed and variable annuities.
- *Brokerage.* Banks may arrange for the purchase and sale of securities on behalf of customers in return for a commission.
- *Corporate and advisory services.* These activities involve advice on mergers and acquisitions, capital raising, and Treasury management in return for a fee.
- *Private banking.* This activity involves investment planning, tax assistance, and credit extensions to wealthy individuals.
- *Private placements.* This activity normally involves the placement of securities on a *best efforts* basis as opposed to an underwriting commitment.
- *Underwriting.* Banks may guarantee to purchase certain allowable securities if they are not fully subscribed to in an offering.
- *401(k) plans and mutual funds.* Banks may distribute mutual funds in a 401(k) plan.

Many of the activities, particularly underwriting, are subject to restriction by regulation as to the type of securities that may be transacted, and separately capitalized subsidiaries may be required. These restrictions are subject to change at the current time and may be significantly relaxed in the near future.

These activities generate fee income that is recorded when earned. Certain activities are conducted in conjunction with credit extension activities, and therefore particular attention is required to ensure that fees generated are appropriately recorded. It is essential to distinguish between fees that may be recorded immediately and fees that are essentially loan origination fees to be accounted for over the life of the loan (SFAS No. 91).

(z) ELECTRONIC BANKING AND TECHNOLOGY RISKS.   Conducting banking by personal computer is a growing area for many institutions. The types of transactions customers can perform online has also increased. For example, customers can transfer funds, pay bills, and apply for loans by using electronic banking.

Additionally, many institutions are using client/server systems and personal computers, rather than mainframe computers, to process customer transactions and maintain bank records. Accordingly, security and database management controls surrounding these client/servers and personal computers becomes very important.

Regulatory agencies have issued guidance addressing the safety and soundness aspects of electronic banking and personal computer bankings and the security risks associated with the Internet and phone banking.

31.3 MORTGAGE BANKING ACTIVITIES

(a) OVERVIEW.   Mortgage banking activities primarily include the origination or purchase, sale, and subsequent long-term servicing of mortgage loans. Mortgage loans are originated or purchased from a variety of sources including applications received directly from borrowers (retail originations) and loans acquired from mortgage brokers or other mortgage lenders (wholesale or correspondent purchases). These loans are then generally sold through the secondary mortgage market to permanent investors or retained by the lender in its own loan portfolio. Typically, loans are sold to permanent investors through conduits, although mortgage loans can also be sold through whole loan sales directly to investors or through public or private securitizations completed by the mortgage banker. Secondary market conduits include government-sponsored entities such as

GNMA, FNMA, and FHLMC, and other private companies involved in the acquisition and securitization of mortgage loans. Loan servicing includes the collection, recording, and remittance to investors of monthly mortgage payments, the maintenance of records relating to the loans, and the management of escrows for taxes and insurance. In return for performing these servicing activities, mortgage servicers earn a fee, which is usually a percentage of the loan's unpaid principal balance. Profits are earned from loan servicing activities if the mortgage banker's cost of performing the servicing of the loans is less than the fee received. The major risks associated with mortgage banking are interest rate risk associated with the loans in the pipeline and warehouse, credit risk associated with loans held for sale or held in portfolio, operational risk associated with performing servicing functions improperly, and prepayment risk associated with mortgage servicing rights.

(b) ACCOUNTING GUIDANCE.   The principal accounting guidance for the mortgage banking industry is found in SFAS No. 65, "Accounting for Certain Mortgage Banking Activities," SFAS No. 91, "Accounting for Nonrefundable Fees and Costs Associated with Originating or Acquiring Loans and Initial Direct Costs of Leases," and SFAS No. 140, "Accounting for Transfers and Servicing of Financial Assets and Extinguishments of Liabilities." SFAS No. 140 supersedes SFAS No. 125. SFAS No. 140 is effective for transfers and servicing of financial assets and extinguishments of liabilities occurring after March 31, 2001, and is to be applied prospectively. Earlier or retroactive application is not permitted. There are also several issues related to the accounting for mortgage banking activities that have been addressed by the EITF.

(c) MORTGAGE LOANS HELD FOR SALE.   Mortgage loans held for sale represent a mortgage banker's "inventory" of loans that have been originated or purchased and are awaiting sale to permanent investors. SFAS No. 65 requires that mortgage loans held for sale be reported at the lower of their cost or market value, determined as of the balance sheet date determined on an individual loan or aggregate basis. The excess of cost over market value is required to be accounted for as a valuation allowance with changes in the valuation allowance included in net income of the period in which the change occurs. SFAS No. 91 requires that loan origination fees and direct loan origination costs be deferred until the related loan is sold. Therefore, any net deferred fees or costs should be included in the cost basis of the loan and considered in determining the required valuation allowance at any balance sheet date. Capitalized costs of acquiring the rights to service mortgage loans associated with the purchase or origination of these assets should be excluded from the cost of the mortgage loans for the purposes of determining lower of cost or market. Likewise, the fair value of the servicing rights associated with the loans included in a mortgage banker's loans held for sale classification should be excluded from the determination of lower of cost or market.

The market value of mortgage loans held for sale shall be determined by type of loan. At a minimum, separate determinations of market value for residential and commercial mortgage loans shall be made. Either the aggregate or individual loan basis may be used in determining the lower of cost or market value for each type of loan under SFAS No. 65. The market value for loans subject to investor purchase commitments shall be based on those commitment prices. The market value for uncommitted loans held on a speculative basis shall be based on the market in which the mortgage banker normally operates.

At any balance sheet date, a mortgage banker will also have outstanding rate commitments, which represent commitments made to loan applicants to fund a loan at a locked-in interest rate provided that loan application eventually closes. These rate commitments make up a mortgage banker's "pipeline." SFAS No. 65 does not specifically address a mortgage banker's pipeline as being subject to a lower of cost or market determination. However, the pipeline should be evaluated for the impact of any adverse commitments. This may be done in conjunction with the lower of cost or market analysis on loans held for sale. The analysis of the pipeline typically would only be done on those commitments expected to become loans (i.e., close) and not on those loans expected to "fallout" (i.e., not close). The existence of losses inherent in the pipeline after adjustment for fallout can often be determined by comparing commitment prices to investor delivery prices for similar loans. If any losses are determined to exist in the mortgage banker's pipeline, the loss should be accrued pursuant to SFAS No. 5.

(d) MORTGAGE LOANS HELD FOR INVESTMENT.   Mortgage loans can be originated or purchased by a mortgage banker with the intention of holding the loan to maturity, or the loans can be transferred into a mortgage banker's "loans held for investment" category from a "loans held for sale" category after it is determined that the loan is unsalable or the mortgage banker decides to retain the loan for investment purposes. SFAS No. 65 requires that mortgage loans held for investment be reported at cost. For mortgage loans transferred into mortgage loans held for investment from loans held for sale, their initial cost basis shall be determined as the lower of the loan's cost or market value on the date of the transfer. A mortgage loan shall not be classified as held for investment unless the mortgage banker has both the intent and the ability to hold the loan for the foreseeable future or until maturity.

If the ultimate recovery of the carrying amount of a mortgage loan held as a long-term investment is doubtful, and the impairment is considered to be other than temporary, the carrying amount of the loan shall be reduced to its expected collectible amount, which then becomes its new cost basis. The amount of the reduction shall be recorded as a loss. A recovery from the new cost basis shall be reported as a gain only at the sale, maturity, or disposition of the loan.

As noted above, SFAS No. 91 requires that loan origination fees and direct loan origination costs be deferred. For mortgage loans held for investment, any net deferred fees or costs should be included in the cost basis of the loan and amortized into interest income on a level yield method.

(e) SALES OF MORTGAGE LOANS AND SECURITIES.   Mortgage bankers typically sell the majority of the loans they originate or purchase to third-party investors in order to remove these loans from their balance sheet and provide funds for the continued origination and purchase of future loans. The sale of mortgage loans results in a gain or loss that should be recognized when the mortgage banker has surrendered control over the assets to a purchaser in a manner such that the transfer of the loans can be accounted for as a sale. SFAS No. 140, which provides guidance concerning the transfers and servicing of financial assets and extinguishments of liabilities, states that a transfer of financial assets in which the transferor surrenders control over those financial assets shall be accounted for as a sale to the extent that consideration other than beneficial interests in the transferred assets have been received in exchange.

The control over financial assets is deemed to have been surrendered under SFAS No. 140 to the extent that all of the following three conditions have been met:

1. The transferred assets have been isolated from the transferor, that is, put presumptively beyond the reach of the transferor and its creditors even in bankruptcy.
2. Each transferee has the right to pledge or exchange the transferred assets, and no condition both constrains the transferee from taking advantage of its right to pledge or exchange and provides more than a trivial benefit to the transferor.
3. The transferor does not maintain effective control over the transferred assets through either: (a) an agreement that both entitles and obligates the transferor to repurchase or redeem them before their maturity, or (b) the ability to unilaterally cause the holder to return specified assets, other than through a clean-up call.

The sale of mortgage loans can occur primarily through one of three methods. Loans can be sold (1) through whole loan or bulk transactions to third-party investors where individual loans or groups of loans are transferred, (2) through government sponsored mortgage-backed securities programs of investors such as FNMA, FHLMC, or GNMA, and (3) through private securitizations where the originator or loan purchaser will securitize and sell directly to third-party investors interests in an underlying pool of mortgage loans.

The most common type of sale utilized by mortgage bankers is the sale of mortgage-backed securities through programs sponsored by FNMA, FHLMC, and GNMA. These sales are relatively straightforward and generally do not have the complex kinds of terms that could call into question sale treatment for the transfer under SFAS No. 140. Whole loan sales are also generally straightforward and do not present complex SFAS No. 140 sales issues; however, in instances where mortgage-backed securities or whole loans are sold through private securitizations or on a recourse basis, surrender of control issues under SFAS No. 140 may be encountered.

Depending on the type of structure utilized in a private mortgage loan securitization, including those with terms where significant interests in securitized pools are retained, those with significant continued involvement of the seller in the securitized pool, and those with unusual legal structures, the attainment of sale accounting under SFAS No. 140 may also not be straightforward and may be difficult to assess. Careful consideration should be given to the requirements of SFAS No. 140 to ensure that a sale of the mortgage loans has occurred before a gain or loss on the transaction can be realized.

(i) Gain or Loss on Sale of Mortgage Loans.   Upon completion of a transfer of mortgage loans that satisfies the conditions of SFAS No. 140 to qualify as a sale, the mortgage banker shall allocate the previous cost basis of the loans, including all deferred SFAS No. 91 costs and fees, between interests sold (i.e., the underlying loans) and interests retained (i.e., the loans' servicing rights, or other retained portions of a securitization such as residual spreads, subordinate bonds, and IO or PO strips) based upon the relative fair value of those components on the date of the sale. The allocated basis assigned to interests in the mortgage loans that are sold should then be derecognized, and a gain or loss calculated as the difference between this allocated basis and proceeds received on the sale, net of any assets or liabilities created in the transaction that should be recorded. Newly created assets and liabilities from the sale should be initially recorded at their fair value and accounted for in accordance with current GAAP for similar assets and liabilities. Interests retained in the sale of mortgage loans are initially recorded at their allocated cost basis and subsequently accounted for in accordance with current GAAP for similar assets and liabilities.

(ii) Financial Assets Subject to Prepayment.   Interest-only strips, loans, and other receivables and retained interests from sales or securitizations of mortgage loans that can be contractually prepaid or otherwise settled in a way such that the holder would not recover substantially all of its recorded investment shall be subsequently measured like investments in debt securities and classified as available-for-sale or trading assets under SFAS No. 115.

(f) MORTGAGE SERVICING RIGHTS.   A mortgage banking entity may purchase mortgage servicing rights separately, or it may acquire mortgage servicing rights by purchasing or originating mortgage loans and selling or securitizing those mortgage loans with the servicing rights retained. When a mortgage banker purchases or originates mortgage loans, the cost of acquiring those loans includes the cost of the related servicing rights. These servicing rights become separate and distinct assets only when their respective mortgage loans are sold with the servicing rights retained.

SFAS No. 140 provides the primary accounting guidance for mortgage servicing rights and requires that servicing assets and other retained interests in the mortgage loans sold be measured by allocating the previous carrying amount of the mortgage loans (as previously discussed) between the mortgage loans sold and the servicing rights retained, based on their relative fair values at the date of the sale. SFAS No. 140 also requires that servicing assets and liabilities be subsequently (a) amortized in proportion to and over the period of estimated net servicing income or loss and (b) assessed for asset impairment or increased obligation based on their fair values.

SFAS No. 140 requires that a mortgage banking enterprise assess its capitalized mortgage servicing rights for impairment based on the fair value of those rights. A mortgage banking enterprise should stratify its mortgage servicing rights based on one or more of the predominant risk characteristics of the underlying loans. Impairment should be recognized through a valuation allowance for each impaired stratum. Each stratum should be recorded at the lower of cost or market value.

(i) Initial Capitalization of Mortgage Servicing Rights. Under SFAS No. 140, each time an entity undertakes an obligation to service mortgage loans, the entity shall recognize either a servicing asset or a servicing liability for that servicing contract, unless it retains the underlying mortgage loans as an investment on its balance sheet. If a servicing asset was purchased or assumed rather than undertaken in a sale or securitization of the mortgage loans being serviced, the servicing asset shall be measured initially at its fair value, presumptively the price paid for the right to service the underlying loans.

Under SFAS No. 140, servicing rights retained in a sale of mortgage loans shall be initially recorded on the balance sheet at their allocated portion of the total cost of the mortgage loans purchased or originated. The allocation of the total cost basis of the mortgage loans shall be based on the relative fair values of the mortgage loans and their respective servicing rights.

(ii) Amortization of Mortgage Servicing Rights. SFAS No. 140 requires that amounts capitalized as servicing assets (net of any recorded valuation allowances) be amortized in proportion to, and over the period of, estimated net servicing income. For this purpose, estimates of future servicing revenue shall include expected late charges and other ancillary revenue, including float. Estimates of expected future servicing costs shall include direct costs associated with performing the servicing function and appropriate allocations of other costs. Estimated future servicing costs may be determined on an incremental cost basis.

(iii) Impairment of Mortgage Servicing Rights. For the purpose of evaluating and measuring impairment of servicing assets, SFAS No. 140 requires that servicing assets be stratified based on one or more of the predominant risk characteristics of the underlying loans. Those characteristics may include loan type, size, note rate, date of origination, term, and geographic location. Historically, note or interest rate has been the predominant prepayment risk characteristic considered by most mortgage bankers because in declining interest rate environments, loans have tended to prepay more rapidly with corresponding impairment to the servicing asset.

Impairment shall be recognized through a valuation allowance for an individual stratum. The amount of impairment recognized shall be the amount by which the carrying value of the servicing assets in a stratum exceeds their fair value. The fair value of servicing assets that have not been recognized through a sale or securitization shall not be used in the evaluation of impairment.

Subsequent to the initial measurement of impairment, the mortgage banking enterprise shall adjust the valuation allowance to reflect changes in the measurement of impairment. Fair value in excess of the amount capitalized as servicing assets (net of amortization), however, shall not be recognized. SFAS No. 140 does not address when a mortgage banking enterprise should record a direct write-down of servicing assets.

(iv) Fair Value of Mortgage Servicing Rights. SFAS No. 140 defines the fair value of an asset or a liability as the amount at which that asset or liability could be bought or sold in a current transaction between willing parties, that is, other than in a forced or liquidation sale. Quoted market prices in active markets are the best evidence of fair value and under SFAS No. 140 shall be used as the basis for the measurement, if available.

If quoted market prices are not available, the estimate of fair value shall be based on the best information available in the circumstances. The estimate of fair value shall consider prices for similar assets or liabilities and the results of valuation techniques to the extent available in the circumstances. Examples of valuation techniques include the present value of estimated expected future cash flows using a discount rate commensurate with the risks involved, option-pricing models, matrix pricing, option-adjusted spread models, and fundamental analysis. Valuation techniques for measuring financial assets and liabilities and servicing assets and liabilities shall be consistent with the objective of measuring fair value. Those techniques shall incorporate assumptions that market participants would use in their estimates of values, future revenues, and future expenses, including assumptions about interest rates, default, prepayment, and volatility. In measuring financial liabilities and servicing liabilities at fair value by discounting estimated future cash flows, an objective is to use discount rates at which those liabilities could be settled in an arm's-length transaction.

Estimates of expected future cash flows, if used to estimate fair value, shall be the best estimate based on reasonable and supportable assumptions and projections. All available evidence shall be considered in developing estimates of expected future cash flows. The weight given to the evidence shall be commensurate with the extent to which the evidence can be verified objectively. If a range is estimated for either the amount or timing of possible cash flows, the likelihood of possible outcomes shall be considered in determining the best estimate of future cash flows.

If it is not practicable to estimate the fair values of assets, the transferor shall record those assets at zero. If it is not practicable to estimate the fair values of liabilities, the transferor shall recognize no gain on the transaction and shall record those liabilities at the greater of:

- The excess, if any, of (1) the fair values of assets obtained less the fair values of other liabilities incurred, over (2) the sum of the carrying values of the assets transferred
- The amount that would be recognized in accordance with SFAS No. 5, "Accounting for Contingencies," as interpreted by FASB Interpretation No. 14, "Reasonable Estimation of the Amount of a Loss"

(v) Sales of Mortgage Servicing Rights.   EITF No. 95-5 provides the primary accounting guidance for sales of mortgage servicing rights. The consensus reached in EITF No. 95-5 states that a sale of mortgage servicing rights should be recognized at the date title passes if substantially all risks and rewards of ownership have irrevocably passed to the buyer and any protection provisions retained by the seller are minor and can be reasonably estimated. If a sale is recognized and minor protection provisions exist, a liability should be accrued for the estimated obligation associated with those provisions. The seller retains only minor protection provisions if (a) the obligation associated with those provisions is estimated to be no more than 10 percent of the sales price and (b) the risk of prepayment is retained by the seller for no more than 120 days. The consensus additionally noted that a temporary subservicing agreement in which the seller would subservice the loans for a short period of time after the sale would not necessarily preclude recognizing a sale at the closing date.

(vi) Retained Interests.   In certain asset sale or securitizations transactions, the mortgage banker may retain an interest in the transferred assets. Examples of retained interests include servicing assets, interest-only strips, and retained (or residual) interests in securitizations. Historically, excess servicing resulted from the sale of loans where the contractual service fee (the difference between the mortgage rate and the pass-through rate to the investor in the loans, after deducting any guarantee fees) was greater than a "normal servicing fee rate." This excess servicing asset was then capitalized separately and subsequently accounted for distinctly from the normal servicing asset recorded. Under SFAS No. 140, the accounting distinction for excess servicing fees was eliminated. In general, under agency servicing contracts, past excess servicing fees represent contractually specified servicing fees as defined under SFAS No. 140 and are combined with servicing rights as a servicing asset. The combined servicing asset will then be subject to the stratified impairment test that was described in Subsection 31.3(f)(iii).

Generally, a servicing fee in excess of a contractually stated servicing fee would only be encountered in an instance where an entity securitizes and sells mortgage loans and creates an interest-only strip above and beyond the compensation allocated to the loan's servicer in the pooling and servicing agreements. If it is determined that an entity's "excess servicing fees" exceed contractually specified amounts, those amounts would be required to be classified as interest-only strips under SFAS No. 140.

Interest-only strips are rights to future interest income from the serviced assets that exceed contractually specified servicing fees. Interest-only strips are not servicing assets, they are financial assets. These assets should be originally recorded at allocated cost and subsequently recorded as an available for sale or trading asset in accordance with FAS No. 115.

Retained or residual interests in securitizations represents the mortgage banker's right to receive cash flows from the mortgage assets that are not required to: (1) pay certificate holders their contractual amounts of principal and interest, (2) fund reserve accounts stipulated in the securitization structure, (3) pay expenses of the securitization, and (4) make any other payments stipulated in the securitization. Such retained interests must be evaluated for impairment pursuant to EITF No. 99-20, "Recognition of Interest Income and Impairment on Purchased and Retained Beneficial Interests in Securitized Financial Assets."

(g) TAXATION.   Mortgage banks are subject to federal income taxes and certain state and local taxes. The taxation of mortgage banks is extremely complex; therefore, a discussion in depth is beyond the scope of this book. However, certain significant factors of mortgage banking taxation are discussed below.

(i) Mortgage Servicing Rights.   The tax treatment of servicing rights changed substantially in 1991 for both mortgage loan originators and subsequent purchasers of mortgage loans. Under Rev. Rule 91-46, a lender selling mortgages while retaining the right to service the loans for an amount in excess of reasonable compensation, is deemed to have two types of income resulting from a servicing contract: "normal" (i.e., reasonable) or "excess" servicing compensation.

Generally, taxable income for normal servicing is recognized as received (i.e., as asset is not created at the time of loan sale as it is for book purposes), thus a book to tax difference will exist upon sale of the underlying loan to a third party. Income deemed received for excess servicing is included in income on a yield-to-maturity basis.

The Treasury has provided safe harbor amounts providing guidance to what is deemed normal or reasonable compensation. Normal compensation is for the performance of general mortgage services, including a contract requiring the servicer to collect the periodic mortgage payments from the mortgagors and remit these payments to the owner of the mortgages.

The safe harbors establish that compensation for the performance of all services under the mortgage servicing contracts should generally be between 25 and 44 basis points, annually, determined more specifically on the type of residential loans. Guidance as to reasonable compensation on commercial mortgages has not been provided; it is the taxpayer's responsibility to establish and support what is reasonable compensation for the services it performs.

Excess servicing is those funds received in excess of reasonable compensation, thus the term *excess servicing rights*. Excess servicing rights have been determined to represent a stripped coupon, while the underlying mortgage that was sold represents a stripped bond. The fair value of the stripped coupon (i.e., servicing right) is determined based on the relevant facts and circumstances.

The mortgage servicing business is fueled by volume, thus it is common for a mortgage bank to be an originator of mortgage loans, a purchaser of mortgage loans, and a purchaser of servicing. If both the loan and the servicing right are purchased, and the loan is subsequently sold with servicing retained, tax treatment will generally follow the same treatment as if the seller originated the mortgage loan.

This treatment is significantly different compared to the purchase of only mortgage servicing rights. Purchased mortgage servicing rights (PMSRs) are amortized over 15 years when acquired in connection with a trade or business or over 108 months when a servicing portfolio is separately acquired. Certain restrictions prevent the recognition of loss in value of a servicing portfolio unless the entire portfolio or individually identified loans within a pool of serviced loans are disposed of, thus taxpayers may have difficulty realizing the loss in value of a servicing portfolio that has significant prepayments until all the underlying mortgages have been paid down.

(ii) Mark-to-Market.   Contrary to normal realization-based tax accounting principles, IRC Section 475 requires "dealers in securities" to recognize gain or loss through "marking-to-market" their securities holdings, unless such securities are validly identified by the taxpayer as excepted from the provisions.

As used in this context, the terms "dealer" and "securities" have very broad application. Virtually all financial institutions are considered dealers in securities for mark-to-market purposes, though regulations provide exceptions for certain institutions not engaging in more than de minimus dealer activities. Securities required to be marked (unless validly identified as excepted) include notes, bonds, and other evidences of indebtedness; stock, notional principal contracts; or any evidence of an interest in or a derivative of such security (other than Section 1256(a) contracts); and any clearly identified hedge of such security.

Securities that may be identified as excepted from the mark-to-market provisions are:

- Securities "held for investment" and property identified as such for tax purposes.
- Notes and other evidences of indebtedness (and obligations to acquire such) that are acquired or originated by the taxpayer in the ordinary course of a trade or business that are "not held for sale."
- Hedges of positions or liabilities that are not securities in the hands of the taxpayer, and hedges of position or liabilities that are exempt from mark-to-market under the two foregoing provisions. This does not apply for hedges held as a dealer.

To be excepted from mark-to-market, the securities must be identified by the taxpayer on a contemporaneous basis (generally day of acquisition) as meeting one of the above exceptions.

Whether or not a security is required to be marked-to-market for financial accounting purposes is *not* dispositive for purposes of determining whether such security is treated as "held for investment" or "not held for sale."

Some financial institutions identify all or a significant portion of their loans to customers as excepted from mark-to-market provisions because they intend to hold these loans to maturity. A possible exception are mortgages that are originated for sale (pipeline or warehoused loans), which do not meet the exception criteria and must be marked-to-market.

31.4 INVESTMENT COMPANIES

(a) BACKGROUND.   An investment company (referred to as a *fund* or a *mutual fund*) generally pools investors' funds to provide them with professional investment management and diversification of ownership in the securities markets. Typically, an investment company sells its capital shares to the public and invests the net proceeds in stock, bonds, government obligations, or other securities, intended to meet the fund's stated investment objectives. A brief history of investment companies is included in paragraphs 1.07 and 1.08 of the *AICPA Audit and Accounting Guide*, "Audits of Investment Companies." One of the more notable distinctions between investment companies and companies in other industries is the extremely high degree of compliance to which registered investment companies must adhere.

(i) Securities and Exchange Commission Statutes.   The SEC is responsible for the administration and enforcement of the following statutes governing investment companies:

- *The Investment Company Act of 1940 (the "1940 Act")*. Regulates registered investment companies and provides extensive rules and regulations that govern record keeping, reporting, fiduciary duties, and other responsibilities of an investment company's management.
- *The Investment Advisers Act of 1940.* Requires persons who are paid to render investment advice to individuals or institutions, including investment companies, to register with the SEC and regulates their conduct and contracts.
- *The Securities Act of 1933.* Governs the content of prospectuses and addresses the public offering and distribution of securities (including debt securities and the capital shares of investment companies).

- *The Securities Exchange Act of 1934.* Regulates the trading of securities in secondary markets after the initial public offering and distribution of the securities under the 1933 Act. Periodic SEC financial reporting requirements pursuant to Section 13 or Section 15(d) of the 1934 Act are satisfied by the semiannual filing of Form N-SAR pursuant to Section 30 of the 1940 Act.

(ii) Types of Investment Companies.   Three common methods of classification are (1) by securities law definition, (2) by investment objectives, and (3) by form of organization.

Classification by Securities Law Definition.   Securities law divides investment companies into three types: management companies, face amount certificate companies, and unit investment trusts. The most common classification is the management company. The term *mutual fund* refers to an open-end management company as described under Section 5 of the 1940 Act. Such a fund stands ready to redeem its shares at net asset value whenever requested to do so and usually continuously offers its shares for sale, although it is not required to do so. A closed-end management company does not stand ready to redeem its shares when requested (although it may occasionally make tender offers for its shares) and generally does not issue additional shares, except perhaps in connection with a dividend reinvestment program. Its outstanding shares are usually traded on an exchange, often at a premium or discount from the fund's underlying net asset value. In addition to open-end and closed-end management companies, there are also management companies that offer the ability for shareholders to periodically redeem their shares on specified dates or intervals.

Other management investment companies include Small Business Investment Companies and Business Development Companies (SBICs and BDCs, respectively). Management companies, at their own election, are further divided into diversified companies and nondiversified companies. A fund that elects to be a diversified company must meet the 75 percent test required under Section 5(b)(1) of the 1940 Act. Nondiversified companies are management companies that have elected to be nondiversified and do not have to meet the requirements of Section 5(b)(1).

The 1940 Act also provides for face amount certificate companies, which are rather rare, and unit investment trusts. Unit investment trusts normally are established under a trust indenture by a sponsoring organization that acquires a portfolio (often tax-exempt or taxable bonds that are generally held to maturity) and then sells undivided interests in the trust. Units of the trust may be offered continuously, such as for a trust purchasing treasury securities, but normally do not make any additional portfolio acquisitions. Units remain outstanding until they are tendered for redemption or the trust is terminated.

Separate accounts of an insurance company that underlie variable annuity and variable life insurance products are also subject to the requirements of the 1940 Act. They may be established as management companies or as unit investment trusts. Variable annuities and variable life products are considered to be both securities subject to the 1933 Act and insurance products subject to regulation by state insurance departments.

Classification by Investment Objectives.   Investment companies can also be classified by their investment objectives or types of investments, for example, growth funds, income funds, tax-exempt funds, global funds, money market funds, and equity funds.

Classification by Form of Organization.   Investment companies can also be classified by their form of organization. Funds may be organized as corporations or trusts (and, to a lesser extent, as partnerships).

Incorporation offers the advantages of detailed state statutory and interpretative judicial decisions governing operations and limited liability of shareholders, and, in normal cases, it requires no exemptions to comply with the 1940 Act.

The business trust, or Massachusetts Trust, is an unincorporated business association established by a declaration or deed of trust and governed largely by the law of trusts. In general, a business trust has the advantages of unlimited authorized shares, no annual meeting requirement, and long duration. However, Massachusetts Trusts have a potential disadvantage in that there is unlimited liability to the business trust shareholders in the event of litigation or other negative factors. Generally, however, the Trust undertakes to indemnify the shareholders against loss.

(b) FUND OPERATIONS.   When a new fund is established, it enters into a contract with an investment adviser (often the sponsoring organization) to manage the fund and, within the terms of the fund's stated investment objectives, to determine what securities should be purchased, sold, or exchanged. The investment adviser places orders for the purchase or sale of portfolio securities for the fund with brokers or dealers selected by it. The officers of the fund, who generally are also officers of the investment adviser or fund administrator, give instructions to the custodian of the fund holdings as to delivery of securities and payments of cash for the account of the fund. The investment adviser normally furnishes, at its own expense, all necessary advisory services, facilities, and personnel in connection with these responsibilities. The investment adviser may also act as administrator; administrative duties include preparation of regulatory filings and managing relationships with other service providers. The investment adviser and administrator are usually paid for these services through a fee based on the value of net assets.

The distributor or underwriter for an investment company markets the shares of the fund—either directly to the public ("no-load" funds) or through a sales force. The sales force may be compensated for their services through a direct sales commission included in (deducted from) the price at which the fund's shares are offered (redeemed), through a distribution fee (also referred to as a *12b-1 plan fee*) paid by the fund as part of its recurring expenses, or in both ways. Rule 12b-1 under the 1940 Act permits an investment company to pay for distribution expenses, which otherwise are paid for by the distributor and not the fund.

A fund has officers and directors (and in some cases, trustees) but generally has no employees, the services it requires being provided under contract by others. Primary servicing organizations are summarized below.

(i) Fund Accounting Agent.   The fund accounting agent maintains the fund's general ledger and portfolio accounting records and computes the net asset value per share, usually on a daily basis. In some instances, this service is provided by the investment adviser or an affiliate of the adviser, or a nonaffiliated entity may perform this service. The fund accounting agent, or in some cases a separate administrative agent, may also be responsible for preparation of the fund's financial statements, tax returns, semiannual and annual filings with the SEC on Form N-SAR, and the annual registration statement filing.

(ii) Custodian.   The custodian maintains custody of the fund's assets, collects income, pays expenses, and settles investment transactions. The 1940 Act provides for three alternatives in selecting a custodian. The most commonly used is a commercial bank or trust company that meets the requirements of Sections 17 and 26 of the 1940 Act. The second alternative is a member firm of a national securities exchange; the third alternative is for the fund to act as its own custodian and utilize the safekeeping facilities of a bank or trust company. Section 17(f) and Rules 17f-1 and 17f-2 of the 1940 Act provide for specific audit procedures to be performed by the fund's independent accountant when either alternative two or three is used.

(iii) Transfer Agent.   The fund's transfer agent maintains the shareholder records and processes the sales and redemptions of the fund's capital shares. The transfer agent processes the capital share transactions at a price per share equal to the net asset value per share of the fund next determined by the fund accounting agent (forward pricing). In certain instances, shareholder servicing—the direct contact with shareholders, usually by telephone—is combined with the transfer agent processing.

(c) ACCOUNTING.   The *AICPA Audit and Accounting Guide*, "Audits of Investment Companies" (May 1, 2001) (the "Audit Guide") provides specific guidance on accounting issues relevant to investment companies. The SEC has set forth in Financial Reporting Policies, Section 404.03,

"Accounting, Valuation, and Disclosure of Investment Securities," its views on accounting for securities by registered investment companies.

Because for federal income tax purposes the fund is a conduit for the shareholders, the operations of an investment company are normally influenced by federal income tax to the shareholder. Accordingly, conformity between book and tax accounting is usually maintained whenever practicable under GAAP. In general, investment companies carry securities, which are their most significant asset, at current value, not at historical cost. In such a "mark-to-market" environment, the deviation between book and tax accounting has no effect on net asset value.

Uniquely, most mutual funds close their books daily and calculate a net asset value per share, which forms the pricing basis for shareholders who are purchasing or redeeming fund shares. SEC Rules 2a-4 and 22c-1 set forth certain accounting requirements, including a one cent per share pricing criterion. Because of this daily closing of the books, mutual funds and their agents must maintain well-controlled and current accounting systems to provide proper records for their highly compliance-oriented industry.

The SEC has promulgated extensive rules under each of the statutes that it administers, including the following:

- *Article 6 of Regulation S-X (Article 3-18 and Article 12-12).* Sets forth requirements as to the form and content of, and requirements for, financial statements filed with the SEC, including what financial statements must be presented and for what periods.
- *Financial reporting policies.* Section 404 relates specifically to registered investment companies.

(d) FINANCIAL REPORTING.

(i) New Registrants. Any company registered under the 1940 Act that has not previously had an effective registration statement under the 1933 Act must include, in its initial registration statement, financial statements, and financial highlights of a date within 90 days prior to the date of filing. For a company that did not have any prior operations, this would be limited to a seed capital statement of assets and liabilities and related notes.

Section 14 of the 1940 Act requires that an investment company have a net worth of at least $100,000. Accordingly, a new investment company is usually incorporated by its sponsor with seed capital of that amount.

(ii) General Reporting Requirements. The SEC reporting requirements are outlined in Section 30 of the 1940 Act and the related rules and regulations thereunder, which supersede any requirements under Section 13 or Section 15(d) of the 1934 Act to which an investment company would otherwise be subject. A registered management investment company is deemed by the SEC to have satisfied its requirement under the 1934 Act to file an annual report by the filing of semiannual reports on Form N-SAR.

The SEC requires that every registered management company send to its shareholders, at least semiannually, a report containing financial statements and financial highlights. Only the financial statements and financial highlights in the annual report are required to be audited.

Some funds prepare quarterly reports to shareholders, although they are not required to do so. They generally include a portfolio listing, and in relatively few cases, they include full financial statements. Closed-end funds listed on an exchange have certain quarterly reporting requirements under their listing agreements with the exchange.

(iii) Financial Statements. Article 6 of Regulation S-X deals specifically with investment companies and requires the following statements:

- A statement of assets and liabilities (supported by a separate listing of portfolio securities) or a statement of net assets, which includes a detailed list of portfolio securities at the reporting date

- A statement of operations for the year
- A statement of changes in net assets for the latest two years

SFAS No. 95 provides that a statement of cash flows should be included with financial statements prepared in accordance with GAAP. SFAS No. 102 exempts investment companies from providing a statement of cash flows, provided certain conditions are met. A statement of changes in net assets should be presented even if the statement of cash flows is presented because a statement of changes in net assets presents the changes in shareholders' equity required by GAAP and by Article 6 of Regulation S-X.

(e) TAXATION.   Investment companies are subject to federal income taxes and certain state and local taxes. However, investment companies registered under the 1940 Act may qualify for special federal income tax treatment as regulated investment companies (RICs) under the IRC and may deduct dividends paid to shareholders. If a fund fails to qualify as a RIC, it will be taxed as a regular corporation, and the deduction for dividends paid by the fund is disallowed. Subchapter M (§§851–855) of the IRC applies to RICs. Chapter 6 of the Audit Guide discusses the tax considerations related to RICs.

To qualify as a RIC, the fund must:

- Be a domestic entity registered under the 1940 Act
- Derive 90 percent of its total income from dividends, interest, and gross gains on sales of securities
- Have 50 percent of its assets composed of cash, U.S. government securities, securities of other funds, and "other issues," as defined
- Have not more than 25 percent of the value of its total assets invested in the securities (other than U.S. government securities or the securities of other regulated investment companies) of any one issuer or of two or more issuers controlled by the fund that are determined to be engaged in the same or similar trades or businesses

In order for a RIC to use its distributions to offset taxable income, it must distribute at least 90 percent of its net investment company taxable income and net tax-exempt interest income to its shareholders. Also, to avoid a 4 percent nondeductible excise tax, a fund must distribute, by December 31 of each year, 98 percent of its ordinary income measured on a calendar year basis and 98 percent of its net capital gains measured on a fiscal year basis ending October 31. Actual payment of the distribution must be before February 1 of the following year.

(f) FILINGS.   SEC registration forms applicable to investment companies include the following:

- *Form N-8A.* The notification of registration under the 1940 Act.
- *Form N-1A.* The registration statement of open-end management investment companies under the 1940 and the 1933 Acts. (It is not to be used by SBICs, BDCs, or insurance company separate accounts.) The Form describes in detail the company's objectives, policies, management, investment restrictions, and similar matters. The Form consists of the prospectus, the statement of additional information (SAI), and a third section of other information, including detailed information on the SEC-required yield calculations. Post-effective amendments on Form N-1A, including updated audited financial statements, must be filed and become effective under the 1933 and 1940 Acts within 16 months after the end of the period covered by the previous audited financial statements if the fund is to continue offering its shares.
- *Form N-SAR.* A reporting form used for semiannual and annual reports by all registered investment companies that have filed a registration statement that has become effective pursuant to the 1933 Act, with the exception of face amount certificate companies and BDCs. BDCs file periodic reports pursuant to Section 13 of the 1934 Act. Management investment

companies file the form semiannually; unit investment trusts are only required to file annually. There is no requirement that the form or any of the items be audited. The annual report filed by a management investment company must be accompanied by a report on the company's system of internal accounting controls from its independent accountant. The requirement for an accountant's report on internal accounting controls does not apply to SBICs or to management investment companies not required by either the 1940 Act or any other federal or state law or rule or regulation thereunder to have an audit of their financial statements.

- *Form N-2.* A registration statement for closed-end funds comparable to Form N-1A for open-end funds. Under Rule 8b-16 of the 1940 Act, if certain criteria are met in the Annual Report of a closed-end fund, the fund may not need to annually update its Form N-2 filing with the SEC.

- *Forms N-1, N-3, N-4, and N-6.* The registration statements for various types of insurance-related products, including variable annuities and variable life insurance.

- *Form N-5.* The registration statement for SBICs, which are also licensed under the Small Business Investment Act of 1958, is used to register the SBIC under both the 1933 Act and the 1940 Act.

- *Form N-14.* The statement for registration of securities issued by investment companies in business combination transactions under the 1933 Act. It contains information about the companies involved in the transaction, including historical and pro forma financial statements.

(g) INVESTMENT PARTNERSHIPS—SPECIAL CONSIDERATIONS.   Investment partnerships may be described generally as limited partnerships organized under state law to trade and/or invest in securities. They are sometimes also referred to as *hedge funds*, which has become a generic industry term for an investment partnership (or another nonpublic investment company), although this may be a misnomer depending on the partnership's investment strategy. Investment partnerships, if certain conditions are met, are generally not required to register under the 1940 Act and are also generally not subject to the Internal Revenue Code rules and regulations that apply to RICs.

An investment partnership is governed by its partnership agreement. This is the basis for legal, structural, operational, and accounting guidelines. The majority of the capital in an investment partnership is owned by its limited partners. The general partner usually has a minimal investment in the partnership, if any at all. Limited partners may be a variety of entities, including private and public pension plans, foreign investors, insurance companies, bank holding companies, and individuals. There are legal, regulatory, and accounting and tax considerations associated with each of the above types of investors. For example, investment in an investment partnership by pension plans may subject the investment partnership to the rules and regulations of the Employee Retirement Income Security Act of 1974 (ERISA) (generally, investment partnerships will not be subject to ERISA if less than 25 percent of the partnership's capital is derived from pension or other employee benefit plan assets); foreign investors may be subject to foreign withholding taxes; and the number of partners in an investment partnership may subject the investment partnership to registration under the 1940 Act (generally, an investment partnership must have fewer than 100 partners [or must have partners who are all "qualified purchasers"] to avoid registration under the 1940 Act).

The limited partners are generally liable for the repayment and discharge of all debts and obligations of the investment partnership, but only to the extent of their respective interest in the partnership. They usually have no part in the management of the partnership and have no authority to act on behalf of the partnership in connection with any matter. The general partner can be an individual, a corporation, or other entity. The general partner usually has little or no investment in the investment partnership (often one percent of total contributed capital) and is responsible for the day-to-day administration of the investment partnership. The general partner, however, usually has unlimited liability for the repayment and discharge of all debts and obligations of the partnership irrespective of its interest in the partnership. The general partner may also be the investment adviser or an affiliate of the adviser.

Although investment partnerships are generally not "investment companies" as defined in federal securities laws, they do meet the definition of investment companies as contained in the Audit Guide. Accordingly, the Audit Guide is generally applicable to investment partnerships. There are, however, certain disclosure requirements in the Audit Guide to which most partnerships have historically taken exception and have not followed. The AICPA clarified the appropriate disclosure for partnerships in its issuance of SOP 95-2, "Financial Reporting for Nonpublic Investment Partnerships," as amended by SOP 01-1, "Amendment to Scope of Statement of Position 95-2," which is applicable for fiscal years beginning after December 15, 1994.

A partnership is classified as a pass-through entity for tax purposes, meaning that the partners, not the partnership, are taxed on the income, expenses, gains, and losses incurred by the partnership. The partners recognize the tax effects of the partnership's operations regardless of whether any distribution is made to such partners. This differs from a corporation, which incurs an entity level tax on its earnings and whose owners (stockholders) incur a second level of tax when the corporation's profits are distributed to them.

(h) OFFSHORE FUNDS—SPECIAL CONSIDERATIONS.   Offshore funds may be described generally as investment funds set up to permit international investments with minimum tax burden on the fund shareholders. This is achieved by setting up the funds in countries with favorable tax laws, as well as in countries with nonburdensome administrative regulations. Popular offshore locations include Bermuda, the Cayman Islands, and the Netherlands Antilles.

An offshore fund's shares are offered to investors (generally non-U.S.) residing outside the country in which the fund is domiciled. Assuming the offshore fund is not publicly sold in the United States and does not have more than 100 U.S. shareholders (or only "qualified purchasers"), the offshore fund will not be subject to SEC registration or reporting requirements. Similar to hedge funds, because of the lack of regulatory restrictions, offshore funds often have higher risk investment strategies than U.S. regulated funds.

A major U.S. tax advantage to non-U.S. shareholders of investing in U.S. securities through an offshore fund as opposed to a U.S. domiciled fund is the avoidance of certain U.S. withholding taxes. By investing through the offshore fund, the shareholder avoids withholding taxes on most U.S.-sourced interest income and short-term capital gains, which would be subject to withholding taxes if the amounts were paid to the non-U.S. shareholder through a U.S. domiciled fund. Offshore funds also avoid the U.S. Internal Revenue Code distribution requirements imposed on U.S. funds. This allows for the potential "roll-up" of income in the fund (i.e., the deferral of income recognition for the shareholder for tax purposes, depending on the tax residence of the shareholder).

Under new tax legislation, a fund's U.S. administrative and other activities, which were previously required to be performed offshore to comply with IRC Reg. Sec. 1.864– 2(c)2 (the "Ten Commandments"), generally will not create tax nexus for U.S. federal income tax purposes. However, depending on the laws of the particular jurisdiction in which its U.S. activities are conducted, those same U.S. activities may under some circumstances create tax nexus in certain state or local jurisdictions. Careful consideration should be given to the potential state and local tax consequences of onshore activities before any activities that were previously recommended to be conducted outside the United States are brought onshore.

Fund managers and advisers should consider several nontax factors before bringing certain functions onshore. These include the following:

- Whether the performance of more operations onshore will make it more likely that the fund, manager, and/or advisers can be subject to the jurisdiction of U.S. courts and/or applicable U.S., state, or local laws and regulations
- The regulatory requirements of the fund's domicile (e.g., Luxembourg, Dublin, and Bermuda require administration and certain other functions to be performed locally)
- The investor's desire for confidentiality
- The potential applicability of federal, state, and local tax or other filing requirements
- The potential effect on prospectus disclosure

31.5 SOURCES AND SUGGESTED REFERENCES

Accounting Principles Board Opinion 30, "Reporting the Results of Operations—Reporting the Effects of Disposal of a Segment of a Business and Extraordinary, Unusual and Infrequently Occurring Events and Transactions." AICPA, New York, 1973.

American Institute of Certified Public Accountants Audit and Accounting Guide "Banks and Savings Institutions." AICPA, New York, 1997.

———, "Audits of Investment Companies." AICPA, New York, 2001.

Cammarano, Nicholas, and James J. Klink Jr. *Real Estate Accounting and Reporting: A Guide for Developers, Investors, and Lenders.* Third Edition. John Wiley & Sons, New York, 1995.

Financial Accounting Standards Board, Statement of Financial Accounting Standards No. 5, "Accounting for Contingencies." FASB, Stamford, CT, 1975.

———, Statement of Financial Accounting Standards No. 15, "Accounting by Debtors and Creditors for Troubled Debt Restructurings." FASB, Stamford, CT, 1977.

———, Statement of Financial Accounting Standards No. 34, "Capitalization of Interest Cost." FASB, Stamford, CT, 1979.

———, Statement of Financial Accounting Standards No. 52, "Foreign Currency Translation." FASB, Stamford, CT, 1981.

———, Statement of Financial Accounting Standards No. 58, "Capitalization of Interest Cost in Financial Statements That Include Investments Accounted for by the Equity Method." FASB, Stamford, CT, 1982.

———, Statement of Financial Accounting Standards No. 65, "Accounting for Certain Mortgage Banking Activities." FASB, Stamford, CT, 1982.

———, Statement of Financial Accounting Standards No. 66, "Accounting for Sales of Real Estate." FASB, Stamford, CT, 1982.

———, Statement of Financial Accounting Standards No. 67, "Accounting for Costs and Initial Rental Operations of Real Estate Projects." FASB, Stamford, CT, 1982.

———, Statement of Financial Accounting Standards No. 72, "Accounting for Certain Acquisitions of Banking or Thrift Institutions (an Amendment of APB Opinion No. 17, an Interpretation of APB Opinions No. 16 and 17, and an Amendment of FASB Interpretation No. 9)." FASB, Norwalk, CT, 1983.

———, Statement of Financial Accounting Standards No. 77, "Reporting by Transferors for Transfers of Receivables with Recourse." FASB, Stamford, CT, 1983.

———, Statement of Financial Accounting Standards No. 80, "Accounting for Futures." FASB, Stamford, CT, 1984.

———, Statement of Financial Accounting Standards No. 91, "Accounting for Nonrefundable Fees and Costs Associated with Originating or Acquiring Loans and Initial Direct Costs of Leases (an Amendment of FASB Statements No. 13, 60, and 65 and a Rescission of FASB Statement No. 17)." FASB, Stamford, CT, 1986.

———, Statement of Financial Accounting Standards No. 95, "Statement of Cash Flow." FASB, Norwalk, CT, 1987.

———, Statement of Financial Accounting Standards No. 102, "Statement of Cash Flows—Exception of Certain Enterprises and Classification of Cash Flows from Certain Securities Acquired for Resale (an amendment of FASB Statement No. 95.)." FASB, Norwalk, CT, 1989.

———, Statement of Financial Accounting Standards No. 104, "Statement of Cash Flows—Net Reporting of Certain Cash Receipts and Cash Payments and Classification of Cash Flows from Hedging Transactions (an Amendment of FASB Statement No. 95)." FASB, Norwalk, CT, 1989.

———, Statement of Financial Accounting Standards No. 105, "Disclosure of Information about Financial Instruments Off-Balance Sheet Risk and Financial Instruments with Concentrations of Credit Risk." FASB, Norwalk, CT, 1990.

———, Statement of Financial Accounting Standards No. 107, "Disclosures About Fair Value of Financial Instruments." FASB, Norwalk, CT, 1991.

———, Statement of Financial Accounting Standards No. 114, "Accounting by Creditors for Impairment of a Loan (an Amendment of FASB Statements 5 and 15)." FASB, Norwalk, CT, 1993.

———, Statement of Financial Accounting Standards No. 115, "Accounting for Certain Investments in Debt and Equity Securities." FASB, Norwalk, CT, 1993.

_____, Statement of Financial Accounting Standards No. 118, "Accounting by Creditors for Impairment of a Loan-Income Recognition and Disclosures (an Amendment of FASB Statement 114)." FASB, Norwalk, CT, 1994.

_____, Statement of Financial Accounting Standards No. 119, "Disclosures about Derivative Financial Instruments and Fair Value of Financial Instruments." FASB, Norwalk, CT, 1994.

_____, Statement of Financial Accounting Standards No. 121, "Accounting for the Impairment of Long-Lived Assets and for Long-Lived Assets to Be Disposed Of." FASB, Norwalk, CT, 1995.

_____, Statement of Financial Accounting Standards No. 122, "Accounting for Mortgage Servicing Rights." FASB, Norwalk, CT, 1995.

_____, Statement of Financial Accounting Standards No. 125, "Accounting for Transfers and Servicing of Financial Assets and Extinguishments of Liabilities." FASB, Norwalk, CT, 1996.

_____, Statement of Financial Accounting Standards No. 126, "Exemption from Certain Required Disclosures about Financial Instruments for Certain Nonpublic Entities (an Amendment of FASB Statement No. 107)." FASB, Norwalk, CT, 1996.

_____, Statement of Financial Accounting Standards No. 127, "Deferral of the Effective Date of Certain Provisions of FASB Statement No. 125 (an Amendment of FASB Statement No. 125)." FASB, Norwalk, CT, 1996.

_____, Interpretation No. 9, "Applying APB Opinions No. 16 and 17 When a Savings and Loan Association or a Similar Institution Is Acquired in a Business Combination Accounted for by the Purchase Method." FASB, Norwalk, CT, 1976.

_____, Interpretation No. 39, "Offsetting of Amounts Related to Certain Contracts." FASB, Norwalk, CT, 1992.

_____, Interpretation No. 41, "Offsetting of Amounts Related to Certain Repurchase and Reverse Repurchase Agreements—An Interpretation of APB Opinion No. 10 and a Modification of FASB Interpretation No. 39." FASB, Norwalk, CT, 1994.

_____, Technical Bulletin 85-2, "Accounting for Collateralized Mortgage Obligations." FASB, Norwalk, CT, 1985.

_____, Technical Bulletin 94-1, "Application of Statement 115 to Debt Securities Restructured in a Troubled Debt Restructuring." FASB, Norwalk, CT, 1994.

Accounting Standards Division, Statement of Position 78-9, "Accounting for Investments in Real Estate Ventures." AICPA, New York, 1978.

_____, Statement of Position 92-3, "Accounting For Foreclosed Assets." AICPA, New York, 1992.

_____, Statement of Position 94-6, "Disclosure of Certain Significant Risks and Uncertainties." AICPA, New York, 1994.

_____, Statement of Position 95-2, "Financial Reporting for Nonpublic Investment Partnerships." AICPA, New York, 1995.

_____, Statement of Position 97-1, "Accounting by Participating Mortgage Loan Borrowers." AICPA, New York, 1997.

_____, Statement of Position 01-1, "Amendment to Scope of Statement of Position 95-2, Financial Reporting for Nonpublic Investment Partnerships," New York 2001.

Financial Accounting Standards Board, EITF Abstracts: A Summary of Proceedings of the FASB Emerging Issues Task Force, EITF Issue No. 84-7, "Termination of Interest Rate Swaps." FASB, Norwalk, CT, 1984.

_____, EITF Abstracts: A Summary of Proceedings of the FASB Emerging Issues Task Force, EITF Issue No. 84-14, "Deferred Interest Rate Setting." FASB, Norwalk, CT, 1984.

_____, EITF Abstracts: A Summary of Proceedings of the FASB Emerging Issues Task Force, EITF Issue No. 84-36, "Interest Rate Swap Transactions." FASB, Norwalk, CT, 1984.

_____, EITF Abstracts: A Summary of Proceedings of the FASB Emerging Issues Task Force, EITF Issue No. 85-6, "Futures Implementation Question." FASB, Norwalk, CT, 1985.

_____, EITF Abstracts: A Summary of Proceedings of the FASB Emerging Issues Task Force, EITF Issue No. 86-25, "Offsetting Foreign Currency Swaps." FASB, Norwalk, CT, 1986.

_____, EITF Abstracts: A Summary of Proceedings of the FASB Emerging Issues Task Force, EITF Issue No. 86-28, "Accounting Implications of Indexed Debt Instruments." FASB, Norwalk, CT, 1986.

_____, EITF Abstracts: A Summary of Proceedings of the FASB Emerging Issues Task Force, EITF Issue No. 87-1, "Deferral Accounting for Cash Securities That Are Used to Hedge Rate or Price Risk." FASB, Norwalk, CT, 1987.

_____, EITF Abstracts: A Summary of Proceedings of the FASB Emerging Issues Task Force, EITF Issue No. 87-26, "Hedging of Foreign Currency Exposure with a Tandem Currency." FASB, Norwalk, CT, 1987.

_____, EITF Abstracts: A Summary of Proceedings of the FASB Emerging Issues Task Force, EITF Issue No. 88-8, "Mortgage Swaps." FASB, Norwalk, CT, 1988.

_____, EITF Abstracts: A Summary of Proceedings of the FASB Emerging Issues Task Force, EITF Issue No. 88-11, "Allocation of Recorded Investment When a Loan or Part of a Loan Is Sold." FASB, Norwalk, CT, 1995.

_____, EITF Abstracts: A Summary of Proceedings of the FASB Emerging Issues Task Force, EITF Issue No. 90-17, "Hedging Foreign Currency Risk with Purchased Options." FASB, Norwalk, CT, 1990.

_____, EITF Abstracts: A Summary of Proceedings of the FASB Emerging Issues Task Force, EITF Issue No. 91-1, "Hedging Intercompany Foreign Currency Risks." FASB, Norwalk, CT, 1991.

_____, EITF Abstracts: A Summary of Proceedings of the FASB Emerging Issues Task Force, EITF Issue No. 91-4, "Hedging Foreign Currency Risk with Complex Options and Similar Transactions." FASB, Norwalk, CT, 1991.

_____, EITF Abstracts: A Summary of Proceedings of the FASB Emerging Issues Task Force, EITF Issue No. 93-10, "Accounting for Dual Currency Bonds." FASB, Norwalk, CT, 1993.

_____, EITF Abstracts: A Summary of Proceedings of the FASB Emerging Issues Task Force, EITF Issue No. 94-7, "Accounting for Financial Instruments Indexed to, and Potentially Settled in, a Company's Own Stock." FASB, Norwalk, CT, 1994.

_____, EITF Abstracts: A Summary of Proceedings of the FASB Emerging Issues Task Force, EITF Issue No. 94-8, "Accounting for Conversion of a Loan into a Debt Security in a Debt Restructuring." FASB, Norwalk, CT, 1994.

_____, EITF Abstracts: A Summary of Proceedings of the FASB Emerging Issues Task Force, EITF Issue No. 94-9, "Determining a Normal Servicing Fee Rate for the Sale of an SBA Loan." FASB, Norwalk, CT, 1994.

_____, EITF Abstracts: A Summary of Proceedings of the FASB Emerging Issues Task Force, EITF Issue No. 95-2, "Determination of What Constitutes a Firm Commitment for Foreign Currency Transactions Not Involving a Third Party." FASB, Norwalk, CT, 1995.

_____, EITF Abstracts: A Summary of Proceedings of the FASB Emerging Issues Task Force, EITF Issue No. 95-5, "Determination of What Risks and Rewards, If Any, Can Be Retained and Whether Any Unresolved Contingencies May Exist in a Sale of Mortgage Loan Servicing Rights." FASB, Norwalk, CT, 1995.

_____, EITF Abstracts: A Summary of Proceedings of the FASB Emerging Issues Task Force, EITF Issue No. 95-11, "Accounting for Derivative Instruments Containing Both a Written Option-Based Component and a Forward-Based Component." FASB, Norwalk, CT, 1995.

_____, EITF Abstracts: A Summary of Proceedings of the FASB Emerging Issues Task Force, EITF Issue No. 96-1, "Sale of Put Options on Issuer's Stock that Require or Permit Cash Settlement." FASB, Norwalk, CT, 1996.

_____, EITF Abstracts: A Summary of Proceedings of the FASB Emerging Issues Task Force, EITF Issue No. 96-2, "Impairment Recognition When a Nonmonetary Asset Is Exchanged or Is Distributed to Owners and Is Accounted the Asset's Recorded Amount." FASB, Norwalk, CT, 1996.

_____, EITF Abstracts: A Summary of Proceedings of the FASB Emerging Issues Task Force, EITF Issue No. 96-10, "Impact of Certain Transactions on the Held-to-Maturity Classification under FASB Statement No. 115." FASB, Norwalk, CT, 1996.

_____, EITF Abstracts: A Summary of Proceedings of the FASB Emerging Issues Task Force, EITF Issue No. 96-11, "Accounting for Forward Contracts and Purchased Options to Acquire Securities Covered by FASB Statement No. 115." FASB, Norwalk, CT, 1996.

_____, EITF Abstracts: A Summary of Proceedings of the FASB Emerging Issues Task Force, EITF Issue No. 96-12, "Recognition of Interest Income and Balance Sheet Classification of Structured Notes." FASB, Norwalk, CT, 1996.

_____, EITF Abstracts: A Summary of Proceedings of the FASB Emerging Issues Task Force, EITF Issue No. 96-13, "Accounting for Derivative Financial Instruments Indexed to, and Potentially Settled in, a Company's Own Stock." FASB, Norwalk, CT, 1996.

_____, EITF Abstracts: A Summary of Proceedings of the FASB Emerging Issues Task Force, EITF Issue No. 96-14, "Accounting for the Costs Associated with Modifying Computer Software for the Year 2000." FASB, Norwalk, CT, 1996.

_____, EITF Abstracts: A Summary of Proceedings of the FASB Emerging Issues Task Force, EITF Issue No. 96-15, "Accounting for the Effects of Changes in Foreign Currency Exchange Rates on Foreign-Currency-Denominated Available-for-Sale Debt Securities." FASB, Norwalk, CT, 1996.

_____, EITF Abstracts: A Summary of Proceedings of the FASB Emerging Issues Task Force, EITF Issue No. 96-19, "Debtor's Accounting for a Substantive Modification and Exchange of Debt Instruments." FASB, Norwalk, CT, 1996.

_____, EITF Abstracts: A Summary of Proceedings of the FASB Emerging Issues Task Force, EITF Issue No. 96-20, "Impact of FASB Statement No. 125 on Consolidation of Special-Purpose Entities." FASB, Norwalk, CT, 1996.

_____, EITF Abstracts: A Summary of Proceedings of the FASB Emerging Issues Task Force, EITF Issue No. 96-22, "Applicability of the Disclosure Required by FASB Statement No. 114 When a Loan Is Restructured in a Troubled Debt Restructuring into Two (or More) Loans." FASB, Norwalk, CT, 1996.

_____, EITF Abstracts: A Summary of Proceedings of the FASB Emerging Issues Task Force, EITF Issue No. 96-23, "The Effect of Financial Instruments Indexed to, and Settled in, a Company's Own Stock of Pooling-of-Interests Accounting for a Subsequent Business Combination." FASB, Norwalk, CT, 1996.

_____, EITF Abstracts: A Summary of Proceedings of the FASB Emerging Issues Task Force, EITF Issue No. 97-3, "Accounting for Fees and Costs Associated with Loan Syndications and Loan Participations after the Issuance of FASB Statement No. 125." FASB, Norwalk, CT, 1997.

_____, EITF Abstracts: A Summary of Proceedings of the FASB Emerging Issues Task Force, EITF Issue No. 97-7, "Accounting for Hedges of Foreign Currency Risk Inherent in an Available-for-Sale Marketable Equity Security." FASB, Norwalk, CT, 1997.

_____, EITF Abstracts: A Summary of Proceedings of the FASB Emerging Issues Task Force, EITF Issue No. 97-9, "Effect on Pooling-of-Interests Accounting of Certain Contingently Exercisable Options or Other Equity Instruments." FASB, Norwalk, CT, 1997.

_____, AICPA Practice Bulletin No. 1, "Purpose and Scope of AcSEC Practice Bulletins and Procedures for Their Issuance (1987), including the following: Exhibit I—ADC Arrangements (1986)—provides guidance in accounting for Acquisition, Development and Construction (ADC) arrangements in which the leader participates in an expected residual profit, such as an equity kicker." AICPA, New York, 1987.

_____, AICPA Practice Bulletin No. 4, "Accounting for Foreign Debt/Equity Swaps." AICPA, New York, 1988.

_____, AICPA Practice Bulletin No. 5, "Income Recognition on Loans to Financially Troubled Countries." AICPA, New York, 1998.

_____, AICPA Practice Bulletin No. 6, "Amortization of Discounts on Certain Acquired Loans." AICPA, New York, 1989.

Securities and Exchange Commission, "Regulation S-X, Article 9, Bank Holding Companies.

_____, Securities Act Guide 3, Statistical Disclosure by Bank Holding Companies.

Securities and Exchange Commission, "Financial Reporting Policies, Section 401 Banks and Holding Companies," Financial Reporting Release No. 1, Section 404.03, "Accounting, Valuation, and Disclosure of Investment Securities," (Accounting Series Release No. 118, "Accounting for Investment Securities by Registered Investment Companies"). Warren, Gorham & Lamont, Boston, MA, 1995.

_____, Staff Accounting Bulletin No. 50, "Financial Statement Requirements in Filings Involving the Formation of a One-Bank Holding Company." SEC, Washington, DC, 1983.

_____, Staff Accounting Bulletin No. 56, "Reporting of an Allocated Transfer Risk Reserve in Filings under the Federal Securities Laws." SEC, Washington, DC, 1984.

_____, Staff Accounting Bulletin No. 59, "Accounting for Noncurrent Marketable Equity Securities." SEC, Washington, DC, 1985.

_____, Staff Accounting Bulletin No. 60, "Financial Guarantees." SEC, Washington, DC, 1985.

_____, Staff Accounting Bulletin No. 61, "Allowance Adjustments." SEC, Washington, DC, 1986.

_____, Staff Accounting Bulletin No. 69, "Application of Article 9 and Guide 3 to Non-Bank Holding Companies." SEC, Washington, DC, 1987.

_____, Staff Accounting Bulletin No. 71 and SAB 71A, "Financial Statements of Properties Securing Mortgage Loans." SEC, Washington, DC, 1987.

_____, Staff Accounting Bulletin No. 75, "Accounting and Disclosures by Bank Holding Companies for a 'Mexican Debt Exchange' Transaction." SEC, Washington, DC, 1988.

_____, Staff Accounting Bulletin No. 82, "Certain Transfers of Nonperforming Assets" and "Disclosures of the Impact of Assistance from Federal Financial Institution Regulatory Agencies." SEC, Washington, DC, 1989.

_____, Staff Accounting Bulletin No. 89, "Financial Statements of Acquired Financial Institutions." SEC, Washington, DC, 1989.

_____, Federal Reporting Release No. 23, "The Significance of Oral Guarantees to the Financial Reporting Process." SEC, Washington, DC, 1985.

_____, Federal Reporting Release No. 28, "Accounting for Loan by Registrants Engaged in Lending Activities." SEC, Washington, DC, 1986.

_____, Federal Reporting Release No. 36, "Management's Discussion and Analysis of Financial Condition and Results of Operations; Certain Investment Company Disclosures." SEC, Washington, DC, 1989.

_____, Federal Reporting Release No. 48, "Disclosure of Accounting Policies for Derivative Financial Instruments and Derivative Commodity Instruments and Disclosure of Quantitative and Qualitative Information About Market Risk Inherent in Derivative Financial Instruments, Other Financial Instruments." SEC, Washington, DC, 1997.

Bank and Savings Institutions' Regulatory Guidance

Selected guidance prepared by the federal bank and savings institutions regulatory agencies is contained in the following documents:

- *Bank Holding Company Supervision Manual,* Federal Reserve System
- *Comptroller's Handbook for National Bank Examiners,* OCC
- *Comptroller's Manual for National Banks,* OCC
- *Comptroller's Handbook for Fiduciary Activities,* OCC
- *Comptroller's Handbook for Compliance,* OCC
- *Federal Reserve Commercial Bank Examination Manual*
- *Thrift Activities Regulatory Handbook,* OTS
- *Instructions—Consolidated Reporting of Condition and Income,* FFIEC
- *Federal Deposit Insurance Corporation (FDIC)FDIC Division of Supervision Manual of Examination Policies*
- *FDIC Trust Examination Manual*
- *Federal Banking Law Reporter,* Commerce Clearing House, Inc.
- *OCC Bank Accounting Advisory Series,* Third Edition (June 1994)

In addition, the OCC, FDIC, FRB, OTS, and FFIEC regularly publish various bulletins, advisories, letters, and circulars addressing current issues.

CHAPTER 32

PRODUCERS OR DISTRIBUTORS OF FILMS

Paul Rosenfield, CPA

32.1 HISTORY OF GUIDANCE

In 1974, the American Institute of Certified Public Accountants (AICPA) issued Industry Accounting Guide *Accounting for Motion Picture Films* and Statement of Position (SOP) 79–4, "Accounting for Motion Picture Films," providing specialized reporting principles for the industry. In 1981, the Financial Accounting Standards Board (FASB) extracted those specialized principles and presented them in its Statement No. 53, "Financial Reporting by Producers and Distributors of Motion Picture Films." Between 1981 and 2000, the origin of the majority of a film's revenue expanded from distribution to movie theaters and free television to those outlets plus, for example, home video, satellite and cable television, and pay-per-view television, and international revenue has become more significant. Also in that period, application of Statement No. 53 has varied significantly. The FASB therefore asked the Accounting Standards Executive Committee (AcSEC) to develop an SOP to replace that Statement.

This chapter was reviewed for the Eleventh Edition by Francis E. Scheuerell Jr., CPA, CMA. Mr. Scheuerell is a Partner, Financial Reporting Services with Callaway Partners, LLC in Atlanta, Georgia.

In response, AcSEC issued SOP 00–2, "Accounting by Producers or Distributors of Films," in June 2000, effective for fiscal years beginning after December 15, 2000, and the FASB simultaneously rescinded its Statement No. 53 in its Statement No. 139, "Rescission of FASB Statement No. 53 and Amendments to FASB Statements No. 63, 89, and 121." This chapter presents the accounting guidance in SOP 00–2.

32.2   REVENUE REPORTING

(a) BASIC REVENUE REPORTING PRINCIPLES.   A film producer or distributor obtains revenue from sale or licensing of its films.

An arrangement to license a single film or multiple films transfers a single right or a group of rights to distributors, theaters, exhibitors, or others exclusively or nonexclusively in a particular market and territory under terms that may vary significantly among different contracts. License fees are commonly fixed in amount or based on a percentage of the customer's revenue, which may include a nonrefundable minimum guarantee payable in advance or over the license period. Direct control over the distribution of a film may remain with the producer or may be transferred to a distributor, exhibitor, or other licensee.

A producer or distributor should report revenue from a sale or licensing arrangement of a film when all of the following five conditions are met:

1. There is persuasive evidence of a sale or licensing arrangement.
2. The film is complete and has been delivered or is available for immediate and unconditional delivery in accordance with the terms of the arrangement.
3. The license period has begun and the customer can begin its exploitation, exhibition, or sale.
4. The arrangement fee is fixed or determinable.
5. Collection of the fee is reasonably assured.

Reporting revenue should be deferred until all of the conditions have been met. A producer or distributor that reports a receivable for advances currently due before the date revenue is to be reported or that receives cash payments before that date should also report an equivalent liability for deferred revenue until all of the conditions have been met. Even a producer or distributor that sells or otherwise transfers such a receivable to a third party should not report revenue before that date. Amounts scheduled to be received in the future based on an arrangement for any form of distribution, exploitation, or exhibition should be reported as a receivable only when they are currently due or the above conditions have been met, if earlier.

(b) DETAILED REVENUE REPORTING PRINCIPLES.

(i) Persuasive Evidence of an Arrangement.   The persuasive evidence of a licensing arrangement needed to report revenue is provided solely by legally enforceable documentation that states, at a minimum, the license period, the film or films covered, the rights transferred, and the consideration to be exchanged. Revenue should nevertheless not be reported if there is significant doubt about the obligation or ability of either party to perform under the terms of the arrangement.

Verifiable evidence required is, for example, a purchase order or an online authorization. It should include correspondence from the customer that details the mutual understanding of the arrangement or evidence that the customer has acted in accordance with the arrangement.

(ii) Delivery.   Revenue should be reported no sooner than delivery is complete if the licensing arrangement requires physical delivery of a product to the customer or if the arrangement is silent about delivery.

In contrast, a licensing arrangement may not require immediate or direct physical delivery of a film to the customer but instead provide the customer with immediate and unconditional access to a film print held by the producer or distributor or authorization for the customer to order a film laboratory to make the film immediately and unconditionally available for the customer's use—known as a *lab access letter*. If the film is complete and available for immediate delivery, the requirement for delivery has been met.

A licensing arrangement may require a producer or distributor to change the film significantly after it is first available to a customer. If so, revenue should be reported only after those changes are made. Significant changes are additive to the film, that is, the producer or distributor is required to create new or additional content, for example, by reshooting a scene or creating additional special effects. Insertion or addition of preexisting film footage, adding dubbing or subtitles, removing offensive language, reformatting to fit a broadcaster's screen dimensions, and adjustments to allow for the insertion of commercials are examples of insignificant changes in this sense.

Costs incurred for significant changes should be added to film costs (discussed below) and later reported as expense when the related revenue is reported. Costs expected to be incurred for insignificant changes should be accrued and reported as expense if revenue is reported before those costs are incurred.

(iii) Availability. The imposition of a street date, the initial date on which home video products may be sold or rented, defines the date on which a customer's exploitation rights begin. The producer or distributor should report revenue no sooner than that date. If conflicting agreements place restrictions on the initial exploitation, exhibition, or sale of a film by a customer in a particular territory or market, the producer or distributor should report revenue no sooner than the date the restrictions lapse.

(iv) Fixed or Determinable Fee. A fee based on a licensing arrangement for a single film that provides for a flat fee is considered fixed and determinable, and the producer or distributor should report it as revenue when the other conditions for reporting revenue have been met.

A flat fee payable on multiple films, including films not yet completed, should be allocated to each individual film, by market and territory, based on relative fair values of the rights to exploit each film under the arrangement. Allocations to films not yet completed should be based on the amounts refundable if the producer or distributor does not complete and deliver the films. The allocations should not be adjusted later. The producer or distributor should report as revenue the amount allocated to an individual film when all of the conditions for reporting revenue have been met for the film by market and territory. If the producer or distributor cannot determine the relative fair values, the fee is not fixed or determinable and the producer or distributor should report revenue no sooner than it can determine them.

Quoted market prices are usually not available to determine fair value for this purpose. The producer should estimate the fair value of a film by using the best information available in the circumstances, with the objective to arrive at an amount it believes it would have received had the arrangement granted the same rights to the film separately. A discounted cash flow model may be used, in conformity with paragraphs 39–71 of FASB Statement of Concepts No. 7, which provide guidance on the traditional and expected cash flow approaches. The rights granted for the film under the arrangement, such as the length of the license period and limitations on the method, timing, or frequency of exploitation, should be observed.

The fee may be based on a percentage of the customer's revenue from exhibition or other exploitation of a film—variable fee. The producer or distributor should report revenue as the customer exhibits or exploits the film if the other conditions for reporting revenue have been met.

If the customer guarantees and pays or agrees to pay the producer or distributor a nonrefundable minimum amount applied against a variable fee on films that are not cross-collateralized—part of an arrangement in which the exploitation results for multiple films are aggregated—the producer or distributor should report the minimum guaranteed amount as revenue when all the other conditions for revenue reporting have been met. If they are cross-collateralized, the minimum guarantee for each film cannot be objectively determined and should be reported as revenue as the customer exhibits or exploits the film if all the other conditions for reporting revenue have been met.

(v) Barter Revenue.   Some licensing arrangements with television station customers provide that the stations may exhibit films in exchange for advertising time for the producers or distributors. The exchanges should be reported in conformity with Accounting Principles Board (APB) Opinion No. 29 as interpreted by Emerging Issues Task Force (EITF) No. 93–11.

(vi) Modifications of Arrangements.   If all of the conditions for reporting revenue are met by an existing arrangement and the parties agree to extend the time for the arrangement, reporting revenue depends on whether a flat fee or a variable fee is involved. The fee should be reported as revenue in conformity with the principles stated above for flat fees or variable fees.

Any other kind of change to a licensing arrangement, for example, the arrangement is changed from a fixed fee to a smaller fixed fee with a variable component, should be reported on as a new licensing arrangement, in conformity with the guidance in this section. The producer or distributor should consider the original arrangement terminated and accrue and expense associated costs and reverse previously reported revenue for refunds and concessions, such as a provision to accept a license fee rate below market.

(vii) Returns and Price Concessions.   A producer or distributor should report revenue on an arrangement that includes a right of return or if its past practices allow for returns in conformity with FASB Statement No. 48, which includes the necessity for the producer or distributor to be able to reasonably estimate the future returns.

Contractual provisions or the producer's or distributor's customary practices may involve price concessions, for example, "price protection," in which the producer or distributor lowers the prices to the customer on product it previously bought based on lowering of its wholesale prices. If so, the producer or distributor should provide related allowances when it reports revenue. If it cannot reasonably and reliably estimate future concessions or if there are significant uncertainties about whether it can maintain its prices, the fee is not fixed or determinable, and it should report revenue no sooner than it can estimate concessions reasonably and reliably.

(viii) Licensing of Film-Related Products.   A producer or distributor should report revenue from licensing arrangements to market film-related products no sooner than the film is released.

(ix) Present Value.   Revenue should be calculated based on the present value of the license fee as of the date it is first reported in conformity with APB Opinion No. 21.

32.3 COSTS AND EXPENSES

Costs incurred by producers and distributors to produce a film and bring it to market include film costs, participation costs, exploitation costs, and manufacturing costs.

(a) FILM COSTS—CAPITALIZATION.   A separate asset should be reported at cost for films in development or in inventory. Interest costs should be reported in conformity with FASB Statement No. 34.

The production overhead component of film costs includes allocable costs of persons or departments with exclusive or significant responsibility for the production of films. It should not include administrative and general expenses, charges for losses on properties sold or abandoned (no full-cost method for films), or the costs of certain overall deals as follows. In an overall deal, a producer or distributor compensates a producer or other creative individual for the exclusive or preferential use of that party's creative services. It should report as expense the costs of overall deals it cannot identify with specific projects over the period they are incurred. It should report a reasonable proportion of costs of overall deals as specific project film costs to the extent that they are directly related to the acquisition, adaptation, or development of specific projects. It should not allocate to specific project film costs amounts it had previously reported as expense.

The costs to prepare for the production of a particular film of adaptation or development of a book, stage play, or original screenplay to which a producer or distributor has film rights should be added to the cost of the rights.

Properties in development should be periodically reviewed to determine whether they will likely ultimately be used in the production of films. When a producer or distributor determines that a property will be disposed of, it should report any loss involved, including allocable amounts from overall deals, as discussed above. A property should be presumed to be subject to disposal if these have not all occurred within three years of the time of the first capitalized transaction: Management has implicitly or explicitly authorized and committed to funding the production of a film, active preproduction has begun, and principal photography is expected to begin within six months. The loss is the excess of the fair value of the project over the carrying amount. If management has not committed to a plan to sell the property, the rebuttable presumption is that the fair value of the property is zero.

Ultimate revenue for an episodic television series can include estimates from the initial market and secondary markets, as discussed below. Costs for a single episode in excess of the amount of revenue contracted for the episode should not be capitalized until the producer or distributor can establish estimates of secondary market revenue, as discussed below. Costs over this limit should be reported as expense and not subsequently restored as capitalized costs. Costs capitalized for an episode should be reported as expense as it reports revenue for the episode. When the producer or distributor can estimate secondary market revenue, as discussed below, it should capitalize subsequent film costs as discussed below and should evaluate the carrying amount for impairment as discussed below.

(b) FILM COSTS—AMORTIZATION AND PARTICIPATION COST ACCRUALS. A producer or distributor should amortize film costs and accrue expense for participation costs using the individual-film-forecast-computation method. That method amortizes costs or accrues expenses in this ratio: the current period actual revenue divided by estimated remaining unreported ultimate revenue as of the beginning of the current fiscal year. Unamortized film costs as of the beginning of the current fiscal year and ultimate participation costs not yet reported as expense are each multiplied by that fraction. Without changes in estimates, this method yields a constant rate of profit over the ultimate period for each film before exploitation costs, manufacturing costs, and other period expenses, thus contributing to stable income reporting (see Chapter 6). A producer or distributor should report a liability for participation costs only if it is probable that it will have to pay to settle its obligation under the terms of the participation agreement. At each reporting date, accrued participation costs should be at least the amounts the producer or distributor has to pay as of that date. Amortization of capitalized film costs and reporting of participation costs as expenses should begin when the film is released and revenue reporting on it begins.

With no revenue from third parties directly related to the exhibition or exploitation of a film, the producer or distributor should make a reasonably reliable estimate of the portion of unamortized film costs that is representative of the utilization of the film in its exhibition or exploitation. It should report those amounts as expense as it exhibits or exploits the film. Consistent with the smoothing objective of the individual film-forecast-computation methods, all revenue should bear a representative amount of the amortization of film costs during the ultimate period.

Results may vary from estimates, of course. A producer or distributor should revise estimates of ultimate revenue and participation costs as of each reporting date to reflect the most current information available. It should determine a new fraction that reflects only ultimate revenue from the beginning of the fiscal year of change. The revised fraction should be applied to the net carrying amount of unamortized film costs and to the film's ultimate participation costs not reported as expense as of the beginning of the fiscal year. The difference between expenses determined using the new estimates and amounts previously reported as expense during the fiscal year should be reported in the income statement in the period such as the quarter in which the estimates are revised.

The individual film-forecast-computation method should be applied to multiple seasons of an episodic television series that meet the conditions stated below to include estimated secondary market revenue in ultimate revenue by treating them as a single product.

(c) ULTIMATE REVENUE.   Ultimate revenue for the denominator of the individual-film-forecast-computation method fraction should include estimates of revenue expected to be reported by the producer or distributor from the exploitation, exhibition, and sale of the film in all markets and territories, subject to these limitations:

- For other than episodic television series, the period covered by the estimate should not exceed 10 years following the film's initial release. For episodic television series, the period should not exceed 10 years from the date of delivery of the first episode or, if still in production, five years from the date of delivery of the most recent episode, if later. For previously released films acquired as part of a film library (individual films whose initial release dates were at least three years before the acquisition date), the period should not exceed 20 years from the date of acquisition.

- For episodic television series, estimates of secondary market revenue for produced episodes only if the producer or distributor can show by its experience or industry norms that the episodes already produced plus those for which a firm commitment exists and the entity expects to deliver can be licensed successfully in the secondary market.

- Estimates from a particular market or territory only if there is persuasive evidence that there will be revenue or if the producer or distributor can show a history of earning revenue there. Estimates from newly developing territories only if an existing arrangement provides persuasive evidence that the producer or distributor will obtain revenue there.

- Estimates from licensing arrangements with third parties to market film-related products only if there is persuasive evidence that an arrangement for the particular film exists, for example, a signed contract with a nonrefundable minimum guarantee or a nonrefundable advance, or if the producer or distributor can show a history of earning revenue from that kind of arrangement.

- Estimates of the portion of the wholesale or retail revenue from sale by the producer or distributor or peripheral items such as toys and apparel attributable to the exploitation of themes, characters, or other contents related to a film only if the producer or distributor can show a history of earning revenue from that kind of exploitation in similar kinds of films, such as the portion of such revenue that it would earn by having rights granted under licensing arrangements with third parties. Estimates should not include the entire amount of wholesale or retail revenue from its sale of peripheral items.

- Estimates should not include revenue from unproven or undeveloped technologies.

- Estimates should not include wholesale promotion or advertising reimbursements; such amounts should be offset against exploitation costs.

- Estimates should not include amounts related to the sale of film rights for periods after those stated in the first bullet.

Ultimate revenue should be discounted to present value to the date that the producer or distributor first reports the revenue and should not include projections for inflation. Foreign currency estimates should be based on current rates.

(d) ULTIMATE PARTICIPATION COSTS.   Estimates of ultimate participation costs not yet reported as expense for the individual-film-forecast-computation method to arrive at current period participation cost expense should be determined using assumptions consistent with the producer's or distributor's estimates of film costs, exploitation costs, and ultimate revenue, limited as discussed in Section 32.3(c). If the reported participation costs liability exceeds the estimated unpaid ultimate participation costs for an individual film at a reporting date, the excess should be reduced with an offsetting credit to unamortized film costs. If an excess liability exceeds unamortized film costs for that film, it should be reported in income.

A producer or distributor should accrue associated participation costs as revenue is reported after its film costs are fully amortized.

(e) FILM COSTS VALUATION. A producer or distributor should assess whether the fair value of a complete or incomplete film is less than its unamortized film costs, for example, if the following occur:

- An adverse change in the expected performance of the film before it is released.
- Actual costs are substantially more than budgeted costs.
- The completion or release schedule is substantially delayed.
- The release plans change; for example, the initial release pattern is reduced.
- Resources to complete the film and market it effectively become insufficient.
- Performance after release does not meet expectations before release.

If the producer or distributor concludes that the fair value of a film is less than its unamortized film costs plus estimated future exploitation costs determined as discussed below, it should report the difference as a loss in income. The write-off should not subsequently be restored.

In determining the current fair value of a film, discounted cash flows may be used based on existing contractual arrangements without consideration of the limitations discussed in Section 32.3(c), considering these factors:

- The film's performance in prior markets
- The public's perception of the film's story, cost, director, or producer
- Historical results of similar films
- Historical results of the cast, director, or producer on prior films
- The running time of the film

The determination should incorporate estimates of necessary future cash outflows such as costs to complete and exploitation and participation costs. The most likely cash flows should be used, probability weighted by period using the mean or average by period.

The discount rate should reflect the risks associated with the film, and therefore these rates should not be used: the producer's or distributor's incremental borrowing rate, liability settlement rates, and weighted cost of capital. In addition to the time value of money, expectations should be incorporated about possible variations in the amount or timing of the most likely cash flows and an element to reflect the price market participants would seek for bearing the uncertainty in such an asset, and other factors, sometimes unidentifiable, including illiquidity and market imperfections.

(f) SUBSEQUENT EVENTS. Evidence that becomes available after the reporting date but before the financial statements are issued of a need for a write-down of unamortized film costs of a film should be assumed to bear on conditions at the reporting date. The assumption can be overcome if the producer or distributor can show that the conditions did not exist then.

(g) EXPLOITATION COSTS. Advertising costs should be reported in conformity with SOP 93–7. All other exploitation costs, including marketing costs, should be reported as expense when incurred.

(h) MANUFACTURING COSTS. Manufacturing or duplication costs of products for sale, such as videocassettes and digital video discs, should be reported as expense on a unit-specific basis when the related revenue is reported. At each reporting date, inventories of such products should be evaluated for net realizable value and obsolescence and needed adjustments reported as expense. The cost of theatrical film prints should be reported as expense over the period benefited.

32.4 PRESENTATION AND DISCLOSURE

If the reporting entity presents a classified balance sheet, it should list unamortized film costs as noncurrent. In any event, it should disclose the following in its notes:

- The portion of the costs of its completed films expected to be amortized in the upcoming operating cycle, presumed to be 12 months.
- The operating cycle if other than 12 months.
- The components of costs of films released, completed and not released, in production, or in development or preproduction, separately for theatrical films and direct-to-television product.
- The percentage of unamortized film costs for released films other than acquired film libraries expected to be amortized within three years of the reporting date. If less than 80 percent, additional information should be provided, including the period over which 80 percent will be reached.
- The amount of remaining unamortized costs, the method of amortization, and the remaining amortization period for acquired film libraries.
- The amount of accrued participation liabilities expected to be paid during the upcoming operating cycle.
- The methods of reporting revenue, film costs, participation costs, and exploitation costs.

Cash outflows for film costs, participation costs, exploitation costs, and manufacturing costs should be reported as operating activities in the statement of cash flows. Amortization of film costs should be included in the reconciliation of net income to net cash flows from operating activities.

CHAPTER 33

REGULATED UTILITIES

Benjamin A. McKnight III, CPA
Arthur Andersen LLP, Retired

Mr. McKnight wishes to acknowledge the assistance provided by Alan D. Felsenthal and Robert W. Hriszko, both formerly of Arthur Andersen LLP.

33.1 THE NATURE AND CHARACTERISTICS OF REGULATED UTILITIES

(a) INTRODUCTION TO REGULATED UTILITIES.   Many types of business have their rates for providing services set by the government or other regulatory bodies, for example, utilities, insurance companies, transportation companies, hospitals, and shippers. The enterprises addressed in this chapter are limited to electric, gas, telephone, and water (and sewer) utilities that are primarily regulated on an individual cost-of-service basis. Effective business and financial involvement with the utility industry requires an understanding of what a utility is, the regulatory compact under which utilities operate, and the interrelationship between the rate decisions of regulators and the resultant accounting effects.

(b) DESCRIPTIVE CHARACTERISTICS OF UTILITIES.   Regulated utilities are similar to other businesses in that there is a need for capital and, for private sector utilities, a demand for investor profit. Utilities are different in that they are dedicated to public use—they are obligated to furnish customers service on demand—and the services are considered to be necessities. Many utilities operate under monopolistic conditions. A regulator sets their prices and grants an exclusive service area, which probably serves a relatively large number of customers. Consequently, a high level of public interest typically exists regarding the utility's rates and quality of service.

Only a utility that has a monopoly of supply of service can operate at maximum economy and, therefore, provide service at the lowest cost. Duplicate plant facilities would result in higher costs. This is particularly true because of the capital-intensive nature of utility operations, that is, a large capital investment is required for each dollar of revenue.

Because there is an absence of free market competitive forces such as those found in most business enterprises, regulation is a substitute for these missing competitive forces. The goal of regulation is to provide a balance between investor and consumer interests by substituting regulatory principles for competition. This means regulation is to:

- Provide consumers with adequate service at the lowest price
- Provide the utility the opportunity, not a guarantee, to earn an adequate return so that it can attract new capital for development and expansion of plant to meet customer demand
- Prevent unreasonable prices and excessive earnings
- Prevent unjust discrimination among customers, commodities, and locations
- Insure public safety

To meet the goals of regulation, regulated activities of utilities typically include these six:

1. Service area
2. Rates
3. Accounting and reporting
4. Issuance of debt and equity securities
5. Construction, sale, lease, purchase, and exchange of operating facilities
6. Standards of service and operation

This chapter covers the historical development of regulated utilities as a monopoly service provider and the regulation of their rates as a substitute for competition. Although many of the historical practices continue, regulated utilities are increasingly operating in a deregulated, competitive environment. Certain industry segments have been more affected than others by the judicial, legislative, and regulatory actions, as well as technological changes, that have produced this shift. These industry segments include long distance telecommunications services, natural gas production and transmission, and electric generation.

33.2 HISTORY OF REGULATION

Some knowledge of the history of regulation is essential to understanding utilities. Companies that are now regulated utilities find themselves in that position because of a long sequence of political events, legislative acts, and judicial interpretations.

Rate regulation of privately owned business was not an accepted practice during the early history of the United States. This concept has evolved because important legal precedents have established not only the right of government to regulate but also the process that government bodies must follow to set fair rates for services. The background and the facts of *Munn v. Illinois* [94 U.S. 113 (1877)] are significant and basic to the development of rate making since the case established a U.S. legal precedent for the right of government to regulate and set rates in cases of public interest and necessity.

(a) MUNN V. ILLINOIS.   In 1871, the Illinois State Legislature passed a law that prescribed the maximum rates for grain storage and that required licensing and bonding to ensure performance of the duties of a public warehouse. The law reflected the popular sentiment of midwestern farmers at that time against what they felt was a pricing monopoly by railroads and elevators. Munn and his partner, Scott, owned a grain warehouse in Chicago. They filed a suit maintaining that they operated a private business and that the law deprived them of their property without due process.

The case ultimately reached the U.S. Supreme Court. The Court decided that, when private property becomes "clothed with a public interest," the owner of the property has, in effect, granted the public an interest in that use and "must submit to be controlled by the public for the common good." The Court was impressed by Munn and Scott's monopolistic position while furnishing a service practically indispensable to the public.

From the precedent of *Munn,* railroads, a water company, a grist mill, stockyards, and finally gas, electric, and phone companies were brought under public regulation. Thus, when utilities finally came into existence in the 20th century, the framework for regulation already was in place and did not have to be decided by the courts. When state legislatures began to set up utility commissions, it was the *Munn* decision that established beyond question their right to do so.

(b) CHICAGO, MILWAUKEE & ST. PAUL RAILROAD CO. V. MINNESOTA EX REL. RAILROAD & WAREHOUSE COMM..   A second important case that began to establish the principle of "due process" in rate making is *Chicago, Milwaukee & St. Paul Railroad Co. v. Minnesota ex rel. Railroad & Warehouse Comm.* [134 U.S. 418 (1890)]. In this case, the courts first began to address the issue of standards of reasonableness in regulation. The U.S. Supreme Court decided that a Minnesota law was unconstitutional because it established rate regulation but did not permit a judicial review to test the reasonableness of the rates. The Court found that the state law violated the due process provisions of the 14th Amendment because the utility was deprived of the power to charge reasonable rates for the use of its property, and if the utility was denied judicial review, then the company would be deprived of the lawful use of its property and, ultimately, the property itself.

(c) SMYTH V. AMES.   A third important case, *Smyth v. Ames* [169 U.S. 466 (1898)], established the precedent for the concept of "fair return upon the fair value of property." During the 1880s, the state of Nebraska passed a law that reduced the maximum freight rates that railroads could charge. The railroads' stockholders brought a successful suit that prevented the application of the lowered rates. The state appealed the case to the U.S. Supreme Court, which unanimously ruled that the rates were unconstitutionally low by any standard of reasonableness.

In its case, the state maintained that the adequacy of the rates should be tested by reference to the present value, or reproduction cost, of the assets. This position was attractive to the state because the current price level had been declining. The railroad was built during the Civil War, a period that was marked by a high price level and substantial inflation, and the railroad believed that its past costs merited recognition in a "test of reasonableness."

In reaching its decision, the Court began the formulation of the "fair value" doctrine, which prescribed a test of the reasonableness and constitutionality of regulated rates. The Supreme Court's opinion held that a privately owned business was entitled to rates that would cover reasonable operating expenses plus a fair return on the fair value of the property used for the convenience of the public.

The *Smyth v. Ames* decision also established several rate-making terms still in use today. This was the first attempt by the courts to define rate-making principles. These four terms include:

1. *Original Cost of Construction.* The cost to acquire utility property.
2. *Fair Return.* The amount that should be earned on the investment in utility property.
3. *Fair Value.* The amount on which the return should be based.
4. *Operating Expenses.* The cost to deliver utility services to the public.

Each of these three landmark cases, especially *Smyth v. Ames,* established the inability of the legislative branch to effectively establish equitable rates. They also demonstrated that the use of the judicial branch is an inefficient means of accomplishing the same goal. In *Smyth v. Ames,* the U.S. Supreme Court, in essence, declared that the process could be more easily accomplished by a commission composed of persons with special skills and experience and the qualifications to resolve questions concerning utility regulation.

33.3 REGULATORY COMMISSION JURISDICTIONS

A view of the overlays of regulatory commissions will be helpful in understanding their unique position and responsibilities.

(a) FEDERAL REGULATORY COMMISSIONS.   The interstate activities of public utilities are under the jurisdiction of several federal regulatory commissions. The members of all federal regulatory commissions are appointed by the executive branch and are confirmed by the legislative branch. The judicial branch can review and rule on decisions of each commission. This form of organization represents a blending of the functions of the three separate branches of government.

- The Federal Communications Commission (FCC), established in 1934 with the passage of the Communications Act, succeeded the Federal Radio Commission of 1927. At that time the FCC assumed regulation of interstate and foreign telephone and telegraph service from the Interstate Commerce Commission, which was the first federal regulatory commission (created in 1887). The FCC prescribes for communications companies a uniform system of accounts (USOA) and depreciation rates. It also states the principles and standard procedures used to separate property costs, revenues, expenses, taxes, and reserves between those applicable to interstate services under the jurisdiction of the FCC and those applicable to services under the jurisdiction of various state regulatory authorities. In addition, the FCC regulates the rate of return carriers may earn on their interstate business.
- The Federal Energy Regulatory Commission (FERC) was created as an agency of the cabinet-level Department of Energy in 1977. The FERC assumed many of the functions of the former Federal Power Commission (FPC), which was established in 1920. The FERC has jurisdiction over the transmission and sale at wholesale of electric energy in interstate commerce. The FERC also regulates the transmission and sale for resale of natural gas in interstate commerce and establishes rates and prescribes conditions of service for all utilities subject to its jurisdiction. The entities must follow the FERC's USOA and file a Form 1 (electric) or Form 2 (gas) annual report.

- The Securities and Exchange Commission was established in 1934 to administer the Securities Act of 1933 and the Securities Exchange Act of 1934. The powers of the SEC are restricted to security transactions and financial disclosures—not operating standards. The SEC also administered the Public Utility Holding Company Act of 1935 (the 1935 Act), which was passed because of financial and services abuses in the 1920s and the stock market crash and subsequent depression of 1929–1935. Under the 1935 Act, the SEC was given powers to regulate the accounting, financing, reporting, acquisitions, allocation of consolidated income taxes, and parent–subsidiary relationships of electric and gas utility holding companies. The Energy Policy Act of 2005 includes the repeal of the 1935 Act, which is effective on February 8, 2006, and will eliminate significant federal restrictions on the scope, structure, and ownership of electric companies. However, the repeal is accompanied by the transfer of certain authority to the FERC and state regulatory commissions.

(b) STATE REGULATORY COMMISSIONS. All 50 states and the District of Columbia have established agencies to regulate rates. State commissioners are either appointed or elected, usually for a specified term. Although the degree of authority differs, they have authority over utility operations in intrastate commerce. Each state commission sets rate-making policies in accordance with its own state statutes and precedents. In addition, each state establishes its prescribed forms of reporting and systems of accounts for utilities. However, most systems are modifications of the federal USOAs.

33.4 THE TRADITIONAL RATE-MAKING PROCESS

(a) HOW COMMISSIONS SET RATES. The process for establishing rates probably constitutes the most significant difference between utilities and enterprises in general. Unlike an enterprise in general, where market forces and competition establish the price a company can charge for its products or services, rates for utilities are generally determined by a regulatory commission. The process of establishing rates is described as rate making. The administrative proceeding to establish utility rates is typically referred to as a *rate case* or *rate proceeding*. Utility rates, once established, generally will not change without another rate case.

The establishment of a rate for a utility on an individual cost-of-service basis typically involves two steps. The first step is to determine a utility's general level of rates that will cover operating costs and provide an opportunity to earn a reasonable rate of return on the property dedicated to providing utility services. This process establishes the utility's required revenue (often referred to as the *revenue requirement* or *cost-of-service*). The second step is to design specific rates in order to eliminate discrimination and unfairness from affected classes of customers. The aggregate of the prices paid by all customers for all services provided should produce revenues equivalent to the revenue requirement.

(b) THE RATE-MAKING FORMULA. This first step of rate regulation, on an individual cost-of-service basis, is the determination of a utility's total revenue requirement, which can be expressed as a rate-making formula, which involves five areas:

$$\text{Rate Base} \times \text{Rate of Return} = \text{Return(Operating Income)}$$
$$\text{Return} + \text{Operating Expenses} = \text{Required Revenue(Cost of Service)}$$

1. *Rate Base.* The amount of investment in utility plant devoted to the rendering of utility service upon which a fair rate of return may be earned.
2. *Rate of Return.* The rate determined by the regulatory agency to be applied to the rate base to provide a fair return to investors. It is usually a composite rate that reflects the carrying costs of debt, dividends on preferred stock, and a return provision on common equity.

3. *Return.* The rate base multiplied by rate of return.

4. *Operating Expenses.* Merely the costs of operations and maintenance associated with rendering utility service. Operating expenses include:

    a. Depreciation and amortization expenses

    b. Production fuel and gas for resale

    c. Operations expenses

    d. Maintenance expenses

    e. Income taxes

    f. Taxes other than income taxes

5. *Required Revenue.* The total amount that must be collected from customers in rates. The new rate structure should be designed to generate this amount of revenue on the basis of current or forecasted levels of usage.

(c) RATE BASE. A utility earns a return on its rate base. Each investor-supplied dollar is entitled to such a return until the dollar is remitted to the investor. Some of the items generally included in the rate base computation are utility property and plant in service, a working capital allowance, and, in certain jurisdictions or circumstances, plant under construction. Generally, nonutility property, abandoned plant, plant acquisition adjustments, and plant held for future use are excluded. Deductions from rate base typically include the reserve for depreciation, accumulated deferred income taxes (ADITs), which represent cost-free capital, certain unamortized deferred investment tax credits, and customer contributions in aid of construction. Exhibit 33.1 provides an example of the computations used to determine a rate base.

(d) RATE BASE VALUATION. Various methods are used in valuing rate base. These methods apply to the valuation of property and plant and include these three:

1. Original cost

2. Fair value

3. Weighted cost

(i) Original Cost. The original cost method, the most widely used method, corresponds to accounting principles generally accepted in the United States (GAAP), which require historical cost data for primary financial statement presentation. In addition, all regulatory commissions have adopted the USOA, requiring original cost for reporting purposes. Original cost is defined in the

NET INVESTMENT RATE BASE	
	In Millions
Plant in service	$350
Less reserve for depreciation	(100)
Net plant in service	250
Add:	
Working capital allowance	3
Construction work-in-progress	33
Deduct:	
Accumulated deferred income taxes	(14)
Advances in aid of construction	(2)
Net investment rate base	$270

Exhibit 33.1   Example of a utility rate base computation.

FERC's USOA as "the cost of such property to the person first devoting it to public service." This method was originally adopted by various commissions during the 1930s, at which time inflation was not a major concern.

(ii) Fair Value.   The fair value method is defined as not the cost of assets but rather what they are really worth at the time rates are established. The following three methods of computing fair value are most often used:

1. *Trended Cost.* Utilizes either general or specific cost indices to adjust original cost.
2. *Reproduction Cost New.* A calculation of the cost to reproduce existing plant facilities at current costs.
3. *Market Value.* Involves the appraisal of specific types of plant.

(iii) Weighted Cost.   The weighted cost method for valuation of property and plant is used in some jurisdictions as a compromise between the original cost and the fair value methods. Under this method, some weight is given to both original cost and fair value. Regulatory agencies in some weighted cost jurisdictions use a 50/50 weighting of original cost and fair value, whereas others use 60/40 or other combinations.

(iv) Judicial Precedents—Rate Base.   In a significant rate base case, *Federal Power Commission v. Hope Natural Gas Co.* [320 U.S. 591 (1944)], the original cost versus fair value controversy finally came to a head. A number of important points came out of this case, including the Doctrine of the End Result. The U.S. Supreme Court's decision did not approve original cost or fair value. Instead, it said a rate-making body can use any method, including no formula at all, so long as the end result is reasonable. It is not the theory but the impact of the theory that counts.

(e) RATE OF RETURN AND JUDICIAL PRECEDENTS.   The rate of return is the rate determined by a regulator to be applied to the rate base to provide a fair return to investors. In the capital market, utilities must compete against nonregulated companies for investors' funds. Therefore, a fair rate of return to common equity investors is critical.

Different sources of capital with different costs are involved in establishing the allowed rate of return. Exhibits 33.2 and 33.3 show the computations used to determine the rate of return.

The cost of long-term debt and preferred stock is usually the "embedded" cost, that is, long-term debt issues have a specified interest rate, whereas preferred stock has a specified dividend rate. Computing the cost of equity is more complicated because there is no stated interest or dividend rate. Several methods have been used as a guide in setting a return on common equity.

COST OF CAPITAL AND RATE OF RETURN

	In Millions
Capitalization	
Stockholder's equity:	
Common stock ($8 par value, 5,000,000 shares outstanding)	$ 40
Other paid-in capital	45
Retained earnings	55
Common stock equity	140
Long-term debt (6.75% average interest rate)	130
	$270

Exhibit 33.2   Example of a utility capitalization structure.

	In Millions	Capitalization Ratios	Annual Cost Rate	Weighted Cost
Long-term debt	$130	48%	6.75%	3.24%
Common stock equity	140	52	13.00	6.76
Cost of capital	$270	100%		10.00%

Exhibit 33.3   Computation of the overall rate of return.

These methods reflect different approaches, such as earnings/price ratios, discounted cash flows, comparable earnings, and perceived investor risk.

The cost of each class of capital is weighed by the percentage that the class represents of the utility's total capitalization.

Two important cases provide the foundation for dealing with rate of return issues: *Bluefield Water Works & Improvement Co. v. West Virginia Public Service Comm.* [262 U.S. 679 (1923)] and the *Hope Gas* case. The important rate of return concepts that arise from these cases include the following five concepts:

1. A company is entitled to, but not guaranteed, a return on the value of its property.
2. Return should be equal to that earned by other companies with comparable risks.
3. A utility is not entitled to a return such as that earned by a speculative venture.
4. The return should be reasonably sufficient to:
   a. Assure confidence and financial soundness of the utility.
   b. Maintain and support its credit.
   c. Enable the utility to raise additional capital.
5. Efficient and economical management is a prerequisite for profitable operations.

(f) OPERATING INCOME.   Operating income for purposes of establishing rates is computed based on test-year information, which is normally a recent or projected 12-month period. In either case, historic or projected test-year revenues are calculated based on the current rate structure in order to determine if there is a revenue requirement deficiency. The operating expense information generally includes most expired costs incurred by a utility. As illustrated in Exhibit 33.4, the operating expense information, after reflecting all necessary pro forma adjustments, determines operating income for rate-making purposes.

Above-the-line and below-the-line are frequently used expressions in public utility, financial, and regulatory circles. The above-the-line expenses on which operating income appears are those that ordinarily are directly included in the rate-making formula; below this line are the excluded expenses (and income). The principal cost that is charged below-the-line is interest on debt since it is included in the rate-making formula as a part of the rate-of-return computation and not as an operating expense. The inclusion or exclusion of a cost above-the-line is important to the utility since this determines whether it is directly includable in the rate-making formula as an operating expense.

A significant consideration in determining the revenue requirement is that the rate of return computed is the rate after income taxes (which are a part of operating expenses). In calculating the revenue required, the equity return component of operating income (the equity return) (equity rate of return times rate base) deficiency must be grossed up for income taxes. This is most easily accomplished by dividing the equity return deficiency by the complement of the applicable income tax rate. For example, if the operating income deficiency is $5,000 and the income tax rate is 40 percent, the required revenue is $5,000/.6, or $8,333. By increasing revenues $8,333, income tax expense will increase by $3,333 ($8,333 × 40 percent), with the remainder increasing equity return by the deficiency amount of $5,000. This concept is illustrated as part of an example revenue

---

COST OF SERVICE INCOME STATEMENT—TEST YEAR
(Twelve Months Ended 12/31/XX)

	In Millions
Operating revenue	$310
Operating expenses	
Commercial	45
Maintenance	45
Traffic	49
General and administrative	61
Depreciation	60
General taxes	20
Income taxes	10
Total operating expenses	290
Operating income	$ 20

Exhibit 33.4   Example of a utility operating income computation.

requirement calculation based on the information presented in Exhibit 33.5. Exhibit 33.6 shows a proof of the revenue requirement calculation.

When the rate-making process is complete, the utility will set rate tariffs to recover $319 million. At this level, future revenues will recover $292 million of operating expenses (including income taxes of $12 million) and provide a return of $27 million. This return equates to a 10 percent earnings level on rate base. The $27 million operating income will go toward paying $9 million of interest on long-term debt ($130 million × 6.75 percent) and leaving net income for the common equity holders of $18 million—which approximates the desired 13 percent return on common equity of $140 million. However, the rate-making process only provides the opportunity to earn at that level. If future sales volumes, operating costs, or other factors change, the utility will earn more or less than the allowed amount.

(g) ALTERNATIVE FORMS OF REGULATION.   As a result of changing market conditions and growing competition, alternative forms of regulation began to emerge in the late 1980s. There are many new and different forms of regulation, but they all generally share a common characteristic. Utilities are provided an opportunity to achieve and retain higher levels of earnings compared with

---

RATE-MAKING FORMULA AND REVENUE REQUIREMENT CALCULATION

(Rate of Return × Rate Base) + Operating
    Expenses = Revenue Requirement

Revenue Requirement Calculation:			In Millions
Test-Year Operating Revenues			$310
Test-Year Operating Expenses Other Than Income Taxes		$280	
Interest Expense Required ($270 × 3.24%)		9	
Equity Return Required ($270 × 6.76%)	$18		
Income Tax Conversion Factor (1–40% Tax Rate)	.6		
Equity Return and Income Taxes		30	
Revenue Requirement			319
Revenue Requirement Deficiency			$ 9

Exhibit 33.5   Example of the revenue requirement computation based on Exhibits 33.1 through 33.4.

Proof of Revenue Requirement Calculation	In Millions
Revenue Requirement	$ (319
— Operating Expenses Other Than Taxes	(280)
— Interest Expenses	(9)
Taxable Income	30
— Income Tax @40%	(12)
Equity Return ($270 × 6.67%)	$ 18

Exhibit 33.6   Shortcut computation of the utility revenue requirement.

traditional regulation. It is believed that this opportunity will fundamentally change the incentives under regulation for cost reductions and productivity improvement. Alternative forms of regulation also are intended, in some cases, to provide needed pricing flexibility for services in competitive markets.

Examples of alternative forms of regulation include:

- Price ceilings or caps
- Rate moratoriums
- Sharing formulas
- Regulated transition to competition

(i) Price Ceilings or Caps.   Price caps are essentially regulation of the prices of services. This contrasts with rate of return or cost-based regulation under which the costs and earnings levels of services are regulated.

The fundamental premise behind price cap regulation is that it provides utilities with positive incentives to reduce costs and improve productivity because shareholders can retain some or all of the resulting benefits from increased earnings. Under rate of return regulation, assuming simultaneous rate making, customers receive all of the benefits by way of reduced rates.

Typical features of price cap plans are these three:

1. A starting point for prices that is based on the rates that were previously in effect under rate of return regulation. Under some plans, adjustments may be made to beginning rates to correct historical pricing disparities with the costs of providing service.
2. The ability to subsequently adjust prices periodically up to a cap measured by a predetermined formula.
3. The price cap formula usually includes three components: the change in overall price levels, an offset for productivity gains, and exogenous cost changes.

    The change in overall price levels is measured by some overall inflation index, such as the Gross National Product—Price Index or some variation of the Consumer Price Index.

    The productivity offset is a percentage amount by which a regulated utility is expected to exceed the productivity gains experienced by the overall population measured by the inflation index. The combination of a change in price levels less the productivity offset can produce positive or negative price caps. As an example, if the change in price levels was +5.5 percent, and the productivity offset was 3.3 percent, a utility could increase its prices for a service by +2.2 percent.

    There are also provisions to add or subtract the effects of exogenous cost changes from the formula. Exogenous changes are defined as those beyond the control of the company. Endogenous changes conversely are those assumed to be included in the overall price level change. Examples of exogenous items in certain jurisdictions might include changes in GAAP, environmental laws, or tax rates. Each regulatory jurisdiction's price cap plan may differ somewhat as to the definition of exogenous versus endogenous cost changes.

In their purest form, price caps are applied to determine rates, and the company retains the actual level of earnings the rates produce. However, most price cap plans also include backstop mechanisms. These include sharing earnings above a certain level with customers or for increasing rates if actual earnings fall below a specified level. Some plans also permit adjustment of rates above the price cap, subject to full cost justification and burden of proof standards.

(ii) Rate Moratoriums.   Rate moratoriums are simply a freeze in prices for a specified period of time. In effect, rate moratoriums function like a price cap where the productivity offset is set equal to the change in price levels, yielding a price cap of 0 percent. Most rate moratorium plans have provisions to adjust prices for specified exogenous cost changes, although the definition of exogenous may be even more restrictive than under price cap plans.

(iii) Sharing Formulas.   Sharing formulas are often paired with traditional rate of return regulation as an interim true-up mechanism between rate proceedings or added to price cap or rate moratorium plans as a backstop.

Sharing usually involves the comparison of actual earnings levels (determined by applying the traditional regulatory and cost allocation processes) with an authorized rate of return. Earnings above specified intervals are shared between shareholders and customers based on some formula.

Sharing is accomplished in a variety of ways. Five of the more common forms are:

1. One-time cash refunds or bill credits to customers
2. Negative surcharges on customer bills for a specified time period
3. Adjustments to subsequent price cap formulas
4. Infrastructure investment requirements
5. Capital recovery offsets

(iv) Regulated Transition to Competition.   Prior to the 2000–2001 energy crisis in California and the western United States, regulators in a number of states had adopted, or were in the process of adopting, legislation to change the traditional approach to the regulation of the generation portion of electric utility operations. The objective of this change was to provide customers with the right to choose their electricity supplier.

In simple terms, this legislation provides for a transition period from cost-based to market-based regulation. During this transition period, customers obtain the right to choose their electricity supplier at market price. Customers might also be charged a transition surcharge during the transition, which is intended to provide the electric utility with recovery of some or all of its electric generation stranded costs.

Stranded costs are often synonymous with high-cost generating units. However, they are more broadly defined to include other assets or expenses that, when recovered under traditional cost-based regulation, cause rates to exceed market prices. These costs can include regulatory assets and various obligations, such as for plant decommissioning, fuel contracts, or purchase power commitments.

At the end of the transition period, customers will be able to purchase electricity at market prices from their chosen supplier and the electric utility will be limited to providing transmission and distribution services at regulated prices.

33.5 INTERRELATIONSHIP OF REGULATORY REPORTING AND FINANCIAL REPORTING

(a) ACCOUNTING AUTHORITY OF REGULATORY AGENCIES.   Regulatory agencies with statutory authority to establish rates for utilities also prescribe the accounting that their jurisdictional regulated entities must follow. Accounting may be prescribed by a USOA, by periodic reporting requirements, or by accounting orders.

Because of the statutory authority of regulatory agencies over both accounting and rate setting of regulated utilities, some regulators, accountants, and others believe that the agencies have the final authority over the form and content of financial statements published by those utilities for their investors and creditors. This is the case even when the stockholders' report, based on regulatory accounting requirements, would not be in accordance with GAAP.

Actually, this issue has not arisen frequently because regulators have usually reflected changes in GAAP in the USOA that they prescribe. For example, the USOA of the FCC has GAAP as its foundation, with departures being permitted as necessary, because of departures from GAAP in ratemaking. But the general willingness of regulators to conform to GAAP does not answer the question of whether a regulatory body has the final authority to prescribe the accounting to be followed for the financial statements included in the annual and other reports to stockholders or outsiders, even when such statements are not prepared in accordance with GAAP.

The landmark case in this area is the *Appalachian Power Co. v. Federal Power Commission* [328 F.2d 237 (4th Cir.), *cert. denied,* 379 U.S. 829 (1964)]. The FPC (now the FERC) found that the financial statements in the annual report of the company were not in accordance with the accounting prescribed by the FPC's USOA. The FPC was upheld at the circuit court level in 1964 and the Supreme Court denied a writ of certiorari. The general interpretation of this case has been that the FPC had the authority to order that the financial statements in the annual report to stockholders of its jurisdictional utilities be prepared in accordance with the USOA, even if not in accordance with GAAP.

During subsequent years, the few differences that have arisen have been resolved without court action, and so it is not clear just what authority the FERC or other federal agencies may now have in this area. The FERC has not chosen to contest minor differences, and one particular utility, Montana Power Company, met the issue of FPC authority versus GAAP, by presenting, for several years, two balance sheets in its annual report to shareholders. One balance sheet was in accordance with GAAP, which reflected the rate making prescribed by the state commission, and one balance sheet was in accordance with the USOA of the FPC, which had ordered that certain assets be written off even though the state commission continued to allow them in the rate base. The company's auditors stated that the first balance sheet was in accordance with GAAP and that the second balance sheet was in accordance with the FPC USOA.

Since then the FERC has allowed a company to follow accounting that the FERC believes reflects the rate making even though the accounting does not comply with a standard of the Financial Accounting Standards Board (FASB). The SEC has ruled that the company must follow GAAP. As a result, the regulatory treatment was reformulated to meet the FASB standard, and so the conflict was resolved without going to the courts.

(b) SECURITIES AND EXCHANGE COMMISSION AND FINANCIAL ACCOUNTING STANDARDS BOARD.   The Financial Accounting Standards Board (FASB) has no financial reporting enforcement or disciplinary responsibility. Enforcement with regard to entities whose shares are traded in interstate commerce arises from SEC policy articulated in ASR No. 150, which specifies that FASB standards (and those of its predecessors) are required to be followed by registrants in their filings with the SEC. Thus, the interrelationship between the FASB and the SEC operates to achieve, virtually without exception for an entity whose securities trade in interstate commerce, the presentation of financial statements that reflect GAAP. Although this jurisdictional issue is neither resolved nor disappearing, it appears that the SEC currently exercises significant, if not controlling, influence over the general-purpose financial statements of all public companies, including regulated utilities.

(c) RELATIONSHIP BETWEEN RATE REGULATION AND GENERALLY ACCEPTED ACCOUNTING PRINCIPLES

(i) Historical Perspective   Rate making on an individual cost-of-service basis is designed to permit a utility to recover its costs that are incurred in providing regulated services. Individual cost-of-service does not guarantee cost recovery. However, there is a much greater assurance of cost recovery under individual cost-of-service rate making than for enterprises in general. This likelihood of cost recoverability provides a basis for a different application of GAAP, which recognizes that rate making can affect accounting.

As such, a rate regulator's ability to recognize, not recognize, or defer recognition of revenues and costs in established rates of regulated utilities adds a unique consideration to the accounting and financial reporting of those enterprises. This unique economic dimension was first recognized by the accounting profession in paragraph 8 of ARB No. 44 (Revised), "Declining-Balance Depreciation":

> Many regulatory authorities permit recognition of deferred income taxes for accounting and/or rate-making purposes, whereas some do not. The committee believes that they should permit the recognition of deferred income taxes for both purposes. However, where charges for deferred income taxes are not allowed for rate-making purposes, accounting recognition need not be given to the deferment of taxes if it may reasonably be expected that increased future income taxes, resulting from the earlier deduction of declining-balance depreciation for income-tax purposes only, will be allowed in the future rate determinations.

A year later, in connection with the general requirement to eliminate intercompany profits, paragraph 6 of ARB No. 51, "Consolidated Financial Statements," concluded:

> However, in a regulated industry where a parent or subsidiary manufactures or constructs facilities for other companies in the consolidated group, the foregoing is not intended to require the elimination of intercompany profit to the extent that such profit is substantially equivalent to a reasonable return on investment ordinarily capitalized in accordance with the established practice of the industry.

(ii) The Addendum to Accounting Principles Board (APB) Opinion No. 2.   In 1962, the APB decided to express its position on applicability of GAAP to regulated industries. The resulting statement, initially reported in The *Journal of Accountancy* in December 1962, later became the Addendum to APB Opinion No. 2, "Accounting for the Investment Credit" (the Addendum), and provided that:

1. GAAP applies to all companies—regulated and nonregulated.
2. Differences in the application of GAAP are permitted as a result of the rate-making process because the rate regulator creates economic value.
3. Cost deferral on the balance sheet to reflect the rate-making process is appropriately reflected on the balance sheet only when recovery is clear.
4. A regulatory accounting difference without ratemaking impact does not constitute GAAP. The accounting must be reflected in rates.
5. The financial statements of regulated entities other than those prepared for regulatory filings should be based on GAAP with appropriate recognition of rate-making consideration.

The Addendum provided the basis for utility accounting for almost 20 years. During this period, utilities accounted for certain items differently than enterprises in general. For example, regulators often treat capital leases as operating leases for rate purposes, thus excluding them from rate base and allowing only the lease payments as expense. In that event, regulated utilities usually treated such leases as operating leases for financial statement purposes. This resulted in lower operating expenses during the first few years of the lease.

Also, utilities capitalize both debt and equity components of funds used during construction, which is generally described as an allowance for funds used during construction (AFUDC). The FASB, under SFAS No. 34, "Capitalization of Interest Cost," allows nonregulated companies to capitalize only the debt cost. Because property is by far the largest item in most utility companies' balance sheets and because they do much of their own construction, the effect of capitalizing AFUDC is frequently very material to both the balance sheet and the statement of income.

Such differences, usually concerning the timing of recognition of a cost, were cited as evidence that the Addendum allowed almost any accounting treatment if directed by rate regulation. There was also some concern that the Addendum applied to certain industries that were regulated, but not on an individual cost-of-service basis. These as well as other issues ultimately led to the FASB issuing SFAS No. 71, "Accounting for the Effects of Certain Types of Regulation," which attempted to provide a clear conceptual basis to account for the economic impact of regulation, to emphasize the concept of one set of accounting principles for all enterprises, and to enhance the quality of financial reporting for regulated enterprises.

33.6 STATEMENT OF FINANCIAL ACCOUNTING STANDARDS NO. 71: "ACCOUNTING FOR THE EFFECTS OF CERTAIN TYPES OF REGULATION"

(a) SCOPE OF STATEMENT OF FINANCIAL ACCOUNTING STANDARDS NO. 71.   SFAS No. 71 specifies criteria for the applicability of the Statement by focusing on the nature of regulation rather than on specific industries. As stated in paragraph 5 of SFAS No. 71:

> [T]his statement applies to general-purpose external financial statements of an enterprise that has regulated operations that meet all of the following criteria:
>
> 1. The enterprise's rates for regulated services or products provided to its customers are established by or are subject to approval by an independent, third-party regulator or by its own governing board empowered by statute or contract to establish rates that bind customers.
> 2. The regulated rates are designed to recover the specific enterprise's costs of providing the regulated services or products.
> 3. In view of the demand for the regulated services or products and the level of competition, direct and indirect, it is reasonable to assume that rates set at levels that will recover the enterprise's costs can be charged to and collected from customers. This criterion requires consideration of anticipated changes in levels of demand or competition during the recovery period for any capitalized costs.

Based on these criteria, SFAS No. 71 provides guidance in preparing general-purpose financial statements for most investor-owned, cooperative, and governmental utilities.

The FASB's sister entity, the GASB, has been empowered to set pervasive standards for government utilities to the extent applicable, and, accordingly, financial statements issued in accordance with GAAP must follow GASB standards. However, in the absence of an applicable pronouncement issued by the GASB, differences between accounting followed under GASB or other FASB pronouncements and accounting followed for rate-making purposes should be handled in accordance with SFAS No. 71.

(b) AMENDMENTS TO STATEMENT OF FINANCIAL ACCOUNTING STANDARDS NO. 71.
After the issuance of SFAS No. 71, the FASB became concerned about the accounting being followed by utilities (primarily electric companies) for certain transactions. Significant economic events were occurring, including these three:

1. Disallowances of major portions of recently completed plants
2. Very large plant abandonments
3. Phase-in plans

All of these events in one way or another prevented utilities from recovering costs currently and, in some instances, did not allow recovery at all. As a result, the FASB amended SFAS No. 71 with SFAS No. 90, "Regulated Enterprises—Accounting for Abandonments and Disallowances of Plant Costs," and SFAS No. 92, "Regulated Enterprises—Accounting for Phase-In Plans." Also,

SFAS No. 144, "Accounting for the Impairment or Disposal of Long-Lived Assets," amended SFAS No. 71 to require a continuing probability assessment for the recovery of regulatory assets.

Due to the increasing level of competition and deregulation faced by all types of rateregu-lated enterprises, the FASB issued SFAS No. 101, "Regulated Enterprises—Accounting for the Discontinuation of Application of FASB Statement 71." SFAS No. 101 addresses the account-ing to be followed when SFAS No. 71 is discontinued. Related guidance is also set forth in the FASB's Emerging Issues Task Force (EITF) Issue No. 97-4, "Deregulation of the Pricing of Electricity—Issues Related to the Application of FASB Statements No. 71, Accounting for the Effects of Regulation and No. 101, Regulated Enterprises—Accounting for the Discontinuation of Application of FASB Statement No. 71."

(c) OVERVIEW OF STATEMENT OF FINANCIAL ACCOUNTING STANDARDS NO. 71. The major issues addressed in SFAS No. 71 relate to the following:

- Effect of rate making on GAAP
- Evidence criteria for recording regulatory assets and liabilities
- Application of GAAP to utilities
- Proper financial statement disclosures

SFAS No. 71 sets forth (pars. 9–12) general standards of accounting for the effects of regulation. In addition, there are specific standards that are derived from the general standards and various examples (Appendix B) of the application of the general standards.

(d) GENERAL STANDARDS. In SFAS No. 71, the FASB recognized that a principal consider-ation introduced by rate regulation is the cause-and-effect relationship of costs and revenues—an economic dimension that, in some circumstances, should affect accounting for regulated enterprises. Thus, a regulated utility should capitalize a cost (as a regulatory asset) or recognize an obligation (as a regulatory liability) if it is probable that, through the rate-making process, there will be a corresponding increase or decrease in future revenues. Regulatory assets and liabilities should be amortized over future periods consistent with the related increase or decrease, respectively, in future revenues.

(i) Regulatory Assets. Paragraph 9 of SFAS No. 71 states that the "rate action of a regulator can provide reasonable assurance of the existence of an asset." All or part of an incurred cost that would otherwise be charged to expense should be capitalized if:

- It is probable that future revenues in an amount approximately equal to the capitalized cost will result from inclusion of that cost in allowable costs for rate-making purposes.
- The regulator intends to provide for the recovery of that specific incurred cost rather than to provide for expected levels of similar future costs.

This general provision is not totally applicable to the regulatory treatment of costs of abandoned plants and phase-in plans. The accounting accorded these situations is specified in SFAS No. 90 and SFAS No. 92, respectively. EITF Issue No. 92-12, "Accounting for OPEB Costs by Rate Regulated Enterprises," addresses regulatory assets created in connection with the adoption of SFAS No. 106, "Employers' Accounting for Postretirement Benefits Other Than Pensions."

With these exceptions, SFAS No. 71 requires a rate-regulated utility to capitalize a cost that would otherwise be charged to expense if future recovery in rates is probable. Probable, as defined in SFAS No. 5, "Accounting for Contingencies," means likely to occur, a very high probability threshold. If, however, at any time the regulatory asset no longer meets the above criteria, the cost should be charged to earnings. This requirement results from an amendment to SFAS No. 71 included in SFAS No. 144. Thus, paragraph 9 mandates a probability of future recovery test to be met at each balance sheet date in order for a regulatory asset to remain recorded.

The terms "allowable costs" and "incurred costs," as defined in SFAS No. 71, also required further attention. The two terms were often applied interchangeably so that, in practice, the provisions of SFAS No. 71, paragraph 9, were interpreted to permit the cost of equity to be deferred and capitalized for future recovery as a regulatory asset. The FASB, in SFAS No. 92, concluded that equity return (or an allowance for earnings on shareholders' investment) is not an incurred cost that would otherwise be charged to expense. Accordingly, such an allowance shall not be capitalized pursuant to paragraph 9 of SFAS No. 71.

An incurred cost that does not meet the asset recognition criteria in paragraph 9 of SFAS No. 71 at the date the cost is incurred should be recognized as a regulatory asset when it meets those criteria at a later date. Such guidance is set forth in EITF Issue No. 93-4, "Accounting for Regulatory Assets." SFAS No. 144 provides for previously disallowed costs that are subsequently allowed by a regulator to be recorded as an asset, consistent with the classification that would have resulted had the cost initially been included in allowable costs. This provision covers plant costs as well as regulatory assets. Additionally, SFAS No. 144 requires the carrying amount of a regulatory asset recognized pursuant to the criteria in paragraph 9 to be reduced to the extent the asset has been subsequently disallowed from allowable costs by a regulator.

(ii) Regulatory Liabilities.   The general standards also recognize that the rate action of a regulator can impose a liability on a regulated enterprise, usually to the utility's customers.

Following are three typical ways in which regulatory liabilities can be imposed:

1. A regulator may require refunds to customers (revenue collected subject to refund).
2. A regulator can provide current rates intended to recover costs that are expected to be incurred in the future. If those costs are not incurred, the regulator will reduce future rates by corresponding amounts.
3. A regulator can require that a gain or other reduction of net allowable costs be given to customers by amortizing such amounts to reduce future rates.

Paragraph 12 of the general standards states that "actions of a regulator can eliminate a liability only if the liability was imposed by actions of the regulator." The practical effect of this provision is that a utility's balance sheet should include all liabilities and obligations that an enterprise in general would record under GAAP, such as for capital leases, pension plans, compensated absences, and income taxes.

(e) SPECIFIC STANDARDS.   SFAS No. 71 also sets forth specific standards for several accounting and disclosure issues.

(i) Allowance for Funds Used During Construction (AFUDC).   Paragraph 15 allows the capitalization of AFUDC, including a designated cost of equity funds, if a regulator requires such a method, rather than using SFAS No. 34 for purposes of capitalizing the carrying cost of construction.

Rate regulation has historically provided utilities with two methods of capturing and recovering the carrying cost of construction:

1. Capitalizing AFUDC for future recovery in rates
2. Recovering the carrying cost of construction in current rates by including construction work-in-progress in the utility's rate base

The computation of AFUDC is generally prescribed by the appropriate regulatory body. The predominant guidance has been provided by the FERC and FCC. The FERC has defined AFUDC as "the net cost for the period of construction of borrowed funds used for construction purposes and a reasonable rate on other funds when so used." The term *other funds*, as used in this definition, refers to equity capital.

The FERC formula for computing AFUDC is comprehensive and takes into consideration these five:

1. Debt and equity funds.
2. The levels of construction.
3. Short-term debt.
4. The costs of long-term debt and preferred stock are based on the traditional embedded cost approach, using the preceding year-end costs.
5. The cost rate for common equity is usually the rate granted in the most recent rate proceeding.

The FCC instructions also provide for equity and debt components. In allowing AFUDC, the FERC and FCC recognize that the capital carrying costs of the investments in construction work-in-progress are as much a cost of construction as other construction costs such as labor, materials, and contractors.

In contrast to regulated utilities, nonregulated companies are governed by a different standard, SFAS No. 34. Under the FASB guidelines:

> [T]he amount of interest to be capitalized for qualifying assets is intended to be that portion of interest cost incurred during the assets acquisition periods that theoretically could have been avoided (for example, by avoiding additional borrowings or by using the funds expended for the assets to repay existing borrowings) if expenditures for the assets had not been made.

Furthermore, SFAS No. 34 allows only debt interest capitalization and does not recognize an equity component.

The specific standard in SFAS No. 71 states that capitalization of such financing costs can occur only if both of the following two criteria are met.

1. It is probable that future revenue in an amount at least equal to the capitalized cost will result from the inclusion of that cost in allowable costs for rate-making purposes.
2. The future revenue will be provided to permit recovery of the previously incurred cost rather than to provide for expected levels of similar future costs.

In practice, many have interpreted the standard under SFAS No. 71 to mean that AFUDC should be capitalized if it is reasonably possible (not necessarily probable under SFAS No. 5) that the costs will be recovered. This same reasoning was also applied to the capitalization of other incurred costs such as labor and materials. Thus, capitalization occurred so long as recovery was reasonably possible and a loss was not probable.

As previously indicated, SFAS No. 90 amends the definition of "probable" included in SFAS No. 71 such that "probable" is now defined under the stringent technical definition in SFAS No. 5. In addition, paragraph 8 of SFAS No. 90 clarified that AFUDC capitalized under paragraph 15 can occur only if "subsequent inclusion in allowable costs for rate-making purposes is probable." Accordingly, the standard for capitalizing AFUDC is different from the standard applied to other costs, such as labor and materials.

The FASB also concluded in SFAS No. 92, paragraph 66, that:

> [I]f the specific criteria in paragraph 15 of SFAS No. 71 are met but AFUDC is not capitalized because its inclusion in the cost that will become the basis for future rates is not probable, the regulated utility may not alternatively capitalize interest cost in accordance with SFAS No. 34.

(ii) Intercompany Profit. Paragraph 16 of SFAS No. 71 generally reaffirms the provision in ARB No. 51 that intercompany profits on sales to regulated affiliates should not be eliminated in general-purpose financial statements if the sales price is reasonable and it is probable that future revenues allowed through the rate-making process will approximately equal the sales price.

(iii) Accounting for Income Taxes.   In paragraph 18 of SFAS No. 71, the FASB recognized that, in some cases, a regulator flows through the tax effects of certain timing differences as a reduction in future rates. In such cases, if it is probable that future rates will be based on income taxes payable at that time, SFAS No. 71 did not permit deferred taxes to be recorded in accordance with APB Opinion No. 11, "Accounting for Income Taxes."

In February 1992, SFAS No. 71 was amended by SFAS No. 109 and paragraph 18 was replaced by the following:

> A deferred tax liability or asset shall be recognized for the deferred tax consequences of temporary differences in accordance with FASB Statement No. 109, "Accounting for Income Taxes."

(iv) Refunds.   Paragraph 19 of SFAS No. 71 addresses the accounting for significant refunds. Examples include refunds granted gas distribution utilities from pipelines and telephone refunds occurring where revenues are estimated in one period and "trued-up" at a later date or where revenues are billed under bond pending settlement of a rate proceeding.

For refunds recognized in a period other than the period in which the related revenue was recognized, disclosure of the effect on net income and the years in which the related revenue was recognized is required if material. SFAS No. 71 provides presentation guidance that the effect of such refunds may be disclosed by displaying the amount, net of income tax, as a line item in the income statement, but not as an extraordinary item.

Adjustments to prior quarters of the current fiscal year are appropriate for such refunds, provided all of the following three criteria are met:

1. The effect is material (either to operations or income trends).
2. All or part of the adjustment or settlement can be specifically identified with and is directly related to business activities of specific prior interim periods.
3. The amount could not be reasonably estimated prior to the current interim period but becomes reasonably estimable in the current period.

This treatment of prior interim periods for utility refunds is one of the restatement exceptions contained in paragraph 13 of SFAS No. 16, "Prior Period Adjustments."

(v) Deferred Costs Not Earning a Return.   Paragraph 20 of SFAS No. 71 requires disclosure of costs being amortized in accordance with the actions of a regulator but not being allowed to earn a return during the recovery period. Disclosure should include the remaining amounts being amortized (the amount of the nonearning asset) as well as the remaining recovery period.

(vi) Examples of Application.   Appendix B in SFAS No. 71 contains examples of the application of the general standards to specific situations. These examples, along with the basis for conclusions (Appendix C), are an important aid in understanding the provisions of SFAS No. 71 and the financial statements of utilities.

Items discussed include the following:

- Intangible assets
- Accounting changes
- Early extinguishment of debt
- Accounting for contingencies
- Accounting for leases
- Revenue collected subject to refund
- Refunds to customers
- Accounting for compensated absences

33.7 STATEMENT OF FINANCIAL ACCOUNTING STANDARDS NO. 90: "REGULATED ENTERPRISES—ACCOUNTING FOR ABANDONMENTS AND DISALLOWANCE OF PLANT COSTS"

(a) SIGNIFICANT PROVISIONS OF STATEMENT OF FINANCIAL ACCOUNTING STANDARDS NO. 90. The provisions of SFAS No. 90 are limited to the narrow area of accounting for abandonments and disallowances of plant costs and not to other assets, regulatory or otherwise.

(i) Accounting for Regulatory Disallowances of Newly Completed Plant. When a *direct disallowance* of a newly completed plant is probable and estimable, a loss should be recorded, dollar for dollar, for the disallowed amount. After the write-down is achieved, the reduced asset forms the basis for future depreciation charges.

An indirect disallowance occurs when, in certain circumstances, no return or a reduced return is permitted on all or a portion of the new plant for an extended period of time. To determine the loss resulting from an indirect disallowance, the present value of the future revenue stream allowed by the regulator should be determined by discounting at the most recent allowed rate of return. This amount should be compared with the recorded plant amount and the difference recorded as a loss. Under this discounting approach, the remaining asset should be depreciated consistent with the rate making and in a manner that would produce a constant return on the undepreciated asset equal to the discount rate.

(ii) Accounting for Plant Abandonments. In the case of abandonments, when no return or only a partial return is permitted, at the time the abandonment is both probable and estimable, the asset should be written off and a separate new asset should be established based on the present value of the future revenue stream. The entities' incremental borrowing rate should be used to measure the new asset. During the recovery period, the new asset should be amortized to produce zero net income based on the theoretical debt, and interest should be assumed to finance the abandonment. FTB No. 87-2, "Computation of a Loss on an Abandonment," supports discounting the abandonment revenue stream using an after-tax incremental borrowing rate.

(iii) Income Statement Presentation. SAB No. 72 (currently cited as SAB Topic 10E) concludes that the effects of applying SFAS No. 90 should not be reported as an extraordinary item. SAB No. 72 states that such charges should be reported gross as a component of other income and deductions and not shown net-of-tax. The following presentation complies with the requirements of SAB No. 72:

Operating income	$XX
Other income (expense)	
Allowance for equity funds used during construction	XX
Disallowed plant cost	(XX)
Income tax reduction for disallowed plant cost	XX
Interest income	XX
Income taxes applicable to other income	XX
Income before interest charges	$XX

33.8 STATEMENT OF FINANCIAL ACCOUNTING STANDARDS NO. 92: "REGULATED ENTERPRISES—ACCOUNTING FOR PHASE-IN PLANS"

(a) SIGNIFICANT PROVISIONS OF STATEMENT OF FINANCIAL ACCOUNTING STANDARDS NO. 92. A phase-in plan, as defined in SFAS No. 92, is a method of ratemaking that meets each of the following three criteria:

1. Adopted in connection with a major, newly completed plant of the regulated enterprise or one of its suppliers or a major plant scheduled for completion in the near future
2. Defers the rates intended to recover allowable costs beyond the period in which those allowable costs would be charged to expense under GAAP applicable to enterprises in general
3. Defers the rates intended to recover allowable costs beyond the period in which those rates would have been ordered under ratemaking methods routinely used prior to 1982 by that regulator for similar allowable costs of that utility

The phase-in definition includes virtually all deferrals associated with newly completed plant, such as rate levelization proposals, alternative methods of depreciation such as a sinking fund approach, rate treatment of capital leases as operating leases, and other schemes to defer new plant costs to the future. SFAS No. 92 specifically states that it applies to rate-making methods developed for "...major newly completed plant of the regulated enterprise or of one of its suppliers..." Accordingly, SFAS No. 92 must be considered with respect to purchase power contracts.

Under the accounting provisions of SFAS No. 92, cost deferral under a phase-in plan is not permitted for plant/fixed assets on which substantial physical construction had not been performed before January 1, 1988. Consequently, for a major, newly completed plant that does not meet the January 1, 1988, cutoff date, post in-service deferrals for financial reporting purposes are limited to a time frame that ends when rates are adjusted to reflect the cost of operating the plant. This limitation, along with the restriction on modifying an existing phase-in plan, as discussed below, are the most important SFAS No. 92 provisions today.

As indicated above, SFAS No. 92 applies to the costs of a major, newly completed plant. There are situations in which a regulator subsequently starts to defer rates intended to recover allowable plant costs after return on and recovery of such costs have been previously provided. One example of this situation would occur when a regulator orders a future reduction in the depreciation rate (and rates charged to customers) of a 15-year-old nuclear generation plant, to factor in a potential 20-year license extension. Assuming that the new depreciation rate adopted by the regulator cannot be supported under GAAP (perhaps because the utility does not believe a license extension will occur), a regulatory deferral of plant costs (i.e., regulatory depreciation expense would be less than depreciation for financial reporting purposes) would result.

If the rate order was issued in connection with a major, newly completed plant, the guidance set forth in paragraph 35 of SFAS No. 92 presumes that the regulatory deferral of the "old" plant is equivalent to the regulatory deferral of the "new" plant. Thus, SFAS No. 92 must be applied. And, under that Statement, because the regulatory action results in a phase-in plan as defined in SFAS No. 92, no costs can be deferred for financial reporting purposes.

However, if the new rate order was not issued in connection with a major, newly completed plant and it is clear that the regulatory deferral relates only to "old" plant, SFAS No. 92 would not apply. Any deferral for financial reporting purposes must meet the requirements of SFAS No. 71, paragraph 9, for establishing and maintaining a regulatory asset. That determination should consider, as noted in paragraph 57 of SFAS No. 92, that the existence of such regulatory cost deferrals calls into question the applicability of SFAS No. 71.

(i) Accounting for Phase-In Plans. If the phase-in plan meets all of the criteria required by SFAS No. 92, all allowable costs that are deferred for future recovery by the regulator under the plan should be capitalized for financial reporting as a separate asset. If any one of those criteria is not met, none of the allowable costs that are deferred for future recovery by the regulator under the plan should be capitalized.

- The plan has been agreed to by the regulator.
- The plan specifies when recovery will occur.
- All allowable costs deferred under the plan are scheduled for recovery within 10 years of the date when deferrals begin.

- The percentage increase in rates scheduled for each future year under the plan is not greater than the percentage increase in rates scheduled for each immediately preceding year.

When an existing phase-in plan is modified or a new plan is ordered to replace or supplement an existing plan, the above criteria should be applied to the combination of the modified plan and the existing plan. Thus, the 10-year period requirement, from when cost deferral commences until all costs are recovered, cannot be extended. If the recovery period is modified beyond 10 years, recorded costs under the phase-in plan should be immediately charged to earnings.

(ii) Financial Statement Classification.   From a financial statement viewpoint, costs deferred should be classified and reported as a separate item in the income statement in the section relating to those costs. For instance, if capital costs are being deferred, they should be classified below-the-line. If depreciation or other operating costs are being deferred, the "credit" should be classified above-the-line with the operating costs. Allowable costs capitalized should not be reported net as a reduction of other expenses. Amortization of phase-in plan deferrals typically should be above-the-line (similar to recovering AFUDC via depreciation). This income statement presentation is consistent with guidance provided by the SEC's staff in the "Official Minutes of the Emerging Issues Task Force Meeting" (February 23, 1989, Open Meeting).

(iii) Allowance for Funds Used During Construction (AFUDC).   SFAS No. 92 clarifies that AFUDC-equity can be capitalized in general purpose financial statements only during construction (based on par. 15 of SFAS No. 71) or as part of a qualifying phase-in plan. Thus, it is clear that, after January 1, 1988, AFUDC-equity can no longer be capitalized in connection with short-term rate synchronization deferrals. It should also be noted that, in connection with the adoption of SFAS No. 92, such deferrals can be recorded only when it is probable—based on SFAS No. 5—that such costs will be recovered in future rates. This is consistent with the discussion on SFAS No. 90 relating to capitalizing AFUDC.

(iv) Interrelationship of Phase-In Plans and Disallowances.   Amounts deferred pursuant to SFAS No. 92 should also include an allowance for earnings on stockholders' investment. If the phase-in plan meets the criteria in SFAS No. 92 and the regulator prevents the enterprise from recovering either some amount of its investment or some amount of return on its investment, a disallowance occurs that should be accounted for in accordance with SFAS No. 90.

(v) Financial Statement Disclosure.   A utility should disclose in its financial statements the terms of any phase-in plans in effect during the year. If a phase-in plan exists but does not meet the criteria in SFAS No. 92, the financial statements should include disclosure of the net amount deferred for rate-making purposes at the balance sheet date and the net change in deferrals for rate-making purposes during the year for those plans. In addition, the nature and amounts of any allowance for earnings on stockholders' investment capitalized for rate-making purposes but not capitalized for financial reporting are to be disclosed.

33.9   STATEMENT OF FINANCIAL ACCOUNTING STANDARDS NO. 101: "REGULATED ENTERPRISES—ACCOUNTING FOR THE DISCONTINUATION OF APPLICATION OF FINANCIAL ACCOUNTING STANDARDS BOARD STATEMENT NO. 71"

The continuing applicability of SFAS No. 71 has been receiving more and more attention over the last 10 years, particularly with price cap regulation in the telecommunications industry and market-based or other alternative forms of pricing taking place in the pipeline and electric industries. Virtually every major telecommunications company that historically applied SFAS No. 71 has now discontinued applying it. Also, electric companies, including some of the largest in the industry, in various regulatory jurisdictions, have discontinued application of SFAS No. 71 for the generation portion of their operations as a result of the industry undergoing various fundamental changes. However, the changes are being revisited by many electric companies and their regulators as a result of the energy crisis in California that occurred in 2000 and early 2001. As a result, some companies have reapplied or are currently evaluating whether to reapply SFAS No. 71.

It is important that companies carefully review *both the current and anticipated future* rate environment to determine continued applicability of SFAS No. 71. In EITF Issue No. 97-4, a consensus was reached that the application of SFAS No. 71 to a segment of a rate-regulated enterprise's operations that is subject to a deregulation transition period should cease no later than the time when the legislation is passed or a rate order is issued and the related effects are known.

(a) FACTORS LEADING TO DISCONTINUING APPLICATION OF STATEMENT OF FINANCIAL ACCOUNTING STANDARDS NO. 71.   SFAS No. 101 gives several examples that may cause an enterprise to no longer meet the criteria for applying SFAS No. 71. Because virtually all regulated utilities are experiencing one or more of the examples cited below, it is important to make an evaluation of the continuing application of SFAS No. 71 at each balance sheet date.

Causes cited in SFAS No. 101 include: deregulation, a change from cost-based rate making to another form of regulation, increasing competition that limits the ability to recover costs, and regulatory actions that limit rate relief to a level insufficient to recover costs. Other stress signs that may indicate that SFAS No. 71 is no longer applicable include these eight:

1. Increasing amounts of regulatory assets, including systematic underdepreciation of assets and deferral of costs

2. Regulatory assets being consistently amortized over long periods, particularly if such assets relate to ongoing operating costs

3. Substantial regulatory disallowances

4. Increasing amounts of deferred costs not earning a return

5. Chronic excess capacity (e.g., generating capacity and/or readily available supplies) resulting in nonearning assets

6. Rates for services or per mcf or kWh which are currently, or forecasted in the future, to be higher than those of neighboring entities and/or alternative competitive energy sources

7. Significant disparity among the rates charged to residential, commercial, and industrial customers and rate concessions for major customers or segments

8. Stress accumulation and/or the actions of other to discontinue application of SFAS No. 71, making the specialized regulatory accounting model no longer creditable

These examples provide warning signs and are not meant as hard and fast rules. Instead, considerable judgment is required to determine when an enterprise ceases to meet the criteria of SFAS No. 71. However, we believe there are two trigger points that generally indicate an enterprise no longer meets the criteria of SFAS No. 71:

1. If the current form of rate regulation results in an extended rate moratorium or a regulatory process that precludes the enterprise for an extended period (in excess of five years) from adjusting rates to reflect the utility's cost of providing service

2. The regulatory process results or is expected to result in the utility earning significantly less (250–300 basis points) than its allowed or a reasonable current rate of return for an extended period of time (three or four years)

(b) REGULATORY ASSETS AND LIABILITIES.   Once a utility concludes that all or a part of a company's operations no longer comes under SFAS No. 71, it should discontinue application of that Statement and report discontinuation by eliminating from its balance sheet the effects of any actions of regulators that had been recognized as assets and liabilities pursuant to SFAS No. 71 but would not have been recognized as assets and liabilities by enterprises in general. The guidance in SFAS No. 101 indicates that all regulatory-created assets and liabilities should be written off unless the right to receive payment or the obligation to pay exists as a result of past events and regardless of expected future transactions.

Five examples of such regulatory-created assets and liabilities include:

1. Deferred storm damage
2. Deferred plant abandonment loss
3. Receivables or payables to future customers under purchased gas or fuel adjustment clauses (unless amounts are receivable or payable regardless of future sales)
4. Deferred gains or losses or reacquisition of debt
5. Revenues subject to refund as future sales price adjustments

SFAS No. 101 specifies that, if a separable portion of a rate-regulated utility's operations within a regulatory jurisdiction ceases to meet the criteria for application of SFAS No. 71, application of SFAS No. 71 to that separable portion should be discontinued. In EITF Issue No. 97-4, a consensus was reached that regulatory assets and liabilities should be recorded based on the separable portion of the operation from which the regulated cash flows to realize and settle them will be derived, rather than based on the separable portion initially incurring such costs. The consensus applies not only to regulatory assets and liabilities existing when the separable portion ceases application of SFAS No. 71, but also to regulatory assets and liabilities or any other costs of that separable portion that are probable of recovery, regardless of when incurred.

(c) FIXED ASSETS AND INVENTORY.   SFAS No. 101 also states:

> However, the carrying amounts of plant, equipment, and inventory measured and reported pursuant to SFAS No. 71 should not be adjusted unless those assets are impaired (as measured by enterprises in general), in which case the carrying amounts of those assets should be reduced to reflect that impairment.

The carrying amount of inventories measured and reported pursuant to SFAS No. 71 would not be adjusted—to eliminate, for example, intercompany profit—absent loss recognition by applying the "cost or market, whichever is lower" rule set forth in Chapter 4, "Inventory Pricing," of ARB No. 43, "Restatement and Revision of Accounting Research Bulletins."

Reaccounting is required for true regulatory assets that have been misclassified as part of plant, such as postconstruction cost deferrals recorded as part of plant, and for systematic underdepreciation of plant in accordance with rate-making practices.

(d) INCOME TAXES.   An apparent requirement of SFAS No. 101 when SFAS No. 71 is discontinued is that net-of-tax AFUDC should be displayed gross along with the associated deferred income taxes. This requirement is based on the notion that the net-of-tax AFUDC presentation is pursuant to industry practice and not SFAS No. 71. The interaction of this requirement along with the SFAS No. 101 treatment of excess deferred income taxes and the transition provision in SFAS No. 109 must be considered in connection with discontinuing the application of SFAS No. 71.

(e) INVESTMENT TAX CREDITS.   A utility might consider changing its method of accounting for investment tax credits in connection with adopting SFAS No. 101. Paragraph 11 of APB Opinion No. 4, "Accounting for the Investment Credit," as well as The Revenue Act of 1971 and U.S. Treasury releases, have required specific, full disclosure of the accounting method followed for ITC—either the flow-through method or the deferral method. Paragraph 16 of APB Opinion No. 20, "Accounting Changes," specifies that the previously adopted method of accounting for ITC should not be changed after the ITC has been discontinued or terminated. Therefore, the method of accounting used for ITC reported in financial statements when the Tax Reform Act of 1986 was signed, and such credits were discontinued, must be continued for those tax credits. Paragraph 4 of Accounting Interpretations of APB No. 4 indicates that the above guidance would apply to old ITC, even if a new similar credit were later enacted.

(f) INCOME STATEMENT PRESENTATION.   The net effect of the above adjustments should be included in income of the period of the change and classified as an extraordinary item in the income statement.

(g) REAPPLICATION OF STATEMENT OF FINANCIAL ACCOUNTING STANDARDS NO. 71. As noted in paragraph 43 of SFAS No. 101, the FASB concluded that the accounting for the reapplication of SFAS No. 71 is beyond the scope of SFAS No. 101. However, there have been several companies that have reapplied SFAS No. 71, including at least one registrant that precleared its accounting with the SEC staff.

When facts and circumstances change so that a utility's regulated operations meet all of the criteria set forth in paragraph 5 of SFAS No. 71, that Statement should be reapplied to all or a separable portion of its operations, as appropriate.

Reapplication includes adjusting the balance sheet for amounts that meet the definition of a regulatory asset or regulatory liability in paragraphs 9 and 11, respectively, of SFAS No. 71. AFUDC should commence to be recorded if it is probable of future recovery, consistent with paragraph 15 of SFAS No. 71. Plant balances should not be adjusted for any difference that resulted from capitalizing interest under SFAS No. 34 instead of AFUDC while SFAS No. 71 was discontinued. Instead, a regulatory asset should be recorded if supportable As provided for in SFAS No. 144, previously disallowed costs that are subsequently allowed by a regulator should be recorded as an asset, consistent with the classification that would have resulted had these costs initially been allowed.

In practice, the net effect of the adjustments to reapply SFAS No. 71 have been classified as an extraordinary item in the income statement.

33.10 ISSUE NO. 97-4

In recent years the SEC's staff has focused on electric utility restructuring and its effect on financial reporting. As a result, the appropriateness of the continuing application of SFAS No. 71 became a serious issue during the 1990s. Specifically, the SEC staff challenged the continued applicability of SFAS No. 71 by registrants in states where plans transitioning to market-based pricing/competition for electric generation were being formulated.

The SEC staff's concerns initially resulted from enacted legislation in California that provided at that time for transition to a competitive electric generation market. These concerns led to the identification of several unresolved issues concerning when SFAS No. 71 should be discontinued and how SFAS No. 101 should be adopted. A consensus was reached on each of the three major issues identified in Issue No. 97-4.

The first issue addresses when an enterprise should stop applying SFAS No. 71 to the separable portion of its business whose product or service pricing is being deregulated. However, this issue was limited to situations in which final legislation is passed or a rate order is issued that has the effect of transitioning from cost-based to market-based rates. In such situations, should SFAS No. 71 be discontinued at the beginning or the end of the transition period?

The EITF concluded that when deregulatory legislation or a rate order is issued that contains sufficient detail to reasonably determine how the transition plan will effect the separable portion of the business, SFAS No. 71 should be discontinued for that separable portion. Thus, SFAS No. 71 should be discontinued at the beginning (not the end) of the transition period.

Once SFAS No. 71 is no longer applied to a separable portion of an enterprise, the financial statements should segregate, via financial statement display or footnote disclosure, the amounts contained in the financial statements that relate to that separable portion.

The scope of the EITF's final consensus for Issue No. 97-4 was limited to a specific circumstance in which deregulatory legislation is passed and a final rate order issued. The EITF did not address the broader issue of whether the application of SFAS No. 71 should cease prior to final passage of deregulatory legislation or issuance of a final rate order.

Some relevant guidance for this situation is set forth in Paragraph 69 of SFAS No. 71, which states:

> The Board concluded that users of financial statements should be aware of the possibilities of rapid, unanticipated changes in an industry, but accounting should not be based on such possibilities unless their occurrence is considered probable. [emphasis added]

Based on this guidance, once it becomes probable that the deregulation legislative and/or regulatory changes will occur and the effects are known in sufficient detail, SFAS No. 101 should be adopted.

If the start of the transition period is delayed and uncertainty exists because of an appeal process, it seems reasonable that the application of SFAS No. 71 should continue until the completion of such process and the change to market-based regulation becomes probable. However, if or when it is probable that the appeal will be denied and the change to market-based regulation ultimately enacted, the discontinuance of SFAS No. 71 and adoption of SFAS No. 101 should not be delayed.

On the second issue, the EITF determined that the regulatory assets and regulatory liabilities that originated in the separable portion of an enterprise to which SFAS No. 101 is being applied should be evaluated on the basis of where (i.e., the portion of the business in which) the regulated cash flows to realize and settle them will be derived. Regulated cash flows are rates that are charged customers and intended by regulators to be for the recovery of the specified regulatory assets and settlement of the regulatory liabilities. They can be, in certain situations, derived from a "levy" on rate-regulated goods or services provided by another separable portion of the enterprise that meets the criteria for application of SFAS No. 71.

Accordingly, if such regulatory assets and regulatory liabilities have been specifically provided for via the collection of regulated cash flows, they are not eliminated until:

- They are recovered by or settled through regulated cash flows, or
- They are individually impaired or the regulator eliminates the obligation, or
- The separable portion of the business from which the regulated cash flows are derived no longer meets the criteria for application of SFAS No. 71.

Finally, the EITF reached a consensus that the source of cash flow approach adopted in the second consensus should be used for recoveries of all costs and settlements of all obligations for which regulated cash flows are specifically provided in the deregulatory legislation or rate order. Thus, the second consensus is not limited to regulatory assets and regulatory liabilities that are recorded at the date SFAS No. 101 is applied.

For example, a regulatory asset should also be recorded for the loss on the sale of an electric generating plant or the loss on the buy out of a purchased power contract that is recognized after SFAS No. 101 is applied to the generation portion of the business, if it is specified for recovery in the legislation or a rate order, and a separable portion of the enterprise that meets the criteria for application of SFAS No. 71 continues to exist.

33.11 OTHER SPECIALIZED UTILITY ACCOUNTING PRACTICES

(a) UTILITY INCOME TAXES AND INCOME TAX CREDITS.   Income tax expense is important to utilities because it generally is one of the largest items in the income statement and usually is a key factor in the determination of cost of service for ratemaking purposes. Deferred income taxes represent a significant element of internally generated funds and a major financing source for the extensive construction programs that utilities have historically experienced. In addition, the complexity of the Internal Revenue Code and of the various regulations to which utilities are subject causes a significant amount of controversy. As a result, the method of accounting for income taxes—"normalization" versus "flow-through" rate making—is often a specific issue in rate proceedings. The rate-making method is an important area of concern to analysts and can be a factor in establishing the cost of equity and new debt offerings.

(i) Interperiod Income Tax Allocation.   GAAP, under SFAS No. 109, require that a "provision for deferred taxes" be made for the tax effect of most of differences between income before income taxes and taxable income. This practice of interperiod tax allocation is referred to in the utility industry as normalization.

The term *normalization* evolved because income taxes computed for accounting purposes on the normalization basis would cause reported net income to be a "normal" amount had the utility not adopted, for example, a particular tax return method for a deduction that created the tax-book difference. Under the deferred tax, or normalization concept, the taxes that would be payable, except for the use of the tax return deduction that created the tax-book difference, are merely deferred, not saved. For example, when tax depreciation exceeds book depreciation in the early years of property life, deferred taxes are charged to expense with a contra credit to a liability account. In later years, when the tax write-offs are lower than they otherwise would be, the higher taxes when payable are charged against this reserve. To illustrate the concept, assume the following facts:

	Year 1	Year 2	Year 3
Revenues	$1,000	$1,000	$1,000
Other expenses	600	600	600
Book depreciation	200	200	200
Tax depreciation	300	200	100
Tax rate	34%	34%	34%

Exhibit 33.7 sets forth how normalized (deferred) tax accounting would be recorded in Year 1 for the tax and book depreciation difference of $100.

(ii) Flow-Through.   "Flow-through" is a concept wherein the reductions in current tax payments from tax deductions, such as received by using accelerated depreciation, are flowed through to customers via lower cost-of-service and revenue requirements. Under this approach, income tax

---

DEFERRED TAX ACCOUNTING

	Income Statement	Tax Return	Timing Difference
Revenue	$1,000	$1,000	$ —
Depreciation	(200)	(300)	100
Other expenses	(600)	(600)	—
Income before taxes	$ 200	$ 100	$100
Federal income taxes:			
Payable currently (34% × $100)	$ 34	$ 34	
Deferred (34% × $100)	34		$ 34
Total	$ 68		
Operating income	$ 132		

Exhibit 33.7   Illustration of "normalized" tax accounting.

expense is equal to the currently payable amount only. No recognition (deferred taxes) is given to the tax effect of differences between book income before income taxes and taxable income. Under a "partial" allocation approach, deferred taxes are provided on certain differences but are ignored on others.

The principal argument used by those who support flow-through accounting is that a provision for deferred taxes does not constitute a current cost and therefore such a deferment should not be made. Income tax expense for the year should only include those taxes legally payable with respect to the tax return applicable to that year, and any provision in excess of taxes payable represents "phantom" taxes or "customer contributed capital." Further, when property additions are growing, and if no changes were made to the tax law, deferred tax provisions in the aggregate would continue to grow and would never turn around (or reverse); thereby the tax timing differences are, in fact, "permanent differences."

Exhibit 33.8 sets forth the initial effect of flow-through tax accounting in Year 1 for the tax and book depreciation difference of $100.

Although Exhibit 33.8 shows a "bottom-line" effect of the elimination of deferred tax expense, such accounting is not acceptable. GAAP requires deferred tax accounting with SFAS No. 71, permitting departures only when regulators affect revenues. To be acceptable, therefore, the regulator would lower revenue requirements due to the omission of deferred tax expense as an element of the utility's cost-of-service for rate-making purposes. The action of the regulator in this case is to defer a cost that will be recoverable through increased rates in the future.

As previously discussed, utility regulators determine operating income first and then add allowable expenses to derive operating revenue. In Exhibit 33.7, $132 is presumed to be the result of multiplying rate base by rate of return. The same operating income of $132 in the normalization example would be developed first under the flow-through concept and, with the elimination of deferred tax expense of $34, only $948 of revenue would be required to produce the $132 of operating income under flow-through. The proper application of flow-through is shown in Exhibit 33.9.

This $52 reduction in revenues (by eliminating only $34 of deferred tax expense) is caused by the tax-on-tax effect, which is discussed under the rate-making formula. In short, the elimination of the deferred tax expense results in a direct reduction of revenues, causing current tax expense also to be reduced. This effect is the primary reason so much attention is focused on normalization versus flow-through rate making for income taxes.

"FLOW-THROUGH" ACCOUNTING ASSUMING NO DECREASE IN CUSTOMER RATES			
	Income Statement	Tax Return	Timing Difference
Revenue	$1,000	$1,000	$ —
Depreciation	(200)	(300)	$100
Other expenses	(600)	(600)	—
Income before taxes	$ 200	$ 100	$100
Federal income taxes:			
Payable currently (34% × $100)	$ 34	$ 34	
Deferred (34% × $0)	—		$ —
Total	$ 34		
Net income	$ 166		

Exhibit 33.8   Illustration of "flow-through" accounting with no effect on customer rates.

"FLOW-THROUGH" ACCOUNTING ASSUMING DECREASE IN CUSTOMER RATES

	Income Statement	Tax Return	Timing Difference
Revenue	$948	$948	—
Depreciation	(200)	(300)	$100
Other expenses	(600)	(600)	—
Income before taxes	$148	$ 48	$100
Federal income taxes:			
Payable currently (34% × $48)	16	16	
Deferred	—		—
Total	$ 16		
Net income	$132		

Exhibit 33.9   Illustration of "flow-through" accounting with a decrease in rates.

The comparison of the normalization and flow-through concepts in Exhibit 33.10 illustrates that operating income continues to be $132 under both methods and that the $52 of savings in revenue requirement in Year 1 due to flow-through is offset by $52 of higher rates in Year 3. For simplicity, this example ignores the rate base reducing effects of deferred taxes.

The comparison illustrates the principal argument for normalization—that revenues are at a level, or normal, amount, whereas revenue varies greatly under flow-through. Advocates of normalization note that normalization distributes income tax expense to time periods, and therefore to customers' revenue requirements, consistently with the costs (depreciation) that are affecting income tax expense. As the rate-making process necessarily involves the deferral of costs such as plant investment and distribution of these costs over time, normalization is used to produce a consistent determination of income tax expense.

Normalization also recognizes that the "using up" of tax basis of depreciable property (or using up an asset's ability to reduce taxes) creates a cost. This cost should be recognized as the tax payments are reduced. Basing tax expense solely on taxes payable without recognizing the cost of achieving reductions in tax payments is not consistent with accrual accounting. Although flow-through rate making ignores this current cost, this cost does not disappear any more than the nonrecognition of depreciation for rate making would make that cost disappear.

(iii) Provisions of the Internal Revenue Code.   Complicating the regulatory treatment and financial reporting of income taxes for utilities are significant amounts of deferred income taxes that are "protected" under provisions of the IRC. That is, normalization is required with respect to certain tax and book depreciation differences if the utility is to remain eligible for accelerated depreciation. A historical perspective of tax incentives and tax legislation, as they relate to the utility industry, is helpful in understanding why the regulatory treatment of income tax is of such importance.

(iv) The Concept of Tax Incentives.   The first significant tax incentive that was generally available to all taxpayers was a provision of the 1954 Code that permitted accelerated methods of depreciation. Prior to enactment of this legislation, tax depreciation allowances were generally limited to those computed with the straight-line method, which is traditionally used for financial reporting and rate-making purposes. The straight-line method spread the cost of the property evenly over its estimated useful life. The accelerated depreciation provisions of the 1954 Code permitted taxpayers to take greater amounts of depreciation in the early years of property life and lesser

COMPARISON OF NORMALIZATION AND FLOW-THROUGH

	Normalization				Flow-Through			
	Year 1	Year 2	Year 3	Total	Year 1	Year 2	Year 3	Total
Revenues	$1,000	$1,000	$1,000	$3,000	$(948)	$1,000	$1,052	$3,000
Depreciation	(200)	(200)	(200)	(600)	(200)	(200)	(200)	(600)
Other expenses	(600)	(600)	(600)	(1,800)	(600)	(600)	(600)	(1,800)
Income before income taxes	200	200	200	600	148	200	252	600
Income taxes								
Payable currently	34	68	102	204	16	68	120	204
Deferred taxes	34	—	(34)	—	16	68	120	204
	68	68	68	204	16	68	120	204
Operating income	$ 132	$ 132	$ 132	$ 396	$132	$ 132	$ 132	$ 396

Exhibit 33.10   Illustration of normalization versus flow-through differences.

amounts in later years. Although accelerated methods permit taxpayers to recover capital investments more rapidly for tax purposes, deductions are limited to the depreciable cost of property. Thus, only the timing, not the ultimate amount of depreciation, is affected.

Because utilities are capital intensive in nature, accelerated depreciation provisions generate significant amounts of tax deferrals. Additionally, other sources of deferred taxes can be relatively small in some industries but are magnified in the utility industry because of its large construction programs. Among the major differences, generally referred to as basis differences, are interest, pensions, and taxes capitalized as costs of construction for book purposes but deducted currently (as incurred) as expenses for tax purposes. Once again, it is the timing, not the ultimate cost, that is affected.

Accelerated methods and lives were intended by the U.S. Congress to generate capital for investment, stimulate expansion, and contribute to high levels of output and employment. The economic benefit to the taxpayer arising from the use of accelerated depreciation and capitalized costs is the time value of the money because of the postponement of tax payments. The availability of what are effectively interest-free loans, obtained from the U.S. Treasury, reduces the requirements for other sources of capital, thereby reducing capital costs. Prior to the Tax Reform Act of 1986, these capitalized overheads represented significant deductions for tax purposes. However, subsequent to that Act, such amounts are now capitalized into the tax basis of the asset and depreciated for tax purposes as well. Thus, the benefits that once resulted from basis differences have, to a large extent, been eliminated.

(v) Tax Legislation.   A brief history of the origin of accelerated tax depreciation and the intent of the U.S. Congress in permitting liberalized depreciation methods is helpful in understanding the regulatory and accounting issues related to income taxes.

Tax Reform Act of 1969.   The accelerated tax depreciation methods initially made available to taxpayers in 1954 were without limitations in the tax law as to the accounting and rate-making methods used for public utility property. However, in the late 1960s, the U.S. Treasury Department and Congress became concerned about larger-than-anticipated tax revenue losses as a result of rate regulatory developments. Although both Congress and the Treasury realized that accelerated tax deductions would initially reduce Treasury revenues by the tax effect, they had not anticipated that flow-through would about double (at the then 48% tax rate) the Treasury's tax loss because of the tax-on-tax effect. Depending on the exact tax rate, about one-half the reduction in payments to the Treasury came from the deduction of accelerated depreciation and the other one-half from the immediate reduction in customer rates from the use of flow-through. It was this second one-half reduction of Treasury revenues that was considered unacceptable. Furthermore, immediate flow-through of these incentives to utility customers negated the intended congressional purpose of the incentives themselves. It was the utility customers who immediately received all of the benefit of accelerated depreciation. Accordingly, the utility did not have all the Treasury "capital" that was provided by Congress for investment and expansion.

Faced with larger-than-anticipated Treasury revenue losses, Congress enacted the Tax Reform Act of 1969 (TRA '69). By adding Section 167(1), it limited the Treasury's exposure to revenue losses by making the accelerated depreciation methods available to public utility properties only if specific qualifying standards as to accounting and ratemaking were met. Although Section 167(1) did not dictate to state regulatory commissions a rate-making treatment they should follow with respect to the tax effects of accelerated depreciation, the Act provided that:

- If a utility had not used accelerated depreciation prior to 1970, it would not be allowed to use accelerated tax depreciation in the future unless it normalized for ratemaking and accounting purposes.
- Utilities that had been using accelerated tax depreciation and were normalizing for accounting and ratemaking purposes would not be allowed to use accelerated depreciation in the future unless they continued to normalize for accounting and ratemaking purposes.

- Companies that were currently on a flow-through basis were allowed to continue on a flow-through basis in the future. However, an election was offered to such companies by which they could elect to be in a position where they would lose accelerated depreciation on future expansion additions unless they were normalizing for rate-making and accounting purposes with respect to such future expansion property additions.

Revenue Act of 1971. The Revenue Act of 1971, signed into law on December 10, 1971, codified the Asset Depreciation Range (ADR) system for determining depreciation for tax purposes. Under ADR, lives were shortened, thereby accelerating tax depreciation even further. The ADR regulations prescribed the same standards regarding normalization versus flow-through rate making as were set forth in TRA '69.

Economic Recovery Act of 1981. The Economic Recovery Act of 1981, signed into law on August 31, 1981, continued to allow acceleration of depreciation tax deductions and included normalization rules for public utility property with respect to depreciation under the Accelerated Cost Recovery System. Normalization is mandatory under the Act for accelerated depreciation taken on all public utility property placed in service after December 31, 1980.

Tax Reform Act of 1986. The Tax Reform Act of 1986 (TRA '86) reduced the acceleration of depreciation tax deductions and continued normalization requirements for public utility property. In addition, the maximum federal tax rate for corporations was reduced from 46% to 34%. This reduction in the federal tax rate not only reduces tax payments currently being made, but will also reduce future tax payments (assuming continuation of the present tax rate) that result from the reversal of previously recorded deferred tax amounts—effectively forgiving a portion of the loan from the U.S. Treasury.

TRA '86 [Section 203(e)] provided that deferred taxes related to certain depreciation method and life differences on public utility property in excess of the new 34% statutory rate be used to reduce customer rates using the average rate assumption method. This method generally requires the development of an average rate determined by dividing the aggregate normalized timing differences into the accumulated deferred taxes that have been provided on those timing differences. As the timing differences begin to reverse, the turnaround occurs at this average rate. Under this method, the so-called excess in the reserve for deferred taxes is reduced over the remaining life of the property.

If a regulatory commission requires reduction in the deferred tax balance more rapidly than under this method, book depreciation must be used for tax purposes. There is no provision in TRA '86 for any protection of other deferred taxes, such as book/tax basis differences, life differences on pre-ADR assets, salvage value on ADR assets, repair allowance, and so on. In addition, the deferred taxes on depreciation method and life differences provided at rates in excess of 46% are not protected under the average-rate assumption method.

(vi) "Accounting for Income Taxes"—Statement of Financial Accounting Standards No. 109. SFAS No. 109 shifts the focus of income tax accounting from the income statement to an asset and liability approach. SFAS No. 109 retains the requirement to record deferred taxes whenever income or expenses are reported in different years for financial reporting and tax purposes. However, it changes the way companies compute deferred taxes by requiring deferred tax assets and liabilities to be adjusted whenever tax rates or other provisions of the income tax law change. This is referred to as the *liability method* of providing deferred income taxes. SFAS No. 109 also requires utility companies to record tax liabilities for all temporary differences (defined as differences between the book and tax bases of assets and liabilities recorded on their respective balance sheets), even those that have previously been flowed through. For many utilities, these amounts are significant.

As a result of adopting SFAS No. 109, utilities adjusted their ADIT balances to the level obtained by multiplying the statutory tax rate by existing temporary differences. Because this amount may be more or less than what has been permitted to be recovered through the rate-making process, regulatory assets or liabilities have also been recorded for financial reporting purposes. These regulatory assets and liabilities represent the future recovery or reduction in revenues as a result of previous income tax policies of regulatory commissions.

To illustrate the unique effects of utilities adopting SFAS No. 109, two significant transactions will be described—recording of amounts previously flowed through as a reduction in customer rates and the effects of a change in tax rates.

1. *Recording of Amounts Previously Flowed Through.* SFAS No. 109 requires utilities to record accumulated deferred taxes using the liability approach for all temporary differences whether normalized or flowed through. Accordingly, paragraph 18 of SFAS No. 71 is superseded by SFAS No. 109. Furthermore, the FASB has concluded that the asset (liability) created by a regulatory promise to allow recovery (or require a settlement) of flow-through amounts is best measured by the expected cash flow to be provided as the temporary difference turns around and is recovered (settled) in rates. Thus, a regulatory asset or liability is established at the revenue requirement level, taking into account the tax-on-tax impact. In the Statement, these regulatory assets/liabilities are characterized as "probable future revenue/probable reduction in future revenue."

   The corresponding ADIT liability represents the income taxes that would result in connection with recovering both the temporary difference itself and the newly recorded regulatory asset. Accordingly, the computation of the amount to be recorded for prior flow-through is:

   Temporary differences flowed through
   × Gross-up (tax-on-tax) factor
   × Tax rate
   _____
   Dr. Regulatory asset/Cr. ADIT liability

   SFAS No. 109 requires the regulatory asset and ADIT liability to be displayed separately for general-purpose financial reporting.

2. *Effects of a Change in Tax Rates.* Under the liability method in SFAS No.109, the ADIT liability is reported at the enacted settlement tax rate. Thus, deferred tax liabilities or assets established at rates in excess of the current statutory rate (35%) should be reduced to that level. Utilities are required to record the reduction in the ADIT liability but presumably will not immediately recognize the reduction in the results of operations because:

   a. The average rate assumption method provision contained in TRA '86 prohibits excess deferred taxes related to protected depreciation differences from being used to reduce customer rates more rapidly than over the life of the asset giving rise to the difference. Under this method, the excess in the deferred tax reserve is not reduced until the temporary differences giving rise to deferred taxes begin to turn around.

   b. Regulators may adopt a similar methodology for nonprotected excess deferred taxes.

   For these reasons, the credit to offset the reduction in the ADIT liability required by the liability method should be reclassified by regulated utilities as a separate liability. Consistent with the asset recovery scenario discussed previously, the FASB measures this separate liability as the cash flow impact of settling the specific liability (i.e., the future reduction in the revenue requirement). Accordingly, a gross-up factor must be applied to the excess deferred tax liability. The concept is illustrated with the following skeleton entry:

Temporary difference
× Enacted tax rate
_____

Required ADIT liability
− Existing deferred taxes on temporary difference
_____

Excess deferred taxes
× Gross-up factor
_____

Dr. ADIT liability/Cr. Other liabilities
_____

Other temporary differences that will result in the recording of ADIT and regulatory assets/liabilities are unamortized ITC balances (see next section), amounts recorded on a net-of-tax basis (SFAS No. 109 prohibits such presentations), and AFUDC-equity (previously recorded on an after-tax basis). Considering the large amounts of construction activity, the AFUDC-equity ADIT and regulatory assets may be significant.

At the time of adoption, paragraph 58 of SFAS No. 109 set forth transitional guidance whereby a single temporary difference between the book and tax bases of plant in service could be computed and the net effect recorded on the balance sheet.

The important concept to consider is that SFAS No. 109, in and of itself, did not alter rate-making/revenue requirements, and therefore SFAS No. 71 requires regulatory assets/liabilities for differences in the recognition of the timing of income tax expense via that process. Thus, flow-through of tax expense may continue for regulatory purposes, but SFAS No. 109 will require financial statements to report the deferred income tax liability with an offsetting regulatory asset to recognize that such cost will be recovered at a future date.

(vii) Investment Tax Credit.   The accounting and rate-making aspects of the ITC are discussed separately because the economics and the effect are different from those of the acceleration in the write-off of costs for tax purposes. The ITC represents a permanent savings in taxes rather than a deferral. Although the tax credit should be used to reduce expense, the accounting and rate-making question is not one of flow-through but rather is a question as to which year's tax expense should be reduced and the benefit passed on to utility customers.

Accounting for ITC. Based on APB Opinion Nos. 2 and 4, the two accounting methods in use are to:

1. Flow the tax reduction through to income over the life of the property giving rise to the investment tax credit (service-life method), or
2. Reduce tax expense in the current year by the full amount of the credit (initial year flow-through method).

Tax Legislation and Regulatory Treatment.   The service-life method is required by the IRC in order for many utilities to claim ITC. In 1964, in connection with the investment credit, the U.S. Congress specifically established certain rate-making requirements, stating that federal regulatory agencies could not use the investment credit to reduce cost of service except over the service life of the related property. Congress also extended the practice of including rate-making requirements in the tax law when it enacted the job development tax credit in 1971 and provided that, except where a special election was made by a limited number of eligible companies, the benefits of the job development credit were to be shared between consumers and investors and that the consumers' share was to be passed on to them over the life of the property.

If the rate making and the accounting are not in accordance with the irrevocable election made by the company pursuant to the 1971 Act, the utility taxpayer can be denied ITC. The four available options were:

1. No portion of the investment credit would be used to reduce cost-of-service for rate purposes, but the unamortized credit could be used to reduce rate base (general rule).

2. The rate-making authority could reduce the cost-of-service for no more than the annual amortization of the investment credit over the book life of the property giving rise to the credit, and the unamortized balance of the credit could not be used to reduce rate base (ratable flow-through).

3. Utilities that were flow-through for accelerated depreciation under the standards of the Tax Reform Act of 1969 were permitted to elect to continue to follow the flow-through method for the investment credit. This election does not preclude the use of a service-life method of amortization of the credit if the regulatory commission agreed.

4. If the appropriate regulatory agency declared there was a shortage of supply, companies in the natural gas or steam heat business would lose the credit if the rate-making body either reduced the cost of service or reduced the rate base.

With few exceptions, electric utilities, gas distribution companies, and telephone companies are now on the service-life amortization method for all or most of the investment credit, in most cases using the rate-making method covered by option 2 above. Natural gas pipeline companies elected the "shortage of supply" option. As a result, no element of the credit could be passed on to customers. They were in the same position as nonregulated companies and could use either the initial year flow-through or service-life method for accounting purposes. However, in 1986, the FERC determined that there was no longer a shortage of gas supply and these companies would follow option 1 for any credits subsequently realized.

The 1986 Act repealed the ITC, generally effective for property placed in service after December 31, 1985. The Act requires that a utility continue to follow its present method of accounting for amortizing the ITC. For failure to continue its present method, a utility will be forced to recapture the greater of (1) ITC for all open years or (2) unamortized ITC of the taxpayer or ITC not previously restored to rate base.

(b) REVENUE RECOGNITION—ALTERNATIVE PROGRAMS. There are various financial reporting issues related to the accounting by rate-regulated utilities for the effects of certain alternative revenue programs adopted in a number of regulatory jurisdictions. Although the specific objectives of various recent programs are intended to address relatively new regulatory policies, the basic form and economic substances of the related regulatory treatment has been widespread and around for many years. The major alternative revenue programs currently in use include the following three:

1. *Weather normalization clauses.* These clauses operate in a manner similar to fuel adjustment clauses and are designed to protect both rate payers and shareholders from the effects of significant changes in unit sales due to weather. Amounts billed or refunded are generally computed by multiplying the difference between actual units sold and units included in the rate-making process times base rates (excluding variable fuel costs). The intent of such a clause is to recover nonfuel cost of service (incurred costs) and return (including equity).

2. *Operating/plant performance measurements.* These programs are designed to hold a utility's management accountable and to effectively reward or penalize shareholders for meeting or not meeting established performance measurements. The reward or penalty can be a specific amount or an amount based on an increase or decrease in the return allowed by the regulator. The amount is usually based on performance for a specific measurement and period (typically an annual period) and billed or refunded to customers prospectively after regulatory review.

3. *Demand side management (DSM).* Many utility companies have implemented various load management and conservation programs that have been designed to address capacity shortages, potential peak demand reductions, money-saving opportunities for customers, and environmental concerns. Such programs include payments made to customers to assist in installation of cost-effective electric load reduction measures, incentives paid to customers for proven conservation and load management measures, retrofit programs directed at large

customers to remodel or update operating equipment, numerous projects to reduce individual customer energy use (such as bill credits for more efficient lighting and water heaters, energy efficient appliances, residential weatherization, and insulation), developing standby generation, and interruptible service rates.

DSM programs reduce sales so regulators are taking various actions to remove this disincentive by:

- Permitting recovery of and return on program costs,
- Permitting compensation for lost revenues, or
- Granting bonuses or incentives for meeting goals and objectives.

These programs typically enable the regulated utility to adjust rates in the future (usually as a surcharge applied to future billings) in response to past activities, transactions, or completed events.

In practice, accounting for amounts due to customers has not been an issue. These amounts represent refunds of revenues collected during the measurement period and are accounted for as contingent liabilities or regulatory liabilities that meet the conditions for accrual under SFAS No. 5 or paragraph 11 of SFAS No. 71, respectively.

The primary accounting question for these programs is whether the economic substance of regulatory actions should be accrued and recorded as assets for financial reporting purposes when it is probable that amounts for program costs and revenue shortfalls will be recovered from customers and no other event is required in the future other than billing. Financial reporting issues related to this question include (1) the limitations on accruing equity return or profit under SFAS No. 71; (2) distinguishing between an incurred and allowable (equity) cost under SFAS No. 71 and situations in which the deferral/capitalization of such costs create regulatory assets for financial reporting purposes; and (3) distinguishing regulatory assets from GAAP assets.

At its May 21, 1992, meeting, the EITF addressed Issue No. 92-7, "Accounting by Rate-Regulated Utilities for the Effects of Certain Alternative Revenue Programs," and reached a consensus that once the specific events permitting billing of the additional revenues under a program have been completed, the regulated utility should recognize the additional revenues if all of the following three conditions are met:

1. The program is established by an order from the utility's regulatory commission that allows for automatic adjustment of future rates. Verification of the adjustment to future rates by the regulator would not preclude the adjustment from being considered automatic.
2. The amount of additional revenues for the period is objectively determinable and is probable of recovery.
3. The additional revenues will be collected within 24 months following the end of the annual period in which they are recognized.

For purposes of applying the consensus, the conditions or accruing revenue effectively determine what accounting model is being followed for asset recognition—a GAAP-based model as followed by enterprises in general or an SFAS No. 71 model. Accordingly, if the conditions of Issue No. 92-7 are met, an asset with many of the characteristics of a GAAP receivable is recorded. In situations where revenue is not accruable as a GAAP asset, paragraph 9 of SFAS No. 71 should be followed to the extent that probable future revenue is being provided to recover a specific *incurred cost* and a regulatory asset exists.

(c) ACCOUNTING FOR POSTRETIREMENT BENEFITS OTHER THAN PENSIONS.   In December 1990, the FASB issued SFAS No. 106, which concludes that such benefits, commonly referred to as *OPEB costs*, represent deferred compensation that should be accounted for on an accrual basis.

Regulators have historically provided regulated utilities rate recovery of OPEB costs on a pay-as-you-go basis. Since SFAS No. 106 was issued, most regulators have allowed SFAS No. 106 expense, or some level of funding above pay-as-you-go, for rate-making purposes. Others, such as the FERC, have specifically issued a policy statement adopting SFAS No. 106-based regulatory treatment for OPEB costs. However, a few regulatory jurisdictions have indicated that they will continue to limit cost recovery through rates to pay-as-you-go or to some other regulatory treatment that will result in significant deferrals of OPEB costs for future recovery in rates. In situations where SFAS No. 106 is not adopted for regulatory purposes, regulatory asset recognition, for the annual difference between SFAS No. 106 costs and costs allowable in rates, would only be appropriate if future rate recovery of the regulatory asset is *probable,* as defined in SFAS No. 5.

In order to provide authoritative guidance as to the appropriate accounting and what constitutes sufficient evidence that a regulatory asset exists, the EITF created Issue No. 92-12, "Accounting for OPEB Costs by Rate-Regulated Enterprises."

The EITF reached a final consensus for Issue No. 92-12 that a regulatory asset related to SFAS No. 106 costs should not be recorded in a regulated utility's financial statements if the regulator continues to *limit inclusion* of OPEB costs in rates *to a pay-as-you-go basis.* Several EITF members noted that the application of SFAS No. 71 for financial reporting purposes requires that a rate-regulated enterprise's rates be designed to recover the specific enterprise's costs of providing the regulated service or product and that enterprise's cost of providing a regulated service or product includes SFAS No. 106 costs.

Further, the EITF reached a final consensus in Issue No. 92-12 that a rate-regulated enterprise *should not* recognize a regulatory asset for financial reporting purposes for the difference between SFAS No. 106 costs and OPEB costs included in the regulated utility's rates unless the company (a) determines that it is *probable* that future revenue in an amount at least equal to the deferred cost (regulatory asset) will be recovered in rates and (b) meets *all* four of the following criteria:

1. The regulated company's regulator has issued a rate order, including a policy statement or a generic order applicable to enterprises within the regulator's jurisdiction, that allows the deferral of SFAS No. 106 costs and subsequent inclusion of those deferred costs in rates.

2. Annual SFAS No. 106 costs, including *normal* amortization of the transition obligation, should be included in rates within approximately five years of SFAS No. 106 adoption. The change to full SFAS No. 106 in rates may take place in multiple steps, but the deferral period should not exceed approximately five years.

3. The combined deferral and recovery period approved by the regulator should not exceed approximately 20 years. If a regulator approves a total deferral and recovery period of more than 20 years, a regulatory asset should not be recognized for any costs not recovered by the end of the approximate 20-year period.

4. The percentage increase in rates scheduled under the regulatory recovery plan for each future year should be no greater than the percentage increase in rates scheduled under the plan for each immediately preceding year. This criterion is similar to that required for phase-in plans in paragraph 5(d) of SFAS No. 92. The EITF observed that recovery of the regulatory asset in rates on a straight-line basis would meet this criterion.

(d) OTHER FINANCIAL STATEMENT DISCLOSURES

(i) Purchase Power Contracts   Many utilities enter into long-term contracts for the purchase of electric power in order to meet customer demand. The SEC's SAB No. 28 (currently cited as SAB Topic 10D) sets forth the disclosure requirements related to long-term contracts for the purchase of electric power. This release states:

> The cost of power obtained under long-term purchase contracts, including payments required to be made when a production plant is not operating, should be included in the operating expenses section of the income statement. A note to the financial statements should present information

concerning the terms and significance of such contracts to the utility company including date of contract expiration, share of land output being purchased, estimated annual cost, annual minimum debt service payment required and amount of related long-term debt or lease obligations outstanding.

Purchasers of power under contracts that specify a level of power to be made available for a specific time period usually account for such contracts as purchase commitments with no recognition of an asset for the right to receive power and no recognition of a liability for the obligation to make payments (i.e., the contracts are accounted for as executory agreements). However, some power purchase contracts may have characteristics similar to a lease in that the contract confers to the purchaser the right to use specific property, plant, and equipment.

The determination of whether a power purchase contract is a lease should be based on the substance of the contract using the guidance set forth in Issue No. 01–8, "Determining Whether an Arrangement Contains a Lease." The fact that an agreement is labeled a "power purchase agreement" is not conclusive. If a contract "conveys the right to use property, plant, and equipment," the contract should be accounted for as a lease. Other power purchase contracts should be accounted for as executory agreements with disclosure as required by SFAS No. 47, "Disclosure of Long-Term Obligations."

(ii) Financing Through Construction Intermediaries.   Utilities using a construction intermediary should include the intermediary's work-in-progress in the appropriate caption of utility plant on the balance sheet. SAB No. 28 (currently cited as SAB Topic 10A) requires the related debt to be disclosed and included in long-term liabilities. Capitalized interest included as part of an intermediary's construction work-in-progress should be recognized as interest expense (with an offset to AFUDC-debt) in the income statement.

A note to the financial statements should describe the organization and purpose of the intermediary and the nature of its authorization to incur debt to finance construction. The note should also disclose the interest rate and amount of interest capitalized for each period in which an income statement is presented.

(iii) Jointly Owned Plants.   SAB No. 28 (currently cited as SAB Topic 10C) also requires a utility participating in a jointly owned power station to disclose the extent of its interests in such plant(s). Disclosure should include a table showing separately for each interest the amount of utility plant in service, accumulated depreciation, the amount of plant under construction, and the proportionate share. Amounts presented for plant in service may be further subdivided into subcategories such as production, transmission, and distribution. Information concerning two or more generating plants on the same site may be combined if appropriate.

Disclosure should address the participant's share of direct expenses included in operating expenses on the income statement (e.g., fuel, maintenance, other operating). If the entire share of direct expenses is charged to purchased power, then disclosure of this amount, as well as the proportionate amounts related to specific operating expenses on the joint plant records, should be indicated.

A typical footnote is as follows:

(x) Jointly Owned Electric Utility Plant

Under joint ownership agreements with other state utilities, the company has undivided ownership interests in two electric generating stations and related transmission facilities. Each of the respective owners was responsible for the issuance of its own securities to finance its portion of the construction costs. Kilowatt-hour generation and operating expenses are divided on the same basis as ownership with each owner reflecting its respective costs in its statements of income. Information relative to the company's ownership interest in these facilities at December 31, 20XX, is as follows:

	Unit 1	*Unit 2*
Utility plant in service	$XXX,XXX	$XX,XXX
Accumulated depreciation	$XXX,XXX	$XX,XXX
Construction work-in-progress	$ XX,XXX	$ XX
Plant capacity—Mw	XXX	XXX
Company's share	XX%	XX%
In-service date	1974	1981

(iv) Decommissioning Costs and Nuclear Fuel. In January 1978, the SEC published SAB No. 19 (currently cited as Topic 10B), which addressed estimated future costs of storing spent nuclear fuel as well as decommissioning costs of nuclear generating plants. SAB No. 19 requires footnote disclosure of the estimated decommissioning or dismantling costs and whether a provision for these costs is being recorded/recognized in rates. If decommissioning or dismantling costs are not being provided for, disclosure of the reasons for not doing so and the potential financial statement impact should be made.

The term *decommissioning* means to safely remove nuclear facilities from service and reduce residual radioactivity to a level that permits termination of the Nuclear Regulatory Commission (NRC) license and release of the property for unrestricted use. The NRC has issued regulations requiring affected utilities with nuclear generation to prepare formal financial plans providing assurance that decommissioning funds in an amount at least equal to prescribed minimums will be accumulated prospectively over the remaining life of the related nuclear power plant. The NRC minimum is based on decontamination of the reactor facility but not demolition and site restoration. The amounts are based on generic studies and represent the NRC's estimate of the minimum funds needed to protect the public safety and are not intended to reflect the actual cost of decommissioning. Companies making annual sinking fund contributions are required by the NRC to maintain external trust funds. SFAS No. 107, "Disclosure About Fair Value of Financial Instruments," and SFAS No. 115, "Accounting for Certain Investments in Debt and Equity Securities," should be addressed with respect to decommissioning trusts.

Financial reporting considerations related to nuclear decommissioning costs have been resolved with the issuance of SFAS No. 143, "Accounting for Asset Retirement Obligations." Generally, the estimated decommissioning obligation for nuclear power plants had been recognized over the life of the plant as a component of depreciation. SFAS No. 143 changed this practice. Instead, an amount for an asset retirement obligation, such as for the decommissioning of a nuclear power plant, is recognized when it is incurred and displayed as a liability. The asset retirement cost is capitalized as part of the plant asset's carrying amount and subsequently allocated to expense over that asset's useful life. SFAS No. 143 includes special provisions for entities that apply SFAS No. 71. Differences between amounts collected through rates and amounts recognized in accordance with SFAS No. 143 were recognized as regulatory assets and liabilities, if the requirements of SFAS No. 71 were met.

SAB No. 19 also suggests disclosure of the estimated future storage or disposal costs for spent fuel recorded as nuclear fuel amortization. The note should also disclose whether estimated future storage or disposal costs and residual salvage value recognized in prior years are being recovered through a fuel clause or through a general rate increase.

(v) Securitization of Stranded Costs, Including Regulatory Assets. In connection with the electric industry restructuring efforts that occurred in a number of states, the legislative or regulatory framework for moving to a competitive marketplace includes provisions for the affected companies to securitize all or a portion of their stranded costs. Generally, such provisions establish a separate revenue stream/tariff that would be the source of recovery from a company's rate payers for the stranded costs. Ultimately, the company would "sell" the stranded costs to a credit-enhanced, bankruptcy remote special-purpose entity or trust established to finance the purchase through the sale of state authorized debt. Collections of the tariff by the company would be passed through to holders of the debt as periodic payments of interest and principal. The transaction would be structured with the objectives of being treated as a sale for bankruptcy purposes and as a borrowing for tax purposes.

The potential benefits to a company from securitizing stranded costs include the opportunity to improve credit quality and to use the proceeds to reduce leverage and fixed charges, or fund the termination of uneconomic contracts. Rate payers should ultimately benefit though lower rates.

In February 1997, the SEC's Office of Chief Accountant provided financial reporting guidance jointly to California's utility registrants for proceeds received in connection with a stranded cost securitization. The SEC staff concluded that the proceeds received should be classified as either debt or deferred revenue based on the guidance in EITF Issue No. 88-18, "Sales of Future Revenues."

EITF Issue No. 88-18 reached a consensus that the presence of any one of six specifically identified factors independently creates a rebuttable presumption that classification of the proceeds as debt is appropriate. The facts and circumstances of stranded cost securitization transactions will typically result in the presence of one or more of the factors set forth in Issue No. 88-18. Thus, securitization proceeds are expected to be classified as debt for financial reporting purposes.

Issue No. 88-18 also concluded that amounts recorded as debt should be amortized under the interest method. Generally, this will result in an increasing amount of stranded cost recognition in income statements during the securitization period. This occurs because the amount recognized will be equal to the principal portion (on a mortgage basis) of the tariffed debt service cost that is billable to customers and recorded as revenue during each period.

In connection with providing classification guidance, the SEC staff also concluded that regulatory assets are not financial assets under SFAS No. 125, "Accounting for Transfers and Servicing of Financial Assets and Extinguishment of Liabilities," which was subsequently replaced by SFAS No. 140, "Accounting for Transfers and Servicing of Financial Assets and Extinguishments of Liabilities." Further, the legislation that provides for the securitization of regulatory assets simply allows the utility's regulator to impose a tariff on electricity sold in the future. The law, however, does not transpose regulatory assets into financial assets. The basis for the SEC staff's conclusion is that the resulting law creates an enforceable right (which is a right imposed on one party by another, such as a property tax) and not a contractual right. The SEC staff, after consulting with the FASB staff, concluded that the FASB specifically limited financial assets to a contractual right, which is essentially a subset of an enforceable right. Thus, enforceable rights that are not contractual rights do not meet the definition of a financial asset under SFAS Nos. 125 and 140.

The SEC staff also concluded that the proceeds received by the utility do not represent cash for assets sold, but cash received for future services. This approach seems to preclude accounting for this type of a transaction as any kind of a sale outside of SFAS Nos. 125 and 140.

Although the above conclusion is based on the facts and circumstances of a specific transaction, the SEC staff indicated that it is doubtful whether this type of transaction could be altered enough to get a different answer.

(vi) Statement of Financial Accounting Standards Nos. 71 and 101—Expanded Footnote Disclosure.   The current relevance of SFAS No. 71 is an often discussed financial reporting topic for rate-regulated enterprises. In SEC staff comment letters, rate-regulated registrants are typically requested to discuss and quantify the effect on the company's financial statements of the application of SFAS No. 71, and what the impact would be of discontinuing SFAS No. 71. Factors that make such discussions meaningful include: (1) deregulation and resulting competition for a variety of services; (2) discounting of approved tariffs; (3) rate designs or new forms of regulation that are not based on the cost of providing utility service; (4) criticism of continual cost deferrals under the provisions of SFAS No. 71 and the financial difficulties experienced by certain entities with significant deferrals; and (5) actual and expected discontinuations of application of SFAS No. 71 by a growing number of entities, particularly telecommunication companies. An example of the footnote disclosure being represented by the SEC staff follows.

NOTE 1: SUMMARY OF SIGNIFICANT ACCOUNTING POLICIES

Regulatory Assets and Liabilities:

The Company is subject to the provisions of Statement of Financial Accounting Standards 71, "Accounting for the Effects of Certain Types of Regulation." Regulatory assets represent probable future revenue to the Company associated with certain costs that will be recovered from customers through the rate-making process. Regulatory liabilities represent probable future reductions in revenues associated with amounts that are to be credited to customers through the rate-making process. Regulatory assets and liabilities reflected in the Consolidated Balance Sheets as of December 31 (in thousands) relate to the following:

	20XX	20XX
Deferred income taxes	$ XX,XXX	$ XX,XXX
Deferred income tax credits	(X,XXX)	(X,XXX)
Energy efficiency costs	XX,XXX	XX,XXX
Order 636 transition costs	XX,XXX	X,XXX
Debt financing costs	XX,XXX	X,XXX
Plant costs	XX,XXX	XX,XXX
Postretirement benefit costs	XX,XXX	XX,XXX
Nuclear plant outage costs	X,XXX	—
Rate case costs	XXX	X,XXX
Environmental costs	X,XXX	X,XXX
Overrecovered fuel adjustment clause	(X,XXX)	(X,XXX)
	$XXX,XXX	$XXX,XXX

As of December 31, 20XX, $XXX,XXX of the Company's regulatory assets and all of its regulatory liabilities are being reflected in rates charged to customers over periods ranging from 5 to 28 years. The Company intends to request recovery of its remaining regulatory assets in a general rate case filing expected in 20XX. For additional information regarding deferred income taxes, Order 636 transition costs, environmental costs, and postretirement benefit costs, see footnotes 3, 4(e), 4(f), and 12, respectively.

If a portion of the Company's operations becomes no longer subject to the provisions of SFAS No. 71, a write-off of related regulatory assets and liabilities would be required, unless some form of transition cost recovery (refund) continues through rates established and collected for the Company's remaining regulated operations. In addition, the Company would be required to determine any impairment to the carrying costs of deregulated plant and inventory assets.

33.12 SOURCES AND SUGGESTED REFERENCES

Accounting Principles Board, "Accounting for the 'Investment Credit,'" APB Opinion No. 4. AICPA, New York, 1964.

———, "Accounting for Income Taxes," APB Opinion No. 11. AICPA, New York, 1967.

———, "Accounting Changes," APB Opinion No. 20. AICPA, New York, 1971.

———, "Reporting the Results of Operations—Reporting the Effects of Disposal of a Segment of a Business, and Extraordinary, Unusual and Infrequently Occurring Events and Transactions," APB Opinion No. 30. AICPA, New York, 1973.

Amble, Joan L., and Cassel, Jules M., "A Guide to Implementation of Statement 87 on Employers' Accounting for Pensions." FASB, Stamford, CT, 1986.

American Institute of Certified Public Accountants, "Restatement and Revision of Accounting Research Bulletins," Accounting Research Bulletin No. 43. AICPA, New York, 1953.

———, "Declining-Balance Depreciation," Accounting Research Bulletin No. 44. AICPA, New York, July 1958.

———, "Consolidated Financial Statements," Accounting Research Bulletin No. 51. AICPA, New York, August 1959.

Financial Accounting Standards Board, "Official Minutes of the Emerging Issues Task Force Meeting." FASB, Norwalk, CT, February 23, 1989.

_____, "Accounting for Contingencies," Statement of Financial Accounting Standards No. 5. FASB, Stamford, CT, 1975.

_____, "Prior Period Adjustments," Statement of Financial Accounting Standards No. 16. FASB, Stamford, CT, 1977.

_____, "Capitalization of Interest Cost," Statement of Financial Accounting Standards No. 34. FASB, Stamford, CT, 1979.

_____, "Accounting for the Effects of Certain Types of Regulation," Statement of Financial Accounting Standards No. 71. FASB, Stamford, CT, 1982.

_____, "Accounting for OPEB Costs by Rate-Regulated Enterprises," Issue No. 92-12. Financial Accounting Standards Board, Emerging Issues Task Force, Norwalk, CT, January 1993.

_____, "Employers' Accounting for Postretirement Benefits Other Than Pension," Statement of Financial Accounting Standards No. 106. FASB, Stamford, CT, December 1990.

_____, "Accounting for Regulatory Assets," Issue No. 93-4. FASB, Emerging Issues Task Force, Norwalk, CT, March 1993.

_____, "Accounting for Income Taxes," Statement of Financial Accounting Standards No. 109. FASB, Norwalk, CT, February 1992.

_____, "Accounting by Rate-Regulated Utilities for the Effects of Certain Alternative Revenue Programs," Issue No. 92-7. FASB, Emerging Issues Task Force, Norwalk, CT, July 1992.

_____, "Regulated Enterprises—Accounting for Abandonments and Disallowances of Plant Costs," Statement of Financial Accounting Standards No. 90. FASB, Stamford, CT, 1986.

_____, "Regulated Enterprises—Accounting for Phase-in Plans," Statement of Financial Accounting Standards No. 92. FASB, Stamford, CT, 1987.

_____, "Regulated Enterprises—Accounting for the Discontinuation of Application of FASB Statement No. 71," Statement of Financial Accounting Standards No. 101. FASB, Norwalk, CT, 1988.

_____, "Accounting for Asset Retirement Obligations," Statement of Financial Accounting Standards No. 143, FASB, Norwalk, CT, June 2001.

_____, "Accounting for the Impairment or Disposal of Long-Lived Assets," Statement of Financial Accounts Standards No. 144, FASB, Norwalk, CT, August 2001.

_____, "Computation of a Loss on an Abandonment," FASB Technical Bulletin No. 87-2. FASB, Stamford, CT, December 1987.

_____, "Deregulation of the Pricing of Electricity—Issues Related to the Application of FASB Statements No. 71, 'Accounting for the Effects of Regulation' and No. 101, 'Regulated Enterprises—Accounting for the Discontinuance of Application of FASB Statement No. 71,'" Issue No. 97-4. FASB, Emerging Issues Task Force, Norwalk, CT, May, July 1997.

_____, "Determining Whether an Arrangement Contains a Lease," Issue No. 01–8. FASB, Emerging Issues Task Force, Norwalk, CT, May 2003.

Securities and Exchange Commission, "Interpretation Describing Disclosure Concerning Expected Future Costs of Storing Spent Nuclear Fuel and of Decommissioning Nuclear Electric Generating Plants," Staff Accounting Bulletin No. 19. SEC, Washington, DC, January 1978.

_____, "Financing by Electric Utilities Through Use of Construction Intermediaries," Staff Accounting Bulletin No. 28. SEC, Washington, DC, December 1978.

_____, "Utilities—Classification of Disallowed Costs or Costs of Abandoned Plants," Staff Accounting Bulletin No. 72. SEC, Washington, DC, November 1987.

CHAPTER 34

STATE AND LOCAL GOVERNMENT ACCOUNTING

Andrew J. Blossom, CPA
KPMG Peat Marwick LLP

Andrew Gottschalk, CPA
KPMG Peat Marwick LLP

John R. Miller, CPA, CGFM
KPMG Peat Marwick LLP

Warren Ruppel, CPA
DiTomasso & Ruppel, CPAs

This chapter has been updated from the previous edition by the editors.

34.1 INTRODUCTION

The rapid changes that have occurred in the environment of state and local governments during the past few years have prompted sweeping changes to governmental accounting practice and theory. The evolution of governmental accounting and reporting standards has made great strides since the formation of the Governmental Accounting Standards Board (GASB) and the Single Audit Act of 1984. Related to the changes is greater scrutiny by federal and state agencies as they begin to realize the importance of audit quality in the governmental environment. Governmental enterprises are no longer the "shoebox" operations imagined by many people. Rather, government is a large business—a very large business. Officials in government need to be and are much more sophisticated now than similar personnel were only a few years ago. In other words, the increasing complexity of the governmental environment, the increasing demands for public accountability, and the challenges and opportunities that face today's governments require accounting systems that provide fast, accurate, and timely information to the government's decision makers.

Going forward and dealing with the challenges of issues like deteriorating infrastructure, an aging workforce, and public health care, including the spread of terrorism are likely to be key concerns of the individuals who operate the state and local governments. However, the nature and organization of a government's daily activities form an important foundation that must be understood in order to deal with the greater challenges of the future.

34.2 THE NATURE AND ORGANIZATION OF STATE AND LOCAL GOVERNMENT ACTIVITIES

(a) STRUCTURE OF GOVERNMENT.   For the most part, government is structured on three levels: federal, state, and local. This chapter deals only with state and local governments.

States are specific identifiable entities in their own right, but accounting at the state level is associated more often than not with the individual state functions, such as departments of revenue, retirement systems, turnpike authorities, and housing finance agencies.

Local governments exist as political subdivisions of states, and the rules governing their types and operation are different in each of the 50 states. There are, however, three basic types of local governmental units: general purpose local governments (counties, cities, towns, villages, and townships), special purpose local governments, and authorities.

The distinguishing characteristics of general purpose local governments are that they:

- Have broad powers in providing a variety of government services, for example, public safety, fire prevention, public works
- Have general taxing and bonding authority
- Are headed by elected officials

Special purpose local governments are established to provide specific services or construction. They may or may not be contiguous with one or more general purpose local governments.

Authorities and agencies are similar to special purpose governments except that they have no taxing power and are expected to operate with their own revenues. They typically can issue only revenue bonds, not general obligations bonds.

(b) OBJECTIVES OF GOVERNMENT.   The purpose of government is to provide the citizenry with the highest level of services possible given the available financial resources and the legal requirements under which it operates. The services are provided as a result of decisions made during a budgeting process that considers the desired level and quality of services. Resources are then made available through property taxes, sales taxes, income taxes, general and categorical grants from the federal and state governments, charges for services, fines, licenses, and other sources. However, there is generally no direct relationship between the cost of the services rendered to an individual and the amount that the individual pays in taxes, fines, fees, and so on.

Governmental units also conduct operations that are financed and operated in a manner similar to private business enterprises, where the intent is that the costs of providing the goods or services be financed or recovered primarily through charges to the users. In such situations, governments have many of the features of ordinary business operations.

(c) ORGANIZATION OF GOVERNMENT.   A government's organization depends on its constitution (state level) or charter (local level) and on general and special statutes of state and local legislatures. When governments were simpler and did not provide as many services as they do today, there was less of a tendency toward centralization. The commission and weak mayor forms of governments were common. The financial function was typically divided among several individuals.

As government has become more complex, however, the need for strong professional management and for centralization of authority and responsibility has grown. There has been a trend toward the strong mayor and council-manager forms of government. In these forms, a chief financial officer, usually called the *director of finance* or *controller*, is responsible for maintaining the financial records and preparing financial reports; assisting the chief executive officer (CEO) in the preparation of the budget; performing treasury functions such as collecting revenues, managing cash, managing investments, and managing debt; and overseeing the tax assessment function. Other functions that may report to the director of finance are purchasing, data processing, and personnel administration.

Local governments are also making greater use of the internal audit process. In the past, the emphasis by governmental internal auditors was on preaudit that is, reviewing invoices and other documents during processing for propriety and accuracy. The internal auditors reported to the director of finance. Today, however, governmental internal auditors have been removing themselves from the preaudit function by transferring this responsibility to the department responsible for processing the transactions. They have started to provide the typical internal audit function that is, conducting reviews to ensure the reliability of data and the safeguarding of assets, and to become involved in performance auditing (i.e., reviewing the efficiency and effectiveness of the government's operations). They have also started to report, for professional (as opposed to administrative) purposes, to the CEO or directly to the governing board. Finally, internal auditors are becoming more actively involved in the financial statement audit and single audit of their government.

(d) SPECIAL CHARACTERISTICS OF GOVERNMENT.   Several characteristics associated with governments have influenced the development of governmental accounting principles and practices:

- Governments do not have any owners or proprietors in the commercial sense. Accordingly, measurement of earnings attributable or accruing to the direct benefit of an owner is not a relevant accounting concept for governments.
- Governments frequently receive substantial financial inflows for both operating and capital purposes from sources other than revenues and investment earnings, such as taxes and grants.
- Governments frequently obtain financial inflows subject to legally binding restrictions that prohibit or seriously limit the use of these resources for other than the intended purpose.
- A government's authority to raise and expend money results from the adoption of a budget that, by law, usually must balance (e.g., the estimated revenues plus any prior years' surpluses need to be sufficient to cover the projected expenditures).
- The power to raise revenues through taxes, licenses, fees, and fines is generally defined by law.
- There are usually restrictions related to the tax base that govern the purpose, amount, and type of indebtedness that can be issued.
- Expenditures are usually regulated less than revenues and debt, but they can be made only within approved budget categories and must comply with specified purchasing procedures when applicable.
- State laws may dictate the local government accounting policies and systems.
- State laws commonly specify the type and frequency of financial statements to be submitted to the state and to the government's constituency.
- Federal law, the Single Audit Act of 1984, defines the audit requirements for state and local governments.

In short, the environment in which governments operate is complex and legal requirements have a significant influence on their accounting and financial reporting practices.

34.3 SOURCE OF ACCOUNTING PRINCIPLES FOR STATE AND LOCAL GOVERNMENT ACCOUNTING

Governmental accounting principles are not a complete and separate body of accounting principles, but rather are part of the whole body of generally accepted accounting principles (GAAP). Since the accounting profession's standard-setting bodies have been concerned primarily with the accounting needs of profit-seeking organizations, these principles have been defined primarily by groups formed by the state and local governments. In 1934, the National Committee on Municipal Accounting published "A Tentative Outline—Principles of Municipal Accounting." In 1968, the National Committee on Governmental Accounting (the successor organization) published *Governmental Accounting, Auditing, and Financial Reporting* (GAAFR), which was widely used as a source of governmental accounting principles. The American Institute of Certified Public

Accountants (AICPA) Industry Audit Guide, "Audits of State and Local Governmental Units," published in 1974, stated that the accounting principles outlined in the 1968 GAAFR constituted GAAP for government entities.

The financial difficulties experienced by many governments in the mid-1970s led to a call for a review and modification of the accounting and financial reporting practices used by governments. Laws were introduced in Congress, but never enacted, that would have given the federal government the authority to establish governmental accounting principles. The Financial Accounting Standards Board (FASB), responding to pressures, commissioned a research study to define and explain the issues associated with accounting for all nonbusiness enterprises, including governments. This study was completed in 1978, and the Board developed SFAC No. 4 for nonbusiness organizations. The Statement defined nonbusiness organizations, the users of the statements, the financial information needs of these users, and the information that is necessary to meet these needs.

(a) NATIONAL COUNCIL ON GOVERNMENT ACCOUNTING. The National Council on Governmental Accounting (NCGA) was the successor of the National Committee reconstituted as a permanent organization. One of its first projects was to "restate," that is, update, clarify, amplify, and reorder the GAAFR to incorporate pertinent aspects of "Audits of State and Local Governmental Units." The restatement was published in March 1979 as NCGA Statement No. 1, "Governmental Accounting and Financial Reporting Principles." Shortly thereafter, the AICPA Committee on State and Local Government Accounting recognized NCGA Statement No. 1 as authoritative and agreed to amend the Industry Audit Guide accordingly. This restatement was completed, and a new guide was published in 1986. Thus NCGA Statement No. 1 became the primary reference source for the accounting principles unique to governmental accounting. However, in areas not unique to governmental accounting, the complete body of GAAP still needed to be considered.

(b) GOVERNMENTAL ACCOUNTING STANDARDS BOARD. In 1984, the Financial Accounting Foundation (FAF) established the GASB as the primary standard setter for GAAP for governmental entities. Under the jurisdictional agreement, GASB has the primary responsibility for establishing accounting and reporting principles for government entities. GASB's first action was to issue Statement No. 1, "Authoritative Status of NCGA Pronouncements and AICPA Industry Audit Guide," which recognized the NCGA's statements and interpretations and the AICPA's audit guide as authoritative. The Statement also recognized the pronouncements of the FASB issued prior to the date of the agreement as applicable to governments. FASB pronouncements issued after the organization of GASB do not become effective unless GASB specifically adopts them.

The GASB has operated under this jurisdictional arrangement since 1984. However, the arrangement came under scrutiny during the GASB's mandatory five-year review conducted in 1988. The Committee to Review Structure of Governmental Accounting Standards released its widely read report in January 1989 on the results of its review and proposed to the FAF, among other recommendations, a new jurisdictional arrangement and GAAP hierarchy for governments. These two recommendations prompted a great deal of controversy within the industry. The issue revolved around the Committee's recommended jurisdictional arrangement for the separately issued financial statements of certain "special entities." (Special entities are organizations that can either be privately or governmentally owned and include colleges and universities, hospitals, and utilities.) The Committee recommended that FASB be the primary accounting standard setter for these special entities when they issue separate, stand-alone financial statements and that GASB be allowed to require the presentation of "additional data" in these stand-alone statements. This arrangement would allow for greater comparability between entities in the same industry (e.g., utilities) regardless of whether the entities were privately or governmentally owned and still allow government-owned entities to meet their "public accountability" reporting objective.

This recommendation and a subsequent compromise recommendation were unacceptable to many and especially to the various public interest groups such as the Government Finance Officers Association (GFOA) who, 10 months after the Committee's report, began discussions to establish a new body to set standards for state and local government. These actions prompted the FAF to consider whether a standard-setting schism was in the interest of the public and the users of financial statements. Based on this consideration, the FAF decided that the jurisdictional arrangement established in 1984 should remain intact.

In response to the jurisdictional arrangement described above, the AICPA issued Statement on Auditing Standards No. 69, "The Meaning of Present Fairly in Conformity with Generally Accepted Accounting Principles in the Independent Auditor's Report," which creates a hierarchy of GAAP specifically for state and local governments. SAS No. 69 raises AICPA Statement of Positions (SOPs) and audit and accounting guides to a level of authority above that of industry practice. As a result, FASB pronouncements will not apply to state and local governments unless the GASB issues a standard incorporating them into GAAP for state and local government. In September 1993, the GASB issued Statement No. 20, "Accounting and Financial Reporting for Proprietary Funds and Other Governmental Entities That Use Proprietary Fund Accounting." The Statement provides interim guidance on business-type accounting and financial reporting for proprietary activities, pending further research by the GASB that is expected to result in the issuance of one or more pronouncements on the accounting and financial reporting model for proprietary activities.

Statement No. 20 requires proprietary activities to apply all applicable GASB Statements as well as FASB pronouncements, Accounting Principles Board (APB) Opinions, and Accounting Research Bulletins issued on or before November 30, 1989, unless those pronouncements conflict or contradict with a GASB pronouncement. A proprietary activity may also apply, at its option, all FASB pronouncements issued after November 30, 1989, except those that conflict or contradict with a GASB pronouncement.

The GASB subsequently issued Statement No. 29, "The Use of Not-for-Profit Accounting and Financial Reporting Principles by Governmental Entities," which amended Statement No. 20 to indicate that proprietary activities could apply only those FASB statements that were developed for business enterprises. The FASB statements and interpretations whose provisions are limited to not-for-profit organizations or address issues primarily of concern to those organizations may not be applied. These actions, along with the increased activity of the FASB in setting standards for not-for-profit organizations, have resulted in increasing differences in GAAP between nongovernmental entities and state and local governments.

These differences also highlight the importance of determining whether a particular entity is a state or local government. While it is obvious that states, cities, and counties are governments, other units of government are less clear. Is a university considered a government if it is supported 70 percent by taxes allocated by the state? What if the percentage is only 15 percent? If a hospital is created by a county but the county has no continuing involvement with the hospital, is the hospital a government? The GASB acknowledged these concerns in the Basis for Conclusions of Statement No. 29 in stating:

> Some respondents believe that the fundamental issue underlying this Statement—identifying those entities that should apply the GAAP hierarchy applicable to state and local governmental entities—will continue to be troublesome until there is an authoritative definition of such "governmental entities." The Board agrees—but does not have the authority to unilaterally establish a definition—and intends to continue to explore alternatives for resolving the issue.

The decision as to whether a particular entity should follow the hierarchy for state and local governments or nongovernmental entities is a matter of professional judgment based on the individual facts and circumstances for the entity in question. The AICPA audit and accounting guide for not-for-profit organizations provides guidance to distinguish between governmental and nongovernmental organizations. It defines governmental organizations as:

> Public corporations and bodies corporate and politic. . . . Other organizations are governmental organizations if they have one or more of the following characteristics:

a. Popular election of officers or appointment (or approval) of a controlling majority of the members of the organization's governing body by officials of one or more state or local governments;

b. The potential for unilateral dissolution by a government with the net assets reverting to a government; or

c. The power to enact and enforce a tax levy.

Furthermore, organizations are presumed to be governmental if they have the ability to issue directly (rather than through a state or municipal authority) debt that pays interest exempt from federal taxation. However, organizations possessing only that ability (to issue tax-exempt debt) and none of the other governmental characteristics may rebut the presumption that they are governmental if their determination is supported by compelling, relevant evidence.

34.4 GOVERNMENTAL ACCOUNTING PRINCIPLES AND PRACTICES

(a) SIMILARITIES TO PRIVATE SECTOR ACCOUNTING.   Since the accounting principles and practices of governments are part of the whole body of GAAP, certain accounting concepts and conventions are as applicable to governmental entities as they are to accounting in other industries:

- *Consistency.* Identical transactions should be recorded in the same manner both during a period and from period to period.
- *Conservatism.* The uncertainties that surround the preparation of financial statements are reflected in a general tendency toward early recognition of unfavorable events and minimization of the amount of net assets and net income.
- *Historical Cost.* Amounts should be recognized in the financial statements at the historical cost to the reporting entity. Changes in the general purchasing power should not be recognized in the basic financial statements.
- *Matching.* The financial statements should provide for a matching, but in government it is a matching of revenues and expenditures with a time period to ensure that revenues and the expenditures they finance are reported in the same period.
- *Reporting Entity.* The focus of the financial report is the economic activities of a discrete individual entity for which there is a reporting responsibility.
- *Materiality.* Financial reporting is concerned only with significant information.
- *Full Disclosure.* Financial statements must contain all information necessary to understand the presentation of financial position and results of operations and to prevent them from being misleading.

(b) USERS AND USES OF FINANCIAL REPORTS.   Users of the financial statements of a governmental unit are not identical to users of a business entity's financial statements. The GASB Concepts Statement No. 1 identifies three groups of primary users of external governmental financial reports:

1. *Those to Whom Government Is Primarily Accountable—The Citizenry.* The citizenry group includes citizens (whether they are classified as taxpayers, voters, or service recipients), the media, advocate groups, and public finance researchers. This user group is concerned with obtaining the maximum amount of service with a minimum amount of taxes and wants to know where the government obtains its resources and how those resources are used.

2. *Those Who Directly Represent the Citizens—Legislative and Oversight Bodies.* The legislative and oversight officials group includes members of state legislatures, county commissions, city councils, boards of trustees, and school boards, and those executive branch officials with oversight responsibility over other levels of government. These groups need timely warning of the development of situations that require corrective action, financial information that can

serve as a basis for judging management performance, and financial information on which to base future plans and policies.

3. *Those Who Lend or Participate in the Lending Process—Investors and Creditors.* Investors and creditors include individual and institutional investors and creditors, municipal security underwriters, bond-rating agencies (Moody's Investors Service, and Standard & Poor's, etc.), bond insurers, and financial institutions.

The uses of a government's financial reports are also different. GASB Concepts Statement No. 1 also indicates that governmental financial reporting should provide information to assist users in (1) assessing accountability and (2) making economic, social, and political decisions by:

- *Comparing Actual Financial Results with the Legally Adopted Budget.* All three user groups are interested in comparing original or modified budgets with actual results to get some assurance that spending mandates have been complied with and that resources have been used for the intended purposes.

- *Assisting in Determining Compliance with Finance-Related Laws, Rules, and Regulations.* In addition to the legally mandated budgetary and fund controls, other legal restrictions may control governmental actions. Some examples are bond covenants, grant restrictions, and taxing and debt limits. Financial reports help demonstrate compliance with these laws, rules, and regulations.
  - Citizens are concerned that governments adhere to these regulations because noncompliance may indicate fiscal irresponsibility and could have severe financial consequences such as acceleration of debt payments, disallowance of questioned costs, or loss of grants.
  - Legislative and oversight officials are also concerned with compliance as a follow-up to the budget formulation process.
  - Investors and creditors are interested in the government's compliance with debt covenants and restrictions designed to protect their investment.

- *Assisting in Evaluating Efficiency and Effectiveness.* Citizen groups and legislators, in particular, want information about service efforts, costs, and accomplishments of a governmental entity. This information, when combined with information from other sources, helps users assess the economy, efficiency, and effectiveness of government and may help form a basis for voting on funding decisions.

- *Assessing Financial Condition and Results of Operations.* Financial reports are commonly used to assess a state or local government's financial condition, that is, its financial position and its ability to continue to provide services and meet its obligations as they come due.
  - Investors and creditors need information about available and likely future financial resources, actual and contingent liabilities, and the overall debt position of a government to evaluate the government's ability to continue to provide resources for long-term debt service.
  - Citizens' groups are concerned with financial condition when evaluating the likelihood of tax or service fee increases.
  - Legislative and oversight officials need to assess the overall financial condition, including debt structure and funds available for appropriation, when developing both capital and operating budget and program recommendations.

With the users and the uses of financial reports clearly defined, the GASB developed the following three overall objectives of governmental financial reporting:

1. Financial reporting should assist in fulfilling a government's duty to be publicly accountable and should enable users to assess that accountability by:
   a. Providing information to determine whether current-year revenues were sufficient to pay for current-year services

    b. Demonstrating whether resources were obtained and used in accordance with the entity's legally adopted budget and compliance with other finance-related legal or contractual requirements

    c. Providing information to assist users in assessing the service efforts, costs, and accomplishments of the governmental entity

  2. Financial reporting should assist users in evaluating the operating results of the governmental entity for the year by providing information:

    a. About sources and uses of financial resources

    b. About how the governmental entity financed its activities and met its cash requirements

    c. Necessary to determine whether the entity's financial position improved or deteriorated as a result of the year's operations

  3. Financial reporting should assist users in assessing the level of services that can be provided by the governmental entity and its ability to meet its obligations as they become due by:

    a. Providing information about the financial position and condition of a governmental entity. Financial reporting should provide information about resources and obligations, both actual and contingent, current and noncurrent, and about tax sources, tax limitations, tax burdens, and debt limitations.

    b. Providing information about a governmental entity's physical and other nonfinancial resources having useful lives that extend beyond the current year, including information that can be used to assess the service potential of those resources.

    c. Disclosing legal or contractual restrictions on resources and risks of potential loss of resources.

    In April 1994, the GASB issued Concepts Statement No. 2, "Service Efforts and Accomplishments Reporting," which expands on the consideration of service efforts and accomplishments (SEA) reporting included in Concepts Statement No. 1. The GASB believes that the government's duty to be publicly accountable requires the presentation of SEA information. Concepts Statement No. 2 identifies the objective of SEA reporting as providing "more complete information about a governmental entity's performance that can be provided by the operating statement, balance sheet, and budgetary comparison statements and schedules to assist users in assessing the economy, efficiency, and effectiveness of services provided." The Concepts Statement also indicates SEA information should meet the characteristics of relevance, understandability, comparability, timeliness, consistency, and reliability. The GASB acknowledges the need for continued experimentation and development of SEA measures prior to the issuance of SEA reporting standards.

(c) SUMMARY STATEMENT OF PRINCIPLES. Because governments operate under different conditions and have different reporting objectives than commercial entities, basic principles applicable to government accounting and reporting have been developed. These principles are generally recognized as being essential to effective management control and financial reporting. In other words, understanding these principles and how they operate is extremely important to the understanding of governments.

    A governmental accounting system must make it possible to both (1) present fairly the financial position and results of financial operations of the government as a whole and of the funds and account groups of the governmental unit in conformity with GAAP, which include full disclosure, and to provide adequately the required supplementary information, including management's discussion and analysis (MD&A); and (2) determine and demonstrate compliance with finance-related legal and contractual provisions. The requirements concerning the government as a whole and MD&A were implemented in GASB Statement No. 34, "Basic Financial Statements—and Management's Discussion and Analysis—for State and Local Governments," issued by the GASB in June 1999.

(i) Government-Wide Financial Statements. Under GASB Statement No. 34, government-wide financial statements should be presented in addition to fund financial statements. They should report information about the reporting government as a whole, except for its fiduciary activities. The statements should include separate columns for governmental activities, business-type activities, total activities, and component units, which are legally separate organizations for which the elected officials of the primary government (PG) are financially accountable, or other organizations for which the nature and significance of its relationship with a PG are such that exclusion from the financial statements of the PG would cause them to be misleading or incomplete. They should be prepared using the economic resources measurement focus and the accrual basis of accounting.

(ii) Fund Accounting Systems. Governmental accounting systems should provide information that permits reporting on a fund basis. A "fund" is defined as a fiscal and accounting entity with a self-balancing set of accounts recording cash and other financial resources, together with all related liabilities and residual equities or balances, and changes therein, which are segregated for the purpose of carrying on specific activities or attaining certain objectives in accordance with special regulations, restrictions, or limitations.

(iii) Types of Funds. The following three types of funds should be used by state and local governments.

Governmental Funds.

1. *The General Fund.* To account for all financial resources except those required to be accounted for in another fund.
2. *Special Revenue Funds.* To account for the proceeds for specific revenue sources (other than expendable trusts, or major capital projects) that are legally restricted to expenditures for specified purposes.
3. *Capital Projects Funds.* To account for financial resources to be used for the acquisition or construction of major capital facilities (other than those financed by proprietary funds and trust funds).
4. *Debt Service Funds.* To account for the accumulation of resources for, and the payment of, general long-term debt principal and interest.
5. *Permanent Funds.* To account for the resources used to make earnings, of which only the earnings may be used for the benefit of the government or its citizenry, such as a cemetery perpetual-care fund.

The GASB Codification also discusses special assessment funds. However, the issuance of GASB Statement No. 6, "Accounting and Financial Reporting for Special Assessments," in January 1987 eliminated the special assessment fund type for financial reporting purposes. The Statement does, however, allow special assessment funds to exist for budget purposes.

Proprietary Funds.

1. *Enterprise Funds.* To account for operations (a) that are financed and operated in a manner similar to private business enterprises, where the intent of the governing body is that the cost (expenses, including depreciation) of providing goods or services to the general public, on a continuing basis, be financed or recovered primarily through user charges; or (b) where the governing body has decided that periodic determination of revenues earned, expenses incurred, and/or net income is appropriate for capital maintenance, public policy, management control, accountability, or other purposes.
2. *Internal Service Funds.* To account for the financing of goods or services provided by one department or agency to other departments or agencies of the governmental unit, or to other governmental units, on a cost-reimbursement basis.

Fiduciary Funds.   Trust and agency funds account for assets held by a governmental unit in a trustee capacity or as an agent for individuals, private organizations, other governmental units, and other funds. These include (1) pension trust funds, (2) investment trust funds, (3) private-purpose funds, and (4) agency funds.

Under GASB Statement No. 34, a government should report separately on its most important, or "major," funds, including its general fund. A major fund is one whose revenues, expenditures/expenses, assets, or liabilities (excluding extraordinary items) are at least 10 percent of the corresponding totals for all governmental or enterprise funds and at least 5 percent of the aggregate amount for all governmental and enterprise funds. Any other fund may be reported as a major fund if the government's officials believe information about the fund is particularly important to the users of the statements. Other funds should be reported in the aggregate in a separate column. Internal service funds should be reported in the aggregate in a separate column on the proprietary fund statements. Separate fund financial statements should be presented for governmental and proprietary funds. A summary reconciliation to the government-wide financial statements should be presented at the bottom of the fund financial statements or in a separate schedule. Fund balances for governmental funds should be segregated into reserved and unreserved categories. Proprietary fund net assets should be reported in the same categories required for the government-wide financial statements. Proprietary fund statements of net assets should distinguish between current and noncurrent assets and liabilities and should display restricted assets.

(iv) Number of Funds.   Governmental units should establish and maintain those funds required by law and sound financial administration. Only the minimum number of funds consistent with legal and operating requirements should be established, however, since unnecessary funds result in inflexibility, undue complexity, and inefficient financial administration.

(v) Accounting for Capital Assets and Long-Term Liabilities.   A clear distinction should be made between (1) proprietary and fiduciary capital assets and general capital assets and (2) proprietary and similar fiduciary long-term liabilities and general long-term debt.

1. Capital assets related to specific proprietary funds should be accounted for through both the government—wide and proprietary funds statements. All other capital assets of a governmental unit should be accounted for only in the government-wide capital account, except for fiduciary fund capital assets that should be accounted for only in the fiduciary funds statements.
2. Long-term liabilities of proprietary funds should be accounted for in those funds. Fiduciary fund long-term liabilities should be reported only in the statement of net assets of the fiduciary fund. All other outstanding general long-term liabilities should be accounted for in the government funds, and in the government activities column in the government-wide statement of net assets.

(vi) Valuation of Capital Assets.   Capital assets should be accounted for at cost or, if the cost is not practicably determinable, at estimated cost. Donated fixed assets should be recorded at their estimated fair value at the time received.

(vii) Depreciation of Capital Assets.   While some assets are not depreciated, such as land, most assets are depreciated over their useful lives. An exception is also those assets accounted for using the modified approach, as outlined in GASB 34. Depreciation of capital assets should be recorded in the government-wide activities statement; the proprietary fund statement of revenues, expense, and changes in fund net assets; and the statement of changes in fiduciary net assets accounts of governmental funds.

(viii) Accrual Basis in Governmental Accounting. The modified accrual or accrual basis of accounting, as appropriate, should be used in measuring financial position and operating results.

- Governmental fund revenues and expenditures should be recognized on the modified accrual basis using the current financial resources measurement focus. Revenues should be recognized in the accounting period in which they become available and measurable. Expenditures should be recognized in the accounting period in which the fund liability is incurred, if measurable, except for outstanding interest on general long-term debt, which should be recognized when due.

- Proprietary fund revenues and expenses should be recognized using the current financial resources measurement focus and the accrual basis. Revenues should be recognized in the accounting period in which they are earned and become measurable; expenses should be recognized in the period incurred, if measurable.

- Fiduciary fund revenues and expenses or expenditures (as appropriate) should be recognized using the current financial resources measurement focus and the accrual basis.

- Transfers should be recognized in the period in which the inter-fund receivable and payable arise.

(ix) Budgeting, Budgetary Control, and Budgetary Reporting. An annual budget should be adopted by every governmental unit. The accounting system should provide the basis for appropriate budgetary control.

(x) Transfer, Revenue, Expenditure, and Expense Account Classification. Interfund transfers should be classified separately from fund revenues and expenditures or expenses.

Governmental fund revenues should be classified by fund and source. Expenditures should be classified by fund, function (or program), organization unit, activity, character, and principal classes of objects.

Proprietary fund revenues and expenses should be classified in essentially the same manner as those of similar business organizations, functions, or activities.

(xi) Common Terminology and Classification. A common terminology and classification should be used consistently throughout the budget, the accounts, and the financial reports of each fund.

(xii) Interim and Annual Financial Reports. Appropriate interim financial statements and reports of financial position, operating results, and other pertinent information should be prepared to facilitate management control of financial operations, legislative oversight, and, where necessary or desired, external reporting.

A comprehensive annual financial report (CAFR) covering all funds and account groups of the governmental unit should be prepared and published, including appropriate combined, combining, and individual fund statements; notes to the financial statements; required supplementary information; schedules; narrative explanations; and statistical tables.

General purpose financial statements may be issued separately from the CAFR. Such statements should include the basic financial statements, notes to the financial statements, and any required supplementary information essential to a fair presentation of financial position and operating results and cash flows of proprietary funds and nonexpendable trust funds.

(d) DISCUSSION OF THE PRINCIPLES. To enable readers to more fully understand the principles, a discussion appears below.

(e) LEGAL COMPLIANCE.   *Principle 1* of governmental accounting (GASB Codification Section 1100.101) states:

> A governmental accounting system must make it possible both: (a) to present fairly and with full disclosure the financial position and results of financial operations of the funds and account groups of the governmental unit in conformity with GAAPs; and (b) to determine and demonstrate compliance with finance-related legal and contractual provisions.

Several state and local governments have accounting requirements that differ from GAAP; for example, cash basis accounting is required, and capital projects must be accounted for in the general fund. Because of this situation, the legal compliance principle used to be interpreted as meaning that, when the legal requirements for a particular entity differed from GAAP, the legal requirements became GAAP for the entity. This interpretation is no longer viewed as sound. When GAAP and legal requirements conflict, governments should present their basic financial report in accordance with GAAP and, if the legal requirements differ materially from GAAP, the legally required reports can be published as supplemental data to the basic financial report or, if these differences are extreme, it may be preferable to publish a separate legal basis report.

However, conflicts that arise between GAAP and legal provisions do not require maintaining two sets of accounting records. Rather, the accounting records typically would be maintained in accordance with the legal requirements but would include sufficient additional information to permit preparation of reports in accordance with GAAP.

(f) FUND ACCOUNTING.   Principle 2, fund accounting, is used by governments because of (1) legally binding restrictions that prohibit or seriously limit the use of much of a government's resources for other than the purposes for which the resources were obtained, and (2) the importance of reporting the accomplishment of various objectives for which the resources were entrusted to the government.

GASB Codification Section 1100.102 defines a fund for accounting purposes as:

> A fiscal and accounting entity with a self-balancing set of accounts recording cash and other financial resources, together with all related liabilities and residual equities or balances, and changes therein, which are segregated for the purposes of carrying on specific activities or obtaining certain objectives in accordance with special regulations, restrictions, or limitations.

Thus a fund may include accounts for assets, liabilities, fund balance or retained earnings, revenues, expenditures, or expenses. Accounts may also exist for appropriations and encumbrances, depending on the budgeting system used.

(g) TYPES AND NUMBER OF FUNDS.   Because of the various nature of activities carried on by government, it is often important to be able to account for certain activities separately from others (i.e., when required by law). Principles 3 and 4 define seven basic fund types in which to account for various governmental activities. The purpose and operation of each fund type differs, and it is important to understand these differences and why they exist. Every fund maintained by a government should be classified into one of these three fund categories:

1. Governmental funds, emphasizing major funds:
   - The general fund
   - Special revenue funds
   - Capital projects funds
   - Debt service funds
   - Permanent funds
2. Proprietary funds:
   - Enterprise funds, emphasizing major funds
   - Internal service funds

3. Fiduciary funds and similar component units
   - Pension and other employee benefit trust funds
   - Investment trust funds
   - Private-purpose trust funds
   - Agency funds

The general fund, special revenue funds, debt service funds, and capital projects funds are considered governmental funds since they record the transactions associated with the general services of a local governmental unit (i.e., police, public works, fire prevention) that are provided to all citizens and are supported primarily by general revenues. For these funds, the primary concerns, from the financial statement reader's point of view, are the types and amounts of resources that have been made available to the governmental unit and the uses to which they have been put.

The enterprise funds and internal services funds are considered proprietary funds because they account for activities for which the determination of net income is important.

The trust and agency funds are considered fiduciary funds. There are basically three types of trust funds: expendable trust funds that operate in a manner similar to governmental funds, nonexpendable trust funds and pension trust funds that operate in a manner similar to proprietary funds, and agency funds that account for funds held by a government entity in an agent capacity. Agency funds consist of assets and liabilities only and do not involve the measurement of operations.

Although a government should establish and maintain those funds required by law and sound financial administration, it should set up only the minimum number of funds consistent with legal and operating requirements. The maintenance of unnecessary funds results in inflexibility, undue complexity, and inefficient financial administration. For instance, in the past, the proceeds of specific revenue sources or resources that financed specific activities as required by law or administrative regulation had to be accounted for in a special revenue fund. However, governmental resources restricted to purposes usually financed through the general fund should be accounted for in the general fund, provided that all legal requirements can be satisfied. Examples include state grants received by an entity for special education. If a separate fund is not legally required, the grant revenues and the grant-related expenditures should be accounted for in the fund for which they are to be used.

Another way to minimize funds is by accounting for debt service payments in the general fund and not establishing a separate debt service fund unless it is legally mandated or resources are actually being accumulated for future debt service payments (i.e., for term bonds or in sinking funds).

Furthermore, one or more identical accounts for separate funds should be combined in the accounting system, particularly for funds that are similar in nature or are in the same fund group. For example, the cash accounts for all special revenue funds may be combined, provided that the integrity of each fund is preserved through a distinct equity account for each fund.

(i) General Fund. The general fund accounts for the revenues and expenditures not accounted for in other funds and finances most of the current normal functions of governmental units: general government, public safety, highways, sanitation and waste removal, health and welfare, culture, and recreation. It is usually the largest and most important accounting activity for state and local governments. Property taxes are often the principal source of general fund revenues, but substantial revenues may also be received from other financing sources.

The general fund balance sheet is typically limited to current assets and current liabilities. The GASB Codification emphasizes this practice by using the terms *expendable assets* and *current liabilities* when describing governmental funds, of which the general fund is one. Thus the fund balance in the general fund is considered available to finance current operations.

A governmental unit, however, often makes long-term advances to independent governmental agencies, such as redevelopment authorities or housing agencies, or provides the capital necessary to establish an internal service fund. The advances are recorded in the general fund as an advance receivable. Although in most cases collectibility is assured, repayment may extend over a number of years. The inclusion of a noncurrent asset in the general fund results in a portion of the general fund's fund balance not being readily available to finance current operations.

To reflect the unavailability of an advance to finance current activities, a fund balance reserve is established to segregate a portion of the fund balance from the general fund in an amount equal to the advance that is not considered currently available. Establishing this reserve does not require a charge to operations; rather, it is a segregation of the fund balance in the available general fund and is established by debiting unreserved fund balance and crediting reserved fund balance. The reserve is reported in the fund balance section of the balance sheet.

(ii) Special Revenue Funds. Special revenue funds should be established to account for the proceeds of specific revenue sources (other than expendable trusts, or major capital projects) that are legally restricted to expenditure for specified purposes and for which a separate fund is legally required. Examples are parks, schools, and museums, as well as particular functions or activities, such as highway construction or street maintenance.

A special revenue fund may have a definite limited life, or it may remain in effect until discontinued or revoked by appropriate legislative action. It may be used for a very limited purpose, such as the maintenance of a historic landmark, or it may finance an entire function of government, such as public education or highways.

A special revenue fund may be administered by the regularly constituted administrative and financial organization of the government; by an independent body or special purpose local district, such as a park board or the board of directors of a water district; or by a quasi-independent body. In some cases, the fund may be administered by an independent board, but the government maintains the accounting records because the independent board does not have the necessary personnel or other facilities.

Some of the activities mentioned above could also be accounted for in an enterprise fund. Deciding which type of fund to use is often difficult. Basically, unless the government determines that the activity should be financed and operated in a manner similar to that for private business enterprises, the activity should be accounted for as a special revenue fund. A special revenue fund is not appropriate, however, when the costs, including depreciation, of providing goods or services to the general public on a continuing basis are to be financed or recovered primarily through user charges. Also, a special revenue fund is not appropriate when the government has decided that periodic determination of revenues earned, expenses incurred, or net income is appropriate for capital maintenance, public policy, management control, accountability, or other purposes.

(iii) Debt Service Funds. Debt service funds exist to account for the accumulation of resources for, and the payment of, long-term debt principal and interest other than that which it is issued for and serviced primarily by an enterprise or similar trust fund. A debt service fund is necessary only if it is legally required or if resources are being accumulated for future payment. Although governments may incur a wide variety of debt, the more common types are described below.

Term (or sinking fund) bonds are being replaced by serial bonds as the predominant form of state and local government debt. For term bonds, debt service consists of annual additions of resources being made to a cumulative "investment fund" for repayment of the issue at maturity. The additions, also called *sinking fund installments*, are computed on an actuarial basis, which includes assumptions that certain rates of interest will be earned from investing the resources accumulating in the investment fund. If the actual earnings are less than the planned earnings, subsequent additions are increased; if the earnings are greater than planned, the excess is carried forward until the time of the final addition of the fund. Because term bond principal is due at the end of the bond's term, the expenditure for repayment of principal is recognized at that time.

Debt service on serial bonds, however, generally consists of preestablished principal payments that are due on an annual basis and interest payments based on either fixed or variable rates that are due on a semiannual basis. No sinking fund is involved in the repayment of serial bonds.

The revenues for a debt service fund come from one or more sources, with property taxes being the predominant source. Taxes that are specified for debt service appear as a revenue of the debt service fund. Taxes for general purposes (i.e., not specified but nevertheless used for debt service) are considered to be an operating transfer to the debt service fund from the fund in which the revenue is recorded, oftentimes the general fund.

Enterprise activity earnings may be another resource for servicing general obligation debt. In these instances, the general obligation debt should be classified as enterprise debt (a liability of the enterprise fund), and the debt service payments should be recorded in the enterprise fund as a reduction of the liability, not in the debt service fund. The debt service transactions would be recorded in the debt service fund only if the enterprise fund was not expected to be responsible for repaying the debt on an ongoing basis. Essentially, if the enterprise fund became unable to service the principal and interest and the general governmental unit assumed responsibility for servicing the debt, then the debt service fund would be used.

More recently, governmental units have been exploring alternative financing activities including lease-purchase arrangements and issuance of zero-coupon or deep discount debt. The issues surrounding lease-purchase arrangements involve legal questions about whether such arrangements constitute debt of a government since they often do not require voter approval prior to incurring the debt. Zero-coupon and deep discount debt issues center on the manner of presenting and amortizing the bond discount amount in the government's financial statements.

Quite often, a refunding bond is issued to replace or consolidate prior debt issues. Determining the appropriate accounting principles to apply to refunding bonds depends primarily on whether the bonds are included in an enterprise fund or in the general long-term debt account group. GASB Statement No. 7, "Advance Refundings Resulting in Defeasance of Debt," outlines the appropriate accounting and reporting principles. For the refunding of debt, the proceeds of the refunding issue become an "other financing source" of the fund receiving the proceeds of the refunding bond (oftentimes a debt service fund created to service the original issue or a capital projects fund). Since the proceeds are used to liquidate the original debt, an "other financing use" is also recorded in the debt service or capital projects fund in an amount equal to the remaining principal, interest, and other amounts due on the original debt.

If, as a result of the refunding, the liability to the bondholders is satisfied, the refunding is referred to as a *legal defeasance of debt* or *current refunding*. However, refundings often do not result in the immediate repayment of the debt but rather assets are placed in a trust to be used to repay the debt as it matures. These refundings are called *advance refundings* or an *in-substance defeasance*. To qualify for an in-substance defeasance, the proceeds of the refunding bonds are placed in an irrevocable trust and invested in essentially risk-free securities, usually obligations of the U.S. Treasury or other government agencies, so that the risk-free securities, together with any premiums on the defeased debt, and expenses of the refunding operation will be sufficient for the trust to pay off the debt to the bondholders when it becomes due. The accounting for an in-substance defeasance is identical to legal defeasances except that payment is made to a trustee rather than to bondholders. The trustee then pays principal and interest to the bondholders based on the maturity schedule of the bond. In addition, the recording of payments of proceeds to the trustee as another financing use is limited to the amount of proceeds.

Advance refundings of debt recorded in a proprietary fund follow the accounting principles outlined in GASB Statement No. 23, "Accounting and Financial Reporting for Refundings of Debt Reported by Proprietary Activities." Statement No. 23 requires that the difference between the reacquisition price and the net carrying amount of the old debt be deferred and amortized as a component of interest expense over the remaining life of the old or the life of the new debt, whichever is shorter.

Regardless of whether the defeased debt was recorded in the government capital account or a proprietary fund, GASB Statement No. 7 requires the disclosure of a description of the refunding transaction; the cash flow gain or loss, which is the difference between the total cash outflow of the new debt (i.e., principal, interest, etc.) and the remaining cash outflow of the old debt; and the economic gain or loss, which is the difference between the present values of the cash flows of the new and old debt.

For advance refundings, each year after the defeasance, the footnotes to the financial statements should disclose the remaining amount of debt principal that the trustee has to pay to bondholders.

(iv) Capital Projects Funds.   The purpose of a capital projects fund is to account for the receipt and disbursement of resources used for the acquisition of major capital facilities other than those financed by enterprise funds. Capital projects are defined as outlays for major, permanent fixed assets having a relatively long life (e.g., buildings), as compared with those of limited life (e.g., office equipment). Capital projects are usually financed by bond proceeds, but they can also be financed from other resources, such as current revenues or grants from other governments.

Capital outlays financed entirely from the direct revenues of the general fund or a special revenue fund and not requiring long-term borrowing may be accounted for in the fund providing such resources rather than in a separate capital projects fund. Assets with a relatively short life—hence not capital projects—are usually financed from current revenues or by short-term obligations and are accounted for in the general or special revenue fund.

Accounting for Capital Projects Fund Transactions.   Bonds are issued and capital projects are started under a multiyear capital program. In some instances, it is necessary to secure referendum approval to issue general obligation bonds. Obligations are then incurred and expenditures made according to an annual capital projects budget.

When a project is financed entirely from general obligation bond proceeds, the initial entry to be made in the capital projects fund when the bonds are sold is:

Cash	$XXX	
Other financing source—		
Proceeds of general obligation bonds		$XXX

Whereas the proceeds of the bonds are accounted for in the capital projects funds, the liability for the face amount of the bonds is recorded in the general long-term debt account group.

If bonds are sold at a premium (i.e., above par value), the premium increases the other financing sources. Often, the premium is transferred—by a debit to "other financing sources" and a credit to "cash"—to the debt service fund established to service the debt for the project. If the bonds are sold at a discount (i.e., below par value), the discount reduces the amount recorded as other financing sources in the capital projects fund. Bond issuance costs either paid out of available funds or withheld from the bond proceeds usually are accounted as debt service expenditures in the capital projects or debt service funds operating statement.

Bond Anticipation Notes (BANs).   Governments sometimes issue BANs prior to the sale of bonds, planning to retire the notes with the proceeds of the bond issue to which the notes are related. The reasons would be:

- The governmental unit wants to accelerate initiation of a project, and issuance of the long-term bonds will require more time than is required to issue BANs.
- The governmental unit does not want to undertake long-term financing until the project is complete and ready for use. Hence BANs are used to provide construction financing.
- The current and projected interest rates make it prudent to issue short-term notes first and to defer issuance of long-term bonds.
- The individual capital projects to be financed from the proceeds of the bond sale are so small as to make the sale of bonds to finance each project impracticable.

The cash proceeds and the liabilities resulting from the sale of BANs should be recorded in the capital projects fund as follows:

Cash	$XXX	
Bond anticipation notes payable		$XXX

When the long-term bonds are sold, an "other financing source" should be recorded and the BANs payable debited in an amount equal to the portion of the BANs redeemed as follows:

Bond participation notes payable	$XXX
Other financing sources	$XXX

If the BANs are not redeemed with long-term bond proceeds or other funds by the end of the year, and the governmental unit has both the intent and the ability (as those terms are defined in Statement of Financial Accounting Standards (SFAS) No. 6, "Classification of Short-Term Obligations Expected to Be Refinanced," pars. 10 and 11) to redeem the BANs with long-term debt, the BANs payable account should be debited and an "other financing source" should be credited. If the governmental unit does not have the intent or ability to redeem the BANs with long-term debt, it is appropriate to leave the liability in the capital projects fund. The ability to redeem the BANs could be demonstrated by a post-balance sheet issuance of long-term debt or the entering into of a long-term financing arrangement for the BANs.

Project Budgets.   When debt is issued to finance an entire capital project, it is usually done so at the beginning of the project in an amount equal to the total estimated project cost. Accordingly, a portion of the proceeds may remain unexpended over a considerable period of time. To the maximum extent possible, these excess proceeds should be invested in interest-bearing investments. However, consideration should be given to the federal arbitrage regulations that limit the amount of interest that can be earned from investing the proceeds of a tax-exempt bond issue. If certain limits are exceeded, the bond's tax-exempt status may be lost or severe penalties could be imposed on the issuer.

Project budgets are typically established for capital projects to control costs and to guard against cost overruns. All expenditures needed to place the project in readiness, that is, indirect as well as direct costs, should be recorded against this budget. The actual expenditures, however, will probably be either less or greater than the amounts authorized. Therefore, in the absence of any legal restrictions, any unspent balance should be transferred to the appropriate sources. If the project was financed only from bond proceeds, the transfer should be to the debt service fund from which the bond issue is to be repaid. If the resources were drawn from more than one source, such as bond proceeds and current revenues, the transfer should be split among the sources in proportion to their contributions. If the expenditures were greater than authorized and a deficit exists, sufficient funds must be transferred to liquidate any commitments.

As construction of the project is completed, the costs should be recorded in the capital account as Construction in Progress and then transferred to the final building account when construction is completed.

(v) Permanent Funds.   Permanent funds should be used to report assets legally restricted so that only earnings, not principal, may be spent for the government's programs, that is, for the benefit of the government or its citizens.

(vi) Proprietary Funds.   Under GASB Statement No. 34 enterprise funds *may be* used to report any activity for which fees are charged to external users in exchange for goods or services. They are *required* to be used if *any one* of the following criteria is met in the context of the activity's principal revenue sources (insignificant activities, such as fees charged for frivolous small-claims suits, are excluded):

- The activity is financed with debt secured solely by a pledge of the net revenues from fees and charges of the activity. (This is met if the debt is secured in part by a portion of its own proceeds.)
- Laws or regulations require that the activity's costs of providing goods or services, including capital costs such as depreciation or debt service, be recovered by its fees and charges, not by taxes or similar revenues.

- The pricing policies of the activity result in fees and charges intended to recover the activity's costs, including capital costs such as depreciation or debt service.
- The primary focus of these criteria is on fees charged to external users.

Proprietary (enterprise) activities are frequently administered by departments of the general purpose government, for example, a municipal water department or a state parks department. They can also be the exclusive function of a local special district, such as a water district, power authority, or bridge and tunnel authority.

User charges are one significant source of enterprise fund resources; revenue bond proceeds are another. Revenue bonds are long-term obligations, the principal and interest of which are paid from the earnings of the enterprise for which the bond proceeds were spent. The enterprise revenues may be pledged to the payment of the debt, and the physical properties may carry a mortgage that is to be liquidated in the event of default.

Revenue bond indentures usually also contain several requirements concerning the use of the bond proceeds, the computation and reporting of revenue bond coverage, and the establishment and use of restricted asset accounts for handling revenue bond debt service requirements. For instance, a revenue bond indenture may require the establishment of various bond accounts including a construction account, operations and maintenance account, current debt service account, future debt service account, and revenue and replacement account. This does not necessarily mean establishing individual accounting funds for each bond issue. Instead, the accounting and reporting requirements can be met through the use of various accounts within an accounting fund.

The revenue bond construction account normally represents cash and investments (including interest receivable) segregated by the bond indenture for construction. Construction liabilities payable from restricted assets should be reported as "contracts payable from restricted assets." As with all restricted accounts, construction assets and the liabilities to be paid from them generally should not be classified as current assets and liabilities. The difference between the restricted construction asset and liability accounts is not required to be reported as a reserve in retained earnings.

A revenue bond operations and maintenance account often is established pursuant to a bond indenture. Resources for this account are provided through bond proceeds and/or operating income or net income. This account generally accumulates assets equal to operating costs for one month. Once this account has been established, additional proceeds from future bond issues generally are necessary only to the extent the costs associated with these expanded operations are expected to increase. This account is normally balanced by a reserve for revenue bond operations and maintenance account in retained earnings.

Bond indentures may also include a covenant requiring the establishment of a restricted account for the repayment of bond principal and interest. Resources for this account also are provided through bond proceeds and/or operating income or net income. Normally, assets accumulated for debt service payments (i.e., principal and interest) due within one year are classified in the revenue bond current debt service account. This account is at least partially associated with the bonds payable—current account and the accrued interest payable account. Any difference between the revenue bond current debt service account and related current bonds payable and accrued interest payable should be reported as reserved retained earnings. When accounts are restricted for debt service payments beyond the next 12 months, a revenue bond future debt service account should be established.

The final restricted account typically established pursuant to a covenant within a bond indenture is the revenue bond renewal and replacement account. Bond proceeds and/or net income are often restricted for payments of unforeseen repairs and replacements of assets originally acquired with bond proceeds. Provided that liabilities have not been incurred for this purpose, the revenue bond renewal and replacement account is balanced by the reserve for revenue bond renewal and replacement account in retained earnings.

The following general rule should be considered when determining the amount of retained earnings to reserve in restricted asset accounts: Unless otherwise required by the bond indenture, retained earnings should only be reserved for amounts of restricted assets in excess of related liabilities.

Another restricted asset often found in enterprise funds is the amount resulting from the deposits customers are required to make to ensure payment of their final charges and to protect the utility against damage to equipment located on the customer's property. These funds are not available for the financing of current operations and, generally, the amount, less the charges outstanding against the account, must be returned to the customer upon withdrawing from the system. Also, these deposits may, depending on legal and policy requirements, draw interest at some stipulated rate.

In some instances, revenue bonds are also secured by the full faith and credit of the governmental unit. This additional security enables the bonds to obtain better acceptance in the securities market. If the bonds are to be serviced by the enterprise activity, the cash, liability, principal, and interest payments should be accounted for in the enterprise fund. Even if the bonds are secured only by full faith and credit and not by a revenue pledge, but the intention is to use enterprise revenues to service the bonds, they should be accounted for as if they were revenue bonds. If, however, general obligation bond proceeds are used to finance the enterprise activity and there is no intention to service the bonds with enterprise fund resources, the amounts provided to the enterprise fund should be recorded as a contribution from the fund recording the proceeds of the bond, typically, the general fund.

Other sources of contributions also provide significant resources for enterprise activities. Such resources include contributions of permanent capital by other funds or other governmental bodies; contributions in aid of construction by customers or other members of the general public; the aforementioned proceeds of a bond issue to be repaid from general fund revenues, federal grants, or state grants; connection charges to users of utility services; payments by real estate developers for installing utility lines; and similar receipts.

If such resources are externally restricted for capital acquisitions or construction, they should be reported as contributed capital. Fixed assets acquired with these contributions should be capitalized at full cost and depreciated over the estimated useful life of the fixed assets. The depreciation on fixed assets acquired by grants, entitlements, and shared revenues received from other governments may be closed to the appropriate contributed capital account rather than retained earnings. If this option is followed, such depreciation is "added back" to the enterprise fund's net income or loss, thereby increasing the net income or reducing the net loss that is closed to retained earnings.

Another resource is the support provided by or to other funds of the government. For instance, an enterprise fund will frequently use the services or commodities of a central facility operated as an internal service fund. Conversely, the general fund departments will use the services of an electric utility fund.

It is important to handle these relationships on a businesslike basis. All services rendered by an enterprise fund for other funds of the government should be billed at predetermined rates, and the enterprise should pay for all services received from other funds on the same basis that is utilized to determine charges for other users. The latter will often include payments in lieu of taxes to the general fund in amounts comparable to the taxes that would have been paid by the enterprise were it privately owned and operated, or an "administrative charge" if the enterprise does not have its own management capacity and instead uses management services provided by the general government. Unless this is done, the financial operations of a government-owned enterprise will be distorted, and valid comparisons of operating results with those for a similar privately owned enterprise cannot be made. However, other considerations, such as the amount of planned idle capacity, have an impact on the comparability of public and private enterprise funds.

Interfund operating transfers may also occur between an enterprise fund and governmental funds. Operating subsidy transfers from the general fund or special revenue fund are possible. There may also be transfers from an enterprise to finance general fund expenditures.

Finally, there are the nonoperating income and expenses, which are incidental to, or by-products of, the enterprise's primary service function. Nonoperating income consists of such items as interest earnings, rent from nonoperating properties, intergovernmental revenues, and sale of excess supplies. Nonoperating expenses include items such as interest expense and fiscal agents' fees.

(vii) Internal Service Funds. Internal service funds finance and account for special activities that are performed and commodities that are furnished by one department or agency of a governmental unit to other departments or agencies of that unit or to other governmental units on a cost-reimbursement basis. The services differ from those rendered to the public at large, which are accounted for in general, special revenue, or enterprise funds. Examples of activities in which internal service funds are established include central motor pools, duplication services, central purchasing and stores departments, and insurance and risk-management activities.

When an internal service fund is established, resources are typically obtained from capital contributions from other operating funds, such as the general fund or an enterprise fund, or from long-term advances from other funds that are to be repaid from earnings. The entry to be made when the fund is created varies depending on the source of the capital.

The cost of services rendered and commodities furnished, including labor, depreciation on all fixed assets used by the funds other than buildings financed from capital projects, and overhead, are charged to the departments served. These departments reimburse the internal service fund by recording expenditures against their budgeted appropriations. The operating objective of the fund is to recover costs incurred to provide the service, including depreciation. Accordingly, the operations of the fund should not result in any significant profit or loss. Whenever it uses the services of another fund, such as an enterprise fund, the fund pays for and records the costs just as if it had dealt with an outside organization.

Since exact overhead charges are usually not known when bills are prepared, the departments being served are usually billed for direct costs plus a uniform rate for their portion of estimated overhead. Any difference in actual overhead expenses may be charged or credited to the departments at fiscal year end or adjusted for in a subsequent year. At the end of each fiscal year, net income or loss must be determined. The excess of net billings to the department over costs is closed to the retained earnings account.

(viii) Fiduciary Funds. The purpose of fiduciary (trust and agency) funds is to account for assets held by a governmental unit in a trustee capacity or as an agent for individuals, private organizations, other governmental units, or other funds.

Trust Funds. Usually in existence for an extended period of time, trust funds deal with substantial vested interests and involve complex administrative problems. The government's records must provide adequate information to permit compliance with the terms of the trust as defined in the trust document, statutes, ordinances, or governing regulations. For instance, if depreciable property were included in a nonexpendable trust fund, depreciation would have to be recorded as an expense and not included in the distributable income, to keep the principal intact. Similarly, gains and losses on the sale of investments may, unless otherwise specified in the trust agreement, be credited or charged to trust principal.

Expendable and Nonexpendable Trust Funds. Within the trust fund category there are expendable trust funds, where the principal as well as the income may be expended, and nonexpendable trust funds, where the principal must be preserved intact. These funds require a precise determination of revenues and expenditures (expenses) in accordance with the trust document so that only the correct net income will be expended.

Pension (and Other Employee Benefit) Trust Funds. Another type of trust fund is the pension (and other employee benefit) trust fund, in which governments account for the money held for the future retirement (defined benefit and defined contribution) benefit(s) of their employees (other postemployment benefits, and other employee benefits). The resources of this fund are the members' contributions, contributions from the government employer, and earnings on investments in authorized securities. The expenses are the authorized retirement allowances and other benefits, refunds of contributions to members who resign prior to retirement, and administrative expenses. Professional actuaries make periodic actuarial studies of the retirement systems and compute the amounts that should be provided so that the benefits can be paid as required.

The proper accounting for pension trust funds has been on the GASB's agenda since its creation. GASB initially allowed governments to choose from three different methods of accounting and financial reporting but required certain disclosures from all governments. The GASB has finally completed its consideration of pensions and issued three statements: Statement No. 25, "Financial Reporting for Defined Benefit Pension Plans and Note Disclosures for Defined Contribution Plans," Statement No. 26, "Financial Reporting for Postemployment Healthcare Plans Administered by Defined Benefit Pension Plans," and Statement No. 27, "Accounting for Pensions by State and Local Government Employers." Statements No. 25 and 26 address issues related to accounting by pension plans and pension trust funds. Statement No. 27 addresses accounting and financial reporting for those employers who participate in a pension plan.

Statement No. 25 establishes two basic financial statements for pension plans: the statement of plan net assets and the statement of changes in plan net assets. These two financial statements are designed to provide current information about plan assets and financial activities. These statements are supplemented by two schedules that provide actuarial information from a long-term perspective: the schedule of funding progress and the schedule of employer contributions. These schedules are reported as required supplemental information. Statement No. 25 sets requirements for note disclosure that include a brief plan description, a summary of significant accounting principles, and information about contributions, legally required reserves, and investment concentrations. Statement No. 25 is effective for fiscal years beginning after June 15, 1996. Statement No. 26 establishes reporting standards for postemployment health care plans that are administered as part of a defined benefit plan and must be implemented concurrently with Statement No. 25.

It is directed at employers which participate in a pension plan and reflects two underlying principles. Statement No. 27 is effective for fiscal years beginning after June 15, 1997. First, the pension cost recognized should be related to the annual required contribution (ARC) as determined by an actuary for funding purposes. Second, the actuarial methods and assumptions used by employers should be consistent with those used by the plan in its separate reporting.

In implementing these basic principles, Statement No. 27 requires the ARC to be recognized as pension expense in proprietary funds and nonexpendable trust funds. Governmental and expendable trust funds will recognize pension expenditure to the extent that the ARC is expected to be liquidated with expendable available resources. The remainder is recorded as a liability in the GLTDAG. If an employer does not contribute the ARC (or has contributed in excess of the ARC), pension expense/expenditure no longer equals the ARC. In these cases the ARC is adjusted to remove the effects of the actuarial adjustments included in the ARC and to reflect interest on previous under or over funding.

Although Statement No. 27 tries to minimize the differences between accounting for pensions and funding pensions, it does place certain limits or "parameters" on the actuary's modified calculation of the ARC. These parameters are consistent with parameters established for accounting for the plan itself in Statement No. 25. These parameters relate to the pension obligation, actuarial assumptions, economic assumptions, actuarial cost method, actuarial valuation of assets, and amortization of unfunded actuarial accrued liability.

Statement No. 27 establishes disclosure requirements that vary depending on whether the government merely participates in a pension plan administered by another entity or includes a pension trust fund. Disclosure requirements also vary for governments with a pension trust fund based on whether the pension plan issues separate publicly available financial statements. These disclosure requirements generally include a plan description, funding policy, pension cost components, actuarial valuation information, and trend data.

Investment Trust Funds.   Investment trust funds should be used by the sponsoring government to report the external part of investment pools, as required by GASB Statement No. 31, paragraph 18.

Private-Purpose Trust Funds.   Private-purpose trust funds, such as one used to report escheat property, should be used to report all other trust arrangements under which principal and income benefit individuals, private organizations, or other governments.

Agency Funds.   Used by governments to handle cash resources held in an agent capacity, agency funds require relatively simple administration. The typical agency funds used by state and local governments include: (1) tax collection funds, under which one local government collects a tax for an overlapping governmental unit and remits the amount collected less administrative charges to the recipient; (2) payroll withholdings, under which the government collects the deductions and periodically remits them in a lump sum to the appropriate recipient; (3) clearance funds, used to accumulate a variety of revenues from different sources and to apportion them to various operating funds; and (4) deferred compensation plans organized under IRC Section 457. Recent changes to IRC Section 457 will result in the assets of deferred compensation plans no longer being reported as assets of the employee. The GASB issued Statement No. 32, "Accounting and Financial Reporting for Internal Revenue Code Section 457, Deferred Compensation Plans," to modify the accounting for these plans when they are changed to place their assets in trust for the participants, to conform with the new requirements of IRC Section 457. The modified deferred compensation plan will then be accounted for as an expendable trust fund.

(ix) Special Assessment Activities.   Special assessment activities pertain to (1) the financing and construction of certain public improvements, such as storm sewers, which are to be paid for wholly or partly from special assessments levied against the properties benefited by such improvements, or (2) the providing of services that are normally provided to the public as general governmental functions and that would otherwise be financed by the general fund or a special revenue fund. Those services may include street lighting, street cleaning, and snow plowing. The payment by the property owners or taxpayers receiving the benefit distinguishes these activities from activities that benefit the entire community and are paid for from general revenues or general obligation bond proceeds. Sometimes, however, a special assessment bond, which is often used to finance the special assessment improvement, also carries the additional pledge of the full faith and credit of the governmental unit.

It should be emphasized that whereas GASB Statement No. 6 eliminated the requirement to report special assessment funds in an entity's general purpose financial statement, accounting for special assessment activities is still an important part of governmental accounting.

Capital improvement special assessment projects have two distinct and functionally different phases. The initial phase consists of financing and constructing the project. In most cases, this period is relatively short in duration, sometimes lasting only a few months, and rarely more than a year or two. The second phase, which may start at the same time as, during, or after the initial phase, consists of collecting the assessment principal and interest levied against the benefited properties and repaying the cost of financing the construction. The second phase is usually substantially longer than the first.

There are many ways of financing a capital improvement special assessment project. Assessments may be levied and collected immediately. Funds will then be available to pay construction costs, and it will not be necessary to issue special assessment bonds. Alternatively, a project may be constructed using the proceeds from short-term borrowing. When the project is complete and the exact cost is known, special assessment bonds are issued to provide the exact amount of money and the short-term borrowings are repaid. A third—and perhaps the most common—financing alternative is for the government to levy a special assessment for the estimated cost of the improvement, issue bonds to provide the funds, construct the improvement using the bond proceeds, and then collect the assessments over a period of years, using the collections to service the bonds.

Five basic types of transactions are associated with a capital project type special assessment:

1. Levying the special assessment
2. Issuing special assessment bonds
3. Constructing the capital project
4. Collecting the special assessment
5. Paying the bond principal and interest

Because the special assessment fund has been eliminated for financial reporting purpose, the transactions related to special assessment activities are typically reported in the same manner, and on the same basis of accounting, as any other capital improvement and financing transaction. Transactions of the construction phase of the project should generally be reported in a capital projects fund, and transactions of the debt service phase should be reported in a debt service fund, if one is required.

At the time of the levy, special assessments receivable should be recognized and offset by deferred revenue; deferred revenue should be reduced as the assessments become measurable and available.

The entry for the retirement of special assessment bonds and for the construction of the special assessment project would follow the accounting principles outlined in the discussion on capital projects. The usual entries are made for expenditures and for encumbrances, if such a system exits. At the end of the year, the revenues and expenditures should be closed to the fund balance to reflect the balance that may be expended in future periods.

Although the accounting for special assessment construction activities is quite similar to other financing and construction activities, the major issue relating to special assessment activities involves the definition of special assessment debt. Special assessment debt is often defined as those long-term obligations, secured by a lien on the assessed properties, for which the primary source of repayment is the assessments levied against the benefiting properties.

However, the nature and composition of debt associated with special assessment-related capital improvements is not always consistent with this definition. Rather, it can vary significantly from one jurisdiction to another. Capital improvements involving special assessments may be financed by debt that is:

- General obligation debt that is not secured by liens on assessed properties but nevertheless will be repaid in part by special assessment collections
- Special assessment debt that is secured by liens on assessed properties and is also backed by the full faith and credit of the government as additional security
- Special assessment debt that is secured by liens on assessed properties and is not backed by the full faith and credit of the government but is, however, fully or partially backed by some other type of general governmental commitment
- Special assessment debt that is secured by liens on assessed properties, is not backed by the full faith and credit of the government, and is not backed by any other type of general governmental commitment; the government is not liable under any circumstance for the repayment of this category of debt should the property owner default

In some cases special assessment debt is payable entirely by special assessment collections from the assessed property owners; in other cases the debt may be repaid partly from special assessment collections and partly from the general resources of the government, either because the government is a property owner benefiting from the improvements or because the government has agreed to finance part of the cost of the improvement as a public benefit. The portion of special assessment debt that will be repaid directly with governmental resources is, in essence, a general obligation of the government. If the government owns property that benefits from the improvements financed by special assessment debt as in item 4 above, or if a public benefit assessment is made against the government, the government is obligated for the public benefit portion and the amount assessed against its property, even though it has no liability for the remainder of the debt issue.

Because the special assessment debt can have various characteristics, the extent of a government's liability for debt related to a special assessment capital improvement can also vary significantly. For example, the government may be primarily liable for the debt, as in the case of a general obligation issue; it may have no liability whatsoever for special assessment debt; or it may be obligated in some manner to provide a secondary source of funds for repayment of special assessment debt in the event of default by the assessed property owners. A government is obligated in some manner for special assessment debt if (1) it is legally obligated to assume all or part of the debt in the event of default or (2) the government may take certain actions to assume secondary liability for all or part of the debt—and the government takes, or has given indications that it will take, those actions.

Stated differently, the phrase "obligated in some manner" is intended to include all situations other than those in which (1) the government is prohibited (by constitution, charter, statute, ordinance, or contract) from assuming the debt in the event of default by the property owner or (2) the government is not legally liable for assuming the debt and makes no statement, or gives no indication, that it will, or may, honor the debt in the event of default.

Debt issued to finance capital projects that will be paid wholly or partly from special assessments against benefited property owners should be reported in one of the following three ways:

1. General obligation debt that will be repaid, in part, from special assessments should be reported like any other general obligation debt.
2. Special assessment debt for which the government is obligated in some manner should be reported in the capital account, except for the portion, if any, that is a direct obligation of a proprietary fund, or that is expected to be repaid from operating revenues of a proprietary fund.
3. Special assessment debt for which the government is not obligated in any manner should not be displayed in the government's financial statements. However, if the government is liable for a portion of that debt (the public benefit portion, or as a property owner), that portion should be reported as above.

(x) Focus on Major Funds.   Governmental and enterprise fund financial statements should focus on major funds, each of which should be presented in the fund statements in a separate column. Other funds should be aggregated and presented in a single column. The general fund or its equivalent should be reported as a major fund. Whether other funds should be reported as major funds depends on whether they meet both of the following criteria:

1. Total assets, liabilities, revenues, or expenditures/expenses excluding extraordinary items of a fund are at least 10 percent of the corresponding element total for all funds of its category (total governmental funds or total enterprise funds).
2. The same element that met the 10 percent criterion in item 1 above is at least 5 percent of the corresponding element for all governmental and enterprise funds combined.

Any other governmental or enterprise fund the government's officials believe is particularly important to financial statement users may be reported as a major fund.

(h) REPORTING CAPITAL ASSETS.   For purposes of GASB Statement No. 34, the term *capital assets* includes land, improvements to land, easements, buildings, building improvements, vehicles, machinery, equipment, works of art and historical treasures, infrastructure, and all other tangible or intangible assets used in operations and that have initial useful lives beyond a single reporting period. Infrastructure assets are capital assets that are normally stationary and normally can be preserved for a significantly greater number of years than most other capital assets, for example, roads, bridges, tunnels, drainage systems, water and sewer systems, dams, and lighting systems. Buildings that are not ancillary parts of networks of infrastructure assets are not infrastructure assets for purposes of GASB Statement No. 34.

Purchased capital assets should be reported at their acquisition costs, which should include ancillary charges needed to place the assets in their intended locations and conditions for use. Ancillary charges include costs directly attributable to asset acquisition, such as freight and transportation charges, site preparation costs, and professional fees. Donated capital assets should be reported at their fair values at their times of acquisition plus ancillary charges.

In general, capital assets should be depreciated. They should be reported net of accumulated depreciation in the statement of net assets, with accumulated depreciation reported on the face of the statement or in the notes. Capital assets not depreciated, such as land and infrastructure assets reported using the modified approach, discussed below, should be reported separately if significant.

Capital assets may also be reported in greater detail, such as infrastructure, buildings and improvements, vehicles, machinery, and equipment. Capital assets should be depreciated over their useful lives based on their net costs less salvage values in a systematic and rational manner unless they are either inexhaustible, such as land and land improvements, or are infrastructure reported using the modified approach. Depreciation, reported in the statement of activities as discussed below, may be calculated for: (a) a class of assets, (b) a network of assets (all the assets that provide a particular kind of service for a government; a network of infrastructure assets may be only one infrastructure asset composed of many components, e.g., a dam composed of a concrete dam, a concrete spillway, and a series of locks), (c) a subsystem of a network (all assets that make up a similar portion or segment of a network of assets, e.g., interstate highways, state highways, and rural roads could each be a subsystem of a network of all the roads of a government), or (d) individual assets.

Eligible infrastructure assets, infrastructure assets that are part of a network or subsystem of a network, need not be depreciated but treated by a modified approach if both of the following are met:

1. The government manages them using an asset management system that has these characteristics:
   ○ Has an up-to-date inventory of eligible infrastructure assets.
   ○ Performs condition assessments of the eligible infrastructure assets and summarizes the results using a measurement scale. The assessments must be documented so they can be replicated—based on sufficiently understandable and complete measurement methods so that different measurers using the same methods would reach substantially similar results—performed by the government or by contract.
   ○ Estimates each year the annual cost to maintain and preserve the eligible infrastructure assets at the condition level established and disclosed by the government.

2. The government documents that the eligible infrastructure assets are being preserved approximately at or above a condition level established and documented by administrative or executive policy or by legislative action and documented by the government. Adequate documentation requires professional judgment and may vary within governments for different eligible infrastructure assets. Nevertheless, documentation should include:
   ○ Complete condition assessments of eligible infrastructure assets performed consistently at least every three years. Statistical sampling may be used, and eligible infrastructure assets may be assessed on a cyclical basis. A complete assessment on a cyclical basis requires all or statistical samples of all eligible infrastructure assets in the network or subsystem to be assessed.
   ○ The three most recent complete condition assessments provide reasonable assurance that the eligible infrastructure assets are being preserved approximately at or above the condition level established and disclosed by the government. The condition level could be measured either by a condition index or as the percentage of a network of infrastructure assets in good or poor condition.

All expenditures other than for additions and improvements made for eligible infrastructure assets that meet the two requirements and are not depreciated should be reported as expense in the periods incurred. Additions and improvements increase the capacity or efficiency of infrastructure assets; expenditures for them should be capitalized. A change from depreciation to the modified approach should be reported as a change in an accounting estimate.

When and if the requirements to report capital assets by the modified approach are no longer met, they should be depreciated in subsequent periods. The change should be reported as a change in accounting estimate.

Governments should in general capitalize individual or collections of works of art, historical treasures, and similar assets at their acquisition costs or fair values at the dates of acquisition or donation (estimated if necessary). They are encouraged but not required to capitalize a collection and all additions to the collection, whether donated or purchased, that meets all three of these conditions (but collections capitalized by June 30, 1999, should remain capitalized and additions to them should be capitalized regardless of whether they meet the conditions):

1. The collection is held for public exhibition, education, or research for public service, not financial gain.

2. The collection is protected, kept unencumbered, cared for, and preserved.

3. The collection is subject to an organizational policy that requires that the proceeds from sales of collection items are used to acquire other items for collections.

Governments that receive donations of works of art, historical treasures, and similar assets should report revenues in conformity with GASB Statement No. 33. Governments should report program expense equal to the revenue reported on donated assets added to noncapitalized collections.

Capitalized collections or individual items of works of art, historical treasures, and similar assets that are exhaustible, such as exhibits whose useful lives decreased because of display or educational or research use, should be depreciated over their estimated useful lives. Depreciation is not required for collections or individual items of works of art, historical treasures, and similar assets that are inexhaustible.

(i) Methods for Calculating Depreciation.   Governments may use any established depreciation method. It may be based on the estimated useful life of a class of assets, a network of assets, a subsystem, a network, or individual assets. Estimated useful lives may be obtained from general guidelines obtained from professional or industry organization, information for comparable assets of other governments, or internal information.

A government may use a composite method, applying one rate, to calculate depreciation, for example, for similar assets or dissimilar assets of the same class, such as all the roads and bridges of the government. Depreciation is determined as the product of the total cost times the rate. The rate can be determined based on a weighted average or an unweighted average estimate of the useful lives of the assets included. Or it may be based on condition assessment or experience with the useful lives of the group of assets. It is generally used throughout the life of the group of assets, but it should be recalculated if the composition of the assets or the estimate of average useful lives changes significantly.

(ii) Subsidiary Property Records.   The maintenance of subsidiary property records aids in the control of fixed assets. The subsidiary records should contain such information as classification code, date of acquisition, name and address of vendor, unit charged with custody, location, cost, fund and account from which purchased, method of acquisition, estimated life, and repair and maintenance data.

(iii) Disposal or Retirement of Capital Assets.   In the disposal or retirement of a capital asset the amount for which the asset is recorded must be removed from the asset side, and an equal amount must be deducted from the investment in fixed assets. If the asset is sold, the amount obtained in cash or by evidence of indebtedness should be recorded in the appropriate governmental fund. The same amount should be credited to a revenue account, such as sale of fixed assets or miscellaneous revenues or other financing sources.

(i) LONG-TERM LIABILITIES.   General long-term liabilities need to be clearly distinguished from fund long-term liabilities. General long-term liabilities are the unmatured principal of bonds, warrants, notes, or other forms of noncurrent or long-term general obligation indebtedness. They may arise from debt issuances, lease–purchase agreements, and other commitments that are not current liabilities properly reported in governmental funds. Other general long-term liabilities include the noncurrent part of capital leases, operating judgments, pensions, special termination benefits, and landfill closure and postclosure care liabilities.

General long-term liabilities should be reported in the governmental activities column in the government-wide statement of net assets, not in governmental funds.

All unmatured long-term indebtedness of the government not directly related to or expected to be repaid from proprietary funds, or similar trust funds, is general long-term debt. General long-term debt is not limited to liabilities arising from debt issuances, but may also include lease purchase agreements, long-term portion of compensated absences, judgments and claims, and other commitments that are not current liabilities properly recorded in the governmental funds. Matured liabilities (other than those associated with proprietary or fiduciary funds) should be reported as governmental fund liabilities. Matured liabilities include (a) liabilities that normally are due and payable in full when incurred and (b) the matured portion of general long-term indebtedness (the portion that has come due for payment), if maintained, or another governmental fund. Long-term indebtedness directly related to and expected to be repaid from proprietary or trust fund resources should be included in those funds. Debt service on formal debt issues (such as bonds and capital leases) generally should be recognized as a governmental fund liability and expenditure when due (matured)—with optional additional accrual as provided in NCGA Statement No. 1, paragraph 72. Compensated absences, claims and judgments, special termination benefits, and landfill closure and postclosure care costs should be recognized as governmental fund liabilities and expenditures to the extent the liabilities are "normally expected to be liquidated with expendable available financial resources." Governments, in general, are normally expected to liquidate liabilities with expendable available financial resources to the extent that the liabilities mature (come due for payment) each period. Examples are compensated absences and landfill closure and postclosure care costs. Modified accrual recognition is independent of the method and timing of resource accumulation.

If there is no explicit requirement to do otherwise, a governmental fund liability and expenditure should be accrued in the period in which the government incurs the liability. They include liabilities that normally are paid in a timely manner and in full from current financial resources, such as salaries, professional services, supplies, utilities, and travel. Unpaid, they represent claims against current financial resources and should be reported as governmental fund liabilities.

Accumulation of earmarked net asset in a governmental fund to later pay unmatured general long-term indebtedness is not an outflow of current financial resources and should not result in the recognition of additional governmental fund liability or expenditure. They should be reported as part of fund balance, for example, as unreserved-designated fund balance.

Unmatured long-term indebtedness includes "Other commitments that are not current liabilities properly recorded in governmental funds" (NCGA Statement No. 1, par. 43). That provides for the possibility that new forms of general long-term indebtedness may be created for which explicit recognition criteria have not yet be established. A fund liability and expenditure should be recognized when such a liability is due, and the remainder should be reported as a general long-term liability.

Typically, the general long-term debt of a state and local government is secured by the general credit and revenue-raising powers of the government rather than by the assets acquired for specific fund resources. Furthermore, just as general fixed assets do not represent financial resources available for appropriation and expenditure, the unmatured principal of general long-term debt does not require current appropriation and expenditure of a governmental fund's financial resources. Thus, to include it as a governmental fund liability would be misleading for management control and accountability functions for the current period.

(j) MEASUREMENT FOCUS AND BASIS OF ACCOUNTING. The accounting and financial reporting treatment applied to a fund is determined by its measurement focus. The measurement focus refers to what is being expressed in reporting an entity's financial performance and position. A particular measurement focus is accomplished by considering not only which resources are measured, but also when the effects of transactions or events involving those resources are recognized (the basis of accounting). Principle 8 describes the basis of accounting used by governments.

(i) Measurement Focus. The government-wide and enterprise funds financial statements should be prepared using the economic resources measurement focus and the accrual basis of accounting. Assets, liabilities, revenues, expenses, and gains and losses that result from exchange transactions and exchange-like transactions should be reported when the transactions occur. (In an exchange-like transaction, the resources or services exchanged, though related, may not be quite equal or the direct benefits may not be exclusively for the parties to the transactions. Nevertheless, the transactions are similar enough to exchanges to justify treating them as exchanges.) Assets, liabilities, revenues, expenses, and gains and losses that result from nonexchange transactions should be reported as discussed elsewhere in this chapter.

Reporting on governmental and business-type activities should conform with all applicable GASB pronouncements plus the following pronouncements issued on or before November 30, 1989, unless they conflict with or contradict GASB pronouncements:

- FASB Statements and Interpretations, except that FASB Statement No. 71 applies to only governments that have qualifying enterprise funds
- APB Opinions; changes in accounting principles, addressed in APB Opinion No. 20, should be reported as restatements of beginning net assets/fund equity
- Accounting Research Bulletins

Governments may apply all FASB Statements and Interpretations issued after November 30, 1989, except for those that conflict with or contradict GASB pronouncements. They are encouraged to apply the same FASB pronouncements for all enterprise funds.

(ii) Basis of Accounting. The basis of accounting determines when revenues, expenditures, expenses, and transfers—and the related assets and liabilities—are recognized in the accounts and reported in the financial statements. Specifically, it relates to the timing of the measurements made, regardless of the measurement focus. For example, whether depreciation is recognized depends on whether expenses or expenditures are being measured rather than on whether the cash or accrual basis is used.

Cash Basis. Under the cash basis of accounting, revenues and transfers in are not recorded in the accounts until cash is received, and expenditures or expenses and transfers out are recorded only when cash is disbursed.

The cash basis is frequently encountered, but its use is not generally accepted for any governmental unit. With the cash basis, it is difficult to compare expenditures with services rendered, because the disbursements relating to those services may be made in the fiscal period following that in which the services occurred. Also, statements prepared on a cash basis do not show financial position and results of operations on a basis that is generally accepted.

Accrual Basis. Under the accrual basis of accounting, most transactions are recorded when they occur, regardless of when cash is received or disbursed. Items not measurable until cash is received or disbursed are accounted for at that time.

The accrual basis is considered a superior method of accounting for the economic resources of any organization because it results in accounting measurements that are based on the substance of transactions and events, rather than merely on the receipt or disbursement of cash.

Modified Accrual Basis. As indicated previously, the financial flows of governments, such as taxes and grants, typically do not result from a direct exchange for goods or services and thus cannot be accrued based on the completion of the earnings process and an exchange taking place. Governments have thus devised the "susceptible to accrual" concept as the criterion for determining when inflows are accruable as revenue. A revenue is susceptible to accrual when it is both measurable and available to finance current operations. An amount is measurable when the precise amount is known because the transaction is completed, or when it can be accurately estimated using past experience or other available information. An amount is available to finance operations when it is: (1) physically available, that is, collectible within the current period or soon enough thereafter to be used to pay liabilities of the current period; and (2) legally available, that is, authorized for expenditure in the current fiscal period and not applicable to some future period.

On the expenditure side, a government's main concern, for governmental funds at least, is to match the financial resources used with the financial resources obtained. This measure of whether current-year revenues were sufficient to pay for current-year services is referred to as *interperiod equity*. A measure of interperiod equity shows whether current-year citizens received services but shifted part of the payment burden to future-year citizens or used up previously accumulated resources. Conversely, such a measure would show whether current-year revenues were not only sufficient to pay for current-year services, but also increased accumulated net resources.

This adaptation of the accrual basis to the conditions surrounding government activities and financing has been given the term *modified accrual*. Modified accrual is currently used in all governmental fund types (i.e., the general fund, special revenue funds, etc.) where the intent is to determine the extent to which provided services have been financed by current resources.

In proprietary funds the objective is to determine net income, and the accounting should be essentially the same as commercial accounting. Hence, proprietary funds use the economic resources measurement focus and the accrual basis without the need for modification described above.

(iii) Revenue Transactions.   The modified accrual basis of accounting is applied in practice for five different revenue transactions as follows:

1. Property taxes are recorded as revenue when the taxes are levied, provided that they apply to and are collected in the current period or soon enough thereafter to finance the current period's expenditures. The period after year end generally should not exceed 60 days. The amount recorded as revenue should be net of estimated uncollectible taxes, abatements, discounts, and refunds. (Property taxes that are measurable but not available—and hence not susceptible to accrual—should be deferred and recognized as revenue in the fiscal year they become available.)

2. Taxpayer-assessed income, gross receipts, and sales taxes should be recorded as revenues when susceptible to accrual.

3. Miscellaneous revenues such as fines and forfeits, athletic fees, and inspection charges are generally recognized when cash is received because they are usually not measurable and available until they are received.

4. Grants should be recorded when the government has an irrevocable right to the grant. If expenditure of funds is the prime factor for determining eligibility for the grant funds, revenue should be recognized when the expenditure is made. A more detailed discussion of grant accounting is provided in Subsection 34.12.

5. Interest earned on special assessment levies may be accrued when due rather than when earned if it approximately offsets interest expenditures on special assessment indebtedness that is also recorded when due.

Escheat property, which is assets reverted to a governmental entity in the absence of legal claimants or heirs, should be reported in government-wide and fund financial statements generally as an asset in the governmental or proprietary fund to which the property ultimately escheats. If held for individuals, private organizations, or another government, it should be reported in a private-purpose trust fund or an agency fund, as appropriate (or in the governmental or proprietary fund in which escheat property is otherwise reported, with a corresponding liability).

Escheat revenue on escheat property reported in governmental or proprietary funds should be reduced and a governmental or proprietary fund liability reported to the extent that it is probable that escheat property will be reclaimed and paid to claimants. The liability should represent the best estimate of the amount ultimately expected to be reclaimed and paid, giving effect to such factors as previous and current trends and anticipated changes in those trends. The liability may differ from the amount specified in law to be held separately for payments to claimants.

Escheat-related transactions reported in the government-wide financial statements should be measured using the economic resources measurement focus and the accrual basis of accounting. Escheat transactions reported in private-purpose trust funds or in agency funds should be excluded from the government-wide financial statements.

(iv) Expenditure Transactions.   Expenditure transactions under the modified accrual basis are treated as follows:

- Interest on long-term debt should be recorded as an expenditure when due.
- Debt issue costs paid from debt proceeds, such as underwriter fees, should be reported as expenditures. Issue costs, such as attorneys' fees, rating agency fees, or bond insurance, paid from existing resources, should be reported as expenditures when liabilities for them are incurred.
- Inventory items may be considered expenditures either when purchased (the purchases method) or when used (the consumption method). Under either method significant amounts of inventory at the end of a fiscal year should be reported as an asset on the balance sheet.
- Expenditures for insurance and similar services extending over more than one accounting period need not be allocated between or among accounting periods, but they may be accounted for as expenditures of the period of acquisition.
- Interest expenditures on special assessment indebtedness may be recorded when due if they are approximately offset by interest earnings on special assessment levies that are also recorded when due.
- Vacation and sick leave benefits should be recorded when a liability has been incurred that is payable from expendable available resources.

(v) Reporting on Nonexchange Transactions.   Similar to a nonreciprocal transaction discussed in APB Statement No. 4, in a nonexchange transaction, a government of any level other than the federal government gives or receives financial or capital resources, not including contributed services, without directly receiving or giving equal value in exchange. They are discussed in four classes:

1. *Derived tax revenues.* This results from assessments imposed by governments on exchange transactions, such as personal and corporate income taxes and retail sales taxes. Some legislation enabling such a tax provides purpose restrictions, requirements that a particular source of tax be used for a specific purpose or purposes, for example, motor fuel taxes required to be used for road and street repairs.

2. *Imposed nonexchange revenues.* This results from assessments on nongovernmental entities, including individuals, other than assessments on exchange transactions, such as property taxes, fines, and penalties, and property forfeitures, such as seizures and escheats. Such a tax is imposed on an act committed or omitted by the payer, such as property ownership or the contravention of a law or a regulation, that is not an exchange. Some enabling legislation provides purpose restrictions; some also provide time requirements, specification of the periods in which the resources must be used or when their use may begin.

3. *Government-mandated nonexchange transactions.* This occurs when a government, including the federal government, at one level provides resources to a government at another level and provides purpose restrictions on the recipient government established in the provider's enabling legislation. Transactions other than cash or other advances are contingent on fulfillment of certain requirements, which may include time requirements, which are called *eligibility requirements.*

4. *Voluntary nonexchange transactions.* This results from legislative or contractual agreements but is not an exchange (unfunded mandates are excluded, because they are not transactions), entered into willingly by two or more parties, at least one of which is a government, such as certain grants, certain entitlements, and donations by nongovernmental entities including individuals (private donations). Providers often establish purpose restrictions and eligibility requirements and require return of the resources if the purpose restrictions or the eligibility requirements are contravened after reporting of the transaction.

Labels such as "tax," "grant," "contribution," or "donation" do not necessarily indicate which of those classes nonexchange transactions belong to and therefore what principles should be applied. Also, labels such as "fees," "charges," and "grants" do not always indicate whether exchange or nonexchange transactions are involved. Principles for reporting on nonexchange transactions depend on their substance, not merely their labels, and determining that requires analysis.

The following expense (or expenditure, for public colleges or universities) reporting principles for nonexchange transactions apply to both the accrual and the modified accrual basis, unless the transactions are not measurable or are not probable of collection. Such transactions that are not measurable should be disclosed.

Time requirements affect the timing of reporting of the transactions. The effect on the timing of reporting depends on whether a nonexchange transaction is an imposed nonexchange revenue transaction or a government-mandated or voluntary nonexchange transaction. Purpose restrictions do not affect the timing of reporting of the transactions. However, recipients should report resulting net assets, equity, or fund balance as restricted until the resources are used for the specified purpose or for as long as the provider requires the resources to be maintained intact, such as endowment principal.

Award programs commonly referred to as *reimbursement-type* or *expenditure-driven* grant programs may be either government mandated or voluntary nonexchange transactions. The provider stipulates an eligibility requirement that a recipient can qualify for resources only after incurring allowable costs under the provider's program. The provider has no liability and the recipient has no asset (receivable) until the recipient has met the eligibility requirements. Assets provided in advance should be reported as advances (assets) by providers and as deferred revenues (liabilities) by recipients until eligibility requirements have been met.

Assets should be reported from derived tax revenue transactions in the period in which the exchange transaction on which the tax is imposed occurs or in which the resources are received, whichever occurs first. Revenues net of estimated refunds and estimated uncollectible amounts should be reported in the period the assets are reported, provided that the underlying exchange transaction has occurred. Resources received in advance should be reported as deferred revenues (liabilities) until the period of the exchange.

Assets from imposed nonexchange revenue transactions should be reported in the period in which an enforceable legal claim to the assets arises or in which the assets are received, whichever occurs first. The date on which an enforceable legal claim to taxable property arises is generally specified in the enabling legislation, sometimes referred to as the *lien date*, though a lien is not formally placed on the property on that date. Others refer to it as the *assessment date*. (An enforceable legal claim by some governments arises in the period after the period for which the taxes are levied. Those governments should report assets in the same period they report revenues, as discussed next.)

Revenues from property taxes, net of estimated refunds and estimated uncollectible amounts, should be reported in the period for which the taxes are levied, even if the enforceable legal claim arises or the due date for payment occurs in a different period. All other imposed nonexchange revenues should be reported in the same period as the assets unless the enabling legislation includes time requirements. If it does, revenues should be reported in the period in which the resources are required to be used or in which use is first permitted. Resources received or reported as receivable before then should be reported as deferred revenues.

The following are the kinds of eligibility requirements for government-mandated and voluntary nonexchange transactions:

- The recipient and secondary recipients, if applicable, have the characteristics specified by the provider. For example, under a certain federal program, recipients are required to be states and secondary recipients are required to be school districts.

- Time requirements specified by enabling legislation or the provider have been met, that is, the period in which the resources are required to be sold, disbursed, or consumed or in which use is first permitted has begun, or the resources are being maintained intact, as specified by the provider.

- The provider offers resources on an "expenditure-driven" basis and the recipient has incurred allowable costs under the applicable program.

- The offer of resources by the provider in a voluntary nonexchange transaction is contingent on a specified action of the recipient, for example, to raise a specific amount of resources from third parties or to dedicate its own resources for a specified purpose, and that action has occurred.

Providers should report liabilities or decreases in assets and expenses from government-mandated or voluntary nonexchange transactions, and recipients should report receivables or decreases in liabilities and revenues, net of estimated uncollectible amounts, when all applicable eligibility requirements have been met (the need to complete purely routine requirements such as filing of claims for allowable costs under a reimbursement program or the filing of progress reports with the provider should not delay reporting of assets and revenues). Resources transmitted before the eligibility requirements are met should be reported as advances by the provider and as deferred revenue by recipients, except as indicated next for recipients of certain resources transmitted in advance. The exception does not cover transactions in which, for administrative or practical reasons, a government receives assets in the period immediately before the period the provider specifies as the one in which sale, disbursement, or consumption of resources is required or may begin.

A provider in some kinds of government-mandated and voluntary nonexchange transactions transmits assets stipulating that the resources cannot be sold, disbursed, or consumed until after a specified number of years have passed or a specific event has occurred, if ever. The recipient may nevertheless benefit from the resources in the interim, for example, by investing or exhibiting them. Examples are permanently nonexpendable additions to endowments and other trusts, term endowments, and contributions of works of art, historical treasures, and similar assets to capitalized collections. The recipient should report revenue when the resources are received if all eligibility requirements have been met. Resulting net assets, equity, or fund balance, should be reported as restricted as long as the provider's purpose restrictions or time requirements remain in effect.

If a provider in a government-mandated or voluntary nonexchange transaction does not specify time requirements, the entire award should be reported as a liability and an expense by the provider and as a receivable and revenue net of estimated uncollectible amounts by the recipients in the period in which all applicable eligibility requirements are met (applicable period). If the provider is a government, that period for both the provider and the recipients is the provider's fiscal year and begins on the first day of that year, and the entire award should be reported as of that date. But if the provider government has a biennial budgetary process, each year of the biennium should be treated as a separate applicable period. The provider and the recipients should then allocate one-half of the resources appropriated for the biennium to each applicable period, unless the provider specifies a different allocation.

Promises of assets including entities individuals voluntarily make to governments may include permanently nonexpendable additions to endowments and other trusts, term endowments, contributions of works of art and similar assets to capitalized collections, or other kinds of capital or financial assets, with or without purpose restrictions, or time requirements. Recipients of such promises should report receivables and revenue net of estimated uncollectible amounts when all eligibility requirements are met if the promise is verifiable and the resources are measurable and probable of collection. If the promise involves a stipulation (time requirement) that the resources cannot be sold, disbursed, or consumed until after a specified number of years have passed or a specific even has occurred, if ever, the recipient does not meet the time requirement until the assets are received.

After a nonexchange transaction has been reported in the financial statements, it may become apparent that (a) if the transaction was reported as a government-mandated or voluntary nonexchange transaction, the eligibility requirements are no longer met, or (b) the recipient will not comply with the purpose restrictions within the specified time limit. If it then is probable that the provider will not provide the resources or will require the return of all or part of the resources already provided, the recipient should report a decrease in assets or an increase in liabilities and an expense, and the provider should report a decrease in liabilities or an increase in assets and a revenue for the amount involved in the period in which the returned resources become available.

A government may collect derived tax revenue or imposed nonexchange revenue on behalf of another government, the recipient, that imposed the revenue source, for example, sales tax collected by a state, part of which is a local option sales tax. The recipient should be able to reasonably estimate the accrual-basis information needed to comply with the above-stated requirements for derived tax revenue or imposed nonexchange revenue. However, if a government shares in a portion of the revenue resulting from a tax imposed by another government, it may not be able to reasonably estimate the accrual-basis information nor obtain sufficient timely information from the other government needed to comply with the above-stated requirements for derived tax revenue or imposed nonexchange revenue. If it cannot, the recipient government should report revenue for a period in the amount of cash received during the period. Cash received afterward should also be reported as revenue of the period, less amounts reported as revenue in the previous period, if reliable information is consistently available to identify the amounts that apply to the current period.

Revenue from nonexchange transactions reported on the modified accrual basis should be reported as follows:

- Recipients should report derived tax revenue in the period in which the underlying exchange transaction has occurred and the resources are available.
- Recipients should report property taxes in conformity with NCGA Interpretation No. 3, as amended.
- Recipients should report other imposed nonexchange revenue in the period in which an enforceable legal claim has arisen and the resources are available.
- Recipients should report government-mandated nonexchange transactions and voluntary nonexchange transactions in the period in which all applicable eligibility requirements have been met and the resources are available.

(k) BUDGETARY ACCOUNTING.   Principle 9 describes the requirements related to budgeting. Budgeting, or the allocation of scarce resources to enable established objectives to be accomplished, is the central element in a government's planning, financial management, control, and public accountability processes. The budget is the financial plan embodied into law, introduced and enacted in the same manner as any other ordinance or statute. Thus it enables governments to demonstrate that they are meeting a major objective of governmental accounting, namely, compliance with the law.

Budgets are the goals of governments in the same way that net income and return on investment are the goals to corporate organizations. A financial report that compares the actual results with the budgeted results is the means by which a governmental unit demonstrates accountability and managerial performance. Accordingly, an annual operating budget is usually developed for and adopted by every governmental fund.

(i) Types of Operating Budgets.   Several types of annual operating budgets are used in contemporary public finance. Among the more common are the following:

- Line item budget
- Program budget

- Performance budget
- Zero-base budget

Line Item Budgeting.   Listing the inputs for resources that each organizational unit requests for each line (or object) of expenditure is referred to as *line item budgeting*. This simple approach produces a budget that governing bodies and administrators can understand, based on their own experience. It provides for tight control over spending and is the most common local government budgeting approach, although this popularity is due primarily to tradition.

Line item budgeting is criticized because it emphasizes inputs rather than outputs, analyzes expenditures inadequately, and fragments activities among accounts that bear little relation to purposes of the government. However, all budgeting systems use objects for the buildup of costs and for execution of the budget.

Overcoming criticisms of a line item budgeting system can be accomplished by:

- Improving the budget structure to encompass all funds and organizational units in a manner that enables the total resources available to a particular organizational unit or responsibility center to be readily perceived
- Developing a level of detail for the object categories that permits adequate analysis of proposed expenditures and effective control over the actual expenditures
- Improving the presentation of historical data to stimulate the analysis of trends
- Providing a partial linking of outputs to the objects of expenditures

Program Budgeting.   Formulating expenditure requests on the basis of the services to be performed for the various programs the government provides is known as *program budgeting*. A program budget categorizes the major areas of citizen needs and the services for meeting such needs into programs. Goals and objectives are stated for each program, normally in relatively specific, quantified terms. The costs are estimated for the resources required (e.g., personnel and equipment) to accomplish the objective for each program. The governing body can then conduct a meaningful review of budget requests by adding or deleting programs or placing different emphasis on the various programs.

Program budgeting has existed for many years, but relatively few governments have adopted it, partly because line item budgeting is so familiar and comprehensible. Lack of acceptance also results from the difficulty of developing operationally useful program budgets that meet the governmental notion of accountability, that is, control of the number of employees and other expense items, rather than achievement of results in applying such resources.

The operational usefulness of program budgeting has also been questioned as a result of the complexity of the program structure, the vagueness of goals and objectives, the lack of organizational or individual responsibility for program funds that span several departments or agencies, and the inadequacy of accounting support to record direct and indirect program costs.

Nevertheless, program budgeting can be an extremely effective approach for a government willing to devote the effort. The steps that departments should take to implement the system are:

- Identify programs and the reasons for their existence
- Define the goals of programs
- Define kinds and levels of services to be provided in light of budgetary guidelines (council- or CEO-furnished guidelines, e.g., budget priorities, budget assumptions, and budget constraints)
- Develop budget requests in terms of resources needed, based on the programs' purposes, the budgetary guidelines, the projected levels of services, and the previous years' expenditure levels for the programs
- Submit budget requests for compilation, review, and approval

Performance Budgeting. Formulating expenditure requests based on the work to be performed is the primary function of performance budgeting. It emphasizes the work or service performed, described in quantitative terms, by an organizational unit performing a given activity; for example, number of tons of waste collected by the Sanitation Department and case workload in the Department of Welfare. These performance data are used in the preparation of the annual budget as the basis for increasing or decreasing the number of personnel and the related operating expenses of the individual departments.

The development of a full-scale performance budget requires a strong budget staff, constructive participation at all levels, special accounting and reporting methods, and a substantial volume of processed statistical data. Primarily for these reasons, performance budgeting has been less widely used than line item budgeting.

The approach to developing a performance budgeting system is as follows:

- Decide on the extent to which functions and activities will be segmented into work units and services for formulation and execution of the budget
- Define the functions in services performed by the government, and assemble them into a structure
- Identify and assemble or develop workload and efficiency measures that relate to service categories
- Estimate the total costs of the functions and services
- Analyze resource needs for each service in terms of personnel, equipment, and so on
- Formulate the first-year performance budget (for the first year, set the budget appropriations and controls at a higher level than the data indicate)
- Perform cost accounting for the functional budget category; initiate statistical reporting of the workload measures; match resources utilized to actual results

Zero-Base Budgeting. In the preparation of a budget, zero-base budgeting projects funding for services at several alternative levels, both lower and higher than the present level, and allocates funds to services based on rankings of these alternatives. It is an appropriate budgeting system for jurisdictions whose revenues are not sufficient for citizen demands and inflation-driven expenditure increases, where considerable doubt exists as to the necessity and effectiveness of existing programs and services, and where incremental budgeting processes have resulted in existing programs and their funding being taken as a given, with attention devoted to requests for new programs.

Zero-base budgeting can be used with any existing budgeting system, including line item, program, or performance budgeting. The budget format can remain unchanged.

The steps to implement zero-base budgeting are as follows:

- Define decision units, that is, activities that can be logically grouped for planning and providing each service
- Analyze decision units to determine alternative service levels, determine the resources required to operate at alternative levels, and present this information in decision packages
- Rank the decision packages in a priority order that reflects the perceived importance of a particular package to the community in relation to other packages
- Present the budget to the governing body for a review of the ranking of the decision packages

(ii) Budget Preparation. The specific procedures involved in the preparation of a budget for a governmental unit are usually prescribed by state statute, local charter, or ordinance. There are, however, certain basic steps:

- Preparation of the budget calendar
- Development of preliminary forecasts of available revenues, recurring expenditures, and new programs

- Formulation and promulgation of a statement of executive budget policy to the operating departments
- Preparation and distribution of budget instructions, budget forms, and related information
- Review of departmental budget requests and supporting work sheets
- Interview with department heads for the purpose of adjusting or approving their requests in a tentative budget
- Final assembly of the tentative budget, including fixing of revenue estimates and the required tax levy
- Presentation of the tentative budget to the legislative body and the public
- Conduction of a public hearing, with advance legal notice
- Adoption of final budget by the legislative body

Revenue and Expenditure Estimates.   The property tax has been the traditional basic source of revenue for local government. The amount to be budgeted and raised is determined by subtracting the estimated nonproperty taxes and other revenues, plus the reappropriated fund balance, from budgeted expenditures. This amount, divided by the assessed valuation of taxable property within the boundaries of the governmental unit, produces the required tax rate.

Many jurisdictions have legal ceilings on the property tax rates available for general operating purposes. Additionally, taxpayer initiatives have forced governments to seek new revenue sources. Accordingly, governmental units have turned increasingly to other types of revenue, such as sales taxes, business and nonbusiness license fees, charges for services, state-collected, locally shared taxes, and grants-in-aid from the federal and state governments. Department heads, however, ordinarily have little knowledge of revenue figures. As a result, the primary responsibility for estimating these revenues usually lies with the budget officer and the chief finance officer.

Most governmental units, as a safeguard against excessive accumulation of resources, require that any unappropriated amounts carried over from a previous year be included as a source of financing in the budget of that fund for the succeeding fiscal year. Most controlling laws or ordinances provide for inclusion of the estimated surplus (fund balance) at the end of the current year, although many require that the includable surplus be the balance at the close of the last completed fiscal year.

Departmental estimates of expenditures and supporting work programs or performance data generally are prepared by the individual departments, using forms provided by the central budget agency. Expenditures are customarily classified to conform to the standard account classification of the governmental unit and thus permit comparison with actual performance in the current and prior periods.

Personal Services.   Generally, personal services are supported by detailed schedules of proposed salaries for individual full-time employees. Nonsalaried and temporary employees are usually paid on an hourly basis, and the budget requests are normally based on the estimated number of hours of work.

Estimates of materials and supplies and other services, ordinarily quite repetitive in nature, are most often based on current experience, plus an allowance, if justified, for rising costs. Capital outlay requests are based on demonstrated need for specific items of furniture or equipment by individual departments.

In recent years, governmental units, particularly at the county, state, and federal levels, have disbursed substantial sums annually that are unlike the usual current operating expenditures. These sums include welfare or public assistance payments, contributions to other governmental units, benefit payments, and special grants. They are properly classified as "other charges." Estimates of these charges are generally based on unit costs for assistance, legislative allotments, requests from outside agencies or governmental units, and specified calculations.

In addition to departmental expenditures, the budget officer must estimate certain nondepartmental or general governmental costs not allocated to any department or organizational unit. Examples include pension costs and retirement contributions, which are not normally allocated, election costs, insurance and surety bonds, and interest on tax notes.

Although most governments still operate under laws that require the budget to be balanced precisely, an increasing number permit a surplus or contingency provision in the expenditure section of the budget. This is usually included to provide a reserve to cover unforeseen expenditures during the budget year.

The expenditure budget may be approved by a board, a commission, or other governing body before presentation to the central budget-making authority.

Presentation of the Budget. To present a comprehensive picture of the proposed fund operations for a budget year, a budget document is prepared that is likely to include a budget message, summary schedules and comparative statements, detailed revenue estimates, detailed expenditure estimates, and drafts of ordinances to be enacted by the legislative body.

The contents of a budget message should set forth concisely the salient features of the proposed budget of each fund and will generally include the following: (1) a total amount showing amounts of overall increase and decrease, (2) detailed amounts and explanations of the increases and decreases, and (3) a detailed statement of the current financial status of each fund for which a budget is submitted, together with recommendations for raising the funds needed to balance the budget of each fund. It should identify the relationship of the operating budget to the capital program and capital budget, which are submitted separately.

Adoption of the Budget. Most states adopt the budget by the enactment of one or more statutes. Many cities require the formality of an ordinance for the adoption of the budget. In other cases, the budget is adopted by resolution of the governing body.

Appropriations. Because appropriations constitute maximum expenditure authorizations during the fiscal year, they cannot be exceeded legally unless subsequently amended by the legislative body (although some governments permit modifications up to a prescribed limit to be made by the executive branch). Unexpended or unencumbered appropriations may lapse at the end of a fiscal year or may continue as authority for subsequent period expenditures, depending on the applicable legal provisions.

It may be necessary for the legislative agency to adopt a separate appropriation resolution or ordinance, or the adoption of the budget may include the making of appropriations for the items of expenditure included therein. Provision for the required general property tax levy is usually made at this time, either by certifying the required tax rates to the governmental unit that will bill and collect the general property tax or by enacting a tax levy ordinance or resolution.

(iii) Budget Execution. The budget execution phase entails obtaining the revenues, operating the program, and expending the money as authorized. The accounts are usually structured on the same basis on which the budget was prepared. Many governments maintain budgetary control by integration of the budgetary accounts into the general and subsidiary ledger. The entry is as follows:

Estimated revenues	$XXX	
Appropriations		$XXX

If estimated revenues exceed appropriations, a credit for the excess is made to "budgetary fund balance"; if they are less the appropriations, the difference is debited to "budgetary fund balance."

Individual sources of revenues are recognized in subsidiary revenue accounts. A typical revenue ledger report is illustrated in Exhibit 34.1. This format provides for the comparison, at any date, of actual and estimated revenues from each source.

To control expenditures effectively, the individual amounts making up the total appropriations are recorded in subsidiary expenditures accounts, generally called *appropriation ledgers.* Exhibit 34.2 presents an example of an appropriation ledger. It should be noted that this format

NAME OF GOVERNMENTAL UNIT
Budget versus Actual Revenue
by Revenue Source
for Accounting Period June 30, 20XX

Fund Type: The General Fund

	Revenues	Budgeted	Actual	Variance
015	Real & per. revenue recognized			
0110	Real & p. prop re.v recognized	$459,449,213	$460,004,317	$ (555,104)
	Revenue class total	459,449,213	460,004,317	(555,104)
020	Motor vehicle & other excise			
0121	M/V taxes—current year	16,000,000	22,727,905	(6,727,905)
0122	M/V taxes—prior 1997	0	2,886,605	(2,886,605)
0123	M/V taxes—1996	0	32,051	(32,051)
0124	M/V taxes—1995	0	45,378	(45,378)
0125	M/V taxes—1994	0	85,393	(85,393)
0126	M/V taxes—1993 and prior	0	2	(2)
0127	Boat excise—cur yr 1998	15,000	40,414	(25,414)
0128	Boat excise—1997	0	155	(155)
0131	M.V. lessor surcharge	200	60	139
	Revenue class total	16,015,200	25,817,963	(9,802,764)
025	Local excise taxes			
0129	Hotel/motel room excise	13,500,000	13,580,142	(80,142)
0130	Aircraft fuel excise	12,400,000	12,960,966	(560,966)
	Revenue class total	25,900,000	26,541,108	(641,108)
030	Departmental & other revenue			
0133	Penalties & int-prop. taxes	1,000,000	1,746,007	(746,007)
0134	Penalties & int.-M/V taxes	525,000	620,124	(95,124)
0135	Penalties & int.-sidewalk	0	115	(115)
0136	Penalties & interest/tax title	5,000,000	3,835,517	1,164,483
0138	Penalties & int./boat excise	0	3	(3)
3101	Data processing services	100	6,849	(6,749)
3103	Purchasing services	50,000	69,038	(19,038)
3104	Recording of legal instruments	150	291	(141)
3105	Registry division—fees	750,000	761,238	(11,238)
3107	City record/sale of publication	10,000	25,353	(15,353)
3108	Assessing fees	1,600	914	686
3109	Liens	400,000	373,410	26,590
3120	City clerk—fees	250,000	231,970	18,030
3130	Election—fees	12,000	10,633	1,367
3140	City council/sale of publication	200	310	(110)
3199	Other general services	35,000	18,691	16,309
3202	Police services	350,000	365,102	(15,102)
3211	Fire services	1,150,000	1,582,355	(432,355)
3221	Civil defense	40,000	161,835	(121,835)
3301	Parking facilities	3,350,000	3,775,810	(425,810)
	Revenue class total	$ 12,924,050	$ 13,585,565	$ (661,515)

Exhibit 34.1   A typical revenue ledger report.

NAME OF GOVERNMENTAL UNIT
Budget versus Actual Expenditures
and Encumbrances by Activity
for Accounting Period June 30, 20XX

Fund Type: The General Fund

Expenditures		**Budgeted**	**Actual**	**Variance**
1100 Human services				
011-384-0384	Rent equity board	$ 1,330,977	$ 1,274,531	$ 56,446
011-387-0387	Elderly commission	2,534,005	2,289,549	244,456
011-398-0398	Physically handicapped comm	180,283	159,768	20,515
011-503-0503	Arts & humanities office	211,916	207,219	4,697
011-740-0741	Vet serv-veterans serv div	2,871,616	2,506,363	365,253
011-740-0742	Vet serv-veterans graves reg	158,270	146,392	11,878
011-150-1505	Jobs & community services	370,053	369,208	845
Activity total		7,657,120	6,953,030	704,090
1200 Public safety				
011-211-0211	Police department	116,850,000	117,145,704	(295,704)
011-221-0221	Fire department	80,594,068	79,587,423	1,006,645
011-222-0222	Arson commission	189,244	175,670	13,574
011-251-0251	Transportation-traffic div	13,755,915	13,707,890	48,025
011-252-0252	Licensing board	542,007	449,825	92,182
011-251-0253	Transportation-parking clerk	7,520,539	7,474,462	46,077
011-261-0260	Inspectional services dept	10,004,470	10,003,569	901
Activity total		229,456,243	228,544,543	911,700
1300 Public works				
011-311-0311	Public works department	64,900,000	60,281,837	4,618,163
011-331-0331	Snow removal	2,250,000	2,360,326	(110,326)
Activity total		67,150,000	62,642,163	4,507,837
1400 Property & development				
011-180-0180	RPD-general administration div	432,740	416,569	16,171
014-180-0183	Real property dept county	1,027,660	354,328	673,332
011-180-0184	RPD-buildings division	6,010,155	6,038,464	(28,309)
011-180-0185	RPD-property division	1,847,650	1,806,427	41,223
011-188-0186	PFD-code enforcement division	504,013	458,984	45,029
011-188-0187	PFD-administration division	4,677,365	4,697,167	(19,802)
011-188-0188	PFD-construction & repair div	3,063,637	2,808,266	255,371
Activity total		$ 17,563,220	$ 16,580,205	$ 983,015

Exhibit 34.2   A typical appropriation ledger report.

provides for recording the budget appropriation and for applying expenditures and encumbrances (see below) relating to the particular classification against the amount appropriated at any date.

When the managerial control purposes of integrating the budgetary accounts into the general ledger have been served, the budgetary account balances are reversed in the process of closing the books at year end. Budgetary accounting procedures thus have no effect on the financial position or results of operations of a governmental entity.

Encumbrances.   An encumbrance, which is unique to governmental accounting, is the reservation of a portion of an applicable appropriation that is made because a contract has been signed or a purchase order issued. The encumbrance is usually recorded in the accounting system to prevent overspending the appropriation. When the goods or services are received, the expenditure is recorded and the encumbrance is reversed. The entry to record an encumbrance is as follows:

Encumbrances	$XXX	
Reserve for encumbrances		$XXX

The entries that are made when the goods or services are received are:

Reserve for encumbrances	$XXX	
Encumbrances		$XXX
Expenditures	$XXX	
Vouchers payable		$XXX

Many governments report encumbrances that are not liquidated at year end in the same way as expenditures because the encumbrances are another use of budgetary appropriations. The total amount of encumbrances not liquidated by year end may be considered as a reservation of the fund balance for the subsequent year's expenditures, based on the encumbered appropriation authority carried over.

Allotments. Another way to maintain budgetary control is to use an allotment system. With an allotment system, the annual budget appropriation is divided and allotted among the months or quarters in the fiscal year. A department is not permitted to spend more than its allotment during the period.

The International City Managers' Association lists the following four purposes of an allotment system:

1. To make sure that departments plan their spending so as to have sufficient funds to carry on their programs throughout the year, avoiding year-end deficiencies and special appropriations
2. To eliminate or reduce short-term tax anticipation borrowing by making possible more accurate forecast control of cash position throughout the fiscal year
3. To keep expenditures within the limits of revenues that are actually realized, avoiding an unbalanced budget in the operation of any fund as a whole
4. To give the chief administrator control over departmental expenditures commensurate with the administrative responsibility, allowing the administrator to effect economies in particular activities as changes in workload and improvements in methods occur

Interim Reports. The last element in the budget execution process is interim financial reports. These are prepared to provide department heads, senior management, and the governing body with the information needed to monitor and control operations, demonstrate compliance with legal and budgetary limitations, anticipate changes in financial resources and requirements due to events or developments that are unknown or could not be foreseen at the time the budget was initially developed, or take appropriate corrective action. Interim reports should be prepared frequently enough to permit early detection of variances between actual and planned operations, but not so frequently as to adversely affect practicality and economy. For most governmental units, interim reports on a monthly basis are necessary for optimum results. With smaller units, a bimonthly or quarterly basis may be sufficient. With sophisticated data-processing equipment, it may be possible to automatically generate the appropriate information daily.

Governmental units should prepare interim financial reports covering the following:

- Revenues
- Expenditures
- Cash projections
- Proprietary funds

- Capital projects
- Grant programs

The form and content of these reports should reflect the government's particular circumstances and conditions.

(iv) Proprietary Fund Budgeting.   The nature of most operations financed and accounted for through proprietary funds is such that the demand for the goods or services largely determines the appropriate level of revenues and expenses. Increased demand causes a higher level of expenses to be incurred but also results in a higher level of revenues. Thus, as in commercial accounting, flexible budgets prepared for several levels of possible activity typically are better for planning, control, and evaluation purposes than are fixed budgets.

Accordingly, budgets are not typically adopted for proprietary funds. Furthermore, even when flexible budgets are adopted, they are viewed not as appropriations but as approved plans. The budgetary accounts are generally not integrated into the ledger accounts because it is considered unnecessary. Budgetary control and evaluation are achieved by comparing interim actual revenues and expenses with planned revenues and expenses at the actual level of activity for the period.

In some instances, fixed dollar budgets are adopted for proprietary funds either to meet local legal requirements or to control certain expenditures (e.g., capital outlay). In such cases, it may be appropriate to integrate budgetary accounts into the proprietary fund accounting system in a manner similar to that discussed for governmental funds.

(v) Capital Budget.   Many governments also prepare a capital budget. A capital budget is a plan for capital expenditures to be incurred during a single budget year from funds subject to appropriation for projects scheduled under the capital program. The annual capital budget is adopted concurrently with the operating budgets of the governmental unit, being subject to a public hearing and the other usual legal procedures.

The capital budget should not be confused with a capital program or capital project budget. A capital program is a plan for capital expenditures to be incurred over a period of years, usually five or six years. The capital project budget represents the estimated amount to be expended on a specific project over the entire period of its construction. The capital budget authorizes the amounts to be expended on all projects during a single year. Controlling this amount is important for the proper use of available funds.

(vi) Budgetary Comparison Information.   Under GASB Statement No. 34, budgetary comparison schedules should present: (1) the original appropriated budgets; (2) the final appropriated budgets; and (3) actual inflows, outflows, and balances, stated on the governmental budgetary basis as discussed in NCGA Statement No. 1, paragraph 154. Separate columns may be provided comparing the original budget amounts with the actual amounts, the final budget amounts with the actual amounts, or both. The original budget is the first complete appropriated budget, which may be adjusted by reserves, transfers, allocations, supplementary appropriations, and other legally authorized legislative and executive changes made before the beginning of the reporting year. It also includes appropriation amounts automatically carried over from prior years by law. The final budget is the original budget adjusted by all legally authorized legislative and executive changes whenever signed into law or otherwise legally authorized. Governments may elect to report the budget comparison information in a budgetary comparison statement as part of the financial statements or as required supplementary disclosure.

(l) CLASSIFICATION AND TERMINOLOGY.   Principles 10 and 11 establish the requirements surrounding classification and terminology. Governmental fund revenues should be classified by fund and source. The major revenue source classifications are taxes, licenses and permits, intergovernmental revenues, charges for services, fines and forfeits, and miscellaneous. Governmental units often classify revenues by organizational units. This classification may be desirable for purposes of management control and accountability, as well as for auditing purposes, but it should supplement rather than supplant the classifications by fund and source.

(i) Classification of Expenditures. There are many ways to classify governmental fund expenditures in addition to the basic fund classification. Function, program, organizational unit, activity, character, and principal class of object are examples. Typically, expenditures are classified by character (current, intergovernmental, capital outlay, and/or debt service). Current expenditures are further classified by function and/or program.

- *Character classification.* Reporting expenditures according to the physical period they are presumed to benefit. The major character classifications are: (1) current expenditures, which benefit the current fiscal period; (2) capital outlays, which are presumed to benefit both the present and future fiscal periods; and (3) debt service, which benefits prior fiscal periods as well as current and future periods. Intergovernmental expenditures is a fourth character classification that is used when one governmental unit makes expenditures to another governmental unit.

- *Function classification.* Establishing groups of related activities that are aimed at accomplishing a major service or regulatory responsibility. Standard function classifications are as follows:

  General government

  Public safety

  Health and welfare

  Culture and recreation

  Conservation of natural resources

  Urban redevelopment and housing

  Economic development and assistance

  Education

  Debt service

  Miscellaneous

- *Program classification.* Establishing groups of activities, operations, or organizational units that are directed at the attainment of specific purposes or objectives, for example, protection of property or improvement of transportation. Program classification is used by governmental units employing program budgeting.

- *Organizational unit classification.* Grouping expenditures according to the governmental unit's organization structure. Organizational unit classification is essential to responsibility reporting.

- *Activity classification.* Grouping expenditures according to the performance of specific activities. Activity classification is necessary for the determination of cost per unit of activity, which in turn is necessary for evaluation of economy and efficiency.

- *Object classification.* Grouping expenditures according to the types of items purchased or services obtained, for example, personal services, supplies, other services, and charges. Object classifications are subdivisions of the character classification.

Excessively detailed object classifications should be avoided since they complicate the accounting procedure and are of limited use in financial management. The use of a few object classifications is sufficient in budget preparation; control emphasis should be on organization units, functions, programs, and activities rather than on the object of expenditures.

(ii) Classifications of Other Transactions. Certain transactions, although not revenues or expenditures of an individual fund or the governmental entity as a whole, are increases or decreases in the equity of an individual fund. These transactions are classified as other financing sources and uses and are reported in the operating statement separately from fund revenues and expenditures. The most common other financing sources and uses are:

- *Proceeds of long-term debt issues.* Such proceeds (including leases) are not recorded as fund liabilities; for example, proceeds of bonds and notes expended through the capital project or debt service funds.
- *Operating transfers.* These include legally authorized transfers from a fund receiving revenues to the fund through which the resources are to be expended; examples are transfers of tax revenues from a special revenue fund to a debt service fund and transfers from an enterprise fund other than payments in lieu of taxes to finance general fund expenditures.

Other interfund transactions are:

- *Interfund loans and advances.* These funds are disbursed by one fund for the benefit of another. If the funds will be repaid shortly, the amount should be reclassified as due from other funds by the lending fund and due to other funds by the receiving fund. When two funds owe each other, the amounts receivable and payable should not be offset in the accounts. However, for purposes of reporting, current amounts due from and due to the same funds may be offset and the net amounts shown in the respective fund balance sheets.

    If the advance is long term in nature and the asset will not be available to finance current operations, a fund balance reserve equal to the amount of the advance should be established.
- *Quasi-external transactions.* These transactions would be treated as revenues, expenditures, or expenses if they involved organizations external to the governmental unit. Examples are payments in lieu of taxes from an enterprise fund to the general fund; internal service fund billings to departments; routine employer contributions from the general fund to a pension trust fund; and a routine service charge for inspection, engineering, utilities, or similar services provided by a department financed from one fund to a department financed from another fund.

    Amounts should be accounted for as revenues in the recipient fund and as expenditures in the disbursing fund.
- *Reimbursements.* These transactions constitute reimbursements of a fund for expenditures or expenses initially made from it that are properly applicable to another fund. An example is an expenditure properly chargeable to a special revenue fund but initially made from the general fund, which is subsequently reimbursed. The transaction should be recorded as an expenditure or expense in the reimbursing fund and as a reduction of an expenditure or expense in the reimbursed fund.

(iii) Residual Equity Transfers.   Another type of interfund transaction, residual equity transfers, is not classified as another financing source or use because it is a change in fund balance that is not considered in the determination of the results of operations. A residual equity transfer is a nonrecurring or nonroutine transfer of equity between funds. Examples are a general fund's contribution of capital to an enterprise fund or an internal service fund; the subsequent return of all or part of such contribution to the general fund; and transfers of residual balances of discontinued funds to the general fund or a debt service fund.

(iv) Classification of Fund Equity.   Fund equity is the difference between a fund's assets and its liabilities. GASB Statement No. 34 requires the equity reported in the government-wide statement of net assets to be called *net assets* and to be displayed in three categories:

- *Invested in capital assets, net of related debt* consists of capital assets, including restricted capital assets, reduced by accumulated depreciation and by any outstanding debt incurred to acquire those assets.
- *Restricted net assets* reports those net assets with restrictions on their use, either by external or internal factors.
- *Unrestricted net assets* consists of all other net assets.

Designations of fund balance identify tentative plans for or restrictions on the future use of financial resources. Such designations should be supported by definitive plans and approved by either the government's CEO or the legislature. Examples of such designations include the earmarking of financial resources for capital projects and contingent liabilities. Management designations for the use of resources should not be reported in the statement of net assets but may be disclosed in notes to the financial statements.

The equity reported in the proprietary fund statement of net assets or balance sheet should be labeled either *net assets* or *fund equity,* using the three net asset components discussed for government-wide net assets.

An important amount in the fund equity account for governmental funds is the amount available for future appropriation and expenditure (i.e., unreserved and undesignated fund balance). The equity reported in the governmental fund balance sheets should be labeled *fund balances* and to be segregated into reserved and unreserved amounts. NCGA Statement 1 notes that fund balance reserves report the portions of the fund balances that are (*a*) legally segregated for a specific use or (*b*) not available for expenditure because the underlying asset is not available for current appropriation or expenditure. Reserves are not intended as valuation allowances, but merely demonstrate the current unavailability of the subject assets to pay current expenditures. Reserves and designations are established by debiting unreserved, undesignated fund balance and crediting the reserve or designation. The reserve is not established by a charge to operations.

GASB Statement No. 34 requires reserved fund balances of non-major governmental funds to be displayed in sufficient detail to disclose the purposes of the reservations, and requires unreserved fund balances of the non-major governmental funds to be displayed by fund type. Management designations of fund balances should be reported as part of unreserved fund balances, and disclosed as separate line items or disclosed in the financial statement notes. Since GASB standards do not identify the legal criteria that would distinguish a reserve from a designation of fund balance, there is diversity in practice as it relates to this issue.

The equity reported in the fiduciary fund statement of fiduciary net assets should be labeled *net assets* but does not require net assets to be categorized into the three components. GASB Statements No. 25, "Financial Reporting for Defined Benefit Pension Plans and Note Disclosures for Defined Contribution Plans;" No. 26, "Financial Reporting for Postemployment Healthcare Plans Administered by Defined Benefit Pension Plans;" and No. 31, "Accounting and Financial Reporting for Certain Investments and for External Investment Pools" contain specific disclosure requirements for these types of funds.

Reconciliations.   The amount of net assets reported for a PG in the government-wide statement of net assets usually will differ from the aggregate amount of equity reported in its fund financial position statements since the funds statements are prepared using the funds flow measurement focus and modified accrual method. There will also be differences between the changes in equity reported in the various activity statements, GASB Statement No. 34, requires summary reconciliations to the government-wide financial statements to be presented on the fund financial statements themselves or in an accompanying schedule. For governmental funds, the total governmental fund balances should be reconciled to the net assets of governmental activities. Also the total changes in the governmental fund balances should be reconciled to the change in net assets of governmental activities. Typical differences that require reconciliation include equity arising from capital assets, deferred revenues, and long-term liabilities). For enterprise funds, (*a*) total enterprise fund net assets should be reconciled to the net assets of business-type activities (however since both are on the accrual basis, there often are no differences) and (*b*) the total change in enterprise fund net assets should be reconciled to the change in net assets of business-type activities, provided there are differences that require reconciliation.

Exhibit 34.4 presents an example from GASB 34 of the balance sheet presentation of the general fund and three major governmental funds. Non-major funds are aggregated in an "Other" column. Note the reconciliation of the balances on the face of the financial statement.

	Budgeted Amounts		Actual Amounts (Budgetary Basis)	Variance with Final Budget Positive
	Original	Final	(See Note A)	(Negative)
Budgetary fund balance, January 1	$ 3,528,750	$ 2,742,799	$ 2,742,799	$ —
Resources (inflows):				
Property taxes	52,017,833	51,853,018	51,173,436	(679,582)
Franchise taxes	4,546,209	4,528,750	4,055,505	(473,245)
Public service taxes	8,295,000	8,307,274	8,969,887	662,613
Licenses and permits	2,126,600	2,126,600	2,287,794	161,194
Fines and forfeitures	718,800	718,800	606,946	(111,854)
Charges for services	12,392,972	11,202,150	11,374,460	172,310
Grants	6,905,898	6,571,360	6,119,938	(451,422)
Sale of land	1,355,250	3,500,000	3,476,488	(23,512)
Miscellaneous	3,024,292	1,220,991	881,874	(339,117)
Interest received	1,015,945	550,000	552,325	2,325
Transfers from other funds	939,525	130,000	129,323	(677)
Amounts available for appropriation	96,867,074	93,451,742	92,370,775	(1,080,967)
Charges to appropriations (outflows)				
General government:				
Legal	665,275	663,677	632,719	30,958
Mayor, legislative, city manager	3,058,750	3,192,910	2,658,264	534,646
Finance and accounting	1,932,500	1,912,702	1,852,687	60,015
City clerk and elections	345,860	354,237	341,206	13,031
Employee relations	1,315,500	1,300,498	1,234,232	66,266
Planning and economic development	1,975,600	1,784,314	1,642,575	141,739
Public safety:				
Police	19,576,820	20,367,917	20,246,496	121,421
Fire department	9,565,280	9,559,967	9,559,967	—
Emergency medical services	2,323,171	2,470,127	2,459,866	10,261
Inspections	1,585,695	1,585,695	1,533,380	52,315
Public works:				
Public works administration	388,500	385,013	383,397	1,616
Street maintenance	2,152,750	2,233,362	2,233,362	—
Street lighting	762,750	759,832	759,832	—
Traffic operations	385,945	374,945	360,509	14,436
Mechanical maintenance	1,525,685	1,272,696	1,256,087	16,609
Engineering services:				
Engineering administration	1,170,650	1,158,023	1,158,023	—
Geographical information system	125,625	138,967	138,967	—
Health and sanitation:				
Garbage pickup	5,756,250	6,174,653	6,174,653	—
				(Continues)

Exhibit 34.3   Budget-to-Actual Comparison Schedule for the General Fund in the Budget Document Format. (Source: Illustration G1 GASB Statement 34.)

	Budgeted Amounts		Actual Amounts (Budgetary Basis) (See Note A)	Variance with Final Budget Positive (Negative)
	Original	Final		
Cemetery:				
Personal services	425,000	425,000	422,562	2,438
Purchases of goods and				
services	299,500	299,500	283,743	15,757
Culture and recreation:				
Library	985,230	1,023,465	1,022,167	1,298
Parks and recreation	9,521,560	9,786,397	9,756,618	29,779
Community				
communications	552,350	558,208	510,361	47,847
Nondepartmental:				
Miscellaneous	—	259,817	259,817	—
Contingency	2,544,049	—	—	—
Transfers to other funds	2,970,256	2,163,759	2,163,759	—
Funding for school district	22,000,000	22,000,000	21,893,273	106,727
Total charges to				
appropriations	93,910,551	92,205,681	90,938,522	1,267,159
Budgetary fund balance,				
December 31	$ 2,956,523	$ 1,246,061	$ 1,432,253	$ 186,192

Exhibit 34.3   Continued.

(m) EXTERNAL FINANCIAL REPORTING.   Prior to 1979, governments traditionally prepared external financial reports by preparing financial statements for every fund maintained by the government. This often resulted in lengthy financial reports. External financial reporting has evolved to require the presentation of financial statements on a more aggregated basis and the inclusion of legally separate entities that have special relationships. Principle 12 relates to financial reporting and is discussed below.

(i) The Financial Reporting Entity.   GASB Statement No. 14, "The Financial Reporting Entity," establishes standards for defining and reporting on the financial reporting entity.

The statement indicates that the financial reporting entity consists of (a) the PG, (b) organizations for which the PG is financially accountable, and (c) other organizations that, if omitted from the reporting entity, would cause the financial statements to be misleading.

The statement also outlines the basic criteria for including organizations in or excluding organizations from the reporting entity. All organizations for which the PG is *financially* accountable should be included in the reporting entity. Such organizations include:

- The organizations that make up the PG's legal entity, and
- Component units. That is, organizations that are legally separate from the PG but:
  ○ The PG's officials appoint a voting majority of the organization's governing board *and*
  ○ Either the PG is able to impose its will on that organization *or* there is a potential for the organization to provide specific financial benefits to, or to impose specific financial burdens on the PG.

A legally separate, tax-exempt organization should be reported as a component unit of a reporting entity if all of the following criteria are met:

	General	HUD Programs	Community Redevelopment	Route 7 Construction	Other Governmental Funds [See H-1]	Total Governmental Funds
ASSETS						
Cash and cash equivalents	$ 3,418,485	$ 1,236,523	$ —	$ —	$ 5,606,792	$ 10,261,800
Investments	—	—	13,262,695	10,467,037	3,485,252	27,214,984
Receivables, net	3,644,561	2,953,438	353,340	11,000	10,221	6,972,560
Due from other funds	1,370,757	—	—	—	—	1,370,757
Receivables from other governments	—	119,059	—	—	1,596,038	1,715,097
Liens receivable	791,926	3,195,745	—	—	—	3,987,671
Inventories	182,821	—	—	—	—	182,821
Total assets	$ 9,408,550	$ 7,504,765	$ 13,616,035	$ 10,478,037	$ 10,698,303	$ 51,705,690
LIABILITIES AND FUND BALANCES						
Liabilities:						
Accounts payable	$ 3,408,680	$ 129,975	$ 190,548	$ 1,104,632	$ 1,074,831	$ 5,908,666
Due to other funds	—	25,369	—	—	—	25,369
Payable to other governments	94,074	—	—	—	—	94,074
Deferred revenue	4,250,430	6,273,045	250,000	11,000	—	10,784,475
Total liabilities [Note 2]	7,753,184	6,428,389	440,548	1,115,632	1,074,831	16,812,584
Fund balances:						
Reserved for:						
Inventories	182,821	—	—	—	—	182,821
Liens receivable	791,926	—	—	—	—	791,926
Encumbrances	40,292	41,034	119,314	5,792,587	1,814,122	7,807,349
Debt service	—				3,832,062	3,832,062
Other purposes	—	"Designations" of unreserved fund balances may			1,405,300	1,405,300
Unreserved, reported in:		be displayed or disclosed in the notes.				
General fund	640,327	—	—	—	—	640,327
Special revenue funds	—	1,035,342	—	—	1,330,718	2,366,060
Capital projects funds	—	—	13,056,173	3,569,818	1,241,270	17,867,261
Total fund balances	1,655,366	1,076,376	13,175,487	9,362,405	9,623,472	34,893,106
Total liabilities and fund balances	$ 9,408,550	$ 7,504,765	$ 13,616,035	$ 10,478,037	$ 10,698,303	

Amounts reported for *governmental activities* in the statement of net assets [A-1] are different because [see Note 4, also]:

Explanations of the reconciling amounts need not be as detailed as the ones illustrated here. In some cases, detailed explanations on the face of the statements may eliminate the need for further descriptions in the notes. On the other hand, long complicated explanations on the statement may distract the users, attention from the other information presented. Preparers should weigh the advantages of eliminating the need for users to refer to the notes against the possible disadvantage of overloading the statement with information. In some situations, however, additional disclosure of reconciling items is required, as discussed in paragraph 77.	Capital assets used in governmental activities are not financial resources and therefore are not reported in the funds.	161,082,708
	Other long-term assets are not available to pay for current-period expenditures and therefore are deferred in the funds.	9,348,876
	Internal service funds are used by management to charge the costs of certain activities, such as insurance and telecommunications, to individual funds. The assets and liabilities of the internal service funds are included in governmental activities in the statement of net assets [see D-1]	2,994,691
	Long-term liabilities, including bonds payable, are not due and payable in the current period and therefore are not reported in the funds [see Note 4a]	[84,760,507]
	Net assets of governmental activities	$ 123,558,874

The reconciliation could be presented on an accompanying page, rather than on the face of the statement. [See the separate reconciliation example in C-3.]

Exhibit 34.4   Balance Sheet Presentation of the General Fund and Three Major Governmental Funds.

- The economic resources received or held by the separate organization are entirely or almost entirely for the direct benefit of the PG, its component units, or its constituents.
- The PG, or its component units, is entitled to, or has the ability to otherwise access,[1] a majority of the economic resources received or held by the separate organization.

---

[1] Ability to otherwise access does not necessarily imply control over the other organization or its resources. It may be demonstrated in several ways. For example, the primary government or its component units historically may have received, directly or indirectly, a majority of the economic resources provided by the organization, the organization may have previously received and honored requests to provide resources to the primary government, or the organization is a financially interrelated organization as defined by FASB Statement No. 136.

- The economic resources received or held by an individual organization that the specific PG, or its component units, is entitled to, or has the ability to otherwise access, are significant to that PG.

Other organizations should be evaluated as potential component units if they are closely related to, or financially integrated[2] with, the PG. It is a matter of professional judgment to determine whether the nature and the significance of a potential component unit's relationship with the PG warrant inclusion in the reporting entity. Organizations not meeting the above criteria are excluded from the reporting entity.

Reporting the inclusion of the various entities comprising the reporting entity can be done using two methods: blending or discrete presentation. Most component units should be included in the financial reporting entity by discrete presentation. Some component units, despite being legally separate entities, are so intertwined with the PG that, in substance, they are the same as the PG and should be "blended" with the transactions of the PG.

Certain other entities are not considered component units because the PG, while responsible for appointing the organization's board members, is not financially accountable. Such entities are considered related organizations. These related organizations as well as joint ventures and jointly governed organizations should be disclosed in the reporting entity's footnotes.

(ii) General Purpose Financial Statements.   Under GASB Statement No. 34, the general purpose financial statements should include a statement of net assets and a statement of activities for the government as a whole. The former "pyramid" concept for external financial reporting has been superseded.

Even though the GASB encourages each governmental entity to prepare a CAFR, the general purpose financial statement constitutes fair presentation of financial position and results of operations in accordance with GAAP and could be opined on as such by an independent auditor. The statements would be suitable for inclusion in an official statement for a securities offering and for widespread distribution to users requiring less detailed information about the governmental unit's finances than is contained in the CAFR.

(iii) Comprehensive Annual Financial Report (CAFR).   The CAFR differs from the GPFS in the level of detail and the quantity of data presented. The additional data are *not* necessary for fair presentation of financial position or results of operation in accordance with GAAP, but they are useful and informative for certain readers of a government's financial report. Furthermore, the CAFR may be the vehicle for providing the necessary information for fulfilling the legal and other disclosure requirements of higher levels of government, bondholders, and similar groups. It is also useful in demonstrating management's stewardship responsibilities, since alongside the comparative budgets it presents in more detail the use of the available resources.

The recommended contents of the CAFR include:

- *Introductory section*

  Title page. Contains the title "Comprehensive Annual Financial Report," the name of the governmental unit, the period of time covered, and the names of the principal government officials. Component units that issue separate statements should indicate the PG of which it is a component.

  A title such as "City Hospital, a Component Unit of City, Any State" is recommended.

  Table of contents. Identifies the presence and location of each item included in the report.

---

[2] Financial integration may be exhibited and documented through the policies, practices, or organizational documents of either the primary government or the other organization.[3] More than one column may be used to display components of a program revenue category. Governments may also provide more-descriptive category headings to better explain the range of program revenues reported therein, for example, *operating grants, contributions, and restricted interest.*

COMPREHENSIVE ANNUAL FINANCIAL REPORT
MANAGEMENT DISCUSSION AND ANALYSIS

	Government-Wide	Fund-Based Reports
Governmental	• Statement of Net Assets • Statement of Activities • *Economic Measurement Focus* • *Accrual*	• Balance Sheet • Statement of Revenues, Expenditures, and Change in Fund Balance • *Current financial resources measurement focus* • *Modified accrual*
Proprietary/ Enterprise	A Component of the Statement of Net Assets and the Statement of Activities	• Statement of Net Assets or Balance Sheet • Statement of Revenues, Expenses, and Change in Net Assets • Statement of Cash Flows • *Economic resources measurement focus* • *Accrual*
Fiduciary	Not Applicable	• Statement of Fiduciary Net Assets • Statement of Change in Fiduciary Net Assets • *Economic resources measurement focus* • *Accrual*

Financial Statement Notes

Required Supplemental Information

Exhibit 34.5   **Relating comprehensive annual financial reporting to the government-wide and fund based reports. (Adapted from Bline, Dennis M., Fischer, Mary M., and Skekel, Ted D,. *Advanced Accounting.* John Wiley & Sons, Inc. Hoboken, NJ. 2004. Pages 484–485.)**

Transmittal letter. From the government's chief finance officer (or CEO), providing significant aspects of financial operations during the period. The letter may include, for example, changes in financial policies; discussion of internal controls; changes in operating results or expected revenues, expenditures, and debt; significant elements of financial management including cash and risk management; financial problems encountered; budget procedures and current budget; and a preview of the significant developments or changes contemplated in the coming year including economic conditions, outlook, and major initiatives.

• *Financial section*

Independent auditor's report.

General purpose financial statements. Includes all required financial statements and related notes as previously described.

Combining financial statements. Used when a governmental unit has more than one fund of a given type.

Individual fund financial statements. Used when this information is not provided in a separate column in a combining statement or it is desirable to present a level of detail that would be excessive for the GPFS or the combining statements. Examples are detail comparisons to budgets that cannot be reflected on the combining statements, comparative data for prior years, or a demonstration of an individual fund's compliance with legal provisions.

Required supplementary information. Included when disclosure is required by the GASB.

Schedules necessary to demonstrate compliance. Included when such are required by state law or by a bond covenant.

Other schedules desired by the government. Used for reporting particular kinds of information that are spread throughout the numerous financial statements and that can be brought together and presented in greater detail than in the individual statements, or that show the details of a specific amount or amounts presented in the GPFS, the combining statements, or the individual fund financial statements.

- *Statistical section*

  Statistical tables cover a period of several years and contain data drawn from more than just the accounting records. Their purpose is to present social, economic, and financial trends, and the fiscal capacity of the governmental unit. The following titles indicate recommended statistical tables for a local government's CAFR:

  General Governmental Expenditures by Function—Last Ten Fiscal Years

  General Revenues by Source—Last Ten Fiscal Years

  Property Tax Levies and Collections—Last Ten Fiscal Years

  Assessed and Estimated Actual Value of Taxable Property—Last Ten Fiscal Years

  Property Tax Rates-All Overlapping Governments—Last Ten Fiscal Years

  Special Assessment Billings and Collections—Last Ten Fiscal Years

  Ratio of Net General Bonded Debt to Assessed Value and Net Bonded Debt Per Capita—Last Ten Fiscal Years

  Computation of Legal Debt Margin (if not in GPFS)

  Computation of Overlapping Debt (if not in GPFS)

  Ratio of Annual Debt Service Expenditures for General Bonded Debt to Total General Government Expenditures—Last Ten Fiscal Years

  Revenue Bond Coverage—Last Ten Fiscal Years

  Demographic Statistics

  Property Values, Construction, and Bank Deposits—Last Ten Fiscal Years

  Principal Taxpayers

  Miscellaneous Statistics

- *Single audit section*

  Although not a required part of a CAFR, some governments include in a separate section the information, including auditor's reports, required by the Single Audit Act Amendments of 1996.

This chapter contains further discussion of the Management's Discussion and Analysis, and Required Supplementary Disclosures. A comprehensive listing of required footnote disclosures and components of the significant accounting policies note can be found in the GASB Codification, Section 2300.

(iv) Certificate of Achievement Program.   Governmental units may submit their CAFRs to the GFOA (180 North Michigan Avenue, Chicago, IL 60601) for evaluation in accordance with the standards of financial reporting established by the GASB and the GFOA. If the report substantially adheres to these standards, the government is awarded a Certificate of Achievement for Excellence in Financial Reporting. The certificate is only valid for one year. It may be reproduced in the government's annual report and should be included in the subsequent year's CAFR. Annually, the GFOA publishes a list of the governments that hold valid certificates.

Many governments endeavor to obtain the certificate. They realize that credit rating agencies and others familiar with governmental accounting and financial reporting recognize that governments holding a certificate typically maintain complete financial records and effectively report their financial information to permit detailed analyses to be performed. This characteristic can improve the government's bond rating.

(v) Popular Reports.   Governments also prepare popular reports to communicate with persons who are neither interested in a complete set of financial statements or able to review them. Popular reports, are also called *condensed summary data.*

There are three types of popular reports. The first is an aggregation of the data from the financial statements that disregards the distinction among fund types and account groups and the different bases of accounting and presents the data as if all the assets, liabilities, equities, revenues, and expenditures (expenses) pertain not to the fund types but to the government as a whole. This results in a presentation similar to that made by corporations and their subsidiaries. In such cases, the government usually eliminates significant interfund transactions before arriving at totals.

The second approach is to visually present the entity's financial information, for instance, by using pie charts or bar graphs. A common presentation is to present one pie to show the composition of revenue by cutting the pie into slices with each slice representing a major revenue source. The size of the slice would reflect the magnitude of the respective revenue source. Similar pie charts can be used to show the major categories of expenditures, the major categories of assets, and the major categories of liabilities.

The third approach, taken by a few governments, is to issue consolidated financial statements, similar to those proposed by the AICPA in a project on experimental financial reporting. Such a consolidated approach replaces the funds and account groups by a single "fund" that is used to report the financial position and results of operations of the entire oversight unit or reporting entity. Intragovernmental transactions are eliminated in the consolidation process and a single basis of accounting (normally accrual) is used for all transactions.

Consolidated financial statements typically include a balance sheet, operating statement, and statement of cash flows. Because the accrual basis of accounting is normally used, fixed assets are reported in the single fund and depreciated. Also, long-term obligations are reported in the single fund, with the result that debt service principal payments are treated as balance sheet rather than operating statement transactions.

(n) REPORTING INTERFUND ACTIVITY.   Interfund activity within and among the three fund categories—governmental, proprietary, and fiduciary—should be classified and reported as follows:

1. Reciprocal interfund activity, which is the internal counterpart to exchange and exchange-like transactions, including:
   ○ *Interfund loans*, which are amounts provided with a requirement for repayment. They should be reported as interfund receivables and payables. They should not be reported as other financing sources or uses in the fund financial statements. If repayment is not expected within a reasonable time, the interfund balances should be reduced and the amount not expected to be repaid should be reported as a transfer from the fund that made the loan to the fund that received the loan.
   ○ *Interfund services* provided and used, which are sales and purchases of goods and services between funds at prices that approximate their external exchange values. They should be reported as revenues in the seller funds and expenditures or expenses in purchases funds, except that when the general fund is used to account for risk-financing activity, interfund charges to other funds should be accounted for as reimbursements.
2. Nonreciprocal interfund activity, which is the internal counterpart to nonexchange transactions, including:
   ○ *Interfund transfers*, which are flows of assets such as cash or goods without equivalent flows of assets in return and without a requirement for repayment. They include payments in lieu of taxes that are not payments for, and are not reasonably equivalent in value to, services provided. They should be reported in governmental funds as other financing uses in the funds making transfers and as other financing sources in the funds receiving transfers. They should be reported in proprietary funds after nonoperating revenues and expenses.
   ○ *Interfund reimbursements*, which are repayments from the funds responsible for particular expenditures or expenses to the funds that initially paid for them. They should not be displayed in the financial statements.

Liabilities arising from interfund activities are not general long-term liabilities and therefore should be reported in governmental funds.

(o) REQUIRED RECONCILIATION TO GOVERNMENT-WIDE STATEMENTS. A government should present a summary reconciliation to the government-wide financial statements at the bottom of the fund financial statements or in a schedule. Brief explanations presented on the face of the statements often are sufficient. However, if aggregated information in the reconciliation obscures the nature of the individual elements of a particular reconciling item, a more detailed explanation should be provided in the notes to financial statements.

Reconciling items include the effects of:

- Reporting capital assets at their acquisition cost and depreciating them instead of reporting capital acquisitions as expenditures when incurred
- Adding general long-term liabilities not due and payable in the current period
- Reducing deferred revenue for amounts not available to pay current-period expenditures
- Adding internal service fund net asset balances
- Reporting revenues on the accrual basis
- Reporting annual depreciation expense instead of expenditures for capital outlays
- Reporting long-term debt proceeds in the statement of net assets as liabilities instead of other financing sources
- Reporting debt principal payments in the statement of net assets as reductions of liabilities instead of expenditures
- Reporting other expenses on the accrual basis
- Adding the net revenue or subtracting the expense of internal service funds

If the amounts reported as net assets and changes in net assets in the proprietary fund financial statements for total enterprise funds differ from the amounts of net assets and changes in net assets of business-type activities in the government-wide statement of activities, they should be explained on the face of the fund statement or in the notes.

(p) REPORTING GENERAL CAPITAL ASSETS.   General capital assets are capital assets of the government that are not specifically related to activities reported in proprietary or fiduciary funds. They are associated with and generally arise from governmental activities and usually result from expenditure of governmental fund financial resources. Nevertheless, they should not be reported as assets in governmental funds; instead, they should be reported in the governmental activities column in the government-wide statement of net assets.

34.5 MANAGEMENT DISCUSSION AND ANALYSIS

Under GASB Statement No. 34, a MD&A should be presented before the financial statements are presented. It should provide an objective and easily readable analysis of the government's financial activities based on facts, decisions, or conditions of which management is aware as of the date of the auditor's report. It should discuss the current-year results and compare them with the results of the prior year, including positive and negative aspects. The use of charts, graphs, and tables is encouraged.

The MD&A should distinguish between information pertaining to the PG and that of its component units, focusing on the PG. Whether to discuss matters related to a component unit should be based on its significance to the total of all discretely presented component units and to the PG.

MD&A requirements in GASB Statement No. 34 are general to encourage effective reporting of only the most relevant information and to avoid boilerplate discussion. The information presented should be confined to the following eight items, including additional details pertaining to those items. Information not related to the items may be provided other than in MD&A, such as in the letter of transmittal or another form of supplementary information.

1. A brief discussion of the basic financial statements, including the relationships of the statements to each other and the significant differences in the information they provide. Analyses should be provided that help users understand why measurements and results reported in fund financial statements either reinforce information in government-wide statements or provide additional information.

2. Condensed financial information derived from government-wide financial statements comparing the current year to the prior year. Governments should present the information needed to support their analysis of financial position and results of operations required in item 3 below, including the following elements, if relevant:

   ○ Total assets, distinguishing between capital and other assets

   ○ Total liabilities, distinguishing between long-term and other liabilities

   ○ Total net assets, distinguishing among amounts invested in capital assets, net of related debt; restricted amounts; and unrestricted amounts

   ○ Program revenues, by major source

   ○ General revenues, by major source

   ○ Total revenues

   ○ Program expenses, at a minimum by function

   ○ Total expenses

   ○ Excess or deficiency before contributions to term and permanent endowments or permanent fund principal, special and extraordinary items, and transfers

   ○ Contributions

   ○ Special and extraordinary items

   ○ Transfers

   ○ Change in net assets

   ○ Ending assets

3. An analysis of the government's overall financial position and results of operations, addressing both governmental and business-type activities as reported in the government-wide financial statements, to help us assess whether the financial position has improved or deteriorated as a result of the year's operations. The analysis should include reasons for significant changes from the prior year. Also, important economic factors, such as changes in the tax year or employment bases, that significantly affected operating results for the year should be disclosed.

4. An analysis of balances and transactions of the individual funds, including the reasons for significant changes in fund balances or fund net assets and whether restrictions, commitments, or other limitations significantly affect the availability of fund resources for future use.

5. An analysis of significant variations between original and final budget amounts and between final budget amounts and actual budget results for the general fund or its equivalent, including any known reasons for such of those variations that are expected to have a significant effect on future services or liquidity.

6. A description of significant capital asset and long-term debt activity (summarizing the required note disclosures on this subject and referring to the notes) during the year, including a discussion of commitments for capital expenditures, changes in credit ratings, and debt limitations that may affect financing of planned facilities or services.

7. A discussion by governments that use the modified approach to report some or all of their infrastructure assets (see below), including:

   ○ Significant changes in the assessed condition of eligible infrastructure assets from previous condition assessments

    ○ How the current assessed condition compares with the condition level the government has established

    ○ Any significant differences from the estimated annual amount to maintain and preserve eligible infrastructure assets compared with the actual amounts spent during the period

8. A description of facts, decisions, or conditions of which management is aware at the date of the independent auditor's report that are expected to significantly affect financial position or results of operations—revenues, expenses, and other changes in net assets.

34.6 GOVERNMENT-WIDE FINANCIAL STATEMENTS

Under GASB Statement No. 34, government-wide financial statements should be presented. They are a statement of net assets and a statement of activities. They should:

- Report overall information about the government without displaying individual funds or fund types
- Not include information about fiduciary activities, including component units that are fiduciary in nature, such as certain public employee retirement systems
- Distinguish between the PG and its discretely presented component units
- Distinguish between governmental activities and business-type activities of the PG
- Measure and report all financial and capital assets, liabilities, revenues, expenses, gains, and losses using the economic resources measurement focus and accrual basis of accounting

(a) FOCUS OF THE GOVERNMENT-WIDE FINANCIAL STATEMENTS. The two PG-wide financial statements, the statement of net assets and the statement of activities, should report information about the reporting government as a whole. The statements should cover the PG and its component units, except for fiduciary funds of the PG and component units that are fiduciary in nature, which should be reported in the statements of fiduciary net assets and changes in fiduciary net assets.

The focus of the government-wide financial statements should be on the PG. The total PG and its discretely presented component units should be distinguished by separate rows and columns. A total column for the government entity as a whole and prior year information are optional.

Governmental and business-type activities of the PG should also be distinguished by separate rows and columns. (An activity need not be set out as a proprietary fund if it is not currently reported as such by the management of the government unless it is required to be reported as an enterprise fund as discussed in Section 34.4(g)(vi).) Governmental and business-type activities are distinguished in general by their methods of financing. Governmental activities are generally financed by taxes, intergovernmental revenues, and other nonexchange-type revenues; they are generally reported in governmental funds and internal service funds. Business-type activities are financed in whole or in part by fees charged for goods or services; they are generally reported in enterprise funds.

(b) STATEMENT OF NET ASSETS. The statement of net assets should report all financial and capital resources and all liabilities, preferably in a format that displays *assets less liabilities equal net assets*, though the format *assets equal liabilities plus net assets* may be used. The difference between assets and liabilities should be reported as *net assets*, not *fund balance* or *equity*.

Governments are encouraged to report assets and liabilities in order of their relative liquidity (and subtotals of current assets and current liabilities may be provided). The liquidity of an asset depends on how readily it is expected to be converted to cash and whether restrictions limit the government's ability to use it. The liquidity of a liability depends on its maturity or on when cash is expected to be required to liquidate it. The liquidity of assets and liabilities may be determined by class, though individual assets or liabilities may be significantly more or less liquid than others in the same class and some may have both current and long-term elements. Liabilities whose average maturities are more than one year should be reported by the amount due within one year and the amount due in more than one year.

Three components of net assets should be reported—*invested in capital assets, net of related debt; restricted*, distinguishing between major categories of restrictions; and *unrestricted*.

(i) Invested in Capital Assets, Net of Related Debt. The amount of this component equals the amount of capital assets, including restricted capital assets, net of accumulated depreciation and less the outstanding balances of bonds, mortgages, notes, or other borrowings attributable to acquiring, constructing, or improving the assets. The portion of debt attributable to significant unspent debt proceeds should be included in the same net assets component as the unspent proceeds, for example, *restricted for capital projects.*

(ii) Restricted Net Assets. Net assets should be reported as restricted if constraints on their use are either:

1. Imposed externally, by creditors, grantors, contributors, or laws or regulations of other governments

2. Imposed by law by constitutional provisions or enabling legislation that both authorizes the government to assess, levy, charge, or otherwise mandate receipt of resources from external providers and includes a legally enforceable requirement to use the resources for only the purposes stated in the legislation

Permanent endowments or permanent fund principal amounts included in restricted net assets should be presented in two components—expendable and nonexpendable. Nonexpendable net assets are those required to be retained in perpetuity.

(iii) Unrestricted Net Assets. Unrestricted net assets are other than net assets invested in capital assets, net of related debt, and other than restricted net assets.

Net assets are often *designated* by the management of the government if they do not consider them available for general operations. Such constraints are internal and can be removed or modified by the management. They are not restricted net assets.

(c) STATEMENT OF ACTIVITIES. Some governments have a single function, program, activity, or component unit (together discussed as functions), as discussed below. Most have more than one function. A government with more than one function should present a statement of activities that reports expenses by each function and revenues specifically pertaining to each function, arriving at net expense or net revenue by function. Net expense or net revenue is sometimes referred to as the *net cost* of a function or program and represents the total expenses of the function or program less its program revenues, that is, charges or fees and fines that derive directly from the function or program and grants and contributions that are restricted to the function or program. That presentation indicates the financial burden (or benefit) each function has on the government's taxpayers and the extent to which each draws on the general revenues of the government or is self-financing. General revenues should be reported after expenses and revenues of the functions, together with contributions to term and permanent endowments, contributions to permanent fund principal, special and extraordinary items, and transfers reported separately, leading to change in net assets for the period.

At a minimum, the statement of activities should present:

- Activities accounted for in governmental funds by function, as discussed in NCGA Statement No. 1, paragraph 112, to coincide with level of detail required in the governmental fund statement of revenues, expenditures, and changes in fund balances.
- Activities accounted for in enterprise funds by different identifiable activities. An activity is identifiable if it has a specific revenue stream and related expenses and gains and losses that are accounted for separately.

(i) Expenses.   All expenses should be reported by function other than special or extraordinary items, defined below. At a minimum, direct expenses, those clearly identifiable with a particular function, should be presented. In addition, some or all indirect expenses of the functions may be reported by function, in columns separate from the direct expenses. A column reporting the total of direct and indirect expenses by function may also be presented. Governments that charge functions for centralized expenses need not identify and eliminate such charges. The fact that they are included in direct expenses should be disclosed in the summary of significant accounting policies.

Depreciation expense on capital assets specifically identifiable with functions should be included in their direct expenses. Depreciation expense on shared capital assets should be assigned ratably to the direct expense of the functions benefiting. Depreciation expense on capital assets that serve all functions, such as city hall, need not be included in the direct expense of the functions but may be reported as a separate line in the statement of activities or as part of the general government function. A government that reports unallocated depreciation on a separate line should state on the face of the statement of activities that this item does not include direct depreciation expenses of the various functions.

Depreciation expense for general infrastructure assets should be reported as a direct expense of the function that the government normally associates with capital outlays for and maintenance of infrastructure assets or on a separate line in the statement of activities.

Interest on long-term liabilities should generally be reported as an indirect expense on a separate line in the statement of activities, clearly indicating that it excludes direct interest expenses, if any, reported in other functions. The amount excluded should be disclosed on the face of the statement or in the notes. However, interest should be included in direct expense on borrowings essential to the creation or continuing existence of a program, such as a new, highly leveraged program in its early stages, if excluding it would be misleading.

(ii) Revenues.   A government obtains revenue essentially from four sources:

1. Entities that buy, use, or directly benefit from the goods or services of programs, including the citizens of the government or others
2. Entities outside the citizens of the government, including other governments, nongovernmental entities, or persons
3. The government's taxpayers, regardless of whether they benefit from particular programs
4. The government itself, for example, from investing

Type 1 is always a program revenue. Type 2 is a program revenue if restricted to specific programs. If unrestricted, type 2 is a general revenue. Type 3 is always a general revenue, even if restricted to specific programs. Type 4 is usually a general revenue.

Program revenues reduce the net cost of program function required to be financed by general revenue. They should be reported separately in three categories:[3] (1) charges for services, (2) program-specific operating grants and contributions, and (3) program-specific capital grants and contributions. For identifying the function to which a program revenue pertains, the determining factor for charges for services is which function generates[4] the revenue. For grants and contributions, the determining factor is the function to which the revenues are restricted.

---

[3] More than one column may be used to display components of a program revenue category. Governments may also provide more-descriptive category headings to better explain the range of program revenues reported therein, for example, *operating grants, contributions, and restricted interest.*

[4] It may sometimes be difficult or impractical to identify a specific function that generates a program revenue. For example, in many jurisdictions fines could be attributed to a public safety or a judicial function. If the source of a program revenue is not clear, the government should adopt a classification policy for assigning those revenues and apply it consistently.

Charges for services is used for a broad category of program revenues from charges to customers, applicants, or others who buy, use, or benefit from the goods, services, or privileges provided or are otherwise directly affected by the services. Such revenues include fees for specific services, such as water use or garbage collection; licenses and permits, such as dog licenses, liquor licenses, and building permits; operating special assessments, such as for street cleaning or special street lighting; and any other charges to service recipients. Fines and forfeitures are also included because they result from direct charges to those who are otherwise directly affected by a program or service, though they receive no benefit. Payments from other governments for goods or services, such as reimbursements by County A to County B for boarding County A's prisoners, are also included.

Program-specific operating and capital grants and contributions consist of revenue from both mandatory and voluntary nonexchange transactions with other governments, organizations, or persons that are restricted for use in particular programs. Grants and contributions of capital assets or resources restricted for capital purposes of specific programs should be reported separately from grants and contributions that may be used for either operating expenses or for capital expenditures at the discretion of the government. Multipurpose grants should be reported as program revenue if the amounts restricted to each program are specified in either the grant award or the grant application on which the grant award was based. Other multipurpose grants should be reported as general revenues.

Earnings of endowments or permanent fund investments should be reported as program revenues if they are restricted to programs specifically identified in the endowments or permanent fund agreements or contracts. Earnings on other investments may also be legally restricted to specific functions or programs, such as earnings on state grants required to be used to support specific programs. Earnings on invested accumulated resources of programs legally restricted for use for the programs should be reported as program revenues.

All other revenues are general revenues, including all taxes and all nontax revenues that do not meet the criteria to be reported as program revenues. General revenues should be reported after total net expense of the government's functions.

The following should be reported separately at the bottom of the statement of activities in the same manner as general revenues, to arrive at the all-inclusive change in net assets for the reporting period:

- Contributions to term and permanent endowments
- Contributions to permanent fund principal
- Special and extraordinary items (see below)
- Transfers between governmental and business-type activities

Other financing sources and uses include face amount of long-term debt, issuance premium or discount, certain payments to escrow agents for bond refundings, transfers, and sales of capital assets (unless the sale meets the criteria for reporting as a special item.

(iii) Special and Extraordinary Items. Special items, significant events within the control of management that are either unusual or infrequent as defined in APB Opinion No. 30, should be reported separately at the bottom of the statement of activities. Extraordinary items, significant events that are both unusual and infrequent, should also be reported separately at the bottom of the statement of activities.

(d) ELIMINATIONS AND RECLASSIFICATIONS. Some amounts reported as interfund activity and balances in the funds should be eliminated or reclassified in aggregating information for the statement of net assets and the statement of activities.

Amounts reported in the funds as interfund receivables and payables should be eliminated in the governmental and business-type activities columns of the PG in the statement of net assets, except for the net residual amount due between the governmental and business-type activities, which should be reported as internal balances. (Amounts reported in the funds as receivable from or payable to fiduciary funds should be reported in the statement of net assets as receivable from and payable to external parties.) Internal balances should be eliminated in the total PG column.

The doubling-up effect of internal service fund activity should be eliminated in the statement of activities. Also, the effects of similar internal events, such as allocations of accounting staff salaries, that are, in effect, allocations of overhead expenses from one function to another or within a single function should be eliminated so that the allocated expenses are reported by only the function to which they were allocated. (The effect of interfund services provided and used between functions should not be eliminated.)

Resource flows between the PG and blended component units (see GASB Statement No. 14, paragraphs 52–54) should be reclassified in accordance with Section 34.4(n) as interfund activity. Resource flows, other than those that affect only the balance sheet, such as loans and repayments, between a PG and its discretely presented component units, should be reported as if they were external transactions, as revenues and expenses. However, amounts receivable and payable between the PG and its discretely presented component units or between those components units should be reported on a separate line.

(e) REPORTING INTERNAL SERVICE FUND BALANCES.   Internal service funds are reported as proprietary funds. Nevertheless, their activities, financing goods and services for other funds, are usually more governmental than business type. Therefore, internal service fund asset and liability balances not eliminated should normally be reported in the governmental activities column of the statement of net assets. However, if enterprise funds are the predominant or only participants in an internal service fund, that fund's residual assets and liabilities should be reported in the business-type activities column.

(f) STATEMENT OF NET ASSETS FORMAT.   The illustrative statement of net assets in Exhibit 34.6 is reprinted by permission from GASB Statement No. 34.

(g) STATEMENT OF ACTIVITIES FORMAT.   The illustrative statement of activities in Exhibit 34.7 is reprinted by permission from GASB Statement No. 34.

34.7 DISCLOSURE REQUIREMENTS

Information essential to fair presentation in the financial statements that cannot be displayed on the faces of the statements should be presented in the notes to the financial statements, which should focus on the PG—its governmental activities, business-type activities, major funds, and nonmajor funds in the aggregate. Information about the government's discretely presented component units should be presented as discussed in GASB Statement No. 14, paragraph 63.

(a) GENERAL DISCLOSURE REQUIREMENTS.   Under GASB Statement No. 34 governments should provide these added disclosures to the extent applicable in their summaries of significant accounting policies, based on the requirements of the Statement:

- A description of the government-wide financial statements, indicating that fiduciary funds and component units that are fiduciary in nature are not included.
- The measurement focus and basis of accounting used in the government-wide statements.
- The policy for eliminating internal activity in the statement of activities.
- The policy for applying FASB pronouncements issued after November 30, 1989, to business-type activities and to enterprise funds of the PG.
- The policy for capitalizing assets and for estimating their useful lives. A government that uses the modified approach for reporting eligible infrastructure assets should describe the approach.

Sample City
Statement of Net Assets
December 31, 2002

Alternatively, the internal balances could be reported on separate lines as assets and liabilities. A notation would need to be added to inform the reader that the "Total" column is adjusted for those amounts (see I-1)

| | Primary Government | | | |
	Governmental Activities	Business-type Activities	Total	Component Units
ASSETS				
Current assets:				
Cash and cash equivalents	$ 13,597,899	$ 8,785,821	$ 22,383,720	$ 303,935
Investments	27,365,221	—	27,365,221	7,428,952
Receivables (net)	12,833,132	3,609,615	16,442,747	4,042,290
Internal balances	175,000	(176,000)	—	—
Inventories	322,149	126,674	448,823	83,697
Total current assets	54,293,401	12,347,110	66,640,511	11,858,874
Noncurrent assets:				
Restricted cash and cash equivalents	—	1,493,322	1,493,322	—
Capital assets (Note 1):				
Land and infrastructure (see G-5)	118,620,361	34,788,333	153,408,694	751,239
Depreciable buildings, property, and equipment, net	51,402,399	116,600,418	168,002,817	36,993,547
Total noncurrent assets	170,022,760	152,882,073	322,904,833	37,744,786
Total assets	$224,316,161	$165,229,183	$389,545,344	$49,603,660
LIABILITIES				
Current liabilities:				
Accounts payable	$ 6,783,310	$ 751,430	$ 7,534,740	$ 1,803,332
Deferred revenue	1,435,599	—	1,435,599	38,911
Current portion of long-term obligations (Note 2)	9,236,000	4,426,286	13,662,286	1,426,693
Total current liabilities	17,454,909	5,177,716	22,632,625	3,268,882
Noncurrent liabilities:				
Noncurrent portion of long-term obligations (Note 2)	83,302,378	74,482,273	157,784,651	27,106,151
Total liabilities	100,757,287	79,659,989	180,417,276	30,375,033
NET ASSETS				
Invested in capital assets, net of related debt	103,711,386	73,088,574	176,799,960	15,906,392
Restricted for:				
Capital projects	11,705,864	—	11,705,864	492,445
Debt service	3,020,708	1,451,996	4,472,704	—
Community development projects	4,811,043	—	4,811,043	—
Other purposes	3,214,302	—	3,214,302	—
Unrestricted (deficit)	(2,904,429)	11,028,624	8,124,195	2,829,790
Total net assets	123,558,874	85,569,194	209,128,068	19,228,627
Total liabilities and net assets	$224,316,161	$165,229,183	$389,545,344	$49,603,660

Net assets restricted for capital projects includes approximately $13 million of capital debt for which the proceeds have not yet been used to construct capital assets (see paragraph 33).

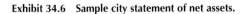

Exhibit 34.6   Sample city statement of net assets.

- A description of the kinds of transactions included in program revenues.
- A description of the policy for allocating indirect expenses to functions in the statement of activities.
- The government's policy for defining operating and nonoperating revenues of proprietary funds.

Sample City
Statement of Activites
For the Year Ended December 31, 2002

The detail presented for governmental activities represents the minimum requirement. Governments are encouraged to provide more details—for example, police, fire, EMS, and inspections—rather than simply "public safety".

Functions/ Programs	Expenses	Charges for Services	Program Revenues Operating Grants and Contributions	Capital Grants and Contributions
Primary government:				
Governmental activities:				
General government	$ 9,571,410	$ 3,148,915	$ 843,617	$ —
Public safety	34,844,749	1,198,855	1,307,693	62,300
Public works	10,128,538	850,000	—	2,252,615
Engineering services	1,299,645	704,793	—	—
Health and sanitation	6,738,672	5,612,267	575,000	—
Cemetery	735,866	212,496	—	—
Culture and recreation	11,532,350	3,995,199	2,450,000	—
Community development	2,994,389	—	—	2,580,000
Education (payment to school district)	21,893,273	—	—	—
Interest on long-term debt	6,068,121	—	—	—
Total governmental activities	105,807,013	15,720,525	5,176,310	4,894,915
Business-type activities:				
Water	3,595,733	4,159,350	—	1,159,909
Sewer	4,912,853	7,170,533	—	486,010
Parking facilities	2,796,283	1,344,087	—	—
Total business-type activities	11,304,869	12,673,970	—	1,645,919
Total primary government	$117,111,882	$28,394,495	$ 5,176,310	$ 6,540,834
Component units:				
Landfill	$ 3,382,157	$ 3,857,858	$ —	$ 11,397
Public school system	31,186,498	705,765	3,937,083	—
Total component units	$ 34,568,655	$ 4,563,623	$ 3,937,083	$ 11,397

General revenues:
  Taxes:
    Property taxes, levied for general purposes
    Property taxes, levied for debt service
    Franchise taxes
    Public service taxes
  Payment from Sample City
  Grants and contributions not restricted to specific programs
  Investments earnings
  Miscellaneous
Special item—Gain on sale of park land
Transfers
    Total general revenues, special items and transfers
      Change in net assets
  Net assets—beginning
  Net assets—ending

(*Continues*)

Exhibit 34.7   Sample city statement of activities.

	Net (Expense) Revenue and Changes in Net Assets			
	Primary Government			
Governmental Activities	**Business-type Activities**	**Total**	**Component Units**
$ (5,580,878)	$ —	$ (5,580,878)	$ —
(32,275,901)	—	(32,275,901)	—
(7,025,923)	—	(7,025,923)	—
(594,852)	—	(594,852)	—
(551,405)	—	(551,405)	—
(523,370)	—	(523,370)	—
(5,087,151)	—	(5,087,151)	—
(414,389)	—	(414,389)	—
(21,893,273)	—	(21,893,273)	—
(6,068,121)	—	(6,068,121)	—
(80,015,263)	—	(80,015,263)	—
—	1,723,526	1,723,526	—
—	2,743,690	2,743,690	—
—	(1,452,196)	(1,452,196)	—
—	3,015,020	3,015,020	—
(80,015,263)	3,015,020	(77,000,243)	—
—	—	—	487,098
—	—	—	(26,543,650)
—	—	—	(26,056,552)
51,693,573	—	51,693,573	—
4,726,244	—	4,726,244	—
4,055,505	—	4,055,505	—
8,969,887	—	8,969,887	—
—	—	—	21,893,273
1,457,820	—	1,457,820	6,461,708
1,958,144	601,349	2,559,493	881,763
884,907	104,925	989,832	22,464
2,653,488	—	2,653,488	—
501,409	(501,409)	—	—
76,900,977	204,865	77,105,842	29,259,208
(3,114,286)	3,219,885	105,599	3,202,656
126,673,160	82,349,309	209,022,469	16,025,971
$123,558,874	$85,569,194	$209,128,068	$19,228,627

Exhibit 34.7   *Continued.*

- The government's policy on whether to first use restricted or unrestricted resources when an expense is incurred for purposes for which both restricted and unrestricted net assets are available.

(b) REQUIRED NOTE DISCLOSURES ABOUT CAPITAL ASSETS AND LONG-TERM LIABILITIES. Details should be disclosed in the notes about capital assets and long-term liabilities of the PG, divided into their major classes and between those associated with governmental activities and those associated with business-type activities. Capital assets not being depreciated should be disclosed separately. The following information should be disclosed about major classes of capital assets:

- Beginning- and end-of-year balances, with accumulated depreciation presented separately from acquisition cost
- Capital acquisitions
- Sales or other dispositions
- Current depreciation expense, including the amounts charged to each of the functions in the statement of activities

Collections of works of art, historical treasures, and similar assets not capitalized should be described and the reasons they are not capitalized should be given. Disclosures as above should be given for collections capitalized.

The following information should be disclosed about long-term debt and other long-term liabilities, such as compensated absences, claims, and judgments:

- Beginning- and end-of-year balances
- Increases and decreases, presented separately
- The portions of each due within one year
- The governmental funds that typically have been used to liquidate other long-term liabilities

Whether to make similar disclosures about capital assets and long-term liabilities of discretely presented component units is a matter of professional judgment, depending on each individual component unit's significance to the total of all discretely presented component units and the component unit's relationship with the PG.

(c) DISCLOSURES ABOUT DONOR-RESTRICTED ENDOWMENTS. The following information should be disclosed about donor-restricted endowments:

- Net appreciation on investments of donor-restricted endowments available for authorization for expenditure by the governing board and how it is reported in net assets
- State law about the ability to spend net appreciation
- The policy for authorizing and spending investment income, such as a spending-rate or total-return policy

(d) SEGMENT INFORMATION. Segment information should be disclosed by governments that report enterprise funds or that use enterprise fund accounting and reporting standards. For purposes of this disclosure, a segment is an identifiable activity (or grouping of activities) reported as or within an enterprise fund or another stand-alone entity for which one or more bonds or other debt instruments (such as certificates of participation) outstanding, with a revenue stream pledged in support of that debt. (Such disclosure is not required for activities whose only outstanding debt is conduit debt for which the government has no obligation beyond the resources provided by related leases or loans, and for individual funds reported as major funds.) In addition, the activity's revenues, expenses, gains and losses, assets, and liabilities are required to be accounted for separately. (The requirement for separate accounting should be imposed by an external party; e.g., accounting and reporting requirements commonly are set forth in bond indentures.) Disclosure requirements for each segment should be met by identifying the types of goods and services provided and by presenting condensed financial information in the notes, including the elements in the three subbullets under the second bullet below:

- The kind of goods or services provided by the segment
- A condensed statement of net assets:
  - Total assets, distinguishing between current assets, capital assets, and other assets, with amounts receivable from other funds or components reported separately
  - Total liabilities, distinguishing between current and long-term amounts, with amounts payable to other funds or components reported separately
  - Total net assets, distinguishing between restricted net assets—with expendable and non-expendable components reported separately, unrestricted net assets, and amounts invested in capital assets, net of related debt
- A condensed statement of revenues, expenses, and changes in net assets:
  - Operating revenues, by major source
  - Operating expenses, with depreciation and amortization identified separately
  - Operating income or loss
  - Nonoperating revenues and expenses, separately reporting major revenues and expenses
  - Capital contributions and additions to permanent and term endowments
  - Special and extraordinary items
  - Transfers
  - Change in net assets
  - Beginning net assets
  - Ending net assets
- A condensed statement of cash flows:
  - *Net cash provided* by:
    - Operating activities
    - Noncapital financing activities
    - Capital and related financing activities
    - Investing activities
    - Beginning cash and cash equivalent balances
    - Ending cash and cash equivalent balances

Whether to provide segment information about component units that use enterprise fund accounting and reporting standards is a matter of professional judgment, depending on each individual component unit's significance to the total of all discretely presented component units and the component unit's relationship with the PG.

Governments are encouraged to present a statement of activities disaggregated for their multiple-function enterprise funds beyond that required for segment reporting. Special-purpose governments in only business-type activities are encouraged to do the same.

34.8 REPORTING COMPONENT UNITS

Under GASB Statement No. 34, discrete presentation of component unit financial information should be given in the statement of net assets and the statement of activities. However, information on component units that are fiduciary in nature should be included only in the fund financial statements, together with the PG's fiduciary funds. Information required by paragraph 51 of GASB Statement No. 14 about each major component unit can be given by:

- Presenting each major component unit other than those that are fiduciary in nature in separate columns in the statements of net assets and activities,
- Including combining statements of major component units (with nonmajor component units aggregated in a single column) with the reporting entity's basic statements after the fund financial statements, or
- Presenting condensed financial statements in the notes.

The "aggregated total" component unit information, as discussed in paragraph 14 of GASB Statement No. 14, should be the entity totals derived from the component units' statements of net assets and activities. (Because component units that are engaged in only business-type activities are not required to prepare a statement of activities, this disclosure should be taken from the information provided in the component unit's statement of revenues, expenses, and changes in fund net assets.)

If component unit information is presented in the notes, the following should be included:

- Condensed statement of net assets:
  - Total assets, distinguishing between capital assets and other assets. Amounts receivable from the PG or from other component units should be reported separately.
  - Total liabilities, distinguishing between long-term debt and other liabilities. Amounts payable to the PG or to other component units should be reported separately.
  - Total net assets, distinguishing between restricted, unrestricted, and amounts invested in capital assets net of related debt
- Condensed statement of activities:
  - Expenses by major functions and for depreciation expense if separately reported
  - Program revenues by type
  - Net program expense or revenue
  - Tax revenues
  - Other nontax general revenues
  - Contributions to endowments and permanent fund principal
  - Special and extraordinary items
  - Change in net assets
  - Beginning net assets
  - Ending net assets

The nature and amount of significant transactions with the PG and other component units should be reported in the notes for each component unit.

34.9 REQUIRED SUPPLEMENTARY INFORMATION OTHER THAN MANAGEMENT'S DISCUSSION AND ANALYSIS

In addition to the information required to be presented as Required Supplementary Information (RSI) by GASB Statement Nos. 10, 25, and 27, other RSI required to be presented by GASB Statement No. 34 includes MD&A, budgetary comparison schedules for governmental funds, and information about infrastructure assets reported using the modified approach.

(a) BUDGETARY COMPARISON INFORMATION.   Under GASB Statement No. 34, budgetary comparison schedules should present: (1) the original appropriated budgets; (2) the final appropriated budgets; and (3) actual inflows, outflows, and balances, stated on the governmental budgetary basis as discussed in NCGA Statement No. 1, paragraph 154.

Information in a separate schedule or in notes to RSI should be provided that reconciles budgetary information to GAAP information. Notes to RSI should disclose excesses of expenditures over appropriations in individual funds presented in the budgetary comparison, as discussed in NCGA Interpretation No. 6, paragraph 4, as amended by GASB Statement No. 37. (If the budgetary comparison information is included in the basic statements, these disclosures should be in the notes to the financial statements rather than as notes to RSI.)

(b) MODIFIED APPROACH FOR REPORTING INFRASTRUCTURE.   A government with eligible infrastructure assets (for subsystems, if any) reported using the modified approach should present as RSI these schedules derived from the asset management systems:

- The assessed condition, based on assessments performed at least every three years, for at least the three most recent complete condition assessments, indicating the dates of the assessments
- The estimated annual amount calculated at the beginning of the year to maintain and preserve the assets at or above the condition level established and disclosed by the government compared with the amounts actually reported as expense for each of the past five reporting periods

The following should be disclosed with the schedules:

- The basis for the condition measurement and the measurement scale used to assess and report condition. For example, a basis could be distresses in pavement surfaces. A scale could range from zero for a failed pavement to 100 for pavement in perfect condition.
- The condition level at which the government intends to preserve its eligible infrastructure assets reported using the modified approach.
- Factors that significantly affect trends in the information reported in the schedules, including any changes in the basis for the condition measurement, the measurement scale, or the condition measurement methods used. Also to be disclosed is an estimate of the effect of a change in the condition level at which the government intends to preserve eligible infrastructure assets of the estimated annual amount to maintain and preserve the assets for the current period.

A government that has asset management systems for infrastructure assets that gather the information required under this subsection but do not use the modified approach are encouraged to disclose it as supplement information.

34.10 BASIC FINANCIAL STATEMENTS REQUIRED FOR SPECIAL-PURPOSE GOVERNMENTS

Special-purpose governments are legally separate entities that are component units or other stand-alone governments, which are legally separate government organizations that (1) do not have separately elected governing bodies and (2) are not component units, plus joint ventures, jointly governed organizations, and pools.

A special-purpose government that is engaged in more than one governmental program or that has both governmental and business-type activities should meet the reporting requirements for governments that are not special-purpose governments. A special-purpose government is engaged in more than one governmental program if it budgets, manages, or accounts for its activities as multiple programs, such as a school district that provides regular instruction, special instruction, vocational education, and adult education.

(a) REPORTING BY SPECIAL-PURPOSE GOVERNMENTS ENGAGED IN GOVERNMENTAL ACTIVITIES. A special-purpose government engaged in a single governmental activity, such as some cemetery districts, levee districts, assessment districts, and drainage districts, may combine its government-wide financial statements and its fund financial statements in a columnar format that reconciles line items of fund financial information to government-wide information in a separate column on the face of the financial statements rather than at the bottom of the statements or in an accompanying schedule. Otherwise, the special-purpose government may present separate government-wide and fund financial statements and may present its government-wide statement of activities in a different format. For example, it may be presented in a single column that reports expenses first followed by revenues by major sources. The difference, net revenue or expense, should be followed by contributions to permanent and term endowments, special and extraordinary items, transfers, and beginning and ending net assets.

(b) REPORTING BY SPECIAL-PURPOSE GOVERNMENTS ENGAGED ONLY IN BUSINESS-TYPE ACTIVITIES. A government engaged in only business-type activities should present only the financial statement required for enterprise funds:

- MD&A
- Enterprise fund financial statements:
  ○ Statement of net assets or balance sheet
  ○ Statement of revenues, expenses, and changes in fund net assets
  ○ Statement of cash flows
- Notes to financial statements
- Applicable RSI other than MD&A

(c) REPORTING BY SPECIAL-PURPOSE GOVERNMENTS ENGAGED ONLY IN FIDUCIARY ACTIVITIES. A special-purpose government engaged in only fiduciary activities should present only the financial statement required for fiduciary funds:

- MD&A
- Statement of fiduciary net assets
- Statement of changes in fiduciary net assets
- Notes to financial statements

A Public Employees Retirement System (PERS) is a special-purpose government that administers one or more defined benefit pension plans and may also administer other kinds of employee benefit plans, such as defined contribution, deferred compensation, and postemployment health care plans. One that administers more than one defined benefit pension plan or postemployment health care plan should present combining financial statements for all such plans and, if applicable, required schedules for each plan. (A PERS that administers one or more agent multiple-employer plans applies these requirement at the aggregate plan level.) It should (1) present a separate column for each plan on the statement of fiduciary net assets and the statement of changes in fiduciary net assets or (2) present combining statements for the plans as part of the basic financial statements.

34.11 IMPLEMENTING THE REQUIREMENTS OF GOVERNMENTAL ACCOUNTING STANDARDS BOARD STATEMENT NO. 34

(a) REPORTING GENERAL INFRASTRUCTURE ASSETS AT TRANSITION. Beginning with the effective dates of GASB Statement No. 34, prospective reporting of general infrastructure assets is required in the statement of net assets. Retroactive reporting is encouraged for all major general infrastructure assets at that date. Such major assets are those that (1) meet the definition of a major asset (2) are associated with and generally arise from governmental activities (not from proprietary funds and special-purpose governments engaged in business-type activities), and (3) are long-lived capital assets that normally are stationary in nature and normally can be preserved for a significantly greater number of years than most capital assets. Retroactive reporting of such assets is required for governments described in footnote 37 as follows:

- Phase 1 governments—fiscal years beginning after June 15, 2005.
- Phase 2 governments—fiscal years beginning after June 15, 2006.
- Phase 3 governments are encouraged but not required to report them retroactively.

If it is not practical to determine the acquisition cost of general infrastructure assets because of inadequate records, a government should estimate and report the acquisition cost of major general infrastructure assets acquired or significantly reconstructed or that received significant improvements in fiscal years ending after June 30, 1980.

Information for networks for which it is available should be reported during the transition period if it is not available for all networks.

During transition, these disclosures should be made:

- Descriptions of the infrastructure assets being reported and of those not being reported
- A description of eligible infrastructure assets the government intends to report using the modified approach

(b) TRANSITION TO THE MODIFIED APPROACH FOR REPORTING INFRASTRUCTURE ASSETS. A government may begin to use the modified approach for reporting eligible infrastructure assets when one complete condition assessment is available and the government documents that the assets are being preserved approximately at or above the condition level the government has established and disclosed. If the three most recent complete condition assessments and the estimated and actual amounts to maintain and preserve the infrastructure assets for the previous five reporting periods required are not initially available, the information required by that section should be reported for as many complete condition assessments and years of estimated and actual expenses as are available.

(c) INITIAL CAPITALIZATION OF GENERAL INFRASTRUCTURE.

(i) Determining Major General Infrastructure Assets. Major general infrastructure assets should be determined at the network or subsystem level based on two criteria:

1. The actual or estimated cost of the subsystem is expected to be at least five percent of the total actual or estimated cost of all general capital assets reported in the first fiscal year ending after June 15, 1999.
2. The actual or estimated cost of the network is expected to be at least 10 percent of the total actual or estimated cost of all general capital assets reported in the first fiscal year ending after June 15, 1999.

(ii) Establishing Capitalization at Transition. If inadequate records make determining acquisition cost at initial capitalization impractical, acquisition cost may be estimated.

(iii) Estimating Acquisition Cost—Current Replacement Cost. If the acquisition costs of assets need to be estimated, their current replacement cost may be determined and reduced back to the acquisition year or estimated acquisition year using public-sector or private-sector price indexes. Accumulated depreciation on assets being depreciated would be determined based on the reduced amounts.

(iv) Estimated Acquisition Cost from Existing Information.   Bond documents used to obtain financing for construction or acquisition of infrastructure assets, expenditures reported in capital project funds or capital outlays in governmental funds, and engineering documents are examples of other information that may provide sufficient support for establishing initial capitalization.

34.12 GRANT ACCOUNTING

(a) DEFINITIONS.   A grant is a contribution or gift of cash, or other assets from another government to be used or expended for a specified purpose, activity, or facility. Some grants are restricted by the grantor for the acquisition or construction of fixed assets. These are capital grants. All other grants are operating grants.

An entitlement is the amount of payment to which a government is entitled pursuant to an allocation formula contained in applicable statutes. A shared revenue is a revenue levied by one government but shared on a predetermined basis with another government. Grants, entitlements, and shared revenues have become major sources of revenues for governments. Frequently, however, special accounting and reporting requirements are associated with these grants.

(b) FUND IDENTIFICATION.   All grants, entitlements, and shared revenues should be accounted for in one of the seven fund types. The identity of the fund should be based on the purpose or requirements of the grant. For instance, grants, entitlements, or shared revenues received for purposes normally financed through the general fund may be accounted for within that fund, provided that applicable legal requirements can be appropriately satisfied. Resources received for the payment of principal or interest on general long-term debt may be accounted for in a debt service fund. Capital grants or shared revenues received for capital acquisitions or construction, other than those associated with enterprise and internal service funds, may be accounted for in a capital projects fund. However, it is not always necessary to establish a separate fund for an individual grant, entitlement, or shared revenue. Existing funds should be used to the extent possible in order to comply with the minimal number of funds principle.

If a grant, entitlement, or shared, revenue may be used for more than one purpose and the recipient has not determined the purposes for which it intends to use the funds, the resources may be accounted for in an agency fund pending determination of their use. When the determination is made, the assets and revenues should be recognized in the appropriate fund and removed from the agency fund. Since most grants, entitlements, or shared revenues are either unrestricted as to purpose or restricted to a specific purpose, there is seldom a need to use an agency fund.

(c) REVENUE AND EXPENDITURE (EXPENSE) RECOGNITION.   Grants, entitlements, and shared revenues recorded in governmental funds should be recognized as revenue when they become susceptible to accrual, that is, measurable and available. Legal and contractual requirements should be carefully reviewed. If the restriction is more form than substance, revenue should be recognized at the time of receipt or earlier. If the grant is earned by the recipient government as funds are expended for a specific restricted purpose, revenue should be recognized when the expenditures are made for that purpose. The latter are called *expenditure-driven* grants.

Grants, entitlements, and shared revenues received before the revenue recognition criteria are met should be reported as deferred revenue and reported as a liability account in the government's financial statements. Resources not received should be reported as a receivable if the revenue recognition criteria have been met. If the resources have not been received and the revenue recognition criteria have not been met, the grants should not be reported on the balance sheet at all. They may, however, be disclosed in the notes to the financial statements.

Grants, entitlements, and shared revenues that are received by a proprietary fund for operating purposes, or that may be used for operations or capital purposes at the discretion of the recipient government, should be recognized as nonoperating revenue when earned. Resources restricted to the acquisition or construction of capital assets should be recorded as contributed capital.

Operating expenses should include depreciation on all depreciable fixed assets, including assets acquired with contributed capital. Depreciation recognized on assets acquired or constructed with contributed capital may be charged to the contributed capital account by "adding back" the depreciation on such assets to net income before closing it to retained earnings.

To promote greater consistency with respect to the accounting and financial reporting for grants and similar financial assistance by state and local governments, the GASB issued Statement No. 24, "Accounting and Financial Reporting for Certain Grants and Other Financial Assistance." Statement No. 24 addresses issues relating to the recognition, measurement, and reporting of grants and other financial assistance received and given by state and local governments including:

- "Pass-through" grants
- Food stamps and similar voucher programs
- "On-behalf" payments of fringe benefits and salaries

34.13 ACCOUNTING PRINCIPLES AND PRACTICES—PUBLIC COLLEGES AND UNIVERSITIES

Public colleges and universities should apply the principles discussed in this chapter.

34.14 AUDITS OF GOVERNMENTAL UNITS

Audits of governmental units with financial statements can be performed in accordance with:

- Generally accepted auditing standards (GAAS)
- *Government Auditing Standards* (the "Yellow Book")
- The Single Audit Act Amendments of 1996 and Office of Management and Budget (OMB) Circular A-133

When performing an audit in accordance with GAAS, the guidance contained in the *AICPA Professional Standards* is followed. This is the same guidance followed by auditors when auditing the financial statement of commercial entities and typically results in the issuance of an opinion of the financial statements and perhaps a management letter. *Government Auditing Standards,* also known as the *Yellow Book* (U.S. Comptroller General, rev. 2003), establishes the concept of an expanded scope audit that includes both financial and compliance features. According to the Yellow Book, a financial audit can help determine whether:

- The financial statements of an audited entity present fairly the financial position and the results of financial operations in accordance with GAAP
- The entity has complied with laws and regulations that may have a material effect on the financial statements

The Yellow Book incorporates the AICPA Professional Standards mentioned above and sets forth additional standards and requirements, including the following six:

1. A review is to be made of compliance with applicable laws and regulations, as set forth in federal audit guides and other applicable reference sources.
2. The auditor reports on the entity's compliance with laws, regulations, contracts and shall also include material instances of noncompliance and instances or indications of illegal acts found during or in connection with the audit.
3. The auditors shall report on their consideration of the entity's internal control structure made as part of the financial audit.

They shall identify as a minimum:

a. Scope of auditor's work in obtaining an understanding of the internal control structure and assessing risk.

b. The reportable conditions including separate identification of material weaknesses identified as a result of the auditor's work.

4. Auditors performing government audits are required to obtain 80 hours of continuing education every two years, of which 24 hours should be directly related to government. At least 20 of the 80 hours should be completed in each year of the two-year period.

5. Audit organizations performing government audits are required to establish an internal quality control system and participate in an external quality control review program.

6. The auditor communicates certain information related to the conduct of the audit to the audit committee or to the individuals with whom they have contracted for the audit.

(a) THE SINGLE AUDIT ACT AMENDMENTS OF 1996.   Many state and local governments are required to obtain a periodic audit of the federal funds they receive—usually once a year. The audits are normally performed by an independent certified public accountant (CPA) or public accountant, or, in some states, by the government's internal audit personnel. A few jurisdictions have an independently elected or appointed auditor who conducts the audit. Single audits are conducted in accordance with GAAS, *Government Auditing Standards,* and the Single Audit Amendments Act of 1996 and its implementing regulation OMB Circular A-133, including its Compliance Supplement. These requirements have been updated for fiscal years beginning on or after July 1, 1997, by the Single Audit Amendments Act of 1996.

The objectives of the Act are:

- To improve the financial management of state and local governments with respect to federal financial assistance programs through improved auditing
- To establish uniform requirements for audits of federal financial assistance provided to state and local governments
- To promote the efficient and effective use of audit resources
- To ensure that federal departments and agencies, to the maximum extent practicable, rely on and use audit work performed pursuant to the requirements of the Single Audit Act

Though the single audit builds on the annual financial statement audit currently required by most state and larger local governments, it places substantial additional emphasis on the consideration and testing of internal controls and the testing of compliance with laws and regulations.

The Single Audit Act and OMB Circular A-128 require the auditor to determine whether:

- The financial statements of the government, department, agency, or establishment present fairly its financial position and the results of operations in conformity with GAAP
- The organization has internal and other control structures to provide reasonable assurance that it is managing federal financial assistance programs in compliance with applicable laws and regulations
- The organization has complied with laws and regulations that may have a material effect on its financial statements and on each major federal financial assistance program

Non-federal entities receiving $500,000 or more in a year in Federal awards are subject to a single audit unless they elect (if qualified) to have a program-specific audit conducted. If less than $500,000 is expended, the entity is exempt from Federal audit requirements for that year, but records must be retained for review or audit, by, for example the General Accountability Office (GAO).

The Single Audit Act provides auditors with guidance on the focus of the audit by defining a level of audit work based on the concept of "major" and "nonmajor" federal assistance programs.

Major programs (not grants) are typically the larger programs in which an entity participates and are determined on a sliding scale by the relationship between the expenditures of the program and the total federal expenditures of the entity. For most small and medium-sized governments, a major program is defined as the larger of $300,000 or three percent of the total federal *expenditures* for all federal programs.

For larger governments whose total federal expenditures exceed $100 million, the Single Audit Act defines a major federal financial assistance program based on a sliding scale.

The Single Audit Act and OMB Circular A-128 require the auditor to issue several reports:

For the entity:

- A report on the audit of the general purpose or basic financial statements of the entity as a whole, or the department, agency, or establishment covered by the audit
- A report on internal control based on an understanding and assessment of the internal control structure obtained as a part of the audit of the general purpose or basic financial statements
- A report on compliance with laws and regulations that may have a material effect on the financial statements

For its federal financial assistance programs:

- A report on a supplementary schedule of the entity's federal financial assistance programs, showing total expenditures for each federal assistance program
- A report on compliance with laws and regulations identifying all findings of noncompliance and questioned costs
- A report on internal control structure used in administering federal financial assistance programs

In March 1990, the OMB issued OMB Circular A-133, "Audits of Institutions of Higher Education and Other Nonprofit Organizations." The audit objectives contained in OMB Circular A-133 are patterned after the Single Audit Act of 1984 (described in the preceding section) and bring under the single audit umbrella nonprofit organizations receiving federal funds. Although the Circular was issued primarily for nonprofit organizations receiving federal funds, institutions of higher education that are operated by a state or local government may elect to conduct a single audit under the provisions of OMB Circular A-133 versus the audit requirements associated with the Single Audit Act of 1984.

In 1995, OMB began a process intended to combine the regulations governing single audits into a single document. As a part of this process, OMB proposed changes to Circular A-133. OMB indicated that these changes would serve as a model for requested changes to the Single Audit Act of 1984 and that, if those changes were made, Circular A-128 would be abolished and that state and local governments would follow Circular A-133. The major proposals in this revision include:

- Use of the concept of risk in determining which programs to audit
- Raising the threshold for an audit to $300,000
- Reduce the time period for submission of the single audit results from 13 to 9 months
- Expansion of the scope to include hospitals

(b) OTHER CONSIDERATIONS.   Most government officials and auditors of governmental units realize that a good audit should furnish more than an opinion on the financial statements. Other services a governmental auditor can provide are pinpointing the key information upon which decisions should be based and contributing to the presentation of this information in a manner that facilitates decision making; uncovering deficiencies in the accounting system and providing suggestions for improving the efficiency and effectiveness of the system; and obtaining and presenting information useful for marketing securities.

Obtaining a qualified auditor, particularly one who can provide the additional services described above, requires that the selection be based on qualifications and experience, and not solely cost.

The National Intergovernmental Audit Forum, in its handbook *How to Avoid a Substandard Audit: Suggestions for Procuring an Audit*, indicates:

> Public entities should never select auditors without considering five basic elements of an effective audit procurement process:
>
> - planning (determining what needs to be done and when),
> - fostering competition by soliciting proposals (writing a clear and direct solicitation document and disseminating it widely),
> - technically evaluating proposals and qualifications (authorizing a committee of knowledgeable persons to evaluate the ability of prospective auditors to effectively carry out the audit),
> - preparing a written agreement (documenting the expectations of both the entity and the auditor), and
> - monitoring the auditor's performance (periodically reviewing the progress of that performance).

This *handbook* provides detailed information about the five elements of procurement listed above as well as the use of audit committees in a government environment and other useful information about the auditor procurement process.

(i) Governmental Rotation of Auditors. The automatic rotation of auditors after a given number of years is a common practice in many governments; however, it is not always beneficial. Many governments have followed this policy, believing that they will (1) receive a fresh outlook from the audit, (2) spread the work among several firms, and (3) encourage lower fees. In actuality, automatic rotation may be harmful in that it could deprive the government of the extensive knowledge of the entity developed by the current auditor. It may also impair auditing effectiveness since a new auditor may need to spend considerable time learning the government's system—the government may actually incur more cost since its personnel will need to spend time explaining the organization, systems, and data to the new auditors, and the new auditors will need to spend valuable time reviewing information that is already part of the previous auditor's workpapers. Although a government should continuously monitor its auditor's performance to assure that the service obtained is commensurate with the cost, the entity should normally change auditors only because of dissatisfaction with services and not for the sake of receiving a lower fee.

(ii) Audit Committees. In recent years, governments have started establishing audit committees similar to those in the private sector. Some appropriate tasks for a local government's audit committee are:

- Reviewing significant financial information for reliability, timeliness, clarity, appropriateness of disclosure, and compliance with GAAP and legal requirements
- Ascertaining that the internal control structure is appropriately designed and functioning effectively
- Evaluating independent audit firms and selecting one for approval by the appropriate body
- Overseeing the scope and performance of the independent audit function
- Ensuring that the auditors' recommendations for improvements in internal controls and operating methods receive management's attention and are implemented on a timely basis
- Providing an effective communications link between the auditors and the full governing board

The primary benefit of an audit committee is in assisting the full governing board to fulfill its responsibilities for the presentation of financial information about the governmental unit. There are also secondary benefits: The other parties involved in the issuance of financial information—management and independent and internal auditors—can perform their roles more effectively if an audit committee is involved in the process. Finally, there are advantages for the government's constituencies—in particular, the taxpayers and bondholders.

34.15 CONCLUDING REMARKS

Governmental accounting and reporting is changing and expanding at an increasing rapid rate. Coupling this with public accountability issues, the federal government's pressure for increased audit quality, and the penalties for substandard audit performance results in increasing levels of audit risk. Government audits, often considered low-risk engagements by many, are quickly becoming areas of extremely high risk. Auditing professionals need to recognize the risk associated with government engagements now and in the future before incurring severe penalties or embarrassment. The technical issues involved in government auditing are on a par with those in the commercial environment but auditors have much less experience and less technical guidance to fall back on.

Dealing with these technical issues requires well-trained, highly motivated individuals and can no longer be left to less experienced members of the audit team. Dealing with the *real* issues governments are facing (e.g., infrastructure, terrorism, prison overcrowding, drugs, etc.) requires even more from the individuals in the profession. Like it or not, government accounting and reporting is being thrust into the spotlight and will be scrutinized by a multitude of individuals and groups. It is imperative that individuals in the industry realize this fact and begin now to prepare for the future.

34.16 SOURCES AND SUGGESTED REFERENCES

American Institute of Certified Public Accountants, "Audits of State and Local Government Units," Industry Audit and Accounting Guide. AICPA, New York, 2004.

_____ , "AICPA Professional Standards." AICPA, New York, 2006.

Financial Accounting Standards Board, "Classification of Short-Term Obligations Expected to Be Refinanced," Statement of Financial Accounting Standards No. 6. FASB, Stamford, CT, 1975.

_____ , "Accounting for Leases," Statement of Financial Accounting Standards Board No. 13. FASB, Stamford, CT, 1975.

_____ , "Objectives of Financial Reporting by Nonbusiness Organizations," Statement of Financial Accounting Concepts No. 4. FASB, Stamford, CT, 1980.

General Accounting Office, "Government Auditing Standards." GAO, Washington, DC, 2003.

Governmental Accounting Standards Board, "Basic Financial Statements—and Management's Discussion and Analysis—for State and Local Governments." GASB Statement No. 34. GASB, Norwalk, CT, 1999.

_____ , "Codification of Governmental Accounting and Financial Reporting Standards." GASB, Norwalk, CT, 2004.

Government Finance Officers Association, "Governmental Accounting, Auditing and Financial Reporting." GFOA, Chicago, IL, 1994. (Study guide available)

Ives, Martin "The Governmental Accounting Standards Board: Factors Influencing Its Operation and Initial Technical Agenda." *Government Accounting Journal*, Spring 2002, V49 (1), 22–27.

APPENDIX 34.1: PRONOUNCEMENTS ON STATE AND LOCAL GOVERNMENT ACCOUNTING

	Government Accounting Standard Board	*Effective Date*
Statement No. 1	Authoritative Status of NCGA Pronouncements and AICPA Industry Audit Guide	On issuance (7/84)
Statement No. 2	Financial Reporting of Deferred Compensation Plans Adopted under the Provisions of Internal Revenue Code Section 457	Financial statements for periods ending after 2/15/86

(Continues)

	Government Accounting Standard Board	*Effective Date*
Statement No. 3	Deposits with Financial Institutions, Investments (including Repurchase Agreements), and Reverse Repurchase Agreements	Financial statements for periods ending after 2/15/86
Statement No. 4	Applicability of FASB Statement No. 87, "Employers' Accounting for Pensions," to State and Local Governmental Employers	On issuance (9/86)
Statement No. 5	Disclosure of Pension Information by Public Employee Retirement Systems and State and Local Governmental Employers	Financial reports issued for fiscal years beginning after 12/15/86
Statement No. 6	Accounting and Financial Reporting for Special Assessments	Financial statements for periods beginning after 6/15/87
Statement No. 7	Advance Refundings Resulting in Defeasance of Debt	Fiscal periods beginning after 12/15/86
Statement No. 8	Applicability of FASB Statement No. 93, Recognition of Depreciation by Not-for-Profit Organizations, to Certain State and Local Governmental Entities	Fiscal periods beginning after 5/15/87
Statement No. 9	Reporting Cash Flows of Proprietary and Nonexpendable Trust Funds and Governmental Entries that Use Proprietary Fund Accounting	Fiscal periods beginning after 12/15/89
Statement No. 10	Accounting and Financial Reporting for Risk Financing and Related Insurance Issues	Pools-Fiscal periods beginning after 6/15/90 Other-Fiscal periods beginning after 6/15/93
Statement No. 11	Measurement Focus and Basis of Accounting—Governmental Fund Operating Statements	Fiscal periods beginning after 6/15/94
Statement No. 12	Disclosure of Information on Postemployment Benefits Other than Pension Benefits by State and Local Governmental Employers	Fiscal periods beginning after 6/15/90
Statement No. 13	Accounting for Operating Leases with Scheduled Rent Increases	Leases with terms beginning after 6/30/90
Statement No. 14	The Financial Reporting Entity	Fiscal periods beginning after 12/15/92
Statement No. 16	Accounting for Compensated Absences	Fiscal periods beginning after June 15, 1993
Statement No. 17	Measurement Focus and Basis of Accounting—Governmental Fund Operating Statements: Amendment of Effective Dates of GASB Statement No. 11 and Related Statements	Immediately
Statement No. 18	Accounting for Municipal Solid Waste Landfill Closure and Post-closure Care Costs	Fiscal periods beginning after June 15, 1993
Statement No. 19	Governmental College and University Omnibus Statement	Fiscal periods beginning after June 15, 1993
Statement No. 20	Accounting and Financial Reporting for Proprietary Funds and Other Governmental Entities That Use Proprietary Fund Accounting	Fiscal periods beginning after December 15, 1993

	Government Accounting Standard Board	*Effective Date*
Statement No. 21	Accounting for Escheat Property	Fiscal periods beginning after June 15, 1994
Statement No. 23	Accounting and Financial Reporting for Refundings of Debt Reported by Proprietary Activities	Fiscal periods beginning after June 15, 1994
Statement No. 24	Accounting and Financial Reporting for Certain Grants and Other Financial Assistance	Fiscal periods beginning after June 15, 1995
Statement No. 25	Financial Reporting for Defined Benefit Pension Plans and Note Disclosures for Defined Contribution Plans	Fiscal periods beginning after June 15, 1996, Statement No. 26 must be implemented simultaneously
Statement No. 26	Financial Reporting for Postemployment Healthcare Plans Administered by Defined Benefit Pension Plans	Fiscal periods beginning after June 15, 1996, Statement No. 25 must be implemented simultaneously
Statement No. 27	Accounting for Pensions by State and Local Governmental Employers	Fiscal periods beginning after June 15, 1997
Statement No. 28	Accounting and Financial Reporting for Securities Lending Transactions	Fiscal periods beginning after December 15, 1995
Statement No. 29	The Use of Not-for-Profit Accounting and Financial Reporting Principles by Governmental Entities	Fiscal periods beginning after December 15, 1995
Statement No. 30	Risk Financing Omnibus	Fiscal periods beginning after June 15, 1996
Statement No. 31	Accounting and Financial Reporting for Certain Investments and for External Investment Pools	Fiscal periods beginning after June 15, 1997
Statement No. 32	Accounting and Financial Reporting for Internal Revenue Code Section 457 Deferred Compensation Plans	Earlier of fiscal periods beginning after December 31, 1998, or amendment of the IRC Section 457 Plan
Statement No. 33	Accounting and Financial Reporting for Nonexchange Transactions	Periods beginning after June 15, 2000
Statement No. 34	Basic Financial Statements—and Management's Discussion and Analysis—for State and Local Governments	(6)
Statement No. 35	Basic Financial Statements—and Management's Discussion and Analysis—for Public Colleges and Universities: Amendment of GASB Statement No. 34	(7)

(Continues)

---

[6] In three phases, based on total annual revenue in the first fiscal year ending after June 15, 1999; Phase 1—governments with total annual revenues of $100 million or more, fiscal periods beginning after June 15, 2001; Phase 2—governments with total annual revenues of $10 or more but less than 100 million, fiscal periods beginning after June 15, 2002; Phase 3—governments with total annual revenues of less than $10 million, fiscal periods beginning after June 15, 2003.

[7] Public institutions that are components of another reporting entity should implement the Statement no later than the same year as their primary government. For public institutions that are not components of another reporting entity, this Statement is effective in the three phases indicated in the preceding footnote.

[8] Simultaneously with Statement No. 34. For governments that implemented Statement No. 34 before Statement No. 37 was issued, Statement No. 37 is effective for periods beginning after June 15, 2000.

	Government Accounting Standard Board	*Effective Date*
Statement No. 36	Recipient Reporting for Certain Shared Nonexchange Revenues: Amendment of GASB Statement No. 33	Simultaneously with Statement No. 33
Statement No. 37	Basic Financial Statements—and Management's Discussion and Analysis—for State and Local Governments: Omnibus	(8)
Statement No. 38	Certain Financial Statement Note Disclosures Discussion and Analysis- for State and Local Governments	(9)
Statement No. 39	Determining Whether Certain Organizations Are Component Units	Periods beginning after June 15, 2003
Statement No. 40	Deposit and Investment Risk Disclosures—An Amendment of GASB Statement No. 3	Periods beginning after June 15, 2004
Statement No. 41	Budgetary Comparison Schedules—Perspective Differences—An Amendment of GASB Statement No. 34	Simultaneously with Statement 34
Statement No. 42	Accounting and Financial Reporting for Impairment of Capital Assets and for Insurance Recoveries	Periods beginning after December 15, 2004
Statement No. 43	Financial Reporting for Postemployment Benefit Plans Other Than Pension Plans	Effective in three phases based on a government's total annual revenues in the first fiscal year ending after June 15, 1999: for periods beginning after December 15, 2005, 2006 and 2007
Statement No. 44	Economic Condition Reporting—The Statistical Section—An Amendment of NCGA Statement 1	Statistical sections prepared for periods beginning after June 15, 2005
Statement No. 45	Accounting and Financial Reporting by Employers for Postemployment Benefits Other Than Pensions	Effective in three phases based on a government's total annual revenues in the first fiscal year ending after June 15, 1999: for periods beginning after December 15, 2006, 2007 and 2008
Statement No. 46	Net Assets Restricted by Enabling Legislation—An Amendment of GASB Statement No. 34	Periods beginning after June 15, 2005.
Statement No. 47	Accounting for Termination Benefits	For termination benefits provided through an existing defined benefit OPEB plan, the provisions of this Statement should be implemented simultaneously with the requirements of Statement 45. For all other termination benefits, this Statement is effective for financial statements for periods beginning after June 15, 2005.

---

[9] In three phases, based on total annual revenue in the first fiscal year ending after June 15, 1999: Phase 1—governments with total annual revenues of $100 million or more, fiscal periods beginning after

	Government Accounting Standard Board	*Effective Date*
Interpretation No. 1	Demand Bonds Issued by State and Local Governmental Entities	Fiscal periods ending after June 15, 1985
Interpretation No. 2	Disclosure of Conduit Debt Obligations	Fiscal periods beginning after December 15, 1995
Interpretation No. 3	Financial Reporting for Reverse Repurchase Agreements	Fiscal periods beginning after December 15, 1995
Interpretation No. 4	Accounting and Financial Reporting for Capitalization Contributions to Public Entity Risk Pools	Fiscal periods beginning after June 15, 1996
Interpretation No. 5	Property Tax Revenue Recognition in Governmental Funds	Fiscal periods beginning after June 15, 2000
Interpretation No. 6	Recognition and Measurement of Certain Liabilities and Expenditures in Governmental Fund Financial Statements: an Interpretation of NCGA Statements 1, 4, and 5, NCGA Interpretation 8, and GASB Statement Nos. 10, 16, and 18	Simultaneously with Statement No. 34
Technical Bulletin No. 84–1	Purpose and Scope of GASB Technical Bulletins and Procedures for Issuance	None
Technical Bulletin No. 87–1	Applying Paragraph 66 of GASB Statement No. 3	On issuance (1/87)
Technical Bulletin No. 94–1	Disclosures about Derivatives and Similar Debt and Investment Transactions	Fiscal periods ending after December 15, 1994
Technical Bulletin No. 96–1	Application of Certain Pension Disclosure Requirements for Employers Pending Implementation of GASB Statement No. 27	Fiscal periods beginning after June 15, 1996
Technical Bulletin No. 97–1	Classification of Deposits and Investments into Custodial Credit Risk Categories for Certain Bank Holding Company Transactions	Fiscal periods beginning after December 15, 1997
Technical Bulletin No. 103–1	Disclosure Requirements for Derivatives Not Reported at Fair Value on the Statement of Net Assets	Financial statements issued after June 15, 2003
Technical Bulletin No. 104–1	Tobacco Settlement Recognition and Financial Reporting Entity Issues	June 15, 2004
Technical Bulletin No. 104–2	Recognition of Pension and Other Postemployment Benefit Expenditures/Expense and Liabilities by Cost-Sharing Employers	Pension transactions: for financial statements for periods ending after December 15, 2004. OPEB transactions: applied simultaneously with the requirements of Statement 45
Concepts Statement No. 1	Objectives of Financial Reporting	None
Concepts Statement No. 2	Reporting Service Efforts and Accomplishments	None
Concepts Statement No. 3	Communication Methods in General Purpose External Financial Reports That Contain Basic Financial Statements	None

(Continues)

June 15, 2001; Phase 2—governments with total annual revenues of $10 million or more but less than $100 million, fiscal periods beginning after June 15, 2002; Phase 3—governments with total annual revenues of less than $10 million, fiscal periods beginning after June 15, 2003.

	National Council on Government Accounting	*Effective Date*
Statement 1	Governmental Accounting and Financial Reporting Principles	Fiscal years ending after 6/30/80
Statement 2	Grant, Entitlement, and Shared Revenue Accounting by State and Local Governments	Fiscal years ending after 6/30/80
Statement 3	Defining the Governmental Reporting Entity (Superseded)	Prospectively for fiscal years ending after 12/31/82
Statement 4	Accounting and Financial Reporting Principles for Claims and Judgments and Compensated Absences	Fiscal years beginning after 12/31/82; ¶20 extended indefinitely by NCGAS 11
Statement 5	Accounting and Financial Reporting Principles for Lease Agreements of State and Local Governments	Fiscal years beginning after 6/30/83
Statement 6	Pension Accounting and Financial Reporting: Public Employee Retirement Systems and State and Local Government Employers	Extended indefinitely by NCGAI 8
Statement 7	Financial Reporting for Component Units Within the Governmental Reporting Entity	Prospectively for fiscal years ending after 6/30/84
Interpretation 1	GAAFR and the AICPA Audit Guide (Superseded)	Issued 4/86; superseded by NCGAS 1
Interpretation 3	Revenue Recognition—Property Taxes	Fiscal years beginning after 9/30/81
Interpretation 4	Accounting and Financial Reporting for Public Employee Retirement Systems and Pension Trust Funds (Superseded)	Fiscal years beginning after 6/15/82; superseded by NCGAS 6 and repealed by NCGAI 8
Interpretation 6	Notes to the Financial Statements Disclosure	Prospectively for fiscal years beginning after 12/31/82
Interpretation 7	Clarification as to the Application of the Criteria in NCGA Statement 3, "Defining the Governmental Reporting Entity"	On issuance
Interpretation 8	Certain Pension Matters	Fiscal years ending after 12/31/83
Interpretation 9	Certain Fund Classifications and Balance Sheet Accounts	Fiscal years ending after 6/30/84
Interpretation 10	State and Local Government Budgetary Reporting	Fiscal years ending after 6/30/84
Interpretation 11	Claim and Judgment Transactions for Governmental Funds	On issuance (4/84)

CHAPTER 35

NOT-FOR-PROFIT ORGANIZATIONS

Ronald F. Ries, CPA

American Express Tax and Business Services, Inc.

Ian J. Benjamin, CPA

American Express Tax and Business Services, Inc.

The authors wish to acknowledge that the exhibits and inspiration for this work were derived from the work *Financial and Accounting Guide for Not-for-Profit Organizations,* Fifth Edition, by Price Waterhouse LLP, Malvern J. Gross Jr., Richard F. Larkin, Roger S. Bruttomesso, and John J. McNally (John Wiley & Sons, Inc., 1995).

35.1 THE NOT-FOR-PROFIT ACCOUNTING ENVIRONMENT

Not-for-profit organizations range from the large and complex to the small and simple. They include hospitals, colleges and universities, voluntary social service organizations, religious organizations, associations, foundations, and cultural institutions. All are confronted with accounting and reporting challenges. All are presently covered by authoritative accounting literature. This chapter discusses not-for-profit accounting and reporting conventions and examines accounting pronouncements, auditing concerns, and the regulatory environment applicable to different types of not-for-profit organizations. Health care organizations are covered in Chapter 36.

As this latest edition of the *Handbook* goes to press, there are many issues within our community, including the accounting environment, which requires all organizations, including not-for-profits, to adhere to accounting policies and principles with the utmost due diligence required to satisfy a scrutinizing public and government regulators.

(a) CURRENT STATUS OF ACCOUNTING PRINCIPLES. Not-for-profit accounting has undergone a period of profound change. In the recent past, authoritative accounting principles and reporting practices were established for many not-for-profit organizations that previously had neither.

In 1972, the American Institute of Certified Public Accountants (AICPA) issued an Industry Audit Guide for hospitals. In 1973, an Industry Audit Guide for colleges and universities was issued. And in 1974, a third not-for-profit Industry Audit Guide, for voluntary health and welfare organizations, was issued. In 1990, the AICPA issued a new audit and accounting guide, "Audits of Providers of Health Care Service," to replace the 1972 hospital audit guide.

In late 1978, the AICPA issued statement of position (SOP 78-10), "Accounting Principles and Reporting Practices for Certain Nonprofit Organizations." SOP 78-10 defines accounting principles and reporting practices for all not-for-profit organizations not covered by earlier guides.

For several years, as the most current broad-scope pronouncement of the accounting profession on not-for-profit accounting, the SOP was the authoritative reference for not-for-profit accounting and reporting questions for the organizations covered, and it was consulted for guidance by other organizations on questions not addressed in their respective audit guides.

These guides and the SOP had a dramatic effect on not-for-profit accounting, as they represented the first authoritative attempt to codify accounting principles and reporting practices for the not-for-profit industry. However, inconsistencies existed among the four guides, and they frequently contradicted one another on key accounting concepts. Also, the accounting principles presented in the guides had limited authority as they constituted generally accepted accounting procedures (GAAP) only until formal standards were set on this subject by the Financial Accounting Standards Board (FASB).

By the early 1980s, persons interested in not-for-profit accounting issues had identified the following key areas of accounting that would have to be considered in unifying the diverse not-for-profit accounting practices:

- Reporting entity (when controlled and affiliated organizations should be included in an entity's financial statements)
- Depreciation
- Joint costs of multipurpose activities, particularly those involving a fund-raising appeal (on what basis such costs should be divided among the various purposes served)
- Revenue recognition for expendable/restricted receipts (when, in which fund, and how such items should be reported as revenue)
- Display (what format should be used to present financial data)
- Valuation of investments
- Contributions (how these should be valued, when and how they should be reported)
- Grants awarded to others (when these should be accrued and expensed by the grantor)

Before accounting principles could be written, concepts had to be developed. The FASB had originally excluded not-for-profits from concepts development, but later started a separate project for not-for-profits. The first concepts statement under this project was issued in 1980. SFACNo. 4, "Objectives of Financial Reporting by Nonbusiness Organizations," proved to be so similar to the corresponding statement for businesses (SFAC No. 1) that the FASB started thinking in terms of only one set of concepts. Indeed, SFAC No. 2 was amended to include not-for-profits; SFAC No. 6, "Elements of Financial Statements" covers both types of entities, although some parts of this statement deal separately with the two sectors.

The FASB identified five areas in which it planned to develop accounting principles for not-for-profits: depreciation, contributions, the reporting entity, financial statement display, and investments, and has issued the following standards that have revolutionized not-for-profit accounting.

- Depreciation is the subject of SFAS No. 93. Effective in 1990, this requires all not-for-profits to depreciate long-lived tangible assets, except that museum collections and similar assets often considered to be inexhaustible need not be depreciated if verifiable evidence of their inexhaustibility is available.

- Accounting for contributions received and made and for museum collections is the subject of FASB Statement No. 116, effective beginning in 1995. Upon adoption it requires a number of significant changes to accounting practices previously followed by many not-for-profit organizations. It requires immediate revenue recognition for all unconditional gifts and pledges, regardless of the presence of donor restrictions and regardless of the intended period of payment (pledges payable in future periods will be discounted to present value (PV). Donors will follow a similar policy for recording expenses and liabilities. Donated services of volunteers will be recorded by charities if certain criteria are met. Museum collection items will be capitalized unless certain criteria are met.

  The requirement for immediate recognition of revenue for purpose and time restricted gifts results from FASB's conclusion in SFAC No. 6 that unspent expendable restricted gifts do not normally meet the definition of a liability (deferred revenue).

- Financial statement format was initially the subject of initial work by an AICPA task force. FASB issued a statement of financial accounting standards No. 117 on financial statement format in June 1993. It became effective in 1995, at the same time as the new standard on contributions (previous bullet).

- In 1995, the FASB issued SFAS No. 124, "Accounting for Certain Investments Held by Not-for-Profit Organizations." Briefly, its requirements are that all marketable securities be reported at current value in the balance sheet, and that unrealized losses be reported in the unrestricted class of net assets (absent donor restrictions or law which would require reporting losses in a restricted class). A more detailed summary of this standard is at Section 35.2(i).

- In 1999, the FASB issued SFAS No. 136, "Transfers of Assets to a Not-for-Profit Organization or Charitable Trust that Raises or Holds Contributions for Others." It differentiates situations in which not-for-profit organizations act as agents, trustee, or intermediaries from situations in which not-for-profit organizations act as donors and donees. It also indicates how organizations that act as agents, trustees, or intermediaries are to report receipts and disbursements of assets if those transfers are not its contributions as defined in SFAS No. 116 and how a beneficiary is to report its rights to the assets held by a recipient organization.

(i) Summary of Statement of Financial Accounting Standards Nos. 116 and 117

Implementation Schedule.   Both Statements were issued in June 1993. They were effective for fiscal years beginning after December 15, 1994 (e.g., for a June 30 year-end entity, for the fiscal year ending June 30, 1996). Adoption of No. 117 must be made retroactively; adoption of No. 116 can be made either retroactively or prospectively. Copies are available from the FASB Order Department: P.O. Box 5116, Norwalk, CT 06856.

Statement of Financial Accounting Standards No. 117 (Display).   Statement No. 117 requires organizations to present aggregated financial data: total assets, liabilities, net assets (fund balances), and change in net assets. Some not-for-profits already do, but many have not done this in the past. Organizations are free to present data disaggregated by classes of net assets (corresponding to funds), but, except for donor-restricted revenue, net assets, and change in net assets, no detail by class is explicitly required.

Three classes of net assets are defined: unrestricted, temporarily restricted, and permanently restricted. Net assets of the two restricted classes are created *only* by donor-imposed restrictions on their use. All other net assets, including board-designated or appropriated amounts, are legally unrestricted, and must be reported as part of the unrestricted class, although they may be separately identified within that class as designated if the organization wishes.

Permanently restricted net assets will consist mainly of amounts restricted by donors as permanent endowment. Some organizations may also have certain capital assets on which donors have placed perpetual restrictions. Temporarily restricted net assets will often contain a number of different types of donor-restricted amounts: unspent purpose-restricted expendable gifts for operating purposes, pledges payable in future periods, unspent explicitly time-restricted gifts, unspent amounts restricted for the acquisition of capital assets, certain capital assets, unmatured annuity and life income funds, and term endowments.

One requirement that is a significant change for many organizations is the reporting of all expenses in the unrestricted class, regardless of the source of the financing of the expenses. As expendable restricted revenue will be reported in the temporarily restricted class, when these amounts are spent, a reclassification (transfer) will be made to match the restricted revenue with the unrestricted expenses.

A second requirement is that all capital gains or losses on investments and other assets or liabilities will be reported in the unrestricted class, no matter which class holds the underlying assets/liabilities, unless there are explicit donor restrictions, or applicable law, which require the reporting of some or all of the capital gains/losses in a restricted class. This practice will often have the effect of increasing the reported unrestricted net asset balance (and decreasing the other net asset balances), compared with previous reporting principles.

All organizations must report expenses by functional categories (program, management, fundraising). Voluntary health and welfare organizations must also report expenses by natural categories (salaries, rent, travel, etc.) in a matrix format; other organizations are encouraged to do so. Reporting in functional categories is new for some organizations, mainly those that do not raise significant amounts of contributions from the general public, such as trade associations, country clubs, and many local churches.

A new financial statement for many organizations is a statement of cash flows, showing where the organization received and spent its cash. Cash flows will be reported in three categories: operating flows, financing flows (including receipt of nonexpendable contributions), and investing flows. This statement has been required for businesses for several years by SFAS No. 95, which should be consulted for further information.

Statement No. 95 permits either of two basic methods for preparing the statement of cash flows: the "direct" or the "indirect" method. Briefly, the indirect method starts with the excess of revenues over expenses and reconciles this number to operating cash flows. The direct method reports operating cash receipts and cash disbursements, directly adding these to arrive at operating cash flows. The authors believe the direct method is much more easily understood by readers of financial statements, and thus recommends its use.

Much of the information used to prepare a statement of cash flows is derived from data in the other two primary financial statements, some of it from the preceding year's statements. Thus, when planning to prepare this statement for the first time, it is helpful to start a year in advance so that the necessary prior-year data is available when needed.

Sample financial statements, illustrating formats that contain the disclosures required by Statement No. 117, are shown in Appendix C to the Statement.

Statement of Financial Accounting Standards No. 116 (Contributions). This document establishes one set of standards for all recipients of contributions, replacing the four different standards in the four AICPA audit guides. It also sets standards for donors of gifts; no explicit standards have heretofore existed, except for private foundations. For-profit organizations are also covered by this part of the document.

Certain types of transactions are not considered contributions: transactions that are in substance purchases of goods or services (even though they may be called grants) and transactions in which a recipient of a "gift" is merely acting as an agent or intermediary for, and passes the gift on to, another organization. Unfortunately, there is not much specific guidance for how to distinguish these two situations from real contributions; organizations will have to use judgment on a case-by-case basis.

SFAS No. 116 explicitly introduces a new concept into accounting for contributions: the conditional promise to give (pledge). This concept has implicitly existed for a long time, but has never before been articulated so clearly. A conditional pledge is one that depends on the occurrence of some specified *uncertain* future event to become binding on the pledgor. Examples of such events are the meeting of a matching requirement by the pledgee, or natural or man-made disasters such as a flood or fire. The mere passage of time is not a condition. Note that the concept of a condition is completely separate from that of a restriction. Conditions relate to events that must occur prior to a pledge becoming binding on the pledgor; restrictions relate to limits on the use of a gift after receipt.

Unconditional pledges are recorded at the time verifiable evidence of the pledge is received. Conditional pledges are not recorded until the condition is met, at which time they become unconditional. Pledges payable in future periods are considered implicitly time-restricted and are reported in the temporarily restricted class of net assets until they are due. Long-term pledges are also discounted to their present value to reflect the time value of money (in accordance with Accounting Principles Board Opinion No. 21); this is a new practice for most organizations. Accretion of the discount to par value will be reported as contribution income.

All contributions are reported as revenue, in the class of net assets (unrestricted, temporarily restricted, or permanently restricted) appropriate to any donor restrictions on the gift, at the time of receipt of the gift. This applies to unconditional pledges as well as cash gifts. The presence or absence of explicit or implicit donor-imposed time or purpose restrictions on the use of a gift do not affect the timing of revenue recognition, only the class in which they are reported. This principle is a significant change in practice for many organizations, which have heretofore deferred donor-restricted gifts and all pledges until a later period when the restriction was met or the pledge collected. The effect is to report higher net asset amounts, mainly in the temporarily restricted class, than under previous principles. This principle has generated a lot of controversy between those who favor retaining the previous deferral method and advocates of the new standard.

Accounting by donors for pledges and other contributions will follow the same principles with respect to recognition and timing as the donees, though of course all the accounting entries are reversed: expense instead of revenue, pledges payable instead of pledges receivable. Also, for-profit donors do not categorize their financial reports into classes because this concept only applies to not-for-profits.

The reporting of the value of donated services of volunteers has changed for many organizations under SFAS No. 116. The new standard requires reporting such a value if either of two criteria is met: (1) the services create or enhance nonfinancial assets, or (2) the services require specialized skills, are provided by persons possessing those skills, and would typically otherwise have to be purchased by the recipient if volunteers were not available. If neither criterion is met, the services may not be recorded. Organizations need to consider which of their volunteer services meet either of the two criteria.

Another matter that was controversial during the process of developing SFAS No. 116 was the question of accounting for museum collections. An early FASB proposal was to require capitalization of such assets. After much discussion of the subject, FASB agreed to allow noncapitalization of these items, if certain conditions relating to the items were met and certain footnote disclosures made.

(ii) Decisions.   Organizations have a number of decisions available to them under SFAS Nos. 116 and 117. These are:
Restricted contributions:

- Do we wish to report restricted contributions whose restrictions are met in the same accounting period as that in which they are received as restricted or as unrestricted support? (Contributions paragraph 14, third sentence.)
- Do we wish to adopt a policy which implies that on gifts of long-lived assets, there exists a time restriction which expires over the useful life of the donated assets? (Contributions paragraph 16.)

Basic financial statement format:

- What titles do we wish to use for the balance sheet and for the statement of activity? (No particular titles are required or precluded by SFAS No. 117.)

- Do we wish to present additional detail in the statement of financial position of assets and liabilities by class? (Display paragraph 156, next-to-last sentence.)
- Which of the sample formats for the Statement of Activities do we wish to follow? (Display paragraph 157 and its examples that follow.)
- Do we wish to present a measure of "operations"? (Display paragraphs 23, 163–167) (See Appendix 35.6 for further guidance.)
- Do we wish to prepare the statement of cash flows using the direct or the indirect method? (SFAS No. 95, "Statement of Cash Flows," paragraphs 27–28.)
- Do we wish to present comparative financial data for prior year(s)? (Display paragraph 70.)

Classification of expenses:

- On the face of the statement of activities, do we wish to categorize expenses by functional or by natural classifications? (Display paragraph 26, second and third lines.)
- If we are not required to disclose expenses in natural categories, do we wish to make such disclosure voluntarily? (Display paragraph 26, last sentence.)
- If expenses have not previously been categorized by function, what categories (beyond the basic categories of program, management, fundraising, membership-development) do we wish to present? (Display paragraphs 26–28.)
- Do we wish to disclose the fair value of contributed services received but not recognized as revenues? (Contributions paragraph 10, last sentence).

Collection items:

- If our organization has assets that meet the definition of collection items at Contributions paragraph 11, do we wish to capitalize these assets or not?
- If we have not previously capitalized but now wish to capitalize these items, do we wish to do so retroactively, or only prospectively? (Contributions paragraph 12.)
- If we choose to capitalize these items retroactively, how do we wish to determine their value for this purpose? (Contributions, footnote 4.)

Do we wish to present nonmonetary information, as discussed in Display footnote 6?

Do we wish to retain our fund accounting system and convert our financial data to the new class structure by worksheets prior to preparing the financial statements, or do we wish to convert our entire accounting system to reflect the three-class structure discussed at Display paragraph 3 and Appendix D?

The division of net assets (formerly called *fund balance*) into three classes—unrestricted, temporarily restricted, and permanently restricted—as set forth in SFAC No. 6, and other matters discussed in that document, has a significant effect on the format of the financial statements of many not-for-profit organizations.

(iii) AICPA Audit Guide and Other Guidance. In 1996, the AICPA issued two new audit guides, one for health care organizations (discussed in Chapter 36 and one for all other not-for-profit organizations. It provides additional implementation guidance for FASB Statements Nos. 116, 117, and 124, as well as other matters affecting not-for-profit organizations. Topics it covers in particular detail include reporting of split-interest gifts and expenses. Its provisions are discussed throughout this chapter.

AICPA Guidance in Specific Areas. The AICPA issues technical practice aids to address questions it receives from practitioners. Preparers of not-for-profit organization financial statements should be familiar with these technical practice aids (TPAs) that are included in the AICPA publication *Technical Practice Aids* at Section 6140.

Important aids that relate to the implementation of SFAS Nos. and 117 include the following:

- *6140.03 Lapsing of Time Restrictions on Receivables that Are Uncollected at Their Due Date.* SFAS No. 116 requires that pledges receivable be recorded as temporarily restricted with an implied time restriction that expires on the due date. Practice is sometimes to release restrictions when a pledge is paid rather than when it comes due. This TPA clarifies that release should occur at the due date; the due date needs to be identified based on the specific circumstances.

- *6140.04 Lapsing of Restrictions on Receivables if Purpose Restrictions Pertaining to Long-Lived Assets Are Met before the Receivables Are Due.* Many organizations raise funds for capital campaigns for building projects with pledges that are payable over a period that extends some time after the building is placed in to service. SFAS No. 116 provides that restrictions expire when the last restriction expires, but the contributions specified for the current period are not considered time restricted. Accordingly, it may be appropriate to release the restrictions on capital campaign pledges when the building is placed into service.

- *6140.05 NPO Accounting for Loans of Cash that Are Interest Free or that Have Below-Market Interest Rates.* The TPA sets out the accounting to be followed to record the contribution of interest at fair value where an organization receives a loan that is interest free or below market. For loans with terms of more than one year, the value needs to be recorded for the full term of the loan at the time of the loan agreement, with recording of interest expense over the term of the loan.

- *6140.06 Functional Category of Costs of Sales of Contributed Inventory.* The TPA recommends that organizations establish a separate classification for such cost of sales as a supporting activity unless the item sold relates to a program activity, in which case it would be reported as such.

- *6140.7 Functional Category of Costs of Special* and *6140.08 Functional Category of the Costs of Direct Donor Benefits.* The TPA clarifies that not all costs of special events, in particular the cost of direct benefits to donors, are fund-raising costs. However, direct benefits to donors are fund-raising costs if the donor has not paid specifically for those benefits in an exchange transaction such as purchasing a ticket to a special event.

- *6140.9 Reporting Bad Debt Losses.* This TPA clarifies that bad debt losses cannot be netted against revenue. It should be noted, though, that losses do not have to be treated the same way as expenses in the statement of activities. Accordingly, to the extent that there is a bad debt loss related to a pledge that has not yet come due, that loss can be recorded as a reduction in temporarily or permanently restricted net assets. This can be helpful to an organization in not increasing the percentage of expenses that relate to supporting activities.

- *6140.10 Consolidation of Political Action Committee Political Action Committee PAC.* This TPA clarifies that SOP 94-3 applies to the consolidation of political action committees (PACs). Accordingly, a PAC should be consolidated when its government committee is appointed by a not-for-profit organization that benefits from its activities.

- *6140.11 Costs of Soliciting Contributed Services and Time that Do Not Meet the Recognition Criteria in FASB Statement No. 116.* This TPA arose from the practice of recording the costs of soliciting volunteers as a program activity. This is of particular importance to the many organizations that use volunteers extensively in meeting their program goals. In many cases the value of these services is not recognized in the financial statements consistent with the requirements of SFAS No. 116. The TPA clarifies that SFAS No. 117 requires that all costs of soliciting contributed services be recorded as fund raising even if the contributed services are not recognized in the financial statements. Organizations with large volunteer departments need to separately identify those costs of soliciting volunteers from the costs of managing volunteers, which may well be program in nature if the volunteers are meeting program goals. If such fund-raising costs are significant, organizations may wish to identify them separately in the financial statements so that readers can relate fund-raising costs with the value of the funds raised.

(iv) Projects in Process.   As of early 2002, the FASB was working on the following additional projects that are particularly applicable to not-for-profit organizations. For current status, refer to the FASB Web site at www.fasb.org.

Combinations of Not-for-Profit Organizations, Goodwill, and Intangible Assets.   The FASB issued Statement No. 141, "Business Combinations," and specifically excluded not-for-profit organizations. SFAS No. 142, "Goodwill and Intangible Assets," delays implementation for not-for-profit organizations until the FASB issues a statement on the combination of not-for-profit organizations.

The FASB tentatively determined that not-for-profit organizations should follow SFAS Nos. 141 and 142 except for circumstances in which a different approach is appropriate because of circumstances unique to not-for-profit organizations. Currently, not-for-profit organizations are required to account for business combinations and acquired intangible assets following the guidance in APB Opinion No. 16, "Business Combinations," and APB Opinion No. 17, "Tangible Assets." However, practice varies considerably and this results principally from combinations where there is no exchange of consideration. Many combinations of not-for-profit organizations have been accounted for using the pooling-of-interest method. The elimination of that method in SFAS No. 141 requires the development of clear guidance for not-for-profit organizations.

The FASB has tentatively concluded that a standard when issued will require identification of the acquiring organization in all combinations. The standard will include criteria to help identify the acquiring organization.

The assets and liabilities, including intangible assets, of the acquired organization will then need to be valued in accordance with the criteria applicable to business organizations in SFAS Nos. 141 and 142.

For combinations with no exchange of consideration, the acquiring organization will record the acquisition as receipt of a contribution in accordance with SFAS No. 116 at fair value.

In situations in which the fair value of the liabilities exceeds the fair value of the assets, the FASB has tentatively concluded that the difference should be accounted for as goodwill. However, the FASB is expected to reconsider this conclusion prior to the issuance of an exposure draft. Alternative approaches would appear to be to reduce the value of acquired assets so as not to exceed the value of the liabilities or to record the excess as an expense at the time of the combination.

For combinations in which there is an exchange of consideration, the FASB would require that SFAS No. 141 be followed. However, if the consideration is only part payment, the fair value of all assets and liabilities would need to be computed and the difference reported as a contribution.

A major difference for most combinations of not-for-profit organizations is the adjustment of values of assets and liabilities of the acquired organizations to fair value and the requirement to record the value of acquired intangible assets, including the value of trademarks and donor lists.

The FASB has not completed its deliberations, and an exposure draft is not expected until the first quarter of 2003.

Consolidations Policy and Procedures.   The FASB has been considering a proposed Statement that would require business enterprises and not-for-profit organizations that control other entities to include those subsidiaries in their consolidated financial statements. "Control" would be defined as the nonshared decision-making ability of one entity to direct the policies and management that guide the ongoing activities of another entity so as to increase its benefits and limit its losses from that other entity's activities.

During 2001, the FASB determined that it had insufficient support to complete this project. FASB members had difficulty agreeing on the definition of "control." Accordingly, the FASB has suspended its work in this area. Not-for-profit organizations cannot expect new guidance in the near future, so the current rules on SOP 94-3 remain applicable (see Section 35.2(k), "Related Organizations.")

(b) GOVERNMENT AUDIT REQUIREMENTS. Not-for-profit entities are increasingly subject to audit requirements imposed by government agencies. These requirements are discussed in Subsection 35.4(f) of this chapter.

35.2 NOT-FOR-PROFIT ACCOUNTING PRINCIPLES AND REPORTING PRACTICES

(a) PRINCIPAL ACCOUNTING AND REPORTING REQUIREMENTS. The various accounting standards discussed in this chapter affect considerably the accounting and financial reporting of all types of not-for-profit organizations. A list of the most significant requirements follows.

Accounting for Contributions (see SFAS No. 116, SFAS No. 136, and the AICPA Audit Guide)

- Pledges are recorded when an unconditional promise to give is communicated to the donee.
- A conditional promise to give is not reported until the condition is met.
  - (The distinction between conditional and restricted gifts is not always clear.)
- Pledges are discounted to their present value and are reported net of an allowance for the estimated uncollectible amount.
- All gifts, including pledges and restricted gifts, are reported as revenue when received.
- Donors (including for-profit donors) must follow the same rules as donees (in reverse—an unconditional pledge must be recorded as an expense and a liability when made). (Fund-raisers should take note of this, as it will affect some donors' willingness to make unconditional pledges.)
- Split-interest gifts are essentially treated as pledges (Audit Guide, Chapter 6); these include:
  - Gift annuities, remainder annuity trusts, unitrusts, pooled income funds (PIF), lead trusts.
  - Irrevocable trusts held by others are reported in the beneficiary's financial statements.
- Gifts-in-kind are recorded at fair value—including property, use of property, equipment, inventory for sale or use, services by other organizations (including bargain purchases).
- Donated services of individual volunteers are recorded only when specified criteria are met:
  - The services create or enhance nonfinancial assets (building something), or
  - The services require specialized skills, the volunteer possesses those skills, and the donee would typically have to purchase the services if the volunteer were not available (the services involve a significant and central activity of the entity).
- A pass-through entity may not be able to record gifts as revenue, depending on the circumstances of the gift.
- A museum does not have to capitalize its collection if certain criteria are met.
- New principles apply to transfers of cash or other financial assets from a donor to a recipient organization that agrees to use the assets on behalf of or transfer the assets to a specified beneficiary.
- If the recipient organization and the specified beneficiary are unaffiliated, the recipient organization reports the assets at fair value and a liability of equal amount. However, if the donor explicitly grants the recipient organization variance power—unilateral power to redirect the use of the assets to another beneficiary—or if the recipient organization and the specified beneficiary are financially interrelated, the recipient organization reports the fair value of the assets as a contribution received.
- A specified beneficiary reports its rights to the assets as an asset at fair value while it has rights to the assets, unless the donor explicitly granted the recipient organization variance power. If the beneficiary and the recipient organization are financially interrelated, the beneficiary reports at fair value its interest in the net assets of the recipient organization and adjusts that

interest for its share of the change in net assets of the recipient organization. However, if the recipient organization is explicitly granted variance power, the specified beneficiary does not report its potential for receipts from the assets held by the recipient organization.

Financial statement format (see SFAS No. 117 and the AICPA Audit Guide)

- Required disclosures are: totals of assets, liabilities, net assets, change in net assets.
- Net assets (formerly, fund balance) and revenue are categorized into three classes:
  - Unrestricted; temporarily restricted; permanently restricted (per donor restrictions only).
  - Restrictions imposed by nondonors do not change category (e.g., contracts).
- Required disclosures for each class are: net assets, change in net assets.
- A statement of cash flows is required (the "direct" method is preferred).
- All expenses are reported in the unrestricted class.
  - Temporarily restricted net assets are reclassified to match related expenses.
- Expenses are reported on a functional basis (program, management, fund raising).
- Revenues and expenses are reported gross, not net (exception: investment management fees).
  - Related items (e.g., sales/cost of sales) may be shown as: gross, deduction, net.
- (See below for treatment of capital gains/losses.)
- Affiliated entities are combined if specified criteria are met (SOP 94-3):
  - For-profit affiliate: criteria based on ownership.
  - Not-for-profit affiliate: criteria based on control and economic interest.

Accounting for Investments (see SFAS No. 117 and 124)

- Marketable securities are reported at current market value.
- Capital gains and losses on endowment are reported mostly in the unrestricted class, unless state law or a donor stipulation specifies otherwise.

Other Matters

- Depreciable assets must be depreciated (see SFAS No. 93).
- Not-for-profits must follow requirements of generally accepted accounting principles (see SOP 94-2).
- Joint costs of multipurpose activities can be allocated to program functions only if certain criteria are met:
  - Purpose; audience; content, including a call to action other than giving (see SOP 98-2, which replaced SOP 87-2).
- Contribution rules in SFAS No. 116 do not affect the timing of revenue recognition for advance payments of earned income: dues, fees, sales, season tickets, and so on—these are still deferred until earned.

(b) BASIS OF ACCOUNTING: CASH OR ACCRUAL.   Not-for-profit organizations frequently maintain their records on a cash basis, a bookkeeping process that reflects only transactions involving cash. On the other hand, most commercial organizations, as well as many medium and large not-for-profit organizations, keep accounts on an accrual basis. In accrual basis accounting, income is recognized when earned and expenses are recognized when incurred. For bookkeeping purposes, either basis is acceptable.

Each accounting basis has certain advantages. The principal advantage of cash basis accounting is simplicity—its procedures are easy to learn and easy to execute. Because of this simplicity, a cash basis accounting system is less complicated and less expensive to maintain than an accrual basis system. A less complicated system will be easier for a volunteer bookkeeper who does not feel comfortable with the more complicated accrual methods. Because there is often no material difference in financial results between cash and accrual basis accounting for small organizations, the incremental cost of an accrual basis system may be unwarranted. In addition, many not-for-profit organizations think it more prudent to keep their books on a cash basis. They often do not want to recognize income prior to the actual receipt of cash.

The principal advantage of accrual basis accounting is that it portrays financial position and results of operations on a more realistic basis—a complex organization with accounts receivable and bills outstanding can present realistic financial results only on the accrual basis. In addition, accrual basis accounting usually achieves a better matching of revenue and related expenses. Also, many individuals who use the financial statements of not-for-profit organizations, such as bankers, local businesspeople, and board members, are often more familiar with accrual basis accounting.

Organizations wanting the accuracy of accrual basis accounting, but not wishing to sacrifice the simplicity of cash basis bookkeeping, have alternatives. They may maintain their books on a cash basis and at year end record all payables, receivables, and accruals. These adjustments would permit presentation of accrual basis financial statements.

An organization can also keep its books on a cash basis, except for certain transactions that are recorded on an accrual basis. A popular type of "modified cash basis" accounting is to record accounts payable as liabilities are incurred, but to record income on a cash basis as received.

(c) FUND ACCOUNTING.   Fund accounting is the process of segregating resources into sets of self-balancing accounts on the basis of either restrictions imposed by donors or designations imposed by governing boards.

In the past, most not-for-profit organizations followed fund accounting procedures in accounting for resources. This was done because many organizations regard fund accounting as the most appropriate means of exercising stewardship over funds. Reporting all the details of funds, however, is not required of all not-for-profit organizations, and in many cases is not recommended. Fund accounting, if carried to its logical extreme, requires a separate set of accounts for each restricted gift or contribution; this leads to confusing financial statements that often present an organization as a collection of individual funds rather than as a single entity. Today, many not-for-profit organizations are combining funds and eliminating fund distinctions for reporting purposes to facilitate financial statement users' understanding of the organization as a whole.

The FASB Standard on financial reporting (SFAS No. 117) specifically requires the reporting of certain financial information by what it calls "classes" rather than funds.

An infinite variety of funds is possible. To limit the number of funds reported, broad fund classifications may be used. One scheme commonly used today is classification of resources by type of donor restriction. Another criterion for classifying funds is the degree of control an organization possesses over its resources. Under this approach, funds are combined for reporting purposes into two groupings—unrestricted and restricted. A third approach classifies resources on the basis of their availability for current expenditure on an organization's programs. Under this approach, funds are combined into two categories, expendable and nonexpendable.

When resources are classified by type of donor restriction, four fund groupings are commonly used—current unrestricted, current restricted, endowment, and fixed asset funds.

The current unrestricted fund contains assets over which the board has total managerial discretion. This fund includes unrestricted contributions, revenue, and other income and can be used in any manner at any time to further the goals of the organization. For all not-for-profit organizations, "board-designated" funds should be included with current unrestricted funds. Board-designated funds are voluntary segregations of unrestricted fund balances approved by the board for specific future projects or purposes.

Current restricted funds are resources given to an organization to be expended for specific operating purposes.

Endowment funds are amounts donated to an organization with the legal restriction that the principal be maintained inviolate either in perpetuity or for a stated period of time and amounts set aside by the organization's governing board for long-term investment. Investment income on such funds is generally unrestricted and should be reported in the current unrestricted fund. Occasionally, endowment gifts stipulate restricted uses for the investment income, and such restricted income should be reported in the appropriate fund.

The fixed asset fund represents the land, buildings, and equipment owned by an organization. Since these assets are usually unrestricted in the sense that the board can employ (or dispose of) them in any manner it wishes to further the goals of the organization, fixed assets need not be reported in a separate fund, and may be reported as part of the current unrestricted fund.

(i) Reclassification of Funds into Classes.   Under SFAS No. 117, organizations must access each component of each fund on an individual basis to determine into which class that fund balance (net assets) should be classified. This assessment, as to the temporarily and permanently restricted classes, is based only on the presence or absence of donor-imposed restrictions. All funds without donor-imposed restrictions must be classified as unrestricted, regardless of the existence of any board designations or appropriations.

Following is a chart showing typical classes into which various types of fund balances will normally be classified:

Funds	Unrestricted	Temporarily Restricted	Permanently Restricted
Endowment	Quasi	Term	Permanent
Specific purpose, or current restricted	Board-designated	Donor-restricted	N/A
Loan	Board-designated	Donor-restricted[1]	Revolving[1]
Split-interest (annuity, life income, etc.)	Voluntary excess reserves	Unmatured	Permanent[2]
Fixed asset	Expended;[3] Board-designated	Donor-restricted unexpended; Expended donated	See note 4
General/Operating	Unrestricted	Donor-time restricted	N/A
Custodian	All (on balance sheet only)[5]	N/A	N/A

[1] A permanently restricted loan fund would be one where only the income can be loaned, or, if the principal can be loaned, repayments of principal by borrowers are restricted to be used for future loans. A loan fund in which principal repayments are available for any use would be temporarily restricted until the loans are repaid, at which time such amounts would become unrestricted.

[2] For example, an annuity fund that, upon maturity, becomes a permanent endowment.

[3] Expended donor-restricted plant funds will be either unrestricted or temporarily restricted, depending on the organization's choice of accounting principle under paragraph 16 of SFAS No. 116.

[4] Fixed assets could be permanently restricted if a donor has explicitly restricted the proceeds from any future disposition of the assets to reinvestment in fixed assets. Museum collection items received subject to a donor's stipulation that they be preserved and not sold might also be considered permanently restricted.

[5] Note that because no transactions related to custodian funds are reported in the income statement of the holder of the assets, and because there is never a fund balance amount (assets are always exactly offset by liabilities), reporting of such funds as separate items becomes an issue only when a balance sheet is disaggregated into classes. The logic for reporting the assets and liabilities of custodian funds in the unrestricted class is that such assets are not the result of donor-restricted gifts, which is a requirement for recording items in one of the restricted classes.

(d) RECLASSIFICATIONS.   The use of fund accounting necessitates transfers in some situations to allocate resources between funds or classes. Financial statement readers often find it difficult to comprehend such reclassifications. In addition, if not properly presented, reclassifications may give the impression that an organization is willfully manipulating amounts reported as income.

To minimize confusion and the appearance of deception, transfers must not be shown as either income or expenses of the transferring fund. Reclassifications of the total organization are merely an internal reallocation of resources and in no way result in income or expense recognition.

Columnar statements, which present the activity of each class in separate, side-by-side columns, facilitate clear, comprehensive presentation of reclassifications.

(e) APPROPRIATIONS.   Appropriations (or designations) are internal authorizations to expend resources in the future for specific purposes. They are neither expenditures nor legal obligations. When appropriation accounting is followed, appropriated amounts should be set aside in a separate account as part of the net assets of an organization.

Appropriation accounting is both confusing and subject to abuse. It is confusing because "appropriation" is an ambiguous term, and many readers do not understand that it is neither a current expenditure nor a binding obligation for a future expenditure. It is subject to abuse because, when treated incorrectly, appropriations can appear to reduce the current year's excess of revenue over expenses to whatever level the board wants. The board can then, at a later date, restore "appropriated" funds to the general use of the organization.

The use of appropriation accounting is not recommended. If an organization wishes to follow appropriation accounting techniques and wants to conform with GAAP, it must be certain that appropriations are not presented as expenses and that they appear only as part of the net assets of the organization. Expenses incurred out of appropriated funds should be charged as expenses in the year incurred, and the related appropriations should be reversed once an expense has been incurred.

Disclosure in notes is an alternative to appropriation accounting. Under this approach, an organization does not refer to appropriations in the body of its financial statements but instead discloses such amounts only in notes to the financial statements.

(f) FIXED ASSETS.   Treatment of fixed assets is sometimes a perplexing accounting issue confronting not-for-profit organizations. There are three reasons some not-for-profit organizations have historically not recorded a value for fixed assets on their balance sheets. First, many not-for-profit organizations have not been as interested in matching income and expenses as are businesses. This being the case, management of these organizations has felt no compelling need to record assets and then charge depreciation expense against current income. Second, the principal asset of some not-for-profit organizations is real estate that was often acquired many years previously. In these inflationary times, many organizations do not wish to carry at cost and depreciate assets now worth several times their original purchase price. Third, many not-for-profit organizations plead poverty as a means of raising funds. By not recording fixed assets, they appear less substantial than they in fact are.

Confusion concerning fixed assets has been heightened by lack of a universally accepted treatment for fixed assets. Historically, there have been three common alternatives for handling fixed assets: immediate write-off, capitalization (with or without depreciation), and write-off, followed by capitalization.

Immediate write-off is the simplest method of treating fixed assets and is used most frequently for small organizations and those on a cash basis. Under this method, an organization expenses fixed asset purchases immediately on the statement of income and expenses.

The principal advantage of this approach is simplicity—the bookkeeping complexities of capitalization are avoided, and the amount of excess revenue over expenses reported on the statement of income and expenses more closely reflects the amount of money at the board's disposal.

The major disadvantage of immediate write-off is that the historical costs of an organization's fixed assets are not recorded, and its balance sheet does not present the true net worth of the organization. Another disadvantage is that expensing fixed assets may produce fluctuations in net income that are largely unrelated to operations. Finally, this approach does not conform with GAAP.

A second alternative available to an organization is to capitalize all major fixed asset purchases. Under this approach, all major fixed assets are reflected on the organization's balance sheet.

The principal advantage of this approach is that it conforms with GAAP and permits an auditor to express an unqualified opinion on an organization's financial statements. It also documents the amount of assets the organization controls, permitting evaluation of management performance, and allows the organization to follow depreciation accounting.

The major disadvantage of capitalization is that it renders financial statements more complex. An unsophisticated statement reader may conclude that an organization has more funds available for current spending than it actually has.

A third alternative is to immediately write off fixed asset purchases on the statement of income and expenses and then capitalize these assets on the balance sheet. This method permits an organization to report expenditures for fixed asset purchases on the statement of income and expenses, thus offsetting any excess of income over expenses that may have been caused by contributions received for fixed assets on its balance sheet.

However, this approach is very confusing, is inconsistent with other accounting conventions, does not permit depreciation accounting in a traditional sense, and does not constitute GAAP. Accordingly, the use of this approach is strongly discouraged.

(i) Fixed Assets Where Title May Revert to Grantors.   Some organizations purchase or receive fixed assets under research or similar grants which provide that, at the completion of the grant period, the right of possession of these fixed assets technically reverts to the grantor. If the grantor is not expected to ask for their return, a fixed asset, whether purchased or donated, should be recorded as an asset and depreciated as with any other asset.

(g) DEPRECIATION.   Depreciation has been as thorny a problem for not-for-profit organizations as the problem of fixed assets. If an organization capitalizes fixed assets, it is immediately confronted with the question of whether it should depreciate them: that is, allocate the cost over the estimated useful life of the assets.

Depreciation accounting is now a generally accepted practice for most not-for-profit organizations, and since 1990, it constitutes GAAP for all not-for-profit organizations. (Prior to that year it was optional for colleges.) SFAS No. 93, "Recognition of Depreciation by Not-for-Profit Organizations," requires not-for-profit organizations to record depreciation on fixed assets. Many arguments in favor of recording depreciation, such as the following, are valid for not-for-profit organizations:

- Depreciation is a cost of operations. Organizations cannot accurately measure the cost of providing a product or service or determine a fair price without including this cost component.
- Most organizations replace at least some fixed assets out of recurring income. If depreciation is not recorded, an organization may think that its income is sufficient to cover costs when, in reality, it is not.
- If depreciation is not recorded, income may fluctuate widely from year to year, depending on the timing of asset replacement and the replacement cost of assets.
- Organizations that are "reimbursed" by a government agency for the sale of goods or services must depreciate fixed assets if they wish to recapture all costs incurred.
- Some not-for-profit organizations pay federal income tax on "unrelated business income." Depreciation should be reported as an expense to reduce income subject to tax.

Depreciation is computed in the same manner as that used by commercial enterprises. Depreciation is reported as an item of expense on the statement of income and expenses, and accumulated depreciation is reported under the "fixed assets" caption on the balance sheet.

If fixed asset purchases are capitalized but not written down through regular depreciation charges in the statement of income and expenses, it may be necessary to periodically write down their carrying value so that the balance sheet is not overstated. The preferred method of achieving this is to report the write-down as an expense on the statement of income and expenses and to reduce the asset value on the balance sheet.

(h) INVESTMENT INCOME.   Dividends and interest earned on unrestricted investment funds, including board-designated funds, should be reported as income in the unrestricted class.

Unrestricted investment income earned on endowment funds should also be reported as income directly in the unrestricted class.

Restricted investment income should be reported directly in the appropriate restricted fund. For example, if the donor of an endowment fund gift specifies that the investment income be used for a particular purpose, investment income should be reported directly in the temporarily restricted class rather than the unrestricted or the permanently restricted class.

(i) GAINS AND LOSSES ON INVESTMENTS.   The FASB reporting standard in Statement No. 117 required many organizations to change their method of reporting gains and losses on endowment funds from the method previously used and described in the seventh edition of this book. Briefly, the new method involves determining which portion of the gains are legally restricted, either by explicit donor restrictions or by applicable laws to which the organization is subject. All gains not so restricted will be reported directly in the unrestricted class rather than in the endowment fund.

Realized gains or losses on unrestricted investment funds should be reported directly in the unrestricted class. Unrestricted capital gains or losses may be reported in the statement of income and expenses as an income item along with dividends and interest, or they may be reported separately from other investment income, above the caption "Change in net assets."

Realized gains or losses on endowment investments were traditionally treated as adjustments to principal of the endowment fund. They have not been considered as income and were thought to possess the same restrictions as those that are attached to the principal. The legal status of gains or losses on endowment funds—as unrestricted income or as a component of restricted principal—is, however, currently discussed in SFAS No. 117. Where permitted by state law, such gains or losses should be treated as income and reported with dividends and interest in the unrestricted class above the caption "change in net assets." Restricted gains or losses may be treated in a similar manner except that they are reported in the appropriate restricted class.

Unrealized gains or losses did not pose accounting questions for not-for-profit organizations prior to 1973 because, before that year, investments could be carried only at cost and gains or losses were realized only at the time investments were sold or otherwise disposed of.

After 1973, the tenor of accounting pronouncements on the carrying value of investments and the treatment of unrealized gains or losses changed dramatically. In 1973 and 1974, the AICPA Industry Audit Guides for colleges and universities and voluntary health and welfare organizations permitted those organizations to carry their investments at either cost or market. Hospitals were required in 1978 to carry equity investments at market if the fair value dipped below cost. SOP 78-10 permitted covered organizations to carry investments at market or the lower of cost or market.

When investments are carried at market, gains and losses are recognized on a continuing basis. Realized and unrealized gains or losses should be reported together in a single caption: "net increase (decrease) in carrying value of investments." It is appropriate to report this increase or decrease in the same section in which investment dividends and interest are reported.

In 1995, SFAS No. 124 was issued. Its requirements include:

- Equity securities that have readily determinable fair market values and all debt securities shall be reported at current fair value.
- In the absence of donor stipulations or law to the contrary:
  - Capital losses shall reduce temporarily restricted net assets to the extent that donor-imposed restrictions on net appreciation of the fund have not yet been met.
  - Any remaining loss shall reduce unrestricted net assets.
  - Gains that restore previous losses shall be reported in the unrestricted class.

Even when investments are carried at cost, if market value declines "permanently" below cost, the carrying value of this investment should be written down to the market value. This is accomplished by setting up a "provision for decline in market value of investments" in the statement of income and expenses in the same section where realized gains or losses are presented.

(j) CONTRIBUTIONS.   Support for a not-for-profit organization can be received in many different forms. Each of the types of contributions will be discussed in a separate section of this chapter.

In 1993, the controversy about proper accounting for contributions was settled by the issuance of SFAS No. 116, "Accounting for Contributions Received and Contributions Made." In brief, it says that all contributions, whether unrestricted or restricted, and in whatever form—cash, gifts-in-kind, securities, pledges, or other forms—are revenue in full immediately upon receipt of the gift or an unconditional pledge. (The practice in many organizations was for restricted contributions not to be deferred until the restriction was met.) The revenue is reported in the class of net assets appropriate to any donor-imposed restriction on the gift (unrestricted, if there is no donor-imposed restriction). It also contains guidance on accounting for donated services of volunteers and an exception to the normal rule when dealing with museum collection objects.

(i) Expendable Current Support

Unrestricted Contributions.   This section discusses simple unrestricted cash gifts. Unrestricted gifts in other forms, such as pledges, gifts of securities, and gifts of equipment and supplies, are discussed in later sections. The general principles discussed here apply to all unrestricted gifts, in whatever form received.

HISTORICAL PRACTICES.   All unrestricted contributions should be recorded in the current unrestricted fund. This principle is fairly well accepted and followed by most not-for-profit organizations. What was not uniformly followed is a single method of reporting such unrestricted contributions. Some organizations followed the practice of adding unrestricted contributions directly to the fund balance either in a separate Statement of Changes in Fund Balances or in the fund balance section where a combined Statement of Income, Expenses, and Changes in Fund Balances was used. Others reported some or all of their contributions directly in an unrestricted investment fund, and worse still, some reported unrestricted contributions directly in the endowment fund as though such amounts were restricted. The result of all these practices was to make it difficult for the readers of the financial statements to recognize the amount and nature of contributions received. Sometimes this was done deliberately in an attempt to convince the readers that the organization badly needed more contributions.

ACCOUNTING FOR UNRESTRICTED CONTRIBUTIONS.   All unrestricted contributions should be reported in the unrestricted class of net assets in a Statement of Income and Expenses or, if a combined Statement of Income, Expenses, and Changes in Net Assets is used, such unrestricted contributions should be shown before arriving at the "Excess of income over expenses" caption. It is *not acceptable* to report unrestricted contributions in a separate Statement of Changes in Net Assets or to report such gifts in a restricted class of net assets.

BARGAIN PURCHASES.   Organizations are sometimes permitted to purchase goods or services at a reduced price that is granted by the seller in recognition of the organization's charitable or educational status. In such cases, the seller has effectively made a gift to the buyer. This gift should be recorded as such if the amount is significant. For example, if a charity buys a widget for $50 that normally sells for $80, the purchase should be recorded at $80, with the $30 difference being reported as a contribution.

It is important to record only true gifts in this way. If a lower price is really a normal discount available to any buyer who requests it, then there is no contribution. Such discounts include quantity discounts, normal trade discounts, promotional discounts, special offers, or lower rates (say, for professional services) to reflect the seller's desire to utilize underused staff or sale prices to move slow-moving items off the shelves.

Current Restricted Contributions.   Current restricted contributions are contributions that can be used to meet the current expenses of the organization, although restricted to use for some specific purpose or during or after some specified time. An example of the former would be a gift "for cancer research" (a "purpose restriction") and, of the latter, a gift "for your 20XX activities" (a "time restriction"). In practice, the distinction between restricted gifts and unrestricted gifts is not always clear. In many cases, the language used by the donor leaves doubt as to whether there really is a restriction on the gift.

Current restricted contributions cause reporting problems, in part because the accounting profession took a long time to resolve the appropriate accounting and reporting treatment for these types of gifts. The resolution arrived at is controversial because many believe it is not the most desirable method of accounting for such gifts.

The principal accounting problem relates to the question of what constitutes "income" or "support" to the organization. Is a gift that can only be used for a specific project or after a specified time "income" to the organization at the time the gift is received, or does this restricted gift represent an amount which should be looked on as being held in a form of escrow until it is expended for the restricted purpose (cancer research in the above example), or the specified time has arrived (20XX in the above example)? If it is looked on as something other than income, what is it—deferred income or part of a restricted net asset balance?

If a current restricted gift is considered income or support in the period received—whether expended or not—the accounting is fairly straightforward. It would be essentially the same as for unrestricted gifts, described earlier, except that the gift is reported in the temporarily restricted class rather than in the unrestricted class of net assets. But if the other view is taken, the accounting can become complex.

The approach required by SFAS No. 116 is to report a current restricted gift as income or support in full in the year received, in the temporarily restricted class of net assets. In this approach, gifts are recognized as income as received and expenditures are recognized as incurred. The unexpended income is reflected as part of temporarily restricted net assets.

Observe, however, that in this approach, a current restricted gift received on the last day of the reporting period will also be reflected as income, and this would increase the excess of support over expenses reported for the entire period. Many boards are reluctant to report such an excess in the belief this may discourage contributions or suggest that the board has not used all of its available resources. Those who are concerned about reporting an excess of income over expenses are therefore particularly concerned with the implications of this approach: a large unexpected current restricted gift may be received at the last minute, resulting in a large excess of income over expenses.

Others, in rejecting this argument, point out that the organization is merely reporting what has happened and to report the gift otherwise is to obscure its receipt. They point out that in reality all gifts, whether restricted or unrestricted, are really at least somewhat restricted and only the degree of restriction varies; even "unrestricted" gifts must be spent realizing the stated goals of the organization, and therefore such gifts are effectively restricted to this purpose even though a particular use has not been specified by the contributor.

There are valid arguments on both sides. This approach is the one recommended in the AICPA Audit Guide for Voluntary Health and Welfare Organizations and therefore has been very widely followed. It will now become the method used by all not-for-profit organizations if they want their independent auditor to be able to say that their financial statements are prepared in conformity with generally accepted accounting principles.

GRANTS FOR SPECIFIC PROJECTS.   Many organizations receive grants from third parties to accomplish specific projects or activities. These grants differ from other current restricted gifts principally in the degree of accountability the recipient organization has in reporting back to the granting organization on the use of such monies. In some instances, the organization receives a grant to conduct a specific research project, the results of which are turned over to the grantor. The arrangement is similar to a private contractor's performance on a commercial for-profit basis. In that case, the "grant" is essentially a purchase of services. It would be accounted for in accordance with normal commercial accounting principles, which call for the revenue to be recognized as the work under the contract is performed. In other instances, the organization receives a grant for a specific project, and while the grantee must specifically account for the expenditure of the grant in detail and may have to return any unexpended amounts, the grant is to further the programs of the grantee rather than for the benefit of the grantor. This kind of grant is really a gift, not a purchase.

The line between ordinary current restricted gifts and true "grants" for specific projects is not important for accounting purposes because the method of reporting revenue is now the same for both. What can get fuzzy is the distinction between grants and purchase of services contracts. Most donors of current restricted gifts are explicit as to how their gifts are to be used, and often the organization will initiate a report back to the donors on the use of their gifts. However, restricted gifts and grants usually do not have the degree of specificity that is attached to purchase contracts. Appendix 35.1 contains a checklist to help readers distinguish between gifts and purchase contracts in practice.

Prepayment versus Cost Reimbursement.   Grants and contracts can be structured in either of two forms: In one, the payor remits the amount up front and the payee then spends that money. In the other, the payee must spend its own money from other sources and is reimbursed by the payor.

In the case of a purchase contract, amounts remitted to the organization in advance of their expenditure should be treated as deferred income until such time as expenditures are made that can be charged against the contract. At that time, income should be recognized to the extent earned. Where expenditures have been made but the grantor has not yet made payment, a receivable should be set up to reflect the grantor's obligation.

In the case of a true grant (gift), advance payments must be recognized as revenue immediately upon receipt, as is the case with all contributions under SFAS No. 116. Reimbursement grants are recognized as revenue as reimbursements become due, that is, as money is spent that the grantor will reimburse. This is the same method as is used under cost-reimbursement purchase contracts.

Some organizations have recorded the entire amount of the grant as a receivable at the time awarded, offset by deferred grant income on the liability side of the balance sheet. This is no longer appropriate under SFAS No. 116. If the entire grant amount qualifies as an unconditional pledge (see below), then that amount must be recorded as revenue, not deferred revenue.

Investment Securities.   Frequently, an organization will receive contributions that are in the form of investment securities: stocks and bonds. These contributions should be recorded in the same manner as cash gifts. The only problem usually encountered is difficulty in determining a reasonable basis for valuation in the case of closely held stock with no objective market value.

The value recorded should be the fair market value at the date received. Marketable stocks and bonds present no serious valuation problem. They should be recorded at their market value on the date of receipt or, if sold shortly thereafter, at the amount of proceeds actually received. However, the "shortly thereafter" refers to a sale within a few days or perhaps a week after receipt. Where the organization deliberately holds the securities for a period of time before sale, the securities should be recorded at their fair market value on the date of receipt. This will result in a gain or loss being recorded when the securities are subsequently sold (unless the market price remains unchanged).

For securities without a published market value, the services of an appraiser may be required to determine the fair value of the gift. See Subsection 35.2(b) for further discussion of investments.

(ii) Gifts-in-Kind

Fixed Assets (Land, Buildings, and Equipment) and Supplies.   Contributions of fixed assets can be accounted for in one of two ways. SFAS No. 116 permits such gifts to be reported as either unrestricted or temporarily restricted income at the time received. If the gift is initially reported as temporarily restricted, the restriction is deemed to expire ratably over the useful life of the asset: that is, in proportion to depreciation for depreciable assets. The expiration is reported as a reclassification from the temporarily restricted to the unrestricted class of net assets. Nondepreciable assets such as land would remain in the temporarily restricted class indefinitely—until disposed of. (Recognizing the gift as income in proportion to depreciation recognized on the asset is not in conformity with generally accepted accounting principles.)

Supplies and equipment should be recorded at the amount that the organization would normally have to pay for similar items. A value for used office equipment and the like can usually be obtained from a dealer in such items. The valuation of donated real estate is more difficult, and it is usually necessary to get an outside appraisal to determine the value.

Despite some controversy over the subject, the new AICPA Audit Guide specifically requires the recording of a value for contributed inventory expected to be sold by thrift shops and similar organizations at the time the items are received. The amount will be an estimate based on the estimated quantities and quality of goods on hand and known statistics for the percentage of the goods that will eventually be sold for cash (versus given away or discarded).

Museum Collections.   SFAS No. 116 makes an exception for recording a value for donated (and purchased) museum collection objects, if certain criteria are met and certain disclosures are made. Owners of such objects do not have to record them, although they may if they wish.

Contributed Services of Volunteers.   Many organizations depend almost entirely on volunteers to carry out their programs and sometimes supporting functions. Should such organizations place a value on these contributed services and record them as "contributions" in their financial statements?

CRITERIA FOR RECORDING.   The answer is yes, under certain circumstances. These circumstances exist only when *either* of the following two conditions is satisfied:

1. The services create or enhance nonfinancial assets; or
2. The services:
   a. Require specialized skills,
   b. Are provided by persons possessing those skills, and
   c. Would typically have to be purchased if not provided by donation.

If neither criterion is met, SFAS No. 116 precludes recording a value for the services, although disclosure in a footnote is encouraged. These criteria differ considerably from criteria in the earlier Audit Guides/SOP.

Creating or Enhancing Fixed Assets.   The first criterion is fairly straightforward. It covers volunteers constructing or making major improvements to buildings or equipment. It would also cover things like building sets or making costumes for a theater or opera company, and writing computer programs, since the resulting assets could be capitalized on the balance sheet. The criterion says "nonfinancial" assets so as *not* to cover volunteer fund-raisers who, it could be argued, are "creating" assets by soliciting gifts.

Specialized Skills.   The second criterion has three parts, all of which must be met for recording to be appropriate. The first part deals with the nature of the services themselves. The intent is deliberately to limit the types of services that must be recorded, thus reducing the burden of tracking and valuing large numbers of volunteers doing purely routine work, the aggregate financial value of which would usually be fairly small. SFAS No. 116 gives very little guidance about how to identify, in practice, those skills that would be considered "specialized," as opposed to nonspecialized. There is a list of skills that are considered specialized, but it merely recites a list of obvious professions, such as doctors, lawyers, teachers, carpenters. What is lacking is an operational definition of specialized that can be applied to all types of services. Appendix 35.2 contains a checklist to help readers make this distinction in practice.

The second part of the criterion will usually cause no problems in practice, as persons practicing the types of skills contemplated should normally possess the skills (if not, why are they performing the services?).

Would Otherwise Purchase. The third part of the criterion will be the most difficult of all to consider, as it calls for a pure judgment by management. Would the organization or would it not purchase the services? This is similar to one in SOP 78-10, which was as follows:

> The services performed are significant and form an integral part of the efforts of the organization as it is presently constituted; the services would be performed by salaried personnel if donated services were not available . . . ; and the organization would continue the activity.

Probably the most important requirement is that the services being performed are an essential part of the organization's program. The key test is whether the organization would hire someone to perform these services if volunteers were not available.

This is a difficult criterion to meet. Many organizations have volunteers involved in peripheral areas which, while important to the organization, are not of such significance that paid staff would be hired in the absence of volunteers. But this is the acid test: If the volunteers suddenly quit, would the organization hire replacements? Appendix 35.3 contains a checklist to help readers assess this criterion.

BASIS ON WHICH TO VALUE SERVICES. An additional criterion that is not explicitly stated in SFAS No. 116 in connection with donated services is that there must be an objective basis on which to value these services. It is usually not difficult to determine a reasonable value for volunteer services where the volunteers are performing professional or clerical services. By definition, the services to be recorded are only those for which the organization would in fact hire paid staff if volunteers were not available. This suggests that the organization should be able to establish a reasonable estimate of what costs would be involved if employees had to be hired.

In establishing such rates, it is not necessary to establish individual rates for each volunteer. Instead, the volunteers can be grouped into general categories and a rate established for each category.

Some organizations are successful in getting local businesses to donate one of their executives on a full- or part-time basis for an extended period of time. In many instances, the amount paid by the local business to the loaned executive is far greater than the organization would have to pay for hired staff performing the same function. The rate to be used in establishing a value should be the lower rate. This also helps to get around the awkwardness of trying to discern actual compensation.

An organization may wish not to record a value unless the services are significant in amount. There is a cost to keep the records necessary to meet the reporting requirements, and unless the resulting amounts are significant, it is wasteful for the organization to record them.

ACCOUNTING TREATMENT. The dollar value assigned to contributed services should be reflected as income in the section of the financial statements where other unrestricted contributions are shown. In most instances, it is appropriate to disclose the amount of such services as a separate line.

On the expense side, the value of contributed services should be allocated to program and supporting service categories based on the nature of the work performed. The amounts allocated to each category are not normally disclosed separately. If volunteers were used for constructing fixed assets, the amounts would be capitalized rather than being charged to an expense category.

Unless some of the amounts are capitalized, the recording of contributed services will not affect the excess of income over expenses, since the income and expense exactly offset each other.

The footnotes to the financial statements should disclose the nature of contributed services and the valuation techniques followed.

Use of Facilities.   Occasionally a not-for-profit organization will be given use of a building or other facilities either at no cost or at a substantially reduced cost. A value should be reflected for such a facility in the financial statements, both as income and as expense. The value to be used should be the fair market value of facilities that the organization would otherwise rent if the contributed facilities were not available. This means that if very expensive facilities are donated, the valuation to be used should be the lower value of the facilities that the organization would otherwise have rented. Implicit in this rule is the ability to determine an objective basis for valuing the facilities. If an organization is given the use of facilities that are unique in design and have no alternative purpose, it may be impossible to determine what they would have to pay to rent comparable facilities. This often occurs with museums that occupy elaborate government-owned buildings.

Where a donor indicates that the organization can unconditionally use such rent-free facilities for more than a one-year period, the organization should reflect the arrangement as a pledge and record the PV of the contribution in the same way as other pledges.

(iii) Support Not Currently Expendable

Endowment Gifts.   Donor-restricted endowment fund contributions should be reported as revenue upon receipt in a restricted class of net assets: temporary in the case of a term endowment gift, otherwise permanent.

Gifts of term endowment are later reclassified to the unrestricted class when the term of the endowment expires. (If, upon expiration of the endowment restriction, the gift is still restricted— likely for some operating purpose—it would not be reclassified until money was spent for that purpose. If upon expiration of the term endowment restriction, the gift becomes permanently restricted, it should be recorded in that class initially.)

Pledges (Promises to Give).   A pledge[1] is a promise to contribute a specified amount to an organization. Typically, fund-raising organizations solicit pledges because a donor either does not want to or is not able to make a contribution in cash in the amount desired by the organization at the time solicited. In giving, as with consumer purchases, the "installment plan" is a way of life. Organizations find donors are more generous when the payments being contributed are smaller and spread out over a period of time.

A pledge may or may not be legally enforceable. The point is largely moot because few organizations would think of trying to legally enforce a pledge. The unfavorable publicity that would result would only hurt future fund raising. The only relevant criteria are: Will the pledge be collected and are pledges material in amount?

If these criteria are satisfied, then there are two accounting questions: Should a pledge be recorded as an asset at the time the pledge is received? If the answer is "yes," the next question is: When should the pledge be recognized as income?

RECORDING AS AN ASSET.   For many organizations, a significant portion of their income is received by pledge. The timing of the collection of pledges is only partially under the control of the organization. Yet over the years most organizations find they can predict with reasonable accuracy the collectible portion of pledges, even when a sizable percentage will not be collected. Accounting literature requires that unconditional pledges the organization expects to collect be recorded as assets and an allowance established for the portion that is estimated to be uncollectible.

---

[1] SFAS No. 116 uses the term *promise to give* to refer to what is more commonly called a *pledge*.

Historically, there was considerable difference of opinion on this subject, with the AICPA Audit Guides and the SOP taking different positions. The College Audit Guide said recording of pledges was optional, and most colleges did not record them until collected. The other three guides required recording pledges, although their criteria and method of recording differed slightly. Now, SFAS No. 116 requires *all* organizations to record unconditional pledges.

CONDITIONS VERSUS RESTRICTIONS.   The requirement in SFAS No. 116 is to record *unconditional* pledges as assets. Unconditional means without conditions. What is meant by conditions? FASB defines a condition as "a future and uncertain event" that must occur for a pledge to become binding on the pledgor. There are two elements to this definition: future and uncertain. Future means it has not happened yet; this is fairly clear. Uncertain is, however, more subject to interpretation. How uncertain? This will be a matter of judgment in many cases.

If a donor pledges to give to a charity "if the sun rises tomorrow," that is not an uncertain event; the sun will rise tomorrow, at a known time. If a donor pledges to give $10,000 to the Red Cross "if there's an earthquake in California," that is very uncertain (a geologist will say the eventual probability of an earthquake happening is 100 percent, but the timing is completely uncertain). This latter pledge would be conditional upon an earthquake occurring. Once an earthquake occurs, then the donor's pledge is unconditional (the condition has been removed), and the pledge would be recorded by the Red Cross.

Another example of a condition is a matching pledge (also known as a *challenge grant*). A donor pledges to give an amount to a charity if the charity raises a matching amount from other sources. (The "match" need not be one for one; it can be in any ratio the donor specifies.) In this case, the charity is not entitled to receive the donor's gift until it has met the required match. Once it does, it will notify the donor that the pledge is now due.

A third type of donor stipulation sounds like a condition, but it may or may not actually be one. A donor pledges to contribute to a symphony orchestra "if they will perform my favorite piece of music [specified by name]." (A cynical person would call this a bribe.) Yes, this is an uncertain future event, since the piece of music has not yet been performed, but how uncertain is it? If the orchestra might very well have played the piece anyway, then the "condition" is really trivial, and the event would not be considered uncertain. However, if the piece were one that the orchestra would be very unlikely to perform without the incentive represented by the pledge in question, then the event would be considered uncertain and the pledge conditional. In this case, the condition is fulfilled when the orchestra formally places the music on its schedule and so informs the donor.

Note that the concept of a condition is quite different from that of a restriction. Conditions deal with events that must occur before a charity is entitled to receive a gift. Restrictions limit how the charity can use the gift after receipt. Unconditional pledges can be either unrestricted or restricted; so can conditional pledges. Donor stipulations attached to a gift or pledge must be read carefully to discern which type of situation is being dealt with. For example, "I pledge $20,000 *if* you play my favorite music" is conditional but unrestricted (the donor has not said the gift must be used to pay for the performance), whereas "I pledge $20,000 *for* [the cost of] playing my favorite piece of music" is restricted, but unconditional. In the latter case, the donor has said the pledge will be paid but can only be used for that performance. The difference in wording is small, but the accounting implications are great. The conditional pledge is not recorded at all until the condition is met; the unconditional restricted pledge is recorded as revenue (in the temporarily restricted class) upon receipt of notification of the pledge. Appendix 35.4 contains a checklist to help readers determine whether an unconditional pledge actually exists. Appendix 35.5 contains a checklist to help distinguish conditions from restrictions.

DISCOUNTED TO PRESENT VALUE.   Prior to SFAS No. 116, pledges were recorded at the full amount that would ultimately be collected. None of the accounting literature for not-for-profit organizations talked about discounting pledges to reflect the time value of money. There had been for many years an accounting standard applicable to business transactions that does require such discounting (APB No. 21), but not-for-profit organizations universally chose to treat this as not applicable to them, and accountants did not object.

SFAS No. 116 does require recipients (and donors) of pledges payable beyond the current accounting period to discount the pledges to their PV, using an appropriate rate of interest. Thus, the ability to receive $1,000 two years later is really only equivalent to receiving about $900 (assuming about a five percent rate of interest) now, because the $900 could be invested and earn $100 of interest over the two years. The higher the interest rate used, the lower will be the PV of the pledge, since the lower amount would earn more interest at the higher rate and still be worth the full $1,000 two years hence.

The appropriate rate of interest to use in discounting pledges will be a matter of some judgment. In many cases, it will be the average rate the organization is currently earning on its investments or its idle cash. If the organization is being forced to borrow money to keep going, then the borrowing rate should be used. Additional guidance is in SFAS No. 116 and APB No. 21.

As the time passes between the initial recording of a discounted pledge and its eventual collection, the PV increases since the time left before payment is shorter. Therefore, the discount element must be gradually "accreted" up to par (collection) value. This accretion should be recorded each year until the due date for the pledge arrives. The accretion is recorded as contribution income. (This treatment differs from that specified in APB No. 21 for business debts for which the accretion is recorded as interest income.)

PLEDGES FOR EXTENDED PERIODS.   There is one limitation to the general rule that pledges be recorded as assets. Occasionally, donors will indicate that they will make an open-ended pledge of support for an extended period of time. For example, if a donor promises to pay $5,000 a year for 20 years, would it be appropriate to record as an asset the full 20 years' pledge? In most cases, no; this would distort the financial statements. Most organizations follow the practice of not recording pledges for future years' support beyond a fairly short period. They feel that long-term open-ended pledges are inherently conditional on the donor's continued willingness to continue making payments and thus are harder to collect. These arguments have validity, and organizations should consider very carefully the likelihood of collection before recording pledges for support in future periods beyond five years.

ALLOWANCE FOR UNCOLLECTIBLE PLEDGES.   Not all pledges will be collected. People lose interest in an organization; their personal financial circumstances may change; they may move out of town. This is as true for charities as for businesses, but businesses will usually sue to collect unpaid debts; charities usually will not. Thus another important question is how large the allowance for uncollectible pledges should be. Most organizations have past experience to help answer this question. If over the years, 10 percent of pledges are not collected, then unless the economic climate changes, 10 percent is probably the right figure to use.

RECOGNITION AS INCOME.   The second, related question is: When should a pledge be recognized as income? This used to be a complicated question, requiring many pages of discussion in earlier editions of this Handbook. Now, the answer is easy: immediately upon receipt of an unconditional pledge. This is the same rule that applies to all kinds of gifts under SFAS No. 116. Conditional pledges are not recorded until the condition is met, at which time they are effectively unconditional pledges. Footnote disclosure of unrecorded conditional pledges should be made.

Under the earlier Audit Guides/SOP, pledges without purpose restrictions were recorded in the unrestricted fund. Only if the pledge has a purpose restriction would it be recorded in a restricted fund. Even pledges with explicit time restrictions were still recorded in the unrestricted fund, to reflect the flexibility of use that would exist when the pledge was collected. Under SFAS No. 116, all pledges are considered implicitly time-restricted, by virtue of their being unavailable for use until collected. Additionally, time-restricted gifts, including all pledges, are now reported in the temporarily restricted class of net assets. They are then reclassified to the unrestricted class when the specified time arrives.

This means that even a pledge not payable for 10 years or a pledge payable in many installments is recorded as revenue in full (less the discount to PV) in the temporarily restricted class in the year the pledge is first received. This is a major change from earlier practice, which generally deferred the pledge until the anticipated period of collection.

Sometimes a charity may not want to have to record a large pledge as immediate revenue; it may feel that its balance sheet is already healthy and recording more income would turn away other donors. If a pledge is unconditional, there is no choice: The pledge must be recorded. One way to mitigate this problem is to ask the donor to make the pledge conditional; then it is not recorded until some later time when the condition is met. Of course, there is a risk that the donor may not be as likely ever to pay a conditional pledge as one that is understood to be absolutely binding, so nonprofit organizations should consider carefully before requesting that a pledge be made conditional.

SFAS No. 116 requires that donors follow the same rules for recognition of the expense of making a gift as recipients do for the income: that is, immediately on payment or of making an unconditional pledge. Sometimes a charity will find a donor reluctant to make a large unconditional pledge but willing to make a conditional pledge. Fund raisers should be aware of the effect of the new accounting principles in SFAS No. 116 on donors' giving habits as well as on recipients' balance sheets.

Bequests.   A bequest is a special kind of pledge. Bequests should never be recorded before the donor dies—not because death is uncertain, but because a person can always change a will, and the charity may get nothing. (There is a special case: The pledge payable upon death. This is not really a bequest, it is just an ordinary pledge, and should be recorded as such if it is unconditional.)

After a person dies, the beneficiary organization is informed that it is named in the will, but this notification may occur long before the estate is probated and distribution made. Should such a bequest be recorded at the time the organization first learns of the bequest or at the time of receipt? The question is one of sufficiency of assets in the estate to fulfill the bequest. Since there is often uncertainty about what other amounts may have to be paid to settle debts, taxes, other bequests, claims of disinherited relatives, and so on, a conservative, and recommended, approach is not to record anything until the probate court has accounted for the estate and the amount available for distribution can be accurately estimated. At that time, the amount should be recorded in the same manner as other gifts.

Thus, if an organization is informed that it will receive a bequest of a specific amount, say $10,000, it should record this $10,000 as an asset. If instead the organization is informed that it will receive 10 percent of the estate, the total of which is not known, nothing would be recorded yet although footnote disclosure would likely be necessary if the amount could be sizable. Still a third possibility exists if the organization is told that while the final amount of the 10 percent bequest is not known, it will be at least some stated amount. In that instance, the minimum amount would be recorded with footnote disclosure of the contingent interest.

SPLIT-INTEREST GIFTS.   The term *split-interest* gifts is used to refer to irrevocable trusts and similar arrangements (also referred to as *deferred gifts*) where the interest in the gift is split between the donor (or another person specified by the donor) and the charity. These arrangements can be divided into two fundamentally different types of arrangements: lead interests and remainder interests. Lead interests are those in which the benefit to the charity "leads" or precedes the benefit to the donor (or other person designated by the donor). To put this into the terminology commonly used by trust lawyers, the charity is the "life tenant," and someone else is the "remainderman." The reverse situation is that of the "remainder" interest, where the donor (or the donor's designee) is the life tenant and the charity is the remainderman, that is, the entity to which the assets become available upon termination (often called the *maturity*) of the trust or other arrangement. There may or may not be further restrictions on the charity's use of the assets and/or the income therefrom after this maturity.

Under both types of arrangement, the donor makes an initial lump-sum payment into a fund. The amount is invested, and the income during the term of the arrangement is paid to the life tenant. In some cases, the arrangement is established as a trust under the trust laws of the applicable state.

In other cases, no separate trust is involved, rather the assets are held by the charity as part of its general assets. In some cases involving trusts, the charity is the trustee; in other cases, a third party is the trustee. Typical third-party trustees include banks and trust companies or other charities such as community foundations. Some arrangements are perpetual, that is, the charity never gains access to the corpus of the gift; others have a defined term of existence that will end either upon the occurrence of a specified event such as the death of the donor (or other specified person) or after the passage of a specified amount of time.

To summarize to this point, the various defining criteria applicable to these arrangements are:

- The charity's interest may be a lead interest or a remainder interest.
- The arrangement may be in the form of a trust or it may not.
- The assets may be held by the charity or held by a third party.
- The arrangement may be perpetual or it may have a defined term.
- Upon termination of the interest of the life tenant, the corpus may be unrestricted or restricted.

LEAD INTERESTS.   There are two kinds of such arrangements as normally conceived.[2] These are:

1. Charitable lead trust
2. Perpetual trust held by a third party

In both of these cases, the charity receives periodic payments representing distributions of income, but never gains unrestricted use of the assets that produce the income. In the first case, the payment stream is for a limited time; in case two, the payment stream is perpetual.

A *charitable lead trust* is always for a defined term, and usually held by the charity. At the termination of the trust, the corpus (principal of the gift) reverts to the donor or to another person specified by the donor (may be the donor's estate). Income during the term of the trust is paid to the charity; the income may be unrestricted or restricted. In effect, this arrangement amounts to an unconditional pledge, for a specified period, of the income from a specified amount of assets. The current value of the pledge is the discounted PV of the estimated stream of income over the term of the trust. Although the charity manages the assets during the term of the trust, it has no remainder interest in the assets.

A *perpetual trust held by a third party* is the same as the lead trust, except that the charity does not manage the assets, and the term of the trust is perpetual. Again the charity receives the income earned by the assets, but never gains the use of the corpus. In effect, there is no remainderman. This arrangement is also a pledge of income, but in this case the current value of the pledge is the discounted PV of a perpetual stream of income from the assets. Assuming a perfect market for investment securities, that amount will equal the current quoted market value of the assets of the trust or, if there is no quoted market value, then the "fair value," which is normally determined based on discounted future cash flows from the assets.

Some may argue that since the charity does not and never will have day-to-day control over the corpus of this type of trust, it should only record assets and income as the periodic distributions are received from the trustee. In fact, that is the way the income from this type of gift has historically been recorded. In the authors' view, this is overcome by the requirement in SFAS No. 116 that long-term unconditional pledges be recorded in full (discounted) when the pledge is initially received by the pledgee. Since SFAS No. 116 requires that the charity immediately record the full (discounted) amount of a traditional pledge, when all the charity has is a promise of future gifts, with the pledgor retaining control over the means to generate the gifts, then the charity surely must record

---

[2] It is also possible to consider both a simple pledge and a permanent endowment fund as forms of lead interests. In both cases, the charity receives periodic payments, but never gains unrestricted use of the assets that generate the income to make the payments. A pledge is for a limited time; an endowment fund pays forever.

immediately the entire amount (discounted) of a "pledge" where the assets that will generate the periodic payments are held in trust by a third party, and receipt of the payments by the charity is virtually assured.

A variation of this type of arrangement is a trust held by a third party in which the third party has discretion as to when and/or to whom to pay the periodic income. Since in this case the charity is not assured in advance of receiving any determinable amount, no amounts should be recorded by the charity until distributions are received from the trustee; these amounts are then recorded as contributions.

REMAINDER INTERESTS.   There are four types of these arrangements. These are:

1. Charitable remainder annuity trust (CRAT)
2. Charitable remainder unitrust (CRUT)
3. Charitable gift annuity (CGA)
4. Pooled income fund (also referred to as a life income fund)

These arrangements are always for a limited term, usually the life of the donor and/or another person or persons specified by the donor—often the donor's spouse. The donor or the donor's designee is the life tenant; the charity is the remainderman. Again, in the case of a trust, the charity may or may not be the trustee; in the case of a CGA, the charity usually is the holder of the assets. Upon termination of the arrangement, the corpus usually becomes available to the charity; the donor may or may not have placed further temporary or permanent restrictions on the corpus and/or the future income earned by the corpus.

In many states, the acceptance of these types of gifts is regulated by the state government—often the department of insurance—since, from the perspective of the donor, these arrangements are partly insurance contracts, essentially similar to a commercial annuity.

A *charitable remainder annuity trust (CRAT)* and *charitable remainder unitrust (CRUT)* differ only in the stipulated method of calculating the payments to the life tenant. An annuity trust pays a stated dollar amount that remains fixed over the life of the trust; a unitrust pays a stated percentage of the then current value of the trust assets. Thus, the dollar amount of the payments will vary with changes in the market value of the corpus. Accounting for the two types is the same except for the method of calculation of the amount of the PV of the life interest payable to the life tenant(s). In both cases, if current investment income is insufficient to cover the stipulated payments, corpus may have to be invaded to do so; however, the liability to the life tenant is limited to the assets of the trust.

A *charitable gift annuity (CGA)* differs from a CRAT only in that there is no trust; the assets are usually held among the general assets of the charity (some charities choose to set aside a pool of assets in a separate fund to cover annuity liabilities), and the annuity liability is a general liability of the charity—limited only by the charity's total assets.

A *pooled income fund (PIF)* (also sometimes called a *life income fund*) is actually a creation of the Internal Revenue Code Section 642(c)(5), which, together with Sec. 170, allows an income tax deduction to donors to such funds. (The amount of the deduction depends on the age(s) of the life tenant(s) and the value of the life interest and is less than that allowed for a simple charitable deduction directly to a charity, to reflect the value that the life tenant will be receiving in return for the gift.) The fund is usually managed by the charity. Many donors contribute to such a fund, which pools the gifts and invests the assets. During the period of each life tenant's interest in the fund, the life tenant is paid the actual income earned by that person's share of the corpus. (To this extent, these funds function essentially as mutual funds.) Upon termination of a life interest, the share of the corpus attributable to that life tenant becomes available to the charity.

ACCOUNTING FOR SPLIT-INTEREST GIFTS.   The essence of these arrangements is that they are pledges. In some cases, the pledge is of a stream of payments to the charity during the life of the arrangement (lead interests). In other cases, the pledge is of the value of the remainder interest. Calculation of the value of a lead interest is usually straightforward, as the term and the payments are well defined. Calculation of remainder interests is more complicated, since life expectancies are usually involved and the services of an actuary will likely be needed.

SFAS No. 116 gives very little guidance specific to split-interests. Chapter 6 of the new AICPA Audit Guide for not-for-profit organizations discusses in detail the accounting for split-interest gifts. Briefly, the assets contributed are valued at their fair value on the date of gift (the same as for any donated assets). The related contribution revenue is usually the PV of the amounts expected to become available to the organization, discounted from the expected date(s) of such availability (in the case of a remainder interest, the actuarial death date of the last remaining life tenant.) The difference between these two numbers is, in the case of a lead interest, the PV of the amount to be distributed at the end of the term of the agreement according to the donor's directions, and, under a remainder agreement, the PV of the actuarial liability to make payments to life tenants.

(iv) Transfers of Assets to a Not-for-Profit Organization or Charitable Trust that Raises or Holds Contributions for Others.   An intermediary, as defined in SFAS No. 116, that receives cash or other financial assets, as defined in SFAS No. 125, should report the assets received and a liability to the specified beneficiary, both measured at the fair value of the assets received. An intermediary that receives nonfinancial assets may but need not report the assets and the liability, provided that the intermediary reports consistently from period to period and discloses its accounting policy. A specified beneficiary of a charitable trust agreement having a trustee with a duty to hold and manage its assets for the benefit of the beneficiary should report as an asset its rights to trust assets—an interest in the net assets of the recipient organization, a beneficial interest, or a receivable—unless the recipient organization is explicitly granted variance power in the transferring instrument—unilateral power (power to act without approval from any other party) to redirect the use of the assets to another beneficiary.

If the beneficiary and the recipient organization are financially interrelated, the beneficiary should report its interest in the net assets of the recipient organization and adjust that interest for its share of the change in the net assets of the recipient organization, similar to the equity method. They are financially interrelated if both of the following are present:

1. One has the ability to influence the operating and financial decisions of the other. That may be demonstrated in several ways:
   ○ The organizations are affiliates.
   ○ One has considerable representation on the governing board of the other.
   ○ The charter or bylaws of one limit its activities to those that are beneficial to the other.
   ○ An agreement between them allows one to actively participate in policy making of the other, such as setting priorities, budgets, and management compensation.
2. One has an ongoing economic interest in the net assets of the other.

If the beneficiary has an unconditional right to receive all or a portion of the specified cash flows from a charitable trust or other identifiable pool of assets, the beneficiary should report that beneficial interest, measuring and subsequently remeasuring it at fair value, using a technique such as PV. In all other cases, a beneficiary should report its rights to the assets held by a recipient organization as a receivable and contribution revenue in conformity with the provisions of SFAS No. 116, paragraphs 6, 15, and 20, for unconditional promises to give.

If the recipient organization is explicitly granted variance power by the donor, the beneficiary should not report its potential for future distributions from the assets held by the recipient organization.

In general, a recipient organization that accepts assets from a donor and agrees to use them on behalf of them, or transfer them, or both to a specified beneficiary is not a donee. It should report its liability to the specified beneficiary and the cash or other financial assets received from the donor, all measured at the fair value of the assets received. In general, a recipient organization that receives nonfinancial assets may but need not report its liability and the assets, as long as the organization reports consistently from period to period and discloses its accounting policy.

A recipient organization that has been explicitly granted variance power acts as a donee.

A resource provider should report as an asset and the recipient organization should report as a liability a transfer of assets if one or more of the following is present:

- The transfer is subject to the resource provider's unilateral right to redirect the use of the assets to another beneficiary.
- The resource provider's promise to give is conditional or otherwise revocable or repayable.
- The resource provider controls the recipient organization and specifies an unaffiliated beneficiary.
- The resource provider specifies itself or its affiliate as the beneficiary and the transfer is not an equity transaction, as discussed next.

A transfer of assets to a recipient organization is an equity transaction if all of the following are present:

- The resource provider specifies itself or its affiliate as the beneficiary.
- The resource provider and the recipient organization are financially interrelated.
- Neither the resource provider nor its affiliate expects payment of the assets, though payment of return on the assets may be expected.

A resource provider that specifies itself as beneficiary should report an equity transaction as an interest in the net assets of the recipient organization or as an increase in a previously reported interest. If a resource provider specifies an affiliate as beneficiary, it should report an equity transaction as a separate line in its statement of activities, and the affiliate should report an interest in the net assets of the recipient organization. A recipient organization should report an equity transaction as a separate line item in its statement of activities.

A not-for-profit organization that transfers assets to a recipient organization and specifies itself or its affiliate as the beneficiary should disclose the following for each period for which a statement of financial position is presented:

- The identity of the recipient organization
- Whether variance power was granted to the recipient organization and, if so, its terms
- The terms under which amounts will be distributed to the resource provider or its affiliate
- The aggregate amount reported in the statement of financial position for the transfers and whether it is reported as an interest in the net assets of the recipient organization or as another asset, such as a beneficial interest in assets held by others or a refundable advance

Exhibit 35.1 demonstrates the process that should be followed to decide how to account for such transfers and the related accounting for them.

Numbers are paragraph references

Examples

Accounting by:

Resource Provider/Donor (A) | Recipient (B) | Beneficiary (C)

Start: Resource provider transfers assets to recipient

One or more of criteria in 17 met?*

- Corporate foundation;
- Revocable trust;
- Endowment fund held by another organization

Refundable advance (92)

Dr. Advance (55;59)
Cr. Asset or Payable (17)

Dr. Asset
Cr. Liability
(Refundable advance (17; 54;58))

Nothing, until all events occur giving C an irrevocable right to a measurable asset; (if C is A, then see A)

All of criteria in 18 met?**

- Endowment fund held by another organization

Equity transaction:
1. C is A
2. C is affiliate of A

1. Dr. Equity interest in B
2. Dr. Change in Net assets #
   Cr. Asset or payable

Dr. Asset
Cr. Change in Net assets #

(1. N/A (C is A))
2. Dr. Equity interest in B
   Cr. change in Net assets #

- separately from revenues and gains (18)

Contribution by A

Dr. Contribution expense
Cr. Asset or payable
(SFAS 116, para. 18)

(for all following scenarios)

(3, referring to 8-16)

Is B an Intermediary? (8;67)

Facilitator

Is B a Trustee for the benefit of C (9)

- Irrevocable trust;
- Some split interests

Dr. Asset
Cr. Liability to C (8;34)

If the assets are nonfinancial, this recipient entry is optional

Dr. Receivable from B (15)
Cr. Revenue (15)

Not specified (9;36;80)

Dr. Interest in assets of B
- receivable (15;36;88)
Cr. Revenue (36)

to second page

* Para. 17 criteria: Any of:
  a. Transfer is subject to resource provider's unilateral right to redirect assets to another beneficiary;
  b. Transfer accompanied by resource provider's conditional promise to give, or is otherwise revocable;
  c. Resource provider controls recipient and specified an unaffiliated beneficiary; or
  d. Resource provider specifies itself or its affiliate as beneficiary, & transfer is not an equity transaction (para. 18)
** - Para. 18 criteria: All of:
  a. Resource provider specifies itself or its affiliate as beneficiary;
  b. Resource provider and recipient are financially interrelated; and
  c. Neither resource provider nor affiliate expects repayment of corpus, but may expect to receive income.

Exhibit 35.1   SFASNo. 136, "Transfer of Assets to a Not-for-Profit Organization or Charitable Trust

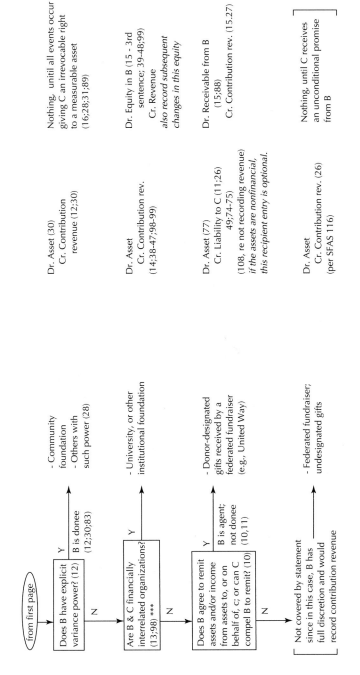

Nothing, until all events occur giving C an irrevocable right to a measurable asset (16;28;31;89)

Dr. Equity in B (15 - 3rd sentence; 39-48;99)
  Cr. Revenue
  also record subsequent changes in this equity

Dr. Receivable from B (15;88)
  Cr. Contribution rev. (15.27)

Nothing, until C receives an unconditional promise from B

Dr. Asset (30)
  Cr. Contribution revenue (12;30)

Dr. Asset
  Cr. Contribution rev. (14;38-47;98-99)

Dr. Asset (77)
  Cr. Liability to C (11;26) 49;74-75)
  (108, re not recording revenue *if the assets are nonfinancial, this recipient entry is optional.*)

Dr. Asset
  Cr. Contribution rev. (26) (per SFAS 116)

- Community foundation
- Others with such power (28)

- University, or other institutional foundation

- Donor-designated gifts received by a federated fundraiser (e.g., United Way)

- Federated fundraiser; undesignated gifts

from first page

Does B have explicit variance power? (12)

Y → B is donee (12;30;83)

N ↓

Are B & C financially interrelated organizations? (13;98) ***

Y →

N ↓

Does B agree to remit assets and/or income from assets to, or on behalf of, c; or can C compel B to remit? (10)

Y → B is agent; not donee (10,11)

N ↓

Not covered by statement since in this case, B has full discretion and would record contribution revenue

*** - Para. 13 definition of "financially interrelated". Both of:
a. One organization has ability to influence operating & financial decisions of the other, such as: by being affiliates; having considerable govering board representation; having the charter or by-laws of one limiting its activities to those which benefit the other; having a formal agreement between them providing for influence in policymaking; and
b. One has an ongoing economic interest in the net assets of the other, which is a residual interest which changes as a result of the activities of the other (as contrasted with a fixed receivable) (102).
(Also consider whether consolidation may be required (100).)

Exhibit 35.1   *Continued*.

(k) RELATED ORGANIZATIONS.   Practice has varied regarding when not-for-profit entities combine the financial statements of affiliated organizations with those of the central organization. Part of the reason for this is the widely diverse nature of relationships among such organizations, which often creates difficulty in determining when criteria for combination have been met.

(i) Definition of the Reporting Entity.   There are two issues here, but they involve the same concepts. First is the question of gifts to affiliated fund-raising entities and whether the affiliate should record the gift as its own revenue, followed by gift or grant expense when their money is passed on to the parent organization, or should record the initial receipt as an amount held on behalf of the parent. Such gifts are often called *pass-through gifts* since they pass through one entity to another entity. Second is the broader question of when the financial data of affiliated entities should be combined with that of a central organization for purposes of presenting the central organization's financial statements. If the data are combined, the question of pass-through gifts need not be addressed since the end result is the same regardless of which entity records gifts initially.

The concept underlying the combining of financial data of affiliates is to present to the financial statement reader information that portrays the complete financial picture of a group of entities that effectively function as one entity. In the business setting, the determination of when a group of entities is really just a single entity is normally made by assessing the extent to which the "parent" entity has a controlling financial interest in the other entities in the group. In other words, can the parent use for its own benefit the financial resources of the others without obtaining permission from any party outside the parent? When one company owns another company, such permission would be automatic; if the management of the affiliate refused, the parent would exercise its authority to replace management.

In the not-for-profit world, such "ownership" of one entity by another rarely exists. Affiliated organizations are more often related by agreements of various sorts, but the level of control embodied in such agreements is usually far short of ownership. The "Friends of the Museum" may exist primarily to support the Museum, but it is likely a legally independent organization with only informal ties to its "parent." The Museum may ask, but the Friends may choose its own time and method to respond. Further, the Museum may have no way to legally compel the Friends to do its bidding if the Friends resist.

The issue for donors is, if I give to the Friends, am I really supporting the Museum? Or if I am assessing the financial condition of the Museum, is it reasonable to include the resources of the Friends in the calculation? Even though the Friends is legally separate, and even though the Friends does not have to turn its assets over to the Museum, isn't it reasonable to assume that if the Museum got into financial trouble, the Friends would help?

Examples of other types of relationships often found among not-for-profits include: a national organization and local affiliates; an educational institution and student and alumni groups, research organizations, and hospitals; a religious institution and local churches, schools, seminaries, cemeteries, broadcasting stations, pension funds, and charities. Since each individual relationship may be different, it requires much judgment to decide which entities should be combined and which should not.

Existing accounting literature includes some guidance, but more is needed. The basic rules for businesses are:

- ARB Opinion No. 51, "Consolidated Financial Statements"
- APB Opinion No. 18, "The Equity Method of Accounting for Investments in Common Stock"
- SFAS No. 94, "Consolidation of All Majority-Owned Subsidiaries"

While, strictly speaking, these rules apply to not-for-profits only in the context of a for-profit subsidiary, the concepts embodied therein and the related background discussions are helpful to someone considering the issue. Rules for not-for-profits are in the AICPA SOP 94-3. These rules focus largely on the question of whether one not-for-profit controls another. Exhibit 35.2 is

Following is a list of factors that may be helpful to not-for-profit organizations in deciding whether to combine financial statements of affiliated organizations and to auditors in assessing the appropriateness of the client's combination decision. Many of these factors are not absolutely determinative by themselves but must be considered in conjunction with other factors.

Factors Whose Presence Indicate Control	Factors Whose Presence Indicate Lack of Control
Organization Relationship	
1. A is clearly described as controlled by, for the benefit of, or an affiliate of R in some of the following:	A is described as independent of R or no formal relationship is indicated.
Articles/charter/by-laws	
Operating/affiliation agreement	
Fund-raising material/membership brochure	
Annual report	
Grant proposals	
Application for tax-exempt status.	
Governance	
2. A's board has considerable overlap in membership with R; common officers.	There is little or no overlap.
3. A's board members and/or officers are appointed by R, or are subject to approval of R's board, officers, or members.	A's board is self-perpetuating with no input from R.
4. Major decisions of A's board, officers, or staff are subject to review, approval, or ratification by R.	A's decisions are made autonomously; or even if in theory subject to such control, R has in fact never or rarely exercised control and does not intend to do so.
Financial	
5. A's budget is subject to review or approval by R.	Budget not subject to R's approval.
6. Some or all of A's disbursements are subject to approval or countersignature by R.	Checks may be issued without R's approval.
7. A's excess of revenue over expenses or fund balances or portions thereof are subject to being transferred to R at R's request, or are automatically transferred	Although some of A's financial resources may be transferred to R, this is done only at the discretion of A's board.
8. A's activities are largely financed by grants, loans, or transfers from R, or from other sources determined by R's board	A's activities are financed from sources determined by A's board.
9. A's by-laws indicate that its resources are intended to be used for activities similar to those of R.	A's by-laws limit uses of resources to purposes which do not include R's activities
10. A's fund-raising appeals give donors the impression that gifts will be used to further R's programs	Appeals give the impression that funds will be used by A.

(Continues)

Exhibit 35.2   Factors related to control that may indicate that an affiliated organization (A) should be combined with the reporting organization (R), if other criteria for combination are met.

Factors Whose Presence Indicate Control	Factors Whose Presence Indicate Lack of Control
Operating	
11. A shares with R many of the following operating functions: Personnel/payroll Purchasing Professional services Fund-raising Accounting, treasury Office space	Few operating functions are shared; or reimbursement of costs is on a strictly arm's-length basis with formal contracts.
12. Decisions about A's program or other activities are made by R or are subject to R's review or approval.	A's decisions are made autonomously.
13. A's activities are almost exclusively for the benefit of R's members.	Activities benefit persons unaffiliated with R.
Other	
14. A is exempt under IRC Section 501(c) (3) and R is exempt under some other subsection of 501(c), and A's main purpose for existence appears to be to solicit tax-deductible contributions to further R's interest.	A's purposes appear to include significant activities apart from those of R.

Exhibit 35.2   *Continued.*

designed to help not-for-profits and their accountants decide whether sufficient control exists to require combination.

In 1994, the AICPA issued a new SOP (94-3) on combining related entities when one is a not-for-profit organization. This SOP requires:

- When a not-for-profit organization owns a majority of the voting equity interest in a for-profit entity, the not-for-profit must consolidate the for-profit into its financial statements, regardless of how closely related the activities of the for-profit are to those of the not-for-profit.
- If the not-for-profit organization owns less than a majority interest in a for-profit but still has significant influence over the for-profit, it must report the for-profit under the equity method of accounting, except that the not-for-profit may report its investment in the for-profit at market value if it wishes. If the not-for-profit does not have significant influence over the for-profit, it should value its investment in accordance with the applicable audit guide.
- When a not-for-profit organization has a relationship with another not-for-profit in which the "parent" both exercises control over the board appointments of and has an economic interest in the affiliate, it must consolidate the affiliate.
- If the not-for-profit organization has either control *or* an economic beneficial interest but not both, disclosure of the relationship and significant financial information is required.
- If the parent controls the affiliate by means other than board appointments, and has an economic interest, consolidation is permitted but not required. If the affiliate is not consolidated, extensive footnote disclosures about the affiliate are required.

(ii) Pass-Through Gifts.   When one organization (C, in Exhibit 35.3) raises funds for another organization (R, in the exhibit), and either C is not required to be consolidated into R under the above rules, or C is consolidated into R, but C also issues separate financial statements, the question of whether C should record amounts raised by it on behalf of R should be reported by C as its revenue (contribution income) or as amounts held for the benefit of R (a liability). If such amounts are reported by C as a liability, C's statement of revenue and expenses will not ever include the funds raised for R. This issue is of considerable concern to organizations such as federated fund-raisers (such as United Ways), community foundations, and other organizations such as foundations affiliated with universities, which raise (and sometimes hold) funds for the benefit of other organizations. Paragraphs 4 and 53 of SFAS No. 116 indicate that when the pass-through entity has little or no discretion over the use of the amounts raised (i.e., the original donor—D in the exhibit—has specified that C must pass the gift on to R), C should not report the amount as a contribution to it. FASB Interpretation No. 42 clarifies that if a resource provider specifies a third-party beneficiary or beneficiaries and explicitly grants the recipient organization the unilateral power to redirect the use of the assets away from the specified beneficiary or beneficiaries—grants it variance power—the organization acts as a donee and a donor rather than as an agent, trustee, or intermediary and should report the amount provided as a contribution. Exhibit 35.3 is a list of factors to be considered in assessing whether a pass-through entity should record amounts raised for others as revenue or as a liability.

"Economic interest" generally means four kinds of relationship: an affiliate that raises gifts for the parent, an affiliate that holds assets for the parent, an affiliate that performs significant functions assigned to it by the parent, or the parent has guaranteed the debt of or is otherwise committed to provide funds to the affiliate.

(l) CASH FLOWS.   SFAS No. 95, which requires businesses to present a statement of cash flows (in lieu of the former statement of changes in financial position), did not apply to not-for-profits. The new FASB standard on financial statements (No. 117) requires the presentation of a statement of cash flows. A sample statement of cash flows, following the example in the Statement, is illustrated in Exhibit 35.4.

(m) GOVERNMENTAL VERSUS NONGOVERNMENTAL ACCOUNTING.   In 1989, the Financial Accounting Foundation, overseer of the FASB and its counterpart in the governmental sector, the (see discussion in "State and Local Government Accounting") resolved the question of the jurisdiction of each body. A question related to several types of organizations, mainly not-for-profits, that exist in both governmental and nongovernmental forms. These types include institutions of higher education, museums, libraries, hospitals, and others. The issue is whether it is more important to have, for example, all hospitals follow a single set of accounting principles, or to have all types of governmental entities do so. This matter was resolved by conferring on GASB jurisdiction over all governmental entities.

35.3 SPECIFIC TYPES OF ORGANIZATIONS

In 1993, the FASB issued two new accounting pronouncements, SFAS No. 116, *Accounting for Contributions Received and Contributions Made,* and No. 117, *Financial Statements of Not-for-Profit Organizations,* which supersede many provisions of the old AICPA Audit Guides.

This chapter summarizes the accounting and reporting principles discussed in the new FASB standards, and, the provisions of the new AICPA not-for-profit Audit Guide. For the most part, the FASB standards prescribe the same accounting treatment for a given transaction by all types of not-for-profit organizations. One exception to that rule is a requirement that voluntary health and welfare organizations continue to present a statement of functional expenses. Other types of organizations are not required to present this statement, although they may if they wish. More detailed discussions of certain accounting and reporting standards in the new FASB documents

Following is a list of factors that may be helpful to:

- Not-for-profit organizations in deciding whether assets received by them are contributions within the meaning of SFAS No. 116, or are transfers in which the entity is acting as an agent, trustee, or intermediary;
- Auditors, in assessing the appropriateness of the client's decision.

No one factor is usually determinative by itself; all relevant factors should be considered together.

D = Original Noncharitable Donor (Individual or Business)
C = Initial Charitable Recipient/Donor (Sometimes there is more than one charity in the chain.)
R = Ultimate Charitable or Individual Recipient

Factors Whose Presence Indicate Recording by C as Revenue and Expense May Not Be Appropriate	Factors Whose Presence Indicate Recording by C as Revenue and Expense May Be Appropriate
General factors—relevant to all gifts:	D has not restricted the gift in this manner. D specifies a third-party beneficiary or beneficiaries and explicitly grants C the unilateral power to redirect the use of the assets away from the specified beneficiary or beneficiaries—grants it variance power.
1. D has restricted the gift by specifying that it must be passed on to R.*	
2. C is controlled by D or by R.	C is not controlled by D nor R.
3. Two or more of D, C, and R are under common control, have overlapping boards or management, share facilities or professional advisors.*	Factor not present.
4. Even without the intermediation of C, D would still easily be able to make the gift to R.	Without such intermediation, D would not easily be able to make a gift to R (D is unaware of existence of R or of R's needs, geographic separation, etc.).*
5. The stated program activities of C and R are similar.	The program activities are not particularly similar.
6. C has solicited the gift from D under the specific pretense of passing it on to R.*	C has solicited the gift ostensibly for C's own activities.
7. C does not ever obtain legal title to the assets composing the gift.*	C does at some time obtain legal title to the assets.
8. D and/or other entities under common control are major sources of support for C.	Factor not present.
9. R and/or other entities under common control are major destinations for C's charitable resources.	Factor not present.
9a. Both factors 8 and 9 are present.*	One but not both present.
10. The "chain" from D to R consists of several Cs.	The chain consists of only one or very few Cs.
11. Gifts passed from D to C are frequently in exactly the same dollar amount (or very close) as gifts subsequently passed from C to R.*	Factor not present.
12. Times elapsed between receipt and disbursement of particular amounts by C are short (less than a month).	Times elapsed are relatively long or variable.

Exhibit 35.3   Factors to be considered in deciding whether a "pass-through" gift is truly revenue and expense to charity (C).

Factors Whose Presence Indicate Recording by C as Revenue and Expense May Not Be Appropriate	Factors Whose Presence Indicate Recording by C as Revenue and Expense May Be Appropriate
13. C makes pledges to R, payment of which is contingent on receipt of gifts from D.	Factor not present.
14. C was created only shortly prior to receiving the gift, and/or C appears to have been created specifically for the sole purpose of passing gifts from D on to R.*	Factor not present.

Factors especially relevant to gifts-in-kind:

15. C never takes physical possession of the gift at an owned or rented facility	C does have physical possession of the items at some time, at a facility normally owned or rented by it.
16. The nature of the items is not consistent with the program service activities of C as stated in its Form 1023, 990, organizing documents, fund-raising appeals, annual report.*	The nature is consistent with C's stated program activities.
17. The gift was not solicited by C.	C specifically solicited the particular items from D.
18. The quantity of items is large in relation to the foreseeable needs of C or its donees.	Factor not present.
19. Factor not present.	Members of the board or staff of C have specific technical or professional expertise about the items, and actively participate in deliberations about where to obtain the items and how best to use them.*
20. D appears to be the only source from which C considers acquiring the item. Same for C/R.	C has several potential or actual sources for the item. Same for R.
21. C receives numerous types of items dissimilar in their purpose or use.	Factor not present.
22. C receives items from D and passes them on to R in essentially the same form.	C "adds value" to the items by sorting, repackaging, cleaning, repairing, or testing them.*
23. C *and* either or both of D and R have little in the way of program services other than distribution of gifts in kind to other charities.	Either C or *both* D and R have significant program services other than distribution of gifts in kind.
24. The value assigned to the items by D or C appears to be inflated.	Factor not present.
25. There is a consistent pattern of transfers of items along the same "chain" (D to C to R, etc.).	Factor not present.
26. Factor not present.	C incurs significant expenses (freight, insurance, storage, etc.) in handling the items.

*Factors considered to be generally more significant.

Exhibit 35.3   *Continued.*

NATIONAL ASSOCIATION OF ENVIRONMENTALISTS
STATEMENT OF CASH FLOWS
For the Year Ended December 31, 20XX

Operating cash flows:	
Cash received from:	
Sales of goods and services	$ 198,835
Investment income	14,607
Gifts and grants:	
Unrestricted	230,860
Restricted	37,400
Cash paid to employees and suppliers	(265,854)
Cash paid to charitable beneficiaries	(83,285)
Interest paid	(350)
Net operating cash flows	132,213
Financing cash flows:	
Nonexpendable gifts	31,500
Proceeds from borrowing	5,000
Repayment of debt	(5,000)
Net financing cash flows	31,500
Investing cash flows:	
Purchase of building and equipment	(38,617)
Purchase of investments	(60,000)
Proceeds from sale of investments	50,000
Net investing cash flows	(48,617)
Net increase in cash	115,096
Cash: Beginning of year	11,013
End of year	$ 126,109

Reconciliation of Excess of Revenues over Expenses to
Operating Cash Flows:

Excess of Revenues over Expenses	$ 161,316
Add: Depreciation expense	13,596
Less: Appreciation of investments	(33,025)
Changes in: Receivables	(6,939)
Payables and deferred income	28,765
Nonexpendable contributions	(31,500)
Operating cash flows	$ 132,213

Exhibit 35.4   Statement of Cash Flows, derived from data included in Exhibits 35.5 and 35.6.

will also be found elsewhere in this chapter. For example, a full discussion of accounting for contributions is in Subsection 35.2(j)(iii).

(a) VOLUNTARY HEALTH AND WELFARE ORGANIZATIONS.   The term "voluntary health and welfare organization" first entered the accounting world with the publication in 1964 of the first edition of the so-called "Black Book," Standards of Accounting and Financial Reporting for Voluntary Health and Welfare Organizations, by the National Health Council and the National Social Welfare Assembly. The term has been retained through two successor editions of that book and was used by the American Institute of Certified Public Accountants in the title of its "audit guide," Audits of Voluntary Health and Welfare Organizations, first published in 1967.

In 1974, the AICPA issued a revised Audit Guide, prepared by its Committee on Voluntary Health and Welfare Organizations. This Audit Guide was prepared to assist the independent auditor in examinations of voluntary health and welfare organizations.

"Voluntary health and welfare organizations" are those not-for-profit organizations that "derive their revenue primarily from voluntary contributions from the general public to be used for general or specific purposes connected with health, welfare, or community services."[3] Note that there are two separate parts to this definition: first, the organization must derive its revenue from voluntary contributions from the general public, and second, the organization must be involved with health, welfare, or community services.

Many organizations fit the second part of this definition, but receive a substantial portion of their revenues from sources other than public contributions. For example, an opera company would not be a voluntary health and welfare organization because its primary source of income is box office receipts, although it exists for the common good. A YMCA would be excluded because normally it receives most of its revenues from dues and program fees. On the other hand, a museum would be excluded, even if it were to receive most of its revenue from contributions, since its activities are educational, not in the areas of health and welfare.

(i) Financial Statements. SFAS No. 117 provides for four principal financial statements for voluntary health and welfare organizations, thus superseding the financial statements discussed in the Guide. Examples are shown in this chapter. These four statements are:

1. Balance Sheet (Exhibit 35.5)
2. Statement of Support, Revenue and Expenses, and Changes in Net Assets (Exhibit 35.6)
3. Statement of Cash Flows (Exhibit 35.4)
4. Statement of Functional Expenses (Exhibit 35.7)

The sample financial statements presented in SFAS No. 117 are for illustrative purposes only, and some variation from the ones presented may be appropriate, as long as the required disclosure elements are shown.

(ii) Balance Sheet. Exhibit 35.5 shows a Balance Sheet for the National Association of Environmentalists. Although SFAS No. 117 only requires (and illustrates) a single-column balance sheet showing the totals of assets, liabilities, and net assets (and net assets by class), many organizations will wish to show more detail of assets and liabilities, but not necessarily by class. This is acceptable.

Funds versus Classes. Note that the columns on the balance sheet reflect the funds used for bookkeeping purposes. This is permissible, as long as the net asset amounts for each of the three classes defined in SFAS No. 117 are shown in the net assets section of the balance sheet.

Comparison Column. In Exhibit 35.5 we have shown the totals for the previous year to provide a comparison for the reader. SFAS No. 117 does not require presentation of a comparison column, but it is recommended.

Designation of Unrestricted Net Assets. While it is a little more awkward to show when the balance sheet is presented in a columnar fashion as in Exhibit 35.5, it is still possible to disclose the composition of the unrestricted net assets of $135,516.

For example, the unrestricted net assets of the National Association of Environmentalists of $135,516 (Exhibit 35.5) could be split into several amounts, representing the board's present intention of how it plans to use this amount. Perhaps $50,000 of it is intended for Project Seaweed,

---

[3] Appendix D of SFAS No. 117.

NATIONAL ASSOCIATION OF ENVIRONMENTALISTS
BALANCE SHEET
December 31, 19X2 and 20XX

| | December 31, 20XX | | | | | December 31, 20XX |
| | Current Funds | | Endowment | Fixed Asset | Total | Total |
ASSETS	Unrestricted	Restricted	Funds	Funds	All Funds	All Funds
Current assets:						
Cash	$ 58,392	$17,151	$ 8,416	$ 2,150	$ 86,109	$ 11,013
Savings accounts	40,000				40,000	
Accounts receivable	3,117				3,117	918
Investments, at market	86,195		226,119		312,314	269,289
Pledges receivable	4,509	1,000			5,509	769
Total current assets	192,213	18,151	234,535	2,150	447,049	281,989
Fixed assets, at cost				111,135	111,135	72,518
Less: Accumulated depreciation				(19,615)	(19,615)	(6,019)
Net fixed assets				91,520	91,520	66,499
Total assets	$192,213	$18,151	$234,535	$ 93,670	$538,569	$348,488
LIABILITIES AND NET ASSETS						
Current liabilities:						
Accounts payable	$ 54,181				$ 54,181	$ 25,599
Deferred income	2,516				2,516	2,333
Total current liabilities	56,697				56,697	27,932
Net assets:						
Unrestricted	135,516			$ 93,670	229,186	124,631
Temporarily restricted		$18,151			18,151	5,915
Permanently restricted			$234,535		234,535	190,010
Total	135,516	18,151	234,535	93,670	481,872	320,556
Total liabilities and net assets	$192,213	$18,151	$234,535	$ 93,670	$538,569	$348,488

Exhibit 35.5   A balance sheet prepared in columnar format.

NATIONAL ASSOCIATION OF ENVIRONMENTALISTS
STATEMENT OF SUPPORT, REVENUE AND EXPENSES, AND CHANGES IN NET ASSETS
For the Year Ended December 31, 20XX

	Unrestricted	Temporarily Restricted	Permanently Restricted	Total
Support:				
Contributions and gifts	$174,600	$38,400	$ 10,000	$223,000
Bequests	60,000		21,500	81,500
Total support	234,600	38,400	31,500	304,500
Revenues:				
Membership dues	20,550			20,550
Research projects	127,900			127,900
Advertising income	33,500			33,500
Subscriptions to nonmembers	18,901			18,901
Dividends and interest income	14,607			14,607
Appreciation of investments	30,000		3,025	33,025
Total revenues	245,458		3,025	248,483
Total support and revenues	480,058	38,400	34,525	552,983
Net assets released from restriction	26,164	(26,164)		
Expenses:				
Program services:				
"National Environment" magazine	110,500			110,500
Clean-up month campaign	126,617			126,167
Lake Erie project	115,065			115,065
Total program services	352,182			352,182
Supporting services:				
Management and general	33,516			33,516
Fund raising	5,969			5,969
Total supporting services	39,485			39,485
Total expenses	391,667			391,667
Excess (deficit) of revenues over expenses	114,555	12,236	34,525	161,316
Other changes in net assets:				
Transfer of unrestricted resources to				
meet challenge grant	(10,000)		10,000	—
Change in net assets	104,555	12,236	44,525	161,316
Net assets, beginning of year	124,631	5,915	190,010	320,556
Net assets, end of year	$229,186	$18,151	$234,535	$481,872

Exhibit 35.6   Income statement that meets the requirements of SFAS No. 117.

and the balance is available for undesignated purposes. The net assets section of the Balance Sheet would appear:

Net assets:	
Designated by the board for Project Seaweed	$ 50,000
Undesignated, available for current purposes	85,516
	$135,516

NATIONAL ASSOCIATION OF ENVIRONMENTALISTS
STATEMENT OF FUNCTIONAL EXPENSES
For the Year Ended December 31, 20XX

	Total All Expenses	Program Services				Supporting Services		
		"National Environment" Magazine	Clean-up Month Compaign	Lake Erie Project	Total Program	Management and General	Fund Raising	Total Supporting
Salaries	$170,773	$ 24,000	$ 68,140	$ 60,633	$152,773	$15,000	$3,000	$18,000
Payroll taxes and employee benefits	22,199	3,120	8,857	7,882	19,859	1,950	390	2,340
Total compensation	192,972	27,120	76,997	68,515	172,632	16,950	3,390	20,340
Printing	84,071	63,191	18,954	515	82,660	1,161	250	1,411
Mailing, postage, and shipping	14,225	10,754	1,188	817	12,759	411	1,055	1,466
Rent	19,000	3,000	6,800	5,600	15,400	3,000	600	3,600
Telephone	5,615	895	400	1,953	3,248	2,151	216	2,367
Outside art	14,865	3,165	11,700	—	14,865	—	—	—
Local travel	1,741	—	165	915	1,080	661	—	661
Conferences and conventions	6,328	—	1,895	2,618	4,513	1,815	—	1,815
Depreciation	13,596	2,260	2,309	5,616	10,185	3,161	250	3,411
Legal and audit	2,000	—	—	—	—	2,000	—	2,000
Supplies	31,227	—	1,831	28,516	30,347	761	119	880
Miscellaneous	6,027	115	4,378	—	4,493	1,445	89	1,534
Total	$391,667	$110,500	$126,617	$115,065	$352,182	$33,516	$5,969	$39,485

Exhibit 35.7 An analysis of the various program expenses showing the natural expense categories making up each of the functional or program categories.

As monies are expended for Project Seaweed in subsequent periods, they would be recorded as an expense in the Statement of Support, Revenue and Expenses, and Changes in Net Assets. At the same time, the amount of the net assets designated by the board for Project Seaweed would be reduced and the amount "undesignated" would be increased by the same amount.

(iii) Statement of Support, Revenue and Expenses, and Changes in Net Assets.   Exhibit 35.6 shows a Statement of Support, Revenue and Expenses, and Changes in Net Assets for the National Association of Environmentalists. This is the format shown in SFAS No. 117, with some modifications (discussed below).

Reporting of Expenses

FUNCTIONAL CLASSIFICATION OF EXPENSES.   Exhibit 35.6 shows the expenses of the National Association of Environmentalists reported on a functional basis. This type of presentation requires management to tell the reader how much of its funds were expended for each program category and the amounts spent on supporting services, including fund raising.

SFAS No. 117 states that this functional reporting is not optional. SFAS No. 117 requires that disclosure of expenses by function must be made either in the primary financial statements or in the footnotes.

In many instances, the allocation of salaries between functional or program categories should be based on time reports and similar analyses. Other expenses such as rent, utilities, and maintenance will be allocated based on floor space. Each organization will have to develop time and expense accumulation procedures that will provide the necessary basis for allocation. Organizations have to have reasonably sophisticated procedures to be able to allocate expenses between various categories. An excellent reference source is the third edition (1988) of the "Black Book," *Standards of Accounting and Financial Reporting for Voluntary Health and Welfare Organizations.*

PROGRAM SERVICES.   Not-for-profit organizations exist to perform services either for the public or for the members of the organization. They do not exist to provide employment for their employees or to perpetuate themselves. They exist to serve a particular purpose. The Audit Guide re-emphasizes this by requiring the organization to identify major program services and their related costs. Some organizations may have only one specific program category, but most will have several. Each organization should decide for itself into how many categories it wishes to divide its program activities.

SUPPORTING SERVICES.   Supporting services are those expenses that do not directly relate to performing the functions for which the organization was established, but that nevertheless are essential to the continued existence of the organization.

The Statement of Support, Revenue and Expenses, and Changes in Net Assets must clearly disclose the amount of supporting services. These are broken down between fund raising and administrative (management and general) expenses. This distinction between supporting and program services is required, as is the separate reporting of fund raising.

Management and General Expenses.   This is probably the most difficult of the supporting categories to define because a major portion of the time of top management usually will relate more directly to program activities than to management and general. Yet many think, incorrectly, that top management should be considered entirely "management and general." The AICPA Audit Guide defines management and general expenses as follows:

> those that are not identifiable with a single program, fund-raising activity, or membership-development activity but that are indispensable to the conduct of those activities and to an organization's existence. They include oversight, business management, general record keeping, budgeting, financing, soliciting revenue from exchange transactions, such as government contracts and related administrative activities, and all management and administration except for direct conduct of program services or fund-raising activities. The costs of oversight and management usually

include the salaries and expenses of the governing board, the chief executive officer of the organization, and the supporting staff. (If such staff spend a portion of their time directly supervising program services or categories of other supporting services, however, their salaries and expenses should be allocated among those functions.) The costs of disseminating information to inform the public of the organization's "stewardship" of contributed funds, announcements concerning appointments, and the annual report, among other costs, should similarly be classified as management and general expenses. The costs of soliciting funds other than contributions, including exchange transactions (whether program-related or not), should be classified as management and general expenses.

Fund-Raising Expenses.   Fund-raising expenses are a very sensitive category of expense because a great deal of publicity has been associated with certain organizations that appear to have very high fund-raising costs. The cost of fund raising includes not only the direct costs associated with a particular effort, but a fair allocation of the overhead of the organization, including the time of top management.

Fund-raising activities involve inducing potential donors to contribute money, securities, services, materials, facilities, other assets, or time. They include publicizing and conducting fund-raising campaigns; maintaining donor mailing lists; conducting special fund-raising events; preparing and distributing fund-raising manuals, instructions, and other materials; and conducting other activities involved with soliciting contributions from individuals, foundations, governments, and others. The financial statements should disclose total fund-raising expenses.

Fund-raising expenses are normally recorded as an expense in the Statement of Activity at the time they are incurred. It is not appropriate to defer such amounts. Thus the cost of acquiring or developing a mailing list that has value over more than one year would nevertheless be expensed in its entirety at the time the list was purchased or the costs incurred. The reason for this conservative approach is the difficulty accountants have in satisfying themselves that costs that might logically be deferred will in fact be recovered by future support related thereto. Further, if substantial amounts of deferred fund-raising costs were permitted, the credibility of the financial statements would be in jeopardy, particularly in view of the increased publicity surrounding fund-raising expenses.

If fund raising is combined with another function it may be possible to allocate the costs among the functions. In order to allocate any such costs to other than fund raising, criteria of purpose, audience and content as defined in SOP 98-2 must be met. These criteria are discussed in the next section.

Cost of Obtaining Grants.   Organizations soliciting grants from governments or foundations have a cost that is somewhat different from fund-raising costs. Where such amounts are identifiable and material in amount, they should be separately identified and reported as a supporting service.

Allocation of Joint Costs of Multipurpose Activities.   In 1998, the ACIPA issued a SOP 98-2 now included in the Audit Guide. This SOP, "Accounting for Cost of Activities of Not-for Profit Organizations and State and Local Government Entities that Include Fund Raising," replaced SOP 87-2. Compliance with SOP 87-2 had been much criticized by charity watchdogs such as the National Charities Information Bureau and the Philanthropic Advisory Services of the Council of Better Business Bureaus (now merged into the BBB Wise Giving Alliance) and by state attorneys general. Charities were criticized that they were allocating costs to program that were really fund raising in nature. The greatest criticism was leveled against charities using significant direct mail campaigns that allocated a significant portion of those costs to program on the basis that it met the program goal of providing educational literature to recipients.

The new SOP, while similar in many ways to the old one, provides a clear step-by-step analysis that must be followed in determining whether costs can be allocated to other than fund raising. If any of the criteria of purpose, audience, and content are not met, all costs of the joint activity must be reported as fund raising. This is so even if some of the costs, if incurred in an activity without fund raising, would be properly allocated to program or management and general costs. One important change from the prior rules is that education about the cause of an organization does not meet the purpose criterion unless it is part of a call for specific action by the audience that will help accomplish the entity's mission. Previously, educational information about the cause was routinely allocated to program costs.

The criteria that must be met for allocation are as follows:

- The *purpose* criterion is met if the purpose of the joint activity includes accomplishing program or management and general functions. To accomplish a program function, there must be a specific call for action, as noted in the previous paragraph. The SOP provides a number of examples and tests for judging whether the purpose criterion is met. Asking the audience to make contributions is indeed a call for action, but not one that helps accomplish the organization's mission.
- The *audience* criterion is designed to ensure that the audience is relevant for the non-fundraising purpose of the activity. In particular, there is a rebuttable presumption that the audience criterion is not met if the audience includes prior donors or has been selected based on its ability or likelihood to contribute.
- The *content* criterion requires that the content meet the program or management and general function and that for program purposes there be a call for specific action to help accomplish the entity's mission.

The SOP does not prescribe or prohibit any specific allocation methods although it does describe some acceptable methods. General cost accounting principles should be used in allocating costs, and they should be consistently applied.

ALL EXPENSES REPORTED AS UNRESTRICTED.   This is a new requirement in SFAS No. 117, and a significant change for almost all not-for-profit organizations (except hospitals). In the past, expenses were reported in the same fund as the revenue that was used to pay for the expenses. Thus unrestricted revenue, and expenses paid for out of that revenue were shown together in the unrestricted fund. Current restricted revenue, and the expenses paid for out of that revenue, were in the current restricted fund. (No expenses could ever be paid out of the permanent endowment fund, due to the nature of the restriction of those amounts.)

With the adoption of SFAS No. 117, all expenses, regardless of the origin of the resources used to finance the expenses, will be shown in the unrestricted class of net assets; no expenses will be in the temporarily restricted class. This is shown in Exhibit 35.6. The method of relating the restricted revenue to the expenses financed out of that revenue is to reclassify an amount of temporarily restricted net assets equal to the expenses to the unrestricted net assets class ($26,164 in Exhibit 35.6).

COLUMNAR PRESENTATION.   The statement presentation is in a columnar format and, as can be observed in Exhibit 35.6, includes all three classes on one statement. It is also possible to present the information in a single column. In this format, information for the three classes is shown sequentially, including the change in net assets for the class, followed by the total change in net assets for the year. An advantage of such a format is the ease of showing comparative prior year information for each class; a disadvantage is the inability to present a total column.

It should be noted that this statement provides a complete picture of all activity of this organization for the year—not just the activity of a single class or fund. Further, by including a "total" column on the statement, the reader is quickly able to see the overall activity and does not have to add together several amounts to get the complete picture. This represents a major advance in not-for-profit accounting.

UNRESTRICTED ACTIVITY IN A SINGLE COLUMN.   One of the most significant features of this presentation is that all legally unrestricted revenues and all expenses are reported in the single column representing the unrestricted class of net assets. The use of a single column in which all unrestricted activity is reported greatly simplifies the presentation and makes it more likely that a nonaccountant will be able to comprehend the total picture of the organization.

Many organizations, of course, will want to continue to keep board-designated accounts within their bookkeeping system. This is fine. But, for reporting to the public, all unrestricted amounts must be combined and reported as indicated in this exhibit.

While not recommended, there would appear to be no prohibition to an organization's including additional columns to the *left* of this total "unrestricted" column to show the various unrestricted board-designated categories of funds that make up the total unrestricted class. However, where an organization does so, it must clearly indicate that the total unrestricted column represents the total unrestricted activity for the year and that the detailed columns to the left are only the arbitrarily subdivided amounts making up this total. Probably an organization is better advised to show such detail in a separate supplementary schedule, if at all.

Where an organization chooses to show its unrestricted class broken into two columns and has only one class with restricted resources, it may be acceptable to eliminate the total unrestricted column in the interest of simplicity. An example of the column headings might be:

Unrestricted			
General Fund	Investment Fund	Temporarily Restricted	Total All Classes

The key to whether this would be acceptable is the extent of activity in the various columns. For example, if the temporarily restricted class in the above illustration were relatively minor in amount, then the total column would largely reflect the unrestricted class (i.e., the general fund and the investment fund). This is a judgment call.

TEMPORARILY RESTRICTED COLUMN.   The "temporarily restricted" column represents those amounts that have been given to the organization for a specified purpose other than for permanent endowment. It should be observed that the amounts reported as revenues in this fund represent the total amount the organization received during the year, and not the amount that was actually expended.

USE OF SEPARATE FIXED ASSET (PLANT) FUND.   SFAS No. 117 does not mention a separate fixed asset category; rather it includes amounts related to fixed assets in the three classes of net assets discussed earlier. Even though a fixed asset fund is maintained in the organization's bookkeeping system, for external financial reporting purposes, the organization would include most of the amounts of the fixed asset fund in the unrestricted class. This has the additional advantage of reducing the number of columns and eliminating the need for certain reclassifications.

Appreciation of Investments.   Appreciation (or depreciation) of investments is shown on the Statement of Support, Revenue and Expenses, and Changes in Net Assets. In this instance, the net appreciation of investments was $33,025. Assuming there were no sales or purchases of investments during the year, this amount would have been determined by comparing the market value of the investments at the end of the year with the market value at the beginning of the year. Normally, however, there will be some realized gain or loss during the year. While there is no technical objection to reporting the realized gain or loss separately from the unrealized appreciation (or depreciation), there seems little significance to this distinction.

OPERATING STATEMENT.   A variation on this statement that some may wish to use is to present a subtotal of "operating" revenue in excess of "operating" expenses. This would focus the reader's attention on what the organization considers its core "operations," as distinguished from matters that it considers peripheral or incidental to its operations. SFAS No. 117 permits, but does not require, this presentation. If an organization chooses this presentation, it will decide for itself what it considers to be its operations, versus other activities. Appendix 35.6 contains a checklist to help organizations decide what they wish to consider as operating versus nonoperating transactions.

(iv) Statement of Cash Flows (Formerly Changes in Financial Position).   A Statement of Cash Flows is a summary of the resources made available to an organization during the year and the uses made of such resources. SFAS No. 117 requires presentation of a Statement of Cash Flows by all not-for-profit organizations. Full discussion of preparation of this statement is in SFAS No. 95.

Exhibit 35.4 shows a Statement of Cash Flows. In some ways it is similar to a Statement of Cash Receipts and Disbursements, in that it presents cash received and spent. It differs by grouping transactions into three groups: Operating, Investing, and Financing cash flows. Also, there is less detail of specific types of operating cash flows, since such detail is already shown for revenue and expenses in Exhibit 35.6.

(v) Statement of Functional Expenses.   Exhibit 35.7 is a statement that analyzes functional or program expenses and shows the natural expense categories that go into each functional category. It is primarily an analysis to give the reader insight as to the major types of expenses involved. In order to arrive at the functional expense totals shown in the Statement of Support, Revenue and Expenses, and Changes in Net Assets, an analysis must be prepared that shows all of the expenses going into each program category. The Statement of Functional Expenses merely summarizes this detail for the reader.

(b) COLLEGES AND UNIVERSITIES.   The AICPA Industry Audit Guide, "Audits of Colleges and Universities," issued in 1973, had been the most authoritative pronouncement on accounting principles and reporting practices for colleges and universities. With the issuance of FASB Statement Nos. 116 and 117, some of the accounting and reporting rules for colleges and universities have changed, as discussed elsewhere in this chapter.

(i) Fund Accounting.   Fund accounting is a prominent element of college and university accounting. Colleges and universities have historically followed fund accounting procedures. Fund accounting continues to find favor at colleges and universities because many gifts and grants that colleges receive possess external restrictions that must be carefully monitored, and also because many colleges voluntarily set aside some current unrestricted funds as "endowment" to produce future income.

The following six fund groupings are generally used for internal bookkeeping by colleges and universities:

Current funds are resources available for carrying out the general activities of an institution. In public reporting, current unrestricted funds are usually reported separately from current restricted funds, that is, funds restricted by donors or grantors for specific current purposes.

Loan funds are resources available for loans to students, faculty, and staff. If only the investment income from restricted endowment funds can be used for loans, only the income should be reported in the loan fund.

Endowment and similar funds consist of three types of endowment resources:

1. True endowment, where the donor stipulates that the principal must be maintained inviolate and in perpetuity, and only the income earned thereon may be expended
2. Term endowment, where the donor stipulates that, upon the passage of time or the incidence of an event, the principal may be used for current operations or specific purposes
3. Quasi-endowment, where the board of trustees voluntarily retains as principal a portion of current funds to produce current and future income

Annuity and life income funds are endowment resources of which the college owns only the principal and not the income earned thereon. In accepting an annuity or life income gift, the college agrees to pay the contributor all income earned or a specific amount for a stated period of time. [See the discussion of split-interest gifts at Subsection 35.2(j)(iii).]

Plant funds consist of four fund groupings, and separate financial data for each are often reported:

1. Unexpended plant funds are used for plant additions or improvements.

2. Renewal and replacement funds are transferred from current funds for future renewal or replacement of the existing plant. These funds provide for the future integrity of the physical plant.

3. Retirement of indebtedness funds are set aside to service debt interest and principal. It is often appropriate to designate which funds are set aside under mandatory contractual agreements with lenders and which funds are voluntarily designated.

4. Investment in plant records the actual cost of all land, buildings, and equipment owned by the college. Donated plant is recorded at market value at the date of the gift.

Agency funds are funds over which an institution exercises custodial but not proprietary authority. An example is funds that are owned by a student organization but are deposited with the college.

(ii) Encumbrance Accounting.   Encumbrance accounting is not acceptable for financial statements of colleges and universities. It is inappropriate to report, as expenditures or liabilities, commitments for materials or services not received by the reporting date. A portion of the current unrestricted fund may be designated to satisfy purchase orders, provided that the designation is made only in the fund balances (net assets) section of the balance sheet.

(c) OTHER NOT-FOR-PROFIT ORGANIZATIONS

(i) Accounting Principles.   Not-for-profit organizations not covered by another AICPA Industry Audit Guide were covered by SOP 78-10. Organizations in this group include professional and trade associations, private and community foundations, religious organizations, libraries, museums, private schools, and performing arts organizations. Most accounting principles applicable to these organizations are discussed elsewhere in this chapter.

Subscription and Membership Income.   Subscription and membership income should be recognized in the periods in which the organization provides goods or services to subscribers or members. This usually requires deferring such amounts when received and recognizing them ratably over the membership or subscription period. Special calculations, based on life expectancy, are required when so-called life memberships are involved.

Grants to Others.   Organizations that award grants should record a grant as a liability and an expense in the period in which the recipient is entitled to the grant. This is usually the period in which the grant is authorized, even though some of the payments may not be made until later periods.

Under SFAS No. 116, grantors account for grants in the same way as grantees—except backward–expense and liability instead of revenue and receivable. See Subsection 35.2(j) for a discussion of accounting for restricted gifts and pledges.

35.4 AUDIT CONSIDERATIONS FOR A NOT-FOR-PROFIT ORGANIZATION

(a) GENERAL CONSIDERATIONS.   An audit of the financial statements of a not-for-profit organization is similar to an audit of a for-profit enterprise, and generally accepted auditing standards should be followed. A not-for-profit organization, however, seeks to provide an optimal level of services, rather than to maximize profits, and its financial statements, accordingly, focus on the activity and balances of different classes and funds. This in turn influences the conduct of the audit.

(b) INTERNAL CONTROL.   Some not-for-profit organizations do not have effective internal control. The size of staff may be inadequate to achieve a proper segregation of duties, and the nature of some transactions often precludes sufficient checks and balances. Internal control deficiencies are often mitigated by adoption of procedures including the following: (1) involvement of senior management and directors in the operation of the organization; (2) restricting check signing to senior management and directors; (3) implementing effective bank reconciliation procedures; (4) preparing annual budgets and promptly investigating variances from budget estimates; and (5) depositing investment securities with independent custodians.

(c) MATERIALITY.   The issue of what is material is equally important for not-for-profit and for-profit organizations. In for-profit enterprises, evaluating materiality involves considering the effect of alternate accounting treatments and disclosures on decisions by investors, and it relates to net income and earnings per share. These measures are generally not applicable to not-for-profit organizations. Instead, evaluating materiality involves considering the effects of accounting treatments and disclosures on decisions by contributors, and it relates to revenue, expenditures, and the cost of individual programs.

(d) TAXES.   Not-for-profit organizations are generally exempt from income taxes and are often exempt from property and sales taxes. Tax liabilities, however, may arise from tax on unrelated business income, tax on net income resulting from a loss of tax-exempt status, or certain excise taxes applicable to private foundations.

(e) CONSOLIDATION.   Not-for-profit organizations do not "own" other organizations in the sense that businesses own other businesses. Not-for-profit organizations, however, may exercise effective control over affiliates or related organizations; in such instances, preparation of combined financial statements may be appropriate.

(f) COMPLIANCE AUDITING.   In recent years, federal and state governments have become more active in requiring recipients of government money to submit auditor reports on various aspects of financial operations. These usually include opinions on financial data for the organization as a whole and, for government grants, reports on internal controls and compliance with laws and regulations. The exact requirements may differ depending on the type of recipient (college, hospital, etc.), the agency that made the grant, whether the money was received directly or through another level of government, and the amount of money received. It is important for the auditor to ascertain any compliance auditing requirements prior to beginning fieldwork, so that the auditor can perform the work necessary to issue the required reports. Specific requirements are contained in a number of different documents including SAS No. 74, "Compliance Auditing Considerations in Audits of Governmental Entities and Recipients of Governmental Financial Assistance"; the Department of Health and Human Services audit guide, "Guidelines for Audits of Federal Awards to Nonprofit Organizations"; various circulars issued by the Office of Management and Budget (principally A-21, A-110, A-122, A-133); and "Government Auditing Standards," issued by the GAO (generally referred to as the "*Yellow Book*"). Compliance auditing requirements are also found in the OMB "Compliance Supplement" (Revised 1997).

Additional guidance for compliance auditing is in a new AICPA SOP to replace SOP 92-9, "Audits of Not-for-Profit Organizations Receiving Federal Awards." Compliance auditing is discussed further in Chapter 32, "State and Local Government Accounting."

(g) UNIQUE AUDITING AREAS.   Auditing areas unique to not-for-profit organizations include the following:

- *Collections of museums, libraries, zoological parks, and similar organizations.* Auditing considerations include valuation of assets, capitalization, accessions and deaccessions, security, insurance coverage, and observation of inventory. Certain procedures are appropriate even though the collection is not capitalized.

- *Contributions.* Auditing considerations include ascertaining that amounts reported as contributions are properly stated. Audit tests for noncash contributions include testing their assigned value. Auditors are particularly concerned about the possibility that contributions that were intended for the organization may never have been received and recorded.

- *Fees for performance of services, including tuition, membership dues, ticket revenue, and patient fees.* Auditing considerations include confirming that revenue is computed at proper rates, collected, and properly recorded for all services provided.

- *Functional allocation of expenses.* Auditing considerations include appropriateness of allocations among functions, reasonableness of allocation methods, accuracy of computations, and consistency of allocation bases with bases of prior periods. These considerations are especially important when joint costs of multipurpose activities (discussed above) are involved.

- *Restricted resources.* Auditing considerations include ascertaining that transactions are for the restricted purpose and are recorded in the proper restricted fund.

- *Grant awards to others.* Auditing considerations include confirming grant awards with recipients and ascertaining that grants are recorded in the proper accounting period.

- *Tax compliance.* Not-for-profits are subject to IRC sections that differ from those regularly applicable to businesses. Auditors must review compliance with these sections. Areas of particular concern are conformity with exempt purpose, unrelated business income, lobbying, status as a public charity (if applicable), and special rules applicable to private foundations.

35.5 SOURCES AND SUGGESTED REFERENCES

American Institute of Certified Public Accountants, Accounting Standards Division, "Accounting for Joint Costs of Informational Materials and Activities of Not-for-Profit Organizations that Include a Fund-Raising Appeal," Statement of Position No. 87-2, 1987. (In process of revision.)

———, Accounting Standards Division, "The Application of the Requirements of Accounting Research Bulletins, Opinions of the Accounting Principles Board, and Statements and Interpretations of the Financial Accounting Standards Board to Not-for-Profit Organizations," Statement of Position No. 94-2, 1994.

———, Accounting Standards Division, "Reporting of Related Entities by Not-for-Profit Organizations," Statement of Position No. 94-3, 1994.

———, Auditing Standards Division, "Compliance Auditing Considerations in Audits of Governmental Entities and Recipients of Governmental Financial Assistance," Statement on Auditing Standards No. 74, 1995.

———, Committee on Not-for-Profit Organizations, "Audits of Not-for-Profit Organizations Receiving Federal Awards," Statement of Position No. 92-9, 1992.

———, Committee on Not-for-Profit Organizations, "Audit and Accounting Guide, Not-for-Profit Organizations," 1996.

———, Health Care Committee, "Health Care Organizations Audit and Accounting Guide, 1996.

Anthony, R. N., *Financial Accounting in Nonbusiness Organizations: An Exploratory Study of Conceptual Issues.* Financial Accounting Standards Board, Norwalk, CT, 1978.

Anthony, R. N., and Young, D. W., *Management Control in Nonprofit Organizations,* Third ed. Richard D. Irwin, Homewood, IL, 1984.

Blazek, J., *Tax Planning and Compliance for Tax-Exempt Organizations: Forms, Checklists, Procedures.* John Wiley & Sons, New York, Second ed., 1993.

Cary, W. L., and Bright, C. B., *The Law and the Lore of Endowment Funds—Report to the Ford Foundation.* New York, 1969.

Daughtrey, W. H., Jr., and Gross, M. J., Jr., *Museum Accounting Handbook.* American Association of Museums, Washington, DC, 1978.

Evangelical Joint Accounting Committee, "Accounting and Financial Reporting Guide for Christian Ministries," Revised edition. Christian Management Association, Diamond Bar, CA, 1997.

Financial Accounting Standards Board, Norwalk, CT:

Statements of Financial Accounting Concepts:

No. 4, "Objectives of Financial Reporting By Nonbusiness Organizations," 1980.

No. 6, "Elements of Financial Statements," 1985.

Statements of Financial Accounting Standards:

No. 93, "Recognition of Depreciation by Not-for-Profit Organizations," Norwalk, CT, 1987.

No. 95, "Statement of Cash Flows," 1987.

No. 116, "Accounting for Contributions Received and Contributions Made," 1993.

No. 117, "Financial Statements of Not-for-Profit Organizations," 1993.

No. 124, "Accounting for Certain Investments Held by Not-for-Profit Organizations," 1995.

FASB Interpretation No. 42, "Accounting for Transfers of Assets in Which a Not-for-Profit Organization Is Granted Variance Power," 1996.

Gross, Larkin, Bruttomesso, and McNally, *Financial and Accounting Guide for Not-for-Profit Organizations,* Fifth ed. New York, John Wiley & Sons, 1995.

Holder, W. W., *The Not-for-Profit Organization Reporting Entity,* Philanthropy Monthly Press, New Milford, CT, 1986.

Hopkins, B. R., *A Legal Guide to Starting and Managing A Nonprofit Organization,* Second ed. New York, John Wiley & Sons, 1993.

———, *The Law of Fund-Raising,* 2nd ed. New York, John Wiley & Sons, 1995.

———, *The Law of Tax-Exempt Organizations,* 7th ed. New York, John Wiley & Sons, 1998.

Hummel, J., *Starting and Running a Nonprofit Organization,* Minneapolis: University of Minnesota Press, 1980.

Larkin, R. F., "Accounting," Chapter 31 of *The Nonprofit Management Handbook—Operating Policies and Procedures.* New York, John Wiley & Sons, 1993; and 1994 Supplement.

———, "Accounting Issues Relating to Fundraising," Chapter 2 of *Financial Practices for Effective Fundraising.* San Francisco, Jossey-Bass, Inc., 1994.

National Association of College and University Business Officers, *Financial Accounting and Reporting Manual for Higher Education.* Washington, DC, 1990.

National Association of Independent Schools, *Business Management for Independent Schools,* Third ed., Boston: Author, 1987.

National Health Council, National Assembly for Social Policy and Development, Inc., and United Way of America, *Standards of Accounting and Financial Reporting for Voluntary Health and Welfare Organizations,* Third ed., NHC, NASPD, and UWA, New York, 1988.

———, *Effective Internal Accounting Control for Nonprofit Organizations.* New York, 1988.

———, *The Audit Committee, the Board of Trustees of Not-for-Profit Organizations and the Independent Accountant.* New York, 1992.

———, *Not-for-Profit Organizations' Implementation Guide for SFAS Statements 116 and 117.* New York, 1993.

United States General Accounting Office, "Government Auditing Standards." GAO, Washington, DC, 1994 Revision.

United States Office of Management and Budget Circulars, OMB, Washington:

No. A-21, "Cost Principles for Educational Institutions," 1996.

No. A-110, "Uniform Administrative Requirements for Grants and Agreements with Institutions of Higher Education, Hospitals, and Other Nonprofit Organizations," 1993.

No. A-122, "Cost Principles for Nonprofit Organizations," 1980. (In process of revision.)

No. A-133, "Audits of States, Local Governments, and Non-profit Organizations," 1997.

United Way of America, *Budgeting: A Guide for United Ways and Not-for-Profit Human Service Organizations.* Alexandria, VA, 1975.

Accounting and Financial Reporting: A Guide for United Ways and Not-For Profit Human Service Organizations, Second ed. Alexandria, VA, 1989.

APPENDIX 35.1: FACTORS TO BE CONSIDERED IN DISTINGUISHING CONTRACTS FOR THE PURCHASE OF GOODS OR SERVICES FROM RESTRICTED GRANTS

Following is a list of factors that may be helpful to not-for-profit organizations in deciding how to account for the receipt of payments that might be considered as being either for the purchase of goods or services from the organization, or as restricted-purpose gifts or grants to the organization (as contemplated in par. 3 of SFAS No. 116). These factors can also be used by auditors in assessing the reasonableness of the client's decision. Additional discussion of this distinction can be found in the instructions to IRS Form 990, lines 1a–c, and in IRS Regulation 1.509(a)–3(g). No one of these factors is normally determinative by itself; all relevant factors should be considered together.

Factors Whose Presence Would Indicate Payment Is for the Purchase of Goods or Services	*Factors Whose Presence Would Indicate the Payment Is a Restricted Grant for a Specific Purpose*
Factors related to the agreement between the payor and the payee:	
1. The expressed intent is for the payee to provide goods/services to the payor, or to other specifically identified recipients, as determined by the payor.	The expressed intent is to make a gift to the payee to advance the programs of the payee.
2. There is a specified time and/or place for delivery of goods/services to the payor or other recipient	Time and/or place of delivery of any goods/services is largely at the discretion of the payee.
3. There are provisions for economic penalties, beyond the amount of the payment, against the payee for failure to meet the terms of the agreement.	Any penalties are expressed in terms of required delivery of goods/services, or are limited to return of unspent amounts.
4. The amount of the payment per unit is computed in a way that explicitly provides for a "profit" margin for the payee.	The payment is stated as a flat amount or a fixed amount per unit based only on the cost (including overhead) of providing the goods/services.
5. The total amount of the payment is based only on the quantity of items delivered.	The payment is based on a line-item budget request, including an allowance for actual administrative costs.
6. The tenor of the agreement is that the payor receives approximately equivalent value in return for the payment.	The payor does not receive approximately equivalent value.
7. The items are closely related to commercial activity regularly engaged in by the payor.	The items are related to the payee's program services.
8. There is substantial benefit to the payor itself from the items.	The items are normally used to provide goods/services considered of social benefit to society as a whole, or to some defined segment thereof (e.g., children, persons having a disease, students), which might not otherwise have ready access to the items.
9. If the payor is a governmental unit, the items are things the government itself has explicitly undertaken to provide to its citizens; the government has arranged for another organization to be the actual service provider.	The government is in the role of subsidizing provision of services to the public by a nongovernmental organization.

Factors Whose Presence Would Indicate Payment Is for the Purchase of Goods or Services	*Factors Whose Presence Would Indicate the Payment Is a Restricted Grant for a Specific Purpose*
10. The benefits resulting from the items are to be made available only to the payor or to persons or entities designated by the payor.	The items, or the results of the activities funded by the payment, are to be made available to the general public, or to any person who requests and is qualified to receive them. Determination of specific recipients is made by the payee.
11. The items are to be delivered to the payor or to other persons or entities closely connected with the payor.	Delivery is to be made to persons or entities not closely connected with the payor.
12. Revenue from sale of the items is considered unrelated business income (IRC Section 512) to the payee.	Revenue is "related" income to the payee.
13. In the case of sponsored research, the payor determines the plan of research and the desired outcome, and retains proprietary rights to the results.	The research plan is determined by the payee; desired outcomes are expressed only in general terms (e.g., to find a cure for a disease), and the rights to the results remain with the payee or are considered in the public domain.
14. The payment supports applied research.	The payment supports basic research.

APPENDIX 35.2: FACTORS TO BE CONSIDERED IN ASSESSING WHETHER CONTRIBUTED SERVICES ARE CONSIDERED TO REQUIRE SPECIALIZED SKILLS (PER PARAGRAPH 9 OF STATEMENT OF FINANCIAL ACCOUNTING STANDARDS NO. 116, "ACCOUNTING FOR CONTRIBUTIONS RECEIVED")

Following is a list of factors that may be helpful to recipients of contributed services of volunteers in assessing whether the skills utilized by the volunteers in the performance of their services are considered to be "specialized" within the meaning of Paragraph 9 of SFAS No. 116. These factors may also aid auditors in assessing the appropriateness of the client's judgment. This list of factors is not intended to be used in determining how to value or account for such services. In some cases, no one of these factors is necessarily determinative by itself; all relevant factors should be considered together.

Eight factors whose presence is often indicative that skills are "specialized":

1. Persons who regularly hold themselves out to the public as qualified practitioners of such skills are required by law or by professional ethical standards to possess a license or other professional certification, or specified academic credentials. Alternatively, if possession of such license/certification/credentials is optional, the person performing the services does possess such formal certification.

2. Practitioners of such skills are required, by law or professional ethics, to have obtained a specified amount of technical prejob or on-the-job training, to obtain specified amounts of continuing professional education, a specified amount of practical work experience, or to complete a defined period of apprenticeship in the particular type of work.

3. Proper practice of the skills requires the individual to possess specific artistic or creative talent and/or a body of technical knowledge not generally possessed by members of the public at large.

4. Practice of the skills requires the use of technical tools or equipment. The ability to properly use such tools or equipment requires training or experience not generally possessed by members of the public at large.

5. There is a union or professional association whose membership consists specifically of practitioners of the skills, as opposed to such groups whose members consist of persons who work in a broad industry, a type of company, or a department of a company. Admission to membership in such organization requires demonstrating one or more of the factors 1, 2, or 3. (Whether the person whose skills are being considered actually belongs to such organization is not a factor in assessing whether the skills are considered to be specialized, though it may be relevant in assessing whether the person possesses the skills.)

6. Practitioners of such skills are generally regarded by the public as being members of a particular "profession."

7. There is a formal disciplinary procedure administered by a government or by a professional association, to which practitioners of such skills are subject, as a condition of offering their skills to the public for pay.

8. Practice of the skills by persons who do so in their regular work is ordinarily done in an environment in which there is regular formal review or approval of work done by supervisory personnel or by professional peers.

APPENDIX 35.3: CHECKLIST—FACTORS TO BE CONSIDERED IN DETERMINING WHETHER AN ORGANIZATION WOULD TYPICALLY NEED TO PURCHASE SERVICES IF NOT PROVIDED BY DONATION

The following is a list of factors that may be helpful to:

- Not-for-profit organizations, in deciding whether contributed services meet the third part of the criterion in paragraph 9b of SFAS No. 116;
- Auditors, in assessing the reasonableness of the client's decision.

No one of these factors is normally determinative by itself; all relevant factors and the strength of their presence should be considered together.

Factors Whose Presence Would Indicate the Services Would Typically Need to Be Purchased	*Factors Whose Presence Would Indicate the Services Would Typically Not Need to Be Purchased*
1. The activities in which the volunteers are involved are an integral part of the reporting organization's ongoing program services (as stated in its IRS Form 1023/4, fund-raising material, and annual report), or of management or fund-raising activities that are essential to the functioning of the organization's programs.	The activities are not part of the reporting organization's program, or of important management or fundraising activities, or are relatively incidental to those activities; the services primarily benefit the program activities of another organization.
2. Volunteer work makes up a significant portion of the total effort expended in the program activity in which the volunteers are used.	Volunteer work is a relatively small part of the total effort of the program.
3. The program activity in which the volunteers function is a significant part of the overall program activities of the organization.	The program activity is relatively insignificant in relation to the organization's overall program activities.
4. The reporting organization has an objective basis for assigning a value to the services.	No objective basis is readily available.

Factors Whose Presence Would Indicate the Services Would Typically Need to Be Purchased	*Factors Whose Presence Would Indicate the Services Would Typically Not Need to Be Purchased*
5. The organization has formal agreements with third parties to provide the program services that are conducted by the volunteers.	Factor not present.
6. The reporting organization assigns volunteers to specific duties.	Assignment of specific duties to volunteers is done by persons or entities other than the reporting organization, or the volunteers largely determine for themselves what is to be done within broad guidelines.
7. The volunteers are subject to ongoing supervision and review of their work by the reporting organization.	The activities of the volunteers are conducted at geographic locations distant from the organization.
8. The organization actively recruits volunteers for specific tasks.	Volunteers are accepted but not actively recruited, or, if recruited, specific tasks are not mentioned in the recruiting materials.
9. If the work of the volunteers consists of creating or enhancing nonfinancial assets, the assets will be owned and/or used primarily by or under the control of the reporting organization after the volunteer work is completed. If the assets are subsequently given away by the organization to charitable beneficiaries, the organization decides who is to receive the assets.	The assets will immediately be owned or used primarily by other persons or organizations.
10. If there were to be a net increase in net assets resulting from the recording of a value for the services (even though in practice, there usually is not), the increase would better meet the criteria for presentation as revenue, rather than a gain, as set forth in SFAC No. 6, par. 78–79, 82–88, and 111–113.	The net increase would better meet the criteria of a gain, rather than revenue.
11. Management represents to the auditor that it would hire paid staff to perform the services if volunteers were not available.	Management represents that it would not hire paid staff; or it is obvious from the financial condition of the organization that it is unlikely that financial resources would be available to pay for the services.

Auditors are reminded that management representations alone do not normally constitute sufficient competent evidential matter to support audit assertions; however, they may be considered in conjunction with other evidence.

Factors particularly relevant in situations where the volunteer services are provided directly to charitable or other beneficiaries of the reporting organization's program services (e.g., Legal Aid Society) rather than to the organization itself:

12. The reporting organization assumes responsibility for the volunteers with regard to workers' compensation and liability insurance, errors or omissions in the work, satisfactory completion of the work.	The organization has explicitly disclaimed such responsibility.
13. The reporting organization maintains ongoing involvement with the activities of the volunteers.	The organization functions mainly as a clearinghouse for putting volunteers in touch with persons or other organizations needing help, but has little ongoing involvement.

APPENDIX 35.4: FACTORS TO BE CONSIDERED IN ASSESSING WHETHER A DONOR HAS MADE A BONA FIDE PLEDGE TO A DONEE

Following is a list of factors that may be helpful to donees, in assessing whether a pledge (unconditional promise to give, as contemplated in pars. 5–7, 22, 23 of SFAS No. 116) has, in fact, been made. These factors may also help auditors in assessing the appropriateness of the client's judgment. This list of factors is not intended to be used in deciding on proper accounting (for either the pledge asset or the related revenue/net assets) or to assess collectibility, although some of the factors may be relevant to those decisions as well. In many cases, no one of these factors is necessarily determinative by itself; all relevant factors should be considered together.

Factors Whose Presence May Indicate a Bona Fide Pledge Was Made	*Factors Whose Presence May Indicate a Bona Fide Pledge Was Not Made*
1. Factors related to the solicitation process:	
____ a. There is evidence that the recipient explicitly solicited formal pledges.	The pledge was unsolicited, or the solicitation did not refer to pledges.
____ b. Public announcement[1] of the pledge has been made (by donor or donee)	No public announcement has been made.
____ c. Partial payment on the pledge has been made (or full payment after balance sheet date).	No payments have yet been made, or payments have been irregular, late, or less than scheduled amounts.
2. Factors related to the "pledge" itself:	
____ a. Written evidence created by the donor clearly supports the existence of an unconditional promise to give. (D)	There is no written evidence;[2] the only written evidence was prepared by the donee, or written evidence is unclear.

____ b. The evidence includes words such as:
       promise
       agree
       will
       binding,	

____ c. The pledge appears to be legally enforceable. (Consult an attorney if necessary.) (Note also factor 4a.)	Legal enforceability is questionable or explicitly denied.
____ d. There is a clearly-defined payment schedule stated in terms of either calendar dates or the occurrence of specified events whose occurrence is reasonably probable.	A payment schedule is not clearly defined, or events are relatively unlikely to occur.
____ e. The calendar dates or events comprising the payment schedule will (are expected to) occur within a relatively short time[3] after the balance sheet date (or in the case of events, have already occurred).	The time (period) of payment contemplated by the donor is relatively far in the future.
____ f. The amount of the pledge is clearly specified or readily computable.	The amount is not clear or readily computable.

Factors Whose Presence May Indicate a Bona Fide Pledge Was Made	*Factors Whose Presence May Indicate a Bona Fide Pledge Was Not Made*
____ g. The donor has clearly specified a particular purpose for the gift, e.g., endowment, fixed assets, loan fund, retire long-term debt, specific program service. The purpose is consistent with ongoing done activities.	The purpose is vaguely or not specified, or inconsistent with donee activities.
3. Factors relating to the donor:	
____ a. There is no reason to question the donor's ability or intent to fulfill the pledge.	Collectibility of the gift is questionable
____ b. The donor has a history of making and fulfilling pledges to the donee of similar or larger amounts.	Factor not present.
4. Factors relating to the donee:	
____ a. The donee has indicated that it would take legal action to enforce collection if necessary, or has a history of doing so.	It is unlikely (based on donee's past practices) or uncertain whether the donee would enforce the "pledge."
____ b. The donee has already taken specific action in reliance on the pledge or publicly[1] announced that it intends to do so.[4]	No specific action has been taken or is contemplated.

(D) This factor, if present, would normally be considered determinative.

[1] The announcement would not necessarily have to be made to the general public; announcement in media circulated among the constituency of either the donor or donee would suffice. Examples include newsletters, fund-raising reports, annual reports, a campus newspaper, and so on. In the case of announcements by the donee, there should be a reasonable presumption that the donor is aware of the announcement and has not indicated any disagreement with it.

[2] Oral pledges can be considered bona fide under some circumstances. Clearly, in the case of oral pledges, much greater weight will have to be given to other factors if the existence of a bona fide pledge is to be asserted. Also, the auditor will have to carefully consider what audit evidence can be relied on.

[3] What constitutes a relatively short time has to be determined in each case. The longer the time contemplated, the more weight will have to be given to other factors (especially 2b, c, 3a and 4a) in assessing the existence of a pledge. In most circumstances, periods longer than three to five years would likely be judged relatively long.

[4] Types of specific action contemplated include:

- Commencing acquisition, construction, or lease of capital assets or signing binding contracts to do so
- Making public announcement of the commencement or expansion of operating programs used by the public (e.g., the opening of a new clinic, starting a new concert series, a special museum exhibit)
- Indicating to another funder that the pledge will be used to match part of a challenge grant from that funder
- Soliciting other pledges or loans for the same purpose by explicitly indicating that "x has already pledged"
- Committing proceeds of the pledge in other ways such as awarding scholarships, making pledges to other charities, hiring new staff, and so on (where such uses are consistent with either the donee's stated purposes in soliciting the pledge or the donor's indicated use of the pledge)
- Forbearing from soliciting other available major gifts (e.g., not submitting an application for a foundation grant) because, with the pledge in question, funding for the purpose is considered complete
- Using pledge as collateral for a loan

APPENDIX 35.5: CHECKLIST—FACTORS TO BE CONSIDERED IN DECIDING WHETHER A GIFT OR PLEDGE SUBJECT TO DONOR STIPULATIONS IS CONDITIONAL OR RESTRICTED (AS DISCUSSED IN STATEMENT OF FINANCIAL ACCOUNTING STANDARDS NO. 116, PARS. 7, 22–23, 57–71, 75–81)

Donors place many different kinds of stipulations on pledges and other gifts. Some stipulations create legal *restrictions* that limit the way in which the donee may use the gift. Other stipulations create *conditions* that must be fulfilled before a donee is entitled to receive (or keep) a gift.

In SFAS No. 116, FASB defines a condition as an uncertain future event that must occur before a promise based on that event becomes binding on the promisor. In some cases, it is not immediately clear whether a particular stipulation creates a condition or a restriction. (Some gifts are both conditional and restricted.) Accounting for the two forms of gift is quite different, so it is important that the nature of a stipulation be properly identified so that the gift is properly categorized.

Following is a list of factors to be considered by:

- Recipients (and donors) of gifts, in deciding whether a pledge or other gift that includes donor stipulations is conditional or restricted
- Auditors, in assessing the appropriateness of the client's decision

In many cases, no one of these factors will be determinative by itself; all applicable factors should be considered together.

Factors Whose Presence in the Grant Document, Donor's Transmittal Letter, or Other Gift Instrument or in the Appeal by the Recipient Would Indicate the Gift May Be Restricted	*Factors Whose Presence in the Communication from the Donor or the Donee-Prepared Pledge Card Would Indicate the Gift May Be Conditional*
Factors related to the terms of the gift/pledge:	
1. The document uses words such as:	The document uses words such as:
If*	Must
Subject to*	For
When	Purpose
Revocable*	Irrevocable
2. Neither the ultimate amount nor the timing of payment of the gift is clearly determinable in advance of payment.	At least one of the amount and/or timing is clearly specified.
3. The pledge is stated to extend for a very long period of time (over, say, 10 years) or is open-ended. (Often found with pledges to support a needy child overseas or a missionary in the field.)	The time is short and/or specific as to its end.
4. The donor stipulations in the document refer to *outcomes* expected as a result of the activity (with the implication that if the outcomes are not achieved, the donor will expect the gift to be refunded, or will cancel future installments of a multiperiod pledge.[1a]* (Such gifts are likely also restricted.)	The donor stipulations focus on the *activities* to be conducted. Although hoped-for outcomes may be implicit or explicit, there is not an implication that achievement of particular outcomes is a requirement.[1b]*

Factors Whose Presence in the Grant Document, Donor's Transmittal Letter, or Other Gift Instrument or in the Appeal by the Recipient Would Indicate the Gift May Be Restricted	*Factors Whose Presence in the Communication from the Donor or the Donee-Prepared Pledge Card Would Indicate the Gift May Be Conditional*
5. There is an explicit requirement that amounts not expensed by a specified date must be returned to the donor.	There is no such refund provision, or any refund is required only if money is left after completion of the specified activities.
6. The gift is in the form of a pledge.	The gift is a transfer of cash or other non-cash assets.
7. Payment of amounts pledged will be made only on a cost-reimbursement basis. (D)	Payment of the gift will be made up front, or according to a payment schedule, without the necessity for the donee to have yet incurred specific expenses.
8. The gift has an explicit matching requirement (D), or additional funding beyond that already available will be required to complete the activity.	Factor not present.

Factors relating to the circumstances surrounding the gift:

9. The action or event described in the donor's stipulations is largely outside the control of the management or governing board of the donee.[2a]*	The action or event is largely within the donee's control.[2b]*
10. The activity contemplated by the gift is one which the donee has not yet decided to do, and it is not yet certain whether the activity will actually be conducted.*	The donee is already conducting the activity, or it is fairly certain that the activity will be conducted.*
11. There is a lower probability that the donor stipulations will eventually be met.	There is a higher probability.
12. As to any tangible or intangible outcomes that are to be produced as a result of the activities, these products will be under the control of the donor. (In such cases, the payment may not be a gift at all; rather it may be a payment for goods or services.)	Any outcomes will be under the control of the donee.

(D) Presence of this factor would normally be considered determinative. Absence of the factor is not necessarily determinative.

* Factors that would generally be considered more important.

[1a] Examples of outcomes contemplated by this factor include:

- Successful creation of a new vaccine
- Production of a new television program
- Commissioning a new musical composition
- Establishing a named professorship
- Reduction in the teenage pregnancy rate in a community
- Construction of a new building
- Mounting a new museum exhibit

[1b] Examples of activities contemplated by this factor include (but see Factor 10**):

- conduct of scientific or medical research
- Broadcasting a specified television program
- Performing a particular piece of music
- Paying the salary of a named professor
- Counseling teenagers judged at risk of becoming pregnant
- Operating a certain facility
- Providing disaster relief

[2a] Examples of events contemplated by this factor include:

- Actions of uncontrolled third parties, for example:
  - other donors making contributions to enable the donee to meet a matching requirement of this gift
  - a government granting approval to conduct an activity (e.g., awarding a building or land use permit, or a permit to operate a medical facility)
  - an owner of other property required for the activity making the property available to the organization (by sale or lease)
- Natural and man-made disasters
- Future action of this donor (such as agreeing to renew a multiperiod pledge in subsequent periods)
- The future willingness and ability of a donor of personal services to continue to provide those services (See SFAS No. 116, par. 70, third sentence.)

(Events outside of the donee's control, but which are virtually assured of happening anyway at a known time and place (e.g., astronomical or normal meteorological events), and the mere passage of time, are not conditions.)

[2b] Examples of events contemplated by this factor include (but see Factor 10**):

- Eventual use of the gift for the specified purpose (e.g., those listed in Note 1b above), or retention of the gift as restricted endowment
- Naming a building for a specified person
- Filing with the donor routine performance reports on the activities being conducted

** There is a presumption here that the right column of Factor 10 applies.

APPENDIX 35.6: CONSIDERATION OF WHETHER ITEMS MAY BE REPORTED AS OPERATING OR NONOPERATING (WITHIN THE CONTEXT OF PAR. 23 OF STATEMENT OF FINANCIAL ACCOUNTING STANDARDS NO. 117)

Paragraph 23 of SFAS No. 117 leaves it to each organization (if it wishes to present a subtotal of "operating" results) to determine what it considers to be operating versus nonoperating items in a statement of activity. If it is not obvious from the face of the statement what items are included or excluded in the operating subtotal, footnote disclosure of that distinction shall be made. Following are some items that might be considered as nonoperating. This is not intended to express any preferences, nor to limit the types of items that a particular organization might report as nonoperating, but merely to provide a list for consideration of various types of items.

Items that would usually be considered nonoperating as to the current period:

- Extraordinary items
- Cumulative effects of accounting changes

- Correction of errors of prior periods
- Prior period adjustments, generally
- Results of discontinued operations

Items that many persons might consider nonoperating in some situations:

- Unrealized capital gains on investments carried at market value
- Unrelated business income (as defined in the Internal Revenue Code Section 512), and related expenses
- Contributions that qualify as "unusual grants," as defined in IRS Regulation Section 1.509(a)–3(c)(3)
- Items that meet some, but not all, of the criteria in APB No. 30/SFAS No. 4 for extraordinary items, or APB No. 30/SFAS No. 16 for prior period adjustments

Items that some persons might consider nonoperating in some situations:

- Bequests and other "deferred gifts" (annuity, life income funds, etc.) received
- Gains and losses, generally (as defined in SFAC No. 6, pars. 82–89)
- Sales of goods/services that, although they are not considered unrelated under the Internal Revenue Code, are nevertheless peripheral to the organization's major activities
- Some "auxiliary activities" of colleges
- Revenue and expenses related to program activities not explicitly listed on the organization's IRS Form 1023
- Revenue and expenses directly related to transactions that are reported as financing or investing cash flows in the statement of cash flows; for example, investment income not available for operating purposes, interest expense, write-offs of loans receivable, nonexpendable gifts (as contemplated by paragraph 30d of SFAS No. 117), adjustment of annuity liability
- Contributions having the characteristics of an "initial capital" contribution to an organization, even though they do not meet the requirements of an extraordinary item or an unusual grant

Notes: The characterization of an item of expense as operating versus nonoperating is not driven by its classification as program, management, or fund-raising expense.

In general, expenses should follow related revenue: For example, if contributions are considered operating, then fund-raising expenses normally would be also, and vice versa.

PROVIDERS OF HEALTH CARE SERVICES

Martha Garner, CPA

PricewaterhouseCoopers LLP

36.1 THE HEALTH CARE INDUSTRY

(a) **OVERVIEW.**   Health care in the United States is provided by entities operating in all sectors of the economy. In the private sector, health care entities may be operated by religious organizations, owned by investors seeking a return on their investment, or sponsored by local communities. Public sector health care entities are operated at the federal, state, and local government levels. Consequently, health care providers may be subject to different accounting and reporting standards depending upon their "ownership" and form of organization.

Traditionally, the primary providers of health care services have been physicians, hospitals, and nursing homes. In the 1980s, cost containment pressures in the industry forced the development of less costly means of delivering certain services. Health maintenance organizations (HMOs) and other prepaid health care plans, home health agencies, ambulatory surgery centers, and specialty hospitals are among the alternative delivery systems and diversifications that have flourished in this climate. The rapidly growing elderly population has also focused attention on senior living communities, particularly those that offer residents health care services ranging from emergency nursing services to long-term inpatient-type care. In short, today's health care providers cover a broad spectrum of activities.

(b) **NOT-FOR-PROFIT PROVIDERS.**   This sector consists mainly of health care entities that are organized, sponsored, or operated by communities, religious groups, or private universities and medical schools. The fees charged by these not-for-profit business-oriented health care providers are intended to help the organization maintain its self-sustaining status rather than to maximize profit for an owner's benefit.

Not-for-profit health care entities are usually exempt from federal and state income taxes if they are operated exclusively for religious, charitable, scientific, or educational purposes and if no part of their net earnings inures to the benefit of any private shareholder or individual. However, they may be subject to taxes on income that is derived from activities not related to their tax-exempt purpose. Tax-exempt providers are allowed to generate profits in order to be able to meet financial obligations, improve patient care, expand facilities, and participate in research, training, education, and other activities that advance the entity's charitable purpose.

Although many tax-exempt health care entities may receive support from religious and fraternal organizations, individuals, corporations, and other donors or grantors, most are essentially self-sustaining; that is, they finance their capital needs primarily from the proceeds of debt issues and their operating needs largely from fees they charge for health care services rendered. As a result, accountability to creditors is more of a driving force in matters pertaining to financial statement presentation and disclosure than it is for nonprofit organizations that rely primarily on outside support. Comparability with financial statements of providers in the investor-owned sectors is also important. Consequently, not-for-profit health care providers must keep up with accounting standards of the business sector as well as the not-for-profit sector.

(c) **GOVERNMENTAL PROVIDERS.**   Governmental health care entities are owned and operated by federal, state, city, or county governments or other political subdivisions. The sponsoring government may participate directly in the operation of the facility, or there may be little interaction between the facility and the governmental unit. Such entities generally receive varying levels of subsidies from their sponsoring governments. This may range from heavy subsidization to no financial support, depending on the entity's circumstances.

Federally sponsored hospitals include hospitals operated by the Veterans' Administration, military hospitals, federal prison hospitals, and certain long-term specialty hospitals. Federal hospitals follow federal accounting guidelines, and are excluded from the scope of this chapter.

The American Institute of Certified Public Accountants (AICPA) audit and accounting guide *Health Care Organizations* defines governmental HCOs as public corporations and bodies corporate and politic. Other organizations are governmental organizations if they have one or more of the following characteristics:

- Popular election of officers or appointment (or approval) of a controlling majority of the members of the organization's governing body by officials of one or more state or local governments;
- The potential for unilateral dissolution by a government with the net assets reverting to a government; or
- The power to enact *and* enforce a tax levy.

Furthermore, organizations are presumed to be governmental if they have the ability to issue directly (rather than through a state or municipal authority) debt that pays interest exempt from federal taxation. However, organizations possessing only that ability (to issue tax-exempt debt) and none of the other governmental characteristics may rebut the presumption that they are governmental if their determination is supported by compelling, relevant evidence.

(d) INVESTOR-OWNED PROVIDERS.   Investor-owned HCOs may be organized as stock corporations (publicly traded or privately held), partnerships, or sole proprietorships. Many investor-owned HCOs are publicly traded, and therefore are also subject to Securities and Exchange Commission (SEC) reporting requirements.

36.2 AUTHORITATIVE PRONOUNCEMENTS

(a) GENERALLY ACCEPTED ACCOUNTING PRINCIPLES—PRIVATE SECTOR.   SAS No. 69, "The Meaning of 'Present Fairly in Conformity with Generally Accepted Accounting Principles' in the Independent Auditor's Report," sets forth the hierarchy of generally accepted accounting procedures (GAAP) for private sector organizations. Its applicability to investor-owned and not-for-profit health care providers is discussed in Chapter 1 of *Health Care Organizations*. Not-for-profit providers with tax-exempt debt should consider the definition of "governmental entity" discussed at Section 36.1(c) in determining whether to follow this GAAP hierarchy or the hierarchy established for governmental organizations.

Generally, not-for-profit HCOs are required to follow the guidance in effective provisions of Accounting Research Bulletins, APB Opinions, and Financial Accounting Standards Board (FASB) Statements and Interpretations, except for specific pronouncements that explicitly exempt not-for-profit organizations, do not apply to not-for-profit organizations by nature of their subject matter, or contain specialized accounting and reporting practices for other industries. Appendixes A to E of Chapter 1 of *Health Care Organizations* list all such pronouncements and the applicability/inapplicability of each to not-for-profit health care entities.

(b) GENERALLY ACCEPTED ACCOUNTING PRINCIPLES—PUBLIC SECTOR.   Since its inception in 1984, the Governmental Accounting Standards Board (GASB) has issued 39 statements and a number of interpretations of financial accounting and reporting standards that set forth accounting principles that must be followed by state and local government entities, including governmental HCOs.

SAS No. 69, "The Meaning of 'Present Fairly in Conformity with Generally Accepted Accounting Principles' in the Independent Auditor's Report," sets forth the hierarchy of GAAP for governmental organizations. Its applicability to governmental health care providers is discussed in Chapter 1 of *Health Care Organizations*.

Most governmental health care providers use enterprise fund accounting and reporting because they are financed and operated in a manner similar to private-sector entities. These organizations are included within the scope of the AICPA audit and accounting guide *Health Care Organizations* as well as the AICPA audit and accounting guide *Audits of State and Local Government Units.* GASB No. 20 states that governmental proprietary organizations should apply all applicable GASB pronouncements as well as any FASB Statements and Interpretations, APB Opinions, and ARBs issued on or before November 30, 1989, that do not conflict with or contradict GASB pronouncements. Furthermore, paragraph 7 of GASB No. 20 provides that governments operated as enterprise funds may apply all FASB Statements and Interpretations issued after November 30, 1989, that do not conflict with or contradict GASB pronouncements.[1] The requirements set forth in *Health Care Organizations* for governmental health care enterprises generally are directed to organizations that apply paragraph 7 of GASB No. 20. However, because those entities should not apply FASB Statements and Interpretations whose provisions are limited to not-for-profit organizations or those that address issues concerning primarily such organizations, they should disregard guidance contained in the Guide that is based on, or provided to implement, FASB Statements Nos. 116, 117, 124, and 136. Generally, such discussions are "flagged" with a footnote or statement citing that proscription.

Other governmental health care facilities (e.g., long-term institutional care of individuals with certain chronic conditions or mental impairments) finance their operating needs primarily from government support. These facilities often use governmental fund accounting and financial reporting because they do not meet the criteria requiring the use of enterprise funds and because user fees are not a principal revenue source for the activity. Consequently, they may be set us as departments under the umbrella of a city, county, or state government. Such organizations are subject to the AICPA audit and accounting guide *Audits of State and Local Government Units.* The guidance in the AICPA audit and accounting guide *Health Care Organizations* does not apply to these organizations, and Chapter 35, rather than this chapter, should be consulted for guidance regarding their accounting and financial reporting considerations.

(c) SECURITIES AND EXCHANGE COMMISSION REQUIREMENTS. Although many investor-owned HCOs are publicly traded, at this time there are no unique SEC rules pertaining specifically to investor-owned health care providers. While not-for-profit and governmental health care entities that issue tax-exempt securities are exempt from the registration and reporting requirements of the federal securities laws, they have to make certain disclosures at the time securities are issued and thereafter on an ongoing basis.[2] In accordance with an SEC rule titled *Municipal Securities Disclosure,* underwriters' agreements require municipal borrowers to provide specific financial information—for example, annual audited financial statements and timely notices of material events, such as rating changes or delays in principal and interest payments—to "repositories" of municipal securities information (similar in some ways to the reporting requirements for SEC registrants). The repositories make the information available to bondholders and prospective bondholders. Additionally, SEC Interpretive Release No. 33-7049, *Statement of the Commission Regarding Disclosure Obligations of Municipal Securities Issuers and Others,* is intended to assist municipal securities issuers, brokers, and dealers in meeting their obligations under the antifraud provisions of the securities laws. These releases are available on the SEC's Web site (www.sec.gov).

(d) HEALTHCARE FINANCIAL MANAGEMENT ASSOCIATION PRINCIPLES AND PRACTICES BOARD. In 1975, the leadership of the Healthcare Financial Management Association (HFMA), a major trade organization that monitors financial issues related to health care providers,

---

[1] The GASB's web site (*www.gasb.org*) contains a list of FASB pronouncements issued since November 30, 1989, and their applicability to enterprises that apply paragraph 7 of Statement 20. This is updated periodically.
[2] The ongoing or "continuing" disclosure requirements apply to securities for which underwriting commitments were executed on or after July 3, 1995.

formed a Principles and Practices Board (P&P Board). The P&P Board is a panel of 12 individuals who are nationally prominent in the area of health care accounting and financial reporting and who set forth advisory recommendations on emerging health care accounting and reporting issues in the form of Statements and Issues Analyses. Although Statements by the P&P Board are advisory in nature, they are of significant value to the industry in that they can be issued relatively quickly to disseminate consensus opinions, along with views on the issues and relevant background information, on topics for which guidance is needed. Once GAAP guidance is provided by a recognized standard-setting body, the statement usually is withdrawn. P&PB Issue Analyses provide short-term assistance on emerging issues. Regulators such as the IRS and the SEC have, in recent years, begun referencing certain of the Statements in correspondence and publications. Information on statements issued by the P&P Board can be obtained from HFMA, Two Westbrook Corporate Center, Suite 700, Westchester, IL 60154 (*www.hfma.org*).

(e) AMERICAN INSTITUTE OF CERTIFIED PUBLIC ACCOUNTANTS AUDIT GUIDE. The American Institute of Certified Public Accountants (AICPA) is the primary source of guidance relating to industry-specific accounting principles and reporting practices for health care organizations (HCOs). Throughout this chapter, the principles outlined herein are those contained in the AICPA audit and accounting guide, *Health Care Organizations,*[3] issued in 1996.

Generally, the Guide applies to all entities whose principal operations involve providing (or agreeing to provide, in the case of prepaid health care arrangements) health care services to individuals. This includes (but is not limited to) hospitals, including specialty facilities such as psychiatric or rehabilitation hospitals; nursing homes; subacute care facilities; HMOs and other providers of prepaid health care services; continuing care retirement facilities (CCRCs); home health companies; ambulatory care companies such as clinics, medical group practices, individual practice associations, and individual practitioners; emergency care facilities; surgery centers; outpatient rehabilitation and cancer treatment centers; and integrated health care delivery systems (also called *health networks*) that include one or more of these types of organizations. It also applies to organizations whose primary activities are the planning, organization, and oversight of entities providing health care services, such as parent or holding companies of health care providers.

There are some exceptions to this general rule, based on the health care organization's ownership characteristics.

- The Audit Guide applies to all such entities described above that are investor-owned.
- With regard to entities described above that operate in the not-for-profit sector, the Guide adds another parameter to the definition: In addition to the provision of health care services, the organization must also derive all or almost all of its revenues from provision of goods and services. This is directed at certain health care organizations that provide health care services, but whose primary source of income is contribution income rather than revenues earned in exchange for providing (or agreeing to provide) health care services. Those types of organizations (defined in SFAS No. 117, par. 168 as "voluntary health and welfare organizations") thereafter would fall within the scope of the AICPA Audit and Accounting Guide Audits of Not-for-Profit Organizations, rather than the Health Care Guide.
- The Guide is specifically applicable to governmental providers that elect to follow GAS No. 20, par. 7, and it was cleared by the GASB prior to issuance. Therefore, it meets the GASB's criteria for classification as category (b) guidance under the governmental GAAP hierarchy. However, governmental health care enterprises are instructed in GAS No. 29 to disregard the provisions of the guide that are based on FAS No. 116, 117, and 124 [see Subsection 36.2(b)].

---

[3] Previous editions were the *Hospital Audit Guide* (1972) and *Audits of Providers of Health Care Services* (1990).

(f) DEFINITION OF "PUBLIC COMPANY" IN THE APPLICATION OF FINANCIAL ACCOUNTING STANDARDS BOARD STANDARDS, HEALTH CARE ORGANIZATIONS, AND AUDITS OF NOT-FOR-PROFIT ORGANIZATIONS. Several recent FASB standards have differentiated between public and nonpublic entities in the application of the standards. Careful consideration should be given to such standards in determining whether an entity whose debt securities trade in a public market (including limited markets) should be considered a public entity for purposes of a particular statement.

36.3 ACCOUNTING PRINCIPLES

(a) CLASSIFICATION AND REPORTING OF NET ASSETS. Not-for-profit and governmental hospitals traditionally have used fund accounting for record-keeping and financial reporting purposes. This accounting technique helps those providers to carry out their fiduciary responsibilities in ensuring that donor-restricted resources are used only for the purposes specified by the donor or grantor. For purposes of external financial reporting, all funds of not-for-profit HCOs must be classified into one or more of three broad classes of net assets: unrestricted, temporarily restricted, or permanently restricted.

For governmental providers, the classes are unrestricted, restricted (expendable or nonexpendable), or "invested in capital assets, net of related debt."

(i) Unrestricted Net Assets. For both not-for-profit and governmental providers, "unrestricted net assets" is the residual component of net assets. For not-for-profit providers, assets and liabilities that are free of any donor-imposed restrictions are included in this classification. The unrestricted components generally include the provider's working capital, long-term debt, and investment in property plant and equipment. It also includes assets whose use is limited to a particular purpose [see Subsection 36.3(b)].

For governmental providers, unrestricted net assets are net assets that do not meet the definition of "restricted" or "invested in capital assets, net of related debt." They are the part of net assets that can be used to finance day-to-day operations without constraints established by debt covenants, donor restrictions, irrevocable trusts, and the like.

(ii) Restricted Net Assets. Not-for-profit and governmental providers have different definitions of "restricted." For not-for-profit providers, assets that are specifically restricted to use for a particular purpose by an external donor or grantor, along with any related obligations, are included in this component. Although donor-imposed restrictions may require individual gifts or grants to be kept separate for record-keeping purposes, as a general rule they may be grouped for financial reporting purposes. Groupings are determined based on whether the restrictions are temporary or permanent, and on the uses for which the resources are intended. The nature of restrictions on donor-restricted resources, if such amounts are material, should be disclosed in the financial statements.

The definition of "restricted" for governmental providers is broader than the not-for-profit definition of "restricted," and it applies to both assets and net assets. Assets are reported as restricted when restrictions on their use change the nature or normal understanding of the availability of the asset. For example, cash and investments held in a separate account that can be used only for specific purposes established by a party external to the organization and that cannot be used to satisfy the organization's general liabilities should be reported as restricted assets.[4] In addition to resources restricted for identified purposes by donors and grants, assets considered to be "restricted" include unexpended debt proceeds held by trustees, bond sinking and debt service reserve funds, and assets set aside to meet statutory reserve requirements. Self-insurance assets held in irrevocable trusts

---

[4] The word "restricted" is not required to be used in labeling the assets themselves; however, the descriptions used on the face of the balance sheet should make it clear that such assets cannot be used to satisfy liabilities other than those that are specifically intended to be satisfied with the restricted assets.

also are considered to be restricted; although the limitation on their use is not externally imposed (because the provider voluntarily enters into the self-insurance arrangement), the irrevocable nature of the trust creates a legally enforceable restriction on the assets, which have irrevocably been set aside for the payment of future malpractice claims and, therefore, cannot be used to satisfy other obligations of the entity.

For a governmental entity, "restricted net assets" represents restricted assets reduced by liabilities related to those assets. A liability relates to restricted assets if (1) the assets resulted from incurring the liability (e.g., unexpended debt proceeds held by a trustee) or (2) the liability will be liquidated with the restricted assets (e.g., bond sinking fund proceeds that will be used to make payments on a particular debt issue). Major categories of restrictions should be reported on the face of the balance sheet (e.g., "restricted for capital acquisitions").

(iii) Invested in Capital Assets, Net of Related Debt.   This net asset class is used only by governmental organizations (because not-for-profit entities include their investments in property and equipment and related liabilities in unrestricted net assets). Its balance is the sum of capital assets (net of accumulated depreciation) less any related debt used to finance those assets.

(b) ASSETS WHOSE USE IS LIMITED.   Health Care Organizations require cash (and claims to cash) that meet any of the following four criteria[5] to be reported separately and excluded from current assets:

1. Are restricted as to withdrawal or use for other than current operations
2. Are designated for expenditures in the acquisition or construction of noncurrent assets
3. Are required to be segregated for liquidation of long-term debt
4. Are required by a donor-imposed restriction that limits their use to long-term purposes (e.g., purchase of capital assets)

(i) Not-for-Profit Providers.   Many not-for-profit health care providers report certain of these noncurrent assets under the balance sheet caption "assets whose use is limited." Generally, assets reported in this manner represent funds that are maintained separately from funds used for general operating purposes. Frequently, they are held by a trustee.

The caption includes funds whose use is contractually limited by external parties, such as:

- Unexpended proceeds of debt issues (or other debt financing instruments) that are held by a trustee and that are limited to use in accordance with the requirements of the financing instrument. (When a financing authority issues tax-exempt bonds or similar debt instruments and uses the proceeds for the benefit of a health care entity, the proceeds are limited to use for project costs. The proceeds of the bond issue are administered under the terms of the indenture by an independent trustee.)
- Funds deposited with a trustee and limited to use in accordance with the requirements of an indenture or similar agreement, such as bond sinking funds.
- Other assets limited to use for identified purposes through an agreement with an outside party other than a donor or grantor. Examples include debt service reserve funds required by bond indentures, malpractice self-insurance trust funds (whether legally revocable or irrevocable), and assets set aside to meet HMO statutory reserve requirements.

This caption may also include assets set aside for specific purposes by the provider's governing board or management, over which they retain control and may, at their discretion, subsequently decide to use for other purposes. Examples include assets set aside that are designated for plant replacement or expansion (a long-standing industry practice referred to as *funded depreciation*).

---

[5] These criteria are based on the guidance in Chapter 3A of ARB No. 43.

This is an acceptable practice under GAAP, based on ARB No. 43's criteria. However, HCOs require providers that report internally designated assets under this caption to distinguish them from assets whose use is contractually limited by external parties. (This distinction is considered important because of the degree of control the organization is able to maintain over the use of those funds.) This may be accomplished either through disclosure in the notes to the financial statements or by presenting separate amounts on the face of the balance sheet.

ARB No. 43 states that where funds are set aside for the liquidation of long-term debts, payments to sinking funds, or similar purposes are considered to offset maturing debt which has properly been set up as a current liability, they may be classified as current assets. Similarly, HCO explicitly requires a portion of malpractice self-insurance funds equal to the amount of assets expected to be liquidated to pay malpractice claims classified as current liabilities to be classified as current assets. A note generally is included in the summary of significant policies (or separately) describing the purpose of the limited-use assets.

(ii) Governmental Providers. Governmental health care entities report these types of limitations as "restrictions" when they arise from external sources or are externally imposed, as discussed in Subsection 36.3(a)(ii).

Management's designation of net assets (i.e., internal limitations indicating that management does not consider them to be available for general operations) are not reported on the face of the balance sheet.

(c) AGENCY TRANSACTIONS. Health care entities may act as agents for other parties; as such, they receive and hold assets that are owned by others. An example of this would be patients' or residents' funds. These are funds held by the facility for the patient's or resident's own personal use, such as for purchasing periodicals, making trips outside the facility, or for other incidentals. Usually, these funds are kept in an account separate from the facility's own cash accounts. In accepting responsibility for these assets, the entity incurs a liability to the owner either to return them in the future or to disburse them to another party on behalf of the owner. Transactions involving agency funds (e.g., disbursements, interest earned) should not have any economic impact on the provider's operations. Consequently, they should not be included in the provider's income statement.

Fund-raising foundations may act as agents in accepting donations on behalf of related HCOs. These situations are discussed in Subsection 36.3(k)(iv).

(d) REVENUE OF HEALTH CARE FACILITIES. A unique aspect of health care operations is that revenue transactions primarily involve more parties than the traditional "buyer" and "seller." As many as four parties may be associated with a revenue transaction involving a health care provider. These include: (1) the individual who receives the care; (2) the physician who orders the required services on behalf of the patient; (3) the health care entity that provides the setting or administers the treatment; and (4) a third-party payer that pays the health care entity, physician, or both on behalf of the patient. The third-party payer may be a government program such as Medicare or Medicaid and/or a commercial insurer such as a managed care plan, a commercial insurance company, a Blue Cross plan, or a preferred provider organization (PPO).

The extent to which third-party payers are involved in paying for services varies by type of health care facility. For hospitals, rehabilitation facilities, and home health companies, the majority of services provided are paid for by third-party payers. In the nursing home sector, roughly half of the patients are considered "private pay" (i.e., the patient or their family pays for the care); for the remainder, Medicaid is the dominant third-party payer (for care provided to low-income individuals). Little commercial insurance coverage presently exists for nursing home care, and Medicare provides very limited nursing home benefits only for short stays. In CCRCs, entrance fees and monthly service fees are paid by the residents themselves, and third-party payer involvement is limited to payment of some services that may be provided in the skilled nursing care portion of the facility.

Third-party payers typically do not pay the health care organization's established rates. The amount paid may be based on government regulations (for Medicare, Medicaid, and other government programs) or contractual arrangements (for PPOs, Blue Cross plans, HMOs, and commercial insurers). The difference between the established charges and the payment rates is referred to as the *contractual allowance* or *contractual adjustment*. Because the amounts received from third party payers bear little relationship to a health care organization's established charges, reporting gross charges in the financial statements is not considered meaningful. Consequently, the Guide instructs providers to report net patient service revenues (i.e., gross changes less contractual adjustments and other deductions from revenue) in the statement of operations.[6]

HCOs that have more than one primary source of revenue (e.g., significant amounts of both patient service revenue and capitation fees) should report them separately in the statement of operations.

(i) Revenue Recognition.   The conceptual basis for revenue recognition is contained in FASB Statement of Financial Accounting Concepts No. 5, "Recognition and Measurement in Financial Statements of Business Enterprises," which states:

> Revenues are not recognized until earned. An entity's revenue-earning activities involve delivering or producing goods, rendering services, or other activities that constitute its ongoing major or central operations, and revenues are considered to have been earned when the entity has substantially accomplished what it must do to be entitled to the benefits represented by the revenues.

With respect to third-party payer arrangements, government regulations or contractual terms will specify what the provider must do in order to be entitled to revenue under the contract or provider agreement. Regulations or contracts will also address payment terms and the degree of risk that is to be assumed by the provider. Consequently, a thorough understanding of the terms of the provider's arrangements with significant third-party payers is important for revenue recognition.

Revenue recognition considerations for broad classes of healthcare revenue and common payment methodologies are discussed below.

Patient Service Revenue.   Patient service revenue is derived from fees earned in exchange for providing services to patients. Payment methodologies include:

- *Fee-for-service.* Under fee-for-service arrangements, payment is made for the specific services that are provided to the patient; therefore, the provider earns revenue as a result of providing those services. Payment may be made at the provider's full established rates, a predetermined discounted rate (e.g., percent of charges), or a fee schedule agreed to by the provider and the third-party payer.
- *Per diem.* Under a per-diem arrangement, the provider is paid a predetermined flat rate per day of inpatient care, regardless of the level of intensity of the care provided. Therefore, revenue is earned as a result of the patient occupying a bed for a particular day. The Medicare prospective payment system (PPS) for skilled nursing facility services is an example of a per-diem methodology.
- *Per case.* Under a per-case arrangement, the provider is paid a predetermined amount based on the patient's "discharge category." The Medicare PPS for hospital inpatient services is an example of a per-case payment methodology involving diagnosis-related groupings. Medicare's PPS for hospital outpatient services is another per-case methodology based on groupings of procedures performed.

---

[6] Health care companies that are SEC registrants may be asked by the SEC staff to provide information related to routine contractual adjustments in Schedule II of Form 10-K (Valuation and Qualifying Accounts). Unlike the types of reserves contemplated in Schedule II, contractual adjustments are intrinsically related to the revenue estimation process. They are not tied to balance sheet accounts and they do not roll forward from year to year. Therefore, such information is not appropriate for inclusion in Schedule II.

- *Episodic.* Under an episodic payment methodology, the provider is paid a predetermined amount for services provided to patients during an "episode of care" (i.e., a stipulated period of time). Revenue is earned based on the passage of time. Medicare's PPS for home health services is an example of an episodic payment methodology.

Capitation. Under the methods discussed above, providers earn revenue as a result of providing services to patients. Under capitation arrangements, the provider earns revenue by *agreeing to* provide covered services to a specific population (e.g., members of a health plan) during a specified time period (usually one month), regardless of whether any services are actually provided or how expensive those services are. The provider is paid a fixed, predetermined amount per member per month.

Capitation revenue is similar to premium revenue earned by HMOs; it is not patient service revenue. Therefore, revenue under capitation contracts should be reported in the period that plan members are entitled to receive health care services. Capitation payments are generally made at the beginning of each month and obligate the provider to render covered services during that month. Therefore, revenue earned under capitation contracts should be recorded by the provider on a month-to-month basis. If capitation payments are received in advance of the month to which they relate, they must be reported as deferred revenue until they are earned. If the provider's accounting system records patient charges and establishes patient receivables as services are rendered, valuation allowances or adjustments must be recorded so only the amount of capitation revenue is reported in the financial statements.

Resident Service Revenue. This represents revenue derived from fees charged to residents of senior living centers such as CCRCs. These types of revenue are discussed at Section 36.4(a).

In addition to Concepts Statement No. 5, the primary sources of accounting guidance on revenue recognition issues associated with patient and resident service revenue are the Guide and AICPA SOP 00-1, "Auditing Health Care Third-Party Revenues and Related Receivables." Sources of accounting guidance on revenue recognition issues associated with prepaid health care arrangements such as capitation contracts include AICPA SOP 81-1, "Accounting for Performance of Construction-Type and Certain Production-Type Contracts" (by analogy) and EITF Issue No. 99–19, "Reporting Revenue Gross as a Principal versus Net as an Agent." Although its status is nonauthoritative, the FASB's 1978 Invitation to Comment, *Accounting for Certain Service Transactions*, may also be helpful in understanding revenue recognition issues associated with contracts.

(ii) Estimating Revenue Related to Governmental Programs. Determining with certainty the amount of cash that ultimately will be received by a health care provider as payment for services rendered during a particular year to Medicare or Medicaid program beneficiaries may take several years. As a result, in the year in which services are rendered, providers must estimate the amount of cash flows ultimately expected to be received for those services and report that amount as revenue. The difference between that amount and the amount of payments received before the balance sheet date is reflected as a receivable or payable in the balance sheet and as a valuation allowance to adjust gross revenues to "net patient services revenues" in the statement of operations. That accrual should be adjusted as events occur that change the estimate of revenue earned.

The amount of revenue earned under arrangements with government programs is determined under complex government rules and regulations that subject the organization to the potential for retrospective adjustments in future years. Because several years may elapse before all potential adjustments related to a particular fiscal year are known, management must estimate the effects of future program audits, administrative reviews, and billing reviews. In making these estimates, management also must take into account the potential for regulatory investigations that may result in denial of otherwise valid claims for payment. These matters are discussed in AICPA SOP 00-1. Among other things, the SOP provides guidance to auditors regarding uncertainties inherent in third-party revenue recognition and regarding reporting on financial statements of health care entities exposed to material uncertainties.

Management's estimates relating to third-party revenue recognition are based on subjective as well as objective factors. This requires judgment that normally is based on management's knowledge of and experience with past and current events and on its assumptions about conditions it expects to exist and courses of action it expects to take. As a result, the extent of management's estimates involving contractual allowances and adjustments may range from relatively straightforward calculations based on information that is readily available, to highly complex judgments based on assumptions as to future events.

All relevant information is used in making these estimates. Approaches vary from entity to entity, depending on individual facts and circumstances. Some entities with significant prior experience may attempt to quantify the effects of individual potential intermediary or other governmental (e.g., Office of Inspector General or Department of Justice) or private payer adjustments, based on detailed calculations and assumptions regarding potential future adjustments. Some may prepare cost report analyses to estimate the effect of potential adjustments. Others may base their estimates on an analysis of potential adjustments in the aggregate, in light of the payers involved, the nature of the payment mechanism, the risks associated with future audits, and other relevant factors. In some cases, the uncertainty surrounding a potential adjustment may be so great that management is unable to make a reasonable estimate of the financial effect for inclusion in the financial statements. In such situations, disclosure regarding such uncertainties should be made in the notes to the financial statements.

Future events (e.g., final settlements, ongoing audits and investigations, or passage of time in relation to the statute of limitations) may differ from management's assumptions and therefore require revision of the balance sheet accrual. The audit and accounting guide *Health Care Organizations* requires that differences between original estimates and subsequent revisions be included in the statement of operations in the period in which the revisions are made and be disclosed, if material; they should not be treated as prior period adjustments unless they meet the criteria for prior period adjustments in SFAS No. 16.

The likelihood of such revisions, coupled with their potential material effect on the financial statements, generally requires disclosure in accordance with SOP 94-6, "Disclosure of Certain Significant Risks and Uncertainties." Such disclosures might include the significance of government program revenues to the entity's overall revenues and a description of the complex nature of applicable laws and regulations, indicating that the possibility of future government review and interpretation exists. SOP 00-1 illustrates this disclosure.

(e) REVENUE OF MANAGED CARE COMPANIES.   In recent years, the line between health care providers and health insurers has blurred substantially. In managed care companies, a third-party payer (e.g., an insurer or health plan) is involved in managing the provider delivery system as well as performing the financing function.

One type of managed care company is the HMO. HMOs are organized health care systems that are responsible for both the financing and the delivery of a broad range of comprehensive health services to an enrolled population. Premium revenue is the primary source of revenue for HMOs. The HMO then provides or arranges for provision of covered services to its members, either by using its own facilities and physicians or by sending members to facilities and physicians with which it has contractual relationships. Payment arrangements with those providers may be based on services provided, or they may involve capitation (under which the providers receive prepayment for services on a per member per month basis).

Specialty managed care companies usually subcontract to comprehensive health plans to provide a specified type of services to an enrolled population. Capitation payments often represent the primary source of revenue for these entities. Issues related to revenue recognition under capitation arrangements are discussed at Subsection 36.3(d)(i).

(i) Reporting Revenue Net or Gross.   Gross versus net reporting of revenue is a significant issue for many managed care organizations, particularly those that subcontract to comprehensive health plans. In those situations, the question is whether the organization's statement of operations should reflect gross revenues and expenses related to the managed care contract, or instead reflect the net amount in income in a caption such as "Network Management Fees Earned."

EITF No. 99-19, "Reporting Revenue Gross as a Principal versus Net as an Agent," addresses situations in which an organization should recognize revenue based on (1) the gross amount billed to the customer because it has earned revenue from the sale of goods or services, or (2) the net amount retained (i.e., the amount billed to the customer less the amount paid to a supplier) because, in substance, it has earned a commission or fee from the supplier. While Issue No. 99-19 states that it excludes transactions involving insurance and reinsurance premiums, that exclusion pertains to contracts covered under authoritative literature for insurance enterprises (e.g., FAS Nos. 60, 97, 113), rather than the prepaid health care arrangements addressed in *Health Care Organizations.*

EITF No. 99-19 concludes that the determination of gross versus net revenue reporting is a matter of judgment that depends on the relevant facts and circumstances, and that each organization's specific facts and circumstances should be evaluated against the following list of indicators that would point toward either gross or net reporting:

Indicators of Gross Revenue Reporting

- Organization is the primary obligor in the arrangement (i.e., responsible for fulfillment, including acceptability of the product or service provided).
- Organization has general inventory risk (for sales of products) or is obligated to compensate individual service providers for work performed (for sales of services).
- Organization has latitude in establishing price for the product or service.
- Organization adds value by changing the nature of the product or by performing part of the service.
- Organization has discretion in supplier selection.
- Organization is involved in the determination of product or service specifications.
- Organization has credit risk.

Indicators of Net Revenue Reporting.

- Supplier (rather than the organization) is the primary obligor in the arrangement.
- Amount the organization earns is a fixed portion of the overall transaction price (i.e., a set dollar amount per transaction; a stated percent of amount billed).
- Supplier (rather than the organization) has credit risk.

The EITF observed that while some of these indicators are stronger than others, no single indicator would provide a presumption that gross or net treatment should be used. The relative strength of all indicators present should be considered.

(f) SETTLEMENTS WITH THIRD-PARTY PAYERS. Payments received under contracts with third-party payers such as Medicare and Medicaid, often are based on estimates. In most cases, these payments are subject to adjustment either during the contract term or afterward, when the actual level of services provided under the contract is known. Final settlements are determined after the close of the fiscal period to which they apply. In the interim, additional information may become available that will necessitate revision of the estimate. Such adjustments have the potential to materially affect the health care entity's financial position and results of operations. The health care entity must make its best estimate of these adjustments on a current basis and reflect these amounts in the Statement of Operations. To the extent that the subsequent actual adjustments are more or less than the estimate, such amounts should be reflected in the Statement of Operations for the period in which the final adjustment becomes known. It is not appropriate to reflect such amounts as prior period adjustments. The Guide requires that amounts receivable from/payable to third-party payers be set forth separately in the balance sheet, if material, and that significant changes in settlement estimates be disclosed in accordance with SOP 94-6. Additional guidance on these matters can be found in SOP 00-1, "Auditing Health Care Third-Party Revenues and Related Receivables."

For health care companies that are SEC registrants, reserves related to third-party settlements represent an area of increased SEC scrutiny, due to SEC's concerns over the potential use of reserves to manipulate earnings by accruing larger-than-necessary reserves under the guise of "conservatism" and then reversing those excess accruals to boost earnings when needed in subsequent periods. Registrants are expected to review the propriety of the reserve amounts each quarter and increase or decrease the accrual based on new events or changes in facts and circumstances. When significant adjustments are reported, the SEC staff may inquire about the registrant's policy on establishing and relieving third-party reserves and ask what new facts and circumstances occurred that triggered the adjustment in the particular period in which it was reported. In some cases, the SEC staff is requiring HCOs to provide detailed disclosures in the notes to the financial statements and the Management Discussions and Analysis (MD&A) on reserve changes and to explain the reasons for reserve adjustments.

(g) BAD DEBTS.   The Guide defines bad debt expense as "the provision for actual or expected uncollectibles resulting from the extension of credit." The provision for bad debts should be determined on an accrual basis and reported as an expense.

(h) CHARITY CARE.   Providers often render services free of charge (or at discounted rates) to individuals who have no means to pay for them. The accounting for the write-off of charges pertaining to charity services is similar to that for bad debts; an allowance for charity services should be established, which is a valuation account related to patient accounts receivable. The provision for charity services should be determined on an accrual basis and accounted for as a deduction from gross revenue.

Special rules apply to the reporting of charity care in the provider's financial statements. According to the Guide, charity care results from an entity's policy to provide health care services free of charge to individuals who meet certain financial criteria. Because no cash flows are expected from these services, charges pertaining to charity services do not qualify for recognition as revenue in the provider's financial statements. The provider is considered to have given away the services, rather than having "sold" them. Receivables reported in the balance sheet for health care services and the related valuation allowance similarly should not include amounts related to charity care. These prohibitions hold true on the face of the financial statements and in any note disclosures or supplemental schedules that accompany the financial statements.

However, the Guide does not intend for all mention of charity care to disappear from the financial statements. Charity care represents an important element of the services provided by many facilities. Accordingly, the Guide requires specific disclosures regarding charity care to be made in the notes to the financial statements. A statement of management's policy with regard to providing charity care, and the fact that charity services do not result in the production of revenue, should be included in the entity's "summary of significant accounting policies." The level of charity care provided for each of the years covered by the financial statements also must be disclosed in the notes to the financial statements. The level of care provided may be measured in a variety of ways, such as at established rates, costs, patient days, occasions of service, or other statistics. The method used to measure the charity care should also be disclosed. These disclosures are applicable to for-profit providers as well as not-for-profit providers.

The Guide recognizes that distinguishing charity care write-offs from bad debt write-offs is not easy in the health care environment. Because charity care results from an entity's policy to provide health care services free of charge to individuals who meet certain financial criteria, the establishment of a formal management policy clearly defining charity care should result in a reasonable determination, according to the Guide.

Some facilities may choose to provide information concerning gross service revenue and deductions from revenue in either the notes to the financial statements or in a supplemental schedule.

If this type of financial statement disclosure is made, the amount shown as gross service revenue may not include charges attributable to services provided to charity patients, and deductions from revenue may not include the provision for charity care.

Contributions, bequests, and grants received that are restricted to be used for care of charity patients are considered to be directly related to the provision of health care services, and are normally classified as "other revenue" when they are expended for their intended purpose, regardless of the provider's accounting policy with regard to other types of contributions and grants. It is not appropriate to account for and report such funds as a reduction of the provision for charity care.

(i) REPORTING REVENUES, EXPENSES, GAINS, AND LOSSES. By definition, income arising from the direct provision of health care services to patients, clients, or residents is classified as revenue, and the cost of providing those services similarly is classified as expense. Similarly, premium income in HMOs is directly related to the provision of, arranging for, or agreeing to provide health care services and therefore should be classified as revenue. Costs related to the provision of, arranging for, or agreeing to provide health care services in a prepaid health care plan should be classified as expense.

Aside from the provision of health care services, a number of other activities are normal in the day-to-day operation of a health care facility. Such income should be accounted for separately from health care service revenue. Examples include:

- Sales of medical and pharmacy supplies to employees, physicians, and others
- Proceeds from sales of cafeteria meals and guest trays to employees, medical staff, and visitors
- Proceeds from sales of scrap, used x-ray film, and so on
- Proceeds from sales at gift shops, snack bars, newsstands, parking lots, vending machines, and other service facilities operated by the entity
- Income from education programs
- Rental of facility space
- Income from transportation services provided to residents
- Investment income

(j) CONCENTRATION OF CREDIT RISK. FASB Statement No. 107, "Disclosure about Fair Value of Financial Instruments," requires disclosure of information about significant concentrations of credit risk from third parties for all financial instruments including trade accounts receivable. Concentration of credit risk is usually an issue for hospitals and physician groups because of the emergency nature of many of the services provided and because they generally tend to treat patients from their local or surrounding communities. An economic event, such as the closing of a large industrial plant, may leave many of the community's residents without insurance. Because an accident or illness requiring an individual to incur hospitalization expense usually is not a matter of choice, many who partake of a provider's services are unable to pay for those services. Hospitals that participate in federal programs cannot deny services to patients who are perceived to be bad credit risks. Therefore, hospitals frequently extend a great deal of unsecured credit. It should be noted that the concentration of credit risk for an individual hospital is different from what it would be for a national multihospital system that includes the individual hospital. When the individual facilities' financial statements are consolidated into statements prepared for the entire system, the credit risk is spread over a much larger geographic area and is therefore not as concentrated.

Some state Medicaid programs are experiencing fiscal problems that may result in inordinately long payment delays or retroactively reduced payment amounts. Such situations may create credit risks for providers with significant concentrations of Medicaid patients or residents.

(k) CONTRIBUTIONS. *Health Care Organizations* "scopes out" (i.e., excludes) health care providers that derive their revenues primarily from contributions from the general public, rather than from fees received in exchange for goods and services. Those organizations instead are required to follow the financial reporting requirements applicable to voluntary health and welfare organizations and other eleemosynary organizations (discussed in Chapter 35).

A health care organization may be the beneficiary of contributions made by donors via a recipient organization, such as an institutionally related foundation. Issues associated with contributions received through such foundations are discussed at Subsection 36.3(k)(iv).

(i) Not-for-Profit Providers.   For not-for-profit providers, the accounting and reporting of contributions received and contributions made is generally governed by FAS No. 116,[7] as modified by certain requirements contained in *Health Care Organizations*. Those modifications are as follows:

- Under FAS No. 116, gifts or grants that are restricted for construction or renovation projects, property or equipment purchases, or capital debt retirement are added to unrestricted net assets when the assets are received. The Guide requires not-for-profit health care providers to exclude such contributions from net income (i.e., report them below the operating indicator in the Statement of Operations).
- The Guide requires providers to recognize the expiration of donor restrictions at the time the asset is placed in service. This is a narrowing of the options available to other types of not-for-profit organizations under FAS No. 116.

(ii) Governmental Providers.   FASB No. 116 does not apply to governmental health care enterprises. Instead, GASB Statement No. 33, "Accounting and Financial Reporting for Nonexchange Transactions," establishes accounting and financial reporting standards for the timing of recognition of nonexchange transactions involving financial or capital resources. It does not apply to noncapital gifts-in-kind or contributed services.

GAS No. 33 defines a nonexchange transaction (e.g., a contribution) as one in which there is no direct and equivalent exchange of value between the resource provider and the recipient of those funds. Governmental health care enterprises classify nonexchange transactions into one of four classes based on their principal characteristics. The predominant form of nonexchange transaction involving governmental HCOs are "voluntary nonexchange transactions," which include certain grants and most donations. Revenue from voluntary nonexchange transactions should be recognized when all applicable "eligibility requirements" have been met. GAS No. 33 specifies four kinds of eligibility requirements: (1) the recipient has the characteristics specified by the resource provider—for example, a certain type of grant that is made only to hospitals with certain characteristics; (2) time requirements have been met; (3) the recipient has complied with any contingencies stipulated by the provider—for example, to qualify for the provider's resources, a potential recipient must first raise a certain amount of resources from third parties; (4) for expenditure-driven grants, the recipient has incurred allowable costs under the resource provider's program.

HCOs should recognize receivables and revenues (net of estimated uncollectible amounts) arising from promises to give (i.e., pledges) when all eligibility requirements are met, provided that the promise is verifiable and the resources are measurable and probable of collection. The only exception to recognition relates to promises of term or permanent endowments, which are discussed in the following paragraph.

If the nonexchange transaction is a term endowment or a permanent endowment, the provider's stipulation that the resources should be maintained intact in perpetuity, for a specified number of years, or until a specific event has occurred (e.g., the donor's death) is a time requirement. In such situations, the time requirement is considered met as soon as the recipient begins to honor the provider's stipulation not to sell, disburse, or consume the resources. The health care organization cannot begin to honor the provider's stipulation until the resources are received; therefore, promises to give term or permanent endowments are not recognized in financial statements. The health care organization should recognize revenues from term or permanent endowments when the resources

---

[7] A comprehensive treatment of FAS No. 116 is contained in Chapter 33.

are received, provided that all other eligibility requirements have been met. The associated net assets should be reported as restricted for as long as the donor's time requirements (and purpose restrictions, if applicable) remain in effect.

GASB Statement No. 34, "Basic Financial Statements—and Management's Discussion and Analysis—for State and Local Governments," provide guidance on how nonexchange transactions should be reported in financial statements. Contributions (both unrestricted and restricted) are reported as nonoperating revenue unless a restriction relates to a capital purpose (e.g., construction, renovation, equipment purchases, capital debt retirement). Contributions related to capital purposes (e.g., contributions of capital assets, or of financial resources that must be used to acquire capital assets) are reported below nonoperating revenue, as are term and permanent endowments.

Governmental entities that receive restricted resources are required to disclose whether, when both restricted and unrestricted resources are available, it is their policy to use restricted or unrestricted resources first.

(iii) Contributions Established Through Trusts. Some donors enter into trusts (or similar agreements) under which providers receive benefits that are shared with other beneficiaries. Examples of such arrangements (termed *split-interest agreements*) include charitable lead trusts, charitable remainder trusts, charitable gift annuities, and pooled life income funds. As a general rule, assets received under split-interest-type agreements should be recorded at their fair value when received. Recognition and measurement principles for these arrangements are discussed in Chapter 35. Additionally, some split-interest agreements may contain an embedded derivative that must be separated from its "host" contract and accounted for separately. This is discussed at Subsection 36.3 (m)(i).

Though not technically a split-interest agreement, perpetual trusts held by third parties are similar, except that the provider is usually the sole beneficiary. Funds contributed to the trust are to be invested in perpetuity under the terms of the trust; the provider is to be the sole beneficiary and is to receive annually the income on the trusts' assets (i.e., the provider has the irrevocable right to receive the income earned on the trust assets in perpetuity, but never receives the assets held in trust). The accounting and reporting issues are similar to those of split-interest agreements. Perpetual trusts held by third parties are quite common among HCOs.

(iv) Contributions Received Through Fund-Raising Foundations. Frequently, health care entities will create separate not-for-profit foundations to raise and hold funds for their benefit. The accounting for contributions received through these not-for-profit foundations depends on the nature of the relationship between the organizations and whether the health care entity is not-for-profit or governmental. Reporting entity issues associated with foundations are discussed at Subsection 36.3(t).

Not-for-Profit Providers. The primary guidance followed by not-for-profit providers in addressing issues related to transactions with related fund-raising foundations is FASB Statement No. 136, "Transfers of Assets to a Not-for-Profit Organization or Charitable Trust That Raises or Holds Contributions for Others." A detailed discussion of FASB No. 136 is provided in Subsection 36.3(k)(v).

Governmental Providers. Governmental health care entities are not subject to FASB Statement No. 136. However, in most cases not-for-profit foundations associated with governmental health care entities will be subject to FAS No. 136 in their stand-alone financial statements. If, under FAS No. 136, the foundation is deemed to be financially interrelated with the health care organization, the foundation recognizes contribution revenue for contributions it receives that are specified for the health care organization. The health care organization recognizes contribution revenue when it receives distributions from the foundation. If GASB No. 39, "Determining Whether Certain Organizations Are Component Units," requires the health care organization to report the foundation as a discretely presented component unit [as discussed at Subsection 30.3(t)(iii)], this may result in double counting revenues—once when they are initially received by the foundation and again (in the health care organization's statements) when the foundation distributes them to the health care organization. The GASB believes that clearly displaying and describing such intra-entity transactions in the notes and on the face of the financial statements should minimize the potential for misunderstanding. The GASB also notes that entities using a side-by-side reporting format also could present a consolidated total for the reporting entity (primary government plus component units) that would reflect the adjustments required to eliminate the effects of double-counting.

When the foundation and the health care organization are not financially interrelated under FAS No. 136, the foundation is presumed to be acting as an agent for the health care organization when it receives contributions that are specified for the health care organization. FASB No. 136 requires nongovernmental beneficiaries to reflect a receivable and contribution revenue for such contributions received by related fund-raising foundations under agency relationships. GASB No. 33, paragraph 21, imposes a similar requirement on governmental beneficiaries to recognize revenue and a receivable for contributions received on their behalf by foundations acting as agents; it states that recipients should recognize receivables and revenues when all eligibility requirements, including time requirements, are met. Distributions made by the foundation are reported as reductions of the receivable if they relate to contributions that are designated for the provider. If the distributions relate to contributions received by the foundation that were not designated for the provider, they are reported as contribution revenue by the provider.

(v) Financial Accounting Standards Board Statement No. 136.   FASB Statement No. 136, "Transfers of Assets to a Not-for-Profit Organization or Charitable Trust that Raises or Holds Contributions for Others," establishes standards for reporting transactions in which a donor makes a contribution by transferring assets to a foundation that agrees to transfer those assets to, or use those assets on behalf of, another organization that is specified by the donor. The reporting of these transactions is based on whether the organizations are "financially interrelated," as that term is defined in FAS No. 136.

Financially Interrelated Organizations.   FAS No. 136 states that a foundation and its beneficiary organization are "financially interrelated" if the relationship between them has both of the following characteristics: One organization has the ability to influence the operating and financial decisions of the other, and one organization has an ongoing economic interest in the net assets of the other. When this type of relationship exists, the foundation recognizes contribution revenue for contributions made by donors to the foundation that specify the health care organization as the intended beneficiary of the gift. Similarly, the health care organization recognizes its rights to those assets held by the foundation as an "interest in the net assets" of the foundation.[8]

When the foundation distributes assets to the provider that are represented by the provider's interest in net assets of the foundation, the provider debits cash and decreases its interest in the net assets. When the foundation distributes assets to the provider that are not represented by the provider's interest in net assets of the foundation (e.g., donations received by the foundation that were not specified for any particular beneficiary), the health care organization that distribution as contribution income.

These concepts are illustrated in the following three examples:

1. *Foundation exists solely to support Hospital.* If Foundation's only beneficiary is Hospital, then donors who make contributions to Foundation implicitly specify that they intend for their gifts to benefit Hospital. Therefore, all contributions made to Foundation are transactions within the scope of FAS No. 136, because they are transfers that involve a specified beneficiary. Because Hospital is the sole beneficiary of Foundation, the two organizations are financially interrelated (clearly, Foundation's activities inure to the benefit of Hospital). Hospital would recognize an asset representing its interest in 100 percent of the net assets of Foundation. When Foundation makes a distribution to Hospital, Hospital credits its interest in net assets and debits cash.

---

[8] That interest would be eliminated if the beneficiary and the recipient organization were included in consolidated financial statements.

2. *Foundation exists primarily to support Hospital but also supports "health-related issues in the surrounding community."* Unlike the previous situation, contributions received by Foundation in this fact pattern do not automatically belong to Hospital. Even though Hospital is the primary beneficiary of Foundation, Foundation may choose to support beneficiaries other than Hospital. Contributions received by Foundation that do not specify a particular beneficiary are not within the scope of FAS No. 136. Hospital would not recognize an asset related to these "undesignated" contributions received by Foundation (even if, historically, Hospital has been the recipient of virtually all of the distributions made by Foundation) because it has no rights to them. Alternatively, if a donor stipulates that his or her gift is to benefit Hospital, those transactions are within the scope of FAS No. 136. In that case, Hospital would recognize its interest in the net assets represented by that gift (Hospital and Foundation are presumed to be financially interrelated). When Foundation distributes some or all of those designated gifts to Hospital, Hospital would credit its interest in net assets and debit cash. When Foundation distributes undesignated contributions to Hospital, Hospital would recognize contribution income.

3. *Foundation exists solely to support Health System; Health System consists of Hospital A, Hospital B, and Hospital C.* In this case, all contributions (including undesignated contributions) received by Foundation are implicitly specified to benefit Health System. Because Health System is the sole beneficiary of Foundation, the organizations are financially interrelated, and Health System would recognize an asset (interest in net assets) related to all contributions held by Foundation. If the individual hospitals in Health System also issue separate-subsidiary financial statements, those hospitals would each reflect assets to the extent that Foundation had received contributions that were specifically designated for them. For example, if a donor gave Foundation $10,000 but did not specify a beneficiary, then none of the hospitals would have rights to that gift, and none would recognize an asset. However, if a donor gave Foundation $10,000 and specified that it was for Hospital B, Hospital B would recognize an asset representing its rights to that gift (either a receivable or an interest in net assets, depending on whether Hospital B and Foundation are financially interrelated[9]) of $10,000. If Hospital B is financially interrelated with Foundation, it recognizes a $10,000 interest in net assets of Foundation. If Hospital B is not financially interrelated with Foundation, Hospital B reflects a $10,000 receivable from Foundation.

When a health care organization has an interest in the net assets of a financially interrelated foundation, it periodically must adjust that interest for its share of the change in the foundation's net assets using a method similar to the equity method of accounting for investments in common stock (see par. 15 of FASB Statement No. 136). The portion of the change in interest resulting from changes in the foundation's restricted net assets is reported below the performance indicator, by analogy to the treatment of "restricted contributions" in paragraph 10.18 of *Health Care Organizations.* The portion of the change in interest resulting from changes in the foundation's unrestricted net assets should be reported above the performance indicator if the health care organization has the ability to influence the timing and amount of distributions from the foundation (e.g., if the health care organization controls the foundation, or if the health care organization does not control the foundation but has such a close working relationship with it that it can, in essence, access the foundation's assets at will). If the health care organization cannot influence the timing and amount of distributions from the foundation, it must imply a time restriction on all assets held by the foundation (including unrestricted net assets). In that situation, the entire change in interest in net assets would be treated as "restricted" and reported below the performance indicator. When restrictions are released (e.g., because a purpose restriction has been satisfied, or because a time restriction ceases to exist), a reclassification is made from restricted net assets to unrestricted assets and reported by the health care organization as "net assets released from restriction."

---

[9] Although Foundation and Health System are financially interrelated (because Health System is the ultimate beneficiary of all gifts to Foundation), there is no presumption that the individual hospitals also are financially interrelated with the foundation.

The AICPA plans to issue guidance regarding the classification of the change in interest in a financially interrelated organization and related issues sometime during 2002. That guidance will be published in Section 6400 the AICPA's *Technical Practice Aids* publication.

Organizations Not Financially Interrelated.   If the foundation and health care organization are not financially interrelated, the foundation is presumed to be acting as an agent when it receives contributions that are designated for the health care organization. In those situations, the provider should recognize an asset and contribution revenue. The asset recorded by the health care organization is based on the nature of the rights to which it is entitled. If the health care organization has an unconditional right to receive all or a portion of the specified cash flows from a charitable trust or other identifiable pool of assets, the health care organization's asset is a *beneficial interest*, which is measured and subsequently remeasured at fair value using a valuation technique such as the present value of the estimated future cash flows. Otherwise, the health care organization should recognize its rights to the assets held by the foundation as a receivable in accordance with the provisions of FASB Statement No. 116 for unconditional promises to give. When the foundation makes distributions to the health care organization from the designated assets, the provider debits cash and decreases the receivable or beneficial interest. If distributions instead represent assets that were not designated for the health care organization (e.g., donations received by the foundation that were not specified for any particular beneficiary), such distributions represent contribution income to the health care organization.

(l) INVESTMENTS.

(i) Investments in Debt Securities and Certain Equity Securities.

- *Investor-owned providers.* For-profit health care enterprises are required to follow the accounting and reporting requirements set forth in FASB Statement No. 115, "Accounting for Certain Investments in Debt and Equity Securities."

- *Not-for-profit providers.* FASB Statement No. 124, "Accounting for Certain Investments of Not-for-Profit Organizations," requires all not-for-profit organizations to report investments in equity securities with readily determinable fair values and all debt securities at fair value on the balance sheet. In addition, the AICPA audit and accounting guide *Health Care Organizations* requires not-for-profit HCOs to report unrestricted investment return using an income recognition approach similar to FASB Statement No. 115 (i.e., to include investment income, realized gains and losses, unrealized gains and losses on trading securities, and other-than-temporary impairment losses in the performance indicator, and report unrealized gains and losses on other than trading securities below the performance indicator). Although paragraph 4.07(a) of the Guide addresses how an other-than-temporary investment loss should be classified in the performance indicator, neither the Guide nor FASB No. 124 provides any guidance on the need to assess whether an other-than-temporary impairment of securities has occurred. By analogy, not-for-profit HCOs should follow an approach similar to that set forth in paragraph 16 of FASB No. 115; that is, when a determination is made that an other-than-temporary impairment has occurred, the cost basis of the individual security should be written down to fair value as a new cost basis and the amount of the writedown should be included in the performance indicator (i.e., accounted for as a realized loss).

- *Governmental providers.* Governmental providers follow the requirements of GAS No. 31, *Accounting and Financial Reporting for Certain Investments and for External Investment Pools.* GAS No. 31 establishes fair value standards for most investments; however, they are permitted to report certain money market investments and participating interest earning investment contracts at amortized cost, provided that the investment has a remaining maturity of one year or less at the time of purchase.

- All investment income (restricted and unrestricted) and all investment gains and losses (realized and unrealized) are reported as nonoperating revenues and expenses, in accordance with

GASB No. 31 and GASB No. 34. Providers with donor-restricted endowments are required to make certain disclosures about their use of investment income generated by those endowments. More detailed guidance about accounting for investments and investment return in governmental organizations is provided in Chapter 35.

(ii) Unconsolidated Affiliates. Investments in unconsolidated affiliates (such as joint ventures) are accounted for in accordance with APB Opinion No. 18.

(iii) Other Securities. Other types of investments not addressed above (such as real estate or oil and gas interests) should be reported at the lower of amortized cost or a reduced amount if an impairment in their value is deemed to be other than temporary.

(m) DERIVATIVES. One of the most common derivatives used by HCOs is the interest rate swap. Prior to FASB No. 133, the only impact of this arrangement on the health care organization's financial statements would be the increased or reduced interest expense reported in the income statement. Under FASB No. 133, the health care organization must also reflect the fair value of the swap contract on its balance sheet, with an offsetting entry to "gain/loss on swap." If the health care organization qualifies (and elects) to use FASB No. 133's hedge accounting provisions, the swaps will be accounted for differently, depending on the type of hedge. A fixed-to-floating swap will be accounted for as a fair value hedge, while a floating-to-fixed swap will be accounted for as a cash flow hedge. A comprehensive discussion of issues related to accounting for derivatives and hedging transactions is included in Chapter 26.

(i) Special Considerations for Not-for-Profit Entities.

Cash Flow Hedge Accounting. In June 2002, AcSEC issued an exposure draft of a proposed Statement of Position, "Accounting for Derivative Instruments and Hedging Activities by Not-for-Profit HCOs, and Clarification of the Performance Indicator." The proposed SOP would resolve diversity in practice created by confusing wording in paragraph 43 of FASB Statement No. 133, which indicates that cash flow hedge accounting is not available to "an entity that does not report earnings as a separate caption in a statement of financial performance (e.g., a not-for-profit organization . . . .)." Because a not-for-profit health care organization's performance indicator generally is analogous to income from continuing operations of a business enterprise, AcSEC concluded that it is appropriate for such organizations to use cash flow hedge accounting. The proposed standard states that not-for-profit HCOs should apply the provisions of FASB Statement No. 133 (including the cash flow hedge accounting provisions) in the same manner as for-profit enterprises. That is, any derivative gains or losses that affect a for-profit enterprise's income from continuing operations should similarly affect a not-for-profit health care organization's performance indicator, and derivative gains or losses that are excluded from a for-profit enterprise's income from continuing operations (such as items reported in other comprehensive income) similarly should be excluded from a not-for-profit health care organization's performance indicator. The proposed SOP would apply only to not-for-profit entities covered by the AICPA audit and accounting guide *Health Care Organizations*; it would not apply to other types of not-for-profit organizations or to governmental HCOs.

Disclosures. The proposed SOP discussed in the previous paragraph would require not-for-profit HCOs to provide all disclosures that are analogous to those required by paragraph 45 of FASB Statement No. 133 for for-profit enterprises, including disclosure of anticipated reclassifications into the performance indicator of gains and losses that have been excluded from that measure and reported in accumulated derivative gain or loss as of the reporting date. Although not-for-profit organizations are not subject to FASB Statement No. 130, "Reporting Comprehensive Income," and therefore do not have the same requirement as for-profit organizations to report changes in the components of accumulated other comprehensive income, the proposed SOP also would require not-for-profit HCOs to separately disclose the beginning and ending accumulated derivative gain or loss that has been excluded from the performance indicator, the related net change associated with current period hedging transactions, and the net amount of any reclassifications into the performance indicator in a manner similar to that described in paragraph 47 of FASB Statement No. 133.

Use of the Short-Cut Method.   FASB Statement No. 138, "Accounting for Certain Derivative Instruments and Certain Hedging Activities (an Amendment of FASB Statement No. 133)," limited application of the shortcut method to interest rate swaps that reference U.S. Treasury rates orLIBOR(London Interbank Offered Rate) as the underlying. Many not-for-profit HCOs use swaps whose underlying is the Bond Market Association Municipal Swap Index (sometimes referred to as the (*BMA*) *Index*). Under FASB No. 138, the BMA Index does not constitute a benchmark interest rate for purposes of applying the shortcut method. Accordingly, if the variable leg of a swap is indexed to the BMA Index (or any rate other than Treasuries or LIBOR), the hedging relationship does not qualify for the short cut method.

Split-Interest Agreements.   As discussed at Subsection 36.3(k)(iii), a split interest agreement is a form of contribution to a not-for-profit organization in which the not-for-profit organization must share the benefits received with other beneficiaries. The amount of the benefit to each beneficiary often will be a function of the fair value of the donated assets over the term of the agreement. When the reporting not-for-profit organization directly receives the donated assets (or is trustee over a trust containing the donated assets), the AICPA audit and accounting guide *Not-for-Profit Organizations* requires that a liability be recognized for the obligation to make future payments to the other beneficiaries of the trust based on the present value of the future expected payments to the beneficiaries. Although that liability may reflect the fair value of the obligation initially, it will not reflect fair value in future periods because the audit guide indicates that the discount rate used in remeasuring the liability each period should not be revised to reflect current interest rates. Because the liability is not measured at fair value, the potential for an embedded derivative exists.

In April 2002, the FASB cleared Derivatives Implementation Group (DIG) Issue No. B35, "Application of Statement No. 133 to a Not-for-Profit Organization's Obligation Arising from an Irrevocable Split-Interest Agreement." Issue No. B35 states that the obligation recognized under a split interest agreement should be analyzed to determine whether there is an embedded derivative; if so, the embedded derivative must be separated from its "host contract" and accounted for separately if certain circumstances are met. In situations where the obligation to make payments to other beneficiaries ceases upon the death of the beneficiary(ies), the split-interest agreement is considered to be "life contingent" and, thus, is excluded from Issue No. B35 under the exception provided in paragraph 10(c) of FASB No. 133 for insurance arrangements. However, under fixed-period arrangements (i.e., those where the payments are made for a specified number of years), if the payments vary based on the investment return from the contributed assets, bifurcation of an embedded derivative will be required.

Issue No. B35 only addresses split-interest agreements that are irrevocable. The author believes that split-interest agreements that are revocable by the donor do not give rise to embedded derivatives under FAS No. 133, as both the assets and the corresponding obligations are recognized at fair value. For similar reasons, situations in which a not-for-profit organization holds a split-interest agreement in the capacity of an independent trustee without having any beneficial interest in the arrangement (i.e., acting similar to a financial institution or fiscal agent) would not appear to be impacted by Issue No. B35.

(ii) Special Considerations for Governmental Entities.

Cash Flow Hedge Accounting.   As discussed at Subsection 36.2(b), governmental entities that have elected to apply paragraph 7 of GASB Statement No. 20, "Accounting and Financial Reporting for Proprietary Funds and Other Governmental Entities that Use Proprietary Fund Accounting," are required to apply all FASB Statements and Interpretations issued after November 30, 1989 (except for those that are limited to not-for-profit organizations or that address issues primarily concerning those organizations) that do not conflict with or contradict GASB pronouncements. FASB Statement No. 133 applies to such organizations to the extent that it does not conflict with the provisions of GASB pronouncements. Because the concept of reporting "other comprehensive income" conflicts with the reporting requirements of GASB Statement No. 34, "Basic Financial Statements—and Management's Discussion and Analysis—for State and Local Governments" (see discussion at Subsection 36.5(d)(iii)); cash flow hedge accounting is not available to those organizations once they have adopted GASB Statement No. 34.

Use of the Shortcut Method. Many governmental HCOs use interest rate swaps whose underlying is the BMA Index. Under FASB Statement No. 138, "Accounting for Certain Derivative Instruments and Certain Hedging Activities (an amendment of FASB Statement No. 133)," the BMA Index does not constitute a benchmark interest rate for purposes of applying the short-cut method. Accordingly, if the variable leg of a swap is indexed to the BMA Index (or any rate other than Treasuries or LIBOR), the hedging relationship does not qualify for the shortcut method.

(n) PROPERTY AND EQUIPMENT. The property and equipment accounts represent the provider's actual investment in plant assets, land, building, leasehold improvements, and equipment. Property that is not used for general operations (such as property held for future expansion or investment purposes) should be presented separately from property used in general operations.

Property and equipment should be recorded at cost, or at fair market value if donated. Where historical cost records are not available, an appraisal at historical cost should be made and the amounts recorded in the provider's books.

The amount of depreciation expense should be shown separately (or combined with amortization of leased assets) in the Statement of Operations. The Guide states that the American Hospital Association's "Estimated Useful Lives of Depreciable Hospital Assets" publication may be helpful in determining the estimated useful lives of fixed assets of health care providers.

Governmental providers also are required to disclose their policy for capitalizing assets and for estimating the useful lives of those assets. In addition, GASB No. 34 requires certain information to be presented about major classes of capital assets, including beginning and ending balances, capital acquisitions, sales or other disposition, current period depreciation expense, and accumulated depreciation.

(i) Capitalizing Costs Associated with Health Insurance Portability and Accountability Act Compliance. The Health Insurance Portability and Accountability Act of 1996 (HIPAA) was enacted by the federal government with the intent to assure health insurance portability, improve the efficiency and effectiveness of the health care system, reduce health care fraud and abuse, help ensure security and privacy of health information, and enforce standards for transacting health information. Among other matters, HIPAA addresses issues of security and confidentiality in the transfer of electronic patient information and establishes standard data content and formats for submitting electronic claims and other administrative transactions.

The costs of modifying computer systems in order to comply with the provisions of HIPAA can be significant. In January 2002, the AICPA Accounting Standards staff released a Technical Practice Aid Q&A (TPA) discussing whether computer systems costs incurred in conjunction with a health care entity's HIPAA compliance efforts can be capitalized.[10] The TPA states that costs associated with upgrading and improving computer systems to comply with HIPAA should follow the guidance set forth in SOP 98-1, "Accounting for the Costs of Computer Software Developed or Obtained for Internal Use." Unless the costs relate to changes that result in "additional functionality" (i.e., that allow the software to perform tasks that it previously could not perform), they should be expensed. Many of the costs associated with HIPAA relate to compliance with the Act and do not result in

---

[10] TPA 6400.34, "Accounting for Computer Systems Costs Incurred in Connection with the Health Insurance Portability and Accountability Act of 1996."

"additional functionality." For example, changes that merely reconfigure existing data to conform to the HIPAA standard and/or regulatory requirements do not result in the capability to perform additional tasks, nor do training costs, data conversion costs (except for costs to develop or obtain software that allows for access to or conversion of old data by new systems), and maintenance costs. However, changes that would increase the security of data from tampering or alteration, or that reduce the ability of unauthorized persons to gain access to the data, represent tasks that the software previously could not perform, and the associated qualifying costs of application development stage activities potentially are capitalizable.

(o) INTANGIBLE ASSETS.   FAS No. 141, "Business Combinations," and FAS No. 142, "Goodwill and Other Intangible Assets," were issued in June 2001. These pronouncements superseded APB Nos. 16 and 17 in providing guidance on accounting for intangible assets. Guidance on evaluating goodwill and other intangible assets for impairment is provided by FAS No. 142 (for goodwill and non-amortizable intangibles) and FAS No. 144 (for amortizable intangibles). A comprehensive discussion of these issues is provided in Chapter 22. Special considerations related to HCOs are discussed below.

(i) Special Considerations for Not-for-Profit Entities.   Issues similar to those deliberated for business organizations in connection with FASB Statement No. 141, "Business Combinations," and FASB Statement No. 142, "Goodwill and Other Intangible Assets," will be deliberated for not-for-profit organizations in the course of FASB's not-for-profit combinations project. As a result, the provisions of FAS Nos. 141 and 142 should not be applied by not-for-profit organizations until the FASB completes the not-for-profit combinations project.[11] Instead, the guidance in Nos. APB 16 and 17 remains in effect for not-for-profit organizations, including continued amortization of goodwill. In addition, when applying APB Nos. 16 and 17, not-for-profit organizations should continue to apply the amendments to those Opinions found in other literature, even though that other literature may have been superseded by FAS Nos. 141 and 142.

Note, however, that the deferred effective date of FAS No. 142 does not apply to for-profit subsidiaries of not-for-profit organizations. Such organizations must follow FAS No. 142 by virtue of their status as for-profit organizations. When the subsidiary's financial statements are rolled up into the consolidated financial statements of the not-for-profit parent, FAS No. 142's principles continue to apply; that is, the subsidiary's financial statements should not be "converted" to the standards followed by the not-for-profit parent as a result of consolidation. Consequently, a portion of the consolidated entity's goodwill and intangible assets may continue to be amortized, while the remainder ceases to be amortized.

The general framework for evaluating impairment of goodwill and other intangible assets for impairment of for-profit HCOs is provided by FAS No. 142 (for goodwill and nonamortizable intangible assets) and FAS No. 121/FAS No. 144[12] (for amortizable intangible assets). Because the effective date of FAS No. 142 is indefinitely deferred for not-for-profit organizations, those organizations must use a different framework for evaluating impairment of intangibles. Prior to the effective date of FAS No. 144 (fiscal years beginning after December 15, 2001), intangible assets of not-for-profit organizations should be evaluated for impairment under either (1) APB No. 17, paragraph 31 (for goodwill associated with assets held for disposal) or (2) FAS No. 121 (all other goodwill and all identifiable intangibles). Once the not-for-profit organization adopts FAS No. 144, all goodwill should be tested for impairment under APB No. 17, paragraph 31. Additionally, because all intangible assets of not-for-profit organizations continue to be amortized until the not-for-profit combinations project is completed, all identifiable intangible assets should be evaluated for impairment under FAS No. 144.

---

[11] Although not-for-profit organizations technically are within the scope of FASB No. 142, its effective date is deferred for those organizations pending completion of the not-for-profit combinations project.
[12] FAS No. 144, "Accounting for the Impairment or Disposal of Long-Lived Assets," will supersede FAS No. 121 in fiscal years beginning after December 15, 2001.

In the not-for-profit combinations project, FASB will evaluate not-for-profit intangibles issues using a "differences-based" approach—that is, it will focus on whether the guidance contained in FASB No. 141 and FASB No. 142 with respect to intangibles make sense when applied to not-for-profit organizations. Any departures from the general framework established in those standards will have to be justified by clear differences in the nature of not-for-profit issues and transactions.

(ii) Special Considerations for Governmental Entities. GAS No. 20, paragraph 7, allows governmental proprietary activities to apply FASB pronouncements except for those that (1) conflict with or contradict GASB pronouncements or (2) those that deal primarily with not-for-profit issues. If a new FASB standard does not fall into one of those categories, governmental entities that have elected the "paragraph 7" option must adopt it unless the GASB issues a standard instructing them not to do so. Governmental health care entities that follow the AICPA audit and accounting guide *Health Care Organizations* generally are "paragraph 7" entities. Consequently, those entities should follow the provisions of FAS Nos. 141 and 142 in accounting for intangible assets.

(iii) Special Considerations for Securities and Exchange Commission-Registered Companies.

Allocation of Purchase Price. FASB No. 141 requires that all identifiable assets purchased in an acquisition transaction be assigned a portion of the cost of the acquired company. The SEC is concerned that in sectors of the industry where tangible assets often are not significant, such as in the health care management sector, such identifiable intangible assets are not being valued separately. As a result, the SEC has increased its scrutiny of allocation of purchase price issues in filings by health care companies. In evaluating the propriety of accounting and reporting of intangibles, the SEC is focusing on allocations to purchased intangibles such as management contracts, covenants not to compete, and so on.

Goodwill Amortization Period. A related area of heightened SEC scrutiny concerns the length of the amortization period assigned to amortizable intangible assets. The SEC has indicated that it believes that a relatively short (up to 25 years) amortization period for capitalized management services agreements(MSAs) in the physician practice management (PPM) sector is appropriate. However, longer lives sometimes are sustained if the facts and circumstances of a particular situation warrant it even though the term of the management agreement may be longer.

Contingent Consideration. Contingent consideration, also referred to as *earn-out arrangements*, provide for additional amounts to be paid to the selling shareholders contingent on the occurrence of specified events or transactions in the future. One accounting question associated with contingent consideration is whether it should be accounted for as additional purchase price or as compensation expense. This issue may be particularly relevant in the acquisition of a health care provider if the owners of the selling company are physicians or other health care professionals who continue to be employed by and provide health care services on behalf of the combined entity after the acquisition. EITF No. 95-8, "Accounting for Contingent Consideration Paid to the Shareholders of an Acquired Company in a Purchase Business Combination," states that the determination of whether contingent consideration should be recorded as part of the purchase price or as compensation expense is a matter of judgment that will depend on the relevant facts and circumstances.

(p) LEASES. HCOs may have access to the use of property and equipment under a variety of arrangements, including lease arrangements. FASB Statement No. 13, "Accounting for Leases," provides accounting guidance for investor-owned, not-for-profit, and governmental providers. In addition, governmental health care entities with certain types of operating leases must follow the additional accounting and disclosure requirements of GASB Statement No. 13, "Accounting for Operating Leases with Scheduled Rent Increases."

(q) TAX-EXEMPT DEBT. For not-for-profit and governmental providers, the tax-exempt bond market is a primary source of capital. The majority of tax-exempt bonds issued by HCOs are revenue bonds (i.e., bonds secured by a pledge of the entity's revenues). Because most providers do not have the ability to issue tax-exempt revenue bonds directly, most borrowings involve issuances through a financing authority. Financing arrangements take many forms. In some cases, a mortgage lien is granted to the governmental entity issuing the bonds; in others, the government may take title to the property and lease it to the provider for an amount sufficient to cover the debt service on the issue.

If the health care organization is responsible for repayment of the bonds, the bonds payable are reported as a liability. If the obligation relates to a lease with a government entity, the provider must determine whether the lease should be classified as operating or capital under FASB Statement No. 13, "Accounting for Leases." If the health care organization has no obligation to make payments of principal and interest on the debt or capital or operating lease payments on related buildings or equipment, the organization should not reflect a liability on its balance sheet. In such circumstances, proceeds from the bond issue are reported as contributions from the sponsoring organization.

In tax-exempt financing transactions, it is common practice for health care entities to create a "pool" of assets as a security vehicle. In a master trust indenture financing, a master trustee holds all of the security in the collateral pool, which is defined as the *obligated group*. For example, a hospital system may place two or three of its facilities in the obligated group as the asset and revenue base the borrowers look to for security.

(i) Municipal Securities Disclosure Requirements. Certain tax-exempt debt issues are subject to disclosure under Rule 15c2-12 of the Securities Exchange Act of 1934. Under these rules, the borrower must provide specific financial information—for example, annual audited financial statements and timely notices of material events, such as rating changes or delays in principal and interest payments—to national repositories for municipal securities information [see Section 36.2(c)].

Many tax-exempt debt agreements involving obligated groups require the health care organization to provide audited, general purpose external financial statements for the obligated group to use in the bond offering document and thereafter to the underwriters on an annual, ongoing basis. Prior to the issuance of *Health Care Organizations* in 1996, these special "carve-out" financial statements were permissible under GAAP because the "reporting entity" in the not-for-profit health care world was loosely defined. Now that *Health Care Organizations* has provided rules on what constitutes the reporting entity under GAAP, anything less than the full reporting entity is no longer a GAAP presentation and must be restricted for limited use. Because a limited-use type report would not be appropriate to include in an official statement nor to submit to a repository, this has created some problems for obligated group issuers [see Subsection 36.3(t)(iii)].

(ii) Funds Held under Bond Indentures. Among the many provisions normally included in tax-exempt debt indentures are requirements to set aside funds annually from operations to ensure that bond principal and interest payments and other requirements are met. Usually these debt reserve funds are placed under the control of a trustee. As discussed in Subsection 36.3(b), not-for-profit HCOs use the balance sheet caption "assets whose use is limited" to report assets such as unexpended proceeds of debt issues and funds of a health care entity deposited with a trustee and limited to use in accordance with the requirements of an indenture or similar document; governmental providers report such assets as "restricted." Regardless of the terminology used, these assets should be reported in the noncurrent section of the balance sheet (except for the portion that is required to satisfy current debt service requirements, which is included in current assets).

(iii) Interest during Construction. FASB Statement No. 34, "Capitalization of Interest Costs," as amended by FASB Statement No. 62, "Capitalization of Interest Cost in Situations Involving Certain Tax-Exempt Borrowings and Certain Gifts and Grants," specifies appropriate practices for accounting for interest expense associated with debt used to finance construction. It provides that capitalized interest cost should be reduced by interest earned on the "borrowed funds" if the proceeds of the tax-exempt borrowing are externally restricted to finance the acquisition of specified qualifying assets or to service the related debt.

(iv) Advance Refundings and Arbitrage. Frequently, providers with tax-exempt debt will restructure their long-term liabilities to take advantage of interest rate changes or to terminate restrictive bond covenants through an advance refunding. In an advance refunding, new debt is issued for the purpose of replacing an existing debt issue. The accounting and reporting requirements for advance refundings entered into by not-for-profit HCOs are provided by APB Opinion No. 26, "Early Extinguishment of Debt," and FASB Statement No. 145, "Rescission of FASB Statements No. 4, 44, and 64, Amendment of FASB Statement No. 13, and Technical Corrections." The difference between the net carrying amount of the extinguished debt (amount due at maturity adjusted for unamortized premium, discount, and cost of issuance) and the reacquisition price (amount paid on extinguishment, including call premium and miscellaneous costs of reacquisition) should be recognized in the determination of net income of the period of extinguishment as a gain or loss and identified as a separate item; it should not be amortized to future periods. Gains or losses on debt extinguishments should not be classified as an extraordinary item unless they meet the criteria of APB No. 30.

FASB Statement No. 40, "Accounting for Transfers and Servicing of Financial Assets and Extinguishments of Liabilities," provides guidance regarding the circumstances that constitute an extinguishment of debt. A liability is extinguished if either of the following conditions is met: (1) the debtor pays the creditor and is relieved of its obligation for the liability (paying the creditor includes delivery of cash, other financial assets, goods, or services, or reacquisition by the debtor of its outstanding debt securities whether the securities are canceled or held as "treasury bonds"); or (2) the debtor is legally released from being the primary obligor under the liability, either judicially or by the creditor. If any debt of an entity is still outstanding that was considered to be extinguished by an in-substance defeasance prior to January 1, 1997, disclosure should be made of a general description of the transaction and the amount of debt that is considered extinguished at the end of the period for as long as that debt remains outstanding.

The accounting, financial reporting, and disclosure requirements for governmental health care entities are provided in GASB Statement No. 23, "Accounting and Financial Reporting for Refundings of Debt Reported by Proprietary Activities," and GASB Statement No. 7, "Advance Refundings Resulting in Defeasance of Debt." Generally speaking, governmental entities are required to amortize any gain or loss resulting from a current or advance refunding to interest expense over the shorter of the life of the new bonds or the remaining life of the old bonds.

Advance refundings involving tax-exempt debt are subject to arbitrage rules under the IRC Section 103(c) and related regulations that, in general, prohibit the yield realized from the investment of the proceeds of the new debt from exceeding the yield on the debt itself. Compliance with those rules is necessary in order for the interest paid to the bondholders to be exempt from federal income tax and, possibly, from state and local tax. The IRS has recently increased its enforcement activities regarding tax-exempt municipal bonds for possible tax law violations. Most of these audits involve questions relating to arbitrage; however, the IRS is also probing the overall level of compliance in municipal bond offerings.

(r) DISCLOSURE OF RISKS, UNCERTAINTIES, AND CONTINGENCIES.

(i) Statement of Position 94–6. "AICPA SOP 946, Disclosure of Certain Significant Risks and Uncertainties," requires organizations to include disclosures in their financial statements concerning the use of estimates in the preparation of the financial statements as well as information about current vulnerability due to certain concentrations. Examples of estimates that often are significant in health care organization financial statements include:

- Provision for contractual allowances
- Estimated third-party settlement reserves

- Provision for bad debts
- Malpractice accruals
- Obligation for future services
- Incurred but not reported (IBNR) accruals involving prepaid health care plans
- Accruals for loss contracts under managed care arrangements

Examples of estimates that are particularly sensitive to changes in the near term (SOP 94-6, par. 18) that may be included in financial statements of HCOs may include:

- Third-party revenue and related receivables (see Subsection 36.3(r)(ii))
- Litigation-related contingencies (e.g., fraud and abuse actions by regulators)
- Assets subject to impairment (e.g., goodwill)
- Estimated risk pool settlements arising from managed care contracting
- Amounts reported for long-term obligations (e.g., pensions and postemployment benefits)
- Estimated net proceeds recoverable, the provisions for expected loss to be incurred, or both, on disposition of a business or assets
- Environmental remediation-related obligations

SOP 94-6 applies governmental HCOs that follow paragraph 7 of GASB No. 20 and to all investor-owned and not-for-profit HCOs.

(ii) Uncertainties Associated with Revenue Recognition. The amount of revenue earned under arrangements with government programs is determined under complex government rules and regulations that subject the organization to the potential for retrospective adjustments in future years. Because several years may elapse before all potential adjustments related to a particular fiscal year are known, management must estimate the effects of future program audits, administrative reviews, and billing reviews. In making these estimates, management also must take into account the potential for regulatory investigations that may result in denial of otherwise valid claims for payment. These matters are discussed in SOP 00-1, "Auditing Health Care Third-Party Revenues and Related Receivables."

The fairness or reasonableness of financial statement presentation of estimates is not dependent on the outcome of the uncertainty (i.e., management's ability to predict the future with accuracy), but rather on the quality and nature of the evidence supporting management's assertions at the time the estimate is made. The fact that future events may differ materially from management's assumptions or estimates should not necessarily lead to a conclusion that management's estimates were not reasonable or valid at the time they were made.

GAAP requires that the uncertainties inherent in significant estimates be disclosed appropriately in the financial statements. If uncertainties associated with revenue recognition are presented in accordance with SOP 94-6, "Disclosure of Certain Significant Risks and Uncertainties," the financial statements are presented fairly in conformity with GAAP. This is true even in situations involving material uncertainties. If a reasonable estimate cannot be made of the outcome of the uncertainty and the circumstances surrounding the uncertainty are adequately disclosed, the financial statements are not deficient from a GAAP perspective. Disclosure, however, is never a substitute for recognition in the financial statements.

The audit and accounting guide *Health Care Organizations* requires that differences between original estimates and subsequent revisions be included in the statement of operations in the period in which the revisions are made and be disclosed, if material. The likelihood of such revisions, coupled with their potential material impact on the financial statements, generally requires disclosure in accordance with SOP 94-6. Such disclosures might include the significance of government program revenues to the entity's overall revenues and a description of the complex nature of applicable laws and regulations, indicating that the possibility of future government review and interpretation exists. SOP 00-1 illustrates this disclosure.

(iii) Illegal Acts Related to Government Programs.   In recent years, the federal government and many states have aggressively increased enforcement efforts under Medicare and Medicaid antifraud and abuse legislation. Broadening regulatory and legal interpretations have significantly increased the risk of penalties for providers; for example, broad interpretations of "false claims" laws are exposing ordinary billing mistakes to scrutiny and penalty consideration. As a result, providers may have significant exposure to allegations of fraudulent activity that potentially could entail multimillion-dollar penalties, fines, and settlements. The far-reaching nature of alleged fraud and abuse violations may represent a significant risk and uncertainty that would require disclosure in accordance with SOP 94-6. If a provider is the target of a government investigation, the need for accruals related to, or disclosure of, contingencies associated with the potential effect of illegal acts must be evaluated.

If the government undertakes an investigation, there are two likely economic consequences to the health care entity:[13] (1) disallowance of certain services previously billed by the entity and paid for by the government; and (2) the imposition of substantial fines or penalties. Consequence (1) is an uncertainty that is involved in the revenue estimation process [discussed at Subsection 36.3(r)(ii)]; it is not a SFAS No. 5 loss contingency. This is a key distinction from a financial reporting perspective. To illustrate, consider that management, in making its best estimate of revenue that will be realized under a contract, may believe that it is appropriate to record a valuation allowance for potential billing adjustments in order to avoid reporting revenues that are uncertain of realization, even though the entity is not currently the subject of a government investigation. If such allowances were accounted for as SFAS No. 5 loss contingencies, the revenue would be recognized, but would carry with it an associated loss contingency that might or might not be accruable in the financial statements. Consequence (2) is a loss contingency under SFAS No. 5, and management must make provision in the financial statements for, or disclose any contingent liabilities associated with, such fines and penalties.

Another potential economic consequence relates to costs the provider may have to incur in future years to demonstrate its compliance with federal laws. When a provider enters into an agreement with the federal government to settle an investigation, such settlement agreements normally impose an obligation on the provider to engage an independent review organization to test and report on compliance with fraud and abuse requirements each year for the following five years. EITF Topic No. D-89, "Accounting for Costs of Future Medicare Compliance Audits," provides the FASB staff's views on whether the expected costs of future audits required as a result of settlement agreements should be accrued as a liability at the time the settlement is agreed to. The staff concluded that a provider should not recognize as liability for the costs of future Medicare compliance audits on the date the settlement is agreed to.

Given the broad scope and draconian penalties of antifraud laws, the ease with which violations (intentional or unintentional) can occur, incentives for whistle-blowers to expose violations, and potential exposure of company executives to criminal charges, it is imperative that health care entities take steps to ensure that their conduct is in compliance with federal and state laws. Implementation of a formal corporate compliance program—a set of written policies and procedures aimed at preventing improprieties in the first place, and detecting them early if they should occur—can help to provide protection from potential fraud and possibly minimize fines and penalties if problems should arise. SOP 99-1, "Guidance to Practitioners in Conducting and Reporting on an Agreed-Upon Procedures Engagement to Assist Management in Evaluating the Effectiveness of Its Corporate Compliance Program," provides additional information on corporate compliance programs, particularly with respect to corporate integrity agreements entered into with the federal government as a result of settlement of fraud and abuse allegations.

(iv) Malpractice Contingencies.   The Guide states that the ultimate costs of malpractice claims should be accrued when the incidents occur that give rise to the claims, if certain criteria are met.

---

[13] There is also the potential for disbarment from participation in the government program, the consequences of which are outside the scope of this discussion.

These criteria include a determination that a liability has been incurred and an ability to make a reasonable estimate of the amount of the loss. In particular, the Guide indicates clearly that health care providers that have not transferred to a third-party all risk for medical malpractice claims arising out of occurrences prior to the financial statement date will probably be required to make an accrual. The Guide provides guidance in accounting for uninsured asserted and unasserted medical malpractice claims, claims insured by captive insurance companies, claims insured under retrospectively rated or claims-made insurance policies, and claims paid from self-insurance trust funds. Governmental health care entities should also consider the accounting and disclosure requirements of GASB Statement No. 10, "Accounting and Financial Reporting for Risk Financing and Related Insurance Issues," with regard to contingencies such as malpractice.

(s) PENSIONS AND OTHER POSTEMPLOYMENT BENEFITS.   Private-sector health care entities follow the same accounting and reporting rules for pensions and other postemployment benefits (OPEB) as do other business enterprises. Governmental health care entities have different pension accounting and disclosure requirements; these are set forth in GASB Statement No. 27, "Accounting for Pensions by State and Local Governmental Employees." With regard to OPEB, GASB Statement No. 12, "Disclosure of Information on Postemployment Benefits Other Than Pension Benefits by State and Local Governmental Employers" provides that state and local government employers are not required to adopt FASB's guidance on accounting and financial reporting of OPEB because the GASB is working on a project dealing with those issues; however, it does not prohibit governmental providers operated as enterprise funds from adopting the FASB's rules, if they desire to do so.

(t) REPORTING ENTITY CONSIDERATIONS.   The health care industry is undergoing significant consolidation and transformation driven by the need to be competitive in the managed care market and the need to respond to reductions in payment for health care services by reducing costs. *Health Care Organizations* contains guidance regarding for-profit and not-for-profit consolidations of parent-subsidiary type relationships,[14] whether evidenced through stock ownership or by other means of control. *Health Care Organizations* describes various forms of control and indicates the circumstances under which those forms of control would require consolidation, as follows:

- Ownership of majority voting interest (or sole corporate membership, if not-for-profit)
- Control of majority voting interest by means other than ownership (i.e., overlapping boards)
- Control through contract or affiliation agreement (e.g., a PPM company)

(i) Not-for-Profit Consolidation/Reporting Entity Requirements.   FAS No. 94 provides very little guidance to not-for-profit health care providers regarding consolidation and the reporting entity, because its provisions generally are tied to ownership of a controlling financial interest as demonstrated by ownership of more than 51 percent of the stock of another entity. Chapter 11 of *Health Care Organizations* provides guidance[15] regarding definition of the not-for-profit reporting entity, including what constitutes "control" in the not-for-profit environment and specific rules regarding consolidation. The consolidation requirements are:

- Reporting entity owns a majority of a for-profit entity's voting stock—consolidate.
- Reporting entity is the sole corporate member of another not-for-profit entity—consolidate.
- Reporting entity controls majority voting interest by means other than ownership and an economic interest exists—consolidate.
- Reporting entity controls a separate not-for-profit entity through a form other than majority ownership or voting interest (e.g., through contract or affiliation agreement) and has an economic interest in that other entity—consolidation permitted but not required.

---

[14] The guidance is not applicable to governmental health care entities, which are required to follow GAS No. 14.

[15] Based on SOP 94-3, "Reporting of Related Entities by Not-for-Profit Organizations."

- Reporting entity has control or economic interest but not both—consolidation prohibited, disclosures required.
- Reporting entity owns 50 percent or less of common voting stock of an investee, and can exercise significant influence over operating and financial policies—use equity method in accordance with APB No. 18.

The guidance in Chapter 11 of *Health Care Organizations* was based, in part, on FAS No. 94. Prior to issuance of FAS No. 144, "Accounting for the Impairment or Disposal of Long-Lived Assets," FAS No. 94 allowed an exception to consolidation for situations where control was temporary. FAS No. 144 eliminated the temporary control exception. Although the health care–specific guidance was based largely on FAS No. 94, it is specialized industry-specific guidance. At this time, the exceptions to consolidation where control is temporary in provided in Chapter 11 of the Guide have not been affected by the issuance of FAS No. 144.

The FASB has on its agenda a project that is addressing the concept of the reporting entity and issues related to consolidations. The above industry-specific guidance will be reconsidered when the FASB completes this project, which may affect the definition of control and other related matters. In 2002, the FASB released an exposure draft of a proposed Interpretation, "Consolidation of Certain Special-Purpose Entities," which does not apply to not-for-profit organizations.

(ii) Governmental Consolidation/Reporting Entity Requirements. GASB Statement No. 14, *The Financial Reporting Entity,* set forth standards for defining and reporting on the governmental financial reporting entity; it also establishes standards for reporting participation in joint ventures. It is applicable to the separately issued financial statements of governmental component units, which specifically includes governmental health care providers; it should also be applied to such component units when they are included in a governmental reporting entity. The Statement also requires certain disclosures about the entity's relationships with organizations other than component units, including related organizations, joint ventures, and jointly owned operations, among others.

According to GASB No. 14, the governmental financial reporting entity consists of (1) a primary government; (2) separate organizations for which the primary government is "financially accountable"; and (3) other organizations that, based on the judgment of the financial statement preparer, have a relationship with the primary government of a nature and significance such that exclusion would cause the reporting entity's financial statements to be misleading or incomplete.

(iii) Not-for-Profit Foundations Associated with Governmental Entities. Legally separate nonprofit organizations may be established to provide financial assistance or other types of support to governmental HCOs.

When a not-for-profit foundation supports a governmental entity, a key issue is determining whether the foundation should prepare its separate financial statements in accordance with GASB or FASB standards. If the governmental health care organization has the right to appoint or approve a controlling majority of the foundation's board, then the foundation meets the definition of a "governmental organization" (see Subsection 36.1(c)). These foundations prepare their financial statements in accordance with GASB standards and report as enterprise funds.

If the board appointment process is not controlled by the governmental health care organization (e.g., if the foundation's board is self-perpetuating), then the foundation is not considered a governmental organization (unless it meets one of the other characteristics contained in the definition, which is highly doubtful). These foundations follow the same guidance in preparing their financial statements as other not-for-profit foundations (FASB Nos. 116, 117, 124, 136, and the *Not-for-Profit Organizations* audit guide). The remainder of this discussion applies to those types of foundations.

If not-for-profit foundations are considered component units of a governmental entity with which they are affiliated, then they must be included in the governmental entity's financial statements. Some foundations fall into category (b) because their governing board is appointed by the primary government (as discussed above), or because they have a "fiscal dependency" on the primary government (as described in pars. 16 through 18 of GASB No. 14); however, most foundations fall into category (c).

GASB No. 39, "Determining whether Certain Organizations Are Component Units," amended GASB No. 14 to accord "component unit" status to legally separate category (c) nonprofit organizations that meet certain criteria that signify a relationship of such nature and significance that inclusion in the governmental reporting entity is required. The application of those criteria to situations involving foundations related to governmental HCOs are as follows:

- *Direct benefit* — The economic resources received or held by the foundation are entirely or almost entirely for the direct benefit of the health care organization or its component units.
- *Entitlement/ability to otherwise access* — The health care organization or its component units are entitled to, or have the ability to otherwise access, a majority of the economic resources received or held by the foundation. The ability to "otherwise access" is not meant to imply or require that the health care organization has control over the foundation or its resources. Rather, it is a broader concept that may be demonstrated in several ways, for example:
- The health care organization or its component units historically may have received (directly or indirectly) a majority of the economic resources provided by the foundation.
- The foundation previously may have received and honored requests to provide resources to the health care organization.
- The foundation is "financially interrelated" with the health care organization under FASB Statement No. 136.[16]
- *Significance* — The resources of the foundation to which the health care organization or its component units are entitled/have the ability to otherwise access are significant to the health care organization.

When all three of these criteria are met, a foundation is deemed to be a component unit of the health care organization's reporting entity. If one or more of the criteria are not met, the foundation may still need to be evaluated for inclusion as a component unit under the "misleading to exclude" standard described in paragraph 41 of GASB No. 14.[17]

When a foundation is deemed to be a "component unit" under GASB No. 39, the nature of its relationship with the health care organization is different from the relationship the health care organization may have with component units that are directly associated with it through the board appointment process or fiscal dependency. The GASB concluded that the special nature of this relationship could best be communicated to users of the financial statements through *discrete presentation* of the foundation's financial data in the health care organization's financial statements. Typically, discrete presentation involves displaying the component unit financial data as a separate column (or columns) in a "side-by-side" presentation with the financial data of the primary government. However, the financial statements of foundations that are includable under the new GASB No. 39 criteria are prepared in accordance with FASB standards, rather than GASB standards. In such situations, the foundation's statements may be presented on separate pages (e.g., the foundation's balance sheet is presented on the page following the health care organization's balance sheet, the foundation's operating statement is presented on the page following the health care

---

[16] Foundations that are not "financially interrelated" with their beneficiary organizations act in an agency capacity when they receive contributions designated for those beneficiaries. Relationships between these foundations and their affiliated health care organizations must also be evaluated for inclusion as "component units" under the three criteria; the only difference is that there is no presumption based on FAS No. 136 that the health care organization has an "ability to otherwise access" in these relationships.

[17] Typically, this evaluation is based on how closely related the foundation is to the entity it supports. GASB No. 39 emphasizes that "closely related organizations" should include those that are "financially integrated" with the primary government in such ways as one entity providing office space and administrative services to the other or participation by employees of the primary government in program activities of the foundation (among others). According to paragraph 6 of GASB No. 39, financial integration may be exhibited and documented through the policies, practices, or organization documents of either the primary government or the foundation.

organization's operating statement, etc.). If a side-by-side presentation is desired, the foundation's financial statements can be converted to a GASB presentation format. This does not, however, also require conversion of the underlying accounting principles used in preparation of the foundation's financial statements to GASB accounting principles.

GASB No. 39 does not require disclosure of the differences between the FASB accounting principles used in preparing the nonprofit organization's financial statements and GASB accounting principles. For example, the net assets of a not-for-profit fund-raising foundation that supports a governmental entity may include permanently restricted endowment funds that are recognizable under FASB Statement No. 116, "Accounting for Contributions Received and Contributions Made," but would not be recognizable under GASB Statement No. 33, "Accounting and Financial Reporting for Nonexchange Transactions." Appendix E of GASB No. 39 illustrates an optional disclosure of a policy note addressing such differences.

For each discretely presented component unit resulting from application of GASB No. 39, the notes to the health care organization's financial statements should include a brief description of the component unit, its relationship to the health care organization, a discussion of the criteria for including the component unit, and how the component unit is reported. For a "major" component unit, the nature and amount of significant transactions between the health care organization and the component unit also must be disclosed.

Additional presentation issues such as differing fiscal year ends (par. 46) and display of component units by governments that are themselves component units of another government (pars. 45 and 56) are addressed in GASB No. 39's Basis for Conclusions.

(iv) Obligated Group Financial Statements. Tax-exempt debt agreements may require preparation of combined financial statements of affiliated entities, the assets or revenues of which serve as collateral for the related debt (e.g., an "obligated group"). ARB No. 51 applies to these situations. However, if debt or other agreements prescribe a financial presentation that varies from GAAP (e.g., exclusion of entities otherwise required to be consolidated), the financial statements must be restricted for limited use. A limited-use-type report on obligated group financial statements would not be appropriate to include in an official statement or to submit to municipal securities information repository (see Subsection 36.2(c)).

In such cases, there may need to be a modification of the agreement with the underwriters. However, quite often the underwriters will accept a consolidated audit report that includes a supplemental schedule showing the entities that add up to the obligated group, with an aggregate column for all other entities, coming up to the consolidated total (i.e., similar to the pro forma financials frequently seen in SEC filings). This should be acceptable to include in an Official Statement or to submit to a repository. Another approach being used in some cases is to provide two sets of financial statements: a set of audited consolidated financial statements and a set of unaudited financial statements that reconcile the obligated group totals to the audited consolidated totals.

(v) Joint Operating Agreements. There has been increased movement toward "virtual mergers" within the health care industry in which two or more organizations or systems agree to share operational responsibilities and profits for their facilities via a joint operating agreement, without actually combining asset ownership. All agree to jointly operate and control certain of their facilities while sharing in the operating results and residual interest upon dissolution, based on an agreed-upon ratio. In these types of arrangements, none of the venturers receives cash or other monetary assets as part of entering into the agreement, and no separate legal entity is created (e.g., a corporation or partnership). They are similar to joint ventures; as such, they typically are characterized by factors such as:

- Common purpose (e.g., to share risks and rewards; to develop a new market, health service, or program; to pool resources)
- Joint funding (all parties contribute resources toward its accomplishment)
- Defined relationship (i.e., typically government by an agreement)
- Joint control (control is not derived from holding a majority of the voting interest)

AICPA Technical Practice Aids, Section 6400, states that since there is joint control in a joint operating agreement (i.e., no party controls the venture), consolidation would not be appropriate. Instead, such agreements should be accounted for similar to a corporate joint venture using the equity method of accounting. Since the transaction would not reflect the culmination of the earnings process, the venturers' basis in the investment would be reported at net book value.

(u) BUSINESS COMBINATIONS. FASB Statement No. 141, "Business Combinations," addresses financial accounting and reporting for business combinations. Detailed considerations related to FASB No. 141 are discussed in Chapter 12 of this book. Considerations related to the applicability of FAS No. 141 to not-for-profit and governmental HCOs are discussed below.

(i) Combinations Involving Not-for-Profit Organizations. Issues similar to those deliberated for business organizations in connection with FASB Statement No. 141, "Business Combinations," will be deliberated in the course of FASB's project on Combinations of Not-for-Profit Organizations. As a result of that project, most combination transactions involving not-for-profit organizations are excluded from the scope of FAS No. 141. These include combination transactions involving two or more not-for-profit organizations or transactions in which a not-for-profit organization acquires a for-profit organization. For these types of combinations, existing GAAP (discussed below) does not change until a final FASB standard on not-for-profit combinations is issued and effective.

Not-for-profit transactions that must be accounted for in accordance with FAS No. 141 include (1) acquisitions of not-for-profit organizations by for-profit organizations and (2) acquisitions made by for-profit subsidiaries of not-for-profit organizations. In the latter case, when the subsidiary's financial statements are rolled up into the consolidated financial statements of the not-for-profit parent, FAS No. 141 continues to apply; that is, the transactions reported in the subsidiary's financial statements should not be "converted" to the standards followed by the not-for-profit parent as a result of consolidation.

Existing GAAP for combinations involving not-for-profit HCOs is provided by APB Opinion No. 16, "Business Combinations," and the health care Guide. Most combinations involving two or more not-for-profit HCOs involve the formation of a new entity without the exchange of any consideration. Chapter 11 of *Health Care Organizations* notes that while APB has been superseded by FAS No. 141, it continues to provide a useful framework when evaluating combination transactions entered into by not-for-profit HCOs. Because the conditions for applying the pooling-of-interests method of accounting under APB No. 16 generally include an exchange of common stock of the combining entities, not-for-profit transactions that do not involve the exchange of consideration generally would not meet APB No. 16's specific conditions for applying the pooling method. Even so, the Audit Guide states that circumstances exist under which reporting on the combination of two or more not-for-profit organizations (or that of a not-for-profit organization with a formerly for-profit entity) by the pooling-of-interests method better reflects the substance of the transaction that reporting by the purchase method. Therefore, not-for-profit organizations are, under some circumstances, permitted to report by the pooling-of-interests method.

Chapter 11 of the Guide provides the following factors to consider when evaluating these transactions.

- If there is an exchange of consideration, exchange of legal title, assumption of liabilities, and so on, the transaction is accounted for similar to a purchase under APB No. 16. For example, in an asset acquisition transaction (a type of purchase accounting), the transferor company's assets pass to the acquirer in accordance with the terms of the contract, and the acquiring company generally is not obligated to pay any of the transferor company's debts or to be responsible for any of the transferor's other liabilities unless it agrees to do so under the acquisition agreement. In practice, however, the purchaser usually assumes at least some of the transferor's liabilities. In many cases, the transferor will be required under bond indentures to arrange for an assumption of its debt by the purchaser (or, instead, to pay off its debt). At closing, the transferor company conveys its assets to the acquirer by bills of sale and assignment, and the acquirer delivers the purchase price. In a complex purchase-type transaction, scores of documents of title, deeds, mortgages, and so forth may pass between the parties.

- If there is simply a change of control, with no exchange of consideration, generally the transaction is accounted for similar to a pooling. An inquiry published in the AICPA's Technical Practice Aids[18] publication attempts to clarify that generally, pooling accounting is used if consideration is not involved. Statutory mergers of not-for-profit health care systems, in which one system will be merged into the other and a new entity formed without the exchange of consideration, would be one illustration of a type of transaction that, generally speaking, would probably fall under the pooling classification. In a statutory merger, the assets and liabilities of the transferor are transferred to the new entity (or the surviving entity, depending on the circumstances) automatically by operation of law. Consequently, there is no need to make the specific transfers of individual assets, rights, and liabilities that is involved in an acquisition of assets. An acceptable practice for reporting such business combinations is to report the assets, liabilities, and net asset balances of the combined entities as of the beginning of the year and disclose the information that would be required to be disclosed for a pooling of interest under APB No. 16.

The above guidance remains in effect until the FASB completes its not-for-profit combinations project; it was not impacted by FAS No. 141's elimination of the pooling method of accounting. The Guide states that when applying the guidance in APB No. 16, not-for-profit HCOs should continue to apply the amendments to APB No.16 made by standards that were superseded by FAS No. 141 or FAS No. 142. Similarly, after FAS No. 144 supersedes FAS No. 121, not-for-profit HCOs should continue to apply the amendments to APB No. 16 made by FAS No. 121.

(ii) Combinations Involving Governmental Entities.   As discussed at Subsection 36.2(b), GAS No. 20, paragraph 7, allows proprietary activities to continue to apply FASB pronouncements except for those that (a) conflict with or contradict GASB pronouncements or (2) deal primarily with not-for-profit issues. If a new FASB standard does not fall into one of those categories, "paragraph 7" entities must adopt it, unless the GASB issues a standard instructing them not to do so. Governmental health care entities that follow the AICPA audit and accounting guide *Health Care Organizations* generally follow paragraph 7 of GAS No. 20. Consequently, those entities must follow the requirements of FAS No. 141 in accounting for combination transactions.

The primary concern this raises for governmental HCOs is FAS No. 141's elimination of the pooling method and requirement to designate an acquirer for all transactions. As with not-for-profit-sector transactions, many governmental mergers do not involve exchange of consideration. If these "merger of mission" transactions are accounted for in accordance with FAS No. 141's negative goodwill provisions, a significant portion of the acquired organization's nonfinancial assets potentially could be written down to zero.

At this time, the GASB has no plans to issue a standard addressing combination transactions. While acknowledging the difficulties that may be involved in adoption of FAS No. 141 by a governmental organization (particularly with respect to combinations that do not involve exchange of consideration), the GASB staff believes that these transactions will be relatively few in number. Absent any further guidance from the GASB, each governmental entity will have to establish a position as to how these transactions should be accounted for under FAS No. 141.

(v) TIMING DIFFERENCES.   For Medicare cost reporting purposes, certain items are accounted for in different periods than they are reported in for financial reporting purposes. The "timing differences" that arise from these items are recognized in the periods in which the differences arise and the periods in which they reverse. Common examples involve deferred compensation arrangements, uses of different depreciation methods for financial reporting and cost reporting purposes, malpractice expense, and reporting of gains or losses on debt extinguishments.

---

[18] Section 6400.33.

36.4 SPECIAL ACCOUNTING PROBLEMS OF SPECIFIC TYPES OF PROVIDERS

(a) CONTINUING CARE RETIREMENT COMMUNITIES.   CCRCs are organizations that provide or guarantee residential and health care services for persons who may reside in apartments, other living units, or a nursing center. They are usually characterized by an obligation to provide future services and some sort of up-front payment on the part of the resident, part of which may be refundable. Unique accounting issues pertaining to CCRCs include: refundable fees, fees repayable to residents from reoccupancy proceeds, nonrefundable fees, the obligation to provide future services, the use of facilities to current residents, and costs of acquiring continuing-care contracts.

(i) Refundable Advance Fees.   Frequently, continuing care contracts provide for some or all of a resident's advance fee (also called an *entrance fee*) to be refunded if the resident dies or withdraws from the CCRC. In many cases, the refundable portion decreases with time or other contractual provisions.

If provisions of the contract allow a refund to be made, an estimate should be made each year of the amount of refundable advance fees that are expected to be refunded to current residents upon death or withdrawal. The estimate would be based on the individual facility's own experience or, if not available, on the experience of comparable facilities. The estimated amount refundable would be reported as a liability. The remainder of the advance fee would be accounted for as deferred revenue. As time passes or other contract provisions cause the amount refundable to decrease, the portion that becomes nonrefundable should be reclassified to deferred revenue and amortized into income. The amortization of this deferred revenue is discussed in Section (iv) below.

The gross amount of contractual refund obligations under existing contracts at the balance sheet date should be disclosed for each year the balance sheet is presented. The CCRC's refund policy should also be disclosed in the notes to the financial statements. Amounts refunded should be classified in the statement of cash flows as a financing transaction.

These conclusions do not apply to refunds that are contingent upon the resale of the unit. Those situations are discussed in Section (iii).

(ii) Nonrefundable Advance Fees.   Most contracts provide that at least some portion of the entrance fee will not be refundable upon the resident's death or withdrawal. Some contracts do not allow any of the entrance fee to be refunded. According to the Guide, nonrefundable fees represent payment for future services to be provided over the life of the resident (unless the contract terms state otherwise). Therefore, nonrefundable amounts should be reported as deferred revenue when received and amortized into income as described in Section (iv) below.

Upon the death or withdrawal of a resident, any unamortized deferred revenue from nonrefundable advance fees pertaining to his or her contract should immediately be reclassified to revenue.

(iii) Fees Refundable to Residents from Reoccupancy Proceeds of a Contract Holder's Unit.   Some contracts provide that entrance fees will be refunded only when and if the contract holder's unit is resold to a new resident. Presumably, each subsequent contract would similarly allow a refund only in the event the unit is again sold. The Guide states that in such situations, the portion of advance fees that is refundable upon reoccupancy should be reported as deferred revenue (provided that law and management policy and practice support the withholding of refunds under this condition).

CCRCs generally structure contracts in this manner to recover the cost of the facilities over their economic lives; therefore, the amount reported as deferred revenue should be amortized to income over the remaining useful life of the facility. The basis and method of amortization should be consistent with the method for calculating depreciation, and should be disclosed in the notes to the financial statements.

No liability for the refund amount exists until the unit is in fact resold. At that time, the liability will be paid from the proceeds of the unit's resale. If the amount received from the new resident is greater than the amount to be refunded to the former resident, the excess also should be considered deferred revenue (provided that the resale contract also contains a provision that refundability is contingent on subsequent resale of the unit).

(iv) Amortization of Nonrefundable Advance Fees. Deferred revenue from nonrefundable advance fees should be amortized into income on a straight-line basis over each individual resident's remaining life expectancy (or the contract term, if it is shorter). The period of amortization would be adjusted annually based on the actuarially determined estimated remaining life expectancy of each individual, or joint and last survivor life expectancy of each pair of residents occupying the same unit. The amortization of each resident's nonrefundable fees should not exceed the amount available to the CCRC under state regulations, contract provision, or management policy.

Although the individual life method may appear to be a time-consuming process that requires substantial record keeping, once the data are developed, calculated, and accumulated, it should not require a significant amount of time to calculate deferred nonrefundable fees for each individual. The individual life method is preferable because it smooths out fluctuations and results in a more accurate accrual of earned revenue than does the group method. (Under the group method, residents are grouped by average age, entry year, type or size of unit, or some other method, and a life expectancy is determined for the group using life expectancy tables.)

CCRCs should assess whether they have sufficient historical information about life expectancies or whether they will have to use regional or national actuarially determined data instead. CCRC-specific data may be the most appropriate, especially for CCRCs that cater to affluent populations. Such groups often are in better health and live longer than average. Whatever statistical information is selected for amortizing deferred revenue must also be used for determining the obligation for future services.

As indicated, the straight-line method should be used to amortize the deferred revenue, except in certain circumstances where costs are expected to be significantly higher in the later years of residence. In those cases, a method that reflects the timing of the costs of the expected services may be used. The amortization method used should be disclosed in a note to the financial statements.

In the income statement, the amortization of deferred revenue from advance fees should be reported in resident fees earned.

(v) Obligation to Provide Future Services. CCRCs generally commit to provide services and the use of facilities to residents for the rest of their lives. Annually, the CCRC needs to assess its contractual arrangements with existing residents to determine whether the expected future revenues from those contracts will be sufficient to cover the costs of providing services and use of facilities over the rest of the residents' lives.

Many CCRCs require residents to pay periodic fees that may be increased, if necessary. CCRCs that have no restrictions on their ability to cover future costs, and those that have a history of profitable operations, may not encounter problems in this area. More likely to be affected are CCRCs that have contracts which restrict the amount of periodic fee increases and CCRCs having contracts that only require residents to pay an advance fee. In this situation, no additional funds can be required to be paid, regardless of how long a resident lives or if the resident requires more services than anticipated.

If the estimated costs of future services are determined to exceed anticipated revenues, the CCRC has entered into a loss contract. Losses resulting from such contracts—the obligation to provide future services—should be recorded in the period in which they are determined to exist. In determining the loss, contracts should be grouped by type, such as "contracts with a limit on annual increases in fees"/"contracts with unlimited fee increases."

According to the Guide, "anticipated revenues" include third-party payments (e.g., those from Blue Cross/Blue Shield), contractually or statutorily committed investment income from sources related to CCRC activities, contributions pledged by donors to support CCRC activities, periodic fees expected to be collected, and the balance of deferred nonrefundable advance fees. Examples of "estimated costs of future services" include costs of resident care, dietary costs, health care facility costs, general and administrative costs, interest expense, depreciation, and amortization costs.

At the time of initial determination that a loss exists, the CCRC would record a liability (the "obligation to provide future services and the use of facilities is excess of amounts received or to be received for such services") and make a corresponding charge to income (the "provision for obligation to provide future services and use of facilities"). The Guide provides a formula for calculating the liability, as follows:

- Present value of future net cash flows
- Minus the balance of unamortized deferred revenue
- Plus depreciation of facilities to be charged related to the contracts
- Plus unamortized costs of acquiring the related initial continuing-care contracts, if applicable

For purposes of determining the present value of future net cash flows, the Guide defines cash inflows as revenue contractually committed to support the residents and inflows resulting from monthly fees, including anticipated increases in accordance with contract terms. Cash outflows are defined as operating expenses, including interest expense but excluding selling and general and administrative expenses. Cost increases resulting from inflation should be factored into the amount of operating expenses included in the computation. The difference between cash inflows and cash outflows should be discounted to present value. The Guide states that the expected inflation rate and other factors should be taken into account in determining the discount rate to be used.

A formula for determining the depreciation of facilities to be charged to current residents is provided in the Guide. Basically, the purpose of this formula is to exclude from the loss computation any depreciation allocable to revenue-producing service areas.

For both the net present value of cash flows and the depreciation of facilities, the computation should be made on a resident-by-resident basis within each contract group, using the resident's remaining life expectancy. The life spans used should be the same as those used in calculating the amortization of deferred revenue.

Each year, the liability should be recalculated. Increases or decreases in the liability would be reported in the income statement as a separate line item, "change in obligation to provide future services and use of facilities," with appropriate note disclosure. In the balance sheet, the obligation to provide future services should be presented separately as a long-term liability, if it is material.

The notes to the financial statements should include a description of the obligation to provide future services, the carrying amount of the liability that is presented at present value (if it is not separately disclosed in the balance sheet), and the interest rate used to discount the liability.

(vi) Costs of Acquiring Initial Continuing Care Contracts.   Most CCRCs regard the costs of obtaining contracts to initially fill a new facility as an investment that will result in future revenues from amortization of nonrefundable advance fees (and future periodic fees, in some cases). The Guide provides guidance on whether "costs of acquiring initial continuing care contracts" (as specifically defined in the glossary of the Guide) should be capitalized or expensed. The glossary states that these are costs incurred to originate a contract that result from and are essential to acquire initial contracts and are incurred through the date of substantial occupancy but no later than one year from the date of completion of construction. They include:

(a) The costs from activities in connection with soliciting potential initial residents (such as model units and their furnishings, sales brochures, semipermanent signs, tours, and grand openings). However, these costs do not include advertising, interest, administrative costs, rent, depreciation, or any other occupancy or equipment costs.

(b) Sales salaries incurred in connection with the activities described in (a).

(c) The costs of processing the contracts, such as evaluating the prospective resident's financial condition; evaluating and recording guarantees, collateral, and other security arrangements; negotiating contract terms; preparing and processing contract documents; and closing the transaction.

(d) The portion of an employee's compensation and benefits that relates to the initial contract acquisitions.

The costs of acquiring initial continuing-care contracts that are described in (a) above and are expected to be recovered from future contract revenues should be capitalized in accordance with FASB Statement No. 67, "Accounting for Costs and Initial Rental Operations of Real Estate Projects," and amortized to expense on a straight-line basis over the average expected remaining lives of the residents under the contract or the contract term, if shorter. Such costs incurred after a CCRC is substantially occupied or one year following completion should be expensed when incurred. Costs that are described in (b) should be expensed, and costs described in (c) and (d) should be accounted for in conformity with the guidance in SOP 98-5, "Reporting on the Costs of Start-Up Activities."

Advertising cost is not a component of "costs of acquiring initial continuing-care contracts." Advertising cost incurred in connection with acquiring initial continuing-care contracts should be accounted for in conformity with the guidance in SOP 93-7, "Reporting on Advertising Costs."

An exposure draft of a proposed SOP, "Accounting for Certain Costs and Activities Related to Property, Plan and Equipment," was issued in 2001 that would amend the guidance regarding capitalization of certain of the costs described in (a).

(b) PREPAID HEALTH CARE PLANS.   Prepaid health care plans provide or arrange for the delivery of health care services to a specified group of individuals in exchange for a fixed, predetermined fee. The most common form of prepaid health care organization is the HMO.

Some have questioned the need for developing specific guidance for the HMO industry when GAAP for insurance companies might be applied to certain similar transactions entered into by HMOs. The fundamental difference noted in the accounting guidance for the two industries is that HMOs undertake to provide (or arrange for the provision of) health care services in addition to their role as a third-party payer. Because FASB Statement No. 60 and other relevant insurance industry principles are applicable only to contracts that involve payment for health care services (not to contracts that extend to the provision of health care services), specialized guidance was needed. That guidance is discussed next.

(i) Expense Recognition Issues.   The event that triggers an HMO to recognize claim expense is the provision of health care services to an enrolled member, not the occurrence of an accident or illness. In order to achieve a proper matching of the HMO's revenues and expenses, as a general rule the costs of providing health care services to HMO members should be reported in the periods in which those services are actually rendered. This is true even if the subscriber is being treated for an illness that requires long-term treatment. It is not appropriate to estimate and accrue the expense of the entire spell of illness in the period in which the diagnosis is made. However, in certain situations it is appropriate for HMOs to accrue the costs of health care services. These are set forth in the following items.

Contractual or Regulatory Obligations.   If an HMO member is hospitalized at the end of the premium period, in situations where the contract or prevailing regulations obligate the HMO to continue to provide care to members after the end of the premium period, the HMO will have to accrue the total costs of these hospitalization services. An example would be if the HMO is contractually obligated to continue to provide coverage for hospital stays that are "in progress" at the end of the premium period.

IBNR Incurred but not Reported Accruals.   "IBNR" accruals must be estimated and reserves recorded for services that have been rendered by providers but not reported to the HMO as of the financial statement date. This will include recurring claims from the HMO's contracted providers, claims from specialists, and claims arising from situations in which a subscriber requires medical care outside of the HMO's service area (such as while traveling). In such cases, the HMO should accrue the costs of any services rendered during the fiscal period for which payment has not been made as of the close of the fiscal period, even if the subcontracting provider has not yet billed the HMO for those services.

The IBNR reserve is one of the key risk areas for an HMO, not only because it has a major effect on an HMO's financial statements but also because it serves as one of the early warning signals of utilization problems. Finance personnel must work closely with utilization management and contacting personnel to analyze cost and utilization data, which is essential to conducting lag schedule analyses and formulating the reserves.

Termination of Contract.   Another situation in which an accrual of health care costs might be required is when a contract between an HMO and an employer is terminated. For instance, a staff model HMO might contract with a major industrial corporation to establish a medical clinic on or near the premises of a plant. In a staff model HMO, the costs of providing health care services to the plant's employees are relatively fixed, because the clinic's physicians and support personnel are generally salaried employees. If the contract with the corporation is terminated, expenses associated with the clinic that the HMO will be unable to avoid, such as guaranteed salaries, rent, or depreciation, should be accrued net of any related anticipated revenues.

(ii) Loss Contracts.   If premiums are set too low or if utilization by the members is unusually high, the HMO will sustain an economic loss in fulfilling that particular contract. Losses should be accrued when an HMO's projected health care costs and maintenance costs pertaining to a particular group of contracts exceed the anticipated premium revenues and stop-loss insurance recoveries under those contracts. The costs considered should include fixed costs as well as variable costs; in other words, the computation should include costs that would be incurred regardless of whether or not a particular contract is in force, such as staff physician's salaries and costs attributable to facilities owned by the HMO. The costs considered should also include all direct costs of the contracts along with indirect costs identifiable with or allocable to the contracts, as is customary in any type of contract accounting. Generally this requires inclusion of all HMO costs other than general and administrative, selling, marketing, and interest.

To determine whether a loss accrual is necessary, an HMO will need to analyze the unexpired contracts in force at the end of each reporting period. Contracts should be grouped in the manner discussed below and the aggregate health care costs, maintenance expenses, premium revenue, and stop-loss recoveries projected for the contracts in each group. If the aggregate expenses for the contract period are expected to exceed the aggregate revenues for the contract period, the amount of the excess should be accrued as a loss on that group of contracts. Furthermore, if any of the contracts in a "loss group" have guaranteed renewal provisions and the HMO is constrained by statutory requirements or community rating practices from increasing the premiums charged on those contracts, the HMO should also accrue any losses it expects to incur attributable to the guaranteed renewal periods.

The groupings used for loss determination correspond with the groupings used by the HMO in establishing its premium rates. For HMOs that use community rating (i.e., one premium rate is established for all members in a given enrollment population; for instance, a particular geographic area or actuarial class), the contracts grouped together for loss determination would be those considered to be part of the same enrollment "pool" for premium determination. HMOs that are experience-rated would group their contracts along the same lines as are used for rate-setting purposes, such as by type of employer. (In an experience-rated HMO, members covered by each contract constitute a separate population base for rate-setting purposes; therefore, premiums are based on the actual or anticipated health care costs of each contract.)

(iii) Risk Pools.   Risk pools provide a vehicle for sharing favorable and unfavorable experiences among providers (and sometimes the payer) by creating incentives for physicians and hospitals to control utilization of services. The type of incentive offered may be positive (gain-sharing pool) or negative (loss-sharing pool), or may combine both positive and negative incentives (combined risk-sharing pool). Risk pool settlements retroactively determine the amount of fees a provider will receive under a given risk contract; therefore, the settlements affect the amount of health care expense that should be recognized by the HMO. The HMO should accrue risk pool settlements payable to physicians, hospitals, and other providers based on relevant factors such as experience to date.

In situations where settlements are due from providers under risk-sharing arrangements, a receivable will exist. Whether or not this receivable can be collected may be a significant item for HMOs, because the amounts can be large relative to net income. It is not uncommon for HMOs ultimately to write such receivables off. Alternatively, some HMOs "recover" the receivable over a period of years by withholding payments from compensation to providers calculated at greater than market rates. Receivables of this nature should be presented net of an allowance for uncollectibles; that allowance may be difficult to estimate due to the factors discussed above. Such receivables may be separately disclosed, if they are material.

(iv) Stop-Loss Insurance. HMOs often purchase stop-loss insurance (also called *excess-of-loss reinsurance*) to protect themselves against the risk of loss incurred in the process of satisfying the claims of HMO subscribers. HMOs should report stop-loss insurance premiums as a health care cost. Stop-loss insurance recoveries should be reported as a reduction of the related premium expense; they should not be reported as revenue. Amounts recoverable (i.e., receivable) from insurers under stop-loss policies should be reported as assets, reduced by appropriate valuation allowances; it is not appropriate to offset such amounts against amounts payable for health care costs.

(v) Acquisition Costs. HMOs incur certain costs in connection with writing contracts and obtaining new members. These costs may be general in nature, such as marketing staff salaries, general promotional literature, and other advertising; or they may be directly related to the acquisition of specific contracts, such as the costs of specialized brochures and advertising and commissions paid to agents or brokers. Acquisition costs other than advertising should be expensed as incurred. Advertising costs should be accounted for in accordance with the guidance in SOP 93-7, "Reporting on Advertising Costs."

(vi) Billing and Reconciliation. It is imperative that an HMO monitor the status of outstanding bills and accounts receivable, that monthly bills be reconciled to amounts received on a timely basis, and that discrepancies be followed up promptly. This facilitates the identification of employers to be terminated for nonpayment but, more importantly, facilitates the identification of retroactive member additions and terminations. This assists in maintaining the integrity of the eligibility database, so that health care services are provided to, and claims and capitation paid only for, enrolled members. Failure to perform this function on a timely basis can seriously threaten the financial stability of an HMO.

(c) PHYSICIAN PRACTICE MANAGEMENT COMPANIES. Physician Practice Management Companies (PPM companies or PPMs) amass physicians into groups that can better contract with managed care companies. Additionally, they manage the business aspects of the medical practices. PPMs' unique accounting and reporting issues are due largely to the presence of state corporate practice of medicine laws. Most states regulate to some degree the form of entity in which a physician or dentist may practice. Typically, state laws permit a medical professional to conduct a medical practice only as an individual, as a member of a partnership, or as an employee of a professional corporation (i.e., a corporation in which all the shareholders are medical professionals) and prohibit, either by specific provisions or as a matter of general policy, a medical professional from conducting a practice as an employee of a general business corporation. These limitations are frequently referred to as *corporate practice of medicine*" prohibitions.

If they cannot buy a medical practice outright, PPMs often "acquire" physician practices by acquiring the practice's nonmedical assets and then entering into long-term (25-to-40-year) management service agreements with the medical entity. This creates some interesting and unusual ownership structures as well as unique financial reporting considerations.

PPM accounting and reporting issues are addressed in EITF Issue No. 97-2, *Application of FAS 94 and APB 16 to Physician Practice Management Entities and Certain Other Management Entities with Similar Circumstances and Arrangements.* EITF Issue No. 97-2 generally applies to medical entities involved in the practice of medicine, dentistry, or veterinary science[19] that enter into transactions with these types of structures, irrespective of whether it is for legal reasons—that is, compliance with corporate practice of medicine laws—or by choice (i.e., for business reasons).

(i) Establishment of Controlling Financial Interest.   EITF Issue No. 97-2 addresses whether a controlling financial interest that requires consolidation can be established through a contractual management agreement, such as a PPM management service agreement. The EITF reached a consensus that a PPM can establish a controlling financial interest in a medical entity solely through contractual arrangements if, via the terms of the contractual arrangement, the PPM has both control over the medical entity and a financial interest in the medical entity that meets six requirements. The requirements are:

a. The contractual arrangement between the PPM and the PC is either (i) the entire remaining life of the physician practice entity; or (ii) for a period of 10 years or more.

b. The contractual arrangement is not terminable by the physician practice except in cases of gross negligence, fraud, or other illegal acts by the PPM, or upon bankruptcy of the PPM.

c. The PPM has exclusive authority over all decision making related to ongoing, major, or central operations of the physician practice, except for the dispensing of medical services.

d. The PPM has exclusive authority over all decision making related to total practice compensation of the licensed medical professionals, as well as the ability to establish and implement guidelines for the selection, hiring, and firing of them.

e. The PPM must have a significant financial interest in the physician practice that is unilaterally salable or transferable.

f. The PPM's significant financial interest must provide the PPM with the right to receive income (both as ongoing fees and as proceeds from the sale of its interest in the physician practice) in an amount that fluctuates based on the performance of the operations of the physician practice and the change in the fair value thereof.

Contract Term.   The first threshold in determining controlling financial interest is to evaluate the "long-term nature of the relationship." In order to be considered "long-term," the contractual agreement between the PPM and the medical entity must be for a period of 10 years or more and may not be terminable by the medical entity except in the event of gross negligence, fraud, or other illegal activities, or bankruptcy of the PPM. The evaluation of whether the contractual arrangement can be considered long term should be based on substance as opposed to form. Therefore, both the original stated contract term and any renewal or cancellation provisions must be considered; for example, an agreement having an initial stated term of five years, with one five-year renewal option exercisable solely at the discretion of the PPM, is considered "long term" because it is collectively a 10-year contract. (*Note:* Defining "long term" as 10 years or more is specific to this particular EITF consensus. It is not intended that this definition be extended to the use of that term in other authoritative accounting literature.)

Control over Medical Entity.   The ability of a PPM to demonstrate control is directly affected by corporate practice of medicine laws. From a structuring perspective, it is generally believed that the most effective way to demonstrate control is through the use of the "nominee shareholder" model.[20] Therefore, the EITF provides a two-pronged approach to evaluating whether control exists, depending on whether or not the contractual arrangement uses the nominee shareholder model.

---

[19] The EITF observed that there may be industries other than the health care industry in which one entity manages another entity under circumstances similar to those addressed in EITF Issue No. 97-2. Therefore, the consensus might impact potentially analogous situations in other industries.

[20] EITF Issue No. 97-2 provides the following description of a "nominee shareholder" arrangement:

When the contractual arrangement between the PPM and the medical practice is structured using the nominee shareholder model, and a majority of the outstanding voting equity instruments of the practice are owned by the nominee shareholder, there is an automatic presumption that the PPM has control over the medical entity. The presumption is rebutted if the PPM, either through a management agreement or through its nominee, has granted rights to others such that the PPM does not have "exclusive decision-making authority." However, it cannot be rebutted if the PPM possesses exclusive decision-making authority.

If the nominee shareholder model is not used, the existence of "control" would be determined based on whether the contractual arrangement meets *both* of the following requirements:

- The PPM has exclusive authority over all decision making related to total compensation of the licensed medical professionals as well as the ability to establish and implement guidelines for their selection, hiring, and termination.
- The PPM has exclusive authority over all decision making related to ongoing, major, or central operations of the medical entity, other than the dispensing of medical services. This includes decision-making authority over scope of services, patient acceptance policy and procedures, pricing of services, negotiation and execution of contracts, and establishment and approval of operating and capital budgets. If debt financing is an ongoing, major, or central source of financing for the medical entity, the PPM must also have exclusive decision-making authority over issuance of debt.

EITF Issue No. 97-2 also discusses whether certain common contractual provisions (e.g., binding arbitration, physician co-signing requirements) result in surrender of some or all of a PPM's "exclusive decision-making authority" in critical areas. There also is discussion regarding the relationship of the "exclusive decision-making authority" requirements and state laws that might appear to impair that decision-making authority, such as patient antidumping laws.

Financial Interest.   As was the case with the "control" criterion, the EITF provided a two-pronged approach to determining whether a financial interest exists based on whether or not the contractual arrangement is based on the "nominee shareholder" model. If the nominee shareholder model is used, and the nominee shareholder owns a majority of the outstanding voting equity instruments of the practice and has exclusive decision-making authority, as discussed above, the PPM is presumed to have a financial interest in the medical entity, as long as the PPM has the power to—at will

---

One or more shareholders whose relationship with the PPM (which can be either the PPM itself or its controlled subsidiaries) perpetually has all of the following characteristics:

Time Frame:
- The PPM can at all times establish or effect a change in the nominee shareholder.
- The PPM can cause a change in the nominee shareholder an unlimited number of times, that is, changing the nominee shareholder one or more times does not affect the PPM's ability to change the nominee shareholder again and again.

Discretion:
- The PPM has sole discretion without cause to establish or change the nominee shareholder.
- The PPM can name anyone as a new nominee shareholder (that is, the PPM's choice of an eligible nominee is not limited).

Impact:
- The PPM and the nominally owned entity incur no more than a nominal cost to cause a change in the nominee shareholder.
- Neither the PPM nor the nominally owned entity is subject to any significant adverse impact upon a change in the nominee shareholder.

and for no or only nominal compensation—reset the terms of its financial interest in the physician practice to a basis that would meet criteria (e) and (f).

If the nominee shareholder model is not used, then the PPM must demonstrate that it has a significant financial interest in the medical entity. The required "significant" level of financial interest of the PPM in the physician practice is intentionally not prescribed. This is meant to convey that what is "significant" must be determined in the context of the facts and circumstances.

A financial interest in a physician practice is the right to share in the change in the fair value of that physician practice. This right must be economically similar to the right a shareholder must possess. For purposes of the financial interest requirements contained in criterion (f), that change in fair value is viewed as consisting of two components: (1) the portion of the change that manifests itself as current operating results and (2) the remainder, which is the portion of the change that manifests itself only upon sale or liquidation of the physician practice. Criterion (f) requires that the PPM have rights to share in both components and that the amounts collectively derived constitute a significant portion of the total change in fair value. If the PPM's arrangement with the physician practice will end before the physician practice is sold or liquidated, the PPM would need to have the right to share in the change in the fair value of the physician practice that arose during the PPM's relationship with it in order to meet the requirement described in criterion (b).

For purposes of determining compliance with criterion (f), the calculation of ongoing fees and the calculation of proceeds from sale are to be evaluated based on their substance as opposed to their form. Determining whether the requirements of criterion (f) are met will require the use of judgment.

(ii) Business Combination Issues.   EITF Issue No. 97-2 also addresses whether such "acquisitions" of medical practices by PPMs qualify as business combinations. The EITF concluded that when a PPM acquires the net assets and enters into long-term management service agreements with the medical entity, the transaction is considered a business combination subject to APB No. 16 if both (1) the medical entity is a "business" that is, it has an existing patient base at the time of the transaction,[21] and (2) the PPM is required to consolidate the medical entity under No. 97-2's consolidation criteria.

(iii) Consolidation and Employee Status.   EITF Issue No. 97-2 also addresses whether physicians employed by the medical practices should be considered employees of the PPM for purposes of determining the appropriate method of accounting for such individuals' stock-based compensation. The EITF observed that that determination should depend on whether the PPM consolidates the physician practice. An employee of a physician practice that is consolidated by the PPM should be considered an employee of the PPM and its subsidiaries, and vice versa. (See also FASB Interpretation No. 44, "Accounting for Certain Transactions Involving Stock Compensation.")

(iv) Financial Reporting Considerations.   Prior to EITF Issue No. 97-2, one of the most perplexing problems faced by PPM companies was characterizing the scope of the company's business in its financial statements. PPMs can own medical practices outright in states that do not prohibit corporate practice of medicine; in such situations, the PPM and the medical practices clearly are components of the same business, and the financial statements will reflect both the medical operations and the practice management operations. However, if a similar business is conducted in a state with corporate practice laws, the PPM legally cannot own stock of the medical practice. In those cases, the PPM will not be able to obtain a controlling financial interest in the usual way (i.e., ownership of more than 50 percent of the medical practice's stock). However, the PPM may be able to determine the direction of the practice's management and policies through the rights provided it in the MSA contract.

---

[21] For example, a dentist who recently graduated and has incorporated, but has yet to establish a practice, would not be considered a "business" for purposes of making this determination.

As discussed in (i), EITF Issue No. 97-2 provides a listing of criteria that, when applied to contractual arrangements between PPMs and medical practices, indicate whether or not the PPM should consolidate the assets and operations of the medical practice. The reporting status creates significant differences in the appearance of the PPM's financial statements, particularly with regard to the income statement, depending on whether the PPM is a "consolidator" or "nonconsolidator."

- "Consolidator" PPMs—those that include the medical entities in their financial statements—characterize their primary business as providing medical care. The top line of their income statement will reflect the revenues derived by the medical practices for patient care. This presentation is based on the rationale that the balance of power (i.e., control) rests with the management company, which is outsourcing the provision of medical services to various medical practices that it controls. This reporting format is illustrated in Exhibit 36.1.
- "Nonconsolidators," on the other hand, characterize their operations as providing business services. Consequently, they begin the income statement with the amount of fees earned under the management service agreement contracts. This presentation is based on the rationale that the balance of power rests with the medical entity, and the PPM is a supplier or vendor to whom the physicians are outsourcing the business functions associated with running their practice. This reporting format is illustrated in Exhibit 36.1.

(v) SEC Reporting Issues.

Inclusion of Separate Financial Statements of Affiliated Medical Practices in IPO Filings. Separate financial statements of a medical practice with which a PPM will consummate, or has recently consummated, a significant management agreement generally are not required in an IPO filing if the PPM does not consolidate the practice and does not guarantee any minimum practice income, extend unusual credit terms, or fund operating losses.

However, if the PPM is expected to have a material dependence on the PC, separate financial information about the practice would be material to investors. For example, if the management fee from the practice is expected to generate more than 20 percent of the PPM's revenues in the next 12 months, the SEC has requested audited financial statements of the practice. However, the SEC has accepted only unaudited summary financial information about the practice for the three most recent fiscal years if audited financial statements are not readily available and its owners are not promoters of the offering being registered.

Historical information about the practice for any period before its ownership by the current owners would not be requested unless the PPM is of the view that a change in an owner does not fundamentally change the underlying business. If the owners of a practice generating 20 percent or more of the PPM's revenues own 10 percent or more of the PPM at the time of its IPO or are promoters of the offering, audited financial statements of that practice for at least its most recent fiscal year ordinarily would be required, unless effects of providing the management services to the practice have been included in the PPM's audited financial statements for at least nine months. If financial information of a managed practice is presented, care should be taken to avoid the impression that an investor is obtaining an interest in the practice or that the historical results are indicative of future results under the altered incentive structure and management affiliates established with the PPM.

Disclosure Issues.   The SEC staff expects PPM registrants to clearly and accurately describe their business and contractual relationships. Financial statement disclosures should address the following:

What is the nature of the PPM's business?

- Describe the contractual relationship among the PPM and the medical practices. Describe the PPM's rights and limitations under the contracts.

Format A— Consolidated Presentation		Format B—Unconsolidated (Standalone) Presentation	

INCOME STATEMENT

Net medical practice revenue	$ 85,000		
Expenses:			
Physician salaries	(30,000)		
Provision for uncollectible			
accounts	(3,000)	Management services revenue	$ 52,000
Clinic costs	(49,000)	Clinic costs	(49,000)
Net Income	$ 3,000	Net Income	$ 3,000

NOTES TO FINANCIAL STATEMENTS

Note A. Basis of Presentation

The consolidated financial statements include the accounts of GoodDocs Inc. ("GoodDocs") and its beneficially owned subsidiary. In response to state corporate practice of medicine statutes, GoodDocs has executed a management service agreement ("MSA") with its related professional corporation ("PC"), Prosperous Internal Medicine Associates. Through the terms of the MSA, GoodDocs has complete control over the PC with the exception of the direct provision of medical services. The MSA substantially restricts the business activities and the rights of the shareholders of the PC. The PC is consolidated because GoodDocs has a controlling financial interest in its assets and business operations and because, notwithstanding the lack of majority ownership, consolidation of the PC is necessary to present fairly the financial position and results of operations of GoodDocs due to the existence of a parent-subsidiary relationship by means other than majority ownership of the PC's voting stock. GoodDocs effectively has perpetual control over the PC and, upon termination of any such agreement by the physicians, GoodDocs intends to exercise its option to purchase the stock of the PC. Fees paid to GoodDocs approximate the operating income of the PC, as defined in the MSA.

Note A. Basis of Presentation

GoodDocs, Inc. ("GoodDocs") provides management support to its related professional corporation, Prosperous Internal Medicine Associates ("PC"), under a 40-year management services agreement (MSA). Under the terms of the MSA, GoodDocs, among other things, bills and collects patient receivables and provides all administrative support services to the PC in exchange for management fees. GoodDocs and the PC are related through common ownership and a common member on both GoodDocs' and PC's Boards of Directors. GoodDocs and the PC structured their business enterprise to comply with state regulatory mandates requiring medical practices to be owned and operated by state-licensed medical professionals.

Note B. Significant Accounting Policies

Net Medical Practice Revenue

Net medical practice revenue is reported at the estimated realizable amounts from patients, third-party payers and others for services rendered. Revenue under certain third-party payer agreements is subject to audit and retroactive adjustments. Provisions for estimated third-party payer settlements and adjustments are estimated in the periods the related services are rendered and adjusted in future periods as final settlements are determined. During the year, X% of net revenue was received under the Medicare program and X% under the Medicaid program. The Medicare and Medicaid programs pay

Note B. Significant Accounting Policies

Management Services Revenue

Management service revenue approximated the operating income of the PC, as defined in the MSA. The following represents amounts included in the determination of management service revenue:

Gross medical billings	$100,000
Contractual allowances	(15,000)
Net medical practice revenue	85,000
Provision for uncollectible accounts	(3,000)
	82,000
Amounts retained by physicians	(30,000)
Management services revenue	$ 52,000

Exhibit 36.1   Comparison of PPM financial presentation formats.

physician services based on fee schedules which are established by the related government agency. GoodDocs has numerous agreements with managed care organizations to provide physician services based on negotiated fee schedules; however, no individual managed care organization is material to the company.

Intangible Assets

Intangible assets include the excess of cost over the fair value of net assets of assets acquired (goodwill), the fair value of acquired third-party payer contracts, and amounts assigned to noncompete agreements. All intangibles are amortized on a straight-line basis with lives between 20 and 40 years for goodwill, 3 to 7 years for payer contracts, and the lives of the agreements for specific noncompete arrangements.

Note C. Contingencies

In addition to the general liability and malpractice insurance carried by the individual physicians, GoodDocs is insured with respect to general liability and medical malpractice risks on a claims-made basis. Management is not aware of any claims against the company. In addition, GoodDocs has not accrued a loss for unreported incidents or for losses in excess of insurance coverage, as the amount, if any, cannot be reasonably estimated and the probability of an adverse outcome cannot be determined at this time. It is the opinion of management that the ultimate resolution of any unasserted claims will not have a material adverse effect on GoodDocs' financial position or results of operations.

Intangible Assets

Intangible assets related to the management service agreement consist of the costs of purchasing the rights to manage the medical practice. Theses costs are capitalized and amortized over the initial noncancelable 40-year terms of the related management service agreement.

Note C. Contingencies

No disclosures related to medical malpractice would be included in the financial statements. The discussion of the business contained in the Form 10-K filed by GoodDocs would probably contain a statement similar to the following: ""The provision of medical services by the physician group with which GoodDocs contracts entails an inherent risk of professional liability claims. GoodDocs does not control the practice of medicine by physicians or the compliance with certain regulatory and other requirements directly applicable to physicians and physician groups.''

Exhibit 36.1   *Continued*

- Disclose how the PPM's fees are determined. If the fees are based on a percentage of certain items, what are those percentages, or what is the range of the percentages? What items affect the calculation?
- Even if the PPM combines the operations of the medical practice group for financial statement purposes or has consolidated subsidiaries that provide the medical services, the PPM must clearly distinguish the services it provides from the practice of medicine.

What is the PPM's relationship with managed care providers?

- Disclose whether the PPM (or an assignee) enters into direct contracts with managed care companies or whether the physician groups contract directly with the managed care companies.
- Identify the party who assumes the risk under managed care contracts (i.e., the PPM or the physician group). If the PPM assumes the contracts, are there any issues relating to medical licensing?
- Who assumes the risk associated with capitated payment contracts? If the PPM assumes the risk, does this subject it to regulation as an insurance company?

Is the PPM subject to any state or federal regulations?

- Describe any state prohibitions on the corporate practice of medicine, and discuss the impact upon the PPM.
- Is the PPM subject to regulation as an insurer?
- What is the effect of federal antikickback and self-referral restrictions?

36.5 FINANCIAL REPORTING PRACTICES

(a) USERS OF FINANCIAL STATEMENTS.   The primary users of health care companies' general purpose financial statements are providers of capital who make rating and investment decisions in competitive capital markets (including investors in tax-exempt debt securities); suppliers of goods and services to the industry with whom health care companies maintain credit relationships; stockholders and other owners; the SEC; and regulators such as state Departments of Insurance and other oversight groups.

(b) BASIC FINANCIAL STATEMENTS.   Investor-owned and not-for-profit health care providers generally prepare four financial statements:

1. Balance sheet
2. Income statement/statement of operations
3. Statement of changes in stockholders' equity/statement of changes in net assets
4. Statement of cash flows

Not-for-profit health care entities are required to follow the financial reporting requirements contained in FAS No. 117, "Financial Statements of Not-for-Profit Organizations," as modified by certain requirements contained in *Health Care Organizations.* Generally speaking, FAS No. 117 provides broad standards of financial reporting with which all not-for-profit organizations (including not-for-profit HCOs) must comply. However, the FASB permitted the AICPA to provide industry-specific implementing guidance for FAS No. 117 through its audit and accounting guides. Although technically the guidance in *Health Care Organizations* stands lower in the GAAP hierarchy than does the FASB guidance, the FASB expects not-for-profit HCOs to apply the requirements of FAS No. 117 in the manner specified by the Audit Guide. Generally speaking, those modifications are intended to keep the financial statements of not-for-profit providers comparable to those of investor-owned providers.

Governmental health care entities are required to follow the financial reporting requirements prescribed by GASB No. 34, "Basic Financial Statements—and Management's Discussion and Analysis—for State and Local Governments." (GASB No. 34's phased-in effective date is discussed at Section 32.11.)

For purposes of applying GASB No. 34, the governmental HCOs included within the scope of the AICPA audit and accounting guide *Health Care Organizations* are considered "special purpose governments engagement in business-type activities." Those entities should present financial statements required for enterprise funds, which consist of:

- Management's Discussion and Analysis (as RSI)
- Statement of net assets (balance sheet)
- Statement of revenues, expenses, and changes in net assets
- Statement of cash flows
- Notes to financial statements
- RSI other than MD&A (if applicable)

Although GASB No. 34 establishes eight required elements of MD&A, many of those elements are not applicable to governmental health care entities. Consequently, MD&A discussion should be limited to only the elements that are applicable.

Health Care Organizations provides illustrative financial statements for investor-owned, tax-exempt, and governmental HCOs. Those statements illustrate the application of the reporting practices contained in the Guide. Specific types of HCOs are presented, but only to illustrate a wide diversity of reporting practices. It is not intended that these illustrations represent either the only types of disclosure nor the only statement formats that would be appropriate. More or less detail should appear in the financial statements or notes, depending on the circumstances.

(c) BALANCE SHEET.   All HCOs must prepare classified balance sheets which segregate assets and liabilities between current and noncurrent categories.[22] Special considerations related to balance sheet reporting of not-for-profit and governmental providers are discussed below.

(i) Not-for-Profit Providers.   Restricted assets and liabilities should not be carved out and presented separately in the balance sheet. Because donor restrictions generally relate to limitations on the use of *net assets* rather than *specific assets* (i.e., the provider normally is not required to physically maintain restricted resources separately from unrestricted resources), "cash is cash" regardless of whether it was received as a specific-purpose gift or generated through operations. As a result, the provider's obligation to use unexpended donor-restricted contributions in accordance with the donor's wishes is reflected by structuring the equity section of the balance sheet into three broad classes: unrestricted net assets, temporarily restricted net assets, and permanently restricted net assets. If the amount of unexpended donor-restricted contributions is material, the nature of restrictions should be disclosed in the notes to the financial statements. The accounting and reporting requirements for donor-restricted contributions is discussed at Section 36.3.

Limitations on the use of assets arising from sources other than donor restrictions are highlighted by using the balance sheet caption "assets whose use is limited." These are discussed at Subsection 36.3(b)(i).

(ii) Governmental Providers.   A governmental provider's balance sheet may be prepared using either the traditional balance sheet format or a net assets format (assets less liabilities equal net assets). The equity section of the balance sheet is structured into three broad classes of net assets: *unrestricted*; *invested in capital assets, net of related debt* (i.e., capital assets reduced by accumulated depreciation and by any outstanding debt incurred to acquire, construct, or improve those assets); and *restricted* (differentiated between expendable and nonexpendable). The provider's obligations to use certain resources for specific purposes is reflected in the balance sheet by (1) presenting those assets separately and (2) reporting any difference between those assets and their related liabilities as "restricted net assets." The word "restricted" is not required to be used in labeling the assets themselves; however, the descriptions used on the face of the balance sheet should make it clear that such assets cannot be used to satisfy the organization's current liabilities (other than any current liabilities that are intended to be satisfied with the restricted assets). Under GASB No. 34, assets are reported as restricted when limitations on their use is externally imposed (e.g., by creditors, grantors, contributors, or the laws or regulations of other governments). Restricted assets should be presented separately in the balance sheet.

Internally imposed limitations (such as specific-purpose designations imposed management or the board) are included in unrestricted net assets.

---

[22] For not-for-profit providers, this is a modification of the guidance provided in FAS No. 117, which requires information about liquidity of assets and liabilities be provided in "some fashion" (e.g., by sequential ranking) within the balance sheet.

(d) OPERATING STATEMENT.   Appendix A of the Guide provides illustrative income statements for investor-owned, not-for-profit, and governmental HCOs. These statements are not intended to establish standards but merely to illustrate the reporting conventions discussed in the Guide. Although income statement reporting requirements differ significantly based on whether a provider is investor owned, not-for-profit, or governmental, all allow flexibility in the amount of detail that is provided. Some providers choose to present a great deal of detail; others present statements that are highly condensed with details, if any, provided in the notes. The Guide allows each provider to determine the level of detail that provides the most meaningful disclosure within the broad parameters established by GAAP.

Significant differences exist in the presentation of extraordinary items, discontinued operations, and cumulative effect of changes in accounting principles depending on whether a provider is investor owned, not-for-profit, or governmental, as follows.

Presentation of

Type of Provider	Extraordinary Items	Discontinued Operations	Cumulative Effect
Investor-owned	Just before net income	Just before net income	Just before net income
Not-for-profit	Just before change in unrestricted net assets, with subtotal	Just before change in unrestricted net assets, with subtotal	Just before change in unrestricted net assets, with subtotal
Governmental	Below nonoperating revenue	See discussion	Adjustment of beginning fund balance

GASB No. 34 is silent on how discontinued operations should be reported. Based on informal discussions with GASB staff, the author believes that reporting of discontinued operations would be part of the detail required by GASB No. 34 for the "Operating revenue" and "Operating expense" sections of the statement of changes in revenues, expenses, and changes in net assets, because both continuing and discontinued operations are part of a HCOs operating activity. The "Operating revenues" section would contain one or more lines identified as "revenue from discontinued operations," with a similar presentation of "expenses from discontinued operations" provided in the "Operating expenses" section. Any gain or loss on disposal of an operation would be reflected as nonoperating revenue or expense (similar to the treatment of other types of gains/losses under GASB No. 34).

(i) Requirements for Investor-Owned Providers.   The income statement reporting requirements for investor-owned health care providers are similar to those for other types of investor-owned service providers. Providers that are SEC registrants sometimes will receive comment letters from the SEC requesting that their income statements display operating expenses at a level of detail "consistent with the AICPA audit guide for health care providers." As stated previously, the sample financial statements included in the Guide are illustrative and are not intended to establish a practice that would require a certain level of disclosure.

(ii) Requirements for Not-for-Profit Providers.   The income statement requirements for not-for-profit health care entities were established by FAS No. 117, as modified by certain requirements contained in *Health Care Organizations*. Those modifications are as follows:

FAS No. 117 Requirement	Modification provided in Health Care Organizations
Presentation of a "statement of activity" that combines the information traditionally presented in an income statement with the information traditionally reported in the statement of changes in net assets.	Subdivides "statement of activity" into two required statements: a "statement of operations" (i.e., income statement) and a "statement of changes in net assets."
Reporting of results of operations (i.e., net income) is permitted but not required.	Must provide "performance indicator" subtotal[23] within the statement of operations.
Contributions of property, plant, and equipment (or of funds expended to purchase such assets) are reported as increases in unrestricted net assets in the statement of activities.	Such contributions should be reported below the "performance indicator" (i.e., excluded from net income) in the statement of operations.

Other requirements imposed on not-for-profit providers that differ from those of investor-owned and governmental providers are as follows:

- Net assets released from restrictions (except those related to long-lived assets) are included in net income.

- All expenses must be reported in the "unrestricted net assets" classification. No expenses may be reported in the statement of changes in net assets for the temporarily or permanently restricted classifications.

- FAS No. 117 requires reporting of expenses by functional categories such as "program," "management," and "fund raising." Administrative allocations to the functional categories should be based on full cost allocations. Normally, providers report expenses classified along revenue/cost center lines (e.g., nursing services, other professional services, general services) or "natural" lines (e.g., salaries and wages, employee benefits, supplies, purchased services). *Health Care Organizations* emphasizes the flexibility allowed in FAS No. 117, which allows reporting the functional information in the notes to the financial statements. Similarly, flexibility is allowed in the degree to which details are presented with regard to functional information. Some providers may choose to present only two categories: "health services" and "general and administrative"; others may desire to report more detailed information.

- APB No. 30 items must be reported below the performance indicator.

The health care guide does not require not-for-profit providers to distinguish between operating and nonoperating activities. If an "income from operations" subtotal is presented and its use is not apparent from the details provided on the face of the statement, note disclosure should be made regarding the nature of the measure or the types of items excluded from that measure.

In June 2002, AcSEC issued an exposure draft of a proposed Statement of Position, "Accounting for Derivative Instruments and Hedging Activities by Not-for-Profit HCOs, and Clarification of the Performance Indicator." The proposed standard would amend the AICPA audit and accounting guide *Health Care Organizations* to clarify that the performance indicator reported by not-for-profit HCOs is analogous to income from continuing operations of a for-profit enterprise. (The analogy is made to a for-profit enterprise's income from continuing operations, rather than net

---

[23] The FASB has objected to use of the term "net income" to refer to the results of operations of not-for-profit health care organizations. Therefore, *Health Care Organizations* uses the generic term "performance indicator" to describe the operating measure.

income, because FAS No. 117 requires "APB No. 30" type items—extraordinary items, cumulative effect of accounting changes, and discontinued operations—to be reported separately from measures of operations such as the performance indicator. In order for the performance indicator to be comparable to net income, APB No. 30 items would need to be included within the performance indicator.) This clarification also provides not-for-profit providers with a clearer concept of "other comprehensive income" reporting. (Not-for-profit organizations were excluded from the scope of FAS No. 130, "Reporting Comprehensive Income," because FAS No. 117 already required them to display the equivalent of total comprehensive income in the Statement of Activities.) Gains and losses that FASB pronouncements classify as elements of other comprehensive income should be excluded from the performance indicator.

(iii) Requirements for Governmental Providers.   The operating statement prepared by governmental HCOs is the "Statement of revenues, expenses, and changes in net assets." The focus of this statement is "all-inclusive"—that is, it presents all changes in net assets, not just those that affect net income. Therefore, it contains all transactions that would be reported in an income statement plus a statement of changes in net assets, including changes in restricted resources.

The statement must be prepared using a specifically sequenced format that distinguishes operating and nonoperating revenues and expenses, and provides an intermediate total for operating income or loss. The prescribed sequence is as follows:

- Operating revenues (detailed)
  - Total operating revenues (required subtotal)
- Operating expenses (detailed)
  - Total operating expenses (required subtotal)
    - Operating income/loss (required subtotal)
- Nonoperating revenues/expenses (detailed)
  - Income before other revenues, expenses, gains, losses, and transfers
- Capital contributions
- Additions to term and permanent endowments
- "Special items"
- Extraordinary items
- Transfers
  - Increase (decrease) in net assets
- Net assets—beginning of period
- Net assets—end of period

Because the focus of this statement is on the change in *total* net assets, rather than changes in classes of net assets, no reclassifications from restricted to unrestricted funds are reported when restrictions are released. The use of restricted funds and expiration of time restrictions are financial statement "nonevents" under GASB No. 34. Balance sheet reclassifications from "restricted" to "unrestricted" and vice versa are not reported anywhere in a governmental entity's financial statements.

Revenues should be reported by major source, and entities are required to separately identify revenues that provide security for revenue bonds. GASB No. 34 links the determination of operating/nonoperating classification to the classification of transactions in the statement of cash flows under GASB No. 9. Transactions related to cash flows that are classified as noncapital financing, capital financing, or investing in the statement of cash flows typically are not classified as "operating" in the statement of revenues, expenses, and changes in net assets. Examples of items that are required to be classified as nonoperating using this approach are contributions received (financing activity), interest expense (financing activity), and interest income (investing activity). Under the all-inclusive format, restricted contributions (other than capital contributions) and restricted investment income are included in nonoperating revenues together with unrestricted contributions and unrestricted investment income). Each organization must establish a policy that defines operating revenues and expenses based on the above parameters and disclose that policy in the notes to the financial statements.

GASB No. 34 established a new category of transaction called *special items*. A special item is a significant transaction or other event that is within the control of management and that meets one (but not both) of the APB No. 30 criteria for classification as an extraordinary item. Similar transactions that are beyond the control of management are not special items. Special items should be reported separately below nonoperating revenues (expenses).

Although governmental health care entities generally are required to apply all FASB pronouncements that apply to for-profit enterprises, the all-inclusive reporting format required by GASB No. 34 conflicts with FASB Statement No. 130, "Reporting Comprehensive Income." Therefore, governmental entities do not have a concept of "other comprehensive income." Gains and losses that FASB pronouncements classify as elements of other comprehensive income should be reported no differently from other gains and losses in the statement of revenues, expenses, and changes in net assets.

(e) STATEMENT OF CHANGES IN NET ASSETS/EQUITY.   A Statement of Changes in Net Assets/Equity should report all changes that have occurred during the reporting period in all equity, net asset, and fund balance accounts maintained by a not-for-profit provider. Governmental providers do not prepare this statement, due to the "all-inclusive" nature of their operating statement as discussed at Subsection 36.5(d)(iii).

(f) STATEMENT OF CASH FLOWS.   Standards for cash flow reporting differ among investor-owned, not-for-profit, and governmental health care entities, as follows:

Type of Provider	Source(s) of Authoritative Guidance	"Cash Flows from Operations" Reconciles To
Investor-owned	FAS No. 95	Net income
Not-for-profit	FAS No. 117/FAS No. 95	Change in net assets
Governmental	GAS No. 9	Income/loss from operations

(i) Considerations for Not-for-Profit Providers.   Unique considerations for not-for-profit providers include the following:

- Because FAS No. 117 reconciles cash flows from operations to change in total net assets, the reconciliation will have to accommodate certain equity items that are not dealt with in cash flow statements prepared for investor-owned companies. These items include equity transfers, contributions of long-lived assets, unrealized gains and losses on certain investments, investment returns restricted by donor or law, and restricted contributions.

- Unrealized gains and losses on investment other than trading securities and contributions of long-lived assets will need to be adjusted out as noncash items.

- Equity transfers, restricted investment income, and restricted contributions (including contributions restricted for purchase of long-lived assets) will need to be "transferred" to the financing category by adjusting them out of operating cash flows and increasing (or decreasing, as appropriate) the financing category by that same amount.

- Purchases, sales, and maturities of trading securities should be classified as cash flows from operating activities; cash flows from purchases, sales, and maturities of other than trading securities should be classified as cash flows from investing activities.

- Cash and cash equivalents reported as "assets whose use is limited" should be excluded from "cash and cash equivalents" reported in the cash flow statement.

(ii) Considerations for Governmental Providers.   Governmental providers follow the guidance in GASB Statement No. 9, "Reporting Cash Flows of Proprietary and Nonexpendable Trust Funds and Governmental Entities That Use Proprietary Fund Accounting," in preparing their statement of cash flows. That statement's requirements differ from those of FASB Statement Nos. 95 and 117 in the following ways:

- The direct method of presenting operating cash flows must be used, with a reconciliation provided of operating cash flows to operating income (loss).
- The GASB cash flow statement has four categories: operating, investing, capital financing, and noncapital financing. The capital financing category is used for acquiring and disposing of capital assets, borrowing money for acquiring capital assets, and repaying the amounts borrowed. All other financing is classified as noncapital.
- Some items are classified differently by the GASB than they are by the FASB. For example, fixed assets are classified as capital financing activities under GASB Statement No. 9, but are considered to be investing activities under FASB Statement No. 95.
- GAS No. 9, par. 8 provides that a statement of cash flows should explain the change in *all* cash and cash equivalents, regardless of any restrictions on their use.
- The total amount of cash and cash equivalents should be easily traceable to similarly titled line items. If it is not, a reconciliation should be provided.

36.6 STATUTORY/REGULATORY REPORTING ISSUES

(a) STATUTORY FINANCIAL STATEMENTS.   Increasingly, HMOs and provider-sponsored networks are coming under regulation by state departments of insurance. Generally speaking, regulated insurers are required by their state of domicile to submit annually a set of audited financial statements that are prepared using that state's prescribed regulatory accounting principles ("statutory financial statements").

In 1999, the National Association of Insurance Commissioners completed a process to codify statutory accounting practices (SAP) for managed care organizations, resulting in a revised *Accounting Practices and Procedures Manual*. Nine of the Statements of Statutory Accounting Principles (SSAPs) included in the Manual have been specifically modified or written to address issues related to managed care. These include SSAP No. 25, "Accounting for and Disclosures about Transactions with Affiliates and Other Related Parties," No. 35, "Guaranty Fund and Other Assessments," No. 47, "Uninsured Plans," No. 50, "Classifications and Definitions of Insurance or Managed Care Contracts in Force," No. 54, "Individual and Group Accident and Health Contracts," No. 55, "Unpaid Claims, Losses and Loss Adjustment Expenses," No. 66, "Retrospectively Rated Insurance Contracts," No. 73, "Health Care Delivery Assets—Supplies, Pharmaceuticals and Surgical Supplies, Durable Medical Equipment, Furniture, Medical Equipment and Fixtures, and Leasehold Improvements in Health Care Facilities," and No. 84, "Health Care Receivables." All other SSAPs should be considered that are applicable to the particular managed care entity.

The Manual is updated annually to reflect revisions or additions to SAP. It is expected that most states will require insurers to comply with most, if not all, provisions of the Manual. States may adopt the Manual in whole, or in part, as an element of prescribed SAP in those states. If, however, the requirements of state laws, regulations, and administrative rules differ from guidance provided in the Manual, those state laws, regulations, and administrative rules preempt the guidance in the Manual.

(b) RISK-BASED CAPITAL FOR MANAGED CARE ORGANIZATIONS.   State laws generally require insurers to maintain minimum levels of capital or surplus. The NAIC has implemented a "risk-based capital" (RBC) formula for managed care organizations under which affected managed care organizations must calculate and report to regulators its capital requirement and total adjusted capital. There are five principal elements to the RBC formula: affiliated investment risk, asset risk, underwriting risk, credit risk, and general business risk. Four action levels (in order of increasingly stringent level of regulatory response) are: company action level, regulatory action level, authorized control level, and mandatory control level. At a minimum, the company action-level event requires the filing of an RBC plan that details conditions leading to the event and proposals of corrective action with the state insurance commissioner.

(c) OFFICE OF MANAGEMENT AND BUDGET CIRCULAR A-133. HCOs that receive financial assistance from a governmental agency may be subject to audit requirements in accordance with the Single Audit Act of 1996 and Office of Management and Budget (OMB) Circular A-133, *Audits of Institutions of Higher Education and Other Nonprofit Organizations.* Financial assistance may take the form of grants, contracts, loans, loan guarantees, property, cooperative agreements, interest subsidies, and insurance or direct appropriations.

36.7 SOURCES AND SUGGESTED REFERENCES

American Institute of Certified Public Accountants, "Health Care Organizations," *Industry Audit and Accounting Guide.* New York, 1996.

———, "Checklists and Illustrative Financial Statements for Health Care Organizations," 1996.

———, "Providers of Health Care Services (Section 6400)." *Technical Practice Aids,* 1997.

Healthcare Financial Management Association, (P&P Board Statements and Issue Analyses are available from HFMA at 1-800–252-4362, ext. 420.) "Accounting and Reporting for Agency Relationships," Principles and Practices Board Statement No. 5. Westchester, IL, 1983.

———, "Accounting and Reporting by Institutional Health Care Providers for Risk Contracts," Principles and Practices Board Statement No. 11, 1989.

———, "Valuation and Financial Statement Presentation of Charity Service and Bad Debts by Institutional Health Care Providers." Principles and Practices Board Statement No. 15, 1993.

———, "Classifying, Valuing, and Analyzing Accounts Receivable Related to Patient Services." Principles and Practices Board Statement No. 16, 1993.

———, "Assessments and Arrangements Similar to Taxes on Tax-Exempt Institutional Health Care Providers," Principles and Practices Board Statement No. 17, 1994.

———, "Public Disclosure of Financial and Operating Information by Health Care Providers," Principles and Practices Board Statement No. 18, 1994.

———, "Transactions Among Affiliated Entities Comprising an Integrated Delivery System," Principles and Practices Board Statement No. 19, 1995.

———, "Healthcare Mergers, Acquisitions, and Collaborations," Principles and Practices Board Statement No. 20, 1997.

———, "Acquisitions of Physician Practices," Principles and Practices Board Issue Analysis No. 95-1, 1995.

———, "Assessing Managed Care Contracting Risk," Principles and Practices Board Issue Analysis No. 97-1, 1997.

Financial Accounting Standards Board, "Application of FASB Statement No. 94, *Consolidation of All Majority-Owned Subsidiaries,* and APB Opinion No. 16, *Business Combinations,* to Physician Practice Management Entities and Certain Other Entities with Contractual Management Arrangements," EITF Issue No. 97-2. Norwalk, CT, 1997.

———, "Accounting for Contributions Received and Contributions Made," Statement of Financial Accounting Standards No. 116, 1993.

———, "Financial Statements of Not-for-Profit Organizations," Statement of Financial Accounting Standards No. 117, 1993.

———, "Accounting for Certain Investments Held by Not-for-Profit Organizations," Statement of Financial Accounting Standards No. 124, 1995.

CHAPTER 37

ACCOUNTING FOR GOVERNMENT CONTRACTS

Margaret M. Worthington, CPA

37.1 UNIQUE ACCOUNTING REQUIREMENTS FOR FEDERAL CONTRACTORS

The federal government operates within a formalized statutory and regulatory framework when it acquires products and services. That process was significantly streamlined and simplified in the 1990s for acquisitions of commercial products and services or awards that are competed among qualified suppliers. For contracts awarded in these circumstances, negotiations are based on prices submitted by offerors in response to government solicitation notices. However, when products or services are custom made and/or awards are not competed, the estimated or actual cost of performance becomes a dominant factor in setting prices. Consequently, systems used by federal contractors in this latter environment must not only maintain information that is necessary to effectively price contracts and control contract incurred costs but also must comply with special cost estimating, cost accounting, billing, and project management requirements. This chapter is designed to provide a practical discussion of those unique federal contracting requirements, which include:

- *Cost Principles.* Federal cost principles contained in Part 31 of the Federal Acquisition Regulation (FAR) provide specific criteria as to the costs that may be included in contract proposals, claims and billings submitted to the government.

- *Cost Accounting Standards (CAS).* Nineteen CAS and disclosure statement filing requirements address disclosure of cost accounting practices and measurement and assignment and allocation of costs.

- *Defective Pricing.* The Truth in Negotiations Act is designed to ensure that the government has the opportunity to review all significant and relevant cost or pricing data available to the contractor when contract prices are being negotiated on the basis of estimated costs of performance. If, after the negotiation, it is determined that current, complete, and accurate data were not submitted, the contract price is subject to downward adjustment for any price increase resulting from the failure to disclose the relevant data.

37.2 MANAGEMENT INFORMATION SYSTEM REQUIREMENTS

To compete effectively in any market, management must have the information necessary to plan and control its business. In the complex federal acquisition environment, companies must have systems and controls that provide adequate accounting, estimating, and project management information. The planning phase begins when a contract proposal is prepared. During that process, contract performance is broken down into meaningful work packages with cost estimates, performance schedules, and performance responsibility assigned to appropriate cost centers. When the contract is awarded, such data should be used to establish the performance and cost baseline for monitoring actual performance. During performance, comparisons of actual and budgeted costs and schedule permit a contractor to take prompt corrective action as unfavorable variances occur.

(a) COST ACCOUNTING SYSTEMS.   Most negotiated federal contracts contain the FAR 52.215-2 clause, "Audit and Records—Negotiation," which provides that "the Contractor shall maintain . . . records and other evidence sufficient to reflect properly all costs claimed to have been incurred or anticipated to be incurred directly or indirectly in performance of this contract." Contractors performing contracts for which cost or pricing data were submitted before contract award must have cost accounting systems that comply with FAR (and perhaps CAS) requirements. Allowable costs form the basis for requests for reimbursement of costs incurred under cost-reimbursement contract billings and fixed-price contract progress payments. For firm-fixed-price contracts requiring submission of cost or pricing data prior to contract award, an adequate cost accounting system is required even though costs incurred on the contract do not affect the remuneration ultimately paid to the contractor upon contract completion. Rather, the cost accounting system is critical for providing data for follow-on contract cost pricing, providing a basis for tracking contract performance and supporting cost-based progress payment requests. To price follow-on contracts, information on the rate of improvement in performing repetitive tasks on subsequent production (i.e., learning curves) is important. Well-designed cost accounting systems can enable estimators to identify the costs or hours incurred on prior contracts or production lots. The ability to segregate nonrecurring costs from recurring costs is also critical for follow-on pricing. Clearly, the design of the accounting system is all-important in providing valuable input for the estimating or planning process for contract costs.

The regulations do not specify that the contractor maintain any specific type of accounting system. Rather, FAR 31.201-1 states that "any generally accepted method of determining or estimating costs that is equitable and is consistently applied may be used." Cost ledgers can be designed in a variety of ways to permit efficient accumulation of costs for billing purposes. In practice, these records vary considerably, based on the individual company's need for information and the complexity of the contract requirements. A key requirement is the existence of adequate audit trails. An accounting system provides satisfactory audit trails if: (1) every transaction is traceable from its origin to its final posting in the books of account; (2) every posting to accounts is susceptible to breakdown into identifiable transactions; and (3) adequate documentation (e.g., time cards or vendors' invoices) is available and accessible to support the accuracy and validity of individual transactions.

In a job-order costing system, costs are collected using a work-order process. Contractors, particularly in a production environment, are not required by the regulations to account for costs by contract (e.g., maintain a job-order cost accounting system). A cost accounting system in a production environment is generally driven by the contractor's products and/or production processes. The cost accounting system should be deemed adequate if production costs are appropriately, equitably, and consistently allocated to all final cost objectives. The obvious necessity is to capture and accumulate costs in a manner that reflects the cost of performance in individual government contracts. To do this, certain costs that can be identified specifically with contracts and/or products are treated as direct costs and are charged in that manner. Typically, direct costs include material, subcontracts, and labor, but they are by no means limited to these. FAR 31.201-4 requires that costs charged directly to contracts be allocated "on a basis of the relative benefits received or other equitable relationship."

Indirect costs, or other costs that benefit more than one contract, must be pooled and allocated to contracts on some equitable basis. According to FAR 31.203(c), the general criteria for establishing indirect cost pools are:

> The contractor shall accumulate indirect costs by logical cost groupings with due consideration of the reasons for incurring such costs. The contractor shall determine each grouping so as to permit use of an allocation base that is common to all cost objectives to which the grouping is to be allocated. The base selected shall allocate the grouping on the basis of the benefits accruing to intermediate and final cost objectives. When substantially the same results can be achieved through less precise methods, the number and composition of cost groupings should be governed by practical considerations and should not unduly complicate the allocation.

FAR 31.203(d) similarly provides flexibility in determining what allocation base to use in distributing costs from the indirect cost pools to contracts:

> Once an appropriate base for allocating indirect costs has been accepted, the contractor shall not fragment the base by removing individual elements. All items properly includable in an indirect cost base shall bear a pro rata share of indirect costs irrespective of their acceptance as Government contract costs. For example, when a cost input base is used for the allocation of G&A costs, the contractor shall include in the base all items that would properly be part of the cost input base, whether allowable or unallowable, and these items shall bear their pro rata share of G&A costs.

Accounting for indirect costs presents a challenge to those uninitiated in government contracting. The government has promulgated specific rules in FAR Part 31 and CAS governing the allocability of indirect costs. However, these rules still permit considerable flexibility in the number and types of pools that can be selected and the methods used for allocating indirect costs.

The allocation of indirect costs in a highly automated environment presents an even greater challenge, since typical overhead allocation bases, such as direct labor, may represent only a minor component of total factory costs. In this environment, the need for multiple cost pools allocated over nonlabor bases, such as machine usage, may be required. This requirement is evident in activity-based costing or advanced cost management systems that have been implemented by some government contractors. In an automated environment, requirements for audit trails still exist; however, additional controls over input to the system and program logic are essential to validate the accuracy of such systems.

For cost-reimbursement, time-and-material, and fixed-price incentive contracts, accurate labor charging by contract is imperative. To make sure of the reliability of recorded labor hours and costs, a contractor must have an adequate internal control system for collecting and distributing labor costs. Accurate labor charging also encompasses accounting for all hours worked. If salaried employees work a significant number of hours in excess of 40 hours per week, a risk of labor mischarging to the government may be asserted if all hours worked are not accounted for. Although no specific regulatory provisions mandate the use of total time accounting, government auditors have long asserted that accounting for all hours worked is a basic requirement of FAR 31.201-4 and CAS 418, which provide that costs should be charged to contracts on the basis of relative benefits received. Proposals for professional or technical services that are acquired on the basis of the number of hours to be provided must identify both uncompensated hours and the uncompensated overtime hourly rate (described in FAR 52.237-10) for direct charge exempt personnel included in the proposal. The accounting practices used to estimate uncompensated overtime must be consistent with the cost accounting practices used to accumulate and report uncompensated overtime hours.

(b) COST ESTIMATING SYSTEMS.   Pursuant to the requirements of FAR Subpart 15.4, cost or pricing data generally must be submitted prior to award of a contract of $550,000 or more unless:

- The prices agreed upon are based on adequate price competition.
- The prices agreed upon are based on prices set by law or regulation.
- Commercial item are being acquired or a contract for commercial items is being modified.
- A waiver has been granted.

In estimating the costs to be incurred on government contracts, contractors' cost estimating systems must incorporate large amounts of data generated from a myriad of sources and departments. These data often include historical data, vendor quotations, projections based on changes in production methods, changes in technology, volume changes, management decisions, and estimates of future costs. FAR 15.407-5 addresses the benefits to both the government and the contractor of using an acceptable estimating system for proposal preparation. The Department of Defense (DOD) Defense FAR Supplement (DFARS), 215-407-5-70(d), applicable to defense contracts and subcontracts, outlines the following characteristics of an acceptable estimating system:

- Clear responsibilities for preparation, review, and approval of cost estimates
- Written description of the organization and duties of personnel responsible for preparing, reviewing, and approving cost estimates
- Sufficient personnel training, experience, and guidance to perform estimating tasks in accordance with established procedures
- Identification of the sources of data, estimating methods, and rationale used in developing cost estimates
- Appropriate supervision throughout the estimating process
- Consistent application of estimating techniques
- Detection and timely correction of errors
- Protection against cost duplication and omissions
- Use of historical experience, where appropriate
- Use of appropriate analytical methods
- Integration of information available from other management systems, where appropriate
- Management review, including review of company estimating policies, procedures, and practices
- Internal review of and accountability for the acceptability of the estimating system, including comparisons of projected and actual results and analyses of variances

- Procedures for timely updates of cost estimates throughout the negotiation process
- Responsibility for review and analysis of the reasonableness of subcontractor prices

The accuracy of the contractor's cost estimating system is critical, since estimating mistakes can only harm the contractor. If the estimate understates costs, the contractor may end up with a loss on the contract. If the proposed costs are overstated, the company may be vulnerable to a downward price adjustment as a result of defective pricing.

Cost proposals must be compatible with the cost accounting system that will be used to measure and accumulate costs during contract performance. To comply with government requirements for some contracts, the cost accounting system must be able to produce information on the specific cost elements and in the same detail as proposed. FAR 15.408 Table 15-2, "Instructions for Submitting Cost/Price Proposals When Cost or Pricing Data Are Required," outlines the documentation needed to support the proposed costs by cost element and contract line item. Table 15-2, Section I—General Instructions, includes a discussion of the requirement for submission of current, complete, and accurate cost or pricing data. Table 15-2, Section II—Cost Elements, identifies specific requirements for presenting and supporting the following elements of cost:

- Materials and services
- Direct labor
- Indirect costs
- Other costs
- Royalties
- Facilities' capital cost of money

Relevant information that becomes available after submitting the proposal must be provided to the contracting officer before final contract negotiation. Contractors should maintain a record of all data provided, the date and to whom provided, and, if feasible, copies of all data provided to the contracting officer and/or the auditor.

(c) MATERIAL MANAGEMENT AND ACCOUNTING SYSTEMS. While no specific cost accounting requirements relating to material costs are contained in FAR, DFARS clause 252.242–7004, "Material Management and Accounting System," addresses "systems for planning, controlling, and accounting for the acquisition, use, issuing, and disposition of material." The clause is included in many defense contracts and subcontracts over $100.00 that are not for the acquisition of commercial items. The clause contains 10 standards that are used in determining whether systems are adequate:

- Adequate system description including policies, procedures, and operating instructions
- Costs of purchased and fabricated material charged or allocated to a contract based on valid time phased requirements as impacted by minimum/economic order quantity restrictions (desired accuracy levels of 98 percent for the bill of material and 95 percent for the master production schedule)
- Mechanism to identify, report and resolve system control weaknesses and manual overrides and identify operational exceptions such as excess/residual inventory as soon as known
- Audit trails and records (maintained for the prescribed record retention periods) necessary to evaluate system logic and to verify through transaction testing that the system is operating as desired
- Adequate levels of record accuracy (desired accuracy level of 95 percent) and reconciliation of recorded inventory quantities to physical inventory by part number on a periodic basis
- Detailed descriptions of circumstances that will result in manual or system generated transfers of parts

- Consistent, equitable, and unbiased logic for costing of material transactions and written policies describing transfer methodologies and loan/payback techniques
- Controls over allocations from common inventory accounts to ensure that: (i) reallocations and credits due are processed no less frequently than the routine billing cycle; (ii) inventories retained for requirements that are not under contract are not allocated to contracts; and (iii) algorithms are maintained based on valid and current data
- Adequate controls to ensure that physically commingled inventories that may include material for which costs are charged or allocated to fixed-price, cost-reimbursement, and commercial contracts do not compromise requirements of any of the above standards
- Periodic internal audits to ensure compliance with established policies and procedures

The accuracy requirements of 98 percent for the bill of materials and 95 percent for the master production schedule are intended to ensure that the right materials are assigned to contracts based on the time-phased requirements. Difficulties arise when the bill of materials and/or production schedule are not updated, thus raising doubt as to whether the materials being procured are actually required and are only procured when they are needed for current production. The 95 percent accuracy standard for physical inventory is intended to ensure that the number of parts reported in the system for government contracts actually is in inventory and that the inventories allocated to defense contracts and included in requests for progress payments have actually been used on those contracts. However, accuracy levels for physical inventories may be difficult to achieve using the gross numbers of items in the inventory. During these periodic counts of physical inventories, defense contractors can stratify inventories based on the value of the items and establish differing accuracy levels for various strata. For example, a high-cost, specialized electronic component may be put in a stratum that requires 100 percent accuracy, whereas an inexpensive bolt may be in a stratum that requires 60 percent accuracy. A potential result of using multiple strata is that inaccuracy in one strata may cause the accuracy of the entire inventory to fall below the 95 percent level; however, using multiple strata may make it easier to demonstrate that DOD has not been harmed due to the lower accuracy in low-value parts. If systems have an accuracy level below 95 percent, the contractor must demonstrate that (1) there is no material harm to the government due to lower accuracy level, and/or (2) the cost to meet the accuracy goal is excessive in relation to the impact on the government.

Because transfers of parts between contracts transfers can affect billings based on cost, transfers must be well documented, consistently applied, and use appropriate and equitable pricing methodologies. Contractors must maintain and disclose a written policy describing the transfer methodologies. The costing methodology may be standard or actual cost, or any of the inventory costing methods permitted under CAS 411. Consistency must be maintained across all contract and customer types and from accounting period to accounting period for initial charging and transfer charging. Loan/payback systems use the principle that contracts that receive transfers of parts due to changed requirements should bear the cost of the parts purchased to replace the items transferred; such systems are permitted only when the loan and the payback are accomplished in the same billing period or, with governments approval, when billings are adjusted to mitigate any overbilling. Where it may not be appropriate to transfer parts and associated costs within the same billing period, use of a "loan/payback" technique must be approved by the administrative contracting officer (ACO). Controls must be in place to ensure that parts are paid back expeditiously; procedures and controls are in place to correct any overbilling that might occur; at a minimum, the borrowing contract and the date the part was borrowed are identified monthly; and the cost of the replacement part is charged to the borrowing contract.

System programming and records must be maintained in machine-readable form for the record retention period outlined in Section 37.2(f). This requirement goes beyond the scope of normal record retention provisions, which require manual or "hard" copies to be retained. This requirement also points out the government's changing view of what constitutes an adequate audit trail.

(d) PROJECT MANAGEMENT SYSTEMS.   The ability to monitor and project costs on government contracts is critical. The government is particularly concerned about overpaying cost-based progress payments and not being forewarned about potential cost overruns.

The preparation of a comprehensive estimate of contract costs at completion is key to assessing progress and determining if problems exist. These estimates should be prepared at least quarterly to ensure the reliability of interim financial statements and to avoid surprises that come too late for effective corrective action. Management must be informed promptly and periodically of the key facts concerning contract performance. Inherent in such systems is a configuration management function that tracks changes to the technical "baseline" of a product. The project management system needs to timely provide information needed, which includes:

- Actual cost to date
- Budgeted cost for work scheduled
- Budgeted cost for work performed
- Estimated cost to complete
- Estimated cost at completion
- Contract amount (including changes)
- Projected overrun or underrun
- Contract scheduled completion date
- Expected completion date
- Projected slippage

To ensure effective monitoring of a contractor's progress on major procurements, DOD inserts the "Earned Value Management System (EVMS)" clause (DFARS 252.234–7001) into certain large contracts requiring compliance with the criteria provided in DOD 5000.2-R, "Mandatory Procedures for Major Defense Acquisitions Programs (MDAPs) and Major Automatic Information System (MAIS) Acquisition Programs. Basically, an EVMS or other type of cost/schedule control system breaks down the contract into work packages, identifies organizations and managers responsible, develops a schedule, and budgets the costs by those work packages.

The "Limitation of Cost" clause (FAR 52.232-20), inserted in fully funded cost-reimbursement contracts, and the "Limitation of Funds" clause (FAR 52.232-22), inserted in incrementally funded cost-reimbursement contracts, obligate the contractor to notify the government when the contractor has reason to believe that within the next 60 days the cumulative cost incurred to date in performing the contract will exceed 75 percent of the estimated cost of, or funds allotted to, the contract. The contractor must also notify the government anytime the total contract cost is expected to be substantially more or less than the estimated cost or allotted funds. The government is not obligated to reimburse the contractor for any cost in excess of the contract estimated cost or funds allotted to the contract. Nor is the contractor obligated to continue performance or incur any costs in excess of the contract estimated costs or funds allotted. The limitation of cost or funds clauses are designed to give the government an opportunity to decide whether it can and will provide additional funds necessary to complete the work. Because of the reporting requirements of these clauses, companies contracting with the government must have an adequate project management system to allow for timely notification of potential cost overruns. Boards of contract appeals and the courts have ruled in numerous instances that inadequate accounting or project management systems are not valid excuses for not providing the notice required by the clauses.

(e) BILLING SYSTEMS.

(i) Cost-Reimbursement Contracts.   The "Allowable Cost and Payment" clause (FAR 52.216-7) provides for reimbursement costs incurred in contract performance that are deemed "allowable" by the contracting officer, in accordance with procurement regulation cost principles and contract terms. The clause provides cost reimbursement of allowable, recorded incurred costs for:

- Items or services purchased directly for the contract and associated financing payments to subcontractors, provided payments are made on a timely basis
- Materials issued from the contractor's stored inventory
- Direct labor
- Direct travel
- Other direct in-house costs
- Properly allocable and allowable indirect costs, except that pension plan contributions must be funded no less frequently that on a quarterly basis

When pension plan contributions are funded less frequently than quarterly, the accrued cost must be excluded from claimed indirect expenses until actually paid. The contractor's cost accounting system is used to determine properly allocable costs. As discussed in Section 37.3(c), the allocation of costs to a government contract may be subject to some or all of the provisions of the Cost Accounting Standards Board (CASB)'s rules, regulations, and standards.

In establishing the allowable indirect costs under a contract, indirect cost rates are applied to allowable contract base costs. Since indirect cost rates can be definitively determined only at the completion of a contractor's fiscal year, estimated rates are required to reimburse contractors on an interim basis. These rates, referred to as *billing rates*, are based on the anticipated final annual rates. To prevent substantial overpayment or underpayment, the billing rates should be adjusted as needed during the year. The contractor must determine the continued appropriateness of previously established billing rates given the passage of time and experience. The ACO or auditor responsible for determining the final indirect cost rates is usually responsible for establishing the billing rates to be used. Final indirect cost rates, which are generally determined after the contractor's fiscal period ends, are used to determine indirect expenses applicable to cost reimbursement–type contracts, as well as fixed-price redeterminable and incentive-type contracts. The contractor is required to submit an adequate final indirect cost rate proposal to the ACO and auditor within six months after expiration of the fiscal year. For guidance on what constitutes an adequate proposal, FAR 42.705-1(b)(1) refers contractors to the Model Indirect Cost Proposal contained in Chapter 6 of the Defense Contract Audit Agency Pamphlet (DCAAP) No. 7641.90, "Information for Contractors."[1]

FAR 42.703-2 and "Certification of Final Indirect Costs" clause (FAR 52.242-4) require execution of the following certification when final indirect cost rate proposals are submitted:

> This is to certify that I have reviewed this proposal to establish final indirect cost rates and to the best of my knowledge and belief:
>
> **1.** All costs included in this proposal (identify proposal and date) to establish final indirect cost rates for (identify period covered by rate) are allowable in accordance with the cost principles of the FAR and its supplements applicable to the contracts to which the final indirect cost rates will apply; and
>
> **2.** This proposal does not include any costs which are expressly unallowable under applicable cost principles of the FAR or its supplements.

The certification must be signed by a senior management official at a level no lower than vice president or chief financial officer. The certification requirements should not be taken lightly. Contractors should ensure that effective internal controls exist to properly screen unallowable costs from indirect expense proposals.

Including expressly unallowable costs in final indirect cost rate proposals subjects the contractor to certain monetary penalties prescribed in FAR 42.709-1 and the "Penalties for Unallowable Costs" clause (FAR 52.242-3).

---

[1] Defense Contract Audit Agency Pamphlet No. 7641.90 can be obtained by contacting Internet address *www.dtic.mil/dcaa/chap5.html.*

(ii) Fixed-Price Contracts. Pursuant to the "Progress Payments" clause (FAR 52.232-16), fixed-price contracts requiring the use of significant contractor working capital for extended periods generally provide for progress payments if the contractor is reliable, is in satisfactory financial condition, and has an adequate accounting and control system. Payments are made as work progresses, as measured by eligible costs incurred, except for construction-type contracts or shipbuilding, conversion, alteration, or repair contracts, which are based on percentage or stage of completion. Progress payments based on eligible costs incurred provide reimbursement of a specified percentage of total allowable costs incurred in performance of the contract, provided that payments for supplies and services purchased directly for the contract are paid on a timely basis. Accrued costs of allowable pension plan contributions must be funded on a quarterly basis.

(f) RECORD-RETENTION REQUIREMENTS. The audit-negotiation clause (FAR 52.215-2), inserted in negotiated contracts, and the audit-sealed bidding clause (FAR 52.214-26), inserted in contracts awarded under sealed bidding, form the basis of the government's access to contractor records, and require contractors to provide the contracting officer, or a representative of the contracting officer who is a government employee, with access to certain records whenever: cost or pricing data is required; a cost reimbursement or flexibly priced contract is used; or cost, funding, or performance reports are required by the contract. The audit clauses must be flowed down to all the subcontracts over $100,000. In these situations, contractors must make available, in their original form, relevant books, records, documents, and other data or evidence, and accounting procedures and practices. The data must be maintained for three years after final payment, except where other retention periods are prescribed in FAR 4.705 for certain specified types of data, as summarized below:

TWO-YEAR RETENTION REQUIREMENT

- Labor cost distribution cards or equivalent documents
- Petty cash records
- Time and attendance cards
- Payroll checks or receipts for wages paid by cash
- Material and supply requisitions

FOUR-YEAR RETENTION REQUIREMENT

- Accounts receivable invoices and supporting data
- Material, work order, or service order files
- Cash advance recapitulations
- Paid, canceled, and voided checks other than payroll checks
- Accounts payable records
- Maintenance work orders
- Equipment property records
- Expendable property records
- Receiving and inspections report records
- Purchase order files for supplies, equipment, materials, or services used in performance of a contract
- Production records of quality control, reliability, and inspection
- Payroll sheets, registers, or their equivalent, of salaries and wages paid to individual employees for each payroll period and tax withholding statements

Records must be maintained for longer than the periods specified in FAR 4.705 if a longer retention period is contractually specified or if the contractor, for its own purposes, retains the records for a longer period.

37.3 SPECIFIC ACCOUNTING REQUIREMENTS

(a) EFFECTS ON CONTRACTORS.   The FAR Part 31 cost principles and CAS affect many companies doing business with the federal government and have significantly affected many accounting systems. In addition to the records needed for financial reporting and tax return preparation, contractors must often maintain records to comply with these requirements. Some contractors tailor their cost accounting practices used for financial reporting purposes to conform with FAR Part 31 and CAS, if such costing techniques are responsive to operational requirements. Other contractors choose to maintain separate memorandum records to establish the cost accounting practices used for government contract costing purposes. The Preamble to CAS 401, discussed in Section 37.3(c)(iv), addresses the use of memorandum records as follows:

> Commentators stated that the purpose of the standards would require each contractor to revise his formal system of accounts in order to maintain them on a basis used for estimating Government contracts. The Board did not intend that requirement. The standard does not contain any requirement that a contractor must revise his formal system of accounts. Cost accounting records are supplemental to, and generally subsidiary to a contractor's financial records. However, it is necessary that the cost accounting records be reconcilable to the contractor's general financial records.

FAR Part 31 and CAS requirements can affect companies' profits and resulting capital accumulation and, if such effect is adverse, can discourage companies from pursuing government work and thus weaken the base of suppliers available to satisfy the government's needs. Industry has continued to express concern that FAR Part 31 and CAS are too detailed and rigid, favor the government, and give little attention to alternatives and that cost/benefit analysis prior to adoption of new requirements is inadequate. Compliance with FAR Part 31 and CAS should not be taken lightly. Failure to comply can result in adverse adjustments of costs and profits.

Positive effects from CAS include: more objective allocation techniques; greater comparability and consistency through limitations on alternative accounting procedures; a more structured framework for effecting changes in cost accounting practices, and a disclosure statement that is useful for gaining a mutual understanding of the practices to be used in costing government contracts.

(b) COST PRINCIPLES.   Cost principles contained in FAR Part 31 and departmental FAR supplement cost principles apply to the pricing of contracts and subcontracts whenever cost analysis is performed and the determination, negotiation, or allowance of costs when required by a contract clause (e.g., "Allowable Cost and Payment" clause—FAR 52.216-7. While concerted efforts over the years have enhanced the uniformity in determining what costs are acceptable, agency differences still exist. Contractors should be aware of such differences so that any proposals, claims, and billings submitted to a particular agency conform to that organization's unique cost principles.

(i) Advance Agreements on Particular Cost Items (Federal Acquisition Regulation 31.109).
Because the cost principles apply broadly to many accounting systems in varying contract situations, the reasonableness and allocability of certain cost items to a given contract may be difficult to determine, particularly when firms or organizational divisions within firms may not be subject to effective competitive restraints. To avoid possible disallowance or dispute based on unreasonableness or nonallocability, contractors are encouraged to seek advance agreement with the government on the treatment to be accorded special or unusual costs. Advance agreements should be negotiated before the cost covered by the agreement is incurred. Agreements must be in writing, executed by both contracting parties, and incorporated in the applicable contracts. Contracting officers are not authorized to enter into advance agreements for the treatment of cost inconsistent with the other provisions of the cost principles.

Restructuring that results from business combinations often causes the incurrence of significant nonrecurring costs (e.g., severance payments, early retirement incentives, idle facilities, and idle capacity) and cost accounting practice changes. Increased overhead costs that are not the result of cost accounting practice changes are not recoverable under existing firm-fixed-price contracts since the prices for these contracts have already been established. Since restructuring decisions benefit future operations, contractors should attempt to negotiate advance agreements to recover such costs over future periods. By amortizing the costs over future years, contractors can recover a portion of such costs in pricing new firm-fixed-price contracts. Advance agreements are required for recovery of restructuring costs on defense contracts; in addition, restructuring costs generally be recoverable only if the Undersecretary of Defense (Acquisition, Technology, and Logistics) or the Principal Deputy determines that the audited projected savings for DOD resulting from restructuring exceeds the restructuring costs by a factor of at lest two to one or the cost allowed and the business combination will result in the preservation of a needed critical capability.

Other costs for which advance agreements may be particularly important include:

- Compensation for personal services
- Use charges for fully depreciated assets
- Deferred maintenance costs
- Precontract costs
- Independent research and development and bid and proposal costs
- Royalties and other costs for use of patents
- Selling and distribution costs
- Travel and relocation costs, as related to: special or mass personnel movements; travel via contractor-owned, -leased, or -chartered aircraft; or maximum per diem rates
- Costs of idle facilities and idle capacity
- Severance pay to employees on support service contracts
- Plant reconversion
- Professional services (e.g., legal, accounting, and engineering)
- General and administrative costs, particularly with regard to construction, job-site, architect-engineer, facilities, and government-owned contractor operated (GOCO) plant contracts
- Costs of construction plant and equipment
- Costs of public relations and advertising
- Training and education costs

Given the potentially controversial nature of many of the costs listed in FAR 31.109, it is readily understandable why they are suggested as items for which advance agreements may be appropriate.

(ii) Composition of Total Allowable Costs. The cost principles of commercial organizations define the "total cost of a contract" as the sum of the allowable direct and indirect costs allocable to the contract, less allocable credits, plus any allocable cost of money. Credits are defined as the applicable portion of income, rebates, allowances, and other credits that relate to allowable costs. Credits can be given to the government as either cost reductions or cash refunds.

The distinction between direct and indirect costs is a significant concept in the cost principles. A direct cost is identifiable with a specific final cost objective (e.g., the contract), whereas indirect costs are incurred for more than one cost objective. However, direct costs of insignificant amounts may be treated as indirect costs for administrative convenience. Consistent application of criteria for identifying costs as either direct or indirect is emphasized. Once a cost is identified as a direct cost to a particular contract, the same type of cost, incurred in similar circumstances, may not be included in any indirect expense pool allocated to that contract or any other contract. The cost principles do not prescribe which costs should be charged as direct as opposed to indirect. The criteria for charging direct versus indirect should be based on an analysis of the nature of the particular contractor's business and contracts. The criteria should be codified into a written statement of accounting principles and practices for classifying costs and for allocating indirect costs to contracts.

(iii) Factors Affecting Allowability (Federal Acquisition Regulation 31.201).   Costs are not allowable merely because they were determined by application of the company's established accounting system. Factors considered in determining the allowability of individual cost items include: (1) reasonableness; (2) allocability; (3) CAS, if applicable, or generally accepted accounting principles (GAAP) and practices appropriate in the particular circumstances; (4) terms of the contract; and (5) limitations specified in the cost; principles. A company should succeed in obtaining reimbursement for incurred costs if the contracting officer believes that all these criteria have been met.

Reasonableness.   Reasonableness has been one of the more difficult concepts in the regulations, and understandably so in view of the substantially subjective nature of the concept. The cost principles consider a cost to be reasonable if, in its nature and amount, it does not exceed that which would be incurred by a prudent person in the conduct of competitive business. The cost principles recognize that reasonableness must often be determined on a case-by-case basis, considering the specific circumstances, nature, and amount of the cost in question. Reasonableness determinations depend on a variety of considerations and circumstances, including whether:

- The cost is generally recognized as ordinary and necessary for conducting business or performing the contract.
- The cost reflects sound business practices, arm's length bargaining, and the requirements of federal and state laws and regulations.
- A prudent businessperson would take similar action, considering his or her responsibilities to the business owners, employees, customers, the government, and the public.
- Significant deviations from established contractor practices inordinately increased contract costs.

Allocability.   Although the concept is not complicated, its application can become extremely difficult and frequently controversial. The cost principles consider a cost to be allocable if it is assignable or chargeable to one or more cost objectives in accordance with the relative benefits received or other equitable relationship. Subject to the foregoing, a cost is allocable to a government contract if it:

- Is incurred specifically for the contract
- Benefits both the contract and other work, or both government work and other work, and can be distributed to them in reasonable proportion to the benefits received
- Is necessary to the overall operation of the business, although a direct relationship to any particular cost objective cannot be shown

If the cost is direct, it is recoverable against a specific contract; if indirect, only an appropriate portion of the expense can be recovered on a given contract. Disagreements often focus on the extent of "benefit" to the government. There is no requirement that benefit to the government be capable of precise measurement.

Cost Accounting Standards or Generally Accepted Accounting Principles.   Certain CAS have been specifically incorporated into the cost principles. A practice inconsistent with those standards is subject to disallowance under the cost principles as well as a finding of noncompliance with the standards. If CAS are not applicable, GAAP may be an authoritative reference for determining appropriate accounting treatment. Although GAAP have been defined for a variety of financial reporting practices, CAS address the allocability of costs to specific final cost objectives (e.g., contracts). Consequently, the courts and boards of contract appeals have generally given considerable weight to GAAP only when more definitive accounting treatment is not prescribed in the acquisition regulations or the contract itself. The boards and courts have cautioned against relying on GAAP to determine the allocability of costs to government contracts by noting that "such principles have been developed for asset valuation and income measurement and 'are not cost accounting principles' as such, although 'cost accounting concepts . . . may evolve out of them.'"[2] When the cost accounting treatment permitted by GAAP is contrary to the criteria provided in the CAS, cost principles, or the contract, these latter criteria generally prevail.

Selected Costs.   The cost principles are revised on occasion to reflect public policy considerations, administrative convenience, and congressional interest. The acquisition regulations require that expressly unallowable costs, plus all directly associated costs, be identified and excluded from proposals, billings, and claims submitted to the government. A "directly associated cost" is a cost that is generated solely as a result of incurring another cost and would not have been incurred had the other cost not been incurred. Salary costs of employees who engage in activities that generate unallowable costs generally are treated as directly associated costs to the extent of the time spent on the proscribed activity. Directly associated costs are only unallowable to the extent that they are material in amount, except where the salary expenses are themselves unallowable. The cost principles do not address each cost that may be incurred. In the absence of a cost principle for a particular cost item, the determination of allowability is to be based on the principles and standards of FAR Subpart 31.2 and the treatment of similar or related selected items in FAR 31.205. Cost items described in the cost principles are listed in Exhibit 37.1, with a brief summary as to whether or not the cost is allowable.

(c) COST ACCOUNTING STANDARDS.   The original CASB was established in 1970 as an agent of Congress. During its turbulent life from 1970 to 1980, CASB promulgated accounting practice disclosure requirements and 19 CAS, which have the full force and effect of law. In 1988, a five-member CASB was reestablished within the executive branch (Office of Federal Procurement Policy—OFPP), and chaired by the OFPP Administrator. The other four members consist of a DOD member, a General Services Administration (GSA) member, an industry member, and a private-sector member knowledgeable in cost accounting matters. The current board, like its predecessor, is authorized by statute to:

- Issue and amend regulations
- Issue standards, and amend existing standards, to achieve uniformity and consistency in the cost accounting principles followed by prime contractors and subcontractors in estimating, accumulating, and reporting costs for pricing, administering, and settling negotiated prime contracts and subcontracts
- Exempt from its standards certain classes or categories of contractors
- Require contractors to disclose in writing their cost accounting principles, including methods of distinguishing direct costs from indirect costs and the basis used for allocating indirect costs
- Require contractors to agree to contract price adjustments in favor of the government, with interest, for any net increased costs resulting from failure either to comply with duly promulgated CAS or to consistently follow their cost accounting principles in pricing contract proposals and in accumulating and reporting cost of contract performance

The CASB's Rules, Regulations, and Standards are codified in Title 48 of the Code of Federal Regulations, Chapter 99.

---

[2] Celesco Industries, ASBCA No. 22401, January 31, 1980, Contract No. 80-1 BCA 14,271.

	FAR 31.205	Allowability Status
Public relations and advertising costs	-1	Substantially unallowable
Bad debts	-3	Unallowable
Bonding costs	-4	Generally allowable
Compensation for personal services	-6	Allowable with restrictions
Contingencies	-7	Unallowable, with regard to conditions that cannot be measured with reasonable accuracy
Contribution and donations	-8	Unallowable
Cost of money	-10	Allowable
Depreciation	-11	Allowable (but see 31.205–52)
Economic planning costs	-12	Allowable
Employee morale, health, welfare, food service, and dormitory costs and credits	-13	Allowable with restrictions
Entertainment costs	-14	Unallowable
Fines and penalties and mischarging costs	-15	Unallowable
Gains and losses on disposition of depreciable property or other capital assets	-16	Allowable (gains limited to depreciation taken)
Idle facilities and idle capacity costs	-17	Allowable with restrictions
Independent research and development and bid and proposal costs	-18	Allowable
Insurance	-19	Allowable with restrictions
Interest and other financial costs	-20	Unallowable
Labor relations costs	-21	Allowable with restrictions
Lobbying and political activity costs	-22	Unallowable
Losses on other contracts	-23	Unallowable
Maintenance and repair costs	-24	Allowable
Manufacturing and production engineering costs	-25	Allowable
Material costs	-26	Allowable, with restrictions
Organization costs	-27	Unallowable
Other business expenses	-28	Allowable
Plant protection costs	-29	Allowable
Patent costs	-30	Allowable with restrictions
Plant reconversion costs	-31	Substantially unallowable
Precontract costs	-32	Allowable with restrictions
Professional and consultant service costs	-33	Allowable with restrictions
Recruitment costs	-34	Allowable with restrictions
Relocation costs	-35	Allowable with restrictions
Rental costs	-36	Allowable with restrictions
Royalties and other costs for use of patents	-37	Allowable with restrictions
Selling costs	-38	Generally allowable
Service and warranty costs	-39	Allowable
Special tooling and special test equipment costs	-40	Allowable
Taxes	-41	Allowable with restrictions
Termination costs	-42	Generally allowable
Trade, business, technical, and professional activity costs	-43	Allowable
Training and educational costs	-44	Allowable with restrictions
Transportation costs	-45	Allowable
Travel costs	-46	Allowable with restrictions
Costs related to legal and other proceedings	-47	Substantially unallowable
Research and development costs	-48	Losses are unallowable
Goodwill	-49	Unallowable
Cost of alcoholic beverages	-51	Unallowable
Asset valuations resulting from business combinations	-52	Unallowable

Exhibit 37.1   FAR 31.205 selected costs.

(i) Contract Coverage.   CAS coverage is determined at the segment or business unit level of a company. A "segment" is defined as a subdivision of an organization, such as a division, product department, or plant, which usually has profit responsibility and/or produces a product or service. A "business unit" can be either an individual segment or an entire business organization that is not divided into segments. Negotiated CAS covered contracts/subcontracts that require submission of cost data and are not eligible for one of the CAS exemptions are subject to either the "full" CAS clause or the "modified" CAS clause.

- Negotiated contracts/subcontracts over $500,000 but less than $50 million are eligible for "modified" coverage if the business unit's total CAS-covered awards in the preceding cost accounting period were less than $50 million. A contractor that is eligible to use "modified" coverage has to elect such coverage; otherwise, "full" coverage will apply.
- Negotiated contracts/subcontracts over $500,000 are subject to "full" coverage if the business unit's total CAS-covered awards in the preceding cost accounting period were $50 million or more.
- A negotiated award of $50 million or more is subject to "full" coverage.

Exemptions and Waivers.   The following categories of contracts and subcontracts are exempt from CAS:

- Sealed bid contracts
- Negotiated contracts and subcontracts not in excess of $500,000
- Contracts and subcontracts with small businesses
- Contracts and subcontracts with foreign governments or their agents or instrumentalities
- Contracts and subcontracts with foreign concerns (exempt from CAS other than 9904.401 and 9904.402)
- Contracts and subcontracts in which the price is set by law or regulation
- Contracts and subcontracts for the acquisition of commercial items that are either firm-fixed priced or fixed price with economic price adjustment not based on actual costs
- Contracts or subcontracts of less than $7.5 million, provided that the business unit is not currently performing any CAS-covered awards valued at $7.5 million or greater
- Contracts and subcontracts award to a U.K. contractor for performance substantially in the United Kingdom, provided a Disclosure Statement has been filed
- Subcontractors under the NATO PHM Ship program to be performed by a foreign concern outside the United States
- Contracts and subcontracts to be executed and performed outside the United States, its territories and possessions
- Firm-fixed price contracts or subcontracts awarded on the basis of adequate price competition without submission of cost or pricing data

Under certain conditions, either the head of an executive agency or the CASB may waive CAS requirements for a contract or subcontract.

Contract Clauses.   An agency implements CAS by including a notice in the solicitation to offerors and inserting a CAS clause in the negotiated contract or subcontract. Awards subject to CASB regulations include either the full-coverage clause or the modified-coverage clause, which determines the number of standards to be applied. Both clauses also contain provisions for handling disputes, examining contractor's records, and flowing down an applicable CAS clause to all covered subcontracts.

FULL COST ACCOUNTING STANDARDS COVERAGE—ORGANIZATIONS OTHER THAN EDUCATIONAL INSTITUTIONS.   The clause applicable to full coverage ("Cost Accounting Standards," FAR 52.230-2) requires a contractor to:

- Disclose in writing its cost accounting practices when a business unit is part of a company that is required to submit a disclosure statement
- Follow its cost accounting practices consistently
- Comply with all CAS in effect either on the date of final agreement on price as shown on the executed certificate or current cost or pricing data
- Comply prospectively with all CAS that become applicable during contract performance
- Agree to an adjustment of contract price, or cost allowance for failure to comply with existing standards or to follow its cost accounting practices and when making changes to its existing practices

MODIFIED COVERAGE—ORGANIZATIONS OTHER THAN EDUCATIONAL INSTITUTIONS.   The clause applicable to modified coverage ("Disclosure and Consistency of Cost Accounting Practices," FAR 52.230-3) requires a contractor not otherwise exempt to:

- Comply with 48 CFR 9904.401 and 9904.402
- Disclose in writing its cost accounting practices when a business unit is part of a company that is required to submit a disclosure statement
- Consistently follow its cost accounting practices
- Agree to an adjustment of contract price, or cost allowance for failure to comply with applicable standards or to follow established cost accounting practices

COST ACCOUNTING STANDARDS COVERAGE—EDUCATIONAL INSTITUTIONS.   The clause applicable to educational institutions not otherwise exempt ("Cost Accounting Standards—Educational Institution," FAR 52.230-5) requires an educational institution to:

- Comply with 9905.501, 9905.502, 9905.505, and 9905.506 (comparable to 9904.401, 9904.402, 9904.405, and 9904.406)
- Disclose in writing their cost accounting practices when required. Consistently follow their cost accounting practices
- Agree to an adjustment of contract price or cost allowance for failure to comply with applicable standards or to follow established cost accounting practices

COST ACCOUNTING STANDARDS ADMINISTRATION CLAUSE.   The clause for CAS coverage is accompanied by an "Administration of Cost Accounting Standards" (FAR 52.230-6) clause.

- CAS requirements must be flowed down to lower-tier subcontractors that are not otherwise exempt from CAS, and the contracting officer must be advised within 30 days, or any other mutually agreed-upon date, of an award of a CAS-covered subcontract.
- The contracting officer must be notified of anticipated cost accounting practice changes. The notification must include a written description of any change to be made, together with a general dollar cost impact showing the shift of costs between CAS-covered contracts by contract type and other work. For changes required to implement a new standard, the description must be provided within 60 days of the date of award of the contract requiring the change. For any other change, it is required not less than 60 days before the effective date of the proposed change. For noncompliance, the written description must be provided within 60 days after the date of agreement of such noncompliance. Other dates for providing the written descriptions may be mutually agreed to by the contracting parties.

- A cost-impact proposal must be submitted within 60 days after the contracting officer's determination of adequacy and compliance of the descriptions submitted above. The proposal must identify the impact of the change on each significant CAS-covered award. The ACO is permitted to withhold up to 10 percent of subsequent payments due under a CAS-covered contract until a required cost-impact proposal is submitted.

(ii) Price Adjustments. Price adjustments are to be negotiated for the impact of changes in cost accounting practices or for correction of noncompliant practices:

- A contract is eligible for equitable adjustment when the contractor (1) is initially required to apply a standard or (2) implements an accounting change that the contracting officer has found to be desirable and not detrimental to the government's interests. Criteria to be used in determining whether an accounting change is desirable encompass the tests of being appropriate, warranted, equitable, fair, or reasonable. The price adjustment is the net increase or decrease in costs resulting from the prospective application of the new standard(s) or desirable changes to all covered contracts. Equitable adjustments may cause the government to pay increased costs to the contractor or may reduce the contract price.
- CAS-covered contracts and subcontracts are adjusted retroactively to reflect a contractor's failure to comply with applicable standards and disclosed practices. Adjustments arising from noncompliance are made only in favor of the government. Payment must include the net resulting increased cost plus interest at the annual rate established by the Internal Revenue Service. Cost increases and decreases may be offset on affected covered contracts.
- CAS-covered contracts and subcontracts are adjusted prospectively for the effect of voluntary changes in practice that the contracting officer has not found to be in the government's interest. The price adjustment is the net increased cost to the government resulting from the application of the revised practice to all covered contracts. Adjustments are made only in favor of the government.

Increased cost is defined as: (1) cost paid by the government that, as a result of a changed practice or a CAS noncompliance, is higher than the cost that would have been paid had the change or noncompliance not occurred; and (2) the excess of the negotiated price on a fixed-price contract over the price that would have been negotiated if the proposal had been priced in accordance with the practices actually used during contract performance.

The primary purpose of the contract adjustment procedures is to hold contractors accountable for the practices used to cost government contracts. To accomplish this important objective, CASB defined a cost accounting practice and a cost accounting practice change.

- *Cost accounting practice* is defined in 48 CFR 9903.302-1 as any accounting method or technique used to measure cost, assign cost to cost accounting periods, or allocate cost to cost objectives. Cost measurement encompasses accounting methods and techniques to define cost components, determine bases for cost measurement, and establish criteria for alternative cost measurement techniques. Cost assignment encompasses the criteria used to determine the cost accounting period(s) to which the cost should be charged, such as accrual versus cash basis of accounting. Cost allocations encompass methods or techniques to accumulate cost, to determine whether a cost is to be directly or indirectly allocated, to determine the composition of cost pools, and to determine the appropriate allocation base.
- *Cost accounting practice change* is defined in 48 CFR 9903.302-2 as an alteration in a cost accounting practice. The initial adoption of a cost accounting practice for the first time a cost is incurred, or a function is created, is not a change in cost accounting practice; neither is the partial or total elimination of a cost or the cost of a function or the revision of a cost accounting practice for a cost that previously had been immaterial.

To clarify the definition, the CASB regulation also provides practical examples of such changes.

(iii) Disclosure Statements.

Purposes and Uses.   The disclosure statement requirement reflects CASB's legislative mandate to require contractors and subcontractors, as a condition of contracting, to disclose in writing their cost accounting principles, including methods of distinguishing direct costs from indirect costs and the basis used for allocating indirect costs. The disclosure statement provides a written, measurable baseline from which to measure compliance and the consistent application of accounting practices. Contractors must adhere to their own certified practices.

To describe and document a contractor's accounting practices, CASB developed a detailed statement—CASB-DS-1 for commercial and nonprofit organizations and CASB-DS-2 for educational institutions. The ACO is designated to review the adequacy of the statements and to notify the contractor of any reporting deficiencies. The ACO delegates this review to Defense Contract Audit Agency (DCAA).

Disclosure statements will not be made public when, as a condition of filing the statement, a contractor requests confidentiality. Contractors should designate those parts of the statement they wish to have kept confidential.

Filing Requirements.   Disclosure statements must be filed by commercial and nonprofit organizations (1) whose negotiated CAS covered prime contracts and subcontracts at all segments totaled $50 million or more during the prior fiscal year, or (2) that receive a single CAS-covered award of at least $50 million. Educational institutions that are listed in Exhibit A of OMB Circular A-21 must submit disclosure statements if (1) CAS covered awards in the prior fiscal year totaled $25 million of more or (2) a single CAS covered award of $25 million is received. Once a noneducational organization has met the filing threshold, a separate disclosure statement must be filed for each segment with CAS-covered contracts, subcontracts, or interorganization orders, unless the segment's CAS-covered awards in the prior cost accounting period were less than 30 percent of the segment's sales and less than $10 million. Amendments to disclosure statements are processed by submitting the changed pages, together with a new cover sheet, to the cognizant ACO and auditor. Subcontractors are permitted to submit disclosure statements to the government instead of to the prime contractor.

Determination of Adequacy.   An agency head may authorize a contract award without obtaining the disclosure statement. Otherwise, submission of an adequate disclosure statement, when required, is necessary before a contract may be legally awarded. The ACO must make a written determination that the statement is adequate (i.e., current, accurate, and complete).

Determination of Compliance.   Neither the CAS regulations nor the acquisition regulations require the ACO to determine, before contract award, that the disclosure statement complies with applicable standards. However, the acquisition regulations require that, after the adequacy determination, the auditor review the disclosed practices for compliance with applicable standards and report the audit findings to the ACO. The ACO is required to obtain a revised disclosure statement and negotiate any required price adjustments if the disclosed practices are determined to be in noncompliance with applicable standards. Some of the items in the disclosure statement pertain to cost accounting practices addressed in specific standards. Prudent contractors should consider the requirements of applicable standards in their disclosure statement responses.

Contents and Problem Areas.   The key to avoiding a deficient disclosure statement is complete disclosure. Auditors are admonished to be alert for vague, incomplete, or ambiguous answers that could lead to alternative accounting interpretations. Materiality is a major factor in determining the level of detail required to be disclosed; consideration should be given to whether a change in accounting procedures would materially affect the flow of costs. Contractors should use the statement's continuation sheets to expand on specific responses and to clearly convey the accounting practices followed. A description of the contents of CASB-DS-1 follows.

- *Cover Sheet and Certification.* Identifies the reporting unit, its address, and the company official to be contacted regarding the statement. A certification of the statement's completeness and accuracy must be executed by an authorized signatory of the reporting unit.
- *General Information (Part I).* Includes industry classification, sales volume, proportion of government business to total, type of cost system, and extent of integration of the cost system with the general accounts.
- *Direct Costs (Part II).* Requests information on direct material, direct labor, and other direct costs and the bases for making direct charges. Accounting for variances under standard costs is explored in depth. In describing classes of labor, sufficient information is required to distinguish the principal labor rate categories.
- *Direct versus Indirect Costs (Part III).* Requests information on how various functions, cost elements, and transactions are treated and, if indirect, what aggregate pools are used.
- *Indirect Costs (Part IV).* Requires descriptions of all overhead, service center, and general and administrative pools, including major functions, activities and element of cost included in the pool, and the makeup of the allocation base.
- *Depreciation and Capitalization (Part V).* Requires identification of the capitalization criteria, the methods of depreciation used, the bases for determining useful lives, and the treatment of gains and losses from disposition.
- *Other Costs and Credits (Part VI).* Covers the methods used for charging or crediting vacation, holiday, sick pay, and other compensation for personal absence.
- *Deferred Compensation and Insurance Costs (Part VII).* Requires information on pension plans and the determination of pension costs, as well as postretirement benefits other than pensions, certain types of deferred compensation, employee stock ownership plan costs, and insurance costs.
- *Corporate or Group Expenses (Part VIII).* Covers pooling patterns and allocation bases for distributing corporate group expenses (home-office expenses) to organizational segments.

A separate disclosure statement (Parts I–VII) must be submitted for each covered segment (e.g., profit center, division, or other organizational unit). A separate Part VIII must be submitted for each group or home office with costs allocated to one or more CAS-covered segment.

The CASB-DS-2 for educational institutions is similar to the CASB-DS-1. It contains a cover sheet and certification and the following seven parts:

1. General Information (Part I)
2. Direct Costs (Part II)
3. Indirect Costs (Part III)
4. Depreciation and Use Allowances (Part IV)
5. Other Costs and Credits (Part V)
6. Deferred Compensation and Insurance Costs (Part VI)
7. Central System or Group Expenses (Part VII)

(iv) The Standards. The 19 standards, including four interpretations, run the gamut from generalized statements providing for little more than consistency in certain circumstances to highly detailed dissertations on the treatment of specific costs. Each standard has an effective date and an applicability date. The effective date designates the point in time when pricing of future covered contracts must reflect the requirements of the standard. Only those contracts existing when a standard becomes effective are eligible for equitable adjustment. The applicability date marks the time by which the contractor's accounting and reporting systems must actually conform to the standard. To fully understand each standard, the entire standard, including prefatory comments (preambles), should be read. Provided below are brief summaries of each standard, discussed in the following order:

	Standards Applicable To	
	Commercial and Nonprofit Organizations	*Educational Institutions*
Consistency Standards	9904.401, 9904.402	9905.501, 9905.502
Allocation Standards	9904.403, 9904.410, 9904.418, 9904.420	
Fixed Asset Standards	9904.404, 9904.409	
Cost of Money Standards	9904.414, 9904.417	
Compensation Standards	9904.408, 9904.412, 9904,413, 9904.415	
Miscellaneous Standards	9904.405, 9904.406, 9904.407, 9904.411, 9904.416	9905.505, 9905.506

Consistency in Estimating, Accumulating, and Reporting Costs (9904.401 and 9905.501). The purpose is to ensure consistency in each of the contractor's cost accounting practices used to estimate, accumulate, and report costs on government contracts. The objective is to enhance the likelihood that a contractor will treat comparable transactions alike. The practices used in estimating costs for a proposal must be consistent with the cost accounting practices followed by the contractor in accumulating and reporting actual contract costs. Like costs may be grouped when it is not practicable to estimate contract costs by individual cost element or function. However, costs estimated for proposal purposes must be presented in such a manner and in sufficient detail so that any significant cost can be compared with the actual cost accumulated and reported. The standards require consistency in: (1) classification of elements or functions of cost as direct or indirect; (2) indirect cost pools to which each element or function of cost is charged or proposed to be charged; and (3) methods used in allocating indirect costs to the contract. Costs presented in proposals do not have to reflect exactly the same detail as the actual costs that are accumulated and reported; however, the practices must be consistent and in sufficient detail to permit a valid comparison. The important consideration is to produce reasonable "trails" from the cost included in the proposal to those accumulated in the accounting records and subsequently reported to the government.

Interpretation No.1 9904.401 requires that percentage factors for scrap and other direct material losses be supported by appropriate accounting, statistical, or other relevant records that document the actual scrap or other losses when a significant part of material cost is estimated by means of such factors.

Consistency in Allocating Costs Incurred for the Same Purpose (9904.402 and 9905.502). The standards require that each type of cost be allocated only once and on only one basis; a contract cannot be charged more than once for the same type of cost. because a cost incurred for the same purpose, in like circumstances, must be classified as either direct cost only or indirect cost only. The standards relate to the system's design as a whole and not necessarily to the treatment on individual contracts. Thus, the standards also prohibit a specific contract from being charged direct for a cost if the same cost incurred in like circumstances is also included in an overhead pool, but not allocated to that contract. The key element is whether the cost is incurred for the same purpose and in like circumstances. If either the purpose or the circumstances differ, then the accounting practices related to the two separate transactions need not be consistent and would not be covered by this standard.

Interpretation No. 1 to 9904.402 notes that bid and proposal (B&P) costs are not always incurred for the same purpose and in like circumstances. B&P costs specifically required by contractual terms and conditions can, on a consistent basis, be properly treated as direct costs, while other contractor B&P costs may be recorded as indirect costs.

Allocation of Home Office Expenses to Segments (9904.403). The standard governs the allocation of the home office expenses to the segments (business units) under its control and divides home office expenses into three categories:

1. Expenses incurred for specific segments, which should be allocated directly to those segments to the maximum extent practical.

2. Expenses incurred for various segments, such as centralized services, certain line and staff management, and centralized payments and accruals, which should be grouped in logical and homogeneous expense pools and allocated on the most objective basis available.

3. Residual expenses incurred to manage the organization as a whole that have no identifiable relationship to any specific segment or segments, which must be allocated to segments either: (1) on the basis of a three-factor formula (payroll dollars, operating revenue, and net book value of tangible capital assets plus inventories); or (2) on any basis representative of the segments' total activity. (The three-factor formula is required when total residual expenses exceed stated proportions of the aggregate operating revenues of all segments for the previous fiscal year.)

A special allocation of home office expenses to particular segments is permitted when it can be shown that the benefits from the expense pool to the segment(s) are significantly different from the benefits accruing to the segments.

Interpretation No. 1 permits use of segment book income as a factor in allocating income tax expense to segments only when the segment book income is expressly used by the taxing jurisdiction in computing the income tax.

Allocation of Business Unit General and Administrative Expenses to Final Cost Objectives (9904.410). The standard narrowly defines G&A expenses to include only expenses that are incurred for the general management and administration of the business unit as a whole and that do not have a directly measurable relationship to particular cost objectives. Home office expenses that meet the definition of segment G&A expense are includable in the receiving segment's G&A expense pool. Insignificant expenses that do not qualify by definition as G&A expenses may be included in G&A expense pools. The G&A expense pool must be allocated to final cost objectives (i.e., contracts) by means of one of three cost input bases: (1) total cost input (total production costs), (2) value-added cost input (total production costs excluding material and subcontract costs), or (3) single-element cost input (direct labor dollars or hours), whichever is most appropriate in the circumstances. A special allocation is permitted when the benefits from G&A expense to a particular final cost objective significantly differ from the benefits accruing to other final cost objectives.

Allocation of Direct and Indirect Cost (9904.418). CAS 418 requires that a contractor have a written policy for distinguishing between direct and indirect costs and that such costs be consistently classified. Indirect costs must be accumulated in homogeneous cost pools. A cost pool is considered homogeneous if: (1) the major activities in the pool have similar beneficial/causal relationships to cost objectives, or (2) separate allocations of costs of dissimilar activities would not result in substantially different amounts. Materiality is a key consideration in whether heterogeneous cost pools must be separately allocated. No changes in the existing indirect cost pool structure are required if the allocations resulting from the existing base(s) are not materially different from the allocations that would result from using discrete homogeneous cost pools. A cost pool that includes a significant amount of direct labor or direct material management activities should be allocated on a base representative of the activity being managed. A cost pool that does not include a significant amount of labor or material management activities should be allocated in accordance with the following hierarchy of preferred bases: (1) a resource consumption measure, (2) an output measure, and (3) a surrogate representative of resources consumed. A special allocation of indirect costs is permitted where a particular cost objective receives significantly more or less benefit from an indirect cost pool than would result from a normal allocation of such costs.

Accounting for Independent Research and Development Costs and Bid and Proposal Costs (9904.420). IR&D refers to technical effort that is neither sponsored by a grant nor required for performance of a contract, and that falls into the area of basic and applied research, development, or systems and other concept formulation studies. B&P costs are those incurred in preparing, submitting, or supporting any bid or proposal that is neither sponsored by a grant, nor required for contractor performance. The standard covers such costs incurred at both the home office and the business unit levels. IR&D and B&P must be identified and accumulated by project, except when the costs of individual projects are not material. IR&D and B&P project costs include all allocable costs except business unit G&A. In essence, IR&D and B&P projects are treated like final cost objectives except for the allocation of G&A expenses. IR&D and B&P projects performed by one segment for another segment are considered final cost objectives of the performing segment, rather than IR&D and B&P projects, unless the work is part of an IR&D or B&P project of the performing segment. In that case, the IR&D or B&P project will be transferred to the home office for reallocation to the benefiting segments. IR&D and B&P costs accumulated at the home office level are allocated to specific segments where projects are identified with such segments; otherwise, the costs are allocated to all segments using the CAS 403 residual expense allocation base. Segment IR&D and B&P costs are allocated to contracts using the G&A base. A special allocation of IR&D and/or B&P costs at either the home office or the segment level is permitted if a particular segment (for home office costs) or a particular final cost objective (for segment costs) receives significantly more or less benefit from IR&D and B&P costs than would result from the normal allocation of such costs.

Capitalization of Tangible Assets (9904.404). Contractors must establish and adhere to a written policy on tangible asset capitalization that: designates the economic and physical characteristics on which the policy is based; identifies the components of plant and equipment that are capitalized when asset units are initially acquired or replaced; and designates minimum service life and acquisition cost criteria for capitalization, not to exceed two years and $5,000, respectively. Tangible capital assets constructed for a contractor's own use must be capitalized at amounts that include G&A expenses when such expenses are identifiable with the constructed assets and are material in amount. When the constructed assets are identical or similar to the contractor's regular product, such assets must be capitalized at amounts that include a full share of indirect costs. Individual low-cost items acquired for the initial outfitting of a tangible capital asset, such as furnishings for an office, which in the aggregate represent a material investment, must be capitalized consistent with the contractor's written policy. Minimum acquisition cost criterion higher in the aggregate than the criterion for such original complements may be designated, provided it is reasonable in the contractor's circumstances. Costs incurred that extend the life or increase the productivity of an asset (betterments and improvements) must be capitalized when they exceed the contractor's specified minimum acquisition cost criterion for betterments and when the asset has a remaining life in excess of two years. The step-up in value of assets acquired in a business combination accounted for under the "purchase method" of accounting is generally prohibited.

Depreciation of Tangible Capital Assets (9904.409). The standard sets forth criteria for assigning costs of tangible capital assets to cost accounting periods and for allocating such costs to cost objectives within such periods. Estimated service lives for contracting purposes must be reasonable approximations of expected actual periods of usefulness, supported by records of past retirements, disposals, or withdrawals from service. Lives based on past experience may be modified to reflect expected changes in physical or economic usefulness, but the contractor bears the burden of justifying estimated service lives that are shorter than those experienced. Assets acquired for which the contractor has no available data or prior experience must be assigned service lives based on a projection of expected usefulness. The depreciation method used for financial accounting purposes must be used for contract costing unless it: (1) does not reasonably reflect the expected consumption of services as measured by the expected activity or physical output of the assets; or (2) is unacceptable for federal income tax purposes. If the method used for financial accounting purposes does not meet these tests, the contractor must adopt a method that best measures the expected consumption of services. Gains or losses on the disposition of assets recognized for contract costing purposes are limited to the difference between the original acquisition cost and the undepreciated balance. The gain or loss, if material in amount, must be allocated in the same manner as depreciation cost; however, if such amounts are immaterial, they may be included in an appropriate indirect cost pool.

Cost of Money as an Element of the Cost of Facilities Capital (9904.414). The standard recognizes facilities capital cost of money (FCCM) as an allocable contract cost. The standard provides criteria for measuring and allocating the cost of capital committed to facilities, which is an imputed cost that is identified with the facilities capital associated with each indirect expense pool. Cost of money is allocated to contracts over the same base used to allocate the other expenses in the cost pool in which it is included. The cost of money rate is based on rates published semiannually by the Secretary of the Treasury. Form CASB-CMF is used for calculating cost of money factors. Procedures for calculating cost of money are:

- The beginning and ending asset balances for the year may be averaged to arrive at the average asset net book values. The values should be the same as those used to generate depreciation or amortization that is allowed for federal contract costing purposes plus the value of land that is integral to the regular operation of the business unit.
- The cost of money devoted to facilities capital for each indirect pool is the product of these net book values and the rates published by the Secretary of the Treasury.
- FCCM factors are computed by dividing the cost of money for each pool by the appropriate allocation base.
- FCCM is separately estimated, accumulated, and reported for each contract.

Once FCCM indirect expense rates are calculated, they must be applied to the base costs incurred or estimated for each contract. Worksheet memorandum records may be used to allocate FCCM to the incurred base costs of flexibly priced contracts.

Cost of Money as an Element of the Cost of Capital Assets Under Construction (9904.417). The standard addresses an imputed cost of money to be included in the capitalized cost of assets constructed for a contractor's own use. The concept is the same as that in CAS 414, which provides criteria for measuring and allocating cost of money as part of the cost of facilities capital. The cost of money to be capitalized must reflect the application of the commercial borrowing rates published semiannually by the Secretary of the Treasury to a representative investment amount for the period that considers the rate at which construction costs are incurred. Other methods for calculating cost of money, such as the method used for financial reporting, may be used, provided the result is not substantially different from the amount calculated as described above.

Accounting for Costs of Compensated Personal Absence (9904.408). The standard provides criteria for measuring costs of vacation, sick leave, holiday, and other compensated personal absences, such as jury duty, military training, mourning, and personal time off. The standard requires that the costs of compensated personal absences be assigned to the cost accounting period or periods in which the entitlement was earned (accrual basis) and that such costs for an entire cost accounting period be allocated pro rata on an annual basis among that period's final cost objectives. Entitlement is determined when the employer becomes liable to compensate the employee for such absence if the employee were terminated. Probationary periods may be included as a part of the service time creating entitlement. An adjustment occasioned by the initial adoption of the standard, the adoption of a new plan, or a change of an existing plan must be carried in a "suspense account" and recognized as a contract cost only to the extent that the suspense account balance at the beginning of the cost accounting period exceeds the ending liability for such compensated absence in a future fiscal year.

Composition and Measurement of Pension Cost (9904. 412).   The standard establishes the components of pension cost, the bases for measuring such cost, and the criteria for assigning pension cost to cost accounting periods. Two types of pension plans are recognized: a defined-contribution plan in which benefits are determined by the amount of the contributions established in advance and a defined-benefit plan in which the benefits are stated in advance and the amount to be paid is actuarially calculated to provide for the future stated benefits. For defined-contribution plans, the components of pension cost for a cost accounting period are the payments made, less dividends, and other credits. For defined-benefit plans, the components are the normal cost, a part of the unfunded liability, plus interest equivalent and adjustment of actuarial gains and losses. Unfunded actuarial liabilities must be consistently amortized in equal annual installments, and such liabilities must be determined by using the same actuarial assumptions as are used for the other pension cost components. Unfunded liabilities for new plans and improvements in existing plans must be amortized within 10–30 years. Actuarial assumptions must be separately identified, but their validity may be evaluated on an aggregate basis. Assumptions used should reflect long-term rather than short-term trends. Pension costs generally may be assigned to a cost accounting period only to the extent funded. SFAS No. 87 and 9904.412 are incompatible is several respects. Consequently, federal contractors that are subject to application of the FAR Part 31 cost principles or full CAS coverage must maintain two sets of pension cost calculations.

Adjustment and Allocation of Pension Cost (9904.413).   The standard provides guidelines for (1) measuring actuarial gains and losses and assigning them to cost accounting periods, (2) valuing pension fund assets, and (3) allocating pension costs to segments. Actuarial gains and losses must be calculated annually and amortized over a 15-year period. The amount included in the current year must include the amortized amount of the gain or loss for the year plus interest for the unamortized balance as of the beginning of the period. Any recognized pension fund valuation method may be used. However, if the method results in a value that is outside a corridor of 80 (120 percent of the assets' market value), the value must be adjusted to the nearest boundary of the corridor. Pension costs for segments generally may be calculated either on a composite basis or by separate computation. However, pension costs must be separately calculated for a segment when the costs at the segment are materially affected by certain conditions. Contractors that separately calculate pension costs for one or more segments have the option of establishing a separate segment for inactive participants, such as retirees. When a segment is closed, the difference between the actuarial liability for the segment and the market value of the assets allocated to the segment as of the closure date must be determined. The difference represents an adjustment of previously determined pension costs. The government's share of the difference is determined by dividing the pension costs allocated to CAS covered awards by total pension costs for a representative period.

Accounting for the Cost of Deferred Compensation (9904.415).   The standard covers deferred compensation awards made in cash, stock, stock options, or other assets and provides criteria for measuring and assigning such costs to cost accounting periods. Deferred compensation costs must be assigned to current cost accounting periods whenever a valid obligation has been incurred (accrual basis) and future funding is assured. A valid obligation for deferred compensation costs has been incurred if: a future payment is required; the payment is to be made in money, other assets, or shares of stock of the contractor; the amount due can be measured with reasonable accuracy; the recipient is known; and there are reasonable probabilities that any conditions required for the payment will occur and any stock options will be exercised. If no obligation is incurred before payment, the cost should be assigned to the period(s) of payment. Amounts to be paid in the future must be discounted to the present value using a commercial borrowing rate published semiannually by the Secretary of the Treasury. For awards that require future service, costs should be assigned to cost accounting periods as the future services are performed. The cost of deferred compensation must be reduced by forfeitures in the cost accounting periods in which the forfeitures occur. The cost assignable for stock awards is the market value of the stock on the date the shares are awarded. The cost assignable for stock options is the excess of the market value of the stock over the option price on the date the options for the specific number of shares are awarded.

Accounting for Unallowable Costs (9904.405 and 9905.505).   The standards do not provide criteria for determining the allowability of costs, which is a function of the appropriate procurement or reviewing authority; rather they establish the accounting treatment and reporting requirements after the costs are determined to be unallowable. Contractors must identify in their accounting records, and exclude from any proposal, billing, or claim, costs specifically described as unallowable either by the express wording of laws or regulations or by mutual agreement of the contracting parties. Contractors must identify: (1) costs designated as unallowable as a result of a written decision by a contracting officer pursuant to contract disputes procedures; (2) any costs incurred for the same purpose and in like circumstances as those specifically identified as unallowable; and (3) the costs of any work project not contractually authorized. Costs that are mutually agreed to be directly associated with unallowable costs must be identified and excluded from proposals, billings, or claims. Costs that are designated as directly associated with unallowable costs pursuant to contract disputes procedures must be identified in the accounting records. Costs specifically described as unallowable, as well as directly associated costs, must be included in any indirect allocation base or bases in which they would normally be included.

Cost Accounting Period (9904.406 and 9905.506).   The standards require a contractor to use its normal fiscal year as its cost accounting period except: when costs of an indirect function exist for only part of a cost accounting period; another fixed annual period other than a fiscal year is an established practice and is consistently used; or when a transitional period is used in connection with a change in fiscal year. The cost accounting period used for accumulating costs in an indirect cost pool must be the same as the period used for establishing related allocation bases. Indirect expense rates used for estimating, accumulating, and reporting costs—including progress payments and public vouchers—should be based on the established annual cost accounting period.

Use of Standard Costs for Direct Material and Direct Labor (9904.407).   The standard provides criteria for establishing and revising standard costs, as well as disposing of variances from standard costs, for those contractors who elect to use such costs in estimating, accumulating, and reporting costs of direct material and direct labor. Standard costs must be entered into the books of account. Standard costs and related variances must be accounted for at the production unit level, which is defined as a group of activities that either uses homogeneous input (e.g., direct labor and material) or yields homogeneous outputs. Practices relating to setting and revising standards, using standard costs, and disposing of variances must be stated in writing and consistently followed. Variances must be allocated to cost objectives at least annually on the basis of material or labor cost at standard, labor hours at standard, or units of output, whichever is most appropriate in the circumstances. If variances are immaterial, they may be included in appropriate indirect cost pools for allocation to applicable cost objectives.

Accounting for Acquisition Costs of Material (9904.411).   The standard sets forth criteria for accumulating and allocating material costs and contains provisions on the use of certain inventory-costing methods. First-in, first-out; last-in, first-out; weighted or moving average; and standard cost are all acceptable methods of inventory costing. The method(s) selected must be used consistently for similar categories of material within the same business unit and must be applied "in a manner which results in systematic and rational costing of issues of materials to cost objectives." Although the last-in, first-out method is not prohibited, the provision that the method used should result in systematic and rational costing has been interpreted to require costing on a reasonably current basis. The cost of units of a category of material can be directly allocated, as long as the cost objective is identified at the time of purchase or production. The cost of material used for indirect functions may be allocated to cost objectives through an indirect cost pool when it is not a significant element of production cost. When the cost of such inventories remaining at the end of any cost accounting period significantly exceeds the cost at the beginning of the period, the difference must be capitalized as inventory and the indirect cost pool reduced correspondingly. Contractors are required to maintain in writing, and consistently apply, their accounting policies and practices for accumulating and allocating costs of materials.

Accounting for Insurance Costs (9904.416).   The standard provides criteria for measuring, assigning, and allocating insurance costs. Insurance cost assigned to a cost accounting period is the projected average loss for that period plus insurance administration expenses. Insurance premiums or payments to a trusteed fund, properly prorated and adjusted for applicable refunds, dividends, or additional assessments, should represent the projected average loss. For exposure to risk of loss not covered by insurance premiums or payments to a trusteed fund, a program of self-insurance accounting must be developed. If insurance can be purchased against the self-insured risk, the cost of such insurance may be used to estimate the projected average loss. If purchased insurance is not available, the projected average loss should be based on the contractor's experience, relevant industry experience, and anticipated conditions using appropriate actuarial principles. Actual losses can only be charged to insurance expense when they are expected to approximate the projected average loss or are paid to retirees under a self-insurance program. Actual loss experience must be evaluated regularly for comparison with the self-insurance cost used to estimate the projected average loss. Insurance costs should generally be allocated on the basis of the factors used to determine the premium or assessment. Necessary records must be maintained to substantiate amounts of premiums, refunds, dividends, losses, and self-insurance charges and the measurements and allocation of insurance costs.

(d) CONTRACT CHANGES AND TERMINATIONS.   One of the unique aspects of federal contracting is that the government has the right to change the terms and conditions of an existing contract or cancel the contract through a contract termination.

(i) Contract Changes.   The "Changes" clause permits an equitable adjustment to the contract for changes made within the general scope of the contract. The purpose of the equitable adjustment is to reimburse either the contractor or the government for the difference in cost of performance with and without the change, while not disturbing the profit or loss that will be experienced on the unchanged portion of the contract. If the contractor cannot estimate the cost of changed work with a sufficient degree of confidence, it may be necessary to wait until after the costs have been incurred to negotiate the equitable adjustment. The use of retroactive pricing places some additional burdens on the contractor to "prove" the incurred cost. Even if incurred costs are presumed to be reasonable, they must be shown to have been incurred specifically for performance of the changed effort or allocable to that effort. Records showing incurred costs are generally needed for the contractor to successfully negotiate the adjustment. Pursuant to the "Change Order Accounting" (FAR 52.243-6) clause, contractors may be directed to segregate change-order costs in their accounting records. FAR 43.203(b) indicates that the following costs are normally segregable and accountable under the terms of the clause: nonrecurring costs; costs of added distinct work caused by the change; and costs of recurring work. While specific accounting records should assist in measuring the impact of changes, preparation of the request for equitable adjustment will also likely require the use of various estimating techniques.

(ii) Contract Terminations.   When a federal contract is terminated for convenience, the contractor is generally entitled to recoup its full cost of performance prior to a termination. However, preparing termination settlement proposals can be both challenging and complex because most cost accounting systems are designed to handle normal operations—contracts performed to completion—not contracts that are prematurely terminated. Thus, when a contract is terminated, established procedures for allocating direct and indirect costs may not be appropriate for determining cost of performance. For example, if a contractor incurs significant costs in setting up a new contract production line and charges such costs to overhead, the contractor's established method of allocating overhead to that contract will not provide equitable recovery of the start-up cost if the contract is terminated at a early stage of performance. However, once a contractor departs from its usual accounting practices, there is an implication of "double counting" (i.e., charging the same type of cost indirectly in one instance and directly in another). Fortunately, FAR and CAS recognize that double counting exists only when "costs incurred for the same purpose, in like circumstances are charged inconsistently" and that terminations constitute different circumstances.

The cost principle on termination costs (FAR 31.205–42) acknowledges that: "Contract terminations generally give rise to the incurrence of costs or the need for special treatment of costs that would not have arisen had the contract not been terminated." The cost principle specifically addresses the allowability of such costs as: lease costs or depreciation that cannot be discontinued as of the date of the termination but that the contractor has taken all reasonable steps to mitigate; initial costs such as initial plant rearrangement, production planning, and training; loss of useful value of special tooling and special machinery and equipment, which cannot reasonably be used on other work and for which the government's interest can be protected (e.g., title passage); and termination settlement costs that are incurred solely because of the termination. The FAR also provides criteria for equitable recovery of costs by permitting costs to be deleted from the indirect costs to which they were originally charged and recovered as a direct costs on the terminated contract. In calculating the costs to be included in termination settlement proposals, the FAR Part 49 termination provisions further discuss a fairness concept in addition to the specific allowability criteria tests found in FAR 31.205–42.

The total amount of the termination settlement is limited to the contract price of the items terminated, plus settlement expenses. If a contractor would have sustained a loss on a fixed-price contract if it were completed, the termination settlement must be reduced by a loss adjustment factor developed by dividing the total contract price by the estimated cost at completion (i.e., total cost incurred before the termination, plus the estimated costs to complete the contract if the termination had not occurred). If the costs incurred on a completely or partially terminated contract have been increased because of government action or inaction, a request for equitable adjustment should be prepared, concurrent with the termination settlement proposal, to demonstrate that the contract price should be increased prior to any calculation of a loss factor.

When contractor personnel are engaged in termination settlement activities, allowable settlement labor should be burdened with applicable indirect costs, such as payroll taxes, fringe benefits, occupancy costs, and immediate supervision. Significant settlement expenses should be accumulated under separate account or work order legal and accounting fees that are charged to the terminated order.

PENSION PLANS AND OTHER POSTRETIREMENT AND POSTEMPLOYMENT BENEFITS*

Vincent Amoroso, FSA

Deloitte Consulting LLP

Jason Flynn, FSA

Deloitte Consulting LLP

Timothy Geddes, FSA

Deloitte Consulting LLP

*This chapter was updated for the Eleventh Edition by the Editors.

38.1 BACKGROUND, ENVIRONMENT, AND OVERVIEW

(a) INTRODUCTION.   The accounting for pensions and other forms of retirement and postemployment benefits underwent dramatic transformation in the 1980s and early 1990s. These changes placed a significant burden on companies and their accountants to understand the intricate concepts of accounting for pension and other types of benefits, assets, obligations, and periodic costs. This chapter has been written to explain those accounting concepts and to assist the reader in understanding and implementing them. The focus will be on the two distinct set of accounting standards that apply to pension and retirement plans—Statement of Financial Accounting Concepts (SFAS) No. 35, "Accounting and Reporting by Defined Benefit Pension Plans," and SFAS Nos. 87 and 88, "Employers' Accounting for Pensions" and "Employers' Accounting for Settlements and Curtailments of Defined Benefit Pension Plans and for Termination Benefits." SFAS No. 35 applies to the preparation of financial statements for the pension plan, as an entity. SFAS Nos. 87 and 88, on the other hand, specify the accounting to be followed in the financial statements of the plan sponsor. They also established new standards for measuring a company's annual pension cost and balance sheet pension obligations. Additionally, the intricacies of SFAS No. 106, "Employers' Accounting for Postretirement Benefits Other Than Pensions," and SFAS No. 112, "Employers' Accounting for Postemployment Benefits," will be explored. SFAS No. 132 revises disclosures about pension and other postretirement benefits. Disclosure requirements are now standardized and presented in one note to the financial statements.

(b) DEVELOPMENT OF THE PRIVATE PENSION SYSTEM. Before consideration of the accounting requirements specified by SFAS Nos. 35, 87, and 88, some background information regarding the pension system may be useful. It will outline why companies sponsor retirement programs and how plans are changing in response to a changing environment.

(i) The Past. The U.S. private pension system traces its origins to 1875, when the first formal plan was established by a company in the railroad industry. In addition to fostering humanitarian objectives, the early plans were established to achieve a well-defined management goal—to affect the age composition of the workforce. By using such plans, manufacturing firms could ease out older workers who were less productive and service industries were able to provide promotion opportunities for younger employees. Pension plans were typically established in conjunction with mandatory retirement policies. Tax-driven motives were noticeably absent because there were no meaningful tax incentives until 1942 when corporate tax rates were increased dramatically to finance World War II.

The private U.S. pension system started during the industrial revolution. Emerging national companies could not continue their past practice of accommodating aged workers with informal ad hoc policies. One by one, big companies with the financial ability to do so adopted formal retirement arrangements to solve this problem. The list includes the Standard Oil Companies, DuPont, U.S. Steel, and Bell Companies. By 1930, nearly 400 major corporations with more than 4 million workers, representing approximately one-sixth of the private workforce, had adopted formal pension plans.

The seeds of federal regulation were sown before the Great Depression. Many plans were implemented and operated by companies to achieve their goals without regard to employee rights. Courts viewed these contracts as one-sided and issued decisions that construed plans as gratuities.

(ii) The Period of Growth. Plan sponsors' motives for providing pensions have become less homogeneous since World War II. During this period of unprecedented economic prosperity, companies have responded in droves to increased taxes and union demands (or threats of organization) by establishing plans.

Higher tax rates coupled with federal wage controls that had been imposed to stifle war-related inflation triggered a spurt of growth in plan formation during the 1940s.

The wide-reaching economic prosperity of the 1950s and 1960s had a profound effect on the pension system; coverage almost tripled during this period. Through collective bargaining, unions succeeded in establishing plans in many booming industries. Companies with unfilled orders willingly paid the price of starting a program. In addition, plans were established for nonunion employees to assure parity with unionized coworkers. In companies without unions, plans were developed to ward off organization drives. As the economic pie grew, the one-company worker came to expect that he would be rewarded with a secure retirement for his loyal and long service. He was not disappointed. By the dawn of the congressional debates that culminated in the passage of pension reform legislation in 1974, pension plans had been adopted by virtually all established large and medium-sized companies. Pension coverage is still spotty, however, in smaller companies that operate on thin margins.

Small professional corporations maintained a proliferation of pension plans as tax shelters during the 1980s. Accumulation of assets and tax savings for the proprietor(s) are the usual goals of these plans. In many ways federal pension regulation has been driven by tax authorities' desire to correct perceived abuses in this segment of the pension system.

(iii) The Present.   The private system is currently under significant pressure from external forces. Through repeated changes over the past two decades, the federal government is reducing available tax incentives and increasing administrative complexity and, therefore, compliance costs. Foreign competition, corporate restructuring and downsizing, and growing merger activity have caused many companies to rethink their pension policies. Changes in the makeup of the labor force are also affecting the makeup of pension programs.

For now, change in plan design and types of plans used for providing retirement income are the only discernible trends in the responses of plan sponsors. Plans such as 401(k) and thrift or matching programs are becoming an increasingly important part of plan sponsors' deferred compensation policies. Younger employees prefer these savings plans because of their visibility, and the predictability of their annual costs appeals to many employers. In response to this preference, some companies are changing their traditional defined benefit pension plans to a "cash balance plan," a hybrid defined benefit plan that has features of both traditional defined benefit pension plans and 401(k)-type defined contribution plans.

(c) PLAN ADMINISTRATION.   Employers still establish plans to affect the age composition of its workforce by providing income security during employees' retirement years. A plan's level of benefit and other important features—such as early retirement provisions—balance the sponsor's management goals and cost tolerance. Once a program is established, its administration is dictated by specific plan language, which in turn is affected significantly by federal law.

The Employee Retirement Income Security Act of 1974 (ERISA) established minimum standards applicable to virtually all employee plans. Certain unfunded nonqualified plans are exempted. Through a succession of amendments since 1974, the original legal standards have been modified and are now considerably more detailed. Employers are not required to start pension plans but, once established, ERISA limits a sponsor's freedom in changing benefits or options. The Internal Revenue Service (IRS) administers most of the minimum standards, including participation, funding, and vesting and accrual of benefits. The Department of Labor (DOL) is responsible for the fiduciary and reporting and disclosure requirements. In addition, the DOL assists participants by investigating alleged infractions and by bringing civil action to enforce compliance, if necessary. The Pension Benefit Guaranty Corporation (PBGC) administers the termination insurance program established by ERISA.

Plan administration can be viewed as three functions: operation, communication, and compliance. Operating a plan in accordance with its terms requires maintaining sufficient data to determine the proper apportionment of benefits to participants, the calculations needed to apply benefits, and an appropriate level of contributions. Communicating information about benefits to participants assists employees' retirement planning and enhances loyalty. Compliance activities include adopting amendments to conform plans to changing federal requirements and to ERISA's reporting and disclosure requirements. The latter include annual and other reporting to the three pension regulatory agencies and to plan participants.

Most defined benefit pension plans are subject to the termination insurance program that was codified by Title IV of ERISA. Covered plans pay annual premiums to the PBGC, which is set as an annual amount per year per participant plus a surcharge applicable to underfunded plans. Within specified time constraints, an employer can terminate a fully funded plan at will. A procedure is prescribed for notifying participants and the PBGC. Underfunded plans maintained by employers in financial distress can transfer responsibility to the PBGC for paying benefits guaranteed by the insurance program.

(d) EVOLUTION OF PENSION ACCOUNTING STANDARDS. SFAS Nos. 35, 87, and 88 were the result of approximately 11 years of deliberations by the Financial Accounting Standards Board (FASB). However, the controversies concerning the accounting for pension plans well preceded that. As noted in the introduction to SFAS No. 87, since 1956 pension accounting literature has "expressed a preference for accounting in which cost would be systematically accrued during the expected period of actual service of the covered employees."

In 1966, APB Opinion No. 8, "Accounting for the Cost of Pension Plans," was issued. Within broad limits, annual pension cost for accounting purposes under APB No. 8 was the same as cash contributions for prefunded plans. Over the years, however, actuarial funding methods have evolved that produce different patterns of accumulating ultimate costs; some are intended to produce level costs, other front-end load costs, and still others tend to back-load costs.

In 1980, the FASB issued SFAS No. 35, which established standards of financial accounting and reporting for the annual financial statements of a defined benefit pension plan. The Statement was considered the FASB's first step in the overall pension project. After SFAS No. 35 was issued, the FASB concluded that the contribution-driven standard prescribed by APB No. 8 was no longer acceptable for employer financial reporting purposes. The proliferation of plans and a total asset pool of nearly $1 trillion (and growing) argued for an accounting approach under which reported costs would be more consistent for a company from one period to the next and more comparable among companies.

SFAS No. 87 and its companion SFAS No. 88 were issued in 1985. These Statements now govern the accounting for virtually all defined benefit pension plans. They prescribe a single method for accruing plan liabilities for future benefits that is independent from the way benefits are funded. Standards are prescribed for selecting actuarial assumptions used for calculating plan liability and expense components. Most importantly, the discount rate used to calculate the present value of future obligations is market-driven and follows prevailing yields in the bond markets. Taken together, these changes are intended to improve the quality of pension accounting information, but further refinements are possible. SFAS No. 87 states:

> This Statement continues the evolutionary search for more meaningful and useful pension accounting. The FASB believes that the conclusions it has reached are a worthwhile and significant step in that direction, but it also believes that those conclusions are not likely to be the final step in that evolution.

38.2 SPONSOR ACCOUNTING

(a) SCOPE OF STATEMENT OF FINANCIAL ACCOUNTING CONCEPTS NO. 87. The goal of the FASB in issuing SFAS No. 87 was to establish objective standards of financial accounting and reporting for employers that sponsor pension benefit arrangements for their employees. The Statement applies equally to single-employer plans and multiemployer plans, as well as pension plans or similar benefit arrangements for employees outside the United States. Any arrangement that is similar in substance to a pension plan is covered by the Statement.

The accounting specified in SFAS No. 87 does not supersede any of the plan accounting and reporting requirements of SFAS No. 35 (see "Plan Accounting"). It does, however, affect sponsor accounting by superseding the accounting requirements to calculate pension cost as described in

APB No. 8, and the disclosure requirements as stated in SFAS No. 36, "Disclosure of Pension Information."

The Statement does not apply to pension or other types of plans that provide life and/or health insurance benefits to retired employees, although the sponsor of a plan that provides such benefits may elect to account for them in accordance with the provisions of SFAS No. 87. The accounting for the obligations and cost of these other postretirement benefits is the subject of SFAS No. 106 (see "Accounting for Postretirement Benefits Other Than Pensions").

(b) APPLICABILITY OF STATEMENT OF FINANCIAL ACCOUNTING CONCEPTS NO. 87.
In substance, there are two principal types of single-employer pension plans: defined benefit plans and defined contribution plans. SFAS No. 87 applies to both kinds of plans; however, most of the provisions of that statement are directed toward defined benefit plans.

Appendix D of SFAS No. 87 defines these two types of pension plans:

Defined benefit pension plan—A pension plan that defines an amount of pension benefit to be provided, usually as a function of one or more factors such as age, years of service, or compensation. Any pension plan that is not a defined contribution plan is, for purposes of this Statement, a defined benefit plan.

Defined contribution pension plan—A plan that provides pension benefits in return for services rendered, provides an individual account for each participant, and specifies how contributions to the individual's account are to be determined instead of specifying the amount of benefits the individual is to receive. Under a defined contribution pension plan, the benefits a participant will receive depend solely on the amount contributed to the participant's account, the returns earned on investments of those contributions, and forfeitures of other participants' benefits that may be allocated to such participant's account.

The paragraphs that immediately follow address the principal accounting and reporting requirements for a sponsor of a defined benefit pension plan. The provisions of SFAS No. 87 that provide standards for other types of pension plans—defined contribution, multiemployer, and multiple employer plans—are discussed in Subsections 38.2(i), 38.2(k), and 38.2(m).

It should be noted that cash balance plans, which have characteristics of both defined benefit plans and defined contribution plans, are currently the subject of significant FASB discussion and evaluation. In 2002, a group of pension professionals formally requested FASB guidance on the appropriate accounting treatment for cash balance plans. Key questions included whether the plans should be accounted for as defined contribution or defined benefit in nature and the appropriate attribution to apply if the decision were to treat them as defined benefit plans. In 2003, the Emerging Issues Task Force (EITF) formally began considering the issue and assigned it the identification EITF Issue 03–4.

The EITF has since reached preliminary conclusions with respect to a distinct subset of cash balance plans (i.e., those with fixed interest crediting rates). These plans are to be treated as defined benefit plans and valued according to the traditional unit credit attribution method, which does not reflect future pay increases.

With respect to the remaining group of cash balance plans which use a variable interest crediting rate, the FASB is still deliberating. Preliminary releases indicate that the FASB prefers that these plans record the sum of the hypothetical account balances as the plan liability. This would be more of a defined contribution accounting approach, in that the expense would include the actual allocations made to the account and the actual interest credited as the service cost and interest cost components. Still further, the FASB may expand the scope of this new approach to include all defined benefit plans that pay an immediately available lump sum on termination. Final FASB guidance is expected on these cash balance issues during the first half of 2005.

For employers with more than one pension plan, SFAS No. 87 generally applies to each plan separately, although the financial disclosures of the plans in the sponsor's financial statements may be aggregated within certain limitations.

(c) BASIC ELEMENTS OF PENSION ACCOUNTING. The intention of the FASB in adopting SFAS No. 87 was to specify accounting objectives and results rather than the specific computational means of obtaining those results. Accordingly, the Statement permits a certain amount of flexibility in choosing methods and approaches to the required pension calculations.

One of the reasons for the flexibility is that in a defined benefit pension plan an employer promises to provide the employee with retirement income in future years after the employee retires or otherwise terminates employment. The actual amount of pension benefit to be paid usually is contingent on a number of future events, many of which the employer has no control over. These future events are incorporated into the defined benefit plan contract between the employer and employee, and form the basis of the plan's benefit formula.

The benefit formula within a pension plan generally describes the amount of retirement income an employee will receive for services performed during his employment. Since accounting and financial reporting are intended to mirror actual agreements and transactions, it is logical that sponsor accounting for pensions should follow this contract to pay future benefits—that is the plan's benefit formula. However, two problems arise from this accounting premise: How will the amount and timing of benefit payments be determined, and over what years of service will the cost of those pension benefits be attributed?

(i) Attribution. When drafting SFAS No. 87, the FASB considered whether the determination of net periodic pension cost should be based on a benefit approach or a cost approach. The benefit approach determines pension benefits attributed to service to date and calculates the present value of those benefits. The benefit approach recognizes costs equal to the present value of benefits earned for each period. Even when an equal amount of benefit is earned in each period, the cost being recognized will nevertheless increase as an employee approaches retirement. The cost approach, on the other hand, projects the present value of the total benefit at retirement and allocates that cost over the remaining years of service. Under the cost approach, the cost charged in the early years of an employee's service is greater than the present value of benefits earned based on the plan's benefit formula. In the later years of an employee's service, the cost is less than the present value of benefits earned so that the cumulative cost by the time the employee retires will be the same as that under the benefits approach.

As noted previously, accounting is intended to mirror actual agreements. In a defined benefit plan contract, the employer's promise to the employee is specified in terms of how benefits are earned based on service. Accordingly, the benefit approach was selected by the FASB and is the single attribution approach permitted by SFAS No. 87. Specifically, the Statement requires:

- For flat benefit plans, the unit credit actuarial method
- For final-pay and career-average-pay plans, the projected unit credit method

(ii) Actuarial Assumptions. The value of plan benefits that form the basis for determining net periodic pension cost are calculated through use of actuarial assumptions. The discount rate reflects the time value of money. Demographic assumptions help determine the probability and timing of benefit payments—for example, assumptions for mortality, termination of employment, and retirement incidence are used to develop expected payout streams. Demographic assumptions are also utilized to establish certain amortization schedules. Prior service costs attributable to plan amendments and experience gains and losses typically are spread over the expected remaining service of active employees. Paragraphs 43–45 of SFAS No. 87 establish standards for selecting assumptions. Each nonfinancial assumption must reflect the best estimate of future experience for that assumption.

(iii) Interest Rates. Under SFAS No. 87, employers are required to apply two interest rates in measuring plan obligations and computing net periodic pension costs—an assumed discount rate and an expected long-term rate of return on plan assets.

As implied by its name, the expected long-term rate of return on assets should reflect the expected long-term yield on plan assets available for investment during the ensuing year, as well as the reinvestment that yield in subsequent years.

The discount rate is a "snapshot" rate determined on the measurement date used for financial reporting. Paragraph 44 of SFAS No. 87 states the following:

> Assumed discount rates shall reflect the rates at which the pension benefits could be effectively settled. It is appropriate in estimating those rates to look to available information about rates implicit in current prices of annuity contracts that could be used to effect settlement of the obligation (including information about available annuity rates currently published by the PBGF). In making those estimates, employers may also look to rates of return on high-quality fixed-income investments currently available and expected to be available during the period to maturity of the pension benefits.

SFAS No. 87 was published in 1985. In December of 1990, SFAS No. 106 was issued, which said the following in Paragraph 186:

> The objective of selecting assumed discount rates is to measure the single amount that, if invested at the measurement date in a portfolio of high-quality debt instruments, would provide the necessary future cash flows to pay the accumulated benefits when due. Notionally, that single amount, the accumulated post-retirement benefit obligation, would equal the current market value of a portfolio of high-quality zero coupon bonds whose maturity dates and amounts would be the same as the timing and amount of the expected future benefit payments.

For SFAS No. 106, the concept of "settling" obligations using annuities is not usually applicable, so the method for selecting discount rates could not use exactly the same method as SFAS No. 87. But both refer to "high-quality" investments. The Chief Accountant of the Securities and Exchange Commission (SEC) announced the following in a 1993 letter to the Chairman of the EITF at the FASB:

> The SEC staff believes that the guidance that is provided in paragraph 186 of FASB 106 for selecting discount rates to measure the post-retirement benefit obligation also is appropriate guidance for measuring the pension benefit obligation.

Thus, the SEC suggests that SFAS No. 106's method for estimating a discount rate should be used for SFAS No. 87 purposes. Paragraph 186 of SFAS No. 106 can be adapted easily for pension purposes by changing "accumulated post-retirement benefit obligation" to "projected benefit obligation" (PBO). The SEC also clarified the term *high quality* in this letter, indicating that any bond receiving one of two highest ratings given by a recognized rating agency (Moody's Aaa and Aa for example) would be deemed to be high quality.

(iv) Consistency. The Statement suggests some consistency among the assumptions used to calculate plan liabilities. In practice this means that identical components of financial assumptions generally should be used. For example, the assumed rate of increase in salaries and the rate of increase in Social Security benefits both have an inflation component, so as one increases due to expected inflation, so should the other.

Notwithstanding the preceding paragraph, the Statement does not require an employer to adopt any specific method of selecting the assumptions. Instead, SFAS No. 87 requires the assumptions to be the employer's best estimates. Therefore, it is not deemed a change in accounting principle, as defined in APB Opinion No. 20, "Accounting Changes," if an employer should change its basis of selecting the assumed discount rate, for example, from high-quality bond rates to annuity purchase rates. The change in liabilities due to a change in assumptions goes into "unrecognized net gain or loss," hence the amount of unrecognized net gain or loss is one of the best indicators of the reasonableness of assumptions under the plan. If the assumptions are reasonable, the gains and losses should offset each other in the long term. Therefore, when a plan has a pattern of unrecognized gains or losses that does not appear to be self-correcting, the assumptions used to measure benefit obligations and net periodic pension cost may be unrealistic. Assumptions that do not appear on the surface to be unreasonable may still be unrealistic if not borne out by experience.

(v) Actuarial Present Value of Benefits.   As noted previously, the FASB determined the SFAS No. 87 accounting would be based on the plan's contractual arrangement—that the projection of ultimate benefits to be paid under a pension plan should be based on the plan's benefit formula. Accordingly, SFAS No. 87 utilizes two different measurements in estimating this ultimate pension liability—the accumulated benefit obligation (ABO) and the PBO. The ABO comprises two components—vested and nonvested benefits—both of which are determined based on employee service and compensation amounts to date. Benefits are vested when they no longer depend on remaining in the service of the employer. The PBO is equal to the ABO plus an allowance for future compensation levels, that is, a projection of the actual salary upon which the pension benefit will be calculated and paid (i.e., projection of the final salary in a "final-pay" plan). The relationship of these two obligations is reflected in Exhibit 38.1.

Consider the example of a plan that provides a retirement pension equal to one percent of an employee's average final five-year compensation for each year of service. The PBO for an employee with five years of service is the actuarial present value of five percent of his projected average compensation at his expected retirement date; whereas his ABO is determined similarly but only taking into account his average compensation to date. Further, assume that this employee would be 60 percent vested in his accrued benefits if his service is terminated today; then his vested benefit obligation is equal to 60 percent of his ABO.

Unless there is evidence to the contrary, accounting is based on the going-concern concept. Accordingly, the PBO is utilized as the basis for computing the service and interest components of the net periodic pension cost since it is more representative of the ultimate pension benefits to be paid than the ABO.

When evaluating a plan's benefit formula to determine how the attribution method should be applied, SFAS No. 87 specifies that the substance of the plan and the sponsor's history of plan amendments should be considered. For example, an employer that regularly increases the benefits payable under a flat-benefit plan may, in substance, be considered to have sponsored a plan with benefits primarily based on employees' compensation. In such cases, the attribution method should reflect the plan's substance, rather than simply conform to its written terms. Similarly, attribution of benefits (and, therefore, recognition of cost) for accounting purposes may differ from that called for in a plan's benefit formula if the formula calls for deferred vesting ("backloading") of benefits. This by far is one of the more subjective areas of SFAS No. 87. Obviously, the determination that there is a commitment by the sponsor to provide benefits beyond the written terms of the pension plan's benefit formula requires careful evaluation and consideration.

If an employer has committed to making certain plan amendments, these amendments should be reflected in the PBO even if they may not have been formally written into the plan or if some of the changes may not be effective until a later date. Collectively bargained pension plans often provide for benefit increases with staggered effective dates. Such a plan may provide a monthly

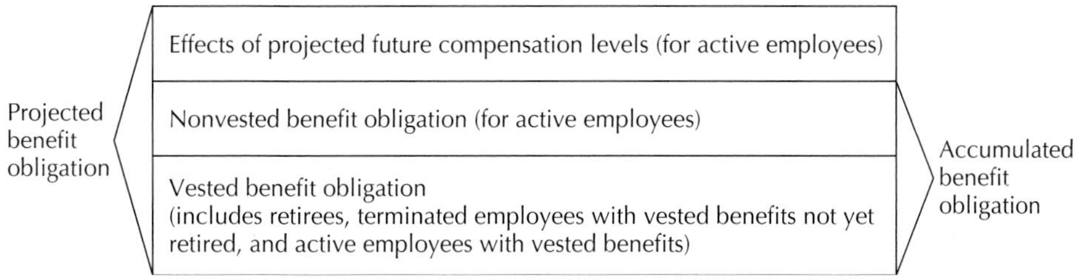

Exhibit 38.1   Relationship of ABO and PBO.

pension equal to $20 per month for each year of service in the first year of a labor contract, $21 in the second year, and $22 in the third. Once the contract has been negotiated, the PBO should reflect the $21 and $22 benefit multipliers for participants assumed to terminate or retire after the first year of the labor contract.

(vi) Measurement Date. The date as of which the plan's PBO and assets are measured—for purposes of disclosure in the employer's financial statements and determination of pension cost for the subsequent period—is known as the *measurement date*. Although SFAS No. 87 contemplates that the measurement date coincides with the date of the financial statements, an alternative date not more than three months prior may be used. However, a change in the measurement date, for example, from September 30 in one year to December 31 in the next year would constitute a change in accounting principle under APB No. 20. Although most employers have one measurement date each year, some employers remeasure their PBO and select the assumed discount rates on a more frequent basis. The frequency of measurement is part of the employer's accounting methods and may not be changed without proper disclosure of the impact.

Although the PBO disclosed in the financial statements is as of the measurement date, it generally is not necessary to determine the PBO using participant data as of that date. Instead the PBO may be estimated from a prior measurement, provided that the result obtained does not differ materially from that if a new measurement is made using current participant data. The fair value of plan assets, on the other hand, should be as of the measurement date.

The period between consecutive measurement dates is known as the *measurement period* and is used for determining the net periodic pension cost. The cost thus determined is used for the related financial reporting period. Events that occur after the measurement date but still within the financial reporting period generally are excluded from the SFAS No. 87 disclosure requirement. If significant, the cost implications thereof should nevertheless be disclosed in a manner similar to other post-year-end events.

(d) NET PERIODIC PENSION COST. Net periodic pension cost represents the accounting recognition of the consequences of events and transactions affecting a pension plan. The amount of pension cost for a specified period is reported as a single net amount in an employer's financial statements. Under SFAS No. 87, net periodic pension cost comprises the following six components:

- Service cost
- Interest cost
- Expected return on plan assets
- Amount of gain or loss being recognized or deferred
- Amortization of unrecognized prior service cost
- Amortization of the unrecognized net obligation or net asset existing at the initial application of the Statement

(i) Service Cost Component. A defined benefit pension plan contains a benefit formula that generally describes the amount of retirement income that an employee will receive for services performed during their employment. SFAS No. 87 requires the use of this benefit formula in the measurement of annual service cost. The service cost component of net periodic pension cost is defined by the Statement as the actuarial present value of pension benefits attributed by the pension benefit formula to employee service during a specified period. Under SFAS No. 87, attribution (the process of assigning pension benefits or cost to periods of employee service) generally is based on the benefit formula (i.e., the benefit attribution approach).

A simplified example will help illustrate this concept. Assume that a pension plan's benefit formula states that an employee shall receive, at the retirement age of 65, retirement income of $15 per month for life, for each year of credited service. Thus, a pension of $15 per month can be attributed to each year of employee service. The actuarial present value of the $15 monthly pension represents the service cost component of net periodic pension cost. Although it is customary to determine the service cost at the end of the year, an equally acceptable practice is to compute the service cost at the beginning of the year and to add the interest thereon at the assumed discount rate to the interest cost component.

In certain circumstances the plan's benefit formula does not indicate the manner in which a particular benefit relates to specific services performed by the employee. In this case, SFAS No. 87 specifies that the benefit shall be considered to be accumulated as follows:

- If the benefit is includable in vested benefits, the benefit shall be accumulated in proportion to the ratio of total completed years of service as of the present to the total completed years of service as of the date the benefit becomes fully vested. A vested benefit is a benefit that an employee has an irrevocable right to receive. For example, receipt of the pension benefit is not contingent on whether the employee continues to work for the employer.

- If the benefit is not includable in vested benefits, the benefit shall be accumulated in proportion to the ratio of completed years of service as of the present date to the total projected years of service. An example of a benefit that is not includable in vested benefits is a death or disability benefit that is payable only if death or disability occurs during the employee's active service.

Some pension plans require contributions by employees to cover part of the plan's overall cost. SFAS No. 87 does not specify how the net periodic pension cost should be adjusted for employee contributions. An often-used approach is to reduce the service cost component directly by the employee contributions, thus possibly resulting in a negative service cost. Under this approach the plan's PBO encompasses both benefits to be financed by employee contributions and those financed by the employer.

(ii) Interest Cost Component.   In determining the PBO of a plan, SFAS No. 87 gives appropriate consideration to the time value of money, through the use of discounts for interest cost. Therefore, the Statement requires that an employer recognize, as a component of net periodic pension cost, interest on the PBO. This interest cost component is equal to the increase in the amount of the PBO due to the passage of time. The accretion of interest on the PBO is based on the assumed discount rate.

Since the assumed discount rate is intended to reflect the interest rate at which the PBO currently could be settled, it is imperative that the discount rate assumption be reevaluated each year to determine whether it reflects the best estimate of current settlement rates. As a rule of thumb, if interest rates are in a period of fluctuation, the discount rate generally should change.

(iii) Expected Return on Plan Assets Component.   SFAS No. 87 requires that an employer recognize, as a component of net periodic pension cost, the expected return on pension plan assets [see Subsection 38.2(e)]. (SFAS No. 87 actually describes an *actual* return on plan assets component in disclosing the net periodic pension cost. However, the difference between actual and expected return was then put into unrecognized gain or loss, so there is no difference between using expected return on assets versus using actual return on assets plus an offsetting unrecognized gain or loss. SFAS No. 132, which amended SFAS No. 87 disclosure requirements, states that expected return is to be disclosed, so that approach is followed here.)

The expected return on plan assets is determined by multiplying the "market-related value of assets" (defined following) by the expected long-term rate of return assumption, and adjusting for interest on contributions and benefit payments expected to be made.

The market-related value of plan assets is used in determining the expected return on pension plan assets. The market-related value of plan assets can be either the actual fair value of plan assets or a "calculated" value that recognizes the changes in the fair value of plan assets over a period of not more than five years. Employers are permitted great flexibility in selecting the method of calculating the market-related value of plan assets. Any method that averages gains and losses over not longer than a five-year period would be acceptable under the Statement, provided it meets two criteria: that the method be both systematic and rational. In fact, changes in the fair value of assets would not have to be averaged but could be recognized in full in the subsequent year's net periodic pension cost, provided that the method is applied consistently to all gains and losses and is disclosed. An employer also may use different methods for determining the market-related values of plan assets in separate pension plans and in separate asset categories within each plan, provided that the differences can be supported. However, a change in calculating the market-related value of plan assets (e.g., going from using fair value of assets to a "smoothed" value, or going from one kind of smoothing to another) would be a change in accounting method under APB No. 20.

The Statement makes no specific allowance for administrative or investment expenses paid directly from the pension fund. These expenses may be reflected in the net periodic pension cost as an offset to the expected return on plan assets, and in such case may also be considered in the selection of the expected long-term rate of return on plan assets. If deemed appropriate, administrative expenses may be treated differently from investment expenses and added to the plan's service cost.

(iv) Amortization of Unrecognized Net Gains and Losses Component.   SFAS No. 87 broadly defines gains and losses as changes in the amount of either the PBO or pension plan assets that generally result from differences between the estimates or assumptions used and actual experience. Gains and losses may reflect both the refinement of estimates or assumptions and real changes in economic conditions. Hence, the gain and loss component of SFAS No. 87 consists of the net difference between the estimates and actual results of two separate pension items: actuarial assumptions related to pension plan obligations (liability gains and losses) and return on plan assets (asset gains and losses).

Liability gains and losses (increases or decreases in the PBO) stem from two types of events: changes in obligation-related assumptions (i.e., discount rate, assumed future compensation levels) and variances between actual and assumed experience (i.e., turnover, mortality). Liability gains and losses generally would be calculated at the end of each year as the difference between the projected value of the year-end pension obligation based on beginning of the year assumptions and the actual year-end value of the obligation based on the end-of-year assumptions.

Asset gains and losses represent the difference between the actual and expected rate of return on plan assets during a period. These gains and losses are entirely experience-related. As noted in the previous section, the actual return on pension plan assets is equal to the difference between the fair value of pension plan assets at the beginning and end of a period, adjusted for any contributions and pension benefit payments made during that period. The expected return on pension plan assets is a computed amount determined by multiplying the market-related value of plan assets (as defined following) by the expected long-term rate of return. The expected long-term rate of return is an actuarial assumption of the average expected long-term interest rate that will be earned on plan assets available for investment during the period.

In order to reduce the potentially volatile impact of gains and losses on net periodic pension cost from year to year, the FASB adopted various "smoothing" techniques in SFAS No. 87—the netting of gains and losses, the market-related value of plan assets, the initial deferral of net gains and losses, and the amortization of the net deferred amount. The impact of the first smoothing technique is obvious; the other techniques are discussed briefly in the following paragraphs.

As noted previously, the market-related value of plan assets is utilized in the determination of the expected return on pension plan assets. The market-related value of plan assets can be either the actual fair value of plan assets or a "calculated" value that recognizes the changes in the fair value of plan assets over a period of not more than five years. Employers are permitted great flexibility in selecting the method of calculating the market-related value of plan assets. Any method that averages gains and losses over not longer than a five-year period would be acceptable under the Statement, provided it met two criteria: that the method be both systematic and rational. In fact, changes in the fair value of assets would not have to be averaged at all but could be recognized in full in the subsequent year's net periodic pension cost provided that the method is applied consistently to all gains and losses (on both plan assets and obligations) and is disclosed. An employer also may use different methods for determining the market-related values of plan assets in separate pension plans and in separate asset categories within each plan, provided that the differences can be supported.

SFAS No. 87 specifies that the net gain or loss resulting from the assumptions or estimates used differing from actual experience be deferred and amortized in future periods. Deferred gains and losses (excluding any asset gains and losses subsequent to the initial implementation of SFAS No. 87 that have not yet been reflected in the market-related value of assets) are amortized as a component of net periodic pension cost if they exceed the "corridor." The corridor is defined as a range equal to plus or minus 10 percent of the greater of either the PBO or the market-related value of plan assets. If the cumulative gain or loss, as computed, does not lie outside the corridor, no amount of gain or loss needs to be reflected in net periodic cost for the current period. However, if the cumulative gain or loss does exceed the corridor, only the excess is subject to amortization. To visualize the concept of the corridor, refer to Exhibit 38.2.

The minimum amortization that is required in net periodic pension cost is the excess amount described above, divided by the average remaining service period of the active employees expected to receive benefits under the plan. Unlike other amortization under SFAS No. 87, the average remaining service period is redetermined each year. The FASB does permit alternative methods of amortization. An employer may decide not to use the corridor method or substitute any alternative amortization method that amortizes an amount at least equal to the minimum. Consequently, an alternative method could recognize the entire amount of the current period's gain or loss in the ensuing period. Any alternative amortization method must be applied consistently from year to year and to both gains and losses, and must be disclosed in the employer's financial statements.

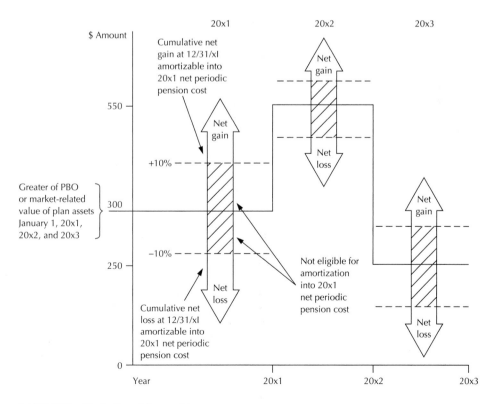

Exhibit 38.2   Illustration of the corridor.

The 10 percent corridor is designed to avoid amortization of relatively small and temporary gains and losses arising in any one year that can be expected to offset each other in the long run. It is not intended to exclude a portion of gains and losses from ever being recognized in the sponsor's income statement. If a substantial amount of net gain or loss remains unrecognized from year to year, or increases in size, it may imply that the PBO and net periodic pension cost have been overstated or understated.

(v) Amortization of Unrecognized Prior Service Cost Component.   Defined benefit pension plans are sometimes amended, usually to provide increased pension benefits to employees. An amendment to a pension plan (or initiation of a pension plan) that grants benefits to employees for services previously rendered generates an increase in the PBO under the plan. This additional PBO is referred to as *prior service cost*. Retroactive pension benefits generally are granted by the employer in the expectation that they will produce future economic benefits, such as increasing employee morale, reducing employee turnover, or improving employee productivity.

Under SFAS No. 87, prior service cost is to be amortized and included as a component of net periodic pension cost. A separate amortization schedule is established for each prior service cost based on the expected future service by active employees who are expected to receive employer-provided benefits under the plan. Instead of a declining amortization schedule, a common practice is to amortize the prior service cost on a straight-line basis over the average future service period. Once this amortization schedule has been established, it will generally not be changed unless the period during which the employer expects to realize future economic benefits has shortened or the future economic benefits have become impaired. Decelerating the amortization schedule is prohibited.

If substantially all of the participants of a pension plan are inactive, the prior service cost from a retroactive amendment should be amortized over the remaining life expectancy of those plan participants.

SFAS No. 87 permits the use of alternative amortization methods that more rapidly reduce the amount of unrecognized prior service cost, provided that the alternatives are used consistently. For example, straight-line amortization of unrecognized prior service cost over the average future service period of active employees who are expected to receive benefits under the plan is acceptable. The immediate recognition of prior service cost, however, generally is inappropriate.

As noted previously, a plan amendment typically increases the cost of pension benefits and increases the amount of the PBO. However, there are situations where a plan amendment may decrease the cost of pension benefits, resulting in a decrease in the amount of the PBO. Any decrease resulting from a plan amendment should be applied to reduce the balance of any existing unrecognized prior service cost using a systematic and rational method [i.e., LIFO (last-in, first-out), FIFO (first-in, first out), or pro rata, unless such reduction can be related to any specific prior service cost]. Any excess is to be amortized on the same basis as increases in unrecognized prior service cost.

Once the employer has committed to a plan amendment, the net periodic pension cost for the remainder of the year should reflect the additional service cost, interest cost, and amortization related to the amendment. Remeasurement based on the current discount rate may also be called for. Pension cost for any prior periods should not be restated merely on account of the amendment, even if the amendment may be effective retroactively to a prior date.

(vi) Amortization of Unrecognized Net Obligation or Net Asset Component.   The unrecognized net obligation or net asset of a pension plan was determined as of the first day of the fiscal year in which SFAS No. 87 was first applied or if applicable, the measurement date immediately preceding that day. The initial unrecognized net obligation or net asset was equal to the difference between the PBO and fair value of pension plan assets (plus previously recognized unfunded accrued pension cost or less previously recognized prepaid pension cost).

A schedule was set up to amortize the initial unrecognized net obligation or net asset on a straight-line basis over the average remaining service period of employees expected to receive benefits under the plan, except under the following circumstances:

- If the average remaining service period was less than 15 years, an employer could elect to use 15 years.
- If the plan was composed of all or substantially all inactive participants, the employer should use those participants' average remaining life expectancy as the amortization period.

(e) PLAN ASSETS. Pension plan assets generally consist of equity or debt securities, real estate, or other investments, which may be sold or transferred by the plan, that typically have been segregated and restricted in a trust. In contrast to SFAS No. 35, for purposes of SFAS No. 87, plan assets exclude contributions due but unpaid by the plan sponsor. Also excluded are assets that are not restricted to provide plan benefits such as so-called rabbi trusts in which earmarked funds are available to satisfy judgment creditors.

Pension plan assets that are held as an investment to provide pension benefits are to be measured at fair value as of the date of the financial statements or, if used consistently from year to year, as of a date not more than three months prior to that date (this date is defined by the Statement as the measurement date).

In the context of SFAS No. 87, fair value is defined as the amount that a pension plan trustee could reasonably expect to receive from the sale of a plan asset between a willing and informed buyer and a willing and informed seller. The FASB believes that fair value is the appropriate measurement for pension plan assets because it provides the more relevant information in assessing both the plan's ability to pay pension benefits as they become due and the future contributions necessary to provide for unfunded pension benefits already promised.

If an active market exists for a plan investment, fair value is determined by the quoted market price. If an active market does not exist for a particular plan investment, selling prices for similar investments, if available, should be appropriately considered. If no active market exists, an estimate of the fair value of the plan investment may be based on its projected cash flow, provided that appropriate consideration is given to current discount rates and the investment risk involved.

Pension plan assets that are used in the actual everyday operations of a plan—buildings, lease-hold improvements, furniture, equipment, and fixtures—should be valued at historical cost less accumulated depreciation or amortization.

(f) RECOGNITION OF LIABILITIES AND ASSETS. SFAS No. 87 retained the requirement of APB No. 8 to reflect either a liability (accrued pension cost) or an asset (prepaid pension cost) in an employer's statement of financial condition for the difference between the pension cost accrued by the employer and the amount actually contributed to the pension plan. However, the Statement introduced a radically new concept to sponsor accounting—the recognition of an additional minimum pension liability.

An additional minimum pension liability must be recorded to the extent that an unfunded ABO (taking into consideration any contribution paid by the employer between the measurement date and the date of the financial statements) exceeds the liability for unfunded accrued pension cost.

There is no additional minimum pension liability in either of the two following situations:

- There is no unfunded ABO (i.e., the fair value of plan assets is greater than the ABO).
- If there is an unfunded ABO and the amount of the accrued pension cost is more than the unfunded ABO.

If a prepaid pension asset and unfunded ABO exist, the minimum liability that is recorded equals the sum of the prepaid amount and the unfunded ABO. If there is an unfunded ABO and the accrued pension cost is more than the unfunded ABO, the minimum liability recorded equals the difference between the accrued pension cost and the unfunded ABO. If an additional minimum liability is recognized, an equal amount of intangible asset should be recorded provided the asset recognized does not exceed any unrecognized prior service cost plus any unrecognized net liability (but not net asset) at the date of initial application of SFAS No. 87. If the additional liability exceeds the sum of the preceding two items, SFAS No. 130 requires the remaining debit balance to be reflected on the balance sheet as accumulated other comprehensive income, net of related tax benefits. The change in accumulated other comprehensive income from the prior year is reflected on the income statement as a charge to other comprehensive income.

The additional liability, intangible asset, and other comprehensive income are reestablished at each measurement date, and the amounts previously presented on the balance sheet are reversed. No amortization of the additional liability or intangible asset is required or permitted.

The additional liability is determined separately for each plan—an employer may not reduce the additional liability for one plan by the excess of plan assets in another.

(g) INTERIM MEASUREMENTS.   Generally, the determination of interim pension cost should be based on assumptions used as of the previous year-end measurements. Similarly, any additional minimum liability recognized in the year-end financial statements should be carried forward, after adjustment for subsequent accruals and contributions. If, however, more recent measurements of plan assets and pension obligations are available, or if a significant event occurs that ordinarily would call for such measurements (i.e., a plan amendment), that updated information should be used.

(h) FINANCIAL STATEMENT DISCLOSURES.   SFAS No. 132, issued in 1998, replaced the disclosure requirements under SFAS No. 87, 88, and 106 in an attempt to make disclosures more "comparable, understandable, and concise." In 2003, SFAS No. 132-R was released, amending the disclosure requirements originally promulgated under SFAS No. 132. Additional disclosures in a number of areas were required and interim reporting was substantially enhanced.

For a defined benefit plan, the following must be disclosed on an annual basis:

- The measurement date
- The ABO
- A reconciliation of the PBO from the beginning of the year to the end of the year
- A reconciliation of the fair value of plan assets from the beginning of the year to the end of the year
- The net amount recognized, shown as a total of:
  ○ The funded status of the plans (calculated as assets minus liabilities), unrecognized actuarial gain or loss, unrecognized prior service cost, and unrecognized obligation or asset existing at the initial application of SFAS No. 87
  ○ The prepaid benefit cost, accrued benefit liability, intangible asset, and accumulated other comprehensive income
- The net periodic benefit cost recognized (separated into its component parts)
- Discount rate used to value liabilities, rate of compensation increase assumed (for pay-related plans), and the expected long-term rate of return on plan assets used to determine the current year's disclosure information, the current year's expense information, the prior year's disclosure information, and the prior year's expense information
- A projection of the benefit payments for each of the subsequent five plan years and in aggregate for plan years six through ten
- A statement of the cash contribution expected to be made
- A schedule showing the current and prior year's asset allocation divided into broad asset classes such as equities, fixed income, real estate, and so on.
- A narrative description of the investment policies and strategies, including target allocation percentages
- A narrative description of the basis used to determine the assumption(s) as to overall expected long-term rate of return on assets

In addition, there are several items that must be disclosed if applicable: securities of the employer in plan assets, alternative amortization methods, substantive commitments (to make future benefit increases, for example), costs and description of special or contractual termination benefits, and an explanation of any other significant change not otherwise apparent in the disclosures.

The disclosures for all of an employer's defined benefit pension plans may be aggregated. However, if disclosures are aggregated, it is required to disclose the aggregate PBO and aggregate fair value of plan assets for plans with PBO in excess of plan assets. In addition, it is required to disclose the aggregate ABO and aggregate fair value of plan assets for plans with ABO in excess of plan assets.

Exhibit 38.3 is a sample disclosure. Footnotes are included for information purposes only and would not need to be included in actual disclosures.

A nonpublic entity may elect a "shorter disclosure." "Nonpublic entity" is defined in SFAS No. 132 as "any entity other than one (a) whose debt or equity securities trade in a public market either on a stock exchange (domestic or foreign) or in the over-the-counter market, including securities

	20X6	20X5
Measurement date	10/1/20X5	10/1/20X4
Accumulated benefit obligation	6,200	5,800
Change in benefit obligation		
Benefit obligation at beginning of year	6,500[1]	6,405
Service cost	90	85
Interest cost	515	490
Actuarial loss	53	(35)
Benefits paid	(460)	(445)
Amendments	264	0
Benefit obligation at end of year	6,962	6,500
Change in plan assets		
Fair value of plan assets at beginning of year	5,850[2]	5,235
Actual return on plan assets	178	260
Employer contributions	550	800
Benefits paid	(460)	(445)
Fair value of plan assets at end of year	6,118	5,850
Funded status	(844)[3]	(650)
Unrecognized actuarial loss	1,192[4]	840
Unrecognized prior service cost	657[5]	450
Net amount recognized	1,005[6]	640
Amounts recognized in the statement of financial position consist of:		
Prepaid benefit cost	1,005	640
Accrued benefit liability	(1,3087)	0
Intangible asset	657	0
Accumulated other comprehensive income	430	0
Net amount recognized	1,005[7]	640[8]
Components of net periodic benefit cost		
Service cost	90	85
Interest cost	515	490
Expected return on plan assets	(493)	(428)
Amortization of prior service cost	57	57
Recognized actuarial loss	16	38
Net periodic benefit cost	185[9]	166

(Continues)

Exhibit 38.3   Sample Disclosure for Public Entity.

	20X6	20X5
Weighted-average assumptions used to determine		
expense for the fiscal year ended December 31		
Discount rate	7.50%	8.25%
Expected return on plan assets	8.50%	8.75%
Rate of compensation increase	5.00%	5.25%
Weighted-average assumptions used to determine		
PBO and other liabilities at December 31		
Discount rate	6.75%	7.50%
Rate of compensation increase	5.00%	5.00%
Expected Benefit Payments		
20X7		350
20X8		325
20X9		330
20(X+1)0		340
20(X+1)1		310
20(X+1)2 − 20y6		1,675
Expected contributions during fiscal 20X7		875

[1.] Several possibilities for change in benefit obligation are not listed here: plan participants' contributions, foreign currency exchange rate changes, business combinations, divestitures, curtailments, settlements, and special termination benefits.

[2.] Several possibilities for change in fair value of assets are not listed here: plan participants' contributions, business combinations, divestitures, settlements, and foreign exchange rate changes.

[3.] For the year ending 20X6, calculated as assets minus liabilities (6,118–6,962).

[4.] Liability loss of 53 during 20X6 (given in "change in benefit obligation"). Asset loss of 315 during 20X6: expected return was 493 (part of the net periodic benefit cost), actual was 178 (part of the change in plan assets), 493 − 178 = 315. Total loss during year of 315 + 53 = 368. Last year's loss was 840, amortized 16 during the year (part of net periodic benefit cost), adding on more loss of 368, gives total unrecognized gain of 840 − 16 + 368 = 1,192.

[5.] 450 in prior service cost last year. Amortized 57 during year (part of the net periodic benefit cost). Added a plan amendment of 264 (part of change in benefit obligation), leaving prior service cost at end of year of 450 − 57 + 264 = 657.

[6.] Net amounts recognized can include unrecognized net obligation or net asset from initial application of FAS No. 87.

[7.] Assume the ABO at 12/31/20X5 is 5,800. Since there is no unfunded ABO, there is no other comprehensive income (no matter how large the prepaid asset).

[8.] Amount of gain or loss due to a settlement or curtailment, if applicable, would be included in the net periodic benefit cost.

Exhibit 38.4   Continued.

quoted only locally or regionally, (b) that makes a filing with a regulatory agency in preparation for the sale of any class of debt or equity securities in a public market, or (c) that is controlled by an entity covered by (a) or (b)."

The "shorter disclosure" must contain the following:

- The measurement date used to determine benefit obligations
- The ABO, PBO, fair value of plan assets, and funded status of the plan (i.e., no reconciliation from the beginning of year to end of year is necessary)

- Employer contributions, participant contributions, and benefits paid
- The net amount recognized, shown as a total of the prepaid benefit cost, accrued benefit liability, intangible asset, and accumulated other comprehensive income
- The net periodic benefit cost recognized
- Discount rate used to value liabilities, rate of compensation increase assumed (for pay-related plans), and the expected long-term rate of return on plan assets used to determine the current year's disclosure information, the current year's expense information, the prior year's disclosure information, and the prior year's expense information
- A projection of the benefit payments for each of the subsequent five plan years and in aggregate for plan years six through ten
- A statement of the cash contribution expected to be made
- A schedule showing the current and prior year's asset allocation divided into broad asset classes such as equities, fixed income, real estate, and so on.
- A schedule showing the current and prior year's asset allocation divided into broad asset classes such as equities, fixed income, real estate, and so on.
- A narrative description of the investment policies and strategies, including target allocation percentages
- A narrative description of the basis used to determine the assumption(s) for overall expected long-term rate of return on assets

In addition, securities of the employer in plan assets must be disclosed (if applicable). Finally, the nature and effect of significant nonroutine events (amendments, divestitures, curtailments, etc.) must be disclosed.

Exhibit 38.4 shows a sample disclosure that could be used for a nonpublic entity instead of the one in Exhibit 38.3.

In addition to the preceding changes to the annual disclosure requirements, SFAS No. 132-R added disclosure requirements in interim financial statements. Public companies must disclose the amount of net periodic benefit cost for the period (separated into its component parts). Public and nonpublic companies must disclose the total amount of the employer's contributions paid, and expected to be paid during the current fiscal year, if significantly different from amounts previously disclosed.

(i) Annuity Contracts. All or part of an employer's obligation to provide pension plan benefits to employees may be effectively transferred to an insurance company by the purchase of annuity contracts. An annuity contract is an irrevocable agreement in which an insurance company unconditionally agrees to provide specific benefits to designated individuals, in return for a fixed consideration or premium. Hence, by purchasing an annuity contract, an employer transfers to the insurer its legal obligation, and the attendant risks, to provide pension benefits. For purposes of SFAS No. 87, an annuity contract does not qualify unless the risks and rewards associated with the assets and obligations assumed by the insurance company are actually transferred to the insurance company by the sponsor.

An annuity contract may be participating or nonparticipating. In a participating annuity contract, the insurance company's investment experience with the funds received for the annuity contract are shared, in the form of dividends, with the purchaser (the employer or the pension fund). The purchase price of a participating annuity is ordinarily higher than that for a nonparticipating annuity, with the excess representing the value of the participation right (i.e., expected future dividends). This excess should be recognized as a plan asset.

Benefits covered by annuity contracts are excluded from the benefit obligations of the plan. The annuity contracts themselves are not counted as plan assets, except for the cost of any participation rights. If any benefits earned in the current period are covered by annuity contracts, the cost of such benefits is equal to the cost to purchase the annuities less any participation right.

	20X6	20X5
Accumulated benefit obligation	6,962	6,500
Projected benefit obligation at December 31	6,962	6,500
Fair value of plan assets at December 31	6,118	5,850
Funded status	(844)	(650)
Prepaid (accrued) benefit cost recognized in the statement of financial position	1,005	640
Amounts recognized in the statement of financial position consist of:		
Prepaid benefit cost	1,005	640
Accrued benefit liability	(1,387)	
Intangible asset	657	
Accumulated other comprehensive income	730	
Net amount recognized	1,005	640
Weighted-average assumptions used to determine expense for the fiscal year ended December 31		
Discount rate	7.50%	8.25%
Expected return on plan assets	8.50%	8.75%
Rate of compensation increase	5.00%	5.25%
Weighted-average assumptions used to determine PBO and other liabilities at December 31		
Discount rate	6.75%	7.50%
Rate of compensation increase	5.00%	5.00%
Components of net periodic benefit cost		
Benefit cost	185	166
Employer contribution	550	800
Plan participants' contributions	0	0
Benefits paid	460	445

Exhibit 38.4   Sample Postretirement Medical Disclosures for a Nonpublic Company.

Annuity contracts issued by a captive insurance company are not considered annuities for the purpose of SFAS No. 87, since the risk associated with the benefit obligations remains substantially with the employer. Similarly, if there is reasonable doubt that the insurance company will meet its obligations under the contract, it is not considered an annuity contract.

Insurance contracts that are not in substance annuity contracts are accounted for as pension plan assets and are measured at fair value. If a contract has a determinable cash surrender value or conversion value, that is presumed to be its fair value.

A pension fund may have structured a portfolio of fixed-income investments with a cash flow designed to match expected benefit payment. Known as a *dedicated bond portfolio*, its purpose is to protect the pension fund against swings in interest rates. For the purposes of SFAS No. 87, a dedicated bond portfolio is not an annuity contract even if it is managed to remove all or most of the investment risk associated with covered benefit payments.

(i) DEFINED CONTRIBUTION PENSION PLANS.   A defined contribution pension plan provides for employer contributions that are defined in the plan. A defined contribution plan maintains individual accounts for each plan participant and contains terms that specify how contributions are allocated among participants' individual accounts. Pension benefits are based solely on the amount available in each participant's account at the time of retirement. The amount available in each participant's account at the time of retirement is the total of the amounts contributed by the employer, the returns earned on investments of those contributions, and forfeitures of other participants' accounts that have been allocated to the participant's account.

Under SFAS No. 87, the net periodic pension cost of a defined contribution pension plan is the amount of contributions for the period in which services are rendered by the employees. If a plan calls for contributions after an individual retires or terminates, the estimated cost should be accrued during periods in which the individual performs services.

An employer that sponsors one or more defined contribution pension plans discloses the following information separately from its defined benefit pension plan disclosures:

- A description of the plan(s) including employee groups covered, the basis for determining contributions, and the nature and effect of significant matters affecting comparability of information for all periods presented
- The amount of pension cost recognized during the period

For the purposes of SFAS No. 87, any plan that is not a defined contribution pension plan is considered a defined benefit pension plan.

(j) NON-U.S. PENSION PLANS. SFAS No. 87 does not make any special provision for non-U.S. pension plans. In some foreign countries it is customary or required for an employer to provide benefits for employees in the event of voluntary or involuntary severance of employment. In this event, if the substance of the arrangement is a pension plan (i.e., benefits are paid for substantially all terminations), it is subject to the provisions of SFAS No. 87.

The discount rate used for valuing liabilities for non-U.S. plans should be based on the yields available on bonds issued in the country where the plan exists. Therefore, most companies with international operations will have discount rates for valuing non-U.S. plans that are well below the rates used for valuing U.S. liabilities.

Plans in Puerto Rico or other U.S. territories are considered U.S. plans.

(k) MULTIEMPLOYER PLANS. A multiemployer plan is a plan to which more than one employer contributes, usually pursuant to a labor union agreement. Under these plans, contributions are pooled and separate employer accounts do not exist. As a result, assets contributed by one employer may be used to provide benefits to the employees of other participating employers.

SFAS No. 87 provides no change in the accounting for multiemployer plans. A participating employer should recognize pension cost equal to the contribution required to the plan for the period. The disclosures required by the Statement for multiemployer plans are similar to those for defined contribution pension plans—a description of the plan, including the employee groups covered and type of benefits provided, and the amount of pension cost recognized in the period.

An underfunded multiemployer plan may assess a withdrawing employer a portion of its unfunded benefit obligations. If this withdrawal liability becomes either probable or reasonably possible, the provisions of SFAS No. 5, "Accounting for Contingencies," apply.

(l) MULTIPLE EMPLOYER PLANS. A multiple employer plan is similar to a multiemployer plan except that it usually does not include any labor union agreement. It is treated under ERISA as a collection of single-employer plans sponsored by the respective participating employers. If separate asset allocation is maintained among the participating employers (even though pooled for investment purposes), SFAS No. 87 applies individually to each employer with respect to its interest and benefit obligations within the plan. If assets are not allocated among the participating employers (e.g., when a number of subsidiaries participate in a plan sponsored by their parent), the organization sponsoring the plan, if one exists, should account for the plan as a single-employer plan, whereas each participating employer should account for this arrangement as a multiemployer plan in its separate financial statements. Disclosure of net periodic pension cost and the reconciliation of the funded status should be for the plan as a whole, with each participating employer further disclosing its own pension cost with respect to this arrangement.

(m) FUNDING AND INCOME TAX ACCOUNTING.   SFAS No. 87 does not address funding considerations, other than to recognize that there may be differences between reported net periodic pension cost and funding. The IRS regulations recognize the projected unit credit method as one of several acceptable funding methods. However, when employing the projected unit credit method and the same explicit assumptions used to calculate net periodic pension cost, the range between the permissible maximum and minimum funding amount may not bracket the net periodic pension cost. This can be caused by the difference in amortization periods for unrecognized pension costs and limitation imposed by the tax law on contributions to relatively well-funded plans. In general, the objective of matching expensing and funding of net periodic pension cost may no longer be appropriate due to tax, legal, and cash flow considerations. In this regard companies must continue to provide deferred taxes, where appropriate, for these differences.

The method of accounting for income taxes—particularly the way deferred taxes are calculated—was changed by SFAS No. 109, "Accounting for Income Taxes." Its focus is on an asset and liability approach, as opposed to an income statement approach. On a simplified basis, deferred taxes are calculated by applying the tax rates enacted for future years to differences between the financial statement carrying amounts and the tax bases of assets and liabilities. These differences are known as *temporary differences*.

Temporary differences frequently will arise as a result of differences between the tax basis of pension assets and liabilities and the amounts recognized under SFAS No. 87. For example, assuming that a company funds the pension cost to the extent deductible for tax purposes, a pension asset (prepaid pension cost) will be recognized when the amount funded is in excess of pension cost determined under SFAS No. 87. A pension liability (accrued pension cost) will be recognized when the amount funded is less than the pension cost determined under SFAS No. 87. In addition, settlement gains and losses recognized under SFAS No. 88 will create temporary differences because the transactions generally are not taxable or deductible at the date recognized for financial reporting purposes. Because of the complexities of accounting for pensions, numerous other situations will result in temporary differences.

38.3 SPONSOR ACCOUNTING FOR NONRECURRING EVENTS

(a) OVERVIEW.   An integral concept of pension accounting is that certain pension obligations should be recognized over time rather than immediately. They include gains and losses from experience different from that assumed, the effects of changes in actuarial assumptions on the pension obligations, the cost of retroactive plan amendments, and any unrecognized net obligation or asset at transition established when the plan first complied with SFAS No. 87. The premise of this delayed recognition is that plan amendments are made in anticipation of economic benefits that the employer may derive over the future service periods of its employees, and that gains or losses already incurred may be reversed in the future. When events happen that fundamentally alter or eliminate the premise for delayed recognition, immediate recognition of previously unrecognized amounts may be required.

Examples of such special events include business combinations, addressed in paragraph 74 of SFAS No. 87; and settlements, curtailments, and termination benefits, the subjects of SFAS No. 88, which is effective simultaneously with SFAS No. 87. Thus an employer generally may not, for instance, follow the SFAS No. 88 accounting for a settlement unless SFAS No. 87 has been adopted. Relevant paragraphs of APB Opinion Nos. 8 and 16 are superseded by these new statements, as is SFAS No. 74 in its entirety.

Although prior accounting opinions and statements, such as APB Opinion No. 8, did require immediate recognition of gains or losses in certain situations, they did not define the methodology by which the special pension recognition should be carried out. As a result, widely divergent practices evolved, with differing effects on the affected employers' subsequent pension costs. In contrast, the new accounting provisions for nonrecurring events are based on standardized measurement methods that are applied within the general framework of SFAS No. 87. As with that

Statement, SFAS No. 88 focuses on proper accounting of events in the future and generally allows plans to begin with a clean slate at the initial compliance date regardless of how such events were handled previously. There is also an exception for immaterial items.

(b) SETTLEMENT. To constitute a settlement, a transaction must (1) be irrevocable, (2) relieve the employer of primary responsibility for a pension benefit obligation, and (3) eliminate significant risks related to the obligations and the assets used to effect the settlement. This is a new accounting concept introduced by SFAS No. 88.

The most common type of settlement is the purchase of nonparticipating annuities for or lump-sum cash payments to plan participants to discharge all or part of the benefit obligation of the plan, which may or may not be connected with a plan termination. (A participating annuity allows the purchaser to participate in the investment performance and possibly other experience—for example, mortality experience—of the insurance company, through dividends or rate credits. It generally costs more than a nonparticipating annuity, which is based on a fixed price.) Although SFAS No. 88 extends condition (2) in the preceding paragraph to include a transaction that relieves the plan of the responsibility for the benefit obligation, that condition is generally not sufficient, for example, if the benefit obligation is transferred to another plan sponsored by the same or a related employer, or if the annuities are purchased from a subsidiary of the employer.

(i) Timing. The timing of the settlement recognition depends on when all three qualifying conditions for a settlement have been met. For example, a commitment to purchase annuity is not sufficient to constitute a settlement until the benefit obligation risk has been transferred to the insurance company and the premium for the annuities has been paid in cash or in kind, except for minor adjustments. Although a dedicated portfolio designed to match the estimated benefit payments under the plan may eliminate the investment risk on assets backing those payments, it does not constitute a settlement because the plan continues to be exposed to the mortality risk on those payments and also because the portfolio is not irrevocable.

(ii) Gain or Loss. The maximum gain or loss subject to settlement recognition is the unrecognized net gain or loss in the plan at the date of settlement, plus any remaining unrecognized net asset (but not a net obligation) at transition. The magnitude of the PBO to be settled, as determined by the employer prior to the settlement, is generally not the same as the cost to discharge that obligation, such as the premium for the annuities, and must first be set equal to the latter. This adjustment in the PBO generates a gain or loss that is added to unrecognized net gain or loss before the settlement recognition is done. The amount of the settlement gain or loss is equal to the maximum gain or loss subject to settlement recognition multiplied by the settlement percentage, which is the percentage of the PBO of the plan being settled. Computations described in this paragraph are generally performed on a plan-by-plan basis rather than by aggregating all of the employer's plans.

(iii) Use of Participating Annuities. Participating annuities are acceptable instruments to effect a settlement, unless their substance is that the employer remains subject to all or most of the risks and rewards associated with the benefit obligation covered by the annuities or the assets transferred to the insurance company. If the purchase of a participating annuity constitutes a settlement, the maximum gain (but not the maximum loss) must first be reduced by the cost of the participation feature. This means that the participation feature of the annuity contract is excluded from the settlement recognition entirely and its value, which is the present value of the future dividends expected from the insurance company, is carried as a plan asset.

SFAS No. 88 also permits a de minimis exemption from settlement recognition if the total cash and annuity settlements in a year do not exceed the sum of the service cost and interest cost components of the net periodic pension cost, provided this accounting practice is followed consistently from year to year.

(c) CURTAILMENT.   A curtailment is an event that significantly reduces the expected years of future service of present employees covered by the plan or eliminates for a significant number of employees covered by the plan the accrual of defined benefit for some or all of their future services. It is possible for an event, such as a window retirement program, to change significantly the benefit obligation but not the total expected future services and, therefore, not to be a curtailment. Unrelated, individually insignificant reductions in future services do not qualify as a curtailment even if they occur in a single year and are significant in aggregate. Conversely, a series of individually insignificant reductions in future services, which are caused by the same event but take place over more than one fiscal year, should be aggregated to determine if the reduction is sufficiently significant to constitute a curtailment.

Examples of curtailment include reduction in workforce, closing of a facility with the employees not employed elsewhere by the employer, disposal of a business segment, window retirement program, termination of a defined benefit plan, or freezing of the benefits thereunder. A process known as *termination/reestablishment*, whereby an employer terminates a defined benefit plan, recovers the surplus plan assets, and then establishes a new plan for the same employees that provides the same overall benefits as the terminated plan when benefits from the terminated plan are taken into account, is not a curtailment because the employer's benefit obligation has not been materially altered. Even if the new plan created through the termination/reestablishment process does not reproduce the same overall benefits, the transaction should be treated as a plan amendment and not a curtailment. Similarly, if the employees are covered by multiple plans and the suspension of their benefit accrual under one plan is wholly or partially balanced by increased benefit accrual under another plan of the same or a related employer (e.g., a supplemental retirement plan providing defined benefits, which is offset by the benefits from the suspended plan), the event should be treated not as a curtailment but as simultaneous amendments to the two plans: one reduces benefits and one increases benefits.

The curtailment gain or loss to be recognized is the sum of the prior service cost recognition and the PBO adjustment, both determined on a plan-by-plan basis rather than by aggregating all of the employer's plans.

According to statements made by the FASB staff, the prior service cost recognition is intended to be the immediate recognition of any unrecognized prior service cost and any remaining unrecognized net obligation (but not a net asset) at transition that relate to those employees whose services have been curtailed. Since these two items are often not available for specific employees or groups of employees, SFAS No. 88 provides a general rule to compute the prior service cost recognition as the product of any unrecognized net obligation at transition, or any prior service cost related to the entire plan, and the applicable curtailment percentages. The curtailment percentage is the percentage reduction in the remaining expected future years of service associated with the prior service cost or the net obligation at transition; it is determined separately for each prior service cost and the net obligation at transition. To reduce computational complexity, it is common practice to use an alternative curtailment percentage such as the percentage reduction in future years of service of all employees immediately prior to the curtailment, provided that the results would not be materially distorted.

The PBO adjustment can be a gain or a loss. If the curtailment reduces the PBO, the reduction is applied first against any unrecognized net loss in the plan and the residual amount is recognized as a gain. If the curtailment increases the PBO, the increase is applied first against any unrecognized net gain and any remaining unrecognized net asset at transition, and the residual amount is recognized as a loss.

The timing of the curtailment recognition depends on whether the net effect is a gain or a loss. A net gain is recognized when the event has occurred, whereas a net loss is recognized when the event appears probable and its effects are reasonably estimable.

Although paragraph 31 of APB Opinion No. 8 had required immediate recognition of any actuarial gains or losses resulting from unusual events, SFAS No. 88 further specifies the conditions necessitating the immediate recognition and the method of determining the amount to be recognized, thus greatly narrowing down the divergence of practice that prevailed prior to SFAS No. 88.

(d) DISPOSAL OF A BUSINESS. When an employer disposes of a business segment, its pension plan may experience a curtailment, due to the termination of some employees' services, and a settlement, if all or part of the benefit obligation is transferred to the purchaser. Certain termination benefits, such as severance payments, may also be involved. The effects of such curtailment, settlement, and termination benefits should be determined in accordance with SFAS No. 88 and then included in the gain or loss on the disposal pursuant to paragraphs 15–17 of APB Opinion No. 30, "Reporting the Results of Operations—Reporting the Effects of Disposal of a Segment of a Business and Extraordinary, Unusual and Infrequently Occurring Events and Transactions," except for the following modifications to the SFAS No. 88 measurements: (1) the curtailment recognition is made regardless of whether the reduction in future services is significant; (2) the de minimis exemption for settlements does not apply; and (3) the difference between any benefit obligation and plan assets transferred to the purchaser is recognized in full as a gain or loss before the settlement percentage is determined. However, if the settlement, by purchasing annuities, for example, could have taken place in the absence of the business disposal, the settlement recognition should not be included in the gain or loss on the disposal.

(e) PLAN MERGER, SPINOFF, AND TERMINATION. The merger of two or more pension plans of the same employer does not require any SFAS No. 88 recognition. Prior service costs should be amortized as before. The remaining unrecognized net obligations or assets at transition should be netted and amortized over a reasonably weighted average of the remaining amortization periods previously used by the separate plans. The unrecognized net gains or losses should be aggregated and the minimum amortization thereof should reflect the average remaining service period of the combined employee group.

Spinoff of a portion of a pension plan to an unrelated employer, as may happen after the sale of a business segment, should be handled as a settlement unless there is reasonable doubt that the purchaser will meet the benefit obligation and the seller remains contingently liable for it. A settlement does not occur if an employer divides a pension plan into two or more plans all sponsored by it. In that case any remaining unrecognized net obligation or asset should be allocated among the plans in proportion to their respective PBOs, as should any unrecognized net gain or loss. Any unrecognized prior service cost should be allocated on the basis of the participants in the surviving plans.

If one of these surviving plans is further transferred to a subsidiary, the employer should reduce its prepaid (accrued) pension cost by the amount of prepaid (accrued) pension cost related to the transferred plan and simultaneously record a decrease (increase) in its stockholders' equity by the same amount. The subsidiary, on the other hand, should record the transferred prepaid (accrued) pension cost as an asset liability and an equal amount as an increase (decrease) in its stockholders' equity.

Prior to SFAS No. 88, the accounting effect of the termination of a defined benefit plan was largely based on the amount of surplus assets or deficit in the plan. If surplus assets were returned to the employer and there was no successor defined benefit plan, the previously unrecognized amount was typically reflected in the employer's earnings over a period of 10–20 years. SFAS No. 88 changed entirely the accounting concept relating to a plan termination. First of all, any remaining unrecognized gain from a prior asset reversion, which had been accomplished through a settlement as defined by SFAS No. 88, was recognized immediately upon the initial application date of the Statement as the effect of a change in accounting principle, to the extent that plan assets plus (minus) accrued (prepaid) pension cost exceeded the PBO. There would be no further amortization of the remaining amount since it was already reflected in the size of the unrecognized net obligation or asset at transition. The second change introduced by SFAS No. 88 is that a plan termination is accounted for as a combination of a curtailment (i.e., elimination of further benefit accrual, assuming that there is not a successor defined benefit plan) and a settlement. Indeed, the asset reversion is no longer the triggering event, and substantially the same accounting effect has been achieved when the benefit accrual is frozen and the benefit obligation settled, even if the plan is not terminated. Any excise tax related to the asset reversion should be recognized at the time of the reversion. As noted in Subsection 32.3(c), the termination/reestablishment of a defined benefit plan does not constitute a curtailment, but it may nevertheless require a settlement recognition.

Withdrawal from a multiemployer plan may result in additional cost to the employer. The effect of the withdrawal should be recognized when it becomes probable or reasonably possible.

(f) TERMINATION BENEFITS.   In 1983, SFAS No. 74, "Accounting for Special Termination Benefits Paid to Employees," was issued ostensibly to address window retirement programs and shutdown benefits. Although it required recognition of the effects of any changes on the previously accrued expenses for those benefits, no recognition method was defined and compliance with the Statement was not widespread.

SFAS No. 88 superseded SFAS No. 74, and as with that Statement, it deals with both pension and nonpension benefits such as severance payments, supplemental unemployment benefits, and life and health insurance benefits, regardless of whether they are paid by a plan or directly by the employer. The amount to be recognized is the amount of any immediate payments plus the present value of any expected future payments. The cost of special termination benefits that are offered only for a short period of time should be recognized when the employees accept the offer and the amount can be reasonably estimated. In contrast, contractual termination benefits, which are required by the terms of a plan only if a specified event (such as a plant closing) occurs, should be recognized when it is probable that employees will be entitled to benefits and the amount can be reasonably estimated.

Keep in mind that a situation involving termination benefits often also involves a curtailment. The curtailment recognition is first determined using the benefit obligation without the termination benefits. The effect of the termination benefits is then the difference between the benefit obligations determined with and without the termination benefits.

It is not unusual, in the measurement of the PBO and the pension cost of a plan, to assume some probability for events that may give rise to termination benefits. In such a situation, the amount of termination benefits to be recognized under SFAS No. 88 is the difference between the PBO including the termination benefits and that measured without any termination benefit. For example, a plan may permit early retirement after age 55 with a reduced pension but provide an unreduced pension regardless of age in the event of a change in control of the employer. When a change in control occurs, the amount of termination benefit to be recognized for an employee who is age 40 is the difference in the value of his unreduced pension commencing immediately and his reduced pension commencing when he will reach age 55. Furthermore, if the situation constitutes a curtailment, the PBO adjustment is the difference between the value of his reduced pension commencing at age 55 and his PBO determined using the regular actuarial assumptions including, if applicable, an allowance for some probability that change-in-control benefits may be invoked. It would not be reasonable to treat the entire change in PBO as a gain or loss or to handle the situation solely as a curtailment, merely because the assumptions used to determine the PBO prior to the change of control included some allowance for change-in-control benefits.

(g) BUSINESS COMBINATIONS.   SFAS No. 141, issued in June 2001, supersedes APB Opinion No. 16 and precludes the use of the pooling-of-interest method for business combinations. Under the Statement, all business combinations must be accounted for under the purchase method. Using the purchase method, the purchaser should record a liability (accrued pension cost) equal to the excess of the acquired PBO over the acquired plan assets, or an asset (prepaid pension cost) equal to the excess of the acquired plan assets over the acquired PBO. Simultaneous with the recording of such purchase accounting liability (asset), goodwill is increased (decreased) by an equal amount. Once these adjustments have been made, any previously existing unrecognized prior service cost, net obligation, or asset at transition and net gain or loss are eliminated and no further amortization of them will be needed. If the acquired company continues to issue its own separate financial statement, after the purchase date, its pension cost may be determined without the purchase accounting adjustment and may therefore be different from the pension cost reported by the parent company on its behalf.

The measurement date for the purchase accounting adjustment is the acquisition date, even if the employer customarily uses a measurement date different from its fiscal year end for all other aspects of SFAS No. 87. In determining the PBO at the acquisition date, the effects of certain postacquisition events should be reflected. Examples of such events include curtailments (without regard to the significance criterion), termination benefits, and plan amendments that were highly probably at the time of the purchase. To be included in the purchase accounting, these events generally must either occur, or be substantially decided upon, within one year of the acquisition date.

Similar purchase accounting adjustments may also be made for postretirement and postemployment benefits. The restructuring of a company including merger of two or more legal entities generally does not trigger a purchase accounting adjustment for pensions.

(h) SEQUENCE OF MEASUREMENT STEPS.   In a year containing one of the unusual events described above, the employer's pension cost comprises (1) the net periodic pension cost for the period prior to the event, determined without regard to the event; (2) the effect of the event such as the curtailment or settlement recognition; and (3) the net periodic pension cost for the period subsequent to the event, fully reflecting the changes resulting from the event. The preevent pension cost in (1) is generally based on the assumptions, such as the discount rate, used for the previous year-end measurement. Updated PBO and plan assets are then determined as of the event date as if the event had not taken place, using assumptions that are appropriate at that date, including, if applicable, any adjustment to the PBO to reflect the actual cost of settling any benefit obligation. The prepaid (accrued) pension cost, as well as any unrecognized prior service cost, net obligation, or asset at transition and net gain or loss, is brought up to date. The effect of the event is next determined on the basis of the updated PBO and plan assets. The postevent pension cost in item (3) is based on the PBO, plan assets, prior service cost, unrecognized net obligation, or asset at transition and net gain or loss that remain after the event.

In determining the postevent pension cost, the remaining amortization period for any unrecognized net obligation or asset at transition will generally not be changed even though the amount to be amortized may have. Similarly, the remaining amortization schedule of any prior service cost will generally remain unchanged, unless the period during which the employer expects to realize future economic benefits from the plan amendment is shorter than originally estimated, or if the future economic benefits have been impaired. Amortization of net gain or loss, on the other hand, should reflect the postevent average remaining service period.

In case of multiple events occurring within one fiscal year, the process described in the preceding paragraphs may need to be repeated more than once, taking the events one at a time in chronological order. For simultaneous events, it is permissible to establish the presumed sequence unless there is compelling reason against the logic of that sequence, provided that the same approach is followed consistently in the future. The sequence selected can materially affect the amount of gain or loss to be recognized. It is also possible for events that originated from the situation to be recognized in different fiscal years, for example, when a plan is terminated in one year but the benefit obligation is not settled until the following year.

Special considerations are needed when the plan's measurement date differs from the employer's fiscal year end. It is generally not practical to measure the effect of the special event on any date other than the date of the event, since such measurement typically involves the changes in the PBO or plan assets on the event date, such as the amounts of benefit obligation and plan assets being transferred to another employer. One approach is to determine the effect of the event using benefit obligation, plan assets, and net gain or loss as of the event date, even though the preevent pension cost was computed using a measurement date different from the fiscal year end, and then determine the postevent pension cost for the period from the event date to the fiscal year end. However, the ensuing year-end measurement may again be done at a measurement date that is consistent with that used in the preceding year.

Gain or loss related to events occurring after the measurement date but prior to the employer's fiscal year end is generally not recognized in the current period, except when it relates to a disposal of business segment that is reflected in the current year or when it results from the termination of a pension plan without a successor defined benefit plan. Even if not recognized, the effect of the event should be disclosed if it is material. The preceding statements apply to quarterly financial statements as well.

(i) DISCLOSURE REQUIREMENTS FOR NONRECURRING EVENTS.   SFAS No. 132 requires the disclosure of nonrecurring events in the following ways:

- The change in PBO due to the nonrecurring event should be included in the reconciliation of PBO from the beginning of the year to the end of the year.
- The change in assets due to the nonrecurring event should be included in the reconciliation of assets from the beginning of the year to the end of the year.
- The amount of gain or loss recognized due to a settlement or curtailment should be included in the disclosure of the amount of net period benefit cost recognized.
- The cost of providing any special or contractual termination benefits recognized should be disclosed, as well as a description of the nature of the event.

Despite the nonrecurring nature of these events, such gain or loss is normally not an extraordinary item as defined in paragraphs 20–22 of APB Opinion No. 30. One exception is when the gain or loss is related to the disposal of a business segment.

(j) ILLUSTRATION—NONRECURRING EVENTS.   Exhibit 38.5 illustrates the application of SFAS No. 88 with respect to settlement, curtailment, and special termination benefits and that of SFAS No. 87 with respect to business combinations accounted for under the purchase method.

38.4 SPONSOR ACCOUNTING FOR NONQUALIFIED PLANS

(a) QUALIFIED VERSUS NONQUALIFIED PLANS.   Qualified pension plans present notable tax advantages to both employer and employee as a form of employee compensation. The immediate advantage to the employer is the ability to deduct currently, within limitations, contributions to

---

BACKGROUND INFORMATION AND ASSUMPTIONS

Company X, which was used to illustrate the application of SFAS No. 87, experienced the following events, all occurring on December 31, 20X3, and in the sequence shown below:

- The PBO for pensioners was $6,000 on December 31, 20X3. Company X purchased participating annuities at a cost of $6,200 to discharge this obligation, $600 of which would be expected to be refunded by the insurance company in the form of dividends in future years.
- Company X closed one of its major manufacturing plants and permanently laid off all its workers. These workers would have represented 20% of the future service of all of Company X's employees. The PBO with respect to these laid-off workers was $1,500 before the layoff and only $800 after the layoff, ignoring the special benefits described below.
- For those laid-off employees who were eligible for early retirement, Company X offered unreduced early retirement pensions and an additional supplemental pension up to age 62. If not for the plant closing, these employees would have been entitled to a reduced early retirement pension only and no supplement. The value of the supplements and the waiver of the early retirement reduction was $400.
- Also on December 31, 20X3, Company X acquired Company Y, which sponsored a defined benefit pension plan with a PBO of $1,000 and plan assets worth $1,400. Company X has not adopted SFAS No. 96.

Exhibit 38.5   Nonrecurring events.

EFFECT ON FUNDED STATUS ON DECEMBER 31, 20X3

	Initial Status	Effect of Settlement[1]	Effect of Curtailment[2]	Special Termination Benefit[3]	Acquisition of Company Y[4]	Revised Status
Projected benefit obligation	$ (16,600)	$ 6,200	$ 700	$(400)	$(1,000)	$(11,100)
Plan assets (fair value)	12,150	(5,600)	0	0	1,400	7,950
Funded status	$ (4,450)	$ 600	$ 700	$(400)	$ 400	$ (3,150)
Unrecognized net loss (gain)	967	(728)	(239)	0	0	0
Unrecognized prior service cost	1,690	0	(338)	0	0	1,352
Unrecognized net obligation at date of initial application	2,200	0	(440)	0	0	1,760
Prepaid (accrued) pension cost	$ 407	$ (128)	$(317)	$(400)	$ 172	$ (266)

[1] Although the price of the annuity contract was $6,200, the cost for SFAS No. 87 purposes is only $5,600 since $600 of future dividends are anticipated. The $600 will be carried as a plan asset.

In accounting for the settlement the following steps are followed:

First, the $16,600 PBO needs to be reevaluated because the PBO for pensioners was discovered to be $5,600 instead of $6,200. The revised PBO, therefore, is $16,000, of which $5,600 was settled through the annuity purchase. The settlement percentage is 35%.

Second, the unrecognized net loss is reduced from the $967 before the settlement by the $600 "savings" from the annuity contract, leaving a net loss of $367)

The settlement loss is $128 (i.e., $367 net loss times settlement percentage of 35%). This loss reduces the prepaid pension cost from $407 to $279.

[2] The 20% reduction in future services expected from the employee is significant enough to constitute a curtailment under SFAS No. 88. The curtailment gain/loss consists of two components—the prior service recognition and the PBO adjustment.

The curtailment loss is calculated as follows:

The remaining unrecognized prior service cost on December 31, 20X3, is $1,690 and the remaining transition obligation is $2,200 for a total of $3,890. The prior service cost recognition is 20% (the curtailment percentage) of the $3,890, or a $778 loss.

The PBO is reduced by $700 on account of the plant closing. However, since the plan still carries an unrecognized net loss of $239 at this point, the $700 saving must first be applied to eliminate the $239 unrecognized loss before the remaining $461 may be recognized as a PBO adjustment gain.

The net curtailment loss is $317 (the $778 prior service cost less the $461 PBO gain). This $317 loss results in an accrued pension cost of $38. The amortization of the prior service cost ($130 in 20X3) will be $160 in 19X4. The respective remaining amortization periods will nevertheless remain unchanged.

[3] The value of the special benefits ($400) is recognized in full immediately and further increases the accrued pension cost from $38 to $438.

[4] Company Y's plan has an excess of $400, the difference between the plan assets of $1,400 and the PBO of $1,000. The $400 excess (less $228 in deferred tax) is recognized in purchase accounting and added to goodwill. Meanwhile the accrued pension cost is reduced by $172, from $438 to $266.

Exhibit 38.5   Continued.

the plan. The employee on whose behalf the contribution is made does not, however, have to report the amount as gross income until it is made available to him. This deferral of tax has an added advantage since, in the typical case, benefits are not distributed until retirement, when the employee may be in a lower income tax bracket. The long-term, and perhaps the most important, tax advantage enjoyed by a qualified plan is that the fund or trust that receives and invests the contributions enjoys tax-exempt status. Investments earnings are not taxed until distributed, thus permitting an accelerated rate of growth for the fund.

For a pension plan to be considered qualified for income tax purposes, it must comply with certain IRC requirements, not only in the design of the plan but also in its operations. Some of these requirements are:

- The plan must not discriminate in favor of employees who are officers or shareholders or highly compensated.
- Benefits under the plan must be reasonable in amount when considered with other forms of compensation.
- Plan operations must be conducted in accordance with the plan document and trust agreement.
- The pension fund must be exclusively for the benefit of participants and their beneficiaries.
- The plan must comply with certain minimum funding and reporting requirements.

Over the years these requirements have become increasingly complex and burdensome, thus adding to the costs of administering qualified plans.

It has always been fairly common for an employer to maintain nonqualified retirement plans or to provide individualized deferred compensation arrangements for a selected group of management and highly compensated employees. There is no precise definition of "highly compensated employees" in this context, and it is not linked to the definition of "highly compensated employees" introduced by the Tax Reform Act of 1986. The primary advantages of such nonqualified arrangements are that (1) the coverage can be limited to only a few selected employees; (2) the benefits can be designed to meet the employer's objectives and the employees' needs without having to worry about the myriad of constraints imposed by ERISA and the Tax Code; and (3) they are exempt from virtually all ERISA reporting and funding requirements except a one-time notice of their existence to the DOL.

During the 1980s, the Tax Code was repeatedly amended to limit the amount of benefit that can be provided by, and the flexibility in the design of, a qualified plan. As a result, nonqualified plans gained increasing importance. Despite these advantages over qualified plans, a nonqualified plan suffers from a serious tax disadvantage. Contributions to the plan, if any, are not currently tax-deductible to the employer as long as the employees' rights to those contributions are subject to a substantial risk of forfeiture. Instead, the employer may deduct the benefits when they are paid. Moreover, there is no tax shelter for any fund that the employer may have set aside to finance the plan. Investment earnings on such fund are taxed directly to the employer, thus retarding the growth of the fund.

An exception to the preceding paragraph is a plan that is funded through a secular trust (also known as a *vesting trust*). In that case, the employer's contribution is tax-deductible to the employer and is taxed as income to the employee when the employee's interest has vested. Investment earnings of the trust are generally taxed to the employer unless distributed to the employee. The use of secular trust as the funding vehicle for a nonqualified plan may subject the plan to the reporting, funding, and other requirements of ERISA and the Tax Code. It is assumed throughout this chapter that the nonqualified plan is not being funded through a secular trust.

(b) NONQUALIFIED PLAN ASSETS. For accounting and tax purposes, any fund that an employer may have set aside to finance a nonqualified plan is treated as an asset of the employer and not as an asset of the plan in the context of SFAS Nos. 87 and 88. Indeed, some plans must be unfunded in order to be exempt from the ERISA funding and reporting requirements. Therefore, such a fund is accounted for like any other general asset of the employer, whereas the cost of the benefits under the plan is determined in accordance with SFAS Nos. 87 and 88 as if there were no plan assets.

In order to improve the security of benefits to the employees, legal devices such as rabbi trusts have been used to prohibit or limit access to the plan fund by the employer or its creditors. Nevertheless, the assets of a rabbi trust are still considered assets of the employer, and the trust accounting is consolidated with the employer's accounting.

(c) NONQUALIFIED DEFINED CONTRIBUTION PLANS.   Pure nonqualified defined contribution plans are relatively uncommon. To constitute a defined contribution plan, the employer's obligation must be limited to its contributions to the plan, with the employees receiving benefits based on those contributions plus investment earnings thereon. Since most nonqualified plans are either unfunded or funded indirectly through vehicles such as corporate-owned life insurance, the mechanism to operate a defined contribution generally does not exist. A deferred compensation plan that promises a certain rate of interest on compensations deferred by employees is not a defined contribution plan, unless the promised rate is equal to the actual after-tax rate of return on the compensations deferred by the employees. This situation is not changed if the promised rate is based, for example, on the projected rate of return on certain life insurance policies used to finance the plan.

The employer's cost for a defined contribution plan is equal to its contribution to the plan.

(d) NONQUALIFIED DEFINED BENEFIT PLANS.   Both SFAS Nos. 87 and 88 apply to nonqualified plans and to any arrangement that is similar in substance to a pension plan regardless of the form or means of financing. For any other individually designed deferred compensation contract, cost should be accrued in accordance with APB Opinion No. 12 in a systematic and rational manner over the employee's period of active employment, starting from the time the contract is entered into, so that the full cost will have been accrued at the end of the term of active employment.

Examples of nonqualified defined benefit plans are (1) supplemental retirement plans for selected employees providing retirement benefits in addition to the employer's qualified pension plans; (2) benefit restoration plans to restore to the employees any benefits that may have been restricted by IRC Section 401(a) or 415, or by Section 401(k) on the maximum amount of compensation that can be deferred; (3) deferred compensation or termination indemnity plans promising to credit a rate of interest that is not equal to the after-tax investment return on the assets set aside to finance the plans. Golden parachutes are generally accounted for as severance payments. Change-of-control pension provisions in a pension plan, which provide certain special benefits in the event of a change in control of the employer, are handled as termination benefits under SFAS No. 88.

In applying SFAS Nos. 87 and 88 to a nonqualified plan, the following factors should be considered: (1) The discount rate should reflect the effect of any tax liability for annuities that may be purchased to discharge the benefit obligation; (2) there is generally no contribution to the plan since any funds set aside to finance the plan remain assets of the employer, except for benefits paid to the employees or payments made to purchase annuities, for example, to discharge benefit obligations; (3) as a result of (2) above, the expected return on plan assets is zero (whereas the investment return on any assets or funds that may have been appropriated to finance the plan would have already been reported elsewhere as income to the employer); (4) as noted under (2) above, benefit payments are also treated as contributions and, therefore, would reduce the employer's accrued pension cost; and (5) a nonqualified plan linked to a qualified plan, such as a supplemental retirement plan providing benefits that are offset by benefits from a qualified pension plan, should nevertheless be accounted for separately from the qualified plan.

38.5 PLAN ACCOUNTING

(a) BACKGROUND.   In March 1980, the FASB issued SFAS No. 35, which established for the first time GAAP for the entity defined as a pension plan. The standard was effective for financial statements for fiscal years beginning after December 15, 1980. SFAS No. 35 was developed only after a great deal of controversy and followed a discussion paper, a public hearing, and two exposure drafts over a period of five years. It applies to all plans, including private plans and those of state and local governments. Coming under the standard are defined benefit pension plans that are subject to the financial reporting requirements of ERISA as well as those that are not. It does not apply to plans that are being terminated.

For nongovernmental plans with 100 or more participants as of the beginning of the plan year, a comprehensive annual report (Form 5500) must be filed in accordance with ERISA. The annual report must include these two items:

1. A set of financial statements prepared in accordance with GAAP, with an audit and opinion by an independent qualified public accountant
2. An actuarial report, including the status of the minimum funding standard account, and opinion by an enrolled actuary

(b) OBJECTIVE AND CONTENT OF FINANCIAL STATEMENTS.   Under SFAS No. 35, the plan itself is the reporting entity, not the trust. The Statement is based on a position that the primary objective of a plan's financial statements is to provide information useful in assessing its present and future ability to pay benefits when due. This objective requires the presentation of information about the economic resources of the plan and a measurement of its participants' accumulated benefits. The Statement leaves unresolved, at least for the time being, the issue of whether accumulated plan benefits are accounting liabilities of the plan. Therefore, it allows flexibility in presenting the actuarial information by providing that the plan's annual financial statements must include the following:

- A statement that includes information regarding net assets available for benefits
- A statement that includes information regarding the changes in net assets available for benefits
- Information regarding the actuarial present value of accumulated plan benefits as of the benefit information date (which can either be at the beginning or end of the year)
- Information regarding the effects, if significant, of certain factors affecting the year-to-year change in the actuarial present value of accumulated plan benefits

The SFAS No. 35 provides that the actuarial information required under the third and fourth bullet points can be presented in separate statements, in the notes to financial statements, or combined with the other required information on the net assets available for benefits and the year-to-year changes therein (provided the information is as of the same date and/or for the same period).

(c) NET ASSETS AVAILABLE FOR BENEFITS.   Plan investments, excluding insurance contracts, must be reported at fair value. Insurance contracts must be reported in accordance with the rules required by certain governmental agencies relating to the plan's annual report filed pursuant to ERISA. Because net assets are the existing means by which a plan can provide benefits, net asset information is necessary to assess a plan's ability to pay benefits when due. Using fair value as the basis to measure a plan's investments provides the most relevant information about resources currently available to pay the participants' benefits. The fair value of an investment is the amount that the plan could reasonably expect to receive for the investment from a current sale between a willing buyer and a willing seller, that is, not in a forced liquidation sale. If there is an active market for the investment, fair value is measured by the *market price* as of the reporting date.

(i) Good Faith Valuations.   Investments that do not have a quoted market price must be valued "in good faith." In determining a good faith value, the following factors should be considered:

- Quoted market prices for similar investments

- Information about transactions or offers regarding the plan's investment
- Forecast of expected cash flows for that investment

(ii) Disclosures for Investments. Information regarding the plan's investments must be presented in the plan's statement of net assets available for benefits in sufficient detail to identify the general types of investment (e.g., as government securities, short-term securities, corporate bonds, common stocks, mortgages, and real estate). In addition, whether fair values have been measured by quoted price in an active market or determined otherwise must be disclosed.

(iii) Operating Assets. Assets used in the plan's operations must be presented at cost, less accumulated depreciation or amortization. Such assets would include, for example, buildings, equipment, furniture and fixtures, and leasehold improvements. Although the DOL's instructions to Forms 5500 and 5500-C/R require the presentation of all assets at fair value, it is believed that the DOL will not object to this presentation in the financial statements.

(iv) Contributions Receivable. The plan's financial statements should include as contributions receivable all amounts due the plan, as of the reporting date, from the employer, participants, and other sources of funding (e.g., state subsidies or federal grants). These receivables would include amounts due pursuant to formal commitments as well as legal or contractual requirements.

(d) CHANGES IN NET ASSETS AVAILABLE FOR BENEFITS. The information about a plan's ability to pay benefits when due, provided by its financial statements, is affected whenever transactions or other events affect the net asset or benefit information presented in those statements. Because a plan's ability to pay participants' benefits normally does not remain constant, users of its financial statements are concerned with assessing the plan's ability to pay participants' benefits not only as of a particular point in time, but also on a continuing basis. For this reason, they need to know the reasons for changes in the net asset and benefit information reported in successive financial statements.

The FASB concluded, therefore, that plan financial statements should include (1) information regarding the year-to-year change in net assets available for benefits and (2) disclosure of the effects, if significant, of certain factors affecting the year-to-year change in benefit information.

SFAS No. 35 requires presentation of the statement of changes in net assets available for benefits in sufficient detail to permit identification of the significant changes during the year. The statement should include these eight, at a minimum:

1. The net change in fair value for each significant class of investments, segregated as between investments whose fair values have been measured by quoted prices in an active market and those whose fair values have been determined otherwise
2. Investment income, excluding the changes of fair value described in item 1
3. Contributions from employers, segregated as between cash and noncash contributions
4. Contributions from participants
5. Contributions from other identified sources such as state subsidies or federal grants
6. Benefits paid
7. Payments to insurance companies to purchase contracts that are excluded from plan assets
8. Administrative expenses

In presenting this information, gains and losses from investments sold are not segregated from unrealized gains and losses relating to investments held at the plan's year end.

(e) ACTUARIAL PRESENT VALUE OF ACCUMULATED PLAN BENEFITS. Accumulated plan benefits are future benefit payments that are attributable, under the plan's provisions, to employees' service rendered prior to the benefit information date—the date as of which the actuarial present value of accumulated plan benefits is presented. Accumulated benefits include benefits for retired or terminated employees, beneficiaries of deceased employees, and present employees or their beneficiaries.

The accumulated benefit information may be presented as of the beginning or end of the plan year. If it is presented as of the beginning of the plan year, the prior year statement of net assets available for benefits and changes therein must also be presented. For example, if the plan year end is December 31, 2002, and the statement of accumulated plan benefits is based on a benefit information date of December 31, 2001, statements of net assets available for benefits and of changes therein also would be presented for 2001.

Measurement of accumulated plan benefits is based primarily on the employees' history of pay, service, and other appropriate factors as of the information date. Future salary changes are not considered, nor is a provision for inflation allowed. However, future increases that are guaranteed under a cost-of-living adjustment (COLA) should be estimated. Future years of service are considered only in determining an employee's expected eligibility for benefits of particular types, such as early retirement, death, and disability benefits. To measure the actuarial present value, assumptions are used to adjust the accumulated plan benefits to reflect the time value of money and the probability of payment between the benefit information date and the expected date of payment. An assumption that the plan is ongoing must underlie those assumptions. Benefit information should relate to the benefits reasonably expected to be paid in exchange for employees' service to the benefit information date.

To the extent possible, plan provisions should apply in measuring accumulated plan benefits. If the benefit for each service year is not determinable from the provisions of the plan, the benefit must be considered to accumulate by years of service rendered in proportion to total years required to earn a particular benefit. Normally, the plan provisions will indicate how to measure accumulated plan benefits. Plan amendments occurring subsequent to the date of the calculation must be excluded from the actuarial computation. In addition, benefits that are guaranteed by a contract with an insurance company (i.e., allocated contracts) are also excluded.

(i) Actuarial Assumptions.   The most important decisions in developing the actuarial present value of accumulated plan benefits are in the selection of actuarial assumptions. The interest return assumption (analogous to the discount rate assumption in the section "Sponsor Accounting") is the single most important issue. It is used to discount future benefit payments, as well as to determine the anticipated rates of return on current and prospective assets. The concept of a best estimate and the principle of an explicit approach are integral to the rationale used in developing actuarial assumptions.

The concept of a "best estimate" is used by the FASB in discussing the actuarial assumptions in SFAS No. 35, possibly because the term is included in the ERISA certification required of an enrolled actuary. The reason is not critical, but it is important to realize that the best estimate requirement under ERISA is being interpreted in several ways. Its use for plan accounting purposes may be quite different from the best estimate for a funding basis. The section on sponsor accounting discusses the concept further.

Although there is no specific discussion of what the FASB intended by "best estimate," there is a discussion in the Statement of what is meant by "explicit approach." It is important to recognize that prior to the Omnibus Budget Reconciliation Act of 1987, the explicit approach, although strongly recommended to actuaries by the American Academy of Actuaries, was not required in developing the ERISA requirements under the minimum funding standard account. Because of the importance of this issue, part of SFAS No. 35 is reproduced here:

> 199. This statement requires that each significant assumption used in determining the benefit information reflect the best estimate of the plan's future experience solely with respect to that assumption. That method of selecting assumptions is referred to as an explicit approach. An implicit approach, on the other hand, means that two or more assumptions do not individually represent the best estimate of the plan's future experience with respect to those assumptions. Rather, the aggregate effect of their combined use is presumed to be approximately the same as that of an explicit approach. The Board believes that an explicit approach results in more useful information

regarding (a) components of the benefit information, (b) changes in the benefit information, and (c) the choice of significant assumptions used to determine the benefit information.

200. The following illustrates the preferability of an explicit approach as it relates to measuring components of the benefit information (that is, vested benefits of participants currently receiving payments, other vested benefits, and nonvested benefits). Under an implicit approach, it might be assumed that the net result of assuming no withdrawal before vesting and increasing assumed rates of return by a specified amount would approximate the same actuarial present value of total accumulated plan benefits as that which would result from using assumed rates of return and withdrawal rates determined by an explicit approach. Even if that were true, increasing assumed rates of return to compensate for withdrawal before vesting might significantly misstate components of the benefit information. Withdrawal before vesting relates only to nonvested benefits. Therefore, discounting vested benefits at rates of return that have been adjusted to implicitly reflect that withdrawal understates that component of the benefit information and correspondingly overstates the nonvested benefit information.

201. The disadvantage of an implicit approach with respect to information regarding changes in the benefit information can be similarly illustrated. Assume that under an implicit approach, assumed rates of return are decreased to implicitly reflect the effects of a plan's provision for an automatic COLA. In that situation, the effect of a plan amendment relating to the automatic COLA, for example, an amendment to increase the "cap" on the COLA from 3% to 4%, might be obscured. If significant, the effect of such an amendment should, pursuant to the requirements of the Statement, be disclosed as the effect of a plan amendment. If an implicit approach is used, however, assumed rates of return would be adjusted to reflect the effects of that amendment and accordingly, some part or all of the effect might be presented as the effect of a change in an actuarial assumption rather than as the effect of a plan amendment (particularly if assumed rates of return are also changed for other reasons).

202. In addition to the foregoing possible disadvantages, an implicit approach might result in less meaningful disclosure of the significant assumptions used to determine the benefit information. For example, disclosure of the assumed rates of return resulting from the implicit approaches described in paragraphs 200 and 201 could mislead users of the financial statements regarding the plan's investment return expectations and could result in noncomparable reporting for two plans with the same investment return expectations. Users might also draw erroneous conclusions about the relationship between the plan's actual and assumed rates of return.

There are economic actuarial assumptions and noneconomic actuarial assumptions. The key issue in developing a plan's economic assumptions is the forecast of long-term inflation. The inflation component should be consistently reflected in all the economic assumptions. For example, if the long-term investment return assumption reflects a five percent inflation component, then the estimate of future salary increases should also reflect a five percent inflation component. In plan accounting, it is not necessary to develop an assumption for future pay increases or future Social Security benefits. Because very few plans provide for automatic postretirement COLAs, that assumption will seldom be required for plan accounting.

It is clear from SFAS No. 35 that the interest assumption used for accounting purposes will frequently, if not usually, be different from that used for funding. The key requirement in developing an interest assumption, and for that matter any other assumption, is to use a sensible rationale. Judgmental elements in the actuary's development of a recommendation should be highlighted and subject to review and approval by the plan's sponsor. The framework and illustration of such a rationale is discussed in "Sponsor Accounting." Although the result may differ as between sponsor and plan accounting, the same approach can be applied in both instances.

The noneconomic assumptions of mortality, withdrawal, disability, and early (late) retirement are referred to in SFAS No. 35, relating to the probability and timing of benefit payments. They are referred to here as *noneconomic* because they are usually not influenced by the long-term economic forecast, although short-term economic conditions can have a marked impact on withdrawal and early retirement experience. The mortality and disability assumptions are more highly technical. The typical plan sponsor will have to rely more heavily on the actuary's judgment and recommendations when adopting them. The impact of variations in mortality and disability assumptions on the actuarial value of accumulated benefits is not generally very large. The withdrawal and early retirement assumptions can vary considerably from one organization to another, because they are affected by the personnel practices and business circumstances of the plan sponsor. Accordingly, more input from the plan sponsor is appropriate with respect to these assumptions. The discussion of these assumptions under "Sponsor Accounting" applies here as well.

(ii) Disclosures for Actuarial Present Value of Accumulated Plan Benefits.   As previously stated, the accumulated benefit information may be presented as a separate financial statement, in a note to the financial statements, or combined with other information in the financial statements. The information must all be located in one place and must be segregated as follows:

- Vested benefits of participants currently receiving benefits
- Other vested benefits
- Nonvested benefits

If employees contribute to the plan, accumulated employee contributions must be disclosed, and, if applicable, accumulated interest credited on the contributions, including the interest rate, must also be disclosed.

(f) CHANGES IN THE ACTUARIAL PRESENT VALUE OF ACCUMULATED PLAN BENEFITS. The FASB requires disclosure of the effects, if significant, of certain factors affecting the year-to-year change in the benefit information. If the benefit information date is the beginning of the year, the required information regarding the year-to-year change in the benefit information would also relate to the preceding year. Consistent with the requirement for accumulated benefit information, the changes therein also may be presented as a separate financial statement, combined with other information in the financial statements, or in the notes to the financial statements. In addition, the information can be presented either in a reconciliation format or in a narrative format. As a minimum, significant effects of the following three factors must be included in the disclosure of the information:

- Plan amendments
- Changes in the nature of the plan, such as a plan spinoff or a merger with another plan
- Changes in actuarial assumptions

Effects that are individually significant should be separately identified.

If only the minimum required disclosure is presented, presentation in a statement format will necessitate an additional unidentified "other" category to reconcile the beginning and ending amounts. Changes in actuarial assumptions are treated as changes in accounting estimates, and therefore previously reported amounts should not be restated.

(g) ILLUSTRATIVE PLAN FINANCIAL STATEMENTS.   Exhibits 38.6 through 38.9 illustrate the financial statements of a defined benefit pension plan. Exhibit 38.6 presents a statement of net assets available for benefits. SFAS No. 35 requires the net asset information to be presented as of the end of the plan year. However, if the information regarding the actuarial present value of accumulated plan benefits is presented as of the beginning of the plan year, the net asset information also must be presented as of that date (i.e., presented as of the end of the current and preceding plan years).

Exhibit 38.7 contains a statement of changes in net assets available for benefits, identifying the significant changes during the plan year. If the information regarding accumulated plan benefits is presented as of the beginning of the plan year, the statement of changes in net assets available for benefits must be presented for two years.

Exhibits 38.8 and 38.9 present a statement of accumulated plan benefits and a statement of changes in accumulated plan benefits. This information can be presented as of a benefit information

	December 31, 20X3
Assets	
Investments, at fair value	
U.S. government securities	$ 350,000
Corporate bonds and debentures	3,500,000
Common stock	
ABC Company	690,000
Other	2,250,000
Mortgages	480,000
Real estate	270,000
	7,540,000
Deposit administration contract, at contract value*	1,000,000
Total investments	8,540,000
Receivables	
Employees' contributions	40,000
Securities sold	310,000
Accrued interest and dividends	77,000
	427,000
Cash	200,000
Total assets	9,167,000
Liabilities	
Accounts payable	70,000
Accrued expenses	85,000
Total liabilities	155,000
Net assets available for benefits	$9,012,000

*Deposit administration contract is reflected at contract value, as opposed to fair value, because such contract was entered into prior to March 1990 (refer to transition provisions of SFAS No. 110).

Exhibit 38.6   Statement of net assets available for benefits.

date that is either the beginning or the end of the plan year. In addition, the information can be presented in a combined statement with the related net asset information or included in the notes to the financial statements. The statement presented in Exhibit 38.9 reconciles the year-to-year change in the actuarial present value of accumulated plan benefits. As an alternative to presenting this information in a statement format, disclosure can be made of only the factors significantly changed in accumulated plan benefits. The information can be disclosed in the notes to the financial statements or presented on the face of the statement of accumulated plan benefits. Factors that usually have a significant effect on accumulated plan benefits include plan amendments, changes in the nature of a plan (e.g., a plan spinoff or merger with another plan), and changes in actuarial assumptions.

(h) ADDITIONAL FINANCIAL STATEMENT DISCLOSURES. Disclosure of the plan's accounting policies must include a description of the methods and significant assumptions used to determine the fair value of investments and the reported value of contracts with insurance companies. In addition, a description of the method and significant actuarial assumptions used to determine the actuarial present value of accumulated plan benefits must be disclosed in the notes to the financial statements. Such disclosure would include any significant changes of methods or assumptions between benefit information dates.

	Year Ended December 31, 20X3
Investment income	
Net appreciation in fair value of investments	$ 207,000
Interest	345,000
Dividends	130,000
Rents	55,000
	737,000
Less investment expenses	39,000
	698,000
Contributions	
Employer	780,000
Employees	450,000
	1,230,000
Total additions	1,928,000
Benefits paid directly to participants	740,000
Purchases of annuity contracts	257,000
	997,000
Administrative expenses	65,000
Total deductions	1,062,000
Net increase	866,000
Net assets available for benefits	
Beginning of year	8,146,000
End of year	$9,012,000

Exhibit 38.7   Statement of changes in net assets available for benefits.

	December 31, 20X3
Actuarial present value of accumulated plan benefits	
Vested benefits	
Participants currently receiving payments	$ 3,040,000
Other participants	8,120,000
	11,160,000
Nonvested benefits	2,720,000
Total actuarial present value of accumulated plan benefits	$13,880,000

Exhibit 38.8   Statement of accumulated plan benefits.

	Year Ended December 31, 20X3
Actuarial present value of accumulated plan benefits at beginning of year	$ 11,880,000
Increase (decrease) during the year attributable to:	
Plan amendment	2,410,000
Change in actuarial assumptions	(1,050,500)
Benefits accumulated	895,000
Increase for interest due to the decrease in the discount period	742,500
Benefits paid	(997,000)
Net increase	2,000,000
Actuarial present value of accumulated plan benefits at end of year	$ 13,880,000

Exhibit 38.9   Statement of changes in accumulated plan benefits.

In addition to disclosing significant accounting policies, SFAS No. 35 requires the following nine disclosures:

1. A brief general description of the plan agreement, including vesting and benefit provisions.

2. A description of significant plan amendments made during the year. If significant amendments occur between the latest benefit information date and the plan's year end and therefore were not reflected in the actuarial present value of accumulated plan benefits, disclosure should be made of this matter.

3. A brief general description of the priority order of participants' claims to the assets of the plan in the event of plan termination and benefits guaranteed by the PBGC.

4. Funding policy and any changes in such policy during the plan year.

5. The policy regarding the purchase of contracts with insurance companies that are excluded from plan assets.

6. Tax status of the plan, if a favorable letter of determination has not been obtained or maintained.

7. Identification of individual investments that represent five percent or more of the net assets available for benefits.

8. Significant real estate or other transactions between plan and the sponsor, employers, or employee organizations.

9. Unusual or infrequent events or transactions occurring subsequent to the latest benefit information date but before issuance of the financial statements, such as a plan amendment occurring after the latest benefit information date that significantly increases future benefits that are attributable to employee service rendered before that date.

(i) DECISION TO PREPARE PLAN FINANCIAL STATEMENTS. The number of accounting decisions required to prepare the plan's financial statements is not large.

For many plans, the first and most important decision will be whether to issue a statement at all. Plans subject to ERISA requirements must issue a statement, but public employee plans and ERISA plans with fewer than 100 participants are not required by ERISA to issue statements. The usual reason for not publishing plan financial statements, particularly for smaller employers, will be to avoid the additional expenses of preparing, auditing, and distributing the statement. The usual reasons for publishing statements when not required by ERISA will include the following four reasons:

1. The employer wishes to present a strong, positive image to employees (or the public) about the administration and financial strength of the plan.

2. The number of participants may not be indicative of the financial values involved. Plan assets could be very significant in relation to the company's net worth.

3. The employer wants to protect the plan's fiduciaries against legal liability.

4. Publication is required by state or local law.

Other reasons for decisions are practical, largely affecting the ease and expense with which financial statements can be prepared. One subtle decision occurs when there have been multiple changes during the year, such as plan amendments and changes in assumptions. The order in which these items are presented can affect the reader's perception of what actually happened during the year. The FASB in SFAS No. 35 commented:

> The Board recognized that the determined effects of factors comprising the net change in the benefit information will vary depending on the order in which the effects are calculated. . . . Thus, the Board concluded that at this time it would not prescribe an order.

This can be cleared up through footnote disclosures as desired. Some of the practical decisions involved include the following:

- Whether to use a benefit information date other than year end. Many plans (if not most) will find it more convenient to use a beginning-of-the-year date. However, that approach does require more information to be furnished regarding both net assets available and changes in such assets during the preceding year. Another approach when the regular actuarial valuation (to determine funding) is performed at the beginning of the year is to value the accumulated benefits at that point, and project to year end, using "reasonable approximation." The FASB makes permissive reference to that type of an approach, provided that the results are substantially the same as those contemplated by SFAS No. 35. For many plans, this approach will produce very acceptable results. An employer that discloses the funded status of its pension plan under SFAS No. 87 in its year-end financial statements may find it convenient to satisfy the SFAS No. 35 disclosure requirements by using the accumulated and vested benefit obligations disclosed under SFAS No. 87.

- Whether to make a more complete disclosure of the plan's circumstances. In the interest of doing so, some plan sponsors may wish to present the benefit value information in more than the three minimum categories specified by SFAS No. 35. For example, the other vested benefit category could be expanded to include the value of vested benefits for employees eligible for normal or early retirement.

(j) DEFINED CONTRIBUTION PLANS.   Although SFAS No. 35 does not cover defined contribution plans, many of the concepts and principles included are applicable to defined contribution plans. Defined contribution plans require the maintenance of individual accounts for each participant, to record each one's share of the total net assets of the plan. Typically, a defined contribution plan will require a certain contribution from the employer without specifying the amount of benefits to be provided to the participants. The types and amounts of benefits, as well as the eligibility requirements, are frequently determined by the plan's trustees, who can be totally "unrelated" to the employer; in other cases, the employer reserves those rights. Employer contributions are based on a formula that may be a certain rate per hour of work or per unit of production, a function of the employee's contribution, a percentage of the employer's annual profitability, or some other specified method. The employer's obligation here differs from that under a defined contribution plan. With a defined contribution plan, the employer is not obligated to make up any shortfalls in actual versus assumed experience. This can be particularly significant, of course, in the case of the investment experience.

(i) Separate Accounts.   Employer contributions, changes in the value of the plan's net assets, and forfeitures, if any, are allocated to individual participant accounts maintained for each participant. In addition, employee contributions, if any, are credited to the account.

(ii) Types of Plans.   Defined contribution plans include the following four:

1. Profit-sharing plans, which provide for an employer contribution based on current or accumulated profits
2. Money purchase plans, which provide for an employer contribution based on employee compensation, units of production, hours worked, or some criterion other than profits
3. Stock bonus and employee stock ownership plans that are qualified profit-sharing plans that invest substantially all the plan's assets in the stock of the employer company
4. Thrift or savings plans, which provide for periodic employee contributions with matching, in whole or in part, by the employer—usually from current or accumulated profits

(iii) Financial Statements.   Financial statements for a defined contribution plan should include a statement of net assets available for benefits and a statement of changes in net assets available for benefits. The disclosures would be similar to those required for a defined benefit pension plan, except for the references to actuarial information.

(k) POSTRETIREMENT MEDICAL BENEFIT FEATURES OF DEFINED BENEFIT PENSION PLANS.   Assets accumulated under Section 401(h) of the Internal Revenue Code to provide a postretirement medical benefit component to a defined benefit pension plan are not available for pensions. They and the associated liabilities should therefore be presented, net, in two places apart from the other amounts in the plan's statement of net assets available for pension benefits: (1) among the assets and (2) among the liabilities. The pension plan's statement of changes in net assets should show only the following related to Section 401(h): (1) qualified transfers to the 401(h) account and (2) any unused or unspent amounts, including allocated income, in the 401(h) account at the end of the year that were qualified transfers of excess pension assets that should have been but were not transferred back to the defined benefit pension plan, or both. Only information concerning pension benefits should be reported as accumulated plan benefits.

The notes to the financial statements of defined benefit pension plans should disclose the nature of the assets related to Section 401(h) and that the assets are available to pay only retiree health benefits. Also, because ERISA requires 401(h) assets to be reported as assets of the defined benefit pension plan in regulatory filings with the U.S. government on Form 5500, a reconciliation of the net assets reported in the plan's financial statements to those reported in Form 5500 should be provided.

38.6 ACCOUNTING FOR POSTRETIREMENT BENEFITS OTHER THAN PENSIONS

(a) BACKGROUND.   On December 21, 1990, the FASB issued SFAS No. 106, "Employer's Accounting for Postretirement Benefits Other Than Pensions." Retiree medical benefits are SFAS No. 106's primary focus, but life insurance and other welfare benefits provided to employees after retirement are also included.

Prior to SFAS No. 106, most employers had recognized the cost of postretirement benefits other than pensions when paid. Under the accounting requirements of SFAS No. 106, postretirement benefits are viewed as a form of deferred compensation that should be recognized on an accrual basis during the periods that the employees render the service needed to qualify for benefits. The specific approach and methodology of SFAS No. 106 closely parallel the pension accounting rules addressed in SFAS Nos. 87 and 88. Their disclosures are similar as well.

The practice of providing postretirement health care benefits took root after the Medicare program was established in 1965. Employers found that, for relatively few dollars, Medicare supplements, as they were called, bought much employee goodwill. The effect of inflation on medical costs, the trend toward earlier retirement, and longer life expectancies have made these benefits increasingly expensive. During recent decades, the cost of medical care has risen at twice the average inflation rate for the same period. These dramatic cost increases have prompted many companies to significantly reduce or even eliminate retiree medical benefits. Retiree health care benefits are now predominantly found at larger employers, as the escalating costs have made these benefits too costly for most midsize and smaller employers.

Although some employers provide benefits only until retirees reach age 65 and become eligible for Medicare, many programs still provide lifetime benefits. Typically, benefits for retirees are similar to those for active employees, including the ability to cover eligible dependents. Many plans provide the same level of benefits regardless of years of service, while other plans provide incremental benefits to employees retiring with longer service periods. Programs for retirees age 65 and over usually are coordinated with Medicare benefits to help contain costs. Furthermore, retirees are now often required to pay some portion of the cost of these benefits. This cost sharing is one of many methods employers have used to help contain their costs. Another commonly used method is cost caps, where the company establishes a fixed dollar amount above which the retiree will cover all costs.

(b) STATEMENT OF FINANCIAL ACCOUNTING STANDARDS NO. 106.   SFAS No. 106
requires employers that provide medical or other affected benefits to follow a prescribed method
in determining the annual expense charge for such benefits and to provide extensive disclosures in
their financial statements. As noted above, much of the guidance in SFAS No. 106 is similar to that
in SFAS No. 87, which is covered in detail in Section 38.2. This section focuses on identifying
the similarities of the two Statements as well as their key differences.

(i) Similarities to Statement of Financial Accounting Standards No. 87.   The measurement
of obligations in a postretirement medical plan closely follows SFAS No. 87 methodology. Unlike
the pension model, where the monthly benefit is fixed at retirement, future medical benefits depend
on the likelihood and cost of future claims. Nonetheless, the basic concept of projecting future
cash flows, assigning a probability of payment, and discounting back to the measurement date
apply. The discounted value of future benefits forms the basic building blocks for the expense and
liability determinations under SFAS No. 106. The attribution of the obligation to an employee's
service period under SFAS No. 106 does differ slightly, as is addressed below.

The annual postretirement benefit expense is composed of all of the same components as the
SFAS No. 87 net periodic pension expense as outlined in Section 38.2(d). This includes service
cost, interest cost, expected return on assets (if funded), and amortization of transition obligation,
prior service costs, and actuarial gains and losses. With minor exceptions, the measurement of
these items is consistent with SFAS No. 87. In particular, most of the allowable amortization
methodologies, including the corridor approach for gains and losses, directly follow SFAS No. 87.

The balance sheet liability or asset under SFAS No. 106 is similar to that under SFAS No.
87. The accrued (prepaid) postretirement benefit expense (asset) represents the accumulated excess
(shortfall) between the amount of expense recorded and the amount the employer has contributed.
For plans that are not prefunded, the employer contributions are equal to the annual benefit payments made to retirees. A prepaid asset attributable to a postretirement welfare plan is somewhat
rare since most postretirement welfare plans are not prefunded.

Many of the actuarial assumptions used to develop SFAS Nos. 87 and 106 liabilities and expense
are similar. In particular, the methodology used to develop the SFAS No. 106 discount rate is the
same as that described in Section 38.2(c)(iii). Each of the significant actuarial assumptions for
SFAS No. 106 is discussed in greater detail later in this section.

Finally, like its pension counterpart, SFAS No. 106 allows a measurement date that is within
three months of the date of the financial statements. SFAS No. 106 applies to both U.S. and
non-U.S. plans.

(ii) Differences from Statement of Financial Accounting Standards No. 87.   While there are
many similarities between SFAS No. 106 and SFAS No. 87, there are some important differences.
SFAS No. 106 introduces the expected postretirement benefit obligation (EPBO). This represents
the discounted value as of the measurement date of all future benefits expected to be paid. SFAS
No. 87 does not define an equivalent liability measurement. This differs from the PBO in pension
accounting in that the EPBO represents the value of all future postretirement benefits, not just those
that have been attributed to employees' service as of the reporting date. The service cost is the
portion of EPBO attributed to the current period. The accumulated postretirement benefit obligation
(APBO) under SFAS No. 106 is determined by apportioning the EPBO over the appropriate
attribution period. Therefore, the APBO represents the portion of the EPBO that is attributable to
prior service, which is equivalent to the PBO under SFAS No. 87. If an employee has reached his
full eligibility date, the APBO would be the same as the EPBO. The concepts are the same but
the terminology is slightly different.

SFAS No. 106 also introduces the term *substantive plan*, which is the plan as understood by the
employer and employee, which may differ from the written plan. This can be a significant issue
because the employer sometimes communicates to covered employees its intent to change certain
plan features, such as the level of employee contributions, in the future. The substantive plan
can thus have a value on the measurement date materially different from the plan as written and

operated. To the extent the substantive plan differs from the written plan, the substantive plan is the basis for accounting under SFAS No. 106. Therefore, great care should be taken to understand the true nature of the benefit promise the employer has made to its retirees. This is a significant difference from SFAS No. 87, since most pension plans require a formal document that serves as the basis for pension accounting.

The substantive plan has become increasingly more important as employers have made changes to their retiree medical plans to control escalating costs. Specifically, both cost sharing and cost cap arrangements are often implemented. These changes can significantly affect the measurement of the plan's obligations, but these measurements are realistic only if the employer implements the cost sharing and caps that have been communicated. To the extent the employer does not implement them, the actual operation of the plan should dictate appropriate accounting treatment.

Unlike SFAS No. 87, SFAS No. 106 gives employers the option of recognizing the entire transition obligation immediately. For employers electing to defer its recognition, SFAS No. 106 allows an amortization period equal to the greater of the average remaining service period for active participants and 20 years. SFAS No. 87 allows deferred recognition of the transition obligation or asset over the greater of the average remaining service period for active participants and 15 years. Both Statements require the use of the average remaining life expectancy of the participants if almost all participants are inactive. Additional amortization of the transition obligation is required if the cumulative cost computed under SFAS No. 106 is less than cumulative benefit payments less any plan assets or unrecognized accrued cost at transition. This provision requires additional amortization for a few mature plans with very high pay-as-you-go costs for the first few years following adoption of the Statement.

The attribution period required by SFAS No. 106 differs slightly from that in SFAS No. 87. As discussed earlier, SFAS No. 87 requires an attribution that accrues the costs from hire date (or service start date) to the expected retirement date, following the accrual pattern specified by the plan formula. SFAS No. 106, in contrast, requires a ratable attribution from hire date (or service start date) to full eligibility date. The end of the attribution period differs for the two Statements.

In many retiree medical plans, employees are eligible to retire with full benefits as early as age 55, assuming they have earned enough service. In this case, SFAS No. 106 would generally require the liability for active employees to be fully accrued by the time they attain age 55. If significant benefits accrue beyond the full eligibility date, as may be the case when additional service provides enhanced benefits, SFAS No. 106 would require an attribution period that is consistent with SFAS No. 87. Overall, SFAS No. 106 generally requires a more rapid accrual of the liability than SFAS No. 87.

As noted above, many of the actuarial assumptions used to develop SFAS Nos. 87 and 106 liabilities and expense are similar. Relevant actuarial assumptions, including assumptions that are unique to SFAS No. 106, are discussed in greater detail later in this section.

SFAS No. 132 governs the financial statement disclosure requirements for SFAS No. 87 and SFAS No. 106. The specific disclosure requirements, including a description of the differences for pension and retiree welfare plans, are included later in this section.

Finally, unlike the pension rules under SFAS No. 87, SFAS No. 106 does not require a minimum balance sheet liability.

(c) ACTUARIAL ASSUMPTIONS.   Many of the actuarial assumptions necessary to develop the SFAS No. 106 expense and liabilities, such as discount rate, mortality, retirement age, and turnover, are similar to those used for SFAS Nos. 87 and 88. The discount rate for SFAS No. 106 purposes is established using the same discounted cash flow methodology described in Subsection 38.2(c)(iii). In practice, most employers will use the same assumptions for SFAS No. 87 and SFAS No. 106 to the extent the plans cover the same group of employees. However, the nature of the benefits covered by SFAS No. 106 requires the use of some unique actuarial assumptions.

Perhaps the most significant of these assumptions is the assumed per capita claims cost. Unlike pension plans that provide monthly cash payments, retiree medical plans typically promise benefits in the form of medical services. Besides variations due to plan provisions that define the level or richness of benefits provided, claims experience varies significantly by age, sex, occupation, and geographic location. This necessitates the development of an assumed set of per capita health care costs, usually stratified by age and gender. This per capita claims estimate should reflect the provisions of the plan and is typically based on historical claims experience of the employer. Since most plans are integrated with Medicare, assumptions must also be made for post-65 participants as to the portion of their benefits that will be provided by the government.

Another assumption unique to SFAS No. 106 is the medical trend assumption. While some retiree medical plans cap benefits at current levels, the more common approach is to provide uncapped benefits that are subject to medical inflation. As noted above, medical inflation has outpaced standard inflation over the past 20 years. Currently, most health care experts expect this trend to continue in the near future. Therefore, the medical trend assumption for most employers reflects a relatively high initial medical trend that decreases each year until it reaches a flat, long-term level. Many employers use different medical trend rates for different benefits that are provided by the plan. In particular, prescription drug inflation has been higher than overall medical trend, and many employers reflect this discrepancy in their assumed trend rates.

There are several other assumptions unique to SFAS No. 106. Since not all employees will elect to be covered by the retiree medical plan, an assumption about the participation level must be made. This is particularly important in plans where retirees must contribute toward the cost of coverage. If these costs become too high, many retirees will decline coverage and rely on Medicare or purchase their own medical coverage. In addition, many retiree medical plans have more than one coverage option, such as a health maintenance organization (HMO), preferred provider organization (PPO), and an indemnity plan. In such a case, an assumption must be made as to which plan a participant will elect when he retires. Actual experience and anticipated employer subsidies must be considered in setting this assumption.

(d) NONRECURRING EVENTS.   SFAS No. 88 addresses the special accounting that is required for settlements, curtailments, and special termination benefits related to pension plans. These events may also affect postretirement medical plans. While the treatment for pension and retiree medical plans is quite similar, SFAS No. 106 directly addresses the accounting for settlements and curtailments and the unique issues related to postretirement welfare benefit plans. The Statement defers to SFAS No. 88 for the accounting for special termination and contractual termination benefits.

As discussed earlier, a settlement is an irrevocable commitment that releases the employer from primary responsibility for some or all of the liability. Settlements are fairly rare in postretirement medical plans due to the nature of the benefit promise. Unlike a pension plan that provides that a nonparticipating annuity contract can be purchased to settle the obligation, there are no viable financial instruments that can settle the promise of lifetime medical coverage. The one instance in which settlements can occur with postretirement medical plans is for companies that have instituted cost caps for their retirees and thereby transformed the liability into a fixed monthly annuity. The settlement accounting prescribed by SFAS No. 106 precisely follows SFAS No. 88.

Curtailments occur when the expected years of future service for covered employees is significantly reduced or the future accrual of benefits is eliminated for future service. In general, curtailment accounting under SFAS No. 106 follows the treatment under SFAS No. 88. However, due to the some of the unique aspects of retiree medical benefits, curtailment accounting for these plans can be complex.

For example, assume we have a company that sponsors a retiree medical plan that covers 100 current retirees ($2 million in APBO) and 500 active employees ($3.5 million in APBO). Further assume that the company chooses to eliminate these benefits for all active employees as of some fixed date. This plan change eliminates both past and future accruals. Since these benefits are not protected by minimum vesting requirements similar to those applicable to pension plans, this is a possible scenario. In fact, many companies have taken this approach as a reaction to escalating retiree medical liabilities.

Under this scenario, there is both a negative plan amendment and a curtailment. The negative plan amendment relates to the change in the APBO that is attributable to past service. Curtailment accounting, in contrast, is focused on any portion of the liability attributable to future service. For a retiree medical plan, all of the APBO is attributable to past service. If the plan included retiree life insurance that was based on final average pay, the portion of the APBO attributable to using projected salary increases would be a curtailment gain. For example, assume the life insurance liability is $200,000 based on covered participants current service and salary. However, SFAS No. 106 requires the APBO to be valued using current service and projected salary. Therefore, the total APBO might be $300,000. If this life insurance benefit were eliminated, $200,000 would be treated as a negative plan amendment and $100,000 as a curtailment gain. Since the typical retiree medical plan is not based on salary, the entire APBO is attributable to prior service. Therefore, the entire reduction in APBO is attributed to the negative plan amendment. There is no curtailment gain subject to immediate recognition. The only effect the curtailment might have is the accelerated recognition of existing unrecognized prior service costs or transition obligation. The negative prior service cost from the current plan change is not subject to accelerated recognition. Therefore, in many cases, the elimination of retiree medical benefits for active employees often results in a curtailment that has no immediate income statement effect. The $3.5 million reduction in APBO from the example must be amortized over the average remaining life expectancy of the 100 retirees. Question and Answer 28 from the SFAS No. 106 Implementation Guide addresses a similar scenario.

(e) DISCLOSURES.   As amended by SFAS No. 132-R, disclosures under SFAS No. 106 are very similar to disclosures under SFAS No. 87. Following are the differences:

- Since there is no "additional minimum" required to be recognized under SFAS No. 106, the breakdown of the net amount recognized as a sum of intangible asset, additional minimum, and so on, is unnecessary.
- One additional assumption must be disclosed: the medical trend assumption. Since the medical trend is assumed to vary over several years, it is acceptable to paraphrase.
- Since the medical trend assumption has a large effect on the benefit obligation, a sensitivity analysis must be performed. This analysis shows the effect on service cost plus interest cost, and the benefit obligation, under a one percentage point increase and decrease in the trend assumptions.

Exhibit 38.10 is a sample disclosure under SFAS No. 106 for a public entity.

For a nonpublic reporting entity, the disclosures can be considerably shortened, similar to disclosures under SFAS No. 87. The only difference between the formats of disclosures under SFAS No. 87 for nonpublic entities versus SFAS No. 106 for nonpublic entities is that the medical trend rate assumption must be disclosed, using a paragraph similar to the one in Exhibit 38.10.

38.7 EMPLOYERS' ACCOUNTING FOR POSTEMPLOYMENT BENEFITS

(a) BACKGROUND.   Issued by the FASB in November 1992, SFAS No. 112, "Employer's Accounting for Postemployment Benefits," established accounting standards for the estimated cost of benefits provided by an employer to former or inactive employees in the window of time after employment but before retirement (hereafter referred to as *postemployment benefits*). Postemployment benefits include such items as salary continuation, supplemental unemployment benefits, disability-related benefits (including workers' compensation), job training, and the continuation of health care benefits and life insurance coverage.

Prior to the issuance of SFAS No. 112, the accounting for the cost of postemployment benefits varied from employer to employer. Although some employers accounted for these benefits under a form of accrual accounting (e.g., terminal accrual accounting—under which the cost of the benefit is accrued at the time the event giving rise to the payment of benefits occurs), most still used a cash basis to recognize the costs associated with such benefits.

	20X6	20X5
Change in benefit obligation		
Benefit obligation at beginning of year	1,825	2,000
Service cost	110	100
Interest cost	110	120
Actuarial loss	55	(45)
Benefits paid	(400)	(350)
Amendments	150	0
Benefit obligation at end of year	1,850	1,825
Change in plan assets		
Fair value of plan assets at beginning of year	0	0
Actual return on plan assets	0	0
Employer contributions	400	350
Benefits paid	(400)	(350)
Fair value of plan assets at end of year	0	0
Funded status	(1,850)	(1,825)
Unrecognized actuarial loss	175	120
Unrecognized prior service cost	360	240
Net amount recognized	(1,315)	(1,465)
Weighted-average assumptions used to determine expense for the fiscal year ended December 31		
Discount rate	7.50%	8.25%
Weighted-average assumptions used to determine benefit obligation at December 31		
Discount rate	6.75%	7.50%

For measurement purposes, a 12% annual rate of increase in the per capita cost of covered health care benefits was assumed for 20X7. The rate was assumed to decrease gradually to 5% for 20(X + 1)4 and remain at that level thereafter.

Components of net periodic benefit cost

	20X6	20X5
Service cost	110	100
Interest cost	110	120
Expected return on plan assets	0	0
Amortization of prior service cost	30	35
Recognized actuarial loss	0	0
Net periodic benefit cost	250	255

Assumed health care cost trend rates have a significant effect on the amounts reported for health care plans. A one-percentage-point change in assumed health care cost trend rates would have the following effects:

	1-Percentage-Point Increase	1-Percentage-Point Decrease
Effect on total of service and interest cost components	12	(10)
Effect on postretirement benefit obligation	190	(175)

Expected Benefit Payments

20X7	275
20X8	250
20X9	225
20(X+1)0	275
20(X+1)1	300
20(X+1)2—20y6	1,175
Expected contributions during fiscal 20X7	275

Exhibit 38.10   Sample Postretirement Medical Disclosures for a Public Entity.

The Board concluded that generally accepted accounting principles required recognition of postemployment benefits on an accrual basis. The Board also concluded that two existing Statements, SFAS No. 43, "Accounting for Compensated Absences," and SFAS No. 5, "Accounting for Contingencies," specified appropriate accounting for postemployment benefits. However, both these Statements specifically excluded postemployment benefits. Therefore, SFAS No. 112 amended SFAS No. 43 and SFAS No. 5 to include postemployment benefits.

(b) STATEMENT OF FINANCIAL ACCOUNTING STANDARDS NO. 112.   As noted above, SFAS No. 112 requires employers to recognize the obligation to provide postemployment benefits under an accrual method of accounting.

(i) Application (Statement of Financial Accounting Standards No. 43 versus Statement of Financial Accounting Standards No. 5).   The method of accrual accounting required under SFAS No. 112 depends on whether the benefit is covered by SFAS No. 43 or SFAS No. 5. Specifically, postemployment benefits that meet each of the following four conditions should be accounted for in accordance with SFAS No. 43:

1. The employer's obligation relating to employee's rights to receive compensation for future absences is attributable to employee services already rendered.
2. The obligation relates to rights that vest or accumulate.
3. Payment of the compensation is probable.
4. The amount can be reasonably estimated.

Postemployment benefits covered by SFAS No. 112 that do not meet these conditions should be accounted for in accordance with SFAS No. 5 so long as it is probable that an event causing the liability has occurred and the cost is reasonably estimable.

In practice, the second item above is the most significant in determining whether SFAS No. 5 or SFAS No. 43 accrual accounting is applicable. Since most postemployment benefits do not vest, accumulation is the key factor. In general, the term *accumulate* means that the benefit varies with an employee's service. In other words, a benefit that increases as an employee renders additional service is said to accumulate. A benefit that is independent of an employee's service does not meet this standard, and SFAS No. 5 treatment should be applied.

An example of a plan that would require SFAS No. 43 accrual accounting is a disability plan that pays income continuation benefits for two weeks for each year of service an employee has rendered at the time of disability. This plan meets each of the four criteria described above. Conversely, if the plan provided 10 weeks of income continuation regardless of seniority at the time of disability, SFAS No. 5 accounting would apply.

As with all of the Statements described in this chapter, SFAS No. 112 need not be applied to immaterial items. Unlike SFAS Nos. 87 and 106, postemployment benefits are much more likely to fall below the materiality threshold for many employers. This is due to the nature of postemployment benefit plans, which often pay relatively small benefits for short periods of time.

(ii) Differences in Accrual Accounting.   For postemployment benefits that are subject to SFAS No. 43, a liability and expense must be accrued for all participants covered by the benefit plan in question. This includes all active employees who are eligible for the benefit as well as participants who are currently in pay status. For active participants, that raises a question regarding attribution. Paragraphs 12 and 13 of SFAS No. 43 appear to be based on an assumption that accumulating postemployment benefits should accrue uniformly over all service. Looking to SFAS Nos. 87 and 106, as SFAS No. 112 suggests, SFAS No. 43 type benefits should accrue uniformly over all service unless the benefit accrual pattern is strongly front-loaded. In this case, the Statements suggest that the expense accrual pattern should follow the benefit accrual pattern. Therefore, a service-based approach following the pattern of benefit accruals should be applied for the attribution of benefits under SFAS No. 43.

SFAS No. 5 requires a terminal accrual approach. Therefore, income is not charged until both of the following conditions are met:

1. Information available before the financial statements are issued indicates that it is *probable* that a liability has been incurred.
2. The amount of the liability can be reasonably estimated.

The importance of the term *probable* in the conditions above is best illustrated with an example. With long-term disability plans, it is often several months between the date a disability occurs and the time at which benefit payments are approved. The time between when the claim is filed and when payment is approved is used to confirm that the disability meets all of the conditions necessary to trigger payment under the terms of the plan. If this adjudication period overlaps a fiscal year end, SFAS No. 5 requires that a liability be accrued for an employee if the employer believes it is probable that disability payments will be made to the employee in question.

Therefore, the liability for such a plan is equal to the actuarial present value of future benefits for all participants currently in pay status plus the liability attributable to employees who have been injured but whose claims have not been fully adjudicated. Since not every disability claim results in payment, an assumption about the number of disability claims that will result in payment should be made. No liability is accrued for currently healthy active employees under SFAS No. 5.

(iii) Measurement Issues. SFAS No. 112 does not specifically address how to measure an employer's postemployment benefit obligation. However, the Board urged employers to utilize guidance provided in SFAS Nos. 87 and 106 on the measurement of postretirement benefit obligations. Since most postemployment benefits are structurally similar to pension and other postretirement benefits, employers have generally adopted the methodology and assumptions guidance provided in these two Statements.

For plans subject to SFAS No. 43 accounting, the annual expense determination is similar to that in SFAS Nos. 87 and 106. The expense is made up of several familiar components: service cost, interest cost, amortization of prior service cost, and amortization of actuarial gains and losses. Paragraph 25 of SFAS No. 112 specifically disallowed delayed recognition of the transition obligation. Therefore, all employers were required to record the entire liability at adoption as the effect of a change in accounting principle.

SFAS No. 112 and SFAS No. 43 provide little or no explicit guidance on delayed recognition of plan amendments and actuarial gains and losses. While a strict reading of SFAS No. 43 seems to preclude delayed recognition of any portion of the liability, in practice many employers have used the Board's advice to rely on SFAS Nos. 87 and 106 to support delayed recognition of these two items. When amortization is used, the amortization period is expected future service until expected payment. This produces a fairly short amortization period, thereby reducing the discrepancy between immediate and delayed recognition.

For plans covered by SFAS No. 5, the balance sheet liability is equal to the actuarially determined value of the benefit obligation as of the financial statement date. Therefore, the income statement expense is equal to the amount to reconcile the prior and current year's reserve, adjusting for actual cash payments during the year.

SFAS No. 112 provides no specific guidance on the use of discounting or other assumptions, other than indicating that discounting of postemployment benefit obligations is permitted but not required. SFAS Nos. 43 and 5 are also silent on this issue. As encouraged by paragraph 23 of SFAS No. 112, employers should look to SFAS Nos. 87 and 106 for guidance in selecting assumptions to the extent they are used. Therefore, employers have used actuarial assumptions such as discount rates, salary scale, mortality, and disability incidence in measuring the SFAS No. 112 liability. In general, these assumptions are the same as those used for measuring liabilities under SFAS Nos. 87 and 106. One exception is the discount rate for workers' compensation, which is based on yields on risk-free securities. Employers have therefore looked to Treasury security yields instead of high-quality corporate debt in setting the discount rate for these purposes.

(iv) Disclosures.   SFAS No. 112 does not include any stringent disclosure requirements. In fact, the Statement requires disclosure only if the obligation for a postemployment benefit plan is not reflected in the financial statements because the amount cannot be reasonably estimated. This may be the case for a postemployment benefit that is triggered by an event that is difficult to predict with any degree of accuracy. Therefore, in practice, employers have not provided detailed financial statement notes like those required under SFAS No. 132 for pension (SFAS No. 87) and other postretirement benefits (SFAS No. 106).

(v) Illustration.   The following is an illustration of the key actuarial results for a typical SFAS No. 112 liability. The plan in question is a long-term disability plan that provides income and

---

Reconciliation of Funded Status

1. Actuarial Liability	
a. Disabled Participants	($12,000,000)
b. Active Participants	($20,000,000)
c. Total	($32,000,000)
2. Fair Value of Assets	$0
3. Funded Status	($32,000,000)
4. Unrecognized Amount at Transition*	$0
5. Unrecognized Net Loss/(Gain)	$6,000,000
6. Unrecognized Prior Service Cost	$0
7. (Accrued)/Prepaid Postemployment Benefit Cost at Year End	($26,000,000)

*SFAS No. 112 did not allow delayed recognition of the transition obligation.

Change in (Accrued)/Prepaid Postemployment Benefit Cost

1. (Accrued)/Prepaid Postemployment Benefit Cost at Prior Year End	($24,400,000)
2. Expense During Year*	
a. Service Cost	$2,200,000
b. Interest Cost	$2,800,000
c. Amortization of Loss/(Gain)	$600,000
d. Total Expense	$5,600,000
3. Payouts During Year**	$4,000,000
4. (Accrued)/Prepaid Postemployment Benefit Cost at Current Year End	($26,000,000)

* Since SFAS No. 43 applies to this plan, the annual expense is explicitly calculated as the sum of the service cost, interest cost, and amortization of unrecognized actuarial losses. Were this a SFAS No. 5 plan, the annual expense would equal the change in the actuarial reserve, adjusted for benefit payments made during the year.
** Since the plan is unfunded, benefit payments are treated as employer contributions.)

Exhibit 38.11   Illustration of SFAS No. 112 accounting.

medical continuation benefits. The amount of benefit is based on a schedule that takes an employee's service at time of disability into account. Since the benefits "accumulate," the plan is subject to the requirements of SFAS No. 43, and therefore, the reporting on it must reflect a liability for both active and disabled participants.

The reconciliation of funded status is reflected in a manner similar to that for SFAS No. 87 and SFAS No. 106 to show the similarities between SFAS No. 112 and these two Statements. However, SFAS No. 112 does not include financial statement note disclosure for this type of plan, so this level of detail need not be presented (see Exhibit 38.11).

38.8 SOURCES AND SUGGESTED REFERENCES

American Academy of Actuaries, "An Actuary's Guide to Compliance with Statement of Financial Accounting Standards No. 87." AAA, Washington, DC, 1986.

———, "Actuarial Compliance Guideline for Statement of Financial Accounting Standards No. 88." Actuarial Standards Board, Washington, DC, 1989.

Accounting Principles Board, "Accounting for the Cost of Pension Plans," APB Opinion No. 8. AICPA, New York, 1966.

———, "Accounting Changes," APB Opinion No. 20. AICPA, New York, 1971.

———, "Reporting the Results of Operation—Reporting the Effects of Disposal of a Segment of a Business, and Extraordinary, Unusual and Infrequently Occurring Events and Transactions," APB Opinion No. 30. AICPA, New York, 1973.

Accounting Standards Executive Committee, "Accounting for and Reporting of Postretirement Medical Benefit (401(h)) Features of Defined Benefit Pension Plans," Statement of Position 99-2. AICPA, New York, 1999.

Financial Accounting Standards Board, "A Guide to Implementation of Statement 87 on Employers' Accounting for Pensions: Questions and Answers." FASB, Stamford, CT, 1986.

———, "A Guide to Implementation of Statement 88: Questions and Answers." FASB, Norwalk, CT, 1988.

———, "Accounting and Reporting by Defined Benefit Pension Plans," Statement of Financial Accounting Standards No. 35. FASB, Stamford, CT, 1980.

———, "Employers' Accounting for Pensions," Statement of Financial Accounting Standards No. 87. FASB, Stamford, CT, 1985.

———, "Employers' Accounting for Settlements and Curtailments of Deferred Benefit Pension Plans and for Termination Benefits," Statement of Financial Accounting Standards No. 88. FASB, Stamford, CT, 1985.

———, "Employers' Accounting for Postretirement Benefits Other than Pension," Statement of Financial Accounting Standards No. 106. FASB, Norwalk, CT, 1990.

———, "Accounting for Income Taxes," Statement of Financial Accounting Standards No. 109. FASB, Norwalk, CT, 1992.

———, "Reporting by Defined Benefit Pension Plans of Investment Contracts," Statement of Financial Accounting Standards No. 110. FASB, Norwalk, CT, 1992.

———, "Employers' Accounting for Postemployment Benefits," Statement of Financial Accounting Standards No. 112. FASB, Norwalk, CT, 1992.

———, "Reporting Comprehensive Income," Statement of Financial Accounting Standards No. 130. FASB, Norwalk, CT, 1997.

———, "Employers' Disclosures about Pensions and Other Postretirement Benefits," Statement of Financial Accounting Standards No. 132 (revised 2003). FASB, Norwalk, CT, 2003.

———, "Business Combinations," Statement of Financial Accounting Standards No. 141. FASB, Norwalk, CT, 2001.

Lorenson, Leonard, and Rosenfield, Paul, "Vested Benefits—A Company's Only Pension Liability," *Journal of Accountancy*, October 1983.

Munnell, Alicia H., *Economics of Private Pensions*. The Brookings Institution, Washington, DC, 1982.

STOCK-BASED COMPENSATION

Peter T. Chingos, CPA

Mercer Human Resources Consulting

Walton T. Conn, Jr., CPA

KPMG Peat Marwick LLP

John R. Deming, CPA

KPMG Peat Marwick LLP

39.1 HISTORY OF ACCOUNTING FOR STOCK-BASED COMPENSATION

The nature and types of stock-based compensation plans and awards have constantly changed over the years. However, the two most significant problems in determining the appropriate accounting for such awards have remained the same:

1. Measurement of compensation cost (i.e., the determination of total compensation cost to be allocated to expense for financial reporting purposes)

2. Allocation of compensation cost (i.e., the determination of the period(s) over which total compensation cost should be allocated to expense and the method of allocation)

To be sure, employees are compensated by being awarded stock options when they contribute services. However, their employers do not incur any cost in compensating them that way, any more than they do in issuing previously unissued shares of their stock when they receive money from new stockholders. The preexisting stockholders are the ones who incur a cost when employees are awarded stock options, first a cost of contingent dilution of their ownership interest and later a cost of actual dilution of their ownership interest. A reporting entity should report the costs it incurs, not costs other entities incur. Ironically, after centering its consideration of reporting in connection with the awarding of employee stock options on the concept of compensation cost, the Financial Accounting Standards Board (FASB) implicitly agreed that the employers incur no cost when compensating the employees when awarding the options, though they do incur a cost in using up the services provided by the employees for which they are awarded options: "... issuances of equity instruments result in the receipt of ... services, which give rise to expenses as they are used in an entity's operations."[1] *Compensation cost* is therefore a misnomer, and attempting to determine the amount and timing of such a nonexistent cost diverts attention away from determining the amount and timing of the cost of using up the services received from the employees. The American Institute of Certified Public Accountants (AICPA) Accounting Standards Division made that point to the FASB when the FASB was considering the issue. The FASB explicitly ignored that advice when it issued its Invitation to Comment: It stated that AcSEC's analysis is "... beyond the scope of this project."[2]

The authoritative accounting literature addresses the accounting for stock-based compensation in two pronouncements which are as follows:

1. APB Opinion No. 25, "Accounting for Stock Issued to Employees" (AICPA, 1972). Also see Interpretation of APB Opinion No. 25, "Accounting for Stock Issued to Employees" (AICPA, 1973).

2. Statement of Financial Accounting Standard No. 123, "Accounting for Stock-Based Compensation" (FASB, 1995).

The APB Opinion No. 25 is applicable "to all stock option, purchase, award, and bonus rights granted by an employer corporation to an individual employee .... "The Opinion contains substantial guidance in the application of its provisions to such plans.

Subsequent to the issuance of APB Opinion No. 25, the trend toward the adoption by enterprises of more complex plans and awards continued. Of particular significance was the increase in the number of combination plans—plans that provide for the granting of two or more types of awards to individual employees. In many combination plans, the employee, or the enterprise, must make an election from alternative awards as to the award to be exercised, thereby canceling the other awards granted under the plan.

Following the issuance of APB Opinion No. 25, there was also a significant increase in the number of plans that provided for the granting of variable awards to employees. A variable award is one that at the date the grant is awarded, either (1) the number of shares of stock (or the amount of cash) an employee is entitled to receive, (2) the amount an employee is required to pay to exercise his rights with respect to the award, or (3) both the number of shares an employee is entitled to receive and the amount an employee is required to pay, are unknown. One of the most popular variable awards is the stock appreciation right (SAR). The SARs are rights granted that entitle an employee to receive, at a specified future date(s), the excess of the market value of a specified number of shares of the granting employer's capital stock over a stated price. The form of payment for amounts earned under an award of SARs may be specified by the award (i.e., stock,

---

[1] FASB, Statement of Standards No. 123, "Accounting for Stock-Based Compensation," par. 89.
[2] Id., Invitation to Comment, "Accounting for Compensation Plans Involving Certain Rights Granted to Employees," May 31, 1984, par. 155.

cash, or a combination thereof), or the award may permit the employee or employer to elect the form of payment.

Notwithstanding the guidance provided in APB Opinion No. 25, considerable disagreement continued to exist as to the appropriate method of accounting for variable awards. As a result, significant differences arose in the methods used by employers to account for variable awards, which led to numerous requests of the FASB for clarification. In December 1978, the FASB provided this clarification through the issuance of FASB Interpretation No. 28, "Accounting for Stock Appreciation Rights and Other Variable Stock Option or Award Plans," an interpretation of APB Opinion No. 25. In paragraph No. 2 of the Interpretation, the FASB specifies that:

> APB Opinion No. 25 applies to plans for which the employer's stock is issued as compensation or the amount of cash paid as compensation is determined by reference to the market price of the stock or to changes in its market price. Plans involving SARs and other variable plan awards are included in those plans dealt with by [APB] Opinion No. 25.

The Interpretation provides specific guidance in the application of APB Opinion No. 25 to variable awards, particularly in those more troublesome areas where the greatest divergence in accounting existed prior to its issuance.

However, APB Opinion No. 25, as interpreted, failed to incorporate criteria that can be consistently applied to all types of plans. As a result, as new types of plans have evolved and changes in the tax laws have occurred, new interpretations and guidance have been required, resulting in a steady stream of pronouncements by the FASB and the Emerging Issues Task Force (EITF) since 1978, as shown in Exhibit 39.1.

The nature and the frequency of these additional pronouncements underscore the difficulties in applying the primary pronouncements to the myriad of stock-based compensation awards that have arisen since their issuance.

To address this problem, the FASB undertook a major project in 1984 to reconsider the accounting for stock-based compensation, whether issued to employees or issued to vendors, suppliers, or other nonemployees. In October 1995, the FASB issued FASB Statement No. 123, "Accounting for Stock-Based Compensation." FASB Statement No. 123 allows companies to retain the current approach set forth in APB Opinion No. 25, as amended, interpreted, and clarified; however, companies are encouraged to adopt a new accounting method based on the estimated fair value of employee stock options. Companies that do not follow the fair value method are required to provide expanded disclosures in the footnotes. Thus, the FASB settled on a compromise solution to a complex issue that had become extremely politicized. The vast majority of entities have not elected the fair value method of accounting for stock options. Therefore, the financial statements of most companies include two presentations of a company's results of operations rather than the normal presentation of a single net income.

FASB Statement No. 123 was preceded by an exposure draft issued by the FASB that would have required a new accounting method that results in reporting expense in connection with virtually all stock options issued to employees. However, those who receive stock options believe a requirement to change to the new method could threaten their stock options: The *Wall Street Journal* reported that "FASB's chairman . . . Dennis Beresford . . . says he scoffed at the doomsday arguments during a heated discussion aboard one corporate jet. The executives he was debating invited him to exit the craft—at 20,000 feet."[3] And Beresford himself reported that ". . . the CEO of one of United States' most successful companies . . . said that if the FASB was allowed to finalize the draft as proposed 'it would end capitalism' "[4]

To prevent this "disaster," the U.S. Congress prepared a bill entitled the Accounting Standards Reform Act, which, if enacted, would have required the Securities and Exchange Commission

---

[3] John Helyar and Joann S. Lublin, "Corporate Coffers Gush with Currency of an Opulent Age," *Wall Street Journal*. August 10, 1998, p. B.5.

[4] Dennis R. Beresford, "How to Succeed as a Standard Setter by Trying Really Hard," *Accounting Horizons*, September 1997, p. 83.

FASB AND EITF PRONOUNCEMENTS SINCE 1978

Year	Issued By	Title
1982	FASB	FASB Technical Bulletin No. 82–2: "Accounting for the Conversion of Stock Options into Incentive Stock Options as a Result of the Economic Recovery Tax Act of 1981"
1984	FASB	FASB Interpretation No. 38: "Determining the Measurement Date for Stock Option, Purchase, and Award Plans Involving Junior Stock," an interpretation of APB Opinion No. 25
1984	EITF	EITF Issue No. 84–13: "Purchase of Stock Options and Stock Appreciation Rights in a Leveraged Buyout"
1984	EITF	EITF Issue No. 84–18: "Stock Option Pyramiding"
1984	EITF	EITF Issue No. 84–34: "Permanent Discount Restricted Stock Purchase Plans"
1985	EITF	EITF Issue No. 85–45: "Business Combinations: Settlement of Stock Options and Awards"
1987	EITF	EITF Issue No. 87–6: "Adjustments Relating to Stock Compensation Plans"
1987	EITF	EITF Issue No. 87–23: "Book Value Stock Purchase Plans"
1987	EITF	EITF Issue No. 87–33: "Stock Compensation Issues Related to Market Decline"
1988	EITF	EITF Issue No. 88–6: "Book Value Stock Plans in an Initial Public Offering"
1990	EITF	EITF Issue No. 90–7: "Accounting for a Reload Stock Option"
1990	EITF	EITF Issue No. 90–9: "Changes to Fixed Employee Stock Option Plans as a Result of Equity Restructuring"
1994	EITF	EITF Issue No. 94–6: "Accounting for the Buyout of Compensatory Stock Options"
1995	EITF	EITF Issue No. 95–16: "Accounting for Stock Compensation Arrangements with Employer Loan Features under APB Opinion No. 25"
1995	FASB	FASB Statement No. 123, "Accounting for Stock-Based Compensation"
1997	EITF	EITF Issue No. 96–18, "Accounting for Equity Instruments That Are Issued to Other Than Employees for Acquiring, or in Conjunction with Selling, Goods or Services"
1997	EITF	EITF Issue No. 97–12, "Accounting for the Delayed Receipt of Option Shares upon Exercise under APB Opinion No. 25"
1997	EITF	EITF Issue No. 97–12, "Accounting for Increased Share Authorizations in an IRS Section 423 Employee Stock Purchase Plan Under APB Opinion No. 25"
1997	FASB	FASB Technical Bulletin 97–1, "Accounting under Statement 123 for Certain Employee Stock Purchase Plans with a Look-Back Option"
1999	EITF	EITF Topic No. D-83, " Accounting for Payroll Taxes Associated with Stock Option Exercises"
2000	EITF	EITF Issue No. 00–8, "Accounting by a Grantee for an Equity Instrument to Be Received in Conjunction with Providing Goods or Services"
2000	EITF	EITF Issue No. 00–18, "Accounting Recognition for Certain Transactions Involving Equity Instruments Granted to Other Than Employees"
2000	FASB	FASB Interpretation No. 44, "Accounting for Certain Transactions Involving Stock Compensation"
2000	EITF	EITF Topic No. 91, "Application of APB Opinion No. 33 and FASB Interpretation No. 44 to an Indirect Repricing of a Stock Option"
2000	EITF	EITF Issue No. 0012, "Accounting by an Investor for Stock-Based Compensation Granted to Employees of an Equity Method Investee"
2000	EITF	EITF Issue No. 00–18, "Classification in the Statement of Cash Flows of the Income Tax Benefit Received by a Company upon Exercise of a Nonqualified Employee Stock Option"
2000	EITF	EITF Issue No. 00–16, "Recognition and Measurement of Employer Payroll Taxes on Employee Stock-Based Compensation"
2001	EITF	EITF Issue No. 00–23, "Issues Related to the Accounting for Stock Compensation under APB Opinion No. 25 and FASB Interpretation No. 44"
2001	EITF	EITF Issue No. 01–1, "Accounting for a Convertible Instrument Granted or Issued to a Nonemployee for Goods or Services or a Combination of Goods or Services and Cash"
2001	EITF	EITF Topic No. 93, "Accounting for Rescission of the Exercise of Employee Stock Options"

Exhibit 39.1   Accounting pronouncements related to stock compensation plans and awards since 1978.

(SEC) to pass on all new standards approved by the FASB. The bill stated, in part: ". . . any new accounting standard or principle, and any modification . . . shall become effective only following an affirmative vote of a majority of a quorum of the member of the [Securities and Exchange] Commission." The bill was proposed simply to pressure the SEC to prevent the FASB from making this particular exposure draft final.

When the FASB was considering accounting for stock-based compensation leading to the issuance of FASB Statement No. 123, it did not address practice issues related to Opinion No. 25, because the Board had planned to supersede Opinion No. 25. Because FASB Statement No. 123 did not supersede Opinion No. 25, the FASB issued its Interpretation No. 44 to address issues on the application of Opinion No. 25 in a number of circumstances. Interpretation No. 44 was developed within the framework of Opinion No. 25 and does not refer to the concepts in FASB Statement No. 123.

Interpretation No. 44 became effective July 1, 2000. Except as noted next, it was to be applied prospectively to new awards, exchanges of awards in business combinations, modifications to outstanding awards, and changes in grantee status that occurred on or after that date.

The guidance about modifications to fixed stock option awards that directly or indirectly reduce the exercise price of an award apply to modifications made after December 15, 1998. The guidance about the definition of an employee applies to new awards granted after December 15, 1998. The guidance about modifications to fixed stock option awards to add a reload feature applies to modifications made after January 12, 2000. To the extent that events covered by the Interpretation discussed in this paragraph occur after the applicable date but before July 1, 2000, the effects of applying the Interpretation are to be recognized only prospectively. Accordingly, no adjustments are to be made on initial application of the Interpretation to financial statements for periods before July 1, 2000. Additional compensation cost measured on initial application of the Interpretation attributable to periods before July 1, 2000, is not recognized.

The initial application of the guidance for awards to an entity's nonemployee board of directors, if previously accounted for as awards to nonemployees and now required by the Interpretation to be accounted for under Opinion No. 25, is to be reported as a cumulative effect of a change in accounting principle.

Since companies continue to use the intrinsic value approach prescribed by APB Opinion No. 25, the authors have separated the chapter into two distinct parts. The first part will cover the application of APB Opinion No. 25 and its related interpretations and EITF issues. The remainder of the chapter will address the application of FASB Statement No. 123.

39.2 SCOPE OF ACCOUNTING PRINCIPLES BOARD OPINION NO. 25

FASB Interpretation No. 44 addresses questions that have been raised as to whether Opinion No. 25 applies to accounting by the grantor of stock compensation to independent contractors or other service providers not employees of the grantor. It states that Opinion No. 25 applies to grantor employers for only stock compensation to those who meet the definition of employee under Opinion No. 25 as amplified by Interpretation No. 44.

For purposes of applying Opinion No. 25, a person is an employee if the grantor consistently represents the person to be an employee under common law, as illustrated in case law and under U.S. Internal Revenue Service Revenue Ruling 87–14. For such a person to be a common law employee, the grantor must represent the person as an employee for payroll tax purposes. However, simply representing a person as an employee for payroll tax purposes is insufficient to indicate that the person is an employee for purposes of Opinion No. 25.

An exception to the guidance in the preceding paragraph involves a grantor of stock compensation to a person who provides services to the grantor under a lease or co-employment agreement between the grantor and another entity under which the grantor is not the employer of record for payroll tax purposes. Such a person is deemed to be an employee of the grantor under Opinion No. 25 if all of the following criteria are met:

a. The person is a common law employee of the grantor, and the other entity is contractually required to pay payroll taxes on the compensation paid to the person for services provided to the grantor.

b. The grantor and the other entity agree in writing to all of the following:

    1. The grantor has the exclusive right to grant stock compensation to the person for the person's services to the grantor.

    2. The grantor has a right to hire, fire, and control the activities of the person. (The other entity may have the same right.)

    3. The grantor has the exclusive right to determine the economic value of the services performed by the person (including wages and the number of units and value of stock compensation granted).

    4. The person can participate in the grantor's employee benefit plans, if any, on the same basis as comparable employees of the grantor.

    5. The grantor agrees to and does remit funds to the other entity sufficient to cover the complete compensation of the person, including all payroll taxes, on or before a contractually agreed date or dates.

A nonemployee member of a grantor's board of directors ordinarily does not meet that definition of an employee. However, application of Opinion No. 25 is required to stock compensation granted to such a person for services provided as a director if the person (a) was elected by the grantor's shareholders or (b) was appointed to a board position to be filled by shareholder election when the existing term expires. Employee status is not involved for awards granted to people for advisory or consulting services in a nonelected capacity or to nonemployee directors for services outside their role as directors, such as legal or investment banking advice or for loan guarantees.

Except as indicated in the preceding paragraph, Opinion No. 25 does not apply to the accounting by a grantor for stock compensation granted to nonemployees. For example, it does not apply to the accounting by a corporate investor of an unconsolidated investee for stock options or awards granted by the investor to employees of the investee accounted for under the equity method.

Whether a person is an employee under Opinion No. 25 is evaluated for consolidated financial statements at the consolidated group level. Stock compensation based on the stock of any consolidated group member is accounted for under Opinion No. 25 if the person meets the definition of an employee for any entity in the consolidated group. For example, Opinion No. 25 applies to the accounting in the consolidated financial statements for awards based on parent stock granted to employees of a consolidated subsidiary, to awards in stock of a consolidated subsidiary granted to employees of the parent, and to awards based on a consolidated subsidiary's stock granted to the employees of another consolidated subsidiary.

Opinion No. 25 does not apply to accounting by an employer for stock compensation granted to its employees (a) by another entity, such as an investee, based on that entity's stock or (b) by the employer based on the stock of another entity. Though that would seem to apply to awards based on the stock of a subsidiary for purposes of reporting in the separate financial statements of the subsidiary, Opinion No. 25 does apply in such circumstances if the subsidiary is part of the consolidated group including the parent company for purposes of preparing its consolidated financial statements.

With a change in status of a grantee to or from that of an employee of the grantor while an outstanding stock option or award is retained by the grantee with no modification of any of its terms, compensation cost under Opinion No. 25 is measured as if the award were newly granted at the date of the change in status. Only the portion of the newly measured cost attributable to the remaining vesting (service) period is recognized as compensation cost prospectively from the date of the change in status. Further, no adjustment is made to compensation cost recognized by the grantor before the change in status unless the award is forfeited unvested because the grantee does not fulfill an obligation. A modification made to a vested award's terms as a result of a change in status has no effect. If the grantee terminates employment before vesting, the cumulative estimate of compensation cost recorded in previous periods is reduced to zero by decreasing compensation cost in the period of forfeiture.

If there is a change in status of a grantee to or from that of an employee of the grantor while an outstanding stock option or award is retained by the grantee with a modification to the award at the time the status is changed, the modified award is treated under Opinion No. 25 as a new award appropriate to the new status of the grantee. Compensation cost thus measured is recognized in full over the remaining vesting (service) period, if any. Compensation cost previously recognized for the forfeited award, if any, is adjusted to zero in the period of forfeiture. A modification is deemed made if its terms would have required it to be forfeited on the change in status and the terms are then modified to continue the award. The modification in effect reinstates or extends the life of the award as a new award to the grantee immediately after the change in status. Similarly, a modification and an effective reinstatement of an award is made if the terms of the award (or underlying plan) provide for the award to continue at the discretion of the grantor and the grantee retains the award after the change in status.

As an exception, a change in grantee status from an employee to a nonemployee as a direct result of a spin-off does not change the grantor's accounting under Opinion No. 25. This applies to only awards granted and outstanding, including adjustments to those awards, at the date of the spin-off. This exception does not apply to other kinds of transactions, such as sale by a parent company of a large enough percentage of the shares of a subsidiary requiring the parent company to deconsolidate the subsidiary.

39.3 APPLICATION OF APB OPINION NO. 25

(a) NONCOMPENSATORY AND COMPENSATORY PLANS.   The APB Opinion No. 25 provides that a plan must have the following four characteristics in order to be considered as noncompensatory:

1. Substantially all full-time employees meeting limited employment qualifications may participate (employees owning a specified percentage of the outstanding stock and executives may be excluded).
2. Stock is offered to eligible employees equally on the basis of a uniform percentage of salary or wages (the plan may limit the number of shares of stock that an employee may purchase through the plan).
3. The time permitted for exercise of an option or purchase right is limited to a reasonable period.
4. The discount from the market price of the stock is no greater than would be reasonable in an offer of stock to stockholders or others.

Because Opinion No. 25 refers to a plan that qualifies under Section 423 of the U.S. Internal Revenue Code as a noncompensatory plan, which permits discounts of up to 15 percent, such a plan has the characteristic required under item 4. Further, for a stock option with an exercise price fixed at the date of grant, a discount of the exercise price of no more than 15 percent from the stock price on that date is reasonable for application of item 4.

Section 423 of the U.S. Internal Revenue Code permits a qualified employee stock purchase plan to contain a look-back option. A look-back option, for example, is a provision in an employee stock purchase plan that establishes the purchase price as the lesser of the stock's market price at the grant date or its market price at the exercise (purchase) date. Because Opinion No. 25 states that a plan that qualifies under Section 423 is noncompensatory, a plan with a look-back option qualifies as noncompensatory under Opinion No. 25.

A compensatory plan is any plan that does not have all four characteristics of a noncompensatory plan. It should be recognized, however, that awards granted under compensatory plans do not necessarily result in recognition of compensation expense by the employer. An employer recognizes compensation expense with respect to awards granted pursuant to a compensatory plan only if the application of the measurement principle results in the determination of compensation cost.

(b) MEASUREMENT OF COMPENSATION: GENERAL PRINCIPLE. Paragraph 10 of APB Opinion No. 25 sets forth the following "measurement principle" for the measurement of compensation cost related to stock option, purchase, and award plans:

> Measurement Principle—Compensation for services that a corporation receives as consideration for stock issued through employee stock option, purchase, and award plans should be measured by the quoted market price of the stock at the measurement date less the amount, if any, that the employee is required to pay.... If a quoted market price is unavailable, the best estimate of the market value of the stock should be used to measure compensation.... The measurement date for determining compensation cost in stock option, purchase, and award plans is the first date on which are known both (1) the number of shares that an individual employee is entitled to receive, and (2) the option or purchase price, if any.

When both of the factors specified in paragraph 10 of APB Opinion No. 25 are known at the grant or award date (i.e., a fixed award), total compensation cost for an award is measured at the grant date. However, when either or both of these factors are not known at the grant or award date (i.e., a variable award), an employer should estimate total compensation cost each period from the date of grant or award to the measurement date based on the quoted market price of the employer's capital stock at the end of each period. This latter point is clarified in FASB Interpretation No. 28, which defines the compensation related to variable plan awards as:

> The amount by which the quoted market value of the shares of the employer's stock covered by the grant exceeds the option price or value specified, by reference to a market price or otherwise, subject to any appreciation limitations under the plan. Changes, either increases or decreases, in the quoted market value of those shares between the date of grant and the measurement date [as defined in APB Opinion No. 25] result in a change in the measure of compensation for the right or award.

(c) APPLICATION OF THE MEASUREMENT PRINCIPLE. A proper understanding of the measurement principle of APB Opinion No. 25 (including the clarification set forth in FASB Interpretation No. 28) is essential to determining the appropriate accounting, including the amount of compensation expense to be recognized. Paragraphs 11(a) through 11(h) of APB Opinion No. 25, as well as subsequent FASB and EITF pronouncements, contain guidance on the application of the measurement principle, as discussed in the following paragraphs.

(i) Measurement of Compensation Cost Based on Cost of Treasury Stock. Paragraph 11(a) states:

> Measuring compensation by the cost to an employer corporation of reacquired (treasury) stock that is distributed through a stock option, purchase, or award plan is not acceptable practice. The only exception is that compensation cost under a plan with all the provisions described in paragraph 11(c) may be measured by the cost of stock that the corporation (1) reacquires during the fiscal period for which the stock is to be awarded and (2) awards shortly thereafter to employees for services during that period.

Thus compensation cost of an award of stock for current services may be measured by the cost of reacquired treasury stock only if the above conditions and those specified in paragraph 11(c) (see below) of the Opinion are met. Otherwise, compensation cost should be measured as of the measurement date otherwise determined in accordance with the criterion set forth in paragraph 10 of the Opinion.

(ii) Vesting Contingent on Continued Employment.   Paragraph 11(b) states:

> The measurement date is not changed from the grant or award date to a later date solely by provisions that termination of employment reduces the number of shares of stock that may be issued to an employee.

This paragraph makes it clear that a requirement that an employee remain employed by the granting enterprise for a specified period of time in order for his rights to become vested under a stock-based compensation award does not preclude a determination, as of the grant or award date, of the total compensation cost to be recognized as an expense by the granting employer.

(iii) Designation of Measurement Date.   Paragraph 11(c) states:

> The measurement date of an award of stock for current service may be the end of the fiscal period, which is normally the effective date of the award, instead of the date that the award to an employee is determined if (1) the award is provided for by the terms of an established formal plan, (2) the plan designates the factors that determine the total dollar amount of awards to employees for the period (for example, a percent of income), although the total amount or the individual awards may not be known at the end of the period, and (3) the award pertains to current service of the employee for the period.

The effect of this paragraph is to allow the designation of the end of a fiscal period as the measurement date when all of the conditions specified in paragraph 11(c) are met, even though the actual awards to individual employees may not be determined until after the close of the fiscal period.

(iv) Impact of Renewals, Extensions, and Other Modifications of Stock Options and Purchase Rights.   Paragraph 11(d) states:

> Renewing a stock option or purchase right or extending its period establishes a new measurement date as if the right were newly granted.

This paragraph reflects a very important concept. Its application could result in measurement of compensation cost with respect to outstanding stock option or purchase rights upon their renewal or extension, even though no compensation cost was ascribable to the original award under the measurement principle of APB Opinion No. 25. For example, any excess of the quoted market price of an employer's capital stock over the exercise price of a stock option at the date of renewal or extension is compensation cost; this may require recognition of compensation cost in addition to any compensation cost associated with the original award.

Paragraph 11(d) addresses "renewals" and "extensions" of stock purchase rights. There are modifications other than renewals and extensions that could also have an impact on the accounting for previously granted awards.

The EITF Issue No. 87–33, "Stock Compensation Issues Related to Market Decline," addresses a series of issues related to modifications to stock option and award plans as a result of market decline. The EITF's consensus on these issues generally precludes reversals of previously recognized compensation expense when outstanding awards are modified because of market value declines and, in many instances, require measurement and recognition of compensation cost for both the original and the modified award.

FASB Interpretation No. 44 addresses several issues related to modifications to stock option and award plans that change the life of the award through an extension of the exercise period or a renewal, decreases the exercise or purchase price of the award, or increases the number of shares the grantee is entitled to receive, including the addition of a reload feature.

A modification that renews a fixed award or extends the award's period (life), including a modification contingent on a future separation from employment, results in a new measurement of compensation cost the same as a newly granted award. Any intrinsic value at the modification date in excess of the amount measured at the original measurement date is recognized as compensation cost over the remaining future service period if the award is unvested, or immediately if the award is vested, for any employee who could benefit from the modification.

A modification that increases the life of an option award on separation from employment, but not beyond the original maximum contractual life of the award, is an extension of the award at the date the separation occurs and the life of the award is extended. The intrinsic value of the award is measured at the date of the modification, and any intrinsic value in excess of the amount measured at the original measurement date is recognized as compensation cost if the separation occurs. If the award vests and is exercised before the separation, any incremental intrinsic value at the date of the modification is not recognized, because the life of the award has not been extended. Attribution of additional compensation cost may require estimates, and adjustment of the estimates may be necessary in later periods.

If the original terms of the award provide for vesting to be accelerated at the discretion of the grantor (or on some other discretionary basis), subsequent acceleration of vesting is a modification. In contrast, if vesting is accelerated based on the occurrence of a specific event or condition in accordance with the original terms of the award, for example, if the original terms of an award specify that vesting is accelerated on retirement, death, or disability, no modification has been made and no new measurement of compensation cost is required.

A fixed stock option award may be subject to a modification by having its exercise price reduced (commonly called *repricing*). The exercise price has been reduced if the fair value of the consideration required to be remitted by the grantee on exercise is less than or potentially less than the fair value of the consideration required of the grantee according to the original terms of the award. Such an award is accounted for as variable from the date of the modification to the date the award is exercised, forfeited, or expires unexercised.

An exercise price can be reduced indirectly. For example, the grantor can give the grantee a cash bonus arrangement that is paid only if and when the award is exercised. This is an example of a combined stock award and cash bonus arrangement, discussed below. Or the grantor can allow the grantee to exercise the award with a full-recourse note that does not bear the market interest rate. If the exercise price has been reduced indirectly, the guidance in the preceding paragraph applies.

A grantor can directly or indirectly modify an award by reducing the exercise price contingent on the occurrence of a specified future event or condition, for example, if a certain earnings target or stock price is achieved in the future. Such a modification causes the award to be variable for the remainder of its outstanding life regardless of whether the triggering event occurs or the contingency provisions expires without the contingency occurring. In contrast, the original terms of a stock option award may provide for a reduction to the award's exercise price if a specified future event or condition occurs. If so, variable accounting is applied from the date of grant. A measurement date would occur and variable accounting would stop when the contingency is resolved or the contingency provision expires.

A grantor can, in effect, cancel an option award, for example, by modifying its terms to reduce or eliminate the likelihood that the grantee will exercise the option, such as by increasing the exercise price or curtailing the remaining life of the award. Any such modification is a cancellation.

A grantor can indirectly reduce the exercise price of a fixed stock option award by canceling or effectively canceling it or settling it for cash or other consideration and granting a replacement award at a lower exercise price, either before or after the cancellation or effective cancellation. If a cancellation and an award are combined that way, the replacement award is given variable accounting until it is exercised, is forfeited, or expires unexercised.

An option award cancellation is combined with another option award with a lower exercise price and results in an indirect reduction to the exercise price of the combined award if the other award is granted to the grantee within one of the following periods:

a. The period before the date of the cancellation that is the shorter of six months or the period from the date of the grant of the canceled option

b. The period ending six months after the date of the cancellation

To identify the replacement award that becomes subject to variable accounting on the cancellation of an award, the grantor first looks back in the period before the cancellation described in (a) above. If the award was granted during that period with an exercise price below that of the canceled award, the award and the canceled award are combined. If canceled options remain that were not combined with a replacement award in the look-back period, the grantor then looks forward to the period described in (b) above. If an award is granted during that period at an exercise price below that of the canceled award, the award and the canceled award are combined. When looking backward and then forward, options granted at dates closest to the date of cancellation are first identified as the replacement award. If the replacement award is identified in the look-back period, variable accounting for the award begins at the cancellation date. Prior-period financial statements are not restated if the award was accounted for as a fixed award in those statements.

Nevertheless, an oral or written agreement or implied promise by the grantor to compensate the grantee for any increase in the market price of the stock after a cancellation but before grant of a replacement award requires variable accounting for the replacement award regardless of the amount of time between the cancellation and the replacement grant. Any agreement between the grantor and the grantee when an option award is granted to cancel at a future date another outstanding option award requires variable accounting for the newly granted award from the date of grant.

The preceding also applies to the cancellation of an option award that has been accounted for as variable because of a reduction to that award's exercise price through a prior modification. But any option award granted during the look-back and look-forward periods, regardless of the exercise price of the replacement award, is eligible to be the replacement award. Thus, any replacement or modified award that has been accounted for as a variable award retains that status.

A cancellation of a fixed stock option award and the grant of stock results in a new measurement of compensation cost for the stock grant. The exercise price has been effectively reduced to zero. Variable accounting does not therefore apply to the replacement award. Any excess of the number of shares underlying the canceled fixed stock option award over the number of shares of the replacement stock award is subject to the guidance in the immediately preceding paragraphs.

An equity restructuring is a nonreciprocal transaction between an entity and its shareholders, such as a stock dividend, spin-off, stock split, rights offering, or recapitalization through a special, large, nonrecurring dividend that causes the market value per share of the stock underlying the option award to decrease. Such a restructuring may adjust the exercise price, the number of shares, or both of outstanding stock options or awards. (Ordinary cash dividends or distributions are not equity restructurings for this purpose.) The grantor may reduce the exercise price, increase the numbers of shares under the award, or both, to offset the decrease in the per share price of the stock underlying the award. No accounting consequence results from such an equity restructuring if both of the following are met:

1. The aggregate intrinsic value of the award immediately after the change is not greater than the aggregate intrinsic award immediately before the change.
2. The ratio of the exercise price per share to the market value per share is not reduced.

If those criteria are not met, the modified award is accounted for under Opinion No. 25 as variable from the date of the modification to the date the award is exercised, is forfeited, or expires unexercised. If they are met but the terms of the original award have also been modified to either accelerate the vesting or extend the life of the award, a new measurement of compensation cost is made at the date of the modification as if the award were newly granted. Cash or other consideration provided to restore the economic position of the grantee as a result of an equity restructuring transaction is recognized as compensation cost. The guidance concerning restructuring is applied without regard to whether the provisions of the stock option or award provide for adjustments to the terms in the event of an equity restructuring.

A modification that increases the number of shares to be issued under a fixed stock option award requires the award to be accounted for as variable from the date of the modification to the date the award is exercised, is forfeited, or expires unexercised.

A grantor that modifies a fixed stock option award to add a reload feature, which provides for the grant of a new option award on the exercise of an existing award if specified conditions are met, applies variable accounting for the modified award from the date of the modification to the date the award is exercised, is forfeited, or expires unexercised. The methods used to determine the exercise price, the number of shares, and the life of the reload grant are irrelevant. Variable accounting is required for each additional grant that includes a reload feature under a reload feature that provides for multiple subsequent grants through further reloads.

Total compensation cost is measured as the sum of the following if a fixed stock option or award is canceled or modified and a new measurement of compensation cost or variable accounting is required as a result of the modification:

a. The intrinsic value of the award (if any) at the original measurement date

b. The intrinsic value of the modified (or variable) award that exceeds the lesser of the intrinsic value of the original award (1) at the original measurement date or (2) immediately before the modification

When a stock option or award is modified and a new measurement of compensation cost or variable accounting is required, the remaining unrecognized original intrinsic value, if any, plus any additional compensation cost measured under (b) above is recognized over the remaining vesting (service) period, if any. If the modified award is fully vested at the date of the modification, any additional compensation cost to be recognized is recognized immediately. Recognized compensation cost for an award forfeited because an employee does not fulfill an obligation is reduced to zero by decreasing compensation cost in the period of the forfeiture.

Additional compensation cost measured as of the modification date for modifications to accelerate vesting or to extend the life of an award on a specified future separation from employment (but not beyond the award's original maximum contractual life) for all awards for which the modification results in an effective term extension or an effective renewal. Attribution of additional compensation cost may require estimates and adjustments of the estimates in later periods.

Compensation cost is adjusted for increases or decreases in the intrinsic value of a modified award that requires variable accounting in subsequent periods until the award is exercised, is forfeited, or expires unexercised. Compensation cost is not, however, adjusted below the intrinsic value (if any) of the modified stock option or award at the original measurement date unless the award is forfeited because the employee does not fulfill an obligation.

If cash is paid to an employee to settle an outstanding stock option, to settle an earlier grant of a stock award within six months after vesting, or to repurchase shares within six months after exercise of an option or issuance, total compensation cost is measured as the sum of the following:

- The intrinsic value of the stock option or award (if any) at the original measurement date
- The amount of cash paid to the employee (reduced by any amount of cash paid by the employee to acquire the shares) that exceeds the lesser of the intrinsic value (if any) of the award (1) at the original measurement date or (2) immediately before the cash settlement

The following guidance differs on whether the entity is a public entity or a private entity for this purpose. For this purpose, a public entity is any entity (a) whose securities trade in a public market either on a stock exchange (domestic or foreign) or in an over-the-counter market, including securities quoted only locally or regionally, (b) that makes a filing with a regulatory agency in preparation for the sale of any class of equity securities in a public market, or (c) that is controlled by an entity that meets criterion (a) or (b). A subsidiary of a public entity or a public entity with thinly traded stock follows the accounting for the public entity. But an entity with publicly traded debt but no publicly traded equity securities follows the accounting for a nonpublic entity.

For public reporting entities other than for shares expected to be repurchased at fair value for required tax withholding, variable accounting is required for a stock option or award with a share repurchase feature if the shares are expected to be repurchased within six months after option exercise or issuance of the shares. For a repurchase feature that is a right held by the employee to sell the shares back to the entity, variable accounting is required for the award if the right can be exercised within six months of issuance of the shares. After an option is exercised, the employee bears the risks and rewards of ownership with respect to those shares (except that if the consideration for exercise is a nonrecourse note, the substance is the same as a stock option and the employee bears no risks or rewards of ownership in the shares received). A subsequent repurchase of the shares by the entity (except within six months after option exercise or share issuance) thus represents a separate transaction to acquire treasury stock that is accounted for apart from the original stock option or award.

If the grantor repurchases shares within six months of issuance or option exercise and the repurchase was not expected by the grantor before the date of the repurchase, the grantor follows the preceding guidance for cash settlement of an earlier award.

If a share repurchase feature gives the employee the right to sell the shares back to the grantor after option exercise or share issuance for a premium that is not fixed or determinable over the then-current stock price, that feature creates an arrangement that requires variable accounting, even if the share cannot be sold back to the entity within six months after option exercise or issuance. If such a feature gives the employee the right to sell shares back to the entity for a fixed dollar amount over the stock price but not within six months of issuance of the shares, the fixed premium is recognized as additional compensation cost over the vesting (service) period.

For nonpublic reporting entities, variable accounting is not required for a stock option or award with one of these share repurchase features:

- The stated share repurchase price is equal to the fair value of the shares at the date of repurchase, the employee cannot require the entity to repurchase the shares within six months of option exercise or share issuance, and the shares are not expected to be repurchased within six months after exercise or share issuance.

- The stated share repurchase price is not the fair value of the shares at the date of repurchase, but the employee has made a substantial investment and must bear risks and rewards normally associated with share ownership for at least six months.

- Shares are repurchased for tax-withholding purposes at the grantor's minimum statutory withholding rates, including payroll taxes, applicable to supplemental taxable income.

A substantial investment has been made for purposes of an award that contains a repurchase feature at other than fair value when the employee invests in a form other than services rendered to the entity an amount equal to 100 percent of the stated share repurchase price calculated at the date of grant. If the award is an option, a substantial investment therefore cannot be made before exercise of the option. Because the award is variable, compensation cost is recognized for any intrinsic value of the option from the date of grant to the date a substantial investment has been made.

For purposes of paragraph 11(g) of Opinion No. 25 for both public and nonpublic entities, to determine the variable amount not required, required tax withholding is defined as the employer's minimum statutory withholding rates for federal and state tax purposes, including payroll taxes applicable to such supplemental taxable income. Withheld amounts in excess of that rate do not represent the employer's required tax withholding for this purpose.

If an election to repurchase shares on exercise in excess of the number necessary to satisfy the employer's required tax withholding is at the discretion of the employee, variable accounting is required from the date the award is granted to the date the award is exercised, is forfeited, or expires unexercised. If the terms of an award are silent on tax withholding, or if the repurchase of shares for tax withholding in excess of the number necessary to satisfy the employer's required tax withholding is at the discretion of the employer, variable accounting is not required. However, in either circumstance, if the employer exhibits a pattern of consistently approving repurchases of excess shares, variable accounting is required from the date of grant for all awards under the plan.

If shares are repurchased on exercise of a fixed option award in excess of the number necessary to satisfy the employer's required tax withholding, a new measurement of compensation cost is required for the entire award.

Changes to the exercise price or the number of share of a fixed stock option award as a result of an exchange of fixed stock option awards in a business combination accounted for by the pooling of interests method have no accounting consequence if both of the following are met at the date of exchange:

a. The aggregate intrinsic value of the options immediately after the exchange is no greater than the aggregate intrinsic value of the options immediately before the exchange.

b. The ratio of the exercise price per option to the market value per share is not reduced.

If those criteria are not met, a new measurement of compensation cost is required.

Vested stock options or awards issued by an acquirer in a business combination accounted for by the purchase method in exchange for outstanding awards held by employees of the acquiree are considered to be part of the purchase price paid by the acquirer for the acquiree and accounted for under FASB Statement No. 141. The fair value of the new (acquirer) awards are included as part of the purchase price.

Unvested stock options or awards granted by an acquirer in a business combination accounted for by the purchase method in exchange for stock options or awards held by employees of the acquiree are considered to be part of the purchase price for the acquiree, and the fair value of the new (acquirer) awards are included in the purchase price. However, to the extent that service is required after the consummation date of the acquisition in order to vest in the replacement awards, a portion of the intrinsic value (if any) of the unvested awards is allocated to unearned compensation and recognized as compensation cost over the remaining future vesting (service) period. The amount allocated is based on the portion of the intrinsic value at the consummation date related to the future vesting (service) period. The amount is calculated as the intrinsic value of the replacement awards at the consummation date multiplied by the fraction that is the remaining future vesting (service) period divided by the total vesting (service) period, which is the vesting period before the consummation date plus the remaining future period required to vest in the replacement award. Any intrinsic value of the replacement awards allocated to unearned compensation cost is deducted from the fair value of the awards for purposes of the allocation of the purchase price to the other assets acquired.

Awards granted under a plan subject to shareholder approval generally are not deemed granted until approval is obtained, and, therefore, no measurement date can occur before then. However, if management and the members of the board of directors control sufficient votes to approve the plan, a grant date and therefore a measurement date may be deemed to have occurred before shareholder approval, because approval then is merely a formality.

Deferred tax assets recognized for temporary differences related to stock options or awards under Opinion No. 25 should not be adjusted for subsequent declines in the stock price. Such assets are determined by the compensation expense recognized for financial reporting rather than by reference to the expected future tax deduction, which would be estimated using the current intrinsic value of the award. A valuation allowance to reduce the carrying amount of the assets is established only if the grantor expects future taxable income to be insufficient to recover the assets in the periods in which the deduction would otherwise be recognized for tax purposes.

A cash bonus and a stock option award are accounted for as a combined award if payment by the grantor or refund by the employee of the cash bonus is contingent on exercise of the option award. A cash bonus that is not fixed and that is contingent on exercise of an option award is accounted for as a variable award. A fixed cash bonus that is contingent on exercise of a fixed option award is accounted for as a combined fixed award with the cash bonus reducing the stated exercise price of the option award. A cash bonus, regardless of whether it is fixed or variable, that is contingent on vesting of a stock option or award is accounted for as compensation cost separate from the stock option or award.

(v) Transfer of Stock or Assets to a Trustee, Agent, or Other Third Party.   Paragraph 11(e) states:

> Transferring stock or assets to a trustee, agent, or other third party for distribution of stock to employees under the terms of an option, purchase, or award plan does not change the measurement date from a later date to the date of transfer unless the terms of the transfer provide that the stock (1) will not revert to the corporation, (2) will not be granted or awarded later to the same employee on terms different from or for services other than those specified in the original grant or award, and (3) will not be granted or awarded later to another employee.

This paragraph reinforces the principle that the measurement date is the first date on which are known both (1) the number of shares that an individual employee is entitled to receive and (2) the option or purchase price, if any. The authors are not aware of any awards that have been structured in a manner that has resulted in an acceleration of the otherwise determined measurement date as a result of the application of paragraph 11(e).

(vi) Awards of Convertible Stock or Rights.   Paragraph 11(f) states:

> The measurement date for a grant or award of convertible stock (or stock that is otherwise exchangeable for other securities of the corporation) is the date in which the ratio of conversion (or exchange) is known unless other terms are variable at that date (paragraph 10b). The higher of the quoted market price at the measurement date of (1) the convertible stock granted or awarded or (2) the securities into which the original grant or award is convertible should be used to measure compensation.

Awards to employees of convertible stock or rights to purchase convertible stock are not common. Nevertheless, this paragraph provides guidance in measuring the compensation cost of such awards. Further guidance can be found in FASB Interpretation No. 38, "Determining the Measurement Date for Stock Option, Purchase, and Award Plans Involving Junior Stock," an interpretation of APB Opinion No. 25.

(vii) Settlement of Awards.   Paragraph 11(g) states:

> Cash paid to an employee to settle an earlier award of stock or to settle a grant of option to the employee should measure compensation cost. If the cash payment differs from the earlier measure of the award of stock or grant of option, compensation cost should be adjusted (par. 15). The amount that a corporation pays to an employee through a compensation plan is "cash paid to an employee to settle an earlier award of stock or to settle a grant of option" if stock is reacquired shortly after issuance. Cash proceeds that a corporation receives from sale of awarded stock or stock issued on exercise of an option and remits to the taxing authorities to cover required withholding of income taxes on an award is not "cash paid to an employee to settle an earlier award of stock or to settle a grant of option" in measuring compensation cost.

The intent of this paragraph seems quite clear. If an earlier award of stock or stock options is ultimately settled by cash payment to the employee, the amount actually paid is the final measure of compensation cost to be recognized by the employer, regardless of the amount of compensation cost previously determined. However, in practice, application of this paragraph has often proved difficult and, as a result, a number of EITF Issues have dealt with cash settlements of awards, as discussed in the following paragraph.

Emerging Issues Task Force Issue No. 84–13, "Purchase of Stock Options and Stock Appreciation Rights in a Leveraged Buyout."   This pronouncement sets forth the EITF's consensus that the "target company" in a leveraged buyout should recognize compensation expense in the amount of cash paid by the target company to acquire outstanding stock options and SARs.

Emerging Issues Task Force Issue No. 85–45, "Business Combinations: Settlement of Stock Options and Awards."   Similar to the consensus in EITF Issue No. 84–13, this consensus indicates that when a target company settles outstanding stock options or awards "voluntarily, at the direction of the acquiring company, or as part of the plan of acquisition, APB Opinion No. 25 requires that the settlement be accounted for as compensation expense in the separate financial statements of the target company."

Emerging Issues Task Force Issue No. 87–6, "Adjustments Relating to Stock Compensation Plans."   This consensus addresses stock option plans that contain a cash bonus feature that provides for a reimbursement to employees of the taxes payable as a result of the exercise of a nonqualified stock option (a "tax-offset bonus"). The consensus indicates that awards under such plans are variable awards. Thus, the existence of a tax-offset bonus related to a stock option award requires that the entire award (the stock option *plus* the cash bonus feature) be accounted for as a variable award, as the option and the tax-offset bonus are viewed as a single variable award. This consensus is consistent with footnote 1 to FASB Interpretation No. 28, "Accounting for Stock Appreciation Rights and Other Variable Stock Option or Award Plans" which states, in part, "Plans under which an employee may receive cash in lieu of stock or additional cash upon the exercise of a stock option are variable plans for purposes of the Interpretation as the amount is contingent upon the occurrence of future events." The significant point here is that two different awards, one being a fixed award and the other a variable award, should be accounted for as a single, variable award.

Emerging Issues Task Force Issue No. 87–23, "Book Value Stock Purchase Plans."   This consensus provides much-needed guidance in accounting for formula-based plans, under which employees purchase shares, or are granted options to acquire shares, of the employer's common stock at a formula price. The formula price is usually based on book value, a multiple of book value, or earnings. Additionally, the employee must sell the acquired shares back to the employer upon retirement or other termination of employment, at a selling price determined in the same manner as the original purchase price.

Privately held companies only:

> No compensation expense should be recognized for changes in the formula price during the employment period "if the employee makes a substantive investment that will be at risk for a reasonable period of time." This consensus applies to plans where the employee is allowed to resell all or a portion of the acquired shares to the company at fixed or determinable dates, as well as plans where the shares are resold to the company only upon retirement or other termination of employment.

Privately held and publicly held companies:

> If options are granted to employees to purchase shares at the formula price and the employees can resell the options, or the shares acquired upon exercise of the options, to the company upon retirement or other termination of employment, or at fixed or determinable dates, the consensus of the EITF is the same for both privately held and publicly held companies. The consensus indicates that compensation expense should be recognized for increases in the formula price from the grant date to the exercise date (i.e., the award should be accounted for as a variable award). The consensus further indicates that the expense previously recognized should not be reversed upon exercise of the option, and that "additional expense would be recognized if the shares are sold back to the company shortly after exercise, as required by paragraph 11(g) of APB Opinion No. 25."

The SEC observer at the EITF provided the following clarification of the SEC staff's views of book value plans for publicly held companies:

> The SEC Observer indicated that the SEC staff views a book value plan for a publicly held company as a performance plan and noted that it should be accounted for like an SAR.

As previously noted, a difference exists between accounting for book value purchase (and other formula-based) awards by privately held and publicly held companies. This difference, of course, raised questions as to the accounting to be applied to these types of awards when a privately held company becomes publicly held. This issue was subsequently addressed in EITF Issue No. 88–6, "Book Value Stock Plans in an Initial Public Offering."

Emerging Issues Task Force Issue No. 87–33, "Stock Compensation Issues Related to Market Decline." This consensus addresses a number of issues related to the October 1987 stock market decline, including "How to account for the repurchase of an outstanding option and the issuance of a 'new' option." The Task Force consensus on this issue was that "paragraph 11(g) of APB Opinion No. 25 does not apply if an existing option is repurchased in contemplation of the issuance of a new option that contains terms identical to the remaining terms of the original option except that the exercise price is reduced . . . ." The consensus also indicates that "the cash paid to repurchase the original option represents additional compensation that should be charged to expense in the current period."

The effect of this consensus is to preclude an employer from decreasing compensation cost associated with a stock option award, by "settling" the award through a cash payment that is less than the amount of compensation cost previously determined, and then granting a "new" option to the same employee that contains terms identical to the remaining terms of the original option except that the exercise price is reduced. In the event such an arrangement were entered into, application of the consensus would (1) require the employer to charge the amount of the cash payment to expense in the current period, (2) prohibit the reversal of previously recognized expense associated with the original option, and (3) require continued amortization of any compensation measured at the original measurement date that had not been amortized and, additionally, could result in the measurement of additional compensation expense associated with the "new" award.

The consensus also requires similar accounting when an option is "repriced," as opposed to the situation described above where an option is canceled and reissued.

Emerging Issues Task Force Issue No. 88–6, "Book Value Stock Plans in an Initial Public Offering." As previously noted, EITF Issue No. 87–23 addresses certain issues related to the accounting for stock purchase awards to employees, where the purchase price is a formula price based on book value or earnings, and where the shares must ultimately be sold back to the company by the employee at a price determined in the same manner as the original purchase price. The consensus set forth in EITF Issue No. 87–23 makes certain distinctions between privately and publicly held companies with respect to the accounting for these types of awards.

In EITF Issue No. 88–6, the Task Force reached a consensus that a book value stock purchase plan of a publicly held company should be viewed as a performance plan and should be accounted for like an SAR (this is consistent with the SEC observer's comment noted under the discussion of EITF Issue No. 87–23 above). Thus, for a publicly held company, compensation expense should be recognized for increases in book value (or other formula price based on earnings) on awards outstanding under such a plan. For a privately held company, however, under the consensus reached in EITF Issue No. 87–23, no compensation expense would be recognized for such increases in the book value or other formula price, regardless of when the awards were granted.

The Task Force also reached consensuses in EITF Issue No. 88–6 related to the recognition and measurement of compensation expense by a privately held company for such awards in the event of a subsequent IPO (i.e., when a privately held company becomes a publicly held company). These consensuses are set forth in Exhibit 39.2.

EITF Issue No. 88–6 also contains certain guidance regarding pro forma disclosures for these types of plans in the event of an IPO, as well as an exhibit that contains "Examples of the Application of APB Opinion No. 25 and the EITF Consensus from Issue Nos. 87–23 and 88–6 in an IPO."

Emerging Issues Task Force Issue No. 94–6, "Accounting for the Buyout of Compensatory Stock Options." EITF Issue No. 87–33 addressed the settling of options and the issuance of new options.

ACCOUNTING FOR BOOK VALUE OPTIONS AND SHARES
OF A PRIVATELY HELD COMPANY AT TIME OF IPO

Type of Award Outstanding	Status at Time of IPO	Accounting
Book value option	Converts to an option to purchase unrestricted (market value) stock	In addition to compensation expense previously recognized for changes in book value, compensation expense should be recognized on successful completion of the IPO for the difference between market value and book value at the date of the IPO, because conversion of the book value option to a market value option results in a new measurement date. Subsequent to the IPO, no further compensation expense would be recognized, assuming the plan otherwise remains a fixed plan under APB Opinion No. 25.
	Remains a book value option	Any change in book value resulting from successful completion of the IPO should be recognized as compensation expense at the time of the IPO in accordance with variable plan (SAR) accounting. Subsequent to the IPO, the plan should continue to be accounted for like an SAR based on the consensus reached in conjunction with EITF Issue No. 87–23.
Book value shares	Converts to unrestricted (market value) stock	No compensation expense should be recognized at the time of the IPO; however, shares issued under the purchase plan within one year of the IPO are presumed to have been issued in contemplation of the IPO and would result in compensation expense for the difference between the book value of those shares and their estimated fair value at date of issuance. Subsequent to the IPO, no further compensation expense would be recognized, assuming the plan remains a fixed plan under APB Opinion No. 25.
	Remains book value stock	No compensation expense should be recognized upon successful completion of the IPO for any impact that the IPO may have on book value; however, shares issued under the purchase plan within one year of the IPO are presumed to have been issued in contemplation of the IPO, and would result in variable award (SAR) accounting for actual changes in book value of the shares since the date of their issuance. Subsequent to the IPO, compensation expense would be recognized for increases in book value after the IPO (variable award accounting).

Exhibit 39.2   Accounting for book value options and book value shares at time of an IPO.

In this issue, the Task Force was asked to address the buyout, or settling, of options without an issuance of new options. In the consensus, the Task Force imposes a rebuttable presumption that options granted within six months of the buyout of the outstanding options would be considered replacement options. In such a case, the issuer would have to consider the implications of EITF Issue No. 87–33.

The Task Force reached a consensus that the total amount of compensation cost to be recognized is the sum of: (1) the compensation cost amortized to the buyout date; (2) the options' intrinsic value, if any, at the buyout date in excess of the compensation cost recognized as expense to the buyout date; and (3) the amount, if any, paid for the options in excess of their intrinsic value at the buyout date. In addition, any remaining unamortized compensation cost related to the original options would not be included in income for any period. Exhibit 94–6A of the EITF Issue No. 94–6 provides examples.

(viii) Combination Plans and Awards.   Paragraph 11(h) states:

> Some plans are a combination of two or more types of plans. An employer corporation may need to measure compensation for the separate parts. Compensation cost for a combination plan permitting an employee to elect one part should be measured according to the terms that an employee is most likely to elect based on the facts available each period.

If more than one type of award is granted to an employee under a plan, the measurement principle must be applied to each award for purposes of measuring compensation cost to an employer. Furthermore, if a combination plan permits an employee to elect one award from a number of alternative awards, compensation cost should be measured in terms of the award the employee is considered most likely to elect in view of the facts available each period. In many combination plans involving alternative awards, an employer retains the right to approve or reject an employee's election under certain circumstances, giving the employer significant control over the determination of the award under which compensation cost will be measured.

FASB Interpretation No. 28 provides additional guidance with respect to combination plans. In that Interpretation, the FASB specifies that in combination plans involving both an SAR or other variable award and a fixed award (e.g., a stock option), compensation cost should normally be measured and allocated to expense under the presumption that the variable award will be elected by the employee. However, this presumption may be overcome if experience or other factors, such as ceilings on the appreciation available to the employee under the variable feature, provide evidence that the employee will elect to exercise the fixed award.

(ix) Stock Option Pyramiding.   Stock option pyramiding is a stock option exercise approach that developed subsequent to the issuance of APB Opinion No. 25. This approach involves the payment by the employee of the option exercise price by transferring to the employer previously owned shares with a current fair value equal to the exercise price. In EITF Issue No. 84–18, "Stock Option Pyramiding," the Task Force reached a consensus that "some holding period" for the exchanged shares is necessary to "avoid the conclusion that the award of the option is, in substance, a variable plan (or a SAR), thereby requiring compensation charges." A majority of the Task Force members indicated that a six-month period would satisfy the holding period requirement.

In a subsequent consensus set forth in EITF Issue No. 87–6, "Adjustments Relating to Stock Compensation Plans," the Task Force addressed a "phantom" stock-for-stock exercise arrangement, under which an employee holds "mature" shares meeting the holding period requirement discussed in EITF Issue No. 84–18. In this consensus, the Task Force indicated that if the exercise is accomplished by the enterprise issuing a certificate for the "net" shares (i.e., the shares issuable upon exercise of the option less the number of shares required to be relinquished to pay the exercise price), as opposed to the enterprise accepting the mature shares in payment of the exercise price and then issuing a new certificate for the total number of shares covered by the exercised option, the plan remains a fixed plan.

Thus, even though the "net" number of shares to be issued under either of the arrangements described above is not known at the date of grant, the use of qualifying mature shares to pay the option exercise price does not, under these two consensuses, change a plan that otherwise qualifies as a fixed plan to a variable plan. As a result, the enterprise is not required to recognize compensation expense for appreciation in shares under option subsequent to the date of grant solely because the award allows for payment of the exercise price of an option by surrendering mature shares owned by the employee or through a phantom stock-for-stock exercise involving mature shares owned by the employee.

(x) Stock Option Gain Deferrals.   Compensation consultants have developed a transaction that they believe enables employees to defer the taxable income derived from the exercise of stock options (and that also delays the employer's tax deduction) by deferring the employees' receipt of the shares of the stock. The transaction, typically referred to as a *stock option gain deferral transaction*, is accomplished by a stock-for-stock exercise. An employee receives new shares equal to the value of the shares tendered, and the remaining shares under option are credited to the employee's deferred compensation account. The employee then receives the shares from the deferred compensation account at retirement or some other future date.

In EITF Issue No. 97–5, "Accounting for the Delayed Receipt of Option Shares upon Exercise under APB Opinion No. 25," the Task Force addressed whether certain characteristics of stock option gain deferral arrangements would cause a new measurement date (or variable plan accounting) for financial reporting purposes under APB Opinion No. 25. An FASB staff announcement resolved the issue prior to the EITF's reaching a consensus. The announcement provides that variable plan accounting would be required if the employee does not meet the necessary six-month holding period set forth in EITF Issue 84–18, "Stock Option Pyramiding," which is discussed above. In addition, the announcement provides that an award that permits diversification into alternative types of investments makes the award subject to variable accounting. Accordingly, if an employee uses "mature" shares in the stock-for-stock exercise and if an award does not permit diversification, the delayed delivery of shares generally would not create a new measurement date or variable plan accounting.

(xi) Use of Stock Option Shares to Cover Required Tax Withholding.   EITF Issue No. 87–6, "Adjustments Relating to Stock Compensation Plans," addresses an issue that is similar to the stock option pyramiding issue discussed under (ix) above. The Task Force reached a consensus that "an option that allows the use of option shares to meet tax withholding requirements may be considered a fixed plan if it meets all the other requirements of APB Opinion No. 25. No compensation needs to be recorded for the shares used to meet the tax withholding requirements. The Task Force noted that this treatment would be limited to the number of shares with a fair value equal to the dollar amount of only the *required* tax withholding." Therefore, even though the net number of shares to be issued would not be known at the date of grant under these circumstances (since the shares to be withheld to cover the required tax withholding will not be known until the exercise date), plans with tax withholding features may be accounted for as fixed plans as long as they meet the other requirements for a fixed plan under APB Opinion No. 25.

(d) ALLOCATION OF COMPENSATION COST: DETERMINING THE SERVICE PERIOD.
APB Opinion No. 25 requires that compensation cost related to "stock option, purchase, and award plans should be recognized as an expense of one or more periods in which an employee performs services.... The grant or award may specify the period or periods during which the employee performs services or the periods may be inferred from the terms or from the past pattern of grants or awards."

FASB Interpretation No. 28 also indicates that compensation cost with respect to variable awards should be allocated to expense over the period(s) in which the employee performs the related services. However, the FASB went a step further in this interpretation by specifying that the service period is presumed to be the vesting period. The vesting period is normally the period from the date of the grant of the rights or awards to the date(s) they become exercisable. These criteria for determining the service period are considerably more definitive than the guidance provided in APB Opinion No. 25 and, in the authors' view, should be used for determining the service period for awards made pursuant to all stock-based compensation awards (i.e., both fixed and variable awards).

(i) Allocation of Compensation Cost Related to Fixed Awards.   Compensation cost related to fixed awards should normally be allocated to expense over the service period on a straight-line basis. On rare occasions, however, circumstances may arise that would justify allocation on another basis. In any event, the method used should be systematic, reasonable, and consistently applied.

(ii) Allocation of Compensation Cost Related to Variable Awards.   Allocating compensation cost related to variable awards to expense is more complex, because the measurement date and, thus, the final determination of compensation cost, occur subsequent to the date of grant. Total compensation cost with respect to a variable award must be estimated from the date of grant to the measurement date, based on the quoted market price of the employer's stock at the end of each interim period. Compensation cost so determined should be allocated to expense in the following manner:

- If a variable award is granted for current and/or future services, estimated total compensation cost determined at the end of each period prior to the expiration of the service period should be allocated to expense over the service period. Changes in the estimated total compensation cost attributable to increases or decreases in the quoted market price of the employer's capital stock subsequent to the expiration of the service period (but prior to the measurement date) should be charged or credited to expense each period as the changes occur.
- If a variable award is granted for past services, estimated total compensation cost determined at the date of grant is charged to expense of the period in which the award is granted. Changes in the estimated total compensation cost attributable to increases or decreases in the quoted market price of the employer's capital stock subsequent to the date of grant (but prior to the measurement date) should be charged or credited to expense each period as the changes occur.

(e) CANCELED OR FORFEITED RIGHTS.   APB Opinion No. 25 states in paragraph 15: "If a stock option is not exercised (or awarded stock is returned to the corporation) because an employee fails to fulfill an obligation, the estimate of compensation expense recorded in previous periods should be adjusted by decreasing compensation expense in the period of forfeiture." Application of this paragraph to a situation where an award is canceled or forfeited because employment is terminated prior to vesting of the award is straightforward; the previously accrued compensation should be eliminated by decreasing compensation expense in the period of cancellation or forfeiture.

However, prior to the issuance of FASB Interpretation No. 28, the application of this paragraph to combination plans was unclear. In a combination plan that permits an employee to elect either a fixed award (e.g., a stock option) or a variable award (e.g., an SAR), FASB Interpretation No. 28 specifies that compensation cost should be accrued based on the presumption that the employee will elect the variable award, unless there is evidence to the contrary. In cases involving combination plans where the employer has accrued compensation based on the presumption that the employee will elect to exercise the variable award and, due to a change in circumstances, it becomes more likely that settlement will be based on the fixed award (e.g., when appreciation in the quoted market price of the employer's capital stock exceeds the maximum appreciation an employee is entitled to receive upon exercise of an SAR), FASB Interpretation No. 28 specifies that the compensation accrued with respect to the variable award should not be adjusted by decreasing compensation expense, but should be recognized as consideration for the stock issued upon settlement of the fixed award. However, FASB Interpretation No. 28 further specifies that, if both the fixed award and the variable award are forfeited or canceled, accrued compensation should be eliminated by decreasing compensation expense during the period of forfeiture or cancellation.

EITF Issue No. 87–33, "Stock Compensation Issues Related to Market Decline," provides further clarification of APB Opinion No. 25, paragraph 15. In this pronouncement, "Task Force members agreed that the reversal of previously measured compensation would be appropriate only if the forfeiture or cancellation of an option or award results from the employee's termination or nonperformance."

(f) ACCOUNTING FOR INCOME TAXES UNDER APB OPINION NO. 25.   Compensation expense associated with stock-based compensation awards is often deductible by the employer for income tax purposes in a different period from when such expense is recognized for financial reporting purposes. Such differences are temporary differences and should be accounted for as specified in FASB Statement No. 109, "Accounting for Income Taxes."

In many instances, however, there is a permanent difference between the amount of compensation expense recognized for financial reporting purposes and compensation expense deductible for income tax purposes. These differences generally arise because an employer is normally entitled to an income tax deduction for such awards equal to the amount of compensation reportable as income by the employee, and this amount is often different from the amount of compensation expense recognized by an employer for financial reporting purposes. In addressing this situation, APB Opinion No. 25 specifies that the reduction in income tax expense recorded by an employer with respect to a stock option, purchase, or award plan should not exceed the proportion of the tax reduction related to the compensation expense recognized by the employer for financial reporting purposes. Any additional tax reduction should not be accounted for as a reduction of income tax expense but, rather, should be credited directly to paid-in capital in the period that the additional tax benefit is realized through a reduction of current income taxes payable.

Occasionally, the amount of compensation expense for financial reporting purposes exceeds the amount of compensation deductible for income tax purposes. In these situations, an employer may, in the period of the tax reduction, deduct from paid-in capital and credit to income tax expense or previously recognized deferred taxes the amount of the additional tax reduction that would have resulted had the compensation expense recognized for financial reporting purposes been deductible for income tax purposes. However, this reduction is limited to the amount of tax reductions attributable to awards made under the same or similar plans that have been previously credited to paid-in capital.

(g) OTHER APB OPINION NO. 25 ISSUES.

(i) Time Accelerated Restricted Stock Award Plan.   One type of plan that possesses certain aspects of a variable award while providing for fixed award accounting is the "TARSAP." Under a TARSAP, restricted stock is awarded to the participant. The plans generally provide for a lifting of the restrictions based on the passage of time (e.g., 20 percent per year for five years, 10 percent per year for 10 years). The restrictions may be lifted quicker based on certain performance criteria; however, they can never be lifted later than the original schedule. The lifting of the restrictions only affects the timing of the recognition of the compensation expense, not the amount of the compensation expense. The earnings per share and balance sheet classification of a TARSAP follow the same rules as any restricted stock plan.

Another form of a TARSAP involves stock options. For example, a company grants stock options, at the market price, with cliff vesting after seven years. The plan provides for accelerated vesting if certain performance criteria are met.

It is important for companies to establish realistic vesting schedules in order to follow fixed plan accounting. If the employee cannot realistically expect to vest in the award, absent the achievement of the performance criteria, then fixed plan accounting would not be appropriate. An example of such a situation would be a stock option that, absent the achievement of performance criteria, does not vest until after the retirement date of the employee or after the expiration of an employment contract.

(ii) Applying APB Opinion No. 25 to Nonemployees.   Generally accepted accounting principles require that the issuance of stock-based awards issued to nonemployees be recorded at fair value. Given this, one might wonder how a company should account for stock-based awards issued to directors or consultants. While directors are not legally employees, they perform services very similar to employees, and, accordingly, practice has extended the application of APB Opinion No. 25 to directors' stock based plans. The accounting for awards granted to consultants is not so clear. Some believe that if the consultant is working essentially as an employee (i.e., on a full-time basis), then APB Opinion No. 25 should be applied. However, if the consultant is truly consulting on a temporary basis, then the award should be recorded at its fair value. Because diversity has developed in practice, the FASB has added to its agenda a project to address the scope of APB Opinion No. 25, including the definition of an employee.

(iii) Nominal Issuances.   If a company issues stock or stock options shortly before an IPO, the SEC staff generally will presume that fair value of the (underlying) stock at the date of issuance for APB Opinion No. 25 purposes is the initial public offering price. This presumption is rebuttable by the company if objective evidence exists to validate the fair value to be something different than the initial public offering price. One other point of interest is that these shares, in certain circumstances, may be considered outstanding for diluted earnings per share computations for all periods presented in a registration statement filed in connection with an IPO. During the periods covered by income statements that are included in such a registration statement or in the subsequent period prior to the effective date of the IPO, a company may issue, for "nominal consideration," common stock, options, or other equity instruments (collectively, "nominal issuances"). The SEC staff has indicated that the determination of whether an equity instrument has been issued for nominal consideration is based on facts and circumstances; however, these situations should be rare. In computing diluted earnings per share for such periods, nominal issuances of common stock and potential common stock should be reflected in a manner similar to a stock split or stock dividend.

39.4 EARNINGS PER SHARE UNDER APB OPINION NO. 25

Computation of the effect of stock-based compensation awards on earnings per share is addressed in FASB Statement No. 128, "Earnings Per Share." FASB Statement No. 128, issued by the FASB in February 1997, superseded APB Opinion No. 15, "Earnings Per Share," and FASB Interpretation No. 31, "Treatment of Stock Compensation Plans in EPS Computations." It replaces the primary and fully diluted earnings per share computations set forth in APB Opinion No. 15 with basic and diluted earnings per share, respectively. Basic earnings per share, unlike primary earnings per share, excludes all dilution, while diluted earnings per share, like fully diluted earnings per share, reflects the potential dilution that could occur if stock options or other contracts to issue common stock were exercised or resulted in the issuance of common stock.

Specifically, basic earnings per share is computed by dividing net income available to common stockholders (the numerator) by the weighted-average number of common shares outstanding (the denominator) during the period. The computation of diluted earnings per share is similar to the computation of basic earnings per share except that the denominator is increased, by application of the Treasury stock method, to include the number of additional common shares that would have been outstanding if the dilutive potential common shares had been issued. In addition, the numerator in the diluted earnings per share computation is adjusted for any impact of assuming the potential common shares were issued, but such adjustments generally do not relate to stock-based compensation.

Stock-based compensation awards impact basic and diluted earnings per share to the extent of compensation expense or credits to compensation expense, net of income tax effects, recognized by the employer for financial reporting purposes. For awards that will be settled by payment of cash to the employee, there is no additional impact on earnings per share, because settlement of the award will not result in the issuance of shares of an employer's common stock. However, when awards will be settled through issuance of shares of common stock, diluted earnings per share may reflect further dilution because of the incremental number of shares of the employer's common stock deemed to be outstanding. Stock-based compensation arrangements that may be settled in either common stock or cash at the election of either the entity or the employee are presumed to be settled in common stock (absent compelling evidence to the contrary), and the resulting potential common shares are included in the computation of diluted earnings per share if the effect is dilutive.

A discussion of basic earnings per share and diluted earnings per share involving various types of stock-based compensation plans follows.

(a) BASIC EARNINGS PER SHARE.   Basic earnings per share does not include consideration of common stock equivalents. Thus, unexercised stock options do not affect the denominator, but the shares issued upon exercise of stock options are included in the denominator for the portion of the period they are outstanding. Similarly, nonvested stock does not affect the denominator until the awards become vested. Contingently issuable shares (shares issuable for little or no cash consideration upon the satisfaction of certain conditions) are considered outstanding common shares and included in the computation of basic earnings per share only beginning with the date that all necessary conditions have been satisfied. Outstanding common shares that are contingently returnable are treated in the same manner as contingently issuable shares. For example, shares that have been issued but that the holder must return if certain performance conditions are not achieved, are treated as contingently issuable shares.

(b) DILUTED EARNINGS PER SHARE.   As previously indicated, the denominator in the diluted earnings per share computation is increased to include the number of additional common shares that would have been outstanding if the dilutive potential common shares had been issued. Accordingly, the dilutive effect of all outstanding options (and their equivalents such as nonvested stock) that are subject only to time-based vesting are reflected in diluted earnings per share by application of the treasury stock method. As discussed in further detail below, stock-based compensation awards that are subject to performance-based vesting are treated as contingently issuable shares.

Dilutive options that are issued during a period or that expire or are canceled during a period are included in the denominator of diluted earnings per share for the period they are outstanding. Similarly, dilutive options exercised during the period are included in the denominator for the period prior to actual exercise. The common shares issued upon exercise of the options or warrants are included in the denominator for the period after the exercise date as part of the weighted-average number of common shares outstanding.

Contingently issuable shares are included in the computation of diluted earnings per share as of the beginning of the period in which the conditions are satisfied (or as of the date of the agreement providing for contingently issuable shares, if later). If all necessary conditions have not been satisfied by the end of the period, the number of contingently issuable shares included in diluted earnings per share is based on the number of shares, if any, that would be issuable if the end of the reporting period were the end of the contingency period. As noted above, stock-based compensation awards that are subject to performance-based vesting are treated as contingently issuable shares. Performance-based vesting describes vesting that depends on both (a) an employee rendering service to the employer for a specified period of time and (b) the achievement of a specified performance target.

In applying the Treasury stock method to stock-based awards, the assumed proceeds is the sum of (a) the amount, if any, the employee must pay upon exercise, (b) the amount of compensation cost attributed to future services and not yet recognized (assumed proceeds does not include compensation ascribed to past services), and (c) the amount of tax benefits (both deferred and current), if any, that would be credited to stockholders' equity assuming exercise of the options. The tax benefit is the amount resulting from a tax deduction for compensation in excess of compensation expense recognized for financial reporting purposes. If the resulting difference in income tax will be deducted from stockholders' equity, such taxes to be deducted are treated as a reduction of assumed proceeds.

(c) DILUTED EARNINGS PER SHARE COMPUTATIONS FOR FIXED AWARDS.   Computations of the impact of fixed awards on diluted earnings per share are relatively straightforward. At the date an award is granted, both the number of shares that an individual employee is entitled to receive (i.e., the shares issuable pursuant to the award) and the option or purchase price, if any, are known. Thus the number of shares issuable pursuant to the award remains constant until the award is settled by issuance of shares. However, the reduction in the number of incremental shares for common shares deemed to be acquired by an employer with the assumed exercise proceeds might vary each period because of changes in (a) the quoted market price of the employer's common stock and (b) the amount of measurable compensation ascribed to future services and not yet charged.

It should be noted that though the issuance of shares pursuant to fixed awards may be contingent on time-based vesting, such shares are not considered to be contingently issuable shares.

(d) DILUTED EARNINGS PER SHARE COMPUTATIONS FOR VARIABLE AWARDS SUB-JECT ONLY TO TIME-BASED VESTING. Computations of the impact of variable awards on diluted earnings per share are considerably more complex than computations involving fixed awards. In the case of variable awards, either (1) the number of shares issuable pursuant to the award, (2) the option or purchase price, if any, or (3) both the number of shares issuable and the option or purchase price are not known at the date the award is granted. For example, in the case of SARs to be settled by issuance of shares of an employer's common stock, there is no option or purchase price. However, the estimated number of shares issuable will vary each period in which an award is outstanding, based on changes in the quoted market price of the employer's common stock. Furthermore, the number of shares deemed to be acquired by the employer from the assumed exercise proceeds will also vary each period in which an award is outstanding, due to changes in (a) the quoted market price of the employer's common stock and (b) the amount of measurable compensation ascribed to future services and not yet charged to expense.

As with fixed awards, shares to be issued pursuant to variable awards subject only to time-based vesting are not considered to be contingently issuable shares.

(e) DILUTED EARNINGS PER SHARE COMPUTATIONS FOR VARIABLE AWARDS SUB-JECT TO PERFORMANCE-BASED VESTING. For stock-based compensation awards subject to performance-based vesting, as with variable awards subject only to time-based vesting, either (1) the number of shares issuable pursuant to the award; (2) the option or purchase price, if any; or (3) both the number of shares issuable and the option or purchase price are not known at the date the award is granted. However, because issuance of performance-based awards is contingent on satisfying conditions in addition to the mere passage of time, these awards are considered to be contingently issuable shares in the computation of diluted earnings per share.

If all necessary conditions have been satisfied by the end of the reporting period (i.e., the performance conditions have been achieved), those shares are included as of the beginning of the reporting period in which the conditions were achieved (or as of the date of the agreement providing for contingently issuable shares, if later).

If all necessary conditions have not been satisfied by the end of the reporting period, the number of contingently issuable shares included in diluted earnings per share is based on the number of shares, if any, that would be issuable if the end of the reporting period were the end of the contingency period and if the result would be dilutive. Those contingently issuable shares are included in the denominator of diluted earnings per share as of the beginning of the reporting period (or as of the date of the agreement providing for contingently issuable shares, if later).

In addition to the foregoing complexities, the estimated number of shares issuable may vary each period in which an award is outstanding, based on changes in the quoted market price of the employer's common stock. Furthermore, the number of shares deemed to be acquired by the employer from the assumed exercise proceeds will also vary each period in which an award is outstanding, due to changes in (a) the quoted market price of the employer's common stock and (b) the amount of measurable compensation ascribed to future services and not yet charged to expense.

39.5 ILLUSTRATIONS OF ACCOUNTING UNDER APB OPINION NO. 25

This section includes: (a) definitions of certain stock-based compensation awards; (b) a summary of the accounting consequences of the awards, including the impact on compensation expense and federal income tax expense to be recognized for financial reporting purposes, and the impact on earnings per share; (c) a summary of the federal income tax consequences of the awards to both the employer and the employee; and (d) exhibits illustrating the accounting and federal income tax consequences of hypothetical awards.

The discussion and exhibits demonstrate the application of the principles and concepts discussed in this chapter. Stock-based compensation plans and awards, however, tend to be unique;

accordingly, the income tax and accounting consequences of any stock-based compensation award should be determined based on the specific terms of the award and the authoritative accounting literature and the tax laws and rulings in effect at the time of the award. State and local income tax consequences of stock-based compensation awards are not addressed in this section; such consequences should be determined pursuant to the tax laws of the applicable state and local governments. Finally, the exhibits ignore any employer withholding tax requirements; however, an employer should institute measures to ensure compliance with any requirements to withhold income taxes from recipients of awards. Failure to comply with applicable withholding requirements could jeopardize the employer's right to a tax deduction with respect to an award.

The discussion and exhibits address the accounting and income tax consequences of a fixed award, a variable award, and a formula award, as follows:

Fixed Award. Nonstatutory stock option (nondiscounted).
Variable Award. SAR.
Variable Award. Performance stock option.
Book Value or Formula Award. Book value share.

(a) FIXED AWARD.

(i) Definition. A nonstatutory stock option is an employee stock option that does not qualify for the special tax treatment afforded incentive stock options under Internal Revenue Code (IRC) Section 422A, or the special tax treatment afforded stock options issued under employee stock purchase plans under IRC Section 423.

A nonstatutory stock option (nondiscounted) entitles an employee to purchase shares of the employer's capital stock for an amount equal to the fair market value of the shares as of the grant date. The employee's right is nontransferable and normally vests over a specified period (e.g., three to five years) although, in some instances, the right is vested at the date of grant. The right to exercise the option expires after a specified period of time (e.g., 10 years).

(ii) Accounting by Employer for Compensation Expense. A nonstatutory stock option (nondiscounted) is a fixed award (i.e., both the number of shares the employee is entitled to receive and the option price are known at the date of grant). However, for financial reporting purposes, there is no compensation expense associated with such an award, since the option exercise price is equal to the fair market value of the employer's capital stock at the date of grant.

(iii) Accounting by Employer for Federal Income Taxes. Upon exercise by an employee of a nonstatutory stock option, the employer is entitled to an income tax deduction for compensation expense, based on the difference between the option exercise price and the fair market value of the shares acquired through exercise, determined as of the exercise date. *(Note:* If the employee qualifies as an "insider" pursuant to the Securities Exchange Act of 1934, the computation of the tax deduction may differ.)

Thus, a difference usually arises between the amount of compensation expense recognized for financial reporting purposes and the amount of compensation expense that is deductible for income tax purposes. Any reduction of income taxes payable resulting from an excess of compensation expense deducted for income tax purposes over compensation expense recognized for financial reporting purposes should be credited to paid-in capital in the period of the reduction.

(iv) Accounting by Employer for Earnings per Share. A reduction of diluted earnings per share occurs as a result of the incremental number of common shares of the employer's stock deemed to be outstanding as a result of such awards if the award is dilutive. The incremental number of outstanding shares, if any, is computed using the treasury stock method in accordance with FASB Statement No. 128.

(v) Illustration of a Fixed Award. Exhibit 39.3 demonstrates the accounting and earnings per share consequences of a hypothetical nonstatutory stock option award (nondiscounted).

FIXED AWARD
Assumptions

Event	Date	Market Price of Employer's Common Stock
Grant of options to acquire common shares	January 1, 1998	$20
Vesting date (i.e., the date options become exercisable)	January 1, 2001	27
Exercise of options	December 31, 2002	42
Options granted	100	
Exercise price (options are nondiscounted, so exercise price equals fair market value at date of grant)	$20	
Par value of employer's common stock	$ 5	
Employer's effective tax rate	40%	

The year-end and average market prices of the employer's common stock between the date of grant and the exercise date (required for purposes of determining the impact of the award on earnings per share) are as follows:

Market Price of Employer's Common Stock

Year Ended December 31	End of Year	Average During the Year
1998	$25	$24
1999	29	27
2000	27	28
2001	34	30
2002	42	36

ACCOUNTING ENTRIES

Date	Description	Debit	Credit
December 31, 2002	Cash	$2,000	
	Common stock		$ 500
	Paid-in capital		1,500
	To record proceeds from exercise of stock option ($20 × 100)		
December 31, 2002	Income taxes payable	880	
	Paid-in capital		880
	To record the federal income tax benefit resulting from the deduction of compensation expense [40% (($42 − $20) × 100)]		

Exhibit 39.3 Accounting for a fixed award.

(b) VARIABLE AWARD—STOCK APPRECIATION RIGHT.

(i) Definition. A Stock Appreciation Right (SAR) is a right granted by an employer to an employee that entitles the employee to receive the excess of the quoted market price of a specified number of shares of the employer's capital stock over a specified value (usually the market price of the specified number of shares of the employer's capital stock at the date the right is granted). An SAR sometimes contains a limitation on the amount an employee may receive upon exercise. Further, an SAR may be the only compensation feature of an award; however, an SAR is often granted as part of a combination award in tandem with a nonstatutory stock option, whereby an

EARNINGS PER SHARE

Basic Earnings per Share

Employee stock options do not affect the denominator in the basic earnings per share calculation.

Diluted Earnings per Share

	Incremental Number of Shares Year Ended December 31				
	1998	1999	2000	2001	2002
Average market price of employer's common stock	$24	$27	$28	$30	$36
Less exercise price	20	20	20	20	20
Difference	4	7	8	10	16
Multiplied by shares issuable	100	100	100	100	100
Tax deductible compensation expense	400	700	800	1,000	1,600
Effective tax rate	40%	40%	40%	40%	40%
Tax benefit to be credited to additional paid-in capital	160	280	320	400	640
Proceeds from employee upon exercise	2,000	2,000	2,000	2,000	2,000
Total assumed proceeds	2,160	2,280	2,320	2,400	2,640
Divided by average market price of employer's common stock	24	27	28	30	36
Shares deemed acquired with assumed proceeds	(90)	(84)	(83)	(80)	(73)
Shares issuable upon exercise	100	100	100	100	100
Incremental shares to be added to the denominator of the primary earnings per share calculation	10	16	17	20	27

Exhibit 39.3 *Continued.*

employee or the employer must make an election to settle the award pursuant to either (but not both) the SAR or the nonstatutory stock option. The form of payment for amounts earned pursuant to an SAR may be specified by the award (i.e., stock, cash, or a combination thereof), or the award may allow the employee or employer to elect the form of payment. If the award is settled in stock, the number of shares issued to the employee is determined by dividing the amount earned by the fair market value of this stock, determined as of the exercise date. The employee's right to exercise an SAR normally vests after a specified period (e.g., 5 years) and the right to exercise expires after a specified period (e.g., 10 years). In the case of an SAR granted in tandem with a nonstatutory award (or other alternate award), the vesting and expiration dates for both awards are usually identical.

(ii) Accounting by Employer for Compensation Expense. An SAR is a variable award, that is, the number of shares, or the amount of cash, an individual is entitled to receive is not known at the date the award is granted. The measurement date and, thus, the determination of total compensation cost associated with an SAR, occur at the exercise date. Total compensation, determined at the exercise date, is equal to the number of rights multiplied by the difference between the quoted market price of the employer's capital stock at the exercise date and the value specified in the award (normally the quoted market price of the employer's capital stock at the grant date).

For purposes of allocating compensation cost to expense of interim periods between the date of grant and the measurement date, compensation cost is estimated at the end of each interim period by multiplying the number of options expected to become exercisable times the intrinsic value of each option as of the end of the period. During the service period, this estimate of compensation cost is allocated to interim periods by recognizing expense (or a decrease in expense) in an amount required to adjust accrued compensation at the end of each period to an amount equal to the percentage of the total service period that has elapsed times the estimated compensation cost.

In some cases, an SAR awarded to an employee vests over various periods (e.g., 25 percent per year for four years). In these situations, each portion of the SAR that vests on a different vesting date is accounted for as a separate award. Thus, compensation cost attributable to each group should be separately determined and allocated to expense of interim periods from the date of grant to the measurement date in the manner set forth in the preceding paragraph. The accounting for an SAR that vests in this manner is illustrated in Appendix B to FASB Interpretation No. 28.

(iii) Accounting by Employer for Federal Income Taxes. When the amount earned by an employee under an SAR is settled by payment of cash, the employer is entitled to a tax deduction for compensation expense, in the year of payment, equal to the amount of cash paid. Accordingly, the entire amount of the tax benefit is credited to previously recorded deferred taxes and/or income tax expense.

When the amount earned by an employee under an SAR is settled by issuance of shares of the employer's capital stock, the employer is entitled to a tax deduction for compensation expense in the year in which the shares to be issued are delivered to the transfer agent. The amount of the deduction is equal to the fair market value of the shares, determined as of the date of delivery to the transfer agent. Thus, the deduction for compensation expense for tax purposes may differ from the amount of compensation expense recognized for financial reporting purposes if shares are delivered to the transfer agent after the measurement date (i.e., the exercise date). The treatment of this difference is discussed in Subsection 39.3(f), "Accounting for Income Taxes under APB Opinion No. 25."

(iv) Accounting by Employer for Earnings per Share. Earnings per share are affected each period from the date of the award of an SAR to the measurement (exercise) date as a result of compensation expense (net of related income taxes) recognized for financial reporting purposes. If the award is expected to be settled in cash, there would be no impact on earnings per share other than the impact due to compensation expense charged against earnings. However, if the award is expected to be settled by issuance of shares of the employer's common stock, additional dilution may occur as a result of the incremental number of shares of the employer's common stock deemed to be outstanding. It should be noted that for SARs "that may be settled in common stock or in cash at the election of either the entity or the holder, the determination of whether that contract shall be reflected in the computation of diluted earnings per share shall be made based on the facts available each period. It shall be presumed that the contract will be settled in common stock and the resulting potential common shares included in diluted earnings per share" if the effect is more dilutive. "The presumption that the contract will be settled in common stock may be overcome if past experience or a stated policy provides a reasonable basis to believe that the contract will be paid partially or wholly in cash." The incremental number of shares, if any, deemed to be outstanding is computed under the treasury stock method in accordance with FASB Statement No. 128. Appendix C of FASB Statement No. 128 includes an illustration of the computation of earnings per share for SARs.

(v) Illustration of a Variable Award. Exhibit 39.4 shows the consequences of a hypothetical SAR award.

(c) VARIABLE AWARD—PERFORMANCE STOCK OPTION.

(i) Definition. A performance stock option is an employee stock option that entitles the employee to purchase shares of the employer's stock subject to the achievement of specified performance criteria. There are numerous different types of performance stock options; however, the most common performance stock option only becomes exercisable upon the achievement of the performance criteria. For example, a typical performance stock option plan might provide for the grant of stock options that would vest and become exercisable if specified performance targets such as return on assets or earnings per share growth are met.

(ii) Accounting by Employer for Compensation Expense. A performance stock option is a variable award since the number of shares the employee is entitled to receive or the exercise price the employee is required to pay is not known at the date of grant. The measurement date and, thus, the determination of total compensation is not determined until the date at which performance ultimately can be measured. Total compensation cost is equal to the number of stock options that become exercisable multiplied by the intrinsic value of each option at the measurement date.

For purposes of allocating compensation cost to expense of interim periods between the date of grant and the measurement date, compensation cost is estimated at the end of each interim period by multiplying the number of options expected to become exercisable times the intrinsic value of each option as of the end of the period. During the service period, this estimate of compensation cost is allocated to interim periods by recognizing expense (or a decrease in expense) in an amount required to adjust accrued compensation at the end of each period to an amount equal to the percentage of the total service period that has elapsed times the estimated compensation cost.

(iii) Accounting by Employer for Federal Income Taxes. Accounting for income taxes for a nonstatutory performance stock option is similar to the accounting for income taxes for a nonstatutory (non performance) stock option addressed above.

(iv) Accounting by Employer for Earnings per Share. Performance-based employee stock options (and performance-based nonvested stock) are treated as contingently issuable shares in diluted earnings per share computations. Contingently issuable shares are included in the computation of diluted earnings per share as of the beginning of the period in which the conditions are satisfied (or as of the date of the agreement providing for contingently issuable shares, if later). If all necessary conditions have not been satisfied by the end of the period, the number of contingently issuable shares included in diluted earnings per share is based on the number of shares,

---

HYPOTHETICAL VARIABLE AWARD

Event	Date	Market Price of Employer's Common Stock
Grant of SAR	January 1, 1998	$20
Vesting of SAR (i.e., the date SAR becomes exercisable)	December 31, 2001	$22
Expiration date of SAR	December 31, 2002	No significance
Exercise of SAR and delivery of shares to the transfer agent	December 31, 2002	$34

	End of Year		Average During the Year
Fair market value of employer's	December 31, 1998	22	21
common stock:	December 31, 1999	26	24
	December 31, 2000	28	27
	December 31, 2001	22	25
	December 31, 2002	34	28
Number of shares/rights covered by award	1,000		
"Base price" of SAR	$20		
Par value of employer's common stock	$ 5		
Employer's effective tax rate	40%		

Share appreciation is payable in stock or cash at the employee's election.

(Continues)

Exhibit 39.4   Accounting for a variable award.

ACCOUNTING BY EMPLOYER (Entries Required)

Date	Description	Debit	Credit
December 31, 1998	Compensation expense	$ 500	
	Accrued compensation		$ 500
	Deferred income taxes	200	
	Income tax expense		200
December 31, 1999	Compensation expense	2,500	
	Accrued compensation		2,500
	Deferred income taxes	1,000	
	Income tax expense		1,000
December 31, 2000	Compensation expense	3,000	
	Accrued compensation		3,000
	Deferred income taxes	1,200	
	Income tax expense		1,200
December 31, 2001	Accrued compensation	4,000	
	Compensation expense		4,000
	Income tax expense	1,600	
	Deferred income taxes		1,600
December 31, 2002	Compensation expense	12,000	
	Accrued compensation		12,000
	Deferred income taxes	4,800	
	Income tax expense		4,800
	To record compensation expense and the related federal income tax effect for each of the years in the 5-year period ended December 31, 2002 (see computation)		
December 31, 2002	Accrued compensation	14,000	
	Income taxes payable	5,600	
	Common stock		2,060
	Paid-in capital		11,940
	Deferred income taxes		5,600
	To record issuance of 412 earned shares ($14,000 ÷ $34) and the related adjustments to accrued compensation and deferred income taxes		

Computation of compensation expense and the related federal income tax effect:

	Year Ended December 31				
	1998	**1999**	**2000**	**2001**	**2002**
Increase in fair market value of employer's capital stock over base price	$ 2%	$ 6%	$ 8%	$ 2%	$ 14%
Shares covered by SAR	× 1,000	× 1,000	× 1,000	× 1,000	× 1,000
Estimated total compensation cost	$2,000	$6,000	$8,000	$2,000	$14,000
Service period elapsed (%)	× 25%	× 50%	× 75%	× 100%	× 100%
Cumulative compensation expense	$ 500	$3,000	$6,000	$ 2,000	$14,000
Accrued compensation— beginning of period	—	−500	−3,000	−6,000	−2,000
Compensation expense— current period	$ 500	$2,500	$3,000	$(4,000)	$12,000
Effective tax rate	× 40%	× 40%	× 40%	× 40%	× 40%
Tax effect	$ 200	$1,000	$1,200	$(1,600)	$4,800

Exhibit 39.4   *Continued.*

EARNINGS PER SHARE

Basic Earnings per Share

SARs do not affect the denominator in the basic earnings per share calculation.

Diluted Earnings per Share

	Incremental Number of Shares Year Ended December 31				
	1998	1999	2000	2001	2002
Market price of employer common stock—end of period	$ 22	$ 26	$ 28	$ 22	$ 34
Less exercise price	20	20	20	20	20
Difference	$ 2	$ 6	$ 8	$ 2	$ 14
Multiplied by unexercised SARs	1,000	1,000	1,000	1,000	1,000
Aggregate compensation expense	$2,000	$6,000	$8,000	$2,000	$14,000
Percentage accrued	25%	50%	75%	100%	100%
Compensation accrued to date	$ 500	$3,000	$6,000	$2,000	$14,000
Average aggregate compensation[1]	$1,000	4,000	$7,000	$5,000	$ 8,000
Divided by average market price of employer common stock	$ 21	$ 24	$ 27	$ 25	$ 28
Shares issuable	48	167	259	200	286
Average assumed proceeds[2]	$ 750	$2,250	$2,500	$1,000	$—
Divided by average market price of employer common stock	21	24	27	25	28
Shares deemed acquired with assumed proceeds	36	94	93	40	—
Shares issuable	48	167	259	200	286
Shares deemed acquired with assumed proceeds	36	94	93	40	—
Incremental shares to be added to the denominator of the diluted earnings per share calculation	12	73	166	160	286

[1] Average aggregate compensation is calculated by averaging aggregate compensation expense at the beginning of the period and the end of the period. For example, the average for 1998 is $1,000 (($0 beginning of year + $2,000 end of year)/2), the average for 1999 is $4,000 (($2,000 beginning of year + $6,000 end of year)/2), and so on.

[2] Average assumed proceeds is calculated as the average of the beginning of the year and end of the year unrecorded aggregate compensation expense. For example, for 1998, average assumed proceeds is $750 = (($0 beginning of year + $1,500 end of year)/2). For 1999, average assumed proceeds is $ 2,250 = (($1,500 beginning of year + $3,000 end of year)/2).

Exhibit 39.4   *Continued.*

if any, that would be issuable if the end of the reporting period were the end of the contingency period.

(v) Illustration of a Performance Award.   Exhibit 39.5 demonstrates the accounting and earnings per share consequences of a hypothetical performance stock option award.

(d) BOOK VALUE OR FORMULA AWARD.

(i) Definition.   Book value shares must be sold back to the company upon retirement or earlier termination of employment, and the arrangement may also permit the employee to sell some or all of his shares back to the company at other fixed or determinable dates. The initial purchase price

---

Hypothetical Performance Award

General: An employer grants 1,000 performance stock options to employees on January 1, 1998. If employer earnings are at least $1,500,000, in the aggregate, for the three years ended December 31, 2000, all of the stock options will vest and become exercisable immediately. If earnings are at least $3,000,000, in the aggregate, for the three years ended December 31, 2000, an additional 1,000 stock options will vest and become exercisable immediately. On December 31, 1998 and 1999, the employer estimates that 1,000 options will vest.

Event	Date	Market Price of Employer's Common Stock
Grant of performance options	January 1, 1998	$10
Vesting of date	December 31, 2000	16
Exercise of options	December 31, 2000	16
Options granted	2,000	
Exercise price	$10	
Par value of employer's common stock	$2	
Employer's effective tax rate	40%	
Earnings for year ended December 31, 1998	$1,200,000	
Earnings for year ended December 31, 1999	500,000	
Earnings for year ended December 31, 2000	1,500,000	

Market Price of Employer's Common Stock

Year Ended December 31	End of Year	Average During the Year
1998	$13	$11
1999	15	12
2000	16	15

ACCOUNTING ENTRIES

Date	Description	Debit	Credit
December 31, 1998	Compensation expense	$1,000	
	Paid-in capital		$1,000
	Deferred income taxes	400	
	Income tax expense		400
December 31, 1999	Compensation expense	2,350	
	Paid-in capital		2,350
	Deferred income taxes	940	
	Income tax expense		940
December 31, 2000	Compensation expense	8,650	
	Paid-in capital		8,650
	Deferred income taxes	3,460	
	Income tax expense		3,460
	To record compensation expense and the related federal income tax effect for each of the years in the 3-year period ended December 31, 2000 (see computation)		

Exhibit 39.5   Hypothetical Performance Award.

Date	Description	Debit	Credit
December 31, 2000	Cash	20,000	
	Income taxes payable	4,800	
	Common stock		4,000
	Paid-in capital		16,000
	Deferred income taxes		4,800
	To record proceeds from exercise of 2,000 stock options and to record the related adjustment to deferred income taxes.		

Computation of compensation expense and the related federal income tax effect:

	Year Ended December 31		
	1998	**1999**	**2000**
Increase in fair market value of employer's common stock over exercise price	$ 3	$ 5	$ 6
Number of performance options expected to vest	× 1,000	× 1,000	× 2,000
Estimated total compensation expense	3,000	5,000	12,000
Service period elapsed	33%	67%	100%
Cumulative compensation expense	1,000	3,350	12,000
Accrued compensation— beginning of period	—	−1,000	−3,350
Compensation expense— current period	1,000	2,350	8,650
Effective tax rate	× 40%	× 40%	× 40%
Tax effect	400	940	3,460

EARNINGS PER SHARE

Basic Earnings per Share

Employee stock options do not affect the denominator in the basic earnings per share calculation.

Diluted Earnings per Share

	Incremental Number of Shares Year Ended December 31,		
	1998[1]	1999	2000
Exercise price		10	10
Shares issuable upon exercise		1,000[2]	2,000[3]
Proceeds from employee upon exercise		10,000	20,000
Average unrecognized compensation expense (see computation below)		1,825	825
Total assumed proceeds[4]		11,825	20,825
Divided by average market price of employer common stock		12	15
Shares deemed acquired with assumed proceeds		(985)	(1,388)
Shares issuable upon exercise		1,000	2,000
Incremental shares to be added to the denominator of the diluted earnings per share calculation		15	612

(Continues)

Exhibit 39.5   Continued.

	Incremental Number of Shares Year Ended December 31,		
	1998[1]	1999	2000
Computation of average unrecognized compensation expense:			
Unrecognized compensation expense— beginning of period—		2,000	1,650
Unrecognized compensation expense— end of period	2,000	1,650	–
Average unrecognized compensation	1,000	1,825	825

[1] Performance options are not included in the computation of earnings per share until the beginning of the period in which the performance conditions are satisfied. In this example, the employer has not reached the first threshold performance condition (net income of $1,500,000). Accordingly, the performance options are not included in the computation of diluted earnings per share for 1998.

[2] In 1999, the first threshold performance condition is met (i.e., cumulative net income of $1,500,000). Accordingly, 1,000 options are included in the diluted earnings per share computation as of the beginning of the year.

[3] In 2000, the second threshold performance condition is met (i.e., cumulative net income of $3,000,000). Accordingly, 2,000 options are included in the diluted earnings per share computation as of the beginning of the year.

[4] Under APB Opinion No. 25, compensation expense for financial reporting generally equals tax compensation expense until the final measurement date (i.e., at December 31, 2000 in this example when the number of shares becomes fixed). Accordingly, there is no tax benefit component in the assumed proceeds. If the example extended to future years after the measurement date, a tax benefit component likely would be included in the computation of assumed proceeds.

Exhibit 39.5   *Continued.*

(or, in the case of a full value award where the employee is not required to pay for the shares, the initial measurement of compensation cost) is equal to the book value of the shares. When the shares are subsequently sold back to the company, the selling price is determined in the same manner as the initial valuation (i.e., book value). An employee-holder of book value shares is entitled to the same voting and dividend rights as other holders of the same class of stock. Shares for which the valuations are based on a multiple of book value, or on another formula based on earnings, are similar to book value shares, and the guidance in this illustration is generally applicable to such shares.

(ii) Accounting by Employer for Compensation Expense. As previously discussed, and as addressed in EITF Issue Nos. 87–23 and 88–6, there is a distinction, for accounting purposes, between book value shares of publicly held and privately held companies. Subsection 39.3(c)(vii) provides a detailed discussion of the accounting for these plans.

(iii) Accounting by Employer for Federal Income Taxes. The federal income tax treatment of book value plans differ based on specific provisions and elections made by the employee. Accordingly, the authors strongly urge companies to consult with their tax advisors. Suffice it to say, the tax deduction can differ from the expense recognized in the financial statements. The treatment of this difference is discussed in Subsection 39.3(f), "Accounting for Income Taxes Under APB Opinion No. 25."

(iv) Accounting by Employer for Earnings per Share. For publicly held companies, book value shares that are viewed as a form of mandatorily redeemable security (see ASR No. 268) should be classified outside of stockholders' equity. As a result, such shares do not increase the number of shares used in the computation of earnings per share for publicly held companies. Private companies are not required to present earnings per share.

(v) Illustration of a Formula Award. Exhibit 39.6 illustrates the consequences of a hypothetical book value purchase award made by a privately held company.

39.6 APPLICATION OF FINANCIAL ACCOUNTING STANDARDS BOARD STATEMENT NO. 123

FASB Statement No. 123 provides elective accounting for stock-based employee compensation arrangements using a fair value model. Companies currently accounting for such arrangements under APB Opinion No. 25, "Accounting for Stock Issued to Employees," may continue to do so; however, FASB Statement No. 123 superseded the disclosure requirements of APB Opinion No. 25 and is applicable to all companies with stock-based compensation arrangements. Companies not electing the fair value accounting method must disclose the pro forma net income and, for public companies, earnings per share as if this method had been elected. The guidance provided by FASB Statement No. 123 applies equally to companies adopting the fair value accounting as to companies determining the pro forma amounts that must be disclosed if a company continues to apply APB Opinion No. 25.

(a) SCOPE OF FINANCIAL ACCOUNTING STANDARDS BOARD STATEMENT NO. 123.
FASB Statement No. 123 applies to all transactions in which an employer grants shares of its common stock, stock options, or other equity instruments to employees, except for employee stock ownership plans (ESOPs). Accounting for ESOPs is specified in AICPA Statement of Position No. 93–6,

---

HYPOTHETICAL FORMULA AWARD
(Privately Held Company)

Assumptions
General: Common shares are acquired by an employee at their net book value. Acquired shares (book-value shares) can be sold back to the employer by the employee at their net book value three years from the date of purchase, or at any time thereafter, but must be resold upon termination of employment. If employment is terminated prior to three years from the date of purchase, the shares must be resold to the employer at a price equal to the lower of their net book value at date of termination or the amount originally paid for the shares.

Date of award and acquisition of shares by employee	January 1, 1998	
Vesting date (i.e., the first date on which shares may be sold back to the employer at net book value)	January 1, 2001	
Number of shares acquired	1,000	
Book value per share of employer's common stock	January 1, 1998	$10
	December 31, 1998	11
	December 31, 1999	13
	December 31, 2000	14
	January 1, 2001	14
	September 30, 2001	17
Effective date as of which employee elects to sell shares back to the employer	September 30, 2001	
Date employer acquires shares from employee (based on book value per share as of September 30, 1997)	November 15, 2001	
Par value of employer's common stock	$5	
Employer's effective tax rate	40%	
Dividends		
Paid between the date shares are acquired by the employee and the vesting date	June 30, 2000	$0.50 per share
Paid between the vesting date and the date shares are sold back to the employer	June 30, 2001	0.50 per share
		(Continues)

Exhibit 39.6 Illustration of a formula award.

ACCOUNTING ENTRIES

Date	Description	Debit	Credit
January 1, 1998	Cash	$10,000	
	Common stock		$5,000
	Paid-in capital		5,000
	To record issuance of 1,000 book-value shares (10 × 1,000)		
June 30, 2000	Retained earnings	500	
	Cash		500
	Income taxes payable	200	
	Paid-in capital		200
	To record dividends paid on book-value shares (0.50 × 1,000) and the related tax benefit [40% (500)]		
January 1, 2001	Income tax payable	1,600	
	Paid-in capital		1,600
	To record reduction of taxes payable due to vesting of book value shares ($4,000 × 40%)		
June 30, 2001	Retained earnings	500	
	Cash		500
	To record dividends paid on book-value shares (0.50 × 1,000)		
November 15, 2001	Treasury shares	17,000	
	Cash		17,000
	To record acquisition of book-value shares		

Exhibit 39.6   Continued.

"Employers' Accounting for Employee Stock Ownership Plans." FASB Statement No. 123 also applies to transactions in which an employer incurs a liability to employees that will be settled in cash based on the market price of the employer's stock or other equity instruments (e.g., cash-based SARs). A company may not elect accounting on a plan-by-plan basis (e.g., elect FASB Statement No. 123 for variable plans and retain accounting under APB Opinion No. 25 for fixed plans).

Shares of stock, stock options, or other equity instruments transferred directly to employees or other provider of goods or services by a principal shareholder (generally a shareholder who owns 10 percent or more of a company's common stock) are subject to the provisions of FASB Statement No. 123, unless the transfer was for a purpose other than compensation. In substance, these arrangements are considered to be capital contributions by a principal shareholder to the entity, with a subsequent award of equity instruments by the entity to its employees or other provider of goods or services.

(b) MEASUREMENT OF AWARDS. FASB Statement No. 123 requires compensation cost for all stock-based compensation awards, including most plans currently considered noncompensatory under APB Opinion No. 25 (i.e., broad-based plans), to be measured by a new fair value-based method of accounting. For those companies adopting the recognition provisions of FASB Statement No. 123, the current accounting distinction between fixed options and performance options will be substantially eliminated.

As discussed earlier in the chapter, compensation cost for fixed and variable stock-based awards under APB Opinion No. 25 is measured by the excess, if any, of the market price of the underlying stock over the amount the individual is required to pay (the intrinsic value). Compensation cost for fixed awards is measured at the grant date, while compensation cost for variable awards is estimated until both the number of shares an individual is entitled to receive and the exercise or purchase price are known (measurement date). Compensation cost under variable awards is ultimately based on the intrinsic value on the vesting or settlement date.

FASB Statement No. 123 calls for different accounting and recognition of compensation cost for stock-based compensation plans, depending on whether an award qualifies as a liability or an equity instrument at the grant date. Inherent in the distinction between a liability and an equity instrument is an expectation as to the manner in which the award will ultimately be settled. A stock-based plan expected to be settled by issuance of equity securities would be considered an equity instrument when it is granted. Accordingly, compensation cost would be based on the stock price at the date of grant and would not be adjusted for subsequent changes in the stock price. In contrast, a stock-based plan that requires settlement in cash, or that allows an employee to require settlement in cash, indicates that the employer has incurred a liability. The amount of the liability for such an award would be measured each period based on the end-of-period stock price, similar to variable plan accounting under APB Opinion No. 25.

FASB Statement No. 123 specifies that measurement of an equity instrument award should be based on its estimated fair value at grant date, with the resulting compensation cost recognized over the employee service period (typically the vesting period). Changes in the stock price subsequent to the grant date will have no impact on determining the value of an award at grant date.

The fair value of a stock option award will be estimated using an option-pricing model that considers certain variables and assumptions. Restricted stock awards (called *nonvested stock* in FASB Statement No. 123) will be measured using the market price of an unrestricted share (or vested share) of the same stock if the stock is publicly traded, or the estimated market price if it is not publicly traded. In other words, shares subject to vesting provisions will not be afforded a discount in measuring compensation cost.

Exhibit 39.7 provides a comparison of compensation cost measured under FASB Statement No. 123 and APB Opinion No. 25 for a fixed stock option and a performance stock award.

(c) MEASUREMENT DATE. FASB Statement No. 123 indicates that the measurement date for stock options or other equity instruments granted to employees as compensation should be the date at which the stock price that enters into measurement of the fair value of an award is fixed. Measurement of compensation cost should be based on the underlying stock price at the date the terms of a stock-based award are agreed to by the employer and the employee (in most cases, the grant date). Awards made under a plan that is subject to shareholder approval are not deemed to be granted until that approval is obtained unless approval is essentially a formality.

The estimated fair value at the grant date should be subsequently adjusted, if necessary, to reflect the outcome of both performance conditions and service-related factors. No compensation cost will be recognized for options that do not vest due to either forfeitures upon termination of service or failure to meet specified performance targets or conditions. Companies may base their accruals of compensation cost on the best estimate of the number of options or other equity instruments expected to vest and revise that estimate, if necessary, to reflect actual forfeitures. Alternatively, for awards subject only to a service requirement, a company may begin accruing compensation cost as if all instruments were expected to vest and recognize the effect of actual forfeitures when they occur. However, vested options that expire unexercised at the end of their contractual terms do not avoid recognition of compensation cost. Only options forfeited because of failure to meet vesting requirements are excluded from determination of compensation cost.

In certain circumstances, due to the terms of a stock option or other equity instrument, it may not be feasible to reasonably estimate the fair value of a stock-based award at the grant date. For example, the fair value of a stock option whose exercise price adjusts by a specified amount with each change in the underlying price of the stock cannot be reasonably estimated using an option pricing model. If the fair value cannot be estimated at the grant date, fair value at the first date at which it is possible to reasonably estimate that value should be used as the final measure of compensation cost. For interim periods during which it is not possible to determine fair value, companies should estimate compensation cost based on the current intrinsic value of the award.

COMPARISON OF COMPENSATION COST RECOGNIZED UNDER
FASB STATEMENT NO. 123 AND APB OPINION NO. 25

Assume the following for stock compensation awards made by Company A, a public company:

Stock price at date of grant (January 1, 2000)	$40
Expected life of options	6 years
Risk-free interest rate	7.0%
Expected volatility in stock price	30%
Expected dividend yield	1.5%
Vesting schedule for options	100% at end of third year
Options expected to vest	
(5,000 forfeited each year)	285,000
Estimated fair value of each option*	$15
Stock price at December 31, 2002	$60

*Fair value calculated using an acceptable pricing model.

Fixed Stock Option Award

On January 1, 2000, Company A grants 300,000 stock options to officers and other employees with a maximum term of 10 years and an exercise price equal to the market price of the stock at date of grant.

	APB Opinion 25	FASB Statement No. 123
Compensation cost recognized:		
Year 2000	$ 0	$1,425,000
Year 2001	0	1,425,000
Year 2002	$ 0	$1,425,000
Total	$ 0	$4,275,000

Performance Stock Award

On January 1, 2000, Company A also grants 30,000 restricted shares to certain employees. The restrictions lapse at the end of three years if certain annual earnings per share targets are met during the three-year period. For purposes of this example, assume the earnings per share targets were met during the three-year period and the restrictions lapsed on December 31, 2002.

	APB Opinion 25	FASB Statement No. 123
Compensation cost recognized	$1,800,000	$1,200,000

Exhibit 39.7   Comparison of Compensation Cost Recognized Under FASB Statement No. 123 and APB Opinion No. 25.

(d) OPTION PRICING MODELS. In addressing the issue of estimating fair value of equity instruments, the FASB noted that it was not aware of any quoted market prices that would be appropriate for employee stock options. Accordingly, FASB Statement No. 123 requires that the fair value of a stock option (or its equivalent) be estimated using an option-pricing model, such as the Black-Scholes or a binomial pricing model, that considers the following assumptions or variables:

- *Exercise price of the option.*
- *Expected life of the option* —Considers the outcome of service-related conditions (i.e., vesting requirements and forfeitures) and performance-related conditions. Expected life is typically less than the contractual term.
- *Current price of the underlying stock* —Stock price at date of grant.

- *Expected volatility of the underlying stock* — An estimate of the future price fluctuation of the underlying stock for a term commensurate with the expected life of the option. Volatility is not required for nonpublic companies.
- *Expected dividend yield on the underlying stock* — Should reflect a reasonable expectation of dividend yield commensurate with the expected life of the option.
- *Risk-free interest rate during the expected term of the option* — The rate currently available for zero-coupon U.S. government issues with a remaining term equal to the expected life of the options.

FASB Statement No. 123 requires that the option pricing model utilized consider management's expectations relative to the life of the option, future dividends, and stock price volatility. Both the volatility and dividend yield components should reflect reasonable expectations commensurate with the expected life of the option. As there is likely to be a range of reasonable expectations about factors such as expected volatility, dividend yield, and lives of options, a company may use the low end of the range for expected volatility and expected option lives and the high end of the range for dividend yield (assuming that one point within the ranges is no better estimate than another). These estimates introduce significant judgments in determining the value of stock-based compensation awards.

During the FASB's discussions prior to issuance of FASB Statement No. 123, those favoring retention of the basic requirements of APB Opinion No. 25 emphasized the imprecision of measuring fair value through option pricing models, particularly in light of the fact that most stock options issued to employees are not transferable and are forfeitable. The Board believes that it has addressed these issues by valuing at zero options that are expected to be forfeited, and by valuing options that vest based on the length of time they are expected to remain outstanding rather than on the stated term of the options.

During the last 20 years, a number of mathematical models for estimating the fair value of traded options have been developed. The most commonly used methodologies for valuing options include the Black-Scholes model, binomial pricing models, and the minimum value method. The minimum value of a stock option can be determined by a simple present value calculation which ignores the effect of expected volatility. (See Exhibit 39.8 for an illustration of the minimum value method.) The fair value of an option exceeds the minimum value because of the volatility component of an option's value, which represents the benefit of the option holder's right to participate in stock price increases without having to bear the risk of stock price decreases.

ESTIMATED OPTION VALUES

Assumptions:

Exercise price—$40 (equals current price of underlying stock)
Expected dividends—0%, 2%, and 4%
Expected risk-free rate of return—7%
Expected volatility—0%, 20%, 30%, and 40%
Expected term—six years

Fair values calculated using a Black-Scholes option pricing model

| Dividend | Volatility | | | |
Rate	0%	20%	30%	40%
0%	$13.35	$15.14	$17.56	$20.16
2%	8.87	11.42	13.98	16.57
4%	4.96	8.45	11.05	13.58

Exhibit 39.8   Estimated option values.

The Black–Scholes and binomial pricing models were originally developed for valuing traded options with relatively short lives and are based on complex mathematical formulas. Option values derived under these models are sensitive to both the expected stock volatility and the expected dividend yield. Exhibit 39.8 illustrates the relative effect of changes in expected volatility and dividend rates using a generalized Black-Scholes option-pricing model. Software packages that include option pricing models are readily available from numerous software vendors.

As demonstrated in Exhibit 39.8, option values increase as expected volatility increases, and option values decrease as expected dividend yield increases. It is interesting to note that in instances where higher expected volatility is coupled with higher dividend yields, the binomial model generally produces higher option values than the Black-Scholes model due primarily to increased sensitivity to compounded dividend yields in the binomial model. Nevertheless, FASB Statement No. 123 permits the use of either model.

(i) Expected Volatility.   Volatility is the measure of the amount that a stock's price has fluctuated (historical volatility) or is expected to fluctuate (expected volatility) during a specified period. Volatility is expressed as a percentage; a stock with a volatility of 25 percent would be expected to have its annual rate of return fall within a range of plus or minus 25 percentage points of its expected rate about two-thirds of the time. For example, if a stock currently trades at $100 with a volatility of 25 percent and an expected rate of return of 12 percent, after one year the stock price should fall within the range of $87 to $137 approximately two-thirds of the time (using simple interest for illustration). Stocks with high volatility provide option holders with greater economic "up-side" potential and, accordingly, result in higher option values under the Black–Scholes and binomial option pricing models.

FASB Statement No. 123 suggests that estimating expected future volatility should begin with calculating historical volatility over the most recent period equal to the expected life of the options. Thus, if the weighted-average expected life of the options is six years, historical volatility should be calculated for the six years immediately preceding the option grant. FASB Statement No. 123 provides an illustrative example for calculating historical volatility. Companies should modify historical stock volatility to the extent that recent experience indicates that the future is reasonably expected to differ from the past. Although historical averages may be the best available indicator of expected future volatility for some mature companies, there are legitimate exceptions including: (1) a company whose common stock has only recently become publicly traded with little, if any, historical data on its stock price volatility, (2) a company with only a few years of public trading history where recent experience indicates that the stock has generally become less volatile, and (3) a company that sells off a line of business with significantly different volatility than the remaining line of business. In such cases, it is appropriate for companies to adjust historical volatility for current circumstances or use the average volatilities of similar companies until a longer series of historical data is available.

FASB Statement No. 123 does not allow for a company with publicly traded stock to ignore volatility simply because its stock has little or no trading history. A company with only publicly traded debt is not considered a public company under FASB Statement No. 123. Subsidiaries of public companies are considered public companies for purposes of applying FASB Statement No. 123's provisions.

(ii) Expected Dividends.   The assumption about expected dividends should be based on publicly available information. While standard option pricing models generally call for expected dividend yield, the model may be modified to use an expected dividend amount rather than a yield. If a company uses expected payments, any history of regular increases in dividends should be considered. For example, if a company's policy has been to increase dividends by approximately three percent per year, its estimated option value should not assume a fixed dividend amount throughout the expected life of the option.

Some companies with no history of paying dividends might reasonably expect to begin paying small dividends during the expected lives of their employee stock options. These companies may use an average of their past dividend yield (zero) and the mean dividend yield of an appropriately comparable peer group.

(iii) Expected Option Lives. The expected life of an employee stock option award should be estimated based on reasonable facts and assumptions on the grant date. The following factors should be considered: (1) the vesting period of the grant, (2) the average length of time similar grants have remained outstanding, and (3) historical and expected volatility of the underlying stock. The expected life must at least include the vesting period and, in most circumstances, will be less than the contractual life of the option.

Option value increases at a higher rate during the earlier part of an option term. For example, a two-year option is worth less than twice as much as a one-year option if all other assumptions are equal. As a result, calculating estimated option values based on a single weighted-average life that includes widely differing individual lives may overstate the value of the entire award. Companies are encouraged to group option recipients into relatively homogeneous groups and calculate the related option values based on appropriate weighted-average expectations for each group. For example, if top level executives tend to hold their options longer than middle management, and nonmanagement employees tend to exercise their options sooner than any other groups, it would be appropriate to stratify the employees into these three groups in calculating the weighted-average estimated life of the options.

(iv) Minimum Value Method. FASB Statement No. 123 indicates that a nonpublic company may estimate the value of options issued to employees without consideration of the expected volatility of its stock. This method of estimating an option's value is commonly referred to as the *minimum value method*. The underlying concept of the minimum value method is that an individual would be willing to pay at least an amount that represents the benefit of the right to defer payment of the exercise price until a future date (time value benefit). For a dividend-paying stock, that amount is reduced by the present value of dividends forgone due to deferring exercise of the option.

Minimum value can be determined by a present value calculation of the difference between the current stock price and the present value of the exercise price, less the present value of expected dividends, if any. Minimum value also can be computed using an option-pricing model and an expected volatility of effectively zero. Although the amounts computed using present value techniques may produce slightly different results than option-pricing models for dividend-paying stocks, the Board decided to permit either method of computing minimum value.

Exhibit 39.9 illustrates a minimum value computation for an option, assuming an expected five-year life with an exercise price equal to the current stock price of $40, an expected annual dividend yield of 1.25 percent, and a risk-free interest rate available for five-year investments of 6 percent.

The FASB Statement No. 123 does not allow public companies to account for employee stock options based on the minimum value method because that approach was considered inconsistent with the overall fair value concept. However, the FASB acknowledged that estimating expected volatility for the stock of nonpublic companies is not feasible. Accordingly, FASB Statement No. 123 permits nonpublic companies to ignore expected volatility in estimating the value of options granted. As a result, nonpublic entities are allowed to use the minimum value method for stock

MINIMUM VALUE METHOD	
Current stock price	$40.00
Less:	
Present value of exercise price	(29.89)
Present value of expected dividends	(2.11)
Minimum value of option[1]	$ 8.00

[1] The $8.00 minimum value was determined by a present value calculation. By way of contrast, application of a Black–Scholes option-pricing model results in a minimum value of $7.70.

Exhibit 39.9 Minimum value computation.

options issued to employees. However, during the EITF's discussion of EITF Issue No. 96–18, "Accounting for Equity Instruments That Are Issued to Other Than Employees for Acquiring, or in Conjunction with Selling, Goods or Services," an FASB staff representative stated that when applying the consensuses in that Issue, the minimum value method is not an acceptable method for determining the fair value of nonemployee awards by nonpublic companies.

(e) RECOGNITION OF COMPENSATION COST.   As previously discussed, FASB Statement No. 123 requires either recognition of compensation cost in an employer's financial statements for those companies adopting the new standard or disclosure of pro forma net income and earnings per share for companies remaining under APB Opinion No. 25 for all awards of stock options and other stock-based instruments. FASB Statement No. 123 applies the same basic accounting principles to all stock-based plans, including those currently considered noncompensatory under APB Opinion No. 25. At the date of grant, compensation cost is measured as the fair value of the total number of awards expected to vest. Adjustments to the amount of compensation cost recognized should be made for actual experience in performance and service-related factors (i.e., forfeitures, attainment of performance goals, etc.). Changes in the price of the underlying stock or its volatility, the life of the option, dividends on the stock, or the risk-free interest rate subsequent to the grant date do not adjust the fair value of options or the related compensation cost.

A stock option for which vesting or exercisability is conditioned upon achievement of a targeted stock price or specified amount of intrinsic value does not constitute a performance award for which compensation expense would be subsequently adjusted. For awards that incorporate such features, compensation cost is recognized for employees who remain in service over the service period regardless of whether the target stock price or amount of intrinsic value is reached. FASB Statement No. 123 does indicate, however, that a target stock price condition generally affects the value of such options. Previously recognized compensation cost should not be reversed if a vested employee stock option expires unexercised.

Awards for past services would be recognized as a cost in the period the award is granted. Compensation expense related to awards for future services would be recognized over the period the related services are rendered by a charge to compensation cost and a corresponding credit to equity (paid-in capital). Unless otherwise defined, the service period would be considered equivalent to the vesting period. Vesting occurs when the employee's right to receive the award is not contingent upon performance of additional services or achievement of a specified target.

Compensation cost for an award with a graded vesting schedule should be recognized in accordance with the method described in FASB Interpretation 28, "Accounting for Stock Appreciation Rights and Other Variable Stock Option or Award Plans," if the fair value of the award is determined based on different expected lives for the options that vest each year, as it would be if the award is viewed as several separate awards, each with a different vesting date. However, if the value of the award is determined based on a composite expected life, or if the award vests at the end of a period (i.e., cliff vesting), the related compensation cost may be recognized on a straight-line basis over the service period, presumed to be the vesting period. FASB Statement No. 123 does require that the amount of compensation cost recognized at any date must at least equal the value of the vested portion of the award at that date.

FASB Statement No. 123 requires that dividends or dividend equivalents paid to employees on the portion of restricted stock or other equity award that is not expected to vest be recognized as additional compensation cost during the vesting period. Also, certain awards provide for reductions in the exercise or purchase price for dividends paid on the underlying stock. In these circumstances, FASB Statement No. 123 requires use of a dividend yield of zero in estimating the fair value of the related award. This provision would have the effect of increasing the fair value of a stock option on a dividend-paying stock.

(f) ADJUSTMENTS OF INITIAL ESTIMATES.   Measurement of the value of stock options at grant date requires estimates relative to the outcome of service- and performance-related conditions. FASB Statement No. 123 adopts a grant date approach for stock-based awards with service requirements or performance conditions and specifies that resulting compensation cost should be adjusted for subsequent changes in the expected or actual outcome of these factors. Subsequent adjustments would not be made to the original volatility, dividend yield, expected life, and interest rate assumptions or for changes in the price of the underlying stock. Exhibit 39.10 illustrates the impact on compensation cost when actual forfeitures resulting from terminations deviate from the rate anticipated at grant date.

A performance requirement adds another condition that must be met in order for employees to vest in certain awards, in addition to rendering services over a period of years. Compensation cost for these awards should be recognized each period based on an assessment of the probability that the performance-related conditions will be met. Those estimates should be subsequently adjusted to reflect differences between expectations and actual outcomes. The cumulative effect of such changes in estimates on current and prior periods should be recognized in the period of change.

(g) MODIFICATIONS TO GRANTS.   FASB Statement No. 123 requires that a modification to the terms of an award that increases the award's fair value at the modification date be treated, in substance, as the repurchase of the original award in exchange for a new award of greater value. Additional compensation cost arising from a modification of a vested award should be recognized for the difference between the fair value of the new award at the modification date and the fair value of the original award immediately before its terms are modified, determined based on the shorter of (a) its remaining expected life or (b) the expected life of the modified option. For modifications of nonvested options, compensation cost related to the original award not yet recognized must be added to the incremental compensation cost of the new award and recognized over the remainder of the employee's service period.

As an example of a modification of a vested option, assume that, on January 1, 2000, Company A granted its employees 300,000 stock options with an exercise price of $50 per share and a contractual term of 10 years. The options vested at the end of three years and 15,000 of the original 300,000 options were forfeited prior to vesting. On January 1, 2004, the market price of Company A stock has declined to $40 per share, and Company A decides to reduce the exercise price of the options. Under FASB Statement No. 123, Company A has effectively issued new options and would recognize additional compensation cost as a result of the reduction in exercise price. The estimated fair value of the original award at the modification date would be determined using the assumptions for dividend yield, volatility, and risk-free interest rate at the modification

---

ADJUSTMENT OF FORFEITURE RATE UNDER FASB STATEMENT NO. 123

Assumptions:

Options granted	10,000
Vesting schedule	100% at end of third year (cliff vesting)
Estimated forfeiture rate	6% per year (upon termination)
Actual forfeiture rate	6% in years 1 and 2; 3% in year 3
Option value at grant date	$10

Estimated fair value of award at grant date: $(10,000 \times .94 \times .94 \times .94) \times \$10 = \underline{\underline{\$83,100}}$

Compensation cost recognized in years 1 and 2: $\$83,100 \div 3 = \underline{\underline{\$27,700}}$

Compensation cost recognized in year 3 (3% forfeiture rate):

Total compensation cost to be recognized: $(10,000 \times .94 \times .94 \times .97) \times \$10 = \$85,700$

Cost recognized in year 1	(27,700)
Cost recognized in year 2	(27,700)
Cost recognized in year 3	$\underline{\underline{\$30,300}}$

Exhibit 39.10   Adjustment of forfeiture rate under FASB Statement No. 123.

MODIFICATIONS TO GRANTS UNDER STATEMENT FASB NO. 123

Assume the following for stock options granted and subsequently modified by Company A, a public company:

	Fair Value of Original Award January 1, 2000	Fair Value of New Award January 1, 2004	Fair Value of Original Award January 1, 2004
Exercise price	$50	$40	$50
Stock price	$50	$40	$40
Expected volatility	30%	35%	35%
Expected dividend yield	1.5%	2.0%	2.0%
Expected option life	6 years	5 years	2 years[1]
Risk-free interest rate	6.5%	5.75%	5.75%
Estimated fair value of each option[2]	$18	$13	$05

[1] Lesser of remaining expected life of original award or expected life of new award.

[2] Fair value calculated using an acceptable pricing model.

The computation of additional compensation cost resulting from this modification would be as follows:

Estimated fair value of new award ($13/option × 285,000)	$ 3,705,000
Estimated fair value of original award at modification date ($5/option × 285,000)	(1,425,000)
Incremental compensation cost of new award	$ 2,280,000

Because the award is fully vested at the modification date, the additional compensation cost of $2,280,000 would be expensed in the period of modification.

Exhibit 39.11   Modifications to grants under FASB Statement No. 123.

date. Exhibit 39.11 illustrates the measurement of additional compensation cost upon modification of the terms of this award.

In certain cases, modifications may be made to options that were granted before FASB Statement No. 123 was effective. Under APB Opinion No. 25, compensation cost would not have been recognized upon initial issuance of an option if the exercise price was equal to the market price on the grant date. Because no compensation cost was recognized for the original options, the modified options are treated as a new grant. For modifications of vested options, compensation cost is recognized immediately for the fair value of the new option on the modification date. However, if the options had intrinsic value on the modification date (i.e., the options were in the money), the intrinsic value would be excluded from the amount of compensation cost recognized because an employee could have exercised the options immediately before the modification and received the intrinsic value without affecting the amount of compensation cost recognized by the company. For modifications to nonvested options, previously unrecognized compensation cost, if any, is added to incremental compensation cost from the new award and recognized over the employee's service period.

Exchanges of options or changes in their terms in conjunction with business combinations, spin-offs, or other equity restructurings are considered modifications under FASB Statement No. 123, with the exception of those changes made to reflect the terms of the exchange of shares in a business combination accounted for as a pooling of interests. This represents a change in practice, as such modifications do not typically result in a new measurement date under APB Opinion No. 25, and, therefore, additional compensation expense is not recorded. However, changing the terms of an award in accordance with antidilution provisions that are designed, for example, to equalize an option's value before and after a stock split or a stock dividend is not considered a modification.

(h) OPTIONS WITH RELOAD FEATURES.   Reload stock options are granted to employees upon exercise of previously granted options whose original terms provide for the use of "mature" shares of stock that the employee has owned for a specified period of time (generally six months) rather than cash to satisfy the exercise price. When an employee exercises the original options using mature shares (a stock for stock exercise), the employee is automatically granted a reload option for the same number of shares used to exercise the original option. The exercise price of the reload option is the market price of the stock at the date the reload option is granted, and the term is equal to the remainder of the term of the original option. Compensation cost related to options with reload features should be calculated separately for the initial option grant and each subsequent grant of a reload option.

In the "Basis for Conclusions" (Appendix A to FASB Statement No. 123), the FASB states its belief that, ideally, the value of an option with a reload feature should be estimated at the grant date, taking into account all of its features. However, the Board concluded that it is not feasible to do so because no reasonable method currently exists to estimate the value added by a reload feature. Accordingly, the Board decided that compensation cost for an option with a reload feature should be calculated separately for the initial option grant and for each subsequent grant of a reload option as if it were a new grant.

(i) SETTLEMENT OF AWARDS.   Employers occasionally repurchase vested equity instruments issued to employees for cash or other assets. Under FASB Statement No. 123, amounts paid up to the fair value of the instrument at the date of repurchase should be charged to equity, and amounts paid in excess of fair value should be recognized as additional compensation cost. For example, a company that repurchases a vested share of stock for its market price does not incur additional compensation cost. A company that settles a nonvested award for cash has, in effect, vested the award, and the amount of compensation cost measured at the grant date and not yet recognized should be recognized at the repurchase date.

A repurchase of vested stock options would be treated in a manner similar to a modification of an option grant. Incremental compensation cost, if any, to be recognized upon cash settlement should be determined as the excess of cash paid over the fair value of the option on the date the employee accepts the repurchase offer, determined based on the remainder of its original expected life at that date. Additionally, if unvested stock options are repurchased, the amount of previously unrecognized compensation cost should be recognized at the repurchase date because the repurchase of the option effectively vests the award. Exhibit 39.12 illustrates the accounting for the repurchase of an award by the employer.

In certain circumstances, awards granted prior to adoption of FASB Statement No. 123 may be settled in cash subsequent to adoption of FASB Statement No. 123. Compensation cost would not have been recognized for the original award under APB Opinion No. 25 if the exercise price equaled the market price on the grant date. Because no cost was previously recognized for the original award, the cash settlement of the vested options is treated as a new grant and recognized as compensation cost on the repurchase date. However, if the original options had been in-the-money and thus had intrinsic value immediately before the settlement, the intrinsic value is excluded from compensation cost, similar to the accounting for a grant modification.

(j) TANDEM PLANS AND COMBINATION PLANS.   Employers may have compensation plans that offer employees a choice of receiving either cash or shares of stock in settlement of their stock-based awards. Such plans are considered tandem plans. For example, an employee may be given an award consisting of a cash SARs and an SAR with the same terms except that it calls for settlement in shares of stock with an equivalent value. The employee may demand settlement in either cash or in shares of stock and the election of one component of the plan (cash or stock) cancels the other. Because the employee has the choice of receiving cash, this plan results in the company incurring a liability. The amount of the liability will be adjusted each period to reflect the current stock price. If employees subsequently choose to receive shares of stock rather than receive cash, the liability is settled by issuing stock.

If the terms of a stock-based compensation plan provide that settlement of awards to employees will be made in a combination of stock and cash, the plan is considered a combination plan. In a combination plan, each part of the award is treated as a separate grant and accounted for separately. The portion to be settled in stock is accounted for as an equity instrument and the cash portion is accrued as a liability and adjusted each period based on fluctuations in the underlying stock price.

REPURCHASE OF AWARD UNDER FASB STATEMENT NO. 123

On January 1, 2000, Company A grants a total of 10,000 "at-the-money" options to employees. The options vest after three years and are exercisable through December 31, 2009. The market price of Company A stock is $50 at grant date. It is expected that a total of 8,500 options will vest, based on projected forfeitures. The fair value of an option at grant date is $18, using an acceptable option pricing model. At grant date, Company A would compute compensation cost of $153,000 (8,500× $18 per option) to be recognized ratably over the service period.

On January 1, 2005, Company A repurchases 2,000 of the vested options for $30 per option. On that date, the market price of Company A's stock is $60 and the option's fair value is $24. Additional compensation cost would be recognized for the difference between the cash paid and the fair value of the option at the date of repurchase.

Calculations:

Repurchase price of options	$30	
Fair value of options at repurchase date	24	
Additional compensation cost	$ 6 × 2,000 options =$12,000	

Journal entry:

Compensation expense	$12,000	
Additional paid in capital[1]	48,000	
Cash		$60,000

[1] Fair value of options repurchased (2,000× $24)

Exhibit 39.12   Repurchase of award under FASB Statement No. 123.

Exhibit 39.13 illustrates the accounting for an award expected to be settled in a combination of cash and stock.

(k) EMPLOYEE STOCK PURCHASE PLANS.   Some companies offer employees the opportunity to purchase company stock, typically at a discount from market price. If certain conditions are met, the plan may qualify under Section 423 of the Internal Revenue Code, which allows employees to defer taxation on the difference between the market price and the discounted purchase price. APB Opinion No. 25 generally treats employee stock purchase plans that qualify under Section 423 as noncompensatory.

Under FASB Statement No. 123, broad-based employee stock purchase plans are compensatory unless the discount from market price is relatively small. Plans that provide a discount of no more than five percent would be considered noncompensatory; discounts in excess of this amount would be considered compensatory under FASB Statement No. 123 unless the company could justify a higher discount. A company may justify a discount in excess of five percent if the discount from market price does not exceed the greater of (a) the per-share discount that would be reasonable in a recurring offer of stock to stockholders or (b) the per-share amount of stock issuance costs avoided by not having to raise a significant amount of capital by a public offering. If a company cannot provide adequate support for a discount in excess of five percent, the entire amount of the discount should be treated as compensation cost.

For example, if an employee stock purchase plan provides that employees can purchase the employer's common stock at a price equal to 85 percent of its market price as of the date of purchase, compensation cost would be based on the entire discount of 15 percent unless the discount in excess of 5 percent can be justified.

If an employee stock purchase plan meets the following three criteria, the discount from market price is not considered stock-based compensation:

1. The plan incorporates no option features other than the following, which may be incorporated:
   (a) employees are permitted a short period of time (not exceeding 31 days) after the purchase

---

COMBINATION PLAN UNDER FASB STATEMENT NO. 123

Company A has a performance-based plan that provides for a maximum of 900,000 performance awards to be earned by participants if certain financial goals are met over a three-year period. Each performance award is equivalent to one share of Company A stock. The terms of the plan call for the awards to be settled two-thirds in stock and one-third in cash at the date the performance goals are attained (the settlement date). This plan may be viewed as a combination plan consisting of 600,000 shares of restricted stock and 300,000 cash SARs.

The market price of Company A stock is $30 at grant date. The Company estimates that 750,000 performance awards will ultimately be earned based on the Company's expectations of meeting benchmark goals and estimated forfeitures. Company A intends to settle the award by issuing 500,000 shares of stock and settling the remaining 250,000 units in cash based on the market price of Company A stock at the settlement date.

The stock portion of the award is accounted for as a grant of an equity instrument. Company A would recognize compensation cost of $15 million (500,000 × $30 per unit) over the three-year service period for the portion of the award expected to be settled in stock.

The cash portion of the award would result in initial compensation cost of $7.5 million (250,000 × $30) to be accrued as a liability over the participants' service period. The amount of the liability will be adjusted each period based on fluctuations in the market price of the stock. If the market price of Company A stock is $36 at the end of the service period, additional compensation cost of $1.5 million would be recognized (250,000 × $6).

Exhibit 39.13   Combination plan under FASB Statement No. 123

price has been fixed in which to enroll in the plan, and (b) the purchase price is based solely on the stock's market price at the date of purchase and employees are permitted to cancel participation before the purchase date.

2. The discount from the market price is five percent or less (or the company is able to justify a higher discount).

3. Substantially all full-time employees meeting limited employment qualifications may participate on an equitable basis.

(l) LOOK-BACK OPTIONS.   Some companies offer options to employees under Section 423 of the Internal Revenue Code, which allows employees to defer taxation on the difference between the market price of the stock and a discounted purchase price if certain requirements are met. One requirement is that the option price may not be less than the smaller of (a) 85 percent of the market price when the option is granted or (b) 85 percent of the market price at exercise date. Options that provide for the more favorable of several exercise prices are referred to as *look-back* options. Under APB Opinion No. 25, Section 423 look-back plans generally are considered noncompensatory.

Under the FASB Statement No. 123, the effect of a look-back feature would be recorded at fair value at the grant date similar to other stock-based compensation. Accordingly, the fair value of a look-back option should be estimated based on the stock price and terms of the option at the grant date by breaking it into its components and valuing the option as a combination position.

For example, on January 1, 2004, a company offers its employees the opportunity to sign up for payroll deductions to purchase its stock at either 85 percent of the stock's current $50 price or 85 percent of the stock price at the end of the year when the options expire, whichever is lower. Assume that the dividend yield is zero, expected volatility is 35 percent, and the risk-free interest rate available for the next 12 months is 7 percent.

The look-back option consists of 15 percent of a share of nonvested stock and 85 percent of a one-year call option. The underlying logic is that the holder of the look-back option will always receive 15 percent of a share of stock upon exercise, regardless of the stock price at that date. For example, if the stock price fell to $40, the exercise price will be $34 (40 × .85), and the holder will benefit by $6 ($40 − $34), or 15 percent of the exercise price. If the stock price exceeds the $50 exercise price, the holder of the look-back option receives a benefit that is more than equivalent to 15 percent of a share of stock. A standard option-pricing model can be used to value the one-year call option on 85 percent of a share of stock represented by the second component.

Total compensation cost at the grant date is computed in Exhibit 39.14.

FASB Technical Bulletin No. 97–1, "Accounting under Statement 123 for Certain Employee Stock Purchase Plans with a Look-Back Option," discusses various types of look-back options and provides illustrations of the related fair value calculations.

(m) AWARDS REQUIRING SETTLEMENT IN CASH. In most cases, an employer settles stock options by issuing stock rather than paying cash. However, under certain stock-based plans, an employer may elect or may be required to settle the award in cash. For example, a cash SAR derives its value from increases in the price of the employer's stock but is ultimately settled in cash. Such plans include phantom stock plans, cash SARs, and cash performance unit awards. In other instances, an employee may have the option of requesting settlement in cash or stock.

Under APB Opinion No. 25, cash paid to settle a stock-based award is the final measure of compensation cost. The repurchase of stock shortly after exercise of an option is also considered cash paid to settle an earlier award and ultimately determines compensation cost. FASB Statement No. 123 indicates that awards calling for settlement in stock are considered equity instruments when issued, and their subsequent repurchase for cash would not necessarily require an adjustment to compensation cost if the amount paid does not exceed the fair value of the instruments repurchased. Awards calling for settlement in cash (or other assets of the employer) are considered liabilities when issued, and their settlement would require an adjustment to previously recognized compensation cost if the settlement amount differs from the carrying amount of the liability. Also, if the choice of settlement (cash or stock) is the employee's, FASB Statement No. 123 specifies that the employer would be settling a liability rather than issuing an equity security; accordingly, compensation cost should be adjusted if the settlement amount differs from the carrying amount of the liability.

FASB Statement No. 123 indicates that the accounting for stock compensation plans, as equity or liability instruments should reflect the terms as understood by the employer and the employee. While the written plan generally provides the best evidence of its terms, an employer's past practices may indicate substantive terms that differ from written terms. For example, an employer that is not legally obligated to settle an award in cash but that generally does so upon exercise of stock options whenever an employee asks for cash settlement is probably settling a substantive liability rather than repurchasing an equity instrument. In that instance, the Statement requires accounting for the substantive terms of the plan.

FASB Statement No. 123 does not change current accounting practice for nonpublic companies with stock repurchase agreements, provided that the repurchase price is the fair value of the stock at the date of repurchase. Alternatively, many nonpublic companies sponsor stock purchase plans that provide for employees to acquire shares in the company at book value or a formula price

---

COMPUTATION OF COMPENSATION COSTS OF A LOOK-BACK OPTION UNDER FASB STATEMENT NO. 123

.15 of a share of nonvested stock (50 × .15)	$ 7.50
Call option on. 85 of a share of stock, exercise price of $50 ($8.48* × .85)	7.21
Total compensation cost at grant date	$14.71

  *Fair value calculated using an acceptable pricing model.

Exhibit 39.14   Computation of compensation costs of a look-back option under FASB Statement No. 123.

based on book value or earnings. In addition, these arrangements frequently require the company to repurchase the shares when the employee terminates at a price determined in the same manner as the purchase price.

Under current practice, a nonpublic company is not required to recognize compensation cost for share repurchases under book value or formula plans if the employee has made a substantive investment that will be at risk for a reasonable period of time. FASB Statement No. 123, however, requires fair value as the basic method of measuring compensation cost for all stock-based plans, including those of private companies. FASB Statement No. 123 indicates that each plan will need to be assessed on a case-by-case basis to determine whether the book value or formula price is a reasonable estimate of fair value and whether the plan is subject to additional compensation cost.

(n) TRANSACTIONS WITH NONEMPLOYEES.   Except for stock-based awards to employees that are currently within the scope of APB Opinion No. 25, FASB Statement No. 123 provides that all transactions in which goods or services are the consideration received for the issuance of equity instruments should be accounted for based on the fair value of the consideration received or the fair value of the equity instruments issued, whichever is more reliably measurable. In some cases, the fair value of goods or services received from suppliers, consultants, attorneys, or other nonemployees is more reliably measurable and indicates the fair value of the equity instrument issued.

If the fair value of goods or services received is not reliably measurable, the measure of the cost of goods or services acquired in a transaction with nonemployees should be based on the fair value of the equity instruments issued. However, FASB Statement No. 123 does not specify the date that should be used to value the equity instruments or the methodology that should be used to determine the total cost to be recognized when the number or terms of the equity instruments are variable. These issues are addressed in EITF Issue No. 96–18, "Accounting for Equity Instruments That Are Issued to Other Than Employees for Acquiring, or in Conjunction with Selling, Goods or Services."

Further, some such transactions are more complex: the exchange may span several periods, the issuance of the equity instruments is contingent on service or delivery of goods that must be completed by the provider of the goods or services in order to vest in the equity instrument, or fully vested, nonforfeitable equity instruments issued to a grantee may contain terms that may vary based on the achievement of a performance condition or certain market conditions. In certain cases, the fair value of the equity instruments to be received may be more reliably measurable than the fair value of the goods or services to be given as consideration.

In EITF Issue No. 00–8, the Task Force agreed that for transactions in which an entity provides goods or services in exchange for equity instruments, the grantee should measure the fair value of the equity instruments using the stock price and other measurement assumptions as of the earlier of either of these dates:

- The date the parties come to a mutual understanding of the terms of the equity-based compensation arrangement and commitment for performance by the grantee to earn the equity instruments (a "performance commitment" in the sense used in EITF Issue No. 96–18) is reached
- The date at which the grantee's performance necessary to earn the equity instruments is complete, which is the vesting date

The Task Force agreed that if on the measurement date the quantity or any of the terms of the equity instrument depend on the achievement of a market condition, the grantee should measure revenue based on the fair value of the equity instruments inclusive of the adjustment provisions, calculated as the fair value of the equity instruments without regard to the market condition plus the fair value of the commitment to change the quantity or terms of the equity instruments if the market condition is met. Footnote 10 to FASB Statement No. 123 indicates that pricing models have been adapted to value many of those path-dependent instruments.

The Task Force agreed that if on the measurement date the quantity or any of the terms of the equity instrument depend on the achievement of grantee performance conditions beyond those for which a performance commitment exists, changes in the fair value of the equity instrument that result from an adjustment to the instrument on the achievement of a performance condition should be measured as additional revenue from the transaction using a methodology consistent with "modification accounting" described in paragraph 35 of FASB Statement No. 123. The adjustment should thus be measured at the date of the revision of the quantity or terms of the instrument as the difference between (a) the then-current fair value of the revised instruments using the then-known quantity and terms and (b) the then-current fair value of the old equity instruments immediately before the adjustment.

EITF Issue Nos. 96–18 and 00–8 do not address the periods or manner in which the fair value of the transactions should be recognized other than to observe that a transaction should be recognized in the same periods and in the same manner as if cash were being exchanged in the transaction instead of the equity instruments.

EITF Issue No. 00–18 addresses those issues but does not readdress the issues addressed by EITF Issue Nos. 96–18 and 00–8.

The Task Force agreed that if fully vested, exercisable, nonforfeitable equity instruments are issued at the date the grantor and grantee enter into an agreement, any obligation on the part of the counterparty to earn the equity instruments has been eliminated, and thus a measurement date has been reached. The grantor should therefore recognize the equity instruments when they are issued, usually when the agreement is entered into. Most of the Task Force generally agreed that the specific facts and circumstances determine whether the corresponding cost is an immediate expense, a prepaid asset, or an amount that should be classified as contra-equity.

The Task Force generally agreed that if fully vested, nonforfeitable equity instruments exercisable by the grantee only after a specified period of time, but the agreement provides for earlier exercisability if the grantee achieves specified performance conditions, the grantor should measure the fair value of the equity instruments at the date of grant and should recognize that measured cost as indicated in the preceding paragraph. Footnote 5 in EITF Issue No. 96–18 should be amended to eliminate the reference to immediate exercisability. Most of the Task Force agreed that if, after the arrangement date, the grantee performs as specified in the agreement and exercisability is accelerated, the grantor should measure and report the resulting increase in the fair value of the equity instruments using "modification accounting."

If a transaction includes a grantee performance commitment with the grantee having a contingent right to receive, on performing under the commitment, grantor equity instruments that are consideration for the grantee's future performance, the grantee treats the arrangement as an executory contract, with no accounting before performance, the same as the grantee would have agreed to pay cash on vesting for the goods or services.

(o) ACCOUNTING FOR INCOME TAXES UNDER FINANCIAL ACCOUNTING STANDARDS BOARD STATEMENT NO. 123.   The cumulative amount of compensation cost recognized that ordinarily results in a future tax deduction under existing tax law is a deductible temporary difference under FASB Statement No. 109, "Accounting for Income Taxes." Under current tax law, incentive stock options do not result in tax deductions for an employer (provided employees comply with requisite holding periods) and, accordingly, do not create a future deductible temporary difference. Tax benefits arising because employees do not comply with requisite holding periods (i.e., disqualifying dispositions) are recognized in the financial statements only when such events occur.

Nonqualified stock options and grants of restricted stock do generate tax deductions for employers. In general, the tax deduction equals the intrinsic value of the award at the date of exercise. Under FASB Statement No. 123, the cumulative amount of compensation cost recognized in a company's income statement is considered to be a deductible temporary difference under FASB Statement No. 109. Deferred tax assets recognized for deductible temporary differences should be reduced by a valuation allowance if, based on available evidence, such an allowance is deemed necessary. The deferred tax benefit or expense resulting from increases or decreases in that temporary difference (e.g., as additional compensation cost is recognized over the vesting period) is recognized in the income statement because those tax effects relate to continuing operations. Similar to the provisions of APB Opinion No. 25 on accounting for the income tax effects of stock compensation awards, the amount of tax benefits recognized in the income statement is limited to the effects of deductions based on reported compensation cost. If the deduction for income tax purposes exceeds the amount of compensation cost recognized for financial reporting purposes, the benefit of the excess tax deduction is credited to additional paid-in capital.

(p) EFFECTIVE DATE AND TRANSITION.   The disclosure provisions of FASB Statement No. 123, as discussed below, are effective for fiscal years beginning after December 15, 1995. However, disclosure of pro forma net income and earnings per share, as if the fair value method had been used to account for stock-based compensation, is required for all awards granted in fiscal years beginning after December 5, 1994.

During the initial phase-in period, the effects of applying FASB Statement No. 123 for either recognizing compensation cost or providing pro forma disclosures may not be representative of the effects on reported net income for future years. Financial statements should include a disclosure to this effect if applicable.

39.7 EARNINGS PER SHARE UNDER FINANCIAL ACCOUNTING STANDARDS BOARD STATEMENT NO. 123

Computation of the impact of stock-based compensation awards on earnings per share is addressed in FASB Statement No. 128, and the same concepts apply to the earnings per share computations regardless of the method of accounting for stock-based compensation. Accordingly, much of the discussion of earnings per share computations for stock-based awards under APB Opinion No. 25 in Section 39.4 is relevant to earnings per share computations for stock-based awards under FASB Statement No. 123. However, the impact of stock-based compensation awards accounted for under FASB Statement No. 123 usually differs from the impact of awards accounted for under APB Opinion No. 25. Net income available to common stockholders (the numerator) frequently differs because of the differences in the methods of determining compensation cost under each of these standards. Furthermore, the weighted-average number of common shares outstanding (the denominator) in computations of diluted earnings per share may differ due to the differences in the determination of assumed proceeds in application of the Treasury stock method. For example, the amount of compensation cost attributed to future services and not yet recognized and the amount of tax benefits that would be credited to stockholders' equity assuming exercise of the options generally would differ depending on whether a company is accounting for stock-based compensation under FASB Statement No. 123 or APB Opinion No. 25. Discussed below are a few other points to consider in computing the impact of stock-based awards on earnings per share.

Under FASB Statement No. 128, forfeitures of stock-based awards do not affect the computation of assumed proceeds in application of the treasury stock method until the forfeitures actually occur. This practice may be inconsistent with the method that a company uses for determining compensation expense since, under FASB Statement No. 123, a company can determine compensation expense based on actual forfeitures as they occur or based on an estimate of forfeitures with adjustments to actual forfeitures.

There also is an inconsistency in when compensation cost for performance awards is included in the numerator of the diluted earnings per share computation pursuant to FASB Statement No. 123 and when the related contingent shares are included in the denominator of the same computation pursuant to FASB Statement No. 128. Interim accruals of compensation cost for performance awards are based on the best estimate of the outcome of the performance condition. In other words, for each reporting period, compensation cost is estimated for the awards that are expected to vest based on performance-related conditions. However, pursuant to FASB Statement No. 128, diluted earnings per share reflects only those awards that would be issued if the end of the reporting period were the end of the contingency period. In most cases, performance awards will not be reflected in diluted earnings per share until the performance condition has been satisfied.

In applying the Treasury stock method to awards accounted for pursuant to FASB Statement No. 123, the awards may be antidilutive even when the market price of the underlying stock exceeds the related exercise price. This result is possible because compensation cost attributed to future services and not yet recognized is included as a component of assumed proceeds upon exercise in applying the Treasury stock method. Since this component represents an amount over and above the intrinsic value of the award at the grant date, it is possible that stock options with a positive intrinsic value would be considered antidilutive and thereby excluded from diluted earnings per share computations under to FASB Statement No. 128.

Exhibit 39.15 illustrates basic and diluted earnings per share computations under APB Opinion No. 25 and FASB Statement No. 123.

39.8 FINANCIAL STATEMENT DISCLOSURES

(a) DISCLOSURE REQUIREMENTS FOR ALL COMPANIES. FASB Statement No. 123 superseded the disclosure requirements under APB Opinion No. 25 and requires disclosure of the following information by employers with one or more stock-based compensation plans regardless of whether a company has elected the recognition provisions or retained accounting under APB Opinion No. 25:

1. A description of the method used to account for all stock-based employee compensation arrangements should be included in the company's summary of significant accounting policies.
2. A description of the plans, including the general terms of the awards under the plans such as vesting requirements, the maximum term of options granted, and the number of shares authorized for grants of options or other equity instruments.
3. The following information should be disclosed for each year for which an income statement is presented:
   a. The number and weighted-average exercise prices of options for each of the following groups of options: (1) those outstanding at the beginning and end of the year, (2) those exercisable at the end of the year, and (3) the number of options granted, exercised, forfeited, or expired during the year.
   b. The weighted-average grant-date fair values of options granted during the year. If the exercise prices of some options differ from the market price of the stock on the grant date, weighted-average exercise prices and fair values of options would be disclosed separately for options whose exercise price (1) equals, (2) exceeds, or (3) is less than the market price of the stock on the date of grant.

EARNINGS PER SHARE UNDER FASB STATEMENT NO. 123 AND APB OPINION NO. 25

For purposes of this example, assume that 2006 is the first year that Company A had a stock option plan.

On January 1, 2001, Company A granted 100,000 options with an exercise price equal to the market price of the stock at that date ($30). The fair value of each option granted was $9, and the options vest at the end of three years. Company A expects that 85,000 options granted in 2001 will vest. Assume a 40% tax rate.

On January 1, 2001, Company A computed compensation cost of $765,000 (85,000 × $9) to be recognized ratably at $255,000 per year pursuant to FASB Statement No. 123. (For this example, compensation cost under FASB Statement No. 123 has been computed based on the number of options expected to vest. Alternatively, the company may have elected to recognize forfeitures as they occur.) During 2001, 5,000 options were forfeited.

Exhibit 39.15   Earnings per share under FASB Statement No. 123 and APB Opinion No. 25

The market price of Company A stock at December 31, 2001, is $42, and the average stock price during 2001 was $36. Net income for 2001 (before recognition of compensation expense related to the option grant) was $2,700,000. Weighted average common shares outstanding are 1,500,000 at December 31, 2001.

Calculation of basic earnings per share for the year ended December 31, 2001:

	FASB STATEMENT No. 123	APB OPINION No. 25
Net income before stock compensation expense	$2,700,000	$2,700,000
Stock-based compensation, net of income taxes[1]	153,000	0
Net income	$2,547,000	$2,700,000
Weighted average shares outstanding	1,500,000	1,500,000
Basic earnings per share	$ 1.70	$ 1.80

	FASB STATEMENT No. 123	APB OPINION No. 25
Assumed proceeds from exercise of options[2]	$2,925,000*	$2,925,000
Average unrecognized compensation cost related to future services[3]	735,000)[1]	0
Tax benefits credited to equity on assumed exercise based on average market price less weighted average exercise price[4]	$ 0*	$ 234,000
Total assumed proceeds	$3,660,500	$3,159,000
Shares assumed issued upon exercise of options	97,500	97,500
Shares repurchased at average market price	$ 101,667	$ 87,750
Incremental shares	$ (4,167)*	$ 9,750
Net income before stock compensation expense	$2,700,000	$2,700,000
Stock-based compensation, net of income taxes[5]	153,000	$0,000,000
Net income	$2,547,000	$2,700,000
Weighted average shares outstanding	1,500,000	1,500,000
Incremental shares	$ 0	$ 9,750
Total weighted average shares outstanding	$1,500,000	$1,509,750
Diluted earnings per share	$ 1.70	$ 1.79

*Impact on earnings per share is antidilutive; therefore, options are excluded from weighted average shares outstanding.
[1] ($765,000 ÷ 3) ×.60 = $153,000.
[2] 97,500 (average options outstanding) × $30.
[3] ($900,000 + $570,000) ÷ 2 = $735,000.
[4] Under FASB Statement No. 123, the tax deduction based upon average market price ($6 per option) is less than the cost recognized for financial statement purposes ($9 per option); therefore, there is no tax benefit upon assumed exercise that would be credited to paid-in capital. Under APB Opinion No. 25, the tax deduction of $6 for each of the 97,500 average outstanding options at a tax rate of 40% would result in a tax benefit of $234,000.
[5] ($765,000 ÷ 3) ×.60 = $153,000.

Exhibit 39.15 *Continued.*

c. The number and weighted-average grant-date fair value of equity instruments other than options (e.g., shares of nonvested stock) granted during the year.

d. A description of the method and significant assumptions used to estimate the fair values of options, including the weighted-average (1) risk-free interest rate, (2) expected life, (3) expected volatility, and (4) expected dividend yield.

e. Total compensation cost recognized in income for stock-based compensation awards.

f. The terms of significant modifications to outstanding awards.

A company that has both fixed and indexed or performance-based plans should provide certain of the foregoing information separately for different types of plans. For example, the weighted-average exercise price at the end of the year would be shown separately for plans with a fixed exercise price and those with an indexed exercise price.

4. For options outstanding at the date of the latest balance sheet presented, disclosure of the range of exercise prices, the weighted-average exercise price, and the weighted-average remaining contractual life. If the range of exercise prices is wide (e.g., the highest exercise price exceeds 150 percent of the lowest exercise price), the exercise prices should be segregated into meaningful ranges. The following information should be disclosed for each range:

a. The number, weighted-average exercise price, and weighted-average remaining contractual life of options outstanding, and

b. The number and weighted-average exercise price of options currently exercisable.

FASB Statement No. 123 provides an extensive example disclosure.

(b) DISCLOSURES BY COMPANIES THAT CONTINUE TO APPLY THE PROVISIONS OF APB OPINION NO. 25.   In addition to the disclosures described above, companies that continue to apply the provisions of APB Opinion No. 25 must disclose the following for each year an income statement is presented:

- The pro forma net income and, for public entities, the pro forma earnings per share, as if the fair value-based accounting method prescribed by FASB Statement No. 123 had been used to account for stock-based compensation cost

- Those pro forma amounts should reflect the difference between compensation cost, if any, included in net income in accordance with APB Opinion No. 25 and the related cost measured by the fair value-based method, as well as additional tax effects, if any, that would have been recognized in the income statement if the fair value-based method had been used

- The required pro forma amounts should reflect no other adjustments to reported net income or earnings per share

FASB Statement No. 123 provides an extensive example disclosure.

39.9 SOURCES AND SUGGESTED REFERENCES

Accounting Principles Board, "Accounting for Stock Issued to Employees," APB Opinion No. 25. AICPA, New York, 1972.

———, "Stock Plans Established by a Principle Stockholder," Accounting for Stock Issued to Employees: Interpretation of APB Opinion No. 25. AICPA, New York, 1973.

Financial Accounting Standards Board, "Purchase of Stock Options and Stock Appreciation Rights in a Leveraged Buyout," EITF Issue No. 84–13. FASB, Stamford, CT, 1984.

———, "Stock Option Pyramiding," EITF Issue No. 84–18. FASB, Stamford, CT, 1984.

———, "Permanent Discount Restricted Stock Purchase Plans," EITF Issue No. 84–34. FASB, Stamford, CT, 1984.

———, "Business Combinations: Settlement of Stock Options and Awards," EITF Issue No. 85–45. FASB, Stamford, CT, 1985.

———, "Adjustments Relating to Stock Compensation Plans," EITF Issue No. 87–6. FASB, Stamford, CT, 1987.

———, "Book Value Stock Purchase Plans," EITF Issue No. 87–23. FASB, Stamford, CT, 1987.

———, "Stock Compensation Issues Related to Market Decline," EITF Issue No. 87–33. FASB, Stamford, CT, 1987.

———, "Book Value Stock Plans in an Initial Public Offering," EITF Issue No. 88–6. FASB, Norwalk, CT, 1988.

———, "Accounting for a Reload Stock Option," EITF Issue No. 90–7. FASB, Norwalk, CT, 1990.

———, "Changes to Fixed Employee Stock Option Plans as a Result of Equity Restructuring," EITF Issue No. 90–9. FASB, Norwalk, CT, 1990.

———, "Accounting for the Buyout of Compensatory Stock Options," EITF Issue No. 94–6. FASB, Norwalk, CT, 1994.

———, "Accounting for Stock Compensation Arrangements with Employer Loan Features under APB Opinion No. 25," EITF Issue No. 95–16. FASB, Norwalk, CT, 1995.

———, "Accounting for Equity Instruments That Are Issued to Other Than Employees for Acquiring, or in Conjunction with Selling, Goods or Services," EITF Issue No. 96–18. FASB, Norwalk, CT, 1997.

———, "Accounting for the Delayed Receipt of Option Shares upon Exercise under APB Opinion No. 25," EITF Issue No. 97–5. FASB, Norwalk, CT, 1997.

———, "Accounting for Increased Share Authorizations in an IRS Section 423 Employee Stock Purchase Plan under APB Opinion No. 25," EITF Issue No. 97–12. FASB, Norwalk, CT, 1997.

———, "Accounting by a Grantee for an Equity Instrument to Be Received in Conjunction with Providing Goods or Services," EITF Issue No. 00–8, FASB, Norwalk, CT, 2000.

———, "Accounting Recognition for Certain Transactions Involving Equity Instruments Granted to Other Than Employees," EITF Issue No. 00–18, FASB, Norwalk, CT, 2000.

———, "Accounting for Stock Appreciation Rights and Other Variable Stock Option or Award Plans," FASB Interpretation No. 28. FASB, Stamford, CT, 1978.

———, "Determining the Measurement Date for Stock Option, Purchase, and Award Plans Involving Junior Stock," FASB Interpretation No. 38. FASB, Stamford, CT, 1984.

———, "Accounting for Certain Transactions Involving Stock Compensation," FASB Interpretation No. 44, FASB, Norwalk, CT, 2000.

———, "Accounting for the Conversion of Stock Options into Incentive Stock Options as a Result of the Economic Recovery Tax Act of 1981," FASB Technical Bulletin No. 82–2. FASB, Stamford, CT, 1982.

———, "Accounting under Statement 123 for Certain Employee Stock Purchase Plans with a Look-Back Option," FASB Technical Bulletin 97–1. FASB, Norwalk, CT, 1997.

———, "Accounting for Income Taxes," Statement of Financial Accounting Standards No. 109. FASB, Norwalk, CT, 1992.

———, "Accounting for Stock-Based Compensation," Statement of Financial Accounting Standards No. 123. FASB, Norwalk, CT, 1995.

———, "Earnings Per Share," Statement of Financial Accounting Standards No. 128. FASB, Norwalk, CT, 1997.

Securities and Exchange Commission, "Codification of Financial Reporting Policies," Financial Reporting Release No. 1, § 211 (ASR No. 268). SEC, Washington, DC, 1982.

CHAPTER 40

PROSPECTIVE FINANCIAL STATEMENTS

Don M. Pallais, CPA

40.1 TYPES OF PROSPECTIVE FINANCIAL STATEMENTS

(a) DEFINITIONS. *Prospective financial information* is future-oriented; that is, financial information about the future. *Prospective financial statements* are future-oriented presentations that present, at a minimum, certain specific financial information.

The American Institute of Certified Public Accountants (AICPA) *Guide for Prospective Financial Information* (2002) defines prospective financial statements as presentations of an entity's financial position, results of operations, and cash flows for the future. In addition to the AICPA Guide, there is also a Statement on Standards for Attestation Engagements No. 10, Attestation Standards: Revision and Recodification: Chapter 3, "Financial Forecasts and Projections" (AT 301), which establishes standards for accountants' services.

Entity means an individual, organization, enterprise, or other unit for which financial statements could be prepared in conformity with generally accepted accounting practices (GAAP). It is not necessary for the entity to have been formed at the time the prospective financial statements are prepared—prospective financial statements may be prepared for entities that may be formed in the future. In fact, before committing capital to proposed entities, prospective investors or lenders often insist on seeing prospective financial statements covering the early years of proposed operations.

Although the AICPA Guide defines prospective financial statements as presentations of future financial position, results of operations, and cash flows, three full financial statements are not always required. Prospective financial statements may be presented in summarized or condensed form. A presentation of future financial data would be considered to be a prospective financial statement if it disclosed at least the following nine items, to the extent they apply to the entity and would be presented in the entity's historical financial statements for the period covered:

1. Sales or gross revenue
2. Gross profit or cost of sales
3. Unusual or infrequently occurring items
4. Provision for income taxes
5. Discontinued operations or extraordinary items
6. Income from continuing operations
7. Net income
8. Basic and diluted earnings per share (required only when disclosure is also required for the entity's historical financial statements)
9. Significant changes in financial position (i.e., significant balance sheet changes not otherwise disclosed in the presentation)

The definition of prospective financial statements does not specify the *length of* the future period. For a presentation to be prospective, however, *some* of the period covered must be in the future even though a part of the period may have expired. Thus, a calendar 20X1 presentation done on December 30, 20X1, would still, in theory, be a prospective presentation since there would still be an unexpired day in the period. Determining the period to be covered by prospective financial statements is discussed in more detail in Subsection 40.3(c)(ii).

There are two kinds of prospective financial statements: financial forecasts and financial projections. In practice, though, prospective financial statements are often given other names, such as "budgets," "business plans," and "studies."

Although the terms "forecast" and "projections" are sometimes used interchangeably in popular usage, in the technical accounting literature, forecasts and projections differ in what they purport to represent. Forecasts represent expectations, whereas projections are hypothetical analyses.

(i) Financial Forecasts. Financial forecasts are defined as prospective financial statements that present, to the best of management's knowledge and belief, an entity's expected financial position, results of operations, and cash flows based on management's assumptions reflecting conditions it expects to exist and the course of action it expects to take. In some cases forecasts can be prepared by persons other than current management, such as a potential acquirer of the entity, but usually the person (or persons) who take responsibility for the assumptions is someone who expects to be in a position to influence the entity's operations during the forecast period. The AICPA Guide refers to the person who takes responsibility for the assumptions as the *responsible party*.

Despite the inherent uncertainty of future events and the softness of prospective data, a forecast cannot be prepared without a *reasonably objective basis*. That is, sufficiently objective assumptions must be capable of being developed to present a forecast. Without a reasonably objective basis, management has no grounds for any expectations; all it would have is guesses.

The determination of whether a reasonably objective basis for a forecast exists is primarily an exercise in judgment. The key question is whether assumptions, based on the entity's plans, made by persons who are informed about the industry in which the entity operates would generally fall within a relatively narrow range. If so, there may be a reasonably objective basis for the forecast. On the other hand, if there is so much uncertainty regarding significant assumptions that consensus would be unlikely to be reached, there may not be a reasonably objective basis, precluding preparation of a forecast (although a projection could be developed). For example, there would be no reasonably objective basis to forecast the winnings of a thoroughbred being reared to race.

If prospective financial data are necessary, but no reasonably objective basis exists to present a forecast, management might hypothesize the assumption that is not subject to reasonable estimation and call the presentation a *projection* or quantify only those assumptions that have a reasonably objective basis and prepare a *partial presentation*. However, both of these alternatives are limited in their usefulness [see Subsections 40.2(a)–(d) for a further discussion].

Exhibit 40.1 presents factors to consider in determining whether there is a reasonably objective basis to present a forecast.

Occasionally, an entity may need to present a forecast but cannot do so because of an uncertainty about the *actions* the *users* of the forecast may take. For example, an assumption may relate to passage of a referendum when the forecast is to be used by voters deciding on the referendum. In those cases, despite the high level of uncertainty, management may select one of the four alternatives as its assumption and then call the presentation a forecast if:

1. The assumption is subject to only two possible outcomes (an either/or situation).
2. The outcome of that assumption is dependent on the actions of the users of the presentation.
3. The alternative selected is not unreasonable on its face.
4. The presentation discloses that the forecast represents management's expectations only if the prospective action of users takes place.

SUFFICIENTLY OBJECTIVE ASSUMPTIONS—MATTERS TO CONSIDER

Basis	Less Objective	More Objective
Economy	Subject to uncertainty	Relatively stable
Industry	Emerging or unstable—high rate of business failure	Mature or relatively stable
Entity		
• Operating history	Little or no operating history	Seasoned company; relatively stable operating history
• Customer base	Diverse, changing customer group	Relatively stable customer group
• Financial condition	Weak financial position; Poor operating results	Strong financial position; Good operating results
Management's Experience With:		
• Industry	Inexperienced management	Experienced management
• The business and its products	Inexperienced management; high turnover of key personnel	Experienced management
Products or Services		
• Market	New or uncertain market	Existing or relatively stable market
• Technology	Rapidly changing technology	Relatively stable technology
• Experience	New products or expanding product line	Relatively stable products
Competing Assumptions	Wide range of possible outcomes	Relatively narrow range of possible outcomes
Dependency of Assumptions on the Outcome of Forecasted Results	More dependency	Less dependency

Exhibit 40.1   Determining a reasonably objective basis. (Source: AICPA, Guide for Prospective Financial Information, Section 7.05.)

Regardless of the need for a reasonably objective basis and management's efforts to present its expectations, a forecast is not a prediction. A forecast is not judged on whether, in hindsight, it came true. A forecast is a presentation intended to provide financial information regarding management's plans and expectations for the future. It augments information in historical financial statements and other sources of data to help prospective investors, lenders, or others make better financial decisions.

(ii) Financial Projections.   Financial projections present, to the best of management's knowledge and belief, an entity's future financial position, results of operations, and cash flows given the occurrence of one or more *hypothetical assumptions*. Financial projections are sometimes prepared to analyze alternative courses of action, as in response to a question such as "What would happen if . . . ?"

The hypothetical assumptions in a projection are those that are not necessarily expected to occur but are consistent with the reason the projection was prepared. There is no explicit limit on the number of hypothetical assumptions used in a projection. However, since a projection is a presentation of expectations based on the occurrence of the hypothetical assumptions, a presentation in which all significant assumptions have been hypothesized would not be a projection because it depicts no dependent expectations. Thus, at some point the number of hypothetical assumptions may grow so large that the presentation is not a projection.

Hypothetical assumptions need not be reasonable or plausible; in fact, they may even be improbable if their use is consistent with the reason the projection is prepared. For example, it is generally improbable that a hotel would experience 100 percent occupancy. But use of that occupancy rate as a hypothetical assumption would be appropriate if the projection were prepared to demonstrate the maximum return on investment of a hotel. However, there are special disclosure rules when hypothetical assumptions are improbable [see Subsection 40.4(c)(ii)].

All the nonhypothetical assumptions in a projection are expected to occur if the hypothetical assumption occurred, which may be different from expecting the nonhypothetical assumption actually to occur. For example, a company may hypothesize adding a new product line and intend to use the resulting projection in deciding whether to do so. As a result of the assumption about a new product line, the projection might include assumptions about hiring new sales personnel. Management may not actually expect to hire new sales personnel, but it would hire them if it started a new product line; thus the assumption is not actually expected, but it is expected given the occurrence of the hypothetical assumption.

(b) OTHER PRESENTATIONS THAT LOOK LIKE PROSPECTIVE FINANCIAL STATEMENTS. A number of presentations look like prospective financial statements but are not, including presentations for wholly expired periods, partial presentations, pro forma financial statements, and financial analyses.

(i) Presentations for Wholly Expired Periods. Prospective financial statements are presentations for a future period. If the period covered by a presentation is wholly expired, such as a prior-year budget, it is not a prospective financial statement.

(ii) Partial Presentations. Partial presentations are presentations of prospective financial information that omit one or more minimum items required of prospective financial statements [see Subsection 40.1(a)]. They are not subject to the same rules as prospective financial statements.

(iii) Pro Formas. Pro forma financial statements are historical financial statements adjusted for a prospective transaction. Although one transaction has not occurred at the time of presentation, the statements are essentially historical ones. In essence, such statements answer the question "What would have happened if...?" Guidance for accountants' reports on pro forma presentations can be found in SSAE No. 10, Chapter 4, "Reporting on Pro Forma Financial Information" (AT 401).

(iv) Financial Analyses. Financial analyses are defined in the AICPA Guide as presentations in which the independent accountant rather than management develops and takes responsibility for the assumptions. Such presentations are normally a by-product of a consulting engagement in which management asks the accountant to analyze a condition and make recommendations about possible or prudent courses of action.

These analyses are not prospective financial statements because the party who takes responsibility for the assumptions (the accountant) is not, and does not expect to be, in a position to influence the entity's operations in the future period. If, however, management adopts the assumptions used, it may present the statements as a forecast or projection.

40.2 LIMITATIONS ON THE USE OF PROSPECTIVE FINANCIAL STATEMENTS

(a) HOW PROSPECTIVE FINANCIAL STATEMENTS ARE USED. The use of prospective financial statements is neither required nor recommended by AICPA literature. Nonetheless, they are used for many purposes in practice. For example, they are used by management in internal planning, by potential suppliers of capital in making investment decisions, and by government agencies for monitoring or approving an entity's operations.

The AICPA Guide (Chapter 4) categorizes all the potential uses of prospective financial statements into two broad classes: *general use*, which refers to passive users, and *limited use*, which refers to use by management only or use by persons who are negotiating directly with management.

The AICPA Guide states that forecasts are appropriate for either general or limited use; projections are generally appropriate only for limited use.

Unlike Securities and Exchange Commission (SEC) registration rules, the type of use is not dependent on the *number* of users of the prospective financial statements. A user is considered a limited user if it is negotiating directly with the entity; if it is not, it is a general user. Thus, even one passive user would constitute general use; whereas an entity may negotiate directly with numerous users, each of whom can change the terms of the transaction, and each would be considered a limited user.

(b) GENERAL USE. General use means use of the prospective financial statements by persons who are not negotiating directly with management. General users are passive users; that is, they can review the prospective financial statements to determine their own course of action, but they cannot affect the company's actions or the terms of their investment. For example, after reviewing an entity's prospective financial statements, a potential investor in a limited partnership can decide whether to invest in it and, if so, how much to invest, but cannot change the terms of the investment; thus the user would be considered a general user. A user who can change the terms of the investment would be considered a limited user.

Because general users cannot negotiate the terms of their involvement with the entity, their information needs are much like those of shareholders in a public company. To make informed decisions, general users would ordinarily be served best by a presentation of management's estimate of future financial results—a forecast.

A presentation of results based on a hypothetical assumption that does not reflect management's expectations (i.e., a projection) would not serve general users because such a presentation would only tell them what is *not* necessarily expected to happen, not what is. This would be analogous to providing shareholders with pro forma financial statements including transactions that did not occur instead of with historical financial statements.

Accordingly, financial projections are not ordinarily issued to general users unless the projections supplement a forecast *for the period covered by the forecast.* Thus, general users may benefit from an analysis of a hypothetical course of action when it supplements a presentation of management's expectations for that period, but not when it stands alone as the only presentation of prospective results for a period.

That forecasts are appropriate for general use, of course, does not suggest that they will meet all the users' information needs. Potential investors or lenders often need to consider other information as well before making economic decisions, just as they do when presented with historical financial statements.

(c) LIMITED USE. Limited use of prospective financial statements means use by the entity itself or use by persons with whom the entity is negotiating directly. Negotiating is an active concept. It includes more than the user's ability to ask questions of the entity; it refers to the user's ability to affect the terms of its business with the entity beyond merely deciding whether to participate and the amount of its participation.

There is no limit on the potential number of limited users in a particular circumstance except for the limit of the number of parties that management can practically negotiate with at any one time. It is also unnecessary to specifically identify the limited users at the time the prospective financial statements are prepared.

Because limited users can negotiate the terms of their involvement and challenge or propose changes to the hypothetical assumptions, they can use presentations that do not present management's best estimates. Accordingly, projections are often useful for limited users.

Similarly, because limited users can demand additional information as a condition of their participation (or, when there is a lack of needed information, increase the cost of capital in response to a perceived increase in risk), it may also be appropriate for limited users to use partial presentations or financial analyses.

Of course, financial forecasts are appropriate for limited users as well as general users.

(d) INTERNAL USE. Internal use means use of the prospective financial statements only by the entity itself. It is a type of limited use. Limitation of the prospective financial statements to internal use does not affect the type of statements that are appropriate in the circumstances, but it affects the type of services that an independent accountant can perform on them. This is discussed in more detail in Subsection 40.9(a).

40.3 DEVELOPING PROSPECTIVE FINANCIAL STATEMENTS

(a) GENERAL GUIDELINES. Chapter 6 of the AICPA Guide presents 11 guidelines for preparation of prospective financial statements. Although forecasts and projections can be developed without adhering to those guidelines, using them often results in more reliable prospective data.

The AICPA guidelines are listed in Exhibit 40.2. They apply to projections as well as forecasts, though in many cases they do not apply to the hypothetical assumptions in projections.

A general approach to developing prospective financial statements involves three steps:

1. Identifying key factors
2. Developing assumptions for each key factor
3. Assembling the prospective financial statements

(b) IDENTIFYING KEY FACTORS. The AICPA Guide (Section 6.28) states: "Key factors are those significant matters upon which an entity's future results are expected to depend. Those factors are basic to the entity's operations and serve as a foundation for the prospective financial statements."

Key factors vary by entity and industry. They are general matters such as manufacturing labor, sales, or capital asset needs. A knowledge of the entity's industry and proposed operations is necessary to identify all the key factors that will form the basis for the prospective financial statements.

Financial forecasts should be prepared in good faith.

Financial forecasts should be prepared with appropriate care by qualified personnel.

Financial forecasts should be prepared using appropriate accounting principles.

The process used to develop financial forecasts should provide for seeking out the best information that is reasonably available at the time.

The information used in preparing financial forecasts should be consistent with the plans of the entity.

Key factors should be identified as a basis for assumptions.

Assumptions used in preparing financial forecasts should be appropriate.

The process used to develop financial forecasts should provide the means to determine the relative effect of variations in the major underlying assumptions.

The process used to develop financial forecasts should provide adequate documentation of both the financial forecasts and the process used to develop them.

The process used to develop financial forecasts should include, where appropriate, the regular comparison of the financial forecasts with attained results.

The process used to prepare financial forecasts should include adequate review and approval by the responsible party at the appropriate levels of authority.

Exhibit 40.2   Guidelines for preparation of prospective financial statements. (Source: AICPA, Guide for Prospective Financial Information, Section 6.08.)

(c) DEVELOPING ASSUMPTIONS.   Assumptions are developed for each key factor. In a forecast, the assumptions represent management's best estimate of future conditions and courses of action. In a projection, the hypothetical assumptions are consistent with the purpose of the projection, and all the other assumptions represent management's best estimate of future conditions and courses of action given the occurrence of the hypothetical assumptions.

Approaches to developing assumptions range from highly sophisticated mathematical models to estimates based on personal opinion. Regardless of the approach taken to quantify the assumptions, to determine whether the assumptions are appropriate, management considers the following six:

1. There appears to be a rational relationship between the assumptions and the underlying facts and circumstances.
2. Assumptions have been developed for each key factor.
3. Assumptions have been developed without undue optimism or pessimism.
4. Assumptions are consistent with the entity's plans and expectations.
5. Assumptions are consistent with each other.
6. Individual assumptions make sense in the context of the prospective financial statements taken as a whole.

It is not always necessary to obtain support for each significant assumption, but developing support often results in more reliable prospective financial information. In any case, the significant considerations in developing a forecast are (1) whether management has a reasonably objective basis [see Subsection 40.1(a)(i)] to base its expectations on and (2) whether the assumptions are consistent with its expectations.

(i) Mathematical Models.   Forecasts may be based on sophisticated mathematical techniques such as regression analysis. However, merely extrapolating historical results into the future does not result in a forecast. To forecast, management satisfies itself that it has identified the conditions and course of action it intends to take in the future period. If, based on consideration of key factors, management believes that historical conditions are indicative of future results, it then might use an estimation technique based on historical results.

(ii) Length of the Prospective Period.   The AICPA Guide states that length of time to be covered by prospective financial statements should be based on the needs of the user and management's ability to estimate future financial results.

In establishing a minimum length, the AICPA Guide (Section 8.33) states that to be meaningful to users, a forecast or projection should include at least one full year of normal operations. For example, an entity forecasting a major acquisition would present at least the first full year following the acquisition; a newly formed entity would show at least the first full year of normal operations in addition to its start-up period.

When the entity has a long operating cycle or when long-term results are necessary to evaluate the investment consequences involved, it may be necessary to forecast farther into the future to meet the needs of users.

Uncertainty increases as to periods farther in the future. At some point, the underlying assumptions become so subjective that no reasonably objective basis exists to present a forecast.

The AICPA Guide (Section 8.33) limits the maximum length of the forecast period to three to five years. It states that ordinarily it would be difficult to establish that a reasonably objective basis for a forecast exists for a longer period. However, the Guide recognizes that, in some cases, forecasts can be presented for longer periods, such as when long-term contracts exist that specify the timing and the amount of revenue and costs can be controlled within reasonable limits (as in the case of real estate projects with long-term leases). It also recognizes that in some cases, it may be hard to justify even a three-year forecast, such as for certain start-up or high-technology companies.

The SEC rules are generally more restrictive than the AICPA's. For prospective financial statements included in SEC filings, the SEC has stated that "[F]or certain companies in certain industries a [forecast] covering a two or three year period may be entirely reasonable. Other companies may not have a reasonable basis for [forecasts] beyond the current year" [Reg. 229.10(b)(2)].

In determining how far into the future it can forecast, management considers the key factors and resulting assumptions for each future period presented. Considering them in detail for, say, one year and merely extrapolating the results for an additional two years beyond that does not result in a three-year forecast, but in a one-year forecast and a two-year projection.

(d) ASSEMBLING THE PROSPECTIVE FINANCIAL STATEMENTS.   Assembling the prospective financial statements involves converting the assumptions into prospective amounts and presenting the amounts and assumptions in conformity with AICPA presentation guidelines. Those guidelines are discussed in more detail in the following sections.

40.4 PRESENTATION AND DISCLOSURE OF PROSPECTIVE FINANCIAL STATEMENTS

(a) AUTHORITATIVE GUIDANCE.   The primary source of guidance for presentation and disclosure of financial forecasts and projections is Chapter 8 of the AICPA Guide. In the absence of Financial Accounting Standards Board (FASB) pronouncements, the Guide establishes the equivalent of GAAP for prospective financial statements.

Although the Guide establishes guidelines for presentation and disclosure, it does not require or recommend the presentation of prospective financial statements in any circumstance. The decision to present prospective financial statements is generally management's, based on its need and desires and those of potential financial statement users.

Other bodies have also established rules concerning presentation and disclosure of forecasts and projections. For example, the SEC, the North American Security Administrators Association, and individual state securities commissions have established rules that are applicable in certain situations. Issuers of prospective financial statements used in offering statements should be aware of those rules as well, but it is beyond the scope of this chapter to discuss all of them.

Occasionally, potential users of prospective financial statements also require a specific form or content for the statements. For example, users may specify the level of detail presented or the period covered, or they may require the completion of prescribed forms. Issuers of prospective financial statements should consider how those requirements compare with those in the AICPA Guide and whether compliance with the user's requirements may cause difficulties in obtaining an independent accountant's services on the statements.

(b) FORM OF PROSPECTIVE FINANCIAL STATEMENTS.   Unlike historical financial statements, the form of prospective financial statements is flexible. Flexibility is permitted to present the most useful information in the circumstances.

Presenting prospective financial statements in the same form as the historical financial statements expected to be issued at the end of the prospective period facilitates later comparison. Accordingly, if later comparison is expected, an entity may issue a prospective balance sheet, income statement, and statement of cash flows.

If no later comparison is intended, or if more aggregated data are desired, the prospective financial statements may be presented in a summarized or condensed format. The amount of condensation or summarization is flexible as long as the following nine minimum items, to the extent they are applicable and would be presented in the historical financial statements, are either presented or otherwise derivable from the presentation:

1. Sales or gross revenue
2. Gross profit or cost of sales

3. Unusual or infrequently occurring items

4. Provision for income taxes

5. Discontinued operations or extraordinary items

6. Income from continuing operations

7. Net income

8. Basic and diluted earnings per share

9. Significant changes in financial position

A summarized presentation should disclose significant cash flows and other significant changes in balance sheet accounts for the prospective period. The specific items to be presented depend on the circumstances, but often include cash flows from operations.

Exhibit 40.3 illustrates a condensed format for a financial forecast.

(i) Amounts Presented.   The prospective financial statements may be presented in terms of single-point estimates or ranges.

Ranges are sometimes presented when management wants to present a forecast but cannot refine its estimate of expected results sharply enough to present a single point as its best estimate. If the prospective financial statements are presented in terms of ranges, the range is not selected in a biased manner. That is, one end of the range is not significantly more likely than the other. In addition, the range is not characterized as representing the best and worst cases, since actual results might fall outside of the range.

XYZ Company, Inc.
Summarized Financial Forecast
Year Ending December 31, 20X3
(in thousands except per-share amounts)

	Forecasted 20X3	Comparative Historical Information* 20X2	20X1
Sales	$101,200	$91,449	$79,871
Gross profit	23,700	21,309	19,408
Income tax expense	3,400	3,267	2,929
Net income	4,500	3,949	3,214
Earnings per share	4.73	4.14	3.37
Significant anticipated changes in financial position: Cash provided by operations	4,100	3,103	4,426
Net increase (decrease) in long-term borrowings	3,400	300	(300)
Dividend (per share 20X3: $1.50; 20X2: $1.35; 20X1: $1.00)	1,400	1,288	954
Additions to plant and equipment	4,400	2,907	2,114
Increase (decrease) in cash	1,400	(334)	1,017

See accompanying Summary of Significant Forecast Assumptions and Accounting Policies [not illustrated in exhibit].

*Comparative historical information is not part of the minimum presentation.

Exhibit 40.3   Illustration of condensed format for prospective financial statements. (Source: AICPA, Guide for Prospective Financial Statements, Section 410.05.)

Any of the following formats for a forecast might be acceptable:

Single-point estimate:

Sales	$XXX
Cost of sales	XXX

Range (from X to Z) showing an intermediate point (Y):

	X	Y	Z
Sales	$XXX	$YYY	$ZZZ
Cost of sales	XXX	YYY	ZZZ

Range showing a one line item only; example assumes the range is based on a forecasted range of sales prices and demand is inelastic:

Sales	$XXX—$YYY
Cost of sales	$XXX

(ii) Titles. The titles of financial forecasts should include the word "forecast" or "forecasted." Financial projections' titles should refer to the hypothetical assumptions. Titles such as "budget" are avoided since they offer no indication whether the presentation is a forecast or a projection.

(c) DISCLOSURES. In addition to the items listed at the beginning of Subsection 40.4(b), the AICPA Guide requires that the following three matters be disclosed in prospective financial statements:

1. Description of what the presentation intends to depict
2. Summary of significant assumptions
3. Summary of significant accounting policies

Each page of the prospective financial statements should direct the readers' attention to the summaries of significant assumptions and accounting policies. A legend such as "The accompanying summaries of significant assumptions and accounting policies are an integral part of the financial forecast" or "See accompanying summaries of significant assumptions and accounting policies" is generally used.

(i) Description of the Presentation. The prospective financial statements should include a description of what management intends the statements to present, a statement that the assumptions are based on management's judgment at the time the prospective information was prepared, and a caveat that the prospective results may not be achieved.

The description is usually presented as the introduction to the summary of significant assumptions.

The introduction to the assumptions for a financial forecast would disclose the necessary information as follows:

> This financial forecast presents, to the best of management's knowledge and belief, the Company's expected financial position, results of operations, and cash flows* for the forecast period. Accordingly, the forecast reflects its judgment, as of [date], the date of this forecast, of the expected conditions and its expected course of action. The assumptions disclosed herein are those that management believes are significant to the forecast. There will usually be differences between the forecasted and actual results, because events and circumstances frequently do not occur as expected, and those differences may be material.

---

* If the presentation is summarized or condensed, this might read "… summary of the Company's expected results of operations and changes in financial position …."

The introduction to the summary of significant assumptions for a financial projection would be similar to that for a forecast except that it would clearly explain the special purpose and limitations on the usefulness of the presentation. Such an introduction might read as follows:

> This financial projection is based on sales volume at maximum productive capacity and presents, to the best of management's knowledge and belief, the Company's expected financial position, results of operations, and cash flows* for the projection period if such volume were attained. Accordingly, the projection reflects its judgment, as of [date], the date of this projection, of the expected conditions and its expected course of action if such sales volume were experienced. The presentation is designed to provide information to the Company's board of directors concerning the maximum profitability that might be achieved if current production were expanded through the addition of a third production shift and should not be considered to be a presentation of expected future results. Accordingly, this projection may not be useful for other purposes. The assumptions disclosed herein are those that management believes are significant to the projection. Management considers it highly unlikely that the stated sales volume will be experienced during the projection period. Further, even if the stated sales volume were attained, there will usually be differences between the projected and actual results, because events and circumstances frequently do not occur as expected, and those differences may be material.

---

* If the presentation is summarized or condensed, this might read "...summary of the Company's expected results of operations and changes in financial position...."

If the presentation is shown as a range, the introduction also makes it clear that presentation is shown as a range, that the range represents managements' expectations, and that there is no assurance that actual results will fall within the range. A sample introduction follows:

> This financial forecast presents, to the best of management's knowledge and belief, the Company's expected financial position, results of operations, and cash flows for the forecast period at occupancy rates of 75% and 95% of available apartments. Accordingly, the forecast reflects its judgment, as of [date], the date of this forecast, of the expected conditions and its expected course of action at each occupancy rate. The assumptions disclosed herein are those that management believes are significant to the forecast. Management reasonably expects, to the best of its knowledge and belief, that the actual occupancy rates achieved will be within the range shown; however, there can be no assurance that it will. Further, even if the actual occupancy rate is within the range shown, there will usually be differences between the forecasted and actual results, because events and circumstances frequently do not occur as expected, and those differences may be material, and the actual results may be outside the range presented by the forecast.

(ii) Significant Assumptions.   The assumptions form the basis for the prospective financial statements; for the statements to be meaningful to users, the assumptions should be disclosed.

Numerous assumptions are made in developing prospective financial statements. Only significant assumptions are required to be disclosed. Significance is generally considered to be measured in terms of the magnitude of an assumption's effect on the prospective financial statements.

Assumptions, however, may be considered significant even though they may not have a direct and large dollar effect on the statements. Four assumptions, which need to be disclosed as well, include:

1. Sensitive assumptions, that is, assumptions about which there is a reasonable possibility of the occurrence of a variation that may significantly affect the prospective results
2. Significantly changed conditions, that is, assumptions about anticipated conditions that are expected to be significantly different from current conditions
3. Hypothetical assumptions used in a projection
4. Other matters deemed important to the statements or their interpretation

The form and placement of assumptions is flexible and can be based on management's judgment in the circumstances. The guiding principle is that the disclosure is understandable by the persons expected to use the statements.

Disclosure of the basis or rationale underlying the assumptions assists users in understanding and making decisions based on prospective financial statements. Such disclosure is recommended, but not required, by the AICPA Guide.

The following examples show the form of disclosure of significant assumptions that might be appropriate in various circumstances:

As a footnote in a formal presentation:

2. *Sales.* Sales of the Company's product in 20X2 are expected to increase 20 percent over those experienced in 20X1 ($1,000,000).

As a footnote in a formal presentation, including basis and rationale:

2. *Sales.* Based on commitments received and its current expansion into the Midwest market, management expects unit sales to increase by 15 percent over the number of units sold in 20X1. In addition, the Company expects to increase sales prices by an average of five percent over the year to cover expected increases in raw material costs. Increasing sales prices is not expected to adversely affect units sold since raw material cost increases will affect the entire industry and management anticipates industry-wide price increases. (Disclosure might also include discussion of other product lines, marketing plans, and other related information.)

Informal, shown on the face of the statements:

Sales (units up 15 percent over 20X1, price up 5 percent) $1,200,000

Informal, shown as output of factors used in an electronic spreadsheet:

Sales = 1.2* 20X1Sal

The appropriateness of each approach would depend on the expected use of the prospective financial statements. The formal presentation that includes the basis and rationale would be most useful for general users; the informal printout of factors from a spreadsheet might be appropriate, and least costly to prepare, for internal use.

The disclosure of significant assumptions should also indicate which assumptions are *hypothetical* and which are *particularly sensitive.*

The *hypothetical* assumptions used in a projection should be specifically identified. In addition, if any of the hypothetical assumptions are considered *improbable,* the disclosure should indicate that.

Particularly sensitive assumptions are those for which there is a relatively high probability of variation that would significantly affect the prospective financial statements. The presentation should indicate which assumptions appeared to be particularly sensitive at the time of preparation of the statements (even though hindsight might indicate that others actually were particularly sensitive).

The disclosure of sensitivity is flexible. Below are examples of disclosures that might be appropriate in the circumstances:

With sensitivity quantified:

9. *Interest Expense.* The forecast assumes that the debt to be placed will carry an interest rate of 10 percent; however, the rate will not be determined until closing. For each 1/4 of one percent that the actual interest rate differs from the rate assumed, forecasted income before income taxes would be raised or lowered by $25,000 and after-tax cash flow would change by approximately $16,000. If the rate exceeds $11\frac{1}{4}$ percent, the forecast would not indicate sufficient cash flow from the new project to service the debt.

Without sensitivity quantification:

9. *Interest Expense.* The forecast assumes the debt to be placed will carry an interest rate of 10 percent. The actual rate will not be determined until closing and may be higher or lower. To the extent that the actual rate exceeds 10 percent, forecasted income would be adversely affected.

Informal, printout of factors in an electronic spreadsheet:

Int exp = 0.1*debt! part. sensitive

(iii) Significant Accounting Principles.   The prospective financial statements should include disclosure of the *significant accounting principles* used in the statements. The basis of accounting and the accounting principles used in the prospective statements are generally those that are expected to be used during the prospective period. Thus, if the prospective statements accompany historical financial statements, this disclosure may be accomplished by referring the reader to the appropriate note in the historical statements.

If the basis of accounting used in the prospective statements is a *comprehensive basis of accounting other than GAAP*, the basis used should be disclosed as well as that it is different from GAAP.

If the basis of accounting used is different from that expected to be used in the historical financial statements for the prospective period (such as presenting cash-flow forecast for an entity that uses GAAP for its historical financial statements), the use of a different basis of accounting in the prospective statements should be disclosed. The differences in prospective results that are caused by the use of the different basis would usually be reconciled in the statements unless the reconciliation would not be useful.

If the accounting principles used differ from those expected to be used (such as in a projection that analyzes the effect of a possible change in accounting principles), the use of a different principle in the projection should be disclosed. The results in the projection may also be reconciled to those that would result from using the principle used in the historical financial statements.

If management expects to change an accounting principle during the prospective period, the change in principle should be reflected in the prospective financial statements the same way it would be in the historical financial statements covering the prospective period. Other specific disclosures required for historical financial statements, such as those regarding pensions and income taxes, are not required for prospective financial statements.

(iv) Other Matters.   The *date* of preparation of the prospective financial statements should be disclosed. This disclosure provides information to users about how current the information underlying the statements is likely to be. The date is generally disclosed in the introduction to the summary of significant assumptions.

Occasionally, management recognizes that users need information for periods beyond its ability to forecast. For example, management may plan a refinancing of debt or the introduction of new products after the end of the forecast period. Or management may expect expiration of a significant contract or future adverse tax consequences to investors.

If users are considered limited users, management may present projections or partial presentations for the more distant periods.

If, however, the users are general users, presentation of a projection outside of the forecast period would be considered inappropriate. The AICPA Guide (Section 8.40) provides guidance for disclosure of significant postforecast-period matters.

Such a disclosure should include the following four items:

1. Include a title indicating that it presents information about periods beyond the financial forecast period.
2. Include an introduction indicating that the information presented does not constitute a financial forecast and indicating its purpose.

3. Disclose significant assumptions and identify those that are hypothetical, as well as the specific plans, events, or circumstances that are expected to have a material effect on results beyond the forecast period.

4. State that (a) the information is presented for analysis purposes only, (b) that there is no assurance that the events and circumstances described will occur, and, if applicable, (c) that the information is less reliable than the forecast.

The disclosures are part of the forecast presentation; they are generally in the summary of significant assumptions. The Guide prohibits presenting them comparative to the forecasted results on the face of the forecast, in related summaries of benefits (such as in a summary of investor benefits), or as a financial projection.

40.5 TYPES OF ACCOUNTANTS' SERVICES

(a) OBJECTIVE OF ACCOUNTANTS' SERVICES.   Companies generally retain independent accountants to provide services on prospective financial statements for either of two reasons: to add credibility to prospective statements expected to be used by third parties or to provide consultation or assistance in developing statements expected to be used primarily by the client. The AICPA performance and reporting standards recognize that the type of service that is appropriate in the circumstances may vary depending on the expected use.

The AICPA standards provide three standard accountants' services for prospective financial statements expected to be used by third parties: *compilation, examination*, and application of *agreed-upon procedures*. (No review or moderate-level assurance service is permitted.) When third-party use is not reasonably expected, the accountant may provide the three standard services or other types of services and reports that more closely reflect the purpose of the engagement.

(b) STANDARD ACCOUNTANTS' SERVICES.   The accountant is required to compile, examine, or apply agreed-upon procedures whenever:

- The presentation includes prospective financial statements.
- The statements are, or reasonably might be, expected to be used by a third party.
- The accountant either (a) submits to the client or others statements that the accountant has assembled or assisted in assembling or (b) reports on the statements.

There are three exceptions to this rule:

1. The accountant need not report on *drafts* of prospective financial statements submitted if they are clearly marked as such.

2. The accountant need not provide one of the standard services when the prospective financial statements are used solely in connection with engagements involving potential or pending litigation before a trier of fact in connection with the resolution of a dispute between two or more parties (often called *litigation support services*). In such circumstances, the accountant's work is ordinarily subjected to detailed analysis and challenge by each party to the dispute. However, the exception does not apply when the prospective financial statements are used by third parties who do not have the opportunity for such analysis and challenge. For example, creditors may not have that opportunity when a financial forecast is submitted to them to secure their agreement to a plan of reorganization.

3. The accountant who submits interim historical financial statements in a document that also contains prospective financial statements need not provide one of the standard services on the prospective statements if the prospective statements are labeled "budget," they do not extend beyond the end of the current fiscal year, the accountant's report states that the accountant did not apply any of the standard services to them, and the accountant's report disclaims an opinion or any other form of assurance on the statements.

(i) Prospective Financial Statements.   If the presentation does not meet the minimum disclosure requirement of prospective financial statements [see Subsection 40.1(a)], it is a *partial presentation* rather than prospective financial statements. In that case, the accountant is not required to provide a standard service on the prospective data. Chapter 23 of the AICPA Guide contains guidelines for compilations, examinations, and application of agreed-upon procedures to partial presentations. It does not *require* those services on partial presentations, but provides guidance for the accountant who is engaged to provide them.

(ii) Third-Party Use.   Third parties generally are any persons outside the entity presenting the prospective financial statements. Sometimes, however, such persons may not need to be considered third parties for the purpose of determining whether the guidance on accountants' services applies.

The AICPA Guide (Section 10.02) provides the following guidelines for determining whether outsiders are considered third parties:

In deciding whether a party that is or reasonably might be expected to use an accountant's report is considered to be a third party, the accountant should consider the degree of consistency of interest between [management] and the user regarding the forecast. If their interests are substantially consistent (e.g., both the [preparer] and the user are employees of the entity about which the forecast is made), the user would not be deemed to be a third party. On the other hand, where the interests of the [preparer] and user are potentially inconsistent (e.g., the [preparer] is a nonowner manager and the user is an absentee owner), the user would be deemed a third party. In some cases, this determination will require the exercise of considerable professional judgment.

In considering whether the statements will be restricted to internal use, the accountant may generally rely on management's oral or written representations, unless something leads the accountant to believe that, despite management's representations, the statements are likely to be distributed to a third party.

(iii) Assemble and Submit.   "Assembly" means the "manual or computer processing of mathematical or other clerical functions related to the presentation of the prospective financial statements" (AICPA Guide, Section 3.16). This refers to converting the assumptions into prospective amounts or putting the amounts into the form of statements. Assembly does not mean merely copying or collating statements prepared by someone else.

(c) INTERNAL USE.   The accountant may provide compilation, examination, or agreed-upon procedures engagements for internal use if engaged to do so. However, for internal use, the accountant has more flexibility to accommodate the varying circumstances of the engagement. Normally, these engagements involve consulting or planning (such as in management-consulting or tax-planning services) rather than third-party reliance. Common reporting options for internal use include *assembly reports* and *plain paper* prospective financial statements. Internal-use services are discussed in more detail in Section 40.9.

(d) PROHIBITED ENGAGEMENTS.   The AICPA Guide prohibits the accountant from submitting or reporting on prospective financial statements intended for third-party use if those statements omit the disclosure of significant assumptions. Similarly, the accountant is prohibited from submitting or reporting on a projection for third-party use if it does not identify the hypothetical assumption or describe the limitations on the usefulness of the presentation.

The accountant also may not submit or report on a financial projection that is intended for general use (unless it supplements a forecast for the same period) because such use is considered inappropriate [see Subsection 40.2(b)]. This prohibition means that the accountant could not assemble and submit such a presentation even if management agreed not to present the accountant's report or refer to the accountant in the document containing the projection that would be presented to general users.

(e) MATERIALITY. Accountants consider *materiality* in conducting engagements on prospective financial statements much as they do for historical financial statements. The AICPA Guide (Section 10.31) states, however, "Materiality is a concept that is judged in light of the expected range of reasonableness of the information; therefore, users should not expect prospective information (information about events that have not yet occurred) to be as precise as historical information."

It follows, then, that materiality criteria would be higher for prospective statements than for the same company's historical statements. That is, an amount that would be material to the historical statements might not be material to the prospectives. There is no consensus in practice, however, as to just how much higher materiality should be for prospective financial statements.

(f) SECURITIES AND EXCHANGE COMMISSION PERSPECTIVE. Relevant SEC rules regarding accountants' services on prospective financial statements in filings subject to the SEC's authority include the Safe Harbor Rule for Projections and as policies stated in equation S-K § 229.10. These rules, however, add relatively little to the requirements for accountants' procedures and reports established by the AICPA Guide. The more significant SEC policies in this area are less formal ones. Two particularly significant positions taken by the SEC involve *compilation services* and *independence rules*.

(i) Compilations in Securities and Exchange Commission Filings. Although not stated in formal SEC rules, the Commission's staff has been reluctant to accept compilations of prospective financial statements. Thus, although that service is allowed under the AICPA literature for both public and nonpublic entities (unlike compilations of historical statements, which are only appropriate for nonpublic companies), they generally are not an option for filings subject to SEC authority.

(ii) Independence. The SEC independence rules differ from those established by the AICPA. As a general rule, AICPA literature considers independence impaired when the accountant either has a direct financial interest in the client or when the accountant is acting in the capacity of management or an employee. Thus, providing a service on prospective financial statements would not, in and of itself, affect the auditor's independence for the audit of its historical financial statements or any other service.

The SEC rules, however, are based on a different concept, which the SEC refers to as "mutuality of interest." The SEC considers that the accountant's assistance in preparing prospective financial statements creates a mutuality of interest in the prospective results. Thus, it has stated that, generally, an accountant who actively participates in the preparation of the prospective data loses the independence necessary to examine and report on that prospective data.

In a letter to an accountant, the SEC staff pursued this reasoning even further, stating that active assistance in the preparation of a company's prospective financial statements would also affect the accountant's independence in regard to its *historical financial statements* for the length of the prospective period. This independence impairment would occur regardless of whether the prospective statements were forecasts or projections or whether they were issued to the public or restricted to internal use.[1]

(g) INTERNAL REVENUE SERVICE PERSPECTIVE. The Internal Revenue Service (IRS) Circular 230 applies to prospective financial statements included in tax shelter offerings. It states that an accountant who reports on prospective financial statements in such offerings must either provide a *tax shelter opinion* or rely on one issued by another professional, such as another accountant or a lawyer.

A tax shelter opinion under Circular 230 states whether, in the professional's opinion, it is more likely than not that an investor will prevail on the merits of each material tax issue that involves

---

[1] Letter from Chief Accountant to Amper, Politzner, and Mattia, April 14, 1987; CCH, 1990, paragraph 7986.

a reasonable possibility of challenge by the IRS and an overall evaluation of the extent to which the material tax benefits are likely to be realized in the aggregate.

40.6 COMPILATION SERVICES

(a) SCOPE OF THE COMPILATION SERVICE.   A *compilation* of prospective financial statements is similar to a compilation of historical financial statements performed subject to SSARS No. 1, "Compilation and Review of Financial Statements" (1978). It relies primarily on an informed reading of the statements with an eye for obvious problems, but it does not provide any assurance on the statements.

The AICPA Guide states that a compilation of prospective financial statements involves these three:

1. Assembling, to the extent necessary, the prospective financial statements based on management's assumptions
2. Performing the required compilation procedures, including reading the prospective financial statements with their summaries of significant assumptions and accounting policies and considering whether they appear to be presented in conformity with AICPA presentation guidelines and not obviously inappropriate
3. Issuing a compilation report

(b) ASSEMBLY.   Assembly, which is defined in Subsection 40.5(b)(iii), refers to performing the necessary mathematics to turn assumptions into prospective financial data and drafting prospective financial statements in the appropriate form. In some cases, such as when the client has a sophisticated financial reporting function and prepares its own statements, assembly may not be required in a compilation. Often, however, assembly assistance is one of the primary benefits the client receives from the accountant.

Assembly does not include identifying key factors or developing assumptions, although accountants often help clients in these areas in a compilation.

(c) COMPILATION PROCEDURES.   The compilation procedures required by AICPA standards are listed in Exhibit 40.4.

There are two principal differences between the procedures done in a compilation of prospective statements and a compilation of historical statements: the requirement to consider the *actual results* for any expired portion of the prospective period and the requirement to obtain *signed representations* from the client.

Another difference between prospective and historical compilations is that *working papers* are required in a compilation of prospective financial statements. The working papers serve mainly to:

- Provide the principal support for the accountant's report, including the representation regarding observance of the standards of fieldwork, which is implicit in the reference in the report to the attestation standards.
- Aid the accountant in the conduct and supervision of the engagement. In this regard, the working papers should be sufficient to (1) enable members of the engagement team with supervision and review responsibilities to understand the nature, timing, extent, and results of procedures performed, and the information obtained and (2) indicate the engagement team member(s) who performed and reviewed the work.

In performing a compilation of prospective financial statements the practitioner should, where applicable—

a. Establish an understanding with the client regarding the services to be performed. The understanding should include the objectives of the engagement, the client's responsibilities, the practitioner's responsibilities, and limitations of the engagement. The practitioner should document the understanding in the working papers, preferably through a written communication with the client. If the practitioner believes an understanding with the client has not been established, he should decline to accept or perform the engagement.

b. Inquire about the accounting principles used in the preparation of the prospective financial statements.

  ○ For existing entities, compare the accounting principles used to those used in the preparation of previous historical financial statements and inquire whether such principles are the same as those expected to be used in the historical financial statements covering the prospective period.

  ○ For entities to be formed or entities formed that have not commenced operations, compare specialized industry accounting principles used, if any, to those typically used in the industry. Inquire about whether the accounting principles used for the prospective financial statements are those that are expected to be used when or if the entity commences operations.

c. Ask how the responsible party identifies the key factors and develops its assumptions.

d. List, or obtain a list of, the responsible party's significant assumptions providing the basis for the prospective financial statements and consider whether there are any obvious omissions in light of the key factors upon which the prospective results of the entity appear to depend.

e. Consider whether there appear to be any obvious internal inconsistencies in the assumptions.

f. Perform, or test the mathematical accuracy of, the computations that translate the assumptions into prospective financial statements.

g. Read the prospective financial statements, including the summary of significant assumptions, and consider whether—

  ○ The statements, including the disclosures of assumptions and accounting policies, appear to be not presented in conformity with the AICPA presentation guidelines for prospective financial statements.[1]

  ○ The statements, including the summary of significant assumptions, appear to be not obviously inappropriate in relation to the practitioner's knowledge of the entity and its industry and, for a Financial forecast, the expected conditions and course of action in the prospective period. Financial projection, the purpose of the presentation.

h. If a significant part of the prospective period has expired, inquire about the results of operations or significant portions of the operations (such as sales volume), and significant changes in financial position, and consider their effect in relation to the prospective financial statements. If historical financial statements have been prepared for the expired portion of the period, the practitioner should read such statements and consider those results in relation to the prospective financial statements.

i. Confirm his understanding of the statements (including assumptions) by obtaining written representations from the responsible party. Because the amounts reflected in the statements are not supported by historical books and records but rather by assumptions, the practitioner should obtain representations in which the responsible party indicates its responsibility for the assumptions. The representations should be signed by the responsible party at the highest level of authority who the practitioner believes is responsible for and knowledgeable, directly or through others, about matters covered by the representations.

  ○ For a financial forecast, the representations should include the responsible party's assertion that the financial forecast presents, to the best of his knowledge and belief, the expected financial position, results of operations, and cash flows for the forecast period and that the forecast reflects the responsible party's judgment, based on present circumstances, of the expected conditions and its expected course of action. The representations should also include a statement that the forecast is presented in conformity with guidelines for presentation of a forecast established by the AICPA. The representations should also include a statement that the assumptions on which the forecast is based are reasonable. If the forecast contains a range, the representation should also include a statement that, to the best of the responsible party's knowledge and belief, the item or items subject to the assumption are expected to actually fall within the range and that the range was not selected in a biased or misleading manner.

(Continues)

Exhibit 40.4   Standard compilation procedures. (Source: AICPA, Statement on Standards for Attestation Engagements, AT 301.)

○ *For a financial projection,* the representations should include the responsible party's assertion that the financial projection presents, to the best of his knowledge and belief, the expected financial position, results of operations, and cash flows for the projection period given the hypothetical assumptions, and that the projection reflects his judgment, based on present circumstances, of expected conditions and its expected course of action given the occurrence of the hypothetical events. The representations should also (1) identify the hypothetical assumptions and describe the limitations on the usefulness of the presentation, (2) state that the assumptions are appropriate, (3) indicate if the hypothetical assumptions are improbable, and (4) if the projection contains a range, include a statement that, to the best of the responsible party's knowledge and belief, given the hypothetical assumptions, the item or items subject to the assumption are expected to actually fall within the range and that the range was not selected in a biased or misleading manner. The representations should also include a statement that the projection is presented in conformity with guidelines for presentation of a projection established by the AICPA.

j. Consider, after applying the above procedures, whether he has received representations or other information that appears to be obviously inappropriate, incomplete, or otherwise misleading and, if so, attempt to obtain additional or revised information. If he does not receive such information, the practitioner should ordinarily withdraw from the compilation engagement.[2] (The omission of disclosures, other than those relating to significant assumptions, would not require the practitioner to withdraw.)

[1] Presentation guidelines for entities that issue prospective financial statements are set forth and illustrated in the AICPA Guide for Prospective Financial Information.

[2] The practitioner need not withdraw from the engagement if the effect of such information on the prospective financial statements does not appear to be material.

Exhibit 40.4   *Continued.*

(d) REPORTING ON A COMPILATION.   The *standard report* on a compilation of prospective financial statements includes:

1. An identification of the prospective financial statements presented by the responsible party
2. A statement that the accountant has compiled the prospective financial statements in accordance with attestation standards established by the AICPA
3. A statement that a compilation is limited in scope and does not enable the accountant to express an opinion or any other form of assurance on the prospective financial statements or the assumptions
4. A caveat that the prospective results may not be achieved
5. A statement that the accountant assumes no responsibility to update the report for events and circumstances occurring after the date of the report
6. The manual or printed signature of the accountant's firm
7. The date of the compilation report

The standard form of compilation report for a financial forecast is as follows:

We have compiled the accompanying forecasted balance sheet, statements of income, retained earnings, and cash flows of XYZ Company as of December 31, 20XX,* and for the year then ending, in accordance with attestation standards established by the AICPA.

A compilation is limited to presenting in the form of a forecast information that is the representation of management and does not include evaluation of the support for the assumptions underlying the forecast. We have not examined the forecast and, accordingly, do not express an opinion or any other form of assurance on the accompanying statements or assumptions. Furthermore, there will usually be differences between the forecasted and actual results, because events and circumstances frequently do not occur as expected, and those differences may be material. We have no responsibility to update this report for events and circumstances occurring after the date of this report.

[Signature]

[Date]

* If the presentation is summarized, the opening sentence of the report would begin, "We have compiled the accompanying summarized forecast of XYZ Company as of December 31, 20X1 . . . ."

The standard form of report for the compilation of a financial projection is as follows:

We have compiled the accompanying projected balance sheet, statements of income, retained earnings, and cash flows of XYZ Company as of December 31, 20XX,* and for the year then ending, in accordance with attestation standards established by the AICPA. The accompanying projection was prepared for [state special purpose, for example, "the purpose of negotiating a loan to expand XYZ Company's plant"].

A compilation is limited to presenting information in the form of a projection that is the representation of management and does not include evaluation of the support for the assumptions underlying the projection. We have not examined the projection and, accordingly do not express an opinion or any other form of assurance on the accompanying statements or assumptions. Furthermore, even if [describe hypothetical assumption, for example, "the loan is granted and the plant is expanded"], there will usually be differences between the projected and the actual results, because events and circumstances frequently do not occur as expected, and those differences may be material. We have no responsibility to update this report for events and circumstances occurring after the date of this report.

The accompanying projection and this report are intended solely for the information and use of [identify specified parties, for example, "XYZ Company and DEF Bank"] and are not intended to be and should not be used by anyone other than these specified parties.

[Signature]

[Date]

* If the presentation is summarized, the opening sentence of the report would begin, "We have compiled the accompanying summarized projection of XYZ Company as of December 31, 20X1 . . . ."

If the presentation is shown as a range, the accountant's report also includes a paragraph that states that management has shown the results of one or more assumptions as a range. The following is an example of such a paragraph:

As described in the summary of significant assumptions, management of XYZ Company has elected to portray forecasted [description of the financial statement element or elements for which the expected results of one or more assumptions fall within a range, and identification of the assumptions expected to fall within a range, e.g., "revenue at the amounts of $XX and $YY, which is predicated upon occupancy rates of XX% and YY% of available apartments"] rather than as a single-point estimate. Accordingly, the accompanying forecast presents forecasted financial position, results of operations, and cash flows [description of the assumptions expected to fall within a range, e.g., "at such occupancy rates"]. However, there can be no assurance that the actual results will fall within the range [description of the assumptions expected to fall within a range, e.g., "occupancy rates"] presented.

(e) PROBLEM SITUATIONS. Potential problems in a compilation engagement include scope limitations, deficiencies in the prospective financial statements, and lack of independence.

(i) Scope Limitations. Scope limitations might include a client's inadequate responses to the limited inquiries required in a compilation or its refusal to supply signed representations. The

AICPA Guide does not allow a scope-limitation compilation report. An accountant who cannot apply all the necessary procedures cannot complete the engagement and ordinarily should withdraw.

(ii) Presentation Deficiencies. Possible deficiencies in the prospective financial statements might affect either the assumptions or the other required disclosures. If the deficiency affects disclosures *other than assumptions*, the accountant may mention it in the compilation report. For example, if management chose to omit the disclosure of significant accounting policies, the accountant might add the following paragraph to the compilation report:

> Management has elected to omit the summary of significant accounting policies required by the guidelines for presentation of a financial forecast established by the AICPA. If the omitted disclosures were included in the forecast, they might influence the user's conclusions about the Company's financial position, results of operations, and cash flows for the forecast period. Accordingly, this report is not intended for those who are not informed about such matters.

If the deficiency affects the disclosure of *assumptions* and the accountant is unable to have it corrected, the accountant is not permitted merely to mention it in the report. In that case, the accountant ordinarily would withdraw from the engagement.

(iii) Independence. Since a compilation provides no assurance, an accountant may compile prospective financial statements when not independent. In that case, the report would indicate the lack of independence, but not the reason for it. The following sentence would be added to the compilation report to indicate the lack of independence:

> We are not independent with respect to XYZ Company.

40.7 EXAMINATION SERVICES

(a) SCOPE OF AN EXAMINATION. An examination of prospective financial statements is similar to an audit of historical financial statements. It is based on evidence-gathering procedures and results in positive assurance about the statements. The main difference between the two services involves the evidence-gathering procedures. Because completed transactions do not generally constitute the bulk of the data underlying prospective financial statements, the accountant's procedures generally consist primarily of inquiry and analysis rather than of document inspection and confirmation.

An examination of prospective financial statements involves the following four evaluations:

1. Evaluating the preparation of the statements
2. Evaluating the support underlying the statements
3. Evaluating the presentation of the statements for conformity with AICPA presentation guidelines
4. Issuing a report as to whether, in the accountant's opinion,
   a. The prospective financial statements are presented in conformity with AICPA presentation guidelines and
   b. The assumptions provide a reasonable basis for the forecast or, for a projection, whether the assumptions provide a reasonable basis given the hypothetical assumptions

(i) Evaluating Preparation. The accountant considers the process that management uses to develop its prospective financial statements to determine how much support will need to be accumulated. This consideration is similar to the consideration an auditor gives to a company's internal control in planning and performing an audit of historical financial statements. The better controlled the process of developing the financial statements, the less work the accountant generally needs to do in obtaining support for them.

In judging the process the entity uses in developing its prospective financial statements, the accountant generally compares the process to the guidelines discussed in Subsection 40.3(a).

(ii) Evaluating Assumptions. The accountant performs procedures to determine whether the assumptions provide a reasonable basis for the prospective financial statements. The accountant can decide that they do if the accountant can conclude that:

- Management has identified all key factors expected to affect the entity during the prospective period.
- Management has developed assumptions for each key factor.
- The assumptions are suitably supported.

To determine whether management has identified all *key factors* and developed assumptions for each one, the accountant needs to possess, or obtain during the engagement, an appropriate knowledge of the industry in which the entity will operate and the accounting principles and practices of that industry.

The accountant can conclude that the assumptions are *suitably supported* if the preponderance of information supports each significant assumption. Preponderance here does not imply a statistical majority of information. A preponderance exists if the weight of available information tends to support the assumption. The AICPA Guide states, however, "Because of the judgments involved in developing assumptions, different people may arrive at somewhat different but equally reasonable assumptions based on the same information."

The accountant need not obtain support for the *hypothetical* assumptions in a projection, since they are not necessarily expected to occur. For a projection, the accountant considers whether the hypothetical assumptions are consistent with the purpose of the projection and whether the other assumptions are suitably supported given the hypothetical assumption.

In evaluating the support for the assumptions, the accountant considers six factors:

1. Whether sufficient pertinent sources of information, both internal and external to the entity, have been considered
2. Whether the assumptions are consistent with the sources from which they are derived
3. Whether the assumptions are consistent with each other
4. Whether the historical financial information and other data used in developing the assumptions are sufficiently reliable for that purpose
5. Whether the historical information and other data used in developing the assumptions are comparable over the periods specified or whether the effects of any lack of comparability were considered in developing the assumptions
6. Whether the logical arguments or theory, considered with the data supporting the assumptions, are reasonable

Support for assumptions may include market surveys, engineering studies, general economic indicators, industry statistics, trends and patterns developed from an entity's operating history, and internal data and analysis, accompanied by their supporting logical argument or theory.

The accountant determines whether the assumptions provide a reasonable basis for the statements but cannot conclude that any outcome is expected because (1) realization of prospective results may depend on management's intentions, which cannot be examined; (2) there is substantial uncertainty in the assumptions; (3) some of the information accumulated about an assumption may appear contradictory; and (4) different but similarly reasonable assumptions concerning a particular matter might be derived from common information.

(iii) Evaluating Presentation. The accountant compares the presentation of the prospective financial statements to the AICPA presentation guidelines [see Subsections 40.4(b) and (c)].

(b) STANDARD EXAMINATION REPORT. The accountant's *standard report* on an examination of prospective financial statements includes six statements:

1. A title that includes the word "independent"

2. An identification of the prospective financial statements presented

3. An identification of the responsible party and a statement that the prospective financial statements are the responsibility of the responsible party

4. A statement that the accountant's responsibility is to express an opinion on the prospective financial statements based on the examination

5. A statement that the examination of the prospective financial statements was conducted in accordance with attestation standards established by the AICPA and, accordingly, included such procedures as the accountant considered necessary in the circumstances

6. A statement that the accountant believes that the examination provides a reasonable basis for the opinion

7. The accountant's opinion that the prospective financial statements are presented in conformity with AICPA presentation guidelines and that the underlying assumptions provide a reasonable basis for the forecast or a reasonable basis for the projection given the hypothetical assumptions

8. A caveat that the prospective results may not be achieved

9. A statement that the accountant assumes no responsibility to update the report for events and circumstances occurring after the date of the report

10. The manual or printed signature of the accountant's firm

11. The date of the examination report

The standard report on the examination of a financial forecast is as follows:

Independent Accountant's Report

We have examined the accompanying forecasted balance sheet, statements of income, retained earnings, and cash flows of XYZ Company as of December 31, 20XX,* and for the year then ending. XYZ Company's management is responsible for the forecast. Our responsibility is to express an opinion on the forecast based on our examination.

Our examination was conducted in accordance with attestation standards established by the AICPA and, accordingly, included such procedures as we considered necessary to evaluate both the assumptions used by management and the preparation and presentation of the forecast. We believe that our examination provides a reasonable basis for our opinion.

In our opinion, the accompanying forecast is presented in conformity with guidelines for presentation of a forecast established by the AICPA, and the underlying assumptions provide a reasonable basis for management's forecast. However, there will usually be differences between the forecasted and actual results, because events and circumstances frequently do not occur as expected, and those differences may be material. We have no responsibility to update this report for events and circumstances occurring after the date of this report.

[Signature]

[Date]

* If the presentation is summarized, the opening sentence of the report would begin, "We have examined the accompanying summarized forecast of XYZ Company as of December 31, 20X1...."

The standard report on the examination of a financial projection is as follows:

Independent Accountant's Report

We have examined the accompanying projected balance sheet, statements of income, retained earnings, and cash flows of XYZ Company as of December 31, 20XX, and for the year then ending.* XYZ Company's management is responsible for the projection, which was prepared for [state special purpose, for example, "the purpose of negotiating a loan to expand XYZ Company's plant"]. Our responsibility is to express an opinion on the projection based on our examination.

Our examination was conducted in accordance with attestation standards established by the AICPA and, accordingly, included such procedures as we considered necessary to evaluate both the assumptions used by management and the preparation and presentation of the projection. We believe our examination provides a reasonable basis for our opinion.

In our opinion, the accompanying projection is presented in conformity with guidelines for presentation of a projection established by the AICPA, and the underlying assumptions provide a reasonable basis for management's projection [describe the hypothetical assumption, for example, "assuming the granting of the requested loan for the purpose of expanding XYZ Company's plant as described in the summary of significant assumptions"]. However, even if [describe hypothetical assumption, for example, "the loan is granted and the plant is expanded"], there will usually be differences between the projected and actual results, because events and circumstances frequently do not occur as expected, and those differences may be material. We have no responsibility to update this report for events and circumstances occurring after the date of this report.

The accompanying projection and this report are intended solely for the information and use of [identify specified parties, for example, "XYZ Company and DEF National Bank"] and are not intended to be and should not be used by anyone other than these specified parties.

[Signature]

[Date]

* If the presentation is summarized, the opening sentence of the report would begin, "We have examined the accompanying summarized projection of XYZ Company as of December 31, 20X1 . . . ."

When the prospective financial statements are presented as a range, the report also includes a separate paragraph describing the range [see Subsection 40.6(d) for an example].

(c) MODIFIED EXAMINATION REPORTS.   There are four types of modified examination reports:

1. A *qualified* report, used when the statements depart from the AICPA presentation guidelines but the deficiency does not affect the assumptions (although if the matter is highly material, the accountant may issue an adverse report)
2. An *adverse* report, used when the statements fail to disclose significant assumptions or when the assumptions do not provide a reasonable basis for the presentation
3. A *disclaimer* used when the accountant is precluded from applying procedures considered necessary in the circumstances
4. A *reference* to another accountant, used when another accountant examines the prospective financial statements of a significant portion of the entity, such as a major subsidiary

(i) Qualified Opinion.   The accountant issues a qualified opinion if there is a material presentation deficiency that does not affect the assumptions. The following is an examination report qualified because of a presentation deficiency:

Independent Accountant's Report

We have examined the accompanying forecasted balance sheet, statements of income, retained earnings, and cash flows of XYZ Company as of December 31, 20XX, and for the year then ending. XYZ Company's management is responsible for the forecast. Our responsibility is to express an opinion on the forecast based on our examination.

Our examination was conducted in accordance with attestation standards established by the AICPA and, accordingly, included such procedures as we considered necessary to evaluate both the assumptions used by management and the preparation and presentation of the forecast. We believe our examination provides a reasonable basis for our opinion.

The forecast does not disclose significant accounting policies. Disclosure of such policies is required by guidelines for presentation of a forecast established by the AICPA.

In our opinion, except for the omission of the disclosure of the significant accounting policies as discussed in the preceding paragraph, the accompanying forecast is presented in conformity with guidelines for presentation of a forecast established by the AICPA, and the underlying assumptions provide a reasonable basis for management's forecast. However, there will usually be differences between the forecasted and actual results, because events and circumstances frequently do not occur as expected, and those differences may be material. We have no responsibility to update this report for events and circumstances occurring after the date of this report.

[Signature]

[Date]

(ii) Adverse Report.   The accountant who believes a significant assumption is unsupported or not disclosed issues an adverse opinion. An adverse opinion is also issued when the accountant believes that a departure from the presentation guidelines not involving the assumptions is serious enough to warrant it. The following is an example of an adverse report issued by the accountant because an assumption was unreasonable:

Independent Accountant's Report

We have examined the accompanying forecasted balance sheet, statements of income, retained earnings, and cash flows of XYZ Company as of December 31, 20XX, and for the year then ending. XYZ Company's management is responsible for the forecast. Our responsibility is to express an opinion on the forecast based on our examination.

Our examination was conducted in accordance with attestation standards established by the AICPA and, accordingly, included such procedures as we considered necessary to evaluate both the assumptions used by management and the preparation and presentation of the forecast. We believe our examination provides a reasonable basis for our opinion.

As discussed under the caption "Sales" in the summary of significant forecast assumptions, the forecasted sales include, among other things, revenue from the Company's federal defense contracts continuing at the current level. The Company's present federal defense contracts will expire in March 20XX. No new contracts have been signed and no negotiations are under way for new federal defense contracts. Furthermore, the federal government has entered into contracts with another company to supply the items being manufactured under the Company's present contracts.

In our opinion, the accompanying forecast is not presented in conformity with guidelines for presentation of a financial forecast established by the AICPA because management's assumptions, as discussed in the preceding paragraph, do not provide a reasonable basis for management's forecast. We have no responsibility to update this report for events and circumstances occurring after the date of this report.

[Signature]

[Date]

There is no caveat about actual results differing from those forecasted since the accountant believes the forecast assumptions to be unreasonable.

(iii) Disclaimer.   The accountant who cannot apply all the procedures deemed necessary to support an opinion on the statements issues a disclaimer. An example of a disclaimer follows:

Independent Accountant's Report

We were engaged to examine the accompanying forecasted balance sheet, statements of income, retained earnings, and cash flows of XYZ Company as of December 31, 20XX, and for the year then ending. XYZ Company's management is responsible for the forecast.

As discussed under the caption "Income from Investee" in the summary of significant forecast assumptions, the forecast includes income from an equity investee constituting 23 percent of forecasted net income, which is management's estimate of the Company's share of the investee's income to be accrued for 20XX. The investee has not prepared a forecast for the year ending December 31, 20XX, and we were therefore unable to obtain suitable support for this assumption.

Because, as described in the preceding paragraph, we are unable to evaluate management's assumption regarding income from an equity investee and other assumptions that depend thereon, the scope of our work was not sufficient to express, and we do not express, an opinion with respect to the presentation of, or the assumptions underlying, the accompanying forecast. We have no responsibility to update this report for events and circumstances occurring after the date of this report.

[Signature]

[Date]

In a disclaimer there is no caveat about differences between actual and forecasted assumptions since the accountant is not satisfied about the reasonableness of the assumptions.

Notwithstanding his scope limitation, if the accountant is aware of material deficiencies in the forecast, those deficiencies should be discussed in the disclaimer.

(iv) Divided Responsibility.   When another accountant is involved in the examination, the principal accountant may refer to the work of the other accountant as a basis, in part, for the principal accountant's own report. The reference is done in essentially the same way divided-responsibility reports are done for audits of historical financial statements.

(d) INDEPENDENCE.   The accountant who examines prospective financial statements is required to be independent. If not, the accountant generally issues a compilation report rather than disclaim an opinion after the examination.

40.8 AGREED-UPON PROCEDURES

(a) SCOPE OF SERVICE.   An engagement to apply agreed-upon procedures to prospective financial statements involves applying the procedures specified by the users of the statements and reporting the results of their application. The level of service is flexible; the accountant's report may only be distributed to the users who specified the procedures. Thus, it is a limited-distribution service.

(b) PROCEDURES.   The procedures applied in an engagement may be limited or extensive, depending on the users' needs. For example, the service may consist of procedures below the level done in a compilation (such as mere assembly) or may be similar to those done in an examination. Alternatively, the service may consist of different levels of procedures applied to different amounts in the statements, such as a high level of work done on forecasted sales and very limited procedures on forecasted expenses.

An accountant may perform an agreed-upon procedures attest engagement on prospective financial statements provided that the following conditions are met:

1. The accountant is independent.

2. The accountant and the specified parties agree upon the procedures performed or to be performed by the accountant. Generally, the accountant's procedures may be as limited or as extensive as the specified parties desire, as long as the specified parties take responsibility for their sufficiency. However, mere reading of a financial forecast does not constitute a procedure sufficient to permit an accountant to report on the results of applying agreed-upon procedures.

3. The specified parties take responsibility for the sufficiency of the agreed-upon procedures for their purposes.

4. The prospective financial statements include a summary of significant assumptions.

5. The prospective financial statements to which the procedures are to be applied are subject to reasonably consistent evaluation against criteria that are suitable and available to the specified parties.

6. Criteria to be used in the determination of findings are agreed upon between the accountant and the specified parties.

7. The procedures to be applied to the prospective financial statements are expected to result in reasonably consistent findings using the criteria.

8. Evidential matter related to the prospective financial statements to which the procedures are applied is expected to exist to provide a reasonable basis for expressing the findings in the accountant's report.

9. Where applicable, the accountant and the specified users agree on any agreed-upon materiality limits for reporting purposes.

10. Use of the report is to be restricted to the specified parties.

(c) REPORTS.   The accountant's report on the results of applying agreed-upon procedures should contain the following elements:

1. A title that includes the word "independent"

2. Identification of the specified parties

3. Reference to the prospective financial statements covered by the accountant's report and the character of the engagement

4. A statement that the procedures performed were those agreed to by the specified parties identified in the report

5. Identification of the responsible party and a statement that the prospective financial statements are the responsibility of the responsible party

6. A statement that the agreed-upon procedures engagement was conducted in accordance with attestation standards established by the AICPA

7. A statement that the sufficiency of the procedures is solely the responsibility of the specified parties and a disclaimer of responsibility for the sufficiency of those procedures

8. A list of the procedures performed (or reference to them) and related findings

9. Where applicable, a description of any agreed-upon materiality limits

10. A statement that the accountant was not engaged to and did not conduct an examination of prospective financial statements; a disclaimer of opinion on whether the presentation of the prospective financial statements is in conformity with AICPA presentation guidelines and on whether the underlying assumptions provide a reasonable basis for the forecast, or a reasonable basis for the projection given the hypothetical assumptions; and a statement that if the accountant had performed additional procedures, other matters might have come to the accountant's attention that would have been reported

11. A statement of restrictions on the use of the report because it is intended to be used solely by the specified parties

12. Where applicable, reservations or restrictions concerning procedures or findings

13. A caveat that the prospective results may not be achieved

14. A statement that the accountant assumes no responsibility to update the report for events and circumstances occurring after the date of the report

15. Where applicable, a description of the nature of the assistance provided by a specialist

16. The manual or printed signature of the accountant's firm

17. The date of the report

The following is an example of a report on the application of agreed-upon procedures:

Independent Accountant's Report
on Applying Agreed-Upon Procedures

Board of Directors—XYZ Corporation
Board of Directors—ABC Company

At your request, we have performed certain agreed-upon procedures, as enumerated below, with respect to the forecasted balance sheet, statements of income, retained earnings, and cash flows of DEF Company, a subsidiary of ABC Company, as of December 31, 20XX, and for the year then ending. These procedures, which were agreed to by the Boards of Directors of XYZ Corporation and ABC Company, were performed solely to assist you in evaluating the forecast in connection with the proposed sale of DEF Company to XYZ Corporation. DEF Company's management is responsible for the forecast.

This agreed-upon procedures engagement was conducted in accordance with attestation standards established by the AICPA. The sufficiency of these procedures is solely the responsibility of the specified parties. Consequently, we make no representation regarding the sufficiency of the procedures described below either for the purpose for which this report has been requested or for any other purpose.

a. With respect to forecasted rental income, we compared the occupancy statistics about expected demand for rental of housing units used in the forecast to occupancy statistics for the following comparable properties. Comparable properties for this purpose are defined as [describe characteristics of comparability, e.g., those located in Sample City with between xxx and yyy rental units, rental prices within z percent of those used in the forecast.]

[List comparable properties]

As a result of performing this procedure, we found occupancy statistics used in the forecast were [describe findings].

b. We traced each amount in the forecast to underlying schedules prepared by management and tested the arithmetical accuracy of management's calculations of rental income, operating income, and income tax expense contained thereon.

We found no differences as a result of these procedures.

We were not engaged to, and did not, conduct an examination, the objective of which would be the expression of an opinion on the accompanying prospective financial statements. Accordingly, we do not express an opinion on whether the prospective financial statements are presented in conformity with AICPA presentation guidelines or on whether the underlying assumptions provide a reasonable basis for the presentation. Had we performed additional procedures, other matters might have come to our attention that would have been reported to you. Furthermore, there will usually be differences between the forecasted and actual results, because events and circumstances frequently do not occur as expected, and those differences may be material. We have no responsibility to update this report for events and circumstances occurring after the date of this report.

This report is intended solely for the information and use of the Boards of Directors of ABC Company and XYZ Corporation and is not intended to be and should not be used by anyone other than these specified parties.

[Signature]

[Date]

40.9 INTERNAL USE SERVICES

(a) SCOPE OF SERVICES.   The accountant who assembles and submits or reports on prospective financial statements for *third-party use*, must compile, examine, or apply agreed-upon procedures to them. However, for *internal use* the accountant's services and reports can be more flexible.

Internal use services generally are provided in the form of consulting, tax planning, or so-called controllership services. In these types of service, the objective of the service is not to lend credibility to the statements and there is no third-party reliance on them, so AICPA guidelines allow the accountant to structure the engagement and report to fit the circumstances.

The accountant may provide compilation, examination, or agreed-upon procedures for internal use prospective financial statements but is not required to do so.

(b) DETERMINING WHETHER USE IS INTERNAL.   The accountant may provide internal use services if the accountant believes that third-party use is not reasonably expected. In arriving at this belief, the accountant may rely on the oral or written representation of management, unless something comes to the accountant's attention to contradict management's representation.

The AICPA Guide (Section 10.02) provides the following guidelines for determining whether outsiders are considered third parties:

In deciding whether a party that is or reasonably might be expected to use an accountant's report is considered to be a third party, the accountant should consider the degree of consistency of interest between [management] and the user regarding the forecast. If their interests are substantially consistent (e.g., both the [preparer] and the user are employees of the entity about which the forecast is made), the user would not be deemed to be a third party. On the other hand, where the interests of the [preparer] and user are potentially inconsistent (e.g., the [preparer] is a nonowner manager and the user is an absentee owner), the user would be deemed a third party. In some cases, this determination will require the exercise of considerable professional judgment.

(c) PROCEDURES.   The procedures applied in an internal use engagement are usually based on the nature of the engagement. They may focus on developing prospective data, or they may focus on improving operations or financial planning with prospective data being only a by-product of the engagement.

(d) REPORTS.   The accountant's report for internal use services is flexible. Such reports sometimes speak solely to the prospective financial statements, but often they focus on alternative or recommended courses of action.

The standard compilation, examination, or agreed-upon procedures reports may be issued for internal use, but often they are not used.

Reports on prospective financial statements for internal use generally take three broad forms: *plain paper*, *legend*, and *formal*. Where there is a report on the statements, it may stand alone or may be incorporated into another report, such as a consultant's report.

(i) Plain Paper.   "Plain paper" means that the accountant provides neither a report on the statements nor any other written communication that accompanies them. In a plain-paper situation, there would be nothing apparent to the reader to associate the accountant with the statements.

(ii) Legend.   When an accountant's written communication (such as a transmittal letter) accompanies the prospective financial statements, the AICPA Guide (Section 22.09) requires that the accountant include (1) a caveat that prospective results may not be achieved and (2) a statement that the prospective financial statements are for internal use only. Many accountants choose to present this as a *legend* on the statement itself.

(iii) Formal Report.   The accountant may decide to issue a report on a service. However, the accountant is not permitted to report on a forecast or projection, even for internal use, if it does not disclose the significant assumptions.

According to the AICPA Guide (Section 22.06), a report for internal use preferably:

- Is addressed to management
- Identifies the statements being reported on
- Describes the character of work performed and the degree of responsibility taken with respect to the statements
- Includes a caveat that the prospective results may not be achieved
- Indicates the restrictions as to the distribution of the statements and report
- Is dated as of the date of the completion of the accountant's procedures
- For a projection, describes the limitations on the usefulness of the presentation

The following is an example of a report on an internal use service consisting of assembly of a forecast:

To Mr. John Doe, President
XYZ Company

We have assembled, from information provided by management, the accompanying forecasted balance sheet, statements of income, retained earnings, and cash flows of XYZ Company as of December 31, 20XX,* and for the year then ending. We have not compiled or examined the financial forecast and express no assurance of any kind on it. Further, there will usually be differences between the forecasted and actual results, because events and circumstances frequently do not occur as expected, and those differences may be material. In accordance with the terms of our engagement, this report and the accompanying forecast are restricted to internal use and may not be shown to any third party for any purpose.

* If the presentation is summarized as discussed in Subsection 40.4(b), the first sentence would read, in part, "We have assembled . . . the accompanying summarized forecast of XYZ Company . . . ."

An example of a report on the assembly of a projection is as follows:

To Mr. John Doe, President
XYZ Company

We have assembled, from information provided by management, the accompanying projected balance sheet, statements of income, retained earnings, and cash flows, and summaries of significant assumptions and accounting policies of XYZ Company as of December 31, 20XX,* and for the year then ending. The accompanying projection and this report were prepared for [description of the special purpose, e.g., "presentation to the Board of Directors of XYZ Company for its consideration as to whether to add a third operating shift"]. We have not compiled or examined the financial projection and express no assurance of any kind on it. Further, even if [description of the hypothetical assumption, e.g., "the third operating shift is added"], there will usually be differences between the projected and actual results, because events and circumstances frequently do not occur as expected, and those differences may be material. In accordance with the terms of our engagement, this report and the accompanying projection are restricted to internal use and may not be shown to any third party for any purpose.

* If the presentation is summarized as discussed in Subsection 40.4(b), the first sentence would read, in part, "We have assembled . . . the accompanying summarized forecast of XYZ Company . . . ."

In addition to the above, the accountant's report on prospective financial statements for internal use would:

1. Indicate if the accountant is not independent with respect to the client (the report would not express any assurance on the statements if there is a lack of independence) and
2. Note any disclosures required under the presentation guidelines (see Subsection 40.4(a)) whose omission comes to the accountant's attention (other than omitted assumptions).

The report might either describe the omitted disclosures or merely note the omission of disclosures in a manner such as:

This financial forecast was prepared to help you develop your personal financial plan. Accordingly, it does not include all disclosures required by the guidelines established by the AICPA for presentation of a financial forecast.

40.10 SOURCES AND SUGGESTED REFERENCES

American Institute of Certified Public Accountants, Accounting and Review Services Committee, "Compilation and Review of Financial Statements," Statement on Standards for Accounting and Review Services No. 1. AICPA, New York, 1978.

———, Auditing Standards Board, "Attestation Standards: Revision and Recodification," Statement on Standards for Attestation Engagements No. 10, AICPA, New York, 2001.

———, *Guide for Prospective Financial Information.* AICPA, New York, 1999.

Commerce Clearing House, *SEC Accounting Rules.* CCH, Chicago, 1990.

Financial Accounting Standards Board, "Statement of Cash Flows," Statement of Financial Accounting Standards No. 95. FASB, Stamford, CT, 1987.

Pallais, Don, and Holton, Stephen D., *Guide to Forecasts and Projections,* Third Edition Practitioners Publishing, Fort Worth, TX, 1998.

CHAPTER 41

PERSONAL FINANCIAL STATEMENTS

William B. Boles, CPA/ABV, ASA, CFP

Lisa A. Ritter, CPA, CFE

Brent W. Emrick, CPA/ABV, MBA, CFP

Michael W. Zelko, CPA/ABV

Boles Metzger Brosius & Ritter PC

Boles, Metzger, Brosius & Ritter, PC is located in Harrisburg, PA. Lisa Ritter, CPA, CFE is a member of the firm's executive committee and a member of the AICPA's Auditing Board. Bill Boles and Brent Emrick are partners in the Firm, Mike Zelko is manager of the firm's Business Valuation Department.

41.1   WHAT ARE THEY? AND WHY DO WE NEED THEM?

(a) WHAT IS A PERSONAL FINANCIAL STATEMENT?   A standard definition of a personal financial statement is: a listing of everything owned or owed presented in a uniform way so that the user of the statement can understand it.

A personal financial statement presents the personal assets and liabilities of an individual, a husband and wife, or a family. It is not a financial statement on a business owned by the person; however, it does contain important information about such business interests.

The essential purpose of a personal financial statement is to measure wealth at a specified date—to take a snapshot of the person's financial condition. It does this by presenting:

- Estimated current values of assets
- Estimated current amounts of liabilities
- A provision for income taxes based on the taxes that would be owed if all the assets were liquidated and all the liabilities paid on the date of the statement
- Net worth

Although both personal and business financial statements are presented for the purpose of informing a reader about the finances of the entity being presented, the statements have many significant differences (see Exhibit 41.1).

The basic personal financial statement containing this information is called a *statement of financial condition*, not a balance sheet. Values and amounts for one or more prior periods may be included for comparison with the current values and amounts, but this is optional. The statement

	Personal	**Business**
Objective	Measurement of wealth	Reporting of earnings; evaluation of performance
Uses	Facilitation of financial planning; Procuring of credit; Provision of disclosures to the public or the court	Procuring of credit; Information for shareholders; Regulatory requirements
Valuation	Current value	Historical cost
Method of accounting	Accrual	Accrual
Classification	None: assets presented in order of liquidity, liabilities in order of maturity	Assets and liabilities classified as current or long-term
Excess of assets over liabilities	Net worth	Equity earnings

Exhibit 41.1   Personal and business financial statements compared.

of changes in net worth is also optional (also, see Section 41.8). It presents the major sources of increase or decrease in net worth (see Exhibit 41.2).

(b) WHOSE FINANCIAL STATEMENT IS IT?   Normally, a personal financial statement is compiled for an individual and their spouse or one or the other individually.

A personal financial statement covering a whole family usually presents the assets and liabilities of the family members in combination, as a single economic unit. However, the members may have different ownership interests in these assets or liabilities. For example, the wife may have a remainder interest in a testamentary trust, whereas the husband may own life insurance with a net cash surrender value. It may be useful, especially when the statement is to be used in a divorce case, to disclose each individual's interests separately. This may be done in separate columns within the statement, in the notes to the statement, or in additional statements for each individual.

Often, an individual covered by the statement is one of a group of joint owners of assets, as with community property or property held in joint tenancy. In this case, the statement should include only the individual's interest as a beneficial owner under the laws of the state. If the parties' shares in the assets are not clear, the advice of an attorney may be needed to determine whether the person should regard any interest in the assets as his or her own, and if so, how much. The statement should make full disclosure of the joint ownership of the assets and the grounds for the allocation of shares.

(c) WHY ARE THEY NEEDED?   Many individuals or families use personal financial statements for investment, tax, retirement, gift and estate planning, or for obtaining credit. A personal financial statement may also be required for disclosure to the court in a divorce case or to the public when the individual is a candidate or an incumbent of public office. Another example of the use of a specialized personal financial statement was where the statement was used in litigation to show the solvency of an individual who had been the holder of a business franchise that was terminated due to an "alleged" insolvency.

(d) CASH, ACCRUAL, OR SOMETHING ELSE?   American Institute of Certified Public Accountants (AICPA) Statement of Position (SOP) 82–1 (see Applicable Professional Standards, Section 41.2(d)) establishes the use of estimated current values and amounts and the accrual basis of accounting as generally accepted accounting principles (GAAP) for personal financial statements. The AICPA *Personal Financial Statements Guide* (the "Guide") allows accountants to prepare, compile, review, or audit personal financial statements on other comprehensive bases of accounting, such as historical cost, tax, or cash. In actual practice, there are many "variations on a theme,"

JAMES AND JANE PERSON
Statements of Financial Condition
December 31, 20X3 and 20X2

	December 31	
	20X3	**20X2**
Assets		
Cash	$ 3,700	$ 15,600
Bonus receivable	20,000	10,000
Investments		
Marketable securities (Note 2)	160,500	140,700
Stock options (Note 3)	28,000	24,000
Kenbruce Associates (Note 4)	48,000	42,000
Davekar Company, Inc. (Note 5)	550,000	475,000
Vested interest in deferred profit-sharing plan	111,400	98,900
Remainder interest in testamentary trust (Note 6)	171,900	128,800
Cash value of life insurance ($43,600 and		
$42,900), less loans payable to insurance		
companies ($38,100 and $37,700) (Note 7)	5,500	5,200
Residence (Note 8)	190,000	180,000
Personal effects (excluding jewelry) (Note 9)	55,000	50,000
Jewelry (Note 9)	40,000	36,500
	$1,384,000	$1,206,700
Liabilities		
Income taxes–current year balance	$ 8,800	$ 400
Demand 10.5% note payable to bank	25,000	26,000
Mortgage payable (Note 10)	98,200	99,000
Contingent liabilities (Note 11)		
	132,000	125,400
Estimated income taxes on the differences		
between the estimated current values of assets		
and the estimated current amounts of liabilities		
and their tax bases (Note 12)	239,000	160,000
Net worth	1,013,000	921,300
	$1,384,000	$1,206,700

The notes are an integral part of these statements.

Exhibit 41.2   Illustrative financial statements. (*Source:* Reproduced with permission from AICPA, Personal Financial Statements Guide, Appendix E: Statement of Position No. 82–1, "Accounting and Financial Reporting for Personal Financial Statements," 1992, pp. 53–58.)

JAMES AND JANE PERSON
Statements of Changes in Net Worth
For the Years Ended December 31, 20X3 and 20X2

	Year ended December 31	
	20X3	**20X2**
Realized increases in net worth		
Salary and bonus	$ 95,000	$ 85,000
Dividends and interest income	2,300	1,800
Distribution from limited partnership	5,000	4,000
Gains on sales of marketable securities	1,000	500
	103,300	91,300
Realized decreases in net worth		
Income taxes	26,000	22,000
Interest expense	13,000	14,000
Real estate taxes	4,000	3,000
Personal expenditures	36,700	32,500
	79,700	71,500
Net realized increase in net worth	23,600	19,800
Unrealized increases in net worth		
Marketable securities (net of realized gains on securities sold)	3,000	500
Stock options	4,000	500
Davekar Company, Inc.	75,000	25,000
Kenbruce Associates	6,000	
Deferred profit-sharing plan	12,500	9,500
Remainder interest in testamentary trust	43,100	25,000
Jewelry	3,500	
	147,100	60,500
Unrealized decrease in net worth		
Estimated income taxes on the differences between the estimated current values of assets and the estimated current amounts of liabilities and their tax bases	79,000	22,000
Net unrealized increase in net worth	68,100	38,500
Net increase in net worth	91,700	58,300
Net worth at the beginning of year	921,300	863,000
Net worth at the end of year	$1,013,000	$921,300

The notes are an integral part of these statements.

(Continues)

Exhibit 41.2   *Continued.*

JAMES AND JANE PERSON
Notes to Financial Statements

Note 1. The accompanying financial statements include the assets and liabilities of James and Jane Person. Assets are stated at their estimated current values and liabilities at their estimated current amounts.

Note 2. The estimated current values of marketable securities are either (a) their quoted closing prices or (b) for securities not traded on the financial statement date, amounts that fall within the range of quoted bid and asked prices.

Marketable securities consist of the following:

	December 31, 20X3		December 31, 20X2	
	Number of Shares or Bonds	Estimated Current Values	Number of Shares or Bonds	Estimated Current Values
Stocks				
Jaiven Jewels, Inc.	1,500	$ 98,813		
McRae Motors, Ltd.	800	11,000	600	$ 4,750
Parker Sisters, Inc.	400	13,875	200	5,200
Rosenfield Rug Co.			1,200	96,000
Rubin Paint Company	300	9,750	100	2,875
Weiss Potato Chips, Inc.	200	20,337	300	25,075
		153,775		133,900
Bonds				
Jackson Van Lines, Ltd. (12% due 7/1/X9)	5	5,225	5	5,100
United Garvey, Inc. (7% due 11/15/X6)	2	1,500	2	1,700
		6,725		6,800
		$160,500		$140,700

Note 3. Jane Person owns options to acquire 4,000 shares of stock of Winner Corp. at an option price of $5 per share. The option expires on June 30, 20X5. The estimated current value is its published selling price.

Note 4. The investment in Kenbruce Associates is an 8% interest in a real estate limited partnership. The estimated current value is determined by the projected annual cash receipts and payments capitalized at a 12% rate.

Note 5. James Person owns 50% of the common stock of Davekar Company, Inc., a retail mail order business. The estimated current value of the investment is determined by the provisions of a shareholders' agreement, which restricts the sale of the stock and, under certain conditions, requires the company to repurchase the stock based on a price equal to the book value of the net assets plus an agreed amount for goodwill. At December 31, 20X3, the agreed amount for goodwill was $112,500, and at December 31, 20X2, it was $100,000.

A condensed balance sheet of Davekar Company, Inc., prepared in conformity with generally accepted accounting principles, is summarized below:

Exhibit 41.2   Continued.

| | December 31 | |
	20X3	20X2
Current assets	$3,147,000	$2,975,000
Plant, property, and equipment—net	165,000	145,000
Other assets	120,000	110,000
Total assets	3,432,000	3,230,000
Current liabilities	2,157,000	2,030,000
Long-term liabilities	400,000	450,000
Total liabilities	2,557,000	2,480,000
Equity	$ 875,000	$ 750,000

The sales and net income for 20X3 were $10,500,000 and $125,000 and for 20X2 were $9,700,000 and $80,000.

Note 6. Jane Person is the beneficiary of a remainder interest in a testamentary trust under the will of the late Joseph Jones. The amount included in the accompanying statements is her remainder interest in the estimated current value of the trust assets, discounted at 10%.

Note 7. At December 31, 20X3 and 20X2, James Person owned a $300,000 whole life insurance policy.

Note 8. The estimated current value of the residence is its purchase price plus the cost of improvements. The residence was purchased in December 20X1, and improvements were made in 20X2 and 20X3.

Note 9. The estimated current values of personal effects and jewelry are the appraised values of those assets, determined by an independent appraiser for insurance purposes.

Note 10. The mortgage (collateralized by the residence) is payable in monthly installments of $815 a month, including interest at 10% a year through 20Y8.

Note 11. James Person has guaranteed the payment of loans of Davekar Company, Inc., under a $500,000 line of credit. The loan balance was $300,000 at December 31, 20X3, and $400,000 at December 31, 20X2.

Note 12. The estimated current amounts of liabilities at December 31, 20X3, and December 31, 20X2, equaled their tax bases. Estimated income taxes have been provided on the excess of the estimated current values of assets over their tax bases as if the estimated current values of the assets had been realized on the statement date, using applicable tax laws and regulations. The provision will probably differ from the amounts of income taxes that eventually might be paid because those amounts are determined by the timing and the method of disposal or realization and the tax laws and regulations in effect at the time of disposal or realization.

The estimated current values of assets exceeded their tax bases by $850,000 at December 31, 20X3, and by $770,300 at December 31, 20X2. The excess of estimated current values of major assets over their tax bases are—

| | December 31 | |
	20X3	20X2
Investment in Davekar Company, Inc.	$430,500	$355,500
Vested interest in deferred profit-sharing plan	111,400	98,900
Investment in marketable securities	104,100	100,000
Remainder interest in testamentary trust	97,000	53,900

Exhibit 41.2   *Continued.*

but the methodologies and approaches should be disclosed and should not be misleading to the user of the statement.

(e) WHICH ASSET/LIABILITY GOES FIRST?   Cash is "king" (and the most liquid of the assets). So cash is at the top of the list. Assets are presented in order of liquidity and liabilities in order of maturity. No distinction is made between current and long-term assets and liabilities because there is no operating cycle on which to base that distinction in a person's financial affairs.

Assets and liabilities of a closely held business that is conducted as a separate entity are not combined with similar personal items in a personal financial statement. Instead, the estimated current net value of the person's investment in the entity is shown as one amount. But if the person owns a business activity that is not conducted as a separate entity, such as a real estate investment with a related mortgage, the assets and liabilities of the activity are shown as separate amounts.

41.2 PRACTICAL TIPS

(a) DUE DILIGENCE IN THE ACCOUNTANT-CLIENT RELATIONSHIP.   As is the case with any potential business relationship, before accepting an engagement involving personal financial statements, the accountant ordinarily would evaluate certain aspects of the potential client relationship.

The accountant may wish to consider facts that might bear on the integrity of the prospective client. Consideration of the character and reputation of the individual helps to minimize the possibility of association with a client who lacks integrity. The extent of the accountant's inquiries before acceptance might depend on his or her previous knowledge of the client and the nature of the client's financial activities. The accountant may want to consult predecessor accountants or auditors, attorneys, bankers, and others having business relationships with the individual regarding facts that might bear on the integrity of the prospective client. This does not suggest that, in accepting an engagement, the accountant vouches for the integrity or reliability of a client. However, prudence suggests that an accountant be selective in determining his or her professional relationships. It is not unknown for a seemingly high profile potential client, complete with private jet and an entourage of assistants, to be a fraudster, destined for more humble quarters in a prison.

The accountant may also wish to consider circumstances that present unusual business risk, such as considering whether an individual is in serious financial difficulty, and if that fact could have a bearing on the integrity of the information presented to the accountant for the preparation of the financial statements.

In addition, the accountant may want to consider up front the effect of any lack of independence on the type of report he may issue in compliance with professional standards. Statements on Standards for Accounting and Review Services (SSARS) No. 1 permits the accountant to issue a compilation report on personal financial statements of an individual with respect to whom he is not independent. However, the accountant must be independent to issue a review report or an audit opinion. For example, if a prospective client requesting a personal financial statement is the co-owner of a business with the spouse of the accountant, the accountant is not independent and can only issue a compilation.

Before accepting an engagement involving personal financial statements, the accountant may want to ask the potential client about the availability of records and consider whether available records provide a basis sufficient for providing the services requested. Incomplete or inadequate accounting records are likely to give rise to problems in compiling, reviewing, or auditing personal financial statements. Because of the informal nature of most personal financial records, the accountant should evaluate the need to perform other accounting services in conjunction with personal financial records. AICPA Interpretation 101–3, *Performance of Nonattest Services*, should be consulted for guidance.

Professional standards require the accountant to attain a certain level of knowledge of his client's financial activities. Before accepting an engagement, the accountant should consider whether he or she can obtain an appropriate understanding of the nature of the prospective client's financial activities and the specialized accounting principles and practices related to any of the client's financial activities.

(b) MAKING SURE THE ENGAGEMENT IS CLEAR TO ALL PARTIES.   Once the accountant has decided to accept an engagement involving personal financial statements, he should establish an understanding with the client, preferably in writing, regarding the services to be performed and the terms and objectives of the engagement. The individuals requesting personal financial statements may not be familiar with the accountant's service or its limitations and may confuse such engagements with audits. It is important that both parties have an understanding of the engagement, and a written understanding is the best one to prevent misunderstandings. An engagement letter would normally include the type of service being provided (review, compilation, audit), the statements to be produced, applicable standards, client and accountant/auditor responsibilities including for items such as errors, fraud and illegal acts, and fees.

(c) THE VALUE OF A WRITTEN UNDERSTANDING.   Talk is cheap and can be easily misconstrued or, in retrospect, be unclear as to facts and circumstances. During an engagement, the client will ordinarily make many representations to the accountant. Documentation of these representations in written form will indicate their continuing appropriateness, and reduce the possibility of misunderstanding. The actual content of the letter will depend upon the circumstances of the particular engagement.

Generally Accepted Auditing Standards (GAAS) require that an independent auditor performing an audit in accordance with GAAS obtain written representations from management for all financial statements and periods covered by the auditor's reports. The representation should be addressed to the auditor and should be made as of a date no earlier than the date of the auditor's report.

SAARS No. 1 as amended by SSARS No. 9, *Omnibus Statement on Standards for Accounting and Review Services—2002,* and SSARS No. 10, *Performance of Review Engagements*, requires that the accountant obtain a representation letter from the client as part of every review engagement as well. Compilation engagements do not contemplate tests of accounting records and of responses to inquiries by obtaining corroborating evidential matter. However, because of the informal nature of most personal financial records, it is advisable to obtain written representation from the client to confirm the oral representations made in all personal financial statement engagements.

(d) THE OPERATING RULES ARE OTHERWISE KNOWN AS THE "APPLICABLE PROFESSIONAL STANDARDS."   The primary authoritative guidance for accountants on the preparation of personal financial statements is SOP 82–1, *Accounting and Financial Reporting for Personal Financial Statements*, issued by the AICPA.

Accountants are often engaged to compile, review, or audit personal financial statements. These different types of engagements are governed by different Standards. Standards for compilation of financial statements prescribed by SSARS No. 1, *Compilation and Review of Financial Statements*, as amended by SSARS 8, *Amendment to Statement on Standards for Accounting and Review Services No. 1*, are applicable to the compilation of personal financial statements in the same manner as to the compilation of other financial statements.

However, a subsequent AICPA release, SSARS No. 6, *Reporting on Personal Financial Statements Included in Written Personal Financial Plans*, allows accountants to prepare personal financial statements that omit disclosures required by GAAP so long as the statement will be used solely in the development of the client's personal financial plan and not to obtain credit or to meet other disclosure requirements. If an accountant prepares a personal financial statement under this exemption, he or she should issue a written report stating the restricted purpose of the statement and noting that it has not been audited, reviewed, or compiled. Nonetheless, SSARS No. 6 does not preclude an accountant from complying with SSARS No. 1, as amended, in such engagements. (Also see Sections 41.8, "Compilation" and 41.9 "Review").

Standards for review of financial statements prescribed by SSARS No. 1, as amended, apply to the review of personal financial statements in the same manner as to the review of other financial statements (also see Section 41.8), and GAAS apply to the audit of personal statements in the same manner as to the audit of other financial statements.

Accountants may also be asked to report on specified elements, accounts, or items of a personal financial statement. In those circumstances, the guidance provided by Statement on Auditing Standards (SAS) No. 62, *Special Reports*, Statements on Standards for Attestation Engagements

(SSAE) No. 10, *Attestation Standards: Revision and Recodification*, Chapter 1, *Attest Engagements*, as amended; Chapter 2, *Agreed-Upon Procedures Engagements*, as amended; or Accounting and Review Services Interpretation No. 8, *Reports on Specified Elements, Accounts, or Items of a Financial Statement*, of SSARS No. 1, *Reports on Specified Elements, Accounts, or Items of a Statement* should be followed, as applicable.

The authors highly recommend the use of the AICPA publication *Personal Statements Guide* (referred to throughout this chapter as *the Guide*). The Guide, which was prepared by the AICPA Personal Statements Task Force, provides excellent guidance about the application of professional standards to personal statement engagements. The Guide was originally published in 1982–1983, but has been updated periodically to include changes resulting from the issuance of authoritative pronouncements since that time.

41.3 RULES AND GUIDANCE IN PRESENTING ASSET VALUES

(a) START BY USING THE ESTIMATED CURRENT VALUE.   According to SOP 82–1, it is recommended that assets be presented at their estimated current values.

The definition of estimated current value as shown in SOP 82–1 is "the amount at which the item could be exchanged between a buyer and a seller, each of whom is well informed and willing, and neither of whom is compelled to buy or sell." Sales commissions and other costs of disposal should be considered if they are expected to be material to the value.

SOP 82–1 recognizes that determining the estimated current value of some assets may be difficult. Judgment should be exercised if the costs of determining the estimated current value of such assets outweigh the benefits. For example, some unique "collections" may not have a readily determinable value, as there are few benchmark transactions or no discernable market for these items (like there is for some stamp, coin and car collections) on which to base a valuation. In such cases, the valuation may be a conservative one, despite the enthusiastic valuation of the assets by their owner.

In general, the best way to determine estimated current value is by reference to recent transactions involving market prices of similar assets in similar circumstances, such as published prices for marketable securities.

If recent market prices are not available, other methods may be used. SOP 82–1 recommends the following:

- Capitalization of past or prospective earnings
- Liquidation value
- Appraisals
- Adjustment of historical cost based on changes in a specific price index
- Discounted amounts of projected cash receipts and payments

Whatever method is used, it should be consistently applied from period to period for the same asset unless there is a change in circumstances. Should there be a change in the method or the circumstances surrounding a particular asset, a disclosure regarding such a change should be made in the notes to the statements.

If the client requests a change in the method used to calculate the value of an asset and it is not supported by a significant change surrounding the circumstances surrounding the asset, this is a departure from GAAP, and the accountant's report should be modified.

(b) WHAT IS OWED BY OTHERS?   Debts or obligations that are owed are called *receivables*. When they represent near term commitments, they often do not carry any provision for interest to be paid, as it would be a nominal amount. The theory however, is that such notes or promises, when they are far in the future, be presented at the discounted (net of interest) amounts of cash expected to be collected, using the prevailing interest rate at the date of the statement to discount these cash flows.

Even though there is no interest noted in an agreement, the face amount of the note showing the balance owed may not be the amount that should be shown on the statement of condition. Within many families and within certain religious, cultural or ethnic groups, the concept of interest is not recognized, and as a result the "face" amount of the amount owed may not appear to specify that there is any interest involved, but may, in fact, include an implicit interest amount. Another issue faced in valuation is the determination of the discount when faced with a risk of collectability. For example, a valuation engagement for an estate involved a note receivable from a corporation that was near bankruptcy. After reviewing the statements of the company the accountant discounted the value of the note by 40 percent, by using a high interest rate to compensate for the risk. In a similar manner a note from one family member to another may be discounted more heavily based on the poor condition of the debtor.

(c) THE STOCK MARKET AND OTHER MARKETS.   Marketable securities are stocks, bonds, unfulfilled futures contracts, options on traded securities, certificates of deposit, and money market accounts for which market quotations are publicly available. The estimated current value of a marketable security is its closing price on the date of the statement, less any expected sales commission to be paid. Individual Retirement Accounts and Keogh accounts should be presented net of the penalty charge for early withdrawal.

- If the security was not traded on that date, but published bid and ask prices are available, SOP 82–1 states that the estimated current value should be within the range of those prices. Using the principal of conservatism, one school of thought suggests that if there is a wide gap between bid and asked amounts, then the selected price should be toward the lower end of the range.

- If bid and asked prices are not available for the date of the statement, the estimated current value is the closing price on the last day that the security was traded, unless the trade occurred so far in the past as to be meaningless by the date of the statement.

- On over-the-counter securities, unfortunately, the market does not speak with a single voice. Different quotations may be given by the financial press, quotation publications, financial reporting services, and various brokers. In such a case, the mean (average) of the bid prices, of the bid and asked prices, or of the prices quoted by a representative sample of brokers may be used as the estimated current value.

- Large blocks of stock may also pose a problem. If a large block of stock was dumped on the market, the price might not hold up. On the other hand, a controlling interest might be worth more, share for share, than a minority interest. Market prices may need to be adjusted for these factors to determine estimated current value. Preparers should consult a qualified stockbroker for an opinion on a particular situation such as this. Discounts for "blockage" as it relates to accounting and fair value are issues of contemporary accounting discussion for large companies as well as smaller ones.

- Restrictions on the transfer of a stock are yet another factor that might call for an adjustment of market prices to determine estimated current value.

- Options values should be reported at published prices. If prices are not available then value should be determined on the basis of the value of the asset subject to option, considering exercise price and the length of the option period.

Because of the importance to taxing authorities, some valuations may result in challenges, even though they may conform to accounting practice. For example, when valuing the transfer of stock for gift tax purposes an accountant discounted the value of the stock by five percent for "blockage." The facts supported the small discount of five percent since, although the stock was regularly traded, it was not traded in large quantities. Unfortunately, the Internal Revenue Service did not agree with the valuation and, in order to avoid a costly appeals process and possible litigation, a lower, compromise discount was proposed and accepted.

(d) LIMITED PARTNERSHIP INTERESTS ARE LIMITED. Since these interests are limited by the terms of the agreement, they should be discounted to reflect the lack of participation and transferability.

Except for publicly traded limited partnerships, accountants may value the asset by taking the value of the assets less liabilities, and discounting the result based upon the nature and extent of restrictions contained in the partnership agreement, also giving consideration to the actual operation of the partnership as it relates to distribution of cash flow. In one engagement we found that in a limited partnership that owned and operated a business, the manager/general partner was underpaid for their duties and responsibilities. After determining the appropriate compensation and adjusting cash flow downward we reduced the value of the partnership interests.

If the interests in a limited partnership are actively traded, the estimated current value of such an interest should be based on the prices of recent trades. If interests in the partnership are not actively traded, the value of reasonably comparable securities, or the current value of the partnership's underlying assets may be used to measure the value of the interest [see Closely Held Businesses, Subsection 41.3(h)]. When this method is used, the person should consider discounting the value of the interest for lack of marketability and lack of control over the general partner. As with the valuation of private equity securities, discounts should not be based on arbitrary rules of thumb, but be based on the facts and circumstances of the valuation. In practice they can vary significantly (e.g., 5 percent to 60 percent) based on the nature and number of the issues.

If it is not feasible to estimate the current value of the partnership's underlying assets (and the interests are not actively traded), and the entity is in an early stage of development, the estimated current value of the interest may be shown as the amount of cash that the person has invested. If the underlying assets of the partnership are considered to be virtually worthless, however, the interest should be valued at zero.

The person's share of the partnership's negative tax basis, if any, should be included in the computation of the provision for income taxes (see Section 41.5).

The statement should disclose the person's share of any recourse debts of the partnership and any commitments for future funding. If the person's interest in the partnership represents a substantial proportion of ownership, it may be useful to disclose summarized financial information about the partnership as an investment in a closely held business [see Subsection 41.3(h)].

(e) GOLD, SILVER, AND OTHER PRECIOUS METALS. The estimated current value of precious metals, like that of marketable securities, is their closing price on the date of the statement, less the expected sales commission.

(f) OPTIONS ON ASSETS OTHER THAN MARKETABLE SECURITIES. Options to buy assets other than marketable securities should first be valued at the difference between the exercise price and the asset's current value. Then this difference should be discounted at the person's borrowing rate over the option period, if this is material. The borrowing rate should reflect the cost of any loan secured by the asset.

Because we are valuing the option not the asset, we need to find out if the option is "in the money." That is would it make economic sense to exercise the option because the current value higher than the exercise price. If it is not higher, then the option has no current value.

(g) LIFE INSURANCE. The estimated current value of a life insurance policy is its cash surrender value, less any loans against it. This information may be obtained from the insurance company.

Disclosure of the face value of the policy is required by SOP 82–1. It may also be useful to disclose the death benefits that would accrue to family members covered by the statement.

(h) A REAL CHALLENGE IS VALUING A CLOSELY HELD BUSINESS.   Can a business with liabilities in excess of it assets have value? Answer. It all depends on the facts. One business that had a negative net worth sold for approximately $4 million dollars due to the intangibles of a customer list and its established name. The challenge is finding those assets. Another company was worth more than it would appear due to its trained and in place work force.

If the person has a material investment in a closely held business that is conducted as a separate entity, the statement should disclose:

- The name of the company
- The person's percentage of ownership
- The nature of the business
- Summarized financial information on the company's assets, liabilities, and results of operations, based on the company's financial statements for the most recent year
- The basis of presentation of the company's statements, such as GAAP, tax, or cash
- Any significant loss contingencies

Determining the estimated current value of an investment in a closely held business, whether a proprietorship, partnership, joint venture, or corporation, is notoriously difficult. The objective is to approximate the amount at which the investment could be exchanged, on the date of the statement, between a well-informed and willing buyer and seller, neither of whom is compelled to buy or sell. This value is presented as a single item in the statement of financial condition, and a condensed balance sheet of the company should be presented in the notes.

SOP 82–1 recognizes several methods, or combinations of methods, for determining the estimated current value of a closely held business:

- Appraisals
- Multiple of earnings
- Liquidation value
- Reproduction value
- Discounted amounts of projected cash receipts
- Adjustments of book value
- Cost of the person's share of the equity of the business

SOP 82–1 says that if there is an existing buy-sell agreement, specifying the amount that the person will receive when he/she withdraws, retires, or sells out, it should be considered, but that it does not necessarily determine estimated current value.

While all of the methods listed above are valid valuation methods, the difficulty is determining which method or methods are most appropriate for the particular business being valued. It is also important to keep in mind that estimated current value is based on the accrual basis of accounting. If the business being valued keeps it books on the cash or tax basis of accounting, the amounts utilized in determining the estimated current value should be adjusted to the accrual basis.

A question that SOP 82–1 does not address is whether an accountant preparing a personal financial statement should try to value a closely held business at all. Competence in valuing businesses requires a considerable degree of specialized knowledge, and often accountants' litigation liability coverage excludes valuations.

In addition, the Professional Ethics Executive Committee (PEEC) of the AICPA has issued Interpretation 101–3—*Performance of Nonattest Services.* This interpretation states that independence would be impaired if a member performs an appraisal or valuation service for an attest client where the results of the service, individually or in the aggregate, would be material to the statements, and the appraisal or valuation involves a significant degree of subjectivity. Since valuations and appraisals generally involve a significant degree of subjectivity, independence would often be impaired if the valuation were performed by the accountant issuing a report on the statement. For these reasons, the CPA may refrain from valuing the business interest himself or herself. qualified appraisers are often readily accessible to value the business.

There are various business valuation accrediting organizations. Some of the best known are the ABA (Accreditation in Business Valuation, by the AICPA) the ASA (Accredited Senior Appraiser of the American Society of Appraisers) the CBA (Certified Business Appraiser, of the Institute of Business Appraisers). Such organizations generally set standards for objectivity and report preparation and require qualifying examinations and appraisal experience to receive the credential. Additionally, to be an ABA, the candidate must be a CPA.

(i) REALTY.

(i) Location, Location, Location.   Estimated current values may be based on the following:

- Sales of similar properties in similar circumstances
- The discounted amounts of projected cash flows from the property
- Appraisals based on estimates of selling prices and selling costs obtained from independent real estate agents or brokers familiar with similar properties in similar locations
- Appraisals used to obtain financing
- Assessed value for property taxes, considering the basis of the assessment and its relationship to market values in the area

The estimated current value of a property should be presented net of expected sales commissions and closing costs.

Pitfalls sometimes encountered with realty include environmental problems, zoning restrictions, flood plains, or other hazardous conditions or encumbrances. For example a property of significant value would be valued at a much lower value because if it was leased by another entity at below market value on a long-term lease.

(j) PERSONAL PROPERTY.   Personal property includes but is not limited to cars, jewelry, antiques, and art. These items should be valued at appraisal values derived from a specialist's opinion or at the values given in published guides such as *Kelley's Blue Book* for automobiles. If the costs of an appraisal seem to outweigh the benefits, and the valuation is not significant to the overall, historical costs are often used. Appraisers can be located through the American Society of Appraisers.

From a practical perspective, personal property which has appreciated in value is generally conservatively valued if the purpose of the statement of condition is collateral for lending purposes. Accordingly, it may often be prudent to simply use the cost basis

(k) INTANGIBLE ASSETS.   Patents, copyrights, and other intangible assets should be presented at the net proceeds of a current sale of the asset or the discounted amount of cash flow arising from its future use. If the amounts and timing of receipts from the asset cannot be reasonably estimated, the asset should be presented at its purchased cost, evaluated for impairment.

The real issue is often to identify such assets. Frequently, they are not visible to the accountant nor recognized by the person engaging the accountant. Questioning and experience are used to identify potential intangibles that might have a recognizable value. For example a patent may be owned and used within a business enterprise without a designated, separate cash flow. Sometimes anomalies arise such as a line of greeting cards being valued at greater than the value of the aggregate business that had created and owned the line of greeting cards. Such situations can arise when some product lines are not profitable.

(l) FUTURE INTERESTS. The following future interests should be shown in a personal financial statement:

- Guaranteed minimum portions of pensions
- Vested interests in pension or profit-sharing plans
- Deferred compensation contracts
- Beneficial interests in trusts
- Remainder interests in property subject to life estates
- Fixed amounts of alimony for a definite future period
- Annuities

Any other future interests should also be shown, so long as they are non-forfeitable rights for fixed or determinable amounts; are not contingent on the holder's life expectancy or the occurrence of a particular event, such as disability or death; and do not require future performance of service by the holder.

The presentation of future interests should be at the discounted amount of estimated future receipts, using an appropriate interest (discount) rate as of the date of the statements.

41.4 RULES AND GUIDANCE IN PRESENTING LIABILITIES

(a) START BY USING THE ESTIMATED CURRENT AMOUNT OF THE DEBT OR LIABILITY.
Payables and other liabilities are presented at their estimated current amount. This is the amount of cash to be paid, discounted by the rate implicit in the transaction in which the debt was incurred. Accounting Principles Board (APB) Opinion No. 21, *Interest on Receivables and Payables*, explains how to determine this rate.

Although certain kinds of liabilities are not discounted in business financial statements, all liabilities should be presented at their discounted amounts in personal financial statements. No distinction is made between current and long-term liabilities.

With some home mortgages and other debts, the person may be able to pay off the debt currently at an amount less than the present value of future payments. If this alternative exists, the debt should be presented at the lower amount, as that is the amount the liability could be satisfied if paid today.

Personal liabilities such as home mortgages are shown separately from investment liabilities such as margin accounts. Obligations related to limited partnership investments should be shown if the person is personally liable for them. Debt that was included in the valuation of an investment in a closely held business, however, should not be shown again in this section of the personal statement.

In addition to discounting because of the terms of the obligation, it may be appropriate to reflect the poor condition of the creditor in the valuation. For example, a 30 percent discount rate was applied to value a $100,000 debt, which was payable over ten years. The discounted value reflected the uncertainty of the later payments, and the reduced valuation was used in creditor negotiations.

(b) FIXED COMMITMENTS. Child support, alimony, pledges to charities, and other noncancelable commitments to pay future sums should be presented as liabilities at their discounted amounts if they have all of these characteristics:

- The commitment is for a fixed or determinable amount.
- The commitment is not contingent on someone else's life expectancy or the occurrence of a particular event, such as death or disability.
- The commitment does not require future performance by others, as an operating lease does.

(c) CONTINGENCIES: WAITING FOR THE OTHER SHOE TO DROP. During life we enter into many open transactions. While we are waiting for the son's or daughter's business to succeed; the lease we co-signed for their business location is the other shoe waiting to drop. Items like this must be disclosed.

Among the contingent liabilities that should be considered for disclosure are:

- Personal guarantees on others' loans
- Liabilities for limited partnership obligations
- Lawsuits against the person
- Inadequate medical insurance coverage
- Noncoverage for personal liability

Statement of Accounting Standards (SFAS) No. 5, *Accounting for Contingencies*, as amended, provides guidance on whether a contingent liability should be recorded, disclosed in a footnote, or omitted. This pronouncement says, in short, that a liability should be recorded if its related contingent loss or range of loss can be estimated and its occurrence is probable. If the amount of loss cannot be estimated but its occurrence is either probable or possible, the related liability should be disclosed in a footnote. If its occurrence is remote, neither recording nor disclosure is required.

(d) PAYING THE DEVIL HIS DUE! INCOME TAXES! Income taxes currently payable include any unpaid income taxes for past tax years, deferred income taxes arising from timing differences, and the estimated amount of income taxes accrued for the elapsed portion of the current tax year to the date of the statement.

If the statement date coincides with the tax year end, then there is obviously no difficulty in estimating the amount for the current year. If the dates do not coincide, the estimate should be based on taxable income to date and the tax rate applicable to estimated taxable income for the whole year. The taxes for the current year should be shown net of amounts withheld from pay or paid with estimated tax returns.

Estimated income taxes are shown after the liabilities but before net worth on the statement of condition.

41.5 PROVISION FOR INCOME TAXES

(a) DEFINITION. The personal financial statement should show an estimate for the income taxes that would be owed if all of the person's assets were sold, and all of his or her liabilities paid, on the date of the statement. This estimate known as a *provision* should be shown under its full title as given in SOP 82–1: "Estimated income taxes on the differences between the estimated current values of assets and the estimated current amounts of liabilities and their tax bases." It is presented in the statement as one amount and is shown between liabilities and net worth. A note discloses the methods and assumptions used to compute it (see Exhibit 41.2).

(b) COMPUTING THE PROVISION FOR INCOME TAXES. Currently applicable income tax laws and regulations, state and local as well as federal, should be used in computing the provision for income taxes. Items for consideration include:

- Recapture of depreciation
- Available carryovers of losses, credits or deductions
- The exclusion for the gain on the sale of a residence
- Deductible state income taxes
- Alternative minimum taxes

Because most of these considerations apply to some assets or liabilities but not to others, the provision for income taxes should be computed separately for each asset and each liability. It is not necessary, however, to disclose all these computations in the note. For example, note 12 in Exhibit 41.2, which is reproduced from SOP 82–1, shows only the excess of estimated current values over the tax bases of major assets.

(c) TAX BASIS.   It is often difficult to determine the tax basis of an asset or liability acquired long ago or by inheritance or trade. In such a case, the preparer may use a conservative estimate of the tax basis in computing the provision for income taxes, with a note disclosing how the estimate was determined.

(d) DISCLAIMER.   SOP 82–1 requires a statement that "the provision will probably differ from the amounts of income taxes that might eventually be paid because those amounts are determined by the timing and the method of disposal, realization, or liquidation and the tax laws and regulations in effect at the time of disposal, realization, or liquidation." This statement should be made in the note (see Exhibit 41.2, note 12).

(e) OMISSION OF DISCLOSURE.   In addition to omitting the deferred tax liability some practitioners will also not estimate the income tax liability for the provision for income taxes. This departure from GAAP must be disclosed in the report. In our experience many personal statements are prepared in connection with bank requirements for loans. We have found that for most of those loans the banks are not concerned with the amount of estimated taxes on appreciation in value of assets. What they are concerned with are the unpaid income tax obligations for the current and prior years and other short-term liquidity issues. If not provided by the client, one technique to obtain the federal tax liability is to obtain a transcript of the individuals' current and prior tax year records. The transcripts are available if a power of attorney, Form 2848, has been filed with the Internal Revenue Service.

41.6 STATEMENT OF CHANGES IN NET WORTH

(a) DEFINITION.   A statement of changes in net worth is an *optional* statement that presents the major sources of change in a person's net worth.

Whereas the statement of financial condition may or may not show amounts for prior periods and thus may not show change in net worth, the statement of changes in net worth should present:

- Increases in net worth produced by income
- Increases in the estimated current values of assets
- Decreases in the estimated current amounts of liabilities
- Decreases in the provision for income taxes
- Decreases in net worth produced by expenses
- Decreases in the estimated current values of assets
- Increases in the estimated current amounts of liabilities
- Increases in the provision for income taxes

The statement of changes in net worth does not attempt to measure net income. It combines income and other changes because the financial affairs of an individual are a mixture of business and personal activities.

The accountant is not precluded from undertaking an engagement to issue a compilation report on a statement of financial condition when a statement of changes in net worth has not been prepared.

(b) USES.   Accountants have often found that lenders do not require a statement of changes in net worth from persons seeking credit; and that credit-seekers, for their part, are not eager to reveal so much information about their standard of living. But a statement of changes in net worth can be very useful in financial planning by providing information about how much an individual will have to increase earnings or decrease consumption to achieve a desired level of wealth—or, on the other hand, how much he or she may decrease earnings or increase consumption and still achieve the same goal.

(c) FORMAT.   The sample statement of changes in net worth shown in Exhibit 41.2, which is reproduced from SOP 82–1, distinguishes realized from unrealized sources of increase or decrease in net worth, thus dividing the sources into four categories: realized increases, realized decreases, unrealized increases, and unrealized decreases.

41.7 DISCLOSURES

SOP 82–1 states that personal statements should include sufficient disclosures to make the statements adequately informative. These disclosures can be made in the body of the statements or in the notes. The following list, although not exhaustive, indicates the nature and type of information that should ordinarily be disclosed:

- A clear indication of the individuals covered by the statement.
- Assets are presented at their estimated current values and liabilities at their estimated current amounts.
- The methods used to determine estimated current values of assets and estimated current amounts of liabilities, and any change in these methods from one period to the next.
- If any assets shown in the statement are jointly held, and the nature of the joint ownership.
- If the person's investment portfolio is material in relation to his or her other assets and is concentrated in one or a few companies or industries, the names of the companies or industries and the estimated current values of the securities.
- If the person has a material investment in a closely held business, the following, at a minimum should be disclosed:
  - The name of the business, the business form (corporation, partnership, etc.) and the person's percentage of ownership.
  - The nature of the business.
  - Summarized information about assets, liabilities, and results of operations for the most recent year based on the statements of the business, including information about the basis of presentation (e.g., GAAP, income tax basis, or cash basis) and any significant loss contingencies.
- Descriptions of intangible assets and their useful lives.
- The face amount of life insurance owned by the individuals.
- Nonforfeitable rights, such as pensions based on life expectancy that do not have the characteristics discussed earlier in the assets section regarding future interests.
- The following tax information:
  - The methods and assumptions used to compute the estimated income taxes on the differences between the estimated current values of assets and the estimated current amounts of liabilities and their tax bases and a statement that the provision will probably differ from the amounts of income taxes that might eventually be paid because those amounts are determined by the timing and the method of disposal, realization, or liquidation.
  - Unused operating loss and capital loss carryforwards.
  - Other unused deductions and credits, with their expiration periods, if applicable.

○ The differences between the estimated current values of major assets and the estimated current amounts of major liabilities or categories of assets and liabilities.

- Maturities, interest rates, collateral, and other pertinent details relating to receivables and debt.

- Related party transactions such as notes receivable or notes payable to other family members.

- Contingencies such as pending lawsuits and loan guarantees.

- Noncancelable commitments, such as operating leases that do not have the characteristics required for inclusion.

- Subsequent events, such as a decline in value of an asset after the statement date.

It is important to reinforce that the disclosures listed are not all inclusive. GAAP other than those discussed in the SOP 82–1 may apply to personal statements. Should a situation arise that is covered by a FASB or other pronouncement, the accountant should look to that source for guidance.

41.8 COMPILATION

The standards applicable to compilations of financial statements in SSARS No. 1 are applicable to personal financial statements.

SSARS No. 1 provides that an accountant should reach an understanding with the client, preferably in writing, about the services to be performed. Such an understanding may avoid disputes and fee disagreements. The AICPA *Personal Statement Guide* includes sample engagement letters for compilations, reviews, and audits in Appendix A.

The accountant should also have a general understanding of the nature of the individual's financial transactions, form of available records, qualifications of accounting personnel, if any, the accounting basis on which the statements are to be presented, and the form and content of the statements. For example, the statements may be on a GAAP, cash, or tax basis.

A compilation requires an understanding of the individual's business and personal records necessary to compile personal financial statements in an appropriate format.

Knowledge required is generally gained through experience with the client's records such as bank statements, tax returns, broker's statements, property insurance policies, wills, leases, safe deposit box contents, records of closely held business and through inquiries. The accountant must consider other services that may be necessary to compile an individual's financial statements, such as utilizing a specialist to determine the value of an asset.

Ordinarily an accountant can compile personal statements based on the individual's representation of the estimated current values of assets and the estimated current amounts of liabilities. The accountant should have a clear understanding of the methods used to determine the estimated current values of significant assets and the estimated current amounts of significant liabilities and be satisfied that those methods are appropriate considering the circumstances of the engagement. The accountant is not an appraiser of assets or an expert in determining present values for items such as pension plans and other assets and liabilities that may appear in personal financial statements. Therefore, it may be appropriate for the accountant to rely on the services of an expert, such as a real estate appraiser or an actuary, in gathering and evaluating client information.

In a compilation, the accountant is not required to make inquiries or perform other procedures to verify, corroborate, or review information supplied by the individual. However, if the accountant has reason to believe that the information supplied by the client is not correct, is incomplete, or is otherwise unsatisfactory to support the compilation of personal financial statements, he should attempt to obtain additional or revised information. If the client refuses to provide additional or revised information, or the accountant cannot otherwise obtain the needed information, he should withdraw from the engagement.

Before issuing the report, the accountant should read the compiled personal statements and consider whether they appear to be appropriate in form and free from obvious material errors.

The term *errors* refers to mistakes (intentional or unintentional) in compiling financial statements, including arithmetical or clerical mistakes, and mistakes in applying accounting standards, which includes inadequate disclosure. Examples of errors that might occur in personal financial statements prepared in conformity with GAAP (SOP 82–1) include: failure to record estimated income taxes on the differences between the estimated current values of assets and the estimated current amounts of liabilities and their tax bases; not disclosing the method utilized to estimate current values and amounts; and presenting asset or liability amounts at an obviously inappropriate value or amount.

Paragraphs 16 through 18 of SSARS No. 1, as amended by SSARS No. 8, permit an accountant to compile financial statements that omit substantially all disclosures required by GAAP. However, if personal financial statements omit disclosure of the use of a comprehensive basis of accounting other than estimated current values and amounts, the accountant should follow the guidance in Interpretation 12 of SSARS No. 1. Also, since GAAP for personal financial statements involve measurement principles different from those for other reporting entities, the accountant should disclose the use of estimated current values and amounts in his report if the disclosure is not provided in the financial statements.

If the accountant believes that the methods used to determine the estimated current values of assets and the estimated current amounts of liabilities are not in accordance with SOP 82–1, or if he believes that the methods are not appropriate in light of the nature of each asset and liability, he should modify his report because of a departure from GAAP or withdraw from the engagement.

If uncertainties are encountered in personal financial statements, the accountant is not required to modify the standard report provided the financial statements appropriately disclose the matter. However, the accountant may wish to draw attention to such uncertainty in an explanatory paragraph of his compilation report. If so, he should follow the guidance in Interpretation No. 11 of SSARS No. 1.

The Guide encourages the use of a representation letters in personal statement compilation engagements.

41.9 REVIEW

Standards for reviews of personal financial statements are established in SSARS No. 1. The following items discussed in the previous section on Compilations, are applicable to reviews: reaching an understanding with the client, gaining an understanding of the individuals' transactions, understanding the methods used to determine estimated current values of significant assets and the estimated current amounts of significant liabilities, becoming satisfied that those methods are appropriate, utilizing the services of an expert when necessary, and reading the statements to ensure they are appropriate in form and free from material error, whether caused unintentionally or due to fraud.

In addition to those items, the accountant must perform inquiry and analytical procedures sufficient to provide a reasonable basis for expressing limited assurance that there are no material modifications that should be made to the client's personal financial statements for them to be in conformity with GAAP or other comprehensive basis of accounting. Analytical procedures include developing an expectation about the relationships between data and comparing recorded amounts to those expectations. The accountant should also consider making inquiries of management concerning their knowledge of fraud in a review engagement. Procedures performed should be documented to support the conclusions reached by the accountant.

Further, before issuing the review report, the accountant should read the reviewed personal statements and consider whether they appear to be appropriate in form and free from obvious material errors, whether unintentional or caused by fraud. The accountant should also consider making inquiries of management concerning their knowledge of fraud.

A review does not include obtaining an understanding of internal control or assessing control risk, tests of accounting records and of responses to inquiries by obtaining corroborating evidential matter, and certain other procedures ordinarily performed during an audit. Thus, a review does not provide assurance that the accountant will become aware of all significant matters that would be disclosed in an audit. However, if the accountant becomes aware of information that appears incorrect, incomplete, or otherwise unsatisfactory, he or she should perform the additional procedures considered necessary to achieve limited assurance that there are no material modifications that should be made to the financial statements for them to be in conformity with the basis of reporting.

As amended, SSARS No. 1 requires a written representation letter in all review engagements. An example representation letter appropriate for a compilation, review, or audit engagement is reproduced in Appendix C of the Guide.

Further, whereas a compilation can be completed without disclosures, a review can not.

41.10 AUDITS

GAAS apply to audits of personal financial statements, as they do to other audit engagements. As with any financial statement, the audit objective in personal financial statement engagements is to attest to the fairness of the assertions embodied in the statements. Special attention must be given to the establishment of estimated current values and amounts in accordance with SOP 82–1.

GAAS requires a study and evaluation of internal accounting control, tests of accounting records and of responses to inquiries, and other evidential procedures considered necessary in the circumstances of the engagement. Because internal control is not usually a consideration, most of the independent auditors' effort in forming an opinion of personal financial statements consists of gathering evidential matter to support the assertions of existence and valuation of assets and the rights and obligations associated with those assets. SAS No. 101 *Auditing Fair Value Measurements and Disclosures* provides important guidance when auditing a personal financial statement, as well as the June 2003 *Journal of Accountancy* Article "The Auditor's Approach to Fair Value."

Often, as a result of the inadequacy of personal financial records, significant restrictions are imposed on the auditor's efforts to obtain needed evidential matter to support an opinion on personal financial statements. Accordingly, expressing an unqualified opinion is not possible. For this reason, most personal financial statement engagements are compilations, with some reviews.

41.11 REPORTS

The Guide discusses specific auditor reports relevant to compilation, review, and audit engagements that incorporate the basic reporting standards in the applicable SSARS and SASs.

Because a statement of financial condition is the only personal financial statement required by SOP 82–1, the accountant is frequently engaged to report on that statement only. Occasionally, an individual will need or want the accountant to report on both the statement of financial condition and a statement of changes in net worth. Usually the accountant is asked to report on current period statements only, although sometimes comparative statements (covering more than one date) are requested.

Reporting standards in the SSARS apply to compilations and reviews of personal financial statements. In a compilation or review engagement, an accountant is required to issue a report whenever the compilation or review is complete; and this requirement is applicable to the personal financial statements of an individual, as specified by SSARS No. 1. However, if an engagement is not completed, a report is unlikely to be issued.

(a) STANDARD COMPILATION REPORT. Personal financial statements compiled by an accountant should be accompanied by a report stating that:

> A compilation has been performed in accordance with Statements on Standards for Accounting and Review Services (SSARS) issued by the American Institute of Certified Public Accountants.

A compilation is limited to presenting in the form of a personal financial statement(s) information that is the representation of the individual.

The financial statement(s) have not been audited or reviewed and, accordingly, the accountant does not express an opinion or any other form of assurance on them.

(SSARS No. 1, paragraph 14, modified for personal financial statements)

Any other procedures the accountant performs in connection with the engagement should not be mentioned in the report.

The compilation report is addressed to the individual whose financial statement(s) are compiled and the date of the report is the date of the completion of the compilation procedures. Also, each page of the statement of financial condition (and the statement of changes in net worth, if presented) should include a reference "See Accountant's Compilation Report."

(b) REPORTING WHEN SUBSTANTIALLY ALL DISCLOSURES ARE OMITTED. An accountant may be asked to compile personal financial statements that omit substantially all disclosures required by GAAP (SOP 82–1), including disclosures that might appear in the body of the statements. Such reporting is appropriate provided the omission of the disclosures is clearly indicated in the accountant's compilation report and the accountant is not aware that the disclosures are being omitted for the purpose of misleading the intended users of the statements. For example, it would not be appropriate to omit from personal financial statements intended for use in obtaining a home mortgage informative disclosures that would be important to the financial institution in making the loan decision. If disclosures are omitted, and certain selected information is presented in the footnotes, for example, information important in obtaining a mortgage loan, such information should be labeled "Selected Information—Substantially All Disclosures Required by GAAP Are Not Included."

If substantially all disclosures are omitted from the personal financial statements and the statements do not disclose that the assets are presented at their estimated current values and that the liabilities are presented at their estimated current amounts, the accountant should include this disclosure in his or her compilation report. If the statements have been presented on a comprehensive basis of accounting other than GAAP, that basis of accounting, if not disclosed in the statements, must be included in the accountant's report.

(c) REPORTING WHEN THE ACCOUNTANT IS NOT INDEPENDENT. An accountant may issue a compilation report on the personal financial statements of an individual even though he or she is not independent with respect to that individual. In such cases, the accountant must modify the compilation report. The specific reason or reasons for the lack of independence, such as a family relationship, need not be discussed. The accountant should add an additional paragraph to the compilation report stating:

I am [we are] not independent with respect to [name of individual].

(d) REPORTING ON PRESCRIBED FORMS. Sometimes an accountant is requested by an individual to assist in assembling data for the completion of a standard preprinted loan form and sign the form, or to sign such a form the client has compiled. SSARS No. 3, *Compilation Reports on Statements Included in Certain Prescribed Forms*, provides an alternative form of standard compilation report when a prescribed form or related instructions call for a departure from GAAP by specifying a measurement principle not in conformity with GAAP or by failing to request the disclosures required by GAAP.

SSARS No. 3 reporting standards are appropriate for prescribed forms that request information from personal financial statements that have been compiled or reviewed by an accountant.

As stated in SSARS No. 3, paragraph 2, a prescribed form is any standard preprinted form designed or adopted by the body to which it is to be submitted, for example, forms used by credit agencies. There is a presumption in SSARS No. 3 that the information required by a prescribed form is sufficient to meet the needs of the body that designed or adopted the form. Therefore, there is no need for that body to be advised of departures from GAAP (SOP 82–1 for personal financial statements on prescribed forms) that are required by the prescribed form or related instructions.

An accountant should not sign a preprinted accountant's report that does not conform to the guidance in SSARS No. 1 regarding the standard compilation report. If the preprinted report form cannot be appropriately revised, the accountant should attach his or her own report following the guidance provided in SSARS No. 3 or SSARS No. 1, as appropriate.

(e) REPORTING WHEN THERE IS A DEPARTURE FROM GENERALLY ACCEPTED ACCOUNTING PRINCIPLES.   An accountant compiling or reviewing personal statements may become aware of a departure from GAAP involving either measurement principles or disclosure principles, or both. If the accountant determines that explaining the GAAP deficiencies in the personal statements in his report will not adequately communicate the problems to potential statement users, the accountant should withdraw from the engagement and issue no report.

If the accountant believes he can appropriately communicate the departure in the compilation or review report, the departure should be described in a separate paragraph of the report. The separate paragraph(s) should explain what GAAP requires, the client's departure, and the effects of the departure on the statements, if such effects have been determined. If the effects have not been determined, this fact should also be disclosed in the separate paragraph(s).

For example, if the client has reported an investment at cost, rather than at fair value as required by GAAP for personal financial statements, and the accountant cannot persuade the individual to change the amount, the accountant's report should explain the GAAP departure.

Some departures from GAAP are not as easy to detect. For example, a client going through a divorce may want to change the method utilized from previous financial statements to estimate the fair value of an asset. If the sole purpose of the change is to manipulate the distribution of property in the divorce, the change in method is a departure from GAAP.

(f) STANDARD REVIEW REPORT.   The standard review report, from the Guide, Chapter 5, paragraph 11 follows:

> I [We] have reviewed the accompanying statement of financial condition of [James and Jane Person] as of [date], and the related statement of changes in net worth for the [period] then ended, in accordance with Statement on Standards for Accounting and Review Services issued by the American Institute of Certified Public Accountants. All information included in these financial statements is the representation of [James and Jane Person].
>
> A review of personal financial statements consists principally of inquiries of the individuals whose financial statements are presented and analytical procedures applied to financial data. It is substantially less in scope than an audit in accordance with generally accepted auditing standards, the objective of which is the expression of an opinion regarding the financial statements taken as a whole. Accordingly, I [we] do not express such an opinion.
>
> Based on my [our] review, I am [we are] not aware of any material modifications that should be made to the accompanying financial statements in order for them to be in conformity with generally accepted accounting principles.

Reviews of personal financial statements are not requested as frequently as compilations. Reviews require inquiry and analytical procedures, and carry more professional responsibility on the part of the accountant than does a compilation engagement. Further, users of these reports may not understand the concept of limited assurance. As a result, the accountant should take care in determining the type of engagement required and in accepting the engagement. As a matter of simple economics, compilations are the least expensive service, but provide the lowest assurance value to the reader, but still may be sufficient for the purpose for which they are prepared.

Audits of personal financial statements are the least common of the three types of engagements primarily because of the general lack of adequate accounting records supporting personal assets and liabilities, and the transactions data affecting those balances. Additionally, the required tests and procedures cause this to be a more costly service. Recent requirements regarding the auditor's responsibility to apply procedures relevant to the detection of fraud (SAS 99) and other requirements such as the assessment of the design of the system of internal controls make little sense in the context of personal statements. Also, the standards requiring presentation of a statement of financial condition with assets at estimated fair values and liabilities at estimated current amounts may create audit difficulties. Fair value estimates involve uncertainty and subjectivity that may not lend themselves to producing evidence which can be efficiently or effectively audited. The auditor may be unable to obtain sufficient competent evidential matter to support an opinion on personal financial statements. Many such engagements that start out as audits end up with a "disclaimer of opinion" because of scope restrictions on the auditor's ability to obtain necessary evidence.

(g) STANDARD AUDIT REPORT.   Following is the auditor's standard report appropriate for personal financial statements (Guide, Chapter 5, paragraph 14):

INDEPENDENT AUDITOR'S REPORT

I [We] have audited the accompanying statement of financial condition of [James and Jane Person] as of [date], and the related statement of changes in net worth for the [period] then ended. These financial statements are the responsibility of [James and Jane Person]. My [Our] responsibility is to express an opinion on these financial statements based on my [our] audit.

I [We] conducted my [our] audit in accordance with generally accepted auditing standards in the United States of America. Those standards require that I [we] plan and perform the audit to obtain reasonable assurance about whether the financial statements are free of material misstatement. An audit includes examining, on a test basis, evidence supporting the amounts and disclosures in the financial statements. An audit also includes assessing the accounting principles used and significant estimates made by [James and Jane Person], as well as evaluating the overall financial statement presentation. I [We] believe that my [our] audit provides a reasonable basis for my [our] opinion.

In my [our] opinion, the financial statements referred to above present fairly, in all material respects, the financial condition of [James and Jane Person] as of [date], and the changes in their net worth for the [period] then ended in conformity with accounting principles generally accepted in the United States of America.

The Guide presents examples of auditor's reports on personal financial statements modified because of scope restrictions (qualified opinions and disclaimer of opinions) and reports modified because of departures from GAAP (qualified opinions and adverse opinions).

SAS No. 62, "Special Reports," paragraphs 9 and 10, provides guidance concerning disclosures in personal financial statements presented on a comprehensive basis of accounting other than GAAP, such as the cash or tax basis of accounting. Similar informative disclosures are appropriate to those required by GAAP for the same or similar item.

SSARS No. 6 provides an exception for the performance and reporting standards in SSARS No. 1 for personal financial statements included in written personal financial plans. Such statements included in written personal financial plans frequently exclude disclosures required by GAAP and contain other GAAP departures. These exceptions exist because the statements are prepared to facilitate the financial plan and not for credit purposes.

An accountant, according to SSARS No. 6, may submit a written personal financial plan containing unaudited personal financial statements to a client without complying with the compilation and review performance and reporting standards when all the following conditions are met:

- An understanding is reached with the client, preferably in writing, that the financial statements, will be used solely to assist the client's advisers to develop the client's personal financial goals and objectives.

- The document will not be used to obtain credit or for any purposes other than developing the personal plan.
- Nothing comes to the accountant's attention during the engagement to cause him or her to believe that the statements will be used to obtain credit or for any purposes other than the personal financial plan or its implementation by an insurance agent, broker, attorney, or like agent.

If the above objectives are met, the following report, from paragraph 26, Chapter 5, of the Guide, may be used in place of the standard compilation report for personal financial statements included in personal financial plans:

> The accompanying statement of financial condition of [James and Jane Person], as of [date], was prepared solely to help you develop your personal financial plan. Accordingly, it may be incomplete or contain other departures from generally accepted accounting principles and should not be used to obtain credit or for any purposes other than developing your financial plan. We have not audited, reviewed, or compiled the statement.

Each of the personal financial statements should include a reference to the accountant's report.

41.12 COMPILED STATEMENTS ONLY FOR CLIENT INTERNAL USE

In accordance with SSARS No. 8, when an accountant submits unaudited financial statements to his client that are not expected to be used by a third party, he should:

1. Issue a compilation report in accordance with the reporting requirements discussed in AR Section 100.11–. 19 of the AICPA Code of Professional Standards, vol. 2
2. Document an understanding with the individual through the use of an engagement letter, preferably signed by the individual, regarding the services to be performed and the limitations on the use of those financial statements. Such an understanding reduces the risk that the accountant or the client may misinterpret the needs or expectations of the other party; if the accountant believes an understanding with the client has not been established, he should decline to accept or perform the engagement.
3. Include a reference on each page of the financial statements restricting their use such as "Restricted for Client's Use Only" or "Solely for the information and use by the client [name of individual] and not intended to be and should not be used by any other party."

The following illustrative personal statement has been reproduced with permission from the AICPA Personal Statement Guide, Appendix E: Statement of Position No. 82–1, "Accounting and Reporting for Personal Statements," 2005, pp. 73–79.

41.13 SOURCES AND SUGGESTED REFERENCES

Accounting Principles Board, APB Opinion No. 21, "Interest on Receivables and Payables." AICPA, New York, 1971.

American Institute of Certified Public Accountants Accounting and Review Services Committee, "Compilation and Review of Financial Statements," Statements on Standards for Accounting and Review Services No. 1, AICPA, New York, 1979.

American Institute of Certified Public Accountants. "Reporting on Personal Financial Statements Included in Written Personal Financial Plans," Statements on Standards for Accounting and Review Services No. 6, AICPA, New York, 1986.

_____ "Accounting and Financial Reporting for Personal Financial Statements," Accounting Standards Division, Statement of Position No. 82–1. AICPA, New York, 1982.

Auditing Standards Board, Statement on Auditing Standards No.101, "Auditing Fair Value Measurements and Disclosures," AICPA, New York, 2003.

Bull, I.O., "Personal Financial Statements—Suggestions for Improvement." *CPA Journal*, December 1984, p.42.

Financial Accounting Standards Board, "Accounting for Contingencies," Statement of Financial Accounting Standards No.5, FASB, Stamford, CT, 1975.

Kinsman, M.D., and Samuelson, B., "Personal Financial Statements: "Valuation Challenges and Solutions." *Journal of Accountancy,* September 1987, p.139.

Menelaides, S.L., Graham, L.E., and Fishbach, G., "The Auditor's Approach to Fair Value," *Journal of Accountancy,* June 2003, p. 73.

Personal Financial Statements Task Force, "Personal Financial Statements Guide, With Conforming Changes as of May 1, 2005." AICPA, New York, 2005.

CHAPTER 42

PARTNERSHIPS AND JOINT VENTURES

Gerard L. Yarnall, CPA
Deloitte & Touche, LLP

Ronald J. Patten, PhD, CPA
DePaul University

The editors wish to acknowledge the previous contribution to this chapter by George N. Dietz, CPA, American Institute of Certified Public Accountants.

42.1 NATURE AND ORGANIZATION OF PARTNERSHIP ENTITY

(a) DEFINITION OF PARTNERSHIP.   The Uniform Partnership Act (UPA), which has been adopted by most of the states, defines a partnership as an association of two or more persons who contribute money, property, or services to carry on as co-owners a business for profit.

A partnership may be general or limited. In the general partnership, each partner may be held personally responsible for all the firm's debts, whereas in the limited partnership, the liability of certain partners is limited to their respective contributions to the capital of the firm. The limited partnership is composed of a general partner and limited partners with the latter playing no role in the management of the business. Limited partnerships are discussed in Section 42.6.

While partnerships remain popular as a form of business organization, they are not as commonly used as they once were. The Tax Reform Act of 1986 has served to dampen the attractiveness of limited partnerships as tax shelters. Similarly, new accounting standards that are more prone to require consolidation of investees have made the use of partnerships and joint venture for purposes such as research and development less advantageous. At the same time, many law firms and public accounting firms that were organized as general partnerships are tending to organize themselves as professional corporations as a result of the favorable tax status that can flow from that structure, as well as the easing of state laws forbidding professional firms to incorporate.

(b) ADVANTAGES AND DISADVANTAGES OF A PARTNERSHIP.   Bogen states:

> The partnership form of organization is superior to the proprietorship because it permits several persons to combine their resources and abilities to conduct a business. It is easier to form than a corporation, and retains a personal character making it more suitable in professional fields.[1]

---

[1] Jules I. Bogen, "Advantages and Disadvantages of Partnership," *Financial Handbook,* Fourth Edition (Ronald Press, New York, 1968), p. 5.

A distinct advantage of a partnership over a corporation is the close relationship between ownership and management. This provides more flexible administration, as well as more management talent with a personal interest in the problems and success of the business.

Historically, the three outstanding disadvantages of the partnership form of organization, as compared with corporate form, were recognized as (1) unlimited liability of the partners for business debts, (2) mutual agency power of each partner as it pertains to business actions, and (3) limited life of the partnerships. However, the existence of a number of large partnerships, particularly in the fields of law, accountancy, and investment banking, indicates that to a great degree many of these disadvantages may be more apparent than real. In addition, partnerships have devised a number of ways to overcome some of the drawbacks. For example, since the partnership is subject to dissolution upon the death, bankruptcy, insanity, or retirement of a partner—events that do not affect the continuity of a corporation—long-term commitments for the business unit are difficult to obtain. Many partnership agreements overcome this drawback by providing for automatic continuation by the remaining partners subject to liquidation of the former partner's interest. In a sense, these partnerships have an unlimited life.

Still, the unlimited liability condition, which creates the possibility of loss of personal assets on the part of each partner, is a retardant to many. This is especially important when one considers that each party is assumed to be an agent for all partnership activities, with the power to bind other partners as a result of his or her actions. Again, however, some partnerships have managed to overcome these difficulties, at least partially, by adopting variations of the partnership form of organizations. Such variants include the following:

Limited Liability Companies. Limited liability companies (LLCs) are a relatively new form of business entity in the United States and have characteristics of both corporations and partnerships. LLCs shield their owners (or members) from personal liability for certain of the entity's debts and obligations, in much the same manner as a corporation. At the same time, a properly organized LLC can be treated as a partnership for federal income tax purposes, enabling it to enjoy the tax item pass-through and other benefits of the standard partnership form.

Registered Limited Liability Partnerships. Registered limited liability partnerships (LLPs), a distant relative of the LLC, are a type of general partnership that protects the partners' personal assets if another of their partners is sued for malpractice. However, the assets of the partnership itself remain at risk, as do the personal assets of the accused partner, and all partners still retain the standard joint-and-several liabilities of the partnership (e.g., lease obligations and bank loans).

Limited Partnerships. The limited partnership form has proliferated in recent years as a vehicle for raising capital for a particular project or undertaking. Limited partnerships are particularly common in the leasing and oil and gas industries. Prior to the Tax Reform Act of 1986, the limited partnership form also served as the organizational structure for a number of tax shelters. Limited partners risk losing their limited liability the more they participate in the management or control of the partnership's activities, thus reducing the attractiveness of the limited partnership structure for some potential partners. See Section 42.6 for further discussion of limited partnerships.

Joint Ventures. Partnerships are often encountered in the formation and operation of joint ventures. In a typical corporate joint venture, two or more entities form a partnership to undertake a specific business project, often for a specific, agreed-upon period. Each party's contributions to the venture may vary widely from case to case. For example, one corporation may provide technology, personnel, or facilities while the other contributes only the cash or other operating capital required for the undertaking. Alternatively, the venturers may jointly provide some or all of these elements. In any event, the entities form an enterprise that will function as a partnership, even if that partnership has the legal status of a corporation. See Section 42.8 for further discussion of joint ventures.

(c) TAX CONSIDERATIONS. Even though a partnership is not considered a separate taxable entity for purposes of paying and determining federal income taxes, it is treated as such for purposes of making various elections and for selecting its accounting methods, taxable year, and method of depreciation.

Under Section 761 (a) of Subchapter K of the Internal Revenue Code (IRC) of 1954, certain unincorporated organizations may be excluded, completely or partially, from treatment as partnerships for federal income tax purposes. This exclusion applies only to those organizations used (1) for investment purposes rather than as the active conduct of a business, or (2) for the joint extraction, production, or use of property, but not for the purpose of selling the products or services extracted or produced.

The use of limited partnerships because of favorable tax considerations has been significantly reduced as a result of the Tax Reform Act of 1986. Prior to passage of that Act, limited partnerships as a form of tax-sheltered investment had been used in real estate, motion picture production, oil drilling, cable TV, cattle feeding, and research and development. The limited partnership gave investors the tax advantages of the partnership such as the pass-through of losses, while at the same time limiting their liability to the original investment. The Tax Reform Act of 1986 changed the situation considerably, however.

IRC Section 465 generally limits a partner's loss to the amount that the partner has "at risk" and could actually lose from an activity. These rules, which apply to individuals and certain closely held corporations, are designed to prevent taxpayers from offsetting trade, business, or professional income with losses from investments in activities that are, for the most part, financed by nonrecourse loans for which they are not personally liable. If it is determined that the loss is deductible under these "at-risk" rules, the taxpayer is subjected to "passive activity" loss rules. Generally, losses from passive trade or business activities, such as in a partnership where the partner is not active, may not be deducted from other types of income such as wages, interest, or dividends according to IRC Section 469.

Some substantial tax benefits can still be enjoyed by investing in a triple net lease limited partnership. These partnerships buy buildings that are used by fast-food, auto parts, and other chains and franchises that do not want mortgage debt on their balance sheet. The partnerships collect rent and pass it along to the partners net of three costs—insurance, upkeep, and property taxes—paid by the tenants.

(d) IMPORTANCE OF PARTNERSHIP.   In the United States, the single proprietorship is the most common form of business organization in terms of number of establishments, and the corporate form does by far the greatest volume of business. Nevertheless, the partnership form of organization holds an important place in both respects and fills a significant need. It is widely employed among the smaller business units and in professional fields such as medicine, law, dentistry, and accountancy, activities in which the partners are closely identified with the operation of the business or profession. Partnerships are also found in financial lines, such as investment banks. Occasionally a substantial trading or other business is conducted as a partnership.

(e) FORMATION OF PARTNERSHIP.   The agreement among the copartners that brings the partnership into existence may be oral or written. The latter is much to be preferred. Note the following from Bedford, Perry, and Wyatt:

> Since a partnership is based on a contract between two or more persons, it is important, although not necessarily a legal requirement, that special attention be given to the drawing up of the partnership agreement. This agreement is generally referred to as the "Articles of Copartnership." In order to avoid unnecessary and perhaps costly litigation at some later date, the Articles should contain all of the terms of the agreement relating to the formation, operation, and dissolution of the partnership.[2]

Each partner should sign the articles and retain a copy of the agreement. It is desirable that a copy of the agreement be filed with the recorder, clerk, or other official designated to receive such documents in the county in which the partnership has its principal place of business. In the

---

[2] Norton M. Beford, Kenneth W. Perry, and Arthur H. Wyatt, *Advanced Accounting—An Organization Approach* (John Wiley & Sons, New York, 1979).

case of a limited partnership, such filing is imperative. There may also be a requirement that the agreement be published in newspapers.

According to Bogen, the following 12 matters should be covered by the articles:

1. Names of partners and the firm name
2. Kind of business to be conducted
3. Capital contribution of each partner
4. Duration of the partnership contract
5. The time to be devoted to the business by each, and any limitation upon outside business interests
6. Method of dividing profits and losses
7. Restrictions upon the agency powers of the partners
8. Salaries to be paid partners, or limitations upon the withdrawal of profits
9. Method of admitting new partners
10. Provision for insurance on lives of partners for benefit of firm
11. Procedure to be followed in voluntary dissolution
12. Procedure upon death or withdrawal of partner, including method of valuation of tangible assets and goodwill, and provision for continuation of the business by the remaining partners[3]

In the event that contributions of assets other than cash are being made to the new firm, the articles should also cover the matter of income tax treatment upon the subsequent disposal of such assets. In general, such assets retain the tax basis of the previous owner so that the taxable gain or loss when ultimately disposed of may be greater or less than the gain or loss to the partnership.

Many partnerships have been plagued, if not entirely destroyed, through disagreements that could have been avoided, or greatly minimized, by the exercising of more care and skill in the drafting of the original agreement.

(f) INITIAL BALANCE SHEET. Section 8 of the UPA states that:

- All property originally brought into the partnership or subsequently acquired by purchase or otherwise, on account of the partnership is partnership property.
- Unless the contrary intention appears, property acquired with partnership funds is partnership property.

It follows that the initial balance sheet should explicitly identify the assets contributed by partners as belonging to the partnership and assign values to these assets that are agreeable to all partners. Debts assumed by the partnership will receive comparable treatment. The initial balance sheet should also show the total initial proprietorship and the partners' shares therein. According to Moonitz and Jordan:

> The most direct manner of accomplishing this result is to include the initial balance sheet in the partnership agreement itself. If it is not expedient to include it as an integral part of the agreement, reference to the initial balance sheet should be made in the agreement, and the balance sheet, as a separate document, should be signed by each partner.[4]

Unambiguous identification of assets and obligations at the inception of the partnership is important for at least two reasons: (1) Partnership creditors have no claim against the assets of

---

[3] Bogen, "Advantages and Disadvantages of Partnership."
[4] Maurice Moonitz and Louis H. Jordan, *Accounting—An Analysis of Its Problems*, 2 vols., rev. ed. (Holt, Rinehart and Winston, New York, 1963).

individual partners until the partnership assets have been exhausted (special cases are discussed in Parts III and VI of the UPA). (2) Unless specifically provided for in the partnership agreement, partnership assets may be used only for partnership purposes; partners' personal assets are, of course, subject to no such limitations.

42.2 ACCOUNTING FOR PARTNERSHIP OPERATIONS

(a) PECULIARITIES OF PARTNERSHIP ACCOUNTING.   In many respects, the accounting problems of the partnership are the same as those of other forms of business organization. The underlying pattern of the accounting for the various assets and current goods and service costs, including departmental classification and assignment, is not modified by the type of ownership and method of raising capital employed. The same is true of the recording of revenues and the treatment of liabilities. The special features of partnership accounting relate primarily to the recording and tracing of capital, the treatment of personal services furnished by the partners, the division of profits, and the adjustments of equities required upon the occasion of reorganization or liquidation of the firm.

(b) METHODS OF DIVIDING PROFITS AND LOSSES.   As stated in Section 18 of the UPA, partnership income is shared equally unless otherwise provided for in the partnership agreement. In some cases, the agreement may specify division of profits in an arbitrary ratio (which of course includes the equal ratio already mentioned), referred to elsewhere in this discussion as the *income ratio*. Such a specified ratio (e.g., 60–40, 2/3–1/3) may or may not be related to the original capital contributions of the respective partners. It is reiterated that the essential point is agreement among the partners as to how they wish profits to be divided.

Another example of profit division by a single set of relationships is afforded by division in proportion to capital balances. Since this phrase is ambiguous, the agreement should specify which of the following bases are intended: (1) original capital, (2) capital at the beginning of the year, (3) capital at the end of the year, or (4) average capital. If the last is specified, the method of computation should be outlined.

(c) EXAMPLE USING AVERAGE CAPITAL RATIO.   The following example shows the division of profits and losses on the basis of average capital ratios.

The Articles of Copartnership of Bracey and Maloney provide for the division of profits on the basis of the average capital balances as shown for the year by the books of the partnership. Effect is to be given to all contributions and withdrawals during the year. The capital accounts for the year appear as follows:

	Bracey		Maloney	
	Debit	*Credit*	*Debit*	*Credit*
January 1		$60,000		$48,000
March 1	$6,000			
April 1			$3,000	
June 1		12,000		
July 1			6,000	
September 1		3,000		21,000
October 1	9,000		9,000	
December 1				6,000

Computation of average capital is as follows:

Bracey

	Debits	Credits	Balance	Time Maintained	Dollar-Months
January 1		$60,000	$60,000	2 mos.	$120,000
March 1	$6,000		54,000	3	162,000
June 1		12,000	66,000	3	198,000
September 1		3,000	69,000	1	69,000
October 1	9,000		60,000	3	180,000
	$15,000	$75,000	$60,000	12 mos.	$729,000
Average capital ($729,000 ÷ 12)					$ 60,750

Maloney

	Debits	Credits	Balance	Time Maintained	Dollar-Months
January 1		$48,000	$48,000	3 mos.	$144,000
April 1	$ 3,000		45,000	3	135,000
July 1	6,000		39,000	2	78,000
September 1		21,000	60,000	1	60,000
October 1	9,000		51,000	2	102,000
December 1		6,000	57,000	1	$57,000
	$18,000	$75,000	$57,000	12 mos.	$576,000
Average capital ($576,000 ÷ 12)					$48,000

If net profit for the year is $36,000, it is distributed as follows:

Bracey	$ 60,750	6,075 ÷ 10,875 × $36,000	$20,110.35
Maloney	$ 48,000	4,800 ÷ 10,875 × 36,000	$15,889.65
	$108,750		$36,000.00

The method above assumes each month to be of equal significance. If the contributions and withdrawals are dated irregularly, it might be desirable to use days rather than months as the time unit.

(d) TREATMENT OF TRANSACTIONS BETWEEN PARTNER AND FIRM.   It has often been pointed out that no single profit-sharing ratio can yield equitable results under all circumstances in view of the various contributions of the partners to the firm activities. Accordingly, the articles may well include provisions regarding allowances for (1) interest on invested capital, (2) salaries for services rendered, and (3) bonuses. The ratio for dividing the profit or loss remaining after applying such provisions must, of course, also be specified.

(i) Interest on Invested Capital.   The partnership agreement should cover at least four points in the matter of allowing interest on invested capital:

1. Specific rate or directions for determining the rate
2. Procedure to be followed if the net income before interest is less than the interest requirement
3. Procedure to be followed if the partnership experiences a loss
4. Capital balance (beginning, closing, or average) on which interest is to be allowed (and, if an average balance, method by which the average is to be determined)

The rate of interest may be stated specifically or it may be determined by reference to the call money market, the yield of certain governmental obligations, the charge made by local banks for commercial loans, or some other available measure.

If the articles provide for a regular interest allowance, there should be included a statement of how to deal with the cases in which the firm operates at a loss or has a net profit of less than the interest. Following are two ways of dealing with these contingencies: (1) the interest allowance may be dropped or reduced (when there is some profit) for the period in question; (2) the full interest may be allowed and the resulting net debit in the income account apportioned in the income (profit-sharing) ratio. The second procedure is customary for cases in which the articles do not cover the point precisely.

(ii) Partners' Salaries. Each working partner should be entitled to a stated salary as compensation for his services, just as each investing partner should receive interest on his capital investment. (The general rule, from a legal standpoint, is that a partner is not entitled to compensation for services in carrying on the business, other than his share in the profits, unless such compensation is specifically authorized in the partnership agreement.) It is always desirable that the articles of partnership specify the amounts of salaries or wages to be paid to partners or indicate clearly how the amounts are to be determined. The agreement regarding salaries should also cover the contingencies of inadequate income and net losses in particular periods.

Charges for salaries designed to represent reasonable allowances for personal services rendered by the partners are often viewed as operating expenses, and this interpretation may be included in the agreement. Under this interpretation, there would seem to be good reason for concluding that regular salaries should be allowed, whether or not the business is operated at a profit. As is the case with interest allowances on capital investments, there is strong presumption that if salaries are authorized in the agreement, they must be allowed, regardless of the level of earnings, in all cases in which a contrary treatment is not prescribed.

Treatment of salary allowances as business expenses is convenient from the standpoint of accounting procedure, particularly in that this treatment facilitates appropriate departmentalization of such charges. On the other hand, it must not be forgotten that partners' salaries, like interest allowances, are essentially devices intended to provide equitable treatment of partners who are supplying unlike amounts of capital and services to the firm; the purpose, in other words, is to secure an equitable apportionment of earnings.

According to Bedford, a distinct rule, "derived from custom and from law," that applies in accounting for partnership owners' equities, is that "the income of a partnership is the income before deducting partners' salaries; partners' salaries are treated as a means of dividing partnership income."[5]

Dixon, Hepworth, and Paton, on the other hand, indicate that the interpretation of partners' salaries should vary with the circumstances:

Where there are a substantial number of partners, and salaries are allowed to only one or two members who are active in administration, there is practical justification for treating such salaries as operating charges closely akin to the cost of services furnished by outsiders. This is especially defensible where the salaries are subject to negotiation from period to period and are in no way dependent upon the presence of net earnings. Where there are only two partners, and both capital investments and contributions of services are substantially equal, there is less need for salary adjustments; if "salaries" are allowed in such a situation it would seem to be reasonable to interpret them as preliminary distributions of net income—an income derived from a coordination of capital and personal efforts in a business venture. Between these two extremes there lies a range of less clear-cut cases....[6]

---

[5] Norman M. Bedford, *Introduction to Modern Accounting* (Ronald Press, New York, 1962).
[6] Robert L. Dixon, Samuel R. Hepworth, and William A. Paton, Jr., *Essentials of Accounting* (Macmillan, New York, 1966).

(iii) Bonuses. Where a particular partner furnishes especially important services, the device of a bonus—usually expressed as a percentage of net income—may be employed as a means of providing additional compensation. The principal question that arises in such cases is the interpretation of the bonus in relation to the final net amount to be distributed according to the regular income ratio, as illustrated in the following example.

Stark and Bruch share profits equally. Per the partnership agreement, Bruch is to receive a bonus of 20 percent of the net income of the firm, before allowing the bonus, for special services to the firm. If in a particular year the credit balance of the expense and revenue account is $27,000 before allowing the bonus, profits are divided as follows:

	Stark	Bruch	Total
Bonus, 20 % of $27,000		$ 5,400	$ 5,400
Balance equally	$10,800	10,800	21,600
	$10,800	$16,200	$27,000

If the bonus is to be treated as an expense item in the computation of the final net income, the $27,000 credit balance of the expense and revenue account represents both the bonus and the final net income. Hence the $27,000 is 120 percent of the net income, and the net income is 100 percent, or $22,500. Under this method the profits are divided as follows:

	Stark	Bruch	Total
Bonus, 20 % of $22,500		$ 4,500	$ 4,500
Balance equally	$11,250	11,250	22,500
	$11,250	$15,750	$27,000

(iv) Debtor–Creditor Relationship. At times, when a partnership is formed, a partner may not be interested in investing more than a certain amount of assets on a permanent basis. He, therefore, may make an advance to the partnership that is viewed as a loan rather than an increase in his capital account. The firm may thus obtain the initial financing it needs without having to negotiate with an outside source on less favorable terms. The loan may be interest bearing and may be repayable in installments. As noted by Meigs, Johnson, and Keller (1966), interest charges on such loans should be treated as an expense of the partnership, and the loan itself should be disclosed clearly as a liability of the firm.

Occasionally, a partner may withdraw a sum from the partnership. This type of transaction should be treated in the manner dictated by the circumstances. If the loan is material relative to the partner's net personal assets, if no repayment terms are stipulated, and if the loan has been long outstanding, the loan is, in effect, a withdrawal and should be viewed as a contraction of the firm's capital. If, on the other hand, the partner has every intention of repaying the sum, the loan may be regarded as a valid receivable.

(v) Landlord–Tenant Relationship. In some cases, a partner may rent property from or to the partnership. Transactions of this type should be handled exactly as rental agreements with others are handled. The only possible difference in recording this type of event would find the rent receivable from a partner being debited to his drawing or capital account instead of to a "rent receivable" account. If the rent was owed to the partner, the payable could be recorded as a credit to either the partner's drawing or capital account. To minimize the possibility of confusion, it is preferable to record rental transactions with partners in the same manner as other rental agreements.

(vi) Statement Presentation.   Receivables and payables arising out of transactions between a partner and the firm of which he is a partner should be classified in the balance sheet in the same manner as are receivables and payables arising out of transactions with nonpartners. However, any such receivables and payables included in the balance sheet should be set forth separately; they should not be combined with other receivables and payables. Statement of Financial Accounting Standards (SFAS) No. 57 indicates that receivables or payables involving partners stem from a related party transaction and, as such, if material, should be disclosed in such a way as to include these four:

1. The nature of the relationship(s) involved
2. A description of the transactions including transactions to which no amounts or nominal amounts were ascribed, for each of the periods for which income statements are presented, and such other information deemed necessary to an understanding of the effects of the transaction on the financial statements
3. The dollar amounts of transactions for each of the periods for which income statements are presented and the effects of any change in the method of establishing the terms from that used in the preceding period
4. Amounts due from or to related parties as of the date of each balance sheet presented and, if not otherwise apparent, the terms and manner of settlement[7]

(e) CLOSING OPERATING ACCOUNTS.   The operating accounts are closed to the expense and revenue account in the usual manner. That account is then closed by crediting each partner's capital account with his share of the net income or debiting it with his share of the net loss. The drawing account of each partner is then closed to the respective capital account.

(i) Division of Profits Illustrated.   The articles of copartnership of (the fictitious firm of) Ahern and Ciecka include the following provisions as to distribution of profits:

Partners' loans. Loans made by partners to the firm shall draw interest at the rate of 6% per annum. Such interest shall be computed only on December 31 of each year regardless of the period in which the loan was in effect.

Partners' salaries. On December 31 of each year, salaries shall be allowed by a charge to the expense and revenue account and credits to the respective drawing accounts of the partners at the following amounts per annum: Ahern $14,400; Ciecka, $12,000. Partners' salaries are to be allowed whether or not earned.

Interest on partners' invested capital. Each partner is to receive interest at the rate of 6% per annum on the balance of his capital account at the beginning of the year. Such interest is to be allowed whether or not earned.

Remainder of profit or loss. The balance of net income after provision for salaries, interest on loans, and interest on invested capital is to be divided equally. Any loss resulting after provision for the above items is to be divided equally.

On December 31, the books of the partnership show the following balances before recognition of interest and salary adjustments:

---

[7] Financial Accounting Standards Board, "Related Party Disclosures," Statement of Financial Accounting Standards No. 57, FASB, Stamford, CT, 1982.

Sundry assets	$309,000	
Sundry liabilities		$ 66,000
Ahern, capital		120,000
Ahern, drawings	15,000	
Ciecka, capital		60,000
Ciecka, drawings	9,000	
Ciecka, loan		30,000
Expense and revenue		57,000
	$333,000	$333,000

Balances of the capital accounts on January 1 were: Ahern $105,000; Ciecka $48,000. The loan from Ciecka was made on April 1. Division of profits is as shown in Exhibit 42.1.

(ii) Statement of Partners' Capitals Illustrated.   Formal presentation of the activity of the partners' capital accounts is often made through the *statement of partners' capitals* (Exhibit 42.2).

(f) INCOME TAXES.   According to Hoffman:

Unlike corporations, estates, and trusts, partnerships are not considered separate taxable entities. Instead, each member of a partnership is subject to income tax on their distributive share of the partnership's income, even if an actual distribution is not made. (Section 701 of Subchapter K of the 1954 Code contains the statutory rule that the partners are liable for income tax in their separate or individual capacities. The partnership itself cannot be subject to the income tax on its earnings.) Thus, the tax return (Form 1065) required of a partnership serves only to provide

AHERN AND CIECKA, PARTNERSHIP
Schedule of Division of Net Income
For the year ended December 31, 20XX

	Total	Ahern	Ciecka
Interest on loan	$ 1,350		$ 1,350
Interest on capital	9,180	$ 6,300	2,880
Salaries allowed	26,400	14,400	12,000
Remainder—equally	20,070	10,035	10,035
Profit earned	$57,000	$30,735	$26,265

Exhibit 42.1   Division of profits.

AHERN AND CIECKA, PARTNERSHIP
Statement of Partners' Capitals
For the year ended December 31, 20XX

	Total	Ahern	Ciecka
Balances: January 1	$153,000	$105,000	$48,000
Add: additional investments	27,000	15,000	12,000
net income for year—per schedule	57,000	30,735	26,265
Total	$237,000	$150,735	$86,265
Less: withdrawals	24,000	15,000	9,000
Investment, December 31	$213,000	$135,735	$77,265

Exhibit 42.2   Sample statement of partners' capitals.

information necessary in determining the character and amount of each partner's distributive share of the partnership's income and expense.[8]

Some states, however, impose an unincorporated business tax on a partnership that for all practical purposes is an income tax.

42.3 ACCOUNTING FOR CHANGES IN FIRM MEMBERSHIP

(a) EFFECT OF CHANGE IN PARTNERS.   From a legal point of view, the withdrawal of one or more partners or the admission of one or more new members has the effect of dissolving the original partnership and bringing into being a new firm. This means that the terms of the original agreement as such are not binding on the successor partnership. As far as the continuity of the business enterprise is concerned, on the other hand, a change in firm membership may be of only nominal importance; with respect to character of the business, operating policies, relations with customers, and so on, there may be no substantial difference between the new firm and its predecessor.

To determine the value of the equity of a retiring partner or the amount to be paid for a specified share by an incoming partner, a complete inventory and valuation of firm resources may be required. Estimation of interim profits and unrealized profits on long-term contracts may be involved. In any event, there should be a careful adjustment of partners' equities in accordance with the new relationships established.

A withdrawing partner may continue to be liable for the firm's obligation incurred prior to his withdrawal unless the settlement includes specific release therefrom by the continuing partners and by the creditors.

A person admitted as a partner into an existing partnership is liable for all the obligations of the partnership arising before his admission as if he had been a partner when such obligations were incurred, except that this liability shall be satisfied only out of partnership property.

(b) NEW PARTNER PURCHASING AN INTEREST.   It is possible for a party to acquire the interest of a partner without becoming a partner. A member of a partnership may sell or assign his interest, but unless this has received the unanimous approval of the other partners, the purchaser does not become a partner; one partner cannot force his copartners into partnership with an outsider. Under the UPA, the buyer in such a case acquires only the seller's interest in the profits and losses of the firm and, upon dissolution, the interest to which the original partner would have been entitled. He has no voice in management, nor may he obtain an accounting except in case of dissolution of the business; ordinarily he can make no withdrawal of capital without the consent of the partners.

To illustrate some of the possibilities in connection with purchase of an interest, assume that the firm of Hirt, Thompson, and Pitts negotiates with Davis for the purchase of a capital interest. Data are as follows:

	Capital Accounts	Income Ratio
Hirt	$20,000	50%
Thompson	12,000	40
Pitts	8,000	10
	$40,000	100%

---

[8] William H. Hoffman, Jr., ed., *West's Federal Taxation: Corporations, Partnerships, Estates and Trusts* (West, St. Paul, MN, 1978).

(i) Purchase at Book Value.   If Davis purchases a one-fourth interest for $10,000, it is clear that he is paying exactly book value, and the entry would be:

Hirt, capital	$5,000	
Thompson, capital	3,000	
Pitts, capital	2,000	
Davis, capital		10,000

The cash payment would be divided in the same manner (i.e., Hirt $5,000, Thompson $3,000, and Pitts $2,000) and would pass directly from Davis to them without going through the firm's cash account.

(ii) Purchase at More than Book Value.   Assume now that Davis agrees to pay $12,000 for a one-fourth interest; this is more than book value. In general, two solutions are possible.

Bonus Method. Under this method, the extra $2,000 paid by Davis is considered to be a bonus to Hirt, Thompson, and Pitts and is shared by them in the income ratio. The entry is:

Hirt, capital	$5,000	
Thompson, capital	3,000	
Pitts, capital	2,000	
Davis, capital		10,000

The cash payment of $12,000 is divided as follows:

	Hirt	Thompson	Pitts	Total
Capital transferred	$5,000	$3,000	$2,000	$10,000
Premium—in income ratio	1,000	800	200	2,000
Cash received	$6,000	$3,800	$2,200	$12,000

Goodwill Method.   That Davis is willing to pay $12,000 for a one-fourth interest indicates that the business is worth $48,000. Existing assets are therefore undervalued by $8,000. Under the goodwill or revaluation of assets method, if specific assets can be revalued, this should be done. If not, or if the agreed revaluation is less than $8,000, the difference may be assumed to be goodwill. Dividing the gain in the income ratio results in this entry:

Sundry, assets and/or goodwill	$8,000	
Hirt, capital		$4,000
Thompson, capital		3,200
Pitts, capital		$4,800

The entry to record Davis's admission would then be:

Hirt, capital	$6,000	
Thompson, capital		$ 3,800
Pitts, capital		2,200
Davis, capital		$12,000

The cash payment will be received in amounts equal to the transfer from the capital accounts.

(iii) Purchase at Less than Book Value.   Assume next that Davis agrees to pay only $9,000 for a one-fourth interest—that is, less than book value. Again two solutions are possible.

Bonus Method.   Under this method, the same transfers are made from the three partners to Davis's capital account as if he had paid book value, but the difference of $1,000 is apportioned to determine the cash settlement, as follows:

	Hirt	Thompson	Pitts	Total
Capital transferred	$5,000	$3,000	$2,000	$10,000
Loss—in income ratio	500	400	100	1,000
Cash received	$4,500	$2,600	$1,900	$ 9,000

Revaluation of Assets Method.   This approach reasons that a price of $9,000 for a one-fourth interest indicates that the business is worth $36,000 and that assets should be revalued downward by $4,000. Where a portion of the write-down can be identified with specific tangible assets, the appropriate accounts should be adjusted. Otherwise, existing goodwill should be included in the write-down.

	(1)	
Hirt, capital	$2,000	
Thompson, capital	1,600	
Pitts, capital	2,400	
Sundry, assets and/or goodwill		$4,000
	(2)	
Hirt, capital	$4,500	
Thompson, capital	2,600	
Pitts, capital	1,900	
Davis, capital		$9,000

(c) NEW PARTNER'S INVESTMENT TO ACQUIRE AN INTEREST.   The admission of a new partner when he makes an investment in the firm to acquire a capital interest is illustrated by the following cases.

Assume that the capital account balances of the partnership of Andrews and Bell prior to the admission of Cohen are:

	Capital Accounts	Income Ratio
Andrews	$18,000	60%
Bell	12,000	40
	$30,000	100%

(i) Investment at Book Value.   If Cohen invests $10,000 in the firm for a one-fourth interest, the entry is:

Cash (or other assets)	$10,000
Cohen, capital	$10,000

(ii) Investment at More than Book Value.   If Cohen is willing to invest $14,000 for a one-fourth interest, the total capital will be $44,000.

Bonus Method.   Under this method, Cohen's share is one-fourth or $11,000, and the $3,000 premium is treated as a bonus to the old partners by the entry:

Cash (or other assets)	$14,000	
Andrews, capital		$ 1,800
Bell, capital		$ 1,200
Cohen, capital		$11,000

Goodwill Method.   If Cohen invests $14,000 for a one-fourth interest, it would seem that the total worth of the firm should be $56,000. Since total capital is $44,000, under the goodwill or revaluation of assets method, there is justification in assuming that existing assets are undervalued to the extent of $12,000. Circumstances may indicate that the $12,000 undervaluation is in the form of goodwill. If it is to be recognized, the entries are as follows:

	(1)	
Goodwill	$12,000	
Andrews, capital		$ 7,200
Bell, capital		4,800

	(2)	
Cash	$14,000	
Cohen, capital		$14,000

If the understatement of the capital of the old partners was attributable to excessive depreciation allowances, land appreciation, an increase in inventory value, or some combination of such factors, an appropriate adjustment of the asset or assets involved would be substituted for the charge to "goodwill."

(iii) Investment at Less than Book Value.

Bonus Method.   If Cohen invests $8,000 for a one-fourth interest, it may indicate the willingness of the old partners to give Cohen a bonus to enter the firm.
   Since the total capital is now $38,000, a one-fourth interest is $9,500 and the entry is:

Cash	$8,000	
Andrews, capital	900	
Bell, capital	600	
Cohen, capital		$9,500

Revaluation of Assets Method.   Under this method, the investment by Cohen of only $8,000 for a one-fourth interest may be taken to mean that the existing net assets are worth only $24,000. The overvaluation of $6,000 could be corrected by crediting the overvalued assets and charging Andrews and Bell in the income ratio.

	(1)	
Andrews, capital	$3,600	
Bell, capital	2,400	
Sundry assets		$6,000
	(2)	
Cash	$8,000	
Cohen, capital		$8,000

(iv) Goodwill Method.   A third method sometimes offered to handle this situation is the goodwill method, which assumes that the new partner contributes goodwill (of $2,000 in this case) in addition to the cash and is credited for the amount of his interest at book value ($10,000 in this case). This seems illogical, however, since it contradicts the original fact that Cohen's investment was to be $8,000.

(d) SETTLING WITH WITHDRAWING PARTNER THROUGH OUTSIDE FUNDS.   The withdrawal of a partner where settlement is effected by payments made from personal funds of the remaining partners directly to the retiring partner is illustrated by the firm of Adams, Bates, & Caldwell:

	Capital Balances	Income Ratio
Adams	$30,000	50%
Bates	24,000	30%
Caldwell	$16,000	20%
	$70,000	100%

(i) Sale at Book Value.   If Caldwell retires, selling his interest at book value to the other partners in their income ratio and receiving payment from outside funds of Adams and Bates, the entry is:

Caldwell, capital	$16,000	
Adams, capital		$10,000
Bates, capital		$6,000

The total payment to Caldwell is $16,000, and payments by Adams and Bates are $10,000 and $6,000, respectively.

(ii) Sale at More than Book Value.   If payment to Caldwell exceeds book value, either the bonus or the goodwill method may be used.

Bonus Method.   If total payment to Caldwell is $18,000, the premium of $2,000 may be treated as a bonus to Caldwell. The entry to record the withdrawal of Caldwell is the same as above, and payment would be as follows:

	Adams	Bates	Total
Capital per books	$10,000	$6,000	$16,000
Premium paid	1,250	750	2,000
Cash required	$11, 250	$6, 750	$18, 000

Goodwill Method.   In the following situation, Adams and Bates are willing to pay a total of $2,000 more than book value for Caldwell's interest. Since the latter receives 20 percent of the profits, this implies that assets are undervalued by $10,000. Under the goodwill or revaluation of assets method, all or part of this amount may be goodwill. The entries to record this situation are:

	(1)	
Goodwill or sundry assets	$10,000	
Adams, capital		$5,000
Bates, capital		3,000
Caldwell, capital		2,000
	(2)	
Caldwell, capital	$18,000	
Adams, capital		$11,250
Bates, capital		6,750

(iii) Sale at Less than Book Value.   If Caldwell should agree to accept $15,000 for his interest, this is $1,000 less than book value.

Bonus Method.   The $1,000 may be considered to be a bonus to Adams and Bates. The entry would be the same as in the first example, but the cash payments would be calculated as follows:

	Adams	Bates	Total
Capital, per books	$10,000	$6,000	$16,000
Less discount allowed	625	375	1,000
Cash required	$9, 375	$5, 625	$15, 000

Revaluation of Assets Method.   In this example, it can be argued under the revaluation of assets approach that the discount of $1,000 for a 20 percent share in firm profits implies an overstatement of book values of assets by $5,000. If this correction is to be made, the entries to adjust the books and record the subsequent withdrawal of Caldwell are:

	(1)	
Adams, capital	$ 2,500	
Bates, capital	1,500	
Caldwell, capital	1,000	
Sundry assets		$5,000
	(2)	
Caldwell, capital	$15,000	
Adams, capital		9,375
Bates, capital		5,625

In preceding examples, the so-called bonus method and revaluation of assets method have been presented as alternatives. Although each method results in different capital account balances in the new firm that comes into being, it should be observed that the partners in the new firm are treated relatively the same under either method. This is subject to the basic qualification that the old partners who remain in the new firm must continue to share profits and losses as between themselves in the same ratio as before.

(e) SETTLEMENT THROUGH FIRM FUNDS.   The withdrawal of a partner where settlement is to be made from funds of the business is illustrated by the firm of Arnold, Brown & Cline.

	Capital Balances	Income Ratio
Arnold	$ 40,000	30%
Brown	50,000	30
Cline	60,000	40
	$150, 000	100%

(i) Premium Paid to Retiring Partner.   Payment is to be made to Cline from the assets of the partnership. Payment is $64,000, to be made one-half in cash and the balance in notes payable. Under one treatment, the premium of $4,000 is viewed as chargeable to the remaining partners in their income ratio. The entry is:

Arnold, capital	$ 2,000	
Brown, capital	2,000	
Cline, capital	60,000	
Cash		$32,000
Notes payable		32,000

A second method treats the $4,000 premium as payment for Cline's share of the unrecognized goodwill of the firm. The following entry would be made:

Goodwill	$ 4,000	
Cline, capital	60,000	
Cash		$32,000
Notes payable		32,000

A third possibility for recording the retirement of Cline is to recognize a total goodwill or asset revaluation implied by the premium paid for the retiring partner's share. Since a $4,000 premium was paid for a 40 percent share, total implied goodwill or asset revaluation is $10,000, and the entries are:

	(1)	
Goodwill or sundry assets	$10,000	
Arnold, capital		$3,000
Brown, capital		3,000
Cline, capital		4,000
	(2)	
Cline, capital	$64,000	
Cash		$32,000
Notes payable		32,000

Many accountants are inclined to approve of the first treatment on the grounds that it is "conservative." Meigs, Johnson, and Keller state that it is "consistent with the current trend toward viewing a partnership as a continuing business entity, with asset valuations and accounting policies remaining undisturbed by the retirement of a partner."[9] The second treatment is supported by

---

[9] Walter B. Meigs, Charles E. Johnson, and Thomas F. Keller, *Advanced Accounting I* (McGraw-Hill, New York, 1966).

reference to the rule that it is proper to set up goodwill only when it has been purchased. The third interpretation relies on the idea that it is inconsistent to recognize the existence of an intangible asset and then to record it at only a fraction of the proper amount.

The accountant may distinguish between a payment for goodwill and one that represents a partner's share of the increase in value of one or more of the firm's assets. In the latter case, it is generally not reasonable to record only the increase attaching to the retiring partner's equity. Suppose, for example, that an inventory of merchandise has a market value on the date of settlement substantially above book value. Clearly, the most appropriate treatment here is that under which the inventory is adjusted to market value—the value at which it is in effect acquired by the new firm; to add to book value only the withdrawing partner's share of the increase would result in figures unsatisfactory from the standpoint both of financial accounting and operating procedure.

(ii) Discount Given by Retiring Partner. Assuming that Cline receives $57,000 for his interest in the firm and payment is made by equal amounts of cash and notes payable, two possible accounting treatments are available.

First, the discount of $3,000 may be credited to the remaining partners in their income ratio:

Cline, capital	$60,000	
Cash		$28,500
Notes payable		28,500
Arnold, capital		21,500
Brown, capital		21,500

In the second method, the implied overvaluation of assets is recognized. Since Cline's share (40 percent) was purchased at a discount of $3,000, the total overvaluation of firm assets may be considered as $7,500. The following entries are made:

	(1)	
Arnold, capital	$2,250	
Brown, capital	2,250	
Cline, capital	3,000	
Sundry assets		$ 7,500
	(2)	
Cline, capital	$57,000	
Cash		$28,500
Notes payable		28,500

(f) ADJUSTMENT OF CAPITAL RATIOS. Circumstances may arise in partnership affairs when it becomes desirable to adjust partners' capital account balances to certain ratios—most often the income ratio. This may happen in connection with the admission of a new partner, the withdrawal of a partner, or at some time when no change in personnel has occurred. Only a simple case involving a continuing firm is illustrated here.

Assume the following data for the firm of Emmett, Frye, and Gable:

	Capital Balances	Income Ratio
Emmett	$50,000	50%
Frye	25,000	30%
Gable	$15,000	20%
	$90,000	100%

If the partners wish to adjust their capital balances to the income ratio without changing total capital, it is obvious that Frye should pay $2,000 and Gable $3,000 directly to Emmett and that the entry should be:

Emmet, capital	$5,000	
Frye, capital		$2,000
Gable, capital		3,000

Adjustment of the capital balances to the income ratio by the minimum additional investment into the firm (as distinguished from the preceding personal settlement) could, of course, be effected by the additional investment of $5,000 each by Frye and Gable.

42.4 INCORPORATION OF A PARTNERSHIP

According to Meigs, Johnson, and Keller:

> Most successful partnerships give consideration at times to the possible advantages to be gained by incorporating. Among the advantages are limited liability, ease of attracting outside capital without loss of control, and possible tax savings.

> A new corporation formed to take over the assets and liabilities of a partnership will usually sell stock to outsiders for cash either at the time of incorporation or at a later date. To assure that the former partners receive an equitable portion of the total capital stock, the assets of the partnership will need to be adjusted to fair market value before being transferred to the corporation. Any goodwill developed by the partnership should be recognized as part of the assets transferred.

> The accounting records of a partnership may be modified and continued in use when the firm changes to the corporate form. As an alternative, the partnership books may be closed and a new set of accounting records established for the corporation . . . .[10]

42.5 PARTNERSHIP REALIZATION AND LIQUIDATION

(a) BASIC CONSIDERATIONS.   A partnership may be disposed of either by selling the business as a unit or by the sale (realization) of the specific assets followed by the liquidation of the liabilities and final distribution of the remaining assets (usually cash) to the partners. A basic principle to be observed carefully in all such cases is that losses (or gains) in realization or sale must first be apportioned among the partners in the income ratio, following which, if outside creditors have been paid in full or cash reserved for that purpose, payments may be made according to the remaining capital balances of the partners.

Discussions of partnership liquidations usually point out that the proper order of cash distribution is: (1) payment of creditors in full, (2) payment of partners' loan accounts, and (3) payment of partners' capital accounts. Actually, the stated priority of the partners' loans appears to be a legal fiction. An established legal doctrine called the right of offset requires that any credit balance standing in a partner's name be set off against an actual or potential debit balance in his capital account. Application of this right of offset always produces the same final result as if the loan or undrawn salary account were a part of the capital balance at the beginning of the process. For this reason, no separate examples are given that include loan accounts. If they are encountered, they may be added to the capital account balance at the top of the liquidation statement. (The existence of partners' loan accounts might have an effect on profit sharing, however, in the sense that interest

---

[10] Id.

on partners' loans is usually provided for and profits might be shared in the average capital ratio; loans would presumably be excluded from the computation.)

Realization of all assets and liquidation of liabilities may be completed before any cash is distributed to partners. Or, if the realization process stretches over a considerable period of time, so-called installment liquidation may be employed.

(b) LIQUIDATION BY SINGLE CASH DISTRIBUTION. The illustration below demonstrates the realization of assets, payment of creditors, and final single cash distribution to the partners. Losses are first allocated to the partners in the income ratio, followed by cash payment to creditors and then to partners.

Rogers, Stevens, and Troy are partners with capital balances of $20,000, $15,000, and $10,000, respectively. Profits and losses are shared equally. On a particular date they find that the firm has assets of $80,000, liabilities of $47,000, and undistributed losses of $12,000. At this point the assets are sold for $59,000 cash. The proper distribution of the cash is as follows:

	Total	Rogers	Stevens	Troy
Capital balances	$45,000	$20,000	$15,000	$10,000
Less undistributed losses	12,000	4,000	4,000	4,000
Adjusted balances	$33,000	$16,000	$11,000	$6,000
Less loss on sale of assets	21,000	7,000	7,000	7,000
Adjusted balances	$12,000	$9,000	$4,000	$(1,000)
Payment by Troy for deficiency	1,000			1,000
Balances before distribution	$13,000	$9,000	$4,000	0
Cash available	$60,000			
Paid to creditors	47,000			
Cash paid to partners	$13,000	$9,000	$4,000	0

In this example, it was assumed that Troy was financially able to make up the $1,000 deficiency that appeared in his capital account. Only by making this payment does he bear his agreed share of the losses. If Troy had been personally insolvent and therefore unable to make the $1,000 payment, the statement from that point on would have taken the following form:

	Total	Rogers	Stevens	Troy
Adjusted balances	$12,000	$9,000	$4,000	$(1,000)
Apportion deficiency in income ratio		(500)	(500)	1,000
Balances before distribution	$12,000	$08,500)	$3,500)	0
Cash available	$59,000			
Paid to creditors	47,000			
Cash paid to partners	$12,000	$8,500	$3,500	0

Troy is now personally indebted to Rogers and Stevens in the amount of $500 each. Just how this debt would rank in the settlement of Troy's personal affairs depends on the state having jurisdiction. Under the UPA, his personal creditors (not including Rogers and Stevens) have prior claim to his personal assets; because he was said to have been personally insolvent, the presumption is that Rogers and Stevens would collect nothing. In a common-law state, a deficiency of this sort is considered to be a personal debt and would generally rank along with the other personal creditors. In this event, Rogers and Stevens would presumably make a partial recovery of the $500 due each of them.

(c) LIQUIDATION BY INSTALLMENTS. It is sometimes necessary to liquidate on an installment basis. Two of the many possible cases are illustrated—in the first there is no capital deficiency to any partner when the first cash distribution is made; in the second there is a possible deficiency of one partner at the time of the first cash distribution. The situation involving a final deficiency of a partner is discussed above in the partnership of Rogers, Stevens, and Troy. If this situation should appear in the winding up of an installment liquidation, its treatment would be the same as described there.

The role of the liquidator is especially important in the case of installment liquidation. In addition to his obvious responsibility to see that outside creditors are paid and to convert the various assets into cash with a maximum gain or a minimum loss, he must protect the interests of the partners in their relationship to each other. Other than for reimbursement of liquidation expenses, no cash payment can be made to a partner, even on loan accounts or undrawn profits, except as the total standing to his credit exceeds his share of total possible losses on assets not yet realized. Improper payment by the liquidator might result in personal liability. Therefore, recovery could not be made from the partner who was overpaid.

(d) CAPITAL CREDITS ONLY—NO CAPITAL DEFICIENCY. Below is the balance sheet of Burns & Mantle as of April 30, when installment liquidation of the firm began. The partners share profits and losses equally.

	Assets		*Liabilities and Capital*	
Cash	$ 6,200	Liabilities	$ 56,000
Other assets	350,000	Burns, capital	220,200
		Mantle, capital	80,000
	$356,200		$356,200

During May, assets having a book value of $220,000 are sold for cash of $198,000, and $39,000 is paid to creditors. During June, the remaining assets are sold for $90,000, the balance due creditors is paid, and liquidation expenses of $8,000 are paid. Distribution of cash to the partners should be made as follows:

	Total	*Burns*	*Mantle*
Capital, per balance sheet	$300,200	$220,200	$80,000
Less realization loss in May	22,000	11,000	11,000
Balance after loss	$278,200	$209,200	$69,000
Cash available to partners	$148,200		
Possible loss divided	$130,000	65,000	65,000
Balances paid in cash		$144,200	$ 4,000
Balances, June 1		$ 65,000	$65,000
Less realization loss in June	40,000	20,000	20,000
Balances after loss	$ 90,000	$ 45,000	$45,000
Less liquidation expense	8,000	4,000	4,000
Final cash payment	$ 82,000	$ 41,000	$41,000

Cash available to partners at May 31 is calculated as follows:

Cash, per balance sheet	$ 6,200	
Received from sale of assets—May	$198,000	$204,200
Paid to creditors—May	$ 39,000	
Reserved for creditors	$ 17,000	$ 56,000
Available for distribution to partners		$148,200

Cash available to partners at May 31 is calculated as follows:

In this example, the first payment of $148,200 reduces the capital claims to the profit and loss ratios, and all subsequent charges or credits to the partners' capital accounts are made accordingly.

BURNS & MANTLE
Statement of Liquidation
May 1 to July 31

	Total	Burns	Mantle
Capital balances, May 1	$300,200	$220,200	$80,000
Less realization loss in May	30,000	15,000	$15,000
Balances after loss, May 31[a]	$270,200	$205,200	$65,000
Less realization loss in June	40,000	20,000	20,000
Balances after loss, June 30	$230,200	$185,200	$45,000
Cash available to partners[b]	060,200		
Possible loss apportioned	$170,000	85,000	85,000
Balances after apportionment		$100,200	$(40,000)
Further possible loss to Burns		(40,000)	40,000
Cash payment to Burns		60,200	
Balances, July 1		$125,000	$45,000
Less realization loss in July	25,000	12,500	12,500
Balances after loss, July 31	$145,000	$112,500	$(32,500)
Less liquidation expense	8,000	4,000	4,000
Final cash payment	$137,000	$108,500	$28,500

[a] No cash was distributed to partners at May 31 because only $200 was available at that time. The calculation:

Cash, per balance sheet	$ 6,200	
Received from sale of assets—May	50,000	$ 56,200
Paid to creditors—May	$ 39,000	
Reserved for creditors	17,000	$ 56,000
Available to partners—not distributed, May 31		$ 200

[b] This amount is the $200 not distributed at May 31 plus the $60,000 received in June from sale of assets.

Exhibit 42.3   Sample statement of liquidation.

(i) Capital Credits Only—Capital Deficiency of One Partner.   This situation is illustrated in Exhibit 42.3 using the previous balance sheet but assuming the following liquidation data:

	Assets Sold	Cash Received	Creditors Paid	Expenses Paid
May	$ 80,000	$ 50,000	$39,000	
June	100,000	60,000	17,000	
July	170,000	145,000		$8,000

In Exhibit 42.3, each partner received in total the balance of his capital account per the balance sheet minus his share (50 percent) of realization losses and expenses, the same as if one final cash payment had been made on July 31. Note that if Mantle had had a loan account of, say, $20,000 and a capital balance of $60,000, the first cash distribution of $60,200 would still have gone entirely to Burns. At this point, after exercising the right of offset, Mantle would still have had a future possible deficiency of $40,000.

(ii) Installment Distribution Plan.   A somewhat different approach to the problem of installment liquidation is illustrated below.

Fox, Green, and Harris are partners sharing profits equally. Following is the partnership balance sheet as of December 31, at which time it is decided to liquidate the firm by installments.

Assets		Liabilities and Capital	
Cash	$ 3,000	Liabilities	$ 24,000
Other assets	186,000	Fox, capital	79,000
		Green, capital	52,000
		Harris, capital	34,000
	$189,000		$189,000

Using the balance sheet above, computation of correct cash distribution is as follows:

	Total	Fox	Green	Harris
Partners' capital balances	$165,000	$79,000	$52,000	$34,000
Loss that would eliminate				
Harris, who is least able				
to absorb	102,000	34,000	34,000	34,000
Balances	$ 63,000	$45,000	$18,000	
Loss that would eliminate				
Green	36,000	18,000	18,000	
Balances	$ 27,000	$27,000		

The amount of the loss that will extinguish each partner's capital account is determined by dividing his capital account by his percentage of income and loss sharing. Hence, for Harris, this amount is $34,000 ÷ 331/3 percent, or $102,000.

From the computations, it is possible to prepare a schedule for the distribution of cash as follows:

	Cash	Liabilities	Fox	Green	Harris
First	$21,000	$21,000			
Next	27,000		All		
Next	36,000		1/2	1/2	
All in excess of	84,000		1/3	1/3	1/3

It is assumed that the $3,000 cash on hand on December 31 is used in payment of liabilities. The following liquidation data are given:

	Assets Sold	Cash Received	Creditors Paid
January	$64,000	$41,000	$24,000
February	60,000	37,000	
March	62,000	54,000	
Totals	$186,000	$132,000	$24,000

Based on these data, the application of the computations already made results in the following payments to creditors and partners:

	Amount	Liabilities	Fox	Green	Harris
January	$41,000	$21,000	$20,000		
February	37,000		7,000		
			15,000	$15,000	
March	54,000		3,000	3,000	
			16,000	16,000	$16,000
Totals	$132,000	$21,000	$61,000	$34,000	$16,000

42.6 LIMITED PARTNERSHIPS

(a) DEFINITION. Limited partnerships are business partnership structures that permit partners to invest capital with the proviso that there will be limited control over business operations and, accordingly, assumption of liability limited to the extent of capital contributions.

In general partnerships, the potential liability that can accrue to individual partners is unlimited. That unlimited liability has always been a major drawback of the partnership structure. Limited partnerships evolved to a great extent in order to overcome that disadvantage.

The legal provisions governing limited partnerships are provided by the Uniform Limited Partnership Act and the Revised Uniform Limited Partnership Act, which have been adopted in some form by each state government.

(b) DIFFERENCES BETWEEN LIMITED PARTNERSHIPS AND GENERAL PARTNERSHIPS. In addition to limitations on the liability of partners, limited partnerships differ from general partnerships in these ways:

- Limited partners have no participation in the management of the limited partnership.
- Limited partners may invest only cash or other assets in a limited partnership; they may not provide services as their investment.
- The surname of a limited partner may not appear in the name of the partnership.

(c) FORMATION OF LIMITED PARTNERSHIPS. The formation of limited partnerships is generally evidenced by a certificate filed with the county recorder of the principal place of business of the limited partnership rather than a partnership agreement such as that described in Subsection 42.1(e). Such certificates include many of the items present in the typical partnership contract of a general partnership. In addition, certificates must include the name and residence of each general partner and limited partner; the amount of cash and other assets invested by each limited partner; provision for return of a limited partner's investment; any priority of one or more limited partners over other limited partners; and any right of limited partners to vote for election or removal of general partners, termination of the partnership, amendment of the certificate, or disposal of all partnership assets.

Interests in limited partnerships are offered to prospective limited partners in units subject to the Securities Act of 1933. Thus, unless provisions of that Act exempt a limited partnership, it must file a registration statement for the offered units with the Securities and Exchange Commission (SEC) and undertake to file periodic reports with the SEC. Large limited partnerships that engage in ventures such as oil and gas exploration and real estate development and issue units registered with the SEC are called *master limited partnerships*. The SEC has provided guidance for such registration and reporting in Industry Guide 5: *Preparation of Registration Statements Relating to Interests in Real Estate Limited Partnerships.*

(d) ACCOUNTING AND FINANCIAL CONSIDERATIONS. As a general rule, the accounting records of limited partnerships are kept on a cash basis. However, the SEC requires that limited partnerships registrants prepare and file basic financial statements in conformity with generally accepted accounting principles (GAAP). For example, SEC Staff Accounting Bulletin Topic 4F requires the equity section of the limited partnership's balance sheet to distinguish between general partner and limited partner equity, with a separate statement of changes in partnership equity for each type of participation provided for each period for which a limited partnership income statement is presented.

The SEC also believes it is appropriate for a limited partnership registrant to include financial data on a tax basis of accounting, with an appropriate reconciliation of differences in major disclosure areas between tax and financial accounting. Whether GAAP-basis financial statements (along with the data necessary for income tax return preparation) should be distributed to the participants of SEC-reporting limited partnerships is a matter covered by the proxy rules.

American Institute of Certified Public Accountants (AICPA) Practice Bulletin No. 14 provides reporting guidance along with guidance on certain accounting issues regarding the application of existing authoritative literature for limited liability companies and limited liability partnerships (jointly referred to herein as *LLCs*).

(i) Financial Statement Reporting Issues.   According to Practice Bulletin No. 14, a complete set of LLC financial statements should include the following:

- Statement of financial position as of the end of the reporting period
- Statement of operations for the period
- Statement of cash flows for the period
- Accompanying notes to financial statements

LLCs should also present information related to changes in members' equity for the period, either in a separate statement combined with the statement of operations or in the notes to the financial statements. The headings of an LLC's financial statements should identify clearly the financial statements as those of a limited liability company.

Practice Bulletin No. 14 stipulates that the financial statements of an LLC should be similar in presentation to those of a partnership. Since the owners of an LLC are referred to as *members*, the equity section in the statement of financial position should be titled "members' equity." If more than one class of members exists, each having varying rights, preferences, and privileges, the LLC is encouraged to report the equity of each class separately within the equity section. If the LLC does not report the amount of each class separately within the equity section, it should disclose those amounts in the notes to the financial statements.

Even though a member's liability may be limited, if the total balance of the members' equity account or accounts described in the preceding paragraph is less than zero, a deficit should be reported in the statement of financial position.

If the LLC maintains separate accounts for components of members' equity (e.g., undistributed earnings, earnings available for withdrawal, or unallocated capital), Practice Bulletin No. 14 permits disclosure of those components, either on the face of the statement of financial position or in the notes to the financial statements.

If the LLC records amounts due from members for capital contributions, such amounts should be presented as deductions from members' equity. Practice Bulletin No. 14 notes that presenting such amounts as assets is inappropriate except in very limited circumstances when there is substantial evidence of ability and intent to pay within a reasonably short period of time.

Presentation of comparative financial statements is encouraged, but not required, by Chapter 2A, "Comparative Financial Statements," of Accounting Research Bulletin (ARB) No. 43, "Restatement and Revision of Accounting Research Bulletins." If comparative financial statements are presented, amounts shown for comparative purposes must be in fact comparable with those shown for the most recent period, or any exceptions to comparability must be disclosed in the notes to the financial statements. Situations may exist in which financial statements of the same reporting entity for periods prior to the period of conversion are not comparable with those for the most recent period presented, for example, if transactions such as spin-offs or other distributions of assets occurred prior to or as part of the LLC's formation. In such situations, sufficient disclosure should be made so the comparative financial statements are not misleading. If the formation of the LLC results in a new reporting entity, the guidance in Accounting Principles Board (APB) Opinion No. 20, "Accounting Changes," paragraphs 34 and 35, should be followed and financial statements for all prior periods presented should be restated.

(ii) Financial Statement Disclosure Issues.   Practice Bulletin No. 14 requires that the following disclosures be made in the financial statements of a limited liability company:

- A description of any limitation of its members' liability.
- The different classes of members' interests and the respective rights, preferences, and privileges of each class. If the LLC does not report separately the amount of each class in the equity section of the statement of financial position, those amounts should be disclosed.
- LLCs subject to income tax should make the disclosures required by Financial Accounting Standards Board (FASB) SFAS No. 109, "Accounting for Income Taxes."
- If the LLC has a finite life, the date the LLC will cease to exist should be disclosed.
- For LLCs formed by combining entities under common control or by conversion from another type of entity, the notes to the financial statements for the year of formation should disclose that the assets and liabilities previously were held by a predecessor entity or entities. LLCs formed by combining entities under common control are encouraged to make the relevant disclosures in paragraph 64 of APB Opinion No. 16, "Business Combinations."

(iii) Accounting Issues.   Practice Bulletin No. 14 requires that an LLC formed by combining entities under common control or by conversion from another type of entity initially should state its assets and liabilities at amounts at which they were stated in the financial statements of the predecessor entity or entities in a manner similar to a pooling of interests.

LLCs generally are classified as partnerships for federal income tax purposes. An LLC that is subject to federal (U.S.), foreign, state, or local (including franchise) taxes based on income should account for such taxes in accordance with FASB Statement No. 109.

Practice Bulletin No. 14 points out that in accordance with FASB Statement No. 109, an entity whose tax status in a jurisdiction changes from taxable to nontaxable should eliminate any deferred tax assets or liabilities related to that jurisdiction as of the date the entity ceases to be a taxable entity. FASB Statement No. 109 requires disclosure of significant components of income tax expense attributable to continuing operations including "adjustments of a deferred tax liability or asset for . . . a change in the tax status of the enterprise."

42.7 NONPUBLIC INVESTMENT PARTNERSHIPS

Statement of Position (SOP) 95–2, "Financial Reporting by Nonpublic Investment Partnerships," provides financial reporting guidance for investment partnerships that are exempt from SEC registration pursuant to the Investment Company Act of 1940 and defined as investment companies in paragraph 1.01 of the AICPA Audit and Accounting Guide, "Audits of Investment Companies," except for:

- Investment partnerships that are brokers and dealers in securities subject to regulation under the Securities Exchange Act of 1934 (registered broker-dealers) and that manage funds only for those who are officers, directors, or employees of the general partner
- Investment partnerships that are commodity pools subject to regulation under the Commodity Exchange Act of 1974

SOP 95–2 provides that the financial statements of an investment partnership, when prepared in conformity with GAAP, should, at a minimum, include a condensed schedule of investments in securities owned by the partnership at the close of the most recent period. Such a schedule should categorize investments by:

- Type (such as common stocks, preferred stocks, convertible securities, fixed-income securities, government securities, options purchased, options written, warrants, futures, loan participations, short sales, other investment companies, etc.)
- Country or geographic region
- Industry

The schedule should report the percentage of net assets that each such category represents and the total value and cost for each type of investment and country or geographic region. The schedule should also disclose the name, shares or principal amount, value, and type of:

- Each investment (including short sales) constituting more than five percent of net assets
- All investments in any one issuer aggregating more than five percent of net assets

In applying the five percent test, total long and total short positions in any one issuer should be considered separately.

Other investments (those that are individually five percent or less of net assets) should be aggregated without specifically identifying the issuers of such investments and be categorized by type, country or region, and industry. Also note that the foregoing information is required when the partnership's proportional share of any security owned by an individual investee exceeds five percent of the reporting partnership's net assets. Disclosure of the required information for such securities may be made either on the schedule itself or in a note thereto.

SOP 95–2 also requires that investment partnerships present their statements of operations in conformity with the requirements for statements of operations of management investment companies as set forth in the AICPA Audit and Accounting Guide, "Audits of Investment Companies," which requires, among other things, separate disclosure of dividend income and interest income and realized and unrealized gains (losses) on securities for the period.

Investment companies organized as limited partnerships typically receive advisory services from the general partner. For such services, a number of partnerships pay fees chargeable as expenses to the partnership, whereas others allocate net income from the limited partners' capital accounts to the general partner's capital account, and still others employ a combination of the two methods. SOP 95–2 states that the amounts of any such payments or allocations should be presented in either the statement of operations or the statement of changes in partners' capital, and the method of computing such payments or allocations should be described in the notes to the financial statements.

42.8 JOINT VENTURES

(a) DEFINITION.   Joint ventures are partnerships formed when two or more parties pool resources for the purpose of undertaking a specific project, such as the development or marketing of a product. Joint ventures are owned, operated, and jointly controlled by a small group of owners or investors as separate business projects operated for the mutual benefit of the ownership group. Joint ventures may take the legal form of partnerships or they may be separately incorporated entities.

The owners or investors (venturers) in a joint venture may or may not have equal ownership interests in the venture. A venturer's share may range from as low as 5 percent or 10 percent to over 50 percent, but no less. All venturers usually participate in the overall management of the venture. Significant decisions generally require the consent of all venturers regardless of the percentage of ownership so that no individual venturer has unilateral control.

(b) ACCOUNTING BY JOINT VENTURES.   Regardless of their legal form of organization, joint ventures must maintain accounting records and prepare financial statements just like any other enterprise. The primary users of the joint ventures financial statements are the venturers, who need to record their share of the profit or loss of the venture and to value their investment in it. Most of the accounting principles and procedures used by joint ventures are the same as those used by other business enterprises.

The most significant accounting issue for most joint ventures is the recording of initial capital contributions, particularly noncash contributions. Such contributions should be recorded on the books of the venture at the fair value of the assets contributed on the date of contribution, unless the fair value of the assets is not readily or reliably determinable or the recoverability of that value is in doubt. This general rule does not apply, however, to assets contributed by a venturer who controls a venture. In those circumstances, the assets should be recorded on the books of the venture at the same amount at which they were carried on the venturer's books because there has been no effective change in control over the assets.

(c) ACCOUNTING FOR INVESTMENTS IN JOINT VENTURES.   Since joint venturers have rights and obligations that may differ from their ownership percentages assuring them of significant influence even at ownership percentages of less than 20 percent, the application of customary equity or consolidation accounting is not always appropriate. Interests in incorporated joint ventures are accounted for in accordance with APB Opinion No. 18, which mandates use of the equity method. Accounting for interests in joint ventures that are organized as partnerships or undivided interests is discussed in an AICPA staff interpretation of APB Opinion No. 18 that states that many of the provisions of that Opinion are appropriate in accounting for such investments.

In 1979, the AICPA's Accounting Standards Executive Committee issued an Issues Paper entitled *Joint Venture Accounting.* The Issues Paper contains the following advisory conclusions:

- The portion of APB Opinion No. 18 dealing with investments in joint ventures should be reexamined.
- The one-line equity method described in APB Opinion No. 18 should be required for investments in joint ventures (whether incorporated or unincorporated) that are subject to joint control, except that the cost method should be permitted for investments that are not material to the investor.
- If an entity that otherwise meets the definition of a joint venture is, in fact, controlled by majority voting interest or otherwise, the entity should be required to be accounted for as a subsidiary of the controlling investor and to be fully consolidated by that investor.
- If an entity that otherwise meets the definition of a joint venture is not subject to joint control, by reason of its liabilities being several rather than joint as in some undivided interests, investments in the entity should be required to be accounted for by the proportionate consolidation method.
- The use of the same method in the balance sheet and income statement should be required.
- Disclosure of supplementary information as to the assets, liabilities, and results of operations should be mandatory if the investments in the aggregate are material.

(i) Financial Statement Presentation.   There are a number of different methods that venturers use to display their interest in joint ventures in their financial statements. The AICPA Issues Paper mentioned previously describes seven different methods, only four of which are considered acceptable. The methods described in the Accounting Standard Executive Committee (AcSEC) advisory conclusions are not interchangeable; that is, each should be applied when specified circumstances exist. The four methods are briefly described in the following paragraphs.

One-Line Equity Method.   This method involves the application of the "traditional" equity method of accounting described in APB Opinion No. 18. The Issues Paper expresses the position that this method should remain the prevalent method of accounting for joint venture investments. Since most joint ventures give each investor significant influence over the venture, the equity method is generally more appropriate than the historical cost method used when an investor has only minor influence. The equity method of accounting is described in Chapter 13 of this *Handbook.*

Many venturers prefer to use the equity method because it reflects the venturer's exposure to only the net liabilities of the venture by presenting the investment as a net position. The equity method also reflects the investor's share of the net income of the venture in the income statement for the period in which the net income is earned by the joint venture. Critics point out that it tends to obscure the nature and volume of the business of investors that conduct significant operation through joint ventures. It also excludes certain assets and liabilities that may be essential to an investor's business from the investor's balance sheet and elements of revenue and expense that arise from the venture's operations from the investor's income statement.

Proportionate Consolidation Method.   Under this method, the investor's proportionate share of the assets, liabilities, revenues, and expenses is combined with similar items in the investor's financial statements. This method is often used in the real estate and oil and gas industries. The Issues Paper on joint venture accounting recommends that the proportionate consolidation method be used only in situations in which venturer's liabilities are several rather than joint. The SEC, however, generally has not favored proportionate consolidation and use of the method in other industries has thus been constrained. AICPA SOP 78–9, "Accounting for Investments in Real Estate Ventures," states that the usual full consolidation or equity methods should be applied to *corporate* joint ventures in the real estate industry.

While the proportionate consolidation method provides information in an entity's financial statements that may be useful to present and potential investors on past and prospective changes in the economic resources and obligations of the entity, its critics point out that it is based on the concept of control over pieces of the joint venture even though such control does not actually exist. Similarly, the method combines net assets in the balance sheet and operations in the income statement that the investor owns and controls directly with those over which the investor may have little or no control.

Full Consolidation.   The Issues Paper recommends that when a venturer has control of a joint venture, the full or traditional consolidation method of accounting be used as described in FASB Statement No. 94, "Consolidation of All Majority-Owned Subsidiaries." That method involves the combination of the assets, liabilities, revenues, and expenses of the joint venture with those of the venturer in the venturer's financial statements. The portion of the venture's net assets owned by the other venturers is shown as a liability on the venturer's balance sheet and is usually described as a *minority interest.*

Cost Method.   Presenting an investment in a joint venture at cost is permissible only for immaterial investments.

(ii) Combination of Methods.   Some investors believe that a combination of these methods is the most appropriate way to present an investment in a joint venture in their financial statements. Those investors might use one method for the balance sheet and another for the income statement. When a combination of methods is used, it generally involves use of the one-line equity method in the balance sheet and the proportionate consolidation method in the income statement. The AICPA Issues Paper recommends against using a combination of methods.

(iii) Income Tax Issues.   Differences may arise between an investor's accounting treatment of an investment in a joint venture for purposes of financial reporting and for income tax purposes. In such circumstances, deferred taxes are required to be recognized. For joint ventures organized as partnerships, investors generally use the equity method for both tax and financial reporting purposes and therefore deferred taxes do not arise. No less, there may be differences between the book and tax carrying amount of the investment. Such differences are *temporary differences* as defined by FASB Statement No. 109, "Accounting for Income Taxes," and therefore do require recognition of deferred taxes. The length of time over which such differences may reverse depends on the specific differences in the carrying method used.

(d) CURRENT DEVELOPMENTS. The FASB currently has on its agenda a project on consolidations and related matters. This group of related projects is intended to cover all aspects of accounting for affiliations between entities along with several other matters that raise similar or potentially related issues about financial statements. The FASB is reconsidering issues relating to ARB No. 51, "Consolidated Financial Statements," APB Opinion No. 18, "The Equity Method of Accounting for Investments in Common Stock," and FASB Statement No. 14, "Financial Reporting for Segments of a Business Enterprise." This area was initially divided into five projects: consolidation policy and procedures, disaggregated disclosures (segments), new basis accounting, unconsolidated entities, and similar matters for not-for-profit entities. At present, the project on consolidation policy and procedures is considering both business enterprises and not-for-profit organizations. In August 1996, the Board removed the new basis project from its agenda because other current projects are perceived as higher priorities. Some new basis issues are in other projects, and the Board may address those issues again. In June 1997, the Board completed the project on disaggregated disclosures resulting in the issuance of FASB Statement No. 131, "Disclosures about Segments of an Enterprise and Related Information."

The unconsolidated entities project addresses presentation in the investor's financial statements and other issues related to investments in noncontrolled corporations and partnerships, including joint ventures and undivided interests. Late in 1996, the FASB's staff began research on the issues. The staff also is participating in development of a paper, "Bases of Reporting Interests in a Joint Venture: Conceptual, Methodological, and Practical Issues." The FASB expects to use that paper to solicit comments on some of the issues in this project. A group of researchers is developing a study with the FASB staff's assistance to determine how users react to different methods of presenting joint venture investments in an investor's financial statements. The FASB's staff also is monitoring the AICPA's progress on a project to develop a new SOP on accounting for real estate ventures.

The initial phase of the consolidation policy and procedures project resulted in the issuance of FASB Statement No. 94, "Consolidation of All Majority-Owned Subsidiaries," in October 1987. A second phase resulted in a Discussion Memorandum, "Consolidation Policy and Procedures," in September 1991; a Preliminary Views, Consolidation Policy, in August 1994; and an Exposure Draft, "Consolidated Financial Statements: Policy and Procedures," in October 1995. The Exposure Draft proposed that a controlling entity (parent) consolidate all entities that it controls (subsidiaries) unless control is temporary at the time that the entity becomes a subsidiary. The proposed Statement, which would apply to business enterprises and not-for-profit organizations, also prescribes certain procedures for preparing consolidated financial statements.

During its redeliberations, the FASB tentatively decided to modify and clarify the Exposure Draft's proposed definition of control and discussion of its characteristics. Control tentatively is defined as the power to direct the policies and management that guide the activities of another entity so as to benefit from its activities. The FASB tentatively decided to retain many of the Exposure Draft's provisions for consolidation procedures, including those on (1) reporting the noncontrolling interest in the consolidated financial statements, (2) accounting for acquisitions and dispositions of control of a subsidiary by a parent, (3) transactions that change a parent's proportionate ownership interest in a subsidiary while maintaining control, and (4) elimination of intercompany transactions and balances. The Board also has decided to make certain changes to the Exposure Draft, including the following:

- Losses attributable to the noncontrolling interest that exceed the noncontrolling interest's equity in a subsidiary would be reported as part of the noncontrolling interest rather than being absorbed by the controlling interest.

- If a parent acquires control of an entity in which the parent previously held an investment, that investment should be remeasured at its fair value on the date the parent-subsidiary relationship is established, and a holding gain or loss on that investment accumulated while it was held as an investment should be recognized in earnings.

- If, upon relinquishing control, a parent retains an investment in a former subsidiary that investment should be measured at its fair value on the date control is relinquished.

The FASB has decided to focus its efforts on developing the consolidation policy and to consider resuming discussion on consolidation procedures after completion of the efforts on consolidation policy. The FASB is focusing its effort on developing criteria for consolidation policy that would be based on both control and benefits, and it has begun but not completed its reconsideration of the level and types of benefit required for consolidation. The FASB has also decided to consider expanding the scope of the proposed Statement to specify the accounting for all rights and obligations stemming from a relationship with a special-purpose or limited-purpose entity that is not consolidated.

The FASB's Emerging Issues Task Force (EITF) has also discussed several matters that may affect the appropriate accounting for investments in joint ventures. Those matters include:

- Issue No. 96–16, "Investor's Accounting for an Investee When the Investor Has a Majority of the Voting Interest but the Minority Shareholder or Shareholders Have Certain Approval or Veto-Rights," which considers whether rights of a minority shareholder should preclude an investor from consolidating when the investor has a majority voting interest in an investee.

- Issue No. 95–6, "Accounting by Real Estate Investment Trust for an Investment in a Service Corporation," which sets forth criteria for determining whether significant influence exists. While the criteria were developed specifically for real estate investment trusts and service corporations, they may be useful in making that determination for other entities as well.

- Issue No. 94–1, "Accounting for Tax Benefits Resulting from Investments in Affordable Housing Projects," which describes the Task Force's consensus position about how an entity that invests in a qualified affordable housing project through a limited partnership should account for its investment.

- Appendix D-46, "Accounting for Limited Partnership Investments," which describes discussion of the SEC staff's position that investments in all limited partnerships should be accounted for pursuant to paragraph 8 of AICPA SOP 78–9, "Accounting for Investments in Real Estate Ventures." That guidance requires the use of the equity method unless the investor's interest "is so minor that the limited partner may have virtually no influence over partnership operating and financial policies."

42.9 SOURCES AND SUGGESTED REFERENCES

American Institute of Certified Public Accountants, "Related Party Transactions," Statement of Auditing Standards No. 45. AICPA, New York, 1983.

Anderson, R. J., *External Audit.*. Pitman Publishing Co., Toronto, Ontario, Canada, 1977. Bedford, Norton M., *Introduction to Modern Accounting.* Ronald Press, New York, 1962.

Bedford, Norton M., Perry, Kenneth W., and Wyatt, Arthur H., *Advanced Accounting—An Organization Approach.* John Wiley & Sons, New York, 1979.

Bogen, Jules I., "Advantages and Disadvantages of Partnership," in *Financial Handbook,* Fourth Edition Ronald Press, New York, 1968.

Defliese, Philip L., Johnson, Kenneth P., and Macleod, Roderick K., *Montgomery's Auditing,* Ninth Edition Ronald Press, New York, 1975.

Dixon, Robert L., Hepworth, Samuel R., and Paton, William A., Jr., *Essentials of Accounting.* Macmillan, New York, 1966.

Financial Accounting Standards Board, "Related Party Disclosures," Statement of Financial Accounting Standards No. 57. FASB, Stamford, CT, 1982.

Hoffman, William H., Jr., ed., *West's Federal Taxation: Corporations, Partnerships, Estates and Trusts.* West, St. Paul, MN, 1978.

Internal Revenue Service & Internal Revenue Code of 1954, Section 761, Subchapter K.

Meigs, Walter B., Johnson, Charles E., and Keller, Thomas F., *Advanced Accounting.* McGraw-Hill, New York, 1966.

Moonitz, Maurice, and Jordan, Louis H., *Accounting—An Analysis of Its Problems,* 2 vols., rev. ed. Holt, Rinehart and Winston, New York, 1963.

CHAPTER 43

ESTATES AND TRUSTS

Philip M. Herr, JD, CPA

Kingsbridge Financial Group, Inc.

43.1 ESTATES—LEGAL BACKGROUND

(a) EXECUTING A WILL.   A will is a revocable instrument whereby a person makes a disposition of his property to take effect at death. A prudent person should secure legal advice upon reaching the age of majority (age 18 in many states). If the attorney deems it advisable, such person should execute a will. In the will, the testator (maker) should spell out in detail who is to inherit his property upon his death. The testator may also name a person to administer the estate and select a guardian (a protector of the body and property of his children, if any). A will can be very simple or very complex depending on the extent of the testator's property and desires. To be valid, the will must be properly executed according to state law. Such state laws normally require the maker to declare that the document is his last will and testament and to sign it in the presence of at least two witnesses, who also sign. Such witnesses, called *subscribing witnesses*, may later be called upon to testify about the maker's appearance of mental competence at the time of the execution of the will.

(b) WILL PROVISIONS.   Every will provision must be adhered to by the executor and the courts unless it is contrary to law or against public policy.

A typical will provides for:

- A statement revoking all prior wills and codicils.
- An instruction to pay all just debts, expenses of administration, funeral expenses, and sometimes final burial instructions. (However, these instructions are better left in a letter of

instruction left with a close family member or friend in case the will should be found after the funeral.)

- General bequests or legacies of money or property to named individuals payable out of the general assets of the estate.
- Devises of real property to specified individuals.
- Specific bequests or legacies of specific property. They fail if the property does not exist at the testator's death.
- Demonstrative bequests or legacies. These are gifts of money or property payable out of a particular fund; if the fund is insufficient, the balance becomes a general legacy.
- Provisions concerning disposal of the residuary estate. The residuary estate is all property not otherwise provided for in the will.
- The duties and powers of the executor (described later in this section).
- The naming of fiduciaries (executors, trustees, guardians, committees for incompetents) and their successors; and often, the exemption of having to post a fidelity bond.
- Definitions of terms used in the will.
- Provisions apportioning federal and state death taxes among the various classes of beneficiaries (marital vs. nonmarital, specific vs. residuary, charitable vs. noncharitable).
- Simultaneous death provision that provides who shall be presumed to have survived whom as between the testator and other beneficiaries taking under the will.
- The terms of any testamentary trusts that might be established under the will (i.e., for a minor beneficiary).
- Signature of testator and subscribing witnesses, which may also be notarized in an attempt to "self-prove" the will.

(c) RULES UNDER INTESTACY. "Intestacy" is defined as the state or condition of dying without having made a valid will, or without having disposed by will of a part of the deceased's property. Thus it arises not only when the deceased died without having made a will, but also if the will is invalid, or if it contains ineffective or no provisions concerning the disposal of the residuary estate.

When an intestacy is present, state law provides who is to receive the property. In effect, state statutes make a will for the deceased. The plan of distribution of the property, sometimes called *intestate succession* or *laws of descent and distribution*, is strictly defined by state statute and is based on degree of relationship to the deceased. New York State, for example, provides that if a decedent dies without a will and leaves a wife and two children, the wife receives $50,000 and one-half of the residuary estate and the children share the other one-half. Under the same circumstances, Oregon allows the spouse one-half of the estate and the children share the other one-half. Distribution plans under state laws vary even more if a spouse or children do not survive the decedent. It could result, for example, in a surviving parent, who may have made lifetime gifts to the decedent for the parent's own estate planning purposes, receiving those assets back. Distribution plans under intestacy do not take into account financial needs or close bonds of a decedent to certain relatives. It may result in relatives with whom a decedent has had no contact for many years inheriting a portion of the property. Absence of a will can result in fights over the appointment of administrators and in custody battles over the guardianship of minor children and their property. The failure to make a will should be a conscious decision of an informed individual to allow state law to make it for him and not a result of ignorance or procrastination.

(d) DOMICILE. Generally most states take the position that the property of a person domiciled in a state at the time of death is subject to court jurisdiction (and the estate and inheritance tax) of that state. Domicile is defined as the place where a person has a true, fixed, and permanent home to which, whenever absent, the person has the intention of returning.

In addition, states generally also claim court jurisdiction over (and estate and inheritance tax on) real and tangible personal property located within their boundaries for persons domiciled outside the state at the time of their death.

These two concepts often force an executor or administrator to bring court proceedings in more than one state. Proceedings brought outside the state of domicile are called *ancillary proceedings*. The distribution by the executor or administrator of ancillary property is governed by the state law of the property's location.

Sometimes more than one state claims that a decedent was domiciled in that state at the time of death. Such a situation can lead to expensive litigation and excessive estate or inheritance tax. A person with dual residences should clearly establish which state he considers to be his domicile. This can be done by consistency in such evidence of domicile as voter registration, automobile registration, state income tax returns, declaration in will, and positions taken in documents executed during life.

Separate issues arise if the decedent is not a U.S. citizen. If the decedent was a resident alien with a U.S. citizen spouse, his estate will be administered and taxed as if a U.S. citizen. The executor or administrator, however, should determine whether the United States has an estate tax treaty with the decedent's country of citizenship, especially if the decedent owned assets in that country, and review the laws of that country to determine if any death taxes are owed to that country. If the surviving spouse is not a U.S. citizen, the executor or administrator must carefully review the estate tax rules relating to this situation. For example, the regular marital deduction rules do not apply. A marital deduction is permitted only if the will provides for a qualified domestic trust or if the spouse elects to become a U.S. citizen.

If the decedent is not a U.S. citizen and not a resident alien, the estate taxation and administration of the estate take on a whole new complexion. The issue of domicile becomes extremely important and could have a major impact on the U.S. taxation of the estate, as well as the number of ancillary international proceedings that may have to be conducted. A situation like this behooves an executor or administrator to seek expert advice and counsel.

(e) PROBATE PROCEDURES: WILL.   The courts having jurisdiction over decedents' estates have different names. Some states call such a court a probate court; others, a surrogate court. Often the same court governs both decedents leaving wills and those dying without wills.

Most wills are drafted by an attorney; however, a holographic will is written entirely in the decedent's handwriting. Most state statutes recognize these wills and impose only minimal requirements to establish their validity. Two universal requirements are that the will be executed with testamentary intent and be signed by the testator. A holographic will need *not* be witnessed to be valid in certain states. A court's determination of whether a holographic will is valid becomes part of the probate process.

A codicil to a will, or will codicil, is an amendment to or modification of an otherwise valid will. Testators will often use a codicil to make minor or modest changes instead of going through the whole process of redrafting the entire will. In certain cases this may be a misconception on their part since a codicil must meet certain statutory requirements of its own and must be executed in the same manner as a will (i.e., signed by the testator and two or more witnesses). In any event, a codicil becomes part of the last will and testament document.

After a decedent's will has been located, it should be presented to the court for probating, that is, proving it valid. The named executor (executrix if a female), if qualified and willing to act, is issued letters testamentary, that is, a document authorizing him to act on behalf of the estate. In some states temporary letters are issued with formal letters issued at a later date.

(f) PROBATE PROCEDURES: FAILURE OF EXECUTOR.   If the executor named in the will is unqualified because of such factors as age, competency, or residency, any named successor if qualified is allowed to take the executor's place. Should all successors fail to qualify or refuse the appointment, any beneficiary of the estate may petition the court for appointment. State laws generally provide an order of priority, the appointment going first to a qualified surviving spouse, then to qualified children (sometimes in age order), then to qualified grandchildren, and so on.

The person who qualifies and accepts the appointment is called an *administrator* (or administratrix) CTA (*cum testamento annexo*, i.e., "with the will annexed"). The administrator CTA has the same duties and powers as an executor and looks to the will for authority to act.

(g) PROBATE PROCEDURES: INTESTACY.   The death of a person without a will necessitates the appointment of an administrator. As mentioned above, appointments are made by interested parties petitioning the court and the court appointing the first person who can qualify in the order of priority outlined under state law. Letters of administration are issued after compliance with the governing statutes. The administrator must distribute the estate in accordance with the laws of intestacy of the state in which he is appointed.

(h) SETTLEMENT OF SMALL ESTATES.   Most state statutes provide special rules for the settlement of small estates with either no court administrative involvement or some form of an abbreviated procedure. The definition of "small" depends on the gross value of the estate. These values can be as low as $5,000 to $15,000, or as high as $50,000 to $60,000. Utilization of these special rules results in greatly reduced administration costs and a quicker settlement of the estate.

(i) FIDUCIARY RESPONSIBILITIES.

(i) Executor versus Administrator.   Although the executor's powers and duties come primarily from the will and secondarily from state law if the will is silent, the administrator of a person dying intestate must look solely to state law for authority to act.

The term *personal representative* or simply *representative* as used in this section encompasses both executors and administrators. The term *fiduciary* includes executors, administrators, guardians, and trustees.

(ii) General Duties of Representatives.   Duties of a representative, stated generally, are to collect the decedent's assets, pay creditors, account for all income and expenses, and distribute the assets remaining according to the provisions of the will or in accordance with state law in the absence of will provisions.

In the performance of these duties, the personal representative must use the "reasonable man" rule, that is, duties must be exercised with the prudence a reasonable person would exercise with his own property. The representative does not guarantee estate assets against loss. However, he is responsible for acting reasonably and can be asked to make good estate losses should he fail to act reasonably. Since the representative is not required to possess the expertise of an accountant, attorney, or investment counselor (although a decedent may often name such a professional in the will), a representative acting in a "reasonable" manner should determine whether the will or state law authorizes the retention of such advisers whenever necessary.

(iii) Preliminary Administration.   Often a death is sudden and unexpected. Determining whether the decedent left a will is sometimes a problem. Finding it and determining whether it is the last will executed may be even bigger problems. A careful search must be made of the decedent's personal papers. If the decedent had an attorney, accountant, banker, or insurance broker, the person may be helpful in ascertaining the existence of a will and locating it. The importance of the will lies not only in carrying out the decedent's plan for distribution of his assets, but also in determining the persons named as executors, trustees, and guardians of minors or others incapable of caring for themselves. Administration of the estate must begin, however, at the moment of death. There are too many important acts, such as carrying out the decedent's instructions for bodily organ donations, arranging for the funeral, and safeguarding valuable or perishable assets, to await the location of the will or formal appointment of a representative. Someone must take responsibility at once. Should it later turn out that another person was named executor or appointed administrator, an orderly transition of authority can be made.

(iv) Specific Duties of Representatives. Twelve other specific duties of the personal representative are to:

1. Arrange to have all estate assets inventoried and title transferred to the name of the executor or administrator.

2. Obtain possession of the decedent's important papers and personal property and arrange for safekeeping.

3. Arrange for adequate insurance coverage for estate assets.

4. Collect all debts owed to the decedent and litigate if necessary.

5. Arrange for an appraisal of all estate assets by qualified appraisers before distributing any assets.

6. Keep clear and accurate records of all estate receipts and disbursements. This is necessary for tax returns and for accountings to courts and beneficiaries.

7. Determine whether assets coming under the control of representatives are sufficient to meet both claims against the estate and legacies allowed by will and/or state law.

8. Review cash requirements to pay legacies, taxes, debts, and administration expenses, and determine whether assets are sufficiently liquid to pay such claims as they become due.

9. Arrange for the preparation of any payment of tax due on the decedent's final income tax returns, federal estate return, state or foreign estate or inheritance tax returns, and estate income tax returns.

10. Advertise for creditors (publish notification of decedent's death, allowing statutory period for claim presentation) and pay all valid claims against the estate.

11. Pay legacies at times specified under state law and distribute the remainder of the estate after payment of all debts and administration expenses to persons directed by will or by state law in the absence of will direction.

12. Prepare interim and/or final accountings for beneficiaries and courts as required by state law.

A graphic outline of the administration of a decedent's estate is presented in Exhibit 43.1.

(v) Possession of Assets. After the appointment of the administrator or executor, the next step is to assemble the property belonging to the estate. The representative is required to exercise due diligence in the discovery of assets and must take all proper legal steps to obtain possession of them.

(vi) Probate versus Nonprobate Assets. Probate assets are those assets whose disposition is controlled by the decedent's will. Nonprobate assets pass to the designated beneficiary by either operation of law (i.e., joint tenancy with right to survivorship, tenants by the entirety) or by operation of contract (i.e., designated beneficiary of an insurance policy, qualified retirement plan, or other form of deferred compensation). Although the value of nonprobate assets is includable in the decedent's gross estate for tax purposes, the administrator or executor is not responsible for the collection of these assets. However, the estate representative's cooperation in assisting a beneficiary obtain possession of these assets is a usual occurrence.

(vii) Personal Property Exemptions. Personal property of the deceased passes directly to the personal representative of the decedent. However, certain items of personal property must be exempted by statute for the benefit of the family of the decedent.

(viii) Real Property. Title to real property passes directly to the heirs, or devisees, and such property does not ordinarily come under the control of the representative unless left to the estate by will, sold by order of the court to pay valid obligations of the estate, or administered by

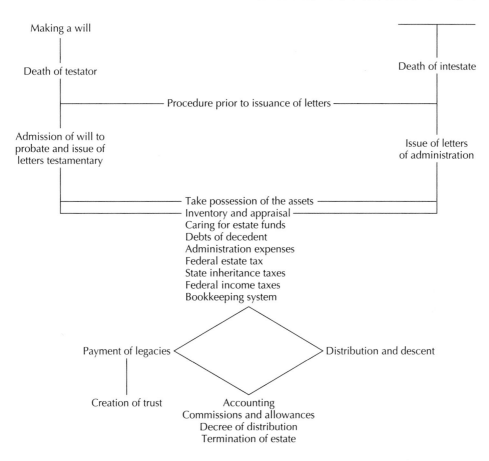

Exhibit 43.1   Graphic outline of the administration of decedent's estate.

the representative as a requirement of state law. If real estate does come under the control of the representative, it is handled in the same manner as personal property. In some states, the representative may manage the real estate and collect rents during the period of administration. The balance due on a land contract receivable is personal property of the estate, although the title to the land passes to the heirs and is retained by them until the contract is paid.

(ix) Inventory of Assets.   A detailed inventory of all assets taken over, which will form the basis of the accounting of the representative, should be prepared and filed with the court. Schedules should be prepared of all cash on hand and on deposit; all furniture, fixtures, and articles of personal use; all claims against others (choices in action); all contract rights that do not involve personal services; all unpaid fees, commissions, and salaries; all life insurance policies payable to the estate; all interest in partnerships; all unpaid dividends of record as of the date of death, or other accrued income; all leases; and all other personal property owned by the decedent. The inventory does not include goods or money held by the decedent for others. Claims canceled by will are included in the inventory, as are articles exempted for the decedent's family and articles of no apparent value. No liabilities are mentioned in the inventory, and assets pledged to secure a loan are listed without deduction for the amount of the loan. Accruals are to be computed up to midnight following the death of the decedent.

(x) Valuation of Assets. The asset values are usually set by appraisers appointed by the court and will presumably be the market values at the time of death. The executor should keep a copy of the inventory and incorporate its details into the bookkeeping system.

(xi) Management of Estate Funds. Generally, the function of the administrator or executor of an estate is to liquidate, whereas the role of the trustee or guardian is to manage. Nonetheless, the administrator or executor may have important managerial functions to perform. Perishable goods, speculative investments, and burdensome property should be disposed of promptly. Unless forgiven in the will, every effort should be made to collect all claims due the estate. Articles of a personal nature are usually distributed among legatees or next of kin at their inventory value but may be sold if such a distribution is not feasible.

All estate funds should be kept in a separate bank account in the name of the representative, with an indication of the fiduciary relationship, and should not be mingled with those of the representatives (except in the case of a trust company). All disbursements should be made by check. Interest should be secured on bank balances if possible. Stock certificates in the name of the decedent should be transferred to the name of the representative in his fiduciary capacity. Adequate insurance should be carried against fire, theft, public liability, and other risks. In general, the representative, to avoid personal liability for loss of funds and property, must care for the assets as diligently as if they were his own, assuming the representative to be a reasonably prudent businessman.

An executor or administrator may not be under legal compulsion to invest the funds of the estate, but it is certainly good business practice to make interim investments in guaranteed obligations, such as short-term U.S. securities or bank savings certificates or savings accounts if significant amounts of cash are accumulated for taxes, expenses, or future distribution. If investments are made, the representative must be guided by the procedure required of trustees (see later discussion).

The representative is not justified in continuing to operate a business owned by the decedent unless authorized to do so by the will. In the case of a closely held business, either a corporation or partnership, the representative will be guided by the provisions, if any, in the partnership or shareholder agreement. The terms of a buy-sell agreement may obligate and bind the representative to sell the decedent's business interest to either the surviving shareholders or partners, or to the corporation or partnership itself. In the absence of any such agreements or provisions, the business should be liquidated by the surviving partners.

(xii) Payments of Debts. The administrator or executor has a duty to satisfy himself as to the validity of the claims made against the estate and should interpose objections to any doubtful claims. A judgment cannot be rejected. A doubtful claim may be settled by a reasonable compromise in good faith. A partial payment of a debt barred by the statute of limitations does not revive the debt.

The representative is not required to pay any debt or make any distribution of assets until the expiration of a statutory period of time. If any payment or distribution is made during the period, the representative may be held responsible for the remaining assets not being sufficient to meet the remaining liabilities.

(xiii) Advertising for Creditors. The representative is permitted to advertise for creditors and should do so for personal protection. Notices are inserted in one or more newspapers published in the county requesting persons who have claims to present them with supporting affidavits and vouchers within a specified time, usually six months. Claims not yet due should be presented for proof so that funds will be set aside for their payment.

(xiv) Order of Debt Payment. When the list of debts is completed and presented to the court, the solvency or insolvency of the estate can be determined. If the estate is solvent, the order of payment is immaterial, but if the liabilities are in apparent excess of the value of the assets, a statutory order must be followed. The following order of payment is, according to Stephenson, representative:

1. Debts that by law have a special lien on property to an amount not exceeding the value of the property
2. Funeral expenses
3. Taxes
4. Debts due to the United States and to the state
5. Judgments of any court of competent jurisdiction, within the state, docketed and in force, to the extent to which they are a lien on the property of the deceased person at death
6. Wages due to any domestic servant or mechanical or agricultural laborer for a period of not more than one year immediately preceding the death
7. Claim for medical services within 12 months preceding death
8. All other debts and demands[1]

(xv) Source of Funds for Debt Payment. Unless the will directs otherwise, six assets of the estate are used in the following order in the payment of debts:

1. Personal property not bequeathed
2. Personal property bequeathed generally
3. Personal property bequeathed specifically
4. Realty not devised
5. Realty devised generally
6. Realty devised specifically

The sale, lease, or mortgaging of real estate to provide funds for the payment of debts must, in the absence of a provision to the contrary in the will, follow a petition to the court for permission to so use the realty, and the court must approve of the disposition made by the representative. Property descended to heirs is usually used before that distributed by will. Land sold by an heir or devisee before the estate is settled is subject to a possible claim for unpaid debts of the estate. All dower or curtsy rights (statutory rights for surviving wife or husband) and estates for life or years are adjusted, and heirs or devisees must be reimbursed if any assets are subsequently discovered from which the debts could have been paid.

In many instances, if the decedent was an owner of a closely held business, he may have entered into some form of a buy sell agreement with his co-owners. The agreement usually provides that the executor shall sell the decedent's interest in the business to one or more co-owners, or to the business entity itself, at the price set forth therein in exchange for cash. Depending on the arrangement, the buy-sell agreement will be referred to as either a *cross purchase* or *entity redemption* (or corporate stock redemption) agreement. The decedent's agreement to be bound by the terms of the agreement contractually binds the executor to sell the decedent's interest in the business pursuant to the terms of the agreement. This sales price also works to establish the estate tax value of the business interest in the gross estate.

The decedent, anticipating his need to provide liquidity for the estate, may have established and funded an irrevocable life insurance trust. In this arrangement, the trust applies for a life insurance policy on the decedent's life. The trustee is both the owner and beneficiary of the policy. Upon the decedent's death, the trustee collects the insurance proceeds. While neither the trustee nor the executor is contractually bound to do so, the trustee usually purchases assets from the estate, hence providing the needed liquidity. This technique also eliminates the need for the executor to sell assets in a rush at liquidation, or "estate sale," prices.

The executor should be sure to review the decedent's personal papers thoroughly, and interview the surviving spouse and business associates or partners, to determine the existence of a buy-sell agreement or irrevocable life insurance trust.

---

[1] G. T. Stephenson and Norman Wiggins, *Estates and Trusts*, Fifth Edition (Appleton-Century-Crofts, New York, 1973).

(xvi) Administration Expenses.   Reasonable and necessary outlays made by the representative in collecting and distributing assets will be allowed by the court. The representative is personally liable for amounts disallowed. The compensation of the representative, court costs, and an allowance for preparing the accounting are allowed specifically when an accounting is made. Attorney's fees, accountant's fees, fire insurance premiums, necessary repairs to property, collection costs, and other ordinary expenses will be allowed. The character and amount of the estate and the complications of the particular situation will govern the decisions of the courts as to the reasonableness or necessity of a particular expenditure.

Most states statutorily regulate attorney's fees by prescribing a set fee schedule based on the size of the probate estate. Should an attorney's fee exceed the statutory maximum, he or she will need to seek the court's approval. In many instances, the estate's attorney may also be one of the executors, or the sole executor. This may entitle the attorney/executor to both a fee and a commission; however, the attorney/executor will have to keep detailed records of time spent and duties performed in order to sustain dual compensation.

(xvii) Distribution of Estate Assets.   After making appropriate provisions for the payment of all claims against the estate, the personal representative proceeds to distribute the remaining assets according to the instructions in the will or in compliance with the laws of descent and distribution.

(xviii) Payment of Legacies.   Legacies are usually payable one year after the death of the testator. General legacies ordinarily draw interest after that date and should be charged with interest for payments prior to the due date. General legacies to the testator's dependent children usually bear interest from the date of death. If the estate appears to be solvent, the executor may pay or deliver legacies at any time but should, for his own protection, take a bond from the legatee providing for a refund to the estate in case the assets prove to be inadequate to meet the prior claims. Otherwise a suit in equity may be necessary to recover the improper payments.

(xix) Abatement of Legacies.   If there are insufficient assets to meet the debts and other prior claims, the legacies are reduced or abated. A complete revocation is referred to as an *ademption*. The four rules governing priority in the abatement of legacies are as follows:

1. A specific legacy takes priority over a general legacy. If the testator bequeaths specific shares of stock to A and $5,000 in cash to B, B's legacy will be diminished or, if necessary, entirely wiped out before the stock left to A is resorted to.
2. A legacy for the support of the testator's widow or children, who are not otherwise adequately provided for, takes priority over legacies to strangers or more distant relatives.
3. In most states, the personal assets of the estate will be used for the payment of debts before resorting to the real estate. As a result, the bequests of money or personal property may be diminished or wiped out, although the devisees of the real property are not affected.
4. Subject to the foregoing rules, all legacies are reduced pro rata in case of a deficiency.

If the will directs that real estate be sold to pay debts, the sale will take place before any legacies are abated.

(xx) Deductions from Legacies.   There may be certain required deductions from legacies, the most common one being state inheritance taxes. A debt due by a legatee to the testator should be deducted, but a debtor who becomes a legatee is not entitled to retain funds applicable to the payment of all charges and legacies.

(xxi) Lapsed Legacies.   A legacy is said to have "lapsed" if the legatee dies before the testator, and the assets involved revert to the undistributed or residuary portion of the estate. An exception is sometimes made when the deceased legatee is a child or other near relative who has left surviving children; the children then receive the legacy.

The children would receive the legacy on either a per stripes or per capita basis. "Per stripes" means that the children of a deceased parent receive an equal share of the deceased parents' share. "Per capita" means that the children of a deceased parent receive their own share. For example: A's will leaves everything to spouse or A's children should spouse predecease. A's spouse and one adult child predecease A. A is survived by a second adult child (B) and the predeceased child's two children (C and D). A per stripes distribution would leave 50 percent to B and 25 percent to each of C and D. A per capita distribution would leave 33 1/3 percent to B, C, and D.

(xxii) Advancement and Hotchpot.   An advancement is a transfer of property by a parent to a child in anticipation of the share of the estate the child would receive if the parent died intestate. If a person indicates in his will that the advances are to be part of the child's legacy, these advances are considered as part of the corpus of the estate and must be taken into account in making the final distribution. An allowance to a widow for the support of the family is not an advance, nor is it a direct charge against items devised or bequeathed to her.

If there is no will and the advancement exceeds the child's distributable shares of the estate, the legatee is entitled to no further distribution but is not required to return the excess; if the advancement is less than the child's share, he is entitled to the difference. Hotchpot, or collation, is the bringing together of all the estate of an intestate with the advancements made to the children in order that it may be divided in accordance with the statutes of distribution.

(xxiii) Surviving Spouse's Right of Election against the Will.   Should a decedent's will completely disinherit a surviving spouse or provide less than a certain percentage of the estate to her, the spouse may petition the court to elect to receive a specified percentage of the estate, normally ranging between 30 percent and 50 percent, "against the will" (e.g., in lieu of the existing dispositive will provisions). The right to make this election will vary among the states depending on whether the probated will was executed before the marriage or during the marriage between the decedent and surviving spouse.

(xxiv) Disclaimers.   It is often recommended that an intended legatee or beneficiary forfeit, give up, or disclaim, an estate distribution. In other words, the legatee or beneficiary waives his or her right to receive all or part of their interest in an estate asset or distribution of assets. The effect of a proper disclaimer is that the intended legatee or beneficiary is presumed to have predeceased the decedent, and the asset is distributed to the contingent legatee or beneficiary. Disclaimers are governed both by state statute and the Internal Revenue Code (IRC) in Sections 2046 and 2518. The requirements of both must be carefully observed in order to obtain the desired result. In general, the following four steps must be observed:

1. The disclaimer must be made in writing.
2. It must be received by the executor and filed with the surrogate or probate court that has jurisdiction of the estate within nine months of the date of death.
3. The intended legatee or beneficiary must renounce all right, title, and interest in the item(s) and must not have received, or be deemed to have received, any economic benefit of the assets being disclaimed.
4. The disclaimed interest must pass to someone other than the disclaiming legatee or beneficiary, and he may not direct to whom the asset will pass in lieu of himself.

(xxv) Decree of Distribution and Postdecree Procedure.   The principal distribution of estate properties is made after the issuance by the court of a decree of distribution. Upon the filing of an acceptable final accounting (see below) and the expiration of the time for objections by interested parties, the court approves the accounting, allows the expenses of preparing the accounting and the representative's commission, and issues a decree that disposes of the balance of the estate according to the will or according to the statutes of descent and distribution in that jurisdiction.

The representative distributes the estate assets according to the decree, pays his commission, settles any other expenses allowed in the decree, closes his books, presents his vouchers to the court, and asks for a discharge from his responsibilities and for the cancellation of his bond.

(xxvi) Funding of Trusts.   It is not uncommon for part of the estate to be distributed to a testamentary trust or to a preexisting inter vivos trust. The distribution to the trust may make up part of a marital, residuary, or charitable bequest. A testamentary trust may also be funded to hold assets for a minor beneficiary. The appointment and approval of the trustee(s), and the distribution of the estate assets to the trust would be included in the courts' decree described above.

(j) POWERS OF ESTATE REPRESENTATIVE.

(i) Executor versus Administrator.   The personal representative's powers, as distinguished from duties, are those acts that he is authorized, rather than required, to perform. As previously mentioned, the powers of an executor or administrator CTA are outlined in the will and are often broader than those allowed to an administrator of an intestate, who must look solely to statutory authority.

The most common statutory and will clause powers of the personal representative are to invest and reinvest estate assets, to collect income and manage the estate property, to sell estate property as he sees fit, to mortgage property (in some states), and to deliver and execute agreements, contracts, deeds, and other instruments necessary to administer the estate. Most properly drawn wills reproduce the statutory powers and add additional desired powers not granted by statute.

(ii) Will Powers Not Conferred by Statute.   Using New York State law as outlined by Harris as an example, the powers listed below, when included in a will of a New York decedent, would grant additional powers not conferred by statute.[2] These 10 powers would not be available to an executor unless enumerated in the will (and are never available to an administrator of an intestate):

1. To distribute the estate immediately after death. Many states require the executor to delay any distribution for as much as one year after letters testamentary are issued.
2. To hold property without regard to the limitations imposed by law on the proper investment of estate assets.
3. To make "extraordinary repairs" to estate assets. New York allows the representative to make only "ordinary repairs"; he has to secure the permission of all beneficiaries and possibly of the court to make "extraordinary repairs" such as replacing a heating system on real estate administered by the estate.
4. To charge the cost of agents such as attorneys, accountants, and investment advisors as estate expenses.
5. To continue a business of decedent.
6. To keep funds uninvested or invested in nonincome-producing assets.
7. To abandon, alter, or demolish real estate.
8. To borrow on behalf of the estate and give notes or bonds for the sums borrowed, and to pledge or mortgage any property as security for the borrowing.
9. To pay all necessary or proper expenses and charges from income or principal, or partly from each as the fiduciary deems advisable. (This important power will be expanded on in the discussion of income and principal of trusts.)
10. To do all acts not specifically mentioned as if the fiduciary were the absolute owner of the property.

---

[2] Homer I. Harris, *Estates Practice Guide*, Fourth Edition (Lawyer's Co-Operative Publishing, Rochester, NY, 1984), Nov. 1994 Suppl.

(iii) Will Powers versus Statutory Powers. It is important to remember that state law is looked to only where the will is silent. Any will provision will be adhered to, even if it is broader or more restrictive than statutory powers, unless such provision is contrary to law or public policy.

(k) COMMISSIONS OF REPRESENTATIVES. Many states make executors' and administrators' commissions statutory. However, with an executor, the first step is to look to the will. Testators may specifically provide the amount of commission or prohibit commissions for fiduciaries. These will provisions will be adhered to, although several states allow an executor to renounce the will provisions and receive statutory commissions. Other states force the executor to renounce the appointment and petition to be appointed administrator, thereby becoming eligible for the statutory commissions of an administrator. Some states do not have statutory commission rates, leaving the awarding of commissions to the court's discretion.

It is important to bear in mind that commissions are allowed only on the probate assets, that is, assets that come under the administration of the personal representative. As previously mentioned, real property does not generally come under the control of the representative and thus is not usually a probate asset. When real property is a probate asset, the representative is entitled to commissions. In several states, specific bequests and the income thereon are treated as nonprobate and thus noncommissionable assets. In addition, if an asset is secured by a liability, only the net equity should enter into the commission base.

Sometimes a will provides for more than one executor. State law must then be examined to determine whether each is entitled to statutory commission or whether one such commission must be shared.

(l) TAXATION OF ESTATES.

(i) Final Individual Income Taxes. One of the responsibilities of the personal representative is to file any unfiled federal and state income tax returns, as well as final income tax returns for the short taxable year that ends on the date of death of the decedent. If the deceased left a surviving spouse, the personal representative can elect to file a joint federal tax return for the year of death. A joint return will normally be prepared on the cash basis for the calendar year, including the decedent's income only through the date of death, and the income of the surviving spouse for the full calendar year. An election in the final return to accrue medical expenses unpaid at death that are paid within one year of death may be made. Accrued interest on U.S. Government Series E Bonds owned by the decedent may be included as income in the final federal income tax return. Expert tax advice should be secured by the representative before making these or various other available elections.

Unused capital loss carryforwards and unused charitable contribution carryforwards of decedent are no longer deductible after the final year. Unused passive activity losses are allowed on the final return to the extent they exceed the estate tax value over the decedent's adjusted basis.

If a joint return is being filed, the tax shown on the return must be allocated between the decedent and the surviving spouse. The allocation will take into account the decedent's withholding tax and his actual payments of estimated tax, leaving the estate of the decedent with either an asset (representing overpayment of taxes) or a liability (representing underpayment of taxes). If the surviving spouse had income or paid some portion of the tax, she would owe the estate or be entitled to reimbursement from it, depending on the relationship of her tax payments to the separate tax liability on her income.

(ii) Federal Estate Tax. Decedents with gross estates valued at over $1 million[3] are required to file a Federal Estate Tax Return, Form 706, regardless of the fact that there may be no federal

---

[3] This is the filing threshold effective for decedents dying on or after January 1, 2002. This threshold is scheduled to increase as follows: in 2004, increases to $1.5 million; in 2006, increases to $2 million; in 2009, increases to $3,500,000; in 2010 the estate tax is repealed, hence no filing requirement; in 2011, the estate repeal "sunsets" and the pre-2002 rules become effective once again, hence the filing threshold is reduced to $675,000 [see Internal Revenue Service Publication 950 (Rev. March 2002), " Introduction to Estate and Gift Taxes"]. See discussion of these changes made by EGTRRA later.

estate tax liability. The federal estate tax is a tax on the value of the decedent's gross estate less certain deductions. Generally, the tax is paid from the estate property and reduces the amount otherwise available to the beneficiaries. Therefore, in the absence of specific directions in a will or trust, taxes are generally apportioned to the property that causes a tax. If property passes without tax because of a marital or charitable deduction, no taxes are chargeable to the property.

The gross estate for tax purposes includes all of the decedent's property as defined in the IRC, not merely probate property. The following are seven examples of property that is part of the gross estate for estate tax purposes, though not part of the probate estate and thus not accounted for in the representative's accounting:

1. Specifically devised real property
2. Jointly owned property passing to the survivor by operation of law
3. Life insurance not payable to the estate when the decedent possessed "incidents of ownership" such as the right to borrow or change the beneficiary of the policy, and policies transferred within three years of death
4. Lump-sum distributions from retirement plans paid to someone as a result of surviving the decedent
5. Gift taxes paid by the decedent within three years of death
6. Fair market value of the principal of any revocable "living" trust of which the decedent was the grantor or settlor
7. Fair market value of the principal of any irrevocable trust in which the decedent, as grantor or settlor, had retained any rights to income, or over the beneficiaries' rights to the use, enjoyment, or possession of the trust principal

In putting a value on the gross estate for estate tax purposes, the representative has an election to value the estate as of the date of death or an alternative date. The alternative date is either six months after the date of death or at disposition of an asset if sooner. If the election to use the alternative date is not made, all property must be valued as of the date of death; if the alternative date is elected, all property must be valued at the alternative valuation date or dates. Alternate valuation is available only if there is a reduction in estate taxes.

Deductions from the gross estate to arrive at the taxable estate include administration expenses (if an election has not been made to deduct them on estate income tax returns), funeral expenses, debts of the decedent, bequests to charitable organizations, and a marital deduction for property passing to a surviving spouse.

The 1976 Tax Reform Act unified estate and gift tax rates by provisions for a unified table to be applied both to taxable gifts made after 1976 and to taxable estates for persons dying after 1976. In computing estate taxes on the taxable estate, gifts made after 1976 are added to the taxable estate and the unified tax is recomputed with credit given for the gift tax previously paid on such gifts. This computation has the effect of treating gift taxes paid as only payments on account of future estate and gift tax brackets. A marital deduction is now available for 100 percent of property passing to the surviving spouse. The property may be left in trust with income to the spouse for life, together with either a general power of appointment, or limited power of appointment. The latter may qualify for the marital deduction if the representative makes a Qualified Terminable Interest Property (QTIP) election with the return. Eventually, the property would be taxable in the surviving spouse's estate and the tax thereon would be payable from the property.

Estates are also allowed an unlimited charitable deduction for bequests left directly to charities. A prorated charitable deduction is allowed for a split-interest bequest to charity either in the form of a remainder interest or an income interest.

The Tax Reform Act of 1997 added a new exclusion or deduction. Effective for decedents dying after December 31, 1997, decedents who owned a "qualified family owned business interest" or family farm may be eligible for this new estate tax exclusion. The amount of the exclusion is correlated with the unified credit, so that in any one year the combination of the taxable estate equivalent of the unified credit and the family owned business exclusion total $1,300,000. The eligibility rules to qualify for this new exclusion are complex and extensive; therefore, they must be closely reviewed before assuming that an estate will be able to avail itself of this exclusion.

A unified credit is allowed against the computed estate tax. The unified credit is subtracted from the taxpayer's estate or gift tax liability. However, the amount of the credit available at death will be reduced to the extent that any portion of the credit is used to offset gift taxes on lifetime transfers. The amount of the credit is equivalent to a taxable estate of $600,000. Therefore, a decedent can have a taxable estate of up to $600,000 before any estate tax is due.

The Tax Reform Act of 1997 increased the unified credit over a period of years. Beginning in 1998, the taxable estate equivalent to the credit was increased to $625,000; and will increase as follows through 2006: 1999, $650,000; 2000 and 2001, $675,000; 2002 and 2003, $700,000; 2004, $850,000; 2005, $950,000; and 2006, $1,000,000.

The Economic Growth and Tax Relief Reconciliation Act of 2001 (EGTRRA), signed into law June 7, 2001, made broad, sweeping changes to several areas of the tax law including the estate, generation-skipping transfer, and gift taxes. In short, the estate and generation-skipping transfer taxes are phased out from 2002 to 2009 and eventually repealed in 2010. The current law, however, "sunsets" on December 31, 2010, and becomes effective again as it did back in 2001. The gift tax is not repealed; however, the rates decrease to 35 percent by 2010. The following is a brief description of the changes made by EGTRRA while they last.

The highest tax rate for all three transfer taxes will reduce as follows from 2002 through 2009: 2002—50 percent, 2003—49 percent, 2004—48 percent, 2005—47 percent, 2006—46 percent, and 2007–2009—45 percent. In 2010, the gift tax is cut to 35 percent while the other two transfer taxes are 0 percent (i.e., repealed). In 2011, the rates return to the 2001 level of 55 percent when the law sunsets. The unified tax credit, or applicable exclusion amount, for the estate tax increases from 2002 through 2009 as follows: 2002–2003—$1 million, 2004–2005—$1.5 million, 2006–2008—$2 million, 2009—$3.5 million. The unified credit, or applicable exclusion amount, returns to the 2001 level of $675,000 in 2011. The unified credit, or applicable exclusion amount, is increased to and remains at $1 million in 2002. This remains constant through 2010, until it returns to the 2001 level of $675,000.

The qualified family-owned business deduction that was added to the law by the Tax Reform Act of 1997 (discussed above) is repealed in its entirety in 2004. It reappears, however, in 2011 when the law sunsets.[4]

Several other credits may be allowed against the computed estate tax. Most common is a credit for state estate and inheritance taxes (described next). Depending upon the nature, situs, and other aspects of certain assets included in the gross estate, the following other credits may be allowed against the computed estate tax: prior transfers, foreign death taxes, death taxes on remainders, and recovery of taxes claimed as credits.

Filing of the Form 706 is due nine months after the decedents' date of death. The executor or administrator may request a six-month extension of time to file the return. If any tax is due with the return, an estimated payment of said tax is due six months from the date of death, with any balance due with the filing of the return.

While payment of the estate tax cannot normally be extended, IRC Section 6166 provides relief for certain estates. Should the estate assets include an interest in a closely held business that exceeds 35 percent of the adjusted gross estate, an election by the executor or administrator would permit the deferral and payment of the estate tax, that is attributable to the inclusion of the closely held business interest in the estate, in installments over several years. The requirements of this code section are strict; therefore, the executor or administrator should carefully consider all available options, advantages, and consequences of making this election.

One of these options, available to closely held corporations, is an IRC Section 303 stock redemption. If funds are available, the corporation may redeem stock held by the executor or

---

[4] For a more detailed discussion of EGTRRA, see Alan D. Kahn, Mark H. Levin, and Robert H. Colson, "The 2001 Tax Act, Estate Tax Repeal?" *The CPA Journal*, September 2001, p. 26.

administrator equal to an amount that may not exceed the sum of the estate taxes, outstanding debts, and administration expenses. While this option does not serve to defer the payment of estate taxes, it is an option that may be used in conjunction with or in lieu of the deferred payments under Section 6166 described above.

(iii) State Estate and Inheritance Taxes.   The estate tax in some states, such as New York, take the form of a tax on the right to transmit wealth that is similar to the federal estate tax. In other states, like New Jersey, an inheritance tax is applied to one's right to receive a portion of a decedent's estate. The state inheritance taxes are paid from estate funds by the representative, who will therefore withhold an appropriate amount from each legacy or establish a claim against those beneficiaries responsible for the tax by the terms of the will or by state law. Kinship of the beneficiary to the decedent is usually the controlling factor in determining exemptions and tax rates, with close relatives being favored.

Other states, such as Florida, assess an estate tax based on the amount of credit for state death taxes claimed on the federal estate tax return.

Almost all states provide for the tax to be at least equal to the federal credit for state death taxes if total inheritance taxes are less.

EGTRRA reduces the state death tax credit by 25 percent in 2002, 50 percent in 2003, and 75 percent in 2004. In 2005, the credit is repealed and replaced with a deduction for state death taxes actually paid. This will require almost every state to enact some form of conforming legislation to coordinate its statute with the federal changes.

The timing of the state's estate or inheritance tax return and payment of any taxes may differ from the federal rules. An executor or administrator should be acquainted with these rules to avoid penalty and interest assessments. A state return may be required to be filed even though no federal return is required if the gross estate is less than $1,000,000, and even if no state tax is due.

(iv) Generation Skipping Transfer Tax.   The Tax Reform Act of 1986 revised and imposes a new generation skipping transfer tax on most transfers made to individuals two generations (i.e., grandchildren) down from the donor or decedent. Most transfers prior to 1987 are exempt. Direct transfers or distributions from trusts to individuals two generations down will be subject to the tax if the transfer exceeds the allowable exemption.

A donor/decedent has a lifetime exemption of $1,000,000. Effective for decedents dying after December 31, 1998, the Taxpayer Relief Act of 1997 provides that the $1,000,000 exemption amount will be indexed for cost-of-living adjustments in $10,000 increments. Transfers in excess of this amount to grandchildren are subject to a flat tax in addition to the estate and gift tax. This flat tax is imposed at the highest marginal estate and gift tax rate, which is currently 55 percent. Consequently, it is conceivable that transferring $100 could cost $110 in estate/gift and generation skipping taxes. The law is relatively new and complex. Therefore, knowledge of the law and planning is important in order to minimize the impact of the tax.

In 2001, the lifetime exemption was indexed up to $1,060,000. It will continue to be indexed for inflation in 2002 (it is currently $1,100,000) and 2003. For 2004 through 2009, the lifetime exemption is equal to the unified credit or applicable exclusion amount. The tax is repealed for 2010 and then returns to the 2001 levels. The tax rate is changed in the same manner as the estate tax rates discussed above. In addition, some of the substantive rules were liberalized effective for transfers made after December 31, 2000.

(v) Estate Income Taxes.   The representative may be responsible for filing annual federal income tax returns for the estate for the period beginning the day after the date of death and ending when the estate assets are fully distributed. The returns are generally prepared on a cash basis and can be prepared on a fiscal year, rather than a calendar year, basis. Such an election is made with the filing of the initial return and is often done to cut off taxable income in the first year of the estate. Maintenance of books on a fiscal year basis and filing the request for an extension of time to file the return will also establish the fiscal year. If returns are not timely filed, the estate will then be required to file on a calendar year basis.

A federal income tax return is due if the estate earns gross income of $600 or more per year. A $600 exemption is allowed in computing the income subject to federal income taxes. Administration expenses, such as executor's commission and legal and accounting fees may be deducted if the representative does not elect to take these expenses on the federal estate tax return. If the estate distributes net income (gross income less expenses), such distributable net income is taxed to the recipient and the estate is allowed a corresponding deduction in computing its taxable income. Any remaining taxable income after deductions for exemption, expenses, and distributions is taxed at a rate specified in a table to be used exclusively for estates and trusts.

The income tax basis of estate assets are stepped up to their estate tax value. Therefore, should the executor or administrator sell any assets to raise cash, the assets' estate tax value is used to determine whether any gain or loss is realized upon the sale. There are, however, certain assets includable in the estate whose income tax basis carries over from the decedent. These assets are called *income* in respect of a decedent, or IRD, and are described in IRC Section 691. The following are examples of IRD: proceeds of U.S. savings bonds in excess of decedent's purchase price, IRAs, tax sheltered annuities and regular annuities, deferred compensation, and final paychecks and other remittances of compensation. Certain IRD give rise to income taxation upon receipt, while others do not cause taxation until they are redeemed or otherwise liquidated. Should an item of IRD be paid directly to an estate beneficiary or be distributed to the beneficiary from the estate, the same rules regarding income tax basis apply. An offsetting deduction is available to the executor or beneficiary who must recognize IRD in his gross income. The deduction is equal to that item's attributable share of the estate tax its inclusion in the estate has caused.

EGTRRA has modified the income tax rules relating to the step-up in basis discussed above beginning in 2010. To make up for the loss of revenue from the estate tax repeal, a new "carryover basis" regime will become effective. Under this regime, property acquired from a decedent will have a basis equal to the lesser of the decedent's basis or the fair market value of the property on the date of the decedent's death. A total $4.3 million of property may, however, still qualify to use the current step-up in basis rules. Up to $3 million of property passing to a surviving spouse, plus up to an aggregate of $1,300,000 of property passing to any beneficiaries will qualify for a step-up in basis. These new rules sunset after 2010, resulting in the modified carryover basis rules ending and the current step-up in basis rules being reinstated in 2011. So just in case, we should all start keeping better records in order to accurately reflect our tax basis in the assets we hold currently.

Estates must now make quarterly estimated tax payments in the same manner as individuals, except that an estate is exempt from making such payments during its first two taxable years. Accordingly, the penalties for underpayment of income tax are applicable to fiduciaries.

Some states also tax the income of estates, and the representative must see to it that such state statutes are complied with.

43.2 ACCOUNTING FOR ESTATES

(a) GOVERNING CONCEPTS.   The general concepts governing the accounting for decedent's estates are for the most part similar to those applicable to trusts, but there are some differences. The underlying equation expressing the accounting relationship is assets = accountability. However, the representative is concerned *not* with the long-term management of property for beneficiaries, but rather with the payment of debts and the orderly realization and distribution of the estate properties. The collection and the distribution of income are incidental to the main function of the estate's fiduciary.

Whenever an estate accounting is prepared, a reconciliation of the gross estate as finally determined for estate tax purposes should be made with the schedule of principal received at the date by the representative. Every difference should be explainable.

(i) Accounting Period.   The accounting period of the estate is determined by the dates set by the fiduciary or by the court for intermediate and final accountings; nevertheless, the books must be closed at least once a year for income tax purposes.

(ii) Principal and Income.   Unless otherwise provided for, the rules outlined below for the trustee should generally be followed by the representative in the allocation of receipts and disbursements to principal and income. Such distinctions, although not called for under the will, are frequently mandated by requirements of estate, inheritance, and income tax laws and regulations.

(iii) Treatment of Liabilities.   The representative picks up only the inventory of assets of the decedent at the inception of the estate. Claims against the estate, after presentation and review, are paid by the representative and are recorded as "debts paid." The payment of such debts reduces in proportion the accountability of the representative.

(b) RECORD-KEEPING SYSTEM.   No special type of bookkeeping system is prescribed by law, but a complete record of all transactions must be kept with sufficient detail to meet the requirements of the courts and of the estate, inheritance, and income tax returns. Much of the information may be in memorandum form outside of the formal accounting system.

The federal estate tax law requires information regarding assets beyond those ordinarily under the control of the representative (e.g., real estate). Such information must be assembled in appropriate form by the representative, who has responsibility for the estate tax return.

(i) Journals.   A single multicolumn journal is usually sufficient. It should incorporate cash receipts, cash disbursements, and asset inventory adjustments. Further, it is important to note and keep track of the distinction between principal and income.

(ii) Operation of a Going Business.   If the decedent was the individual proprietor of a going business and if the court or the will instructs the administrator or executor to continue the operation of the business, the bookkeeping procedure becomes somewhat complicated. The books of the business may be continued as distinct from the general estate books, or the transactions of the business may be combined with other estate transactions in one set of records. The best procedure, if the business is of at least moderate size, is to keep the operations of the business in a separate set of books and to set up a controlling accounting in the general books of the executor or administrator.

As soon as the representative takes charge of the business, the assets should be inventoried and the books closed, normally as of the date of death. The liabilities should be transferred to the list of debts to be paid by the representative, leaving the assets, the operating expenses and income, and the subsequently incurred liabilities to be recorded in the books of the company. An account should be opened in the books of the business for the representative that will show the same amount as the controlling account for the business in the books of the representative.

(iii) Final Accounting.   The "final" accounting is the report to the court of the handling of the estate affairs by the representative, if required. It presents, among other things, a plan for the distribution of the remainder of the assets of the estate and a computation of the commission due the representative for his services. If the court approves the report, it issues a decree putting the proposals into effect.

(c) REPORTS OF EXECUTOR OR ADMINISTRATOR.   The form of the reports of the fiduciary will vary according to the requirements of the court and to the character of the estate. In general, however, the representative "charges" himself with all of the property received and subsequently discovered plus gains on realizations, and "credits" (or discharges) himself with all disbursements for debts paid, expenses paid, legacies distributed, and realization losses. Each major item in the charge and discharge statement should be supported by a schedule showing detailed information. At any time during the administration of the estate, the excess of "charges" over "credits" should be represented by property in the custody of the fiduciary. It may be necessary to show the market value of property delivered to a legatee or trustee at the date of delivery, in which case the investment schedule will show the increase or decrease on distribution of assets, as well as from sales. The income schedule, when needed, should be organized to show the total income from each investment, the expenses chargeable against income, and the distribution of the remainder.

ESTATE OF JOHN SMITH
Charge and Discharge Statement
A. L. White, Executor
From April 7, 20XX, to December 15, 20XX

First, as to Principal:
The Executor charges himself as follows:

With amount of inventory at the date of death, April 7, Schedule A	$xxx	
With amount of assets discovered subsequent to date of death, Schedule B	xxx	
With gain on realization of assets, Schedule C	xxx	
		$xxx

The Executor credits himself as follows:

With loss on realization of assets, Schedule C	$xxx	
With amount paid for funeral and administrative expenses, Schedule D	xxx	
With amount paid on debts of the estate, Schedule F	xxx	
With distributions to legatees, Schedule G	xxx	
		xxx
Leaving a balance of principal, Schedule C, of		$xxx

Second, as to Income:
The Executor charges himself as follows:

With amount of income received, Schedule H	$xxx	

The Executor credits himself as follows:

With amount of administrative expenses chargeable to income, Schedule D	$xxx		
With distribution of income to legatees, Schedule I	xxx	xxx	
Leaving a balance of income, Schedule J			xxx
Leaving a balance of principal and income of			$xxx

Balance of principal and income to be distributed to those entitled
thereto, subject to the deduction of the Executor's commissions,
legal fees, and the expenses of this accounting, Schedule K.

Exhibit 43.2   Sample charge and discharge statement.

Exhibit 43.2 is typical of the charge-and-discharge statement, each item being supported by a schedule.

43.3 TRUSTS AND TRUSTEES—LEGAL BACKGROUND

(a) NATURE AND TYPES OF TRUSTS.   The trust relationship exists whenever one person holds property for the benefit of another. The trustee holds legal title to the property for the benefit of the beneficiary, or *cestui que trust*. The person from whom trust property is received is known as the *grantor*, *donor*, *settlor*, *creator*, or *trustor*.

An express trust is one in which the trustee, beneficiary, subject matter, and method of administration have been explicitly indicated. An implied trust may be created whether language of an instrument indicates the desirability of a trust but does not specify the details or when the trust relationship is assumed in order to prevent the results of fraud, breach of trust, or undue influence. The terms "constructive," "resulting," and "involuntary" trust are sometimes applied to such situations.

A testamentary trust is one created by a will. A living trust, or *trust inter vivos,* is created to take effect during the grantor's lifetime. Trusts are sometimes created by court order, as in the case of a guardianship.

A private trust is created for the benefit of particular individuals, while a public or charitable trust is for the benefit of an indefinite class of persons. Charitable trusts are discussed in Chapter 35.

A simple trust directs the trustee to distribute the entire net income of the trust to the named beneficiary. A complex trust gives the trustee the discretionary authority to distribute or accumulate the trust net income to or on behalf of the named beneficiary. In some instances, the trust may start off as complex and then convert to a simple trust upon the happening of a specified event, that is, the beneficiary's attainment of age 21 or 25.

A grantor trust exists when both the grantor and beneficiary are the same individual. A grantor trust may be implied if the grantor retains sufficient rights or controls over disposition of trust income and/or principal.

When a grantor establishes an irrevocable *trust inter vivos* and transfers assets to it, the grantor has made a completed gift of the property transferred for income, gift, and estate tax purposes. Should the grantor retain any of the rights enumerated in IRC Sections 671–679, however, the grantor will be continue to be treated as the grantor or owner of the trust property for income tax purposes only. The grantor will be taxed on the income of the trust instead of the trust or trust beneficiaries (even if they receive a distribution of this trust income). This is referred to as an *intentionally defective grantor trust* (IDGT) and can be used as an effective estate and financial planning tool.

A trust may include a spendthrift clause that prohibits the beneficiary from assigning his interest before receiving it or prevents creditors from enforcing their claims against the income or principal of a trust fund, or both.

Trusts are often used for business purposes, as when property is transferred by a deed of trust instead of a mortgage, when trustees are appointed to hold title and perform other functions under a bond issue, or when assets are assigned to a trustee for the benefit of creditors. Bankruptcy and insolvency are discussed in Chapter 45.

(i) Limitations on Private Trusts.   A public trust may be established for an indefinite period, but a trust may not suspend indefinitely the power of anyone to transfer the trust property. The common law rule, otherwise known as the *Rule against Perpetuities*, limits the duration of a private trust to 21 years after the death of some person who is living when the trust is created. Another common limitation in certain states is "two lives in being" at the origin of the trust.

Accumulation of the income of a trust is also restricted by state law. A common provision, for example, is that in the case of a trust created for the benefit of a minor, the income can be accumulated only during the minority of the beneficiary. Even the income of a charitable trust cannot be accumulated for an "unreasonable" period.

(ii) Revocation of Trusts.   A completed trust cannot be revoked without the consent of all the beneficiaries unless the right to revoke has been expressly reserved by the grantor. Trusts are therefore sometimes classified as "revocable" or "irrevocable."

(b) APPOINTMENT AND REMOVAL OF TRUSTEES.   In general, anyone competent to make a will or a contract is competent to create a trust. The trustee must be one who is capable of taking and holding property and who has the legal capacity and natural ability to execute the trust.

(i) Choice of Trustee.   The decedent's will usually names the trustee for a testamentary trust. A grantor who is establishing an inter vivos trust will usually appoint one or more of the following to act as trustee: a relative; his professional adviser, that is, attorney, accountant, broker; a business associate; or an institutional entity, such as a bank or trust company. Each type of trustee has its pros and cons; however, the most important concern is not to choose a trustee that will cause adverse income tax consequences.

(ii) Methods of Appointment.   Seven of the means by which trustees are appointed are:

1. *By deed or declaring of trust.* The creator of the trust names the trustees in the instrument.
2. *By will.* The same person may be both executor and trustee under a will, but this dual capacity should be clearly indicated.
3. *By agreement.*

4. *By the court.* The court will appoint a trustee when a trust may fail for lack of a trustee, when a trustee refuses to serve or has died, or when a vacancy from any cause exists and no other means have been provided for filing the vacancy.

5. *By implication of law.*

6. *By self-perpetuating boards.* When vacancies occur, they are filed by the remaining members of the board.

7. *By the exercise of a power of appointment.* The instrument creating the trust may give the remaining trustees, beneficiaries, or any other person the power to appoint a trustee to fill a vacancy. Specific instructions should be included in the instrument as to the situation establishing a vacancy, the persons who may be appointed, and the manner of making the appointment.

(iii) Acceptance or Disclaimer. Acceptance of an appointment as trustee may be made by positive statement, by qualifying as executor if the appointment is by will, by the acceptance of property of the trust, or by other acts from which acceptance may be presumed. An individual may refuse to accept an appointment as a trustee and should execute and deliver a disclaimer expressing rejection of the appointment.

(iv) Resignation of Trustee. According to the Restatement of the Law of Trusts 2d (1 Trusts A.L.I. 234):

A trustee who has accepted the trust cannot resign except (a) with the permission of a proper court; or (b) in accordance with the terms of the trust; or (c) with the consent of all the beneficiaries, if they have capacity to give such consent.

(v) Removal of Trustee. The court has power to remove a trustee and appoint a successor under certain circumstances. Scott cites, among others, the following six grounds upon which trustees have been removed:

1. Failure to exercise discretion
2. Self-dealing
3. Failure to keep proper accounts, and mingling with trustee's own funds
4. Incompetency and neglect of duty
5. Conversion of trust property
6. Refusal to obey orders of the court[5]

(c) POWERS AND DUTIES OF TRUSTEES. The powers of trustees are obtained both from the provisions and implications of the instrument creating the trust and from the general laws pertaining to the trust relationship. The instrument may either expand or restrict the general powers, except that it may not relieve the trustee from liability for gross negligence, bad faith, or dishonesty. The powers of a trustee may be either (1) imperative or mandatory or (2) permissive or discretionary. In other words, they must either be exercised definitely and positively within a given length of time or upon the occurrence of some contingency, or they may be exercised at the discretion of the trustee.

(i) General Powers. The nine general powers of a trustee, which include all necessary incidental powers, are:

1. To take and retain possession of the trust property
2. To invest trust funds so as to yield a fair income

---

[5] A. W. Scott, *The Law of Trusts*, Fourth Edition (Little Brown, 1987), 1995 Supplement.

3. To sell and reinvest when necessary

4. To sell and convey real estate when necessary to carry out the provisions of the trust

5. To release real estate so that it may earn income

6. To pay for repairs, taxes, and other such expenses in connection with trust property

7. To sue or defend suits when necessary

8. To make contracts that are necessary to carry out the purposes of the trust

9. To pay over and distribute the trust property to those entitled to it

The trustee secures possession of the trust property and holds title in his own name. All debtors should be notified of the change in ownership of claims against them in order to hold them directly liable to the trustee. All debts due the trust estate should be collected promptly. Trust property must be kept separate from the property of anyone else. The trustee will be liable for any loss occurring as a result of their mingling of funds or other property. An exception is usually made when a trust company is acting as trustee; it may deposit cash in trust funds with itself or may mingle various trust funds and deposit same with designated depositories.

(ii) Duties.   The 14 duties of the trustee are outlined by Scott as follows:

1. To administer the trust as long as he continues as trustee

2. To administer the trust solely in the interest of the beneficiary (the duty of loyalty as a fiduciary)

3. Not to delegate to others the performance of acts which the trustee sought personally to perform

4. To keep clear and accurate accounts

5. To give to beneficiaries upon their request complete and accurate information as to the administration of the trust

6. To exercise such care and skill as a man of ordinary prudence would exercise in dealing with his own property; and if the trustee possesses greater skill than that of an ordinary prudent man, he must exercise the skill he has

7. To take reasonable steps to secure control of trust property and to keep control of it

8. To use care and skill to preserve the trust property. The standard of care and skill is that of a man of ordinary prudence

9. To take reasonable steps to realize on claims which he holds in trust and to defend claims of third persons against the trust estate

10. To keep the trust property separate from his own property and separate from property held upon other trusts; and to designate trust property as property of the trust

11. To refrain in ordinary circumstances from lending trust money without security

12. To invest trust funds so that they will be productive of income

13. To pay the net income of the trust to the beneficiary at reasonable intervals; and if there are two or more beneficiaries he must deal with them impartially

14. Where there are several trustees, it is the duty of each of them, unless otherwise provided by the trust instrument, to participate in the administration of the trust, and each trustee must use reasonable care to prevent the others from committing a breach of trust[6]

(d) PROPER TRUST INVESTMENTS.   The trustee is under a duty to invest funds in such a way as to receive an income without improperly risking the loss of the principal. The only general rule as to investment is that the trustee is under a duty to make such investments as a prudent man (the "prudent man" rule or "Massachusetts" rule) would make of his own property, having primarily

---

[6] Id.

in view the preservation of the estate and the amount and regularity of the income to be derived. In some states ("legal-list" states), the legislatures tell trustees in what they must or may invest funds unless the terms of the trust otherwise provide.

Eight kinds of investments that are almost universally condemned are summarized by Scott as follows:

1. Purchase of securities on margin
2. Purchase of speculative shares of stock
3. Purchase of bonds selling at large discount because of uncertainty of repayment at maturity
4. Purchase of securities in new and untried enterprises
5. Use of trust property in the carrying on of a trade or business, even though it is not an untried enterprise
6. Purchase of land or other things for the purpose of resale, unless authorized by the terms of the trust
7. Purchase of second and other junior mortgages
8. Making unsecured loans to individuals or firms or corporations[7]

Three types of investments that are almost universally permitted include:

1. Bonds of the United States or of the state or of a municipality thereof
2. First mortgages on land
3. Corporate bonds of a high investment grade

In 1990, the American Law Institute adopted the Uniform Prudent Investor Act (the UPIA) and published it in the *Restatement of the Law of Trusts*, Third Edition. The UPIA incorporates a new Prudent Investor Rule that has since been adopted by a significant majority of the states in a form that is similar to, or somewhat comparable to, the scope of these new rules. The Restatement embodies three main themes:

1. Although it is thought that a trustee may not delegate any of his duties, other than certain ministerial duties, this position is relaxed in that a trustee should, or even must, delegate investment authority to skilled professionals should they lack the required expertise or experience to properly manage the assets within the trust.
2. The costs incurred by the trustee in performing his duties must be reasonable.
3. A trustee is now charged with the responsibility for maintaining the trust portfolio so as to keep pace with inflation. In other words, trustees should invest for the maximum total return on investment without regard for distinctions between principal and income. This is referred to as *modern portfolio theory*, permitting trustees to invest for capital appreciation as well as current income in the form of interest, dividends, rents, and so forth.

(e) TRUSTEE'S PERSONAL LIABILITIES AND LIABILITY FOR ACTS OF CO-TRUSTEE. A trustee is liable to the beneficiary for failure to fulfill his duties under the statutes, general rules of equity, or the provisions of the trust indenture.

A trustee must be particularly circumspect in all matters affecting his own property or benefit. He is personally liable for torts committed by himself or his agents and, unless his agreement states otherwise, is personally liable on all contracts made on behalf of the trust.

A trustee is not responsible for loss by theft, embezzlement, or accident if he has taken all the precautions that a careful businessman takes in guarding his own property, and if he is strictly following his line of duty as a trustee. If a trustee is not insolvent and mixes trust property with his

---

[7] Id.

own, the beneficiary may take the whole, leaving the trustee to prove his own part. If the trustee is insolvent, the beneficiary shares with the other creditors unless definite property can be identified as belonging to the trust. Interest will be charged against a trustee who has mingled trust funds with his own. If bank deposits are made in the individual name of the trustee, he will be treated as a guarantor of the solvency of the bank, even though he uses care in his choice of the bank and has not in any way misused the funds.

In general, a trustee is not liable for losses caused by the default or negligence of a co-trustee unless he has cooperated with the trustee who is at fault, or has known of the trustee's misconduct and has not taken any steps to prevent it. If, however, each trustee should have interested himself in the matter in question, such as the proper investment of funds, each would be responsible even though he took no part in or knew nothing of the misconduct. All trustees should act together in handling the trust property and should apply to the court for instructions in case they cannot agree. Unanimity is usually required for all important decisions in the case of private trusts, but a majority of a board of trustees may act for a charitable trust.

In certain circumstances, a trustee may become personally liable for the unpaid estate taxes of a decedent under the theory of transferee liability. Ordinarily, the beneficiary of an estate or trust is ultimately liable for any unpaid estate or gift taxes due on the transfer. The liability is equal to the value of the property received by the recipient as of the date of transfer. A review of IRC Sections 6324 and 6901, primarily, is in order. For example, the trustee of an inter vivos trust that is included in the gross estate for estate tax purposes could result in the trustee being personally liable, as opposed to the beneficiaries, for payment of any attributable estate taxes. Certain trust distributions trigger the GSTT, discussed in Subsection 43.1(l), requiring the trustee to pay this tax. As a result of this possibility, a trustee should consider maintaining a reserve until he is satisfied that all such taxes are satisfied. Upon making distributions, the trustee should also consider requesting that the beneficiaries indemnify him for any taxes that may be assessed against him.

(f) GUARDIANS.   If a person is incompetent to manage his own property because of a disability such as infancy or mental incompetency, a guardian will be appointed by the probate or other appropriate court. The court must approve the appointment of a guardian by will. A guardian is a trustee in the strictest sense of the term. He is directly under the supervision of the court. If possible, only the income from the property should be used for the maintenance and education of the beneficiary; permission must be granted by the court before the principal can be used for this purpose. Any sale of real estate must be authorized by the court. A guardian should have the authorization of the court or the direction of a will before paying money to a minor or to anyone for the minor; otherwise he may be compelled to pay the amount again when the minor becomes of age.

(g) TESTAMENTARY TRUSTEE.   The work of the trustee appointed by a will begins when the executor sets aside the trust fund out of the estate assets. One person may serve as both executor and trustee under a will.

The testamentary trustee has slightly more freedom in handling the funds than does the executor, and his responsibility may be made less rigorous by provisions of the will. He holds, invests, and cares for the property, and disposes of it or its income as directed by the will. A trustee should have specific authority of a will or the court, or the consent of everyone interested, before carrying on a business. If there are several executors, one can act alone, but trustees must act jointly.

(h) COMPENSATION OF TRUSTEES.   Trustees are usually allowed compensation for their work, either by provision of the trust instrument or by statute. The statutory provision is usually a graduated percentage of the funds handled.

A trustee is entitled to be repaid expenditures reasonably and properly incurred in the care of trust property. The compensation is usually allocated to principal and income in accordance with the specific provision of the indenture or as provided by statute or rules of law.

(i) RIGHTS OF BENEFICIARY.   The beneficiary has an equitable title to the trust property, that is, he can bring suit in a court of equity to enforce his rights and to prevent misuse of the property by the trustee. Unless the instrument by which the trust is created provides otherwise, the beneficiary, if of age, can sell or otherwise dispose of his equitable estate in the property.

The beneficiary has the right to inspect and take copies of all papers, records, and data bearing on the administration of the trust property and income that are in the hands of the trustee. The beneficiary may have an accounting ordered whenever there is any reason for suspicion, or any failure to allow inspection or to make satisfactory reports and statements. Whenever it seems advisable, a court of equity will order an accounting.

The beneficiary may have an injunction issued to restrain the trustee from proceeding with any unauthorized action, if such action will result in irremediable damage. The beneficiary may present a petition to the court for the removal of a trustee but must be able to prove bad faith, negligence, lack of ability, or other such cause for the removal. The trustee is entitled to a formal trial.

The beneficiary can, if it is possible to do so, follow the trust property and have it subjected to the trust, even if a substitution has been made for the original property, unless it comes into the hands of an innocent holder for value. If the trust property cannot be traced or is in the hands of an innocent holder for value, the beneficiary may bring action against the trustee in a court of equity for breach of trust.

If the beneficiary is of age and mentally competent, he may approve or ratify acts of the trustee that would otherwise be a violation of the trustee's duties or responsibilities.

(j) DISTINCTION BETWEEN PRINCIPAL AND INCOME.   Probably the most difficult problem of the trustee is to differentiate between principal (corpus) and income. The intention of the creator of the trust is binding if it can be ascertained, but in the absence of instructions to the contrary the general legal rules must be followed.

The life tenant (the present beneficiary) is entitled to the net income and the remainderman (the future beneficiary) to the principal, as legally determined. The principal is the property itself that constitutes the trust fund, and the income is the accumulation of funds and other property arising from the investment or other use of the trust principal. Increases or decreases in the value of the assets that constitute the trust fund affect only the principal. The income determined under these rules is not always the same as taxable income or income as determined by generally accepted accounting principles (GAAP). The life tenant is entitled to receive only the net income from all sources for the entire term of his tenancy. He is not allowed to select the income from only those investments that are lucrative.

The existing rules regarding principal and income are based on the Uniform Principal and Income Act of 1962 (UPAIA). These rules are, to a great extent, at odds with a trustee's ability to comply with the modern portfolio theory contained in the Uniform Prudent Investor Act described earlier. As one commentator noted,[8] the incompatibility of the UPIA and UPAIA were reconciled in 1997 by the National Conference of Commissioners on Uniform State Laws. The revised UPAIA accomplishes:

> this result by way of an adjustment power conferred upon trustees, pursuant to which the trustee is empowered to allocate traditional trust accounting income (e.g., interest, dividends, rents) to principal and perhaps more importantly, to allocate to income what is typically considered principal. Thus, a trustee can increase the amount currently distributable to a beneficiary, for example, by allocating capital appreciation to income. Some states (New York, New Jersey, Delaware, and Missouri) added an alternative approach to their respective adoptions of the new UPAIA: an optional unitrust provision. Instead of being limited to the annual accounting income

---

[8] The commentator is Linda B. Hirschon, Esq., of Greenberg Tauig LLP, New York, in an updated version of her article "The Unitrust Alternative, A Framework for Total Return Investing," *Tax Management Memorandum*, Vol. 42, No. 23 (November 5, 2001). The updated version of the article appeared in a NYS Bar Association CLE publication entitled, "New York's New Principal and Income Act, the Power of Adjustment Between Principal and Income and the New 4% Unitrust Option."

actually realized by the trust in any year, the current beneficiary of a unitrust is entitled to an amount equal to a fixed percentage of the value of the trust's assets determined annually. As a result, the trustee is free to invest for total return absent the need to produce sufficient income to satisfy the current beneficiary. By adopting the unitrust alternative, the trustee is relieved of the obligation to determine each year whether an equitable adjustment is warranted. In addition, the unitrust approach provides the current beneficiary with the certainty of knowing what he or she is entitled to each year instead of having to await the trustee's possible exercise of its discretionary adjustment power.

All of the statutes give testators and grantors the ability to opt out of the statutory language by defining how they want principal and income to be recognized and charged. The UPAIA in effect in a given state is operative only if the trust document or will is silent. The U.S. Treasury Department and Internal Revenue Service have recognized this new trend in trust accounting and have issued Proposed Treasury Regulation Section 1.643(a) through (d).

The following describes the principal and income rules under the UPAIA of 1962. Trustees are advised to seek to professional counseling to determine whether the 1962 or 1997 revised rules are in effect in their respective state.

(i) Receipts of Principal.   The following ten receipts of cash or other property have been held to be part of the corpus of the trust and therefore to belong to the remainderman or persons entitled to the corpus:

1. Interest accrued to the beginning of the trust. Bond coupons are not apportioned in the absence of a statute providing for such a division.
2. Rent accrued to the beginning of the trust. Under the common law, rent was not apportioned according to the time expired.
3. Excess of selling price of trust assets over their value in the original inventory or over its purchase price. Appreciation, in general, belongs to the trust corpus.
4. The value of assets existing at the time the original inventory was taken but not included in the inventory.
5. Dividends (see discussion below).
6. Proceeds of the sale of stock rights.
7. Profit from the completion of executory contracts of a decedent.
8. Profits earned prior to the beginning of the trust on the operations of a partnership or sole proprietorship.
9. Insurance money received for a fire that occurred prior to the date of the beginning of the trust, or after that date if the property is in the hands of the trustee for the benefit of the trust in general.
10. If trust property is mortgaged, the proceeds may be said to be principal assets, although there is no increase in the equity of the remainderman.

(ii) Disbursements of Principal.   The following 12 payments, distribution, and exhaustion of assets have been held to be chargeable to the corpus:

1. Excess of the inventory value or purchase price of an asset over the amount realized from its sale.
2. Payment of debts owed, including accruals, at the date of the beginning of the trust.
3. Real estate taxes assessed on or before the date of the beginning of the trust. In the case of special assessments made during the administration of the trust, the remainderman may pay the assessment and the life tenant may be charged interest thereon annually during the life of the trust, or else some other equitable adjustment will be made between them.

4. Any expenditures that result in improvements of the property, except those made voluntarily by a life tenant for his own benefit, and all expenditures on newly acquired property that are necessary to put it into condition to rent or use.

5. Wood on the property that the life tenant uses for fuel, fences, and other similar purposes. The life tenant may operate mines, wells, quarries, and so on, that have been opened and operated on the property.

6. Losses due to casualty and theft of general trust assets.

7. Expenses of administration except those directly pertaining to the administration of income. For example, legal expenses incurred in defending the trust estate are chargeable to principal; however, the expenses of litigation in an action to protest only the income are payable out of income.

8. Trustee's commissions in respect to the receipts or disbursements out of principal. Commissions computed on income are ordinarily payable out of income.

9. Brokerage fees and other expenses for changing investments should generally be chargeable to principal, since they are a part of the cost of purchase or sale.

10. Income taxes on gains made from disposition of principal assets.

11. Carrying charges on unproductive real estate, unless the terms of the trust direct the trustee to retain the property even though it is unproductive.

12. Cost of improvements to property held as part of the principal.

(iii) **Receipts of Income.**   The following six receipts have been held to be income and to belong to the life tenants or persons entitled to the income:

1. Interest, rent, and so on, accruing after the date of the beginning of the trust. The proceeds of a foreclosed mortgage may be apportionable between principal and income. Interest includes the increment in securities issued at a discount.

2. Increase in value of investments made by the trustee from accumulated undistributed income.

3. Dividends (see discussion below).

4. Crops harvested during the trust.

5. Royalties or other income from operation of mines, quarries, or wells that were made productive prior to the beginning of the trust, or were developed or leased in cooperating with the remainderman.

6. Net profit from the operation of a business.

(iv) **Disbursements of or Charges to Income.**   The following eight items have been held to be chargeable against the income of the trust:

1. Interest payable, accruing during the life of the trust

2. Any expenses incurred in earning or collecting income, caring for trust property, or preserving its value, and an appropriate share of administration fees and expenses

3. Income tax except those levied on gains from sale of principal assets

4. Premiums on trustee's bond

5. Provision for amortization of wasting property, including leasehold interests, royalties, oil and gas wells, machinery, and farm implements (see discussion of depreciation below)

6. Provision for amortization of improvements to trust property when such improvements will not outlive the duration of the trust

7. Losses of property due to the negligence of the life tenant

8. Losses due to casualty and theft of income assets

(k) PRINCIPAL AND INCOME—SPECIAL PROBLEMS. The distinction between principal and income also involves a consideration of such problems as unproductive property, accruals, dividends, bond premium and discount, and depreciation and depletion.

(i) Unproductive Property. When the trustee is required to sell unproductive property and the sale is delayed, the net proceeds of the sale should be apportioned between principal and income. The net proceeds are allocated by determining the sum that, with interest thereon at the current rate of return on trust investments, would equal the net proceeds, and the sum so determined is treated as principal and the balance as income (Restatement of Trusts 2d, § 241). Apportionment between principal and income is generally applicable to real estate, but it has been applied in the case of personal property also. It does not matter whether the property is sold at a gain or a loss.

(ii) Accruals. There are two dates at which the matter of accruals becomes significant. The first is the date at which the trust begins. Income and expenses accrued at that date belong to the corpus of the estate. The second date is the one when the life interest terminates. Income and expenses accrued at that date belong to the life tenant or his estate.

Larsen and Mosich provide a summarization of the general rule of accrual as applied to certain items, from which the following is taken:

1. *Interest.* Interest accrued on receivables and investments at the date the trust is established is considered part of the trust corpus. Exceptions are interest on (a) savings accounts when the interest is paid only if the deposit remains until the end of the interest period, and (b) coupon bonds when the payment is contingent upon the owner presenting the coupon, in which case the date of receipt is controlling. Similar rules apply to the accrual of interest expense.

2. *Rent.* The accrual of rent prior to the beginning of the trust is considered by many states as a portion of a trust corpus. Any rent accruing between the date of the establishment of the trust and the termination of the tenancy belongs to the income beneficiary. Rent expense is handled similarly.

3. *Dividends.* Ordinary cash dividends are not divisible. If the dividend is declared and the date of record has passed before the trust is created, the dividend is a part of the corpus. Otherwise it is considered income to the trust. A stock dividend is treated in the same manner in many states . . . . [For a discussion of special treatment of cash and stock dividends under the Massachusetts and Pennsylvania rules, see below.]

4. *Property taxes.* Taxes which have been levied on trust property prior to the beginning of the trust are charges against the principal. Any taxes assessed on the basis of trust property held for the benefit of the income beneficiary are chargeable against income. Special assessments made during the administration of the trust are usually paid by the remainderman, although in some cases where the assessment is for improvements that benefit the life tenant, a part or all of the assessment may be charged against income. When the assessment is paid from the corpus, interest on the funds advance may be charged against income.

5. *Profits.* Income earned by a partnership or proprietorship does not accrue. The income that is earned prior to the creation of the trust is considered a part of the principal of the trust. In many cases a partnership is dissolved upon the death of a partner, and there may be no income earned after the trust is established. In the event that the business continues by specific direction of the grantor or provision of the partnership agreement, any income earned after the trust is created is income of the trust.

6. *Executory contracts.* Any profits earned on the completion of an executory contract by the trustee is an addition to the principal of the trust.

7. *Livestock and crops.* Any livestock born during the tenancy under the trust is considered income, except to the extent that the herd must be maintained as directed by the grantor, in which case the increase must be divided between principal and income in a manner which honors this intention. If the principal includes land, any crops harvested during this tenancy are considered income of the trust.

8. *Premium returns.* Any return of premium or dividend on insurance policies which was paid prior to the creation of the trust is a part of the principal. This is considered realization of assets.

9. *Royalties.* Royalties or other income from the operation of mines or other natural resource deposits which were made operative before the trust was created or which were developed in cooperation with the remainderman are income to the trust. [9]

(iii) Dividends.   The determination of whether a dividend is principal or income involves a consideration of applicable state laws. Ordinary cash dividends declared during the period of the trust belong to the income beneficiary. An ordinary stock dividend is usually regarded as income except in states that follow the Massachusetts rule. This rule holds that all cash dividends are treated as income and that stock dividends are entirely principal.

Some states follow the Pennsylvania rule, which holds that, in regard to extraordinary dividends, it is not the form of the dividend but its source that determines whether and to what extent it is income or principal. Generally, under this rule extraordinary dividends are income if declared out of earnings accruing to the corporation during the period of the trust, but they are principal if declared out of earnings accruing prior to the creation of the trust. Thus, if such dividends cause the book value of the corporation's stock to be reduced below the book value that existed at the creation of the trust, that portion of the dividend equivalent to the impairment of book value is principal and only the remainder is income. The present Pennsylvania law provides that stock dividends of six percent or less "shall be deemed income" unless the instrument provides to the contrary.

Although there is still wide diversity among the courts and state statutes in the apportionment of corporate distributions, Scott points out that the recent trend has been in favor of the Massachusetts rule.[10] The Uniform Principal and Income Act (Uniform Laws Annotated, Vol. 7B, § 5) follows the essence of the Massachusetts rule in treating cash and other property dividends as income and stock dividends as principal.

(iv) Premium and Discount on Bonds.   The necessity of accumulating bond discount or amortizing bond premium in order to determine the correct interest income still gives rise to a great deal of confusion in trust and estate administration. In general, it appears that most courts support the amortization of premium on bonds purchased by the trustee, but there has been little or no support of the accumulation of discount. Any difference between the inventory value and the face value of the bonds taken over by the trustee is usually treated as an adjustment of principal.

In the event of redemption before maturity, it has been held that the proper procedure is to amortize the premium to the date of redemption; the unamortized balance is a loss borne by principal. If a bonus is received, it should be credited to principal.

Scott suggests:

> It might well be held that the whole matter [of amortizing premium and discount] should be left to the discretion of the trustee, and if he is not guilty of an abuse of discretion in unduly favoring some of the beneficiaries at the expense of the others, the court should not interpose its authority. This, of course, is the result reached where such discretion is expressly conferred upon the trustee by the terms of the trust.[11]

(v) Depreciation and Depletion.   In determining whether provision must be made for depreciation and depletion, it is essential to consider carefully the intentions and wishes of the trustor. If the trustor intended to give the full, undiminished income to the life tenant even though the principal would thereby be partially or completely exhausted, no deduction from income for depletion or

---

[9] E. J. Larsen and A. N. Mosich, *Modern Advanced Accounting*, Sixth Edition (Shephards McGraw-Hill, New York, 1994).

[10] Scott, *The Law of Trusts.*

[11] Id.

depreciation is allowed. If, however, there is an expressed or implied intention to preserve the principal intact, the trustee is required to withhold from income an amount sufficient to maintain the original property of the trust.

When the trustor's intentions regarding the receipts from wasting property cannot be determined from the trust instrument, then, according to Scott, the inference is that the trustor did not intend that the life beneficiary should receive the whole income at the expense of the principal.[12] Thus, when the trustee holds wasting property, including royalties, patents, mines, timberlands, machinery, and equipment, he is under a duty to make a provision for amortization of such property. The general rule has been applied to new buildings erected and improvements made by the trustee; however, the courts have generally held that buildings that were part of the trust estate at the beginning of the trust need not be depreciated. The courts have, in effect, refused to treat the buildings as wasting property.

The trend appears to be in the direction of adopting principles of depreciation followed in accounting practice. For example, the position taken in Section 13 of the Revised Uniform Principal and Income Act is that, with respect to charges against income and principal, there shall be:

> . . . a reasonable allowance for depreciation under generally accepted accounting principles, but no allowance shall be made for depreciation of that portion of any real property used by a beneficiary as a residence or for depreciation of any property held by the trustee on the effective date of this Act for which the trustee is not then making an allowance for depreciation.

(l) TAX STATUS OF TRUST. Unless the trust qualifies as an exempt organization (charitable, educational, etc.), or unless the income of the trust is taxable to the grantor (revocable, or grantor retains substantial dominion and control), the income of the trust is subject to the federal income tax in a manner similar to the case of an individual. In general, the trust is treated as a conduit for tax purposes and is allowed a deduction for its income that is distributed or distributable currently to the beneficiaries. The trust may also be subject to state income taxes, personal property taxes, and so on. A tax service should be consulted for the latest provisions and rulings as to deductions, credits, rates, and filing requirements.

It is important to note that although trusts and estates are taxed similarly, there are two major differences. Trusts must be operated on a calendar year basis, whereas estates may operate on a fiscal year, usually tied to the decedent's date of death. Secondly, trusts must pay estimated taxes in the same fashion as individuals. Estates, on the other hand, are exempt from this requirement, but only for their first two tax years.

The impact of the Revenue Reconciliation Act of 1993 (RRA) substantially compressed the income tax rates applicable to trusts and estates. Indexed from its original level effective for tax years beginning in 1993, trusts reach the top 38.6 percent marginal bracket at $9,200 of taxable income in 2002. Compare this to married individuals filing jointly, for example, where the 38.6 percent top marginal bracket is not reached until taxable income exceeds $307,050 in 2002. That is quite a disparity. Trustees of existing trusts need to consider their responsibility to take this disparity into consideration when reviewing the mix of assets in the current trust portfolio and when exercising their discretion to make discretionary distributions of income. In certain cases, where older trusts were established with a different rate structure in mind, and where state law permits, a trustee may want to consider bringing a court proceeding to reform the terms of the trust accordingly. If the settlor is still alive, all of the beneficiaries are adults, and trust is irrevocable, it may be possible under state law, as it is in New York, to revoke the trust and create a new one if the gift tax cost is not excessive.

(m) TERMINATION OF TRUST. A trust may be terminated by the fulfillment of its purpose or by the expiration of the period for which the trust was created. A trust may also be terminated under a power reserved by the grantor or by the consent of all beneficiaries unless continuance of the trust is necessary to carry out a material purpose for which it was created.

---

[12] Id.

When the trust is terminated, the trustee is discharged when he has transferred the property to those entitled to it according to the terms of the trust instrument. The trustee, to protect himself, may secure a formal release of all claims from all who receive any of the property and are competent to consent, may require a bond of indemnity from the beneficiaries, or may refuse to act without a decree of court.

43.4 ACCOUNTING FOR TRUSTS

(a) GENERAL FEATURES.   Generally, accounting for a trust is the same as accounting for an estate. The emphasis for a trust, however, is that principal or corpus versus income should be properly distinguished. Two interests, that is, current or life versus future or remainder, usually serve different parties. One party may have a current or income interest whereas another party holds a future or remainder interest. Therefore, allocation between principal and income is important. See discussion at Section 43.3(j) for an update on these issues.

(i) Accounting Period.   The accounting period for a trust depends somewhat on the nature of the trust and the provisions of the trust instrument. Reports may be required by the court or may be submitted to other interested parties at various intervals during the life of the trust.

(ii) Recording Principal and Income.   A careful distinction must be made between principal (corpus) and income in recording the transactions. The legal theory seems to be that the principal of a trust is not a certain amount of monetary value but is a certain group of assets that must be capable of isolation from the assets that compose the undistributed income. Actual separation of cash and investments is difficult because of such factors as accrued interest and amortization of bond premium and discount. Ordinarily it is sufficient to keep one account for cash and one for each type of investment, and to indicate the claims of the principal and income in the total.

Accounts should be kept with the beneficiaries to show the amounts due and paid to each.

The trustee should keep records that will meet both the requirements of the income tax law and regulations and the law relating to principal and income. There are apt to be conflicts at various points in the determination of taxable income and of income belonging to the life tenant. The only solution is to keep sufficiently detailed records so that all of the information is available for both purposes. In some cases, it may be necessary to prepare reconciliation schedules in order to keep a record of the differences between the income tax calculation of net income and the application of trust accounting principles of accounting income.

See discussion at Section 43.3(j) for an update on these issues.

(iii) Accounting for Multiple Trusts.   Several trusts may be created by a single instrument, such as trusts originating through the provisions of a will, and a single trustee may have to keep his accounts so as to be able to prepare a report of the administration of the estate as a whole and also a separate report of each trust.

(iv) Treatment of Liabilities.   In some cases, trust property will be encumbered with an unpaid mortgage or other obligation of which the trustee must keep a record. It is also possible that in handling the business of the trust some liabilities will be incurred. These are usually current in character, and the entry made at the time of payment, charging the amount to an asset or expense account, is usually sufficient.

(b) RECORD-KEEPING SYSTEM.   The bookkeeping system requirements for the trust, like those for any other enterprise, vary with the complexity of the situation. The trustee should keep a complete record of all transactions relating to the trust in order to protect himself, to make reports to the court, to prepare income tax returns, and to give the beneficiaries of the trust an adequate accounting. No special type of bookkeeping system is prescribed by law, but a complete record of all transactions must be kept in such a way that the reports required by the courts can be prepared. All records should be kept in permanent form and should be carefully preserved and filed for possible future reference.

(i) Journals. In a comparatively simple situation, one multicolumn journal may be satisfactory, but in most cases a set of various journals should be kept.

(ii) Principal and Income Accounts. It is necessary to distinguish carefully between principal and income in the administration of trusts. The Trust Principal account and the Undistributed Trust Income account record the net worth or capital of the trust. It will usually be necessary to analyze those accounts for income tax purposes, just as equity is analyzed in corporation accounts to obtain all of the information required for the income tax return. There may be some conflicts between income as defined by the law relating to the administration of trusts and taxable income as defined by the income tax law and regulations.

(iii) Opening Books of Account. If an inventory has been filed with the court, such as an executor's or guardian's inventory, the trustee must record the same values in his accounts. If no such inventory was filed, the trustee should have one prepared that will serve as the basis of his property accounting. Whenever possible, the inventory should contain the same values as those required for income tax purposes in determining the gain or loss from the sale of property. In any case, a record of such values must be available.

(iv) Amortization of Bond Premium or Discount. When bonds are taken over in the inventory at more or less than their face value, the difference between the inventory value and the amount received at maturity is ordinarily treated as a loss or gain on realization; but when bonds are purchased at a premium or discount, the difference between the amount paid and the amount to be received at maturity should be treated as an adjustment of the interest earned and should be written off during the remaining life of the bond. If the amount is not large, the "straight-line" method may be used, that is, the total premium or discount is divided by the number of remaining interest payments to obtain the amount to be written off at each interest date. If the amount is large, amortization tables may be used in which the effective rate of interest is applied to the present value of the bond to obtain the income due to the life tenant.

(v) Depreciation. Except for buildings forming part of the inventory at the date of origin of the trust, or in trusts where contrary provisions were intended by the grantor, wasting assets, including buildings and equipment, should be preserved by reflecting depreciation as a charge to income, if allowed by the trust instrument or state law. Many states have no provision for depreciation.

If all of the trust income is distributed to beneficiaries without regard for depreciation, the entire periodic deduction for depreciation is taken for income tax purposes by the beneficiaries, and the trustee has no occasion to record depreciation in his records. In all instances, the trustee should be guided by the provisions of the trust instrument or state law in his handling of depreciation.

(vi) Payments of Expenses. A distinction must be made between expenses chargeable to principal and income. In the absence of direction in the instrument, the fiduciary should rely on state law as to allocation of trust expenses. Generally if an expense is recurring each year, it is usually charged to income. It could also be allocable one-half to principal and one-half to income. If an expense is attributable to corpus, it should be charged to principal. If the expense was to maintain and collect income, then it should be charged to income. For example, capital gains are allocated to principal, and the income tax paid by the trustee on capital gains should also be charged to principal; however, when a bank assesses an annual fee for a custody account, the custody fee could be charged to income or split 50/50 between income and principal.

(c) TRUSTEE'S REPORTS.   Trustee's reports vary in form and in frequency according to the nature and provisions of the trust, and whether it is being administered under the jurisdiction of a court. Moreover, the form of the report varies among jurisdictions. Before preparing the report, the accountant should ascertain from the court whether a particular form is required. The valuations to be used must always be the same as those appearing on the inventory unless specific permission has been granted to change them. If assets have been written off as worthless, they must nevertheless appear in the new inventory without value.

If income and principal cash accounts have been properly maintained, the balance of the undistributed income would be represented by an equal amount of cash in the bank. If specific investments have been made with the intention that the funds used were still to be considered as undistributed income, the assets acquired should be shown as assets belonging to the trust income account.

The reports consist primarily of an analysis of the principal and income accounts. In addition, a statement showing the changes in the investments, an inventory of the property at the date of the report, and supporting schedules of various items will be required. A reconciliation of cash receipts and disbursements is also often prepared.

43.5 SOURCES AND SUGGESTED REFERENCES

Denhardt, J.G., Jr., and Denhardt, J.W., *Complete Guide to Trust Accounting and Trust Income Taxation.* Prentice-Hall, Englewood Cliffs, NJ, 1977.

Denhardt, J.G., Jr., and Grider, John D., *Complete Guide to Estate Accounting and Taxes,* Fourth Edition Prentice-Hall, Englewood Cliffs, NJ, 1988.

———, *Complete Guide to Fiduciary Accounting.* Prentice-Hall, Englewood Cliffs, NJ, 1981.

Executors and Administrators, 31 Am Jur 2d (rev.), Lawyer's Cooperative Publishing. Rochester, NY, 1989, April 1995 Cum. Suppl.

Federal Taxes Weekly Alert, *Effect of Death on an Individual's Income Tax Attributes,* November 16, 1995 Practice Alert, Research Institute of America.

Ferguson, M. Carr, Freeland, James J., and Ascher, Mark L., *Federal Income Taxation of Estates, Trusts and Beneficiaries,* Second Edition Little, Brown, Boston, 1993.

Gillett, Mark R., and Stafford, Joel D., "Steps to Prepare and File Estate Tax Returns Effectively," *Estate Planning,* May/June 1995. Warren Gorham & Lamont.

Harris, Ann C., "Proper Disposition if IRD Items Can Produce Tax Savings," *Estate Planning,* September/October 1994. Warren Gorham & Lamont.

Harris, Homer I., *Estates Practice Guide,* Fourth Edition Lawyer's Cooperative Publishing, Rochester, NY, 1984, November 1994 Suppl.

Harrison, Louis S., "Coordinating Buy-Outs and Installment Payment of Estate Tax," *Estate Planning,* May/June 1995. Warren Gorham & Lamont.

Herr, Philip M., and Etkind, Steven M., "When and How an Interest in a Tax Shelter Should Be Disposed of Before Death," *Estate Planning,* September/October 1990. Warren Gorham & Lamont.

Larsen, E. J., and Mosich, A. N., *Modern Advanced Accounting,* Sixth Edition Shephards McGraw-Hill, New York, 1994.

Nossman, Walter L., Wyatt, Joseph L., Jr. and McDaniel, James R., *Trust Administration and Taxation,* rev. Second Edition Matthew Bender, New York, 1988, August 1995 Cum. Suppl.

Peschel, John L. and Spurgeon, Edward D., *Federal Taxation of Trusts, Grantors and Beneficiaries,* Second Edition Warren, Gorham & Lamont, New York, 1989, 1995 Cum. Suppl.

Restatement 3rd Trusts (Prudent Investor Rule) §§ 227–229. American Law Institute, 1990.

Restatement, Second, Trusts. American Law Institute, 1959.

Sages, Ronald A., "The Prudent Investor Rule and the Duty Not to Delegate," *Trust & Estates,* May 1995.

Schlesinger, Sanford J., and Weingast, Fran Tolins, "Income Taxation of Estates and Trust: New Planning Ideas," *Estate Planning,* May/June 1995. Warren Gorham & Lamont.

Scott, Austin Wakeman, *The Law of Trusts,* Fourth Edition Little, Brown, Boston, 1987, 1995 Suppl.

Share, Leslie A., "Domicile Is Key in Determining Transfer Tax of Non-Citizens," *Estate Planning*, January/February 1995. Warren Gorham & Lamont.

Stephens, Richard B., Maxfield, Guy B., Lind, Stephen A., and Calfee, Dennis A., *Federal Estate and Gift Taxation*, Sixth Edition Warren, Gorham & Lamont, New York, 1991, 1995 Cum. Suppl. No. 3.

Stephenson, G. T., and Wiggins, Norman, *Estates and Trusts*, 5th ed. Appleton-Century-Crofts, New York, 1973.

Tractenberg, Beth D., "Transferee Liability Can Reach Trustee as Well as a Beneficiary," *Estate Planning*, September/October 1994. Warren Gorham & Lamont.

Trusts & Estates Staff, "Uniform Laws Provide a Road Map for Estate Planners," *Trust & Estates*, May 1994.

Trusts, 76 Am Jur 2d (rev.). Lawyer's Cooperative Publishing, Rochester, NY, 1992, April 1995 Cum. Suppl.

Turner, George M., *Trust Administration and Fiduciary Responsibility,* Shephards McGraw-Hill, New York, 1994.

Uniform Principal and Income Act. American Laws Annotated, Vol. 7.

Uniform Probate Code. American Laws Annotated, Vol. 8, 8A and 8B.

Waggoner, Lawrence W., "The Revised Uniform Probate Code," *Trust & Estates*, May 1994.

CHAPTER 44

VALUATION OF NONPUBLIC COMPANIES

Allyn A. Joyce

Allyn A. Joyce & Co., Inc.

Jacob P. Roosma, CPA

Willamette Management Associates

44.1 DEFINITION OF VALUE

(a) DEFINITION OF NONPUBLIC. A public company is one whose common stock has widespread ownership and investment interest and such active trading that market quotations ordinarily represent fair market value. In contrast, the common stock of a nonpublic company generally has concentrated ownership and such few trades that the transactions do not provide reliable indications of fair market value.

(b) PURPOSES FOR VALUATIONS. The need for valuing the common stock of a nonpublic or closely held company arises on many occasions. Among the more important situations requiring the valuation of nonpublic stock are filing estate and gift tax returns, transactions involving estate planning, financial planning, employee stock ownership plan transactions and reports, granting stock options, drawing stock purchase agreements, marital dissolutions, structuring recapitalizations, sales, mergers, and divestitures, and litigation.

(c) FAIR MARKET VALUE. Briefly stated, fair market value is that value at which a willing buyer and a willing seller, both well informed and neither under any compulsion to act, would arrive in an arm's-length sale of the asset in question. Such value is always determined as of a specific date and is based on all pertinent facts and conditions that are known or reasonably might be anticipated on that date. The existence of a willing buyer and a willing seller is assumed in the very definition of fair market value.

44.2 GENERAL PROCEDURE FOR VALUATION

(a) COMPILE BACKGROUND INFORMATION ABOUT THE COMPANY. In valuing the common stock of a nonpublic company, it is necessary to become as informed as the well-informed buyer and seller assumed in the definition of value.

The appraiser should review the history of the corporation, including date and state of incorporation, the products originally made, evolutionary developments to the present, and changes in control over the years. A list of stockholders, directors, and a listing of officers' names, salaries, ages, and experience should be obtained.

The appraiser must understand the nature of the company's products and/or services, raw materials used, and the methods of manufacture. A facilities tour is helpful. He should inquire as to how technologically advanced (or backward) the company is and review anticipated capital expenditures.

Information on the size of the labor force, the existence of collective bargaining agreements, and background information on employee relations as well as the corporation's strike experience should be obtained. The risk of customer loss during a strike must be evaluated.

The analyst should carefully analyze the structure of the industry, including the identity of existing competitors, barriers to entry and exit, and the bargaining position of customers and suppliers.

Obtain information on the sales force, including its size, structure, methods of compensation, and radius of distribution. Information on markets, including principal industries served and principal customers served, is also important. Any material dependence on a single industry (25 percent or more of sales) or on a single customer (10 percent or more of sales) should be carefully reviewed and the risk of a sudden loss evaluated. The nature of the markets served (e.g., replacement versus original equipment market or job shop versus proprietary) should be examined. The economic forces that give rise to demand for the company's products or services should be understood. Market share data, when available, can be helpful. Price, quality, and service as competitive factors should be assessed. The role of patents and proprietary or secret technology in the competitive structure of the industry should be examined, and if these are important, the possible effects of patent expirations should be reviewed. Research and development projects under way should be reviewed with management.

Changes in the industry, particularly those of a technological or marketing nature, must be analyzed in terms of the company's outlook. The analyst should obtain a "feel" for the industry. Background information can usually be obtained from trade sources. The analyst should understand the growth and cyclical characteristics of the industry. He should review the performance of the company relative to its industry, and he should understand the reasons for any pronounced differences in trends between the company and its industry.

(b) COMPILE FINANCIAL INFORMATION REGARDING THE COMPANY. The appraiser should obtain audit reports for the past five years. Some situations may require a complete audit of the books or even the services of a forensic accountant. The appraiser should disclose the source of the financial information upon which he has relied.

The appraiser should review the historical income accounts, including such areas as officers' compensation, the company's relationship with affiliated entities, and travel and entertainment.

It is helpful to restate the income account in ratios, as this may disclose trends in cost-price relationships that should be discussed with management. Margins by product lines should be reviewed for a multiline company. The appraiser should obtain the latest interim statement and interview management with regard to the company's outlook. It is useful to get the interim statement for the same period of the previous year.

It is helpful to review a five-year comparison of the balance sheets, to analyze changes that may be occurring in financial position, and to evaluate its capacity to finance future growth. The balance sheet may indicate the existence of nonoperating assets, which, if material, should be segregated and valued separately. The potential existence of hidden assets or hidden liabilities should be discussed in interviews with management. The capital structure must be carefully reviewed, as well as the terms of any stock purchase agreements or stock options.

The appraiser should get sales, income, and dividend data to review both the growth and cyclical characteristics of the company, as well as its long-term dividend policy. It is important to review the long-term outlook with management and to obtain financial projections if available.

(c) SELECT GUIDELINE COMPANIES. Having reviewed the quantitative and qualitative factors discussed above, the appraiser must translate this complex array of facts into value. This requires an analysis of the most relevant facts from the actual marketplace. This is ordinarily done through the selection and analysis of guideline companies that can be used to formulate objective guidelines for the evaluation of the subject company. Guideline companies are publicly held companies that come as close as possible to the investment characteristics of the company being valued. Ideally, they are in the same industry. Frequently, however, there are no public companies in the same industry, so it is necessary to select companies with an underlying similarity of investment characteristics based on markets, products, growth, cyclical variability, and other factors.

Such companies were traditionally called *comparative companies*, a term that seems to connote companies "just like" the company being valued. It is seldom, if ever, possible to find publicly held companies "just like" the company under consideration. Appraisers have come to generally use the term *guideline companies* as a more appropriate term than *comparative companies*.

The importance of a thorough, objective selection of guideline companies cannot be overestimated. The credibility of any valuation analysis is dependent on the demonstrated objectivity of the selection of guideline companies.

There are numerous sources for identifying public companies by industry. In recent years, many appraisers have switched from printed sources of information on possible guideline companies to computerized databases. It must be recognized that the breadth and depth of coverage and the accuracy of the information contained in such services will affect the results. Although they are far more efficient than the traditional printed sources, if such databases are not comprehensive in the number of companies they cover or in the way they classify businesses, some actively traded companies that meet the criteria established for the selection of guideline companies may be missed.

The appraiser must clearly state the criteria used in selecting guideline companies. A description of each guideline company finally selected should be part of the report.

(i) Compile Data on Guideline Companies.   It is necessary to compile financial and operating data on the guideline companies. Annual reports should be obtained on the guideline companies, and 10-K reports often are helpful. As much information as possible must be gleaned from official reports, trade sources, prospectuses, and so on, regarding products, markets, and customer dependence, for each of the guideline companies. Balance sheet and income account comparisons are recommended. Where possible, adjustments should be made to the income and balance sheets of the guideline companies and/or the subject company to minimize differences in accounting when such differences are material.

Generally, public companies compute depreciation on the straight-line basis for financial reporting purposes. If the company being valued uses accelerated depreciation, its income and net worth should be adjusted to a straight-line basis when the difference is substantial (10 percent or more of average income over the past five years).

Adjustments should be considered when there is a difference in inventory accounting method between the subject company and the guideline companies. The most common difference is that most or all of the guideline companies are on last-in, first out (LIFO) and the subject company is on first-in, first-out (FIFO).

The income accounts of the subject company should be carefully reviewed and the management interviewed with regard to extraordinary factors affecting income, such as inventory write-downs, uninsured losses, plant moving expenses, or anything of a substantial and nonrecurring nature. Adjustments should be made to eliminate the effects of these extraordinary, nonrecurring items.

(ii) Calculate Market Value Ratios.   Next, the appraiser should calculate the market values of the guideline companies by multiplying the number of shares outstanding by the price per share on the valuation date. If the company has preferred stock outstanding, include it in this computation.

It is necessary to compute the price-earnings ratio. The period selected must be the one that best measures the earning power of the subject company relative to the earning power of the guideline group. Generally, median ratios are used to avoid the distorting effect of extremes on the arithmetic average.

Compute the average cash flow (net income plus noncash charges) for each of the guideline companies using the same period. Compute the median price-cash flow ratio of the guideline group.

Compute the price-dividend ratio of each of the guideline companies. Generally, the dividend of the latest year is suitable for this purpose. However, if there has been an abrupt change in the dividend rate in a recent quarter, the new rate may be more indicative of dividend expectations. Compute the median price-dividend ratio of the guideline group.

Compute market-value-to-book-value ratios and the median of these ratios.

(d) ESTIMATE DIVIDEND-PAYING CAPACITY.   The use of the price-dividend ratio raises the question of the significance of the actual dividend payments of a nonpublic corporation. In many cases, even though the company has the capacity to pay dividends, it pays small ones or none at all. This inevitably raises the question of whether actual dividend payments or dividend-paying capacity should be capitalized. That dividend-paying capacity must be considered is quite clearly the position of the Internal Revenue Service (IRS) (Rev. Rul. 59–60, ¶ 3e), but the courts have not always been as clear.

In estimating dividend-paying capacity, the guideline companies are useful. Compute the payout ratio (dividends as a percentage of net income) of the guideline companies and derive the median payout ratio of the group. Then examine the financial position of the company being valued relative to that of the guideline companies. Consider also that the company being valued, as a closely held company, does not have the same access to capital markets for equity capital as the guideline companies and must, therefore, rely on the retention of earnings to a greater extent than publicly held companies. When the financial position of the company being valued is weaker than that of the guideline companies, the dividend-paying capacity is correspondingly less. If the financial position of the company being valued is significantly stronger than that of the guideline companies, it may have a dividend-paying capacity equal to or greater than that of the guideline companies, despite its inferior access to capital markets.

A second part to this question is: If dividend-paying capacity should be capitalized, how? Does a dollar of dividend that could be paid, but is not paid, have a value to the minority interest investor equal to a dollar of dividend that is actually paid? One reasonable procedure is to capitalize actual dividend payments at the same rate as the guideline companies and capitalize unpaid dividend-paying capacity (the excess of the capacity to pay dividends over the actual dividends paid) at half the multiplier derived from the guideline companies. This procedure recognizes that the minority interest investor does benefit from that unpaid dividend-paying capacity because the company builds its equity base faster than it would if such dividends were paid. However, it also recognizes that the benefit is not as direct nor as immediate as the actual payment of dividends.

(e) JUDGMENTAL MODIFICATION OF THE VALUATION RATIOS.   These market value ratios provide useful valuation guidelines. However, they are nothing more than guidelines and must inevitably be combined with the appraiser's judgment in arriving at a sound valuation conclusion. The appraiser must, after careful consideration of all relevant factors, come to one of three possible conclusions:

1. Investors would find the subject company to be more attractive than the group of guideline companies. (In this case, a premium must be added to the median valuation ratios.)
2. Investors would find the subject company to be less attractive than the guideline companies. (In this case, a discount from the median valuation ratios is required.)
3. Investors would regard the subject as being neither more nor less attractive than the group of guideline companies. (In this case, the use of the median ratios would be appropriate.)

This decision requires a careful comparative analysis of the subject company and the guideline companies in terms of both qualitative and quantitative differences.

In addition to the basic nature of the product, qualitative considerations may include such factors as market position, geographic, product, and market diversification, patent protection, depth of management, research and development capabilities, and many others. Often, but by no means always, public companies are larger and more diversified, and have more professional management. When they are used as guideline companies for the valuation of a smaller, weaker, less diversified company, a judgmental adjustment to the valuation ratios may be necessary. However, in making these judgmental adjustments, care must be taken to avoid "counting the same trick twice." For instance, in valuing a company with low earnings, one should not take a discount for poor management, if it is the poor management that causes the low earnings. That would obviously be "doubling up."

In terms of quantitative differences, the appraiser should first look to long-term trends and outlook for sales and income. Place the sales and income of each of the guideline companies on an index basis, selecting a base period that is not affected by abnormal factors. Determine the median sales index of the group of guideline companies and compare it to the company being valued. Charts of these comparisons are particularly helpful.

Differences in trends may be properly reflected in the valuation procedure through the use of a weighted average. However, a pronounced long-term inferiority of sales trend, and particularly of income trend, may require a further discount to the valuation ratios derived from the guideline companies. Conversely, a decided long-term superiority of trends may require an upward adjustment to those valuation ratios.

The appraiser should also look to the factor of variability. A company with high variable earnings is less attractive to investors than a company with a stable earnings trend. However, be careful in comparing the trend of earnings of a single company to that of the group average or median. The averaging process tends to have a stabilizing influence, and it may therefore be desirable to make a comparison on an individual company basis.

A comparison of financial ratios is also recommended. This should include the current ratio (current assets divided by current liabilities), liquidity ratio (current assets as a percentage of total assets), and leverage ratios (total liabilities as a percentage of total assets and net worth as a percentage of total assets). Differences in financial position can be appropriately reflected in the estimation of dividend-paying capacity. In most cases, the use of dividend-paying capacity as a valuation factor makes a reasonable allowance for differences in financial position. When there are extreme differences, some further adjustment may be necessary. The financial position of the company being valued may be so weak that the nonpayment of dividends does not adequately reflect its poor financial position. In this case, an appraiser must make a judgmental negative adjustment to the valuation ratios. On the other hand, a strong financial position is normally adequately reflected through either liberal dividend payments or a strong dividend-paying capacity. A company with an extremely strong financial position relative to the guideline companies represents an unusual situation, which is covered in Subsection 44.3(h).

Operating ratios, including sales times net worth, net income as a percentage of sales, and income as a percentage of net worth, should be computed and charted. These ratios should be reviewed with particular attention to the profit margin. A profit margin that is well below average may indicate a high-cost operation and, when accompanied by highly variable earnings, may require some discount to the valuation ratios. However, frequently a low profit margin is accompanied by a high ratio of sales to net worth, and together these characteristics are symptomatic of integration lesser than that of the guideline companies.

Finally, examine the fundamental assumption in the valuation procedure that the earnings outlook of the subject company is roughly similar to that of the guideline companies. If there are strong indications that such an assumption is not reasonable, make an appropriate adjustment to the valuation ratios.

(f) APPLICATION OF THE MARKET VALUE RATIOS. At this point, the appraiser has derived four valuation ratios that have been derived from the guideline companies: price-net worth ratio, price-earnings ratio, price-cash flow ratio, and price-dividend ratio. The application of the four ratios provides four indicators of value, and there may be considerable variation among them. This inevitably raises the question of their relative importance. There is close to universal acceptance of the notion that, except under unusual circumstances, earnings are the most important valuation factor.

Some appraisers and some courts completely ignore the concept of cash flow. The use of cash flow in valuation analysis is most appropriate when the company has large assets that do not necessarily decline in value with time and are not "used up" in production. An obvious example is a real estate holding company. The use of cash flow in the valuation of companies with very little investment in depreciable assets (service companies, for instance) is somewhat redundant in that cash flow may be almost identical to earnings, and its use is simply a repetition of the price-earnings ratio analysis.

If the subject company is significantly more or less capital intensive than the guideline companies, the cash flow approach should be modified or eliminated.

Some appraisers completely ignore dividends and dividend-paying capacity. Some give no weight to the book value factor.

The necessity of translating these indicators into a value presents a dilemma to the appraiser. If he uses specific weights, he must defend these as reasonable and not constituting a formula. On the other hand, deriving a value from only one of these factors also constitutes a weighting procedure because it assigns a weight of 100 percent to that one factor and zero to the others. Some appraisers cope with this problem by simply stating that "all things considered, I think the value is X," but they must face the obvious question: What factors did you consider and how much weight did you give to them?

For the most part, courts do not specify the weight they accord to these various valuation factors. In the few cases where the courts have been specific, they have tended to ascribe primary importance to earnings rather than do dividends, and they have demonstrated a tendency to give more weight to earnings than to dividends. The factor of book value has generally received relatively little weight in court decisions involving industrial companies. However, it is not totally ignored.

Whatever weights are used, the appraiser must thoughtfully analyze the resulting value for reasonableness. If this stock were publicly traded at this price, would it be more attractive than the shares of the guideline companies? Would it be significantly less attractive than shares of the guideline companies? If the appraiser can answer both of these questions in the negative, he has probably arrived at a reasonable result.

(i) Discount for Lack of Marketability. The value derived from the guideline analysis is the freely traded price, that is, the price at which the common stock of the subject company would trade if it had an active public market.

Clearly, lack of ready marketability makes a stock considerably less attractive than it would be if it were readily marketable. This was recognized by the IRS in its Rev. Rul. 77–287 when, in discussing the value of unregistered shares of public companies, it stated: "The discount from the market price provides the main incentive for a potential buyer to acquire restricted securities."

In recent years, appraisers have generally used transactions in the restricted shares of public companies as the best guideline for determining the appropriate discount for lack of marketability. A number of studies have been made of this market, and they indicate a rather wide dispersion of discounts but most indicate a median discount of about 35 percent. The two seminal studies, those of Maher and Moroney, indicated median discounts of 34.73 percent and 33 percent respectively.[1] More recent studies have been made by Willamette Management Associates (median 31.2 percent) and Standard Research Consultants (45 percent). The change in the required holding period of restricted stock has limited the usefulness of this evidence in the valuation of nonpublic companies.

Willamette Associates has also analyzed the relationship of original public offering prices to arm's-length trades during the three years preceding the public offering, which suggests discounts in the 40 percent to 60 percent range.

(ii) Discount for Minority Interest. The discount for lack of marketability should not be confused with a discount for minority interest. This chapter has explained the use of publicly held guideline companies in making a judgment as to the value of stock in a nonpublic company. The prices at which the common stocks of those guideline companies sell reflect minority interest values; therefore, the comparative analysis enables the appraiser to express an opinion about the price at which the stock of the subject closely held company would trade if it had an active public market (the freely traded value). It is therefore a minority interest value to begin with, and a minority interest discount is inappropriate. However, the stock of a closely held company is lacking in marketability, and a discount for lack of marketability is appropriate.

(g) DISCOUNTED FUTURE BENEFITS APPROACHES. A discounted future benefits valuation involves two fundamental, difficult, and very imprecise steps:

1. The long-term projection of the benefit
2. The determination of an appropriate discount rate, by which the future benefits may be reduced to present value

It is essential that the discount rate and the benefit be matched. That is, a dividend or net-free cash flow discount rate must be applied to projected dividends or net-free cash flow. An earnings discount rate must be applied to projected earnings. The use of a net cash flow discount rate to discount earnings, for instance, is erroneous.

Data on past rates of return on publicly traded common stocks are readily available and can be used as a reference point in estimating the appropriate rate of return (dividend or net-free cash flow discount rate) of a subject company. As a result, discounted future benefits valuations are almost always done on the basis of cash flow. The term *net cash flow* is often used, usually in the context of an enterprise valuation. Because net cash flow is the total cash flow of the business

---

[1] J. Michael Maher, "Discounts for Lack of Marketability for Closely-Held Business Interests," *Taxes—The Tax Magazine,* September 1976, pp. 562–571. Robert E. Moroney, "Most Courts Overvalue Closely Held Stocks," *Taxes—The Tax Magazine,* March 1973, pp. 144–154.

minus its capital (fixed assets and working capital) needs, it is essentially the same as dividends or dividend-paying capacity.

The projection of net-free cash flow or dividends is a three-step procedure:

1. Project total cash flow (total revenues less cash expenses)
2. Project the capital needs of the business
   a. Project required capital expenditures
   b. Project required net working capital changes
3. Compute dividend-paying capacity (total cash flow minus total capital needs)

The general theory used in estimating the expected rate of return is that investors' return expectations are based on past returns. In establishing the required rate of return for a nonpublic company, practitioners almost invariably use long-term stock return data compiled by Ibbotson Associates, whose *Annual Yearbook* includes series of stock return data.

In deriving the required rate of return for a subject company, it is first necessary to estimate the rate of return investors expect on the small companies themselves on the valuation date. Then, if the appraiser believes that an investment in the subject company is riskier than in the small companies, he must add an increment to their rate of return to reflect that greater risk. Conversely, if the appraiser believes the risk is less, the rate of return must be reduced.

The value of stock is the present value of future returns in perpetuity. This axiom requires, at least theoretically, that future dividends or net-free cash flows be projected and their present value be determined in perpetuity or, as a practical matter, so far into the future that present value increments become insignificant. There are three ways of doing this:

1. The arithmetic method
2. The algebraic method
3. The semialgebraic method

Under the arithmetic method, each year's dividend is projected and its present value determined using the expected rate of return. This is done for all future years until the annual present value increments become insignificant. Then the present values are totaled to give value.

In the algebraic method, the appraiser used the Gordon Model, which is:

$$\text{value} = \frac{D}{ROR - g}$$

where D = dividends for the first year after the valuation date, ROR = the expected rate of return, and g = expected rate of growth in perpetuity.

The algebraic method produces the same value as the arithmetic method. It is simply a computational shortcut. It can be used only if the assumed growth rate of dividends is constant.

In the semialgebraic method, dividends or net-free cash flows are projected for a few years, usually five, and then present value is determined. Then the Gordon Model is used to determine the value at the end of the projection period, and the present value of that "terminal value" is added to the present value of the cash flows during the projection period.

Appraisers rarely use the arithmetic method because it tends to highlight the fact that their valuation depends on a projection of dividends decades into the future. Also, appraisers do not commonly use the algebraic method, possibly because it seems embarrassingly simple. By far the most common method used is the semialgebraic, probably because it gives the appearance of suitable complexity and tends to obscure the inherently infinite nature of the projection. However, unlike the algebraic method, it can accommodate changes in the growth rates and capital needs during the projection period.

The discounted future net-free cash flow or dividends approach, as a valuation model, is eminently sound. However, the problems inherent in its application to a specific fact situation, primarily the inexactitude of the two major inputs, return and benefits, render the results obtained only as good as the assumption incorporated in its application.

If the guideline company approach and the discounted future benefits approach produce substantially different values, the appraiser should carefully analyze the reasons for the difference. Such differences usually indicate that the investing public is using a different discount rate and/or growth rate from those used by the appraiser in his discounted benefits approach.

(h) USE OF FORMULAS.   Rev. Rul. 59–60, the courts, and the Employees Stock Ownership Plan (ESOP) Association have discredited the use of valuation formulas. The ESOP Association made the point very clearly: "Formula appraisals are totally unacceptable, because they will virtually always result in an unfair, if not absurd, appraisal at some time in the future."

Valuation formulas can be as simple as "Value = net book value," "Value = net asset value," or "Value = 10× earnings." On the other hand, they can be so complex as to defy comprehension. Doctors and engineers seem particularly enamored of complex valuation formulas.

The most widely employed type of formula still in use by some business appraisers is the "excess earnings formula." The original formula of this type was ARM-34, which was used for many years by IRS in the valuation of closely held companies.

ARM-34 was as follows:

$$\text{Value} = \text{book value} + \text{capitalized excess earnings}$$

Generally, excess earnings were defined as earnings in excess of 10 percent of net worth, and a 20 percent capitalization rate was generally used in capitalizing excess earnings so that, in practice, the formula was:

$$\text{Value} = \text{book value} + 5 \text{ learnings} - 2$$

The formula has long since been discredited and abandoned by the IRS as well as the courts because it is arbitrary and not market oriented and can therefore produce very unrealistic values.

However, a variation of ARM-34 is still in use by some appraisers. The basic formula is the same:

$$\text{Value} = \text{book value} + \text{capitalized excess earnings}$$

Excess earnings are defined as the earnings in excess of the industry's average rate of earnings on stockholders' equity. Typically, these excess earnings are capitalized at 20 percent (or multiplied by 5). The shortcomings of this approach are fundamentally the same as ARM-34. The underlying assumption that a company is worth its book value if it has an average rate of earnings on net worth for its industry is arbitrary, unsupported, and often absurd. In fact, companies in industries marked by low rates of earnings on book value will tend, on average, to have values in excess of book value, sometimes by a factor of 4 or 5.

(i) NET ASSET VALUE APPROACH.   Net asset value is simply computed by adjusting all assets to a market value basis and deducting all liabilities. Fundamentally, this is yet another formula approach, the formula being "Value = net asset value." There is ample evidence in the marketplace that the common stocks of industrial companies can sell appreciably above or below net asset value. This is not surprising because the normal expectation of investors is that the benefits of ownership will be received by them by way of dividends and a rising market price. However, if the liquidation of a company is pending, net asset value is of paramount importance.

Net asset value has greater relevance to the appraisal of holding companies, notably investment companies and real estate holding companies. Even here, however, the evidence of the marketplace is that the stocks of such companies almost always trade below net asset value.

44.3 SPECIAL SITUATIONS

(a) **WHOLESALE AND RETAIL COMPANIES.**   The valuation of wholesale and retail companies is essentially similar to that of an industrial company as described above. Attention should be given to costs of store openings as well as to credit and inventory management. Particular attention should be paid to the factor of geographic diversification in valuing distribution companies. For example, a supermarket chain whose stores are concentrated in a single city involves greater investment risk than a regional supermarket company operating in a number of cities, and special allowance should be made for such differences.

(b) **VALUATION OF SERVICE COMPANIES.**   The U.S. economy is increasingly dominated by companies engaged in the performance of services for their customers as opposed to manufacturing. Service companies range in the size and scope of activities from small businesses having a considerable dependence on one or a few specialized employees to large businesses such as the major payroll/computer service businesses. The size and scope of activities will determine the valuation method employed. Since the value of a business engaged in the provision of services typically attaches to human resources as opposed to capital assets, the factor of size of capital generally is accorded less weight than size of the financial benefits of ownership in the valuation of an industrial or manufacturing company. Moreover, the factor of cash flow may in many instances simply be duplicative of earnings in service businesses having modest capital needs.

Smaller businesses having a particular dependence on relatively few employees and a special market niche may not lend themselves to the publicly traded guideline company approach. Services providing limited information on small company transactions exist and can be helpful in delineating valuation parameters provided the business in question is reasonably similar to the businesses reported on in these services. The appraiser ordinarily will use a capitalization of earnings approach employing an appropriate risk-adjusted capitalization factor giving consideration to the special risks associated with their small size. Such capitalization factors inevitably involve a considerable injection of professional judgment on the part of the appraiser.

(c) **COMPANIES WITH LOW EARNINGS.**   The valuation of a company with a very low rate of earnings on stockholders' equity can present a particular problem. The extreme form of this is a company that over a period of years has had no earnings and no capacity to pay dividends. The use of the valuation procedure described earlier can be misleading in this instance, since primary weight is given to evidence of earning power. Obviously, the company with no earnings has no value based solely on the factor of earning power. These cases must be carefully judged on their own merits. If liquidation is certain, or even probable, liquidating value is governing. If not, a going-concern valuation is called for, recognizing that companies that are "worth more dead than alive" because of chronically low earnings may go on for years without liquidating, and the minority interest investor cannot force a liquidation.

In estimating going-concern value, it is helpful to examine the range of the ratios of market value to book value of the guideline companies. Frequently there are, among the guideline companies, two or three companies with low rates of earnings on stockholders' equity (5 percent or less), and these tend to have low price-book value ratios. In a group where the median price-book value ratios might be 80 percent or 90 percent, there may very well be two or three companies earning less than five percent on capital, which may have price-book value ratios of 40 percent or 50 percent. Under such circumstances, these data would lead to the conclusion that the company with no earnings at all should be valued below that 40 percent or 50 percent.

The influence of judgment in this situation can be reduced through the use of a statistical regression technique. Examine the relationship between the market value-book value ratio and the rate of earnings on book value of the guideline companies. Generally there is a definite relationship that can be described precisely through the use of a simple linear correlation. This technique makes it quite clear that the companies with high rates of earnings on stockholders' equity tend to have high price-book value ratios, and the companies with low rates of earnings on stockholders' equity tend to have low market price-book value ratios. The statistical definition of this relationship can constitute a satisfactory basis for the valuation of a company with little or no earnings.

(d) HOLDING COMPANIES.   The guideline company technique is also used in valuing holding companies, that is, companies whose assets consist largely of securities. Guideline companies must be selected that parallel, to the extent possible, the nature of the assets of the company being valued. If the holding company being valued has a diversified portfolio of common stocks, it is desirable to select closed-end diversified investment companies. The analyst can then examine the relationship between the market value of the stocks of such companies and underlying net asset values. The relationships of market value to earnings and of market value to dividends should also be reviewed. However, the ratio of market value to net asset value is generally conceded to be the primary determinant of value, and, as a practical matter, this ratio generally shows far greater consistency than the price-earnings or price-dividends ratios of closed-end investment companies. In determining the net asset value of the holding company, the capital gains tax on unrealized capital gains may be deducted as a way to reflect the tax disadvantage of the holding company vis-à-vis regulated investment companies. However, some simply modify the median price to net asset value derived from comparatives on the theory that the subject company, unlike the guideline companies, may be "locked in" to some investments by virtue of the capital gains tax.

The procedure involving a nondiversified investment company is essentially similar to that just described for diversified companies, except that nondiversified investment companies are selected for comparison. The other difference is that some of the nondiversified investment companies may be taxed as ordinary corporations; therefore, the holding company may not be at a tax disadvantage relative to such guideline companies.

If the portfolio of the subject company is concentrated in just a few investments, it may be difficult to find public companies so lacking in diversification. Under these circumstances, it will be necessary to apply a discount to the ratios derived from the guideline companies.

If the investment portfolio is largely debt securities of good quality, the appraiser should examine the relationship between market value and underlying net asset value of closed-end bond funds. As a general rule, the market value-net asset value ratio among these companies is quite close to net asset value.

(e) REAL ESTATE COMPANIES.   The valuation of a minority interest in a real estate holding company requires an appraisal of the underlying assets by a qualified real estate appraiser.

The net asset value of the real estate holding company can then be computed by adjusting stockholders' equity for the difference between the appraisal value of the real estate and net book value.

The appraiser should select publicly held real estate companies owning similar types of real estate, which disclose the estimated appraised value of their assets. This can be used in calculating net asset value. This, in turn, can be used to calculate the price-net asset value relationship. It is also recommended that the relationship among market value and earnings, cash flow, and dividends be examined.

In applying such ratios to the company being valued, primary weight should be given to the market price-net asset value ratio. However, the factors of earnings, cash flow, and dividends certainly should not be ignored.

In applying these ratios, judgment must be brought to bear on qualitative differences between the guideline companies and the subject company. Diversification by property and neighborhood must be considered. A comparison of financial position and the operating record is important.

(f) COMPANIES WITH NONOPERATING ASSETS.   Industrial companies with large nonoperating assets present a particular valuation problem. The company whose cash clearly exceeds its operating needs by a substantial margin is a case in point. Another is a company owning a large portfolio of securities. Still another example is a company owning valuable real estate unrelated to its basic business. In these instances, it is best to remove such assets from the balance sheet and deduct the related earnings, with an appropriate tax adjustment, from reported earnings. Dividends must also be adjusted. Value the company as though it did not own the nonoperating assets. It is then necessary to determine the appropriate increment to the value of the stock determined on an operating basis. If the nonoperating assets are securities, the best procedure is that recommended for an investment company [see Subsection 44.3(d)]. Similarly, if such assets are real estate, the procedure used in valuing a minority interest in a real estate company is appropriate.

(g) LIFE INSURANCE PROCEEDS.   In valuing common stock for estate tax purposes, it is necessary to reflect any windfall to the company arising from any life insurance on the deceased. This may be done by considering the company's improved financial position and its higher earning power related to the proceeds. If the proceeds result in a level of cash beyond the needs of the business, then the excess should be treated as a nonoperating asset, as reviewed above.

If the deceased was a key man, it may be necessary to apply a special discount to reflect the higher risk related to his loss.

(h) COMPANIES WITH AN EXTREMELY STRONG FINANCIAL POSITION.   A company with an extremely strong financial position can present a particular valuation problem. An example is a real estate company with no long-term debt. The publicly held companies that might be used for comparative purposes, without exception, have large amounts of long-term debt outstanding. Thus any price-earnings ratio or price-net asset value ratio that can be derived from them reflects the way in which the investing public values a real estate company with significant leverage.

An appraiser might approach this problem in the usual way and then adjust the valuation ratios derived from publicly held real estate companies to reflect the superior financial position of the subject company. However, the influence of the appraiser's judgment can be minimized by changing to the "total invested capital technique," to quantify better the effect of extreme superiority in financial position.

In employing the total invested capital technique, the total market value of all preferred and common stock is combined with the total market value of all the outstanding long-term debt of each of the guideline companies. That represents the total market value of the total invested capital. That amount is then related to the book value of that total invested capital (net worth plus long-term debt), adjusted for underlying asset values in the case of real estate companies.

Similarly, the total market value of the total invested capital is related to the earnings available for that total invested capital (net income plus interest on long-term debt), to the cash flow available for that invested capital (net income plus noncash charges, plus interest on long-term debt), and finally to the earnings paid out on that total invested capital (dividends plus interest on long-term debt). The application of these ratios to a company with a decidedly stronger financial position is recommended when the company being valued is stronger than the guideline companies by a very wide margin, a circumstance that tends to occur in the valuation of real estate companies but may be encountered in the valuation of an industrial company.

One important drawback of this technique should be noted. It is necessary to ascertain the market value of the long-term debt of the guideline companies and, when the debt is not publicly traded, it is necessary to estimate its market value. This introduces an element of judgment that the basic procedure does not entail.

(i) PREFERRED STOCK.   A standard preferred stock is a security that has the following seven features:

1. The right to receive a stated cumulative cash dividend before any cash dividends are paid to the company's common stock
2. The right to receive a stated amount upon liquidation of the company before any proceeds are distributed to the company's common stock
3. No voting rights in normal circumstances
4. No participation rights in dividends or liquidation proceeds beyond its stated preferences

5. No conversion rights

6. No redemption rights at the option of the holder; may be callable by the company

7. No sinking fund or other feature that provides a definite maturity

There are two key elements in the valuation of a standard preferred stock:

1. The probability that the company will meet the obligations of the preferred stock. This entails consideration of:
    a. The earnings coverage for the dividend preference
    b. The asset coverage for the liquidation preference
    c. The characteristics of the corporation, which could affect these coverages, particularly its prospective growth, financial position, and stability
2. The yields available from comparable fixed income investments

The valuation of preferred stock requires the selection and analysis of publicly traded preferred stocks that can be used to formulate the best possible valuation guidelines. There are surprisingly few actively traded standard preferred stocks of industrial companies, and it is not possible to confine comparatives to a single industry. It is necessary to compute the earnings coverage of each of these securities. Earnings coverage is computed as follows:

$$\frac{\text{Earnings before interest and taxes}}{\text{Interest} + \left(\dfrac{\text{preferred dividend requirement}}{1 - \text{tax rate}}\right)}$$

Asset coverage is measured relative to both current assets and total assets and is computed as follows:

$$\text{Current assets coverage} = \frac{\text{Current assets}}{\text{Total liabilities} + \text{par value of preferred}}$$

$$\text{Total assets coverage} = \frac{\text{Total assets}}{\text{Total liabilities} + \text{par value of preferred}}$$

Compute the yield (dividend divided by market price) on each of these securities, looking for a relationship between the yield and the earnings and asset coverages of the comparative preferreds. Qualitative factors should also be considered. Precise relationships are seldom ascertainable. However, a careful review of the data should provide a good base for the exercise of informed judgment in determining the freely traded value.

A discount to the freely traded value is required. General practice among appraisers is to apply a discount of 15 percent to 20 percent for lack of marketability of standard preferred stocks.

It is sometimes necessary to appraise a preferred stock that deviates in significant ways from a standard preferred stock. An exhaustive list of such preferred stocks is not practical. However, five of the more common variations are as follows:

1. *Noncumulative preferred stock.* Some increase in the yield is warranted for the risk that the dividend may be skipped and "gone forever."
2. *Preferred stock with share convertibility.* This is preferred stock that is convertible into a specified number of shares of common stock. It is necessary to determine the fair market value of the common stock into which the preferred is convertible. If the conversion value (the value of the common stock into which the preferred is convertible) is substantially less than the value as a standard preferred, the premium for convertibility is small or even nonexistent. On the other hand, if the conversion value exceeds the value as a standard preferred stock, the market value is equal to the conversion value plus a small premium.

3. *Preferred stock with dollar convertibility.* This type of preferred is typically convertible into an amount of common stock having a specified dollar value, usually $100, on the conversion date. Even though its dividend may not warrant a value of $100, the conversion feature may give it a value close to or at the conversion price, depending on the assurance that the owner of the preferred can convert and receive $100 worth of common stock at any time.

4. *Preferred stock with participation rights.* This type of preferred is entitled to the standard fixed dividend and liquidation preferences plus a share of the residual dividends or asset values, or both, which would otherwise pass to the common stock. Such rights give the preferred some of the attributes of a common stock and these attributes should be valued in a similar manner.

5. *Preferred stock with an adjustable dividend rate.* The dividend rate on such preferreds is typically adjusted quarterly to reflect prevailing market yields. This adjustment feature, depending on its specific structure, generally maintains the value of these preferreds at or near par. Many public companies have issued adjustable rate preferred stocks, but they are uncommon among nonpublic companies.

(j) EMPLOYEE STOCK OWNERSHIP PLANS.   There has been an enormous growth in the number of companies with employee stock ownership plans. The trust established under an ESOP requires a determination of fair market value for a variety of reasons, including these five:

1. Contributions of stock by the company or sales by its stockholders to the ESOP
2. Sales of stock by the ESOP to third parties
3. Transfer of shares from the ESOP to a beneficiary
4. Repurchase of shares from a beneficiary exercising his or her put
5. Reports required by the Employee Retirement Income Security Act (ERISA)

The appraiser of ESOP shares should be familiar with the Department of Labor (DOL) proposed regulations regarding ESOP appraisals. These regulations stress the requirement that the appraiser be independent of all parties to the transaction other than the plan. They also stress the requirement of a fully documented appraisal. The proposed regulation affirms Rev. Rul. 59–60 as a reasonable statement of general valuation principles, but the DOL seems to go out of its way to mandate the use of guideline companies.

The valuation of ESOP shares is fundamentally the same as valuation for other purposes except that the put obligation, providing it is enforceable, constitutes a kind of marketability that may reduce or even eliminate the lack of marketability discount that would otherwise be required. The appraiser, in deriving the freely traded value of the shares, will have used publicly held guideline companies as valuation guidelines. If the appraiser concludes that the put gives the beneficiary about the same assurance of marketability that he would enjoy if the trust held stock of the guideline companies, then little discount is necessary. However, if the business risks of the subject company are such that the assurance of marketability is less, then some discount for lack of marketability is required. The size of such discount depends on the appraiser's assessment of the probability that the company will be financially able to honor put obligations. This requires an analysis of the company's growth, stability, financial position, and cash flow—all factors that the appraiser will have considered in the basic process. Consideration should also be given to the timing and size of stock distributions to terminating employees since these factors could affect the company's ability to honor its put obligations.

Some appraisers believe that an additional discount is required for the lack of marketability of the stock in the hands of the trust, because the put does not affect the marketability of shares until they are distributed out of the trust. Others, viewing the trust as a device by which stock is held for ultimate distribution to terminating employees, conclude that the degree of marketability to the trust need not be reflected in valuing the stock.

There has been considerable discussion within the appraisal profession as to the effect that the stock repurchase liability may have on the fair market value of the stock. ("Stock repurchase liability" is not a liability in the normal sense of the word because it is an obligation to purchase an asset at its market value.) To date, no consensus has developed, and most appraisers seem to ignore the issue or list it as "a factor that has been considered."

Leveraged ESOPs present additional problems to the appraiser beyond the scope of this book.

(k) VALUATIONS FOR MARITAL DISSOLUTIONS. The classic definition of fair market value is not always appropriate for a business valuation to be used in a divorce proceeding. This is particularly true in the case of professional practices that cannot be sold. The standard of value may not be clear from the statutes or the case law. It is imperative that the appraiser should seek guidance from an attorney with regard to the standard of value and the ways in which that standard can be applied to the case at hand.

The date as of which the marital estate is to be valued frequently is not clear from the statutes or case law and can, in some states, be set at the discretion of the trier of fact.

(l) RESTRICTIVE AGREEMENTS. The existence of certain restrictive agreements can be determinative of value for estate tax purposes. If such an agreement restricts the sale of the stock during the stockholder's lifetime and obligates the estate to sell after death, and if the price is readily ascertainable from the agreement (and was reasonable at the time the agreement was signed), then the agreement is normally determinative of the value for estate tax purposes. However, where the parties to the agreement are family members, there is the possibility that Internal Revenue Code (IRC) Chapter 14, Special Valuation Rules, will apply and require a different valuation standard. This question should be resolved by the attorney for the estate.

(m) S CORPORATIONS. There is no consensus among appraisers as to the effects of the Subchapter S election on value. Some appraisers simply adjust the earnings of the S corporation to a C corporation basis. These methods assume that the S election has no effect on value. Other appraisers have concluded that the premium can be as much as 100 percent or more, depending on the payout ratio (Schackelford, 1988). The premium, if any, attributable to a minority interest in an S Corporation is derived from the tax benefit associated with the avoidance of the corporate level income tax.

Any such calculation of the tax advantage associated with the avoidance of corporate tax must inherently assume that the S advantage will remain unchanged in perpetuity. In fact it can be lost by changes within the legal structure of the company or its ownership or by changes in the tax code. Moreover, because it reduces the type and number of possible purchasers of the stock, an increment to the discount for lack of marketability seems warranted.

(n) START-UP COMPANIES. Start-up companies are all future, no past; therefore, the guideline company approach will be of limited use in appraising a start-up company. Some form of discounted future benefit approach must be used. The projections will be of the utmost importance, and, in the case of a high-technology company, the appraiser will need significant input from an expert familiar with the technology and its market potential. The present value discount rate associated with an unproven business is used. Venture capitalists typically employ expected rates of return ranging upward of 20 percent to 40 percent in determining the value of a start-up business, depending on the nature of the contemplated enterprise and the perceived degree of risk.

(o) NONVOTING STOCK. Many corporations have a voting and a nonvoting common stock, which presents a valuation problem. One Securities and Exchange Commission (SEC) study indicates a value differential of about eight percent between high vote and low vote common shares where voting power is the only difference in the rights of each class.

Courts have been erratic on this question. In one case, the court held that the voting stock, which constituted 1 percent of the equity, had 40 percent of the value. However, in other cases, the courts were more moderate, and a number of cases have used relatively modest discounts for nonvoting stock, generally about five percent. A 5 percent to 10 percent differential seems reasonable in considering minority interest blocks.

(p) VALUATION OF A CONTROLLING INTEREST.   The ultimate controlling interest is the 100 percent interest. The value of such an interest is the greater of the liquidating value of the corporation or the price it would fetch as a going concern in a sale or merger. If the company has relatively low earnings, the liquidating value should be estimated. Liquidating value may differ substantially from book value. Receivables may be difficult to collect by a company in liquidation, particularly if the company has granted credit to a large number of small accounts. The value of inventories tends to vary with the complexity of the inventory. An inventory of raw material, steel or copper, for example, has a fairly ascertainable value. On the other hand, a complex inventory of plumbing supplies, for example, can generally be sold only at a deep discount.

An appraisal should be obtained for real estate as well as machinery and equipment. Standard machinery, a machine tool for instance, has an established market, and an experienced machinery and equipment appraiser can readily ascertain its value. Special machinery may have no more than scrap value. Consideration must be given to operating costs during the wind-up period and to severance pay and pension obligations under the ERISA. If liquidating value exceeds going-concern value, then the value of the 100 percent interest is the present value of the estimated proceeds of liquidation.

Most companies are worth more as going concerns than they are in liquidation, and, under those circumstances, it is necessary to estimate the value of the company as a going concern. This presents essentially the same problem as a minority valuation in the sense that the appraiser must make a judgment as to the proper capitalization of earnings. It is desirable to examine the objective evidence of the marketplace. The preferred approach is to analyze available data on similar companies that have been involved in a sale or merger. There are numerous sources of information to be used in obtaining information on such transactions.

These sources should reveal a number of companies of a similar nature that have been sold or merged near the valuation date. Often it is not possible to obtain extensive details on such transactions. However, when the analyst can obtain a minimum of information, such as the sale price of the company, combined with a recent balance sheet and at least one year's income account, the transaction can serve as a useful guideline in the valuation of a 100 percent interest. When the acquiring company reports to the SEC, 10-K and S-4 reports may contain useful information.

Frequently this "direct approach" to the valuation of a 100 percent interest is not feasible because there have been no transactions involving similar companies or because information cannot be obtained on the transactions that have occurred. In that case, standard practice is to determine a minority interest value, following essentially the procedure outlined previously. Having determined this minority interest value, it is necessary to apply an appropriate premium to derive the value of a 100 percent interest. A useful guideline in this respect can be developed from the premiums that have been paid for publicly held industrial companies generally in recent months. This premium can be derived by examining the relationship between the sale price of the stock of each company and its stock price before the pending merger was influencing its market value. If this is done on a sufficient number of companies, a useful guideline to an appropriate merger premium for the company being valued can be obtained. However, there tends to be considerable variation among merger premiums, and the appropriate merger premium for the subject company is essentially a matter of judgment. The merger premium analysis is a very rough guideline, but it is a very useful one.

Lesser percentages of ownership can constitute absolute control. In some states, 50 percent plus one share can force the sale, merger, or liquidation of a company. In other states, it is two-thirds plus one share. Blocks of stock having legal absolute control are worth a substantial premium over minority interest values. However, some large companies have a policy of avoiding less than 100 percent acquisitions because they may prevent consolidation for income tax purposes or involve possible minority interest or dissenting stockholder problems. Therefore, a block of stock, substantially less than 100 percent, but legally constituting absolute control, has a per share value greater than that of a minority interest but somewhat less than that of a 100 percent interest.

In some states (Illinois, Ohio, Minnesota, and others) a two-thirds majority is required for sale, merger, or liquidation. In these states, it is possible to own more than 50 percent of the voting securities and still not have absolute control. In these states, the owner of, for example, 55 percent of the voting securities has working control, but not absolute control. He can control the dividend-paying policy of the company, its operating policies, and its employment policies. The owner of that 55 percent block is certainly in a better position than the owner of a minority interest. However, because he cannot force the sale or liquidation of the company, the 55 percent interest is not proportionately as valuable as an interest that can force the sale or merger of the company.

The premium that should be attached to a minority interest value to reflect this kind of working control tends to vary from company to company, and considerable judgment must be used by the appraiser in reflecting this factor. The premium should be 10 percent or more, but it should be significantly less than the premium for absolute control.

(q) FIFTY PERCENT INTEREST.   Sometimes it is necessary to value a block of stock that represents exactly 50 percent of the voting power. Obviously, this block of stock is not a controlling interest. However, 50 percent of the vote does have "veto power." Although it cannot force any number of basic moves that may be deemed desirable, it can prevent the remaining half from undertaking action it deems to be undesirable. A holder of a 50 percent interest is in a better position than an owner of a minority interest; therefore, a 50 percent block should have some premium in value over a minority interest value. This premium should be small, certainly no more than 10 percent.

44.4 COURT DECISIONS ON VALUATION ISSUES

The U.S. Tax Court probably hears more business valuation cases than any other court. However, looking to Tax Court opinions for guidance with regard to "factors considered," discounts, premiums, and so on can be a rather frustrating exercise because the opinions are not always clear. The best summary of court decisions related to business valuations is the *Federal Tax Valuation Digest.*

An analysis of cases is beyond the scope of this book. However, two developments in court decisions should be mentioned.

For many years, the U.S. Tax Court seemed to reflect a "split it down the middle" attitude, which fostered extreme valuations by the government as well as by taxpayers. This was explicitly changed by a series of decisions in the early 1980s. The most important of these was *Buffalo Tool & Die v. Commissioner* (74 TC 441, 1980), in which the court indicated that it would lean heavily toward the party that presents the better appraisal. Subsequent cases that made the same point include *Donald Strutz v. Commissioner* (40 TCM 757, 1980), *Sirloin Stockade, Inc. v. Commissioner* (40 TCM 928, 1980), and *Hooker Industries v. Commissioner* (44 TCM 258, 1982). The cumulative effect of these cases, together with the imposition of tax penalties for overappraisal or underappraisal (see IRC pars. 6659 and 6660) has been to increase drastically the risk of relying on a poorly documented or poorly reasoned appraisal.

The second development concerns the definition of what constitutes a minority interest, as opposed to a controlling interest, in a family-owned corporation. In the early 1980s, the IRS took the position in Rev. Rul. 81–253 that individual minority interest blocks of stock owned by family members in a family-controlled corporation should be valued as parts of a control block. This theory has not been accepted by any court so far [see, e.g., *Estate of Bright v. U.S.,* 658 F. 2d 999 (5th Cir. 1981); *Estate of Andrews,* 79 TC 938 (1982); *Victor J. Minahan v. Commissioner,* 88 TC 492 (1987)].

The Service has finally acknowledged the existence of minority interests in family corporations with the issuance of Rev. Rul 93-12.

Valuations in matrimonial cases vary greatly among jurisdictions and may involve a standard of value different from the classic definition of fair market value.

44.5 SAMPLE CONDENSED VALUATION ANALYSIS

(a) COMPANY BACKGROUND.   The following abbreviated valuation of a company is presented for illustrative purposes. Many of the facts and most of the tables and charts used in a full valuation analysis have been omitted here for the sake of brevity. The subject company and the guideline companies are fictional.

The purpose of the appraisal is to determine the fair market value of a 20 percent interest in ABC Snack Foods Inc., as of March 31, 20XX.

The ABC Snack Foods, Inc. (hereinafter referred to as *ABC*) is a producer of potato chips, tortilla and corn chips, and popcorn. The company has two plants, one of 205,000 sq. ft. in Houston, Texas, and a second of 100,000 sq. ft. in Amarillo, Texas, which was opened in 20XX.

Products are distributed through 350 routes, of which 225 are company owned and 125 are independent distributors. In each of its major markets ABC is either the first or second brand. Advertising, which averages 1.75 percent of sales, is done primarily by TV and radio and, to a lesser extent, by billboards. Promotions normally account for 2.5 percent of sales. No single customer accounts for more than 5 percent of sales.

The analysis indicated that ABC was growing somewhat faster than both the potato chip and the popcorn industries. Both the potato chip and popcorn businesses are marked by fairly intense competition in terms of price, promotions, distribution, and advertising. The company competes with several companies that are substantially larger than ABC, as well as with a large number of small local firms, some of which are industry leaders in their locality.

Financial and income data with appropriate adjustments are shown for ABC Snack Foods in Exhibit 44.1.

(b) SELECTION OF GUIDELINE COMPANIES.   In selecting guideline companies, certain criteria were established:

- The common stock must be publicly held and actively traded.
- The stock must trade above $2.00 per share. This criterion was established to eliminate very cheap stocks whose prices frequently do not have realistic relationships to basic determinants of value.
- Guideline companies must be primarily engaged in the production and sale of dessert and snack foods.

In searching for companies that would meet these criteria, we reviewed all companies classified as food companies in *Standard Corporation Records* and in *Moody's Industrial Manual* and *Moody's OTC Industrial Manual*. These sources published financial data concerning virtually all securities in which there is sufficient public interest to warrant such publication. All the companies in the industry classifications listed were reviewed, and eight were selected as being the best possible companies that could be used as a valuation guideline. The reasons for the exclusion of the others were given. A very brief description of each of these companies follows:

Alabaster Ice Cream, Inc., manufactures premium ice cream for distribution throughout the West and in several major cities in the Midwest.

Hi-Grade Enterprises, Inc., manufactures and distributes potato chips, fried pork skins, peanut butter crackers, and popcorn. Products are sold throughout the South.

Hudson Foods Corp., produces meat sticks and beef jerky under the names Slim Jim and Pemmican. Distribution is national.

Interlaken Foods Corp. is primarily a producer of chocolate and confectionary products distributed nationally.

ABC SNACK FOODS, INC.
Condensed Balance Sheets and Computations of Total Net Worth
Net Income, Cash Flow, and Dividends
(Figures in Thousands of Dollars)

Fiscal Years Ending March 31,	2004	2005	2006	2007	2008	2009
Condensed Balance Sheets						
Assets:						
Current assets						
Cash and equivalent	$ 3,827	$ 4,818	$ 4,578	$ 3,130	$ 4,259	$ 4,157
Accounts receivable	3,599	5,433	7,627	7,289	7,203	9,552
Inventories	1,385	2,402	2,408	2,236	2,576	3,861
Other current assets	909	419	434	843	914	1,322
Total current assets	9,720	13,072	15,047	13,498	14,360	18,892
Net fixed assets	7,615	8,665	9,254	13,949	17,464	16,875
Net fixed assets	7,615	8,665	9,254	13,949	17,464	16,875
Other assets	131	178	176	1,075	454	426
Other assets	131	178	176	1,075	454	426
Total assets	$17,467	$21,915	$24,477	$28,522	$32,278	$36,193
Capital and liabilities:						
Current liabilities	$ 3,501	$ 4,613	$ 4,008	$ 4,382	$ 4,313	$ 5,070
Current liabilities	3,501	4,613	4,008	4,382	4,313	5,070
Other credits	—	—	—	—	—	—
Other liabilities	784	989	1,103	1,593	2,004	2,524
Total net worth	13,180	16,314	19,369	22,545	25,963	28,599
Total capital and liabilities	$17,465	$21,916	$24,480	$28,520	$32,280	$36,193
Computation of Total Net Worth						
Preferred stock	$ —	$ —	$ —	$ —	$ —	$ —
Common stock	2,045	2,045	2,045	2,045	2,045	2,045
Additional paid-in capital	3,554	3,554	3,554	3,554	3,554	3,554
Retained earnings	7,581	10,716	13,771	16,946	20,365	23,001
Treasury stock	—	—	—	—	—	—
Adjustments:						
Total net worth	$13,180	$16,314	$19,369	$22,545	$25,963	$28,599
Additional Information						
Total liabilities	$ 4,285	$ 5,602	$ 5,111	$ 5,975	$ 6,317	$ 7,594
Net working capital	6,219	8,459	11,040	9,116	10,047	13,822
Net sales	51,581	58,880	62,376	66,037	70,671	76,499
Computation of Adjusted Net Income and Cash Flow						
Reported net income		$ 3,481	$ 3,431	$ 3,679	$ 3,924	$ 4,386
Adjustments:						
Flood loss (net)		—	—	—	—	843
Adjusted net income		3,481	3,431	3,679	3,924	5,229
Depreciation & amortization		1,140	1,479	1,825	2,023	2,197
Cash flow		$ 4,620	$ 4,911	$ 5,504	$ 5,947	$ 7,426
Computation of Total Dividends						
Preferred stock dividends		$ —	$ —	$ —	$ —	$ —
Common stock dividends		342	376	505	505	686
Total dividends		$ 342	$ 376	$ 505	$ 505	$ 686

Exhibit 44.1   Adjusted financial and income data.

King Foods Inc. produces and markets soft pretzels, baked cookies, and semifrozen carbonated beverages and frozen juice treats and desserts. Distribution is national.

Munchies, Inc., produces and distributes snack items including peanut butter or cheese-filled cracker sandwiches, cookie sandwiches, potato chips, popcorn, and fried pork skins. Sales are primarily through the company's own sales organization to service stations and drug stores in 35 states, primarily east of the Mississippi River.

Sweetgoods Corp. produces sweet goods, including single portion cakes, frozen cakes and pies, doughnuts, and cookies. Distribution is primarily in 23 eastern and southeastern states.

Tri-State Snacks Corp. is a producer of candy and other snack items, primarily under its own brand names. Products are marketed nationally.

The market value of each of the guideline companies has been computed by simply multiplying the closing price on March 31, 2009, by the number of shares outstanding. That market value appears on Column I of Exhibit 44.2.

Column II shows the weighted average earnings of each company during the five years preceding the valuation date. (The weighting procedure places a weight of one on 2004, two on 2005, up to five on the earnings of 2008.) Column III shows the price-earnings ratios. The median price earnings ratio is 16.8. The next column shows the five-year weighted average cash flow over the same period and shows that the median market price to cash flow ratio is 10.7 times. Column VI shows the dividends of each company in the year preceding the valuation date and this is followed by the price dividend ratio. The median is 41.0. Column VIII shows the payout ratio of each company, indicating that the median payout ratio is 42.5 percent. Finally we show the total net worth of each company, and that is followed by the market value to net worth percentage.

These market value ratios provide useful guidelines for the valuation of ABC. However, they are nothing more than guidelines and must inevitably be combined with the appraiser's judgment

MARKET VALUE RATIOS

Company	I 3/31/09 Total Market Value	II Latest 5-Year Weighted Average Earnings	III Market Value Times Latest 5-Year Weighted Average Earnings	IV Latest 5-Year Weighted Average Cash Flow
	($000)[(a)]	($000)		($000)
Alabaster Ice Cream, Inc.	$ 112,258	$ 5,076	22.1	$ 10,252
Hi-Grade Enterprises, Inc.	121,617	6,957	17.5	14,143
Hudson Foods Corp.	63,129	4,153	15.2	6,091
Interlaken Foods Corp.	2,389,938	116,487	20.5	161,127
King Foods Inc.	75,842	4,784	15.9	8,191
Munchies, Inc.	561,257	38,060	14.7	53,736
Sweetgoods Corp.	137,542	7,291	18.9	12,372
Tri-State Snacks Corp.	235,345	14,518	16.2	17,144
Guideline company median			16.8	

NOTE: (a) On a minority interest basis.

Exhibit 44.2   Market value data for the guideline companies.

MARKET VALUE RATIOS

V	VI	VII	VIII	IX	X
Market Value Times Latest 5-Year Weighted Average Cash Flow	Latest Year Dividends	Market Value Times Latest Year Dividends	Latest Year Dividends as a % of Latest 5-Year Weighted Average Earnings	Total Net Worth	Market Value as a % of Net Worth
	($000)			($000)	
10.9	$ 1,421	79.0	28.0	$ 29,888	375.6
8.6	4,097	29.7	58.9	58,914	206.4
10.4	1,537	41.1	37.0	24,935	253.2
14.8	58,530	40.8	50.2	679,284	351.8
9.3	2,037	37.2	42.6	33,113	229.0
10.4	20,999	26.7	55.2	201,593	278.
11.1	3,096	44.4	42.5	50,651	271.5
13.7	4,077	57.7	28.1	42,693	551.2
10.7		41.0	42.5		275.0

Exhibit 44.2 *Continued.*

in arriving at a sound valuation conclusion. The appraiser must, after careful consideration of all relevant facts, come to one of three possible conclusions:

1. Investors would find ABC to be more attractive than the group of guideline companies. (In this case, a premium must be added to the median valuation ratios.)
2. Investors would find ABC to be less attractive than the guideline companies. (In this case, a discount from the median valuation ratios is required.)
3. Investors would regard ABC as being neither more nor less attractive than the group of guideline companies. (In this case, the use of the median ratios would be appropriate.)

(c) **QUALITATIVE CONSIDERATIONS.** ABC has an excellent trade name in its marketing territory as evidenced by the fact that it is the number one or number two brand in all its major markets. We think that the ABC trade name, in its markets, is as good as some of the guideline companies and inferior to several of them. On balance we think that this is a small negative consideration for ABC.

In terms of size, ABC is at the low end of the range of the guideline companies, and it has less geographic diversification than the group of guideline companies. This is a small negative consideration for ABC.

ABC's new plant in Amarillo positions it to expand geographically and results to date exceed expectations. We think that this is a positive factor.

ABC uses two commodities, potatoes and corn, and both of these commodities are subject to rather considerable price variability. However, some of the guideline companies' businesses are as vulnerable as ABC to price changes of a limited number of commodities.

Mr. A.B. Caldwell, the founder of the company, is 64 and in ill health. Mr. John Grundy, the company's executive vice president, has been groomed to succeed Mr. Caldwell. However, there is no one other than Mr. Grundy with the depth of experience needed to run the company. We conclude that ABC has somewhat less depth of management than the guideline companies and that this is a negative consideration.

(d) QUANTITATIVE CONSIDERATIONS.   A comparison of sales and income growth appears in Exhibit 44.3. The sales of each company were placed on an index basis with the years 2005–2006 equal to 100, and the group median was determined. The upper portion of that chart shows that the sales growth of ABC has been similar to that of the guideline companies.

The lower portion of that chart shows that the long-term trend of ABC's net income has been close to the group of guideline companies.

A comparison of certain operating ratios is shown in Exhibit 44.4. The top section shows that in 2004 and 2005, ABC was generating more sales per dollar of equity capital than the group of guideline companies. However, during the last three years, ABC has been almost identical to the group median.

The middle portion of the chart shows that ABC's net profit margin has remained fairly constant at about 6 percent, whereas the guideline companies have declined from 7.7 percent in 2004 to 5.2 percent in 2008.

The lower portion of that chart shows that ABC's rate of earnings on stockholders' equity was above the group median in 2004 but has been slightly inferior to the group median since then. Since 2004, the trends have been parallel.

ABC's current ratio of 3.7 times is considerably better than the group median of 2.2 times. Both ABC and the guideline companies have about 50 percent of their assets in the form of current assets and about 50 percent in fixed assets. In terms of leverage, ABC is significantly better than the group median. ABC's ratio of total liabilities to total assets is 21 percent, compared to the group median of 43 percent. We conclude that the overall financial position of ABC is better than the group of guideline companies.

The quantitative analysis revealed no important differences between ABC and the group of guideline companies that would require modification of the median ratios. Its growth rates were not significantly different. The comparison of operating ratios did not reveal any significant differences that would require adjustment. The analysis did reveal that ABC has significantly less leverage than the guideline companies. However, that low leverage has enabled ABC to pay out about the same percentages of its earnings as the guideline companies (40 percent versus 42.5 percent) despite its inferior access to capital markets. We think that the better financial position is reasonably reflected through the capitalization of dividends.

We summarize as follows:

NEGATIVE DIFFERENCES

- Slight inferiority in trade name
- Inferior depth of management
- Less geographic diversification

POSITIVE DIFFERENCES

- ABC's promising geographic expansion

We think that, on balance, these differences make ABC somewhat less attractive than the guideline companies and are appropriately reflected by a 10 percent reduction in the median valuation ratios.

(e) APPLICATION OF THE VALUATION RATIOS.   The valuation ratios are applied to ABC's own figures on Exhibit 44.5. Primary weight (60 percent) is applied to the value derived from earnings and 20 percent each to the values derived from cash flow and dividends. This weighting procedure results in a value of $62,382,000.

It should be noted that the value of $62,382,000 is 218 percent of ABC's book value of $28,599,000. This is well within the range of the guideline companies and is reasonable. No separate weight has been given to the guideline companies' ratio of market value to book value

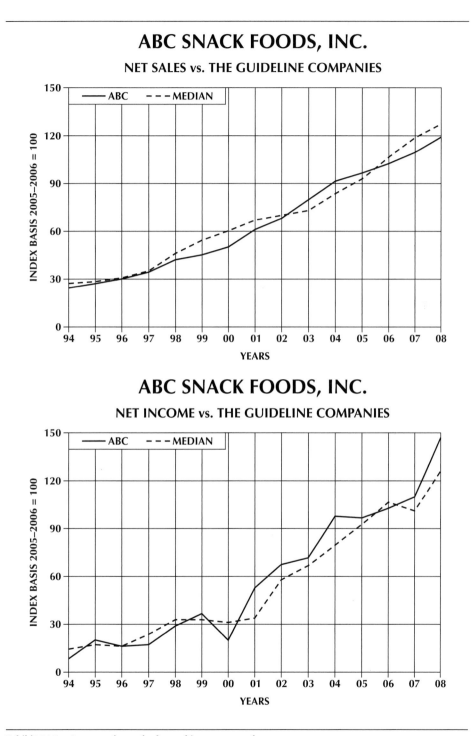

Exhibit 44.3   A comparison of sales and income growth.

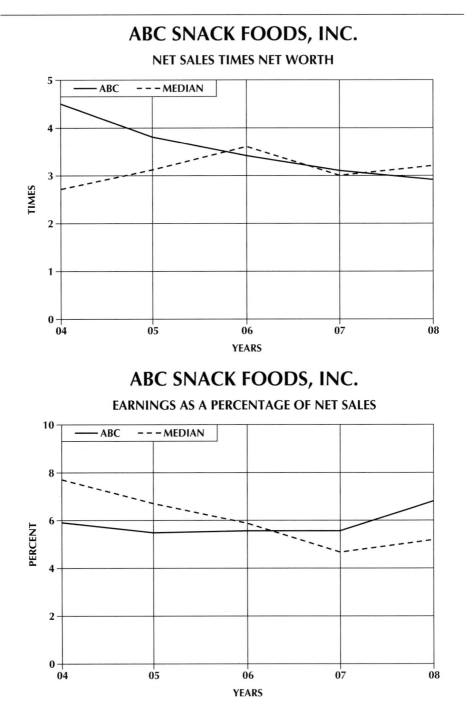

(Continues)

Exhibit 44.4 A comparison of certain operating ratios.

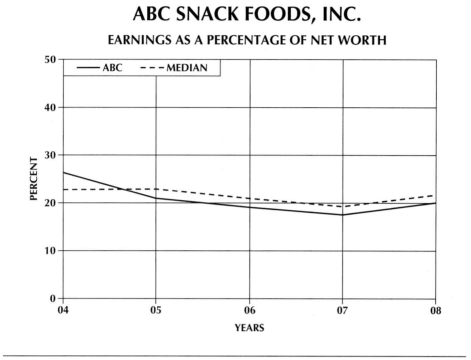

ABC SNACK FOODS, INC.
EARNINGS AS A PERCENTAGE OF NET WORTH

Exhibit 44.4   *Continued.*

VALUATION OF THE COMMON STOCK OF ABC SNACK FOODS, INC.
Modified Valuation Ratios Derived on Exhibit 44.2

	Median Ratios	Modified Valuation Ratios	
Market value × 2004–2008 weighted average earnings	16.8	15.1	
Market value × 2004–2008 weighted average cash flow	10.7	9.6	
Market value × 2008 dividends	41.0	36.9	
Application of valuation ratios to ABC's earnings, cash flow, and dividends			
15.1 × ABC's 2004–2008 weighted average earnings of $4,214,000 = $63,631,000 × a weight of 60%			$38,179,000
9.6 × ABC's 2004–2008 weighted average cash flow of $6,125,000 = $58,800,000 × a weight of 20%			11,760,000
36.9 × ABC's 2008 dividends of $1,686,000 = $62,213,000 × a weight of 20%			12,443,000
			$62,382,000
Freely traded value per share (based on 100,000 shares issued and outstanding)			$ 624
Less: Discount for lack of marketability (30%)			$ 187
Fair market value per share			$ 437

Exhibit 44.5   **Valuation of the common stock of ABC Snack Foods, Inc., as of March 31, 2009.**

because we believe that investors give little, if any, weight to book value in appraising the securities of companies with the high rates of earnings on capital that are characteristic of this industry.

It should also be noted that we have not used a discounted future benefits approach because ABC's prospective growth rates are roughly comparable to those of the guideline companies. The adjusted valuation ratios are, therefore, a reflection of both the growth rate and the capitalization rate appropriate to ABC Snack Foods, Inc., on the valuation date.

Dividing the preliminary value of $62,382,000 by the 100,000 shares outstanding results in a freely traded value (the price at which the stock would trade in an active market) of $624 per share.

The fact that the ABC stock lacks ready marketability must be reflected by a discount for lack of marketability. We think that a discount of 30 percent is appropriate. This results in a value for the common stock of $437 per share.

It is our conclusion that a block of 20,000 shares had a fair market value of $437 per share as of March 31, 2009, or $8,740,000 for the entire block.

44.6 SOURCES AND SUGGESTED REFERENCES

Blackman, L., *The Valuation of Privately-Held Businesses.* Probus Publishing, Chicago, 1986.

Brown, Ronald L., *Valuing Professional Practices and Licenses: A Guide for the Matrimonial Practitioner.* Prentice-Hall, Englewood Cliffs, NJ, 1987.

Burke, Frank M., Jr., *Valuation and Valuation Planning for Closely-Held Businesses.* Prentice-Hall, Englewood Cliffs, NJ, 1981.

Ibbotson, Roger A., *Stocks, Bonds, Bills and Inflation.* Ibbotson Associates, Chicago, 1989.

Internal Revenue Service, *IRS Valuation Guide for Income, Estate & Gift Taxes.* Commerce Clearing House, Chicago, 1985.

————, Revenue Ruling No. 59–60. U.S. Treasury Dept., Washington, DC.

Maher, J. Michael, "Discounts for Lack of Marketability for Closely-Held Business Interests," *Taxes—The Tax Magazine,* September 1976, pp. 562–71.

Moroney, Robert E., "Most Courts Overvalue Closely Held Stocks," *Taxes—The Tax Magazine,* March 1973, pp. 144–154.

Pratt, Shannon P., ed., *Readings in Business Valuation.* American Society of Appraisers Educational Foundation, 1986.

————, *Valuing Small Businesses and Professional Practices.* Dow Jones-Irwin, Homewood, IL, 1986.

————, *Valuing a Business,* Second Edition Dow Jones-Irwin, Homewood, IL, 1989.

Schackelford, Aaron L., "Valuation of S Corporations," *Business Valuation Review,* December 1988, pp. 159–162.

Schnepper, J. A., *The Professional Handbook of Business Valuation.* Addison-Wesley, Reading, MA, 1982.

Smith, Gordon V., *Corporate Valuation.* John Wiley & Sons, New York, 1988.

Standard & Poor's Corporation, *Standard Corporation Records.* Standard & Poor's, New York, annual update.

CHAPTER 45

BANKRUPTCY

Grant W. Newton, PhD, CPA, CIRA

Pepperdine University

45.1 OVERVIEW

This chapter contains a brief description of the Bankruptcy Code, a discussion of the services that can be rendered by the accountant, and an introduction to the problems faced by accountants working in the bankruptcy area.

45.2 ALTERNATIVES AVAILABLE TO TROUBLED COMPANIES

The debtor's first alternatives are to locate new financing, to merge with another company, or to find some other basic solution to its situation that avoids the necessity of discussing its problems with representatives of creditors. If none of these alternatives is possible, the debtor may be required to seek a remedy from creditors, either informally (out of court) or with the help of judicial proceedings.

(a) OUT-OF-COURT SETTLEMENTS.   The informal settlement is an out-of-court agreement that usually consists of an extension of time (stretch-out), a pro rata cash payment for full settlement of claims (composition), an issue of stock for debt, or some combination. Developing an out-of-court settlement may take several forms. For example, the debtor, through counsel or credit association, calls an informal meeting of the creditors for the purpose of discussing its financial problems. In many cases, the credit association makes a significant contribution to the out-of-court settlement by arranging a meeting of creditors, providing advice, and serving as secretary for the creditors' committee.

A credit association is composed of credit managers of various businesses in a given region. Its functions are to provide credit and other business information to member companies concerning their debtors, to help make commercial credit collections, to support legislation favorable to business creditors, and to provide courses in credit management for members of the credit community.

At the creditors' meeting, the debtor describes the causes of failure, discusses the value of assets (especially those unpledged) and unsecured liabilities, and answers any questions the creditors may ask. The main objective of this meeting is to convince the creditors that they would receive more if the business were allowed to operate than if it were forced to liquidate and that all parties would benefit from working out a settlement.

In other situations, the debtor or its representative will not negotiate with the creditors as a group, but rather will work individually with, for example, the secured lenders, and attempt to reach a tentative agreement or at least develop a possible agreement and then move on to the unsecured lenders and talk with them. The debtor may continue the process, meeting with individual creditors or groups of similar creditors until an agreement is reached.

(i) Appointment of Creditors' Committee.   To make it easier for the debtor to work with the creditors, a committee of creditors is normally appointed during the initial meeting of the debtor and its creditors, providing, of course, the case is judged to warrant some cooperation by the creditors. It should be realized that the creditors are often as interested in working out a settlement as is the debtor. The creditors' committee serves as the bargaining agent for the creditors, supervises the operation of the debtor during the development of a plan, and solicits acceptance of a plan once the committee has approved it. Generally, the creditors' committee meets immediately after appointment for the purpose of selecting a presiding officer and counsel.

(ii) Plan of Settlement.   Provided there is enough time, it is often advisable that the accountant and the attorney assist the debtor in preparing a suggested plan of settlement for presentation and discussion at the first meeting with creditors. Typically only the largest creditors and a few representatives of the smaller creditors are invited so that the group is a manageable size for accomplishing its goals.

There is no set pattern for the form that a plan of settlement proposed by the debtor must take. It may call for 100 percent payment over an extended period of time, payments on a pro rata basis in cash for full settlement of creditors' claims, satisfaction of debt obligations with stock, or some combination. A carefully developed forecast of projected operations, based on realistic assumptions developed by the debtor with the aid of its accountant, can help creditors determine whether the debtor can perform under the terms of the plan and operate successfully in the future.

(b) ASSIGNMENT FOR BENEFIT OF CREDITORS.   A remedy available under state law to a corporation in serious financial difficulties is an assignment for the benefit of creditors. In this instance, the debtor voluntarily transfers title to its assets to an assignee, who then liquidates them and distributes the proceeds among the creditors. Assignment for the benefit of creditors is an extreme remedy because it results in the cessation of the business. This informal liquidation device (although court-supervised in many states) is like the out-of-court settlement devised to rehabilitate the debtor, in that it requires the consent of all creditors or at least their agreement to refrain from taking action. The appointment of a custodian over the assets of the debtor gives creditors the right to file an involuntary bankruptcy court petition.

Proceedings brought in the federal courts are governed by the Bankruptcy Code. Normally it is necessary to resort to such formality when suits have been filed against the debtor and its property is under garnishment or attachment or is threatened by foreclosure or eviction.

(c) BANKRUPTCY COURT PROCEEDINGS.   Bankruptcy court proceedings are generally the last resort for the debtor whose financial condition has deteriorated to the point where it is impossible to acquire additional funds. When the debtor finally agrees that bankruptcy court proceedings are necessary, the liquidation value of the assets often represents only a small fraction of the debtor's total liabilities. If the business is liquidated, the creditors get only a small percentage of their claims. The debtor is discharged of its debts and is free to start over; however, the business is lost and so are all the assets. Normally, liquidation proceedings result in large losses to the debtor, the creditors, and the business community in general. Chapter 7 of the Bankruptcy Code covers the proceedings related to liquidation. Another alternative under the Bankruptcy Code is to seek some type of relief so that the debtor, with the help of the bankruptcy court, can work out agreements with creditors and be able to continue operations. Chapters 11, 12, and 13 of the Bankruptcy Code provide for this type of operation.

(i) Title 11—Bankruptcy Code.   Title 11 U.S. Code contains the bankruptcy law. The code is divided into eight chapters:

Chapter 1	General Provisions
Chapter 3	Case Administration
Chapter 5	Creditors, the Debtor, and the Estate
Chapter 7	Liquidation
Chapter 9	Adjustment of Debts of a Municipality
Chapter 11	Reorganization
Chapter 12	Adjustment of Debts of a Family Farmer with Regular Income
Chapter 13	Adjustment of Debts of an Individual with Regular Income

Chapters 1, 3, and 5 apply to all proceedings under the code except Chapter 9, where only specified sections of Chapters 1, 3, and 5 apply. A case commenced under the Bankruptcy Code—Chapters 7, 9, 11, 12, or 13—is referred to as a *Title 11* case. Chapter 13, which covers the adjustment of debts of individuals with regular income, is beyond the scope of this presentation because it can be used only by individuals with unsecured claims of less than $307,675 and secured claims of less than $922,975. The dollar amount of the debt limits for a Chapter 13 petition are to be increased to reflect the change in the Consumer Price Index for All Urban Consumers on April 1 every third year. The amounts are to be rounded to the nearest $25 multiple. The next three-year-period adjustment will be made on April 1, 2007. Provisions relating to Chapter 11 are discussed in detail in a separate section.

(ii) Chapter 7—Liquidation.   Chapter 7 is used only when the corporation sees no hope of being able to operate successfully or to obtain the necessary creditor agreement. Under this alternative, the corporation is liquidated and the remaining assets are distributed to creditors after administrative expenses have been paid. An individual debtor may be discharged from liabilities and entitled to a fresh start. A corporation's debt is not discharged.

The decision as to whether rehabilitation or liquidation is best also depends on the amount that can be realized from each alternative. The method resulting in the greatest return to the creditors and stockholders should be chosen. The amount received from liquidation depends on the resale value of the firm's assets minus the costs of dismantling and legal expenses. The value of the firm after rehabilitation must be determined (net of the costs of achieving the remedy). The alternative leading to the highest value should be followed.

Financially troubled debtors often attempt an informal settlement or liquidation out of court; if it is unsuccessful, they will then initiate proceedings under the Bankruptcy Code. Other debtors, especially those with a large number of creditors, may file a petition for relief in the bankruptcy court as soon as they recognize that continuation of the business under existing conditions is impossible.

As soon as the order for relief has been entered, the U.S. trustee appoints a disinterested party from a panel of private trustees to serve as the interim trustee. The functions and powers of the interim trustee are the same as those of an elected trustee. Once an interim trustee has been appointed, the creditors meet to elect a trustee that will be responsible for liquidating the business. If a trustee is not elected by the creditors, the interim trustee may continue to serve in the capacity of the trustee and carry through with an orderly liquidation of the business.

The objective of the trustee is to liquidate the assets of the estate in an orderly manner. Once the property of the estate has been reduced to money and the security claims have been satisfied to the extent allowed, then the property of the estate is distributed to the holders of the claims in the order specified by the Bankruptcy Code. The first order, of course, is priority claims; when they have been established, the balance goes to unsecured creditors. After all the funds have been distributed, the remaining debts of an individual are discharged. As mentioned earlier, if the debtor is a corporation, the debts are not discharged. Thus it is necessary for the corporation to cease existence. Any funds subsequently coming into the corporate shell would be subject to attachment.

(iii) Chapter 12—Adjustment of Debt of a Family Farmer with Regular Annual Income.
To help farmers resolve some of their financial problems, Congress passed Chapter 12 of the Bankruptcy Code. It became effective November 26, 1986, and was scheduled to expire several times and on a few occasions, the legislation expired before Congress extended it for an additional time period. The 2005 Act provided for Chapter 12 to be permanent and was expanded to include fisherman with regular income.

Prior to Chapter 12, a family farmer in need of financial rehabilitation had to file either a Chapter 11 or 13 petition. Most family farmers, because they have too much debt to qualify, cannot file under Chapter 13 and are limited to Chapter 11. Many farmers have found Chapter 11 needlessly complicated, unduly time-consuming, inordinately expensive, and, in too many cases, unworkable. Chapter 12 is designed to give family farmers an opportunity to reorganize their debts and keep their land. According to legislative history, Chapter 12 gives debtors the protection from creditors that bankruptcy provides while, at the same time, it prevents abuse of the system and ensures that farm lenders receive a fair repayment.

In order to file a petition, an individual or an individual and spouse engaged in farming operations must have total debt that does not exceed $3,237,000, and at least 50 percent of noncontingent, liquidated debts (excluding debt from principal residence unless debt arose out of family operations) on the date the petition is filed must have arisen out of farming. Additionally, more than 50 percent of the petitioner's gross income for the taxable year prior to the filing of the petition must be from farming operations.

A corporation or partnership may file if more than 50 percent of the outstanding stock or equity is owned by a family and:

- More than 80 percent of the value of its assets consist of assets related to farming operations.
- The total debts do not exceed $3,237,000 and at least 50 percent of its noncontingent, liquidated debts on the date the case is filed arose out of farming operations.
- The stock of a corporation is not publicly traded.

Similar provisions apply to family fisherman except that the aggregate debt limit is $1,500,000 and at least 80 percent of it debt is from commercial fishing operations.

Only the debtor can file a plan in a Chapter 12 case. The requirements for a plan in Chapter 12 are more flexible and lenient than those in Chapter 11. In fact, only four requirements are set forth in Section 1205 of the Bankruptcy Code. First, the debtor must submit to the supervision and control of the trustee all or such part of the debtor's future income as is necessary for the execution of the plan. Second, the plan must provide for full payment, in deferred cash payments, of all priority claims unless the creditors agree to a different treatment. Third, where creditors are divided into classes, the same treatment must apply to all claims in a particular class unless the holder of a claim or interest agrees to less favorable treatment. The Fourth requirement, added by the 2005 Act, provides that less than full payment of domestic support obligations that are a priority claim may be provided for in the plan, if all of the debtors disposal income over a five year period is used to make the payments required under the plan. The plan can alter the rights of secured creditors with an interest in real or personal property, but there are a few restrictions. To alter the right of the secured claim holder, the debtor must satisfy one of the following three requirements:

1. Obtain acceptance of the plan.
2. Provide in the plan that the holder of such claim retain the lien and as of the effective date of the plan provide that the payment to be made or property to be transferred is not less than the amount of the claim.
3. Surrender the property securing such claim.

If a holder of an allowed unsecured claim does not accept the plan, then the court may not approve the plan unless the value of the property to be distributed is equal to at least the amount of the claim and the plan provides that all of the debtor's projected disposable income to be received within three years, or longer if directed by the court, after the first payment is made will be a part of the payments under the plan.

To facilitate the operation of the business and the development of a plan, Section 1206 of the Bankruptcy Code allows family farmers to sell assets not needed for the reorganization prior to confirmation without the consent of the secured creditor, provided the court approves such a sale.

(iv) Prepackaged Chapter 11 Plans.   Before filing a Chapter 11 plan, some debtors develop a plan and obtain approval of the plan by all impaired claims and interests. The court may accept the voting that was done prepetition provided that the solicitation of the acceptance (or rejection) was in compliance with applicable nonbankruptcy laws governing the adequacy of disclosure in connection with the solicitation. If no nonbankruptcy law is applicable, then the solicitation must have occurred after or at the time the holder received adequate information as required under Section 1125 of the Bankruptcy Code.

It is often necessary for a Chapter 11 plan to be filed for several reasons including the following three:

1. Income from debt discharge is taxed in an out-of-court workout to the extent that the debtor is or becomes solvent. While some tax attributes may be reduced in a bankruptcy case, the gain from debt discharged is not taxed.
2. A larger percent of the net operating loss may be preserved if a Chapter 11 petition is filed. For example, the provisions of Sections 382(l)(5) and 382(l)(6) of the Internal Revenue Code (IRC) dealing with net operating losses only apply to bankruptcy cases.
3. A smaller percentage of creditor approval is needed in Chapter 11. Only two-thirds of the dollar amount of debt represented by those creditors voting and a majority in number in each class are necessary in Chapter 11. However, for any out-of-court workout to succeed, the percentage accepting the plan must be much greater. For example, some bond indenture agreements provide that amendments cannot be made unless all holders of debt approve the modifications. Since it is difficult, if not impossible, to obtain 100 percent approval, it is necessary to file a bankruptcy plan to reduce interest or modify the principal of the bonds.

Since the professional fees and other costs, including the cost of disrupting the business, of a prepackaged plan are generally much less than costs of a regular Chapter 11 bankruptcy, a prepackaged bankruptcy may be the best alternative.

The use of a *prenegotiated plan* is common among public companies today. A prenegotiated plan is a modification of the prepackaged bankruptcy in that the voting is completed after the petition has been filed rather than before the plan is filed. In a prenegotiated plan, the debtor reaches an agreement with the major creditors and then files a plan either at the time or shortly after the Chapter 11 petition is filed. For public companies, the filing of the petition before voting allows all documents related to the plan to be filed with the bankruptcy court and eliminates the need to follow the Securities and Exchange Commission (SEC) requirements in the voting process.

(d) THE ACCOUNTANT'S SERVICES IN PROCEEDINGS.   One of the first decisions that must be made at an early meeting of the debtor with bankruptcy counsel and accountants is whether it is best to liquidate (under provisions of state law or Bankruptcy Code), to attempt an out-of-court settlement, to seek an outside buyer, or to file a Chapter 11 petition. To decide which course of action to take, it is also important to ascertain what caused the debtor's current problems, whether the company will be able to overcome its difficulties, and, if so, what measures will be necessary. Accountants may be asked to explain how the losses occurred and what can be done to avoid them in the future. To help with this determination, it may be necessary to project the operations after a 30-day period over at least the next three to six months, and to indicate the areas where steps will be necessary in order to earn a profit.

For existing clients, the information needed to make a decision about the course of action to make may be obtained with limited additional work; however, for a new client, it is necessary to perform a review of the client's operations to determine the condition of the business. Once the review has been completed, the client must normally decide to liquidate the business, attempt an informal settlement with creditors, or file a Chapter 11 petition, unless additional funds can be obtained or a buyer for the business is located. For example, where the product is inferior, the demand for the product is declining, the distribution channels are inadequate, or other similar problems exist that cannot be corrected, either because of the economic environment or management's lack of ability, it is normally best to liquidate the company immediately.

The decision whether a business should immediately file a Chapter 11 petition or attempt an out-of-court settlement depends on several factors. Among them are the following eight:

1. Size of company
   a. Public
   b. Private
2. Number of creditors
   a. Secured
   b. Unsecured
   c. Public
   d. Private
3. Complexity of matter
   a. Nature of debt
   b. Prior relationships with creditors
4. Pending lawsuits
5. Executory contracts, especially leases
6. The impact of alternatives selected
7. Nature of management
   a. Mismanagement
   b. Irregularities
8. Availability of interim financing

45.3 GENERAL PROVISIONS OF BANKRUPTCY CODE

(a) FILING OF PETITION.   A voluntary case is commanded by the debtor's filing of a bankruptcy petition under the appropriate chapter.

An involuntary petition can be filed by three or more creditors (if 11 or fewer creditors, only one creditor is necessary) with unsecured claims of at least $10,000 and can be initiated only under Chapter 7 or 11. An indenture trustee may be one of the petitioning creditors. The Court allows a case to proceed only if (1) the debtor generally fails to pay its debts as they become due, provided such debts are not the subject of a bona fide dispute; or (2) within 120 days prior to the petition a custodian was appointed or took possession. The latter excludes the taking of possession of less than substantially all property to enforce a lien.

(b) TIMING OF PETITION—TAX CONSIDERATIONS.   The timing for filing the petition is important. For example, if the debtor delays filing the petition until the creditors are about to force the debtor into bankruptcy, the debtor may not be in a position to effectively control its destiny. On the other hand, if the petition is filed when the problems first develop and while the creditors are reasonably cooperative, the debtor is in a much better position to control the proceeding. If possible, it is best to file the petition near the end of the month or, even better, near the end of the quarter, to avoid a separate closing of the books.

Tax factors should also be considered in deciding when to file the petition. For example, if a debtor corporation that has attempted an unsuccessful out-of-court settlement decides to file a petition, the tax impact of the out-of-court action should be considered. If, in the out-of-court agreement, the debtor transferred property that resulted in a gain and a substantial tax liability, it would be best for the debtor to file the petition after the end of the current taxable year. By taking this action, the tax claim is a prepetition tax claim and not an administrative expense. If the tax claim is a prepetition claim, interest and penalties stop accruing on the day the petition is filed and the debtor may provide in the plan for the deferral of the tax liability up to six years. If the tax claim is an administrative expense, penalties and interest on any unpaid balance will continue to accrue and the provision for deferred payment of up to six years does not apply.

(c) ACCOUNTING SERVICES—DATA REQUIRED IN THE PETITION.   The accountant must supply the attorney with certain information necessary for filing a Chapter 11 petition. This would normally include the following:

- *List of Largest Creditors.* A list containing the names and addresses of the 20 largest unsecured creditors, excluding insiders, must be filed with the petition in a voluntary case. In an involuntary situation, the list is to be filed with the petition in a voluntary case. In an involuntary petition, the list is to be filed within two days after entry of the order for relief. See Bankruptcy Rule 1007 and Bankruptcy Form 4.

- *List of Creditors.* The debtor must file with the court a list of the debtor's creditors of each class, showing the amounts and character of any claims and securities and, so far as is known, the name and address or place of business of each creditor and a notation whether the claim is disputed, contingent, or unliquidated as to amount, when each claim was incurred and the consideration received, and related data.

- *List of Equity Security Holders.* It is necessary to provide a list of the debtor's security holders of each class showing the number and kind of interests registered in the name of each holder and the last known address or place of business of each holder.

- *Schedules of Assets and Liabilities.* The schedules that must accompany the petition (or filed within 15 days after the petition is filed—unless the court extends the time period) are sworn statements of the debtor's assets and liabilities as of the date the petition is filed under Chapter 11. These schedules consist primarily of the debtor's balance sheet broken down into detail, and the accountant is required to supply the information generated in the preparation of the normal balance sheet and its supporting schedules. The required information is supplied on Schedules A through C, which include a complete statement of assets, and Schedules D through F, which are a complete statement of liabilities. Schedule G requires the debtor to list all executory contracts and unexpired leases. It is crucial that this information be accurate and complete because the omission or incorrect listing of a creditor might result in a failure to receive notice of the proceedings, and consequently the creditor's claim could be exempted from a discharge when the plan is later confirmed. Also omission of material facts may be construed as a false statement or concealment.

- *Statement of Financial Affairs.* The statement of affairs, not to be confused with an accountant's usual use of the term, is a series of detailed questions about the debtor's property and conduct. The general purpose of the statement of affairs is to give both the creditors and the court an overall view of the debtor' operations. It offers many avenues to begin investigations into the debtor's conduct. The statement (Official Form No. 7) consists of 25 questions to be answered under oath concerning the following areas:
  1. Income from employment or operation of business
  2. Income other than from employment or operation of business
  3. Payments to creditors
  4. Suits, executions, garnishments, and attachments
  5. Repossessions, foreclosures, and returns
  6. Assignments and receiverships
  7. Gifts
  8. Losses
  9. Payments related to debt counseling or bankruptcy
  10. Other transfers
  11. Closed financial accounts
  12. Safe deposit boxes
  13. Setoffs
  14. Property held for another person
  15. Prior address of debtor
  16. Spouses and former spouses
  17. Environmental issues
  18. Nature, location, and name of business
  19. Books, records, and financial statements
  20. Inventories
  21. Current partners, officers, directors, and shareholders
  22. Former partners, officers, directors, and shareholders
  23. Withdrawals from a partnership or distributions by a corporation
  24. Tax consolidation group
  25. Pension funds
- *Exhibit "A" to the Petition.* This is a thumbnail sketch of the financial condition of the business listing total assets, total liabilities, secured claims, unsecured claims, information relating to public trading of the debtor's securities, and the identity of all insiders.

The debtor must also file any additional reports or documents that may be required by local rules or by the U.S. trustee.

(d) ADEQUATE PROTECTION AND AUTOMATIC STAY. A petition filed under the Bankruptcy Code results in an automatic stay of the actions of creditors. The automatic stay is one of the fundamental protections provided the debtor by the Bankruptcy Code. In a Chapter 7 case, it provides for an orderly liquidation that treats all creditors equitably. For business reorganizations under Chapter 11, 12, or 13, it provides time for the debtor to examine the problems that forced it into bankruptcy court and to develop a plan for reorganization. As a result of the stay, no party, with minor exceptions, having a security or adverse interest in the debtor's property can take an action that will interfere with the debtor or his property, regardless of where the property is located, until the stay is modified or removed. Section 362(a) provides a list of eight kinds of acts and conduct subject to the automatic stay.

Under Section 362 of the Bankruptcy Code, a tax audit, a demand for a tax return, or the issuance of a notice and demand for payment for such assessment are not considered a violation of the automatic stay.

The stay of an act against the property of the estate continues, unless modified, until the property is no longer the property of the estate. The stay of any other act continues until the case is closed or dismissed, or the debtor is either granted or denied a discharge. The earliest occurrence of one of these events terminates the stay.

(i) Relief from the Stay.   The court may grant relief after notice and hearing, by terminating, annulling, modifying, or conditioning the stay. The court may grant relief for cause, including the lack of adequate protection of the interest of the secured creditor. With respect to an act against property, relief may be granted under Chapter 11 if the debtor does not have any equity in the property and the property is not necessary for an effective reorganization.

Section 361 identifies acceptable ways of providing adequate protection. First, the trustee or debtor may be required to make periodic cash payments to the entity entitled to relief as compensation for the decrease in value of the entity's interest in the property resulting from the stay. Second, the entity may be provided with an additional or replacement lien to the extent that the value of the interest declined as a result of the stay. Finally, the entity may receive the indubitable equivalent of its interest in the property.

The granting of relief when the debtor does not have any equity in the property solves the problem of real property mortgage foreclosures where the bankruptcy court petition is filed just before the foreclosure takes place. It was not intended to apply if the debtor is managing or leasing real property, such as a hotel operation, even though the debtor has no equity, because the property is necessary for an effective reorganization of the debtor.

The automatic stay prohibits a secured creditor from enforcing its rights in property owned by the debtor until the stay is removed. Without this right, a creditor could foreclose on the debtor's property, collect the proceeds, invest them, and earn income from the investment, even though a bankruptcy petition has been filed. Since the Bankruptcy Code does not allow this action to be taken, the creditor loses the opportunity to earn income on the proceeds that could have been received on the foreclosure. The courts refer to this as *creditor's opportunity costs.*

Four circuit courts have looked at this concept of opportunity cost. Two circuits (ninth and fourth) have ruled that the debtor is entitled to opportunity cost, the eighth circuit ruled that under certain conditions opportunity costs may be paid, and the fifth circuit ruled that opportunity cost need not be paid. In January 1988, the Supreme Court held in *In re Timbers of Inwood Forest Associates* [484 U.S. 365 (1988)] that creditors having collateral with a value less than the amount of the debt are not entitled to interest during the period that their property is tied up in the bankruptcy proceeding. Because of the extended time period during which the creditors' interest in the property is tied up in bankruptcy proceedings, this decision will most likely encourage creditors to properly collateralize their claim and may in limited ways restrict the granting of credit.

If relief from the stay is granted, a creditor may foreclose on property on which a lien exists, may continue a state court suit, or may enforce any judgment that might have been obtained before the bankruptcy case.

(ii) Accounting Services—Determining Equity in Property.   The accountant may assist either the debtor or the creditor in determining the value of the collateral to help determine if there is any equity in the property. As a result of the *Timbers* decision, the court is more closely considering the prospects for successful reorganization. In cases where there is considerable question about the ability of the debtor to reorganize, courts are now allowing the stay to be removed, providing there is no equity in the property. The debtor, creditors' committee, or secured creditor(s) may ask accountants to provide evidences as to the ability of the debtor to reorganize.

(e) EXECUTORY CONTRACTS AND LEASES.   Section 365(a) provides that the debtor or trustee, subject to court approval, may assume, assign, or reject any executory contract or unexpired lease of the debtor. For nonresidential real property leases the debtor must make a decision to assume, assign, or reject the lease within 120 days after the petition is field. Only a 90-day extension will be granted, unless the landlord agrees to a larger extension. If a lease is not assumed by the end of the time period, it is presumed that the lease is rejected. A decision regarding all other leases must be made prior to confirmation of a plan in Chapter 11. In the case of a Chapter 7 petition, the decisions must be made regarding the assumption or rejection of all leases within 60 days, unless an extension is granted.

Executory contracts are contracts that are "so far unperformed that the failure of either [the bankrupt or nonbankrupt] to complete performance would constitute a material breach excusing the performance of the other."[1] Countryman's definition seems to have been adopted by Congress in the statement that "executory contracts include contracts under which performance remains due to some extent on both sides."[2] However, before a contract can be assumed, Section 361 indicates that the debtor or trustee must:

- Cure the past defaults or provide assurance they will be promptly cured.
- Compensate the other party for actual pecuniary loss to such property or provide assurance that compensation will be made promptly.
- Provide adequate assurance of future performance under the contract or lease.

(i) Limitations on Executory Contracts.   To be rejected, the contract must still be an executory contract. For example, the delivery of goods to a carrier before the petition is filed, under terms that provide that the seller's performance is completed upon the delivery of the goods to the carrier, would not be an executory contract in Chapter 11. Furthermore, the seller's claim would not be an administrative claim. On the other hand, if the terms provide that the goods are received on delivery to the buyer, the seller under Uniform Commercial Code (UCC) Section 2–705 would have the right to stop the goods in transit and the automatic stay would not preclude such action. If the goods are delivered, payment for such goods would be an administrative expense.

The damages allowable to the landlord of a debtor from termination of a lease of real property are limited to the greater of one year or 15 percent of the remaining portion of the lease's rent due not to exceed three years after the date of filing or surrender, whichever is earlier. This formula compensates the landlord while not allowing the claim to be so large as to hurt other creditors of the estate. The damages resulting from the breach of an employment contract are limited to one year following the date of the petition or the termination of employment, whichever is earlier.

(ii) Accounting Services—Rejection of Executory Contracts.   The accountant may render several services relating to the rejection of executory contracts, including these three:

1. Estimating the amount of the damages that resulted from the lease rejection for either the debtor or landlord.
2. Evaluating for the landlord the extent to which the debtor has the ability to make the payments required under the lease.
3. Assisting the debtor in determining (or evaluating for the creditor's committee) the leases that should be rejected. To the extent possible, this assessment should be made at the beginning of the case to help reduce the expenses of administration during the Chapter 11 case. Amounts paid for rent for the period after filing petition to the date of rejection are considered administrative expenses. Each lease needs to be analyzed to determine if there is equity in the lease or if the debtor needs it to successfully reorganize.

---

[1] See Countryman, "Executive Contracts in Bankruptcy," *Minnesota Law Review*, Vol. 57. (1973), pp. 439, 460.
[2] See S. Rep. No. 95–989, 95th Cong., 2nd Sess. (1977).

(f) AVOIDING POWER. The Bankruptcy Code grants to the trustee or debtor in possession (DIP) the right to avoid certain transfers and obligations incurred. For example, Section 544 allows the trustee to avoid unperfected security interest and other interests in the debtor's property. Thus if the creditor fails to perfect a real estate mortgage, the trustee may be able to avoid that security interest and force the claim to be classified as unsecured rather than secured.

The trustee needs these powers and rights to ensure that actions by the debtor or by creditors in the prepetition period do not interfere with the objective of the bankruptcy laws, to provide for a fair and equal distribution of the debtor's assets through liquidation—or rehabilitation, if this would be better for other creditors involved.

In addition the trustee has the power to avoid preferences, fraudulent transfers, and postpetition transfers.

(g) PREFERENCES. A preferential payment as defined in Section 547 of the Bankruptcy Code is a transfer of any of the property of a debtor to or for the benefit of a creditor, for or on account of an antecedent debt made or suffered by the debtor while insolvent and within 90 days before the filing of a petition initiating bankruptcy proceedings, when such transfer enables the creditor to receive a greater percentage of payment than it would receive if the debtor were liquidated under Chapter 7. Insolvency is presumed during the 90-day period. A transfer of property to an insider between 90 days and one year before the filing of the petition is also considered a preferential payment. An officer, director, or person in control of the corporation would be considered an insider. Action to recover a preferential payment received by a third party that benefited an officer or other insider may only be taken against the officer or other insider and not against the third party. For example, if a president paid off a loan that he personally guaranteed six months before the petition was filed, the payment would be recoverable as a preference from the president, but not from the bank. Preferences include the payment of money, a transfer of property, assignment of receivables, or the giving of a mortgage on real or personal property.

A preferential payment is not a fraud but rather a legitimate and proper payment of a valid antecedent debt. The voidability of preferences is created by law to effect equality of distribution among all the creditors. The 90-day period (one year for transactions with insiders) prior to filing the bankruptcy petition has been arbitrarily selected by Congress as the time period during which distributions to the debtor's creditors may be redistributed to all the creditors ratably. During this period, a creditor who accepts a payment is said to have been preferred and may be required to return the amount received and later participate in the enlarged estate to the pro rata extent of its unreduced claim.

(i) Exceptions to Preferential Transfers. Section 547(c) contains eight exceptions to the power the trustee has to avoid preferential transfers. Five of the assumptions are discussed below.

1. *Contemporaneous exchange.* A transfer intended by the debtor and creditor to have a contemporaneous exchange for new value given to the debtor and that is in fact a substantially contemporaneous exchange is exempted. The purchase of goods or services with a check would not be a preferential payment, provided the check is presented for payment in the normal course of business.

2. *Ordinary course of business and ordinary business terms.* The second exemption protects payments of debts that were incurred in the ordinary course of business or financial affairs of both the debtor and the transferee when the payment is made in the ordinary course of business according to ordinary business terms.

3. *Purchase money security interest.* The third exception exempts security interests granted in exchange for enabling loans when the proceeds are used to finance the purchase of specific personal property. For example, a debtor borrowed $75,000 from a bank to finance a computer system and subsequently purchased the system. The "transfer" of this system as collateral to the bank would not be a preference provided the proceeds were given after the signing of the security agreement, the proceeds were used to purchase the system, and the

security interest was perfected within 20 days after the debtor received possession of the property.

4. *New value.* This exception provides that the creditor is allowed to insulate from preference attack a transfer received to the extent that the creditor replenishes the estate with new value. For example, if a creditor receives $10,000 in preferential payments and subsequently sells to the debtor, on unsecured credit, goods with a value of $6,000, the preference would be only $4,000. The new credit extended must be unsecured and can be netted only against a previous preferential payment, not a subsequent payment.

5. *Inventory and receivables.* This exception allows a creditor to have a continuing security interest in inventory and receivables (or proceeds) unless the position of the creditor is improved during the 90 days before the petition. If the creditor is an insider, the time period is extended to one year. An improvement in position occurs when a transfer causes a reduction in the amount by which the debt secured by the security interest exceeds the value of all security interest for such debt.

A two-point test is to be used to determine if an improvement in position occurred: The position 90 days (one year for insiders) prior to the filing of the petition is compared with the position as of the date of the petition. If the security interest is less than 90 days old, then the date on which new value was first given is compared to the position as of the date of the petition. The extent of any improvement caused by transfers to the prejudice of unsecured creditors is considered a preference.

To illustrate this rule, assume that on March 1, the bank made a loan of $700,000 to the debtor secured by a so-called floating lien on inventory. The inventory value was $800,000 at that date. On June 30, the date the debtor filed a bankruptcy petition, the balance of the loan was $600,000 and the debtor had inventory valued at $500,000. It was determined that 90 days prior to June 30 (date petition was filed), the inventory totaled $450,000 and the loan balance was $625,000. In this case there has been an improvement in position of $75,000 ($600,000–$500,000)–($625,000–$450,000), and any transfer of a security interest in inventory or proceeds could be revoked to that extent.

(ii) Accounting Services—Search for Preferential Payments. The trustee or DIP will attempt to recover preferential payments. Section 547(f) provides that the debtor is presumed to be insolvent during the 90-day period prior to bankruptcy. This presumption does not apply to transfers to insiders between 91 days and one year prior to bankruptcy. This presumption requires the adverse party to come forth with some evidence to prove the presumption. The burden of proof, however, remains with the party in whose favor the presumption exists. Once this presumption is rebutted, insolvency at the time of payment is necessary, and only someone with the training of an accountant is in a position to prove insolvency. The accountant often assists the debtor or trustee in presenting evidence showing whether the debtor was solvent or insolvent at the time payment was made. In cases where new management is in charge of the business or where a trustee has been appointed, the emphasis is often on trying to show that the debtor was insolvent in order to recover the previous payments and increase the size of the estate. The creditors' committee likewise wants to show that the debtor was insolvent at the time of payment to provide a larger basis for payment to unsecured creditors. Of course, the specific creditor recovering the payment looks for evidence to indicate that the debtor was solvent at the time payment was made.

Any payments made within the 90 days preceding the bankruptcy court filing and that are not in the ordinary course of business should be very carefully reviewed to see if the payments were preferences. Suspicious transactions would include anticipations of debt obligations, repayment of officers' loans, repayment of loans that have been personally guaranteed by officers, repayment of loans made to personal friends and relatives, collateral given to lenders, and sales of merchandise made on a countraaccount basis.

In seeking to find voidable preferences, the accountant has two crucial tasks: to determine the earliest date on which insolvency can be established within the 90-day period (one year for insiders), and to report to the trustee's attorney questionable payments, transfers, or encumbrances that have been made by the debtor after that date. It is then the attorney's responsibility to determine the voidable payments. However, the accountant's role should not be minimized, for it is the accountant who initially determines the suspect payments. See Newton (2000) for a discussion of the procedures to follow in a search for preferences.

(h) FRAUDULENT TRANSFERS. Fraudulent transfers and obligations are defined in Section 548 and include transfers that are presumed fraudulent regardless of whether the debtor's actual intent was to defraud creditors. A transfer may be avoided as fraudulent when made within one year (two years for petitions filed on or after April 20, 2006) prior to the filing of the bankruptcy petition, if the debtor made such transfer or incurred such obligation with actual intent to hinder, delay, or defraud existing or real or imagined future creditors. Also avoidable are constructively fraudulent transfers where the debtor received less than a reasonably equivalent value in exchange for such transfer or obligation and (1) was insolvent on the date that such transfer was made or such obligation was incurred, or became insolvent as a result of such transfer or obligation; (2) was engaged in business, or was about to engage in business or a transaction, for which any property remaining with the debtor was an unreasonably small capital; or (3) intended to incur, or believed that the debtor would incur, debts that would burden the debtor's ability to pay as such debts matured.

Under Section 544 of the Bankruptcy Code, fraudulent transfers may also be recovered under state law for payments made between one and six years. Section 546 provides that any action to recover a preference or a fraudulent transfer under Section 548 through the Bankruptcy Code or under Section 544 through state law must commence the action within two years after the order for relief or if a trustee is appointed during the second year after the petition is filed within one year after the trustee is appointed.

In the determination of fraudulent transfers, insolvency is defined by Section 101(32) as occurring when the present fair salable value of the debtor's property is less than the amount required to pay its debts. The fair value of the debtor's property is also reduced by any fraudulently transferred property, and for an individual, by the exempt property under Section 522.

(i) Leveraged Buyout as a Fraudulent Transfer. A fraudulent transfer may occur in a leveraged buyout (LBO). For example, in a LBO transaction where the assets of the debtor were used to finance the purchase of the debtor's stock and the debtor became insolvent, operated with an unreasonably small capital, or incurred debt beyond the ability to repay, a fraudulent transfer may have occurred. Note that the transfer may have been made without adequate consideration because the debtor corporation received no benefit from the proceeds from the loan that were used to retire former stockholder's stock.

(ii) Accounting Services—Search for Fraudulent Transfers. It is important for the accountant to ascertain when a fraudulent transfer has in fact occurred because it represents a possible recovery that could increase the value of the estate. It can, under certain conditions, prevent the debtor from obtaining a discharge. To be barred from a discharge as the result of a fraudulent transfer, the debtor must be an individual and the proceedings must be under Chapter 7 liquidation or the trustee must be liquidating the estate under a Chapter 11 proceeding.

In ascertaining if the debtor has made any fraudulent transfers or incurred fraudulent obligations, the independent accountant would carefully examine transactions with related parties within the year prior to the petition or other required period, look for the sale of large amounts of fixed assets, review liens granted to creditors, and examine all other transactions that appear to have arisen outside the ordinary course of the business.

(i) POSTPETITION TRANSFERS. Section 549 allows the trustee to avoid certain transfers made after the petition is filed. To be avoidable, transfers must not be authorized either by the court or by an explicit provision of the Bankruptcy Code.

(i) Adequate Value Received. The trustee can avoid transfers made under Section 303(f) and 542(c) of the Bankruptcy Code even though authorized. Section 303(f) authorizes a debtor to continue operating the business before the order for relief in an involuntary case. Section 549 does, however, provide that a transfer made prior to the order for relief is valid to the extent of value received. Thus, the provision of Section 549 cautions all persons dealing with a debtor before an order for relief has been granted to evaluate the transfers carefully. Section 542(c) explicitly authorizes certain postpetition transfers of real property of the estate made in good faith by an entity without actual knowledge or notice of the commencement of the case.

(ii) Accounting Services—Preventing Unauthorized Transfers. To prevent unauthorized transfers, the procedures that the accountant should see are operative include the following three:

1. Establishing procedures to ensure that prepetition debt payments are made only with proper authorization
2. Designating an individual to handle all requests for prepetition debt payments
3. Acquainting accounting personnel with techniques that might be used to obtain unauthorized prepetition debt payments

(j) SETOFFS. Setoff is that right existing between two parties to net their respective debts where each party, as a result of unrelated transactions, owes the other an ascertained amount. The right to setoff is an accepted practice in the business community today. When one of the two parties is insolvent and files a bankruptcy court petition, the right to setoff has special meaning. Once the petition is filed, the debtor may compel the creditor to pay the debt owed and the creditor may in turn receive only a small percentage of the claim—unless the Bankruptcy Code permits the setoff.

The Bankruptcy Code gives the creditor the right to offset a mutual debt, providing both the debt and the credit arose before the commencement of the case. Major restriction on the use of setoff prevents the creditor from unilaterally making the setoff after a petition is filed. The right to setoff is subject to the automatic stay provisions of Section 362 and the use of property under Section 363. Thus, a debtor must obtain relief from the automatic stay before proceeding with the setoff. This automatic stay and the right to use the amount subject to setoff is possible only when the trustee or DIP provides the creditor with adequate protection. If adequate protection—normally in the form of periodic cash payments, additional or replacement collateral, or other methods that will provide the creditor with the indubitable equivalent of its interest—is not provided, then the creditor may proceed with the offset as provided in Section 553.

(i) Early Setoff Penalty. Section 553(b) contains a penalty for those creditors who, when they see the financial problems of the debtor and threat of the automatic stay, elect to offset their claim prior to the petition. The Code precludes the setoff of any amount that is a betterment of the creditor's position during the 90 days prior to the filing of the petition. Any improvement in position may be recovered by the DIP or trustee. The amount to be recovered is the amount by which the insufficiency on the date of offset is less than the insufficiency 90 days before the filing of the petition. If no insufficiency exists 90 days before the filing of the petition, then the first date within the 90-day period where there is an insufficiency should be used. Insufficiency is defined as the amount by which a claim against the debtor exceeds a mutual debt owing to the debtor by the holder of such claim. The amount recovered is considered an unsecured claim.

(ii) Accounting Services—Setoffs. In addition to developing a schedule that helps determine the amount of the penalty, the accountant may assist in determining the amount of debt outstanding.

(k) RECLAMATION. One area where the avoiding power of the trustee is limited is in a request for reclamation. Section 546(c) provides that under certain conditions, the creditor has the right to reclaim goods if the debtor received the goods while insolvent during the 45 days prior to the filing of the petition. To reclaim these goods, the seller must demand in writing, within 20 days after the petition was filed. If the seller does not make a timely demand for reclamation, the seller has to right to an administrative expense claim for goods delivered within 20 days prior to bankruptcy.

(l) U.S. TRUSTEE.   Chapter 30 of Title 28, U.S. Code, provides for the establishment of the U.S. trustee program. The Attorney General is responsible for appointing one U.S. trustee in each of the 21 regions, and one or more assistant U.S. trustees perform the supervisory and appointing functions formerly handled by bankruptcy judges. They are the principal administrative officers of the bankruptcy system. The judicial districts of Alabama and North Carolina were not to be a part of the expansion of the U.S. Trustee program until 1992. The Judicial Improvements Act of 1990 (P.L. 101–650) extended the time period in which the six districts must be a part of the system to October 1, 2002. In these districts, some of the functions performed by the U.S. trustee in other districts are assigned to an administrator in the bankruptcy court.

The U.S. trustee establishes, maintains, and supervises a panel of private trustees that are eligible and available to serve as trustee in cases under Chapter 7 or 11. Also, the U.S. trustee supervises the administration of the estate and the trustees in cases under Chapters 7, 11, 12, or 13. The intent is not for the U.S. trustee system to replace private trustees in Chapters 7 and 11. Rather, the system should relieve the bankruptcy judges of certain administrative and supervisory tasks and thus help to eliminate any institutional bias or the appearance of any such bias that may have existed in the prior bankruptcy system.

The U.S. trustees are responsible for the administration of cases. They appoint the committees of creditors with unsecured claims and also appoint any other committees of creditors or stockholders authorized by the court. If the court deems it necessary to appoint a trustee or examiner, a U.S. trustee makes this appointment (subject to court approval) and also petitions the court to authorize such an appointment.

U.S. trustees monitor applications for compensation and reimbursement for officers and accountants and other professionals retained in the case, raising objections when deemed appropriate. Other responsibilities include monitoring plans and disclosure statements, creditors' committees, and the progress of the case.

45.4 HANDLING OF CLAIMS UNDER CHAPTER 11

A claim antedating the filing of the petition that is not a priority claim or that is not secured by the pledge of property is classified as an unsecured claim. Claims where the value of the security interest is less than the amount of the claims are divided into a secured and an unsecured part.

(a) PROOF OF CLAIMS.   A proof of claim or interest is deemed filed in a Chapter 11 case provided the claim or interest is listed in the schedules filed by the debtor, unless the claim or interest is listed as disputed, contingent, or unliquidated. A creditor is thus not required to file a proof of claim if it agrees with the debt listed in the schedules. It is, however, advisable for creditors to file a proof of claim in most situations. Creditors who for any reason disagree with the amount admitted on the debtor's schedules, such as allowable prepetition interest on their claims, or creditors desiring to give a power of attorney to a trade association or lawyer, should always prepare and file a complete proof of claim. Special attention must also be devoted to secured claims that are undersecured.

(b) UNDERSECURED CLAIMS.   Section 506 provides that if a creditor is undersecured, the claim will be divided into two parts. The first part is secured to the extent of the value of the collateral or to the extent of the amount of funds subject to setoff. The balance of the claim is considered unsecured. The value to be used to determine the amount of the secured claim is, according to Section 506(a), to "be determined in light of the purpose of the valuation and of the proposed disposition or use of such property, and in conjunction with any hearing on such disposition or use or on a plan affecting such creditors' interest." Bankruptcy Rule 3012 provides that any party in interest may petition the court to determine the value of a secured claim.

Thus, the approach used to value property subject to a lien for a Chapter 7 may be different from that for a Chapter 11 proceeding. Even within a Chapter 11 case, property may be valued differently. For example, fixed assets that are going to be sold because of the discontinuance of operations may be assigned liquidation values, whereas assets that will continue to be used by the debtor may be assigned going concern values. Although courts have to determine value on a case-by-case basis, it is clear that the value is to be determined in light of the purpose of the valuation and the proposed disposition or use of the property.

Section 1111(b) allows a secured claim to be treated as a claim with recourse against the debtor in Chapter 11 proceedings (i.e., where the debtor is liable for any deficiency between the value of the collateral and the balance due on the debt) whether the claim is nonrecourse by agreement or by applicable law. This preferred status terminates if the property securing the loan is sold under Section 363 or is to be sold under the terms of the plan, or if the class of which the secured claim is a part elects application of Section 1111(b)(2).

Another available section under Section 1111(b) is that a class of undersecured creditors can elect to have its entire claim considered secured. A class of creditors will normally be only one creditor. For example, in Chapter 11 cases where most of the assets are pledged, very little may be available for unsecured creditors after paying administrative expenses. Thus, the creditor might find it advisable to make the Section 1111(b)(2) election. On the other hand, if there will be a payment to unsecured creditors of approximately 75 cents per dollar of debt, the creditor may not want to make this election.

The purpose of the election is to provide adequate protection to holders of secured claims where the holder is of the opinion that the collateral is undervalued. Also, if the treatment of the part of the debt that is accorded unsecured status is so unattractive, the holder may be willing to waive his unsecured deficiency claims. The class of creditors making this election has the right to receive full payment for its claims over time. If the members of the class do not approve the plan, the court may confirm the plan as long as the plan provides that each member of the class receives deferred cash payments totaling at least the allowed amount of the claim. However, the present value of these payments as of the effective date of the plan must be at least equal to the value of the creditors' interest in the collateral. Thus, a creditor who makes the election under Section 1111(b)(2) has the right to receive full payment over time, but the value of that payment is only required to equal the value of the creditor's interest in the collateral.

(c) ADMINISTRATIVE EXPENSES.   The actual, necessary costs of preserving the estate, including wages, salaries, and commissions for services rendered after the commencement of the case, are considered administrative expense. Any tax including fines or penalties is allowed unless it relates to a tax-granted preference under Section 507(a)(8). Compensation awarded a professional person, including accountants, for postpetition services is an expense of administration. Expenses incurred in an involuntary case subsequent to the filing of the petition but prior to the appointment of a trustee or the order for relief are not considered administrative expenses. They are, however, granted second priority under Section 507. Administrative expenses of a Chapter 11 case that is converted to Chapter 7 are paid only after payment of Chapter 7 administrative expenses.

(d) PRIORITIES.   Section 507 provides for the following priorities:

1. Allowed unsecured claim for prepetition domestic support obligations
2. Administrative expenses
3. Unsecured claims in an involuntary case arising after commencement of the proceedings but before an order of relief is granted

4. Wages earned within 180 days prior to filing the petition (or the cessation of the business) to the extent of $10,000[3] per individual

5. Unsecured claims to employee benefit plans arising within 180 days prior to filing petition limited to $10,000 times the number of employees covered by the plan less the amount paid in (4) above and the amount previously paid on behalf of such employees

6. Unsecured claims of grain producers against a grain storage facility or of fishermen against a fish storage or processing facility to the extent of $4,925

7. Unsecured claims of individuals to the extent of $2,225 from deposits of money for purchase, lease, or rental of property or purchase of services not delivered or provided

8. Claims for debts to a spouse or former spouse or child for alimony, maintenance, or support payments

9. Unsecured tax claims of governmental units:
   a. Income or gross receipts tax, provided tax return was due (including extension) within three years prior to filing petition, tax is assessable after commencement of the case; or tax was assessed within 240 days before petition was filed, exclusive of any time during which an offer in compromise was outstanding during the 240-day period plus 30 days and any time a stay of proceeding against collections was in effect in a prior case during the 240-day period, plus 90 days.
   b. Property tax last payable without penalty within one year prior to filing petition
   c. Withholding taxes
   d. Employment tax on wages, and so forth, due within three years prior to the filing of the petition
   e. Excise tax due within three years prior to the filing of the petition
   f. Customs duty on merchandise imported within one year prior to the filing of the petition
   g. Penalties related to a type of claim above in compensation for actual pecuniary loss

10. Allowed unsecured claims based on any commitment by the debtor to the Federal depository institutions regulatory agency (or predecessors to such agency), to maintain the capital of an insured depository institution

11. Allowed claims for personal injury or death resulting from the use of a motor vehicle or vessel if the operator was untoxicated.

Priority claims in a Chapter 11 case must be provided for in the plan.

(e) PROCESSING OF CLAIMS.   Several accounting firms and other businesses have developed models to handle the processing of claims of both small and large debtors. Some of their features include these six:

1. Capture of all the various formats of claims needed by the bankruptcy court
2. Information needed for management to review and evaluate each claim
3. Mailing lists and labels
4. Creditor statements
5. Online update and inquiry capability
6. Modeling and decision analysis capability that enables management to evaluate settlement alternatives efficiently

One system uses a multifield data base to help debtors deal with the complexities of a bankruptcy. Creditors' files can be sorted in terms of classes of creditors, priorities of claims, and so on, and

---

[3] The dollar amounts for priority claims will be adjusted every three years to reflect the changes in the Consumer Price Index for All Urban Customers. The next adjustment will be made on April 1, 2007.

then alphabetically within these categories. Notices sent to creditors include all the necessary information, such as the amount of a claim and its current status. Ongoing information that changes over time is constantly updated. This could include the extent to which proofs of claim differ from the recorded debt, the assessment of market values of collateral pledged as security, other assets that are not pledged as security, distributions made during the course of a Chapter 11 case, and changes to or withdrawals of claims. Automatically prepared and mailed notices keep creditors current on the proceedings of a case. The system, through automatic mailings, answers telephone inquiries as they are entered.

45.5 OPERATING UNDER CHAPTER 11

No order is necessary under the Bankruptcy Code for the debtor to operate the business in Chapter 11. Sections 1107(a) and 1108 grant the debtor all the rights, powers, and duties of a trustee, except the right to compensation under Section 330, and provide that the trustee may operate the business unless the court directs otherwise. Thus, the debtor will continue to operate the business unless a party in interest requests that the court appoint a trustee. Until action is taken by management to correct the problems that caused the adverse financial condition, the business will most likely continue to operate at a loss. If the creditors believe new management is necessary to correct the problem, they will press for a change in management or the appointment of a trustee.

In most large bankruptcies as well as in many smaller cases, the management is replaced, often by turnaround specialists, who have particular expertise in taking over troubled companies. They often eliminate the unprofitable aspects of the company's operations, reduce overhead, and find additional financing as part of the turnaround process. Once the plan has been confirmed, turnaround specialists frequently move on to other troubled companies. In small cases where management is also the stockholders, creditors are apt to be uncomfortable with existing management, which may have created the problems.

(a) USE OF PROPERTY. The debtor or trustee must be able to use a secured party's collateral, or in most situations there would be no alternative but to liquidate the business. Section 363(c) gives the trustee or debtor the right to use, sell, or lease property of the estate in the ordinary course of business without a notice and a hearing. As a result of this provision, the debtor may continue to sell inventory and receivables and use raw materials in production without notice to secured creditors and without court approval. The use, sale, or lease of the estate's property other than in the ordinary course of business is allowed only after notice and an opportunity for a hearing. Under Section 363 of the Bankruptcy Code, companies, with court approval, may sell all of a large percent of the assets of the company. As noted below, the sale of all or a large percentage of the debtor's assets is viewed as a very viable option to the development of a plan.

(i) Cash Collateral. One restriction on the use of the property of the bankruptcy estate is placed on the trustee or debtor where cash collateral is involved. Cash collateral is cash, negotiable instruments, documents of title, securities, deposit accounts, or other cash equivalents where the estate and someone else have an interest in the property. Also included would be the proceeds of noncash collateral, such as inventory and accounts receivable and proceeds, products, offspring, and rents, profits, or property subject to a security interest, if converted to proceeds of the type defined as cash collateral, provided the proceeds are subject to the prepetition security interest.

To use cash collateral, the creditor with the interest must consent to its use, or the court, after notice and hearing, must authorize its use. The court may authorize the use, sale, or lease of cash collateral at a preliminary hearing if there is a reasonable likelihood that the DIP will prevail at the final hearing. The Bankruptcy Code also provides that the court is to act promptly for a request to use cash collateral.

(ii) Accounting Services—Assisting Debtor in Providing Information to Secured Lender.   In many cases, a company cannot operate unless it can obtain use of its cash collateral. For example, cash in bank accounts subject to setoff or collections from pledged receivables and inventory prior to the filing of the petition are not available for use until the company obtains the consent of the appropriate secured creditor or of the court.

Thus, an immediate concern of many companies that need to file a Chapter 11 petition is how to procure enough cash to operate for the first week or so after filing the petition. Often the best way to obtain the use of the cash is to get approval from the secured creditor prior to the filing of the petition. Accountants can work with the debtor in putting together information for the secured lender that may result in the pledge of additional property or an extension of a receivable or inventory financing agreement for the release of cash to allow operation of the business once the petition is filed.

(b) OBTAINING CREDIT.   In most Chapter 11 proceedings, the debtor must obtain additional financing in order to continue the business. Although the debtor was allowed to obtain credit under prior law, the power granted to the debtor under the Bankruptcy Code is broader. Section 364(a) allows the debtor to obtain unsecured debt and to incur unsecured obligations in the ordinary course while operating the business. This right is automatic unless the court orders otherwise. Also the holder of these claims is entitled to first priority as administrative expenses.

If the debtor is unable to obtain the necessary unsecured debt under Section 364(a), the court may authorize the obtaining of credit and the incurring of debt by granting special priority for claims. These priorities may include the following:

- Giving priority over any or all administrative expenses
- Securing the debt with a lien on unencumbered property
- Securing the debt with a junior lien on encumbered property

DIP financing may be obtained from the existing lender or from a new lender. Most all major banks are involved in DIP financing as well as several other financial entities, including funds that are established to make loans to companies in Chapter 11 and on emergence from Chapter 11. At times existing creditors will lend to the Chapter 11 debtor in order to prevent other lenders from obtaining a position that may be superior to that of the existing lender. The bankruptcy court may allow the debtor to prime the position of the existing lender. However, for the court to authorize the obtaining of credit with a lien on encumbered property that is senior or equal to the existing lien, the debtor must not be able to obtain credit by other means and the existing lien holder must be adequately protected.

Credit obtained other than in the ordinary course of business must be authorized by the court after notice and a hearing. Where there is some question whether the credit is related to the ordinary course of business, the lender should require court approval.

The number of 363 sales has recently increased compared to the number of plans approved. Banks and other financial institutions are less willing to lend funds for the time period necessary for businesses to reorganize, but may be willing to provide funds for a shorter period while the debtor implements a 363 sale. Additionally, creditors appear to be less patient today than they were in the 1980s and early 1990s, asking debtors to sell the business or in some cases filing a motion asking the court to provide for a 363 sale.

Asset sales are not restricted to the middle market or smaller cases. For example, companies like Polaroid (received $56.5 million cash for assets of its Identification Systems Business Division), Fruit of the Loom (business operations purchased by Berkshire Hathaway, Inc.), and LTV Corporation (sold its integrated steel assets to WL Ross & Co.) completed significant asset sales as a part of their Chapter 11 filing.

(c) APPOINTMENT OF TRUSTEES.   The Bankruptcy Code provides that a trustee can be appointed in certain situations based on facts in the case and not related to the size of the company or the amount of unsecured debt outstanding. The trustee is appointed only at the request of a party in interest after a notice and hearing. A party in interest includes the debtor, the trustee (in other contexts), creditors' or stockholders' committees, creditors, stockholders, or indenture trustees. Also, a U.S. trustee, while not a party in interest, may petition the court for an appointment of a trustee.

Section 1104(a) states that a trustee be appointed:

1. For cause, including fraud, dishonesty, incompetence, or gross mismanagement of the affairs of the debtor by current management, either before or after the commencement of the case, or similar cause, but not including the number of holders of securities of the debtor or the amount of assets or liabilities of the debtor; or

2. If such appointment is in the interest of creditors, any equity security holders, and other interests of the estate, without regard to the number of holders of securities of the debtor or the amount of assets or liabilities of the debtor.

The U.S. trustee is responsible for the appointment of the trustee from a panel of qualified trustees, once the appointment has been authorized by the court. It also appears that the U.S. trustee would have the right to replace trustees who fail to perform their functions properly.

The Bankruptcy Code, as originally enacted, provided that in a Chapter 7 case, the interim trustee appointed by the U.S. trustee would serve as the trustee unless a trustee is elected by a majority of at least 20 percent of the unsecured creditors voting in an election at a meeting of creditors under Section 341 of the Bankruptcy Code. In most Chapter 7 cases, the interim trustee serves as the trustee. The Bankruptcy Reform Act of 1994 modified Section 1104 of the Bankruptcy Code to provide that on request of a party in interest (made within 30 days after the court authorized the appointment of a trustee), the U.S. trustee must call a meeting of unsecured creditors for the purpose of electing a Chapter 11 trustee. This change might encourage more creditors to petition the court for the appointment of a trustee in a Chapter 11 case because the creditors now have some impact as to who is appointed.

(d) APPOINTMENT OF EXAMINER.   Under the Bankruptcy Code, the trustee's major functions are to (1) operate the business and (2) conduct an investigation of the debtor's affairs. Under certain conditions, it may be best to leave the current management in charge of the business, without resolving the need for the investigation of the debtor. The Code provides for the appointment of an examiner to perform this function. Section 1104(b) states that if a trustee is not appointed:

... [O]n request of a party in interest, and after notice and hearing, the court shall order the appointment of an examiner to conduct such an investigation of the debtor as is appropriate, including an investigation of any allegations of fraud, dishonesty, incompetence, misconduct, mismanagement, or irregularity in the management of the affairs of the debtor of or by current or former management of the debtor, if

1. Such appointment is in the interest of creditors, any equity security holders, and other interests of the estates; or

2. The debtor's fixed, liquidated, unsecured debts, other than debts for goods, services, or taxes, or owing to an insider, exceed $5 million.

(i) Functions of Examiner.   The function of the examiner is to conduct an investigation into the actions of the debtor, including fraud, dishonesty, mismanagement of the financial condition of the debtor and the operation of the business, and the desirability of the continuation of such business. The report is to be filed with the court and given to any creditors' committee, stockholders' committees, or other entities designated by the court. In addition to these two provisions, Section 1106(b) also states that an examiner may perform other functions as directed by the court.

In some cases, the court has expanded the role of the examiner. For example, the bankruptcy judges may prefer to see additional controls exercised over the management of the debtor, but may not see the need to incur the costs of the appointment of a trustee. These functions are assigned to the examiner.

(ii) Accountants as Examiners.   Accountants may serve as examiners, and in some regions U.S. trustees have expressed a preference for appointing accountants in certain situations. Where a financial investigation is needed, an accountant may be the most qualified person to perform as an examiner. In many cases where the role of the examiner has been expanded, accountants were serving as examiners.

(e) OPERATING STATEMENTS.   Several different types of reports are required while the debtor is operating the business in a Chapter 11 reorganization proceeding. The nature of the reports and the time period in which they are issued depend to some extent on local rules and on the type of internal controls of the debtor and the extent to which large losses are anticipated.

Districts establish local bankruptcy rules that generally apply to all cases filed in that particular district. These rules cover some of the procedural matters that relate to the handling of a bankruptcy case, including appearance before the court, forms of papers filed with the court, assignment of case, administration of case, employment of professionals, and operating statements. The rules for the filing of operating statements have become primarily the responsibility of the U.S. trustee and, as a result, the specific procedures for these statements are those of the U.S. trustee.

One statement required by all regions is an operating statement—profit and loss statement. This statement may include, in addition to the revenue and expense accounts needed to determine net income on the accrual basis, an aging of accounts payable (excluding prepetition debts) and accounts receivable, status of payments to secured creditors, analysis of tax payments, analysis of insurance payments and coverage, and summary of bankruptcy fees that have been paid or are due.

The U.S. trustee also requires cash receipts and disbursement statements. In some cases, it may be necessary to prepare this statement for each bank account of the debtor. For example, the U.S. trustee for the central district of California requires that the debtor, in addition to the regular account, establish separate accounts for payroll and taxes. Separate cash receipts and disbursement statements are also required for each account.

An independent accountant may assist the debtor in the preparation of these monthly operating reports. See Section 45.7(c) of this chapter.

(f) REPORTING IN CHAPTER 11.   In November 1990, the American Institute of Certified Public Accountants (AICPA) issued Statement of Position (SOP) 90–7, *Financial Reporting by Entities in Reorganization Under the Bankruptcy Code,* which represents the first major pronouncement to be issued on financial reporting by companies in bankruptcy. The SOP applies to any company that files a Chapter 11 petition after December 31, 1990. In addition, the provisions regarding fresh start reporting apply to any entity that has its plan confirmed after June 30, 1991.

The SOP was designed to eliminate some of the significant divergences in accounting for bankruptcies and to increase the relevance of financial information provided to debtors, creditors, stockholders, and other interested parties who make decisions regarding the reorganization, especially the reorganization plan, of the debtor. The SOP applies to financial reporting by companies that have filed Chapter 11 petitions and expect to reorganize as going concerns, and to companies that emerge from Chapter 11 under confirmed plans. It does not apply to companies that are restructuring their debt outside of Chapter 11 or to those that adopt Chapter 11 plans of liquidation. It deals with how to report the activities of the Chapter 11 company during the reorganization proceeding and how to report the emergence of the company from Chapter 11.

A major objective of financial statements issued by the debtor in Chapter 11 should be to reflect the financial evolution of the debtor during the proceeding. Thus, for financial statements issued in the year the petition is filed and in subsequent years, a distinction should be made between transactions and events directly associated with the reorganization, as opposed to those related to the ongoing operations of the business. This principle is reflected in several significant areas of the financial statements.

(i) Balance Sheet.   Paragraphs 23–26 of the SOP provide specific guidance for the preparation of the balance sheet during the reorganization.

Liabilities subject to compromise should be separated from those that are not and from postpetition liabilities. Liabilities that are subject to compromise include unsecured claims, undersecured claims, and fully secured claims that may be impaired under a plan. Paragraph 23 indicates that if there is some uncertainty as to whether a secured claim is undersecured or will be impaired under the plan, the entire amount should be included with prepetition claims subject to compromise.

In view of this, it is expected that most prebankruptcy claims will be reported initially as liabilities subject to compromise. There are a number of reasons for this. For example, at the time the balance sheet is prepared, the collateral may not have been appraised. Also, it might be determined as the case progresses that estimated cash flows from property are less than anticipated. All security interests may not have been fully perfected. Due to these and other factors, it is not unusual for claims that appeared fully secured at the onset of a case to be found to be compromised during the proceedings.

Paragraph 26 also indicates that circumstances arising during the reorganization may require a change in the classification of liabilities between those subject to compromise and those not subject to compromise.

The principal categories (such as priority claims, trade debt, debentures, institutional claims, etc.) of the claims subject to compromise should be disclosed in the notes to the financial statements. Note that the focus of the reporting requirement is on providing information about the nature of the claims rather than whether the claims are current or noncurrent.

Liabilities that are not subject to compromise consist of postpetition liabilities and liabilities not expected to be impaired under the plan. They are reported in the normal manner and thus should be segregated into current and noncurrent categories if a classified balance sheet is presented.

Liabilities that may be affected by the plan should be reported at the amount expected to be allowed even though they may be settled for a lesser amount. For example, once the allowed amount of an existing claim is determined or can be estimated, the carrying value of the debt should be adjusted to reflect that amount. Paragraph 25 provides that debt discounts or premiums as well as debt issue costs should be viewed as valuations of the related debt. When the allowed claim differs from the net carrying amount of the debt, the discount or premium and deferred issue costs should be adjusted to the extent necessary to report the debt at the allowed amount of the claim. If these adjustments are not enough, then the carrying value of the debt will be adjusted. The gain or loss resulting from the entries to record these adjustments is to be reported as a reorganization item as described below.

Prepetition claims that become known after the petition is filed, such as a claim arising from the rejection of a lease, should also be reported on the basis of the expected amount of the allowed claim and not at an estimate of the settlement amount. Paragraph 48 of the SOP suggests that these claims should be reported at the amount allowed by the court because that is the amount of the liability until it is settled and the use of the allowed amount is consistent with the amounts at which other prepetition liabilities are stated.

Financial Accounting Standards Board (FASB) Statement No. 5, *Accounting for Contingencies,* applies to the process of determining the expected amount of an allowed claim. Claims that are not subject to reasonable estimation should be disclosed in the notes to the financial statements based on the provisions of FASB Statement No. 5. Once the accrual provisions of FASB Statement No. 5 are satisfied, the claims should be recorded.

(ii) Statement of Operations.   The objective of reporting during the Chapter 11 case is to present the results of operations of the reporting entity and to clearly separate those activities related to the normal operations of the business from those related to the reorganization. Thus, revenues, expenses (including professional fees), realized gains and losses, and provisions for losses resulting from the Chapter 11 reorganization and restructuring of the business should be separately reported. According to paragraph 27 of SOP 90–7, items related to the reorganization (except for the reporting of discontinued operations which are already reported separately) should be reported in a separate category within the income (loss) from operations section of the statement of operations. Appendix A in SOP 90–7 contains an example of the form to use for operating statements issued during a Chapter 11 case. The part of the operating statement that relates to the reporting of reorganization items is as follows:

Earnings before reorganization items and income tax benefits	47
Reorganization items:	
Loss on disposal of facility	(60)
Professional fees	(50)
Provision for rejected executory contracts	(10)
Interest earned on accumulated cash resulting from Chapter 11 proceeding	1
	(119)
Loss before income tax benefit and discontinued operations	(72)

Note that the reader of the statement of operations is able to determine the amount of income generated from continuing operations without the impact of the reorganization being reflected in these totals. While it will involve some judgment on the part of management to determine the part of income that relates to ongoing operations, a reasonable estimate of the segregation will be much more beneficial to the reader than including all items in the same category as is current practice.

A summary of the provisions relating to the operating statements includes these five:

1. Gains or losses as a result of restructuring or disposal of assets directly related to the reorganization are reported as a reorganization item (unless the disposal meets the requirement for discontinued operations). The gains or losses include the gain or loss on disposal of the assets, related employee costs, and other charges related to the disposal of assets or restructuring of operations. Note that the reporting of a reduction in business activity does not result in reclassification of revenues or expenses identified with the assets sold or abandoned, unless the transaction is classified as a disposal of a discounted business under Statement No. 144 *Accounting for the Impairment or Disposal of Long-Lived Assets.*

2. Professional fees are expensed as incurred and reported as a reorganization item.

3. Interest income that was earned in Chapter 11 that would not have been earned but for the proceeding is reported as a reorganization item.

4. Interest expense should be reported only to the extent that it will be paid during the proceeding or to the extent that it may be allowed as a priority, secured, or unsecured claim. The extent to which the reported interest expense differs from the contractual rate should be reflected in the notes to the operating statement or shown parenthetically on the face of the operating statement (the SEC prefers the latter). Under current practice, some debtors have accrued interest even though this procedure has been somewhat questionable. This practice should cease under the new SOP.

5. Income from debt discharge (forgiveness) in a Chapter 11 case where fresh start reporting is required should be shown as a reorganization item unless it meets the conditions for an extraordinary item under Accounting Principles Board (APB) Opinion No. 30, paragraph 26 dealing with unusual items and infrequently occurring items. Paragraph 41 (as revised) of the SOP indicates that this should also be the case for debtors not qualified for fresh start reporting.

(iii) Statement of Cash Flows. Paragraph 31 of the SOP indicates that reorganization items should be disclosed separately within the operating, investing, and financing categories of the statement of cash flows. The SOP also indicates that reorganization items related to operating cash flows are better reflected if the direct method is used to prepare the statement of cash flows. An example of the statement of cash flows issued during a Chapter 11 case using the direct approach is found in Appendix A of the SOP.

The SOP indicates that if the indirect method is used, the details of the operating cash receipts and payments resulting from the reorganization should be disclosed in a supplementary schedule or in the notes to the financial statement. The footnote or supplementary schedule should include the information from the reorganization section of the statement of cash flows that is presented above.

It would also be acceptable to reflect this information in the cash flow statement as shown next:

Net loss	$(118)
Adjustment to determine net cash provided by operating items before reorganization items:	
Depreciation	20
Loss on disposal of facility	60
Provision for rejection of executory contracts	10
Loss on discontinued operations	56
Increase in postpetition liabilities and other liabilities	250
Increase in accounts receivable	(180)
Reorganization items	49
Net cash provided by operating activities before reorganization items	147
Reorganization items:	
Interest received on cash accumulated because of the Chapter 11 proceeding	1
Professional fees paid for services rendered in connection with the Chapter 11 proceeding	(50)
Net cash provided by reorganization items	(49)
Net cash provided by operating activities	98

Any reorganization items included in financing and investing activities should also be disclosed separately.

45.6 CHAPTER 11 PLAN

The accountant advises and gives suggestions to the debtor and attorney in drawing up a plan. Section 1121 of the Bankruptcy Code provides that only the debtor may file a plan of reorganization during the first 120 days of the case (unless a trustee has been appointed). This period may be extended; however, the 2005 Act provides that the time period may not be extended beyond 18 months after the petition was filed. This breathing period permits the debtor to hold lawsuits and foreclosures in status quo and to determine economic causes of its financial predicament while developing a plan. Using the schedules of assets and liabilities, statement of affairs, and past and projected financial statements, the debtor and its accountant examine the liabilities of the debtor and the value of the business and explore sources of funding for the plan such as enhanced profitability, partial liquidation, issuing debt securities, or outside capitalization. They outline the classes of debt that cannot be deferred or reduced and negotiate with the rest.

(a) CLASSIFICATION OF CLAIMS. Section 1122 provides that claims or interests can be divided into classes provided each claim or interest is substantially similar to the others of such class. In addition, a separate class of unsecured claims may be established consisting of claims that are below or reduced to an amount the court approves as reasonable and necessary for administrative convenience. For example, claims of less than $1,000, or those creditors who will accept $1,000 as payment in full of their claim, may be placed in one class, and the claimants will receive the lesser of $1,000 or the amount of their claim. All creditors or equity holders in the same class are treated the same, but separate classes may be treated differently.

Generally, all unsecured claims, including claims arising from rejection of executory contracts or unexpired leases, are placed in the same class except for administrative expenses. They may, however, be divided into different classes if separate classification is justified. The Bankruptcy Code does not require placing all claims that are substantially the same in the same class.

Courts have stated that Section 1122(a) "does not require that similar claims must be grouped together, but merely that any group created must be homogeneous."

(b) DEVELOPMENT OF PLAN. The items that may be included in the plan are listed in Section 1123. Certain items are listed as mandatory and others are discretionary. The seven mandatory provisions are:

1. Designate classes of claims and interests.
2. Specify any class of claims or interest that is not impaired under the plan.
3. Specify the treatment of any class of claims or interest that is impaired under the plan.
4. Provide the same treatment for each claim or interest in a particular class unless the holders agree to less favorable treatment.
5. Provide adequate means for the plan's implementation, such as:
   - Retention by the debtor of all or any part of the property of the estate.
   - Transfer of all or any part of the property of the estate to one or more entities.
   - Merger or consolidation of the debtor with one or more persons.
   - Sale of all or any part of the property of the estate, either subject to or free of any lien, or the distribution of all or any part of the property of the estate among those having an interest in such property of the estate.
   - Satisfaction or modification of any lien.
   - Cancellation or modification of any indenture or similar instrument.
   - Curing or waiving any default.
   - Extension of a maturity date or a change in an interest rate or other term of outstanding securities.
   - Amendment of the debtor's charter.
   - Issuance of securities of the debtor, or of any entity involved in a merger or transfer of the debtor's business for cash, for property, for existing securities, or in exchange for claims or interests, or for any other appropriate purpose.
6. Provide for the inclusion in the charter of the debtor, if the debtor is a corporation, or of any corporation referred to in (5) above, of a provision prohibiting the issuance of nonvoting equity securities, and providing, as to the several classes of securities possessing voting power, an appropriate distribution of such power among such classes, including, in the case of any class of equity securities having a preference over another class of equity securities with respect to dividends, adequate provisions for the election of directors representing such preferred class in the event of default in the payment of such dividends.
7. Contain only provisions that are consistent with the interests of creditors and stockholders and with public policy with respect to the selection of officers, directors, or trustee under the plan.

In addition to these requirements, the plan may also include these five:

1. Impair or leave unimpaired any class of unsecured or secured claims or interests.
2. Provide for the assumption, rejection, or assignment of executory contracts or leases.
3. Provide for settlement or adjustment of any claim or interest of the debtor or provide for the retention and enforcement by the debtor of any claim or interest.
4. Provide for the sale of all of the property of the debtor and the distribution of the proceeds to the creditors and stockholders.
5. Include any other provision not inconsistent with the provisions of the Bankruptcy Code.

In determining the classes of creditors' claims or stockholders' interests that must approve the plan, it is first necessary to determine if the class is impaired. Section 1124 states that a class of claims or interest is impaired under the plan, unless the plan leaves unaltered the legal, equitable, and contractual rights of a class, cures defaults that led to acceleration of debts, or pays in cash the full amount of their claims.

(c) DISCLOSURE STATEMENT.   A party cannot solicit the acceptance or rejection of a plan from creditors and stockholders affected by the plan unless they receive a written disclosure statement containing adequate information as approved by the court. Section 1125(b) requires that the court must approve this disclosure statement, after notice and a hearing, as containing adequate information.

(i) Definition of Adequate Information.   Section 1125(a) states that adequate information means information of a kind, and in sufficient detail, as far as is reasonably practicable in light of the records, that would enable a hypothetical reasonable investor typical of holders of claims or interests of the relevant class to make an informed judgment about the plan. This definition contains two parts. First it defines adequate information and then it sets a standard against which the information is measured. It must be the kind of information that a typical investor of the relevant class, not one that has special information, would need to make an informed judgment about the plan.

Section 1125(a)(1) provides that adequate information need not include information about other possible proposed plans.

(ii) Content.   As noted above, the information disclosed in the statement should be adequate to allow the creditor or stockholder to make an informed judgment about the plan. The following seven paragraphs describe the types of information that might be included.

1. *Introduction.* The statement should provide information about voting on the plan as well as background information about the debtor and the nature of the debtor's operations.
2. *Management.* It is important to identify the management that will operate the debtor on emergence from bankruptcy and to provide a summary of their background.
3. *Summary of the plan of reorganization.* Typical investors want to receive a description of the terms of the plan and the reasons the plan's proponents believe a favorable vote is advisable.
4. *Reorganization value.* Included in the disclosure statement should be the reorganization value of the entity that will emerge from bankruptcy. One of the first, as well as one of the most difficult, steps in reaching agreement on the terms of a plan is determining the value of the reorganized entity. Once the parties—debtor, unsecured creditors' committee, secured creditors, and shareholders—agree on the reorganization value, this value is then allocated among the creditors and equity holders. Thus, before determining the amount that unsecured creditors, secured creditors, or equity holders will receive, it is necessary to determine the reorganization value. An unsecured creditors' committee or another representative of creditors or equity holders is generally unable, and often unwilling, to agree to the terms of a

plan without any knowledge of the emerging entity's reorganization value. It also appears that if this value is needed by the parties that must agree on the terms of a plan, it is also needed by each unsecured creditor to determine how to vote on the plan.

Paragraph 37 of SOP 90–7 states that while the court determines the adequacy of information in the disclosure statement, entities that expect to adopt fresh start reporting should report information about the reorganization value in the disclosure statement. The reporting of this value should help creditors and shareholders make an informed judgment about the plan.

The SOP suggests that the most logical place to report the reorganization value is in the pro forma balance sheet that shows the financial position of the entity as though the proposed plan was confirmed.

5. *Financial information.* Among several types of information that may benefit creditors and stockholders considerably in assessing the potential of the debtors' business are the following: audited reports of the financial position as of the date the petition was filed or as of the end of a recent fiscal year, and the results of operations for the past year; a detailed analysis by the debtor of its properties, including a description of the properties, the current values, and other relevant information; and a description of the obligations outstanding with identification of the material claims in dispute. If the nature of the company's operations is going to change significantly as a result of the reorganization, historical financial statements for the past two to five years are of limited value.

In addition to the historical financial statements, it may be useful to present a pro forma balance sheet showing the impact that the proposed plan, if accepted, will have on the financial condition of the company. Included should be the source of new capital and how the proceeds will be used, the postpetition interest obligation, lease commitments, financing arrangements, and so forth.

To provide the information needed by creditors and stockholders for effective evaluation of the plan, the pro forma statement should show the reorganization value of the entity. Thus the assets would be presented at their current values, and, if there is any excess of the reorganization value (going concern value) over individual assets, this value would be shown. Liabilities and stockholder's equity should be presented at their discounted values based on the assumption that the plan will be confirmed. If appraisals of the individual assets have not been made, it appears appropriate to reflect the differences between the book value and reorganization value as an adjustment to the asset side of the pro forma balance sheet.

If the plan calls for future cash payments, the inclusion of projections of future operations will help the affected creditors make a decision as to whether they believe the debtor can make the required payments. Even if the plan calls for no future cash payments, it may still be advisable to include the financial information in the disclosure statement that will allow creditors and stockholders to see the business's potential for operating profitably in the future. These projections must, of course, be based on reasonable assumptions, and the assumptions must be clearly set forth in the projections accompanying the disclosure statement.

6. *Liquidation values.* Included in the disclosure statement should be an analysis of the amount that creditors and equity holders would receive if the debtor were to be liquidated under Chapter 7. In order to effectively evaluate the reorganization alternative, the creditors and equity holders must know what they would receive through liquidation. Also, the court, in order to confirm the plan, must ascertain, according to Section 1129 (a)(7), that each holder of a claim or interest who does not vote in favor of the plan must receive at least an amount that is equal to the amount that would be received in a Chapter 7 liquidation.

Generally, it is not acceptable to state that the amount provided for in the plan exceeds the liquidation amount. The presentation must include data to support this type of statement.

7. *Special risk factors.* In any securities that are issued pursuant to a plan in a Chapter 11 proceeding, certain substantial risk factors are inherent. It may be advisable to include a description of some of the factors in the disclosure statement.

(d) CONFIRMATION OF PLAN.   Prior to the confirmation hearing on the proposed plan, the proponents of the plan will seek its acceptance. Once the results of the vote are known, the debtor or other proponent of the plan will request confirmation of the plan.

The holder of a claim or interest, as defined under Section 502, is permitted to vote on the proposed plan. Voting is based on the classification of claims and interests. A major change from prior law is that the acceptance requirements are based on those actually voting and not on the total value or number of claims or interests allowed in a particular class. The Secretary of the Treasury is authorized to vote on behalf of the United States when the United States is a creditor or equity security holder.

A class of claim holders has accepted a plan if at least two-thirds in amount and more than one-half in number of the allowed claims for that class that are voted are cast in favor of the plan. For equity interests, it is only necessary that votes totaling at least two-thirds in amount of the outstanding securities in a particular class that voted be cast for the plan. The majority in number requirement is not applicable to equity interests.

(e) CONFIRMATION REQUIREMENTS.   Section 1129(a), which contains the requirements that must be satisfied before a plan can be confirmed, is one of the most important sections of the Bankruptcy Code. The provisions follow:

1. *The plan complies with the applicable provisions of Title 11.* Section 1122 concerning classification of claims and Section 1123 on the content of the plan are significant sections.

2. *The proponents of the plan comply with the applicable provisions of Title 11.* Section 1125 on disclosure is an example of a section that is referred to by this requirement.

3. *The plan has been proposed in good faith and is not by any means forbidden by law..*

4. *Payments are disclosed.* Any payment made or to be made for services, costs, and expenses in connection with the case or plan has been approved by, or is subject to the approval of, the court as reasonable.

5. *There is disclosure of officers.* The proponent of the plan must disclose the persons who are proposed to serve after confirmation as director, officer, or voting trustee of the reorganized debtor. Such employment must be consistent with the interests of creditors and equity security holders and with public policy. Also, names of insiders to be employed and the nature of their compensation must also be disclosed.

6. *Regulatory rate has been approved.* Any governmental regulatory commission that will have jurisdiction over the debtor after confirmation of the plan must approve any rate changes provided for in the plan.

7. *The plan satisfies the best-interest-of-creditors test.* It is necessary for the creditors or stockholders who do not vote for the plan to receive as much as they would if the business were liquidated under Chapter 7.

8. *The plan has been accepted by each class.* Each class of creditors or stockholders impaired under the plan must accept the plan. Section 1129(b), however, provides an exception to this requirement—the "Cram Down."

    This section allows the court under certain conditions to confirm a plan even though an impaired class has not accepted it. The plan must not discriminate unfairly, and it must be fair and equitable with respect to each impaired class of claims or interest that has not accepted the plan. The Code states conditions for secured claims, unsecured claims, and stockholder interests that would be included in the "fair and equitable" requirement. It should be noted that because the word "includes" is used, the meaning of fair and equitable is not restricted to these conditions. A discussion of the "cram down" provision is found in Section 5.33 of Newton's *Bankruptcy and Insolvency Accounting.*

9. *Priority claims have been satisfied.* This requirement provides that priority claims must be satisfied with cash payment as of the effective date of the plan unless the holders agree to a different treatment. An exception to this general rule is allowed for taxes. Taxes must be

paid over a period of six years from date of assessment with a present value equal to the amount of the claim.

10. *At least one class accepts the plan.* If a class of claims is impaired under the plan, at least one class that is impaired, other than a class of claims held by insiders, must accept the plan.

11. *Plan is feasible.* Confirmation of the plan is not likely to be followed by liquidation or by the need for further financial reorganization unless the plan provides for such liquidation or reorganization.

12. *Payment of fees.* The filing fees and quarterly fees must be paid or provided in the plan that they will be paid as of the effective date of the plan.

13. *Retiree benefit continuation.* The plan must provide, as of the effective date, for the continuation of all retiree benefits as defined under Section 1114 and at the level established under Section 1114.

(f) ACCOUNTING SERVICES—ASSISTANCE TO DEBTOR.   Accountants can provide considerable services to their client relating to the formulation of the plan, some of which are described in the following subsections.

(i) Liquidation Value of Assets.   Section 1129(a)(7) provides that each holder of a claim must either accept that plan or receive or retain interest in property of a value that is at least equal to the amount that would have been received or retained if the debtor were liquidated under Chapter 7. Accountants can help the debtor establish these values.

(ii) Projections of Future Operations.   Section 1129(a)(11) contains the feasibility standard of Chapter 11 requiring that confirmation of the plan of reorganization is not likely to be followed by liquidation or further reorganization (unless contemplated). The accountant may assist the debtor or trustee to formulate an acceptable plan by projecting the ability of the debtor to carry out and perform the terms of the plan. To establish feasibility, the debtor must project the profitability potential of the business. Where the plan calls for installment payments, the accountant may be requested to prepare or review projected budgets, cash flow statements, and statements of financial position. The creditors must be assured by the projected income statement and cash flow statement that the debtor will be in a position to make the payments as they become due. The forecast of the results of operations and financial position should be prepared on the assumption that the proposed plan will be accepted, and the liability and asset accounts should reflect the balance that would be shown after all adjustments are made relative to the debt forgiveness. Thus, interest expense is based on the liabilities that will exist after the discharge occurs.

(iii) Reorganization Value.   Not only are cash projections needed for the feasibility test as mentioned in the previous paragraph, but they are an important part of the negotiation process. The creditors want to receive the maximum amount possible in any Chapter 11 plan and often want the payment in cash as of the effective date of the plan. The creditors realize, however, that if their demands are beyond the ability of the debtor to make payments, the plan will not work and they will not receive the payments provided for in the plan. Cash flow projections assist both parties in developing reasonable conclusions regarding the value of the entity emerging from Chapter 11. In some reorganizations, there is considerable debate over cash flow projections and the discount rate to be used in determining the value of the debtor's continuing operations, to which must be added the amount to be realized on the sale of nonoperating assets plus excess working capital. Once the debtor and its creditors' committee can agree on the basic value of the entity, it is easier to negotiate the terms of the plan.

During the formulation of the plan, the accountant can assist the debtor considerably by helping to determine the reorganized value of the debtor or by helping the debtor to assess the valuation of an investment banker or other specialists. If the accountant develops the cash projections supporting the valuation, the accountant will be precluded from being independent for SEC purposes. Once the debtor has determined an estimate of the value of the entity that will emerge from bankruptcy, the accountant can provide assistance to the debtor in negotiating the terms of the plan with the creditor.

(iv) Pro Forma Balance Sheet.   Also of considerable help in evaluating a plan is a pro forma balance sheet showing how the balance sheet will look if the plan is accepted and all provisions of the plan are carried out. By using reorganization models or simulation models, the pro forma balance sheet may be prepared based on several possible courses of action that the debtor could take. The pro forma balance sheet illustrates the type of debt equity position that would exist under different alternatives.

This pro forma balance sheet should reflect the debts at discounted values. Assets are generally presented at their historical cost values unless the debtor has made a decision to apply the concept of quasi reorganization. A pro forma balance sheet that reflects the reorganized values of the entity is of considerable benefit to the debtor in developing the terms for a plan.

Once the terms of the proposed plan have been finalized, the pro forma balance sheet based on historical values reflecting these terms is generally included in the disclosure statement that must be submitted prior to or at the time votes are solicited on the plan. The pro forma balance sheet reflecting reorganized values, however, provides information for the creditors and stockholders that is much more relevant in making an informed judgment about how to vote on the plan.

(v) Reorganization Model.   Accountants can develop a model to help the debtor in developing a plan. The outcome of a reorganization plan depends on a variety of assumptions, including the creditors' willingness to accept different mixes of cash and securities, economic trends, possible sources for financing continuing operations or acquisitions, and many other factors. Using a model, these assumptions can be altered one at a time with all else held constant, and the possible courses of action can be analyzed according to the needs of management. Using this technique, creditors or the debtor can identify potential problem areas and request clarifications. Once these have been received and entered into the system, a new set of comparisons is made and the process is repeated until both sides are satisfied that the most favorable course is being pursued. Breakdowns of reorganization plans by computer models allow debtors and creditors to focus on the financial data most relevant to the case at hand.

(g) ACCOUNTING SERVICES—ASSISTANCE TO CREDITORS' COMMITTEE.   The following subsections describe several of the services that the accountant can render for the creditors' committee or for a committee of equity holders.

(i) Assistance in the Bargaining Process.   One of the basic functions performed by the creditors' committee is to negotiate a settlement and then make its recommendation to the other creditors. The accountant should be familiar with the bargaining process that goes on between the debtor and the creditors' committee in trying to reach a settlement. Bargaining can be both vigorous and delicate. The debtor bargains, perhaps, for a settlement that consists of a small percentage of the debt, demanding only a small immediate cash outlay, with payments to be made in the future. The debtor may want the debts outstanding to be subordinated to new credit or may ask that the agreement call for partial payment in preferred stock. The creditors want a settlement that represents a high percentage of the debt and consists of a larger cash down payment with the balance to be paid as soon as possible. In cases where there is very little cash available for debt repayment on confirmation, unsecured creditors may be interested in obtaining most of the outstanding stock of the company. In the past 10 years, the creditors of public companies have received an increasing interest in the ownership of the debtor. It is not unusual for the creditors to own between 80 percent and 95 percent of the outstanding stock of the emerging entity. For example, Wickes' creditors received 84 percent ownership, and the existing equity of Emmons Industries retained only 3 percent interest whereas creditors received the balance. The shareholders of failed LBOs often receive no equity interest in the reorganized entity.

The services that the accountant may render for the creditors' committee in the negotiations with the debtor vary significantly depending on several factors, including the size of the debtor, the experience of the members of the creditors' committee, the nature of the debtor's operations, and the creditors' committee confidence in the debtor and in the professionals—especially attorneys and accountants—who are helping the debtor. The committee in most cases, to varying degrees, depends on the accountant to help evaluate the debtor's operations, the information provided about those operations, and the terms of a proposed plan. Often accountants may be engaged to investigate selected aspects of the debtor's operations and to obtain an overall understanding of the debtor's problems and possible solutions.

(ii) Evaluation of Debtor's Projections. Of primary significance to a creditors' committee is determining whether the projections and forecasts submitted by the debtor are realistic. The representatives of the largest unsecured creditors on the committee typically are not accountants and thus may need assistance in evaluating the financial data prepared by the debtor. The accountant for the creditors' committee may be in a strong position to evaluate the debtor's projections and to make recommendations. The intention is not to perform an audit of such data but rather to review the information to determine whether the projections can be supported to some extent by hard evidence. The level of involvement by the accountant for the creditors' committee will vary, depending on the sophistication of the company or of the financial people who prepared the data. The review in some cases could be limited to a discussion of the data with those who prepared the projections, to determine whether the forecasts seem to make sense. In other situations, however, the accountant may find that the preparation of this information has been somewhat loose or vague. In these circumstances, the accountant for the committee may need to get involved in the preparation or to perform a review of the appropriate accounting records to see whether the basic underlying data have some foundation in fact.

(iii) Reorganization Value. In some cases accountants for the creditors' committee develop their own models of the debtor's operations. Cash flow projections can then be prepared for determining the reorganized entity's value. Operational changes made by the debtor are entered in the model as are proposed sales or other major actions, providing a basis for the committee's response to the debtor's proposals. Evaluation by the creditors' committee focuses on the impact these actions will have on the value of the reorganized entity and on the amount of potential settlement.

(iv) Review of Plan and Disclosure Statement. As was noted earlier, the accountant for the debtor provides advice and assistance in the formulation of a plan of reorganization in a Chapter 11 proceeding and a plan of settlement in an agreement out of court. An important function of an accountant employed by the creditors is to help evaluate the proposed plan of action. In a Chapter 11 case where the debtor has not proposed a plan within 120 days, a proposed plan has not been accepted within 180 days after the petition was filed, or where the trustee has been appointed, the accountant may assist the creditors in developing a plan to submit to the court. The accountant is able to provide valuable assistance to the committee because of familiarity with the financial background, nature of operations, and management of the company gained during the audit. In committee meetings, a great deal of discussion goes on between the committee members and the accountant concerning the best settlement they can expect and how it compares with the amount they would receive if the business were liquidated.

The creditors are interested in receiving as much as possible under any reorganization plan. The accountant may work with the creditors' committee to see that the amount proposed under the plan is reasonable and fair based on the nature of the debtor's business. First, it must be determined that the plan provides for at least as much as would be received in a Chapter 7 liquidation. Second, the creditors must leave for the debtor enough assets to operate the business after reorganization. If a reasonable basis does not exist for future operations, the judge may not confirm the plan because it is not feasible.

If an audit has not been performed, the accountant for the creditors' committee must rely on the information contained in the disclosure statement and in other reports that have been issued.

Thus, the content of the disclosure statement may be most important. Also, since the disclosure statement serves as the basic report used by the creditors to evaluate the plan, it is critical that it be properly prepared and contain the type of information that allows the creditors to effectively evaluate the proposed plan.

The accountant for the creditors' committee may be asked to evaluate the disclosure statement. If, in the accountant's opinion, it does not contain adequate information, the deficiencies may be conveyed to the debtor informally (normally through creditors' committee counsel) prior to submission of the plan to the court, or an objection to the content of the statement may be raised at the disclosure hearing.

In evaluating the information in the disclosure statement, the accountant for the creditors' committee may be asked to review the financial statements contained in the disclosure statement or others that were issued by the debtor. Special consideration must be made in reviewing pro forma and liquidation statements of financial condition. The pro forma statement provides the creditors with an indication of the debtor's likely financial condition if the plan is accepted. This statement should show that the creditors will receive more if they accept the plan than they would receive if the debtor were liquidated. The pro forma statement also should demonstrate that the plan is feasible in that, after satisfying the provisions of the plan, the debtor retains an asset base with which to operate. In reviewing the pro forma statement prepared by the debtor, special consideration must be given to the analysis of the assumptions used to prepare it and to the evaluation of the value of the assets (which may differ from book values). If the pro forma statements are based on historical costs, the accountant for the creditors' committee may want to restate them to reflect the reorganized values of the entity. The creditors' committee will be able to evaluate the terms of the plan more effectively if it can compare the terms to pro forma statements containing the reorganized value of the entity rather than historical values.

Liquidation statements show what the unsecured creditors would receive if the business were liquidated. The assumptions used in the adjustments to book values must be evaluated carefully. The accountant for the creditors' committee may be asked to review statements of this nature and to provide advice as to the reasonableness of the analysis. There may be a tendency for the debtor to understate liquidation values in order to make the terms of the plan more appealing to the unsecured creditors.

(h) ACCOUNTING FOR THE REORGANIZATION.   SOP 90–7 explains how the debtor emerging from Chapter 11 should account for the reorganization both when fresh start reporting should be adopted and when it is not allowed. Fresh start reporting requires the debtor to use current values (going concern or reorganization values) in its balance sheet for both assets and liabilities and to eliminate all prior earnings or deficits.

(i) Requirements for Fresh Start Reporting.   The two conditions that must be satisfied before fresh start reporting can be used are:

1. The reorganized value of the emerging entity immediately before the confirmation of the plan is less than the total of all postpetition liabilities and allowed claims.
2. Holders of existing voting shares immediately before confirmation retain less than 50 percent of the voting share of the emerging entity.

Paragraph 36 of the SOP indicates that the loss of control contemplated by the plan must be substantive and not temporary. Thus, the new controlling interest must not revert to the shareholders existing immediately before the plan was confirmed. For example, a plan that provides for shareholders existing prior to the confirmation to reacquire control of the company at a subsequent date may prevent the debtor from adopting fresh start reporting.

Debtors that meet both of the above conditions will report the assets and liabilities at their going concern (reorganization) values. Reorganization value is defined as the "fair value of the entity before considering liabilities and approximates the amount that a willing buyer would pay for the assets of the entity immediately after the restructuring." The focus in determining the reorganization value is on the value of the assets. The value is normally determined by discounted future cash flows. However, the value from the discounting of cash flows is defined as enterprise value. To get from enterprise value to reorganization value, current liabilities (ignoring current portion of funded debt) are added to the enterprise value.[4] The reorganization value of the entity may be determined by several approaches depending on the circumstances.[5] In most cases, it is not the responsibility of the accountant to determine the reorganization value of the debtor, but to report in the financial statements the value that is determined through the negotiations by the debtor, creditors' and stockholders' committees, and other interested parties.

Professionals involved in bankruptcy cases have been aware of the limited usefulness of book values for some time. For example, market values are required in the schedules that are filed with the bankruptcy court, and fair market value of assets are determined under Section 506 of the Bankruptcy Code for assets pledged.

Reorganization values will be used only when both conditions for a fresh start are satisfied. For example, fresh start reporting will not be used by most nonpublic companies because in most cases there is no change of ownership. Thus, the provisions of the SOP will primarily apply to public companies.

(ii) Allocation of Reorganization Value.   For entities meeting the criteria discussed above (reorganization value less than liabilities and old shareholders own less than 50 percent of voting stock of the emerging entity), fresh start reporting will be implemented in the following three ways:

1. The reorganization value is to be allocated to the debtor's assets based on the market value of the individual assets. The reorganization value is to be allocated to the debtor's assets based on the market value of the individual assets. The allocation of value to the individual assets should generally follow the guidelines of FASB Statement No. 141. Any part of the reorganization value not attributable to specific tangible assets or identifiable intangible assets should be reported as an intangible asset (goodwill) and is not amortized but, in accordance with FASB Statement No. 142, will be written down if impaired. Goodwill will be tested for impairment at a level of reporting referred to as a *reporting unit* at least annually and more often if an event occurs that would more likely than not reduce the carrying value of a reporting unit below its carrying value. FASB Statement No. 142 (pars. 19–20) indicates that a two-step impairment test should be used (1) to identify potential goodwill impairment and (2) to measure the amount of the impairment loss to be recognized.

2. Liabilities that survive the reorganization should be shown at present value of amounts to be paid determined at appropriate current interest rates. Thus, all liabilities will be shown at their discounted values (the practice of discounting debt has not always been followed in the past).

3. Deferred taxes are to be reported in conformity with generally accepted accounting principles. Benefits realized from preconfirmation net operating loss carryforwards should be used to first reduce reorganization value in excess of amounts allocable to other intangibles. Once the balance of the intangible assets is exhausted, the balance is reported as a direct addition to the additional paid-in capital.

SOP 90–7 indicates that three basic entries are needed to record the adoption of fresh start reporting in the accounts:

---

[4] If the appraiser reduced the enterprise by the amount of cash or excess cash, this amount should also be added with current liabilities to determine reorganization value.

[5] Grant W. Newton, *Bankruptcy and Insolvency Accounting*, Sixth Edition (John Wiley & Sons, New York, 2000, updated annually).

1. Entries to record debt discharge
2. Entries to record exchange of stock for stock
3. Entries to record the adoption of fresh start reporting and to eliminate the deficit

(iii) Disclosure Requirements.   Paragraph 39 of the SOP indicates that when fresh start reporting is adopted, the notes to the initial financial statement should disclose the following:

- Adjustments to the historical amounts of individual assets and liabilities
- The amount of debt forgiven
- The amount of prior retained earnings or deficit eliminated
- Significant matters relating to the determination of reorganization value

The SOP indicates that the following are some of the other significant matters that should be disclosed:

- The method or methods used to determine reorganization value and factors such as discount rates, tax rates, the number of years for which cash flows are projected, and the method of determining terminal value
- Sensitive assumptions (those assumptions about which exists a reasonable possibility of the occurrence of a variation that would significantly affect measurement of reorganization value)
- Assumptions about anticipated conditions that are expected to be different from current conditions, unless otherwise apparent

(iv) Reporting by Debtors Not Qualifying for Fresh Start.   Debtors that do not meet both of the conditions for adopting fresh start reporting should state any debt issued or liabilities compromised by confirmed plans at the present values of amounts to be paid. Thus, the debtor will no longer have the option to elect to discount or not to discount debt issued in a Chapter 11 case.

These provisions apply only to Chapter 11 cases. However, in out-of-court workouts where liabilities are generally restated, it will be difficult to justify accounting for issuance of new debt in a manner different from the discounting procedure described in the SOP.

(i) ACCOUNTING FOR THE IMPAIRMENT OF LONG-LIVED ASSETS UNDER CHAPTER 11.
Companies that qualify for fresh start reporting will value all of the assets at their fair value. If a company does not qualify for fresh start reporting, the provisions of FASB Statement No. 144, *Accounting for the Impairment or disposal of Long-Lived Assets and for Long-Lived Assets to Be Disposed Of,* must be followed. FASB Statement No. 142, as described above, provides guidance for the reporting of the impairment of goodwill.

The accounting for impairment of assets follows a three-step approach for financial statement recognition and valuation:

1. *Evaluate conditions.* Initially, the person who prepares the financial statements considers whether conditions exist that indicate an inability to fully recover the carrying amount of an asset held and used.
2. *Review for impairment.* If such conditions exist, the company will look for possible impairment by estimating the future cash flows from the asset. The estimated cash flows are undiscounted and without interest.
3. *Recognition of loss (determination of trigger).* If the sum of the estimated future cash flows is less than the asset's carrying amount, generally an impairment loss must be recognized in earnings.

The loss from impairment of the assets will be the difference between the carrying amount and the fair value of the assets. For example, assume that a manufacturing facility is potentially impaired by use of the plant to manufacture a product different from the original design for plant use. This change in the nature of the product was caused by technological advancements in the industry. The company reviews for impairment by estimating the expected future net cash flows for the asset undiscounted and without interest. For example, if the carrying value of the plant is $3 million and the further cash flows are less than $3 million, then the asset is impaired. The plant is written down to its fair value based on the concept of a "willing buyer and willing seller" as used in FASB Statement No. 15. For example, if the future cash flows were expected to be $2.5 million and the fair value of the plant was determined to be $1.7 million, a loss of $1.3 million would be reflected even though the difference between the cash flows and the carrying value of the plant is only $.5 million. This process is viewed as one only of cost allocation; as a result, subsequent increases in the value of the asset may not be reflected in the accounts.

The rules described here also apply to assets that will be disposed of. Prior practice allowed the entity to reflect these assets to be disposed of at their net realizable value; if there was an increase in their value, a gain was reflected in the accounts to the extent of a previous write-down. This practice will no longer be allowed, except in a case in which FASB Statement No. 144. In the case of disposition of assets associated with discontinued operations, under Statement No. 144 the assets will continue to be measured at their realizable value. At the time a bankruptcy petition is filed, it may appear that assets are impaired and carrying value should be materially reduced. However, with the filing of the petition, there will be a complete analysis of the viability of the business and of the various segments of the business. Until the assessment is complete, the company should avoid the impulse to materially reduce the carrying value of assets.

45.7 REPORTING REQUIREMENTS IN BANKRUPTCY CASES

Accountants often issue various types of reports and schedules as part of services rendered in the bankruptcy and insolvency area. These services include the preparation of operating reports, evaluation or development of a business plan, valuation of the business, and search for preferences. Many of the reports or schedules produced would generally be classified as financial statements. Because financial statements are issued, the accountant must determine if a compilation, review, or audit report must be issued, or if the service that generated the statements is exempted from professional standards related to compilation of financial statements from the records and the attestation standards. This issue has involved considerable controversy among accountants that practice in the bankruptcy and insolvency area.

(a) LITIGATION SERVICES. When the accountant begins an engagement involving bankruptcy or insolvency issues, a decision needs to be made as to application of the attestation standards. Section 9100.48 of *Attestation Engagements Interpretation,* "Applicability of Attestation Standards to Litigation Services," excludes litigation services that "involve pending or potential formal legal or regulatory proceedings before a trier of fact in connection with the resolution of a dispute between two or more parties...." Guidance in this area is provided by the AICPA's Management Consulting Division, in *Consulting Services Special Report 903–1,* "Litigation Services and Applicable Professional Standards" (CSSR03–1). This report concludes in paragraph 76/105.03 that "[b]ankruptcy, forensic accounting, reorganization, or insolvency services, as practiced by certified public accountants ((CPA's), generally are acceptable as forms of litigation services."

CSSR 03–1 notes that the role of the accountant in a litigation engagement is different from the role in an attestation services engagement. When involved in an attestation engagement, the CPA firm expresses "a conclusion about the reliability of a written assertion of another party." In the performance of litigation services, the accountant helps to "gather and interpret facts and must support or defend the conclusions reached against challenges in cross-examination or regulatory examination and in the work product of others."

Appendix G of CSSR 03–1 describes the delivery of reorganization services to include items such as the following:

- Preparing or reviewing valuations of the debtor's business
- Analyzing the profitability of the debtor's business
- Preparing or reviewing the monthly operating reports required by the bankruptcy court
- Reviewing disbursements and other transactions for possible preference payments and fraudulent conveyances
- Preparing or reviewing the financial projections of the debtor
- Performing financial advisory services associated with mergers, divestitures, capital adequacy, debt capacity, and so forth
- Consulting on strategic alternatives and developing business plans
- Providing assistance in developing or reviewing plans of reorganization or disclosure statements[6]

CSSR 03–1 then concludes that bankruptcy services similar to those listed above that are provided by CPA's generally are accepted as a form of litigation services. Appendix G of CSSR 03–1 provides that:

> This acceptance is due to many fundamental and practical similarities between bankruptcy services and the consulting services associated with other forms of litigation. Bankruptcy law, as promulgated by the Bankruptcy Code and case law, is applied by bankruptcy judges and lawyers to resolve disputes between a debtor and its creditors (for example, distribution of the debtor's assets). Bankruptcy cases frequently include actions related to claims for preferential payments and fraudulent conveyances; negligence of officers, directors, or professionals engaged by the debtors; or other allegations common to commercial litigation. The bankruptcy court has the power and authority to value legal claims and resolve such common litigation as product liability, patent infringement, and breach of contract. The decisions of bankruptcy judges can be appealed as can the decisions of other courts.

The above guidelines according to CSSR 03–1 should also apply to services rendered in an out-of-court workout, as described in the following paragraph from Appendix G:

> Out-of-court restructuring holds the potential for litigation. Therefore, the settlement process is generally conducted with the same scrutiny, due diligence, and intense challenge as that of a formal court-administered process. Furthermore, bankruptcy services provided by CPAs are typically not three-party attest services (the three parties in attest services are the asserter, the attester, and the third party). Instead, affected parties have the opportunity to question, challenge, and provide input to the bankruptcy findings and process.

For services to be exempted, they must be rendered in connection with the litigation, and the parties to the proceeding must have an opportunity to analyze and challenge the work of the accountant. For example, when the CPA expresses a written conclusion about the reliability of a written assertion by another party, and the conclusions and assertions are for the use of others who will not have the opportunity to analyze and challenge the work, the professional standards would apply. Also, when the CPA is specifically engaged to perform a service in accordance with the attestation standards or accounting services standards (SAARS), professional standards are applicable.

(b) DISCLOSURE REQUIREMENTS. If it is determined that the analysis or report that will be issued comes under the guidelines as a form of litigation services, it is advisable to explain both the association and the responsibility, if any, through a transmittal letter or a statement affixed to documents distributed to third parties. Appendix 71/B of CSSR 93–1 suggests the following

---

[6] CSSR 03–1 notes that the words "review" and "reviewing" are not intended to have the same meaning as they do in the AICPA SSARSs.

format for a statement that would explain the association of the CPAs and their responsibility, if any:

> The accompanying schedules (projected financial information; debt capacity analysis; liquidation analysis) were assembled for your analysis of the proposed restructuring and recapitalization of ABC Company. The aforementioned schedules were not examined or reviewed by independent accountants in accordance with standards promulgated by the AICPA. This information is limited to the sole use of the parties involved (management; creditors' committee; bank syndicate) and is not to be provided to other parties.

If it is determined that the service does not qualify as litigation service, any financial statements that might be issued from the services rendered should be accompanied with an accountant's report based on the compilation of the financial statements. Prior to the issuance of a compilation report, the format and nature of the report must be cleared with the firm administrator.

(c) OPERATING REPORTS.   Another area where there is considerable uncertainty is in the issuance of operating reports. All regions of the U.S. trustee require monthly operating reports be submitted to the court as well as annual operating reports. Among those items that were listed in CSSR 03–1 that might fall under litigation services was the preparation or review of the monthly operating reports required by the bankruptcy court. These reports, especially for larger public companies, are often prepared in accordance with generally accepted accounting principles, including SOP 90–7. For example, in the region of New York, Connecticut, and Vermont, the U.S. trustee has issued guidelines that require the statements to conform to SOP 90–7. Other U.S. trustees have on request by the accountant allowed the statements to be prepared in the format that conforms to the manner in which the accountant normally prepares monthly financial statements. Additionally, the accountant is asked to prepare supplemental data not generally presented in monthly financial statements such as an aging schedule of postpetition payables and a schedule of postpetition taxes paid and accrued.

As noted above in CSSR 03–1, the professional standards would apply under two conditions:

1. When the CPA expresses a written conclusion about the reliability of a written assertion by another party, and the conclusions and assertions are for the use of others who will not have the opportunity to analyze and challenge the work
2. When the CPA is specifically engaged to perform a service in accordance with the attestation standards or accounting services standards

In most situations, the second requirement—specifically engaged to perform attestation or compilation services—is not satisfied. Thus, based on this condition, the professional standards would not apply. Certified public accountants are generally engaged to prepare the operating reports that the U.S. trustee and the bankruptcy court require and not specifically to perform an audit or review of the financial records or even compile the financial statements in accordance with the professional standards.

It is the first requirement—expressing a written conclusion about the reliability of a written assertion by another party who will not have the opportunity to analyze and challenge the work—that needs further consideration by the profession. While no specific hearing is scheduled to review the reports, creditors or other parties in interest might raise objections to the content of the reports. Objections to the operating reports have been raised, but rarely. The preparation or the review of monthly operating reports that are required by the court is one of the items listed in the services that are rendered by accountants in the performance of reorganization services. CSSR 03–1 notes that "[b]ankruptcy services provided by CPAs generally are accepted as a form of litigation services."

Since operating reports are considered a form of litigation services, a compilation report should not be issued on the reports. Rather, the following statement should be included in a transmittal letter or affixed to the operating reports:

> The accompanying operating reports for the month of were assembled for your analysis of the proposed restructuring of the ABC Company under Chapter 11 of the Bankruptcy Code. The aforementioned operating reports were not examined or reviewed by independent accountants in accordance with the standards promulgated by the AICPA. This information is limited to the sole use of the parties in interest in this Chapter 11 case and is not to be provided to other parties.

If, on the other hand, it is determined in a particular engagement that professional standards are applicable and the CPA is associated with the financial statements, then a compilation report should be issued based on the prescribed form as set forth in SAARS No. 3. As noted above, prior to the issuance of a compilation report the format and nature of the report must be reviewed for conformity to applicable standards.

(d) INVESTIGATIVE SERVICES. Preference analysis or other special investigative services performed in a bankruptcy proceeding, receivership, or out-of-court settlement are considered a litigation service. As a result, the accountant is not required to issue an agreed-upon procedures report. This would not preclude the professional from issuing a report that described the procedures performed and the results ascertained from the performance of the stated procedures. For example, using the above format, a report issued to a trustee based on an analysis of preferences might be worded:

> The accompanying analysis of preferential payments was assembled (or prepared) for your analysis (or consideration) in conjunction with the proposed reorganization of under Chapter 11 of the Bankruptcy Code. The aforementioned analysis of preferential payments was not examined or reviewed by independent accountants in accordance with standards promulgated by the AICPA. This information is limited to the sole use of the trustee in this Chapter 11 case and is not to be provided to other parties.

(e) FINANCIAL PROJECTIONS. Section 200.03 of the AICPA, "Statements on Standards for Attestation Engagements," states that the standards for prospective financial statements do not apply for engagements involving prospective financial statements used solely in connection with litigation support services. CSSR 03–1 clearly indicates that prospective financial information qualifies as a litigation service. CSSR 03–1 states that parties-in-interest can challenge prospective financial information during negotiations or during bankruptcy court hearings often dealing with the plan's feasibility and adequacy of disclosure. Projections that are included in a disclosure statement would not be subject to the attestation standards since there is a hearing on the disclosure statement and the court must approve the disclosure statement before votes for the plan can be solicited. Parties-in-interest have an opportunity to challenge the prospective information included. Any projections provided for the debtor or for the creditors' committee that is used in the negotiations of the plan would also not fall under the attestation standards.

CSSR 03–1 does, however, indicate that in situations where the users of the prospective financial information cannot challenge the CPA's work, the attestation standards apply. CSSR 03–1 suggests that the attestation standard might apply in situations where exchange offers are made to creditors and stockholders with whom the company has not negotiated or who are not members of a creditor group represented by a committee. Section 200.03 of the AICPA, "Statements on Standards for Attestation Engagements," indicates that if the prospective financial statements are used by third parties that do not have the opportunity to analyze and challenge the statements, the litigation exception does not apply.

Section 200.02 of the AICPA, "Statements on Standards for Attestation Engagements," indicates that when an accountant submits, to his client or others, prospective financial statements that he has assembled (or assisted in assembling) or reports on prospective financial statements that might be expected to be used by third parties, a compilation, examination, or agreed-upon procedures engagement should be performed. Thus, for prospective financial statements that do not qualify for the litigation exception, the engagement must be in the form of a compilation, examination, or agreed-upon procedures if the accountant is associated with the financial statements.

The determination of the reorganization or liquidation values to be included in the disclosure statement or to be used by the debtor or creditors' committee in the negotiations of the terms of a plan, as well as other services that involve financial projections, would fall under the litigation exception. If it is determined that the report regarding the issuance of financial projections would not fall under litigation services, the format and nature of the report must be reviewed for conformity to applicable standards.

The following wording might be in the transmittal letter or in a statement affixed to the documents:

> The accompanying projected financial statements (or information) were assembled for your analysis of the proposed restructuring and reorganization of under Chapter 11 of the Bankruptcy Code. The aforementioned statements were not examined or reviewed by independent accountants in accordance with standards promulgated by the AICPA. This information is limited to the sole use of and is not to be provided to other parties.

45.8 SOURCES AND SUGGESTED REFERENCES

Accounting Principles Board, "Interest on Receivables and Payables," Accounting Principles Board Opinion No. 21. AICPA, New York, 1971.

_____, Accounting Standards Executive Committee, Statement of Position (SOP) No. 90–7, "Financial Reporting by Entities in Reorganization Under the Bankruptcy Code." AICPA, New York, 1990.

_____, Business Valuation in Bankruptcy.

_____, Providing Bankruptcy and Reorganization Services.

Behrenfield, William H., and Biebl, Andrew R., "Bankruptcy/Insolvency," *The Accountant's Business Manual.* AICPA, New York, 1989.

Countryman, "Executory Contracts in Bankruptcy," *Minnesota Law Review,* Vol. 57 (1973), pp. 439, 460.

Financial Accounting Standards Board, "Reporting Gains and Losses from Extinguishment of Debt," Statement of Financial Accounting Standards No. 4. FASB, Stamford, CT, 1975.

_____, "Accounting for Contingencies," Statement of Financial Accounting Standards No. 5. FASB, Stamford, CT, 1975.

_____, "Business Combinations," Statement of Financial Accounting Standards No. 141. FASB, Norwalk, CT. 2001.

FASB, FASB Statement No. 144, "Accounting for the Impairment or Disposal of Long-Lived Assets," Norwalk, CT 2001.

_____, "Goodwill and Other Intangible Assets," Statement of Financial Accounting Standards No. 142. FASB, Norwalk, CT. 2001.

_____, "Accounting by Debtors and Creditors for Troubled Debt Restructurings," Statement of Financial Accounting Standards No. 15. FASB, Stamford, CT, 1977.

King, Lawrence P., ed., *Collier Bankruptcy Manual.* Matthew Bender, New York, 1994.

Newton, Grant W., *Bankruptcy and Insolvency Accounting,* Sixth Edition John Wiley & Sons, New York, 2000 (updated annually).

_____, *Corporate Bankruptcy: Tools, Strategizing, and Alternatives*, John Wiley & Sons, Hoboken, NJ, 2002.

Patterson, George F., Jr., and Newton, Grant, "Accounting for Bankruptcies: Implementation SOP 90–97," *Journal of Accountancy,* Vol. 46, April 1993.

Securities and Exchange Commission, 'Push Down' Basis of Accounting for Parent Company Debt Related to Subsidiary Acquisitions," Staff Accounting Bulletin No. 73. SEC, Washington, DC, 1987.

_____, "Views Regarding Certain Matters Relating to Quasi-Reorganizations, Including Deficit Eliminations," Staff Accounting Bulletin No. 78. SEC, Washington, DC, 1988.

CHAPTER 46

FORENSIC ACCOUNTING AND LITIGATION CONSULTING SERVICES

Dennis S. Neier, CPA

American Express Tax and Business Services, Inc.

Margaret R. Kolb, CPA

American Express Tax and Business Services, Inc.

This chapter has been updated from the previous edition by the Editors.

46.1 INTRODUCTION

Forensic accounting can broadly be defined as the application of accounting principles, theories, and discipline to facts and hypotheses at issue in a legal context. This legal context is generally litigation, but any dispute resolution proceeding (e.g., arbitration or mediation) is a candidate for the application of forensic accounting. Litigation consulting services involve any professional assistance nonlawyers provide to lawyers in the litigation process in connection with pending or potential formal legal or regulatory proceedings before a trier of fact in connection with the resolution of a dispute between two or more parties. A trier of fact is a court, regulatory body, or government authority; their agents; a grand jury; or an arbitrator of a dispute. Litigation consulting services include the application of specialized disciplines to the issues involved in a matter in order to express an expert opinion that would help the trier of fact reach an informed conclusion.

Forensic accounting and litigation consulting services apply to both civil and criminal litigation. The principal focus of this chapter will be civil litigation because it is by far the most frequent dispute resolution proceeding in which the professional accountant will be involved.

The terms "forensic accounting," "dispute analysis," "litigation support," or "litigation consulting" are sometimes used as synonyms. For purposes of this chapter, "forensic accounting" and "litigation consulting services" include all financial and accounting analysis performed by a professional accountant to assist counsel in connection with its investigation, assessment, and proof of issues in a dispute resolution proceeding.

This chapter provides a brief description of the litigation process and a discussion of the accountant's role in, and contribution to, that process. In this chapter, the terms *accountant*, *practitioner*, *Certified Public Accountant* (*CPA*), and *litigation consultant* are used interchangeably to describe an accountant who is providing litigation consulting services. It includes a description of the types of cases in which professional accountants typically get involved, the types of services accountants usually provide, and a discussion of the professional standards relevant to litigation consulting services. Section 46.7, "Testimony," provides suggestions as to how to prepare and deliver deposition and trial testimony.

Discussions of issues of expert testimony in this chapter are extended in Chapter 47, "Financial Expert Witness Challenges and Exclusions: Results and Trends in Federal and State Cases since Kumho Tire." Additionally, Chapter 48, "Introduction to E-Discovery," provides insight into the tools and techniques of modern forensic analysis. Finally, Chapter 49, "Detecting Fraud" provides an overview of the subject of fraud.

46.2 THE LEGAL CONTEXT

(a) THE ADVERSARIAL PROCESS.   In civil disputes, it is generally up to the parties (the plaintiff and defendant), not the court, to initiate and prosecute litigation, to investigate the pertinent facts, and to present proof and legal argument to the adjudicative body. The court's function, in general, is limited to adjudicating the issues that the parties submit to it, based on the proofs presented by them.

(b) STAGES IN A CIVIL SUIT.   There are three basic phases or stages in a civil suit, barring appeal. These stages are the same for virtually all adversarial proceedings, whether in a federal, state, or administrative court.

(i) Pleadings.   A lawsuit is started by a complaint that is filed with the clerk of the trial court and served on the defendants. The complaint lays out the facts and causes of action alleged by the plaintiff. The defendants may file a motion to dismiss (arguing that the defendant is not legally liable even if the alleged facts are true) or an answer to the complaint. The answer may contain a denial of the allegations or an affirmative defense (e.g., statute of limitations has expired). The defendant also may file a counterclaim which presents a claim by the defendant (counterplaintiff) against the plaintiff (counterdefendant).

(ii) Pretrial Discovery.   The purpose of pretrial discovery is to narrow the issues that need to be decided at trial and to obtain evidence to support legal and factual arguments. It is essentially an information-gathering process. Evidence is obtained in advance to facilitate presentation of an organized, concise case as well as to prevent any surprises at trial. This sharing of information often will result in the settlement of the case before trial.

The first step in discovery typically involves the use of interrogatories and document requests. Interrogatories are sets of formal written questions directed by one party in the lawsuit to the other. They are usually broad in nature and are used to fill in and amplify the fact situation set out in the pleadings. Interrogatories are also used to identify individuals who may possess unique knowledge or information about the issues in the case.

Requests for production of documents identify specific documents and records that the requesting party believes are relevant to its case and that are in the possession of and controlled by the opposing party. The opposing party is only required to produce the specific documents requested. Accordingly, when drafting these requests, care must be taken to be as broad as possible so as to include all relevant documents but narrow enough to be descriptive. It is not unusual for more than one set of interrogatories and document requests to be issued during the course of a lawsuit. The accountant is often involved in developing interrogatories and document requests on financial and business issues.

Depositions are the second step in the discovery process. They are the sworn testimony of a witness recorded by a court reporter. During the deposition, the witness may be asked questions by the attorneys for each party to the suit. The questions and answers are transcribed, sworn to, and signed. The testimony will allow the party taking the deposition to better understand the facts of the case and may be used as evidence in the trial. The accountant expert witness may be heavily involved at this stage, both in being deposed and in developing questions for the deposition of opposing witnesses.

(iii) Trial.   The third stage of the litigation/adversarial process is the trial. It is the judicial examination and determination of issues between the parties to the action. In a jury trial, the trial begins with the selection of a jury. The attorneys for each party then make opening statements concerning the facts they expect to prove during the trial. Then the plaintiff puts forth its case, calling all of the witnesses it believes are required to prove its case. Each witness will be subject to direct examination and then cross-examination by the opposing party's attorney. After the plaintiff has called all of its witnesses and presented all of its evidence, the defendant will then present its case in the same manner. The plaintiff then has an opportunity to present additional evidence to refute the defendant's case in a rebuttal. The defendant can respond in a surrebuttal. Finally, each party has the opportunity to make a closing statement before the court.

(iv) Settlement.   At any time in the litigation process, the parties can attempt to settle the dispute without the intervention of the court. This can be accomplished by participating in settlement discussions or by using alternative methods of dispute resolution.

(c) ALTERNATIVE DISPUTE RESOLUTION.   Alternative dispute resolution encompasses mediation, arbitration, facilitation, and other ways of resolving disputes focused on effective communication and negotiation, rather than using adversarial processes such as the courtroom. Two basic types of alternative dispute resolution exist. There are nonbinding methods, such as mediation, negotiation, or facilitation, which assist in reaching, but do not impose a resolution of the dispute. There are also more binding methods, such as arbitration or adjudication, in which a neutral decision maker rules on the issues presented. Combinations of these methods also exist. Alternative dispute resolution is often used because it is the vehicle prescribed in an agreement or contract for the resolution of a dispute.

The U.S. Constitution and most state constitutions provide for the right of trial by jury in most cases. This right does not have to be exercised, and many cases are tried without a jury (i.e., a bench trial where the judge is the trier of fact). In most states and in federal courts, one of the parties must request a jury or the right is presumed to be waived.

(d) REQUIRED PROOFS.   In order for a plaintiff to succeed in a claim for damages, it must satisfy three different but related proofs: liability, causation, and amount of damages if applicable. If the burden of proof is not met on any one of these, the claim will fail.

(i) Liability.   The plaintiff must prove that one of its legal rights has been transgressed by the defendant. It will present evidence attempting to prove that the actions of the defendant were in violation of the plaintiff's legal rights. Similarly, the defendant will present evidence in an effort to prove that the plaintiff's rights were not violated, or at least were not violated by the defendant.

(ii) Causation.   If the plaintiff proves that the defendant has violated one of its legal rights, it must be shown that this violation resulted in some harm to the plaintiff. Here, attorneys for the plaintiff and defendant will try to prove or disprove the nexus between the defendant's actions and some harm to the plaintiff.

(iii) Damages.   After presenting the evidence relating to the liability and causation issues, the parties' next step in most cases is to prove damages.

Damages are one of a number of remedies that may be available to a prevailing plaintiff. Other types of remedies include specific performance (performance of the act that was promised), injunctions (an order by the court forbidding or restraining a party from doing an act), and restitution (the return of goods, property, or money previously conveyed). Damages are the only type of remedy discussed in this chapter.

The general principle in awarding damages is to put the plaintiff in the same position it would have been in if its legal rights had not been transgressed. There are three main categories of damages: compensatory, consequential, and punitive. Compensatory damages compensate the injured party only for injuries or losses actually sustained and proved to have arisen directly from the violation of the plaintiff's rights. Consequential damages are foreseeable damages that are caused by special circumstances beyond the action itself. They flow only from the consequences or results of an action. Punitive damages are intended to penalize the guilty party and to make an example of the party to deter similar conduct in the future. They are awarded only in certain types of cases (e.g., fraud).

The quantification of damages is primarily a question of fact. The burden of proving the damage amount normally falls on the plaintiff. Although accountants can be used in cases in which damages are not an issue, accountants are most frequently used in cases in which damages are an issue.

46.3 THE ACCOUNTANT'S ROLE IN THE LITIGATION PROCESS

Typically the accountant is hired by attorneys representing either the plaintiff or the defendant. In some cases, however, an accountant may be engaged directly by one of the parties to the action. No matter who engages the accountant, a number of possible roles might be played. A litigation consulting practitioner can work as a testifying expert, a consultant, a trier of fact (e.g., an arbitrator), a special master (working for the court), or a court-appointed neutral party (an expert, not for the parties to the dispute, but to the court as a neutral party). A detailed discussion of the role of the testifying expert and the consultant follows.

(a) THE TESTIFYING EXPERT. Frequently, the accountant's purpose in the case will be to develop and render an opinion regarding financial or accounting issues. Ordinarily, only facts and firsthand knowledge can be presented by witnesses at trial. The only exception to this rule is the testimony of experts, which can include an expression of the expert's opinions.

According to the courts and the law, experts are those who are qualified to testify authoritatively because of their education, special training, and experience. Clearly, a professional accountant can qualify as an expert in issues relating to accounting and financial data.

As discussed in Subsections 46.4 and 46.5, the accountant as expert may be asked to develop and present evidence in support of any or all of the required proofs. For example, the accountant can review and offer an opinion as to the adequacy of the work performed by another accountant in a professional liability suit (proof of liability). Or the accountant might review the financial records and the business environment of a company to determine whether a bank's withdrawal of credit caused the company to go out of business (proof of causation). Most commonly, the accountant will be asked to provide an opinion regarding the economic loss suffered by the plaintiff in the case or to rebut the damages alleged by the plaintiff on behalf of the defendant (proof of damages).

(b) NONTESTIFYING CONSULTANT. In certain situations, the accountant will be asked to be a consultant rather than a testifying expert. The accountant will take on more of an advisory role and will not provide testimony. The work the accountant performs for the attorney as a consultant is generally protected by the attorney's work product privilege and as such is not discoverable by the opposing party. For this reason, accountants are often engaged initially as consultants. This enables the attorney to explore avenues and conduct analyses from which he might want to shield his testifying expert. However, once the accountant has been designated as an expert, all work products may be subject to discovery.

(c) COMPARING LITIGATION CONSULTING SERVICES TO ATTEST SERVICES. The role of the practitioner in a litigation consulting engagement is different from that in an attestation engagement, where the CPA expresses a conclusion about the reliability of a written assertion of another party. In a litigation consulting engagement, the practitioner is the asserter and must support and defend any conclusions reached against challenge.

In an attestation engagement, the audience is composed of all persons relying on the accountant's report, whereas in a litigation consulting engagement, the audience for the litigation consulting practitioner's opinion and work product is generally limited to the trier of fact and the parties to the dispute who have the opportunity to evaluate and question the practitioner's conclusions, working papers, documents, and methodology.

The standards for attestation engagements do not envision the practitioner as the asserter and were established to provide assurance to third parties about the assertion of another party. Litigation consulting engagements and attestations engagements differ in the purpose in engaging the practitioner and in the use of the practitioner's conclusions. Also, unlike an attestation engagement, there are usually no uninformed third parties in a litigation consulting engagement because all the parties (if the practitioner is an expert) generally have access to the working papers of, and other documents relied on by, the practitioner and can question the conclusions.

(d) CASE ANALYSIS AND PLANNING.   Whether in the role as testifying expert or nontestifying consultant, the litigation consulting practitioner can provide valuable assistance throughout the litigation process.

In many circumstances, the accountant can be of use to the attorney before the complaint is even filed. The accountant can help the attorney understand the accounting, financial, and economic issues involved in the case and can also assess the potential value of the claim by providing an estimate of the amount of damages. In certain cases, the accountant may actually help to identify causes of action to be included in the complaint.

Once a case has been filed, the accountant can help the attorney understand and evaluate critical accounting, financial, and economic issues and assist with the formulation of an appropriate strategy. Strategy formulation is a continual process; as new information is received and additional issues uncovered, the overall strategy is revised. During the planning phase, the accountant will evaluate alternative approaches and determine the most reasonable approach to take based on all available information. At the same time, the accountant will assess the strengths and weaknesses of the opponent's case. The accountant's involvement in this phase will help the attorney to focus on those issues that have the greatest impact on proving the case.

(e) DISCOVERY.   Discovery is the information-gathering stage of the litigation process. During discovery, each party attempts to identify and obtain all the information and documents necessary to prove its case. The accountant's initial assistance may be in formulating specific accounting and financially oriented questions to be included in interrogatories. The accountant will also assist in drafting document requests by identifying in a very specific manner the types of documents (particularly accounting records and reports) that would be of interest and that the opposing party is likely to have retained. The more specific the requests are, the more likely the response will be useful. The accountant will also be able to assist the attorney with the preparation of responses to the opposing party's interrogatories and document requests.

A significant role that the litigation consulting practitioner can play during the discovery phase is in the review and analysis of the documents. During this review, the litigation consulting practitioner identifies key documents that are helpful or harmful to the parties that have retained him. It is also during this phase that the litigation consulting practitioner identifies documents requiring further explanation that can be provided during deposition. Depending on the legal forum in which the case is being tried, expert reports are usually drafted, issued, and exchanged with the opposing party during or just after the discovery phase.

Depositions provide each side with an opportunity to elicit relevant facts and to identify weaknesses in an opponent's argument. The accountant can be helpful in this area by assisting the attorney in identifying subjects to be explored and in developing specific deposition questions, especially when financial executives or experts are being deposed. Frequently, an attorney will request the accounting expert to be present at these key depositions. Here the accountant can help the attorney understand and interpret the deponent's responses and formulate follow-up questions to probe more deeply into the subject area. Having the accountant present at the deposition will enable the attorney to completely understand and consider the financial issues.

The accountant who will be a testifying expert may be subject to deposition by the opposing attorney. The opposition will attempt to gain a thorough understanding of the accountant's analysis and conclusions and, when possible, identify weaknesses and lay the groundwork for attack at trial. Section 46.9 presents a description of the deposition process and some pointers for giving deposition testimony.

(f) SETTLEMENT ANALYSIS. Settlement negotiations can occur at any point during the litigation process. They can be greatly facilitated by the use of an accounting expert. The accountant can be instrumental in evaluating existing alternatives and terms as well as in proposing other strategic approaches. The accountant's evaluation may involve (1) the determination of economic value and feasibility of various strategies or (2) an analysis of the strengths and weaknesses of the two sides' positions.

When determining value and evaluating feasibility, the accountant can estimate damages under various scenarios and help to assess the probability of occurrence for each, thereby giving the attorney a better understanding of the risks involved. Just as importantly, the accountant can evaluate the true economic value of various settlement alternatives and determine possible tax effects of each. This will enable the attorney and client to make a more informed decision regarding settlement options and perhaps offer alternatives that benefit both parties.

The accountant also can provide an evaluation of the relative strengths and weaknesses of both the plaintiff's and the defendant's positions, thereby helping the attorney strengthen his bargaining position and anticipate potential problems.

(g) PRETRIAL. When preparing for trial, the accountant can assist the attorney by: (1) preparing courtroom graphics, presentations, and exhibits; (2) preparing witnesses for trial testimony; (3) preparing for the cross examination of opposing witnesses; and (4) fine-tuning the overall case strategy.

(h) TRIAL. If the case does not settle, the final role of the accountant will be to assist during the trial itself. The accountant's testimony in court is a key part of this role. In testimony, the accountant presents the opinions developed as a result of his information gathering, review, and analysis. This role is clearly the most important one the accountant will play in the process. It is imperative that the accountant present opinions in a straightforward, cogent, and concise manner. The last section of this chapter describes the course of direct testimony and suggests ways to enhance the effectiveness of the testimony.

Although opinion testimony is of paramount importance at the trial stage, the accountant can play other valuable roles. For example, the accountant can be of tremendous value to attorneys during the cross-examination of opposing experts and financial witnesses. The accountant can work with the attorney to prepare cross-examination questions in an effort to undermine the testimony or the credibility of the witness. The accountant will be important in this phase because of his ability to formulate accounting and financially oriented questions that will be difficult for the witness to evade or deflect. More importantly, the accountant will be able to assess the responses and provide follow-up questions to "close the loop" on important issues.

(i) Credentials and Certifications. The expert or consultant in a litigation case brings to the table their skills and past experience. Increasingly, individuals are obtaining professional certifications to reflect those attributes. Along with societal and regulatory increased attention to fraud, as evidenced in the passage of the Sarbanes-Oxley Act of 2002, various professional organizations are increasingly offering professional certifications in forensic and fraud related subject matters. Fraud specific specialty certifications, in most instances, are obtained as a supplement to the widely recognized designation of CPA, but holding a CPA designation may not be a prerequisite to holding other certifications.

One of the best recognized certifications is the Certified Fraud Examiner (CFE) designation of the 36,000 member Association of Certified Fraud Examiners (ACFEs). The American Institute of Certified Public Accountants (AICPA) and ACFE have been working together for some years to leverage expertise and develop joint training programs. The American College of Forensic

Examiners Institute of Forensic Science (ACFEI) offers certifications such as the Certified Forensic Consultant (CFC) and Certified Forensic Accountant (Cr.FA), as well as specialized certifications in Homeland Security and aspects of forensic medical practice. The National Association of Certified Valuation Analysts (NACVA) supports the business valuation, litigation consulting, and fraud deterrence disciplines. It offers the Certified Forensic Financial Analyst (CFFA) and Certified Fraud Deterrence (CFD) Analyst credentials. The Forensic CPA Society was founded 2005, and offers a Forensic Certified Public Accountant certification to those CPAs passing an examination who also demonstrate relevant practical experience. There are other certification organizations other than those mentioned here.

Most certifications require candidates to pass a written examination, have prerequisite experience requirements and annual continuing education requirements as well as requiring adherence to a code of professional ethics.

46.4 TYPES OF SERVICES

The corporate frauds of the late 1990s and early into the new century such as at Enron, Worldcom, and Tyco Industries highlight the continuing need to have controls in place to prevent fraud and sophisticated services to detect, correct, and value the effects of fraud that have occurred.

Accountants and auditors have been long associated with the evaluation of systems of internal control, and have assisted companies in their design and implementation of systems and controls as an advisory service. While independence rules today may preclude certain services involving audit clients, accountants are still active in consulting on the design and implementation of controls and systems.

On the professional standards side, auditing standards such as Statement on Auditing Standards No.99, "Consideration of Fraud in a Financial Statement Audit" require auditors to make inquiries and perform procedures to identify fraud risks or detect material fraud that may cause a material misstatement of the financial statements. An Exhibit attached to that Standard discusses specific actions and programs companies might adopt to address corporate fraud concerns. Beginning in 2004, many large public companies began reporting explicitly on the effectiveness of their systems of internal control under Public Company Auditing Oversight Board (PCAOB) Auditing Standard No. 2 "An Audit of internal Control Over Financial Reporting in Conjunction with an Audit of Financial Statements." AS 2 makes it clear that companies should have controls and a program in place to deter and prevent fraud. Chapter 4 in this edition "Introduction to Internal Control Reporting and Assessment," discusses reporting on internal control under AS 2. These requirements for public companies arose as a result of the Sarbanes-Oxley Act of 2002. In 2007, new AICPA auditing standards for private companies will require an assessment of controls design and controls implementation for major business processes as part of every audit, and will require auditors to report annually to management and those changed with governance any significant deficiencies or material weaknesses identified.

As a result of the Forensic services units of some CPA Firms as well as CPAs in smaller practices offer in-house services to the audit teams, helping them to brainstorm risks of fraud on their clients. To companies where there are no independence issues, these Firms offer services to design and implement or even monitor anti-fraud programs that many companies are now putting in place.

As the pace of business intensifies and the scope of business activities expand, disputes seem to arise more frequently. In addition the testimony and investigative services, a broad array of new forensic related services have developed. The trends of increasing globalization of the world economy, challenges of cross-border law enforcement and different cultural attitudes, the "information age" where "bricks and mortar" are no longer the yardstick in the valuation of an entity, and the increasing reliance on Information Technology to protect and store information have created demands for a multi-discipline and "high tech" forensic practice.

The following are a few examples of the broad categories of services that currently are being offered by forensic specialists:

Litigation Support Services such as general contract disputes, lost profits and value analysis, post-acquisition disputes, securities matters, professional liability claims, marital disputes and valuations, lease disputes and expert witness testimony.

Forensic Investigative Services, which may include corporate internal investigations for fraud and misappropriation, financial reporting related misrepresentations, business intelligence investigations, intellectual property investigations, patent infringement claims and anti-money-laundering, Foreign Corrupt Practices Act and USA Patriot Act advice.

Corporate Fraud Prevention Program Design, which often includes employment screening, ethics policy development, employee awareness and training programs, and the set up and/or monitoring of anonymous fraud "hot line" services.

Analytic and Computer Forensic Services including data recovery and reconstruction, data imaging, evidence preservation, data mining and data analysis, statistical modeling and statistical inference analysis, electronic discovery. Chapter 48, "Introduction to E-Discovery," provides insight into the tools and techniques of modern forensic analysis

Industry Tailored Forensic Services, such as;

- ○ Services to help health care health care providers and payors comply with federal and state regulations and avoid fraud and associated penalties

- ○ Services to recover royalty and revenue due to increasingly complex business arrangements such as intellectual property licensing, profit sharing, joint ventures, Variable Interest Entities, and distribution agreements

- ○ Strategies to assist entertainment and media companies meet the challenges surrounding intellectual property rights, piracy, security, and rights management

- ○ Investigating construction disputes that usually revolve around technical agreement issues and substantiating the related costs

- ○ Investigative assistance that may help quantify a claim for losses arising from the delivery of contaminated or inferior materials in industries such as the food or pharmaceutical industries

These services and the role of the accountant in their performance are discussed next.

(a) GENERAL ROLE OF ACCOUNTANT.   An accountant may provide services in almost any case where there are accounting, financial, bankruptcy, or fraud issues. Since most civil lawsuits involve one or more of these issues, an accountant may be involved in almost any type of litigation.

Accountants are also used as experts in cases that require a knowledge of business records and transactions. However, there are certain types of cases in which accountants more likely to be involved.

A lawsuit typically requires proof of liability, causation, and damages. An accountant may be involved in any or all of these areas. Cases requiring an accountant's testimony on liability typically revolve around professional liability (e.g., was the audit performed properly?) or investigatory accounting (e.g., can the accountant determine what really happened?). Cases involving an accountant's testimony on damages usually involve the computation of lost economic value, including lost profits, lost royalties, or loss of asset value. The following section discusses the types of services that typically involve accountants and the roles that the accountant might play in those types of cases. Litigation engagements often begin with an extensive investigative phase to establish facts and opinions for the case. An engagement that starts out as an engagement may evolve into a litigation case, thus blurring in real-life the distinctions made in the categorization of the types of services.

(b) EXAMPLES OF LITIGATION AND INVESTIGATORY SERVICES.   The accountant's work often involves business disputes. This section presents a summary of common types of cases and the accountant's role.

(i) Breach of Contract. Typically, the plaintiff has a contract with the defendant that the defendant is accused of breaching. For example, the contract may call for the defendant to buy a certain quantity of product for a certain price. The defendant, however, fails to make the required purchases. Or the defendant may be accused of breaching a warranty on its goods or services. The accountant may be asked to quantify the damages suffered by the plaintiff as a result of the breach. Usually, the damages are measured by lost profits, that is, the additional profits the plaintiff would have earned but for the defendant's breach. Among the issues the accountant may address are lost revenues, avoided costs, available capacity, and possible mitigating actions, including sale of the product to others.

(ii) Business Interruption. A business interruption claim may arise from an accident, fire, flood, strike, or other unexpected event. It may even arise from a contract or warranty claim where the defendant's breach has caused the plaintiff to suspend operations. Typically, these claims are filed by a business against its insurance carrier, though a claim against the entity causing the event is possible. In a business interruption case, the plaintiff claims the event caused the business to suffer losses.

Often, the accountant is asked to quantify the loss. Elements to be considered may include lost profits, loss of tangible assets, loss of intangible assets (including goodwill), loss of an entire business or business line, cost to repair or reestablish the business, cost of downtime, or cost of wasted effort (time spent fixing the problem instead of generating operating profits).

(iii) Intellectual Property. Intellectual property disputes involve the rights to use patents, copyrights, and trademarks. The plaintiff claims that the defendant infringed on the plaintiff's intellectual property by illegally using the patent, copyright, or trademark. For patents, damages are defined by law to be plaintiff's lost profits (if reasonably provable), but not less than a reasonable royalty. Damages in a copyright case are the market value of the infringed work, the profits that the owner lost or will lose as a result of the infringement, or the defendant's profit. In a trademark case, where the mark has been registered with the Patent and Trademark Office, the owner may recover actual damages and also the infringer's profits.

Often computations are made separately for lost profits and for reasonable royalties. Sometimes the accountant can perform both analyses. Other times the accountant's opinion on reasonable royalty may be supplemented by another expert with experience in negotiating royalties in the particular industry.

(iv) Antitrust. The plaintiff in antitrust litigation may be either the government or a private party. The government usually brings suit to oppose a merger or to break up a monopolist. Government suits are usually not for monetary damages. Experts in these suits, particularly in liability issues involving monopolistic practices, relevant market share, and the like, are often economists, not accountants.

In a private suit, the plaintiff accuses the defendant of violating antitrust laws, resulting in injury to competition, including (or especially) injury to the plaintiff. The accountant's role again may be the computation of lost profits.

A company may be accused of violating antitrust laws by selling the same goods at different prices to different parties in the same channel of distribution. This ostensibly discriminatory pricing may be refuted if the defendant can show that the price differences are justified by differences in cost of production, service, freight, and so on. An accountant may conduct these cost justification studies.

Accusations of predatory pricing also fall under the antitrust laws. The defendant in a predatory pricing case is accused of pricing so low that competitors lose money and are driven out of business. Once the competition is eliminated, the defendant presumably raises prices and enjoys monopoly profits. One legal standard for predatory pricing is pricing below cost of production. Depending on the law, the standard may be either incremental costs or fully allocated costs. An accountant may help establish or refute this claim by studying product pricing and production costs and measuring the resulting profit margins.

(v) White-Collar Crime and Fraud.   This is a growing field within the area of litigation consulting and covers a wide range of cases. Examples of fraud and white-collar crime cases are schemes by executives, employees, and customers to siphon funds from financial institutions for their personal use, check kiting, lapping, computer fraud, embezzlement, defense procurement fraud, costing fraud, schemes involving kickbacks, income tax frauds, charity and religious frauds, money laundering, insider trading cases, and fraudulent bankruptcy actions. Additional examples include investigations of "boiler room" operations that solicit funds from investors based on promises of high investment return and Ponzi arrangements (i.e., arrangements in which there are no real profits; instead, funds from new investors are used to pay investment returns to existing investors, giving the impression of profits).

The accountant's work in this area centers on investigating what happened and establishing liability. After the investigation is completed, the accountant may be asked to quantify the amount of the loss attributable to the fraud or crime.

The accountant will typically review and analyze many types of data, including correspondence, e-mail, journal entries, financial statements, and financial schedules. Many times, the accountant commences his investigation with little to no detail as to the extent of the situation and must put the pieces of a puzzle together. This involves developing and testing hypotheses throughout the investigation. Therefore, when reviewing documents and other data, it is important to keep an open mind and not dismiss any reasonable possibilities. Very often, an investigation in one area will lead to other problem areas.

Although most litigation takes place in an unfriendly environment, this is especially true in cases involving white-collar crime or fraud. The accountant may conduct or assist the attorney in conducting interviews of relevant parties. Often, the accountant or attorney is attempting to obtain information from the persons who are the subject of the investigation and are attempting to conceal their activities. As such, the accountant should maintain the highest level of professional skepticism throughout the investigation.

Since the accountant's investigation, work product, and conclusions may form the basis of evidence in the case, it is critical to understand the importance of obtaining and preserving evidence and seek guidance from the retaining attorney about such matters whenever necessary. In addition, the accountant may have to coordinate efforts with other areas of law enforcement that may have an interest in the matter.

The circumstances of each engagement are unique. Depending on the circumstances, the accountant or retaining attorney may need to engage other specialists or experts. Computer specialists are frequently used in these types of cases to extract data that have been removed from computer drives or to search the contents of computer disks using key word searches. Private investigators can also be of great assistance in performing detailed background checks or surveillance of potential suspects.

The following are specific examples of tasks that the accountant might perform in different types of white-collar crime cases.

In white-collar crime cases where Ponzi schemes are suspected, the accountant will want to document how the enterprise was structured and to develop organizational charts and flow charts. Tracing transactions from the receipt of investor funds to their ultimate investment or disposition will be required. Analyses that illustrate the lack of any positive cash flow other than by raising additional investor funds will be useful to the attorney in proving liability. Documenting the flow of all cash transactions or custodial arrangements is all within the accountant's scope.

The accountant should also analyze cash disbursements to see whether any patterns indicating self-dealing emerge or to identify possible related entities or personal use or benefit of company assets. Unusual expenses should be vouched, and particular attention should be devoted to traditionally sensitive areas, such as travel and entertainment expenses. Some suspicious transactions are easily detected. Many illegal activities involve disguised transactions, but it is just as likely that the paid bills and supporting evidence will be fairly explanatory.

In the case of a penny stock fraud scheme, the accountant may shift greater attention to the financial results and reports to shareholders, press releases, and the like to determine if evidence exists that such data were incorrect or inaccurate. Income recognition abuses or improper capitalization of expenses are typical categories of abuses used by penny stock promoters to misstate the operating results and mislead investors. In addition, the accountant should analyze key contracts, employment agreements, and other consulting arrangements. A time-line analysis that reflects all key "publicized events" should be developed and used to determine if such events did occur. From the time line it can be determined whether, in the same time frame, all acquisitions or dispositions of assets and other financial transactions were accounted for properly.

(vi) Securities Act Violations. Lawsuits in this area usually involve alleged violations of the federal acts, specifically Sections 11 and 12(2) of the Securities Act of 1933 and Section 10(b) of the Securities and Exchange Act of 1934. These sections concern making false or misleading public statements about a company or omitting a material fact (either in a prospectus or in public statements, including financial statements), resulting in an alleged overvaluing of the company's stock. Typically, when the correct information becomes public, the value of the stock drops. Plaintiffs claim that, but for the misleading statements, they would not have bought the stock or they would have bought at a lower price. These lawsuits are often brought against Officers, directors, investment bankers, lawyers, accountants, and others who may have been party to misstatements.

Accountants may be involved in the liability, causation, and damages portions of securities cases. Involvement with liability issues is most common when an auditor has been accused of violating Section 10(b)5 by failing to perform a generally accepted auditing standards (GAAS) audit and/or by giving a clean opinion to non- generally accepted accounting principles (GAAP) financial statements. Cases involving public company audits dated after the effective date of PCAOB Auditing Standard No. 1 "References in Auditor's Reports to Standards of the Public Company Auditing Oversight Board" will reference the standards of the PCAOB in lieu of GAAS. The accountant will review the auditor's work papers and other relevant materials to reach a conclusion as to the adequacy of the audit of the financial statements.

The causation and damages phases of securities cases are closely linked. They consist of determining whether the information had any impact on the stock price and quantifying the losses suffered by the plaintiff investors as a result. Typically, this involves determining what the stock price would have been if the proper information had been released at the proper time. The methods for doing this are beyond the scope of this chapter; see de Silva et al. for a treatment of this subject.[1]

(vii) Bankruptcy and Bankruptcy Frauds. Bankruptcy matters may require an accountant's services for many different tasks. The role of the accountant and scope of services to be performed are influenced by the size of the company and by whether the accountant is working for the trustee, debtor in possession, secured creditors, or the creditors' committee(s).

Accountants for the debtor in possession may be asked to prepare analyses supporting the solvency or insolvency of the debtor, which may affect creditors' claims, recoveries, or security interests. Such accountants also may be involved in preparing prospective financial information filed with the U.S. Trustee's Office or used in negotiating plans of reorganization with the parties of interest. Another important role may require making analyses to support a debtor's use of cash collateral and analyses showing that adequate protection is available to the secured creditor.

An accountant for the creditors' committee, in addition to reviewing any analyses prepared for the debtor, will have additional responsibilities. The accountant may initially be asked to determine the cause for the business failure and may need to determine quickly whether the debtor's operation may be further depleting the assets available for creditors. The creditors' accountants also may need to investigate the conduct of the debtor. The scope and depth may vary significantly based on the relationship and confidence the creditors have with existing management. At a minimum, a review

---

[1] Harinda de Silva, Nancy N. Low, and Tara N. Nells, "Securities Act Violations: Estimation of Damages," in *Litigation Services Handbook: The Role of the Accountant as Expert*, ed. Roman L. Weil, Michael J. Wagner, and Peter B. Frank (John Wiley & Sons, New York, 1995).

to determine possible preferential payments, fraudulent conveyances, and insider transactions is usually performed. The roles, definitions, and exceptions to preferences and fraudulent conveyances are detailed in the Bankruptcy Code as well as in Newton.[2]

The work required to establish liability in bankruptcy cases is similar to that discussed in the subsection on white-collar crime. One difference is that liability issues in bankruptcy have the benefit of explicit rules in the Bankruptcy Code (Title 11 USC, more specifically, Subsections 543–549). These sections of the Bankruptcy Code detail the powers of a trustee to avoid transfers that defraud, hinder, or delay creditors, give preferential treatment to certain creditors, or do not give the bankrupt person or entity fair value for the transfer. Since these Code sections define the scope of the trustee's power, an accountant engaged by the trustee should first read and understand the relevant provisions before planning the work. In addition, an accountant must obtain an understanding of certain sections of the Uniform Commercial Code and in particular the Uniform Fraudulent Transfer Act of the state where the business is situated. The location of the business may influence the scope of the work since the time period under the bankruptcy statute only allows for recovery one year prior to the bankruptcy, whereas state laws vary from 3 to 10 years.

Once the appropriate time period and scope have been determined, the accountant needs to review all material transactions to gain an understanding as to the economic benefit of the exchange to the bankrupt, including all monetary and nonmonetary exchanges. In addition, the accountant needs to determine the timing and explanation for any liens or other security interest granted or recorded during the time period. This review should include any asset sales, purchases, foreclosures, and tax assessments. Transactions between related entities or commonly controlled entities or their affiliates must be reviewed. In a bankruptcy case, the accountant is trying to develop any evidence that might show fraud or fraudulent intent.

A preferential payment analysis covers a review of transactions within 90 days (one year for insiders) prior to bankruptcy wherein a creditor is paid for an antecedent debt at a time the debtor is insolvent and such payment is not in the ordinary course of business. The definition of insolvency for this purpose is the fair value of assets compared with the fair value of liabilities—a balance sheet approach. "Ordinary course of business" is not defined except by reference to case precedents. For example, if creditors are routinely paid in 90 days but certain creditors get paid just before bankruptcy within 30 days, such payments are probably not in the ordinary course of business.

Certain leveraged buyouts (LBOs) have encountered financial difficulty shortly after consummation, and some creditors have used various security law and bankruptcy law theories to unwind these transactions and seek recoveries from selling shareholders, secured creditors, and others.

The accountant's work in establishing or defending liability is critical. Analyses that show the cash flow of the entity before and after the LBO help establish whether sufficient capital or working capital was available to the company. Changes in a company's borrowing, especially where a significant amount of assets have been recently pledged, also illustrate the potential damage to unsecured creditors. The accountant's ability to distinguish operating losses caused by the form and structure of the buyout from losses due to the economy or other competing companies will also assist counsel in determining whether the LBO can be attacked as a fraudulent transfer.

(viii) Lender Liability. Common law verdicts in numerous states have established a duty requiring banks to act in good faith and to provide a reasonable time period for a customer to arrange alternative financing should the bank no longer wish to continue the relationship. Other cases involve inaccurate or incomplete responses from banks to inquiries by third parties or failure to honor financing commitments. In some situations the bank's activity, either as a member of the business's board of directors, or in selecting those members, or the bank's insistence on designating workout consultants, places them in a position of being too close to operating the business; and they may find themselves accountable for its losses or ultimate bankruptcy.

---

[2] Grant W. Newton, *Bankruptcy and Insolvency Accounting,* (John Wiley & Sons, New York, 1994).

The accountant's role is to assist with liability, causation, and damage issues. With respect to liability issues, the accountant may develop financial data to determine whether the borrower was in compliance with various loan covenants at various intervals during the banking relationship, including at its commencement. A review of debt and equity items in the financial statements could identify differences in definitions or inconsistencies between GAAP and the bank loan document terminology.

Accounting consultants working with defendants to lender liability actions may provide useful information to show the bank was acting prudently in calling a loan or in refusing to extend it based on the results of a financial analysis of the debtor. On the causation issue, the accountant can determine whether the bank's actions caused the business failure or whether other circumstances were involved.

The accountant's role in damages is important for both the plaintiff and defendant. Damage theories may include both the actual cost of the termination of the credit relationship and more complex damages, including punitive and racketeer influenced corrupt organizations (RICOs) claims where business failure occurs.

(ix) Employment Litigation.   Employment litigation typically involves claims of employment discrimination (including discrimination on the basis of age, race, or gender) or wrongful discharge. Claims may involve discrimination in hiring, promotion, or wages.

The accountant may be involved in both liability and damages phases of employment claims. For liability, the accountant may compile hiring rates, promotion rates, salary levels, or similar historical information to prove or refute a claim of differential treatment. This liability work often may be performed in conjunction with a statistician.

On damages, the accountant may determine what the plaintiff's income would have been had the alleged discrimination not occurred. The accountant will consider the proper level of earnings, the likely duration of the earnings, and any offset from amounts actually earned. The issues are very similar to loss of earnings claims in personal injury cases. Although specific approaches are not discussed in this chapter, the methods are logically similar to lost profits claims.

(x) Accountant's Liability.   Most litigated claims against accountants have arisen from audit work. Recently, significant litigation has come from compilation, review, and prospective financial statement engagements.

Litigation over audited financial statements generally involves allegations that GAAP was not applied or that the audit was not conducted in accordance with GAAS, or both. In class action securities litigation, noncompliance with Securities and Exchange Commission (SEC) Regulations S-X and S-K as well as Financial Reporting Releases may also be alleged.

During the discovery process, the accountant has the opportunity to explore the underlying documents and associate the facts with the accounting pronouncements. The accountant will refer to a company's general accounting records and documents as well as to the work papers of the independent auditor. Such a review process requires the expert either to be an auditor or to have some auditing background. Issues related to the auditing firm's consideration of GAAP, their consultation with parties in their firm who provide technical expertise, and the extent to which they have researched a specific area of accounting should be documented in the auditor's work papers.

The accountant may review and assess potential violations of GAAS or other applicable professional standards. Such violations may range from the failure of the defendant auditing firm to adequately observe the physical inventory, to not confirming sufficient accounts receivable, to not performing an adequate subsequent events review. Liability issues related to a failure to perform an audit in accordance with GAAS are usually not unearthed until a review of the auditing firm's work papers has taken place.

In order to adequately address GAAP and GAAS issues, the accountant must stay current with accounting and auditing literature issued by the Financial Accounting Standards Board (FASB), the AICPA, and the SEC. With these types of cases, it often becomes necessary to consult with an accountant with relevant industry expertise.

(xi) Contractual Purchases Litigation.   Litigation often results from the purchase of a company. With such purchases, the audited financial statements are used as the basis for the purchase or condition of the sale. The issues often center on the valuation of assets or the quantification and disclosure of liabilities in those financial statements. Asset values in dispute may include such issues as proper use of last-in, first-out (LIFO) or first-in, first-out (FIFO), inventory write-downs, unrecorded liabilities, accounting for impaired assets, amortization of goodwill, replacement cost versus book value, and realizable value of accounts receivable.

Many purchase and sale agreements contain a "postclosing adjustment" provision. This provision allows for the purchase price to be adjusted based on events that occur or become known after the closing. The accountant can serve as the expert for the buyer or seller with respect to the arguments as to why the purchase price should or should not be adjusted. The accountant can also serve as the arbitrator or mediator on such cases.

The expert in these cases is usually called on to review the working papers of the independent auditor of the financial statements. From these working papers and the notes to the financial statements, the expert can determine what accounting methods were employed and whether they are in conformity with GAAP and common industry practice.

Liabilities are of critical importance since the buyer needs to be alerted to all potential and contingent debts and encumbrances. The accountant would determine whether there was adequate disclosure of the liabilities in the financial statements that were either issued or relied on by the buyer. The accountant may also need to evaluate whether subsequent events were reasonably foreseeable.

Contracts for the purchase and sale of a company sometimes include a provision regarding a material adverse change in the business. In these cases, an accountant may be asked to review the financial records of the company to search for any adverse changes in the business.

(xii) Breach of Fiduciary Duty.   These cases involve the issue of whether a trustee, executor, Officer, director, or other fiduciary has breached his fiduciary duties, thus causing damages to the trust estate or corporation. The accountant can play a vital role in proving or rebutting liability on the part of the fiduciary by demonstrating that the fiduciary acted correctly or incorrectly with respect to accounting, financial, or economic issues or transaction.

(a) NonBusiness Cases. Important nonbusiness issues include marital dissolution, and personal injury matters.

(xiii) Marital Dissolution.   In many states, the financial aspects of a marital dissolution are governed by family law statutes that establish rules for sharing of income and the division of property. The tax laws have also greatly influenced the allocation of income and assets during and after a marital dissolution. Most states divide assets "equitably"; a few states are governed by community property rules. Awareness of the local rules and practices is of critical importance to accountants in their financial analyses.

In cases governed by community property laws, the accountant's role is often to trace assets, receipts, and disbursements to determine which assets are community property. In cases governed by equitable distribution law, the accountant may be asked to analyze the assets in order to determine which assets are subject to equitable distribution. He may also be asked to help an equitable distribution of marital assets.

The "liability" role of the accountant is to identify all assets and liabilities of the parties so that a fair and equitable distribution of assets results. Most family law courts are equity oriented, so the substance of transactions should carefully be considered when analyzing financial data. The forensic accountant has to examine financial data with concern for diversion of assets, improper cash transactions, and padded payroll and other fringe benefits and perks that may deprive the nonworking spouse of a fair share of the business's net worth as well as a share of spousal support.

If financial statements do not exist for closely held companies, such financial statements may need to be prepared. The accountant must be familiar with the local state family law. The accountant must also be familiar with tax implications of various asset transfers or split-ups so that neither spouse later finds unexpected tax consequences. The accountant should be aware of the proper handling of pension plan assets, individual retirement accounts, 401(k) plans, and the like, so that each party receives a fair share of assets and so that income tax or excise taxes are not triggered unnecessarily.

In community property states, the existence of separate property and the impact of prenuptial agreements may also require analysis. significant tracing of funds may become necessary if a total segregation of separate property assets has not been maintained. The marital community may have rights to a contribution for increased value of separate property that arises from services provided by the community after marriage. Lastly, the community may have some interest in separate property if joint tax returns have been filed and no separate tax cost was allocated to each category of assets.

Accountants often are asked to determine the value of the assets owned by the litigants as well as the income sources from which spousal and child support can be calculated. The valuation of assets often includes business valuation and, in the case of professionals, the value of their shareholdings, partnership interest, or professional licenses. Issues such as professional goodwill or celebrity goodwill are important and contested often in marital dissolution litigation.

(ii) Partnership Dissolution.   Partnerships sometimes break up in a manner similar to a divorce. The accountant's work is also similar, focusing on tracing, valuation, and fair apportionment of assets and liabilities, usually pursuant to the terms of the partnership agreement, if one exists.

(iii) Personal Injury.   Personal injury cases stem from automobile accidents, slip-and-falls, and the like. Typically, damage components include medical expenses, pain and suffering, lost earnings, and loss of consortium to the injured party's spouse. The accountant is usually involved in the calculation of lost earnings and in calculations regarding the interest components of the judgment. For identification of the issues involved, see Subsection 46.4(b)(ix).

46.5 CALCULATING DAMAGES

(a) GENERAL CONCEPTS.   In proving liability, the plaintiff must demonstrate that the defendant's actions were in violation of the plaintiff's legal rights. In moving from liability to causation, the plaintiff must demonstrate that the illegal actions caused injury to the defendant. Only then can damages be calculated. In discussing damages, we rely on the concept of the "but-for" world. The but-for world is the economic and physical environment that would have existed "but for" the actions of the defendant. In other words, it is the "undamaged" world, in contrast to the "actual," damaged world that did occur and in which the defendant performed the alleged illegal acts.

(b) MEASURING DAMAGES.   Depending on the case, there are many different standards by which damages are measured, including the following four:

- Lost profits (past profits, prospective profits, or both, including increased costs)
- Lost asset value (the appraised value of identified assets, including goodwill, or other intangibles)
- Lost personal earnings (wages, salary, etc.)
- Lost royalties or licensing fees (amounts due for use of the plaintiff's assets or rights) or share of profits pursuant to participation agreements

In most cases, these approaches are all attempts to compute the difference between the but-for world and the actual world. That is, they attempt to measure the difference between what should have happened and what actually did happen.

Lost profits are the most common standard for business cases. Valuations are used in both business disputes and marital dissolution proceedings. Personal earnings is the damages standard for the economic component of personal injury suits. (Other components are medical costs and pain and suffering.) Reasonable royalty is used in intellectual property disputes, especially patent cases.

(c) MITIGATION. A plaintiff has the obligation to mitigate damages. This means that the plaintiff must take reasonable steps to minimize the damages suffered. More specifically, the courts (and damages experts) will compute damages as if the plaintiff mitigated, whether the mitigation really occurred or not.

In many cases, reasonable mitigation will have occurred, and the expert may look at the difference between what should have occurred and what did occur as the measure of damages. After all, the plaintiff's recovery through litigation is uncertain, and plaintiff has every incentive to reduce damages to itself. However, if reasonable mitigation did not occur, the accountant should make the necessary adjustments.

(d) INTEREST ON DAMAGE AWARDS. Some or all of most damage awards are to compensate for past losses. In order to be made whole in economic terms, it might be supposed that the plaintiff should earn interest on past losses from the date of loss to the date of payment. However, the law does not always allow interest, and when it does, the interest rate is not always the rate applicable to the economic circumstances.

In general, the treatment of interest is governed by the applicable law. The courts distinguish between prejudgment interest (accrued between the date of loss and the date of trial or final judgment) and postjudgment interest (accrued from the date of judgment to the date of payment, which can be years if the judgment is appealed). In some jurisdictions, the rate of interest is set by law. Depending on the case, some jurisdictions do not allow prejudgment interest; most allow postjudgment interest.

Some interest awards are within the province of the court. Some judges may allow calculations of interest to go to the jury as part of the damage claim; others may reserve the right to separately compute interest (either at the statutory rate or at a rate depending on proof) after the jury awards damages. If the court allows economic testimony as to the amount of interest, what is the proper approach? The accountant should determine interest by recreating what would have happened to the plaintiff had the money been received at the times the damage claim asserts. The issues to be analyzed include the following:

- *The amount of cash that would have been received.* This is not necessarily the amount of net income. Adjustments should be made for changes in working capital, capital expenditures, depreciation, repayment of principal, and so on.

- *The income taxes that would be paid on the income.* Interest should be calculated on aftertax cash available for investment, as that is the amount that would be available in the but-for world. Only if net income approximates cash flow would a calculation based on net income be acceptable.

- *The interest rate that would make the plaintiff whole.* The courts reject any "speculative" damage claim, including a speculative interest rate. This means that it is normally inappropriate to treat interest as equivalent to a lost investment opportunity (since the results of that investment may be speculative), thereby computing interest as a return on equity. Appropriate interest rates may include a risk-free (short-term or long-term government rates such as Treasury bills or bonds), money market rates, the plaintiff's or defendant's borrowing rate (if the plaintiff or defendant has debt outstanding), or the prime rate. The choice of rate depends on circumstances.

- *Taxes to be paid on interest earned.* Interest earned is subject to taxes. If a before-tax interest rate is used, taxes must be subtracted before compounding the interest in future periods. Alternatively, an after-tax interest rate may be used. For more on the treatment of taxes, see below.

(e) PRESENT VALUE AND INFLATION.   Time is a factor in most damage claims. A violation typically occurs sometime prior to the loss suffered by the plaintiff; the loss can continue into the future (e.g., lost earnings in a personal injury case); the trial can occur either after the entire loss has been suffered or prior to the full recovery from the effects of the violation; and the award may not be paid until sometime after the trial. Thus, a damage award must compensate the plaintiff for both past and future losses, but it must be made in full at the present time. This requires that the accountant accumulate both past and future lost profits to the present. This accumulation is accomplished by discounting the projected lost profits to the date of violation using a rate of interest and compounding the resulting amount to the present at some prejudgment interest rate. The choice of discount rate depends on circumstances. A nominal discount rate (such as the Treasury bill rate, the prime rate, or any other market rate) includes both a real rate of interest and an inflation premium. If the damages into the future are computed in constant (uninflated) dollars, then discounting at a real rate (net of inflation) may be appropriate. If inflation has been built into the projected damage figures, a nominal interest rate is correct. In either case, the appropriate discount rate should include an adjustment for risk.

For more on determining the present value of a damage award, see Kabe and Blonder.[3]

(f) INCOME TAXES.   Under the law, some damage awards are taxable to the recipient, whereas others are tax-free. In computing damages, the goal is to properly account for taxes so the plaintiff is in the same position as it would have been if the liability act had never occurred.

If the award is taxable, then the damages should be computed on a before-tax basis. The plaintiff then receives the damage award, pays taxes, and is in the proper after-tax position. If the amount is tax-free, only the after-tax amount should be assessed as damages.

Complications arise in the two areas: (1) if prejudgment interest is due, and (2) if tax rates have changed from the damage date to the payment date. As discussed above, prejudgment interest is computed on the after-tax amount, since that is the amount the plaintiff would have had to invest. However, if the award is taxable, the damages must be expressed in pretax dollars. The solution is simple. Compute the entire award, including damages and interest, in after-tax dollars. Then gross up the award by the tax rate in the year of payment. When the plaintiff receives this amount and pays tax on it, plaintiff will be in the proper after-tax position. This approach, although accurate, has been relatively untested in court.

A similar situation arises if tax rates have changed. If pretax damages are used, the change in tax rates will result in an incorrect after-tax award. The solution is again to compute the after-tax amounts, then gross up the award for the current tax rate.

46.6 SUPPORT FOR OPINIONS

(a) SOURCES OF INFORMATION.   The accountant must be aware of the many facts and statistics that relate to the subject and issues of the case and must have adequate data to authoritatively support opinions or conclusions. The data should be of high reliability since the accountant is subject to cross-examination.

There are two basic sources for data: the litigating parties (either the plaintiff or the defendant) and external sources, such as industry publications, economic statistics, and so on. The former is obtained through the discovery phase discussed previously. The latter is discussed here.

Many reference books list sources of business information. Also, computer databases are widely available and eliminate the need for data entry as the information can be downloaded into a computer file.

Often, an accountant may need to call on other experts or persons knowledgeable in the particular industry. This expertise may be found within a different practice area of the accountant's firm, or the accountant may need to obtain expertise outside his firm.

---

[3] Elo R. Kabe and Brian L. Blonder, "Discounting Concepts and Damages," in *Litigation Services Handbook,* 1996 Suppl., ed. Roman L. Weil, Michael J. Wagner, and Peter B. Frank (John Wiley & Sons, New York, 1986).

(b) RELIANCE ON OTHERS. The accountant as an expert witness may rely on the work of employees as well as personal research or sources in forming his opinion. Although the expert may rely on work performed by others, he must ultimately adopt all opinions and conclusions contained in the expert report as his own. Federal Rule of Evidence No. 703 describes permissible bases on which expert testimony may be founded: (1) information acquired through firsthand observation, (2) facts observed by, or presented to, the expert witness at the trial or at the hearing, and (3) data considered by the expert witness outside of court. Rule 703 permits an expert to rely on facts that are not normally admissible in evidence if they are of a type reasonably relied on by experts in the field. "Reasonably" means trustworthy. "Type relied on" is left to the discretion of the trial judge. In turn, the judge may question the accountant-witness as to the appropriate degree of reliance.

(c) DOCUMENTATION. All materials prepared, accumulated, or referred to by the accountant acting as an expert witness in a case may be made available to the opposing side. At the outset, the attorney and accountant should develop a clear understanding of exactly what the accountant will be preparing and retaining for the engagement. Then the accountant should carefully control the content of work papers and correct or avoid collecting materials that are irrelevant to forming an opinion. This should be an ongoing process, as the accountant may not be able to remove anything after receiving a subpoena. All work products of an expert may be discoverable and could be thoroughly scrutinized by the opposing party. Errors, inconsistencies, and irrelevant materials may form the basis for an effective challenge to the testimony of the accountant.

Since all drafts prepared by the accountant prior to his final report may be discoverable, the accountant and his firm should have a policy regarding the retention of such draft reports. This policy may differ from the firm's record retention policy regarding documents prepared in other types of engagements. Once a policy regarding the retention of draft reports in a litigation consulting engagement is established, it must be communicated to the attorney and consistently applied.

(d) ENGAGEMENT LETTERS. The accountant may feel that it is appropriate to issue an engagement letter specifying the engagement's purpose, the tasks that need to be performed, and the terms of compensation. If the accountant is identified as an expert witness, the opposing party can discover the engagement letter. If, due to subsequent events, tasks enumerated in the engagement letter are not completed or are completed with adverse consequences to the accountant's client, opposing counsel may use this information to imply that the accountant's opinion is defective or that the accountant did not perform all the analyses required to substantiate the conclusions presented. Accordingly, under many circumstances, the engagement letter should describe the tasks in general terms only.

46.7 TESTIMONY

Testimony is the ultimate result of expert witness work. This section provides advice on giving deposition and trial testimony and suggestions for the expert.

(a) GIVING DEPOSITION TESTIMONY. A deposition of an expert witness is part of the discovery process in which counsel seeks to fulfill several major objectives. The most obvious objective is to find out what opinions the expert is going to offer at trial, and why. A deposition is also an opportunity to commit the expert to sworn testimony that can later be used for impeachment purposes, should the expert try to change his opinion. Additionally, counsel will use the deposition to assess the expert's effectiveness as a witness and the strength of the case for purposes of settlement negotiation and development of trial strategy. Consequently, expert depositions may be more important than the trial testimony and should be regarded with due respect.

Adequate preparation is crucial to giving an effective deposition. Naturally, a thorough review of the expert's opinions and underlying support is in order. The expert should also review any prior writings and testimony for previous positions that may be construed as contradictory. Being caught unaware in an apparent contradiction can have a debilitating effect on the credibility of a deponent's testimony. Know the information and sources relied on, the various analyses performed, the opinions reached, and the strengths as well as the weaknesses of the case. Above all, tell the truth.

Finally, insist on a detailed predeposition briefing with counsel. This briefing should include a conclusion regarding disclosure strategy. If the objective is to cause a settlement to occur, a complete disclosure of all the strengths of the case should be made. If the case is likely to proceed to trial, then a restrictive approach may be called for, in which the expert should answer only the question asked and should not volunteer related issues to opposing counsel.

There are some general rules an expert should follow when giving a deposition:

- *Bring no documentation unless required or advised by counsel.* To do so will only make opposing counsel more effective in conducting discovery and provide additional avenues of questions. Of course if the deposition is in response to a subpoena, all documents identified in that subpoena must be provided.

- *Think before answering and do not answer unless you are sure you understand the question.* Word crafting is an attorney's stock in trade. If a question is not totally understood, at best the answer will be unresponsive. At worst, the accountant may fall into a trap. Or the attorney may not even understand his own question, and the response will only serve to lead the attorney to more effective questioning.

- *Answer questions directly—then stop.* Do not fill dead air, ramble, or volunteer information. The "pregnant pause" is a favorite gambit to elicit additional information when opposing counsel is not quite sure what to ask next and wants the expert's help.

- *Stop talking and listen when your counsel objects.* The question may be improper, or the accountant's counsel may have noticed the infamous "trick" question. Common trick questions include the use of compound questions, double negatives, absolute terms, and prefacing a question with a misstatement of prior testimony.

  Absolute terms are typified by questions such as "Were those all the documents you reviewed?" or "Are those all your opinions regarding this case?" An affirmative answer may preclude a temporarily forgotten item that is important to the case from later being cited at trial. Consequently, if appropriate, qualify with responses such as "Those are the items that I recall at the present time."

  A question asked with the objective of misstating prior testimony typically starts with, "Earlier you testified . . . " and ends with a question that is often not directly related to the mischaracterized testimony. By answering the question while failing to correct the mischaracterization, an argument can be made that the witness agrees with the misstatement.

- *Refuse to engage in speculation.* Either the expert knows the answer or does not know. Opposing counsel may have the fact in hand and is hoping to trap the expert in a conflict. Being asked to interpret an unfamiliar document can be particularly treacherous. Likewise, an incorrect guess on a forgotten minor detail can be as damaging as an error on a major one. Do not be afraid to respond "I don't know" or "I don't recall." No one knows everything and very few, if any, people have perfect recall.

- *Resist being provoked into anger or arguing with counsel.* Chances are the provocation is calculated, and there is no upside potential. Anger will cloud reasoned logic and possibly blind the expert to a trap that is just about to open.

- *Review the court reporter's transcript, correct all errors and typographical errors, and sign.* Once the deposition has been completed and the court reporter has prepared a transcript, the accountant should read his testimony carefully. If he said something he did not mean, now is the only time he will have to change it. Changes to deposition testimony should be taken seriously. The accountant should have good reasons for changing his testimony. If the changes are extensive, the accountant may be deposed a second time.

(b) GIVING TRIAL TESTIMONY

(i) Direct Testimony.   The objective of direct testimony is to present an opinion in a manner such that it will be understood and believed by the judge and jury or other trier of fact. The testimony will begin by reviewing the witness's qualifications, which provide the prerequisite skill and training enabling the witness to provide the court with expert testimony. Opposing counsel will then have the opportunity to "voir dire" the expert and to challenge his qualifications as an expert. The judge will then decide if the court will qualify the accountant as an expert.

The expert's opinions then will be solicited. It is imperative that the expert not appear to be an advocate for the plaintiff or defendant but rather appear fair and unbiased. The job of advocacy should be reserved for the attorney. Violation of this precept will tend to undermine the expert's credibility.

Finally, the basis for the expert's opinion will be presented. The engagement scope is reviewed, including who retained the expert and why, documents reviewed, interviews conducted, the engagement team, manner of supervision and time spent, compensation, and any engagement scope limitations imposed. Next the methodology employed is explained, which leads to the conclusions and opinions reached. Typically any weaknesses are acknowledged and explained in a preemptive fashion to reduce potential damage on cross-examination.

The key to persuasive and effective testimony is communication. The expert's position may be a technical marvel, but it is worthless if the jury does not understand the testimony or is not convinced. Therefore, the expert should speak English and eliminate accounting and financial jargon. Concepts should be explained by way of common, everyday occurrences. Condescending or patronizing speech is inappropriate.

The expert's job is to educate the jury and the court in an interesting fashion. This job can be facilitated by the use of and reference to trial exhibits. Trial exhibits are used to lead the jury, court, and the expert himself through the basis of the opinion, as well as to keep everyone's attention focused. Like the language used in testimony, the exhibits should be kept clear and simple so the point is unmistakable and memorable. In many jurisdictions, the jury cannot take notes, and visual exhibits are the most effective method to ensure a point or conclusion is remembered.

(ii) Cross-Examination.   The purpose of cross-examination is to cast doubt on or, if possible, undermine the expert witness's credibility and testimony. One of the simpler ways to accomplish this objective is through impeachment. Consequently, a thorough review of prior testimony, writings, and the deposition transcript is required. The expert must make sure not to be on record as holding a view that is or appears to be contrary to the one he is now presenting, or he must be able to provide an explanation.

Be calm and polite, even if opposing counsel is manipulating responses. The expert is in the attorney's ballpark, and any anger will be turned against the witness. Cross-examining attorneys will frequently use "yes/no" questions to manipulate an opposing expert. The expert should generally resist the tendency to provide lengthy qualifications to such questions, as a skilled attorney may succeed in having the expert admonished by the court to answer only the question asked. An admonishment will taint the expert in the jury's mind as well as leave the expert with less maneuvering room during the remainder of cross-examination. However, this is not to suggest the expert should timidly follow the yes/no trail. Make explanations when necessary.

Another favored approach is the hypothetical question. Care must be taken not to appear too defensive or restrictive when answering a hypothetical question. Select the appropriate moment to cleanly sever the link between the hypothetical and the reality of the case at hand. Finally, remember that redirect examination can rehabilitate mischaracterizations by opposing counsel. So even if the expert must admit something that appears damaging, he will have a chance to explain why the admission is irrelevant in the current context.

If opposing counsel has discovered an error, the expert should acknowledge the error, but not necessarily the implications or conclusions drawn by counsel. Again, redirect examination can salvage errors, especially immaterial errors.

It is important to know the opposing expert's opinion and basis and the key differences between both experts' work. The ultimate objective of cross-examination is to get the expert to agree with the opposing expert's opinion and basis. Nearly as damaging is an acknowledgment that the opposing expert is a leading expert in the field. Failing this, an admission that reasonable minds can differ is a likely parting shot.

The expert must also be prepared for questions concerning fees and any scope limitations, especially if opposing counsel has not engaged an expert witness. A comfortable, matter-of-fact response is called for. The expert is a professional who has been asked to conduct certain analyses and offer an opinion. This is not unlike any other engagement an accountant conducts, and the expert should not feel guilty about being compensated for his time and effort.

Finally, the expert must stay within his field of expertise. By straying, the expert will end up in unnecessary difficulties.

(iii) Redirect Examination. The purpose of redirect examination is to rehabilitate points made by the opponent and clarify responses and mischaracterizations. It is generally counterproductive to a witness's credibility to argue with opposing counsel or to resist answering questions that, to the jury, appear reasonable and straightforward. An evasive witness generally is a less credible witness. The expert is back in friendly hands during redirect, and this is the time to mitigate real or perceived damage.

During the redirect examination, the attorney will typically select two or three areas where additional explanation is necessary to counter the points made on cross-examination. This is the witness's opportunity to clearly explain why the points made during cross-examination are irrelevant and have no bearing on the expert's opinion.

46.8 PROFESSIONAL STANDARDS RELEVANT TO LITIGATION CONSULTING

Throughout the litigation process, the accountant will be asked to provide input, conduct analyses, and offer advice or opinions regarding facts at issue in the case. Clearly, the attorney-client will expect that appropriate standards of care are followed by the accountant during the course of the engagement. However, although the litigation process itself is a formal, structured process with many rules and procedures that must be followed, the nature of the accountant's work is typically very unstructured and loosely defined.

However, the accountant should recognize that there is a hierarchy of standards that apply to litigation consulting services as follows:

- AICPA Code of Professional Conduct
- AICPA Statement on Standards for Consulting Services (SSCS)
- AICPA Consulting Services Practice Aids

(a) AMERICAN INSTITUTE OF CERTIFIED PUBLIC ACCOUNTANTS CODE OF PROFESSIONAL CONDUCT. The AICPA Code of Professional Conduct applies to all professional services rendered by AICPA members. Certain sections of the Code of Professional Conduct have particular applicability to litigation consulting services; they are the guiding principles of this practice area. A greater understanding and appreciation of the importance of the existing standards contained in the Code will assist practitioners in their efforts to provide opinions that are relevant and reliable and that assist the trier of fact.

(i) Rule 101: Independence. When performing a litigation service engagement, independence is not required. However, the practitioner should be sensitive to the appearance of independence so that the trier of fact will accept conclusions and judgments as objective and impartial.

(ii) Rule 102: Integrity and Objectivity.   Although independence is not required in a litigation consulting engagement, the accountant is required to comply with Rule 102 of the AICPA Code of Professional Conduct. Rule 102 requires that members shall, in the performance of any professional service, maintain objectivity and integrity, shall be free of conflicts of interest, and shall not knowingly misrepresent facts or subordinate their judgment to others. The accountant should be aware of situations that would cause the trier of fact to question his integrity and objectivity; for example, current, prior, or possible future relationships with either the attorneys or the parties to the dispute, the rendering of contradictory opinions on the same subject matter at issue in the litigation, or having knowledge of facts obtained outside the normal discovery process could impair integrity and objectivity.

The accountant must also recognize how the roles and responsibilities of attorneys differ from those of CPAs in the litigation process. The litigating attorney is the client's advocate. "The litigation process demands that the attorney take every available advantage for the client, put the client's case in the best possible light, not offer evidence that is harmful to the client (with some exceptions) and challenge everything possible in the opponent's case."[4]

The accountant as an expert witness has a role that differs from that of an attorney. The accountant-expert does not serve as an advocate but rather is presented to the trier of fact as someone with specialized knowledge, training, and experience in a particular area and presents positions with objectivity. The function of the accountant as an expert witness is to assist the trier of fact in understanding complex or unfamiliar concepts. The accountant-expert is not expected to single-mindedly and one-sidedly offer only evidence and opinions that help the client. The accountant expert is expected to offer an objective opinion, based on knowledge and experience, of how the issues at hand should be interpreted by the trier of fact.[5] When acting as a consultant, the accountant can provide assistance that is more like that of an advocate.

(iii) Conflicts of Interest.   In a litigation services engagement, a conflict of interest exists when a litigation consulting practitioner's ability to objectively evaluate and present an issue for a client will be impaired by current, prior, or possible future relationships with parties to the litigation. The criterion for evaluating whether a conflict of interest is involved in a litigation services engagement is the ability of the accountant to maintain integrity and objectivity. A conflict of interest is based in fact, rather than appearance. However, the accountant should be mindful of and deal with appearances of conflicts before accepting the engagement.

Unlike the legal profession, the accounting profession has developed little formal guidance on conflicts of interest. An attorney has a well-defined and documented concept of what constitutes a conflict in the legal profession. Consequently, this concept may be applied inappropriately to the accountant. The standards of the legal profession concerning conflicts of interest should not be applied to the accounting profession because the roles of the attorney and the accountant in litigation are entirely different.

If a conflict of interest does not exist in fact, the accountant must decide if a conflict in appearance exists of if business issues would prevent acceptance of the engagement. For example, the accountant may decline to perform services because the position required by the prospective client conflicts with the business interests of an existing client. These determinations are based on the accountant's judgment.

Before accepting a litigation services engagement, the accountant should perform procedures that will enable him to determine if a conflict exists with any parties to the litigation. All conflicts and potential conflicts must be disclosed to the retaining attorney for his evaluation. Interpretation 102.2 of the AICPA Code of Professional Conduct provides that if a conflict exists and is disclosed to the client and other appropriate parties, the accountant can accept the engagement with the

---

[4] AICPA Consulting Services Special Report No. 93–2, "Conflicts of Interest in Litigation Services Engagements," ¶ 2/105.16, AICPA, 1993.
[5] Id., ¶ 2/105.21.

consent of all parties. The accountant should be aware that new federal regulations prohibit the performance of litigation consulting services for any audit client that is an SEC Registrant. For more information regarding conflicts of interest refer to AICPA Consulting Services Special Report No. 93–2, "Conflicts of Interest in Litigation Services Engagements."

(iv) Rule 201: General Standards. The four general standards, professional competence, due professional care, planning and supervision, and sufficient relevant data, under Rule 201 of the Code of Professional Conduct apply to litigation consulting services. In fact, these four standards are included in SSCS No. 1 and are discussed in more detail below.

(v) Rule 202: Compliance with Standards. Pursuant to Rule 202 of the Code of Professional Conduct, the accountant must comply with the standards promulgated by the Consulting Services Executive Committee.

(vi) Rule 203: Accounting Principles. Rule 203 requires the accountant to demonstrate an understanding of GAAP. To the extent that GAAP is applicable, the accountant shall apply the appropriate accounting principles.

(vii) Rule 301: Confidential Client Information. Pursuant to Rule 301, the CPA in public practice may not disclose Confidential client information without the client's consent. In litigation consulting services engagements, Confidential client information obtained in prior engagements must be protected. Thus, the accountant has the dual responsibility to be both truthful and honest while preserving past and present client confidences. Before the accountant relies on specific information obtained in an unrelated prior engagement and uses that information as the basis for his opinion, he must either obtain the consent of the prior client to reveal its confidences or abandon any effort to use such information as the basis of his opinion.

(b) STATEMENT ON STANDARDS FOR CONSULTING SERVICES. Litigation consulting services are consulting services as defined in SSCS No. 1. SSCS No. 1 sets standards that must be followed for all consulting engagements.

(i) General Standards. The general standards defined in Rule 201 of the AICPA Code of Professional Conduct are applicable to litigation consulting engagements.

- *Professional competence.* The practitioner should accept only those engagements he or the CPA firm can reasonably expect to complete with professional competence. The practitioner must have adequate knowledge, skills, training, and experience so that duties can be performed in accordance with appropriate professional standards. Litigation consulting services involve many diverse issues. As a result, the practitioner may need to rely on the assistance of other individuals with the required education and experience in order to comply with this standard. For example, a practitioner may have the required expertise to develop a model for computing damages to a restaurant chain in a breach of contract litigation. However, he may need the assistance of someone in the restaurant industry to provide key components that will be used in the model, for example, the gross profit margin that is typical in the industry.
- *Due professional care.* The practitioner should make a conscientious effort in his performance of the engagement by obtaining sufficient relevant data and applying reliable principles and methods to the facts of the dispute before reaching conclusions and findings and should be able to present his conclusions and findings to the trier of fact in a concise, clear, and correct manner.
- *Planning and supervision.* Planning and supervision have different implications for the litigation consulting practitioner than for many of the other services a CPA may be engaged to provide. A litigation consulting services engagement is usually far more dynamic than other engagements. The facts and circumstances of each litigation consulting engagement are

unique. Planning is essential in a litigation consulting engagement to control costs and focus the practitioner's work product on the engagement requirements. Plans continually change in a litigation engagement and are usually not written because of the dynamic nature of the litigation process.

- *Supervision ensures the quality of the engagement performance.* Since the testifying expert must express the opinions and conclusions reached as his own, the testifying expert should closely supervise the ongoing work that is performed by others.
- *Sufficient relevant data.* The practitioner needs to base his conclusions and judgments on sufficient relevant data. It is not only the practitioner's opinion that is evaluated by the trier of fact, but also the relevancy, sufficiency, and verifiability of the underlying evidence supporting the opinion. The practitioner can generally rely on documents that have been authenticated by the parties to the proceeding or that are acceptable to the court under the various rules of evidence. It is important to communicate to the attorney what evidence is necessary to properly support the practitioner's conclusions and judgments, and it is incumbent upon the practitioner to advise the attorney of possible missing or questionable documents and the lack of relevant data upon which to reach an opinion.

Generally, the practitioner may look to the guidance of generally accepted auditing and other attestation standards with respect to the sufficiency, relevancy, and reliability or evidential matter.

(ii) Consulting Standards.   In addition to the general standards, SSCS No. 1 also establishes specific consulting standards for consulting services.

- *Client interest.* The accountant should serve the interests of the client while maintaining objectivity and integrity. In addition, when acting as an expert, the accountant also has a duty to the trier of fact.
- *Understanding with the client.* The accountant should establish a written understanding with the client about the responsibilities of the parties and the nature, scope, and limitation of the services to be provided.
- *Communication with client.* The client should be informed about:
  - ○ conflicts of interest
  - ○ significant reservations concerning the scope or benefits of the engagement
  - ○ significant engagement findings or events

When acting as an expert, the accountant should be aware that all of his communications with the client, written or oral, are subject to discovery and must be provided upon request by the opposing party. All of the accountant's work product, including draft reports and schedules, notes, supporting schedules, and correspondence, can be requested as part of the discovery process.

(c) AMERICAN INSTITUTE OF CERTIFIED PUBLIC ACCOUNTANTS CONSULTING SERVICES PRACTICE AIDS.   The AICPA has published nonauthoritative educational guidance for practitioners, including Consulting Services Special Report No. 931, "Application of AICPA Professional Standards in the Performance of Litigation Services," Report 93–2, "Conflicts of Interest in Litigation Services Engagements," Report 93–3, "Comparing Attest and Consulting Services: A Guide for the Practitioner," Report 93–4, "Providing Litigation Services," Consulting Services Practice Aid 95–2, "Communicating Understandings in Litigation Services: Engagement Letters," Consulting Services Practice Aid 96–3, "Communicating in Litigation Services: Reports," Consulting Services Practice Aid 97–1, "Fraud Investigations in Litigation and Dispute Resolution Services," Consulting Services Practice Aid 98–1, "Providing Bankruptcy and Reorganization Services," Consulting Services Practice Aid 98–2, "Calculation of Damages from Personal Injury, Wrongful Death, and Employment Discrimination," Consulting Services Practice Aid 99–1, "Alternative Dispute Resolution Services," Consulting Services Practice Aid 99–2, "Valuing Intellectual

Property and Calculating Infringement Damages," and Consulting Services Practice Aid 02–01, "Business Valuation in Bankruptcy."

46.9 FEDERAL RULES OF EVIDENCE

(a) FEDERAL RULE OF EVIDENCE 702. Most witnesses who testify in a litigation are fact witnesses. A fact witness can provide testimony based on what he has seen, heard, or otherwise observed. A fact witness may not offer opinions. By contrast, an expert witness by reason of education or specialized experience possesses superior knowledge about a subject and as such may offer opinions at trial. An accountant may testify as an expert witness if his opinion will assist the trier of fact in understanding the evidence or determining the issues in a case.

Federal Rule of Evidence 702 governs the admissibility of expert opinion testimony. Rule 702 states that "if scientific, technical, or other specialized knowledge will assist the trier of fact to understand the evidence or to determine a fact in issue, a witness qualified as an expert by knowledge, skill, experience, training, or education, may testify thereto in the form of an opinion or otherwise."

(b) EFFECT OF DAUBERT V. MERRELL DOW PHARMACEUTICALS. In *Daubert v. Merrell Dow Pharmaceuticals*, 113 S. Ct. 2796 (1993), the Supreme Court addressed the rules pertaining to the admission of expert testimony.

Since 1923, based on *Frye v. United States*, 293 F.1013 (D.C. Cir 1923), the federal courts applied a test (the general acceptance test) by which scientific expert opinions should be admitted into evidence. Under this standard, an opinion was admitted only if it was based on generally accepted methodology within the industry.

In the *Daubert* decision, the Supreme Court determined that in order for expert witness opinions to be admitted under 702, they did not have to meet the *Frye* general acceptance test and clarified that Rule 702 does not establish general acceptance as a criteria for admissibility. The *Daubert* decision clarified the trial court's role in determining the admissibility of expert testimony. In doing so, the court need not determine whether the methodology meets the general acceptance test but must assess the validity of the methodology used and the applicability of that methodology to the specific facts of the case. Discussions of issues of expert testimony are extended in Chapter 47 "Financial Expert Witness Challenges and Exclusions: Results and Trends in Federal and State Cases since Kumho Tire."

(c) FEDERAL RULE OF CIVIL PROCEDURE 26. If the accountant has been engaged to serve as a testifying expert witness, he must become aware of the effect of Rule 26 of the Federal Rules of Civil Procedure, which deals with the procedure for written disclosure of expert testimony.

Pursuant to Rule 26, the identity of one side's potential testifying experts, as well as information about the expected testimony, must be voluntarily disclosed at the outset of a case, without receipt of a formal discovery request.

In addition, Rule 26 provides that the expert prepare and sign a written report. This report must be disclosed to the other parties before the expert will be allowed to testify at trial. Unless the date by which disclosure of the written report must be made is decided by the trial judge, rules of the local court, or by agreement of the parties, the report must be disclosed at least 90 days before the date of trial. If an expert is retained solely to rebut the testimony of an opposing expert, the report of the rebuttal witness must be disclosed within 30 days of the disclosure of the other expert's report.

Generally, the expert witness will not be permitted to testify at trial to his opinions unless the opinions are contained in the expert witness's written report. Therefore, the content of the expert's report should contain all of his opinions and the bases for the opinions. In addition, once the expert's report is disclosed to the other side, any changes to the report must be disclosed before the commencement of trial.

Rule 26 requires that the expert's report contain:

- A complete statement of the opinion to be expressed and the bases and reasons therefore
- The data or other information the witness considered in forming the opinions
- Any exhibits to be used as a summary of or as support for the opinions
- qualifications of the witness, including a list of publications the witness authored within the preceding 10 years
- The compensation to be paid to the witness for the study and testimony
- A list of all other cases in which the witness has testified as an expert at trial or in deposition within the preceding four years
- Signature of the expert

Pursuant to Rule 26, once the expert's written report required by Rule 26 has been disclosed, the opposing side has the right to take the deposition of any person who has been identified as an expert whose opinions may be presented at trial.

The accountant who is engaged as an expert witness in a matter to be tried in a federal court should ascertain the current status of Rule 26 in the applicable federal district and discuss compliance with Rule 26 with the counsel retaining him.

It is important to point out that the Federal Rules of Civil Procedure give local courts the option of not complying with certain provisions, including the provisions of Rule 26 discussed above. The accountant should consult with the retaining attorney to ascertain whether the case is to be tried in federal or local court and the local rules that apply to the case.

46.10 SOURCES AND SUGGESTED REFERENCES

American Institute of Certified Public Accountants, Code of Professional Conduct. AICPA, New York, 1988.

———, *Statement on Standards for Consulting Services (SSCS) No. 1*, "Consulting Services: Definitions and Standards." AICPA, New York, 1986.

———, Auditing Standards Board, *Statement on Standards for Accountants' Services on Prospective Financial Information,* "Financial Forecasts and Projections." AICPA, New York, 1985.

———, Auditing Standards Board, *Statement on Auditing Standards No. 99* "Consideration of Fraud in an Audit of Financial Statements," AICPA, New York, 2001.

———, *Application of AICPA Professional Standards in the Performance of Litigation Services.* AICPA Special Report 93–1, n.d.

———, *Conflicts of Interest in Litigation Services Engagements.* AICPA Consulting Services Special Report 932, n.d.

———, *Comparing Attest and Consulting Services: A Guide for the Practitioner.* AICPA Consulting Services Special Report 93–3, n.d.

———, *Providing Litigation Services.* AICPA Consulting Services Practice Aid 93–4, n.d.

———, *Communicating Understandings in Litigation Services.* AICPA Consulting Services Practice Aid 95–2, n.d.

———, *Communicating in Litigation Services: Reports,* AICPA Consulting Services Practice Aid 96–3, n.d.

———, *Codification of Statement on Standards for Attestation Engagements,* AICPA, New York, 2003.

Black, Henry C., *Black's Law Dictionary,* Fifth Edition West Publishing, St. Paul, MN, 1979.

Crain, Michael A., Goldwasser, Dan L., and Harry, Everett P., "Liability: Expert Witness—In Jeopardy?" *Journal of Accountancy,* Vol. 42. AICPA, December 1994.

de Silva, Harindra, Lo, Nancy N., and Nells, Tara N., "Securities Act Violations: Estimation of Damages," *In Litigation Services Handbook: The Role of the Accountant as Expert,* ed. Roman L. Weil, Michael J. Wagner, and Peter B. Frank, John Wiley & Sons, New York, 1995.

Dunn, Robert L., *Recovery of Damages for Lost Profits,* Fourth Edition, Lawpress, Tiburon, CA, 1992.

Dykeman, Francis C., *Forensic Accounting: The Accountant as Expert Witness.* John Wiley & Sons, New York, 1982.

Federal Rules of Evidence: 703.

Federal Rules of Civil Procedure: 26, 30, 33, 34, 36, 45.

Frank, Peter B., and Wagner, Michael J., "Computing Lost profits and Reasonable Royalties," *AIPLA Quarterly Journal,* Vol. 15, No. 4. AIPLA, Arlington, VA 1987, pp. 391–425.

Kabe, Elo R., and Blonder, Brian L., "Discounting Concepts and Damages," *In Litigation Services Handbook: The Role of the Accountant as Expert,* 1996 Supplement ed. Roman L. Weil, Michael J. Wagner, and Peter B. Frank, John Wiley & Sons, New York, 1996.

Kinrich, Jeffrey H., "Cost Estimation," *Litigation Services Handbook: The Role of the Accountant as Expert.* ed. Roman L. Weil, Michael J. Wagner, and Peter B. Frank, John Wiley & Sons, New York, 1995.

Knapp, Charles L., *Commercial Damages.* Matthew Bender, New York, 1986.

Kraft, Melvin D., *Using Experts in Civil Cases.* Practicing Law Institute, New York, 1977.

Newton, Grant W., *Bankruptcy and Insolvency Accounting,* Fifth Edition John Wiley & Sons, New York, 1994.

Public Company Accounting Oversight Board. *An Audit of Internal Control Over Financial Reporting Performed in Conjunction With an Audit of Financial Statements.* Auditing Standard No. 2. PCAOB, Washington, D.C. 2004.

———, *References in Auditor's Reports to the Standards of the Public Company Accounting Oversight Board.* Auditing Standard No.1. PCAOB, Washington, D.C. 2003.

Sims, Raymond S., and Haller, Mark W., "Lost profits: Covering All the Bases in the 'But For' World," *Inside Litigation,* Vol. 2, No. 4. Prentice-Hall Law & Business, New York, February 1988.

United States Congress, *The Sarbanes-Oxley Act of 2002,* (HR 3763). 2002.

Wagner, Michael J., and Frank, Peter B., *Litigation Services: Management Advisory Services Technical Consulting Practice Aid No. 7.* AICPA, New York, 1986.

Weil, Roman L., Wagner, Michael J., and Frank, Peter B., eds., *Litigation Services Handbook: The Role of the Accountant as Expert,* Second Edition John Wiley & Sons, New York, 1995.

CHAPTER 47

FINANCIAL EXPERT WITNESS CHALLENGES AND EXCLUSIONS: RESULTS AND TRENDS IN FEDERAL AND STATE CASES SINCE *KUMHO TIRE*

Lawrence F. Ranallo, CPA

PricewaterhouseCoopers LLP

Keith R. Ugone, PhD

Analysis Group, Inc

47.1 INTRODUCTION[1]

Complex business disputes often require complex financial expert witness testimony. Depending on the nature of the case or the cause of action, financial expert witness testimony could cover a very broad range of accounting, financial, and economic topics. These topics might include historically based analyses, such as the insolvency date of a business or the past profitability of a business. Alternatively, the financial expert witness might testify regarding certain counterfactuals, such as

---

[1] We wish to thank Sharon Freeman, Na Dawson, and Aijun Besio for research assistance. The information contained in this chapter does not represent the views of either Pricewaterhouse-Coopers, LLP, or Analysis Group, Inc.

the profitability of a business in the absence of an alleged wrongful act. Finally, a financial expert witness might even testify on economic causation issues, including the impact of market-related events (i.e., industry downturns or increased competition) on the profitability of a business.[2]

Hence, depending on the facts and circumstances of a business dispute, financial expert witnesses could have a number of interwoven important roles. The financial expert witness could provide the trier of fact with guidance as to the economic harm the plaintiff may have suffered. Alternatively, the financial expert witness could provide guidance as to the existence/nonexistence of a financial causal linkage between the alleged wrongful conduct and the claimed economic harm.[3] A certified public accountant (CPA), a financial analyst, an economist, or a statistician, depending on the facts and circumstances of the dispute, could be equally well qualified to render these types of opinions.

The requirements for expert witness qualification in federal cases are provided in certain federal rules, and, since 1993, in the *Daubert* case and its case progeny.[4] The requirements for expert witness qualification in state cases vary by jurisdiction; some states follow the *Daubert* criteria while other states apply requirements similar to the older *Frye* criteria.[5]

Rule 702 of the Federal Rules of Evidence provides for the admissibility of expert testimony as follows:

> If scientific, technical, or other specialized knowledge will assist the trier of fact to understand the evidence or to determine a fact in issue, a witness qualified as an expert by knowledge, skill, experience, training, or education, may testify thereto in the form of an opinion or otherwise, if (1) the testimony is based upon sufficient facts or data, (2) the testimony is the product of reliable principles and methods, and (3) the witness has applied the principles and methods reliably to the facts of the case.[6]

In its *Daubert* opinion, the Supreme Court established four now commonly cited nonexclusive criteria for the admissibility of scientific and technical expert testimony. These criteria were developed to assist the trial judge to "make a preliminary assessment of whether the testimony's underlying reasoning or methodology is scientifically valid and properly can be applied to the facts at issue."[7] The criteria are:

1. Whether the theory or technique in question can be (and has been) tested
2. Whether the theory or technique has been subjected to peer review and publication
3. Whether the theory or technique has a known or potential error rate and the existence and maintenance of standards concerning its operation
4. Whether the theory or technique has attracted widespread acceptance within a relevant scientific community

---

[2] This list is illustrative only and is not intended to be all-inclusive. It is quite common for financial experts to testify on these or similar subjects in securities-related matters, antitrust matters, intellectual property matters, breach of contract disputes, purchase price disputes, and loss of earnings matters, among others.

[3] Here we make a distinction between economic or financial causation versus legal causation (e.g., whether a wrongful act occurred).

[4] See, for example, *William Daubert, et ux., etc., et al. v. Merrell Dow Pharmaceuticals, Inc.* (92–102), 509 U.S. 579 (1993) and *Kumho Tire Company, LTD., et al. v. Patrick Carmichael, etc., et al.* (97–1709), 526 U.S. 137 (1999).

[5] See *Frye v. United States*, 292 F. 1013 (1923). See also, for example, the Supreme Court of Texas case captioned *E.I. du Pont de Nemours and Company, Inc. v. C. R. Robinson and Shirley Robinson* (94–0843), 923 S.W.2d 549 (1995).

[6] Rule 702, Federal Rules of Evidence (Including Amendments Effective December 1, 2000), 2000–2001 Edition, p. 113. As implied by Rule 702, the expert witness must use a reliable methodology and a methodology that fits the facts and circumstances of the case.

[7] *Daubert*, 113 Supreme Court Reporter, 509 U.S. 579, p. 2790.

The *Kumho Tire* case in 1999 clarified that the nonexclusive "*Daubert* criteria" were also applicable to financial experts such as CPAs, financial analysts, economists, and statisticians, among others, in federal cases.

Consequently, financial expert witnesses must be aware of the criteria being used to judge the admissibility of their work and opinions. Since *Kumho Tire,* there has been a particular focus on how courts have applied the "*Daubert* criteria" to financial experts—especially since financial experts are often used in the liability aspects of cases involving accounting and auditing issues and are used for damage quantification and related economic causation issues.

47.2 METHODOLOGY AND OVERVIEW OF OBSERVATIONS AND CONCLUSIONS

In this chapter we present our findings from an analysis of *published opinions* of federal and state cases relating to challenges and exclusions of financial expert witnesses over the 2000–2002 time period (i.e., post-*Kumho Tire*). It is important to note that our search criteria included published opinions that referenced the *Kumho Tire* case decision explicitly—which we used as a primary indicator of matters likely to involve challenges to nonscientific experts such as CPAs, financial analysts, economists, and statisticians. (See Exhibit 47.1.)[8] Our sample included 895 challenges identified through published opinions meeting these criteria.[9] Financial experts were named in 165 of these 895 challenges, with 68 financial experts being excluded either in whole or in part.[10]

Several interesting conclusions can be drawn from the opinions reviewed, including the following:

- *The number of challenges to experts of all types is increasing.* In 2000, there were 250 challenges to expert witnesses in general.[11] This number increased to 289 in 2001 and 356 in 2002. This trend is to be expected. The exclusion of a litigant's expert is often devastating to that party's case. Hence, challenging the admissibility of an expert's opinion is an increasingly utilized weapon in the arsenal of opposing counsel.

- *Once challenged, the rate at which financial experts are excluded in whole or in part is decreasing.* Based on our sample of cases, 22.0 percent of the challenges in 2000 involved financial expert witnesses. The corresponding figures in 2001 and 2002 were 15.2 percent and 18.5 percent, respectively. Hence, the relative proportion of challenges between financial and nonfinancial expert witnesses has not appreciably changed between 2000 and 2002.[12] Interestingly, however, the percentage of financial experts excluded in whole or in part (once challenged) over this same time period declined from 54.5 percent to 40.9 percent to 30.3 percent. While at first this result may appear paradoxical, we believe it is the natural result of the increased emphasis on challenging the admissibility of the opposing financial expert's opinions. Two forces are creating this result. To the extent a *Daubert* challenge is a strategy increasingly utilized by opposing counsel, the quality of challenges and the likelihood of exclusion may not be as high at the margin when increasing numbers of challenges are made.[13] In addition, to the extent it is likely a financial expert has to withstand both a

---

[8] Although broader search criteria would identify additional cases in federal and state jurisdictions, the expert challenges identified using the stated search criteria provided interesting and meaningful insights into certain trends regarding challenges to financial expert witness testimony since *Kumho Tire.*

[9] We conducted research on cases citing *Kumho Tire* (526 U.S. 137) in the Lexis Nexis federal and state court cases database.

[10] Some identified published opinions addressed the proposed testimony of more than one expert.

[11] Using the *Kumho Tire* search criteria previously described.

[12] The purpose of this chapter is to identify and discuss certain observations and trends relating to expert witness challenges and exclusions. We have not analyzed whether statistically significant differences exist between certain percentages we report.

[13] Restated, in the aggregate, it is likely there are diminishing returns to *Daubert* challenges.

	Total Challenges	Federal Challenges*		State Challenges**	
		Number	% Total	Number	% Total
2000					
Expert witness challenges	250	196	78.4%	54	21.6%
Financial expert witness challenges	55	47	85.5%	8	14.5%
2001					
Expert witness challenges	289	254	87.9%	35	12.1%
Financial expert witness challenges	44	38	86.4%	6	13.6%
2002					
Expert witness challenges	356	295	82.9%	61	17.1%
Financial expert witness challenges	66	63	95.5%	3	4.5%
2000 D 2002 Grand Total					
Expert witness challenges	**895**	**745**	**83.2%**	**150**	**16.8%**
Financial expert witness challenges	**165**	**148**	**89.7%**	**17**	**10.3%**

Notes:

*Federal courts searched included the U.S. Supreme Court, various circuit courts, Court of International Trade, Claims Court, Administrative and Agency Court, U.S. Tax Court, National Labor Relations Board, and Military Justice court.

**State courts searched included state courts, state supreme courts, and state appellate courts.

Exhibit 47.1   Jurisdiction analysis (cases citing *Kumho Tire vs. Carmichael*) annual; 2000–2002.

Daubert challenge and cross-examination, financial experts are more inclined (at the margin) to perform higher-quality investigations, to use generally accepted methodologies, and to use methodologies that fit the facts and circumstances of the particular matter. In other words, financial experts have appropriately responded to the incentives created by the likelihood of a *Daubert* challenge. Diminishing returns to financial expert witness challenges and financial expert witness response to the *Daubert* environment have caused the percentage of financial experts excluded in whole or in part to decline.

- *Plaintiff side financial experts are challenged and excluded more frequently than defense side financial experts.* Based on our sample of cases, plaintiff financial experts are two to three times as likely to be challenged relative to defense financial experts. In 2000, 76.4 percent of financial expert challenges involved plaintiffs' financial experts. The corresponding figures in 2001 and 2002 were 68.2 percent and 71.2 percent, respectively. These trends carry over to actual exclusions as well. In 2000, 79.3 percent of financial expert exclusions were plaintiff financial experts. This number increased to 83.3 percent in 2001 and 90.0 percent in 2002. Again, in many respects, these results are not surprising. First, a defendant can survive without its financial expert witness better than a plaintiff can survive without its financial expert witness. (The plaintiff needs a financial expert to put forth a claimed damages figure, whereas a defendant could always just cross-examine the plaintiff's financial expert without putting its own expert on the witness stand.) Hence, at the margin, there is a greater incentive to challenge the plaintiff's financial expert than the defendant's financial expert. In addition, the plaintiff's financial expert often is building or constructing a damage model, while the defendant's financial expert is often just evaluating the work of the plaintiff's financial expert. In terms of pure numbers, the plaintiff's financial expert has many more assumptions and inputs to justify relative to defendant's financial expert, leading to a greater likelihood of a challenge. For the same reason, there is a greater likelihood the plaintiff's financial expert will ultimately be excluded in whole or in part.

The rate of challenges to accountants/CPAs as testifying experts appears to be lower than that for other types of financial experts. The success rate of excluding accountants/CPAs is lower as well.[14] Of the 165 challenges to financial experts, 18 related to accountants/CPAs, 41 related to economists, and 17 related to statisticians.[15] Only three of the accountants/CPAs were excluded in whole or in part, while 21 of the economists and eight of the statisticians were excluded in whole or in part. Care should be exercised when interpreting these figures, however. These figures should not be interpreted as meaning a financial expert with a CPA is necessarily less susceptible to challenges and exclusions relative to financial experts with a PhD in economics (for example). To the contrary, these figures are likely the product of (a) the nature of the engagements traditionally assigned to different types of financial experts, (b) the data that may be available to properly conduct the required analysis in the engagements traditionally assigned to different types of financial experts, and (c) the degree to which the required testimony deviates from the interpretation of historical data toward projecting business performance under an alternative set of conditions. CPAs, in certain types of engagements, may be assessing accounting rules, using accounting rules to support their opinions, or opining on issues relating to the actual past performance of a business. In contrast, the majority of the challenges and exclusions relating to economists pertained to antitrust cases. (See Exhibit 47.2.) Defining a relevant market and/or hypothesizing as to prices, output, market shares, and profits in the absence of an alleged monopolization may place the economist at greater

---

[14] While some courts identified the expert in question as a CPA, others simply identified the expert as an accountant. Consequently, the statistics reported in this article may include both CPAs and non-CPA accountants.

[15] The remaining financial experts were classified as "other financial experts" in our analysis. In some challenges, not enough information was reported to identify these "other financial experts" as CPAs, economists, or statisticians. In other challenges, "other financial experts" included financial analysts and appraisers, among others.

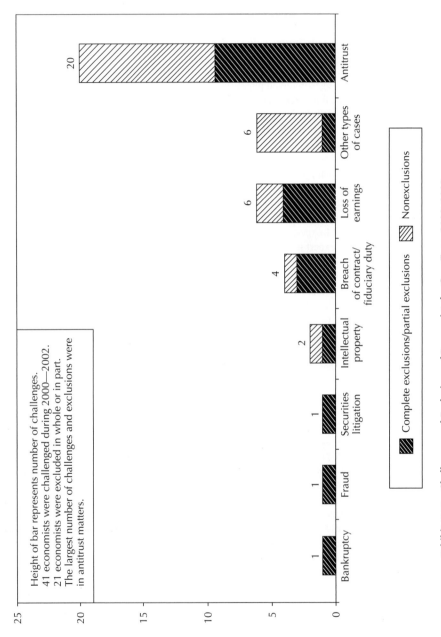

Height of bar represents number of challenges.
41 economists were challenged during 2000—2002.
21 economists were excluded in whole or in part.
The largest number of challenges and exclusions were
in antitrust matters.

Complete exclusions/partial exclusions **Nonexclusions**

Exhibit 47.2 Challenges and Exclusions of Economists by Case Type; 2000–2002.

risk of challenge and possible exclusion than an accountant/CPA functioning as a financial expert in matters that do not involve these components. Hence, we believe it is the nature of the cases and the required analyses that explain the different exclusion rates of CPAs and economists rather than alternative explanations.[16]

Other details to our study are presented in the remainder of this chapter, followed by additional conclusion.

47.3 EXPERT WITNESS CHALLENGES AND EXCLUSIONS: 2000–2002

Reported in Exhibit 47.3 is the number of challenges relating to the admissibility of financial and nonfinancial expert witnesses over the January 2000 through December 2002 time period. The results of these challenges are also reported in Exhibit 47.3. Our investigation indicates that:

- Of the 895 challenges identified using our search criteria, financial experts were challenged a total of 165 times (18.4 percent) while 730 challenges (81.6 percent) involved nonfinancial experts.
- When financial experts were challenged, their testimony was excluded in whole or in part in 68 cases or 41.2 percent of the time.[17] In contrast, nonfinancial experts were excluded in whole or in part in 336 cases or 46.0 percent of the time.[18]
- Financial and nonfinancial experts have their testimony excluded entirely at a higher rate than excluded in part. Our investigation reveals 72.1 percent of the financial expert exclusions and 76.8 percent of the nonfinancial expert exclusions were in whole rather than in part.

Based on the above data, once challenged, financial and nonfinancial experts appear to be excluded in roughly the same proportions.

The annual number of challenges and rate of exclusions of financial and nonfinancial expert witnesses over the 2000–2002 time period is presented in Exhibit 47.4. Based on annual data:

- The number of challenges of experts has trended upward. The total number of expert challenges increased by 15.6 percent in 2001 (from 250 in 2000 to 289 in 2001) and increased by 23.2 percent in 2002 (from 289 in 2001 to 356 in 2002).
- Financial expert challenges have stayed relatively steady as a percentage of the total number of challenges over this three-year period. In 2000, 55 of the 250 challenges (22.0 percent) were challenges of financial experts. In 2002, 66 of the 356 challenges (18.5 percent) were challenges of financial experts.

---

[16] It is interesting to note the reasons given for the exclusion of the three accountants/CPAs discussed in the text. *In re: Bonham* (2000 Bankr. Lexis 727), a bankruptcy court judge excluded the CPA "based on substantial factual mistakes, speculation, innuendo, and inferences which are not supported by full explanations and analysis." *In United States v. Sparks* (2001 U.S. App. Lexis 8002), the circuit court judge upheld the exclusion of an accountant "because there was no indication of authenticity [of documents relied on], however, [the accountant's] testimony, which was based on those documents, did not 'rest on a reliable foundation' and had to be excluded under Rule 702. *Daubert,* 509 U.S. at 597." *In United States v. Rockwell Space Operations* (2002 U.S. Dist. Lexis 6650), the district court judge wrote, "As a consequence, the accuracy of [the CPA's] damage assessment is entirely dependent upon the accuracy and the credibility of [the plaintiff's] non-expert and unreliable estimates. [The CPA's] opinion is not reliable because it was built upon a faulty foundation: the uncorroborated and unreliable estimates of [the plaintiff]." [Bracketed terms have been added for clarity.]

[17] Financial experts were excluded in whole 49 times and excluded in part 19 times.

[18] Nonfinancial experts were excluded in whole 258 times and excluded in part 78 times.

Type of Expert	Number of Challenges*	Partial Exclusions	Complete Exclusions	Total Number of Exclusions	Exclusions as a Percent of Challenges
Financial experts	165	19	49	68	41.2%
Nonfinancial experts**	730	78	258	336	46.0%
Total	**895**	**97**	**307**	**404**	**45.1%**

Note:
*Multiple experts could be challenged in the same case.
**Nonfinancial experts include medical doctors, engineers, forensic scientists, psychologists, and psychiatrists, among others.

Exhibit 47.3   Expert Witness Challenges (Cases Citing *Kumho Tire vs. Carmichael*); January 2000–December 2002.

- The rate at which financial experts have been excluded, once challenged, has declined from 54.5 percent in 2000 to 40.9 percent in 2001 to 30.3 percent in 2002.[19] As discussed previously, this is likely the result of two forces. At the margin, with increases in the number of challenges, the likelihood of a successful challenge to a financial expert witness may be less. Also, at the margin, the quality of work prepared by financial expert witnesses may have improved in response to increased scrutiny stemming from tightened admissibility guidelines. Both of these forces likely explain the decline in the exclusion rate over the 2000–2002 time period.[20]

Interestingly, based on the data in Exhibit 47.4, it appears as though a crossover has occurred with respect to the rate of exclusions of financial and nonfinancial expert witnesses once challenged. Whereas in 2000, when challenged, financial experts were excluded at a higher rate than nonfinancial experts, by 2002 nonfinancial experts were excluded at a higher rate.[21] In 2000, 54.5 percent of the challenges of financial experts resulted in a partial or complete exclusion, declining to 30.3 percent in 2002. In contrast, 46.2 percent of the challenges of nonfinancial experts resulted in a partial or complete exclusion in 2000, declining only slightly to 43.8 percent in 2002.

47.4 REASONS FINANCIAL EXPERTS WERE EXCLUDED: RELEVANCE, RELIABILITY, AND QUALIFICATIONS

We next determined the reasons financial experts were excluded or partially excluded.[22] This analysis was done in the context of the Rule 702 focus on the qualifications of the proposed expert as well as the relevance and reliability of the planned testimony. When financial experts are excluded, it is more likely to be as a result of the lack of reliability in the planned testimony than as a result of relevance issues or the qualifications of the expert. While multiple reasons were often given for the exclusions of the financial experts studied, reliability was mentioned in over 80 percent of the exclusions, relevance was mentioned in half of the exclusions, and qualifications were mentioned in a quarter of the exclusions. Finally, when financial expert testimony is determined to be unreliable, it is more likely to be a result of problems with the quantity or validity of the data used by the expert than with any of the *Daubert* criteria.

47.5 EXCLUSION OF PLAINTIFF FINANCIAL EXPERTS

Reported in Exhibits 47.5, 47.6, and 47.7 is an analysis of challenges and exclusions by the party engaging the financial expert. Our analysis of the data shows:

- Of the 165 financial expert challenges identified, 119 (or 72.1 percent) were engaged by the plaintiff. (See Exhibit 47.5.) Thus, it is more likely that a financial expert will be challenged when engaged by the plaintiff than the defendant.

---

[19] The rate at which nonfinancial experts have been excluded, once challenged, increased slightly in 2001 and then declined in 2002. However, the rate at which nonfinancial experts have been excluded did not decline to the same extent in 2002 as compared to the figures for financial experts.

[20] Analysis of future exclusions will provide insights as to whether the exclusion rate has reached its steady state or equilibrium level. While not part of this study, the case filings mix could also impact the exclusion rate of financial experts over time.

[21] In whole or in part.

[22] Based on a reading of the published opinions reviewed, reasons for the exclusion of financial experts were categorized as relating to relevance issues, reliability issues, and/or qualification issues. A particular expert may have been excluded for more than one reason.

Type of Expert	Number of Challenges*	Partial Exclusions	Complete Exclusions	Total Number of Exclusions	Exclusions as a Percent of Challenges
2000					
Financial experts	55	7	23	30	54.5%
Nonfinancial experts**	195	26	64	90	46.2%
Subtotal	**250**	**33**	**87**	**120**	**48.0%**
2001					
Financial experts	44	5	13	18	40.9%
Nonfinancial experts**	245	28	91	119	48.6%
Subtotal	**289**	**33**	**104**	**137**	**47.4%**
2002					
Financial experts	66	7	13	20	30.3%
Nonfinancial experts**	290	24	103	127	43.8%
Subtotal	**356**	**31**	**116**	**147**	**41.3%**

Note:
*Multiple experts could be challenged in the same case.
**Nonfinancial experts include medical doctors, engineers, forensic scientists, psychologists, and psychiatrists, among others.

Exhibit 47.4   Expert Witness Challenges (Cases Citing *Kumho Tire Co. vs. Carmichael*) Annual; 2000–2002.

	Number of Challenges	Plaintiff's Financial Expert	Percent Plaintiff	Defendant's Financial Expert	Percent Defendant
Partially excluded	19	17	89.5%	2	10.5%
Completely excluded	49	40	81.6%	9	18.4%
Not excluded	97	62	63.9%	35	36.1%
Total	**165**	**119**	**72.1%**	**46**	**27.9%**

Exhibit 47.5 Plaintiff and Defendant Financial Expert Challenges; January 2000–December 2002.

	Number of Challenges	Plaintiff's Financial Expert	Percent Plaintiff	Defendant's Financial Expert	Percent Defendant
2000	55	42	76.4%	13	23.6%
2001	44	30	68.2%	14	31.8%
2002	66	47	71.2%	19	28.8%
Total	**165**	**119**	**72.1%**	**46**	**27.9%**

Exhibit 47.6 Plaintiff and Defendant Financial Expert Challenges Annual; 2000–2002.

- The number of challenges of plaintiff financial experts relative to defense financial experts has remained consistent in each year. (See Exhibit 47.6.) At least two out of every three challenges to financial experts are plaintiff side in each year.
- Once challenged, plaintiff financial experts are more likely to be excluded in whole or in part than defense financial experts. (See Exhibit 47.7.) Although 72.1 percent of the challenges are plaintiff side, 83.8 percent of the exclusions or partial exclusions are plaintiff side. In contrast, while 27.9 percent of the challenges are defense side, only 16.2 percent of the exclusions in whole or in part are defense side.

Notably, while the rate at which financial experts are excluded is declining (as previously discussed), such observations are not quite descriptive of the rate at which plaintiff financial experts are excluded (once challenged) relative to defendant financial experts.

The data reported in Exhibit 47.6 suggests plaintiff financial experts are consistently challenged at a rate two to three times that of defendant financial experts. Annually, over the 2000–2002 time period, 68.2 percent to 76.4 percent of the challenges to financial experts were to the plaintiff's financial expert. The data reported in Exhibit 47.7 suggests plaintiff financial experts are consistently excluded at a rate four to nine times that of defendant financial experts. Annually, over the 2000–2002 time period, 79.3 percent to 90.0 percent of the exclusions of financial experts were to the plaintiff's financial expert.

Exhibits 47.6 and 47.7 combined demonstrate that plaintiff and defendant financial experts have experienced declines in the proportion of exclusions, once challenged. However, the percentage of plaintiff financial experts excluded in whole or in part has not declined to the same extent as defense financial expert exclusions. In 2000, 24 exclusions occurred relating to the 42 plaintiff financial expert challenges (57.1 percent). In 2002, 18 exclusions occurred relating to the 47 plaintiff financial expert challenges (38.3 percent). In comparison, in 2000, 6 of 13 challenged defendant financial experts were excluded (46.2 percent). This figure was reduced to 2 of 19 challenged defendant financial experts being excluded in 2002 (10.5 percent).

47.6 TYPES OF FINANCIAL EXPERTS EXCLUDED

Next we looked at the composition of financial expert challenges and exclusions in the context of the particular financial expertise involved. While the pool of financial experts identified in cases is diverse,[23] we have separately analyzed the challenges and exclusions of economists, statisticians, and accountants/CPAs. This data is reported in Exhibit 47.8. Note that because our analysis is focused only on those cases in which a challenge was made in federal and state cases referring to *Kumho Tire,* it is not possible to calibrate the rate of a particular expert exclusion to the many other cases in which a financial expert is not challenged and provides testimony. However, we have found:

- Among financial experts, accountants/CPAs appear to be among the least frequently challenged financial experts.
- Among financial experts, accountants/CPAs appear to have the lowest proportion of exclusions. Out of 68 financial expert exclusions in whole or in part, only three CPAs have been excluded. In contrast, each of the other categories of financial experts—economists, statisticians, and other financial experts—has a higher percentage of exclusions when challenged than accountants/CPAs.

However, as previously discussed, care must be exercised when interpreting these figures. The empirical data presented does not support the proposition that when two functionally different but

---

[23] Financial experts in this context refer to economists, statisticians, accountants/CPAs, appraisers, finance professors, and so on.

	Number of Challenges	Plaintiff's Financial Expert	Percent Plaintiff	Defendant's Financial Expert	Percent Defendant
2000	30	24	79.3%	6	20.7%
2001	18	15	83.3%	3	16.7%
2002	20	18	90.0%	2	10.0%
Total	**68**	**57**	**83.8%**	**11**	**16.2%**

*Includes partial and complete exclusions.

Exhibit 47.7   Plaintiff and Defendant Financial Expert Exclusions* Annual; 2000–2002.

Type of Expert	Number of Challenges	Completely/Partially Excluded	% Being Completely/Partially Excluded
Accountant/CPA	18	3	16.7%
Economist	41	21	51.2%
Statistician	17	8	47.1%
Other financial	89	36	40.4%
Total	**165**	**68**	**41.2%**

*Includes partial and complete exclusions.

Exhibit 47.8   Financial Expert Challenges and Exclusions* by Expert Type; January 2000–December 2002.

equally qualified experts are being considered for retention, and the nature of the assignment is such that the talents of either type of expert are appropriate, the CPA will have a lower probability of being challenged or excluded.

To the contrary, the figures reported above are likely the product of (a) the nature of the engagements traditionally assigned to different types of financial experts, (b) the data that may be available to properly conduct the required analysis in the engagements traditionally assigned to different types of financial experts, and (c) the degree to which the required testimony deviates from the interpretation of historical data toward projecting business performance under an alternative set of conditions. Hence, we believe it is frequently the nature of the cases and the required analyses that explain the different exclusion rates of CPAs and economists rather than alternative explanations.

47.7 JUNE 30, 2003 UPDATE: THE MOST RECENT OBSERVATIONS

The trends identified over the three-year survey period largely continued in the six-month period ended June 30, 2003, with some important exceptions. Reported below are notable results in the first six months of 2003.

- Financial expert testimony was wholly or partially excluded in 24 situations (or 55.8 percent of the financial expert challenges). The exclusion rate in the first six months of 2003 was greater than the exclusion rate for the year 2002.

- For these financial expert exclusions, there are a higher number of partial exclusions (17 cases) than complete exclusions (7 cases). This is a reversal of prior trends.

- The reliability of the financial expert's opinion (based on the underlying facts and data considered and the methodology used to formulate an opinion) was again the predominant reason for exclusion. Deficiencies relating to the reliability of the proposed testimony were cited in nearly 80 percent of the 24 exclusions. The qualifications of the financial expert were cited in only one exclusion.

- Of 43 total challenges, 30 (or 69.8 percent) were directed to plaintiff financial experts. Of these 30 challenges, plaintiff financial experts were excluded 63.3 percent of the time. This is in contrast to defense financial experts, who were excluded in 38.5 percent of the challenges reviewed.

- Accountants/CPAs did not fare as well in the first six months of 2003. Whereas only 4 of the 43 financial expert challenges related to accountants or CPAs, all 4 of such experts were wholly or partially excluded, more than the total number of exclusions for this type of expert in all of the prior three years surveyed.[24]

---

[24] The reasons for these four exclusions are as follows. *In re: EZ Dock, Inc. v. Schafer Sys* (2003 U.S. Dist. Lexis 3634), the circuit court judge determined that "In his expert report, therefore, [the CPA] has not himself formed an opinion as to the existence of a 'two supplier' market; he has simply adopted Wortley's opinion regarding the nature of the market . . . . His proposed opinions regarding the existence of a demand for the patented product and the absence of non-infringing alternative products is 'not based upon sufficient facts or data' as required by Rule 702." *In re: Valentino v. Proviso Twp.* (2003 U.S. Dist. Lexis 11574), the circuit judge found that "[The CPA] stated he thought this analysis was widespread knowledge; however, neither [plaintiff's] response to the motion nor [the CPA's] subsequent affidavit makes mention of anything to support his assertion that his borrowing history analysis is widespread knowledge or a reliable method to determine the borrowing ability of a Township." *In re: Space Maker Designs, Inc. v. Weldon F. Stump and Company, Inc.* (2003 U.S. Dist. Lexis 3941), the district judge found that "Expert reports should be 'detailed and complete' so as 'to avoid the disclosure of 'sketchy and vague' expert information." Sierra Club at 571 . . . . Under the terms of the Agreed Amended Scheduling Order, Defendants were required to file a complete statement of all opinions to be expressed and the basis and reasons therefore. [The CPA's] expert report falls short of that standard." As to the CPA's

47.8 SUMMARY AND CONCLUSIONS

In summary, certain observations and trends stand out in the analysis of federal and state cases over the past three years where the admissibility of the financial expert witness's opinions has been challenged:

- The number of challenges to experts of all types is increasing.
- Once challenged, the rate at which financial experts are excluded in whole or in part decreased over the 2000–2002 time period.
- Plaintiff financial experts are challenged and excluded more frequently than defense financial experts.
- The rate of challenges to accountants/CPAs as testifying experts appears to be lower than that for other types of financial experts. The success rate of excluding accountants/CPAs is lower as well.[25]

47.9 FINAL COMMENTS RELEVANT TO THE CERTIFIED PUBLIC ACCOUNTANT DESIGNATION

As discussed, we believe it is the nature of the cases and the required analyses that explain the different exclusion rates of CPAs and other financial experts rather than alternative explanations. However, it is worth mentioning, admittedly with a mix of both fact and intuition, that because the CPA designation is well established and well known, it may be qualifying in *certain types* of litigation roles and cases. While the designation is not a sine qua non for the admissibility of testimony, the accreditation of a CPA—which embodies completion of defined education, examination, experience, and annual continuing education requirements—is an established basis for qualification of the financial expert in a suitable litigation context.[26]

CPAs are often chosen for certain defined types of roles in a litigation context that are customarily and commonly within the province of CPAs. For example, the historical cost focus of accountants/CPAs is conducive to the evaluation of historical accounting data in a litigation context. This may be a factor explaining the lower rate of challenges and exclusions of CPAs relative to non-CPAs who conduct analyses outside of traditional historical accounting analyses.

Finally, CPAs may benefit from the professional standards to which they must adhere when faced with a *Daubert* challenge. Since the *Daubert* criteria include peer review and general acceptance of a methodology, the CPA can turn to the codified professional standards of the American Institute of Certified Public Accountants (AICPA) and other standard-setting organizations, among other information, as a basis on which professional opinions may be drawn. Such accounting standards

---

licenses, the court found that "None of those licenses make him qualified to opine on economic trends and their likely effect on profits." *In re: JRL Enterprises, Inc. v. Procorp Associates, Inc.* (2003 U.S. Dist. Lexis 9397) the district court found that the expert's calculations were based solely on projections found in the agreement. The district court noted that the expert performed no market analysis to verify the reasonableness or accuracy of the projections in the DA Agreement. 1998 U.S. Dist. LEXIS 15414 at *1. The court found that this failure established that the expert's calculations could not be evaluated for accuracy. Furthermore, the court found that the expert had failed to establish that the expert's numbers had any basis in reality. The court found that "the expert had failed to offer any evidence of general acceptance, or known rate of error for his methods; finally, the court said that the plaintiff had shown no evidence that the expert's calculations were anything more than an exercise in arithmetic based on inherently unreliable values. 1998 U.S. Dist. LEXIS 15414 at *4." [Bracketed terms have been added for clarity.] Footnote citations have been removed.

[25] Subject to the caveats discussed in this article.

[26] This is not true in all types of litigation contexts. For example, a CPA designation would not provide a shield to a *Daubert* challenge if a CPA was attempting to opine on relevant market issues in an antitrust case.

have heretofore been the result of an established process that largely includes focused research, public input, exposure of issues and standards for open comment, and expert deliberative decision making by members of panels and boards.

In a litigation context, the CPA is able to rely not only on generally accepted accounting principles (GAAP), but also on the standards defined by the AICPA related to audit, consulting (including litigation or business valuation services) or attestation engagements to perform the analysis needed to support opinions relating to liability or economic damages. In contrast, other types of financial experts, though highly skilled and trained, do not have a set of technical standards as codified as those of CPAs. Of course, as a cautionary note, the protections these standards provide the CPA are only applicable to CPAs who are retained on matters where these standards play a role or are relevant to the nature of the inquiry being made. To the extent statistical, economic, or econometric analyses are required, the standards on which a CPA often relies may not be as directly relevant.

CHAPTER **48**

INTRODUCTION TO E-DISCOVERY

Jack Moorman

PricewaterhouseCoopers LLP

Greg Schaffer

PricewaterhouseCoopers LLP

48.1 COMPUTERS? NOW THAT CHANGES EVERYTHING!

At the beginning of the information age, computers were not likely targets for the interests of lawyers or courtrooms. Indeed, their use was so cumbersome that only the most complex mathematical problems were addressed via these room-sized, punch-card-reading behemoths. These machines "crunched numbers" and were not particularly useful for anything else. Needless to say, the integration of computers into society has come a very long way. While visionaries and science fiction writers continue to imagine a world in which computers are even more intertwined with the day-to-day lives of human beings, it is evident that the business world is already utterly dependent on computers today.

Whether you support this reality (carrying cell phone, personal digital assistant, and wireless network card clipped to your belt or tucked in your purse) or eschew it (clinging to the dictation and shorthand world only recently abandoned by the rest of us), one thing is clear: There is no turning back. Although the predictions of a paperless world have never quite come to pass, the computer has changed the way society conducts its business in fundamental ways. These changes make it nearly impossible to run the world without the assistance of silicon chips, keyboards, and hard drives (or the next generation of computing technology that is likely to replace these devices with something that is faster, better, and cheaper).

48.2 SHIFT TO DIGITAL DATA STORAGE AND COMMUNICATION

With the advent of computers, one of the key changes has been the shift to digital storage of virtually everything we create. One hundred years ago the intellectual property of our societies was primarily stored on a single medium: paper. Moreover, it was stored in the most analog of analog forms: handwriting. Handwriting is distinct and variable from person to person. The ability to read and correctly understand every word in a letter, for instance, especially one that had traveled for weeks from one location to another, was questionable at best.

Today we can store and reliably reproduce virtually any form of intellectual property, from music to photographs to manuscripts to handwritten notes, in a digital format that can be reliably and perfectly reproduced at virtually any location on the globe almost instantly. Ben Franklin, a forward thinker in his time, could not have imagined the possibility, but today's four-year-olds, armed with broadband access to the Internet and a parent on business travel, cannot imagine a world without such wonders.

And because we can perform these acts, once considered miracles or magic, with such ease, we do take advantage of the technologies that are available to us, eagerly and often. For example, recent statistics show that over 11 trillion e-mails were sent in 2003.[1] Studies have shown that as much as 93 percent of a modern society's intellectual output is stored digitally.

48.3 INCREASING DATA VOLUMES

It is not just the storage and distribution of data that have changed; it is also our access to it. Imagine what would have been necessary years ago if you wanted to maintain ready access to the amount of data stored on an average desktop computer on sale at any office supply store in United States today (say with a 40-gigabyte hard drive). First, you would have needed a warehouse. Forty gigabytes of data is roughly equivalent to 6 million printed pages.[2] Your basic small-town library probably does not store as much information in analog form. Second, like that library, you would need a staff of employees to index, catalog, and maintain the data over time. Now imagine the data stored on a small business's network of 40 PCs and three servers. Your small-town library

---

[1] *www.spamfilter.com*, 31 billion e-mails per day times 365 days.
[2] Based on Microsoft Word document format.

is now more like the entire library system of a major metropolitan city. And now consider the data stored on a Fortune 100 company's network with literally tens of thousands of desktop and laptop computers and thousands of servers, many with huge storage arrays of disk drives. The U.S. Library of Congress, with its analog collection of more than 120 million items on approximately 530 miles of bookshelves, would never fill this much storage space.[3]

The simple truth is that, as a society, we are pack rats, retaining as much as we can within the limits of our storage capacity. As that capacity has increased through the availability of ever cheaper digital storage technologies, our tendency not to throw things away has taken over. The bottom line is that we could not manage the data we have stored today without the benefit of the digital technologies we have developed for that storage.

48.4 INCREASED VALUE OF DIGITAL DATA

It should not be surprising to learn that the value of our digital data is enormous. In our increasingly service-oriented economy, our ideas are often more valuable than the things they are designed to enable. Imagine the mining company that develops new methodologies for extracting ore from stone, but owns very little ore-bearing land. The methodology, stored as zeros and ones on a hard drive thousands of miles away from any precious gems, may be worth far more than the inventing company's mining results. And this scenario is repeated time and again in American businesses in every sector of the economy.

48.5 GOING AFTER EVIDENCE

With so much valuable information stored on computer systems, and so much of our vital communications passing through computer networks, it is no surprise that our massive communication and storage networks are the target of attorneys looking for proof to support their positions when businesses find themselves in complex commercial disputes. Lawyers increasingly engage in electronic discovery for a simple, straightforward reason: because that is where the data is. And it is not just more of the same data once available to counsel in analog form. Electronically stored information has some special properties that in many ways make it a better source of proof. An understanding of the tools and techniques of computer forensics practitioners can provide an attorney with a wealth of information to review that would otherwise be unavailable. And in a litigation setting, more information is generally a good thing (especially if the information is about the other side).

48.6 THE LEGAL SETTING

The Federal Rules of Civil Procedure make it clear that this wealth of information is generally discoverable, but provide certain limitations. For instance, Rule 26 of the Federal Rules of Civil Procedure specifies that "any matter, not privileged, that is relevant to the claim or defense of any party" is discoverable.[4] Rule 34 provides a mechanism, "the discovery request," that permits service by one party on another of a request for documents:

> Any party may serve on any other party a request (1) to produce and permit the party making the request, or someone acting on the requestor's behalf, to inspect and copy, any designated documents.[5]

---

[3] Of course, today the Library of Congress also stores a sizable amount of digital data on its own very extensive computer network.
[4] Fed. R. Civ. P. 26(b)(1).
[5] Fed. R. Civ. P. 34.

The definition of what constituted a document was extended to include electronic documents in the 1970 amendments to Rule 34 of the Federal Rules.[6] Indeed; the federal courts have been in agreement for years that electronic data is discoverable. For instance, in 1995 the Federal District Court for the Southern District of New York wrote: "it is black letter law that computerized data is discoverable if relevant";[7] as early as 1985 the Federal District Court for the Central District of Utah had declared that "information in computers should be [as] freely discoverable as information not stored in computers";[8] and the Federal District Court for the Southern District of Indiana reiterated this point in 2000: "[C]omputer records . . . are documents discoverable under Fed. R. Civ. P. 34."[9] Although discoverable, electronic documents face the same limitations under the Federal Rules as do paper documents. Rule 26(b)(2) limits discovery where:

> (i) the discovery sought is unreasonably cumulative or duplicative, or is obtainable from some other source that is more convenient, less burdensome, or less expensive; (ii) the party seeking discovery has had ample opportunity by discovery in the action to obtain the information sought; or (iii) the burden or expense of the proposed discovery outweighs its likely benefit, taking into account the needs of the case, the amount in controversy, the parties' resources, the importance of the issues at stake in the litigation, and the importance of the proposed discovery in resolving the issues.

As the three sections of Federal Rules of Civil Procedure (FRCP) 26(b)(2) clearly indicate, there are a host of factors that come into play when making and responding to a discovery request. Suffice it to say that the common law duty to preserve evidence that may be relevant to pending or threatened litigation provides fertile ground for the requesting side to seek to preserve and discover evidence through preservation orders, motions to compel, motions for sanctions, and so on. This places a burden on the responding side, but respondents can attack the request on several fronts, such as relevancy, unreasonably cumulative or duplicative, overly broad, and unduly burdensome. Oftentimes, this leads to legal haggling that can take weeks, months, or years to play out. However, the courts are becoming increasingly sophisticated in dealing with electronic discovery requests and disputes. As a practical matter, there is broad consensus that "the preservation and production of electronic data and documents" should be discussed by the parties, and agreements reached to the extent possible, during their conference under Rule 26(f), if not sooner.[10]

One of the key issues being addressed in recent cases involving digital evidence regards the question of cost shifting; which party should bear the expenses associated with various aspects of the electronic discovery process? As United States District Judge Shira A. Scheindlin recently wrote in *Zubulake v. UBS Warburg LLC*, 2003 U.S. Dist. LEXIS 12643 (S.D.N.Y. July 24, 2003), the "presumption is that the responding party must bear the expense of complying with discovery requests," and requests that run afoul of the Rule 26(b)(2) proportionality test may subject the requesting party to protective orders under Rule 26(c), "including orders conditioning discovery on the requesting party's payment of the costs of discovery." A court will order such a cost-shifting protective order only on a motion of the responding party to a discovery request, and for good cause shown.[11] In *Zubulake*, Judge Scheindlin distinguished accessible electronic data from

---

[6] The Advisory Committee Notes for the 1970 amendments to the Federal Rules of Civil Procedure reflect the inclusive nature of the term *document*: The inclusive description of "documents" is revised according with changing technology. It makes clear that Rule 34 applies to electronic data compilations from which information can be obtained only from detection devices, and that when data can, as a practical matter, be made usable by the discovering party only through the respondent's devices, respondent may be required to use his devices to translate the data into usable form.

[7] *Anti-Monopoly, Inc. v. Hasbro, Inc.*, 94 CIV 2120, 1995 WL 649934, at *2 (S.D.N.Y. Nov. 3, 1995).

[8] *Bills v. Connect Corp.*, 108 F.R.D 459 (C.D. Utah 1985).

[9] *Cf. Simon Property Group L. P. v. my Simon,* 194 F.R.D. 639, 640 (S.D. Ind. 2000).

[10] *Observations on "The Sedona Principles,"* John L. Carroll and Kenneth J. Withers, *www. thesedonaconference.org/miscfiles/carroll/download.*

[11] *Zubulake v. UBS Warburg LLC,* 2003 U.S. Dist. LEXIS 12643 (S.D.N.Y. July 24, 2003), also quoting *Oppenheimer Fund, Inc. v. Sanders*, 437 U.S. 340, 358 (1978).

inaccessible data and held that cost shifting is "potentially appropriate only when *inaccessible* data is sought."[12] *Zubulake* sets forth a new seven-factor test to determine if costs should be shifted to the requesting party when inaccessible data is sought in discovery. In doing so, Judge Scheindlin reversed the trend (as she saw it[13]) of cost shifting to favor the responding party as articulated in *Rowe Entertainment, Inc. v. William Morris Agency, Inc.*[14] The cornerstone of the seven-factor test in *Zubulake* is the marginal utility test announced in *McPeek v. Ashcroft*:

> The more likely it is that the backup tape contains information that is relevant to a claim or defense, the fairer it is that the [responding party] search at its own expense. The less likely it is, the more unjust it would be to make the [responding party] search at its own expense. The difference is "at the margin."[15]

Employment of the seven-factor test will likely reduce the frequency of "fishing expedition" electronic discovery requests since the costs of such endeavors are more likely to be shifted to the requesting party. However, before the court can apply the test, it must have a factual basis on which to opine. In determining that basis, the court may consider, as in *Zubulake*, sampling a subset of the available universe of electronic data or other measures intended to determine the probative value of the requested materials and the likely costs of comprehensive retrieval, review, and production.[16]

Zubulake further points out that inaccessible data (i.e., backup tapes) can be quite expensive to restore, but once restored should be considered as readily accessible as any other data. Consequently, *Zubulake* also establishes a new rule:

> The responding party should always bear the cost of reviewing and producing electronic data once it has been converted to an accessible form.[17]

Thus, under *Zubulake*, cost shifting is generally not appropriate where the responding party has ready access to information in databases, e-mail systems, or other on-line electronic storage mechanisms. And post-*Zubulake*, accessible data presumably includes e-mails and other files restored from less accessible media such as backup tape, even when such restoration was conducted for purposes of e-discovery in another litigation matter. Since Judge Scheindlin is considered knowledgeable in the area, and is from the influential Southern District of New York, *Zubulake* is likely to influence other courts.[18] This will also have a significant impact on the electronic discovery marketplace, making the subject of this chapter all the more topical. Since there is no end in sight to the need for electronic discovery services, there will likely be a continued push for better, faster, and cheaper[19] electronic discovery tools and a need for best practices standards.

---

[12] See *Zubulake I*, 2003 WL 21087884, at *12 ("A court should consider cost-shifting only when electronic data is relatively inaccessible, such as in back-up tapes.").

[13] See *Zubulake I*, 2003 WL 21087884, at *7 ("Courts must remember that cost-shifting may effectively end discovery, especially when private parties are engaged in litigation with large corporations. As large companies increasingly move to entirely paper-free environments, the frequent use of cost-shifting will have the effect of crippling discovery in discrimination and retaliation cases. This will both undermine the 'strong public policy favoring resolving disputes on their merits,' and may ultimately deter the filing of potentially meritorious claims.").

[14] 205 F.R.D. 421, 429 (S.D.N.Y.), aff'd 2002 WL 975713 (S.D.N.Y. May 9, 2002).

[15] 202 F.R.D. 31, 34 (D.D.C. 2001).

[16] See *Zubulake I*, Id. at *13.

[17] *Zubulake v. UBS Warburg LLC*, 2003 U.S. Dist. LEXIS 12643 (S.D.N.Y. July 24, 2003), at 26.

[18] Indeed, a recent Federal District Court opinion from the Northern District of California, (*Open TV vs. Liberate Technologies*, C 02 0655 JSW (MEJ), decided November 18, 2003) adopted and applied the *Zubulake* seven-factor test to determine if cost shifting should be applied to a request for production of computer source code stored in electronic form.

[19] See Section 48.10.

48.7 TODAY'S USE OF ELECTRONIC DISCOVERY TECHNIQUES

Today the use of electronic discovery techniques is still generally limited to certain classes of cases, typically those that do not suffer from what is sometimes referred to as the *reciprocity is hell* problem. The fact is that a lack of understanding of the costs and benefits of modern forensic processes has led many lawyers to believe that making an electronic discovery request is like launching a thermonuclear attack against your opponent. In other words, they believe their opponent will respond in kind, leading to mutually assured destruction through huge processing costs. This has meant that most electronic discovery requests today are being made by government prosecutors, regulatory agencies, and class action plaintiff's counsel. These are parties that generally do not have significant relevant electronically stored data that can be requested by their opponents. It also means that the requests are usually quite broad, since these litigants are not concerned about in-kind responses. In the end, this has perpetuated the perception that electronic discovery is expensive and dangerous in the typical company versus company litigation.

The truth is that electronic discovery has come a long way. As the case law makes clear, and as this chapter will highlight, there are significant amounts of information to be gained through electronic discovery that are not available anywhere else. Moreover, the processes and procedures employed by computer forensic practitioners today can dramatically reduce the overall cost of the discovery process, especially in large cases. Finally, as many attorneys who have dipped their toes into the electronic discovery waters have learned, "there's gold in them there pools."

48.8 MORE/BETTER SUBSTANTIVE INFORMATION (METADATA)

Metadata is one of the prime examples of the benefits of working with electronic evidence. Imagine two litigators working the same case, one based only on paper evidence, one working with the original electronic files that were the source of the paper documents found in the company's files. There can be little question which lawyer will have the better set of data to work with.

When computers store information for later retrieval, the operating systems necessarily create certain data about the stored information in order to facilitate ongoing processing. Such information typically includes the name of the file being stored (e.g., alternateAR.xls), the date the file was created and last modified, and the size of the file.

Many programs automatically add other metadata to the file, such as the type of file being stored, the location the file was stored to, the name of the author, the name of the person who last saved the file, and the number of revisions the file has gone through. Some programs also allow users to add their own metadata to a file, such as a document title, the subject of the file, the name of the author of the document, the name of the manager responsible for the document, and the name of the company that owns the document.

Some programs permit a user to assign metadata to a document in order to facilitate later retrieval. This type of metadata can include assignment of the document to a particular category (i.e., "supplier contract" or "workflow protocol"), inclusion of searchable key words, or a description of the document's contents.

In addition to these explicit types of metadata, there are other variations that are less obvious. For example, spreadsheets and databases can contain complex mathematical formulas and links among fields that are responsible for calculation of the numbers that appear in various cells. Typically the printed spreadsheet will show only the result of the calculation, not the formula that was used to calculate the result. Similarly, modern word processing documents can contain links and references to various types of other electronic files, such as pictures, charts, spreadsheets, and sound files. These linked files may be stored in the same location as the main document or halfway around the world on another computer linked by a proprietary network or the Internet. The printed document may show the content of the other files without revealing that the content is not part of the printed document at all, but rather just linked data. The electronic document will necessarily contain the code needed to connect to the data in the linked files and may give an investigator pointers to additional sources of relevant information. This in turn may lead to additional witnesses, such as the author of the linked document in the remote—and heretofore undisclosed—location.

The key thing about all of this metadata, or data about the files, is that none of it typically appears on the page when the files are printed to paper or converted to an image format such as a TIFF or PDF file.[20] There can be no question that access to this additional information will be useful to anyone investigating alleged misconduct.

48.9 AUDIT TRAILS (TRAFFIC DATA)

In addition to the metadata created at the file level, many computer systems generate significant amounts of traffic data when information is manipulated within a computer or across a computer network. This traffic data, often referred to as *audit trails,* can be particularly useful when trying to tie activity back to a particular user or set of users. Imagine finding a smoking gun document describing a planned fraud sitting out on a network file server accessible to 50 employees in a particular department. An analysis of the metadata associated with the file may give clues as to its authorship, but network traffic data (if it is being stored) may indicate which user account was responsible for storing the document to that location.

There are many types of traffic data that may be available to an investigator. For example, most general ledger systems can be configured to record the user name associated with the last change to any value in the system. Some systems allow users to record the user names responsible for every change to a value over time. Similarly, many e-mail systems retain information about the dates and times associated with transmissions of each e-mail and attachment. Some of these systems also record the date and time of message deletions. Operating systems may maintain dates associated with accessing, moving, or deleting files. All of this information can be extremely useful during the course of an investigation into a legal dispute.

It is important to note, however, that traffic data can only take an investigation so far. It is sometimes said that the last inch in a cyber investigation[21] is the hardest. What we mean by this is that electronic audit trails may indeed lead an investigator back to a particular computer as having been responsible for a given set of activity (e.g., a particular change to a general ledger system). But this does not tell you who was sitting at the keyboard of that computer at the moment the change was made. Proving who was there—making the one-inch jump from keyboard to fingers—is often the hardest part of a cyber investigation and will often require the application of traditional gumshoe and forensic accounting techniques.

48.10 FASTER/BETTER/CHEAPER

Even without the metadata and traffic data, electronic files have one huge advantage over paper documents when conducting discovery. Simply put, a computer can search, sort, and manipulate an electronic document in a fraction of the time necessary for a human to perform the same tasks. In a case involving hundreds of thousands or millions of pages of printed materials, human review and searching for specific information can be tedious and imprecise work. But computer searches across the same volume of electronic files can reliably discover every instance of a particular word or combination of words in short order. Similarly, a computer can instantly sort a large volume of information by date, file name, author, storage location, or any number of other criteria, thereby lifting the cream to the top of an investigator's stack of documents for review.

---

[20] The tagged image file format (TIFF) is a widely used format for storing image data. The Portable Document Format (PDF) was developed by Adobe Corporation to allow efficient electronic distribution of large documents.

[21] A computer-enhanced investigation.

48.11 THE ROLE OF COMPUTER FORENSICS

Computer forensics refers to the process of preserving and analyzing electronically stored information for presentation in a legal proceeding. Over the past 10 years computer forensics has evolved from an arcane hobby of an eclectic group of law enforcement officers to a growing litigation support industry. Where it was once necessary for practitioners to cobble together collections of various disk utilities and shareware programs to perform specific computer forensic tasks, there are now relatively mature software suites that integrate and automate some of the most common computer forensic operations. But in the end forensics is not just about the tools. It is about process, documentation, and the ability to demonstrate that a given result is accurate, reliable, and repeatable.

48.12 EVIDENCE PRESERVATION

One of the key goals of the computer forensic process is the preservation of evidence. Computer data has certain unique and paradoxical properties. It is simultaneously very hard to fully destroy and very easy to manipulate. Once again a comparison to paper is illuminating. Imagine the existence of two sets of very incriminating documents. One set consists of a notepad containing handwritten notes on paper and the other is a collection of documents stored on a floppy disk. Which set is most easily destroyed? Which is most easily modified?

There can be no question that destruction of the paper documents will be easier. Place the pad in a barbecue, apply lighter fluid, apply match. It is as simple as that. As long as the notes had not been copied, destruction is complete. Do the same to the floppy disk and you still have many questions to consider. What computer(s) was used to create and store the files before they were placed on the disk? Were those computers' hard drives backed up to some other storage media? Were the files ever printed or copied to other locations (on a network or through an e-mail attachment)? Have those printed or forwarded materials also been located and destroyed?

The question of modification is also fairly easy to answer. Attempting to reliably alter a handwritten document in a manner that will escape all detection is relatively difficult. Handwriting analysis and forensic analysis of inks and paper are all mature technologies well understood by science and the courts. But electronic files consist of zeros and ones, long lists of binary markings stored on some type of electrical, optical, magnetic, or other media. Bits are bits. Changes are often hard to detect unless you have taken some steps to lock down the data and verify that it has not been changed.

The forensic process is designed to do precisely that; it takes preexisting data and preserves it in a reliable fashion so that litigants and courts can confidently make use of it at a later time.

48.13 PHYSICAL IMAGING VERSUS LOGICAL BACKUPS

Once the goal of the computer forensic process is understood, the advantages of physical imaging of electronic storage media over the logical backing up of data become clear. *Physical imaging* is the term used to describe the process of making a full bit-for-bit copy of all of the data on a given piece of storage media. It is the equivalent of copying every page in a legal pad, including pages that have no writing, pages that are only partially full, pages from the back end of a note for which the front end was ripped out for copying, and pages that have been slashed through (marked for deletion). This is distinguished from a *logical backup,* in which only the pages containing the full text of the documents being actively used by the owner of the pad would be copied and everything else would be ignored.

This simple explanation makes plain why a litigator should prefer to have access to a physical image. The simple fact is that the files the user has chosen to retain are not the only potential pieces of evidence on the legal pad, and the same is true on a hard drive. Because of the way modern computer operating systems work, hard drives and other storage media often contain significant amounts of data in addition to the active files being retained by the user. The drive is likely to contain full versions of files the user has chosen to delete. It is also likely to contain bits and pieces of deleted files captured within the slack space of existing active files.

Most computer users today have heard of the concept of slack space but do not have a detailed understanding of how data from deleted files comes to be stored in "slack." This process is fairly straightforward. Imagine again that your legal pad is a computer hard drive. Imagine that you have a rule that only one active note can be placed on each page. Imagine also that you are an efficient user of legal pads and do not like to waste storage space, so you reuse pages by "deleting" old notes with a slash mark and writing new notes on pages containing deleted notes to the extent there is room to do so. This is almost exactly what a computer does when storing and "deleting" files. Slack space is simply the space in a cluster (a cluster being a legal pad page in our analogy) that is not being used by the active file (note) that is stored on that cluster. Any data previously stored on that cluster beyond the end of file marker[22] for the active file is data "stored in slack." The computer, being efficient, does not overwrite this data but simply ignores it. A forensic expert does just the opposite.

But a logical backup of the hard drive or other storage media does not contain any of the data beyond the logical size of each active file, and therefore analysis of file slack, unallocated disk areas (containing erased but recoverable data), or deleted directory entries is impossible based on a logical backup. Conversely, a physical image of a drive preserves all of this data in slack and allows an investigator to view material that may have been "deleted" months or years before the examination is conducted. Moreover, there is little incremental cost involved in preparing a physical image. Today software and hardware tools exist that allow for very efficient and cost-effective imaging. Whereas imaging an average sized hard drive in 2000 typically took four to six hours of computer time, the much larger drives used today (2004) can often be imaged in two to three hours or less. It is likely that the time necessary to image drives will continue to shrink as new and better imaging tools become available.

This is not to suggest that a physical image must be made in every case. The volume of data that can be stored on modern hard drives can present an analysis challenge. Searches across hundreds of gigabytes of data (or terabytes in some cases) can take days and result in millions of search hits unless the search criteria used are carefully tailored to focus in on very specific categories of information. In such cases analysis of only the logical user-created files and deleted but fully recoverable materials (exclusive of slack space, unallocated space, and system files) may be more appropriate. In other cases the likelihood of discovering material from slack and unallocated space may be remote (e.g., when the data on a device was recently restored from a logical backup). In such cases the incremental cost of making and examining a physical image may not be justified.

48.14 FORENSIC RECORD KEEPING

It is not good enough to simply create physical images of the relevant data. It is also necessary to adequately document (to the greatest extent possible) what data was imaged, from which machines, at what point in time, and by what methodology. Without such documentation there is the potential for an opposing party in a legal dispute to launch a collateral attack against the results of any analysis of the data by challenging the authenticity of the evidence. This is particularly important to keep in mind during the early stages of an investigation when companies are often inclined to ask their IT staff to "take a quick look" at computers expected to contain relevant information. Unless the IT staff is trained in forensic procedures, and have access to the necessary forensic hardware and software tools, a "quick look" can result in significant damage to otherwise useful evidence. Stated differently, the reliability of the evidence collected could be called into question.

---

[22] Or beyond the logical size of the active file in file types that do not use end of file markers.

48.15 ACQUISITION NOTES

During the process of acquiring data for forensic analysis (whether via physical imaging of media, creation of logical backups, or the simple collection of backup tapes from system administrators) examiners will typically record information about the acquisition process. This information should generally include details about the computer the data was collected from, such as the make, model, and serial number of the PC, laptop, server, or other device. It should also include information about the media itself, such as the type, size, and serial number of the drive or disk. Examiners will often photograph the evidence as well.

It is also important to document information about the equipment used to store the copy of the data to be examined by the forensic specialist (if for no other reason than to be able to find the image or logical copy at a later point in time). Other information typically retained from the acquisition process includes the date and time of the acquisition and the name of the examiner.

Examiners will also often retain notes about the acquisition process, especially to the extent that a problem with the hardware or software resulted in a deviation from normal processes. For example, if the examiner's normal process involves booting the target computer to a forensic boot disk[23] but the floppy drive on the computer is not functional, an alternative process would need to be deployed (or a repair would need to be implemented). If all other drives in the case were imaged via a boot disk, and this one drive was imaged via another process, opposing counsel might try to attack the deviation from procedure. This is far less likely to be an effective attack against the evidence if the acquisition paperwork notes the reason for the deviation and documents the alternative process used. Such notes can be especially helpful when counsel seeks to introduce evidence found through a forensic process several years after the actual acquisition at a time when the original examiner is no longer available to testify.

Many modern computer forensic software and hardware tools automate the process of collecting much of this information by extracting some of the data directly from the media and allowing the examiner to input some of the data as part of the acquisition process. Collecting and storing the acquisition data directly in the forensic software is a significant improvement over legacy processes in that retention of the evidentiary data will necessarily result in retention of the associated acquisition information.

48.16 CHAIN OF CUSTODY DOCUMENTATION

In addition to notes about the acquisition, it is important that the forensic examiner maintain information about the chain of custody of the evidence once it comes into his or her possession. As noted above, electronic evidence is easily altered. It is therefore important to be able to establish that the evidence was maintained in a forensically sound manner. This is accomplished through chain of custody documentation that tracks the movement and storage of the data from the time of acquisition until the time of trial.

In addition to traditional chain of custody paperwork, technology has also provided a means to ensure that the data acquired by a forensic examiner was not changed while in storage. Many of the forensic software programs in wide use today provide a means for "hashing" the data found on a particular piece of media and using the hash value as a means of detecting any change in the data over time. Hashing a file or set of data simply involves applying a mathematical formula to the data and storing the resultant hash value. Because the formula operates on every bit of data in the target set, even a one-character change in the data will result in a change in the hash value.

By comparing a hash value calculated at the time of acquisition with a hash value calculated at the time the data is being analyzed, an examiner can ensure (to a very significant degree of probability) that no changes to the data have occurred in the intervening period. Thus, use of a hash value can serve as a means of quickly detecting any alteration or corruption of the data collected and can serve to authenticate the data and the analysis of it.

---

[23] A boot disk stores the files necessary to start up a computer and its operating system, whereas a forensic boot disk starts up a computer and enables access without changing data on the target computer's hard drives.

48.17 ANALYSIS WORK PAPERS

In addition to acquisition and chain of custody documentation, most computer forensic examiners will prepare various reports during the course of their examination. Such reports can take a wide range of forms including printouts of data recovered from the target media, time line charts of relevant files, notes detailing searches conducted and analysis performed, and various reports from the forensic software tools.

While there are no strict rules regulating what types of work papers should be created during the course of a forensic examination, as a general proposition the notes should be sufficient to allow an examiner to repeat the processes that resulted in the discovery of critical evidence.

Obviously computer forensics is not just about preserving the evidence. It is also about analyzing the evidence and discovering relevant materials. But before data analysis can begin, some preliminary considerations are important.

48.18 GET THE "WHOLE ENCHILADA"

To the greatest extent possible (and practical), computer forensic investigations should be conducted on all available relevant data, rather than a mere subset of the data. While this can be difficult, it is nonetheless potentially very important. For instance, consider what happened in a capital murder case in California. The electronic source file for a press release and related memorandum that had been issued by the police department was important to the case but could not be readily located. Prior to the forensic search, but after the memo and release had been written, the police department's network file server had been upgraded. The replacement file server did not contain a copy of the press release. Fortunately, forensic examiners determined that the old file server was sitting in a warehouse and had not been used in over three years. The server was reassembled and started, and the press release was found. Interestingly, the fact that the active server contained a file with the same name in the same path, but with drastically different contents from the original memo, indicates that a cover-up may have been attempted.

During the initial interviews on a case, an effort should be made to identify all potential sources of relevant information. Although a decision may be made to limit the analysis of certain data sets in the first instance, preservation of all relevant data should be a goal. Failure to identify relevant data sets can literally have life-and-death consequences.

Similarly, a good forensic examiner should verify, whenever possible, the answers to questions provided by IT staff. Consider the case of the class action lawsuit where members of the class had to be identified from the defendant's proprietary database system. The defendant's programmer modified an existing computer program to extract the list of potential class members. When the program code was later reviewed by a forensic examiner, it was discovered to contain documentation that seemed to indicate that records were inadvertently being bypassed by a section of the code. Testing revealed that the program had indeed ignored hundreds of thousands of rows of the database and the class list was ultimately revised.

Another example of the need to independently confirm IT staff assumptions comes from a case involving a key executive who had deleted many e-mail and calendar entries from his mail file. Examining the mail file showed a reference to another copy of his e-mail file on a different server. The forensic examiner was told that this alternate server did not store any mail files. When IT was asked to inspect the server anyway, it was determined that there was indeed one mail file on the server, the executive's. Apparently, the server had been a migration or fail-over[24] server for this particular user at one time. The file had not been updated by the executive's deletion activity and consequently contained documents that were several years old, including some of the data erased from the active mail server. This discovery assisted the forensic team to identify messages that had recently been deleted by the user.

---

[24] A fail-over server is a server on standby to step in for a primary server in the event that the primary server fails.

There is one additional point to be mentioned about these processes before we discuss the analysis process itself. Many attorneys and investigators would like to be able to review all of the electronic data relevant to a case in a single unified process. They would prefer to find, sort, search, and review e-mail and attachments, word processing documents, spreadsheets, presentation slides, and financial data all from a single computer terminal. While we are closer to this goal today than ever before, this is still generally not practical in most cases.

The reason is that the electronic files associated with certain types of data do not lend themselves to the same processes as simple word processing or spreadsheet files. For example, e-mail messages are generally not stored as distinct files but instead are aggregated into a data store generally thought of as the user's "mailbox." Searches across all of the files on a user's hard drive will hit very often on these e-mail data stores, but that is generally useless to the investigator because he or she is interested in *which* e-mail contained the relevant data. The only way to answer that question is to parse the e-mail file and search across all the individual e-mail messages and attachments. The same problem exists with respect to compressed volumes such as ZIP and TAR files,[25] databases, and various other file types.

As a practical matter this generally means that the processing of electronic data necessarily happens on parallel tracks, with e-mail and other special file types being handled separately from other simpler file types. Within each track, similar (but not identical) processes are performed. In some cases the results of these separate processing streams can eventually be brought together into a unified review or presentation tool. But the exigencies of modern litigation practice, combined with the very large volumes of data associated with electronic discovery, often dictate that data reviews begin as soon as any data is available rather than waiting for multiple processes to be completed.

48.19 EVIDENCE DISCOVERY

While the analysis process deployed in each case tends to depend on the facts at issue, the nature of the available evidence, and the resources of the examining party, most computer forensic investigations involve undertaking at least some of the processes described below.

(a) DE-DUPLICATION.   One of the problems for forensic examiners is that multiple copies of various materials may be recovered as part of the investigative process. Because of the expense involved in reviewing such duplicative materials, de-duplication of the recovered data sets is often the first order of business after the data has been copied and the acquisition documentation has been completed.

One might suspect that de-duplication would be a straightforward process; however, there are several variations of the process that need to be considered before the work can begin. First the examiner must decide what qualifies as a duplicate. Do all of the fields of data need to match exactly, or should two e-mail messages be considered duplicates if the subject and body are identical without regard to the date and routing information? If you require all of the data to match exactly, then any message with a bcc will appear at least twice since the bcc field will only show up in the bcc recipient's mailbox and not in the other recipients'. Similarly, if the time stamp is off by a second, the message will appear more than once in the review data.

Second, the practitioner must decide which universe of documents should be subjected to de-duping. Consider an investigation involving the e-mail of 25 employees, one e-mail server, and four sets of backup tapes. There are likely to be at least six sets of data available for each employee (four sets of mail from the backup tapes, one set from each individual's office computer, and one from the active server), and there could be many more depending on a variety of variables (i.e., data from one or more additional laptop or desktop computers, Blackberry devices, pagers, e-mail-enabled cell phones, home PCs, etc.).

---

[25] ZIP is a file format where the files are compressed (referred to as zipped). Using a file compression program (e.g., PKZip for DOS, or Winzip for Windows), a ZIP file could be created from one or more original files. TAR is a Unix archive file format. TAR files may also be compressed.

De-duplication of this data could proceed based on the entire universe of data (so that each message would be reviewed by investigators only once), or across the data related to each user (so that each message would appear only once in each user's mailbox, but might be reviewed up to 25 times by investigators if all 25 targets received a copy of the same message), or across a subset of the entire universe (e.g., all employees from a certain department).

Each of these choices has advantages and disadvantages. De-duplication across the entire universe of messages may be the most efficient process in terms of limiting the amount of time it will take to review the data, but it also poses challenges. If the reviewers are divided into teams, with each team focusing on the activities of one of the targets (a typical arrangement) and only one copy of a message sent to seven people will appear in the review data, then which team will see the message? Should one target be considered the prime suspect such that all messages sent to him or her and other targets will appear only in his or her data? And if so, won't this make the review of the other targets' data nonsensical since many of the messages will appear out of context with all duplicated messages not appearing in the secondary subject's data set? As a practical matter these issues require the examiner and the entire investigative team to map out their approach in advance and choose a process that is consistent with the particular project's needs.[26]

De-duplication can dramatically reduce the cost of reviewing a large data set. In one recent investigation 5 terabytes (and nearly 21 million files) of e-mail and user file data recovered from backup tapes was reduced to less than 900 gigabytes of data (and less than 5 million files) through the de-duplication process, thereby cutting the attorney review time by over 75 percent.

(b) DATA SORTING. Although the ability to sort investigative data is mundane, it can also be essential to the project goal, especially when millions of e-mail messages or pages of file documents must be reviewed. Data sorting allows the investigator to separate the data into more manageable subsets for review and analysis.

(i) Date/Time. Date and time sorts are the most common forms of data sorting in investigations. The key factor to keep in mind when sorting computer data is that many dates may be associated with a single document or data point. It is important to understand exactly what a particular date means before drawing conclusions about the data. In a typical Windows environment you may find up to five dates associated with each file (file created, last accessed, last written, deleted, entry modified). All of these dates will not necessarily be available for each file. And each date has a different meaning. Without going into detail, the general meaning of these date references are as follows:

- *File Created Date.* This is a record of when a particular file was created at the particular location where it is found. Thus a file created on a floppy disk just before Christmas in December 1999 may have a file created date in January 2000 if it is found by investigators on the desktop hard drive to which it was copied "after the holidays."

- *Last Accessed Date.* This date refers to the last time the file was accessed, either by viewing, dragging, or even right clicking. A file does not have to be changed for the last accessed date to change. It is important to note that certain automated processes, such as backup routines and virus checking software, can change last accessed dates.

- *Last Written Date.* This date refers to the last time that a file was opened, changed, and saved. Merely accessing the file without making changes will not change the last written date.

- *Entry Modified Date.* Some file systems (notably New Technology Filing System (NTFS) and Linux) can store the date when a file's size last changed. Changes to the file that do not affect its size will not change the entry modified date.

---

[26] Some of these concerns can be obviated if all of the reviewers have access to the same centralized and duplicated database, but this is not always possible or practical.

It is important to note that different programs may use different criteria when assigning dates of various types. It may therefore be necessary to research the particulars of a given set of dates if timing is important to an investigation.

(ii) Owner/Author.   As noted, many programs either automatically insert author information or allow users to input author information into the metadata associated with files. It is often helpful to sort documents subject to an investigation by author. It is, however, important to understand the limitations of reliance on the author data.

First, if the data is input automatically every time a document is created, then every document produced on a certain person's computer will indicate that he or she is the author of the documents. But what if another person was using that computer for some reason? It is also possible that a computer initially issued to one employee was later assigned to another individual without changing the default author setting.

Sometimes a document created by one user becomes a form for documents created by many other users. In this circumstance the author information for all of the documents created from the form will reflect the original author of the form.

If the author information is input manually, there are obvious potential manipulation possibilities.

(iii) File Types/Extension.   It is often very useful to sort the data found on a computer by file type or extension. This allows the investigator to segregate all of the word processing documents, spreadsheets, presentation slides, and other user-created files from program files, dynamic link libraries, and system files. It is important, however, to understand that users can attempt to hide documents by adding false extensions to make a spreadsheet look like an executable program (or any other file type).

Forensic practitioners can get around this problem by performing what is called a *signature analysis* on the files. Many programs require that certain specific programming codes be placed in the initial bytes of data in files used by the program. These codes are sometimes referred to as *file signatures*. Forensic tools can search for these bits of code and compare them to the file extensions used in the file name. If the code does not match the file extension, the software can report a file signature mismatch. Moreover, if the file signature is of a known file type, the software may be able to report what the file actually is (as opposed to what the file extension falsely suggests it is).

While file signature analysis cannot guarantee that all relevant materials will be reviewed by investigators, it will increase the likelihood that user-created files are found and reviewed.

48.20 DATA SEARCHING

Searching the data collected is obviously one of the most basic steps in the investigative process, and there are a variety of ways to conduct such searches. Some of the most basic are discussed below.

(a) KEY WORD SEARCHES.   Key word searching is the most basic type of search that can be conducted across a set of electronic data. It simply involves asking the computer to look for a string of characters appearing in a certain order. Some programs index all of the data on a particular piece of media in order to expedite the search process and allow the investigator to perform complex Boolean[27] searches based on multiple key words, word proximity, and other criteria. Other tools will allow searches based on various wild cards and variations.

There are two key things to keep in mind when conducting key word searches. First, computers are precise. They will only find *exactly* what you tell them to look for within the data set. A search for "Robert P. Smith" will not find "Robert Smith," "Bob P. Smith" or "Robert.P.Smith@aol.com."

---

[27] English mathematician George Boole developed a logical combinatorial system (as Boolean algebra) that represents symbolically relationships (as those implied by the logical operators AND, OR, and NOT) between entities.

You can fashion searches that will find these variants, but doing so requires precision and a clear understanding of the search syntax of the particular program being used by the investigator.

For instance, in an investigation for a large distributor, over 4 terabytes of e-mail and user files from personal computers, file servers, and e-mail servers were collected and had to be searched for relevant documents. Users did not use private or home directories on the corporate network, but had instead saved the majority of their files in common or group directories accessible to a large number of people. This resulted in having to search several million files. Complex search terms were used instead of single key words. This helped to identify the most relevant documents quickly. Out of the several million initial files, 200,000 files were identified as relevant in a 10-week span.

Another thing to keep in mind is that certain terms are almost useless as key words. Virtually any search term of four characters or less will result in massive false positive[28] results. This does not mean that such searches should never be run if you have the human resources necessary to separate the wheat from the chaff, but longer, more complex searches will likely be more fruitful.

(b) KNOWN FILE SEARCHES (HASH VALUES).   In some cases it may be possible to search large sets of data very efficiently without using key words at all. If an investigator is looking for a known electronic file within a set of data (e.g., a memo that an executive claims he or she never received), a hash value search may be the best way to proceed.

Hash values are unique numbers calculated by performing a fixed mathematical formula or algorithm against all of the data in a file. The resulting "hash" of the file is a very long unique value that identifies the file and can be used to search for additional copies of the file within a large data set.

Hashing every file in a large data set will allow an investigator to identify a known file by searching for its hash value. Once the hash values are calculated, this type of search is much faster than searching through the file data itself.

Hash values are also useful for identifying identical files within a data set. An investigator merely needs to sort the data by hash value to find files that are identical even though the file names may be different. (Hash values are generally calculated on the file data only, not on the associated metadata such as file names and dates.) This is particularly useful for identifying all copies of an incriminating file even if a user has changed the file name.

One caveat about hash values is that they will only identify two files as identical if the contents of the file are absolutely the same. If one comma, space, or letter is changed within the file, the hash value will also change.

48.21 DELETED/SLACK/UNALLOCATED SPACE

Up to this point our discussion has centered on active files stored on a computer system, backup tape, server, or other electronic media. One of the beauties of computer forensics is that an investigator is not limited to examining these active files. When files are "deleted" from a computer hard drive, the operating system typically just removes references to the data in the file system. The actual file data is typically not removed from the drive until the operating system needs the space to store other data. Although this "unallocated" space generally cannot be seen using normal operating system tools (e.g., Windows Explorer), it can be seen, searched, and sorted by computer forensic tools. Some data in unallocated space will be fully recoverable as if it were never deleted. Other data may consist of file fragments that have been partially overwritten. While such data may not be fully recoverable, it may still provide clues about the computer user's activities.

Such tools can also search through the space at the end of files between the end-of-file marker and the end of the cluster in which the active file data resides. This slack space that is not being used by any active file may contain bits of data from files long ago marked for deletion from the hard drive. Forensic tools can search for and find data stored in these spaces that might otherwise go undetected.

---

[28] Unintended matches returned from search.

However, there are several potential limitations to the use of data discovered in slack and unallocated space. First, it may not always be possible to accurately attribute dates to such information because the normal operating system dates will not typically be available. Second, highly fragmented data found in slack or unallocated space may be hard to place in context, and therefore drawing conclusions about the data may be difficult in some cases. Third, it may be hard to attribute data found in slack or unallocated space to a particular user, especially if the computer being examined was used by more than one person.

Notwithstanding these potential limitations, the ability to review data that has been marked for deletion by a user is one of the key advantages of a forensic approach to the review of electronic data. Just knowing that a user attempted to erase certain files prior to the investigation may provide significant clues to the investigative team.

48.22 CONCLUSION

Many of the computer forensic techniques described in this chapter were considered exotic just a few years ago, but today they have become routine practices in major investigations. Given our society's dependence on computers, it is reasonable to anticipate that five years from now these procedures will necessarily be performed in virtually every large litigation matter and many smaller ones as well. We can also anticipate that new and better tools and techniques will be brought to bear over time. Indeed, the only constant in computer forensics is rapid change. By making use of the most up-to-date practices and procedures, it is hoped that investigators can stay one step ahead of those who are up to no good.

CHAPTER 49

DETECTING FRAUD

W. Steve Albrecht
Brigham Young University

Conan C. Albrecht
Brigham Young University

49.1 INTRODUCTION

Fraud is different from most crimes in that it is seldom observed. Traditional crimes usually leave evidence that can be seen. For example, if a bank is robbed, there are usually witnesses, physical

From *Fraud Examination,* First Edition by Albrecht. © 2003. Reprinted with permission of South-Western, a division of Thomson Learning: www.thomsonrights.com. Fax 800–730–2215.

Both Steve and Conan Albrecht are professors in the Marriott School of Management at Brigham Young University.

money is missing, and the entire episode is often captured on video. Similarly, the discovery of a body that is obviously the victim of murder leaves little question about whether a crime has been committed. With fraud, however, it is not usually obvious that a crime has been committed. Only fraud symptoms or indicators, called *red flags*, are observed. In addition, these red flags can often be caused by nonfraud factors, such as unintentional control weaknesses or missing documents, so significant investigation is required before investigators can know for certain that fraud has occurred.

To detect fraud, managers, auditors, employees, and examiners must learn to recognize these red flags and pursue them until sufficient evidence has been collected. Investigators must discover whether the symptoms resulted from actual fraud or were caused by other factors. Unfortunately, in many cases, many fraud symptoms go unnoticed, and even symptoms that are recognized are often not vigorously pursued.

49.2 TYPES OF FRAUD

Before discussing the detection of fraud, it is important to discuss the different types of frauds. Statement on Auditing Standards (SAS) No. 99 discusses two types of fraud: (1) fraudulent financial reporting and (2) misappropriation of assets. *Fraudulent financial reporting* includes manipulation of the financial statements as intentional misrepresentation in or omission of material events, transactions or other information; intentional misappropriation of generally accepted accounting principles (GAAP); or falsification or manipulation of accounting records or documents. *Misappropriation of assets* includes the theft of assets, such as cash, from an organization by its employees, vendors, customers, or others. In addition to these two types, there are many other types of fraud, including investment scams, identity theft, telemarketing fraud, bankruptcy fraud, money laundering, and others. In this chapter, we focus our discussion on fraudulent financial reporting and misappropriations.

49.3 FIGHTING FRAUD—AN OVERVIEW

The three primary activities in fighting fraud are:

1. *Fraud prevention:* deterring or preventing fraud from occurring
2. *Fraud detection:* finding fraud predication, defined as searching for and discovering red flags (indicators or symptoms)
3. *Investigating fraud:* once predication is present, following up on discovered red flags to determine if they represent actual fraud and, if so, determining who committed the fraud, how much was taken, which accounts were manipulated, and other elements of the fraud

Accountants can be involved in all three of the above activities. For example, one of the best ways to prevent fraud is through the implementation of effective internal controls. Preventive and detective controls eliminate or reduce the opportunities for fraud—making fraud harder to commit and conceal. Accountants, through Section 404 and other control work, are highly involved in establishing, testing, and evaluating the adequacy of internal controls.

All accountants should be involved in fraud detection. Whether accountants are performing tax-related, systems-related, consulting, or auditing work, they should always be alert for fraud symptoms or red flags. Although they are not expected to be fraud experts or forensic accountants, all accountants should understand fraud symptoms and be able to recognize when additional investigation is necessary.

Fraud investigation involves following up on fraud predication to determine whether fraud has actually occurred and, if it has, who the perpetrators were, how much was taken or manipulated, how the fraud was concealed, why the fraud occurred, and what the impact of the fraud was on the organization and its financial statements. Fraud investigation is usually time-consuming and is performed by forensic accountants, fraud examiners, investigators, and attorneys. Of the three fraud activities (prevention, detection, and investigation), it is usually fraud detection that is most difficult but most important to perform. Even though extremely effective controls and other preventive approaches deter fraud, some fraud will still occur because perpetrators will intentionally work around the system or will perpetrate collusive fraud involving forgery that is hard to prevent. If fraud symptoms or red flags are not recognized, fraud investigation cannot occur. Only when there is predication, based on fraud detection, can fraud investigation determine whether red flags were caused by fraud or by other factors.

49.4 FRAUD DETECTION—THE EARLIEST APPROACHES

Historically, most frauds were detected by luck or chance. Fraud symptoms were not categorized or made explicit in the literature and there were no proactive approaches to detect fraud. Fraud was investigated if someone with knowledge or suspicion provided a tip or if the fraud became so egregious that other symptoms were recognized. In fact, most fraud detection studies, such as those performed by the Association of Certified Fraud Examiners[1] or KPMG,[2] find that fraud is still most commonly detected through luck, tips, or other factors outside the auditor's direct control.

The most effective way to find fraud through tips or complaints is to have an effective whistle-blowing system, as required of public companies by the Sarbanes-Oxley Act of 2002. Although whistleblowing systems often generate spurious claims, effective systems provide opportunities for those with knowledge of actual or suspected fraud to come forward with information.

49.5 FRAUD DETECTION—THE RED FLAG APPROACH

Recent accounting standards and fraud literature, however, have focused on the red-flag approach to detecting fraud. With this approach, examples and categories of fraud symptoms are proposed, and accountants and auditors are cautioned to watch for these symptoms in their work. No specific type of fraud is predicted or hypothesized, but if symptoms are observed, they are investigated to determine if fraud is the cause.

Fraud symptoms can be separated into six groups: (1) analytical anomalies, (2) accounting anomalies, (3) internal control weaknesses, (4) extravagant lifestyles, (5) unusual behavior, and (6) tips and complaints. These six categories of symptoms are inclusive of all types of frauds, regardless of type. Obviously, some symptoms are more common with specific types of fraud. For example, lifestyle symptoms are more relevant for fraud perpetrated for personal gain, such as employee or vendor fraud against organizations, than for financial statement fraud. However, every fraud symptom can be categorized as one of these six types, regardless of whether the fraud being examined is financial statement fraud (usually perpetrated on behalf of an organization) or irregularities (usually perpetrated against an organization). The following are descriptions of the six red-flag types:

1. *Analytical symptoms:* Analytical anomalies are amounts, ratios, or other factors that are out of the ordinary or otherwise unusual. Analytical symptoms include amounts that are too high or too low or that are increasing too fast or too slow; they include events that are unusual or do not make sense within the context of the business; they include actions taken by the wrong people or at the wrong time; they include financial statement ratios that are unusual. In short, anything that is unusual or unexpected is an analytical anomaly.

---

[1] *www.cfenet.com/resources/rttn.asp*, accessed on November 26, 2004.
[2] *www.kpmg.com.sg/publications/survey/fraud_survey.pdf*, accessed on November 26, 2004.

2. *Accounting or documentary symptoms:* These anomalies are organizational records that are not appropriate or that are questionable. Examples include photocopies where an original should exist, a ledger that does not balance, altered or forged documents, stale items on bank reconciliations, missing records, fraudulent documents hidden on computers, and email, memoranda, or correspondence between co-conspirators. Accounting or documentary anomalies can be paper or electronic, formal or informal.

3. *Internal control symptoms:* Internal control weaknesses include the overriding or absence of internal controls. Fraud occurs only when there is a complete fraud triangle, comprised of (1) perceived pressure, (2) perceived opportunity, and (3) some way to rationalize the fraudulent actions as acceptable. The absence or overriding of an internal control creates a real or perceived opportunity that often completes the fraud triangle. When accountants see control weaknesses or the overriding of internal controls, they should not only remediate the control but also determine if it has been abused.

4. *Lifestyle symptoms:* When people commit fraud—especially when they steal assets—they rarely save what they misappropriate. Almost always, they use the stolen funds to meet the financial need that created the perceived pressure; they then continue to steal and spend to enhance their lifestyle. Sudden lifestyle changes, such as purchases of new cars, homes, boats, cabins, or other large, expensive items; spending lavishly on travel or other things; or giving of extravagant gifts are often excellent fraud symptoms, especially of irregularities. Remember, it is not high spending that is the symptom, but rather the *change* in spending patterns.

5. *Behavioral symptoms:* Most fraud perpetrators are first-time offenders. As a result, they usually feel tremendous guilt about their actions and fear getting caught. These feelings of guilt and fear are addressed with changed behavior. For example, people who were nice and congenial may suddenly become irritable or difficult (the opposite could also be true). People who used to come to work late may start arriving early and staying late. Remember, it is not personal behavioral idiosyncrasies that represent symptoms; rather, it is *changes* in behavior.

6. *Tips and complaints:* Tips and complaints are excellent indicators of possible fraud. The receipt of a tip does not automatically mean that there is fraud. It is important to know what motivated the tip or complaint. Sometimes, tips or complaints are forwarded to get even with someone, to get someone in trouble, to camouflage or defer attention from someone else, or for other personal reasons. Often, however, tips signal real fraud and are a great source of predication.

To correctly identify fraud, accountants must understand the context in which the symptom was observed. Fraud symptoms are real symptoms only in context, meaning that the same observation could be taken as a symptom for one person but not by another, because of the differing context or knowledge of the two individuals.

Although the symptoms just described relate to all types of fraud, to better understand how these symptoms relate to financial statement fraud, accountants must clearly understand the operations and nature of the organization they are examining, as well as the nature of the industry and the organization's competitors. Accountants must have a good understanding of the organization's management and its motivations. It is important to understand how the company is organized and have an awareness of relationships the company has with other parties, including the influence that each of those parties has on the client and its officers.

Fraudulent financial statements are rarely detected solely by analyzing the financial statements. Rather, financial statement fraud is usually detected when the information in the financial statements is compared with (1) the real-world referents those numbers are supposed to represent, (2) the context in which management is operating and being motivated, and (3) how the financial statements compare with past financial statements and with those of similar organizations. Fraud is often detected by focusing on the changes in reported assets, liabilities, revenues, and expenses from period to period or by comparing company performance to industry norms. In most financial

Management and Directors	Relationships with Others
	Fraud Exposure Rectangle
Organization and Industry	Financial Results and Operating Characteristics

Exhibit 49.1   The fraud exposure rectangle.

statement fraud cases, for example, each period's financial statements look correct when viewed as stand-alone statements. It is only when changes in assets and revenues from period to period are examined, and when assets and revenues reported in the financial statements are compared with past periods and with other organizations and physical assets, that it can be determined that the financial statements are incorrect.

The exposure rectangle shown in Exhibit 49.1 is useful in thinking about financial statement fraud symptoms. The first corner of the rectangle represents the management and directors of the company. The second corner represents the relationships the company has with other entities. The third corner represents the nature of the organization you are examining and the industry in which that organization operates. The fourth corner represents the financial results and operating characteristics of the organization.

Although accountants have traditionally focused almost entirely on the financial statements and results of operations to perform generally accepted accounting standards (GAAS) audits and detect financial statement fraud, each of these four areas presents fraud exposures that must be examined.

49.6 MANAGEMENT AND THE BOARD OF DIRECTORS

Top management, including the Chief Executive Officer (CEO) and Chief Financial Officer (CFO), is almost always involved when financial statement fraud occurs. Unlike embezzlement and misappropriation, financial statement fraud is usually committed by the highest individuals in an organization, and most often it occurs on behalf of the organization as opposed to against the organization. Because members of management are usually involved, the organization's management and the directors must be investigated to determine their exposure to and motivation for committing fraud. Fraud is not committed by financial statements; rather, it is perpetrated by management or other top officers or directors! In detecting financial statement fraud, accountants must gain an understanding of management and their motivations; this understanding is at least as important as understanding the financial statements. In particular, three aspects of management should be investigated:

1. Management backgrounds
2. Management motivations
3. Management influence in making decisions for the organization

With respect to backgrounds, you should understand what kinds of organizations and situations managers and directors have been associated with in the past. With today's computerized interconnections and databases (e.g., the World Wide Web), it is easy to conduct simple searches on individuals. One way to perform such searches is to type the individual's name into Google or another search engine. The search engine will list all the references to the person's name, including past proxy statements and 10-Ks the person has been affiliated with, newspaper articles about the person, articles written by the person, positions held, and so forth. More in-depth searches can be done with pay-for-use sites such as Lexis/Nexis, ChoicePoint, and many other online services. If Web searches prove insufficient, it does not cost very much to hire a private investigator to perform custom research on members of management.

It is also important to know what motivates directors and managers. Are their personal assets tied up in the organization? Are they under pressure to deliver unrealistic results? Is their compensation primarily performance-based? Do they have a habit of guiding Wall Street to higher and higher expectations? Have they grown through acquisitions or internally? Are there debt covenants or other financial measures that must be met? Are managers' jobs at risk? These questions are examples of what must be asked and answered to properly understand management's motivations. Many financial statement frauds have been perpetrated because management needed to report positive or high income to support stock prices, show positive earnings for a public stock or debt offering, or report profits to meet regulatory or loan restrictions.

Finally, management's ability to influence decisions for the organization must be understood, because perpetrating fraud is much easier when one or two individuals have primary decision-making power than when an organization has a more democratic leadership. Most people who commit financial statement fraud are first-time offenders, and being dishonest the first time is difficult for them. Therefore, it is much more difficult for two or even three individuals to simultaneously conduct dishonest acts. When decision-making ability is spread among several individuals, or when the board of directors takes an active role in the organization, fraud is much more difficult to perpetrate. Most financial statement frauds do not occur in large, historically profitable organizations. Rather, they occur in smaller, public or private organizations where one or two individuals have almost total decision-making control, in companies that have experienced very rapid growth, or where the board of directors and audit committee do not take an active role in financial matters (note that new corporate governance standards have made it very difficult for board members to remain aloof of the financial matters of their companies). An active board of directors and/or audit committee that gets involved in the major decisions of the organization can do much to deter management fraud. In fact, it is for this reason that National Association of Securities Dealers Automated Quotations (NASDAQ) and New York Stock exchange (NYSE) corporate governance standards require that the majority of board members be independent and that some of the key committees, such as audit and compensation, be comprised entirely of independent directors.

Once members of management decide to commit fraud, the particular schemes used are usually determined by the nature of their business operations. In searching for red flags, some of the key questions that must be asked about management and the directors are as described in the following subsections.

(a) UNDERSTANDING MANAGEMENT AND DIRECTOR BACKGROUNDS.

1. Have any of the key executives or board members been associated with other organizations in the past? If so, what was the nature of those organizations and relationships?
2. Were key members of management promoted from within the organization or recruited from the outside?
3. Have any key members of management had past regulatory or legal problems, either personally or with organizations they have been associated with?
4. Have there been significant changes in the makeup of management or the board of directors?
5. Has there been a high turnover of management and/or board members?
6. Do any members of management or the board have criminal backgrounds?
7. Are there any other issues related to the backgrounds of key members of management and the board of directors?
8. Are the majority of the board members independent?
9. Is the chairman of the board separate from the CEO?
10. Does the company have independent audit, compensation, and nominating committees?

(b) UNDERSTANDING MANAGEMENT AND DIRECTOR MOTIVATIONS.

1. Do any of the key executives have personal worth tied up in the organization?
2. Is management under pressure to meet earnings or other financial expectations, or does management commit to analysts, creditors, and others to achieve what appear to be unduly aggressive forecasts?
3. Is management's compensation primarily performance-based (bonuses, stock options, etc.)?
4. Are there significant debt covenants or other financial restrictions that management must meet?
5. Is the job security of any key members of management at serious risk?
6. Is the organization's reported financial performance decreasing?
7. Is management excessively interested in maintaining or increasing the entity's stock price?
8. Does management have an incentive to use inappropriate means to minimize reported earnings for tax reasons?
9. Are there any other significant issues related to the motivations of managers and board members?

(c) UNDERSTANDING THE DEGREE OF INFLUENCE OF KEY MEMBERS OF MANAGEMENT AND THE BOARD OF DIRECTORS.

1. Which key members of management and the board of directors have the most influence?
2. Are there one or two key people who have dominant influence in the organization?
3. Is the management style of the organization autocratic or democratic?
4. Is the organization's management centralized or decentralized?
5. Does management use ineffective means of communicating and supporting the entity's values or ethics, or do they communicate inappropriate values or ethics?
6. Does management fail to correct known reportable conditions in internal control on a timely basis?
7. Does management set unduly aggressive financial targets and expenditures for operating personnel?
8. Does management have too much involvement in or influence over the selection of accounting principles or the determination of significant estimates?
9. Are there any other significant issues related to the degree of influence of key members of management and the board of directors?

49.7 RELATIONSHIPS WITH OTHERS

Financial statement fraud is rarely perpetrated without the help of other real or fictitious organizations. Enron's fraud was conducted primarily through what is known as *special purpose* or *variable interest entities* (SPEs)—business interests formed solely to accomplish some specific tasks. SPEs are not of themselves illegal, but were used in Enron's case to hide debt, manipulate income, hide losses, and conduct other illegitimate activities.

Though relationships with all parties should be examined to determine if they present management fraud opportunities or exposures, relationships with financial institutions, related organizations and individuals, external auditors, lawyers, investors, and regulators should always be carefully considered. Relationships with financial institutions and bondholders are especially important because they indicate the extent to which the company is leveraged. Examples of the kinds of questions that should be asked about debt relationships include:

- Is the company highly leveraged, and with which financial institutions?

- What assets of the organization are pledged as collateral?
- Is there debt or other restrictive covenants that must be met?
- Do the banking relationships appear normal, or are there strange relationships with financial institutions, such as using institutions in unusual geographical locations?
- Are there relationships between the officers of the financial institutions and your client organization?

Relationships with related organizations and individuals (related parties) should be examined, because structuring non-arm's-length and often unrealistic transactions with related organizations and individuals is one of the easiest ways to perpetrate financial statement fraud. These kinds of relationships are usually identified by examining large or unusual transactions, often occurring at strategic times (i.e., at the end of a period) that make the financial statements look better. The kinds of relationships and events that should be examined include:

- Large transactions that result in revenues or income for the organization
- Sales or purchases of assets between related entities
- Transactions that result in goodwill or other intangible assets being recognized in the financial statements
- Transactions that generate nonoperating, rather than operating, income
- Loans or other financing transactions between related entities
- Any transaction that appears to be unusual or questionable for the organization, especially transactions that are unrealistically large

Analysis of the relationship between a company and its auditors is important for several reasons. If there has been an auditor change, there is probably a good reason for the change. Auditing firms do not easily give up clients, and the termination of an auditor-auditee relationship is most often caused by failure of the client to pay, an auditor-auditee disagreement, fraud or other problems suspected by the auditor, or the auditee's belief that the auditor's fees are too high. Although some of these reasons, such as high fees, may not signal a potential fraud problem, auditor-auditee disagreements, failure to pay an audit fee, and suspected problems can all suggest a financial statement fraud problem. The fact that an auditor was dismissed or resigned, together with the difficulty of discovering financial statement fraud for a first-time auditor, is cause for concern any time there is an auditor change. In examining a company for possible financial statement fraud, it is important to know who its auditor is and how long that relationship has existed.

Relationships with lawyers pose even greater risks than relationships with auditors. Auditors are supposed to be independent and must resign if they suspect that financial results may not be appropriate; in contrast, lawyers are usually advocates for their clients. Lawyers will often follow and support their clients until it is obvious that fraud has occurred. In addition, lawyers usually have information about a client's legal difficulties, regulatory problems, and other significant occurrences. Like auditors, lawyers rarely give up a profitable client unless something is obviously wrong. Thus, a change in legal firms without an apparent reason is often a cause for concern. Unlike a change of auditors, for which an 8-K must be filed for public companies, a change of lawyers requires no such reporting.

Relationships with investors are important because financial statement fraud is often motivated by a debt or equity offering to investors. In addition, knowledge of the number and kinds of investors (public or private company, major exchange or small exchange, institutional or individual, etc.) can often provide an indication of the degree of pressure on and public scrutiny of the management of the company and its financial performance. If an organization is publicly held, there are usually investor groups or investment analysts that follow the company very closely and often can provide information or indications that something is wrong with the company. For example, "short" investors are always looking for bad news about an organization that will make its stock go down. If they suspect that something is not right, they will often contact management or even the auditors (or press) to vent their concerns. Investor groups often focus on information very different from that used by auditors, and sometimes the fraud symptoms are more obvious to them than they are to auditors, especially auditors who focus solely on the financial statements. Short sellers have a unique perspective that has allowed them to discover financial statement frauds. Because short sellers often focus on bad news, there have been instances in which they were the first ones to put the pieces of the fraud puzzle together. With Enron, for example, the first one to come forward with negative information about the company was Jim Chanos of Kynikos Associates, a highly regarded firm specializing in short selling, who stated publicly in early 2001 that "no one could explain how Enron actually made money." He noted that Enron had completed transactions with related parties that "were run by a senior officer of Enron" and assumed it was a conflict of interest. (Enron would not answer questions about LJM and other partnerships.) Then, in its March 5, 2001, issue, *Fortune* magazine ran a story about Enron that stated: "To skeptics, the lack of clarity raises a red flag about Enron's pricey stock . . . [t]he inability to get behind the numbers combined with ever higher expectations for the company may increase the chance of a nasty surprise. Enron is an earnings-at-risk story." Unfortunately, investors kept ignoring this bad news until late in 2001, when a misguided earnings release led skeptics to start selling the stock. The company declared bankruptcy in late 2001.

Finally, accountants must understand a client's relationship with regulators. If a client is a publicly held company, accountants should find out whether the Securities and Exchange Commission (SEC) has ever issued an enforcement release against it; whether the Public Company Accounting Oversight Board (PCAOB), through its inspection of Certified Public Accounting (CPA) firms, has focused on the company; or whether the Internal Revenue Service (IRS) or another government agency is investigating or has disputes with the company. For example, in its report pursuant to Section 704 of the Sarbanes-Oxley Act, the SEC stated that during the five-year period from July 31, 1997 to July 30, 2002, it had filed 515 enforcement actions involving 869 named parties, 164 entities, and 705 individuals. Accountants also need to know if all annual, quarterly, and other reports have been filed on a timely basis. If a client is in a regulated industry, such as banking, it is important to discover the nature of its relationship with the corresponding regulatory bodies, such as the Federal Deposit Insurance Corporation (FDIC), Federal Reserve, and Office of the Controller of the Currency. Are there any problematic issues related to those bodies? Does the organization owe any back taxes to the federal or state government or to other taxing districts? Because of the recourse and sanctions available to taxing authorities, organizations usually do not fall behind on their payments unless something is wrong or the organization is having serious cash-flow problems. The following subsections present some of the questions that should be asked about a company's relationships with others when searching for red flags.

(a) RELATIONSHIPS WITH FINANCIAL INSTITUTIONS.

1. With what financial institutions does the organization have significant relationships?
2. Is the organization highly leveraged through bank or other loans?
3. Are there loan or debt covenants or restrictions that pose significant problems for the organization?
4. Do the banking relationships appear normal, or are there unusual attributes about the relationships (strange geographical locations, too many banks, etc.)?
5. Do members of management or the board have personal or other close relationships with officers of any of the major banks used by the company?
6. Have there been significant changes in the financial institutions used by the company? If so, why?

7. Are there significant bank accounts or subsidiary or branch operations in tax-haven jurisdictions for which there appears to be no clear business justification?

8. Have critical assets of the company been pledged as collateral on risky loans?

9. Are there any other questionable financial institution relationships?

(b) RELATIONSHIPS WITH RELATED PARTIES.

1. Are there significant related-party transactions not in the ordinary course of business or with related entities not audited or audited by another firm?

2. Are there large or unusual transactions at or near the end of a period that significantly improve the reported financial performance of the company?

3. Are there significant receivables or payables between related entities?

4. Has a significant amount of the organization's revenues or income been derived from related-party transactions?

5. Is a significant part of the company's income or revenues derived from one or two large transactions?

6. Are there any other questionable related-party relationships?

7. Have relationships with other entities resulted in the reporting of significant amounts of nonoperating income?

(c) RELATIONSHIPS WITH AUDITORS.

1. Have there been frequent disputes with the current or predecessor auditors on accounting, auditing, or reporting matters?

2. Has management placed unreasonable demands on the auditor, including unreasonable time constraints?

3. Has the company placed formal or informal restrictions on the auditor that inappropriately limit the auditor's access to people or information or ability to communicate effectively with the board of directors or the audit committee?

4. Is there domineering management behavior in dealing with the auditor, especially involving attempts to influence the scope of the auditor's work?

5. Has there been an auditor change? If so, for what reason?

6. Are there any other questionable auditor relationships?

(d) RELATIONSHIPS WITH LAWYERS.

1. Has there been significant litigation involving the company in matters that could severely and adversely affect the company's financial results?

2. Has there been an attempt to hide litigation from the auditors or others?

3. Has there been a change in outside counsel? If so, for what reasons?

4. Are there any other questionable lawyer relationships?

(e) RELATIONSHIPS WITH INVESTORS.

1. Is the organization in the process of issuing an initial or secondary public debt or equity offering?

2. Are there any investor-related lawsuits?

3. Are there any problematic or questionable relationships with investment bankers, stock analysts, or others?

4. Has there been significant short selling of the company's stock? If so, why?

5. Are there questionable investor relationships?

(f) RELATIONSHIPS WITH REGULATORY BODIES.

1. Does management display a significant disregard for regulatory authorities?
2. Has there been a history of securities law violations or claims against the entity or its senior management alleging fraud or violations of securities laws?
3. Have any 8-Ks been filed with the SEC? If so, for what reasons?
4. Are there any new accounting, statutory, or regulatory requirements that could impair the financial stability or profitability of the entity?
5. Are there significant tax disputes with the IRS or other taxing authorities?
6. Is the company current on paying its payroll taxes and other payroll-related expenses, and is the company current on paying other liabilities?
7. Are there any other questionable relationships with regulatory bodies?

49.8 ORGANIZATION AND INDUSTRY

Perpetrators sometimes mask financial statement fraud by creating an organizational structure that makes it easier to hide fraud. The attributes of an organization that can act as red flags include such things as an unduly complex organizational structure, an organization without an internal audit department, a board of directors with no or few outsiders on the board or audit committee, an organization in which one or a small group of individuals control related entities, an organization that has offshore affiliates with no apparent business purpose, an organization that has made numerous acquisitions and has recognized large merger-related charges, or an organization that is new. Accountants should gain an understanding of who the owners of an organization are. Sometimes silent or hidden owners are using the organization for illegal or other questionable activities.

The COSO-sponsored study[3] of the attributes of firms committing financial statement fraud concluded:

> The relatively small size of fraud companies suggests that the inability or even unwillingness to implement cost-effective internal controls may be a factor affecting the likelihood of financial statement fraud (e.g., override of controls is easier). Smaller companies may be unable or unwilling to employ senior executives with sufficient financial reporting knowledge and experience.

> The concentration of fraud among companies with under $50 million in revenues and with generally weak audit committees highlights the importance of rigorous audit committee practices even for smaller organizations. In particular, the number of audit committee meetings per year and the financial expertise of the audit committee members may deserve closer attention.

> Investors should be aware of the possible complications arising from family relationships and from individuals (founders, CEO/board chairs, etc.) who hold significant power or incompatible job functions.

The industry of the organization must also be carefully examined. Some industries are riskier than others. For example, in the 1980s, the savings and loan (S&L) industry was extremely risky—to the extent that some accounting firms would not audit an S&L client. More recently, technology companies, especially dot.com-type Internet companies with new and unproven business models, and telecom companies have been extremely risky. With any company, however, the organization's performance relative to that of similar organizations in the same industry should be examined. The following kinds of questions should be asked to understand the exposure to management fraud:

---

[3] *www.theiia.org/iia/index.cfm?doc_id=97*, accessed on November 26, 2004.

1. Does the company have an overly complex organizational structure involving numerous or unusual legal entities, managerial lines of authority, or contractual arrangements without apparent business purpose?
2. Is there a legitimate business purpose for each separate entity of the business?
3. Is the board of directors comprised primarily of officers of the company or other related individuals?
4. Is the board of directors passive, or active and independent?
5. Is the audit committee comprised primarily of insiders or outsiders?
6. Is the audit committee passive, or active and independent?
7. Does the organization have an independent and active internal audit department?
8. Does the organization have offshore activities without any apparent business purpose?
9. Is the organization a new entity without a proven history?
10. Have there been significant recent changes in the nature of the organization?
11. Is there adequate monitoring of significant controls?
12. Is there an effective accounting and information technology staff and organization?
13. Is there a high degree of competition or market saturation, accompanied by declining margins?
14. Is the client in a declining industry with increasing business failures and significant declines in customer demand?
15. Are there rapid changes in the industry, such as high vulnerability to rapidly changing technology or rapid product obsolescence?
16. Is the performance of the company similar or contrary to that of other firms in the industry?
17. Are there any other significant issues related to organization and industry?

49.9 FINANCIAL RESULTS AND OPERATING CHARACTERISTICS

Much can be learned about exposure to financial statement fraud by closely examining management and the board of directors, relationships with others, and the nature of the organization. Investigation of these three elements is always a good idea, but it usually involves the same procedures for all kinds of financial statement frauds, whether the accounts manipulated are revenue accounts, asset accounts, liabilities, expenses, or equities. What differs from fraud scheme to fraud scheme are the kinds of exposures and red flags identified by the financial statements and operating characteristics of the organization. In examining financial statements to assess fraud exposures, a nontraditional approach to the financial statements must be taken. Fraud symptoms are most often manifested through changes in the financial statements. For example, financial statements that contain large changes in account balances from period to period are more likely to contain fraud than financial statements that exhibit only small, incremental changes in account balances. A sudden, dramatic increase in receivables, for example, is often a signal that something is wrong. In addition to changes in financial statement balances and amounts, the footnotes to the financial statements should be studied. Many times, the footnotes strongly hint that fraud is occurring, but what is contained in the footnotes is not clearly understood by auditors and others.

When assessing fraud exposure through financial statements and operating characteristics, the balances and amounts must be compared with those of similar organizations in the same industry, and the real-world referents to the financial statement amounts must be determined. If, for example, an organization's financial statements report that the company has $2 million of inventory, then the inventory has to be located somewhere. Depending on the type of inventory it is, it should require a certain amount of space to store it, forklifts and other equipment to move and ship it, and people to manage it. Are the financial statement numbers realistic, given the actual inventory that is on hand?

Using financial relationships to assess fraud exposures requires that accountants know the nature of the client's business, the kinds of accounts that should be included, the kinds of fraud that could occur in the organization, and the kinds of symptoms those frauds would generate. For example, the major activities of a manufacturing company could probably be subdivided into sales and collections, acquisition and payment, financing, payroll, and inventory and warehousing. Accountants should break an organization down into various activities or cycles such as these and then, for each cycle, identify the major functions performed, the major risks inherent in each function, the kinds of abuse and fraud that could occur, and the kinds of symptoms those frauds would generate. An examiner can then use proactive detection techniques to determine if there is a likelihood of fraud in those cycles. This proactive approach is similar to hypothesis testing done by researchers: auditors repetitively hypothesize that a type of fraud might be occurring and investigate whether symptoms in the financial statements support each hypothesis. The following are some of the critical questions that must be asked about financial statement relationships and operating results when searching for red flags:

1. Are there unrealistic changes or increases in financial statement account balances?
2. Are the account balances realistic given the nature, age, and size of the company?
3. Do actual physical assets exist in the amounts and values indicated on the financial statements?
4. Have there been significant changes in the nature of the organization's revenues or expenses?
5. Do one or a few large transactions account for a significant portion of any account balance or amount?
6. Are there significant transactions near the end of the period that positively affect the results of operations, especially transactions that are unusual or highly complex or that pose substance-over-form questions?
7. Do financial results appear consistent on a quarter-by-quarter or month-by-month basis, or are there unrealistic amounts in a subperiod?
8. Is there an inability to generate cash flows from operations while reporting earnings and earnings growth?
9. Is there significant pressure to obtain additional capital necessary to stay competitive, considering the financial position of the entity—including the need for funds to finance major research and development or capital expenditures?
10. Are reported assets, liabilities, revenues, or expenses based on significant estimates that involve unusually subjective judgments or uncertainties or that are subject to potential significant change in the near term in a manner that may have a financially disruptive effect on the entity (i.e., ultimate collectibility of receivables, timing of revenue recognition, realizability of financial instruments based on the highly subjective valuation of collateral or difficult-to-assess repayment sources, or significant deferral of costs)?
11. Is there unusually rapid growth or profitability, especially compared with that of other companies in the same industry?
12. Is the organization highly vulnerable to changes in interest rates?
13. Are there unrealistically aggressive sales or profitability incentive programs?
14. Is there a threat of imminent bankruptcy, foreclosure, or hostile takeover?
15. Is there a high possibility of adverse consequences on significant pending transactions, such as a business combination or contract award, if poor financial results are reported?
16. Is there a poor or deteriorating financial position when management has personally guaranteed significant debts of the entity?
17. Does the firm continuously operate on a crisis basis or without a careful budgeting and planning process?
18. Does the organization have difficulty collecting receivables or have other cash-flow problems?

19. Is the organization dependent on one or two key products or services, especially products or services that can quickly become obsolete? Do other organizations have the ability to adapt more quickly to market swings?

20. Do the footnotes contain information about difficult-to-understand issues?

21. Are there adequate disclosures in the footnotes?

22. Are there questionable or suspicious factors relating to financial results or operating characteristics?

49.10 STRATEGIC FRAUD DETECTION

The red-flag approach to fraud detection just described typically begins with an anomaly or indication that something is not right, such as anonymous tips, unusual financial statement relationships, or control overrides. The red flags observed provide predication that fraud may exist. Management, auditors, or fraud examiners then investigate the indicators to determine whether the red flags observed represent real fraud or are being caused by other factors. This approach can be viewed as an inductive method: it begins with anomalies brought to someone's attention or found proactively (without a specific fraud in mind) and continues by researching additional events and data until it is determined that fraud may be causing the indicators.

Developments in technology and the widespread use of electronic databases to record transactions have made it possible to reverse the traditional red-flag approach; that is, focusing first on specific types of fraud and moving forward to determine whether indicators or red flags of those specific frauds exist. It is now possible to specifically target different types of frauds, analyze entire populations, and proactively detect fraud before traditional indicators become egregious enough to be observed or predication exists. This strategic approach to fraud detection is a proactive approach that targets industry- and company-specific fraud anomalies and patterns and mines data for indicators of specific fraud types. Exhibit 49.2 describes the six steps involved in the strategic fraud detection model.

Step 1. Understand the Business. Strategic fraud detection starts with an understanding of the business or unit being examined. Because each business environment is different—even within the same industry or firm—strategic fraud detection is an analytical process. The same fraud detection procedures cannot be applied generically to all businesses or even to different units of the same organization. Rather than rely on generic fraud detection methods or generic queries, strategic fraud examiners must gain intimate knowledge of each specific organization and its processes. Having a detailed understanding of the business process underlies the entire strategic fraud detection process. Understanding processes in an organization or unit is similar to the activities undertaken when performing business process reengineering.

Step 2. Identify Possible Frauds That Could Exist. Once accountants feel confident that they understand the business, they must determine what possible frauds could occur in the operation being examined. This risk assessment step requires an understanding of the nature of different frauds, how they occur, and what symptoms they exhibit. The fraud identification process begins by conceptually dividing the business unit into its individual functions. For example, accountants might decide to focus directly on the manufacturing plant, the collections department, or the purchasing function.

In this step, people knowledgeable about the business functions (internal auditors, managers, security directors, etc.) are interviewed. Accountants ask questions such as: Who are the players? What types of employees, vendors, or contractors are involved? How do insiders and outsiders interact with each another? What types of fraud could be committed against the company or on behalf of the company? How could employees or management acting alone commit fraud? How could vendors or customers acting alone commit fraud? How could

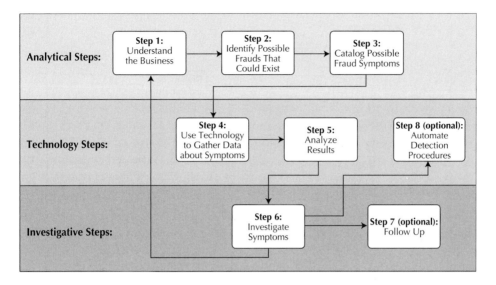

Exhibit 49.2   Strategic fraud detection.

vendors or customers working in collusion with employees commit fraud? What motivations are there to commit fraud on behalf of the organization or against the organization? During this stage, accountants should brainstorm potential frauds by type and participant. The likely occurrence of the various frauds is considered, and a laundry list of frauds that will be considered is developed.

Step 3. Catalog Possible Fraud Symptoms for Each Type of Fraud. This step in strategic fraud detection involves careful consideration of whether variations of the six types of symptoms discussed earlier could be present in the cataloged frauds identified in Step 2. A matrix, tree diagram, or mind map should be created that correlates specific symptoms with specific possible frauds. For example, fraud involving kickbacks from vendors to buyers might be characterized as shown in Exhibit 49.3. This step is extremely important because it makes operational the list of frauds hypothesized in the previous step.

Step 4. Use Technology and Other Means to Gather Data about Symptoms. Once symptoms are defined and correlated with specific frauds, data are extracted from corporate databases, online Web sites, interviews, and other sources. Traditional fraud-search procedures prescribe sampling data, but it is preferable to run fraud-detection queries against full transaction populations. Summarization or sampling limits the power of the detection process. Sampling can miss important transactions within which fraud has been hidden.

Because of the large size of typical organizational data stores, many queries are actually composed of several extractions combined with algorithms programmed in scripting languages. Small scripts, quickly written and executed, allow accountants to analyze large numbers of transactions and perform repeated analyses. For example, ACLScript, the scripting language within ACL, provides significantly more power to the user than using ACL from the menu options alone. Other popular scripting languages include IDEAScript (IDEA), Visual Basic (Microsoft Excel or Access), PowerScript (PowerBuilder), and Python.

Step 5. Analyze and Refine Results. Once relevant data are retrieved, they are compared against expectations and models. These algorithms examine records and highlight anomalies, unknown values, suggestive trends, or outliers that can then be analyzed directly by examiners. These algorithms must be company- and data-specific to be valuable. Data analysis

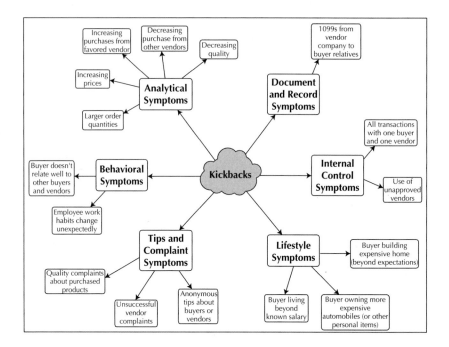

Exhibit 49.3   Example of strategic fraud detection with kickbacks.

techniques, such as time trending, regression, cusum, fuzzy text matching, stratification and summarization, z-score distancing and comparisons, time axis standardization, and relation matching should be used for analysis. (Discussion of these and other appropriate techniques is important but beyond the scope of this chapter.)

Although specific analyses are unique to the business being examined and the type of fraud being searched for, most searches include time series models. This is because fraud is often discovered by examining changes over time. Historical patterns within the data, rather than outside factors, often set the standard against which data are measured. Sharp and unexpected increases in spending, purchases, labor, or even account balances often signal possible fraud. Generated norms that allow the data to speak for themselves are often useful to determine whether observed values are anomalies or fall within expected ranges.

Step 6. Investigate Symptoms. Once anomalies are highlighted and determined to be indicators of fraud, they are investigated using either traditional or strategic approaches. The advantage to the strategic approach, however, is that now the investigation is targeted and specific. Based on the strategic red flags observed, fraud examiners can now, in a cost-effective way, focus their investigation efforts.

49.11 CONCLUSION

It is no longer necessary to wait until fraud symptoms become so egregious as to be observed to detect fraud. Fraud can now be detected either through inductive search for red flags or through deductive, strategic fraud detection. Once fraud occurs, there are no winners. Everyone, including the victim organization, the perpetrators, the auditors, and others, loses. These losses are minimized if fraud can be detected early. Every accountant should understand both the importance of fraud detection and the nature of fraud symptoms. Frauds will never be eliminated completely, but those who understand the nature of fraud and how to detect its occurrence will minimize their losses and, it is hoped, avoid expensive lawsuits, negative exposure, and financial losses.

INDEX